ONE WHO LOVES KNOWLEDGE

MATERIAL AND VISUAL CULTURE OF ANCIENT EGYPT

Series Editors
Joshua A. Roberson
Christina Geisen

NUMBER SIX

ONE WHO LOVES KNOWLEDGE:
STUDIES IN HONOR OF RICHARD JASNOW

ONE WHO LOVES KNOWLEDGE

STUDIES IN HONOR OF RICHARD JASNOW

Edited by
Betsy Bryan
Mark Smith
Christina Di Cerbo
Marina Escolano-Poveda
Jill S. Waller

LOCKWOOD PRESS
COLUMBUS, GEORGIA
2022

ONE WHO LOVES KNOWLEDGE
STUDIES IN HONOR OF RICHARD JASNOW

ISBN: 978-1-948488-35-8

Cover design by Susanne Wilhelm. Cover image by Susan Lezon.

Cataloguing-in-Publication Data

Names: Bryan, Betsy Morrell, editor. | Smith, M. (Mark), 1951- editor. | Di Cerbo, Christina, editor. | Escolano Poveda, Marina, editor. | Waller, Jill S., editor. | Jasnow, Richard, honouree.
Title: One who loves knowledge : studies in honor of Richard Jasnow / edited by Betsy Bryan, Mark Smith, Christina Di Cerbo, Marina Escolano-Poveda, Jill S. Waller.
Other titles: Studies in honor of Richard Jasnow | Material and visual culture of ancient Egypt ; no. 6.
Description: Columbus, Georgia : Lockwood Press, 2022. | Series: Material and visual culture of ancient Egypt ; number six | Includes bibliographical references and index.
Identifiers: LCCN 2022004065 (print) | LCCN 2022004066 (ebook) | ISBN 9781948488358 (hardcover) | ISBN 9781948488365 (pdf)
Subjects: LCSH: Egyptology. | Egyptian philology. | Egyptian language--Papyri, Demotic. | Semitic philology. | Egypt--Antiquities. | LCGFT: Festschriften.
Classification: LCC PJ1026.J37 O54 2022 (print) | LCC PJ1026.J37 (ebook) | DDC 493/.1--dc23/eng/20220505
LC record available at https://lccn.loc.gov/2022004065
LC ebook record available at https://lccn.loc.gov/2022004066

This paper meets the requirements of ANSI/NISO Z39.48-1992 (Permanence of Paper).

Contents

Acknowledgments

The editors first want to thank the contributors to the Festschrift project. This has taken us far longer than we imagined, largely due to the pandemic of 2020 and 2021, and we wish that this could have appeared sooner for Richard's sake and for that of the authors. This is a rich group of articles, and all those who have written have done so with enormous enthusiasm and have waited with great patience for their contributions to appear. It is important that we acknowledge the work of Jill Waller whose name we have added to the list of editors. She has been our rock and consistency throughout this period. Other graduate students in Near Eastern Studies have also helped with the preparation of this volume, particularly Morgan Moroney and Tori Finlayson, both of whom were instrumental in the editing process. We also would like to thank the staff of Near Eastern Studies, past and present: Vonnie Wild and Glenda Hogan in the earlier days and now also Jenny Wohl. The cover image for the book is a figurine of the god Thoth from the Myers Eton College collection on loan to the Johns Hopkins University Archaeological Museum. We thank Associate Director and Curator Sanchita Balachandran for their assistance, as well as Kate Gallagher, Registrar and Assistant Curator. We also thank Tina Di Cerbo for the excellent photographs of Richard which we include with the Introduction. Billie Jean Collins of Lockwood Press deserves our greatest appreciation. Her design for the cover is absolutely beautiful, and her professionalism is a standard to admire. We consider ourselves fortunate in every way to have had a collaborator like her in producing this volume.

Betsy M. Bryan
Mark Smith
Marina Escolano-Poveda
Christina Di Cerbo
Jill S. Waller

Preface – Betsy Bryan

Richard Jasnow has been my colleague since 1995 when he came to Johns Hopkins University from the Epigraphic Survey of the University of Chicago's Chicago House in Luxor, where he was Assistant Director and Senior Epigrapher. Although I did not know Richard extremely well before he arrived, we had become acquainted at the Wilbour Library of the Brooklyn Museum in the years before I left New York for Hopkins in 1986. Once I gave him a ride to Port Authority after we left the Library, and he still refers to it because it was out of my way home. One of Richard's characteristics, which all who get to know him are aware of, is his enjoyment of repeating favorite phrases ("où sont les neiges de hier [sic]?") and recalling incidents from the past, always with the same words ("Remember when you let me into the flow of traffic?") That ride into Manhattan is one of Richard's many repeated recollections, and even very good comedians would have a hard time getting laughs from repeating the same phrases and incidents day in and day out for decades. However, Richard is far more than a very good comedian. He's a demotist comic who has managed to make his Demotic lectures at the annual meetings of the American Research Center in Egypt standing room only because of his hilarious delivery of highly technical philological discussions. Richard is unique and a treasure for the field of Egyptology. His academic prowess needs no further accolade than the list of essays in his honor that we here present.

A product of the University of Wisconsin's Classics B.A. program, Richard then worked with Professors George Hughes and Jan Johnson at the Oriental Institute of the University of Chicago from 1977 until he received his doctorate in 1988. But after he earned his M.A. in September of 1986, Richard immediately found himself in Würzburg as Prof. Karl-Theodor Zauzich's Wissenschaftlicher Assistent as he wrote his dissertation, which he completed in 1988. He continued his three-year stint as Assistent through September of 1989 after which he joined Chicago House, where Tina still works and where Richard returns each winter (except 2020–2021) to seek and study Demotic graffiti, inscriptions, ostraca, or whatever texts he can put his hungry hands on. His research and publication of the Book of Thoth, together with Prof. Zauzich, on which he has spent more than three decades, must certainly be one of Richard's best recognized academic endeavors.

In the many years that Richard and I have been colleagues at Johns Hopkins, we have been fortunate to be able to teach together as well as advise, coach, and mentor our students collaboratively. For more than twenty-five years now we have co-taught Middle Egyptian Texts in a three-hour seminar on Thursday mornings with a short break in the middle that Richard refers to as "legally mandated." We enjoy bringing our separate areas of strength to bear in considering grammatical and lexical problems, allowing the students to consider the patterns of earlier Middle Egyptian as well as those of the late texts. We have been blessed with excellent students over the years, and Richard has worked with them to sharpen their language skills, when necessary. Such excellent scholars as Katherine Davis and Marina Escolano-Poveda, to name but two of the many represented in this volume, had the benefit of Richard's patient and persistent time with texts, as did many others whom we taught. Richard is a superb teacher whose students are dedicated to him. Undergraduates frequently have written how much they love his classes—for example, his "Gods and Monsters in Ancient Egypt" always brings enrollment of one hundred or more. Here is what one student wrote about Richard's class: "Every Monday, Wednesday, and Friday I look forward to this class. Every lecture is some middle ground between history, standup comedy, and performance art (don't worry, more on the side of history). He is extremely caring, just a lovely person, and so much fun to talk with. I highly recommend taking at least one class with him, if not more!"

I hope that most of you who read this preface will already know Richard Jasnow personally, because there is no way to describe him adequately. He is in many ways a Renaissance man: he is a musician, doing classical guitar entirely for his own enjoyment, he reads constantly, enjoying biographies particularly. Indeed, his interest in the lives and careers of individuals from every walk of life is also emblematic of his interest in early Egyptologists. He not only collects books and photographs of early academics in our field, he often reaches out to find letters and biographical details about the early pioneers of the field. Richard's hero is Wilhelm Spiegelberg, but he becomes excited about learning new bits of information about any of the famous or the nearly invisible practitioners of the field.

I have been blessed with the brother that I never had, both Egyptologically and personally, in Richard Jasnow, and I know that my fellow editors, Mark Smith, Christina (Tina) Di Cerbo, Marina Escolano-Poveda, and Jill S. Waller join me in offering, together with the many authors here represented, a hearty "thank you" to Richard as a scholar and, perhaps even more, as a simply superb human being.

Preface – Mark Smith

My friendship with Richard began in the late nineteen seventies, more than forty years ago, when he and I worked together on the Chicago Demotic Dictionary. Along with other colleagues, we occupied a small office at the end of a corridor on the first floor of the Oriental Institute, where we spent our time going through Demotic texts sentence by sentence and word by word, transliterating, translating, and annotating them for eventual incorporation in that work. A portrait of Wilhelm Spiegelberg adorned one wall from which he oversaw our activities with a facial expression which we hoped was benign but, with hindsight, would probably better be described as inscrutable.

Like many of us who emerged from this Demotic crucible, Richard came away with a lifelong passion for texts written in the most cursive script ever devised by the ancient Egyptians. Since those early days in Chicago, he has gone on to great success, winning the esteem and admiration of colleagues in Egyptology and related subjects around the world. His career has led him on a peripatetic journey from Chicago to Luxor to Würzburg (with frequent return visits to each), and finally to Baltimore, where he has been based since 1995, rising through the academic ranks of Johns Hopkins University until his well-deserved appointment as Professor of Egyptology in 2004.

In seeking to describe Richard's contribution to Egyptology here, I would like to focus upon his research and scholarly publications. My co-editor Betsy Bryan has already spoken of his impact as a teacher and departmental colleague. The bibliography included elsewhere in this volume will reveal how prolific Richard has been as an author. One thing that stands out there is the breadth of subjects which he has covered in his published work, encompassing virtually every period of Egyptian history and many different types of text written in a variety of scripts. In response to questions, Richard is fond of saying "What do I know? I'm only a Demoticist." Yet a glance at his bibliography shows that this modest disclaimer should be taken with a pinch of salt. Richard's first monograph was the *editio princeps* of a hieratic wisdom text in the Brooklyn Museum, and he has published several other hieratic texts since then. As a member of the Epigraphic Survey he collaborated in producing records of the scenes and hieroglyphic inscriptions in Theban temples. He has also deciphered hieroglyphic texts on smaller objects, including some from sites outside of Egypt, for example, a Late Bronze Age clay jug discovered at Lachish. In addition, he has co-edited or contributed to volumes on Egyptian and ancient Near Eastern law and written an insightful study of humour in ancient Egypt. Not bad for a mere Demoticist.

But wide-ranging as he is, both in interests and expertise, those who know Richard well can affirm that Demotic studies remain closest to his heart. Perhaps only those who do not limit themselves to Demotic can truly love it. Richard has enriched the discipline with a remarkable number of first editions of new Demotic texts, as well as studies and notes devoted to the elucidation of previously known ones, all of the highest quality and written with a style uniquely his. Chronologically, these extend from the Persian to the Roman period and include graffiti, legal and economic documents, hymns and other religious compositions, and literary works, inscribed on ostraca, papyri, stelae, and the walls of temples and tombs.

Among all these texts, I suspect that Richard's favorite is the Book of Thoth. This composition, attested by multiple witnesses dating to the Roman period, larger or smaller pieces of which are now scattered among museums and libraries throughout the world, records a dialogue between a teacher and his disciple, designated as "one who loves knowledge." Through a series of questions, the master tests the disciple's suitability for initiation into the mysteries of priestly and scribal lore. Richard, in collaboration with Karl-Theodor Zauzich, published the *editio princeps* of this text under the title *The Ancient Egyptian Book of Thoth* in two magisterial volumes containing more than 600 pages and plates in 2005, the fruits of decades of painstaking study and research. In 2014, they published an updated translation of it designed for a nonspecialist readership, entitled *Conversations in the House of Life*. (I can still recall lengthy discussions as to which direction the figure of Thoth on the cover should face.) Richard and Zauzich published a third volume devoted to these, along with a revised transliteration and translation of the entire text and facsimiles of the papyri, in 2021. Independently, Richard has also written numerous articles and has lectured widely on different aspects of the Book of Thoth, and no doubt will continue to do so. New fragments of this fascinating composition continue to come to light. Thus, the text shows every sign of becoming a permanent fixture in his life. The Book of Thoth is not only one of the most difficult texts to have survived from ancient Egypt but one of the most important surviving monuments of ancient Egyptian thought as well. Among Richard's many other achievements, the role he has played in making this challenging work available to scholarship will rank among the highest.

The reader will note that much of the research described above is of a collaborative nature. This is another salient feature of Richard's scholarly work, the frequency and success with which he has collaborated with others, whether in the US, Canada, England, Germany, Egypt, or Japan. Richard is very much an international figure, and the fact that he is so frequently sought out as a partner in collaborative projects reflects not only the degree to which his expertise and organisational skills are valued by others, but how much pleasure his colleagues derive from working with him as well. His enthusiasm for tackling even the most difficult project is both inspirational and infectious. I myself have collaborated with Richard on more than one occasion, and I describe how much I enjoyed the experience elsewhere in this volume.

But publications are by no means the whole story. There is more to Richard than these, and more to him than just Egyptology. At a relatively early stage in our acquaintance, he mentioned to me that he was a guitarist. With characteristic modesty, he underplayed his musical ability. It was only from subsequent conversations with Richard's brother Michael that I learned the extent of his skills and the depth of his knowledge of the guitar, which he actually studied at one time with a view to having a professional career, and found out how close music's gain came to being Egyptology's loss. On one visit to Baltimore several years ago, I had a few hours to spare before going to the airport to catch my flight back to the UK. We spent them in Richard's apartment playing records by the guitar genius Charlie Christian, and it was a privilege to hear these in company with such an acute and sensitive listener.

Over the years, Richard and I have developed a habit of recommending books to each other. Whenever he reads a book which he thinks I might enjoy, he recommends it to me, and I do the same for him. The books in question have been on a wide variety of subjects, but all have one thing in common: they have nothing to do with Egyptology. The most recent book which Richard has recommended to me is *Let's Play Two* by Ron Rapoport, a biography of Ernie Banks, legendary shortstop and first baseman for the Chicago Cubs baseball team from 1953 until 1971. The title of this book was his catchphrase; such was his love for baseball that he was ready to play two games even if only one was scheduled. As I have noted above, Richard brings the same infectious enthusiasm to Egyptology, particularly the reading and translation of difficult Demotic texts. I cannot recall ever hearing him say "Let's decipher two!," but it would not surprise me if one day I do.

EGYPTOLOGICAL BIBLIOGRAPHY OF RICHARD JASNOW

Books

With K.-Th. Zauzich. *The Ancient Egyptian Book of Thoth II: Revised Transliteration and Translation, New Fragments, and Material for Future Study*. Wiesbaden: Harrassowitz, 2021.

With G. Widmer, eds. *Illuminating Osiris: Egyptological Studies in Honor of Mark Smith*. Atlanta: Lockwood, 2017.

With C. Di Cerbo, *On the Path to the Place of Rest: Demotic Graffiti Relating to the Ibis and Falcon Cult from the Spanish-Egyptian Mission at Dra Abu el-Naga (TT 11, TT12, Tomb -399-, and Environs)*. With Contributions by José M. Galán, Francisco Bosch-Puche, and Salima Ikram. Atlanta: Lockwood, 2021.

With J. G. Manning, K. Yamahana, and M. Krutzsch. *The Demotic and Hieratic Papyri in the Suzuki Collection of Tokai University*. With the assistance of Katherine E. Davis, François Gerardin, and Andrew Hogan. Atlanta: Lockwood, 2016.

With K. M. Cooney, eds. *Joyful in Thebes: Egyptological Studies in Honor of Betsy M. Bryan*. Atlanta: Lockwood, 2015.

With K.-T. Zauzich. *Conversations in the House of Life: A New Translation of the Ancient Egyptian Book of Thoth*. Wiesbaden: Harrassowitz, 2014.

With The Epigraphic Survey. *Medinet Habu IX: The Eighteenth Dynasty Temple; Part I: The Inner Sanctuaries*. Chicago: The Oriental Institute of the University of Chicago, 2009.

With K.-T. Zauzich. *The Ancient Egyptian Book of Thoth: A Demotic Discourse on Knowledge and Pendant to the Classical Hermetica*. 2 vols. Wiesbaden: Harrassowitz, 2005.

With R. Westbrook, eds. *Security for Debt in Ancient Near Eastern Law*. Leiden: Brill, 2001.

With The Epigraphic Survey. *Reliefs and Inscriptions at Luxor Temple, Volume 2: The Façade, Portals, Upper Register Scenes, Columns, Marginalia, and Statuary in the Colonnade Hall*. Chicago: The Oriental Institute of the University of Chicago, 1998.

With G. R. Hughes. *The Oriental Institute Hawara Papyri: Demotic and Greek Texts from an Egyptian Family Archive in the Fayum (Fourth to Third Century BC)*. OIP 113. Chicago: The Oriental Institute of the University of Chicago, 1997.

With The Epigraphic Survey. *Reliefs and Inscriptions at Luxor Temple, Volume 1: The Festival Procession of Opet in the Colonnade Hall*. Chicago: The Oriental Institute of the University of Chicago, 1994.

A Late Period Hieratic Wisdom Text: P. Brooklyn 47.218.135. Chicago: The Oriental Institute of the University of Chicago, 1992.

Book Chapters, Articles, and Other Contributions

2021

"A Sadly Neglected Demotic Graffito from Western Thebes (Černý-Sadek Graffito 3434)." In *Up and Down the Nile: Ägyptologische Studien für Regine Schulz*, ed. M. Ullmann, G. Pieke, F. Hoffmann, and C. Bayer, with collaboration of S. Gebhardt, 209–13. ÄAT 97. Münster: Zaphon, 2021.

2020

"Demotic Texts." In *The Oxford Handbook of Egyptology*, ed. I. Shaw and E. Bloxam, 1072–95. Oxford: Oxford University Press, 2020.

2019

"P. Tebt. Frag. 14,433+14,434: A Demotic Theological Composition on the Conflict between Re and Apophis." *Enchoria* 36 (2018/2019): 37–66.

With K.-T. Zauzich. "A Demotic Version of the Hieratic Offering Formula in P. BM EA 10209, 4/1–20 (Ostracon LACMA M.80.202.200)." *Enchoria* 36 (2018/2019): 67–94.

With C. Di Cerbo. "Building Dipinti at Medinet Habu (with an Appendix on Remains of Color Decoration in the Palace)." In *En détail – Philologie und Archäologie im Diskurs: Festschrift für Hans-Werner Fischer-Elfert* 1, ed. M. Brose, P. Dils, F. Naether, L. Popko, and D. Raue, 239–59. Berlin: de Gruyter, 2019.

2018

"A Temple Record Dealing with the Distribution of Precious Metals." In *Hieratic, Demotic and Greek Studies and Text Editions: Of Making Many Books There Is No End; Festschrift in Honour of Sven P. Vleeming*, ed. K. Donker van Heel, F. A. J. Hoogendijk, and C. J. Martin, 198–204. Leiden: Brill, 2018.

2017

"A Ptolemaic Grain Account Papyrus (P. Vienna D. 13.534)." In *Essays for the Library of Seshat: Studies Presented to Janet H. Johnson on the Occasion of Her 70th Birthday*, ed. R. Ritner, 53–62. SAOC 70. Chicago: The Oriental Institute of the University of Chicago, 2017.

"The Book of Thoth." *Religion Compass* (2017); 11:e12236. https://doi.org/10.1111/rec3.12236.

"On the Scribal Stylus as a Lance in the Book of Thoth." *GM* 251 (2017): 5–6.

With K.-T. Zauzich. "Another Praise of the Goddess Ait (O. Sommerhausen 1)." In *Illuminating Osiris: Egyptological Studies in Honor of Mark Smith*, ed. R. Jasnow and G. Widmer, 155–62. Atlanta: Lockwood, 2017.

2016

With C. Di Cerbo. "Demotic Block Notations and Mason's Marks / Assembly Marks from the Small Temple of Medinet Habu." In *Sapientia Felicitas: Festschrift für Günter Vittmann zum 29. Februar 2016*, ed. S. L. Lippert, M. Schentuleit, and M. A. Stadler, 89–105. Montpellier: Université Paul Valéry, 2016.

"Between Two Waters: The Book of Thoth and the Problem of Greco-Egyptian Interaction." In *Greco-Egyptian Interactions: Literature, Translation, and Culture, 500 BCE–300 CE*, ed. I. Rutherford, 317–56. Oxford: Oxford University Press, 2016.

2015

"'From Alexandria to Rakotis': Progress, Prospects and Problems in the Study of Greco-Egyptian Literary Interaction." In *Proceedings of the Tenth International Congress of Egyptologists: University of the Aegean, Rhodes, 22–29 May 2008*, ed. P. Kousoulis and N. Lazaridis, 2:1363–93. Leuven: Peeters, 2015.

With M. Smith. "New Fragments of the Demotic Mut Text in Copenhagen and Florence." In *Joyful in Thebes: Egyptological Studies in Honor of Betsy M. Bryan*, ed. R. Jasnow and K. M. Cooney, 239–82. Atlanta: Lockwood, 2015.

2014

"P. Vienna D 13766: A Fragmentary Demotic Wisdom Text." In *Gehilfe des Thot: Festschrift für Karl-Theodor Zauzich zu seinem 75. Geburtstag*, ed. S. L. Lippert and M. A. Stadler, 55–60. Wiesbaden: Harrassowitz, 2014.

2013

" Greco-Roman Period Demotic Texts from the Faiyum and Their Relationship to *The Book of the Faiyum*." In *Egypt's Mysterious Book of the Faiyum*, ed. H. Beinlich, R. Schulz, and A. Wieczorek, 79–87. Dettelbach: Röll, 2013.

With C. Di Cerbo. "Two Late New Kingdom or Early Third Intermediate Period Hieratic Graffiti in the Temple of Khonsu at Karnak." *JARCE* 49 (2013): 33–44.

2012

"Birds and Bird Imagery in the Book of Thoth." In *Between Heaven and Earth: Birds in Ancient Egypt*, ed. R. Bailleul-LeSuer, 71–76. Chicago: 2012.

2011

With M. Smith. "'As for Those Who Have Called Me Evil, Mut Will Call Them Evil': Orgiastic Cultic Behavior and Its Critics in Ancient Egypt (PSI Inv. [provv.] D 114a + PSI Inv. 3056 verso)." *Enchoria* 32 (2010/2011): 9–53.

"'Caught in the Web of Words': Remarks on the Imagery of Writing and Hieroglyphs in the Book of Thoth." *JARCE* 47 (2011): 297–317.

With C. Di Cerbo. "Recent Documentation of Medinet Habu Graffiti by the Epigraphic Survey." In *Perspectives on Ptolemaic Thebes: Papers from the Theban Workshop 2006*, ed. P. F. Dorman and B. M. Bryan, 35–51. Chicago: The Oriental Institute of the University of Chicago, 2011.

2010

"On Sothis and the So-Called Clepsydra (?) in the Book of Thoth (B02, 3/16 - 4/11)." In *Honi soit qui mal y pense: Studien zum pharaonischen, griechisch-römischen und spätantiken Ägypten zu Ehren von Heinz-Josef Thissen*, ed. H. Knuf, C. Leitz, and D. von Recklinghausen, 237–43. Leuven: Brill, 2010.

2009

With M.-A. Pouls Wegner. "Demotic Ostraca from North Abydos." *Enchoria* 30 (2009): 21–52.

2008

"A Demotic Stela from the First Court of Luxor Temple." In *Servant of Mut: Studies in Honor of Richard A. Fazzini*, ed. S. H. D'Auria, 130–33. Leiden: Brill, 2008.

"A Note on the Epithet of Thoth, *hbhb št3.w*, 'He-Who-Traverses-Mysteries,' in the Book of Thoth." *GM* 216 (2008): 101–2.

2007

"'Through Demotic Eyes': On Style and Description in Demotic Narratives." in *The Archaeology and Art of Ancient Egypt: Essays in Honor of David B. O'Connor*, ed. Z. A. Hawass and J. E. Richards, 1:433–48. Cairo: Conseil Suprême des Antiquités de l'Égypte, 2007.

2004

"The Dispute in the Hawara Necropolis Reopened (P. Cairo 50127)." In *Res severa verum gaudium: Festschrift für Karl-Theodor Zauzich zum 65. Geburtstag am 8. Juni 2004*, ed. F. Hoffmann and H. J. Thissen, 261–81. Leuven: Peeters, 2004.

With P. Magrill and P. Kyle McCarter Jr. "Section C: A Newly Discovered Egyptian Inscription." In *The Renewed Archaeological Excavations at Lachish (1973–1994)*, ed. D. Ussishkin, 3:1618–25. Tel Aviv: Emery and Claire Yass Publications in Archaeology, 2004.

2003

"Response to J. Baines." In *Egyptology at the Dawn of the Twenty-First Century: Proceedings of the Eighth International Congress of Egyptologists, Cairo, 2000*, ed. Z. Hawass and L. Pinch Brock, 3:22–37. Cairo: The American University of Cairo, 2003.

"Egypt: Old Kingdom and First Intermediate Period." In *A History of Ancient Near Eastern Law*, ed. R. Westbrook, 1:93–140. Leiden: Brill, 2003.

"Egypt: Middle Kingdom and Second Intermediate Period." In *A History of Ancient Near Eastern Law*, ed. R. Westbrook, 1:255–88. Leiden: Brill, 2003.

"Egypt: New Kingdom." In *A History of Ancient Near Eastern Law*, ed. R. Westbrook, 1:289–359. Leiden: Brill, 2003.

"Egypt: Third Intermediate Period." In *A History of Ancient Near Eastern Law*, ed. R. Westbrook, 2:777–818. Leiden: Brill, 2003.

2002

"Recent Trends and Advances in the Study of Late Period Egyptian Literature." *JARCE* 39 (2002): 207–16.

2001

"'And Pharaoh Laughed…': Reflections on Humor in Setne 1 and Late Period Egyptian Literature." *Enchoria* 27

(2001): 62–81.

"Pre-Demotic Pharaonic Sources." In *Security for Debt in Ancient Near Eastern Law*, ed. R. Westbrook and R. Jasnow, 35–43. Leiden: Brill, 2001.

"The Name *Pꜣ-wr-ḏl* in P. Louvre 2414." *Enchoria* 27 (2001): 202–3.

1999

"Remarks on Continuity of Egyptian Literary Tradition." In *Gold of Praise: Studies on Ancient Egypt in Honor of Edward F. Wente*, ed. E. Teeter and J. A. Larson, 193–210. Chicago: The Oriental Institute of the University of Chicago, 1999.

1998

With K.-T. Zauzich. "A Book of Thoth?" In *Proceedings of the Seventh International Congress of Egyptologists, Cambridge, 3–9 September 1995*, ed. C. J. Eyre, 607–18. Leuven: Peeters, 1998.

1997

"A Demotic Omen Text? (P. BM 10238)." In *Essays on Ancient Egypt in Honour of Herman te Velde*, ed. J. van Dijk, 207–18. Groningen: Styx, 1997.

"The Greek Alexander Romance and Demotic Egyptian Literature." *JNES* 56 (1997): 95–103.

1996

"A Note on Pharaoh *Sꜣ-sbk* in Papyrus Vandier." *Enchoria* 23 (1996): 179.

With C. Di Cerbo. "Five Persian Period Demotic and Hieroglyphic Graffiti from the Site of Apa Tyrannos at Armant." *Enchoria* 23 (1996): 32–38.

1994

"A Lexicographical Note on the Medinet Habu Inscription of Year 11." *JEA* 80 (1994): 201–2.

"The Hieratic Wooden Tablet Varille." In *For His Ka: Essays Offered in Memory of Klaus Baer*, ed. D. P. Silverman, 99–112. Chicago: The Oriental Institute of the University of Chicago, 1994.

1993

With Günter Vittmann. "An Abnormal Hieratic Letter to the Dead (P. Brooklyn 37.1799 E)." *Enchoria* 19–20 (1992–1993): 23–43.

"Isis, the-Mistress-of-the-Road." *Enchoria* 19–20 (1992–1993): 219.

"*sp.t* = 'Statue-Base' in Demotic." *Enchoria* 19–20 (1992–1993): 220.

With J. C. Darnell. "On the Moabite Inscriptions of Ramesses II at Luxor Temple." *JNES* 52 (1993): 263–74.

1991

"A Demotic Wisdom Papyrus in the Ashmolean Museum (P. Ashm. 1984.77 Verso)." *Enchoria* 18 (1991): 43–54.

1990

"Demotic Texts from the Carnegie Museum of Natural History." *Enchoria* 17 (1990): 89–96.

1988

With R. A. Fazzini. "Demotic Ostraca from the Mut Precinct in Karnak." *Enchoria* 16 (1988): 23–48.

1987

"Serpot 9/8 = Onkhsheshonqy 11/8?." *Enchoria* 15 (1987): 203.

1986

"A Note on *ꜥš-sḥn*." *GM* 92 (1986): 65–67.

1985

"A Misunderstood Group in P. Spiegelberg." *Enchoria* 13 (1985): 211.

1984

"Demotic Graffiti from Western Thebes." In *Grammata demotika: Festschrift für Erich Lüddeckens zum 15. Juni 1983*, ed. H.-J. Thissen and K.-T. Zauzich, 87–105. Würzburg: Gisela Zauzich Verlag, 1984.

"Three Notes on Demotic Lexicography." *Enchoria* 12 (1984): 7–13.

1983

"Evidence for the Deification of Tuthmosis III in the Ptolemaic Period." *GM* 64 (1983): 33–34.

1982

"Two Demotic Papyri in the Oriental Institute." *Enchoria* 11 (1982): 17–22.

"An Unrecognized Parallel in Two Demotic Wisdom Texts." *Enchoria* 11 (1982): 111.

"The Fourth Lower Egyptian Nome in Demotic." *Enchoria* 11 (1982): 112.

1981–1982

"Recording the Graffiti of Western Thebes." *OIAR* (1981–1982): 25–30.

Book Reviews

The Narrative Literature from the Tebtunis Temple Library, by Kim Ryholt. *Enchoria* 36 (2018–2019): 221–25.

Soknopaiou Nesos Project, I (2003–2009), edited by M. Capasso and P. Davoli. Bryn Mawr Classical Review, http://bmcr.brynmawr.edu/2013/2013-09-38.html

Einführung in die altägyptische Rechtsgeschichte, by S. Lippert. *Enchoria* 32 (2010–2011): 149–53.

Verzeichnis der orientalischen Handschriften in Deutschland. Band XIX.4. *Ägyptische Handschriften*, Teil 4, by H.-W. Fischer-Elfert and G. Burkard. *JNES* 60 (2002): 54–55.

The Nile Mosaic Of Palestrina: Early Evidence of Egyptian Religion in Italy, by P. G. P. Meyboom. *Journal of the American Oriental Society* 119 (1999): 79–81.

The Liturgy of Opening the Mouth for Breathing, by M. Smith. *Enchoria* 24 (1997/98): 178–85.

The Sage in Israel and the Ancient Near East, edited by J. G. Gammie and L. G. Perdue. *JNES* 55 (1996): 215–16.

Literarische Ostraka der Ramessidenzeit in Übersetzung. By H.-W. Fischer-Elfert. *JAOS* 111(1991): 832–33.

Le Mythe de l'Oeil du Soleil, by F. de Cenival, *Enchoria* 18 (1991): 205–15.

Grabung in Asasif 1963–1970. Band III. Die Papyrusfunde, by G. Burkard. *Enchoria* 17 (1990): 169–71.

Late Egyptian Wisdom Literature in the International Context, by M. Lichtheim. *Bibliotheca Orientalis* 44 (1987): cols. 103–9.

Les Graffites du Gebel Teir, by D. Devauchelle and G. Wagner. *Enchoria* 14 (1986): 171–73.

Ostraca démotiques du musée du Louvre, Tome I: reçus, by D. Devauchelle. *Serapis* 8 (1985): 53–54.

From the Records of a Priestly Family from Memphis, by E. A. E. Reymond. *JAOS* 105 (1985): 339–41.

Greek and Demotic Texts from the Zenon Archive, by P. W. Pestman. *JEA* 71 (1985) *Reviews Supplement*, p. 71.

Ostraca démotiques du Musée du Louvre, by D. Devauchelle. *Serapis* 9 (1984–85): 53–54.

Cahiers de Recherches de l'Institut de Papyrologie et d'Egyptologie de Lille 6 (1981). *JNES* 45 (1986): 305–7.

List of Figures

Shirley

Stadler

Tait

Vittmann

ABBREVIATIONS

GENERAL

///	indicates damage to the text
AbB	Altbabylonische Briefe
Abb.	Abbildung, (illustration)
Abt.	Abteilung
Akk	Akkadian
ÄMUL	Ägyptisches Museum – Georg Steindorff – der Universität Leipzig
ANAsh Mus	Antiquities section, Ashmolean Museum
Anm.	Anmerkung
Arb	Arabic
Arm	Aramaic
AUC	The American University in Cairo
BCE	Before Common Era
BD	Book of the Dead
Bd.	(German) Band, (volume)
BM	British Museum, London
BM EA	British Museum, Egyptian Antiquities section
bzw.	beziehungsweise
ca.	circa, approximately
Cat.	catalog
CBS	University of Pennsylvania Museum of Archaeology and Anthropology, catalog of the Babylonian section
CDLI	Cuneiform Digital Library Initiative
CE	Common Era
CES RAS	Center for Egyptological Studies of the Russian Academy of Sciences
cf.	confer, compare
Chr	Book of Chronicles
cm	centimeter(s)
CNI	Carsten Niebuhr Institute
col(s).	column(s)
CT	Coffin Text
d.h.	das heißt
DAAD	Deutscher Akademischer Austauschdienst
DAHT	Demotic and Abnormal Hieratic Texts
DeM	Deir el Medina
Dem	Demotic
ders.	derselbe
det.	determinative
Deut	book of Deuteronomy

dies.	dieselbe
diss.	dissertation
DMP	Demotic Magical Papyri
Dyn.	Dynasty
e.g.	exempli gratia
ECM	Eton College Myers
ed.	edition; edited by
EEF	Egypt Exploration Fund, London
EES	Egypt Exploration Society, London
EM	(Egypt Exploration Society) Excavation Memoir
EU	Egyptologische Uitgaven
esp.	especially
et al.	et alii
etc.	et cetera, and so forth
ex.	example
Exod	book of Exodus
Ezek	book of Ezekiel
fasc.	fascicle
fem.	feminine
ff.	following
fig(s).	figure(s)
FN	footnote. Also fn. or Fn. (Fußnote).
frag(s).	fragment(s)
Fs.	Festschrift
ggf.	gegebenenfalls
GR	Greco-Roman (period)
Hbw	Hebrew
HALMA	Histoire, Archéologie et Littérature des Mondes Anciens
Hg(g.)	Herausgeber (singular and plural)
HO	Hieratic Ostracon
HPBM	Hieratic Papyri in the British Museum
i.e.	id est
i.S.v.	im Sinne von
IFAO	Institut français d'archéologie orientale (Cairo)
ined.	ineditus, unpublished
insbes.	insbesondere
inv.	inventory
JE	Journal d'Entrée (Cairo Museum)
JHU	Johns Hopkins University
JHUAM	Johns Hopkins University Archaeological Museum
JPS	Jewish Publication Society
Kol.	Kolumne
KV	Valley of the Kings
l(l).	line(s)
Lev	book of Leviticus
lit.	literally

LXX	Septuagint
m	meter
m.	masculine
m.E.	meines Erachtens
MK	Middle Kingdom (period)
MMA	Metropolitan Museum of Art
MN	Magical Names
MS	manuscript
n(n).	note(s)
NATN	Neo-Sumerian Archival Texts Primarily from Nippur in the University Museum, The Oriental Institute and the Iraq Museum
NCBT	Newell Collections of Babylonian Tablets
Neh	book of Nehemiah
NK	New Kingdom (period)
NN	nomen nescio, name unknown
no(s).	number(s)
Nr.	Nummer
Num	book of Numbers
n(s).	number(s)
NWS	Northwest Semitic
O.	ostracon
o.J.	ohne Jahr
OAD	Oracular Amuletic Decrees
ODeM	Ostraca, Deir el Medina
ODL	Ostraca démotiques du Musée du Louvre
OC	Old Coptic
OI	Oriental Institute, Chicago
OIM	Oriental Institute Museum, Chicago
OK	Old Kingdom
Oxy.	Oxyrhynchus
p(p).	page(s)
P.	Papyrus (e.g., P. Loeb = Papyrus Loeb).
pers. comm.	personal communication
PGM	Papyri Graecae Magicae (Graeco-Egyptian magical papyri)
PhD	Doctor of Philosophy
PIFAO	Publications de l'Institut français d'archéologie orientale du Caire (Cairo)
pl(s).	plate(s)
PT	Pyramid Texts
Ptol.	Ptolemaic / Ptolemy
PTT	Private Tombs at Thebes
rev.	revised
RSV	Revised Standard Version (of the Bible)
rt./ro.	recto
S.	Seite
S.	Stela
scil.	scilicet, namely

s.n.	sine numero, without number
s.u.	siehe unten
s.v.	*sub verbo*, under the word
SBL	Society of Biblical Literature, Atlanta
SMDAN	Spanish Mission in Dra Abu el-Naga
SOV	Subject-Object-Verb; word order in a sentence
s.v.	sub voce
Syr	Syriac
Tab.	Tabelle
Taf.	Tafel(n) (German)
Tebt.	Tebtunis
TIP	Third Intermediate period
trans.	translated by
TT	Theban Tomb
u.a.	unter anderem/n; und andere
UCL	University College London
Ugr	Ugaritic
UMR	Unité Mixte de Recherche
Ur III	Third Dynasty of Ur, ca. 2112–2004 BCE
Urk.	Urkunden
v.	
var.	variant
vel sim.	vel similia, or the like
vgl.	vergleiche
vol.	volume
vs./vo.	verso
VSO	Verb-Subject-Object; word order in a sentence
WS	West Semitic
z.B.	zum Beispiel
z.T.	zum Teil

BIBLIOGRAPHIC

ÄA	Ägyptologische Abhandlungen. Wiesbaden, 1960–.
ÄAT	Ägypten und Altes Testament. Wiesbaden, 1979–.
AAWL	Abhandlungen der Sächsischen Akademie der Wissenschaften zu Leipzig, Philologisch-Historische Klasse. Leipzig, Stuttgart, 1915–.
ABD	Freedman, David N., ed. *The Anchor Bible Dictionary*. 6 vols. New York: Doubleday, 1992.
AcOr	*Acta Orientalia*
AegLeod	Aegyptiaca Leodiensia. Liège, 1987–.
AEO	Gardiner, Alan H. *Ancient Egyptian Onomastica*. 3 vols. Oxford: Oxford University Press, 1947.
ÄF	Ägyptologische Forschungen. Glückstadt, Hamburg, New York, 1936–.
AfO	*Archiv für Orientforschung*
ÄgLev	*Ägypten und Levante*
AH	Aegyptiaca Helvetica. Geneva, then Basel, 1974–.

AHAW Phil.-hist. Kl. Abhandlungen der Heidelberger Akademie der Wissenschaften. Phil-hist. Klasse, Heidelberg, 1913–.
AHw *Akkadisches Handwörterbuch.* Wiesbaden, 1959–1981.
AMun *Magazin für die Freunde ägyptischer Museen und Sammlungen, Berlin*
AnnEPHE Ve sect. Annuaire de l'École pratique des hautes études, section des sciences religieuses. Paris, 1964–.
AOAT Alter Orient und Altes Testament. Kevelaer, Neukirchen-Vluyn, Münster, 1969–.
AoF *Altorientalische Forschungen*
ÄOP Ägyptische und Orientalische Papyri und Handschriften des Ägyptischen Museums und Papyrussammlung Berlin, 2012–.
AOS American Oriental Series. New Haven, 1925–.
APAW Abhandlungen der Preußischen Akademie der Wissenschaften. Berlin, 1804–1907.
APF *Archiv für Papyrusforschung und verwandte Gebiete*
APFB Archiv für Papyrusforschung und verwandte Gebiete Beiheft. Leipzig, 1901–.
ArOr *Archiv Orientální*
ARG *Archiv für Religionsgeschichte*
ASAE *Annales du Service des Antiquités de l'Égypte*
ASE Archaeological Survey of Egypt. London, 1893–.
AuOr *Aula Orientalis*
AV Archäologische Veröffentlichungen/ Deutsches Archäologisches Institut, Abteilung Kairo. Berlin, Mainz am Rhein, 1970–.
BA *Biblical Archaeologist*
BaM *Baghdader Mitteilungen*
BAR-IS British Archaeological Reports. International Series. Oxford, 1974–.
BAR-SS British Archaeological Reports Supplementary Series. Oxford, 1975–1978.
BASOR *Bulletin of the American Schools of Oriental Research*
BASP *Bulletin of the American Society of Papyrologists*
BDB Brown, Francis, S. R. Driver, and Charles A. Briggs. *A Hebrew and English Lexicon of the Old Testament with an Appendix Containing the Biblical Aramaic Based on the Lexicon of William Gesenius as Translated by Edward Robinson.* Oxford: Clarendon, 1907.
BdÉ Bibliothèque d'étude. Cairo, 1908–.
BES Brown Egyptological Studies. Oxford/Providence, 1954–.
BFA *Bulletin of the Faculty of Arts*
BGU Berliner griechische Urkunden. Berlin, 1895–.
BiAe Bibliotheca Aegyptiaca. Brussels, 1932–.
BICS *Bulletin of the Institute of Classical Studies*
BIE *Bulletin de l'Institut égyptien* (later *Bulletin de l'Institut d'Égypte*). Cairo, 1859–1950.
BiEtud Bibliothèque d'étude. Cairo, 1908–.
BIFAO *Bulletin de l'Institut français d'archéologie orientale*
BiGen Bibliothèque générale. Cairo, 1959–.
BiOr *Bibliotheca Orientalis*
BMMA *Bulletin of the Metropolitan Museum of Art*
BMOP British Museum Occasional Papers. London, 1978–.
BMSAES British Museum Studies in Ancient Egypt and Sudan. London, 2002–.
BSAE British School of Archaeology in Egypt. London, 1905–1953.
BSEG *Bulletin de la Société d'Égyptologie, Genève*
BSFE *Bulletin de la Société française d'égyptologie*

BZÄS Beiträge zur Zeitschrift für Ägyptische Sprache und Altertumskunde. Berlin/Leipzig, 2013–.
CA Colloquium Africanum: Beiträge zur Interdisziplinären Afrikaforschung. Köln, 1994–.
CAD Gelb, Ignace J., et al., eds. *The Assyrian Dictionary of the Oriental Institute of the University of Chicago*. 21 vols. Chicago: The Oriental Institute of the University of Chicago, 1956–2010.
CAENL Contributions to the Archaeology of Egypt, Nubia and the Levant, 2012–.
CANE Sasson, Jack, ed. *Civilizations of the Ancient Near East*. New York: Scribner, 1995.
CASAE Cahiers. Suppléments aux ASAE. Cairo, 1946–.
CCdE *Cahiers Caribéens d'Égyptologie*
CD Crum, Walter E. *A Coptic Dictionary*. Oxford: Clarendon, 1939.
CDA *Concise Dictionary of Akkadian*. Wiesbaden: Harrassowitz, 2000–.
CDD Johnson, Janet H., ed. *The Demotic Dictionary of the Oriental Institute of the University of Chicago*. 2001–. https://oi.uchicago.edu/research/publications/demotic-dictionary-oriental-institute-university-chicago
CdÉ *Chronique d'Égypte. Bulletin périodique de la Fondation Égyptologique Reine Élisabeth*
CDLI Cuneiform Digital Library Iniative. https://cdli.ox.ac.uk/wiki/doku.php?id=start
CDPBM Catalogue of Demotic Papyri in the British Museum. London, 1939–.
CED Černý, Jaroslav. *Coptic Etymological Dictionary*. Cambridge: Cambridge University Press, 1976.
CENiM Cahiers de l'Égypte Nilotique et Méditerranéenne. Montpellier, 2008.
CG Catalogue Général des Antiquités Égyptiennes du Musée du Caire. Cairo, 1901–.
CHANE Culture and History of the Ancient Near East. Leiden, 2000–.
ChronÉg *Chronique d'Égypte. Bulletin périodique de la Fondation Égyptologique Reine Élisabeth*
CLE Frédéric Colin. *Les Libyens en Egypte*. Université Libre de Bruxelles, 1996.
CNIP The Carsten Niebuhr Institute of Ancient Near Eastern Studies. Publications. Copenhagen, 1986–.
CRIPEL *Cahiers de Recherches de l'Institut de Papyrologie et d'Égyptologie de Lille*
CUSAS Cornell University Studies in Assyriology and Sumerology. Bethesda, 2008–.
DCH Clines, David J. A. *The Dictionary of Classical Hebrew*. Sheffield: Sheffield Academic Press, 2001.
DDD Lippert, Sandra, and Maren Schentuleit. *Demotische Dokumente aus Dime*. 3 vols. Wiesbaden: Harrassowitz, 2006–2010.
DemNb Lüddeckens, Erich, et al. *Demotisches Namenbuch*. Wiesbaden: Reichert, 1980–2000.
DemStud Demotische Studien. Leipzig: Hinrichs, 1901–1928. Continued, Sommerhausen: Gisela Zauzich Verlag, 1988–.
DFIFAO Documents de fouilles de l'Institut français d'archéologie orientale. Cairo, 1934–.
DG Erichsen, Wolja. *Demotisches Glossar*. Copenhagen: Munksgaard, 1954.
DGE Gangutia Elícegui, Elvira, and Francisco Rodríguez Adrados. *Diccionario Griego-español*. Madrid: Consejo Superior de Investigaciones Científicas, Instituto "Antonio de Nebrija," 1980.
Diosc. Dioscorides Pedanius. *De Materia Medica*.
DÖAWW Denkschrift der Österreichischen Akademie der Wissenschaften in Wien. Vienna, 1850–.
DPAA Dissertazioni della Pontificia Accademia romana di archeologia. Rome, 1821–1921.
DPB Spiegelberg, Wilhelm. *Demotische Papyrus aus den Königlichen Museen zu Berlin*. Leipzig: Giesecke and Devrient, 1902.
Edfou M. de Rochemonteix, continued by É. Chassinat, continued by S. Cauville and D. Devauchelle, *Le Temple d'Edfou*. 14 vols. Cairo: IFAO, 1897–.
Edfou I M. de Rochemonteix, continued by É. Chassinat, continued by S. Cauville and D. Devauchelle, *Le Temple d'Edfou*, vol. 1. 2nd ed. Cairo: IFAO, 1984.
EA Egyptian Archaeology, The Bulletin of the Egypt Exploration Society. London, 1991–.

EA	Rainey, Anson F. *The El-Amarna Correspondence: A New Edition of the Cuneiform Letters from the Site of El-Amarna Based on Collations of All Extant Tablets.* Handbook of Oriental Studies Vol. 110/1–2. Edited by William Schniedewind and Zipora Cochavi-Rainey. Leiden: Brill, 2015.
EES EM	Egypt Exploration Society Excavation Memoirs. London, 1885–.
EES GRM	Egypt Exploration Society Graeco-Roman Memoirs. London, 1922–.
EES TEM	Egypt Exploration Society Texts from Excavations, Memoirs. London, 1975–2011.
EI	*Eretz Israel: Archaeological, Historical and Geographical Studies*
Enchoria	*Enchoria: Zeitschrift für Demotistik und Koptologie*
EPRO	Études préliminaires aux religions orientales dans l'empire romain, Leiden, 1961–1992.
EQÄ	Einführungen und Quellentexte zur Ägyptologie. Münster, 2003–.
Esna	Sauneron, Serge. *Le Temple d'Esna.* 8 vols. IFAO. Cairo, 1959–1982.
EVO	*Egitto e Vicino Oriente*
FAO	Freiburger Altorientalische Studien. Freiburg, 1975–.
FIFAO	Fouilles de l'Institut français d'archéologie orientale du Caire. Cairo, 1921–.
FolOr	*Folia Orientalia*
G&T	Griffith, F. L., and H. Thompson. *The Demotic Magical Papyrus of London and Leiden.* Vols. 1–3. London: H. Grevel and Co., 1904, 1905, 1909.
GAG	Soden, Wolfram von. *Grundriss der akkadischen Grammatik.* Rome: Pontificium Institutum Biblicum, 1952.
Gardiner	Gardiner, Alan H. *Egyptian Grammar: Being an Introduction to the Study of Hieroglyphs.* Oxford: Oxford University Press, 1950.
Gauthier, *DG*	Gauthier, Henri. *Dictionnaire des noms géographiques contenus dans les textes hiéroglyphiques.* 7 vols. Cairo: IFAO, 1925–1931.
GHP Egyptology	Golden House Publications Egyptology. London, 2004–.
GM	*Göttinger Miszellen: Beiträge zur ägyptologischen Diskussion*
GOF	Göttinger Orientforschungen (IV. Reihe: Ägypten), Göttingen, 1973–.
HÄB	Hildesheimer ägyptologische Beiträge. Hildesheim, 1976–.
HALOT	Koehler, Ludwig, Walter Baumgartner, and Johann J. Stamm. *The Hebrew and Aramaic Lexicon of the Old Testament.* Trans. and ed. under the supervision of Mervyn E. J. Richardson. 4 vols. Leiden: Brill, 1994–1999.
HAT	Handschriften des altägyptischen Totenbuches. Wiesbaden, 1995–.
HdO	Handbuch der Orientalistik, erste Abteilung: Der Nahe und Mittlere Osten. Leiden, 1952–.
HEMGR	Hautes Études du monde gréco-romain. Genève, 1965–.
HES	Harvard Egyptological Studies. Leiden and Boston, 2015–.
Holladay	Holladay, William L. *A Concise Hebrew and Aramaic Lexicon of the Old Testament.* Leiden: Brill, 1971.
HSAO	Heidelberger Studien zum Alten Orient. Heidelberg, 1988–.
HSS	Harvard Semitic Studies. Winona Lake, 1976–.
HUCA	*Hebrew Union College Annual*
IBAES	Internet-Beiträge zur Ägyptologie und Sudanarchäologie. Berlin, London, 1998–.
IPN	Noth, Martin. *Die israelitischen Personennamen im Rahmen der gemeinsemitischen Namengebung.* Stuttgart: Kohlhammer, 1928.
JAC	*Journal of Ancient Civilizations*
JAEI	*Journal of Ancient Egyptian Interconnections*
JANER	*Journal of Ancient Near Eastern Religion*
JANES	*Journal of Ancient Near Eastern Studies*

JAOS	*Journal of the American Oriental Society*
JAR	*Journal of Archaeological Research*
JARCE	*Journal of the American Research Center in Egypt*
JBL	*Journal of Biblical Literature*
JCS	*Journal of Cuneiform Studies*
JCSSup	Journal of Cuneiform Studies Supplemental Series
JEA	*Journal of Egyptian Archaeology*
JEOL	*Jaarbericht Ex Oriente Lux*
JHUSA	The Johns Hopkins University Studies in Archaeology. Baltimore, 1924–1950.
JJP	*Journal of Juristic Papyrology*
JNES	*Journal of Near Eastern Studies*
JSSEA	*Journal of the Society for the Study of Egyptian Antiquities*
KÄT	Kleine ägyptische Texte. Wiesbaden, 1969–.
KB[1]	Koehler, Ludwig, and Walter Baumgartner. *Lexicon in Veteris Testamenti Libros*. Leiden: Brill, 1951.
KB[3]	Koehler, Ludwig, and Walter Baumgartner. *Hebräisches und Aramäisches Lexikon zum Alten Testament*. 3rd ed. Leiden: Brill, 1974.
KHw	Westendorf, Wolfhart. *Koptisches Handwörterbuch*. Heidelberg: Winter, 1977.
KRI	Kitchen, Kenneth A. *Ramesside Inscriptions: Historical and Biographical*. 8 vols. Oxford: Blackwell, 1968–1999.
KTU	Dietrich, Manfried, Oswald Loretz, and Joaquín Sanmartín, eds. Die keilalphabetischen Texte aus Ugarit. Münster: Ugarit-Verlag, 2013.
LÄ	Helck, Wolfgang, Eberhard Otto, and Wolfhart Westendorf, eds., *Lexikon der Ägyptologie*. 7 vols. Wiesbaden: Harrassowitz, 1972–1992.
LD	Lepsius, Richard. *Denkmäler aus Ägypten und Äthiopien*. 12 vols. Berlin: Nicolai, 1849–1856.
LGG	Leitz, Christian, et al., eds. *Lexikon der ägyptischen Götter und Götterbezeichnungen*. 8 vols. Orientalia Lovaniensia Analecta 110–116 and 129. Leuven: Peeters, 2002–2003.
LingAeg	*Lingua Aegyptia*
LingAeg SM	Lingua Aegyptia Studia Monographica. Hamburg, Göttingen, 1994–.
LSJ	Liddell, Henry George, and Robert Scott. *A Greek-English Lexicon*. Oxford: Oxford University Press, 1843.
Lucentum	Lucentum: Anales de la Universidad de Alicante; Prehistoria, Arqueología e Historia Antigua. Alicante, 1982–.
MBPR	Münchner Beiträge zur Papyrusforschung und antiken Rechtsgeschichte. Munich, 1915–.
MDAIK	Mitteilungen des Deutschen Archäologischen Instituts, Abteilung Kairo. Mainz/Cairo/Berlin/Wiesbaden, 1930–.
MEEF	Memoir of the Egyptian Exploration Fund. London, 1885–1936.
MIFAO	Mémoires publiés par les membres de l'Institut français d'archéologie orientale du Caire. Paris, Cairo, 1902–.
MIO	Mitteilungen des Instituts für Orientforschung der deutschen Akademie der Wissenschaften zu Berlin. Berlin, 1953–.
MMAF	Mémoires publiés par les membres de la Mission archéologique française au Caire. Cairo, 1889–.
MMJ	*Metropolitan Museum Journal*
Möller	Möller, Georg. *Hieratische Paläographie: Die ägyptische Buchschrift in ihrer Entwicklung von der fünften Dynastie bis zur römischen Kaiserzeit*. 3 vols. Leipzig: Hinrichs, 1909–1912.

MPER NS	Mitteilungen aus der Papyrussammlung der Österreichischen Nationalbibliothek, Neue Serie. Vienna, 1932–.
MVCAE	Material and Visual Culture of Ancient Egypt. Atlanta, 2015–.
NABU	*Nouvelles Assyriologiques Brèves et Utilitaires*
NAC	Numismatica e antichità classiche: quaderni ticinesi. Lugano, 1972–.
NATN	Owen, David I. *Neo-Sumerian Archival Texts Primarily from Nippur in the University Museum, The Oriental Institute and the Iraq Museum.* Winona Lake, IN: Eisenbrauns, 1982.
NEA	*Near Eastern Archaeology*
NeHeT	Revue numérique d'Égyptologie. Paris, 2014–.
NIDB	Sakenfeld, Katherine Doob, ed. *The New Interpreter's Dictionary of the Bible.* Nashville: Abingdon, 2006–2009.
OBO	Orbis Biblicus et Orientalis. Fribourg, Göttingen, 1973–.
OIMP	Oriental Institute Museum Publications. Chicago, 1941–.
OIP	Oriental Institute Publications. Chicago, 1924–.
OIS	Oriental Institute Seminars. Chicago, 2004–.
OLA	Orientalia Lovaniensia Analecta. Leuven, 1975–.
OLP	Orientalia Lovaniensia Periodica. Leuven, 1970–
OMRO	Oudheidkundige mededelingen uit het Rijksmuseum van Oudheden te Leiden. Leiden, 1907–.
Or	*Orientalia*
ORA	Orientalische Religionen in der Antike. Tübingen, 2009–.
OrAnt	*Oriens Antiquus*
OrSuec	*Orientalia Suecana*
PALMA	Papers on Archaeology of the Leiden Museum of Antiquities. Turnhout, 2005–.
PapBrux	Papyrologica Bruxellensia. Brussels, 1962–.
PdÄ	Probleme der Ägyptologie. Leiden, 1953–.
PEFA	The Palestine Exploration Fund Annual. Leeds, 1911–.
PEQ	*Palestine Exploration Quarterly*
PLB	Papyrologica Lugduno-Batava. Leiden, 1941–.
PM I.1	Porter, Bertha, and Rosalind L. B. Moss. *Topographical Bibliography of Ancient Egyptian Hieroglyphic Texts, Reliefs, and Paintings.* Vol. 1: *The Theban Necropolis. Part 1: Private Tombs.* 2nd ed. Oxford, 1960.
PM I.2	Porter, Bertha, and Rosalind L. B. Moss. *Topographical Bibliography of Ancient Egyptian Hieroglyphic Texts, Reliefs, and Paintings.* Vol. 1: *The Theban Necropolis. Part 2: Royal Tombs and Smaller Cemeteries.* 2nd ed. Oxford, 1964.
PM II.1	Porter, Bertha, and Rosalind L. B. Moss, assisted by E. Burney. *Topographical Bibliography of Ancient Egyptian Hieroglyphic Texts, Reliefs, and Paintings.* Vol. 2: *Theban Temples.* 2nd ed., rev. and augmented. Oxford, 1972.
PM III.1	Porter, Bertha, and Rosalind L. B. Moss, assisted by E. Burney. *Topographical Bibliography of Ancient Egyptian Hieroglyphic Texts, Reliefs, and Paintings.* Vol. 3: *Memphis. Part 1: Abu Rawash to Abusir.* 2nd ed., rev. and augmented by J. Málek. Oxford: Griffith Institute, Ashmolean Museum, 1974.
PM III.2 fasc. 1	Porter, Bertha, and Rosalind L. B. Moss, assisted by E. Burney. *Topographical Bibliography of Ancient Egyptian Hieroglyphic Texts, Reliefs, and Paintings.* Vol. 3: *Memphis. Part 2: Saqqara to Dahshur.* Fascicle 1 (III.2, 393–574). 2nd ed., rev. and augmented by J. Málek. Oxford: Griffith Institute, Ashmolean Museum, 1978.

PM III.2 fasc. 2	Porter, Bertha, and Rosalind L. B. Moss, assisted by E. Burney. *Topographical Bibliography of Ancient Egyptian Hieroglyphic Texts, Reliefs, and Paintings.* Vol. 3: *Memphis. Part 2: Saqqara to Dahshur.* Fascicle 2 (III.2, 575–776). 2nd ed., rev. and augmented by J. Málek. Oxford: Griffith Institute, Ashmolean Museum, 1979.
PM III.2 fasc. 3	Porter, Bertha, and Rosalind L. B. Moss, assisted by E. Burney. *Topographical Bibliography of Ancient Egyptian Hieroglyphic Texts, Reliefs, and Paintings.* Vol. 3: *Memphis. Part 2: Saqqara to Dahshur.* Fascicle 3 (III.2, 777–1014). 2nd ed., rev. and augmented by J. Málek. Oxford: Griffith Institute, Ashmolean Museum, 1981.
PM IV	Porter, Bertha, and Rosalind L. B. Moss. *Topographical Bibliography of Ancient Egyptian Hieroglyphic Texts, Reliefs, and Paintings.* Vol. 4: *Lower and Middle Egypt (Delta and Cairo to Asyut).* Oxford, 1934.
PM V	Porter, Bertha, and Rosalind L. B. Moss. *Topographical Bibliography of Ancient Egyptian Hieroglyphic Texts, Reliefs, and Paintings.* Vol. 5: *Upper Egypt: Sites (Deir Rîfa to Aswan, Excluding Thebes and the Temples of Abydos, Dendera, Edfu, Esna, Kôm Ombo, and Philae).* Oxford, 1937.
PM VI	Porter, Bertha, and Rosalind L. B. Moss. *Topographical Bibliography of Ancient Egyptian Hieroglyphic Texts, Reliefs, and Paintings.* Vol. 6: *Upper Egypt: Chief Temples.* Oxford, 1939.
PM VII	Porter, Bertha, and Rosalind L. B. Moss, assisted by E. Burney. *Topographical Bibliography of Ancient Egyptian Hieroglyphic Texts, Reliefs, and Paintings.* Vol. 7: *Nubia, The Deserts, and Outside Egypt.* Oxford, 1952.
PMCDPA	Davies et al. *The Paper Museum of Cassiano dal Pozzo: A Catalogue Raisonné: Drawings and Prints in the Royal Library at Windsor Castle, the British Museum, the Institut de France and Other Collections.* London: Royal Collection, 2013.
PMMAEE	Publications of the Metropolitan Museum of Art Egyptian Expedition. New York, 1926–.
PTA	Papyrologische Texte und Abhandlungen. Bonn, 1968–.
PtoLex	Wilson, Penelope. *A Ptolemaic Lexikon.* OLA 78. Leuven: Peeters, 1997.
RA	*Revue d'assyriologie et d'archéologie orientale*
RAPH	Recherches d'archéologie, de philologie et d'histoire. Institut français d'archéologie orientale du Caire. Cairo, 1930–.
RAR	Rendiconti della Pontificia Accademia Romana di Archeologia. Rome, 1921–.
RdÉ	*Revue d'égyptologie*
RechPap	*Recherches de Papyrologie*
RecTrav	*Recueil de travaux relatifs à la philologie et à l'archéologie égyptiennes et assyriennes*
RGRW	Religions of the Graeco-Roman World. Leiden, 1992–.
RHR	*Revue de l'histoire des religions*
RPN	Ranke, Hermann. *Die ägyptischen Personennamen.* Glückstadt: Augustin, 1935.
RR	Recherches et Rencontres. Genève, 1990–.
SAGA	Studien zur Archäologie und Geschichte Altägyptens. Heidelberg, 1990–.
SAK	*Studien zur altägyptischen Kultur*
SANER	Studies in Ancient Near Eastern Records. Berlin, 2012–.
SAOC	Studies in Ancient Oriental Civilization. Chicago, 1931–.
SArchClass	Volumi di Supplemento di Archeologia Classica. Rome, 1956–.
SAT	Studien zum altägyptischen Totenbuch. Wiesbaden, 1998–.
SAWM	Sitzungsberichte der Bayerischen Akademie der Wissenschaften zu München. Munich.
SCCNH	Studies in the Civilization and Culture of Nuzi and the Hurrians. Winona Lake, IN, 1981–.
SEAP	Studi di egittologia e di antichità puniche. Bologna and Pisa, 1987–.

SERaT	System zur Erfassung von Ritualszenen in altägyptischen Tempeln. https://www.serat.aegyptologie.uni-wuerzburg.de/
SHR	Studies in the History of Religions. Leiden, 1954–.
SRaT	Studien zu den Ritualszenen altägyptischer Tempel. Dettelbach, 2007–.
SSA	Series Syro-Arabica. Córdoba, Beirut, 2012–.
SSEA	Society for the Study of Egyptian Antiquities. Toronto, 1977–.
SSR	Studien zur spätägyptischen Religion. Wiesbaden, 2010–.
StudDem	Studia Demotica. Leuven, 1987–.
StudHell	Studia Hellenistica. Leuven, 1942–.
SWGS	Schriften der Wissenschaftlichen Gesellschaft Strassburg. Berlin, 1920–1929.
TDOT	*Theological Dictionary of the Old Testament.* Edited by G. Johannes Botterweck and Helmer Ringgren. Translated by John T. Willis et al. 8 vols. Grand Rapids: Eerdmans, 1974–2006.
Thots	Infoheft des Collegium Aegyptium e.V.: Förderkreis des Instituts für Ägyptologie der Uni München. München, 2008–.
TLA	Thesaurus Linguae Aegyptiae. Berlin-Brandenburg, 2004. http://aaew.bbaw.de/tla/
TUAT	Texte aus der Umwelt des Alten Testaments. Gütersloh, 1982–2001.
TUAT NF	Texte aus der Umwelt des Alten Testaments, Neue Folge. Gütersloh, 2004–.
UCLAEE	*UCLA Encyclopedia of Egyptology*. Los Angeles, 2010–. https://escholarship.org/uc/nelc_uee
UF	*Ugarit-Forschungen: Internationales Jahrbuch für die Altertumskunde Syrien-Palästinas*
UPZ	Wilcken, Ulrich. *Urkunden der Ptolemäerzeit (ältere Funde)*. 2 vols. Berlin, Leipzig, 1927–1957.
Urk. IV	Sethe, Kurt. *Urkunden der 18. Dynastie.* Urkunden des ägyptischen Altertums 4, fasc. 1–16. Leipzig: Hinrichs, 1906–1909. 2nd rev. ed., 1927–1930. Continued by Wolfgang Helck, fasc. 17–22. Berlin, 1955–1958.
Urk. VI	Schott, Siegfried. *Urkunden mythologischen Inhalts.* Leipzig: Hinrichs, 1929–1939.
UZK	Untersuchungen der Zweigstelle Kairo des Österreichischen Archäologischen Institutes. Vienna, 1975–.
VIO	Veröffentlichungen des Institut für Orientforschung, Deutsche Akademie der Wissenschaften zu Berlin. Berlin, 1968–.
VOHD	Verzeichnis der orientalischen Handschriften in Deutschland. Wiesbaden, Göttingen, 1971–1994
WAW	Writings from the Ancient World. Atlanta, 1990–.
Wb.	Erman, Adolf, and Hermann Grapow, eds. *Wörterbuch der ägyptischen Sprache.* 7 vols, plus 5 vols. Belegstellen. Berlin: Akademie-Verlag, 1926–1963.
WdO	*Die Welt des Orients*
WZKM	*Wiener Zeitschrift für die Kunde des Morgenlandes*
YES	Yale Egyptological Studies. New Haven, 1986–.
ZÄS	*Zeitschrift für ägyptische Sprache und Altertumskunde*
ZA	*Zeitschrift für Assyriologie und Vorderasiatische Archäologie*
ZPE	*Zeitschrift für Papyrologie und Epigraphik*

Book of the Dead Scholarship in Ptolemaic Egypt: The Case of P. Brooklyn 37.1484E

Yekaterina Barbash

I first met Richard Jasnow at Johns Hopkins University, where I came for graduate studies in 1998. His care for students, warmth, and an unparalleled sense of humor made the graduate school experience magical. I feel tremendously lucky to have studied with Richard Jasnow, to have worked with him as my dissertation advisor, and to have gotten to know him as a professor, a mentor, and a friend. His passion for learning and willingness to share his knowledge are akin to descriptions of the god Thoth. He is an excellent scribe, skilled in knowledge, who is always cool of mouth while advising, and who can lecture with his eyes closed. In Richard's honor, I offer a study of one spell in a very curious Book of the Dead. This manuscript appropriately holds clues to understanding ancient Egyptian scholarship. My contribution discusses the famous BD spell 125 that concerns events at the judgment hall of Osiris, which were diligently recorded by the god who loves knowledge.

The Book of the Dead of Herw (P. Brooklyn 37.1484E)[1] measures 23 feet in length and comprises a sequence of spells from 100 to 153 with some spells omitted.[2] Its hieratic script, enclosed with double lined margins on all sides along with the black outline vignettes in the top registers, place the papyrus among a group of BD manuscripts belonging to high-ranking priests from the Saite and early Ptolemaic periods.[3]

The manuscript was made for the God's father Herw,[4] son of Takhabes. Herw's other titles are recorded in hieroglyphs in the Weighing of the Heart vignette of spell 125 (fig. 1). These include King's Familiar, Servant of Ptah, *wab*-priest of the Gods of the Temples of Memphis, *Hm* priest of Min, Scribe of Ptah, and Chamberlain of the King.[5] Several members of a Memphite priestly family from the Ptolemaic period held almost exactly the same titles. Herw

1. The papyrus came to the Brooklyn Museum in 1937 from the New York Historical Society. Prior to that, it belonged Dr. Henry Abbott, who allegedly purchased it in Saqqara in the nineteenth century.

2. Several small fragments from the beginning of the scroll are held by the Penn University Museum, and another fragment appeared in a Sotheby's sale in 2009.

3. These parameters fit Style 2, see Malcolm Mosher, "Theban and Memphite Book of the Dead Traditions in the Late Period," *JARCE* 29 (1992): 150–51, and nn. 39–40.

4. The name and titles were written at the same time as the primary inscription. The name, spelled in several ways, is well attested in the Late and Greco-Roman periods, Hermann Ranke, *Die Ägyptischen Personennamen I* (Glückstadt: Augustin, 1935), 230.

5. Chamberlain of the King appears to have been added after the original inscription in the vignette. For the title *ẖry-tp nsw.t,* well attested since the OK, see Dilwyn Jones, *An Index of Ancient Egyptian Titles, Epithets and Phrases of the Old Kingdom,* BAR International Series 866 (Oxford: Archaeopress, 2000), 2:788, no. 2874; *Wb.* III:396, 2. Hans Goedicke, "Titles for Titles," in *Grund und Boden in Altägypten: Rechtliche und sozio-ökonomische Verhältnisse; Akten des internationalen Symposiums, Tübingen 18.–20. Juni 1990,* ed. Shafik Allam (Tübingen: Allam, 1994), 227–34, argues that this title (in the OK) should rather be read *tpy ẖrt-nsw.t,* "One upon Royal Property." The argument is partly based on the semantic relationship of *ẖr* and (*n*)*sw* and the adjacent position of these signs in the writing of this title, which is clearly not the case in Herw's papyrus.

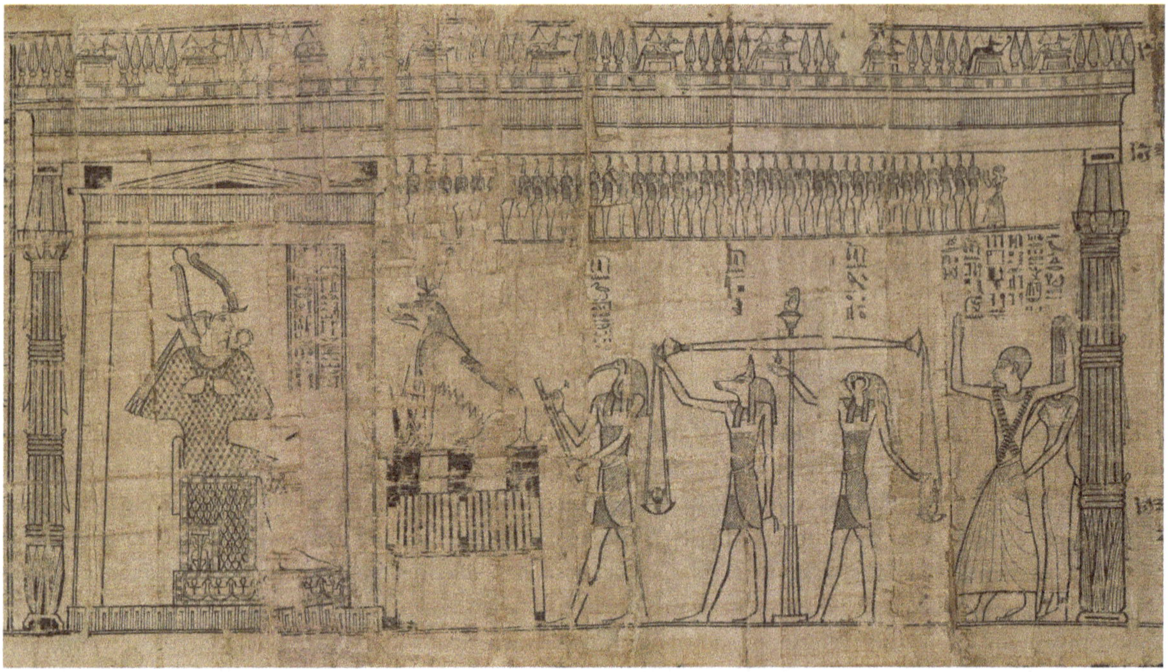

Figure 1. Weighing of the Heart in the Book of the Dead of Herw, pBrooklyn 37.1484E. Image courtesy of the Brooklyn Museum.

must have been part of this family in the very early Ptolemaic period.[6] Judging by the list of titles and the stylistic parallels, this papyrus was certainly made in Memphis, which is a relatively rare origin for such texts.[7]

The most striking feature of Herw's papyrus is the scholarly tendency of its scribe. Eighteen out of the twenty-six textual spells preserved on the Brooklyn portion of Herw's BD include an unusually high number of variants, marked by the phrase *ky-ḏd*. While it is quite typical for Books of the Dead to occasionally incorporate variants, our scribe took this practice to the extreme, at times listing several variants in a row. Spell 125, as it appears in our manuscript, contains sixteen variants—an extraordinarily large number.[8] I compared this spell with over fifty Books of the Dead.[9]

6. Eberhard Otto, "Eine memphitische Priesterfamilie des 2. Jh. v. Chr.," *ZÄS* 81 (1956): 108–29, discusses this family and suggests that the list of titles likely identified the priestly rank, rather than referred to specific posts. At least three persons by the name of Herw belong to this priestly family, but no other Herw with a mother named Takhabes is known, see Otto, "Eine memphitische Priesterfamilie." None of the attested members of this family include the title *ḥry-tp nsw.t*. Carbon 14 analysis performed at the University of Arizona confirmed a range of 360–200 BCE.

7. Mosher, "Theban and Memphite Book of the Dead Traditions," 145 and n. 21, describes the manuscripts in his corpus as follows: "of the nearly 200 documents ... the vast majority come from Thebes and only five can be assigned a Memphite provenance." The situation is compounded by the lower chance of preservation of papyrus in the "shallow sands of the Saqqara desert," Martin Raven, "Book of the Dead Documents from the New Kingdom Necropolis in Saqqara," *BMSAES* 15 (2010): 257. There are 49 papyri with BD from Saqqara, compared to 527 from Thebes in the database of the Totenbuch-Projekt, http://totenbuch.awk.nrw.de/. The provenance of many manuscripts remains undetermined, Marcus Müller-Roth, "From Memphis to Thebes: Local Traditions in the Late Period," *BMSAES* 15 (2010): 175.

8. For example, the famous papyrus of Iufankh only includes one variant in BD 125, Richard Lepsius, *Das Todtenbuch der Ägypter nach dem hieroglyphischen Papyrus in Turin* (Leipzig: Wigand, 1842), pl. XLVI–XLVII. Interestingly, this spell in the Saite papyrus of Iahtesnakht incorporates eight *ky-ḏd* variants, also a considerable number, but none of them correspond to ours, Ursula Verhoeven, *Das Saitische Totenbuch der Iahtesnacht: P. Colon. Aeg. 10207*, 2 vols. (Bonn: Habelt, 1993), 2:79–85.

9. The published papyri include Günter Lapp, *Totenbuch Spruch 125* (Basel: Orientverlag, 2008); Charles Maystre, *Les déclarations d'innocence: Livre des morts, chapitre 125* (Cairo: Institut français d'archéologie orientale, 1937); Martin von Falck, *Das Totenbuch*

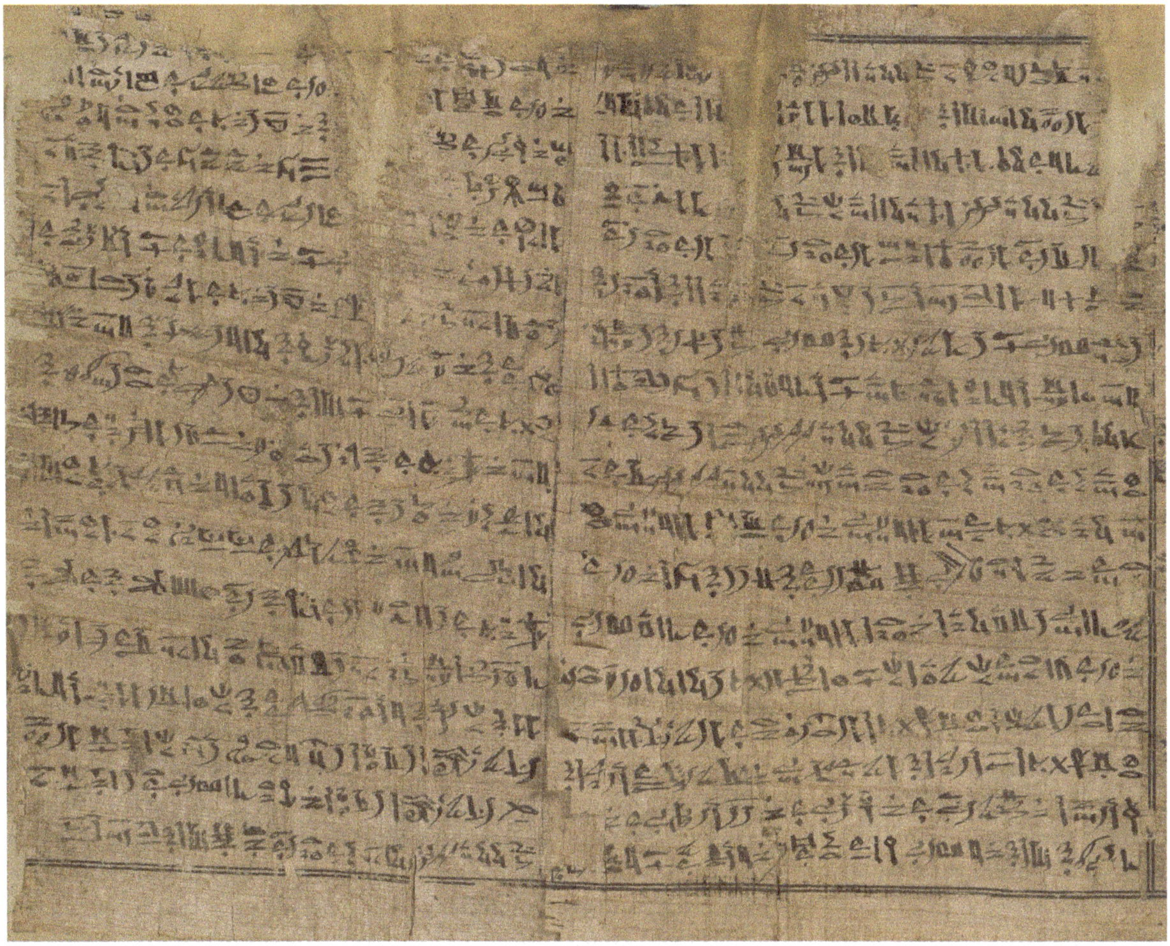

Figure 2. Columns x+13 – 14, pBrooklyn 37.1484E. Image courtesy of the Brooklyn Museum.

Most of the comparanda date from the Late and Ptolemaic periods, with a smaller selection of earlier texts.[10] The comparable papyri cover most of Egypt, including Thebes, Memphis, as well as sites in Middle Egypt.

The initial variant of BD 125 occurs as the deceased addresses Osiris in the very beginning of the spell (fig. 2):

der Qeqa aus der Ptolemäerzeit (pBerlin P.3003), HAT 8 (Wiesbaden: Harrassowitz, 2006); Annie Gasse, *Le Livre des morts de Pacherientaihet au Museo Gregoriano Egizio* (Vatican: Monumenti, Musei e Gallerie Pontificie, 2001); Lepsius, *Das Todtenbuch der Ägypter*; Günter Lapp, *The Papyrus of Nu*, Catalogues of the Books of the Dead in the British Museum I (London: British Museum Press, 1997); Irmtraut Munro, *Der Totenbuch-Papyrus des Hor aus der frühen Ptolemäerzeit: pCologny Bodmer-Stiftung CV + pCincinnati Art Museum 1947.369 + pDenver 1954.61* (Wiesbaden: Harrasowitz, 2006); Irmtraut Munro, *Das Totenbuch des Pa-en-nesti-taui aus der Regierungszeit des Amennemope (pLondon BM 10064)*, HAT 7 (Wiesbaden: Harrassowtiz, 2001); Paul O'Rourke, *An Ancient Egyptian Book of the Dead: The Papyrus of Sobekmose* (New York: Thames & Hudson, 2016); Verhoeven, *Das Saitische Totenbuch der Iahtesnacht*. Access to the unpublished examples is provided by the immensely useful Totenbuch Project, http://totenbuch.awk.nrw.de/.

10. The BD manuscripts in my list of comparanda range in dates from Dynasty 18 to the GR period.

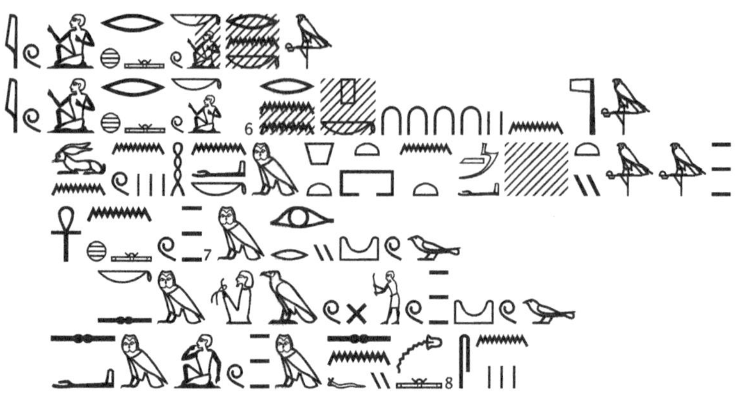

I know your name.
I know the name(s) of your 42 gods
who exist with you in the broad hall,
who live on those who do evil;
variant: those who guard evil;
who swallow their blood.
(Col. x+13, 5–8)

Both versions of this epithet—"those who do evil," and "those who guard evil"—point to one of the functions of the 42 gods in Osiris' court—that of keeping evil at bay. The first epithet, *ỉry ḏw*, "those who do evil," depicts these gods as devourers of evildoers. Surprisingly, this direct and seemingly clear version does not occur in any of the parallels. The epithet that follows *ky-ḏd, sꜣw ḏw*, "those who guard evil," extends the gods' function to the next level, painting them as the eradicators of the protectors of evil. It is this broader version—once removed from directly living off evil—that is the more common one. This version occurs in all of the parallels consulted. The scribe of Herw's manuscript must have deemed the epithet "those who guard evil" insufficient, and supplied *ỉry ḏw*, which points to the heart of the issue. This unique epithet possibly stems from a misreading due to the similarity of hieratic signs for *sꜣw*, (Gardiner's A47), and (Gardiner's A48), which may be read as *ỉry*. A copyist may have seen the ambiguous sign on a master copy, and to be sure, wrote both words, spelling *ỉry* phonetically with an eye, for clarity.[11]

The clause that follows immediately after continues the string of epithets of the 42 gods:

(on) that day of reckoning your character;
variant: veiling the face in the presence Wennefer.
(Col. x+13, 8)

There is no question that the entire clause describes the day of the Osirian judgment. The initial version, *ḥsb ḳd.w*, is what predominantly appears in the parallel papyri. Most modern editors translate this phrase as "reckoning (or

11. While *ỉry* is typically spelled phonetically, the eye (Gardiner's D4) does occur occasionally in this word, see Penelope Wilson, *A Ptolemaic Lexikon: A Lexicographical Study of the Texts in the Temple of Edfu*, OLA 78 (Leuven: Peeters, 1997), 91.

calculating) the character(s)," in the sense of "settling up" during judgment.[12] In the immediate context of spell BD 125 and its adjacent Weighing of the Heart scene, the phrase *ḥsb ḳd.w* forms a pun on *ḥsb ḳd.t*, "counting the kite (i.e., measures of weight)."[13] The pun suggests that the Osirian judgment and the weighing of the heart literally concern calculating the number of kites needed to balance the scale against the weight of one's heart.

Because the verbs *ḥsb* and *ḥbs* use the same consonants, the variants in this line at first appear to be an intentional pun. Only one papyrus, a Ptolemaic-period BD from Memphis, has *ḥbs* in place of *ḥsb*: 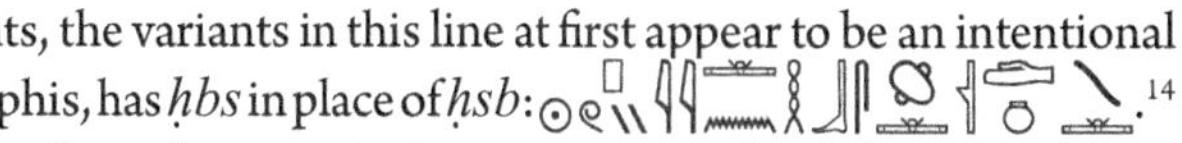.[14] Nevertheless, since in this example *ḥbs* is spelled phonetically with a pustule determinative and is followed by *ḳdw.t*, it is most likely a mistake. The scribe of this manuscript probably rearranged the spelling of the verb *ḥsb* accidentally. The presence of *ḥbs* in Herw's papyrus, however, may be explained as a scribal attempt to correct a text that he was collating. When another scribe—perhaps the scribe of Herw's papyrus himself—was faced with the erroneous writing of *ḥsb*, he deemed it significant to record the frankly odd word and to justify it.[15] Our scribe supplied the variant *ḥbs* with *ḥr*, "face."[16] The phrase *ḥbs ḥr* is typically used in literary and biographical texts with the sense of "ignoring" or "turning away from" people in need or from wrongdoing. For instance, the Eloquent Peasant says: "if you avert your face (*ḥbs ḥr*) from violence, who then shall punish wrongdoing?"[17] Consequently, the variant *ḥbs ḥr*, placed in the middle of the clause, introduces a wholly new nuance to the process of Osirian judgment. "Covering the face in the presence of Wennefer" points to an act of ignoring or turning away from Osiris and does not sound appropriate for the circumstance. However, the notion is not as audacious as it seems at first glance. Spell BD 30, which appears on heart scarabs and addresses one's heart and consciousness, does suggest that some deception may be in order, as it requests that the heart not bear witness against the deceased.[18] Herw's scribe perhaps reveals a hidden truth: that some details should best be ignored or omitted even in front of Osiris.

Next, as the deceased denies wrongdoing and describes his positive qualities, he says:

12. See for instance, O'Rourke, *Ancient Egyptian Book of the Dead*, 101; Verhoeven, *Das Saitische Totenbuch der Iahtesnacht: P. Colon. Aeg. 10207* (Bonn: Habelt, 1993), 1:228; Stephen Quirke, *Going Out in Daylight – prt m hrw. The Ancient Egyptian Book of the Dead. Translations, Sources, Meanings*, (London: Golden House Publications, 2013), 270. For *ḥsb*, "to reckon, count, calculate," see *Wb.* III:166, 11–167, 15. For *ḳd*, "form, character," see *Wb.* V:75, 3–77, 11.

13. *ḳd.t*, "a weight, kite," *Wb.* V:79, 15–80, 3. John Gee, "Of Heart Scarabs and Balance Weights: A New Interpretation of Book of the Dead 30B," *JSSEA* 36 (2009): 1–15, points out that in Dynasties 18 and 19 the Weighing of the Heart scene was associated with BD 30B, which is typically inscribed on heart scarabs. He further demonstrates that the weight of many heart scarabs corresponds to standard weight amounts, particularly to the kite weights.

14. P. Wien Vindob. Aeg. 65 is stylistically similar to the BD of Herw, but inscribed in a distinctly different hand.

15. Daniel Werning, "Inner-Egyptian Receptions of a Theological Book between Reproduction, Update, and Creativity: The Book of Caverns from the 13th to the 4th Century BCE," in *(Re)productive Traditions in Ancient Egypt: Proceedings of the Conference Held at the University of Liège, 6th–8th February 2013*, ed. Todd Gillen (Liège: Presses Universitaires de Liège, 2017), 57–58, interprets such emendations as belonging to a "reproductive" rather than a "creative" working mode.

16. Terence DuQuesne, *At the Court of Osiris, Book of the Dead Spell 194: A Rare Egyptian Judgment Text* (London: Darengo Publications, 1994), 30, offers examples of the confusion between *ḥbs* and *ḥsb* in the phrase *ḥbs-ḥr* as seen in various sources of BD 194.

17. Miriam Lichtheim, *Ancient Egyptian Literature: A Book of Readings* (Berkeley: University of California Press, 1973), 1:176. The phrase is also representative on two MK stelae. Stela of Mentuwoser, MMA 12.184: *n ḥbs=ỉ ḥr r nty m bꜣk.w*, "I have not hid my face from the one who is in servitude," Kurt Sethe, *Aegyptische Lesestücke zum Gebrauch im akademischen Unterricht: Texte des mittleren Reiches* (Leipzig: Hinrichs, 1924) 79, 13–14; and Stela of Intef, BM EA 581: *ỉnk ḥḏ-ḥr ꜣw-ḏrt nb ḏfꜣ šw m ḥbs ḥr*, "I'm bright faced, open-handed, an owner of food who does not cover his face," Lichtheim, *Ancient Egyptian Literature*, 122 and n. 6; Sethe, *Aegyptische Lesestücke*, 80, 21–22. For the phrase *ḥbs ḥr*, see *Wb.* III:64, 13–14. DuQuesne, *At the Court of Osiris*, 17 and 30, points to the similar *ḥbs-tp* in the context of the ritual wearing of masks, such as the jackal mask of Anubis.

18. See for example, BD 30A: "... My heart of my mother, my heart from when I was upon the earth. Do not stand against me as my witness at the side of the lord of offerings. Do not say against me: he has done it in truth (about) what I have done ..."; O'Rourke, *Ancient Egyptian Book of the Dead*, 125.

I have not acted as the leader of any people (at) any moment;

variant: (on) the day (of) working in view of what he has done.

(Col. x+13, 14)

This sentence seems convoluted and many translators have supplied words to make sense out of it.[19] Notably, none of the parallels consulted have *ꜣt nb.t*, "any moment."

Following just three more lines, we encounter another *ky-ḏd*:

I have not caused hunger;

variant: beaten.

(Col. x+13, 18)

This variant introduces a completely different concept from the initial verb. *sḳr* appears in only three parallel texts where it replaces *sḥḳr*. None of these three parallels are Memphite.[20] Since both verbs do not appear together in any other manuscript that I consulted, the variants *sḥḳr* and *sḳr* are either puns or result from an accidental omission of the phoneme "*ḥ*," which was at some point reinterpreted into a different verb that was also appropriate for the context.

Several lines later, the scribe added two variants in a row. Unfortunately, as often happens in the most interesting places, one of the variants is lost in a lacuna, with only the sparrow determinative  (Gardiner's G37) surviving:

I have not ...;

variant: I have not calculated;

variant: destroyed the plummet of the sca[le].

(Col. x+14, 6–7)

19. The most common translations of the line point to not increasing the workload of one's employees, see O'Rourke, *Ancient Egyptian Book of the Dead*, 101n73.

20. The early Ptolemaic pLouvre N. 3115 and the Ptolemaic-period P. Berlin P. 3039 are both Theban. The third occurrence of *sḳr* in this line is in the Saite Period papyrus of Iahtesnakht, pCologne 10207, which is allegedly from Herakleopolis, Verhoeven, *Das Saitische Totenbuch der Iahtesnacht*, 1:6.

Many papyri agree on *nn (s)nmḥ=i*, "I have not tempered with the plummet of the scale," which was likely the verb in the lacuna of Herw's papyrus. Oddly, none of the parallels show either *ḥsb* or *ḥtm*.[21] Other parallels use a number of different verbs, pointing to the broad range of options for tempering with the plummet and the scale.[22]

The following *ky-ḏd* appears only two lines later:

(I) have not snared the birds of the reeds;
variant: the gods.
(Col. x+14, 8–9)

Of the consulted parallels only one fully corresponds to Herw's version, including both nouns and the *ky-ḏd*.[23] In this Saite-period manuscript from Thebes, the variant *nṯr.w* is added above the line, suggesting that *nṯr.w* was meant to replace *ꜣpd.w* here. Most other manuscripts choose either *ꜣpd ḳs(n)*, with *ḳs* written as "bird," "reed" or "harpoon,"[24] or as *ꜣpd nṯr.w*. Interestingly, such Theban manuscripts as the Eighteenth Dynasty papyrus of Nu, the Twenty-First Dynasty papyrus of Paennestitawy, as well as the Saite papyrus of Iahtesnakht, which were created in rather distant locations and time periods from each other, use both modifiers in a slightly different order. And yet, they all result in a similar translation "I have not caught birds in the reeds of the gods."[25]

The next two columns record 125B, known as the Negative Confession (fig. 3). In Herw's manuscript this portion is, in fact, not a confession but rather a mere address to the 42 gods because all the denials have been omitted. All other papyri among my comparisons contain the negative statements.[26] The scribe of Herw's papyrus nevertheless deemed it necessary to include a number of variants among the epithets of the deities:

21. For *ḥtm*, spelled , "to destroy," see *Wb*. III:197. The BD of Iahtesnakht (54, 3) also includes a *ky-ḏd* in this line, but it does not correspond to our text: *nn sẖsẖs=i ky-ḏd swsr m tẖ n mẖꜣ.t*, "I have not weakened; variant: strengthened the plummet of the scales." This reading appears without the *ky-ḏd* in other versions. Chloé Ragazzoli, "Beyond Authors and Copyists: The Role of Variation in Ancient Egyptian and New Kingdom Literary Production," in Gillen, *(Re)productive Traditions*, 102, discusses lexical variation based on phonetic associations.

22. "Measures were probably often altered deliberately or deemed to be unreliable," Pierre Grandet, "Weights and Measures," in *The Oxford Encyclopedia of Ancient Egypt*, ed. Donald Redford (New York: Oxford University Press, 2001), 493. For an in-depth discussion of the ancient Egyptian scale, see Hippolyte Ducros, "Étude sur les balances égyptiennes," *ASAE* 9 (1908): 32–53; Hippolyte Ducros, "Deuxième étude sur les balances égyptiennes," *ASAE* 10 (1910): 240–53; Hippolyte Ducros, "Troisième étude sur les balances égyptiennes," *ASAE* 11 (1911): 251–56; Eva Martin-Pardey, "Waage," *LÄ* 6:1081–86. Colleen Manassa, "Judgment Hall of Osiris in the Book of Gates," *RdÉ* 57 (2006): 57, describes the plummet as the hypostasis of Thoth, as an indicator of balance.

23. P. Cairo CG 40024, the BD of the God's Father Ankhefenkhonsu.

24. The spelling of *ḳsn* with the sparrow, (Gardiner's G37), leads to the clearly erroneous reading "difficult, painful," *Wb*. V:69, 7–70, 16. The parallels, however, do not include this determinative. *ḳsn* may conceivably be a writing of *gnw*, "bird," *Wb*. V:69, 6, which also does not make sense here.

25. See the translation by Quirke, *Going Out in Daylight*, 271, of the early NK Theban papyrus of Nu: *n sẖt=i ꜣpd.w n ḳs.w nṯr.w* (Lapp, *Papyrus of Nu*, pl. 65, lines 4–5): "I have not the snared birds of the thickets(?) of the gods." The BD of Paennestitawy, also from Thebes reads: *nn sẖt=i ꜣpd.w ḳs.w n nṯrw*, Munro, *Das Totenbuch des Pa-en-nesti-taui*, pl. 52. The papyrus of Iahtesnakht reads: *nn sẖt=i ꜣpd.w nṯr.w ḳs.w*, "Ich habe nicht Vögel <im> Röhricht der Götter gefangen," Verhoeven, *Das Saitische Totenbuch der Iahtesnacht* 1:230, 2:80. The Ptolemaic, Theban papyrus of Hor, line 284 offers a variation of this: *n sẖt=i ꜣpd.w=k n nṯrw ḳs.w*, Munro, *Der Totenbuch-Papyrus des Hor*, pl. 12. See also Raymond Faulkner, *The Ancient Egyptian Book of the Dead* (London, British Museum Publications, 1972), 31: "I have not trapped the birds from the preserves of the gods." And see the Eighteenth Dynasty BD of Sobekmose: *nn sẖ.t=i ꜣpd.w n ḳs.w nṯr.w*, "I have not trapped birds belonging to the harpoons of the gods," O'Rourke, *Ancient Egyptian Book of the Dead*, 102.

26. Most early examples record the invocations and applicable negative statements in a table-like arrangement. In KV9 only the

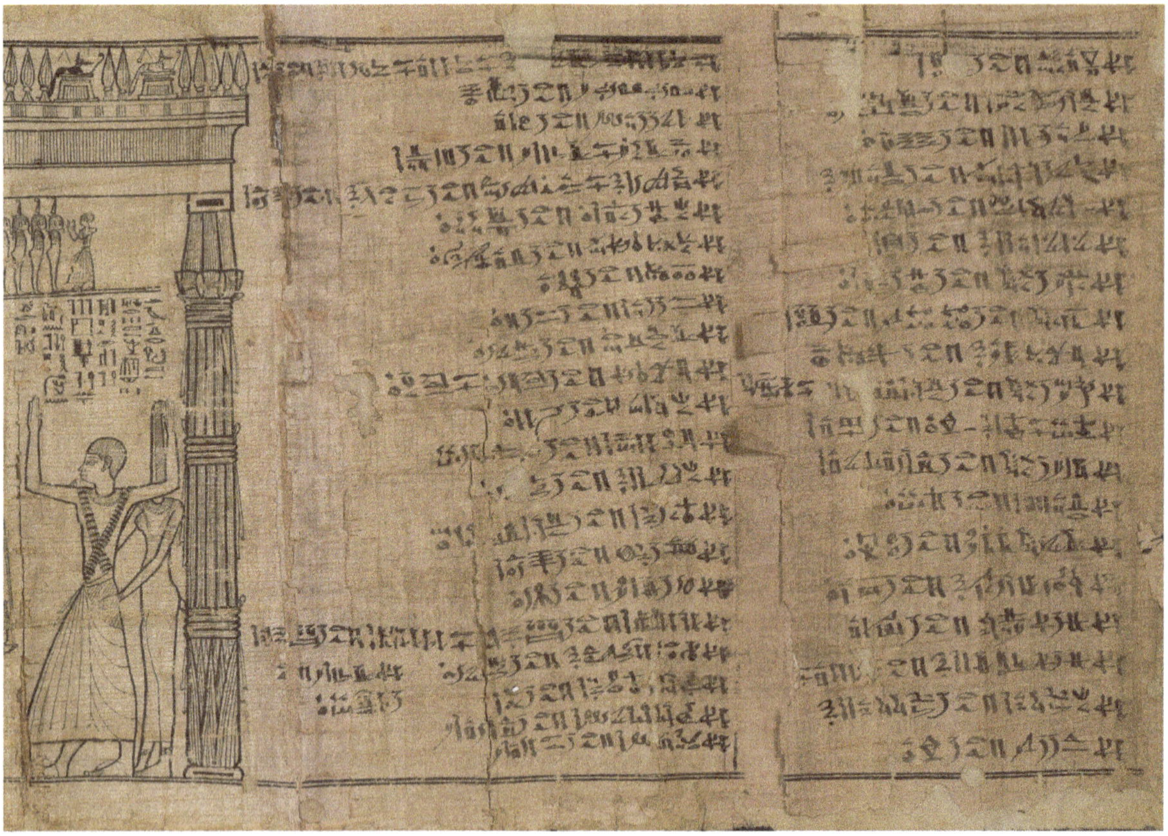

Figure 3. Columns x+15 – 16, pBrooklyn 37.1484E. Image courtesy of the Brooklyn Museum.

O, one whose breath is fire, who came from Memphis;
variant: one who emits flame.
(Col. x+15, 10)

While the sense of the two epithets (*ṯ3w=f m ḫt* and *w3ḏ nsr*) in this first example remains similar, the variants introduce a nuance. *w3ḏ nsr*, "one who emits flame," is the preferred epithet in NK Books of the Dead.[27] The epithet also appears in three Ptolemaic-period parallels that repeat this line word for word, including the *ky-ḏd*. These three manuscripts come from Memphis, Akhmim, and Thebes.[28] Because most epithets in this spell are typically followed

texts of the invocation are arranged schematically in a column, while the negative statements are horizontal, see Lapp, *Totenbuch Spruch 125*, xi. It is possible that our scribe worked from a master copy that was unconventionally arranged akin to the example in KV9 and accidentally (rather than intentionally) omitted the horizontal portion. Other instances of exceptional similarities of BD spells in Herw's papyrus and those recorded in KV9 (and KV2) should be noted. However, these details are outside the scope of this paper.

27. Maystre, *Les déclarations d'innocence*, 73; Lapp, *Totenbuch Spruch 125*, 82–83.

28. P. Louvre N. 3081 is Memphite; P. Berlin P. 10478 A-N is from Akhmim; pLouvre N. 3096 is Theban and dated to Dynasty

by the place of origin of the invoked deity, it is interesting to note that the variant in Herw's text is inserted after the location clause, "who came from Memphis."

The invocation of the following line contains yet another variant:

11

O, one of the necropolis;
variant: one united with Bubastis who came from the crypt.
(Col. x+15, 11)

The barely noticeable nuance of spelling of the two epithets results in a palpable difference in meaning. The variant "one united with Bubastis" also appears in a Ptolemaic-period papyrus from Memphis, which was likely made for a member of Herw's family, or at least created in the same milieu.[29] Most parallels choose "one of the necropolis of Bubastis," suggesting that the name of this city was intended to modify both variants in the papyrus of Herw, that is, "O, one of the necropolis (of Bubastis); variant: one united with Bubastis who came from the crypt."

The next example includes a string of variants, which are again hindered by a lacuna.

Col. 16. 1

O, pale one;
variant: ...
variant: portal;
variant: beautiful one(?) who came from [Heliopolis].
(Col. x+16,1)

All of these variants are clearly alliterative puns, but each produces a considerably different meaning. Most parallel papyri prefer the first version, *ꜥꜣd*.[30]

Two lines later, the variants use the same verb *in*, but result in a different sense:

30–Ptolemaic period. The latter parallel inserts the *ky-ḏd* in a more logical place, before *pr m ḥwt-kꜣ-ptḥ*. The BD of Hor, P. Cologne Bodmer-Stiftung CV, also offers a variant in this line, but it is distinct from ours: *ṯꜣw=f m st k(y)-ḏd wḏ.tw st pr m ḥwt-kꜣ-ptḥ*, Munro, *Der Totenbuch-Papyrus des Hor*, 34, and pl. 13.

29. P. Berlin P. 3149 + 14376 belongs to an *it-nṯr ḥm-nṯr* Horhep, son of Renpetnefret, and generally resembles P. Brooklyn 1484E in style and layout.

30. For *ꜥꜣdy*, "Der Glänzende(?)", see *LGG* II, 75; For *ꜥꜣd*, "to be pale," in *Wb*. I:168, 15. For alternative interpretations of this line in the parallels, see Maystre, *Les déclarations d'innocence*, 78–79. The Memphite Ptolemaic-period BD of Hor, P. Cairo JE 32887 also includes a variant in this line: *i ꜥdy ky-ḏd ꜥ...y pr m iwnw*.

O, one who sees what he has brought;
variant: one who brings his portion who came from the house of Min.
O, chief of the elders;
variant: one who is near the elders who came from Naret, who comes from Mendes.
(Col. x+16, 4–5)

Because the variants in each line are close in meaning to the initial versions, they must be based on an alternative *Vorlage* or a mistake. None of the manuscripts I consulted use the epithets that appear as the variants, that is, "one who brings his portion," or "one who is near the elders." Notably, *in-ꜥ=f* also appears as the last deity invoked in 125B where he is said to come from *i͗grt*.[31]

In another line the variant simply names an alternate toponym:

O, argument-settler who came from Wenes;
variant: Wenut.
(Col. x+16, 11)

Both Theban and Memphite parallels vary as to the origin of the argument-settler. Earlier examples, primarily from the NK and TIP, identify the origin of this deity as *wryt*. The later manuscripts alternate between the phonetically similar *wns* and *wnt*.[32]

In the last example of this spell a pun creates the variant:

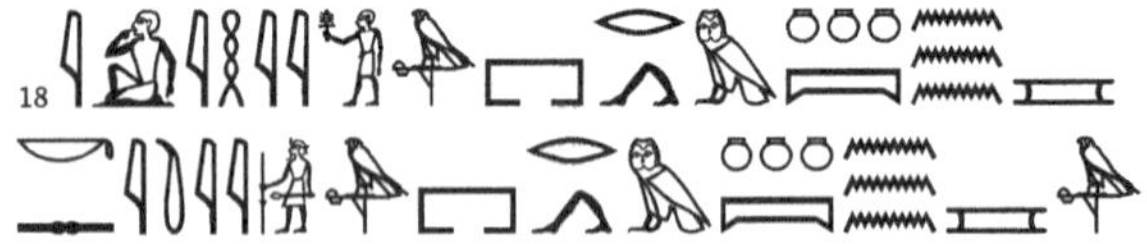

O, musician who came from the deep;
variant: O, sovereign who came from the deep.
(Col. x+16, 18)

31. *LGG* I, 371–72. Compare an alternative passive in the corresponding line of the BD of Iahtesnakht, 55,1: *i͗.mꜣꜣ.n.tw=f m pr-mn*, "Oh du, der gesehen worden ist, der aus dem Tempel des Min <hervorgeht>," Verhoeven, *Das Saitische Totenbuch der Iahtesnacht* 1:232; 2:81.

32. Emily Cole, "Interpretation and Authority: The Social Functions of Translations in Ancient Egypt" (PhD diss., University of California, 2015), 164–67 and 201, discusses the cultural significance in the changes of the names of deities and geographical locations.

This is clearly not only an alliterative but also a graphic pun as both words are formed with four tall vertical signs. Only a handful of parallels, none of them Memphite, prefer the sovereign here.[33] Unlike most previous examples with variants the scribe repeated the line in full—adding the clause "who came from the deep" each time.

Conclusion

The extreme use of the *ky-ḏd* by the scribe of Herw's papyrus is, as far as I know, exceptional. The phrase *ky-ḏd* is used in several situations in spell 125. It can offer a synonym, or a clause that elaborates upon a term, or it can introduce a completely different notion in an otherwise similar context.[34] Some variants replace one mere word, while others substitute an entire clause. Variants can appear as a word that follows *ky-ḏd* in the middle or end of a sentence. Otherwise, the scribe can add a *ky-ḏd* and repeat the same sentence from the beginning using one different word. The scribe of Herw's BD utilizes the full range of variants. Moreover, many of the variants show either phonetic or visual similarity and thus present intentional puns.

Variants have often been explained as scribal attempts to correct a mistake or a lacuna,[35] to update a text,[36] or to reconcile two very different master versions.[37] Certainly, in many instances variants may have stemmed from scribal misunderstanding or skepticism regarding a word's meaning that resulted in an intentional effort to clarify the text. It is undeniable that our scribe deemed it important to resolve the passages that had errors and lacunae and to interpret those that were simply difficult to understand.

The examples examined here demonstrate that variants were not added simply out of necessity to "correct" the text. The unprecedented number of variants in this manuscript suggests that its scribe exerted a tremendous effort to compile as many versions as possible. The significant number of words or phrases that serve as variants in Herw's papyrus but appear as part of the main text in other manuscripts, can only be explained by the fact that our scribe consulted numerous different sources. As a priest of Ptah, Herw likely had access to the accumulations of texts in

---

33. *ity* appears in three Ptolemaic-period manuscripts: two Theban papyri are pLouvre N. 3096 and the papyrus of Hor, pCologny CV, Munro, *Der Totenbuch-Papyrus des Hor*, as well as P. Berlin P. 10478 from Akhmim. Both *ity* and *iḥy* could serve as an epithet of Osiris, among other gods, see *LGG* I, 588–90 and *LGG* I, 542, respectively.

34. Gwyn Griffiths, "Allegory in Greece and Egypt," *JEA* 53 (1957): 97–99, lists diverse uses of *ky-ḏd* including as an introduction of an alternative or a similar reading, a change in subject matter, an interpretation, or an entirely different spell, such as in the case of BD 69 and 70. For an in-depth discussion of the critical examination of texts by scribes, as well as a list of diverse types of *ky-ḏd* (lexical variation, synonym, record of an alternative tradition, etc.), see Pascal Vernus, "L'écrit et la canonicité dans l'Égypte pharaonique," in *Problems of Canonicity and Identity Formation in Ancient Egypt and Mesopotamia*, ed. Kim Ryholt and Gojko Barjamovic (Copenhagen: Museum Tusculanum Press, 2016), 287–90, and *passim*.

35. Maystre, *Les déclarations d'innocence*, 7–8.

36. Alexandra von Lieven, "Closed Canon vs. Creative Chaos: An In-Depth Look at (Real and Supposed) Mortuary Texts from Ancient Egypt," in Ryholt and Barjamovic, *Problems of Canonicity*, 64, discusses scholarly restoration of ancient texts. The desire to modernize a text by substituting a new word or grammatical form is also an important factor in the creation of variants, Pascal Vernus, "Modeling the Relationship between Reproduction and Production of 'Sacralized' Texts in Pharaonic Egypt," in Gillen, *(Re)productive Traditions*, 486–90. Richard Jasnow and Karl-Theodor Zauzich, *The Ancient Egyptian Book of Thoth* (Wiesbaden: Harrassowitz, 2005), 1:118, also discuss scribes "updating" a composition with more contemporary language.

37. Malcolm Mosher, "Transmission of Funerary Literature: Saite through Ptolemaic Periods," in *Book of the Dead: Becoming God in Ancient Egypt*, ed. Foy Scalf (Chicago: The Oriental Institute of the University of Chicago, 2017), 94 and 96, does not believe there were intentional attempts to interpret, but suggests that all variants stem from something unclear or different in an already existing copy. At the same time, he acknowledges the scribal desire to improve and correct the text. Because textual errors are often blamed on misinterpreted dictation, Ogden Goelet, "Observations on Copying and the Hieroglyphic Tradition in the Production of the Book of the Dead," in *Offerings to the Discerning Eye: An Egyptological Medley in Honor of Jack A. Josephson*, ed. Sue D'Auria (Leiden: Brill, 2010), 123, shows that scribes copied texts, and perhaps memorized portions thereof, rather than having them dictated.

the temple of Ptah at Memphis.[38] Arguably, this scribe employed not only so-called *Vorlage*, but also examples of other BD texts that were available to him.[39] This scribe appears to have had access to more BD examples than usual. Perhaps he sought them out deliberately. It was a great surprise to find that a number of the rare variants—not used in most papyri—appear in manuscripts that were not necessarily Memphite in origin but rather came from a broad range of places throughout Egypt. This serves as yet another piece of evidence for an exchange of BD copies among workshops in the Late and Ptolemaic periods.[40]

Furthermore, the fact that the initial version—the one that comes before the word *ky-ḏd*—is frequently less attested among the parallels shows that the scribe not only intentionally pursued sources but also that he listed them according to his own logic. Moreover, he may have supplied new variants on his own accord, as some variants prove an utter lack of parallels. Many of the variants without attested parallels are alliterative or homophonic puns on the terms and phrases that more commonly occur in the parallel texts.[41] The presence of conspicuous graphic and phonetic puns indicates intentional contemplation on the part of the scribe and perhaps his belief in divinely inspired interpretation.

The scribe's fervent collection of numerous versions, as well as the new additions, serves as undeniable evidence of scribal and priestly scholarship.[42] Scholarship and knowledge were clearly valued by the ancient Egyptians.[43] The

---

38. Cole, "Interpretation and Authority," 86, uses the temple of Ptah in Memphis as an example of an institution where scribes were tasked with copying and accumulating textual variants and interpreting ritual texts.

39. The scribe likely incorporated BD versions from both papyri and tomb walls. The fact that comparable Ptolemaic Memphite BD did not include many of the variants seen in Herw's manuscript argues against the notion of a "master book" containing all of the variants being the source of our BD. Furthermore, the inclusion of Herw's name, titles and mother's name, suggests that our manuscript should not be seen as a *Vorlage*, itself. For a detailed discussion of BD *Vorlage*, see Ursula Rössler-Köhler, "Bemerkungen zur Totenbuch-Tradierung während des Neuen Reiches und bis Spätzeitbeginn" in *Religion und Philosophie im Alten Ägypten: Festgabe für Philippe Derchain zu seinem 65. Geburstag am 24. Juli 1991*, ed. Ursula Verhoeven and Erhart Graefe, OLA 39 (Leuven: Peeters, 1991).

40. For the transfer of CT and BD traditions from Thebes north, see Irmtraut Munro, "Evidence of a Master Copy Transferred from Thebes to the Memphite Area in Dynasty 26," *BMSAES* 15 (2010): 207–8. See also Ursula Verhoeven, *Untersuchungen zur späthieratischen Buchschrift* (Leuven: Peeters, 2001), 341. Rössler-Köhler, "Bemerkungen zur Totenbuch-Tradierung," 279–82 and 284, in turn, discusses the transfer of manuscripts, originating in Thebes to Memphis in the New Kingdom. Éva Liptay, "From Funerary Papyrus to Tomb Wall and Vice Versa: Innovation and Tradition in Early Third Intermediate Period Funerary Art," in Gillen, *(Re)productive Traditions*, 582–83 and *passim*, discusses the exchange of iconography and more generally cultural interaction among contemporaneous religious centers in the Ramesside period and TIP. For local adaptation of religious texts, see Vernus, "Modeling the Relationship," 486.

41. The puns, found in literary texts, or in other religious compositions are often understood as a form of exegesis. For an overview of the types of wordplay and their role in mortuary liturgies, see Yekaterina Barbash, "Wordplay's Place in Mortuary Liturgies. Scribal Devices in Papyrus W551," in *Liturgical Texts for Osiris and the Deceased in Late Period and Greco-Roman Egypt. Proceedings of the Colloquiums at New York (ISAW), 6 May 2011, and Freudenstadt, 18–21 July 2012*, ed. Burkhard Backes and Jacco Dieleman, Studien zur Spätägyptischen Religion 14 (Wiesbaden: Harrasowitz, 2015). Annie Gasse, *Un papyrus et son scribe: Le Livre des morts Vatican, Museo Gregoriano Egizio 48832* (Paris: Cybèle, 2002), 41–48, demonstrates alternative interpretations of texts based on confusions stemming from graphic similarity of signs.

42. Griffiths, "Allegory in Greece and Egypt," 98–100, views BD 17, as well as other BD spells where *ky-ḏd* is used, as evidence that its composers intentionally interpreted, disagreed, and supplied additional, often allegorical meaning. Dimitri Laboury, "Tradition and Creativity: Toward a Study of Intericonicity in Ancient Egyptian Art," in *(Re)productive Traditions in Ancient Egypt: Proceedings of the Conference Held at the University of Liège, 6th–8th February 2013*, ed. Todd Gillen (Liège: Presses Universitaires de Liège, 2017), 247–48, demonstrates that the variations in visual representations are systematic and intentional, and thus should not be considered as mistakes but rather as "sources and expressions of creativity." His discussion of interpictoriality, that defines and acknowledges an image's meaning and shape within the network of other images, should be applied to textual analysis, as well. Cole, "Interpretation and Authority," 71–75, discusses the task of unraveling and interpreting, reflected by the term *wḥꜥ*, as "a persistent intellectual pursuit of the well-educated scribe."

43. The professional expertise of priests and scholars is often described by the word for "craft," *ḥmw*, Chloé Ragazzoli, "The Pen Promoted My Station: Scholarship and Distinction in New Kingdom Biographies," in *Problems of Canonicity and Identity Formation in Ancient Egypt and Mesopotamia*, ed. Kim Ryholt and Gojko Barjamovic (Copenhagen: Museum Tusculanum Press, 2016), 158; Laurent

tradition of scribal scholarship is evident through textual collation of such religious compositions as the Coffin Texts and underworld books.[44] The priest scribes were seen as responsible not only for copying, but also for clarifying and interpreting the texts for their human and divine audiences. Despite its "canonization," the BD was not a fossilized text even in the Ptolemaic period. As the example of Herw's papyrus shows, scribes strove to emend and add to the content when copying the BD.[45]

This manuscript is a scholarly attempt to gather as many versions as possible, likely to add others based on phonetic and graphic similarities and to interpret the text from all perspectives. The manuscript illustrates that, in the Egyptian mind, scholarship was not necessarily about finding the one correct answer but was concerned with the process of exploring as many solutions as possible. Just as any effort to explain or simply understand something entails a repetition, an approach from several directions, our Ptolemaic scribe strove to clarify the spells for Herw, and perhaps for himself.

Coulon, "Rhétorique et stratégie du discours dans les formules funéraires: Les innovations des textes des sarcophages," in *D'un monde à l'autre: Textes des pyramides & textes des sarcophages: Actes de la Table ronde internationale "Textes des Pyramides versus Textes des Sarcophages"; IFAO, 24–26 Septembre 2001*, ed. Susanne Bickel and Bernard Mathieu, BdÉ 139 (Cairo: Institut français d'archéologie orientale, 2001), 121–25. Vernus, "L'écrit et la canonicité," 303. Cole, "Interpretation and Authority," 88–89, argues that textual commentary such as annotating passages and gathering variants was intended to expand the understanding of a text.

44. Daniel Werning, "Inner-Egyptian Receptions of a Theological Book," 44–48, and n. 19, proposes the term "archeophililogists," for the scribes who copied and reproduced longer texts. David Silverman, "Textual Criticism in the Coffin Texts," in *Religion and Philosophy in Ancient Egypt*, ed. James Allen (New Haven: Yale Egyptological Seminar, 1989), 43, attributes textual criticism and revisions in the CT primarily to mistakes of copyists. On the contrary, John Gee, "Glossed Over: Ancient Egyptian Interpretations of Their Religion," in *Evolving Egypt: Innovation, Appropriation, and Reinterpretation in Ancient Egypt*, ed. Kerry Muhlestein (Oxford: Archaeopress, 2012), 73, regards the presence of glosses in the earliest copies of CT 335, and increasing in number as the spell transforms into BD 17, as evidence of scribal interest in improving the meaning and function of religious texts through scholarly revisions.

45. Ragazzoli, "Beyond Authors and Copyists," 95–96, describes the "productive aspect" of the transmission of texts. Von Lieven, "Closed Canon vs. Creative Chaos," 67–68 and 72, argues that the BD is a ritual text and thus does not provide knowledge. Nevertheless, she points out that it is the preliminary information, necessary for the ritualist that "contained pieces of divine knowledge." These fragments of knowledge in turn became significant to scholarship, as is evident in the variations within the BD. Vernus, "Modeling the Relationship," 485 and 490–91, discusses "knowledge texts" being viewed as open to modification or renewal (*sm3wy*). See also Vernus, "L'écrit et la canonicité," 299–304.

Dein sei die Maat, Thot verleihe sie dir

Horst Beinlich

Das Überreichen der Maat gehört sicherlich zu den häufigsten und wohl auch wichtigsten Ritualhandlungen des ägyptischen Königs.[1] In den weitaus meisten Fällen geschieht das Überreichen der Maat so, daß der ägyptische König eine Maat-Figur auf der linken oder rechten Hand hält und sie mit der anderen Hand weiht. Die Maat kann aber auch auf andere Weise für die Gottheit wirksam werden.

Man sieht das in sechs Ritualszenen aus Dendara: («111019», Abb. 1), («111025», Abb. 2), («110428», Abb. 3), («110452», Abb. 4), («142316», Abb. 5), («142317», Abb. 6). Bei all diesen Ritualszenen fällt auf, daß die Maat nicht explizit dargebracht wird. Sie ist bereits da. Sie hockt auf einem mehr oder weniger hohen Sockel vor der Gottheit, vor Hathor – oder im Fall des Isis-Tempels von Dendara – auch einmal vor Isis, die mit Hathor hier mehr oder weniger wesensgleich ist. Daß die Sockel der Maat unterschiedlich groß sind, liegt daran, daß sie in vier Fällen in gleicher Augenhöhe mit der Gottheit ist. Nur in den beiden Fällen («111025»), («111019»), wenn der König den Schrein der Göttin öffnet (Ritual: „das Gesicht öffnen") und der mögliche Augenkontakt zwischen Göttin und König eine Rolle spielt, ist sie auf einem so niedrigen Sockel, daß sie diesen Kontakt nicht stört.

Bei den sechs Szenen handelt es sich um zentrale Szenen des Tempels. Zwei Szenen sind im hinteren Sanktuar (J) des Hathortempels direkt neben der Nische, in die die Kultfigur gehört («110428»), («110452»). Zwei Szenen sind im Zentrum des Dach-Kiosks, in der die jährliche Erneuerung der Kultfigur zelebriert wird («111019»), («111025»). Zwei Szenen sind im Sanktuar des Isis-Tempels («142316»), («142317»).

Die beiden Darstellungen im Zentrum des Dachtempels geben anscheinend die reale Situation wieder. Die Figur der Göttin sitzt in einem tragbaren Schrein. Es ist die Hauptfigur des Tempels, sie hat ein Was-Szepter in der Hand. Vor ihr innerhalb des Schreins sieht man einen Kindgott, in («111025») ist es „Ihi-wab", in der korrespondierenden Szene («111019») Ihi-nun. Hinter diesen Kindgöttern ist, ebenfalls im Schrein, die Maat auf ihrem Sockel. Szene («110452») aus dem Sanktuar des Hathor-Tempels gibt die gleiche Szene wieder. Hier öffnet der König allerdings keinen Schrein – diese Handlung hat schon stattgefunden, sondern er übergibt der Göttin zwei Tuchstreifen (Kleidung). In der korrespondierenden Szene («110428») erhält die Göttin Salbe und der Ihi-wab ist zum König hin dargestellt. Die Aussage ist m.E. klar: Die Maat ist bei der Göttin, sie entfernt sich nicht von ihr.[2]

Auch bei den beiden Szenen im Isis-Tempel finden wir fast das gleiche Bild. Der Unterschied ist dabei, daß in beiden Fällen hinter der Göttin ein weiterer Gott thront. Hinter Isis ist es Harsomtus («142317»), hinter Hathor Horus von Edfu («142316»). Isis hält auch in («142316») nicht das Was-Szepter, sondern faßt mit der Hand das Sistrum an, das ihr Ihi-wer überreicht. In Szene («142317») reicht Hor-Ihi der Hathor das Sistrum. Es sei nochmals betont,

1. Siehe dazu: H. Beinlich, *Handbuch der Szenentitel in den Tempeln der griechisch-römischen Zeit Ägyptens. Die Titel der Ritualszenen, ihre korrespondierenden Szenen und ihre Darstellungen*, 2 Bde., SRaT 3 (Dettelbach: Röll, 2008), 1:288; H. Beinlich und J. Hallof, *Einführung in das Würzburger Datenbanksystem*, SRaT 1 (Dettelbach: Röll, 2007), 103–7. (This book explains the database system. With the free programme one can call up the illustrations, comments and picture credits.)

2. Siehe dazu z.B. É. Chassinat, *Le temple d'Edfou* VII, 2. Aufl., Mémoires publiés par les membres de la Mission archéologique française au Caire 24 (Kairo: Institut français d'archéologie orientale, 2009), 90, 10–16; Jean-Claude Goyon, *Le papyrus d'Imouthès, fils de Psintaês au Metropolitan Museum of Art de New-York (Papyrus MMA 35.9.21)* (New York: Metropolitan Museum of Art, 1999), 56.

Abbildung 1. «111019»

Abbildung 2. «111025»

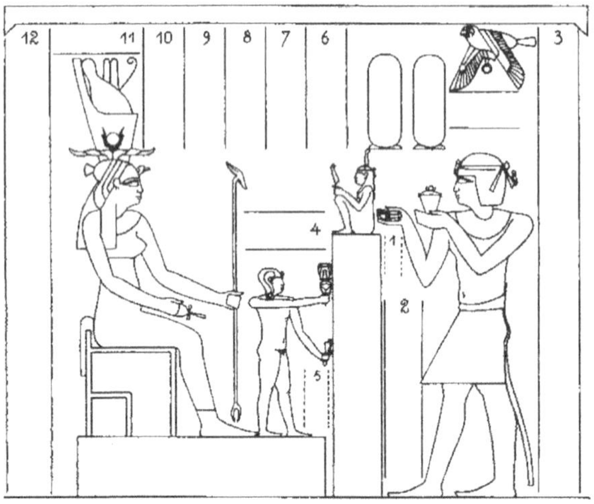

Abbildung 3. «110428»

Abbildung 4. «110452»

Abbildung 5. «142316»

Abbildung 6. «142317»

daß in keiner der hier genannten sechs Darstellungen der König Maat an die Göttinnen gibt. Die Maat – sie wird hier als Große Maat bezeichnet – ist schon da. Dabei ist die Wahrscheinlichkeit groß, daß diese Maat real als Figur der Kultfigur der Göttin beigegeben ist.

In der untersten Krypte auf der Südseite des Hathor-Tempels von Dendara wird eine Maat-Figur auf einem Sockel abgebildet («110526», Abb. 7). Sie sitzt in Front zu einer Hathor-Figur ganz genau so, wie sie z.B. in Szene («111025») gezeigt ist. Begleitet wird die Hathor-Figur von der Figur eines Kindgottes (Ihi-wer). Bei Hathor und Ihi handelt es sich nach der Beischrift um Figuren aus Gold, die eine Elle hoch sind.[3] Die Größe und das Material der Maat – sie wird hier ebenfalls als Große Maat bezeichnet – ist nicht angegeben, aber aus der Zusammenstellung ergibt sich, daß es sich auch um eine Statuette handeln muß. Die drei Figuren sind also so zusammengestellt, wie sie es auch im Kult sind. Daß die Größe der Maat dem entspricht, was die Darstellung in der Krypte vorgibt, darf bezweifelt werden. Die Darstellungen im Dach-Kiosk («111019»), («111025») dürften der Realität näher kommen, aber das läßt sich nicht beweisen.

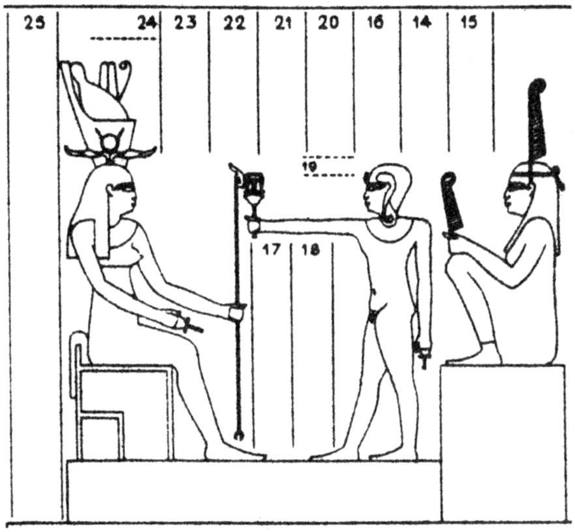

Abbildung 7. «110526»

Es wäre natürlich möglich, daß das Überreichen der Maat in den Ritualszenen mit der Stiftung einer solchen Figur zusammenhängt. Ich meine aber, daß beides voneinander unabhängig ist. Der König garantiert mit dem Überreichen der Maat in den Ritualszenen, daß die Maat im Tempel existiert. Die Figur ist dabei nur ein Ausdruck der Garantie der rechten Weltordnung. Man muß aber damit rechnen, daß eine real existierende Figurengruppe als Vorbild für Darstellungen in Ritualszenen genommen wird.

Eine weitere Möglichkeit, die Maat an die Götter zu überreichen, ist es, die Maat als Göttin selbst agieren zu lassen. Dabei gibt es mehrere Möglichkeiten der Darstellung und auch mehrere Möglichkeiten der Deutung.

3. Siehe dazu und zu den Statuetten in Dendara allgemein: S. Cauville, „Les statues cultuelles de Dendera d'après les inscriptions pariétales", *BIFAO* 87 (1987): 73–117, bes. 80 und 95.

Abbildung 8. «142329»

Abbildung 9. «142346»

1. Die Göttin Maat steht allein vor einer Gottheit

Bis auf eine Ausnahme stammen all diese zehn Darstellungen aus Dendara (s.u.): («111225», Abb. 10), («111232»), («111748», Abb. 11), («130032»), («130051», Abb. 12), («145506»), («145512»), («345051», Abb. 20). Nur zwei zeigen die Maat vor Göttern, die nicht zu den beiden Hauptpersonen des Tempels, Hathor und Isis, gehören: («142329», Abb. 8), («142346», Abb. 9). Bei («142329») ist es Amun-ren-ef; bei («142346») ist es Ptah. Beide werden nach den Texten in ihren Kapellen verehrt.[4] Maat ist nach den Texten auf Dauer bei diesen Göttern und wird sich nicht von ihnen entfernen. Man könnte sich also vorstellen, daß die beiden Darstellungen so interpretiert werden könnten, wie das Bild der Hathor mit der Maat in ihrem Schrein (s.o.). Anders als bei den weiteren sieben Darstellungen steht Maat vor den Göttern und hat die beiden Arme neben sich herabhängen. Dies ist eine Haltung, die man beim König meist mit dem Betreten eines Schreins, dem Anbeten oder dem Erdeküssen verbindet.[5] Der Thronsockel des Ptah ist eine Maat-Hieroglyphe.

Die typische Darstellung vor Hathor oder Isis in Dendara sieht anders aus («111225»), («111232»), («111748»), («130032»), («130051»), («145506»), («145512»). Hier steht Maat mit beiden zur Adoration erhobenen Armen vor der Göttin. Stets ist ein Kindgott anwesend. In den Szenen («111225»), («111232») thront der Kindgott Ihi-wer bzw. Harsomtus in Größe eines Erwachsenen hinter der Göttin Hathor. Bei den anderen Szenen stehen ein oder zwei kleine Kindgötter zwischen Maat und Hathor, in Szene («130051») Isis.

Bei den Szenen («130032») und («130051») steht die Maat vor einer Teiltriade mit Isis und Tenen («130051») bzw. Hathor und Horus von Edfu («130032»). Die vollständigen Triaden hatte ich in einer früheren Arbeit als

4. Siehe dazu: S. Cauville. *Dendara: Le temple d'Isis* (Kairo: Institut français d'archéologie orientale, 2007), 99, 14 und 126, 51 (*ḥḏ*).
5. Siehe dazu Beinlich, *Handbuch der Szenentitel* 2:8f.

Abbildung 10. «111225»

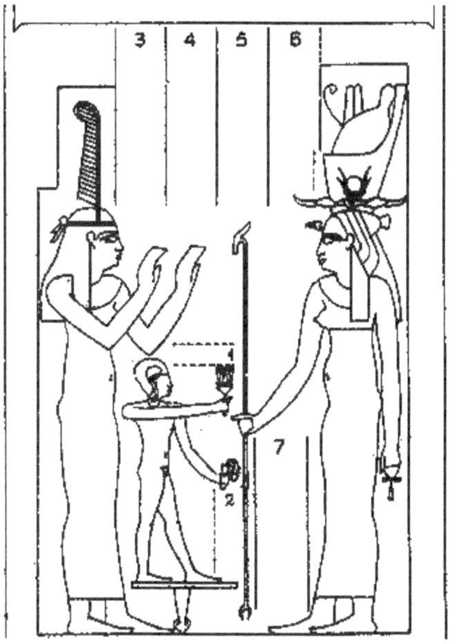

Abbildung 11. «111748»

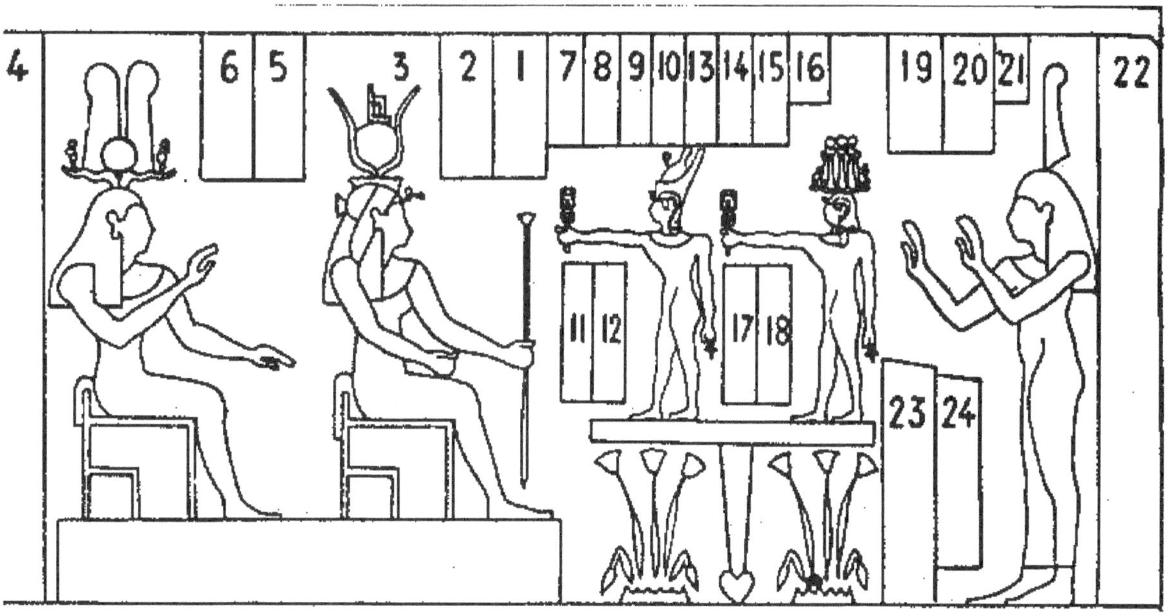

Abbildung 12. «130051»

Krönungstriaden bezeichnet.[6] Dabei entspricht die Hathor-Triade der Isis-Triade bzw. umgekehrt. In den beiden Szenen stehen jeweils zwei Kindgötter vor Hathor bzw. Isis. Im Prinzip haben wir also wieder die Göttergruppe der schon behandelten Szene («110526») der untersten Krypte auf der Südseite des Hathor-Tempels.

6. Beinlich, *Einführung in das Würzburger Datenbanksystem*, 69–89.

Auch auf der Innenseite des Türsturzes des Harsomtus-Tores («145512»), also an prominenter Position, finden wir die Konstellation „Maat und Kindgott vor Hauptgöttin (wohl Hathor)". In Szene «145506» steht Maat-Weret mit Ihi-wer vor Hathor-Isis (S. Cauville, *Porte d'Horus* [Le Caire: IFAO, 2021], 35–36), in Szene «145512» steht Maat mit Harsomtus vor Isis-Hathor (Cauville, 35–36).

2. Die Göttin Maat steht vor einer Gottheit, dahinter steht der König

Wie schon oben gesagt, kann die Maat vor einer Gottheit besagen, daß die Maat beständig bei dieser Gottheit ist. Daß sie vom König garantiert wird, zeigen jene Darstellungen, die den König beim Opfer einer Maat-Figur darstellen. Zu diesem Inhalt gehören wohl auch die Darstellungen, die eine Maat als Göttin zeigen, hinter der noch der König abgebildet ist. Klar wird dies vor allem, wenn der König in seiner Hand eine Maat-Figur opfert: («110816»), («110854», Abb. 13), («111458»), («111474»), («120053»). Die Maat ist dabei in beidhändiger Adorationshaltung dargestellt. Ein Kindgott kann der Szene beigegeben sein. Die Doppelung der Maat, die sich durch die menschengroß dargestellte Göttin und die kleine Figur in der Hand des Königs ergibt, ist allerdings nicht zwingend, wie die Szene («111411», Abb. 14) zeigt.[7] Hier hält der König zwei Men-Gefäße in seinen beiden Händen, während

Abbildung 13. «110854»

Abbildung 14. «111411»

7. Die Haltung des Königs in Szene («142262») ist wegen der Zerstörung nicht eindeutig zu klären. Mir scheint, daß er wie in den Szenen («110432») und («110446») die Arme gesenkt hält.

Abbildung 15. «422045 »

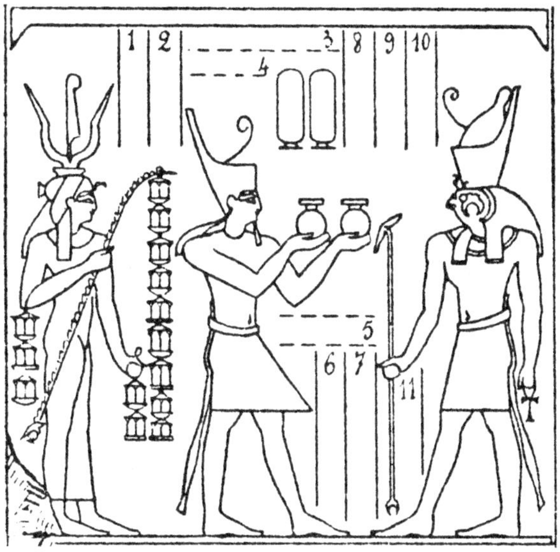

Abbildung 16. «901577»

vor ihm in Adorationshaltung (mit beiden Armen) Maat in Richtung auf die Krönungstriade der Hathor steht. Dazwischen sieht man noch zwei Kindgötter.

Es fällt auf, daß alle bisher genannten Darstellungen der Hathor aus Dendara stammen und man kann sich fragen, ob das daher kommt, daß hier die Konstellation des Sanktuars Pate stand, in der der König vor einen Schrein tritt, in dem sich Hathor, Kindgott und Maat befinden.

In den anderen Tempeln steht die Göttin Maat hinter dem agierenden König. Im Hathor-Tempel von Deir el-Medineh steht sie hinter Ptolemaios IV., der dem Gott Month Wein darreicht. Hinter dem König steht Maat und hält mit der Rechten eine Jahresrispe mit Sed-Fest. Mit der Linken führt sie den einarmigen Adorations-Gestus aus. Die Handlung der Maat ist eindeutig auf den König ausgerichtet. Sie verleiht ihm hunderttausende Jahre.

Abbildung 17. «440013»

Abbildung 18. «111916»

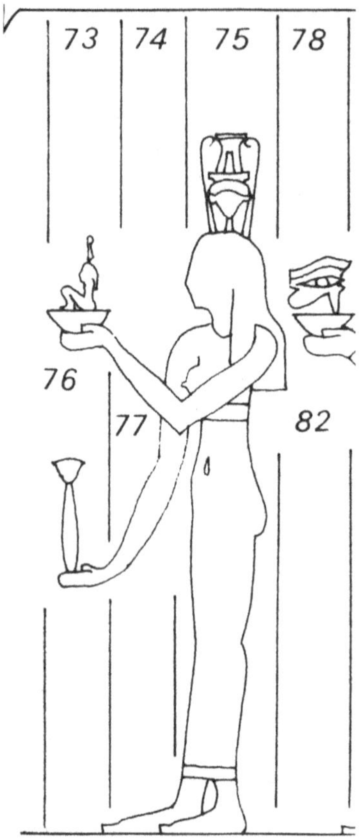

Abbildung 19. «111608»

In Edfu finden wir das gleiche Motiv und zwar ebenfalls aus der Zeit Ptolemaios IV. Die Vielzahl der Jahre wird hier durch eine größere Zahl von Sed-Fest-Symbolen unterstrichen, die die Maat z.T. mit der Linken hält. Auffällig ist, daß die Maat-Feder auf dem Kopf der Göttin mit einem Kuh-Gehörn abgebildet ist. (Die Feder ist in der Zeichnung seitenverkehrt). Wahrscheinlich meint das Kuhgehörn nur „*wp.t* – Scheitel", es könnte aber auch eine Anspielung auf „*wp-rnp.t* – das Jahr eröffnen" sein.

Maat wird auch mit Jahresrispen dargestellt, wenn nur die Götter in einer Szene handeln («142262»). Möglicherweise ist in dieser Szene, in der das Mekes übergeben wird, ihre enge Bindung an Thot ausschlaggebend gewesen.

Auf dem Türsturz des Bab el-Abd im Month-Tempel von Theben wird der König dargestellt, wie er an die Triade des Tempels die Maat übergibt («440013», Abb. 17). Hinter ihm stehen drei Frauen: Berenike, Maat und Waset. In der korrespondierenden Szene («440014») ist Waset durch Niut ausgetauscht, was aber die gleiche Göttin meint. Die ersten beiden Frauen haben ihre beiden Hände zur Adoration erhoben. Die Feder der Maat ist mit einer Sonnenscheibe kombiniert.

Abbildung 20. «345051»

Maat erscheint auf der Seite des Königs auch dann, wenn ganze Götterreihen dargestellt werden. Neben der normalen Darstellung («111916», Abb. 18) – beidhändig adorierend mit Maat-Feder auf dem Kopf – gibt es da auch die Darstellung («111608», Abb. 19), die die Göttin bei der Inthronisation des Horus zeigt. Sie hat dabei ein Hathor-Kapitell auf dem Kopf, trägt in ihrer Linken eine Maat-Figur und in ihrer Rechten eine Papyrus-Pflanze.

Ganz ausgefallen ist die Darstellung im Bibliotheksraum der 2. Ostkolonnade von Philae. Hier steht Maat vor Thot und bietet ihm mit der Rechten eine Schreibpalette dar.

Tafel 1. Bildnachweis und Auflösung der SERaT-Chiffren.

«110428»	Abb. 3	=	Émile Chassinat, *Le temple de Dendara 3* (Kairo: Institut français d'archéologie orientale, 1935), 82, Taf. 190 und 198; Sylvie Cauville, *Dendara III: Traduction*, OLA 95 (Leuven: Peeters, 2000), Taf. 45.
«110432»	s. SERaT	=	Chassinat, *Le temple de Dendara 3*, 77, Taf. 190; Cauville, *Dendara III: Traduction*, Taf. 39.
«110446»	s. SERaT	=	Chassinat, *Le temple de Dendara 3*, 66, Taf. 180; Cauville, *Dendara III: Traduction*, Taf. 29.
«110452»	Abb. 4	=	Chassinat, *Le temple de Dendara 3*, 71, Taf. 190; Cauville, *Dendara III: Traduction*, Taf. 35.
«110526»	Abb. 7	=	Émile Chassinat, *Le temple de Dendara 5* (Kairo: Institut français d'archéologie orientale, 1952), 135, Taf. 424 und 427–28.
«110816»	s. SERaT	=	Émile Chassinat, *Le temple de Dendara 4* (Kairo: Institut français d'archéologie orientale), 1935, 259, Taf. 311; Sylvie Cauville, *Dendara IV: Traduction*, OLA 101 (Leuven: Peeters, 2001), Taf. 205.
«110854»	Abb. 13	=	Chassinat, *Le temple de Dendara 4*, 241, Taf. 311; Cauville, *Dendara IV: Traduction*, Taf. 184.
«111019»	Abb. 1	=	Émile Chassinat und François Daumas, *Le temple de Dendara 8* (Kairo: Institut français d'archéologie orientale, 1978), 28, Taf. 705.
«111025»	Abb. 2	=	Chassinat und Daumas, *Le temple de Dendara 8*, 23, Taf. 705 und 708.
«111225»	Abb. 10	=	Sylvie Cauville, *Le temple de Dendara 12* (Kairo: Institut français d'archéologie orientale), 2007, 17, Taf. 15.
«111232»	s. SERaT	=	Cauville, *Le temple de Dendara 12*, 34, Taf. 24.
«111411»	Abb. 14	=	Sylvie Cauville, *Dendara: Les fêtes d'Hathor*, OLA 105 (Leuven: Peeters, 2002), Taf. 45; Sylvie Cauville, *Le temple de Dendara 15*, o.J., 307, Taf. 169, https://www.ifao.egnet.net/publications/catalogue/Temples-Dendara/.
«111458»	s. SERaT	=	Sylvie Cauville, *Le temple de Dendara 14*, o.J., 28, Taf. 24, https://www.ifao.egnet.net/publications/catalogue/Temples-Dendara/.
«111474»	s. SERaT	=	Cauville, *Le temple de Dendara 14*, 71, Taf. 55.
«111608»	Abb. 19	=	Sylvie Cauville, *Le temple de Dendara 10* (Kairo : Institut français d'archéologie orientale, 1997), 55, Taf. 16, 32.
«111748»	Abb. 11	=	Chassinat, *Le temple de Dendara 5*, 58, Taf. 358 und 365.
«111916»	Abb. 18	=	Sylvie Cauville, *Le temple de Dendara 13*, o.J., 110, Taf. 92–96, https://www.ifao.egnet.net/publications/catalogue/Temples-Dendara/.
«120053»	s. SERaT	=	François Daumas, *Les mammisis de Dendara*, PIFAO (Kairo: Institut français d'archéologie orientale, 1959), 57, Taf. 9, Tab. 3 I.
«130032»	s. SERaT	=	Daumas, *Les mammisis de Dendara*, 112, Taf. 58, 4e reg.
«130051»	Abb. 12	=	Daumas, *Les mammisis de Dendara*, 133, Taf. 58, 4e reg.
«142262»	s. SERaT	=	Sylvie Cauville, *Dendara: Le temple d'Isis* (Kairo: Institut français d'archéologie orientale, 2007), 341, Taf. 273.
«142316»	Abb. 5	=	Cauville, *Dendara: Le temple d'Isis*, 92, Taf. 97.
«142317»	Abb. 6	=	Cauville, *Dendara: Le temple d'Isis*, 119, Taf. 116.
«142329»	Abb. 8	=	Cauville, *Dendara: Le temple d'Isis*, 99, Taf. 102.
«142346»	Abb. 9	=	Cauville, *Dendara: Le temple d'Isis*, 126, Taf. 120.
«145506»	s. SERaT	=	Sylvie Cauville, „Dendara: Le domaine d'Horus et la nécropole d'Osiris", *GM* 259 (2019): 58.
«145512»	s. SERaT	=	Cauville, „Dendara: Le domaine d'Horus", 58.
«345051»	Abb. 20	=	Horst Beinlich, *Die Photos der Preußischen Expedition 1908–1910 nach Nubien, Teil 5*, SRaT 18 (Dettelbach: Röll, 2012), Photo 842-843, WB-Zettel 2937-2941.
«422045»	Abb. 15	=	Pierre du Bourguet, *Le temple de Deir al-Médîna*, MIFAO 121 (Kairo: Institut français d'archéologie orientale, 2002), Nr. 28.

«440013»	Abb. 17	=	Sydney Aufrère, *Le propylône d'Amon-Rê-Montou à Karnak-Nord*, MIFAO 117 (Kairo: Institut français d'archéologie orientale, 2000), 424.
«440014»	s. SERaT	=	Aufrère, *Le propylône d'Amon-Rê-Montou*, 430.
«901577»	Abb. 16	=	Maxence de Rochemonteix, *Le temple d'Edfou I*, MMAF 10 (Kairo: Institut français d'archéologie orientale, 1897), 365, Taf. 31c.

A Little Thoth Goes a Long Way

Betsy M. Bryan

There is no need to explain why I would dedicate a brief article about the god Thoth to Richard Jasnow who, together with Karl-Theodor Zauzich, has made the Book of Thoth a household title in the field of Egyptology.[1] There is surely nothing about the god that I can offer to enlighten Richard further, but instead I will attempt to use a small figurine of Thoth to clarify the position of this faience image in the context of personal and cultic worship embodied in the terms "amulet" and "votive."

The Form of Thoth's Image

The Eton College in Windsor, England loaned a large number of Egyptian objects to the Johns Hopkins University Archaeological Museum for a twenty-year period through 2030. Colonel Joseph Myers was the collector of the majority of these pieces and was very fond of faience, particularly of blue color. This small piece, ECM [Eton College Myers] 625 represents the god Thoth in a striding pose, preserved but for his lower legs and possibly a socle[2] (fig. 1). The measurements set its incomplete height at 8.1 cm, its width at 3.8 cm, and its thickness at 4.7 cm. The original height would have been approximately 11.05 cm, without a socle.[3] The god wears a headdress appearing to consist of a tripartite wig with a circlet atop it and an *atef* crown springing from the modius. At the back of the crown is a loop that could have enabled the figure to be worn as a pendant. The *atef* crown has a cylindrical center element similar to those worn by *muu* dancers and by Osiris (broken at the top) and a sun disk (front and back) at the base of the two feathers resting upon the ram's horns. It also has a uraeus topped by a sun disk at the end of each twisted horn. According to Sandra Collier's descriptions of royal *atef* crowns, these elements are common among examples of the crown from the Twenty-First to Thirtieth Dynasties (and earlier as well).[4]

Thoth's hands cradle a *wedjat* eye, the proper right atop the eye and the left hand below. His long beak touches the top of the brow, a feature that both visually contributes to the protective embrace of the eye but also was an element of the intricate openwork molding that created the figurine. The wig or headdress has been skillfully joined to the beak, which was likely a separate piece connected in the mold with the body and eye. The black colorant (see further

1. Richard Jasnow and Karl-Theodor Zauzich, *The Ancient Egyptian Book of Thoth: A Demotic Discourse on Knowledge and Pendant to the Classical Hermetica*, 2 vols. (Wiesbaden: Harrassowitz, 2005).

2. Measurements of the figure are as follows, all in centimeters (thanks to Kate Gallagher of the JHUAM): height of crown 2.35; greatest depth of crown 0.96; width of crown 3.73; width of shoulders 3.52; bottom of the buttock to shoulder L 3.18, R 3.01; shoulder to top of headdress in rear 3.90; length of beak from headdress to wedjat 1.99 (measured horizontally); length of brow on wedjat 2.13; width of waist 1.95; width of hips 2.26; height of loop in rear 1.10; thickness of loop 0.78; height from top of knee to shoulder L 4.38, R 4.14.

3. Utilizing the older proportional grid of 18 squares to the hairline. But given its date, see also Gay Robins, "Standing Figures in the Late Grid System of the 26th Dynasty," *SAK* 12 (1985): 101–16.

4. Sandra Collier, "The Crowns of Pharaoh: Their Development and Significance in Ancient Egyptian Kingship" (PhD diss., University of California, 1996), 37–38, table 5 on p. 44.

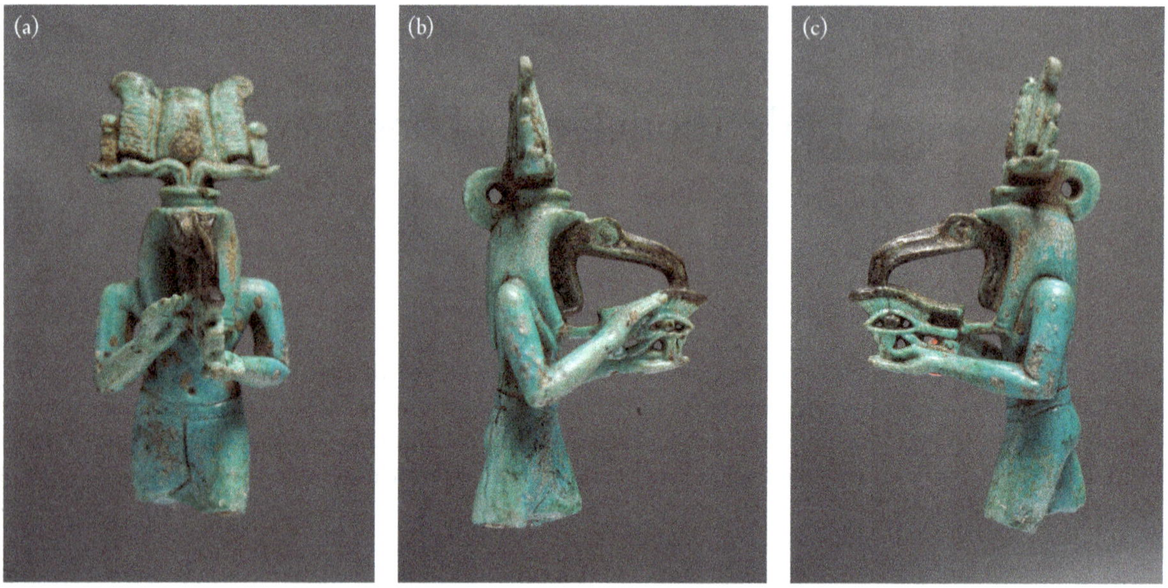

Figure 1. Faience figurine of Thoth, Eton Myers Collection (ECM) 625: (a) front view; (b) left view; (c) right view.

for an analysis) for the beak and brow was able to create a homogenous appearance, while the headdress and beak appear to be quite separate from one another. Thoth seems to be "wearing" a wig or headdress. The eye held by the god would primarily be understood as a left, or "lunar" eye because Thoth's left hand does not obscure its view at all, although his right one does cover a full view of the right eye. Still, both are present in the openwork element and should be evaluated in the iconography of the figurine. A discussion below of possible meanings for this eye will be offered.

Some specific elements of the style of the figure include the coloration, the proportions, the broad and jutting elbows of Thoth that form the greatest width of the object, and the general bodily proportions of the god. All of these contribute to a more precise dating for the figurine than "Late period, Ptolemaic" given in the Eton database. Perhaps the coloration is the strongest element that argues for an earlier date than "Late period, Ptolemaic." The bichromatic turquoise blue and black or brown faience glazing is frequently found on faience amulets and figurines dating to the Third Intermediate period (Dynasties 21–25), perhaps continuing decorative styles from the New Kingdom.[5] During the Twenty-Fifth Dynasty and throughout the Saite era, the penchant for black or brown details on figurines gave way to the monochromatic green glazes, which could be close to matte in finish; still later, blue glazes were common again and can be highly glassy. Nicholson notes that glass production and the use of antimony and other materials used in that industry had also returned during the later Saite era and may have influenced the glazing of some faience as well.[6]

The colorant uses are visible alongside the proportional differences between Third Intermediate period and Late-period figurines, as seen, for example in Eton College Myers Collection ECM 1587[7] (fig. 2). That figure, glazed

5. Paul T. Nicholson and Ian Shaw, eds., *Ancient Egyptian Materials and Technology* (Cambridge: Cambridge University Press, 2000), 184; Paull T. Nicholson, "Faience Technology," in *UCLAEE*, 7, http://escholarship.org/uc/item/9cs9x41z; Florence Friedman et al., eds., *Gifts of the Nile: Ancient Egyptian Faience* (New York: Thames & Hudson, 1998), 155, catalogue number 153, shabtis of Senkamenisken, Museum of Fine Arts, Boston Expedition, 1921.2654, 2679, 2677; Carol Andrews, *Amulets of Ancient Egypt* (London: British Museum Press, 1994), 46 (a) and (h) in particular, compare to the eye on ECM 625.

6. Nicholson and Shaw, *Ancient Egyptian Materials*, 184–85.

7. Friedman et al., *Gifts of the Nile*, entry by Robert Bianchi, catalogue number 169, pp. 146, 271; Meg Swaney and Morgan Moroney,

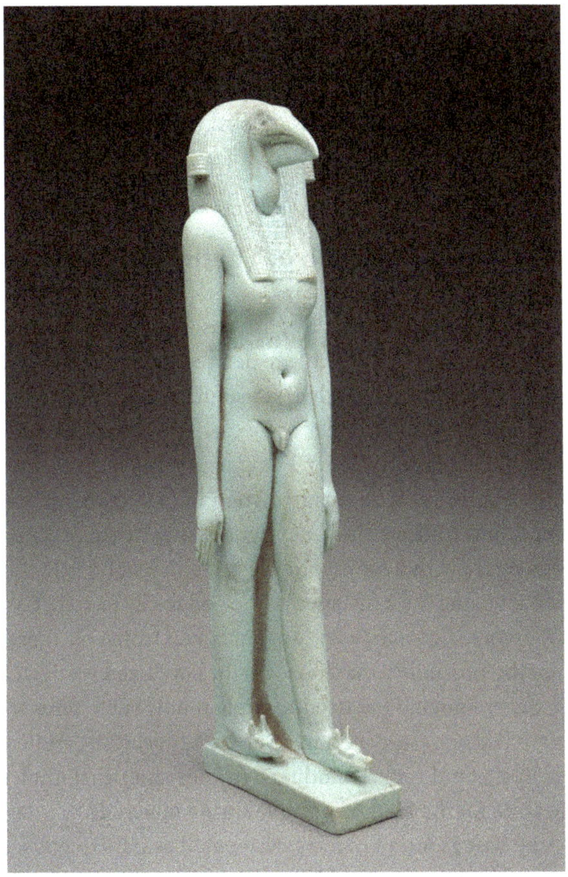

Figure 2. Faience figurine of Thoth. H. 13.5 cm, W. 4.5 cm, D. 3.5 cm. Eton Myers Collection (ECM) 1587.

in a pale green color, was representative of the god as a naked child deity, the Hermopolitan creator, and has protective jackal heads emerging from his feet. The pouchy belly reflects the body type seen on numerous Late-period and Ptolemaic images, for example, on MMA 26.7.860, where it is the lowest part of an adult male abdomen. Russmann discussed the bipartite and tripartite body types seen on royal figures of the Late period; here a male child's, as yet undeveloped, abdomen results in the pouch of the belly without the definition of the upper torso.[8] On the Thoth figurine under discussion, the proportions are quite distinctive—broad shoulders and jutting elbows contrast with an undifferentiated torso. The highly active upper body and arms are the focus of the image emphasizing the eye held by the god. This compares well with the figures in metal discussed by Hill in her exhibition of votive offerings, particularly catalog numbers 17, 19, 20, and 22.[9] Late-period examples of high quality are frequently more refined in style and proportions, and although they commonly display bent arms in active poses, the bodies are more compressed,

eds., *Selections from the Eton College Myers Collection*, Johns Hopkins University Archaeological Museum April to August 2016 (Baltimore: Johns Hopkins University Archaeological Museum, 2016), entry by P. Montgomery, pp. 47–49.

8. Edna R. Russmann, "Late Period Sculpture," in *A Companion to Ancient Egypt*, ed. Alan B. Lloyd (Chichester: Wiley-Blackwell, 2010), 2:950–69 at 650.

9. Marsha Hill, "Heights of Artistry: The Third Intermediate Period (1070–664 B.C.E.)," in *Gifts for the Gods: Images from Egyptian Temples*, ed. Marsha Hill (New York: Metropolitan Museum of Art, 2007), 51–65. The examples were perhaps intended primarily to illustrate Old Kingdom influence, but the results also show active posing and frequently bent arms holding implements. See, in particu-

without the broad shoulders and jutting elbows that we see on the energetic gestures seen on Third Intermediate period images.[10] An assignment of ECM 625 to the Third Intermediate period appears to be demanded from the comparative material available. That body of material agrees well with Carol Andrews's observation that amulets of Thoth carrying the eye "first appear in non-royal burials of IIIrd Intermediate Period date, although superbly modelled ones are characteristically Saite."[11]

The Function of Thoth's Image

Scholars have frequently applied familiar functional designations, such as votive and amulet, to objects such as the Thoth figurine under consideration here. It is not possible to define these categories with precision, but the frequency with which we use them suggests that they are nonetheless useful. Amulets are most often understood to have protective power and to be generally small enough to wear or be carried on one's person; words modernly translated as "amulet" are associated with guarding and protection.[12] Funerary amulets, for example, might be very small indeed, as little as a centimeter or less in length; yet if an image carried on a person could be amuletic, then considerably larger objects could be so defined, and Andrews includes figures larger than 10 cm as amulets. A particularly large one in Berlin is a silver Nefertem figure with a loop, some 26.1 cm in height.[13] The Thoth figurine here, then, could have been apotropaic in function invoking the assistance of the god for its bearer. Based on form, however, Andrews eliminated reliquaries without loops and figurines with loops at ankles from consideration.[14] Diana Patch and Marsha Hill, on the other hand, consider the possibility that loops might have been vestigial artifacts on votive-type objects developed from amuletic ones, thus removing the need to explain how such items were "worn."[15] Likewise, in what are defined as votive caches from Sakkara, deposited in a variety of locations and contexts, items with loops occur among metal objects that range in size and type, including figurines and ritual implements, and even parts of larger elements.[16] Pinch indicated the same for the Hathoric votive shrine materials.

Votive figurines are among the vast group of objects designated as gifts to gods, and their function is as loosely described as the protective one ascribed to amulets. Helmut Brunner considered that a votive gift betrayed a vow to a deity, either as a promise in return for a requested intervention or as a gift in expectation of divine action.[17] In the absence of inscriptional material, however, the intention and anticipation of a donor is outside our knowledge base, and we are left with the donation itself. Indeed, even the identity of the donee may not be certain without provenance or text, despite the form of the figure. Bussmann has recently made this point, and it is a necessary caution that should be kept in mind.[18] In other words, the form of the uninscribed figurine of Thoth holding the eye cannot be linked to

---

lar, the Osorkon I from Brooklyn, 57.92 and the gold figure of Amun, MMA 26.7.1412, pp. 82–89, as well as the copper alloy Nefertem statuette, catalog 20, pp. 52–53.

10. Marsha Hill, "Casting About: The Late Period (664–332 B.C.) and the Macedonian-Ptolemaic Period (332–30 B.C.)," in Hill, *Gifts for the Gods*, 115–52.

11. Andrews, *Amulets of Ancient Egypt*, 49.

12. Andrews, 6; William M. F. Petrie, *Amulets Illustrated by the Egyptian Collection in University College, London* (London: Constable, 1914), 1–4; Adolf Klasens, "Amulett," in *LÄ* 1:232–36; Dows Dunham, "Amulets of the Late Period," *Bulletin of the Museum of Fine Arts* 28.170 (1930): 117–23.

13. Ägyptisches Museum und Papyrussammlung, Staatliche Museen zu Berlin (E 11001); Diana Patch, "Nefertem," in Hill, *Gifts for the Gods*, 143–46.

14. Andrews, *Amulets of Ancient Egypt*, 14.

15. Patch, "Nefertem," 143–46; Hill, "Loops and Metal Statuary," in Hill, *Gifts for the Gods*, 87–88.

16. Sue Davies, "Bronzes from the Sacred Animal Necropolis at North Saqqara," in Hill, *Gifts for the Gods,* 183; Geraldine Pinch, *Votive Offerings to Hathor* (Oxford: Griffith Institute, 1993), 282–300.

17. Helmut Brunner, "Votivgaben," *LÄ* 6:1077–81.

18. Richard Bussmann, "Practice, Meaning and Intention: Interpreting Votive Objects from Ancient Egypt," in *Perspectives on Lived*

the intention of the votive offerer, if this was a gift to a deity, or to the bearer of the amulet, if it was worn in life or after death. To judge very generally from the size of the figurine and from the presence of the loop at the rear of the crown, this image of the ibis-headed Thoth could have been worn or easily borne by a worshiper. Thus by category it would normally be termed as an amulet, but it is unlikely that such a protective image would not also have been an appropriate gift from a hopeful or grateful offerer, as has been noted for the Sakkara animal cemeteries and the Hathoric shrines.[19]

Andrews opined that nearly all images of Thoth presenting the eye, from the Third Intermediate period onward, were funerary in use. That surmise was based on the eye itself as a protective element for the deceased.[20] It is certainly true that the left eye, that is the lunar or Horus eye that endured mutilation, was highly significant for the healing and soundness of the body as required by any person facing the journey to the afterlife. And the gesture of Thoth here, with right hand atop, is common in the examples so far collected. Examples also show the eye parallel to the body of the god, with the eye facing the viewer, and the right hand still atop.[21] These could be either right or left eyes.[22] This is consistent with eye amulets generally, which occur as both right and left eyes but strongly favor the right, solar, eye.[23] The same point was made by Ana Maria Rosso in her discussion of the wedjat eyes from Tell el-Ghaba in the northern Sinai, where thirty-five examples were of the right eye and thirteen of the left.[24]

Other indicators that the image may indeed be primarily funerary are noted by Claas Bleeker, who mentions Pyramid Texts and Book of the Dead spells that specify Thoth's role in guaranteeing the health and wholeness of the deceased.[25] Among the texts that he cites is BD 160 whose vignette shows Thoth handing the deceased a block with the caption: *rdit wꜣḏ n nšmt*, "giving a *wadj* of feldspar.[26]" The spell itself is more suggestive: "I have/am a *wadj* of feldspar which has no negative condition and which the arm of Thoth supports. (For) he hates damage. If it is healthy (*wḏꜣ*), I am healthy (*wḏꜣ*)."[27] Further in the spell Thoth provides the deceased with the Horus eye and makes him live (PT 830). Yet, given the larger size of this faience image of Thoth, it is perhaps not entirely certain that this is a purely funerary amulet rather than one worn during lifetime and perhaps buried with the owner as well.

Religion Practices—Transmission—Landscape, ed. Nico Staring, Huw Twiston Davies, and Lara Weiss (Leiden: Sidestone, 2019), 73–84, esp. 79–80.

19. Davies, "Bronzes," 178.

20. Andrews, *Amulets of Ancient Egypt*, 49.

21. CG 38680. Georges Daressy, *SStatues de divinités*

Daressy, Georges, Statues de divinités: Nos 38001-39384, 2 vols., Catalogue général des antiquités égyptiennes du Musée du Caire (Cairo: Imprimerie de l'Institut français d'archéologie orientale, 1905–1906), 2:pl. XXXVI.

22. Andrews, *Amulets*, fig. 38h. British Museum EA60481 is a copper alloy figure of Thoth holding a left eye.

23. Petrie, *Amulets*, pls. XXIV–XXV demonstrates this.

24. Ana Maria Rosso, "Le symbolisme réligieux des oudjats de Tell el-Ghaba: Les problèmes techniques de leur préservation," in *Egyptology at the Dawn of the Twenty-First Century: Proceedings of the Eighth International Congress of Egyptologists*, ed. Zahi Hawass (Cairo: American University in Cairo Press, 2000), 380–386, at 383.

25. See Claas J. Bleeker, *Hathor and Thoth: Two Key Figures of the Ancient Egyptian Religion*, SHR 26 (Leiden: Brill, 1973), 146, where he mentions Pyramid Texts and Book of the Dead spells that specify Thoth's role in guaranteeing the health and wholeness of the deceased.

26. Günther Lapp, *The Papyrus of Nebseni (EA 99900)* (London: British Museum Press, 2004), pl. 30.

27. Lapp, *Papyrus of Nebseni*, pl. 30, for photograph of hieroglyphic text. Author's translation. Edouard Naville, *Das aegyptische Todtenbuch der XVIII. bis XX. Dynastie* (Berlin: Asher, 1886), 2:437, chapter 160. There are definite oddities about the text, which is based in Naville's case on the British Museum papyrus of Nebseny, Eighteenth Dynasty, ca. 1400 BCE. However, there is nothing at all improved by T. G. Allen's translation based on OIM 9787, P. Ryerson = R in his publication, Thomas G. Allen, *The Egyptian Book of the Dead Documents in the Oriental Institute Museum at the University of Chicago* (Chicago: University of Chicago Press, 1960), 283. The translation in Raymond O. Faulkner, *The Ancient Egyptian Book of the Dead* (London: British Museum Publications, 1985) 155–56, is far preferable. The reading of *iwty šsr.f* rather than *iwty šs*(*w*) *n.f*, which is what the text of Nebseny shows and which Allen incorrectly stated was written *šsr.f*, is nonsensical. Allen translated "uncoated." The *šs* in question is found in *Wb*. IV:543, 1, "Als krankhaften Zustand des Herzens."

The funerary setting is even more relevant for our Eton College Thoth figure as we consider BD 175 the title of which is *r n tm.t mwt m wḥm m ẖrt-nṯr*, "a spell for not dying again in the necropolis."[28] The vignette accompanying this spell depicts a seated ibis-headed Thoth in mummiform guise with an *ankh* sign atop his upright knee. The god sits atop a shrine and faces the adoring deceased, for the spell contains a serious set of questions where Atum addresses Thoth and the deceased beseeches Atum and Re in the role of Osiris. The background subject is the mythological rebellion of humans against the gods and Thoth's role in punishment, while the deceased then learns how Osiris will live in his prepared netherworld even after the world is destroyed.[29]

In some rubrics to this spell, its effectiveness was to be enhanced by the addition of the following: "Words to say over an image of Thoth which will be made of faience and which will be placed in the hand of the person. That allows endurance on earth and not dying quickly. That will save him."[30] Almost immediately we may wonder whether this Thoth statuette was not exactly one placed in the hand of a deceased person at the time of burial—its size would fit in a fisted hand quite comfortably. We might, therefore, be at the close of our discussion.

Yet, questions still remain that we might consider. How might the addition of a figure of Thoth made of faience have improved the probability that the deceased would not die again? The possible symbolism of Thoth's presence in a faience image may be better elucidated through discussion of the substance itself as means of answering this question.

The Material(ity) of Thoth's Image

A great deal has been written on the identification of *ṯḥnt* as faience and just as much, perhaps, on the meaning and symbolic valences of the substance.[31] A survey of how faience was utilized in tombs of all socioeconomic levels led Patch to conclude that "faience (or glazed steatite) was used not because of its inexpensiveness or easy availability—that is in imitation of more precious substances—but because of its color and finish; the choice of faience was integral to the function of the finished product." This view follows that of Sydney Aufrère who argued that the sparkling shine of faience was its characteristic, most particularly as a self-glazing synthetic material.[32]

What is interesting is that the Egyptians themselves appear to have viewed faience as a magical material that, like their most mysterious and cosmically powerful deities, was self-created in the fire of the kiln and had the properties of twinkling stars and dazzling blinding sunlight.[33] They name it with a word that appears to describe its twinkling glazed surface and classify it with a depiction of a bead hanging ornament, probably consisting of faience. It is described as an article made of faience beads in *Wb.* V:390–91; the *Wb. Belegstellen* V:58, for 390n9 cites Heinrich Schäfer, who notes that the pendant beaded classifier preceded the use of a heaven sign with rays(?) streaming from it, and then concludes that *ṯḥnt*, "faience" derived from the meaning of *ṯḥn* as "shining" before it was connected to solar rays.[34] Although the writing of *ṯḥnt*  utilizing the sky sign did appear later than the classifier showing

28. Edouard Naville, *Das aegyptische Todtenbuch der XVIII. bis XX. Dynastie* (Berlin: Asher, 1886), 1:203.

29. See, for example, the text translation by Raymond Faulkner of BD 175 in the Book of the Dead of Any. Faulkner, *Book of the Dead*, 175.

30. P. Barguet, *Le livre des morts des anciens Egyptiens* (Paris: Cerf, 1967), 261; cited by Sydney H. Aufrère, *L'univers minéral dans la pensée égyptienne, Vol. 2: Les minérais, les métaux, les minéraux et les produits chimiques* (Cairo: Institut français d'archéologie orientale, 1991), 261.

31. John R. Harris, *Lexicographical Studies in Ancient Egyptian Minerals* (Berlin: Akademie, 1961), 135–38; Aufrère, *L'univers* mineral, 2:521–37; Diana Patch, "By Necessity or Design: Faience Use in Ancient Egypt," in Friedman et al., *Gifts of the Nile*, 32–45.

32. Patch, "By Necessity or Design," 43, 45n111, citing Aufrère, *L'univers mineral*, 2:32–45.

33. Aufrère, *L'univers minéral*, 2:530–31, 533.

34. *Wb.* V:390–91; the *Wb. Belegstellen* V:58.; Heinrich Schäfer, "Altes und Neues zur Kunst und Religion von Tell el-Amarna," *ZÄS* 55 (1918): 26n2.

a pendant bead ornamentation , it is difficult to maintain a clear distinction in meaning. Old Kingdom textual examples from the Pyramid Texts connect *ṯḥnt* to the sun, for example, PT 301, 24 = W 454a. The spell contains an encouragement to the "eastern Horus" to whom Unis has brought the great eastern eye: "you should ascend to it [the eye] in this your identity as the sun" (*ṯḥnḥn.k im.s mm nṯrw m rn.s pw n ṯḥnt*), "and you should be dazzling by means of it among the gods in this its name of faience."[35] So, just as the connection of faience to the eastern eye (of Horus) was established already in the Old Kingdom, so too was the immensely complicated interconnection of the two eyes—the solar and lunar; the Horus and Re, and the Wedjat—healthy and wounded—equally linked to Thoth from that early moment.[36] "The sky has fortified the sunlight for Pepi. So, this Pepi shall ascend to the sky as the Sun's eye, and this Pepi shall stand at the eastern eye of Horus by means of which the gods' case is hear.... Pepi has become clean in the cleaning that Horus made for his eye. Pepi is Thoth, who tended you, (eye); Pepi is not Seth, who took it."[37]

The complicated relationship between the eyes, Thoth, and faience as well, was further elaborated in later funerary literature, as, for example, in BD 17. Thoth completed the *wedjat* eye following the violence between Horus and Seth, and when it raged against Re, he also lifted the hair from over the eye of Re and returned it, alive, sound, and healthy.[38] In lines 96 to 98 of chapter 17, the deceased's claim not to be an enemy of the sun god is addressed to Khepri. He rather asserts the right to a meal of faience which is in the Tjenenet cavern. The glosses explain further that "as for faience, it is the eye of Horus. As for the Tjenenet cavern, it is the tomb of Osiris."[39] Thomas G. Allen noted that the equivalence of faience with the eye of Horus is the same as that identified in PT 301 cited above.[40] The allusions to faience may, therefore, contribute to bringing the two eyes together mythologically and symbolically. The ability of faience to evoke both starry sky and glistening sunlight accompanies its frequently cool coloration of blue-green, a color of peace and verdancy.[41] It is also one of its magical properties pointed to by Aufèrè who notes that Horus uses bread loaves of faience to counteract the actions of Seth and observes that it could appease the deities in the manner of turquoise. He further points to a couplet from Ptahhotep that contrasts how a lustful man sees a (forbidden) woman—her body is first of glistening faience (*ṯḥnt*), but momentarily later it is of carnelian (*ḥrst*).[42] The primary distinction here is that between the description of glistening (perhaps oiled) limbs and the reddened flesh so frequently referred to in the New Kingdom love songs by the word *inm/inw*, whose meaning should be "complexion" or "tone" as it relates to the human body when stimulated.[43] In sum, it may not surprise that the magical

---

35. Kurt Sethe, *Die altägyptischen Pyramidentexte nach den Papierabdrücken und Photographien des Berliner Museums*, 4 vols. (Leipzig: Hinrichs, , 1908–1922), 1:233. PT 301: 452b; 454a. Translation after James Allen, *The Ancient Egyptian Pyramid Texts*, WAW 23 (Atlanta: Society of Biblical Literature, 2007), W 206, 55–56.

36. Bleeker, *Hathor and Thoth*, 146. Bleeker refers to Thoth as the "psychopomp" and lists his various types of assistance to the dead. Sethe, *Die altägyptischen Pyramidentexte*, PT 448. Vol. 1:462; PT 359, 1:317–19. In PT 359 Thoth carries the king and other gods across the sky on his wing to the eastern sky so that they can contend against Seth over the eye of Horus.

37. Allen, *Ancient Egyptian Pyramid Texts*, 162, Pepi 471.

38. Thomas G. Allen, *Egyptian Book of the Dead*, section 11. Translation on p. 89. Naville, *Todtenbuch*, vol. 1, ll. 29–34: *iw mḥ.n wsir N wḏ3t m-ḫt hk.s hrw pwy n ʿḥ3 rḥwy ptr rf sw hrw pfy n ʿḥ3 ḥr ḥnʿ stḫ m wd.f st3w n ḥr m iṯ.n ḥr ḫrwy n stḥ ir gr ḏḥwty ir nn m ḏbʿw.f ḏs.f iw ṯs.n wsir N šn.f m wḏ3t m tr nšn ptr rf sw irt twy wnmy nt rʿ m nšn.f m-ḫt h3b.f sy in grt ḏḥwty ṯs šnw.f in.f s ʿnḫ wḏ3 snb nn bg3.s r nb.s ky ḏd wnn irt.f pw mr.s m wnn.s ḥr rm n snnw.s ʿḥʿ.n ḏḥwty ḥr pgs.s*. See also Bleeker, *Hathor and Thoth*, 120–21.

39. Naville, *Todtenbuch*, vol. 1, pl. XXVI, ll. 96–98. *Ir ṯḥn.t irt.ḥr pw ir šb ṯnn.t ḥ3t pw nt Wsir*.

40. Allen, *Egyptian Book of the Dead*, 99 n. az.

41. Aufrèrè, *L'univers minéral* 2:531.

42. Aufrèrè, 531nn113–14; Zbyněk Žába, *Les maximes de Ptaḥḥotep* (Prague: Éditions de l'Académie Tchécoslovaque des Sciences, 1956), 139, ll. 285–286.

43. Bernard Mathieu, *La poésie amoureuse de l'Egypte ancienne: Recherches sur un genre littéraire au Nouvel Empire* (Cairo: Institut français d'archéologie orientale, 1996), 51n139, 219, paragraph 119, for erotic language and referencing the tints of the skin (*inw/inm*); 91n303; pl. 16, ll. 3–4: "the young sycomore ... hung with notched and unnotched figs which are redder than jasper; its leaves are

properties of the material strengthens the action of Thoth as guarantor of all the eye's (eyes')promise. The figurine is thus predominantly an amuletic image. Long may the god continue to offer the eye to my colleague Richard Jasnow.

---

like turquoise, and they have the complexion of faience" (*tšrt sw r ẖnmt nꜣy.s gꜣb mi͗ mfkꜣt i͗ntw mi͗ pꜣ ṯ[ḥ]n.t*). As Manniche notes, cosmetics were sometimes used to heighten the reddening of lips and cheeks, and perhaps other more sexual parts of the body; Lise Manniche, *Sexual Life in Ancient Egypt* (London: Kegan Paul, 1987), 46, 107–11. Compare, e.g., the reddened lips of Nefertiti's bust and Nefertari's lips and cheeks in her tomb representations with the images from the Turin "erotic" papyrus where the priestess is applying makeup and offering her unclad vulva at the same time.

Finding Nitocris: Patterns of Female Rule at the End of Egypt's Old Kingdom

Kathlyn M. Cooney

Scholars discuss the end of the Old Kingdom (Dynasties 3–6) at length. Many have said it fell because of the long reign of Pepi II. Others have said it fell because of corruption. Or, it may have ended, in part, because of female rule, though this is not a scholarly hypothesis, rather one of mythology and story. If the latter were true, it would not have been an isolated occurrence. The end of the Twelfth Dynasty shows rule by the female king Neferusobek. The end of the Eighteenth Dynasty is punctuated by the much-debated rule of the (possibly female) king Ankhkheperure Smenkhkare, perhaps none other than Nefertiti herself. The end of the Nineteenth Dynasty was in the hands of a female king, a certain Tawosret, ousted from power by Setnakht. And the end of Egypt's native rule before it was brought into the Roman Empire as a mere province was defined by the extraordinary rule of the female monarch Cleopatra. Why do we see female rule connected to crisis, to the end of dynasties in Egypt? The answer is that in risk-averse Egypt, royal women—wives, sisters, mothers, daughters—were often the safest repositories of power and the last, best choice as a dynasty ground on into its sixth or seventh generation, probably riddled with (unmentioned) inbreeding. Female rule at the end of a dynasty fits a typical Egyptian pattern.

Indeed, there are tales of just such an Egyptian queen from the end of the Sixth Dynasty, albeit only preserved in later histories written in Greek. In the fifth century BCE, thousands of years after her lifetime, the Greek historian Herodotus spoke of a Queen Nitocris who avenged her murdered brother, husband, and king by inviting all the co-conspirators to a grand banquet in an underground hall. When they were all happy eating and drinking, she unleashed floodgates through a secret channel, drowning them all in Nile waters. She then threw herself into a fiery pit so that no one could exact their retribution on her[1] (although one is left wondering if the fiery pit was really any better than whatever torture they could have meted out). Herodotus' narrative continues:

> Next, they read me from a papyrus the names of three hundred and thirty monarchs, who (they said) were his successors upon the throne. In this number of generations there were eighteen Ethiopian kings, and one queen who was a native; all the rest were kings and Egyptians. The queen bore the same name as the Babylonian princess, namely, Nitocris. They said that she succeeded her brother; he had been king of Egypt, and was put to death by his subjects, who then placed her upon the throne. Bent on avenging his death, she devised a cunning scheme by which she destroyed a vast number of Egyptians. She constructed a spacious underground chamber, and, on pretense of inaugurating it, contrived the following: Inviting to a banquet those of the Egyptians whom she knew to have had the chief share in the murder of her brother, she suddenly, as they were feasting, let the river in upon them by means of a secret duct of large size. This and this only did they tell me of her, except that, when she had done as I have said, she threw herself into an apartment full of ashes, that she might escape the vengeance whereto she would otherwise have been exposed.[2]

1. See Jürgen von Beckerath, "The Date of the End of the Old Kingdom of Egypt," *JNES* 21 (1962): 140–47; Percy E. Newberry, "Queen Nitocris of the Sixth Dynasty," *JEA* 29 (1943): 51–54.

2. Herodotus 2.100. See vol. 1 of the translation by George Rawlinson, *The History of Herodotus*, trans. George Rawlinson, 2 vols. (London: Tudor, 1956).

A few centuries later, the third-century BCE Egyptian priest Manetho, compiler of Egypt's most comprehensive, albeit latest and most far removed, king list, puts Nitocris as the last king of the Sixth Dynasty, starting off a pattern of female rulers who closed out Egyptian dynasties. Manetho adds the details that this Queen Nitocris had very light skin, rosy cheeks, was very beautiful, reigned twelve years and had the Third Pyramid built for herself. This last historical element is quite unspecific given the hundreds of pyramids built over the centuries in Egypt for its kings and queens. The section reads:

The Sixth Dynasty consisted of six kings of Memphis:

1. Othoes, for 30 years: he was murdered by his bodyguard
2. Phius, for 53 years
3. Methusuphis, for 7 years
4. Phiops, who began to reign at the age of six, and continued until his hundredth year
5. Menthesuphis, for 1 year
6. Nitocris, the noblest and loveliest of the women of her time, of fair complexion, the builder of the third pyramid, reigned for 12 years. Total, 203 years. Along with the forementioned 1294 years of the first five dynasties, this amounts to 1497 years.[3]

The third century BCE Eratosthenes(?) quoted in Manetho says Nitocris was the twenty-second ruler of Thebes, that she was a queen whose name meant "Athena is Victorious," and that she ruled for six years.[4] Most compellingly, the name *Nt-ikrt*, or Nitocris, appears on one of the fragments of the Turin king list written during the Ramesside period, the name set within a cartouche like all the other leaders and called King of Upper and Lower Egypt.[5]

Thus, we have no contemporary evidence for this queen from the Sixth Dynasty itself—not one burial location, no statuary, no texts, no monuments or stelae, nothing to prove that she was more than a historian's fancy. More recently, Egyptology has even swung to the opinion that this queen may have never existed at all and that all of these tales of a beautiful, fair-skinned woman are just a fantasy concocted when ancient historians messed up one of the names on one of the king lists from which the Turin papyri were copied (presumably easy to do given that two thousand years had already passed since the rulers in question by the time the list was recorded). The fragment had been placed by Egyptologists at the end of the Sixth Dynasty, fitting exactly with the later renditions of a female king closing out the dynasty,[6] but recently Kim Ryholt has found problems with this location, reassigning the fragment to another section and arguing that the name is a corruption. So, according to the most current Egyptological thinking, the female ruler Nitocris never existed at all and was instead a man.[7]

And yet later ancient historians preserved some pretty salacious details for a woman who never existed at all. Is it not too convenient that cultural memory would invent a ruler—a female ruler, at that—from whole cloth, from a miscopy of a name by a scribe or historian, only to see her fictionally aggrandized by later writers? Perhaps we can

3. This being the section from Africanus. William G. Waddell, *Manetho* (London: Heinemann, 1940), 53–55.

4. Waddell, *Manetho*, 221.

5. Kim Ryholt, "The Late Old Kingdom in the Turin King-List and the Identity of Nitocris," *ZÄS* 127 (2000): 87–100.

6. The Turin king list papyrus is in pieces, and Egyptologists have spilled much ink determining which pieces go where. See Jürgen von Beckerath, *Chronologie des pharaonischen Ägypten: Die Zeitbestimmung der ägyptischen Geschichte von der Vorzeit bis 332 v. Chr*, Münchner Ägyptologische Studien 46 (Mainz: von Zabern, 1997); see Kim Ryholt, "The Turin King-List or So-Called Turin Canon (*TC*) as a Source for Chronology," in *Ancient Egyptian Chronology*, ed. Erik Hornung, Rolf Krauss, and David A. Warburton (Leiden: Brill, 2006), 26–32. Kim Ryholt, "The Turin King-List," *Ägypten und Levante / Egypt and the Levant* 14 (2004): 135–55. Kim Ryholt, "The Late Old Kingdom in the Turin King-List and the Identity of Nitocris," *ZÄS* 127 (2000): 87–100.

7. Indeed, Kim Ryholt has stated, "Accordingly the female king Nitocris never existed but was instead a male king with the prenomen Netjerkare and the nomen Siptah..." continuing that "...his prenomen had become corrupt by a false etymology in the Turin King-list..." and, "Unfortunately for King Siptah, it was the tradition of the Turin King-list that survived until the Late Period and upon which the Classical authors based themselves. This destined King Siptah to be remembered as a woman, albeit a beautiful one, for more than two millennia." Ryholt, "Late Old Kingdom in the Turin King-List," 93.

see such cultural memory as made of stronger stuff. Furthermore, we see some extraordinarily familiar patterns to her story that repeat for other female rulers of Egypt, in particular the fact that a woman was usually only allowed to rule at the end of a dynasty when there were no suitable heirs, not to mention the oft-held perception that females in such positions might resort to deceit and trickery to gain rule, rather than exhibit political straightforwardness (when she lies to get the men into the banquet hall). There is enough to Nitocris's legend to suspect some kernels of truth embedded in the romanticized cultural memory, the details of which have come down to us imperfectly, fragmented, and dramatized. If such a female ruler existed, her time was an unstable one for Egypt, not the rock-solid centralized kingship of the Fourth Dynasty when the Great Pyramids on the Giza Plateau were built. No, Nitocris's Egypt would have been teetering on the brink of social collapse; it was a time when elites were pulling more and more political and economic advantage from their king.

Indeed, archaeologists and historians have often documented the balance of royal-elite power through the dynasties by comparing the tombs of the king with those of his courtiers, analyzing the amount of resources expended upon each.[8] We first see an increase in the size of the royal tombs from the First through the Fourth Dynasties, when the king's sepulcher continued to grow bigger and bigger, reaching an apex with the Great Pyramids at Giza built for Khufu, Khafre, and Menkaure. The Fourth Dynasty tombs of their elites and family members were clustered around such monstrous creations in the same necropolis, as if their safety in the afterlife depended on their proximity to their lord, not to mention showing their own social power to their peers. The queens were granted small pyramids of their own, the high elites large rectangular blocks of stone masonry replete with statuary and inscriptions in the chapels and shafts inside, with none of these women's burial places approaching the size of their lord, the king.

But at the end of the Fourth Dynasty, the king's relative power began to shift. Smaller royal tombs advertise the beginning of declining fortunes for the Egyptian monarchs vis-à-vis their elites. From Dynasties 4 to 6, the tombs of the kings shrank in comparison to what was before and in comparison to the tombs of the elites. By the Fifth Dynasty, the pyramids of the kings were no longer built of stone through and through but only of a rubble core cased with a fine white limestone outer skin, a building that only retains its triangular shape when the outer casing stone is preserved on the monument. The last king of the Fifth Dynasty—Unas—may have even attempted to counter the obvious growing power of his elites by including in his burial chamber carved hieroglyphic incantations of transformation and protection, which Egyptologists call the Pyramid Texts and which were previously kept top secret.[9]

Meanwhile, starting with Dynasty 5, the mastaba tombs of the elites became larger and grander, including complicated and colorful scenes in the tomb chapels.[10] Many of the elites decided they didn't even need to have themselves buried in proximity to their lord anymore, instead returning in death to their provincial hometowns, the real sources of their power economically—to places like Abydos, or Elephantine, wherever their family lands and military forces were based.[11] Elite power was now so little based on kingly largesse that wealthy Egyptian men followed their own father-to-son successions for their own mini scribal, priestly, or territorial professional dynasties, building tombs in a horizontal stratigraphy, side by side.

The kings of the Sixth Dynasty suffered the indignity of commissioning and being buried in the smallest pyramids Egypt had ever seen.[12] The age of the infallible kings who could build mountains of white stone was over. It was the

---

8. For example, see Juan Carlos Moreno García, *The State in Ancient Egypt: Power, Challenges and Dynamics,* Debates in Archaeology (London: Bloomsbury Academic, 2020), 31–36.

9. Carina van den Hoven, "The Pyramid of Unas: The King's Journey from Death to New Life as Reflected in Pyramid Texts and Architecture," *Saqqara Newsletter* 6 (2008): 28–32.

10. Massimiliano Nuzzolo, "Patterns of Tomb Placement in the Memphite Necropolis: Fifth Dynasty Saqqara in Context, in *Abusir and Saqqara in the Year 2015,* ed. Miroslav Barta, Filip Coppens, and Jaromír Krejci, (Prague: Czech Institute of Egyptology, 2018), 257–92.

11. Janet Richards, "Text and Context in Late Old Kingdom Egypt: The Archaeology and Historiography of Weni the Elder," *JARCE* 39 (2002): 75–102.

12. Mark Lehner, *The Complete Pyramids* (London: Thames & Hudson, 1997), 156–63.

age of the landowning elite, the provincial lord, the bureaucrat, when the rich perhaps did not even view their god-king as holding the unassailable power their forefathers had. As a group, these elites could and did challenge their king.

Ironically, it may have even been the invention of the pyramid itself that spelled the beginning of the end for Old Kingdom royal power. To create Djoser's Stepped Pyramid, the first monumental construction ever built on this planet of the Third Dynasty, or to erect the first straight sided pyramid of Sneferu at Dahshur in the Fourth Dynasty, and to engineer the fifty-story-high great pyramid of Khufu on the Giza plateau, complete with corbel-vaulted gallery of granite suspended in its limestone interior, the Egyptian kings were forced to create, train, and nurture skilled engineers, mathematicians, tax-collectors, artisans, and administrators.[13] As the kings' power grew, they wanted to reify it, to display it, to show it off, to manifest it physically, and in so doing the kings were forced to pay officials more than they had ever been paid and provide incentives and job security like never before.[14] Thus, it was the kingship itself that created a class of officials capable of competing with that selfsame authority, perhaps eventually taking the centralized monarchy down entirely.

The pyramid—the symbol of Egyptian divine kingship par excellence, the thing that proved a king's divine status in the eyes of every Egyptian—could be seen as the very thing that upset the balance of power in Egypt. Once the straight-sided, fifty-story pyramid was invented and perfected, the kings themselves diminished as power brokers. No longer were their courtiers expendable. Now, these skilled men needed to be rewarded with power of their own. They needed to be kept happy, to be placated. In fact, it was soon after the first monumental pyramid was invented—for King Djoser in Dynasty 3—that noble tombs first started their rise in size and glory.[15] And as the Egyptians moved into Dynasties 5 and 6, these elite tombs just got bigger, while the royal tombs became smaller. By Dynasty 6, the pyramids of the kings were just sad heaps of rubble, cased in white limestone. Later third-century BCE historian Manetho even records that by the late Sixth Dynasty, the institution of kingship was so disrespected that one of its last kings—Othoes, perhaps to be understood as Teti in the Egyptian sources—was murdered by his bodyguard.[16] Our memory of Egypt's Sixth Dynasty is of it heading down a rocky road of instability and turmoil in the absence of a strong king.

We should remind ourselves here that even a powerful and growing elite likely wanted the monarchy to remain strong and centralizing—because they also benefitted from that balance, limiting the need to fight with other elites and decreasing the need to raise private armies that invaded other provincial elite's territories, laying waste to villages, fields, and homes. Strong kingship kept Egypt's wealthy peaceful and prosperous, something that just about every landowner wanted, though we have little understanding of the million or so peasants who had no political voice of which we can speak. Egyptian kingship was still at the pinnacle of this patriarchal society, a thing worthy of preservation by a risk-averse Egyptian population, if only to provide stability and keep from fighting each other. If the royal dynasty failed, the entire game was up, for the elite landowners too. State monopolization of gold and mineral mines for granite, quartzite, turquoise, carnelian, and natron would be compromised; state-run trade with the Levant, Syria, and the northern Mediterranean would stop.[17] Egyptian elites, it seemed, would go along with anything to see the dynasty continue peacefully—even if a given succession crisis demanded the intercession of a royal woman, like

13. Kara Cooney, *The Good Kings: Absolute Power in Ancient Egypt and Today* (Washington, DC: National Geographic Press, 2021).

14. Moreno García, *State in Ancient Egypt*, 53–60 and 111–20.

15. For example, Wendy Wood, "A Reconstruction of the Reliefs of Hesy-re," *Journal of the American Research Center in Egypt* 15 (1978): 9–24; William M. F. Petrie, Ernest Mackay, and Gerald Wainwritght, *Meydum and Memphis (III)* (London: British School of Archaeology in Egypt, 1910); Yvonne Harpur, *The Tombs of Nefermaat and Rahotep at Maidum: Discovery, Destruction and Reconstruction* (Prestbury, Cheltenham: Oxford Expedition to Egypt, 2001).

16. Waddel, *Manetho*, 53.

17. Moreno Garcia deals with the waxing and waning of state monopolization of mining and trade throughout *The State in Ancient Egypt*.

Nitocris, who later sources claim was beautiful and fierce, even conniving, when she acted to avenge her murdered brother-king. In some ways, the best evidence that Nitocris is a remnant of actual events is that her story was so often repeated in Egypt where elites would allow the rule of a female king before seeing their beloved Nile Valley descend into anarchy.

Though there is no physical evidence for a female king Nitocris, the last few kings of the Old Kingdom show an increased reliance on female power; a series of king's mothers took prominent, yet informal, leadership positions as queen-regents because so many Sixth Dynasty kings came to the throne young and unready. Pepi I must have been quite young when he was crowned as he had a fifty-year reign, perhaps demanding that his mother Iput make decisions for him in the palace as regent.[18]

Egypt was in decline economically in Dynasty 6. Historical texts talk about a series of low Nile floods, meaning not enough farmland was inundated for successful harvests.[19] The entire Mediterranean was being thrust into a drying event that caused a cascade of mass migrations and government destabilization everywhere, not just in Egypt.[20] Even though Pepi I had a fifty-year reign, his pyramid is one of the smallest ever built by an Egyptian king. It was certainly not because he lacked the time to build.

Not only that, Pepi I and II may have lived too long, destabilizing their dynasty. Although it has now become unfashionable among Egyptologists to blame state collapse on a king's long reign,[21] it is nonetheless remarkable that the Sixth Dynasty ended with the kingship of Pepi I that was fifty-years long and then that of Pepi II, which was even longer, twice as long according to some (disputed) king lists. If it is overly deterministic to argue that an extended reign could destroy a dynasty outright, a long reign might still have been destabilizing. A reign lasting longer than the lifetime of most royal sons and even grandsons disrupted the movement of administrative positions to the next generation, disallowing a reorganization of power among court elites. Indeed, by the time Pepi I handed over his kingship to his chosen son, his eldest sons would have been in their forties or dead, with succession scattered among a multiplication of candidates.

Astoundingly, even after his astounding fifty-year reign, Pepi I handed the kingship off to two very young sons in succession, both of whom must have demanded intercession by female regents. Why choose boys so young? There must have been other, older sons who required no help from their mothers to rule.[22] It looks as if the Egyptians were actively avoiding competing elite agendas by choosing royal female power, thus systematically selecting young heirs who required the guidance of queen-regents and maybe even female administrators, rather than face the potentially destabilizing choice between strong adult king's sons who may have had land, armies, weapons, and great wealth at their disposal to make trouble competing among themselves.[23]

---

18. Iput may have died, however, before his reign, or shortly into it, as suggested in Vivienne G. Callender, *In Hathor's Image I: The Wives and Mothers of Egyptian Kings from Dynasties I–VI* (Prague: Charles University in Prague, 2011), 221–27.

19. Karl Butzer, *Early Hydraulic Civilization in Ancient Egypt: A Study in Cultural Ecology* (Chicago: University of Chicago Press, 1976), 51–56.

20. Peter B. deMenocal, "Cultural Responses to Climate Change During the Late Holocene," *Science* 292.5517 (2001): 667–73; Helge W. Arz, Frank Lamy, and Jürgen Pätzold, "A Pronounced Dry Event Recorded around 4.2 ka in Brine Sediments from the Northern Red Sea," *Quaternary Research* 66 (2006): 432–41.

21. For example, see Kathryn A. Bard, "State Collapse in Egypt in the Late Third Millennium B.C.," *Annali, Istituto universitario orientale* 54 (1994): 275–81; Nigel Strudwick, *The Administration of Egypt in the Old Kingdom: The Highest Titles and Their Holders* (London: KPI, 1985), 346.

22. For a similar case in the later Eighteenth Dynasty, see Peter Der Manuelian, "The End of the Reign and the Accession of Amenhotep II," in *Thutmose III: A New Biography*, ed. Eric H. Cline and David O'Connor (Ann Arbor: University of Michigan Press, 2006), 413–29.

23. Callender, *In Hathor's Image*, 238–41.

Even with no outright evidence for the female king Nitocris, the Sixth Dynasty was an age of royal women; indeed, court females arguably hadn't seen this kind of influence since the days of Merneith.[24] The vast majority of royal women—royal daughters, royal sisters, or king's wives ostensibly given as girls to the king by important officials and landed elites—remain invisible to history unless they were documented in burial. Only with funerary installations can we see the hierarchy of the feminine side of the court. There was always a pecking order, it seems. One important Sixth Dynasty queen named Inekek-Inti even had the title of vizier,[25] a first for a woman in ancient Egypt and something that most Egyptologists nonetheless doubt was a real title of actual administration.[26] But perhaps we should lend this female influence more credence because so many of the king's wives and daughters were receiving new and fabulous tombs during the reign of Pepi I.[27]

Funerary monuments may even preserve remnants of competition between females for political court power. The burials of two Sixth Dynasty queens, one named Khuit and the other Iput, are a case in point.[28] Khuit was granted a pyramid tomb very close to her dead husband, King Teti. She was interred in a costly granite sarcophagus from Aswan. Her burial chamber was gabled and large, an ostentation that few other Sixth Dynasty queens received. The (rival?) queen Iput was given a mastaba tomb located father from her husband Teti's pyramid. She was buried within a limestone sarcophagus with the remains of an imported cedar inner coffin inside of it. Yet it was Queen Iput whose son would become king as Pepi I, and when that happened, her position changed monumentally, in a physical way that archaeologists can document with repeated modifications to her burial space. Her mastaba tomb was altered into a pyramid, modified from the low rectangular block that had already been built. Granite false doors and decorations were added to the existing architecture. A series of courts and offering halls were placed before her temple. All of these modifications were extraordinarily expensive, demanding scarce resources and precious labor to complete. They were also publicly displayed to every Egyptian courtier. All of these additions were done, ostensibly, by her son Pepi I after he had become king, to honor his mother.[29] This funerary architecture illustrates the kind of power a woman could amass when her son reached the pinnacle of Egyptian society; Iput must have had the same kind of influence at court, vis-à-vis her competitors and even over her son's decision making. One has to assume that the same kind of rivalry – expressed here in mortuary stone – was something much more human and palpable among the living in a palace context.

There are some telltale signs informing us just how destabilized the Egyptian elites already were when trying to determine who among Pepi I's sons would become king next. In fact, a plot seems to have been hatched in Pepi I's harem, led by one of the king's many wives.[30] We only know about it because an official named Weni, buried at the

24. Callender, 238–41.

25. Audran Labrousse, "Huit épouses du roi Pépy Ier," in *Egyptian Culture and Society: Studies in Honour of Naguib Kanawati*, ed. S. Binder, A. McFarlane, and Alexandra Woods (Cairo: Conseil Suprême des Antiquités, 2010), 238–41.

26. Callender, *In Hathor's Image*, 240, states: "Whatever the reason for the title, it is unlikely to have had an administrative function for the queen."

27. Callender, *In Hathor's Image*, 238–41.

28. Vivienne G. Callender, "Some Sixth Dynasty Queens: An Historical Perspective," in *Abusir and Saqqara in the Year 2015*, ed. Miroslav Bárta, Filip Coppens, and Jaromír Krejčí (Prague: Faculty of Arts, Charles University, 2017), 39.

29. For this funerary comparison made with intricate precision, see Callender, *In Hathor's Image*, 226.

30. See Kara Cooney, Chloe Landis, and Turnadot Shayegan, "The Body of Egypt: How the Harem Connected a King with His Elites," in *(Re)Constructing Ancient Egyptian Society: Challenging Assumptions, Exploring Approaches*, ed. Danielle Candelora, Nadia Ben-Marzouk, and Kathlyn M. Cooney (London: Routledge, forthcoming). Despite recent criticism of the term harem (Jan Picton, "Living and Working in a New Kingdom 'Harem Town,'" in *Women in Antiquity: Real Women across the Ancient World*, ed. Stephanie Lynn Budin and Jean MacIntosh Turfa [London: Routledge, 2016], 229–42; Virginia Emery, "The Architecture of Ancient Egyptian Harems," paper presented at the Annual Meeting of the American Research Center in Egypt, Tucson, Arizona, 2018), the term remains, in my opinion, the most useful word for the institution of many wives serving a king, short of calling it something like an institution of biological intensification for the king. Much of the discourse surrounds the physical space where the women would have resided rather than the institution and social sphere of the women's lived experiences. The debate as to how to translate the Egyptian words perpetuates

Figure 1. Autobiography of Weni (Egyptian Museum, Cairo). Image source: E. Grébaut and G. Maspero, eds., *Le Musée égyptien: Recueil de monuments et de notices sur les fouilles d'Égypte*, vol. 1 (Cairo: Institut français d'archéologie orientale 1890), pls. XXVII–XVIII; public domain.

necropolis of Abydos, was called to investigate a secret charge against this royal wife in the harem.[31] Weni was quite proud to brag that he was the most trusted official to deal with such a sensitive matter and that he did this top secret work alone and with the king's full trust (fig. 1). One woman was apparently found guilty of acting against the king in some way, although typically, all of the salacious details are shrouded in secrecy. What was the queen accused of doing? Egypt never preserves any realpolitik on its idealized temple carvings or funerary biographies. Maybe she tried to harm other wives and their sons in the harem, making deals with other courtiers, breaking a path for their own son to become the next king. Perhaps the woman was caught scheming with court officials and her now adult (?) son, working to maneuver him to the top of the pecking order by subterfuge and by force. This king's wife pushed a bit too hard, it seems, and in so doing she lost everything. But it is important to see such scheming as evidence of real power held by female courtiers in the royal Egyptian court.

What were the repercussions for this female political player? We have no idea, but given what we know about Egyptian crime and punishment in later harem conspiracies of the New Kingdom, she may have received the ultimate sentence of death, including the loss of her tomb and even precious afterlife existence.[32] Important officials, including

a discourse that ignores the complexities of the institution of the harem, not to mention the sexual and social exploitation and inequality of the women who served therein. The word "harem" conjures up exploitation and negativity in an instance, much like the words "slave" or "enslaved" or "plantation," and thus should be retained.

31. Miriam Lichtheim, *Ancient Egyptian Literature, The Old and Middle Kingdoms* (Berkeley: University of California Press, 1975), 1:18–22.

32. For such a theory, see Callender, *In Hathor's Image*, 232–37.

the vizier, were also removed from power; many had been pulled into this feeding frenzy, it seems. No matter what the details were, we can say that the court of Pepi I was in turmoil, anxiously anticipating the death of their long-lived king, watching the time pass as royal sons grew older and more established, more able to compete with one another outright, possibly even violently. In this highly charged political climate of conspiracies and trials, it was likely thought that it was in everyone's best interest to skip over all of the king's sisters and their older sons and instead focus on a new biological beginning. Pepi I was thus succeeded by two young sons, ostensibly among the youngest members of the royal nursery, King Merenre who ruled just a few years, and then King Pepi II who came to the throne very young, given his own extraordinary reign length (at the age of six according to Manetho)[33], presumably conceived by a king in the twilight of his years.

Who were the mothers of these two young kings? Outsiders. This new beginning not only bypassed all the king's grown sons but his own royal sisters and daughters as well. Merenre and Pepi II stemmed from two sisters unrelated to the royal family, girls from the nome of Abydos. When they entered the harem, they seem to have brought with them their brother, who was made the new vizier, a man called Djau. Strangely, both sisters bore the same name – Ankhenespepi – which means "She made an oath for Pepi," perhaps an overt declaration of loyalty to the king in a time of conspiracy, but also the cause, for Egyptologists at least, of no end of grief as they determine which Ankhenespepi bore King Merenre and which bore King Pepi II. No matter which was which; they were both from outside of the royal court, daughters not of incest but of wealthy landowners in the province of Abydos.[34]

Royal incest, it could be argued, had the effect of granting great political power to the king's female relatives in the palace. Apparently, it was time to push back against these royal women, to clean house, so to speak, and skip over the whole lot of them. King Pepi I seems to have had enough of his influential sisters and brought in girls from the outside who would be loyal to *him* alone. Pepi I rewarded the sisters beyond all the other women in his harem, according to the funerary evidence available to us.[35] He may have even named Merenre as his co-regent,[36] teaching the young co-king how to rule by his side, marking his heir in advance of his death, a small piece of evidence that this king distrusted that his orders would be followed after his death.

When Pepi I died, he had placed a chosen successor on the throne already and cleverly bypassed the established royal family—grown sons and their mothers. Pepi I's co-kingship with Merenre may have served as a useful adaptation to a king who needed to take power back from royal sisters, wives, and mothers.

Pepi II was just a small boy when he took the throne, and his mother, Ankhenespepi II,[37] who had married her own nephew King Merenre, was now, if we have the genealogies correct, called upon to rule as queen-regent while her son grew into his own kingship.[38] The honors given to her were arguably more fabulous than anything bestow upon a king's wife and mother thus far. Her pyramid complex at Saqqara rivaled the size of her husband and son. The granite entrance lintel placed her names front and center, taking precedence even over the king's. She was the first woman to

33. Von Beckerath, *Chronologie des pharaonischen Ägypten*, 151.

34. Audran Labrousse, "Une épouse du roi Mérenrê Ier: La reine Ânkhesenpépy II," in *Abusir and Saqqara in the Year 2000*, ed. Miroslav Bárta and Jaromír Krejčí (Prague: Academy of Sciences of the Czech Republic, Oriental Institute, 2000), 485–90. Callender, "Some Sixth Dynasty Queens," 41.

35. Callender, "Some Sixth Dynasty Queens," 39–51.

36. Étienne Drioton, "Un corégence de Pepi Ier et de Merenre," *ASAE* 45 (1947): 55–56. Also see Callender, *In Hathor's Image*, 256.

37. Confusingly, this seems to be the same queen as Ankhenesmeryre II. She uses both names. For instance, in her Pyramid Texts, she uses the name Ankhenespepi ninety-five times and Akhenesmeryre eight times. For more on this woman, see the discussion by Callender, *In Hathor's Image*, 258–71.

38. There is disagreement among scholars about Pepi II's parentage. Was his father Pepi I, making him a brother to the previous king Merenre, or was his father Merenre II, making him the product of an aunt–nephew incestuous relationship between Ankhenespepi II and her sister's son Merenre? Jean Leclant and Audran Labrousse, "Les reines Ankhnespépy II et III (fin de l'ancien empire): campagnes 1999 et 2000 de la MAFS," *Comptes rendus de séances de l'Académie des Inscriptions et Belles-Lettres* (2001): 367–84; for more, see Callender, *In Hathor's Image*, 269.

ever have the sacred and secret Pyramid Texts inscribed in her pyramid's burial chamber.[39] This was a woman with real unadulterated power—both religiously and politically. A famous statuette now in the Brooklyn Museum of Art shows the queen holding Pepi II on her lap. She is even depicted of greater stature and size than her small son, as Isis would have been shown holding the living king Horus on her lap. In other words, the queen regent was depicted as no less than the goddess Isis, she who was great of magic and protective power.[40]

Whatever the queen mother's training of him, Pepi II ended up with the longest reign in Egyptian history, clocking in at either 64 or 94 years, depending on historical opinion or text decipherment, an astounding number, either way.[41] By the time Pepi II died, just how old were *his* sons, his grandsons, his great-grandsons? Was he able to produce young sons in his infirm years with lovely young harem beauties, like his father? How much infighting had already occurred when he died at 70, or alternatively, as a centenarian? A long reign may not fully account for a dynasty's fall, but it could not help but destabilize the patriarchal succession. Most royal sons would have long since died. Those sons and grandsons who were left had dug into their own competing agendas, using lands and income to fight each other. By the end of Dynasty 6, power in Egypt was truly decentralized, most of it moving to independent landowners, now warlords, away from the capital city of Memphis.[42] And then there is that important detail that Egypt was suffering from a series of low Niles,[43] translating into crop failures and famines throughout the land. Scarce resources were now even scarcer, even for Egyptian elites. This was even a global event, resulting in invasions from across the Sinai of hungry west Asians, refugees on the move in mass migrations.[44] And this was the inauspicious time when the female king Nitocris would have ruled, if she existed at all, at least according to Manetho.

Locking Queen Nitocris down with any certainty has proved impossible to Egyptologists thus far. A Queen Neith did indeed exist as King's Wife and King's Mother, and she was granted extraordinary honors including a pyramid complex of her own replete with the sacred and protected Pyramid Texts to vault her into the heavenly sky as a god, but she was a daughter of Pepi I and wife of Pepi II.[45] She lived too early to have been the Nitocris we are seeking. Her lifetime ended too soon to have fulfilled the role of the king's wife who tried to hold together the fragments of a shattered dynasty. We also have the added complication that when Pepi II died, king lists recorded a series of sons who took over the kingship, each ruling only ephemerally. Maybe one of these short-lived rulers had a wife named Neithikeret, maybe even one who was called in to avenge regicide. But there is no record of it.

Perhaps it is better to understand the story of Nitocris the way we understand the story of the Exodus—as a cultural memory of a series of real events for which the details have gotten muddled, lost, and dramatized. The end of the Sixth Dynasty was a time period of warring factions, civil war, and invasions—not one of court historians carefully detailing the events of their dynasty. It was a time of endings, not beginnings, and of survival, not record keeping. The details are forever lost to us.

If we try to reconstruct something of the shreds of the Sixth Dynasty, a Nitocris who was her husband's sister, then she was perhaps a granddaughter of Pepi II, giving her the legitimacy to take on the rule of Egypt as king when there was no man left standing. Pepi II could not have been her husband; another, later, less well-known, more ephemeral king was her husband and brother—maybe the last known king of Dynasty 6, Merenre II, who is also mentioned in the same Turin king list. Perhaps Merenre II really was killed by competitors, as the Herodotus story goes, and maybe

39. Callender, "Some Sixth Dynasty Queens," 43.

40. James F. Romano, "Sixth Dynasty Royal Sculpture," in *Les critères de datation stylistiques à l'Ancien empire*, ed. Nicolas Grimal (Cairo: Institut français d'archéologie orientale, 1998), 235–303.

41. Hans Goedicke, "The Death of Pepi II—Neferkare," *SAK* 15 (1988): 111–21.

42. Jaromir Malek, "The Old Kingdom (c. 2686–2125 BC)," in *The Oxford History of Ancient Egypt*, ed. Ian Shaw (Oxford: Oxford University Press, 2000), 89–117.

43. Malek, "The Old Kingdom," 89–117.

44. Juan Carlos Moreno García, "Trade and Power in Ancient Egypt: Middle Egypt in the Late Third / Early Second Millennium BC," *JAR* 25 (2017): 87–132.

45. Callender, *In Hathor's Image*, 271–80.

this woman then stepped in to fill the vacuum of power as sister and wife of the dead king, keeping Egypt as safe as she could under her protection, until she met her own doom, demanding that we leave the stories of diverted Nile floodwaters and burning rooms to the overdramatization of ancient historians, just as we should Moses's parting of the Red Sea.

Epiphany or Erudition? The Inception of Atonism

John Coleman Darnell

Since early in the reign of Ramesses II, those moving through the Ramesside First Court of Luxor Temple—from priests, officials, festival participants, and adorants at the bark shrine; to the later members of the Roman garrision, worshippers in the Coptic church and the mosque of Abu el-Haggag; to the much more recent archaeologists, tourists, and epigraphers (among whom Richard and I numbered ourselves for several seasons in the late 80s and early 90s of the last century)—have passed by or near an interesting Year 3 text of Ramesses II.[1] The inscription occupies several lines on the lower portion of the south face of the east tower of the pylon that forms the river-north facade of Luxor Temple. In that composition, complete with complex cryptographic segments, the young ruler describes his quest in the temple library, searching for cosmographic knowledge that will allow him properly to complete his architectural and decorative program at Luxor Temple.[2] Following the exercise in royal erudition, Ramesses addresses "his nobles who are in his entourage," and dispenses the results of his research. What he learns bears on the cosmic significance of Thebes, and his own status as ruler:

ꜥḥꜥ.n ḏꜥr ḥm=f ỉs n(y) sẖꜣ.w
pgꜣ.n=f sẖꜣy.w pr-ꜥnḫ
rḫ.n=f ỉmn.wt nyw p.t sštꜣ nb nyw(sic) *tꜣ*

gm.n=f Wꜣs.t ỉr.t-Rꜥ m ḳꜣꜣ ḫpr <m> ḥꜣ.t
    wn tꜣ pn [...] *[Ỉ]mn-Rꜥ m nsw.t*

        ḥꜣy=f ḥr.t psd=f šnw
            ḥr mꜣꜣ s.t sḫn.t=f ꜣḫ.t=f
wnm.t=f Wꜣs.t m nỉw.t Ỉwnw šmꜥ
ỉꜣb.t=f m ḥḳꜣ-ꜥnḏw spꜣ.t Ỉwnw Mḥw
nsw.t-bỉty Ỉmn-Rꜥ
nḥḥ rn=f ḏ.t sšm=f kꜣ=f wnn.t nb.t
ḏd nsw.t-bỉty Wsr-Mꜣꜥ.t-Rꜥ stp.n-Rꜥ n šps.w=f wnn.w m-ḫt=f

1. *KRI* 2:346, 5–9; see also Donald B. Redford, "The Earliest Years of Ramesses II, and the Building of the Ramesside Court at Luxor," *JEA* 57 (1971): 110–19; Donald B. Redford, *Pharaonic King-Lists, Annals and Day-Books: A Contribution to the Study of the Egyptian Sense of History*, SSEA Publications 4 (Mississauga: Benben, 1986), 91; Mahmud Abd el-Razik, "The Dedicatory and Building Texts of Ramesses II in Luxor Temple. II: Interpretation," *JEA* 61 (1975): 125–27.

2. John C. Darnell, "New Kingdom Cryptography: Graphic Hermeneutics," in *Enigmatic Writing in the Egyptian New Kingdom: Revealing, Transforming, and Display in Egyptian Hieroglyphs*, ed. David Klotz and Andreas Stauder, ZÄS Beihefte 12/1 (Berlin: de Gruyter, 2020), 1:21–24; John C. Darnell, "Alchemical Landscapes of Desert and Temple," in *Ritual Landscape and Performance*, ed. Christina Geisen, YES 13 (New Haven: Yale Egyptology, 2019), 123–26.

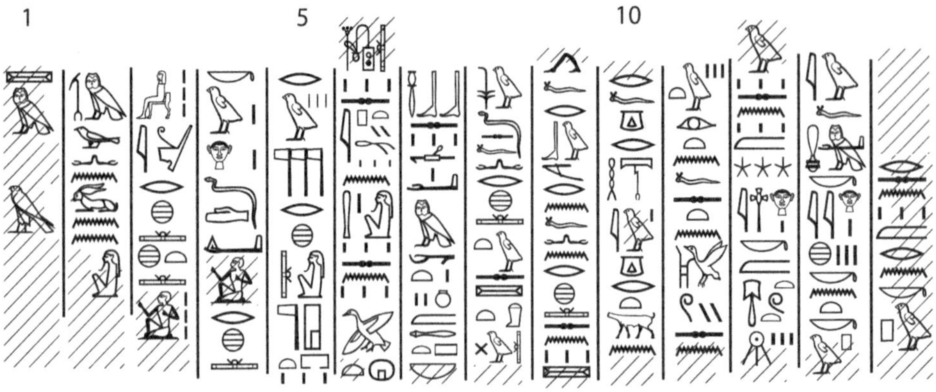

Figure 1. Typeset copy of hieroglyphic text on Akhenaten Temple Project block X 1/5, from the Tenth Pylon of Karnak Temple.

His majesty sought out the library ("chamber of writings").
No sooner did he unroll the writings of the House of Life,
than he became aware of the hidden matters of heaven, and every secret of the earth.

What he discovered was: Thebes, the Eye of Re, was a primordial highland,
when this land was …, Amun-Re being king,
illumining heaven and brightening the circuit (of the sun),
looking for a place where he might set down his luminous eye
(his right eye—the Theban nome—is in the city of Upper Egyptian Heliopolis,
his left eye is in the Heliopolitan nome, namely Lower Egyptian Heliopolis)
As for the king of Upper and Lower Egypt, Amun-Re:
his name is cyclical eternity, his image is linear eternity,
all that exists is his *ka*-spirit.

The king of Upper and Lower Egypt, Usermaatre-setepenre speaks to his nobles who are in his entourage …

What Ramesses discovers in his research is in many ways similar to what Amenhotep IV/Akhenaton earlier claimed regarding his god Aton, his own divine kingship, and the cosmic city of Akhet-Aton that he reared for himself and for the divine solar disk. According to the Year 3 inscription at Luxor Temple, Ramesses II has come to understand the cosmic significance of Thebes, the city that is a solar-Heliopolitan eye of the supreme deity, just as Akhenaton understood the site of his new city of Akhet-Atonto be the chosen horizon of the solar disk. Ramesses states clearly that his personal study of earlier treatises has revealed a metropolitan microcosm to him, whereas Akhenaton, in the texts of his boundary stelae at Akhet-Aton, more vaguely claims that the Aton advised him, without relating how. However, a block from the Tenth Pylon at Karnak Temple preserves a portion of an inscription of Akhenaton while he was yet Amenhotep IV in which that ruler also appears to describe a royal scholarly response to a cult situation that requires research into some divine inventory. That text, heretofore misunderstood, suggests that Amenhotep IV may have come by his revolutionary understanding of the solar religion more through research than revelation.

Ramesses II, following his research, then imparted his knowledge to those in his following, and gave instructions for the carrying out of his work. This should come as no surprise, considering that the king of Egypt was the chief embodiment of solar wisdom, with the gamut of his knowledge, authority, and responsibilities succinctly summarized in the text known as the King as Solar Priest. After describing how the king knows the "mysterious language of the baboons"—the solar worship of the spirits of the eastern horizon—that treatise describes the royal knowledge that can connect transcendental beings and meanings with terrestrial places and more concrete representations:[3]

§4 *ỉw=f rḫ bs=sn ḫpr.w=sn nỉw.wt ỉmy.wt tȝ-nṯr*
ỉw=f rḫ bw ꜥḥꜥ=sn ỉm
    ḫft šsp Rꜥ tp-wȝ.wt

§4He knows their emerging and their forms,
    and their cities that are in the divine land.
He knows the place(s) in which they are stationed,
    after Re takes up the head of the roads.

An expectation of royal research, a resulting royal cosmographic knowledge, and the concrete applications of that research are already well attested on the stela of Neferhotep I and are known for other rulers as well (see below). Akhenaton—for whom the most remarkable change in divine imagery is attested, the ruler known for making the most abrupt and profound reinterpretation of religious architecture and divine landscape—has not seemed to leave more than one fragmentary indication of the origin of his revolutionary changes to Egyptian kingship and religion. That brief text has been taken to present a revelation on the part of Akhenaton, describing the failure of traditional religious imagery. The fragmentary inscription appears, however, on closer examination, to describe the result of royal erudition similar to what Ramesses II describes in his Year 3 text at Luxor Temple.

The background to the inception of Atonism has fascinated scholars, novelists, and enthusiasts of the Amarna period since Akhenaton emerged into the Egyptological consciousness during the nineteenth century. Presentations both popular and scholarly have tended to suggest that Akhenaton had imbibed a revolutionary theology during his childhood, even under the influence of his mother, or have assumed that the concept somehow entered the pharaonic mind with revelatory speed and insistence. The following quotes reveal both divergent opinions and demonstrate the embellishments—both imaginary and more informed—that the Amarna period seems to invite. The second passage is based on the inscription that forms the subject of this brief discussion:

> The court officials blindly followed their young king, and to every word which he spoke they listened attentively. Sometimes the thoughts which he voiced came direct from the mazes of his own mind; sometimes perhaps he repeated the utterances of his deep-thinking mother; and sometimes there may have passed from his lips the pearls of wisdom which he had gleaned from the wise men of his court. At his behest the dreamers of Asia had probably related to him their visions; the philosophers had made pregnant his mind with the mystery of knowledge; the poets had sung to him harp-songs in which echoed the beliefs of the elder days; the priests of strange gods had submitted to him the creeds of strange people. ... The fertile brain of the Pharaoh, it seems probable, was thus sown at an early age with the seed of all that was wonderful in the world of thought.
> A. E. Weigall[4]

> It would be difficult to deny that the event recorded in the 10th pylon block inscription marks a watershed in Akhenaten's Theban sojourn. The king herein is describing for the benefit of his court a determination, if not a downright revelation, having to do with the cessation of activity on the part of all the gods save one. The 10th pylon inscription is a *manifesto.* The king refers to ruination and annihilation, ancestors(?) and wise men, the forms(?) of the gods and their temples. Akhenaten herein lays claim to recondite knowledge about the gods' iconic forms on earth as represented in the *sỉpty* <*wr*> (the "<great> inventory," the cult blue-book) and the reality and validity of this norm. His father in his great mortuary temple had revealed

3. Jan Assmann, *Der König als Sonnenpriester: Ein kosmographischer Begleittext zur kultischen Sonnenhymnik in den thebanischen Tempeln und Gräbern* (Glückstadt: Augustin, 1970), 18; translation by the author.
4. Arthur E. Weigall, *The Life and Times of Akhnaton, Pharaoh of Egypt*, rev. ed. (London: Butterworth, 1922), 68–69.

> the gods in tangible, earthly form and won their approbation and that of Amun. But here one senses a negative assessment: they have ceased operation, ceding place to one whose goings and form were *not* covered by the Great Inventory. There is an embryonic rejection here of all erstwhile normative regulations. And thus, obviously, does Pharaoh justify his future concentration on this unique—surviving!—manifestation of the supernatural, the Sun. It is from this royal séance, as a *terminus a quo*, that we must date all scenes in painting or relief showing the king worshiping the falcon-headed Re-Harakhty alone.
> D. B. Redford[5]

Akhenaton's Religious Revolution—Epiphany or Realization?

How Akhenaton came to champion the worship of a sole solar deity, without cult image so far as we know, remains a mystery. Was Akhenaton struggling against the power of the Amun priesthood, as many have suggested? Was he above all seeking to exalt a solar deity to quasi-monotheistic prominence and power? Is either of these reconstructions of events even partially correct? Some modern authors have assumed that the origins of the undeniably radical aspects of Akhenaton's reign must lie in a long process of experience and thought, perhaps stretching back to childhood experiences, or be the result of an event early during his reign that burst like a thunderclap into the mind of the young ruler.

Only one source has been interpreted as recording the words of Akhenaton with reference to the inception of his new solar religion. A block reused in the Tenth Pylon at Karnak temple, one of two belonging to the early reign of Amenhotep IV and published first and provisionally in 1981, has seemed to provide direct evidence for an epiphany on the part of the king. According to the interpretation of the text offered in the original publication of the blocks, Amenhotep IV there describes his recognition that the traditional images of the gods of Egypt had ceased to function.

Two Blocks from the Tenth Pylon

From the fill of the Tenth Pylon at Karnak, the Akhenaten Temple Project identified two sandstone blocks (X 1/5 and 30/70) that once belonged to a monument from the early phase of Amenhotep IV's reign, before the king had adopted the styles, iconography, and terminology of his longer, Atonist phase.[6] The two blocks appear to belong to the same composition, beginning (on block 30/70) with a depiction of a deity to the left—probably the deity Horakhty to whom the inscription refers—followed by an introductory text giving the full titulary of Amenhotep IV, and referencing "Re-Horakhty, who rejoices in the horizon in his name of Shu [who is in the disk]." The blocks present fragments of one of two royal decrees that appear to derive ultimately from the Hout-Benben at Karnak. The other fragmentary decree dates to the tenth day of some month of the *Akhet*-season during one of the first three regnal years of Amenhotep IV,[7] and the fragmentary decree preserved on blocks X 1/5 and 30/70 may well also be an event from the earliest regnal years of Amenhotep IV.

---

5. Donald B. Redford, "Akhenaten: New Theories and Old Facts," *BASOR* 369 (2013): 14–15.

6. The *editio princeps* is Donald B. Redford, "A Royal Speech from the Blocks of the 10th Pylon," *Bulletin of the Egyptological Seminar* 3 (1981): 87–102; a photograph by the CFEETK appears in Claude Traunecker, "Le dromos perdu d'Amenhotep IV et de Néfertiti à Karnak—espaces cultuels et économiques au service de l'atonisme," in *Les édifices du règne d'Amenhotep IV-Akhenaton, urbanisme et revolution—The Buildings from the Reign of Amenhotep IV-Akhenaten, Urbanism and Revolution*, ed. Marc Gabolde and Robert Vergnieux, CENiM 20 (Montpellier: Université Paul-Valéry Montpellier 3, 2018), 188. See also Donald B. Redford, *Akhenaten: The Heretic King* (Princeton: Princeton University Press, 1984), 172–73; William A. Murnane, *Texts from the Amarna Period in Egypt*, Writings from the Ancient World 5 (Atlanta: Scholars Press, 1995), 31; James K. Hoffmeier, *Akhenaten and the Origins of Monotheism* (Oxford: Oxford University Press, 2015), 160–61; Dimitri Laboury, *Akhénaton* (Paris: Pygmalion, 2010), 125 and 391.

7. Jean-Luc Chappaz, "Le prémier édifice d'Aménophis IV—Karnak," *BSEG* 8 (1983): 31 (NRJ).

Block 1/5 preserves the longest—albeit fragmentary—section of a statement of Amenhotep IV that begins already in column 4 of block 30/70. This is the inscription on the basis of which Akhenaton, already while still Amenhotep IV, has been assumed to have recognized the failure of the old gods and their divine images. An examination of the text reveals, however, that Amenhotep IV is in fact demonstrating his proper royal understanding of the need for cultic renewals, a following and expected reference to royal erudition, and the resulting renewal that is the prerogative and responsibility of every Egyptian ruler. At the beginning of the surviving text on block 1/5 is a probable mention of the name of Horus (fig. 1).[8]

The Need

$^{x+1}$[…] ⸢*Ḥr*⸣(?) […] $^{x+2}$[… *w3y r*(?)] *w3s* (written *ḏꜥm*) *nn wnn*(*y*)*.w* […] $^{x+3}$[…] ⸢*šps.wt*⸣ [*-nsw.t*](?) *i.n rḫw.w-iḫ.t* […] $^{x+4}$[…]

$^{x+1}$[…] ⸢Horus⸣ (?) […] $^{x+2}$[… temples(?) fallen into] ruin,[a] without any (divine) beings[b] […] $^{x+3}$[… royal(?)] ⸢august ones⸣ (?),"[c] so say the knowledgable ones[d] […] $^{x+4}$[…]

Text Notes

[a] As Redford, "Royal Speech," 90 n. B, observed, the verb "to fall into ruin" generally describes structures and may appear in a stereotypical historical retrospective in which the construction works of the active, living ruler are all the more necessary, laudable, and impressive as the older works were neglected, desecrated, and decaying. For the "time of troubles" topos, to which such descriptions of derelict sacred constructions belong, see Redford, *Pharaonic King-Lists*, 259–75; Colleen Manassa, *The Great Karnak Inscription of Merneptah: Grand Strategy in the 13th Century BC*, YES 5 (New Haven: Yale Egyptology, 2003), 110–13; Colleen Manassa, *Imagining the Past: Historical Fiction in New Kingdom Egypt* (Oxford: Oxford University Press, 2013), 45, 64, 169, and 222n109.

[b] Redford, "Royal Speech," 90 n. C suggests reading *nn wn* with the sign A40 determining [*ḥm*]or [*nṯr*], which is possible. If the indication of damage is accurate, the word could rather be *wnn*(*y*)[*.w*] with divine determinative, a slightly archaic usage designating the deities of the temple: Rainer Hannig, Ägyptisches *Wörterbuch I* (Mainz: von Zabern, 2003), 343; Penelope Wilson, *A Ptolemaic Lexikon: A Lexicographical Study of the Texts in the Temple of Edfu*, OLA 78 (Leuven: Peeters, 1997), 232.

[c] Redford, "Royal Speech," 90 n. D, suggested that a term for ancestors might take the august-man sign at the top of l. 3, but one might also suggest "august ones" or "royal august ones"—compare Hatshepsut's text referencing *šps.wt-nsw.t wnny.w m-ḫt=f*, "royal august ones who were in his entourage": Pierre Lacau and Henri Chevrier, with Marie-Ange Bonhème and Michel Gitton, *Une chapelle d'Hatshepsout à Karnak* (Cairo: Institut français d'archéologie orientale, 1977), 1:107, l. 17; Dimitri Meeks, *Année lexicographique, Égypte ancienne 1 (1977)* (Paris: Cybele, 1980), 89 (no. 77.0919). The *šps.w wnn.w m-ḫt=f* are those to whom Ramesses II describes the results of his research in the Year 3 inscription in the First Court of Luxor Temple: *KRI* 2:346, 9.

[d] Though *in rḫw.w-iḫ.t* could represent "it is the knowledgeable ones" or "by the knowledgable ones," as an address of the king follows, this is perhaps more plausibly *i.n rḫw.w-iḫ.t*, "so say the knowledgable ones," concluding a speech to which the king replies.

8. The accompanying version of the text collates the handcopy of Redford, "Royal Speech," 102 with the photograph in Traunecker, "Le dromos perdu," 188. A facsimile copy is much to be desired.

The mention of "knowledgable ones" recalls a passage from a "time of troubles" inscription of Hatshepsut at the Speos Artemidos. That earlier Eighteenth Dynasty ruler bemoans a preexisting lack of knowledgable people in the cult of Thoth, a problem with which she says that she herself, and already her father Thutmosis I, had occupied themselves.[9] A sort of parallel may appear in a text from the Red Chapel at Karnak, in another inscription of Hatshepsut, a composition in which the august ones of the king say they do not understand, and the great ones of the palace are equally perplexed.[10] Under Hatshepsut, in particular, the knowledge of the ruler is emphasized, serving to reinforce a sense of the closeness between the ruler and the divinity.[11] In the text of Akhenaton, the "knowledgble ones" appear just after a description of ruination and may themselves be either lacking or deficient in their knowledge. That the "knowledgable ones" appear to have been speaking suggests that they have relayed to the ruler the fact of cultic collapse, a priestly version of the more militaristic *iw=tw* known from some royal novels.

The Solution

⸢mk⸣.wi ḥr ḏd di=i rḫ[=ṯn ...] $^{x+5}$*[...] ⸢ḫprw.w⸣ nṯr.w rḫ=i ḥw.wt-nṯr [...]* $^{x+6}$*[...] ⸢sš.w⸣ sip.ty n ḥm.w=sn ⸢pꜣw.t⸣ [...]* $^{x+7}$*[...] ꜣbb=s<n> wʿ m-ḫt sn.nw m ʿꜣ.t nb[.t šps.t ...]*

⸢Behold,⸣ I am speaking that I might cause [you] to know[e] [...] $^{x+5}$[...] ⸢manifestations⸣ of the gods, so that I might understand the temples [...] $^{x+6}$[...] ⸢writings⸣ of the inventory of their majesties,[f] the ⸢antiquity⸣ [...] $^{x+7}$[...] which they desire,[g] one after another, out of all [precious] stones [...]

Text Notes

[e] The king may dispense knowledge by means of a royal decree, and such a statement may relay information from a deity. For the decree see Pascal Vernus, "The Royal Command (*wḏ-nsw*): A Basic Deed of Executive Power," in *Ancient Egyptian Administration,* ed. Juan Carlos Moreno García, Handbuch der Orientalistik 104 (Leiden: Brill, 2013), 259–340; for the statement, compare *Urk.* IV:352, 16–17; for the Karnak text of Amenhotep IV placing a version of the *in(.n)=tw n=k r di.t rḫ=k ...* formulation in the mouth of the king, see Vernus, "The Royal Command," 290n141. Other "I cause you to understand/know" texts are discussed in Manassa, *Great Karnak Inscription,* 27–29, with such followed by an expression of royal cognitive prowess. The passage on the Karnak block, describing trouble with following royal pronouncement to what appear to be assembled courtiers, combines the *ḥms.t-nsw.t* royal sitting with the "time of troubles" topos, as does the historical retrospective in the Great Harris Papyrus.[12]

[f] For the inventory, see Redford, "Royal Speech," 92–94 n. J; Pierre Grandet, *Le Papyrus Harris I.,* BdÉ 109/1 (Cairo: Institut français d'archéologie orientale, 1994), 1:95–96 and 130 (n. 24). A close parallel here—and to this section of the block as a whole—is on the stela of Neferhotep I: Wolfgang Helck, *Historisch-biographische Texte der 2. Zwischenzeit und neue Texte der 18. Dynastie,* KÄT 6, 1 (Wiesbaden: Harrassowitz, 2002), 21 [l. 3 of the stela]; see further below. The use of the determinative V12 indicates the concrete and archived inventory document. Compare

9. James P. Allen, "The Speos Artemidos Inscription of Hatshepsut," *Bulletin of the Egyptological Seminar* 16 (2002): pl. 2, ll. 25–26.

10. Lacau and Chevrier, *Une chapelle d'Hatshepsout,* 9.

11. See Susanne Bickel, "Worldview and Royal Discourse in the Time of Hatshepsut," in *Creativity and Innovation in the Reign of Hatshepsut,* ed. José M. Galán, Betsy M. Bryan, and Peter Dorman, SAOC 69 (Chicago: Oriental Institute of the University of Chicago, 2014), 25–26.

12. Redford, *Pharaonic King-Lists,* 267. A parallel for such a combination also appears in the Year 8 Inscription of Ramesses III in his temple at Medinet Habu: Epigraphic Survey, *Medinet Habu 1: Earlier Historical Records of Ramses III,* OIP 8 (Chicago: University of Chicago Press, 1930), pl. 46, ll. 12–15.

Arlette David, *Syntactic and Lexico-Semantic Aspects of the Legal Register in Ramesside Royal Decrees,* GOf IV/38 (Wiesbaden: Harrassowitz, 2006), 210–11.

[g] As noted in Redford, "Royal Speech," 95, the verb *ꜣb,* "to cease," appears in the reduplicating form *ꜣbb* in the (late) New Kingdom copies of the Instruction of Any: see Joachim F. Quack, *Die Lehren des Ani: Ein neuägyptischer Weisheitstext in seinem kulturellen Umfeld,* OBO 141 (Fribourg: Presses Universitaires; Göttingen: Vandenhoeck & Ruprecht, 1994), 117n121; and in the Tale of Woe, see Ricardo A. Caminos, *A Tale of Woe: From a Hieratic Papyrus in the A. S. Pushkin Museum of Fine Arts in Moscow* (Oxford: Oxford University Press, 1977), 16 and 19. However, that verb should have walking legs as a determinative, which the verb on the Karnak block lacks, and normally *ꜣb,* "to cease," does not reduplicate. According to Redford, "Royal Speech," 95, reading *ꜣbb* on the Karnak block as "to cease," "it seems to me, is distinctly preferable in a context which speaks of [forms] of the gods, books of cult prescriptions and ruination of temples; moreover, the inclusion of the phrase *wꜥ m-ḫt sn.nw,* 'one after another,' suits the sense of progressive cessation much better than any meaning of 'desire.'" When *ꜣb,* "to cease," is part of a divine epithet, the verb appears with the negation *nn* to reference a deity's unceasing carrying out of some action—see *LGG* I, 8; in the hymn on the stela of Suty and Hor from the reign of Amenhotep III, the two overseers of works of Amun describe Re as "one who shines in the early morning without ceasing" (Alexandre Varille, "L'hymne au soleil des architectes d'Aménophis III Souti et Hor," *BIFAO* 41 [1941]: 26 [ll. 1–2]). Alone *ꜣb,* "to cease," might reference "pausing, remaining in a place": *LGG* I, 8, *ꜣb-ḫr-mnw,* "one who pauses among the trees"; note also the letter of Ramose from the reign of Akhenaton (P. Robert Mond 1, l. 20: Thomas E. Peet, "Two Letters from Akhetaten," *Annals of Archaeology and Anthropology, University of Liverpool* 17 [1930]: pls. 19 and 24) in which the author says *ꜣbw=f ḫr=ꞽ r pr-Mry.t-ꞽtn,* "let him remain with me at the domain of Merytaton." However, describing the state of a deity or a statue thereof, as suggested for the verb on the Karnak block, one would expect a stative form.

In spite of Redford's preference, *Wb.* VI:24 notes that *ꜣbꞽ,* "wünschen," can appear without a determinative, like *ꜣbb* on the Karnak block and on the Akhet-Aton Boundary Stelae, an orthography that seems more unusual for *ꜣb,* "to cease." For the *ꜣbꞽ*-wish of the Aton in the Boundary Stelae at Akhet-Aton, see below. The passage on the Karnak block could represent a relative form, or be a reference to something or some place *n ꜣbb=sn,* "of their desiring"—compare l. 26 of the Nauri Decree of Sety I: *KRI* 1:50, 5.

The best parallel to this passage is the introductory statement of the king in the text of the stela of Neferhotep I:[13]

ḏd.<ꞽn> ḥm=f n sꜥḥ.w smr.w wnny.w m-ḫt=f sš.w mꜣꜥ n mdw-nṯr ḥr(y).w-tp štꜣ.w nb

ꞽw ꜣb.n ꞽb=ꞽ mꜣꜣ sš.w pꜣw.t tp.t n.t ꞽtm
pgꜣ n=ꞽ r sꞽp.ty-wr
ꞽmꞽ rḫ(=ꞽ) nṯr m ḳmꜣ=f psḏ.t m ḳꞽ.w=sn
mꜣꜥ(=ꞽ) n=sn ḥtpw-nṯr
[wdn(=ꞽ)] šꜥ[.wt] ḥr wḏḥ.w
rḫ=ꞽ nṯr m ꞽrw=f
ms=ꞽ sw mꞽ tp.t-ꜥ=f

<Then> his majesty spoke to the nobles, the companions, those who were in his entourage, the true hieroglyphic scribes who were in his following, those over all the secrets:

My heart has desired to see the writings of the first antiquity of Atum.
Open up for me the great inventory;

13. Helck, *Historisch-biographische Texte,* 21–22 (ll. 2–4 of the stela); see also Maya Müller, "Die Königsplastik des Mittleren Reiches und ihre Schöpfer: Reden über Statuen—wenn Statuen reden," *Imageo Aegypti* 1 (2005): 27–78; Helen Neale, "The Neferhotep Stela, Revisited: Kingship, Authority and Legitimacy in the Abydos Stela of Neferhotep I" (MA thesis, Macquarie University, 2016), 34–36.

let me come to know the god in his form, the ennead in their shapes,
so that I might present to them the divine offerings,
and [offer] ca[kes] upon the offering tables;
so that I might come to know the god in his visible form,
and fashion him like his former condition.

Later inspections involving the *sỉp.ty-wr* are attested at several of the sites of the actual inspection. Two inscriptions from the reign of Merneptah at Thebes, one from the bark shrine of the Eighteenth Dynasty temple at Medinet Habu (regnal year 2) and the other from the upper court of the temple of Hatshepsut at Deir el-Bahari (regnal year 3), reference specifically the making of a *sỉp.ty-wr*. A series of five inscriptions from the reign of Ramesses III (at Karnak, Tod, Elkab, Edfu, and Elephantine) records the king's ordering of the carrying out of a *sỉp.ty wr*.[14] According to the texts of Ramesses III, such inspections involved purification and rebuilding, as well as the more economically significant inspections of treasuries, granaries, and offerings; the prosaic realities of such *sỉp.ty* temple inventories find parallels in the accounting of fortresses.[15] All of this is consistent with an interest at least significantly if not predominately of a physical and economic nature. Amenhotep IV may himself be more interested in the economies and physical infrastructures of the cults he discusses than in more cosmographic aspects of royal research.

The Solar Deity

[x+8][...] ⸢*ms*⸣ *sw ḏs=f nỉ rḫ=tw sštꜣw*[*=f* ...] [x+9][... *ỉw*]*=f r bw mr.n=f nn rḫ=sn š*[*m.t=f* ...] [x+10][...] *r=f grḥ ỉw=ỉ gr.t ḥn*[...] [x+11][...]*.wt(?) ỉr.t.n=f stn.wy sn* [...] [x+12][...]*.w=sn m sbꜣ.w ỉnḏ ḥr=k m st.wt* [...] [x+13][...] *ỉw=f mỉ m ky ḥr ḫw=k ntk* [...] [x+14][...] ⸢*r=sn m rn=k pw*⸣ [...]

[x+8][...] ⸢who bore⸣ himself, [whose] secrets cannot be known[h] [...] [x+9][...] he [coming(?)] to the place he has desired.[j] They will not know his ⸢going⸣ [...] [x+10][...] night; but I approach(?) [...] [x+11][...] which he made, how exalted are they [...] [x+12][...] their [...]s as stars.[k] Hail to you in your rays [...] [x+13][...] What is he like, another like you?[l] You are [...] [x+14][...] ⸢they/them⸣ [...] ⸢in that your name⸣ [...]

Text Notes

[h] Line x+8 appears to begin a section describing a solar creator deity. For *nỉ rḫ=tw sštꜣw*[*=f*], compare David Klotz, *Adoration of the Ram: Five Hymns to Amun-Re from Hibis Temple,* YES 6 (New Haven, CT: Yale Egyptology, 2006), 81–83, ll. 7–8 of the Great Amun Hymn at Hibis: *štꜣy nỉ rḫ=tw sštꜣw=f*, "mysterious one, whose secrets cannot be known" (translation Klotz, *Adoration*, 82). The self begotten aspect of the creator appears also in Klotz, *Adoration*, 71, ll. 1–2 of the Great Amun Hymn.

[j] The reference to "the place he has desired" may relate directly to the deity, within a cultic setting, perhaps during a procession, taking possession of the temple or other site in a festival setting. See Klotz, *Adoration,* 113 and n. 295.

14. See conveniently David, *Syntactic and Lexico-Semanrtic Aspects*, 207–14.

15. Compare a rock-cut stela at Aswan, in which a *ḫtmw kfꜣ-ỉb* Hepu explains that he came: "to perform an inventory in the fortresses of Lower Nubia"—Jacques de Morgan et al., *Catalogue des monuments et inscriptions de l'Égypte antique I.1* (Vienna: Holzhausen, 1894), 25 (no. 178); Andreas Hutterer "Nochmals zur Lesung der Felsstele des *'Ipw* bei Assuan," in *Texte—Theben—Tonfragmente: Festschrift für Günter Burkard*, ed. Dieter Kessler, Regine Schulz, Martina Ullmann, Alexandra Verbovsek, and Stefan J. Wimmer, ÄAT 76 (Wiesbaden: Harrassowitz, 2009), 214–22.

[k]The reference to stars could also be consistent with the cosmic duties of a solar creator—compare Klotz, *Adoration,* 140–41 and n. c to l. 5.

[l]For the structure of the rhetorical question, see *Urk.* IV:1344, 9, cited in Deborah Sweeney, "What's a Rhetorical Question?," *Lingua Aegyptia* 1 (1991): 325. The question apparently expects the answer "no one" (compare Sweeney, "What's a Rhetorical Question?," 327n61). A possible parallel is in l. 20 of the Great Amun Hymn of Hibis Temple: *n[i]m sw nṯr miti=k ntk Rˁ ḥri nṯr.w,* "Who is he, a deity like you? You are Re, chief of the gods": Klotz, *Adoration,* 100–101 and n. c. The passage could belong to a laudatory reply by the courtiers who spoke at the beginning of the passage: compare Anthony J. Spalinger, *The Great Dedicatory Inscription of Ramesses II: A Solar-Osirian Tractate at Abydos,* CHANE 33 (Leiden: Brill, 2008), 50–51.

The import of the text on the X 1/5 block of Amenhotep IV rests greatly on how unique it may truly be, or how much it may in fact find parallels in inscriptions of other rulers less pronouncedly "heretical" and "revolutionary" than Akhenaton. The interpretation of what information the fragmentary Tenth Pylon text actually conveys in turn hinges on how one understands the word that the text's editor has initially and thereafter taken to mean that the images of the gods have "ceased," an interpretation in which others have followed him. According to Redford, the passage in question reads:

> [...] they have ceased, one after the other, whether of precious stones, [gold]
> [...]

The word Redford reads as "to cease" is written *ꜣbb,* without determinative. Redford considered the possibility that this might be the word *ꜣbi,* "to desire, to wish," but decided against this due to his interpretation of the context. As discussed above, although a reduplicating *ꜣbb* of the usual *ꜣb,* "to cease," does appear in later New Kingdom texts, the verb should take walking legs as a determinative, whereas *ꜣbi,* "to wish, desire," may appear without a determinative, as on the Karnak block, and may reduplicate in several verbal forms. The verb *ꜣbi,* "to wish," occurs twice in the text of the Akhet-Aton Boundary Stelae, both passages describing what the Aton desires:[16]

> [xix]*ptr itn i[w] ꜣby pꜣ itn r ir.t [s.t] n=f m mnw ḥr rn nḥḥ ḏ.t*
> Behold Aton! The Aton desires to make [it] for himself as a monument in an eternal and everlasting name.
>
> [14] [...] *m tꜣy ꜣḫ.t itn n pꜣ itn ꜣby.t.n=f ḏs=f hry=f ḥr=s r nḥḥ ḥnˁ ḏ.t*
> [...] in this Horizon of Aton for the Aton, which he himself has desired that he become happy therein forever and ever

On the Karnak block Akhenaton discusses what the whole host of Egypt's deities *ꜣbi*-desire, and in the Earlier Proclamation on the Boundary Stelae, he is only concerned with what the Aton *ꜣbi*-desires. On both accounts, however, Akhenaton is concerned with fulfilling the divine desire, initially of the many and then of the one.

The verb *ꜣb* indeed appears in a context referring to the cessation of a cult, in the great dedicatory inscription of Ramesses II for Sety I at Abydos, but the construction there refers to "cessation having occurred in its divine offerings." In that same passage, the ineffective state of the cult statue is described not by reference to a function or the cessation thereof, but rather through reference to its position: the *sšmw*-statue was on the ground.[17] The passage in

16. William J. Murnane and Charles C. van Siclen, *The Boundary Stelae of Akhenaten* (London: KPI, 1993), 20 (K: xix) and 24 (K: 14); Norman de G. Davies, *Rock Tombs of El-Amarna, Part V: Smaller Tombs and Boundary* Stelae, ASE 17 (London: Egypt Exploration Fund, 1908), pls. 29, l. xix; and 30, l. 14.

17. Spalinger, *Great Dedicatory Inscription,* 26–27 and 59–64.

the Abydos inscription describes the inefficacy of a statue which had not been properly fashioned and the offering endowments of which had ceased. The description of Hatshepsut's benefices within her Speos Artemidos inscription appear to describe a fortunate cult as having a properly made divine image, and properly arranged and appropriately timed offerings, festivals, and rites (ll. 6–7). Had Akhenaton intended to reference cessation, he might reference festivals or rituals, but less probably statues as the subjects of the cessation.

On the Tenth Pylon block, Amenhotep IV appears to describe his knowledge, based on royal research of the *sipty*, and how he will employ that knowledge to correct what is damaged. The ruler appears to be concerned with some thing or things that the gods desire and goes on to describe a solar creator deity. Amenhotep IV's text, as damaged as it is, appears to be a slightly syncopated version of the royal novel describing heroic royal erudition that first appears in the Stela of Neferhotep I and occurs again in such interesting form in the text of Ramesses II on the south side of the east tower of the pylon at Luxor Temple. In layout the Karnak block presents an address of some group to Amenhotep IV, describing cultic troubles; the king's erudite response; and, finally, a paean to a creator deity of solar aspect.

Already during the early Twelfth Dynasty, Sesostris I provides an example of what, during the New Kingdom, will become a recurring theme in a number of royal building inscriptions—the "time of troubles" topos, which Redford so well introduced into the Egyptological discussion (see the references above). These "time of troubles" texts describe a ruined building, damaged statues, malfunctioning cult, or some combination of these situations, and the ruler's remedying of the situation. Although the descriptions and the solutions may be formulaic, and rely on repetitions of certain concepts and phrases, they appear for the most part to have been inspired by some actual problem that the ruler addressed (even though the description of the problem seems in some occasions a bit extreme).

Texts describing the royal response to such a "time of troubles" may provide information on the king's scholarship and the resulting personal ordering of work both sculptural and architectural. The Abydos stela of Neferhotep I is a Late Middle Kingdom version of the *Königsnovelle* focused on heroic royal scholarship. The text describes how Neferhotep I not only finds the book, does not merely order the creation of a proper statue, but personally supervises the artistry that transforms precious materials into the divine image that ultimately derives from royal research. The Speos Artemidos inscription of Hatshepsut likewise presents a personal royal intervention into matters for which those who should have known were both incapable and incompetent. The Year 3 inscription of Ramesses II at Luxor Temple describes a similar royal visit to a library to seek out the original pattern for planned work at Luxor Temple, and records how the king personally issues the order for the work.

The Karnak block of Amenhotep IV/Akhenaton from the Tenth Pylon describes not a revelation from outside, but a royal response to a "time of troubles," mediated through royal research. Particularly on the basis of what Ramesses II relates in his Year 3 text at Luxor Temple, this royal research—like the priestly study recorded in the initiatory inscriptions of early first-millennium BCE date from Karnak, and the later version of the same in evidence in the *Book of Thoth*[18]—takes the researcher beyond the bounds of the imminent world. The researcher understands celestial mysteries against the backdrop of cosmographic vistas, just as Ramesses II saw the city of Thebes as the eye of the creator deity. Akhenaton's study, in response to the "time of troubles," may have revealed similar cosmic vistas to the king. Out of his traditional response of directing royal erudition to the topos of cultic chaos, Akhenaton may well have acquired the complete overview of all of Egypt's cults that would ultimately see the king first tax their wealth and then physically attack their temples and divine images. Akhenaton may at the same time, like Ramesses II, have acquired an understanding of cult topography and solar arcana, an understanding that for Akhenaton must have led to the iconography of the many-armed Aton as sole deity, and the great urban and cultic metropolis that he would construct for the Aton on the plain of Akhet-Aton.

That a *sip.ty*-inventory is referenced on the X 1/5 block from the Tenth Pylon increases the interest of the text, as that very inventory may be related to the list of cults and the imposts on those cults in the favor of the Aton, recorded

18. Richard Jasnow and Karl-Theodor Zauzich, *The Ancient Egyptian Book of Thoth* (Wiesbaden: Harrassowitz, 2005), 58–59.

in a series of blocks that once formed part of Akhenaton's ensemble of structures at Karnak.[19] The list—possibly dating to about Akhenaton's third regnal year—provides a gazetteer of Egyptian temples from Elephantine in the south to Sema-Behdet in the north, recording how they all are now taxed to the advantage of the cult of Aton. Amenhotep IV in the Karnak block may well refer to the inventory that resulted in the monumental list of temples and their taxes for the Aton. Rather than referencing a revelation that statues do not function, Amenhotep IV appears to cite an inventory of temples and their goods that will ultimately fund his new Aton cult, all as the outcome of expected royal research into the nature of the Egyptian cosmos and the physical appearance of the statues and temples of its deities.

The Karnak block does not make clear if Akhenaton was simply interested in an inventory of the cults of Egypt in order properly to fashion needed images, as he appears to suggest, nor does it specify that the king already harbored a desire and a plan to redistribute that divine wealth in the favor of a new imagining of the solar deity. The Karnak block does reveal a traditional background of the erudite ruler consulting the records in order properly to attend to the needs of the cults of Egypt; if it is a manifesto for Atonism, then it reveals erudition, even a cult-economic basis, as the origin of the worship of the Aton.

---

19. Claude Traunecker, "Amenhotep IV—Percepteur du disque," in *Akhénaton et l'époque amarnienne* (Paris: Éditions Khéops et Centre d'Égyptologie, 2005), 145–82; Traunecker, "Le dromos perdu," 188–90.

Silent Signs: Determinatives as Markers of Scribal Knowledge

Katherine E. Davis

Among Richard Jasnow's many contributions to Egyptology, not the least of which are his teaching and mentoring,[1] his publication, together with Karl-Theodor Zauzich, of the Book of Thoth[2] stands out as a triumph of Demotic decipherment and as a crucial step forward in understanding the intellectual history of ancient Egypt. The Book of Thoth relates a dialogue concerning initiation into the House of Life and places a particular emphasis on the nature of written language itself. Given Richard's abiding interest in scribal culture, I offer this modest contribution in honor of all his support, guidance and generosity from which I, as well as so many other Egyptologists, have benefited.

A wealth of evidence attests to the Egyptians' awareness of their own language.[3] From the multilingual Greco-Roman handbooks, like the Book of Nut,[4] to Demotic verbal paradigms,[5] scribes can justifiably be thought of as scholars. Nor is this a phenomenon restricted to the later periods, as recent studies have shown New Kingdom scribal engagement with alphabetic and grammatical systems in ways that parallel the later texts.[6] Yet, Egyptian interest in language does not lie only in the realm of grammar but also in the writing system. Texts like the Tanis Sign Papyrus and P. Carlsberg 7 from the Roman period make it clear that the writing system itself became a site for scribal investigation and knowledge production.[7] A major theme of this late scribal engagement with the writing system is the tension between what a sign visually represents and its phonetic realization.[8] The Tanis Sign Papyrus, despite its

1. This article is a revised version of a paper presented at the ARCE annual meeting in Tuscon, AZ in 2018. I must thank Richard Jasnow who first brought many of the topics discussed in this paper to my attention during our conversations about scribal practice.

2. Richard Jasnow and Karl-Theodor Zauzich, *The Ancient Egyptian Book of Thoth* (Wiesbaden: Harrassowitz, 2005).

3. Sami Uljas, "Linguistic Consciousness," *UCLAEE*, http://digital2.library.ucla.edu/viewItem.do?ark=21198/zz002dn8xd; Katherine E. Davis, "Conceptions of Language: Egyptian Perspectives on Writing and Grammar in the Late Period and Greco-Roman Period" (PhD diss., Johns Hopkins University, 2016).

4. Alexandra von Lieven, *Grundriss des Laufes der Sterne: Das sogenannte Nutbuch*, Carlsberg Papyri 8 (Copenhagen: Museum Tusculanum Press, 2007).

5. E.g., Aksel Volten, "An 'Alphabetical' Dictionary and Grammar in Demotic," *ArOr* 20 (1952): 496–508.

6. Hans-Werner Fischer-Elfert, "'Namen bilden' (*ir.t-rn.w*): Ein Beitrag zur paradigmatischen Anthroponymie des Neuen Reichs," in *The Cultural Manifestation of Religious Experience: Studies in Honour of Boyo G. Ockinga*, ed. Camilla Di Biase-Dyson and Leonie Donovan (Münster: Ugarit, 2017), 311–25; Hans-Werner Fischer-Elfert and Manfred Krebernik, "Zu den Buchstabennamen auf dem Halaḥam-Ostrakon aus TT 99 (Grab des Sennefri)," *ZÄS* 143 (2016): 169–76; Ben Haring, "Halaḥam on an Ostracon of the Early New Kingdom?," *JNES* 74 (2015): 189–96; Thomas Schneider, "A Double Abecedary? Halaḥam and ʾabgad on the TT99 Ostracon," *BASOR* 379 (2018): 103–12.

7. Francis Llewellyn Griffith and William Flinders Petrie, *Two Hieroglyphic Papyri from Tanis*, MEEF 9 (London: Trübner, 1889); Erik Iversen, *Papyrus Carlsberg Nr. VII: Fragments of a Hieroglyphic Dictionary*, Historisk-filologiske Skrifter 3, no. 2 (Copenhagen: Munksgaard, 1958).

8. So, too, do we find New Kingdom scribes articulating a discourse around the scribal arts through emphasizing hands/fingers and mouths, aka writing and reading, graphic and oral. See Chloe Ragazzoli, "Weak Hands and Soft Mouths: Elements of a Scribal Identity in the New Kingdom," *ZÄS* 137 (2010): 157–70.

apparent simplicity, exemplifies this: it lists hieroglyphic signs, their hieratic counterpart, and short hieratic explanations for what the signs represent. These explanations are purely focused on the identification of the visual form, not the phonetic value. The broad organization of the signs relies on thematic category, very similar to a modern sign list. However, sandwiched between the thematically organized sections is a group of signs arranged alphabetically.[9] The entries are uniliteral signs (or originally biliteral signs long used in New Kingdom group writing and whose Ptolemaic and Demotic successors function uniliterally), and while the explanatory third column still merely notes what the sign represents visually, the sequence speaks to a phonetic consciousness on the part of the scribe. Thus, the text juxtaposes two methods of organization: one based on the visual form of the sign and how the thing it represents should be classified in the world and the other based purely on the phonetic value, organized according to an alphabetic order.

While modern scholars have long realized that the tension between the graphic and the spoken underlies the origin of hieroglyphic writing itself (the rebus principle), as well as later scribal creativity such as the phenomenon of Ptolemaic hieroglyphs, the mechanisms by which Egyptian scribes themselves thought about this tension or the extent to which they did is also of interest. The processes of reading and writing are complex, and written texts are not a simple encoding of linguistic data.[10] Written signs do not always even represent language.[11] In many ways, the writing system itself can be understood as a type of knowledge, one that has no clear parallel in modern academic fields, but one that the Egyptians themselves found salient.[12]

This is, of course, a massive topic, one which spans the entire length of Egyptian history across scripts and language stages and beyond the scope of a single article. Unusual uses of determinatives, however, may shine some light on this complex topic and provide a case study for understanding scribal attitudes toward the writing system. The determinative is the written element par excellence; it has no parallel in spoken Egyptian, yet it is persistently and pervasively present throughout Egyptian textual history in all native scripts. Therefore, where determinatives deviate from accepted norms, they may provide evidence for how Egyptian scribes consciously perceived and exploited the writing system and its relationship to spoken language. To this end, I evaluate anomalous uses of determinatives in three specific areas, focusing on larger sections of texts, not individual words: visually and orthographically distinct determinatives, determinatives in non-standard writing contexts, and the exclusion of determinatives. And finally, possible meta-references to determinatives are considered. My goal here is not to examine how determinatives fit with modern linguistic or cognitive theories,[13] but rather to understand whether scribes viewed determinatives as an

9. There is extensive bibliography on the *halaḥam* alphabet in the Egyptian textual tradition. For overviews, see most recently Didier Devauchelle, "L'alphabet des oiseaux," in *A Good Scribe and an Exceedingly Wise Man: Studies in Honour of W. J. Tait*, ed. Aidan Dodson, Janet J. Johnston, and W. Monkhouse, GHP Egyptology 21 (London: GHP, 2014), 57–65; and Joachim F. Quack, "Die spätägyptische Alphabetreihenfolge und das 'südsemitische' Alphabet," *LingAeg* 11 (2003): 163–84; also potential New Kingdom evidence mentioned in n. 5.

10. Christopher Eyre, "The Material Authority of Written Texts in Pharaonic Egypt," in *The Materiality of Texts from Ancient Egypt: New Approaches to the Study of Textual Material from the Early Pharaonic to the Late Antique Period*, ed. F. A. J. Hoogendijk and Steffie van Gompel, Papyrologica Lugduno-Batava 35 (Leiden: Brill, 2018), 1–11.

11. Ben Haring, *From Single Sign to Pseudo-Script: An Ancient Egyptian System of Workmen's Identity Marks*, Culture and History of the Ancient Near East 93 (Leiden: Brill, 2018).

12. In many ways the cuneiform lexical tradition is an instructive parallel on this subject, see Niek Veldhuis, *History of the Cuneiform Lexical Tradition*, Guides to the Mesopotamian Textual Record 6 (Münster: Ugarit-Verlag, 2014).

13. There has been much recent scholarship on determinatives through lens of "classifiers", most significantly by Orly Goldwasser. See, e.g., Orly Goldwasser, *Prophets, Lovers and Giraffes: Wor(l)d Classification in Ancient Egypt*, Classification and Categorization in Ancient Egypt 3, GOF, 4. Reihe: Ägypten 38 (Wiesbaden: Harrassowitz, 2002); Frank Kammerzell, "Egyptian Verb Classifiers," in *Proceedings of the Tenth International Congress of Egyptologists: University of the Aegean, Rhodes, 22–29 May 2008*, ed. P. Kousoulis and N. Lazaridis, OLA 241 (Leuven: Peeters, 2015), 2:1395–1416.; see also Orly Goldwasser and Colette Grinevald, "What Are 'Determinatives' Good For?," in *Lexical Semantics in Ancient Egyptian*, ed. Eitan Grossman, Stéphane Polis, and Jean Winand, Lingua Aegyptia, Studia Monographica 9, (Hamburg: Widmaier, 2012), 17–53 and the references therein. Grinevald's work, as well as that of others,

explicit or implicit category within a graphic system, and if so, the parameters of that knowledge and what ramifications it might have had on scribal practice.

Anomalous Uses of Determinatives

Visually and Orthographically Distinct Determinatives

The practice of writing a determinative separate from the phonetic base of the word is well attested across a broad range of genres and time periods.[14] Most notably, the Ramesseum Onomasticon,[15] dating to the Late Middle Kingdom, employs this format: entries are listed in columns, with each entry occupying its own line and its corresponding determinative separated into an adjacent column (fig. 1). Given that onomastica are linked to the production of scribal knowledge,[16] it is tempting to see this as evidence for deliberate scribal categorization. But there are several caveats. First, no other onomastica use this format. Second, like the later onomastica, the Ramesseum Onomasticon is roughly organized by theme, with topics including liquids, plants, animals, fortresses, towns, and more. But this organization is not always linear, as, for example, entries 122–133 list types of birds (all determined by a bird), entries 134–152 give fish (all determined by a fish), and then entries 153–161 return to birds (again determined by a bird). While entries with the same determinative are naturally clustered together, as one might expect with a thematic organization, it is clear that the determinative itself is not the sole organizing principle since entries with the same determinative may occur scattered throughout the text.[17] And third, every tenth entry is numbered, providing a running total, and a full total is given at line 325.[18] This numbering evokes a more administrative context.

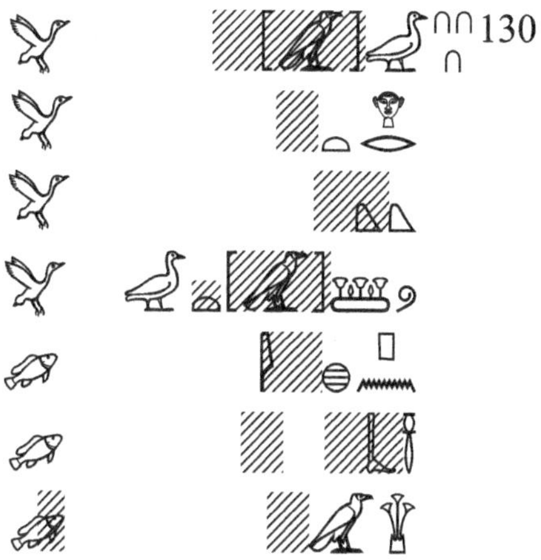

Figure 1. Entries 130–136 from the Ramesseum Onomasticon. After Gardiner, *AEO*, pl. 1A.

---

seeks to link the Egyptian written phenomenon of determinatives with that of oral classifier languages. The major focus of this work has been in the realm of cognitive structures, which is beyond the scope of this article.

14. Friedhelm Hoffmann, "Aufzählungen, Listen, Kataloge und Tabellen im alten Ägypten—formale und inhaltliche Aspekte," in *Die Liste: Ordnungen von Dingen und Menschen in Ägypten*, ed. Susanne Deicher, Ancient Egyptian Design, Contemporary Design History and Anthropology of Design 1 (Berlin: Kadmos, 2015), 87–123.

15. *AEO*, 6–23, pl. I–VI. For the larger context of the find to which the onomasticon belongs, see Richard Bruce Parkinson, *The Tale of the Eloquent Peasant* (Oxford: Griffith Institute, Ashmolean Museum, 1991), xi–xiii.

16. Christian Leitz, "Altägyptische Enzyklopädien," in *Altägyptische Enzyklopädien: Die Soubassements in den Tempeln der griechisch-römischen Zeit*, ed. Alexa Rickert and Bettina Ventker, Studien zur spätägyptischen Religion 7 (Wiesbaden: Harrassowitz, 2014), 2:1017–45; Jürgen Osing, "La science sacerdotale," in *Le décret de Memphis: Colloque de la Fondation Singer-Polignac à l'occasion de la célébration du bicentenaire de la découverte de la Pierre de Rosette*, ed. Dominique Valbelle and Jean Leclant (Paris: Fondation Singer-Polignac, 2000), 127–40.

17. Nor is the determinative the sole organizing principle for later texts either, although again words with the same determinative do cluster together. For example, the persons/professions section of the Onomasticon of Amenemope employs a variety of determinatives and simply leaves out determinatives on titles that usually do not receive them, see *AEO*, 13*–141*. Similarly, the Tebtunis Onomasticon, see Jürgen Osing, *Hieratische Papyri aus Tebtunis I*, CNIP 17 (Copenhagen: Museum Tusculanum Press, 1998).

18. It also appears that the determinative column was written after the column with the base of the word, as a determinative is omitted from entry 268 and an extraneous determinative was added at entry 295. This may of course simply be a product of the copying process. *AEO*, 8.

Although the Ramesseum Onomasticon is the only attested onomasticon with such an arrangement, this practice does not occur in isolation. Similar layouts are paralleled in other genres and other time periods.[19] Moreover, even within the same box of papyri that contained the Ramesseum Onomasticon, two other texts show separated determinatives: P. Ramesseum A with the Eloquent Peasant and P. Ramesseum V with magical-medical texts.[20] In the beginning of the Eloquent Peasant, the items that the peasant loads onto his donkey are listed in a similar format to the Ramesseum Onomasticon with each entry laid out on its own line and the determinatives to the side.[21] Though the Eloquent Peasant is a literary text, Parkinson has noted "the list is presented here as a naturalistic touch: it is a practical document, embedding the peasant in the real world of trade, lists and accounts."[22] As Parkinson's comment indicates, contemporaneous account documents also display this format, such as the P. UC 32179 verso, which lists an assortment of products and goods,[23] and P. UC 32163 and P. UC 32165, which are household census lists that separate the person determinative from names of individual household members.[24] Just like the list in the Eloquent Peasant, the Ramesseum Onomasticon employs the style of such accounts, not simply by the layout, but also by the numbering of entries.

That the separation of determinatives has a practical purpose is further shown by the medical prescriptions on the Twelfth Dynasty cursive-hieroglyphic P. Ramesseum V.[25] Every prescription is organized into a tabular format where each short vertical column contains the name and quantity of an ingredient. The determinatives, plural strokes, and quantity markers rest at the bottom of the column. For longer names of ingredients, the signs fill the allotted space normally; but for short names, a space is created between the base of the word and the determinative at the bottom. In a prescription that contains several types of animal fat (fig. 2), the arrangement reveals that the separated determinative acted as the determinative for the substance as a whole. Thus in column 20, the phrase *mrḥt pnw*, "fat of a mouse" is written with the animal hide determinative directly after the phonetic spelling of *pnw*, while the pot determinative is taken out of its normal position directly after the phonetic base of *mrḥt* and placed at the bottom of the column after both words. The practical implication of this is clear. The user of such a papyrus is looking for a substance contained in a pot, not an actual mouse, lion, donkey, or crocodile; and the quantity is measured in terms of substances contained in pots. Similarly, while not written in a tabular format, many of the prescriptions in the Ebers Papyrus also show a separation between the phonetic base of an ingredient and the determinative/quantity.[26] The inclusion of the quantity again links the format to the genre of accounts and the practical necessity of accessing specific information to produce the desired result, that is, the correct prescription.

Perhaps the best attested separation of determinatives comes, even earlier, from Old Kingdom offering lists. These lists, such as the one from the tomb of Debeheni, often employ an elaborate tabular format where the phonetic

19. Hoffmann, "Aufzählungen," 91–95.

20. Parkinson, *Tale of the Eloquent Peasant,* xi–xii.

21. Richard Bruce Parkinson, *The Tale of the Eloquent Peasant: A Reader's Commentary*, LingAeg SM 10 (Hamburg: Widmaier, 2012), 29–35.

22. Parkinson, *Tale of the Eloquent Peasant: A Reader's Commentary,* 30.

23. Mark Collier and Stephen Quirke, *The UCL Lahun Papyri: Accounts,* BAR International Series 1471 (Oxford: Archaeopress, 2006), 26–27. For the layout of documents more generally, see Christopher Eyre, *The Use of Documents in Pharaonic Egypt* (Oxford: Oxford University Press, 2013), especially 41–52.

24. Mark Collier and Stephen Quirke, *The UCL Lahun Papyri: Religious, Literary, Legal, Mathematical and Medical,* BAR International Series 1209 (Oxford: Archaeopress, 2004), 110–11 and 114–15.

25. Alan Gardiner, *The Ramesseum Papyri: Plates* (Oxford: Oxford University Press, 1955), pls. 15–17; John Barns, *Five Ramesseum Papyri* (Oxford: Oxford University Press, 1956), pl. 21; Hoffmann, "Aufzählungen," 102.

26. For example, see prescriptions in Columns 7–13, 15–18 and 21. Georg Ebers, *Papyros Ebers: Das hermetische Buch über die Arzneimittel der alten Ägypter in hieratischer Schrift* (Leipzig: Engelmann, 1875), pls. 2–5; also, Wolfhart Westendorf, *Handbuch der altägyptischen Medizin*, HdO 36 (Leiden: Brill, 1999), 1:22.

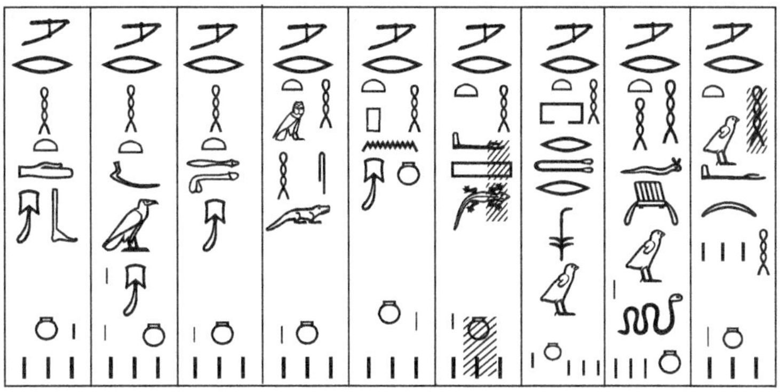

Figure 2. P. Ramesseum V, columns 16–24 (upper). After Barns, *Five Ramesseum Papyri,* pl. 21.

base of offering (often a food, oil, or cloth), the determinative, and the amount each occupy their own cell.[27] Less elaborately tabulated versions from nearly all periods[28] rely on a layout similar to that of P. Ramesseum V, such that items with longer spellings fully occupy the allotted space, while shorter writings result in a space between base and determinative.[29] Just as with the medical prescriptions, the determinatives in the offering lists blur the line between determinative and countable quantity, such that a single determinative might appear when the count is one, but two for a count of two. Beyond offering lists, similar patterns occur in later funerary contexts as well. In the Book of the Dead of Ani, the names of the deities from the Gliedervergottung list in BD 42 occupy vertical columns with the divine determinatives (A40, the seated god; C6, the jackal-headed god; and I12, the cobra) resting on the ground line of the column, separated in all but the longest spellings from the phonetic base of the name.[30]

The distribution of separated determinatives is intriguing. It occurs in a broad range of genres from administrative accounts to funerary texts; yet, despite the fact that onomastica are closely tied to the production of scribal knowledge, no onomastica with such a format have survived after the Ramesseum Onomasticon. Yet spacing does remain a scribal tool in later periods,[31] but usually to separate paragraphs or sections,[32] not to demarcate determinatives. The extensive Roman-period Tebtunis onomasticon often shows some slight spacing between entries along with a coterie of commentary marks, but no spacing within an entry or word.[33] However, the vagaries of preservation being what

27. *LD* II, 35. Winifried Barta, *Die altägyptische Opferliste von der Frühzeit bis zur griechisch-römischen Epoche* (Berlin: Hessing, 1963), 47–67, and 181–82 (figs. 4–5); see also Selim Hassan, *Excavations at Giza 6: 1934–1935, Part 2: The Offering-List in the Old Kingdom* (Cairo: Government Press, 1948), 62.

28. For example, from as late as the Ptolemaic period, the offering list in the Birth House at Kom Ombo. Jacques de Morgan et al., *Catalogue des monuments et inscriptions d'Égypte antique: Kom Ombos,* vol. 2, part 1 (Vienna: Holzhausen, 1895), 41, no. 39. Others do not separate determinatives: for example most entries in an offering list from Edfu, Edfou I, 4, 493.

29. Barta, *Opferliste,* 135–52 (Abb. 6–8); also Hoffmann, "Aufzählungen," 95–96.

30. Raymond Faulkner and Ogden Goelet, *The Egyptian Book of the Dead: The Book of Going Forth by Day, Being the Papyrus of Ani (Royal Scribe of Divine Offerings)*, 3rd ed. (San Francisco: Chronicle Books, 2015), pl. 32-A.

31. Kim Ryholt, "Scribal Habits at the Tebtunis Temple Library: On Materiality, Formal Features, and Palaeography," in *Scribal Repertoires in Egypt from the New Kingdom to the Early Islamic Period,* ed. Jennifer Cromwell and Eitan Grossman (Oxford: Oxford University Press, 2018), 183; William J. Tait, "Guidelines and Borders in Demotic Papyri," in *Papyrus: Structure and Usage,* ed. Morris L. Bierbrier, BMOP 60 (London: British Museum, 1986), 66–67.

32. For example, P. Carlsberg 677. Joachim Friedrich Quack and Kim Ryholt, *Demotic Literary Texts from Tebtunis and Beyond,* CNIP 36 (Copenhagen: Museum Tusculanum Press, 2019), 243–51, pl. 21.

33. Osing, *Hieratische Papyri,* 31–37.

they are, and as more late papyri are being published, we cannot exclude the possibility that evidence for the continuation of this practice may yet come to light.[34]

Thus, scribal use of separated determinatives does not necessarily constitute conscious "linguistic" or "scholarly" engagements with the nature of determinatives. Instead, such a layout both serves a practical purpose and functions as a means of display as the medical texts and offering lists make clear. It allows for easy access to information and easy adaptation into other formats.[35] The concrete nature of the nouns in these contexts, all of them physical things that existed in the world, meant that the determinative, even as it was an element of written language, could represent these (frequently countable) things independent from the phonetic coding. Moreover, particularly in ritual contexts, text, determinative, and image are intertwined and interdependent.[36] The latter issue is, of course, a long-acknowledged element of the complex relationship between text and image, as Henry Fischer has discussed at length.[37]

Nonetheless, the separation of determinative from phonetic base hints at an awareness on the part of scribes that the determinative functioned differently from phonetic signs. While the separation in these contexts lies in the realm of practicality, an understanding of the adaptability of Egyptian script still underpins these uses because it is predicated on a divide between signs functioning phonetically and signs functioning as a determinative. It speaks to a graphic awareness, an awareness that not all aspects of the written form were indexed to speech and an awareness that may have been a precursor to more complex manipulation of the script in later periods.

Determinatives in Nonstandard Writing Contexts

One of the curious, although infrequently attested, linguistic phenomena that occurs in Egyptian texts is the use of an Egyptian script to write out phrases or texts in a foreign language.[38] Distinct from a singular loanword[39] that occurs in an otherwise Egyptian text, these represent the transliteration of larger units of a foreign language. Hieroglyphic, hieratic, and Demotic examples have survived, largely from the New Kingdom and later, but scholars often disagree on their interpretation, the degree to which Egyptian scribes understood the foreign phrases, and sometimes even the original language.[40] Many of these texts display an unusual use of determinatives, which is the focus here. In the

34. For example, a photo of P. Carlsberg 556, an unpublished fragment of a hieratic ritual text, included by Ryholt as part of a discussion about framing lines, appears to show several lines with a divine determinative separated out from the rest of the text. See Ryholt, "Scribal Habits," 165, fig. 7.7c.

35. Friedhelm Hoffmann has made precisely this point with regards to medical prescriptions: "Die Abtrennbarkeit der Determinierung macht es leicht, Listen in Tabellen zu überführen." Hoffmann, "Aufzählungen," 94.

36. Hoffmann, "Aufzählungen," 98–100.

37. In particular, the ways in which two-dimensional images and three-dimensional states can function as determinatives. Henry George Fischer, "Redundant Determinatives in the Old Kingdom," *MMJ* 8 (1973): 7–25; Henry George Fischer, *L'écriture et l'art de l'Egypte ancienne: quatre leçons sur la paléographie et l'épigraphie pharaoniques* (Paris: Presses universitaires de France, 1986), 26–29.

38. Joachim F. Quack, "Egyptian Writing for Non-Egyptian Languages and Vice Versa: A Short Overview," in *Idea of Writing: Play and Complexity*, ed. Alex de Voogt and I. L. Finkel (Leiden: Brill, 2009), 317–25.

39. At the word level, foreign loanwords are extremely well attested from the Old Kingdom through the Greco-Roman period. For an up-to-date summary of research on the topic of foreign words in Egyptian, see Joachim Friedrich Quack, "From Group-Writing to Word Association: Representation and Integration of Foreign Words in Egyptian Script," in Voogt and Finkel, *Idea of Writing*, 73–92. Phrases can also occur within foreign personal names. For Near Eastern personal names, see Thomas Schneider, *Asiatische Personennamen in ägyptischen Quellen des Neuen Reiches*, OBO 114 (Fribourg: Presses Universitaires, 1992); for Meroitic and Nubian, see Karola Zibelius-Chen, *"Nubisches" Sprachmaterial in hieroglyphischen und hieratischen Texten: Personennamen, Appellativa, Phrasen vom Neuen Reich bis in die napatanische und meroitische Zeit*, Meroitic 25 (Wiesbaden: Harrassowitz, 2011).

40. An overview can be found in Quack, "Egyptian Writing," to which the difficult passages from the Pyramid Texts (PT 232–238 and 281–287) that have been treated by Steiner as early Northwest Semitic might be added: Richard C. Steiner, *Early Northwest Semitic Serpent Spells in the Pyramid Texts*, HSS 61 (Winona Lake, IN: Eisenbrauns, 2011). However, nothing in the spells explicitly identifies them as foreign speech (in contrast to most of the New Kingdom hieratic texts, which do), and there is a lack of scholarly consensus

texts where there is some agreement on content and word division, Niv Allon has identified three basic strategies for determinatives: normal distribution of determinatives, repetitive determinatives, and omission of determinatives.[41] The uses from these better-understood texts—New Kingdom hieratic examples from two spells in P. BM 10042,[42] seven spells in P. BM 10059,[43] and a phrase in P. Anastasi;[44] and the extensive Aramaic text in Demotic script P. Amherst 63[45]—illustrate the exploitation of the writing system. Examples of normal and repetitive determinatives are shown below, while the omission of determinatives is treated in the following section.

Spell 21 in P. BM 10059, a magical-medical text from the Eighteenth Dynasty, displays a normal use of determinatives, that is, most words within the foreign transliterated text bear a determinative that matches the semantic category of the word.

Incantation 21, P. BM 10059, VII, 6–7[46]

šnt smn w-b-q[pustule] *s-t*[Ø] *s-b-j*[Ø] *y-ḏ*[walking legs] *ḥ-m-k-t*[man] *r-p-y*[divine] *p3 wr j-m-j*[divine] *dd.tw r zp 4*

"Incantation of *samanu*: *wbq st sbj yḏ ḥmkt rpy* the great one *jmj*. Spell is to be said four times."

Per Incantation 15, which begins this series of spells, the language is foreign.[47] The content of Incantation 21 includes two Egyptian words, *p3 wr*, but the rest is non-Egyptian written in the typical group spelling.[48] The determinatives

around their interpretation. For example, Allen treats them as pure Egyptian and translates as such, see James P. Allen, *The Ancient Egyptian Pyramid Texts*, WAW 23 (Atlanta: Society of Biblical Literature, 2005).

41. Niv Allon, "At the Outskirts of a System: Classifiers and Word Dividers in Foreign Phrases and Texts," *LingAeg* 18 (2000): 1–17.

42. Section Q and Z, see Christian Leitz, *Magical and Medical Papyri of the New Kingdom*, Hieratic Papyri in the British Museum VII (London: British Museum Press, 1999), 42, pl. 18 and 49–50, pl. 23. For section Z, see also Thomas Schneider, "Mag. p.Harris XII, 1–5: Eine kanaanäische Beschwörung für die Löwenjagd?" *GM* 112 (1989): 53–63.

43. Incantation 15–21, see Leitz, *Magical and Medical Papyri*, 61–63, pl. 31–32. Note that Incantation 19 is largely in Egyptian except for two words. See also Richard C. Steiner, "Northwest Semitic Incantations in an Egyptian Medical Papyrus of the Fourteenth Century B.C.E." *JNES* 51 (1992): 191–200 and Richard C. Steiner, "The London Medical Papyrus," in *The Context of Scripture: Canonical Compositions from the Biblical World*, ed. William Hallo and K. Lawson Younger (Leiden: Brill, 1997), 328–29.

44. Hans-Werner Fischer-Elfert, *Die satirische Streitschrift des Papyrus Anastasi I: Textzusammenstellung*, KÄT (Wiesbaden: Harrassowitz, 1983), 138.

45. There is extensive scholarly treatment of this difficult text and much disagreement. Most recently, see Karel van der Toorn, *Papyrus Amherst 63*, AOAT 448 (Münster: Ugarit-Verlag, 2018), which includes full photos of the text; and Tawny Holm, "Nanay and Her Lover: An Aramaic Sacred Marriage Text from Egypt," *JNES* 76 (2017): 1–37, and relevant bibliography, particular n. 9 in Holm. Several key publications must also be mentioned: Charles Nims and Richard C. Steiner, "A Paganized Version of Psalm 20:2–6 from the Aramaic Text in Demotic Script," *JAOS* 103 (1983): 261–74; Charles Nims and Richard C. Steiner, "You Can't Offer Your Sacrifice and Eat It Too: A Polemical Poem from the Aramaic Text in Demotic Script," *JNES* 43 (1984): 89–114; Charles Nims and Richard C. Steiner, "Ashurbanipal and Shamash-Shum-Ukin: A Tale of Two Brothers from the Aramaic Text in Demotic Script, Part 1," *Revue biblique* 92 (1985): 60–81; Sven Vleeming and Jan Wesselius, "An Aramaic Hymn from the Fourth Century BC," *BiOr* 39 (1982): 501–9; Sven Vleeming and Jan Wesselius, *Studies in Papyrus Amherst 63: Essays on the Aramaic Texts in Aramaic/Demotic Papyrus Amherst 63*, 2 vols. (Amsterdam: Juda Palache Instituut, 1985–1990).

46. Steiner translates the foreign speech as "and through the vomiting up of the drunken demon, let ḥ-m-k-tu go out, (O) my healer, great one, mother." Steiner, "London Medical Papyrus," 329.

47. Incantation 15 (P. BM 10059, VI, 6) is labeled *ḏd n ḫ3st* "foreign speech" and seems to apply to the subsequent spells, see Leitz, *Magical and Medical Papyri*, 61, pl. 31.

48. Steiner identifies the language of this group of spells, with the exception of Incantation 20 labeled within the text as Cretan, as "a mixture of Northwest Semitic dialects (Canaanite and Aramaic) ... and a few Akkadian terms thrown in for good measure." Steiner, "London Medical Papyrus," 328. But as the preceding spell (Incantation 20, P. BM 10059, VII, 4–6) is in fact explicitly labeled "in the speech of Crete," other scholars have argued the language of Incantation 21 is also Cretan, see, e.g., Peter W. Haider, "Minoische Sprach-

accord with the proposed meanings of the words,[49] while *st sbj*, be it one word or two,[50] omits the determinative(s). This use of determinatives follows the traditional use of determinatives in regular Egyptian, in which most but not all words take a semantic determinative, but it is the only clearly preserved example of this strategy.

The second strategy for determinatives is repetitive determinatives in which many different foreign words receive the same determinative. Repetitive determinatives occur in Section Q and Z of P. BM 10042, in the phrase from P. Anastasi I, and most famously in P. Amherst 63. Section Z in P. BM 10042, the Harris magical papyrus, is clearly non-Egyptian although the text does not label it as such. Schneider has argued that the language is Canaanite and the content a spell for lion hunting.[51] The text is 4 lines long and stands alone on the verso of a sheet. Only two determinatives are used throughout the text: the T14 throw-stick followed by a diagonal stroke after most words and the bookroll after the word *sm*.[52] The first line from the text shows this distribution:[53]

Section Z, P. BM 10042, rt. XII, 1[54]

j-d-r[throw-stick/] *j-d-s-n*[throw-stick/·] *j-d-r-g-h*[throw-stick/] *j-d-s-n*[throw-stick/·] *s-m*[bookroll] *m-t-m*[throw-stick/] *j-d-s-n*[throw-stick/·]

After nearly every word, the throw-stick and slash appear, except for the bookroll determinative for the word *sm*. While the throw-stick frequently occurs as a determinative indicating foreignness, it typically applies only to words or names for foreign peoples or places, not generally to any foreign word.[55] Moreover, this is the only attested text where it is used in such a repetitive fashion. In addition to the throw-stick as a repetitive determinative, the A2 man-with-hand-to-mouth is also used in such a manner. In the midst of the many foreign loanwords that occur in P. Anastasi I, a full non-Egyptian sentence also appears:

P. Anastasi I, 23, 5[56]

j-b-t[man-with-hand-to-mouth] *k-m*[man-with-hand-to-mouth] *j-y-r*[animal] *m-h-r*[man-with-stick] *n-ʿ-m*[man-with-hand-to-mouth]

denkmäler in einem ägyptischen Papyrus medizinischen Inhalts," in *Das Ägytpische und die Sprachen Vorderasiens, Nordafrikas, und der Ägäis: Akten des Basler Kolloquiums zum ägyptisch-nichtsemitischen Sprachkontakt, Basel 9.–11. Juli 2003*, ed. Thomas Schneider (Münster: Ugarit-Verlag, 2004), 417–18. A summary of these issues and complete list of references for this spell can be found in Susanne Beck, *Sāmānu: Ein vorderasiatischer Dämon in Ägypten*, ÄAT 83 (Münster: Ugarit-Verlag, 2015), 95. Word divisions are the same in either interpretation.

49. Steiner, "London Medical Papyrus," 328–29 and Steiner, "Northwest Semitic Incantations," 198.

50. Leitz's transliteration *stsbj* merely reflects the fact that there is no determinative, as he "follows purely formal criteria, with a space after each determinative," Leitz, *Magical and Medical Papyri*, 62n99, 63. While Steiner does not attempt to translate this portion of the spell in "Northwest Semitic Incantations," 198, he does suggest dividing it into two words *šēdi sabūʾi* "the drunken demon," in Steiner, "London Medical Papyrus," 329. Beck follows Steiner's later interpretation, see Beck, *Sāmānu*, 95.

51. Schneider, "Mag. P. Harris XII, 1–5."

52. Schneider takes *sm* to mean "(fest)setzen, bestimmen," see Schneider, "Mag. P. Harris XII, 1–5," 56.

53. Note that Schneider divides the words slightly differently. For example, he reads *j-d-r-g-h* as two words *jdr gh*. Schneider, "Mag. P. Harris XII, 1–5," 54.

54. Schneider proposes the following translation for this line: "Mächtiger: möge ich doch niedertreten! Mächtiger an Rettung: möge ich doch niedertreten! Der die Grube festsetzt: möge ich doch niedertreten!" Schneider, "Mag. p.Harris XII, 1–5," 54.

55. Quack, "From Group-Writing," 78.

56. Varying translations have been suggested for this line. See James E. Hoch, *Semitic Words in Egyptian Texts of the New Kingdom and Third Intermediate Period* (Princeton: Princeton University Press, 1994), 20–21. Fischer-Elfert has suggested reading it as "Du irrst umher wie ein Schaf, lieber Maher," in Hans-Werner Fischer-Elfert, *Die satirische Streitschrift des Papyrus Anastasi I: Übersetzung und Kommentar*, ÄA 44 (Wiesbaden: Harrassowitz, 1986), 198–99.

Here two words are determined with semantically appropriate determinatives, the animal hide for *j-y-r* meaning lion or lamb and the man with a stick for *m-h-r* meaning officer. The other words have the A2 man-with-hand-to-mouth determinative. While the repetitive use of determinatives here is not as clear as in Section Z of P. BM 10042, there are other instances of the A2 man-with-hand-to-mouth determinative used in such a manner. Section Q of P. BM 10042, which cannot be understood as normal Egyptian and may be either magical words or a foreign language, also uses this sign repetitively as a presumed determinative, although word divisions are not clear.

Most famously, the A2 man-with-hand-to-mouth determinative occurs pervasively in P. Amherst 63. This Aramaic text in Demotic script is much later than the New Kingdom magical spells and likely dates to the fourth century BCE.[57] P. Amherst 63 stands out from all other transliterated foreign texts for its sheer length, twenty-three preserved columns. The length confirms the pervasiveness and repetitiveness of the determinative[58] but also poses a dilemma for scholars to explain how the text came into being, why it was written in Demotic, and how it was actually used.[59] The text also poses a difficulty in identifying the Aramaic vocabulary because certain Aramaic phonemes are not distinguished in Demotic. Despite these difficulties, it is clear that while the A2 determinative usually marked the end of a word, cases where it was applied incorrectly in the middle of a word or missing from an actual word division do occur. Nor is the A2 determinative the only determinative used in the text, although none with the same frequency.[60]

The most common interpretation of these repetitive determinatives is that they are word dividers.[61] In Section Z of P. BM 10042, the presence of the slash alongside the throw-stick bolsters this argument, as it seems to be purely a paratextual mark, not a sign to be read.[62] Moreover, P. Amherst 63 clearly shows that at least part of the function of the A2 determinative was as a word divider, albeit one that occurs persistently but not always regularly. Even in non-foreign-language contexts, the determinatives' role as word divider has long been noted, particularly for Late Egyptian. Junge comments that in regard to common determinatives like the bookroll or man with hand to mouth: "While the determinatives seem to lose significance as indicators of meaning, their role as word separators increases."[63] So too has Quack posited that the "overuse" of the plural determinative in P. Boulaq 4 marked word divisions.[64]

However, in looking at this group of transliterations, Niv Allon[65] has proposed another interpretation: that the repetitive determinative acted not simply a word divider but rather functioned as a metatextual indicator of a foreign-language environment. In other words, the repetitive determinative marked the section as non-Egyptian and so "the reader is signaled to abandon the decoding and word-recognition processes relevant to ancient Egyptian, and to

---

57. Nims and Steiner, "Paganized Version of Psalm 20:2–6," 261 and Vleeming and Wesselius, "Aramaic Hymn," 501. However, the dating is based purely on paleography and the exceptional nature of the text makes dating difficult.

58. The only other possible Aramaic text in Demotic is a graffito from Wadi Hammamat, and it also appears to use the A2 determinative, but there is disagreement on its interpretation. See Richard C. Steiner, "The Scorpion Spell from Wadi Hammamat: Another Aramaic Text in Demotic Script," *JNES* 60 (2001): 259–68.

59. For example, Quack, "Egyptian Writing," 319–20.

60. For example, Holm, "Nanay and Her Lover," 37, particularly "Appendix 4—Independent Determinatives."

61. Karl-Theodor Zauzich, "Abrakadabra oder Ägyptisch? Versuch über einen Zauberspruch," *Enchoria* 13 (1985): 126–27.

62. While the slash may be related to the Z5 sign used in place of complicated determinatives, its use is so unusual here that it perhaps should be treated as a mark specific to this text. Per Quack, "We have the sign of the throw-stick followed by a slash as a unique determinative ... no longer serving as a signal of specific meaning, but only as a word-divider plus an indication that this is foreign." Quack, "From Group-Writing," 78.

63. Friedrich Junge, *Late Egyptian Grammar: An Introduction*, trans. David Warburton, 2nd ed. (Oxford: Griffith Institute, 2005), 34.

64. Joachim Friedrich Quack, *Die Lehren des Ani: Ein neuägyptischer Weisheitstext in seinem kulturellen Umfeld*, OBO 141 (Fribourg: Presses Universitaires; Göttingen: Vandenhoeck & Ruprecht, 1994), 59–60. As Quack notes, this evokes the use of two or three dots as a word divider in Meroitic. See Claude Rilly and Alex de Voogt, *The Meroitic Language and Writing System* (Cambridge: Cambridge University Press, 2012), 7–8.

65. Allon, "At the Outskirts."

apply others when possible."[66] This is a compelling argument because writing down a foreign language in an Egyptian script would not have represented standard scribal operating procedure, nor would reading a transliterated foreign language have followed the normal process of reading Egyptian phrases. Foreign languages, even if transliterated to the best of a scribe's ability, do not share identical phonemes, nor the same pattern of stress and accent, as Egyptian.[67] As the separation of determinatives described in the previous section shows, scribes were conscious of the ability to graphically manipulate determinatives and thus it makes sense that the determinative as a sign that had no parallel in the spoken pronunciation might play a metatextual and metalinguistic role. Similarly, its potential role as a metatextual marker of foreign-language environment does not obviate its role as a word divider. As neither of these functions is a typical element of the writing system, the inconsistency of application should not be surprising.

Transliteration of a foreign language is not the only kind of transliteration that occurs in Egyptian texts. There is a small group of mostly religious texts from the late Ptolemaic to Roman periods whose grammar and vocabulary is to varying degrees that of earlier Egyptian/*Égyptien de tradition* but whose script is Demotic.[68] These instances of language/script mismatch do not follow the pattern of the earlier hieratic texts that transliterate foreign speech with group writing, nor do they quite follow the pattern of P. Amherst 63;[69] instead they use "unetymological" writings. They render some archaic vocabulary and grammatical forms alphabetically, but they also frequently employ entire Demotic words in place of a similar sounding older construction for which there was no accepted Demotic spelling. When these presumably homophonous words were used, their determinative was typically kept.[70] For example, *pꜣ wt Wsjr*, in which *wt* is written as the Demotic word for papyrus complete with the papyrus determinative, functions as a spelling of *pꜣ wt Wsjr,* "the embalmer Osiris" in P. Berlin 6750. That same Demotic word *wt,* "papyrus" with the papyrus determinative is also used in the phrase *pꜣ wt tp* (which looks like "the one who is green of head") for *pꜣw.t-tpy.t,* "first primeval time" in the same text.[71] These unetymological writings consist of two groups: one in which the normal Demotic meaning evoked by the orthography has no bearing on the text, and the other in which the orthography may be an attempt to layer multiple meanings into a single phrase (as the two examples above may be), although there is some debate about whether the second category truly reflects a deliberate scribal choice.[72] Despite the fact that Demotic unetymological writings are far later (and in a different script) than the New Kingdom transliterations and still several centuries later than P. Amherst 63, intra-Egyptian transliteration provides an instructive

66. Allon, 11.

67. While it is probable that not all users (maybe even most) of these texts would have understood the foreign language(s), even a bilingual scribe would have had to employ different decoding processes for the two languages. For evidence that some Egyptian scribes learned Akkadian during the New Kingdom, see Matthias Müller, "Akkadian from Egypt," *UCLAEE,* http://digital2.library.ucla.edu/viewItem.do?ark=21198/zz002jjz3z, and the references therein.

68. The bibliography on this topic is extensive and growing: Ghislaine Widmer, "Une invocation à la déesse (tablette démotique Louvre E 10382)," in *Res severa verum gaudium: Festschrift für Karl-Theodor Zauzich zum 65. Geburtstag am 8. Juni 2004,* ed. Friedhelm Hoffmann and Heinz-Joseph Thissen, Studia Demotica 6 (Leuven: Peeters, 2004), 651–86; Ghislaine Widmer, *Résurrection d'Osiris—Naissance d'Horus: Les papyrus Berlin P. 6750 et Berlin P. 8765,* témoignages de la persistance de la tradition sacerdotale dans le Fayoum à l'époque romaine, ÄOP 3 (Berlin: de Gruyter, 2015), and the references therein; Joachim Quack, "Old Wine in New Wineskins? How to Write Classical Egyptian Rituals in More Modern Writing Systems," in *The Idea of Writing: Writing across Borders,* ed. Alex de Voogt and Joachim Friedrich Quack (Leiden: Brill, 2011), 219–43.

69. While some Demotic sign groups are used in P. Amherst 63, the majority of the Demotic is single-consonant signs.

70. But not always. For example, the Demotic spelling for *tꜣ* "land" is used to write the older *ḏw* "evil" but uses the bad determinative not the place determinative in Louvre E 10382, 11 (Widmer, "Une invocation," 664 and 677) and has no determinative in P. Carlsberg 182 (Osing, *Hieratische Papyri,* 202, pl. 17A). See also, Quack, "Old Wine," 227–28.

71. Widmer, "Une invocation," 678 and Widmer, *Résurrection d'Osiris,* 225 and 390.

72. Widmer calls these two usages "écritures phonétiques" and "reécritures non étymologique," see the two contrasting lists in Widmer, *Résurrection d'Osiris,* 45–46; also Mark Smith, *Traversing Eternity: Texts for the Afterlife from Ptolemaic and Roman Egypt* (Oxford: Oxford University Press, 2009), 392–93. Quack is more skeptical that scribes ever intended multiple meanings, see Quack, "Old Wine," particularly 232–33.

contrast to the transliterated foreign texts, because intra-Egyptian transliteration does not manipulate determinatives as word dividers or metatextual marks. Moreover, this intra-Egyptian style appears to rely on scribes processing the Demotic orthography in a normal manner to produce a particular phonetic realization, one that only then points to another, more archaic meaning. If the scribal intent is also to add an additional layer of meaning, then the normal processes of decoding Demotic are all the more important so that both meanings can be achieved.

Absence of Determinatives

In parallel to the repetition of a determinative, the frequent omission of determinatives also occurs in transliterations of foreign-language phrases. While Allon's main argument primarily focused on the presence of determinatives as a metatextual marker, he also hints that their absence may play a similar role.[73] Of the seven foreign-language spells from P. BM 10059, one has normal determinatives (see Incantation 21 above), three are broken and seem to show some foreign words with determinatives and some without (Incantation 15–17), one has only two foreign words within the spell both with determinatives (Incantation 19), and two (Incantation 18 and 20) seem to omit determinatives almost completely.

Incantation 18, P.BM 10059, VII, 2-3

kt šnt fnt s-b-k-n-j-m-r-s-k-n$^{\emptyset}$ *zp sn j-m-r*$^{\emptyset}$ *n-ḫ-r-s-n*$^{\emptyset}$ *dd.tw r pn zp 4*
Another incantation of the worm: *sbknjmrskn* (twice) *jmr nḫrsn*. This spell is to be said four times.

Identifying where word divisions occur in this section is difficult precisely because of the lack of determinatives. The above division follows Leitz, however Steiner prefers *sbkn*$^{\emptyset}$ *jmr*$^{\emptyset}$ *skn*$^{\emptyset}$ *jmrn*$^{\emptyset}$ *ḫrsn*$^{\emptyset}$. Regardless of where the divisions are drawn, determinatives are absent from the foreign-language portion of the spell, while the Egyptian title retains a normal use. A similar situation occurs in Incantation 20. The Cretan words are largely undetermined and the two determinatives that do occur may have been included simply because the writing resembled a short Egyptian word; hence they represent a phonetic unit, not a complete word with appropriate determinative.[74] Omission, like repetition, of determinatives would have stood out to an ancient scribe, just as it does to modern scholars, and both likely indicated the same thing: the phonetic environment of the unusually determined section was irregular because the language was not Egyptian.

Cryptography provides another instance where the lack of determinatives may play a metatextual function to indicate an abnormal phonetic environment, suggesting that determinatives are not simply a tool for foreign languages but play a broader phonetic role. Cryptographic texts are of course standard Egyptian in terms of grammar and language, but signs frequently represent non-standard phonetic values.[75] Not only are rarer signs used in place of

73. "Even in such an abundantly classified text, like P. BM EA 10059, the shift to a classifierless or to a sporadically classified spell indexes its foreign linguistic environment." Allon, "At the Outskirts," 11.

74. P. BM 10059, VII, 4–6. So Quack on this spell, "hardly any determinatives at all are used and the only ones occurring are visibly derived from the association of short Egyptian words serving to write parts of the phonetic sequence." See Quack, "From Group-Writing," 79.

75. Overviews of cryptography can be found in John Coleman Darnell and Colleen Manassa Darnell, *The Ancient Egyptian Netherworld Books*, Writings from the Ancient World 39 (Atlanta: SBL Press, 2018), 50–55; Andrés Diego Espinel, "Play and Display in Egyptian High Culture: The Cryptographic Texts of Djehuty (TT 11) and their Sociocultural Contexts," in *Creativity and Innovation in the Reign of Hatshepsut*, ed. José Galan, Betsy Bryan, and Peter Dorman, SAOC 69 (Chicago: The Oriental Institute, 2014), 297–335; John

more common signs, but common signs are often given uncommon phonetic values. Even the arrangement of signs can be jumbled in an effect called "perturbation." Thus, cryptography represents an unusual phonetic environment not because the language itself is unusual, but because the written form does not yield the expected phonetic value.

This cryptographic composition from the second shrine of Tutankhamun shows the typical absence of determinatives that characterizes most cryptographic texts:

Second Shrine of Tutankhamun, Side One, Scene 4

nn n nṯrw m sḫr pn m qr(r)wt=sn jmjwt ḥrjt wnn ẖ3t(?)=sn m kkw

"These gods are in this fashion in their caverns which are in the Upper Region: Their corpses(?) exist in the darkness."[76]

Not a single word bears a semantic determinative; the only determinative that does occur is the plural strokes. It is certainly possible to understand the omission of determinatives as an attempt to prevent confusion; but while most cryptographic texts omit the determinatives, some do retain determinatives largely as normal and others occasionally employ determinatives.[77] The significance of the phonetic environment is also highlighted in cryptographic texts because one of the strategies for cryptographic orthography is to spell words according to their actual pronunciation in contrast to the far more conservative *Normalschrift*. Thus, an "*r*" at the end of a word, which had weakened completely by the New Kingdom, was frequently dropped in cryptographic spelling: such as *nṯj* for *nṯr*.[78] Even though this writing reflected contemporaneous pronunciation and Late Egyptian orthographies were wont to do the same, Middle Egyptian texts typically preferred the more conservative spelling.[79] Therefore, one potential reason for the unusual omission of the determinative in cryptographic texts as compared to other contemporaneous hieroglyphic texts may have been to mark the phonetic environment as unusual.[80]

The unusual omission of determinatives is also associated with Saite-period hieroglyphic inscriptions, particularly in conjunction with an alphabetic spelling of the phonetic base.[81] In Peter Der Manuelian's study of royal Saite

---

Coleman Darnell, *The Engimatic Netherworld Books of the Solar-Osirian Unity: Cryptographic Compositions in the Tombs of Tutankhamun, Ramesses VI and Ramesses IX*, OBO 198 (Fribourg: Presses Universitaires; Göttingen: Vandenhoeck & Ruprecht, 2004), 14–34.

76. Following Darnell, *Enigmatic Netherworld Books*, 64–69.

77. For example, west wall of Seti I's Cenotaph, see Joshua Aaron Roberson, *The Ancient Egyptian Books of the Earth*, Wilbour Series 1 (Atlanta: Lockwood, 2012), 94; see also Darnell and Darnell, *Ancient Egyptian Netherworld Books*, 52.

78. Darnell, *Enigmatic Netherworld Books*, 34.

79. See also the comparison of the spelling of the Khepri in the Amduat, which has parallel plain text and cryptographic text: Daniel A. Werning, "Aenigmatische Schreibungen in Unterweltsbüchern des Neuen Reiches: Gesicherte Entsprechungen und Ersetzungsprinzipien," in *Miscellanea in honorem Wolfhart Westendorf*, ed. Carsten Peust, Göttinger Miszellen Beihefte 3 (Göttingen: Seminar für Ägyptologie und Koptologie, 2008), 130–31.

80. That cryptography represents a departure from the normal system of writing is clarified by the later phenomenon of Ptolemaic hieroglyphs. Many cryptographic values survive in the monumental hieroglyphic writings of Greco-Roman temples, but this style is not cryptographic because it represents the hieroglyphic norm of that period. Ptolemaic hieroglyphs omit determinatives not infrequently, but again, this now represents the norm (see Dieter Kurth, *Einführung ins Ptolemäische: Eine Grammatik mit Zeichenliste und Übungsstücken; Teil 1* [Hützel: Backe, 2009], 83). And, in fact, there is a cryptographic version of Ptolemaic hieroglyphs, as the crocodile and ram hymns from Esna show. Interestingly, these cryptographic hymns employ some determinatives, see Christian Leitz, "Die beiden kryptographischen Inschriften aus Esna mit den Widdern und Krokodilen," *SAK* 29 (2001): 251–76 and Ludwig Morenz, "Schrift-Mysterium: Gottes-Schau in der visuellen Poesie von Esna: Insbesondere zu den omnipotenten Widder-Zeichen zwischen Symbolik und Lesbarkeit," in *Ägyptische Mysterien?*, ed. Jan Assmann and Martin Bommas (Munich: Fink, 2002), 77–94.

81. "There are relatively few words, aside from the purely alphabetic spellings, which omit determinatives altogether" and "one absolutely cannot speak of a universal Saite preference for alphabetic spellings in some sort of unswervingly devoted imitation of Old

inscriptions, the majority of writings that omitted determinatives were alphabetic spellings from a single text known from two copies: the Shellal/Karnak stelae of Psamtik II.[82] Slightly later, the Naukratis stela along with the Thonis-Heracleion copy, both from the Thirtieth Dynasty, also display a predilection for alphabetic spellings and omitted determinatives, as well as playful writings that may have a display of scribal virtuosity, all largely restricted to the section of the text expressing praise of king, not the content of the decree itself.[83] While the debate about whether these orthographies represent archaism or a precursor to Ptolemaic writing is beyond the scope of this article,[84] what is noteworthy is the link between alphabetic spelling and a lack of determinatives. The omission clearly does not function as a metatextual marker of an unusual phonetic environment (as may be the case for foreign-language texts and cryptographic texts) because, while some of the alphabetic spellings are unusual, the phonetic values are normal and the language is normal, if archaic Egyptian. Yet the link between alphabetic spelling and a lack of a determinative still hints at the determinative functioning as a site for scribal manipulation, particularly when the phonetic decoding of a particular graphic form was at issue.

There is one question that remains if we suggest that scribes thought of the determinative as a potential mediator of phonetic environment: To what extent were scribes concerned with the texts being spoken out loud? For the foreign-language transliterations, particularly the New Kingdom medical spells, it is clear that pronunciation of the written word was essential. After all, the paratextual instructions for many explicitly require the spell to be "said four times," as in Incantation 18 from P. BM 10059. Even the ones that do not contain the specific instruction, such as Section Z from P. BM 10042, still belong to the magical genre for which recitation constituted effective magical practice.[85] The cryptographic texts, on the surface, complicate this because their graphic form restricts the ability of people to read them and most are located in physically restricted royal tombs.[86] However, restricted though many cryptographic texts are "these texts were intended properly to reveal their secrets to the initiated reader who should not reveal such hard-won and cosmically significant knowledge."[87] Even though cryptography restricts access, the information was still intended to be potentially accessible to select individuals and therefore a concern for recitation exists.

Thus, both the repetition of a determinative and the pervasive omission of determinatives suggest that scribes, at times, used the determinative to mediate the intersection of graphic possibility, phonetic realization, and reader understanding. The variation and inconsistency in this phenomenon indicate that scribes were not following an established practice. By no means was the repetition of a determinative a requirement for the transliteration of a foreign language, nor was the omission of determinatives a requirement for the same or for a cryptographic text. In P. BM 10059, Incantation 21 uses determinatives normally, while Incantation 18 and 20 omit determinatives. Section Z of P. BM 10042 stands out for its otherwise unparalleled use of the throw-stick determinative and slash. Sporadic use

---

Egyptian." Peter Der Manuelian, *Living in the Past: Studies on Archaism of the Egyptian Twenty-Sixth Dynasty* (London: Kegan Paul, 1994), 87 and 99.

82. Der Manuelian, *Living in the Past,* 81 and 337–63.

83. Anne-Sophie von Bomhard, *The Decree of Saïs: The Stelae of Thonis-Heracleion and Naukratis,* Oxford Centre for Maritime Archaeology Monograph 7 (Oxford: Oxford Centre for Maritime Archaeology, 2012), particularly 90–92. See the bibliography therein for earlier scholarship, but particularly Georges Posener, "Notes sur la stèle de Naucratis," *ASAE* 34 (1934): 141–48.

84. Der Manuelian, *Living in the Past,* 81 and 98; von Bomhard, *Decree of Saïs,* 90; Simon D. Schweitzer, "Zur Herkunft der spätzeitlichen alphabetischen Schreibungen," in *Basel Egyptology Prize 1: Junior Research in Egyptian History, Archaeology, and Philology,* ed. by Susanne Bickel and Antonio Loprieno, Aegyptiaca Helvetica 17 (Basel: Schwabe, 2003), 371–86. Quite unlikely is the earlier theory of Greek influence, see Battiscombe Gunn, "Notes on the Naukratis Stela," *JEA* 29 (1943): 55–59.

85. Robert Kriech Ritner, *The Mechanics of Ancient Egyptian Magical Practice,* SAOC 54 (Chicago: Oriental Institute of the University of Chicago, 1993), 35–50.

86. However, while cryptography is best attested in the funerary books from royal tombs, it also occurs in private tombs and graffiti, including, as is the case for the tomb of Djehuty (TT 11), in the most public part of the tomb chapel. See Espinel, "Play and Display," 299–303.

87. Darnell and Darnell, *Ancient Egyptian Netherworld Books,* 54.

of the man-with-hand-to-mouth determinative occurs in P. BM 10042 and P. Anastasi I; and then hundreds of years later in a different script, P. Amherst 63 uses it. Similarly, even though cryptographic texts of the New Kingdom often adhere to a general set of practices, the expression of the determinative varies: often omitted, sometimes retained. The manipulation of the determinative, therefore, likely represents a conscious scribal choice in response to a difficult task. That many of their solutions to an anomalous phonetic process centered upon the manipulation of the determinative reveals a broader understanding of the determinative within the writing system.

Scribal Discourse

The unusual uses of determinatives described above hint at the idea that scribes perceived determinatives as a distinct category of sign and deliberately exploited it, but did Egyptian scribes ever describe, in their own words, their understanding of determinatives? The Egyptian language does not have a word for determinative, nor is there a convenient and explicit philosophical treatise on language. The closest term is the general word for hieroglyphic sign *tjt*, which might apply to any sign.[88] Yet this does not preclude the existence of such a category in the Egyptian mind. Among the many references to scribal activity and the role of hieroglyphs generally,[89] there are several potential oblique allusions to the role of signs, which may encompass ideas about determinatives.

In the tomb of Rekhmire (TT100), vizier to Thutmose III, an inscription records a praise of the king specifically referencing the king's scholarly prowess in terms of language:[90]

Urk. IV:1074, 2–9
jst ḥm=f rḫ ḫprt nn wn ḫmt.n=f rsy ḏḥwty pw m ḫt nb nn mdt tmmt.n=f ʿrq [*sy* ...] *jm.f mj sḫrw n ḥmt sš3t šbšb=f tjt r b3k=s mj nṯr š3 st jr st*
His Majesty knew what happened, there was nothing at all which he did not know. He was Thoth in all things. There was no word which he did not understand [...] in it, after the manner of the majesty of Seshat. He could divide a sign with respect to its use, like the god who commanded it and made it.

The phrase "he could divide a sign with respect to its use" is intriguing. The term *šbšb* means "to divide correctly," mostly used in terms of months and days, particularly with the sense of time divided into smaller parts.[91] Given this association, it is tempting to link this concept of division to that of word division, and hence determinatives' role as word dividers. But the phrase relates this division to *b3k*, "work, use," which raises the possibility that this refers to either: (1) the multivalent phonetic potential that a sign may possess or (2) the different roles (ideogram, phonogram, or determinative) that a sign can play. Rekhmire also speaks of his own intellectual ambitions in similar terms: "there was no sign (*tjt*) whose use (*b3k*) I did not know, forms which had no[t been written?]."[92] Such a statement evokes the slightly earlier claim of Senenmut, "The signs (*tjwt*) which I made from the devising of my heart and of (my own) accord, which were not found in the writings of the ancestors," written next to a cryptogram which he may have, in

88. *Wb.* V:239, 1–240, 11; see also *PtoLex*, 1125.

89. See, e.g., Manfred Weber, *Beiträge zur Kenntnis des Schrift- und Buchwesens der alten Ägypter* (Cologne: Wienand, 1969), 59–79.

90. Donald B. Redford, *Pharaonic King-Lists, Annals and Day-Books: A Contribution to the Study of the Egyptian Sense of History*, SSEA Publications 4 (Mississauga: Benben, 1986), 166–67.

91. *Wb.* IV:442, 4–7 "richtig einteilen." For its use in the context of dating, see, for example, *šbšb sw*, "the fixing of dates" in "The Admonitions of Ipuwer," P. Leiden I 344 rt, 11,4: and *šbšb dw3w r tr 2*, "who divides the hours into two periods" in the Ptolemaic biography of Harkhebi; Georges Daressy, "La statue d'un astronome," *ASAE* 16 (1916): 2; Jacco Dieleman, "Stars and the Egyptian Priesthood in the Graeco-Roman Period," in *Prayer, Magic, and the Stars in the Ancient and Late Antique World*, ed. Scott Noegel, Joel Walker, and Brannon Wheeler (University Park: Pennsylvania State University Press, 2003), 151–52. Also used at Edfu in this manner: *PtoLex*, 999.

92. *Urk.* IV:1082, 2–4; see also, Redford, *Pharaonic King-Lists*, 166.

fact, designed.[93] Thus, the specific context of these statements may be the development of cryptographic writing[94] and the *bꜣk*, "use" indicates the cryptographic phonetic values. Whether or not any of these individuals possessed such scribal skill is beside the point. The rhetoric of such boasts reveals a direct engagement with the writing system, even if these phrases do not directly address a sign functioning as a determinative.

A similar, tantalizing but problematic statement comes from a series of epithets for Thoth from Edfu.

Edfu I, 164, 13
ḏḥwty nṯr špsm Bḥdt nb sẖꜣ wḏꜥ mdt šꜣꜥ tjt nḫb ḥkꜣw qmꜣ wnnt nb m tꜣ
Thoth, the noble god in Behedet, the lord of writing, the one who separates the words, the one who invents the signs, who assigns the magical spells, and who creates everything that exists on earth.

Here Thoth is given the well-attested epithet *wḏꜥ mdw*, "the one who judges."[95] However, it is sandwiched between two other epithets that emphasize Thoth's role as a god of language. The literal meaning of *wḏꜥ mdw* is simply "to divide words/matters" and it is not impossible that such a meaning could exist here,[96] or even that both meanings were deliberately implied.[97] Yet, while a reference to word division, and hence a potential reference to the role determinatives might have played in such, is possible, that interpretation remains inconclusive, and the preponderance of evidence lies on the side of the traditional reading.

Perhaps the strongest, yet still uncertain potential reference comes from the Book of Thoth.[98] This is hardly surprising as the hieroglyphic signs themselves play a crucial role in the text. For example, the vulture list describes the fourty-two nomes of Egypt as vultures and many of the actions of the vultures seem to describe the design of the nome standard (the hieroglyphic sign for the nome) itself.[99] Moreover, figurative language and metaphors involving animals function as rhetoric devices for speaking of hieroglyphic writing.[100] One passage asserts: "The signs[101] revealed their forms. He called to them. They answered to him. He knew the form of speech of the baboons and the ibises. He went about truly in the path of the dog. He did not restrain their barkings. He understood the barking of these and these cries of the vizier."[102] A dual emphasis on the visual form (the baboons, ibises, and dogs) and on pho-

93. *Urk.* IV:406, 10 (from two statues of Senenmut and Neferure, Ägyptisches Museum, Berlin 2296 and Cairo CG 42114); see Peter Dorman, "The Career of Senenmut," in *Hatshepsut from Queen to Pharaoh,* ed. Catharine H. Roehrig (New York: Metropolitan Museum of Art, 2005), 117; Étienne Drioton, "Deux cryptogrammes de Senenmout," *ASAE* 38 (1938): 231–38.

94. The expansion of non-standard phonetic values for signs into a fuller system of cryptographic writing is tied to the New Kingdom. Darnell, *Ancient Egyptian Netherworld Books,* 50–51.

95. "Der Richter," *LGG* II, 651.

96. Mathieu translates this epithet in precisely such a manner: "Thot, le dieu auguste de Béhédet, le maître de l'écriture, qui a séparé les mots, inventé les signes, fixé les formules magiques et créé tout ce qui existe sur terre." Bernard Mathieu, "Grammaire et politique: Réflexions sur quelques empreintes idéologiques dans la terminologie linguistique des grammaires de l'égyptien ancient," in Ägyptologen und Ägyptologien zwischen Kaiserreich und Gründung der beiden *deutschen Staaten: Reflexionen zur Geschichte und Episteme eines altertumswissenschaftlichen Fachs im 150. Jahr der Zeitschrift für Ägyptische Sprache und Altertumskunde,* ed. Susanne Bickel et al., ZÄS Beiheft 1 (Berlin: Akademie Verlag, 2013), 447.

97. Youri Volokhine notes that the phrase *rdj mdw drf,* also associated with Thoth, could deliberately be read in two ways: "the one who causes the writing to speak" and "the one who gives speech and writing." Youri Volokhine, "Le dieu Thot et la parole," *RHR* 221 (2004): 147–48; the potential for dual readings was also noted earlier in Weber, *Beiträge zur Kenntnis,* 64–65.

98. Richard Jasnow, naturally, first drew my attention to this line.

99. Jasnow and Zauzich, *Book of Thoth,* 340–58; Richard Jasnow and Karl-Theodor Zauzich, *Conversations in the House of Life: A New Translation of the Ancient Egyptian Book of Thoth* (Wiesbaden: Harrassowitz, 2014), 175–87; Christian Leitz, "Geierweibchen des Thothbuches in den 42 Gauen Ägyptens," *RdÉ* 63 (2012): 137–86.

100. Richard Jasnow, "'Caught in the Web of Words': Remarks on the Imagery of Writing and Hieroglyphs in the Book of Thoth," *JARCE* 47 (2011): 297–317.

101. *ṯyꜣ* for older *tjt*; Jasnow, "'Caught in the Web of Words,'" 304–5.

102. B02, 10/7–10. Jasnow and Zauzich, *Conversations,* 131; Jasnow and Zauzich, *Book of Thoth,* 260–62.

netic value (form of speech, barking, and cries)[103] takes center stage. With this context in mind, Jasnow and Zauzich have suggested that the following passage could be a reference to hieroglyphs:

P. Berlin 15531 (=B02), 9/11[104]
mꜣꜣ=y wꜣy ḥnꜥ nḏs ẖr-rt ḥ̭mt rꜣ=w ꜣm=sn
Let me see the great and small, and the disciples who shut their mouth between them.

Here the disciple has just asked to enter into the Chamber of Darkness (which is the House of Life) and to learn about what is within, namely the sacred writings. Thus the "great and small" may reference the writings themselves. As the speech and sounds of the metaphorical hieroglyphic signs (and the sacred writings more generally) are frequently invoked, "shutting the mouth" evokes its opposite, the silent signs. Therefore the silent "disciples" (determinatives) stand in between the "great and small" that presumably speak (phonograms). While the overall context of the Book of Thoth makes this interpretation plausible, the line is still fairly obscure, particularly as this line is only attested in two other manuscripts, one of which does not repeat the same expression.[105] Nonetheless, the Book of Thoth makes clear that scribes were deeply concerned with graphic form and with spoken pronunciation, precisely the same issues that occur in texts with unusual determinatives.

Conclusion

The threads I have drawn together here are disparate, dating from across Egyptian history and from a variety of genres. I do not mean to suggest that they all represent the same scribal actions and goals, nor that any clear line can be drawn from one practice to the next, from one time period to another. But while each has a specific context and purpose, they hint at an underlying awareness of and at times a preoccupation with the mediation between written form and phonetic realization. It suggests a knowledge of the malleability of the written system and the particular role determinatives can play. On one level, this is hardly surprising. The sheer iconity of the hieroglyphic system, with its attendant multivalent, polysemous possibilities, seems to demand such a response. Yet, the diverse uses of written language reveal that scribes often had a choice in how to exploit their script and that while written language represents spoken language, the relationship can be complex. Moreover, it suggests that scribes themselves thought about the writing system. If we are to understand the framework of knowledge that Egyptian scribes created and developed about their own language and writing system, such topics are worthy of study.

Although determinatives are mute and silent signs, they traverse the border between written form and spoken realization. In addition to the fact that they can be separated from the phonetic base of a word, their repeated presence or deliberate absence in specific circumstances may play a role in metatextually identifying an anomalous phonetic environment. While not a terribly common occurrence, it speaks to the creative and scholarly engagement on the part of scribes to negotiate the complex relationship between a nonstandard sound value and a sign. Finally, although there are no conclusive references to determinatives in a scribe's own words, there might be the whispers of a discourse among scribes concerning these silent signs, a discourse nonetheless dominated, as the Book of Thoth might say, by the voices of the baboons and ibises.

103. "The author possibly considered the language of the animals to be the phonetic value attached to the signs," Jasnow, "'Caught in the Web of Words,'" 306.

104. Jasnow and Zauzich, *Book of Thoth*, 251–52 and pl. 9; Jasnow and Zauzich, *Conversations*, 126–27.

105. B04 states "while the disciples serve the masters among them," Jasnow and Zauzich, *Conversations*, 127; Jasnow and Zauzich, *Book of Thoth*, 251 and 257.

The First Days of School in Mesopotamia: Preliminary Thoughts on the Personal Name List Inana-teš

Paul Delnero

One of my first encounters with the ancient world and the "mysteries of the past" was at the Treasures of Tutankhamun Exhibition at the Field Museum in Chicago in 1977. Even though I was just a child, and probably spent the duration of the time at the exhibit sleeping in a stroller, I vividly recall one moment that has stayed with me ever since. While the crowds were swarming around the famous golden mask, and all of the other scintillating gold treasures on display, my gaze was transfixed on an unadorned, and otherwise visually unspectacular stela inscribed in Egyptian hieroglyphs. I was so enthralled by the delicate curves of birds, feathers, baboons, waves, and other images I had previously only encountered in coloring books, that I became aware that they must conceal an important message from a distant time and place, and I insisted that my parents translate them for me. Since the description of the object did not include a translation, I felt the first of what was to be many disappointments caused by not being able to understand an ancient text. It is therefore with great admiration, and more than a little envy, that I dedicate these preliminary observations on a comparatively simple Mesopotamian text, to one of the few Egyptologists who can read a text as complex and fraught with difficulties as the *Book of Thoth*.

In a time like the present, when knowledge is valued primarily as a means to an end, the difference between practical knowledge and other forms of knowledge is clear and essentially tautological. Practical knowledge can be applied to produce a tangible result, and knowledge that is not practical cannot. From an educational perspective, practical knowledge is the knowledge necessary to practice a profession, and everything else that is learned, including knowledge that is abstract, factual, speculative, historical, or perceived to be culturally significant, may be intellectually valuable, but is not considered useful beyond the institution in which it is acquired.

A similar distinction is often made between practical and intellectual knowledge in ancient Mesopotamia. There were numerous administrative, legal, scholarly, and religious practices in Mesopotamia, including medicine, divination, accounting, and the performing of cultic rituals, that required both the ability to write and a wide range of additional skills. Evidence for how scribes were trained exists for nearly every period, but it is especially abundant for the early second millennium, or the period known as the Old Babylonian period (ca. 2000–1595 BCE). Although some of the lists and texts copied as scribal exercises in this period were clearly intended to teach how to read and write cuneiform, it has also been observed that many contained more words and cuneiform signs than a professional scribe would have needed to know to copy and produce texts.[1] Niek Veldhuis, in his recent book on the Mesopotamian lexical tradition, attributed this apparent excess to the emergence of a new scribal elite that sought to distinguish itself from the royal family by defining themselves as specialists in a new field of knowledge, writing:

1. For this view, see in particular Niek Veldhuis, "Elementary Education at Nippur: The Lists of Trees and Wooden Objects" (PhD diss., Rijksuniversiteit Groningen, 1997), 82: "Comparing the training in Sumerian with the skills needed to be a competent scribe shows that the pupils learned far too much. The Sumerian business documents a trained scribe had to produce are relatively simple and straightforward. They mainly consist of a standard set of formulas to be filled in with numbers and names. Moreover, for non-standard formulas the scribe could fall back on Akkadian."

> Within a practice-theoretical framework we may understand that Old Babylonian scribal education, excessive as it may seem from the point of view of the job requirements for a future scribe, was imminently practical in that it introduced the novice scribe to the kinds of knowledge he needed for being a plausible member of this elite. This education inculcated the dispositions and beliefs that were part of the scribal habitus, while providing the newly minted scribe with the cultural capital he needed. It really does not matter whether these scribes were ever going to write a single sign after graduating—they have gone through the motions that defined the scribal or scholarly elite. It is well possible (and perhaps likely) that most of the letter writing and the production of administrative documents in this period was not done by these elite scribes; that there were other paths to literacy that were more affordable and that more directly addressed such things as (Akkadian) epistolography and the proper layout of an administrative text.[2]

In arguing that much of what scribes learned during their training was not directly useful in professional practice, Veldhuis's view presupposes the same dichotomy between practical and intellectual knowledge that characterizes current perceptions of education. Knowledge is either practical in so far as it is professionally useful, or it is intellectual, and serves no other purpose than to provide membership to an elite group. If, however, Mesopotamian scribal educational was predominantly intellectual, how did the practitioners of professions in which writing and texts played a critical role learn the requisite practical skills needed to carry out their professional responsibilities? In this article I would like to reconsider the extent to which scribal training was intellectual, as opposed to practical, by comparing how much practical knowledge of cuneiform was taught during the earliest stages of elementary education with how much cuneiform professional cultic lamenters would have needed to know to produce copies of Sumerian laments.

In ancient Mesopotamia, lamenting belonged to a set of cultic practices that were used to prevent or remove individual and collective misfortune. Sumerian laments were performed by cultic officials known in Sumerian as gala s, and in Akkadian as *kalûs*.[3] By examining Old Babylonian administrative documents pertaining to gala-officials, Dahlia Shehata was able to show that there was one head gala, or gala-mah-official, associated with the temple of the main city god in every important cultic center.[4] Gala-mahs had a wide range of professional responsibilities, which included overseeing the activities of other galas, and their high social standing is reflected by their frequent appearance in legal documents pertaining to temple offices, loans, fields, and different types of property. The occurrence of gala-mahs in administrative documents from many cities, including Ur, Larsa, Nippur, Isin, Sippar, Dilbat, and Kish, is also a clear indication that cultic activities involving galas, including the performance of laments, were widespread in Mesopotamia in the early second millennium.[5]

Mesopotamian laments are written in a special linguistic register known as Emesal.[6] Emesal is clearly derived from standard Sumerian but differs substantially from it in pronunciation and also in its use of a relatively limited set of alternate lexical items, like u$_3$-mu-un for en, "lord" and ga-ša-an for nin, "lady," which are specific to Emesal and

---

2. Niek Veldhuis, *History of the Cuneiform Lexical Tradition*, Guides to the Mesopotamian Textual Record 6 (Münster: Ugarit-Verlag, 2014), 225.

3. For a recent discussion of the cultic responsibilities of gala-officials, particularly with respect to their role in the performance of Mesopotamian cultic laments, see Uri Gabbay, *Pacifying the Hearts of the Gods: Sumerian Emesal Prayers of the First Millennium BC*, Heidelberger Emesal-Studien 1 (Wiesbaden: Harrassowitz, 2014), 63–79.

4. Dahlia Shehata, *Musiker und ihr vokales Repertoire: Untersuchungen zu Inhalt und Organisation von Musikerberufen und Liedgattungen in altbabylonischer Zeit*, Göttinger Beiträge zum Alten Orient 3 (Göttingen: Universitätsverlag, 2009), 63–66.

5. Shehata, *Musiker und ihr vokales Repertoire*, 117–222.

6. Emesal is a register of the Sumerian language that is used in some Sumerian literary compositions (such as Inana's Descent to the Netherworld) to record the speech of female deities such as Inana. It is most commonly attested, however, in Sumerian laments, presumably because this was the register of language in which the gala-officials, who performed laments, sung the texts. Emesal is both orthographically and phonologically distinct from the normal dialect of Sumerian and is characterized by shifts such as the pronunciation of /ĝ/ as /m/ and /g/ as /b/. For a detailed discussion of the nature of Emesal and the phonetic and orthographic shifts it involves see Manfred Schretter, *Emesal-Studien: Sprach- und literaturgeschichtliche Untersuchungen zur sogenannten Frauensprache des Sumerischen* (Innsbruck: Verlag des Instituts für Sprachwissenschaft der Universität Innsbruck, 1990). For the use of Emesal in Sumerian laments specifically, see Anne Löhnert, *"Wie die Sonne tritt heraus!" Eine Klage zum Auszug Enlils mit einer Untersuchung zu Komposition und*

do not occur in the main dialect of the language. Although cultic laments were probably performed over the course of most of Mesopotamian history, written sources for the laments are known only from the second and first millennia. Since Sumerian was no longer spoken when the laments were copied, however, it is improbable that many people beyond the cultic specialists who performed these texts understood their semantic content, even if they might have known, through other channels of transmission, what it meant. The presumed obscurity of Emesal, and the difficulties in reconstructing and understanding the content of the laments, many of which are fragmentary, incomplete, and replete with words and expressions that do not occur in other Sumerian texts, has led to the assumption that these compositions would have also been difficult to copy and perform.

The question of how gala-officials learned Emesal is addressed directly by Anne Löhnert in her book, "*Wie die Sonne, tritt heraus!*," which contains editions of the Enlil laments ^{d}utu-gin$_{7}$ e$_{3}$-ta and zi-bu-u$_{2}$ zi-bu-u$_{2}$ and an overview of lamenting in the early second millennium.[7] Noting that the standard curriculum of the Old Babylonian period seems to have contained very little Emesal beyond a few isolated entries in lexical lists and a small group of proverbs about galas written in Emesal, Löhnert argued that after completing their scribal education, gala-officials must have received additional, specialized training to learn the language of the laments, writing:

> In einer Zeit, da das Akkadische Alltagsprache war, zeichnete sich ein intelligenter Schreiber durch die Beherrschung des Sumerischen (im Hauptdialekt) aus, dessen Erlernen ihn durch seine Schulausbildungszeit begleitete. Da sich eine gleichwertige Konzentration auf das Studium von Emesal nicht erkennen lässt, ist zu vermuten, dass dies in einem speziellen Ausbildungsteil erfolgte. Die besondere sprachliche Herausforderung zeigt sich auch in den vielfach belegten syllabischen Schreibungen und Glossen, die auch als Sprachhilfe in der kultischen Praxis zu verstehen sein könnten.[8]

While it is likely that apprentice scribes received minimal training in Emesal, the assumption that it was a "besondere sprachliche Herausforderung" and that scribes would have required a specialized education to learn it has yet to be fully considered. How much cuneiform did a scribe need to know to produce a copy of a lament, and would scribes really have been incapable of copying texts of this type after completing the standard curriculum? To address this question, it is necessary to determine how much cuneiform was taught during scribal training, and then to examine how much more knowledge would have been needed to copy the laments.

Since the publication of Niek Veldhuis's groundbreaking dissertation, Old Babylonian scribal education has been the subject of numerous studies.[9] According to Veldhuis's now very well-known reconstruction of the sequence of the curriculum at Nippur, apprentice scribes began their training with elementary sign lists, syllabaries, and thematic lexical lists, and then continued with more complex sign lists and texts with simple sentences, like proverbs, model contracts, and metrological tables, before concluding their education by copying Sumerian literary and mythological compositions.[10] The most conclusive evidence for the earliest stages of this sequence is the correlation between the types of texts that occur on the obverses and reverses of tablets known as Type II tablets.[11] As Veldhuis has convinc-

Tradition sumerischer Klagelieder in altbabylonischer Zeit, AOAT 365 (Münster: Ugarit-Verlag, 2009), 4n17, with references to previous literature.

7. Löhnert, "*Wie die Sonne tritt heraus!*," 82–87.

8. Löhnert, 85–86.

9. Veldhuis, "Elementary Education at Nippur." For a recent treatment of Mesopotamian scribal education during the Old Babylonian period, with an excellent synthesis and comprehensive bibliography of previous treatments of the topic, see Jay Crisostomo, *Translation as Scholarship: Language, Writing, and Bilingual Education in Ancient Babylonia*, SANER 22 (Boston: de Gruyter, 2019), 41–43.

10. Veldhuis, "Elementary Education at Nippur," 41–66.

11. In contrast to most multicolumn tablets with Sumerian texts, which contain a single, continuous text copied by one scribe, the tablets known as Type II tablets contain a short model extract from a list or text written in the hand of the teacher followed by an adjacent blank space on the tablet for the pupil to copy the model on the obverse, and a longer extract from the same or a different text written entirely by the pupil on the reverse. For a detailed discussion of Type II tablets and their role in Mesopotamian scribal education, see Veldhuis, "Elementary Education at Nippur," 32–37.

ingly shown, the obverses of Type II tablets contain model extracts from texts that were learned after the texts on the reverse, which were copied by pupils reviewing earlier exercises.[12] By correlating the exercises on both sides of Type II tablets, Veldhuis was able to establish that in the first and most elementary stage of scribal education, pupils learned basic cuneiform signs by copying the lists Syllable Alphabet B and Tu-ta-ti. Then, after completing these texts, they copied lists of personal names, and in particular, a list known by its first entry as Inana-Teš.[13]

The personal name list Inana-teš is preserved in 190 sources, all of which, with the possible exception of a school lentil in the Plimpton Collection at Columbia University, are from Nippur. Close to 60 of these sources were identified and published in hand copies by Edward Chiera in 1916 in the first volume of Publications of the Babylonian Section 11, which also contains the first and only edition of the list.[14] Many of the other sources were identified along with numerous joins by Jeremiah Peterson in an article published in 2011, which includes a complete list of all of the sources for the personal name lists from Nippur and a brief description of their content.[15] By comparison, the ten texts in the Decad, which were learned as a group at the beginning of the final phase of the curriculum, and which were copied more frequently as scribal exercises than any other Sumerian literary compositions learned in advanced education, are attested in an average of fourty to fifty sources from Nippur.[16]

The popularity of Inana-teš as an elementary school exercise is also reflected in a reference to the list in the Sumerian literary composition, Edubba D, in which a pupil boasts of everything he has learned at the beginning of his education, saying:

> I have written and recited all of the Sumerian and Akkadian (tablets?) from *a-a me-me* (Syllable Alphabet B) until . . . ; I wrote all the entries from *Inana-teš* through *lu*$_2$*-šu* (the Professions List), including *niğ*$_2$*-zi-ğal*$_2$*-edin-na* ("The Wild Animals of the Steppe," the name of a section of division three of the thematic lexical list *ur*$_5$*-ra*).[17]

The placement of Inana-teš in a sequence after Syllable Alphabet B, and before the thematic list of wild animals and the professions list in the cited passage, also provides additional evidence that Inana-teš was learned after Syllable Alphabet B and before the thematic and more advanced signs lists learned in the following stages of elementary scribal education.

Chiera's edition of Inana-teš,[18] which dates to 1917, is no longer reliable for reconstructing and interpreting the content of the list, in large part because its editor conflated the content of at least three different personal name lists into a single list, including many entries that occur in other personal name lists in his edition of Inana-teš. Additionally, because sources containing sections of the list that were not in any of the sources available to Chiera have since been identified, it is now possible to reconstruct numerous entries that were omitted in Chiera's list. Lastly and most

12. Veldhuis, 41–63.

13. Veldhuis, 41–46.

14. Edward Chiera, *Lists of Personal Names from the Temple School of Nippur: A Syllabary of Personal Names*, Publications of the Babylonian Section 11/1 (Philadelphia: University Museum, 1916), 49–85.

15. Jeremiah Peterson, "The Personal Name Lists in the Scribal Curriculum of Old Babylonian Nippur: An Overview," *ZA* 101 (2011): 246–73.

16. For the group of ten Sumerian literary compositions known as the Decad (which comprises the texts Shulgi Hymn A, Lipit-Eshtar Hymn A, The Song of the Hoe, The Exaltation of Inana, Enlil in the Ekur, The Kesh Temple Hymn, Enki's Journey to Nippur, Inana and Ebih, The Nungal Hymn, and Gilgamesh and Huwawa Version A) and its role in the Old Babylonian scribal curriculum, see Paul Delnero, *The Textual Criticism of Sumerian Literature*, JCSSup 3 (Boston: American Schools of Oriental Research, 2012), 11–15, which includes references to previous literature; and Steve Tinney, "On the Curricular Setting of Sumerian Literature," *Iraq* 61 (1999): 159–72.

17. Edubba D, ll. 11–14: [dub] ki-en-gi ki-uri-ke$_4$ a-a me-me-ta // [. . .]-še$_3$ i$_3$-šid u$_3$ i$_3$-sar // mu didli ^{d}inana-teš$_2$-ta // en-na niĝ$_2$-zi-ĝal$_2$-edin-na za$_3$ lu$_2$-šu-ka-še$_3$ i$_3$-sar. For an edition and translation of Edubba D, see Miguel Civil, "Sur les 'livres d'écolier' à l'époque paleo-babylonienne," in *Miscellanea Babylonica: Mélanges offerts à Maurice Birot*, ed. Jean-Marie Durand and Jean-Robert Kupper (Paris: Recherche sur les civilisations, 1985), 67–78, which includes a discussion of the lines cited here.

18. Chiera, *Lists of Personal Names*.

problematically, however, is that Chiera was working during a time when knowledge of the cuneiform writing system, the cuneiform syllabary, and the Sumerian and Akkadian onomastica was much less advanced than it is now, and as a result there are an extensive number of mistakes that preclude a proper understanding of the content and structure of the list. For this reason, it was necessary to compile a new edition of Inana-teš by transcribing all of the 190 sources in the list compiled by Peterson[19] in order to reconstruct the content of the text and to reanalyze and translate all of the names misunderstood by Chiera. This work was conducted over a period of three months (April–June 2019) working initially from digital photographs of the sources and then consulting the original cuneiform tablets, all but one of which is housed in the tablet collection of The University of Pennsylvania Museum of Archaeology and Anthropology in Philadelphia.[20] Unless otherwise indicated, all of the forms, figures, entry-numbers, and other evidence pertaining to Inana-teš cited throughout the remainder of the article are based directly on the score (a line-by-line transcription of the entire text in which all of the sources containing each line are transcribed in a list that resembles a musical score) that resulted from this work, and the subsequent reanalysis of all of the entries in the newly reconstructed list.[21]

Inana-teš occurs on all of the types of sources associated with the beginning stages of the scribal curriculum at Nippur. One hundred and fifty, or almost 80 percent of the sources are Type II tablets, the main tablet type associated with elementary education. The obverses of thirty-two of the Type II sources contain model extracts from the list. The other 118 have longer extracts on the reverse, copied by pupils reviewing sections of the list they had already begun to learn. Moreover, all but one of the Type II sources with Inana-teš on the obverse have either an earlier section of the same list or Syllable Alphabet B and Tu-ta-ti on the reverse, providing further evidence that these two lists were learned before Inana-teš at the beginning of the curriculum. Of the remaining sources, six are small, rectilinear Type III, or one-column extract tablets that are distinct from the longer and more convex Type III tablets associated with advanced education; ten are school lentils containing short two- to three-line extracts; eleven are multicolumn or Type I sources containing the entire list; one is a prism; and ten sources have tablet types that could not be identified.

Another decisive indication that Inana-teš was copied at the very beginning of scribal education is the low quality of writing on the reverses of Type II tablets. The multicolumn tablets and the prism are copied in a careful, well-executed script, and may even have served as master copies compiled by advanced scribes to teach or review the list. Examples include, but are not limited to, the signs in the prism, CBS 7832, and the Type I sources, CBS 6442 and CBS 6457, which are perfectly aligned, proportional, and accurately rendered with the correct wedges. By contrast, the reverses of Type II tablets are, without exception, poorly written. More often than not, the signs on this tablet type are often large, not aligned with the dividing lines on the tablet between entries, out of proportion to the other signs in the entry, and incorrectly executed, sometimes to the point of being unrecognizable.

Inana-teš has 312 entries, nearly all of which are completely preserved. The most defining feature of the list is that it consists of groups of three entries that share one or more common elements. One example is the first three entries—^{d}inana-teš$_2$(UR), ^{d}inana-KA, and ^{d}inana-ur-sağ—which all begin with the divine name, ^{d}inana, and contain the signs UR and KA, which occur with a different reading and in a slightly modified form in the third entry in the sequence. Another example is the next set of entries, DI.KU$_5$-*i*$_3$-*li*$_2$ (entry four), DI.KU$_5$-*i*$_3$-*li*$_2$-*a* (entry five), and DI.KU$_5$-*i*$_3$-*li*$_2$-*šu* (entry six), which begin with the same two signs and end with different pronominal forms of *i*$_3$-*li*$_2$, a sequence that is also repeated with *dan*- in entries 10–12, *nu-ur*$_2$- in entries 46–48, and *ṭab*- in entries 49–51. Other shared elements include *ri-iš*- in the entries *ri-iš*-AN, *ri-iš-e*$_2$-*a*, and *ri-iš-be*$_2$-*li*$_2$ (13–15), niğ$_2$- in niĝ$_2$-du$_{11}$-ga-ni, niĝ$_2$-^{d}ba-U$_2$, and niĝ$_2$-gur$_{11}$-^{d}nanna (34–36), šeš in šeš-ba-tuku, šeš-kal-la, and šeš-ki-lu$_5$-la (103–105)

19. Peterson, "Personal Name Lists."

20. Special thanks are owed to Grant Frame, the cuneiform tablet collection's curator, for permitting me to visit the collection and carry out this work.

21. The complete score of Inana-teš will be published, along with a new edition of the list, in a forthcoming book on the earliest stages of scribal education at Nippur.

and the sequence of gods, AN, e_2-a, and ^{d}adad which occur after *i-ṣur-*, *i-tur$_2$-*, *u$_2$-tul-*, and *ib-ni-*, in entries 40–42, 94–96, 115–117, and 118–120, respectively. Although nearly all of the groupings in the list share at least one common sign, the ways in which entries are grouped is sometimes also more complex. In the entries, *li-tur$_2$*, *li-tur$_2$-SA$_6$*, and en$_3$(LI)-ĝu$_{10}$-ḫe$_2$-tar-re (97–99), for example, the sign LI has the Akkadian syllabic reading "li" in the first two entries, but the Sumerian reading "en$_3$" in the third entry. Additionally, graphic and phonological similarity can also serve as organizing principles, as illustrated by the entries ur$_5$-bi, temen(TE)-bi, and uru-bi (79–81), where the signs "ḪUR", "TE", and "URU" are graphically similar, and ^{d}*sîn-re'û*(SIPA), ^{d}*sîn-re-me-ni*, and ^{d}*sîn-re-ṣu$_2$-šu* (109–111) which contain the phoneme /re/ in all three forms.

Inana-teš is an elementary list that was used to teach the basic signs and values that occur in Sumerian and Akkadian personal names. For this reason, it very likely reflects the number and types of cuneiform signs that scribes learned at the beginning of their training. To approximate how many additional signs a scribe would have needed to know to copy a lament, I counted and catalogued the signs that occur in Inana-teš and the lament Uruamairabi.

There are 1,161 occurrences of signs in Inana-teš. Among these, a total of 144 different signs occur throughout the entire list. Nearly all of the signs in the list are common and include AB, BA, BI, KA, NU, TA, TI, ZU, and many other signs that occur frequently in both Akkadian and Sumerian texts. Moreover, the frequency with which each sign appears in other cuneiform texts is also more often than not reflected in the number of times the sign occurs in the list. The signs A, AN, BA, BI, E$_2$, KI, NI, and ŠU, which are among the most frequently used signs in the cuneiform corpus, each occur between 23 to 82 times, whereas signs like LUL, SIG$_5$, SUR$_3$, ŠUTUL$_5$ (UR*xšeššig*), and URU$_4$, which are less common, occur only once. Also, while many of the signs in the list are used in both Sumerian and Akkadian names, they are almost always used with their most common value. The only exceptions are signs with multiple values that occur frequently in cuneiform texts. The sign AN, for example, occurs 59 times as a divine determinative, 13 times to write the name of the divinity AN, twice to write the Sumerian word dingir for "god," once to write the copula –am$_3$ (written A.AN), and six times with the Akkadian syllabic reading /an/. Similarly, the sign NI occurs 23 times with the reading "i$_3$," 29 times as "li$_2$," 14 times with the Akkadian syllabic value "ni," and 4 times as the Sumerian possessive suffix –ni.

Uruamairabi, which is a long thirty-three-section lament in which Inana laments the destruction of her city Uruk and the loss of her lover, Dumuzi, was one of the most widely copied and performed laments during the early second millennium.[22] One of the main sources for this composition is NCBT 688, an almost completely preserved tablet in the Yale Babylonian Collection, which contains the first five sections of the Old Babylonian version of the lament. To establish a common basis for comparison, the first 1161 occurrences of signs, which comprise the first 106 lines of the 125-line source, were counted and cataloged. Among these there is a total of 148 different signs, or 4 more than the number of different signs in Inana-teš. Furthermore, only 56 signs, or less than 38 percent, occur in Uruamariabi but not Inana-teš. However, when the occurrences of individual signs are counted, the number of signs common to both texts is even more substantial. Nine hundred ninety-nine of the 1161 occurrences of signs in Uruamairabi, or over 86 percent, are signs that also occur in Inana-teš, whereas only 162, or less than 14 percent, are signs that occur only in Uruamaribi. In other words, a scribe who had only completed elementary scribal education, up to and includ-

22. A complete edition of the Old Babylonian and first-millennium versions of Uruamairabi based on a preliminary list of sources was published by Mark Cohen, *The Canonical Lamentations of Ancient Mesopotamia* (Potomac, MD: Capital Decisions Ltd., 1988), 536–603, with important corrections and additions by Antoine Cavigneaux, review of *The Canonical Lamentations of Ancient Mesopotamia*, by M. Cohen, *JAOS* 113 (1993): 254–57. A revised list of sources for both versions of the text was published by Konrad Volk, *Die Balaĝ-Komposition Uru$_2$ am$_3$-ma-ir-ra-bi: Rekonstruktion und Bearbeitung der Tafeln 18 (19'ff.), 19, 20 und 21 der späten, kanonischen Version*, FAO 18 (Stuttgart: Steiner, 1989), 5–8, together with a new edition of tablets 18–21 of the first millennium version of the composition and the sections of the Old Babylonian source H2, which correspond to these tablets. For a new edition of the first five Kirugus of Uruamairabi see Paul Delnero, *How to Do Things with Tears: Ritual Lamenting in Ancient Mesopotamia*, SANER 26 (Berlin: de Gruyter, 2020), 307–77).

ing Inana-teš, would have already learned a sufficient number of signs to copy all but a very small percentage of the signs that occur in the first 106 lines of Uruamairabi. Moreover, nearly all of the signs in this section of Uruamairabi that do not occur in Inana-teš are common signs (like AL, BAL, DAM, GA_2, GU, ḪUL, IL_2, LA_2, NAM, and SA). These signs would have been encountered shortly after Inana-teš in the elementary stages of the curriculum. They would have also occurred in a few instances in specialized words like amaš (sheepfold), tur_3 (cattlepen), u_5 (the Emesal word for oil), and $sila_4$ (lamb) that are attested with great frequency in the laments and could have been learned easily through repetition.

The high percentage of signs and values that occur in both Inana-teš and the lament Uruamairabi is consistent with the results of a study of personal name lists and Old Babylonian letters that was conducted by Marine Béranger.[23] Comparing the sign values of specific signs that occur in Chiera's 1916 reconstruction of the Old Babylonian personal name lists with those that occur in Old Babylonian letters from Mari dating to the reign of the ruler Zimri-lim and letters from Babylon dating to the reign of the ruler Hammurapi, Béranger also observed that many sign values that are otherwise unique to the personal names in the corpus of Old Babylonian letters she examined also occur in Old Babylonian personal name lists. The equally frequent occurrence of signs and values in Inana-teš in laments like Uruamairabi, as observed here, provides further evidence that the signs learned in personal name lists like Inana-teš taught practical knowledge of writing that could be applied later in the professional careers of scribes.

The number of signs common to both Inana-teš and the lament Uruamairabi strongly suggests that Mesopotamian scribal education was more practical than has been previously assumed. This is, of course, not to claim that scribes who had only completed elementary scribal training would have been able to copy the laments as well as professional scribes. It does however seem that the basis for being able to copy the laments could have been acquired early and easily, and that galas would have required very little, if any, additional training to copy the signs in the texts they performed. Moreover, a no less important conclusion that can be drawn from this preliminary study is this: when the emphasis is placed on the role learning how to write played in scribal education—as opposed to the intellectual and allegedly ideological aspects of this training, such as the apparent excess of words scribes learned that they would never need to use again and the learning of texts in a dead language that was no longer written or spoken—there is still much to be learned about why Mesopotamian scribes were taught what they were taught and what skills they acquired by learning it.

23. Marine Béranger, "Développement des pratiques d'écriture et de l'expression écrite: Recherches sur les lettres de l'époque amorrite (2002–1595 av. J.-C.)" (PhD diss., L'École Pratique des Hautes Études, 2018), 129–53.

L'ostracon Louvre E 11037 : Une lettre à un mort en démotique ?

Didier Devauchelle et Ghislaine Widmer*

L'ostracon démotique Louvre E 11037 (fig. 1) est composé de trois fragments qui ont été récemment rassemblés et restaurés.[1] Entré au Louvre en 1904, il faisait partie de la collection Urbain Bouriant ;[2] il fut vraisemblablement acquis à Louxor, puisque le texte mentionne les dieux de Thèbes (l. x + 7 et peut-être l. x + 1). Remarquable autant par sa grande taille[3] que par la qualité de la main du copiste, il l'est également par sa « mise en page » et son contenu : ce tesson pourrait être le témoignage d'une promesse ou d'un serment fait par un fils au nom du Chay et de la Chepeset de son père défunt(?) concernant des pratiques rituelles qui restent à accomplir. Nous dédions la publication de ce curieux document à Richard, en écho à son intérêt toujours enthousiaste et contagieux pour les textes inédits et insolites ; le thème de cet ostracon lui rappellera peut-être un certain graffito de la montagne thébaine édité il y a quelques années...[4]

Le texte, noté sur un tesson de grand récipient, sans doute une jarre,[5] comporte aujourd'hui neuf lignes inscrites à l'encre noire.[6] L'examen céramologique tout comme la paléographie nous incitent à dater ce document de l'époque

* Université de Lille / UMR 8164 HALMA (CNRS, Univ. Lille, MC).

1. Cet objet porte le numéro d'inventaire Louvre E 11037 + 11037A + 11037B correspondant respectivement à ODL 759, 1537 et 499. Dans l'index de Didier Devauchelle, *Ostraca démotiques du Musée du Louvre* I, 2, BiEtud XCII/2 (Le Caire : Institut français d'archéologie orientale, 1983), 15, corriger ODL E 11097 B en E 11037 B et supprimer ODL E 11087. Nous remercions Vincent Rondot, Directeur du Département des Antiquités égyptiennes pour l'autorisation de publication, ainsi que Marc Étienne, Sophie Duberson, Christian Décamps, Julien Siesse et Audrey Viger, du Musée du Louvre, pour l'aide apportée. Nous savons gré à Thomas Nicq (UMR 8164 HALMA) pour son savoir-faire enthousiaste et nous devons à l'amitié de Sue Davies et d'Harry S. Smith, ainsi qu'à nos discussions à Huntingdon, l'idée qu'il puisse effectivement s'agir d'une « lettre au mort ».

2. Le Registre d'entrée du Musée du Louvre précise qu'il a été acquis le 29 février 1904 auprès de H. Welter, libraire, « qui s'est substitué à M. Pierre Bouriant, fils de l'ancien directeur de l'École du Caire » ; sur le verso des deux petits fragments on voit encore la mention suivante portée au crayon de bois : « Collection Bouriant » accompagnée, dans un cas, d'un numéro d'inventaire(?) que l'on croit pouvoir lire « B 65 ».

3. H. 28,5 cm ; larg. 31 cm ; ép. 1,3–1,5 cm.

4. Richard Jasnow, « Demotic Graffiti from Western Thebes », dans *Grammata Demotika : Festschrift für Erich Lüddeckens zum 15. Juni 1983*, éd. Heinz-Josef Thissen, Karl-Theodor Zauzich (Würzburg : Zauzich, 1984), 89–91 n° 4, graffito 3548 ; cf. plus récemment Sven P. Vleeming, *Demotic Graffiti and Other Short Texts Gathered from Many Publications (Short Texts III 1201–2350)*, StudDem 12 (Leuven : Peeters, 2015), 166–67 n°1554. Nous n'oublions pas non plus sa publication en collaboration avec Günter Vittmann : Richard Jasnow et Günter Vittmann, « An Abnormal Hieratic Letter to the Dead (P. Brooklyn 37 1799 E) », *Enchoria* 19/20 (1992/1993) : 23–43 et pl. 2–3.

5. Terre cuite de pâte calcaire vraisemblablement ; la paroi externe, sur laquelle sont peintes les inscriptions, est soigneusement polie en bandes. Nous remercions Catherine Defernez des informations céramologiques qu'elle nous a fournies à partir des photographies que nous lui avons transmises.

6. Dans la mesure où le texte commence de manière abrupte et que deux petites traces d'encre semblent visibles dans la partie supérieure de l'ostracon, nous supposons qu'il faut restituer au moins une ligne en tête de ce document.

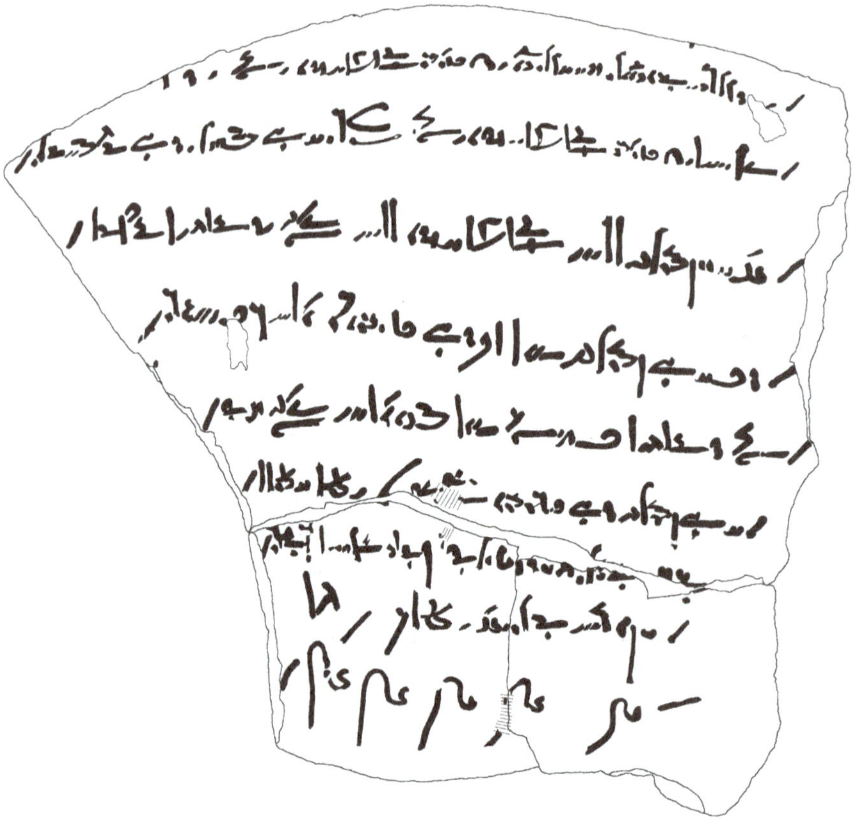

Figure 1. Fac-similé de l'ostracon Louvre E 11037. © Didier Devauchelle / Ghislaine Widmer.

ptolémaïque sans pouvoir être plus précis.[7] Le chiffre 11, en fin de ligne x + 8, qui semble avoir été ajouté après coup (il est situé, un peu en décalage, après le trait oblique et paraît plus épais) fait penser à une marque d'enregistrement ou de classification plutôt qu'à une indication chronologique.

L'écriture du texte est régulière[8] et la main du scribe assurée, révélant une personne expérimentée. On relève, à cinq reprises sur la face externe, des empreintes de corde qui traversent verticalement l'objet, probablement des éléments de décoration, ainsi que diverses incrustations dans la pâte, qui ont parfois gêné le copiste. On note aussi quelques idiosyncrasies comme l'ajout d'un point derrière les déterminatifs du pavois divin et de l'homme qui porte la main à la bouche, et sous certains signes. Plus étonnants sont les traits obliques qui flanquent chacune des lignes du texte rappelant les *check-marks* que l'on rencontre principalement sur des documents administratifs.[9] De même, les cinq serpents quasi-figuratifs qui occupent la dernière ligne sont déroutants (voir plus bas le commentaire).

7. La main semble être du début ou du milieu de l'époque ptolémaïque, malgré quelques graphies qui paraissent plus tardives.

8. Compte tenu de la forme légèrement bombée du tesson et de sa taille, la première et les trois dernières lignes semblent plus petites sur notre fac-similé et sur la photographie que dans la réalité.

9. Voir Mohamed Abd el-Halim Nur-el-Din, « Checking, Terminal, Stress Marks, Partition Indications and Margin Lines in Demotic Documents », *Enchoria* 9 (1979) : 50–51. Toutefois, ces marques sont généralement attestées dans des documents comptables (listes de noms par exemple) et le plus souvent en début de lignes seulement. Nur el-Din (p. 51) mentionne un cas de signes obliques en fin de celles-ci dans une liste de témoins, cf. Françoise de Cenival, « Deux papyrus inédits de Lille avec une révision du P. dém. Lille 31 »,

Translittération et traduction

(x + 1) / *r tꜣ ntr.t ꜥꜣ.t irm pꜣ ntr ꜥꜣ r di.t-ḥr qse.t r-ir=k r nꜣ n[tr.w (Niw.t?)* /]
/ La grande déesse et le grand dieu veilleront aux rites funéraires qui te concernent. Les d[ieux (de Thèbes ?) /]

(x + 2) / *tr.w r di.t-ḥr qse.t r-ir=k ẖr pꜣy=k Šy tꜣy=k Špš.t* /
/ au complet veilleront aux rites funéraires qui te concernent. Par ton Destin (et) ta Destinée, /

(x + 3) / *Ḥr pꜣy(=y) it̯ iw=y <ir(?)> qse.t iw=y ṯꜣi.t̯=k r nꜣ ꜥwy.w-(n-)ḥtp* /
/ ô Hor mon père, j'<assurerai(?)> les rites funéraires, je te tirerai vers les lieux de repos, /

(x + 4) / *nꜣ nty pꜣy=k it̯ n-im=w ḥnꜥ tꜣy=k mw.t ꜥn tw=y s⸢mꜥ⸣y* /
/ ceux dans lesquels se trouvent ton père avec ta mère également. Je te bénis(?) /

(x + 5) / *(r-)ir=k (n?) nꜣ ꜥwy.w nty-iw iw=k n-im=w šꜥ-tw=y ṯꜣi.t̯=k .?.* /
/ (dans ?) les lieux dans lesquels tu te trouves jusqu'à ce que je te tire auprès(?) de /

(x + 6) / *pꜣy=k it̯ tꜣy=k mw.t ⸢gtg(?)⸣ r-ẖrw pꜣ ẖrw* /
/ ton père (et) ta mère, rapidement(?), sur l'injonction de(?) la voix(?) /

(x + 7) [/] *⸢Is.t irm Wsir irm nꜣ ntr⸣.w Niw.t tr.w* … /
[/] d'Isis et d'Osiris et des dieux de Thèbes au complet … /

(x + 8) / *sẖ Ḥyq sꜣ Ḥr r-ẖrw=f* / *11*
/ A écrit Hyq fils de Hor sur son ordre. / 11

(x + 9) /  /

Notes

Ligne x + 1

(a) Le texte débute par deux traits obliques : le premier est une sorte de *check-mark* que l'on retrouve en début et en fin de chaque ligne (voir note 9), le second, plus petit, est le morphème du Futur III avec sujet nominal. Nous

Enchoria 7 (1977) : 3 et pl. 1–2. En revanche, nous n'avons trouvé aucun parallèle à la pratique qui consiste à « cocher » une ligne de part et d'autre, et cela sur toute la longueur du texte. On pourra toutefois faire un rapprochement avec l'ostracon Hor n° 4 (John D. Ray, *The Archive of Ḥor*, Texts from Excavations 2 [Londres : Egypt Exploration Society, 1976], 29–32 et pl. V), auquel on peut ajouter le n° 66 (John D. Ray, « Observations on the Archive of Ḥor », *JEA* 64 [1978] : 113–15 et pl. XVIII text n° 66), deux tessons qui sont pourvus de traits obliques au début de presque chaque ligne. Ray (« Observations on the Archive of Ḥor », 114–15) avait émis, avec réserve, l'hypothèse que ces marques servaient à pointer l'avancement de la copie du texte par le scribe, peut-être sur un autre ostracon. Dans le cas présent, nous nous demandons si elles ne seraient pas liées à une pratique magico-religieuse, d'autant plus que la dernière ligne est constituée d'une série de signes quasi-hiéroglyphiques répétés comme sur de nombreux phylactères. Toutefois, vu que le contenu du texte reste sujet à débat, nous préférons nous aussi rester prudents. On notera enfin que ces traits semblent avoir été tracés au moment de la copie puisqu'ils ne présentent pas de cas d'insertion supra-linéaire (due à un éventuel manque de place) et que le texte en fin de ligne n'est pas « compressé ».

avons choisi de traduire ce temps comme un simple futur, mais il est possible qu'une notion injonctive soit sous-entendue, surtout lorsque la forme verbale est à la première personne du singulier, comme à la ligne x + 3.

(b) « La grande déesse et le grand dieu » désignent vraisemblablement Isis et Osiris mentionnés plus bas l. x + 7.

(c) Pour *di.t-ḥr*, cf. CDD *Ḥ*2 (2009), 196 ; ici comme à la ligne x + 2, on attendrait la préposition *r* ainsi que l'article devant *qse.t*, mais la présence de *r-ir=k* pour préciser ce mot compense vraisemblablement l'absence de *tꜣ*.

(d) Sur le sens de *qse.t*, voir René L. Vos, « Demotic Mummy Labels Containing Permission to Bury, Adressed to Totoès, A *ḥrj sšṯ* of the Sacred Buchis at Hermonthis », dans *Textes grecs, démotiques et bilingues*, éd. E. Boswinkel et P. W. Pestman, PLB 19 (Leyde : Brill, 1978), 265 § 4 et Isabelle Régen, « À propos du sens de *qrs*, 'enterrer' », dans *Verba manent : Recueil d'études dédiées à Dimitri Meeks*, éd. Isabelle Régen et Frédéric Servajean, CENiM 2 (Montpellier : Université Paul Valéry Montpellier III, 2009), 387–99 ; pour des graphies de *qse.t* avec la pointe de harpon en démotique, on renverra, par exemple, à Mohamed Abd el-Halim Nur el-Din et Pieter W. Pestman, « Demotic Mummy Labels Containing Permission for Burial », dans Boswinkel et Pestman, *Textes grecs, démotiques et bilingues*, 173, 4a. Voir aussi, plus récemment, Maria Cannata, *Three Hundred Years of Death : The Egyptian Funerary Industry in the Ptolemaic Period*, Culture and History of the Ancient Near East 110 (Leyde : Brill, 2020), 521–38 (Appendix 1).

(e) *r-ir=k* : nous avions d'abord pensé à une forme verbale relative avec le verbe *ir*, mais l'absence d'article défini et le sens nous ont fait opter pour une graphie de la préposition *r* devant le pronom suffixe.

(f) Nous avons restitué dans la lacune *nꜣ ntr.w Niw.t(?)*, cf. plus bas l. x + 8.

Ligne x + 2

(a) *ḫr* pour *ꜥnḫ*, « Que vive... », cf. CDD ꜥ (2003), 82–83 (*s.v.* *ꜥnḫ*). Sur le recours au serment à l'intérieur des lettres démotiques, voir Mark Depauw, *The Demotic Letter*, DemStud 14 (Sommerhausen : Zauzich, 2006), 281–83.

(b) Pour l'association en démotique de Chaï et de Chepeset, cf. CDD *Š*2 (2010), 13–15 et 111, Thomas M. Dousa, « Imagining Isis : On Some Continuities and Discontinuities in the Image of Isis in Greek Isis Hymns and Demotic Texts », dans *Acts of the 7th Conference of Demotic Studies*, éd. Kim Ryholt, CNI Publications 25 (Copenhague : Carsten Niebuhr Institute of Near Eastern Studies, 2002), 178–79 et Jan Quaegebeur, *Le dieu égyptien Shaï dans la religion et l'onomastique*, OLA 2 (Louvain : Leuven University Press, 1975), 159–60. L'emploi du pronom suffixe individualisant le destin est plus inhabituel ; le *TLA* en mentionne trois exemples dont celui de l'ostracon Hor n° 3, l. 4 où *pꜣy=k Šy* est utilisé en parallèle à *tꜣy=k Špšy* (John D. Ray, *The Archive of Ḥor*, Texts from Excavations 2 [Londres : Egypt Exploration Society, 1976], 21, 25, 26 et le commentaire 157, 14). On ajoutera un autre exemple tiré de l'ostracon Sommerhausen 1, l. 9 (*pꜣy=w Šy tꜣy=w Špšy*), cf. Richard Jasnow et Karl-Theodor Zauzich, « Another Praise of the Goddess Ait (O. Sommerhausen 1) », dans *Illuminating Osiris : Egyptological Studies in Honor of Mark Smith*, éd. Richard Jasnow et Ghislaine Widmer, Material and Visual Culture of Ancient Egypt 2 (Atlanta : Lockwood), 157 et 161. Pour des attestations en hiératique où Renenet occupe la place de Chepeset, voir, par exemple, les décrets oraculaires (Quaegebeur, *Le dieu égyptien Shaï*, 128 note 2) et, notamment, le papyrus Caire CG 58035, l. 54–60, dans lequel sont mentionnés en parallèle *tꜣy=f Šps(.t)*, *pꜣy=f Šy*, *tꜣy=f Rnn.t*, parmi d'autres concepts en lien avec la destinée de l'homme (Iorwerth E. S. Edwards, *Oracular Amuletic Decrees of the Late New Kingdom*, HPBM 4 [Londres : Trustees of the British Museum, 1960], 96–97) ; l'ostracon hiératique inédit cité par Quaegebeur (*Le dieu égyptien Shaï*, 118) a été publié depuis par Bernadette Letellier (« La destinée de deux enfants, un ostracon ramesside inédit », dans *Livre du Centenaire 1880–1980*, MIFAO 104 [Le Caire : Institut français d'archéologie orientale, 1980], 127–33 et pl. IX : *pꜣy=w Šꜣy tꜣ(y)=w Rnn.t*).

Ligne x + 3

(a) Nous avons interprété « Hor mon père » comme un vocatif, dans la mesure où le protagoniste semble s'adresser à lui tout au long du texte, à la deuxième personne du singulier ; voir aussi plus loin le commentaire.

(b) La séquence *ỉw=y qse.t* présente plusieurs difficultés d'interprétation. Nous l'avons considérée comme un Futur III malgré l'omission de la préposition *r*, qui était pourtant notée aux lignes x + 1 et x + 2 (avec sujet nominal il est vrai) ; cf. aussi *ỉw=y ṯꜣy.ṱ=k* qui suit. Le groupe *qse.t* est écrit comme le substantif (cf. l. x + 1 et x + 2), alors que l'on attendrait un verbe à l'infinitif ; c'est la raison pour laquelle nous proposons de restituer (même si le scribe semble faire peu d'erreurs) le verbe *ỉr* dans la construction bien attestée *<ỉr> qse.t* (cf., par exemple, Didier Devauchelle, « Notes sur l'administration funéraire égyptienne à l'époque gréco-romaine », *BIFAO* 87 (1987) : 148–51, et les deux ostraca de Deir el-Medineh publiés en annexe ci-après).

(c) Il est difficile de déterminer si *ỉw=y ṯꜣy.ṱ=k r nꜣ ʿwy.w-(n)-ḥtp* est redondant par rapport à *ỉw=y qse.t* ou s'il s'agit de deux moments distincts, la racine *q(r)s* pouvant servir à résumer toutes les étapes depuis le décès jusqu'à la mise au tombeau, y compris l'emmaillotage (voir plus haut note (d) de la ligne x + 1).

(d) « Les lieux de repos » dans lesquels se trouvent les grands-parents font sans doute référence à la tombe familiale, qui semble également mentionnée, mais de manière abrégée, à la ligne x + 5. On note l'emploi du pluriel qui, du moins dans les stèles des Mères d'Apis, paraît désigner les catacombes là où le singulier renvoie aux caveaux individuels, cf. Harry S. Smith, « The Death and Life of the Mother of Apis », dans *Studies in Pharaonic Religion and Society in Honour of J. Gwyn Griffiths*, éd. Alan B. Lloyd, Occasional Publications 6 (Londres : Egypt Exploration Society, 1992), 202, et plus généralement, pour la bibliographie, Cary J. Martin, *Demotic Papyri from the Memphite Necropolis : In the Collections of the National Museum of Antiquities in Leiden, the British Museum and the Hermitage Museum*, PALMA 5 (Turnhout : Brepols, 2009), 58. Pour le souhait de rejoindre la sépulture des ancêtres, voir, par exemple, Richard Jasnow, « Demotic Graffiti from Western Thebes », dans *Grammata Demotika : Festschrift für Erich Lüddeckens zum 15. Juni 1983*, éd. Heinz-Josef Thissen et Karl-Theodor Zauzich (Würzburg : Zauzich, 1984), 89–91.

Ligne x + 4

(a) Noter l'emploi de *ḥnʿ* entre *pꜣy=k ỉṱ* et *tꜣy=k mw.t*, alors qu'à la ligne x + 6 le scribe juxtapose simplement ces mêmes termes (cf. aussi l. x + 2) ; en revanche, en x + 1 et x + 7, il utilise *ỉrm*. Pour un exemple de *ỉrm* et *ḥnʿ* dans le même document, voir la remarque de Pieter W. Pestman, avec la collaboration de Jan Quaegebeur et René L. Vos, *Recueil de textes démotiques et bilingues* III (Leyde : Brill, 1977), 78 n° 596.

(b) Le déterminatif de la chair dans *mw.t* est attesté plutôt à l'époque romaine, mais quelques exemples ptolémaïques sont recensés par le CDD M (2010), 69–70 ; voir aussi la note de Jasnow, « Demotic Graffiti from Western Thebes », 90–91 (E).

(c) À partir de *tw=y* et jusqu'à la fin de l'ostracon, le sens général devient plus difficile à établir du fait de groupes problématiques et des différentes possibilités de construction qui s'offrent à nous. Les choix que nous avons faits sont ceux qui nous semblent le moins amender le texte, mais ils sont loin d'être satisfaisants. Le groupe *tw=y* peut être interprêté soit comme la première personne du Présent I, soit comme la forme *sḏm=f* du verbe *dỉ*. La lecture *sm* « saluer, bénir » est la plus plausible, d'autant plus que le verbe semble suivi de la préposition *r*, qui est la construction classique ; on la rencontre parfois dans les lettres comme formule de courtoisie, le plus souvent adressée « devant » une divinité (Depauw, *Demotic Letter*, 175–83). Nous avions également considéré la possibilité de traduire *tw=y sm (r-)ỉr=k* comme « J'ai donné la louange / salutation te concernant » (cf. ϯ ⲤⲘⲞⲨ en copte, ainsi que le papyrus BM EA 10507, l. 10, 1 et 2 : Mark Smith, *The Mortuary Texts of Papyrus BM 10507*, CDPBM III (Londres : British Museum Publications, 1987), 48 et 86, note (a) de la ligne 21) qui utilise le verbe *dỉ* avec *sm* au lieu du *ỉr* habituel ; l'emploi de (*r*)-*ỉr=k* au lieu de *n=k* resterait difficile à expliquer, mais on pourrait le rapprocher de la séquence *qse.t r-ỉr=k* (l. x + 1 et x + 2).

Ligne x + 5

(a) L'absence du *r* initial dans l'écriture de (*r*)-*ỉr*=*k* pourrait s'expliquer par la présence du trait oblique en début de ligne, à condition que ce dernier ait bien été tracé au moment de la rédaction du texte de l'ostracon. On notera encore que Wolja Erichsen, *Demotisches Glossar* (Copenhague : Munksgaard, 1954), 237 et Wilhelm Spiegelberg, *Demotische Grammatik* (Heidelberg : Winters, 1925), 127 enregistrent une graphie *ỉr*=*k* sans *r* initial, mais datant de l'époque romaine.

(b) Il est vraisemblable que *nꜣ ꜥwy.w* soit ici une abréviation de *nꜣ ꜥwy.w*-(*n*-)*ḥtp* (l. x + 3), autrement le scribe aurait plutôt employé le terme *mꜣꜥ* ; la personne à laquelle s'adresse la « salutation honorifique » (*sm*) semble donc décédée, attendant de rejoindre sa tombe définitive.

(c) Compte tenu de la forme terminative *šꜥ*-*tw*= et du texte des lignes x + 3 – x + 4, nous avons compris ce passage comme une allusion au fait que la dépouille du père n'avait pas encore rejoint la tombe familiale. Malheureusement, nous ne pouvons pas proposer de lecture satisfaisante pour le dernier groupe de la ligne ; la graphie rappelle celle du pronom sujet première personne du pluriel du Présent I (*ỉnn*) et du Présent circonstanciel (*ỉw*=*n*), voire de *ỉw*(=*y*) *ỉn*, qui ne s'expliquent pas. Nous préférerions y voir une préposition marquant la proximité (*ỉ*-*ỉr*-*ḥr*, *ỉrm*, etc.), mais rien ne semble convenir (comparer *ỉrm* aux lignes x + 1 et x + 7). Nous avons également pensé à une particule initiale (*ỉn*), au verbe « apporter, amener » à l'impératif (*r*-*ỉn*), voire à une lecture *tp*, mais sans succès.

Ligne x + 6

(a) Une nouvelle difficulté réside dans la lecture du mot déterminé par le signe de l'ennemi couché (?) : 
Si l'on considère qu'il s'agit d'un verbe ayant pour sujet *pꜣy*=*k ỉṯ tꜣy*=*k mw.t*, on comprend mal quelle action ou état négatif, qui plus est sans marque du pseudo-participe, pourrait être envisagé. Pour cette raison, nous nous sommes résolus à lire (*n*) *gtg* « rapidement » (un déterminatif similaire est parfois attesté pour ce terme), mais avec beaucoup de réticences. D'autres hypothèses sont envisageables (par exemple *gb*, « être faible, être fatigué », avec déterminatifs de l'oiseau du mal et de l'ennemi couché), mais compte tenu de l'état de conservation du tesson à cet endroit et du nombre de possibilités, nous avons renoncé à en faire la liste.

(b) La séquence *r*-*ẖrw pꜣ ẖrw* (noter l'ajout d'un deuxième trait vertical en fin de ligne qui semble distinguer la seconde mention de *ẖrw* de la première) n'est pas attestée à notre connaissance et reste difficile à traduire vu l'incertitude dans laquelle nous sommes par rapport au mot qui précède et à celui qui semble terminer la phrase à la ligne x + 7. Il est tentant de rapprocher *r*-*ẖrw pꜣ ẖrw ꞽIs.t ỉrm Wsỉr ỉrm nꜣ nṯr.w Nỉw.t tr.w* de *r*-*ẖ*(.*t*) *pꜣ ḥn* (*n*) *ꞽIs.t* attesté sur deux ostraca démotiques de Deir el-Medineh (voir *infra*).

Ligne x + 7

(a) Seul le trait oblique devant le nom d'Isis est en lacune au début de la ligne. En dépit de la cassure, les restitutions semblent assurées.

(b) Le groupe  en fin de ligne présente une nouvelle difficulté. Le premier élément pourrait être la ligature *wꜥ* et l'on serait alors tenté de lire *sp* (*n wꜥ sp*, « ensemble »), mais les traces ne correspondent pas. Le dernier signe est peut-être le déterminatif de l'homme qui porte la main à la bouche, accompagné du petit point caractéristique de la main de ce scribe ; l'ensemble qui précède doit être une ligature (*rn*, *tn*, etc.), mais nous n'avons aucune solution satisfaisante à proposer.

Ligne x + 8

(a) L'anthroponyme *Ḥyq* n'est pas attesté tel quel ; il faut sans doute le rapprocher de *Ḥkꜣ*, cf. Mark Depauw et Willy Clarysse, « When a Pharaoh Becomes Magic », *ChronÉg* 77/153–154 (2002) : 60–61. L'écriture fait songer au substantif *ḥq* (< *ḥkꜣ*) « magie », qui présente une variante *ḥyq* (ϩⲓⲕ ; Günter Vittmann, « Zum Gebrauch des *kꜣ*-Zeichens im Demotischen », *SEAP* 15 [1996] : 3) attestée plus souvent dans des textes d'époque romaine. Dans ce contexte onomastique, il est possible qu'il s'agisse plutôt d'une référence au dieu-enfant Heka.

(b) Pour *r-ḫrw* après *sẖ*, cf. Michel Malinine, « Taxes funéraires égyptiennes à l'époque gréco-romaine », dans *Mélanges Mariette*, BiEtud 32 (Le Caire : Institut français d'archéologie orientale, 1961), 146 (d) ; on rencontre parfois cette tournure en fin de serment, mais cela semble rare, cf. Françoise de Cenival, « Deux serments démotiques concernant des comptes de bétail », *RechPap* 4 (1967) : 103 note l (P. Sorbonne inv. 2301, l. 12).

(c) Pour le chiffre 11 écrit après le trait oblique et qui doit donc être compris comme une insertion postérieure, voir *supra* p. 2.

Ligne x + 9

(a) La dernière ligne du texte est occupée par une série de cinq serpents figuratifs, rappelant les signes hiéroglyphiques (yeux-*oudjat*, scarabées, crocodiles, barques, etc.) accompagnant certaines incantations magiques et souvent placés en fin de document (cf., en dernier lieu, Jacco Dieleman et Hans-Werner Fischer-Elfert, « A Textual Amulet from Theban Tomb 313 [MMA 26.3.225] », *JARCE* 53 [2017] : 255–56 plus particulièrement). Le motif du serpent (cobra ?) à une seule boucle semble plus rare dans ce contexte, mais on le rencontre, par exemple, sur un papyrus-amulette découvert enroulé et ficelé à Tebtynis (deux cobras affrontés, cf. Nicole Brix, « 163. Amulette aux cobras en papyrus », dans *Trésors inattendus : 30 ans de fouilles et de coopération à Tebtynis [Fayoum]*, éd. Claudio Gallazzi et Gisèle Hadji-Minaglou, BiGen 57 [Le Caire : Institut français d'archéologie orientale, 2019], 243, ainsi que dans un collège de 4 sur le papyrus magique Chester Beatty V [v° col. 6, entre l. 4 et 5] associé, entre autres, à quatre yeux-*oudjat* ; voir aussi les amulettes prenant la forme de cet animal dans Carol Andrews, *Amulets of Ancient Egypt* [Austin : University of Texas Press ; Londres : British Museum Press, 1994], 75–76). La répétition par cinq du pictogramme paraît également inhabituelle, mais ce chiffre a tout de même une valeur symbolique importante dans l'imaginaire égyptien, cf. Kurt Sethe, *Von Zahlen und Zahlwörtern bei den alten Ägyptern und was für andere Völker und Sprachen daraus zu lernen ist*, SWGS 25 (Strasbourg : Trübner, 1916), 22–23, 24–26 et 38, et Jean-Claude Goyon, « Nombre et univers : Réflexions sur quelques données numériques de l'arsenal magique de l'Égypte pharaonique », dans *La Magia in Egitto ai tempi dei Faraoni*, éd. Alessandro Roccati et Alberto Siliotti (Milan : Arte e Natura Libri, 1987), 58–59. Enfin, il est possible que le choix de ce motif soit lié à la mention du Chaï et de la Chepeset, pour suggérer leur aspect d'*agathoï daimones* ; toutefois, comme ce signe en démotique, surtout à l'époque romaine il est vrai, sert de déterminatif aux entités divines, on peut aussi se demander s'il ne s'agit pas plus simplement de l'évocation d'un groupe de cinq dieux. Enfin, une dernière hypothèse serait d'y voir une graphie de *nfr* répété cinq fois avec valeur propitiatoire (suggestion de Mark Smith).

Commentaire

L'ostracon Louvre E 11037 est un document remarquable, mais qui, comme d'autres textes démotiques non stéréotypés, s'avère particulièrement frustrant. Sa grande taille, son écriture claire et régulière, ainsi que son état de conservation pouvaient laisser penser que le contenu serait facile à interpréter, mais deux ou trois expressions problématiques entachent la compréhension générale du texte au point que des explications parfois totalement contradictoires peuvent être avancées. L'absence de formule initiale, peut-être en lacune,[10] précisant le contexte et les parties prenantes, en est également la cause. Ainsi, un doute subsiste quant à l'identité du « je » et du « tu » ; nous avons émis l'hypothèse que le signataire Hyq, fils de Hor, est le « je », fils de Hor, lui-même qualifié de « mon père » à la ligne x + 3, bien que cela puisse relever de la coïncidence, l'anthroponyme Hor étant très courant.

Une première difficulté est de déterminer à quel type de document nous avons affaire. La présence des cinq serpents de la dernière ligne fait penser à un texte magique, mais aucun autre élément ne semble aller dans ce sens. En revanche, plusieurs détails le rattachent indirectement à la catégorie des serments promissoires (la particule *ḫr* = *ʿnḫ* + noms divins et l'emploi du Futur III)[11], même si le formulaire est différent et que l'inscription ne comporte pas de date. Le document est clairement structuré avec la mention, au début (l. x+ 1–2) et à la fin (l. x + 7), de « la Grande déesse (var. Isis) et le grand dieu (var. Osiris) et tous les dieux de Thèbes ».[12] En revanche, les entités divines aux noms desquelles le serment est prêté sont « ton Chaï et ta Chepeset », ce qui est sans parallèle à notre connaissance et dénoterait une adaptation à des fins plus personnelles, comme cela se produit dans certaines lettres.[13]

Comme hypothèse de travail, nous proposons de comprendre qu'un fils (Hyq) promet à son père (Hor) de s'occuper de lui après sa mort.[14] La question est de savoir si, au moment de cet engagement, le père est vivant ou décédé. L'allusion aux lieux (de repos ?) dans lesquels il se trouve (l. x + 5) semble indiquer qu'il n'est plus de ce monde : le serment aurait donc été prêté *post mortem*. Le corps du père repose peut-être dans l'atelier d'embaumement ou dans un caveau provisoire.

L'ostracon Louvre E 11037 peut donc être considéré comme une missive adressée à un défunt, ce qui ferait de ce texte le représentant le plus récent de la catégorie des « lettres aux morts ».[15] La disparition vraisemblable de l'en-tête ne permet malheureusement pas de s'en assurer, mais plusieurs éléments plaident en faveur de cette hypothèse, notamment la taille de l'objet[16] et certaines de ses tournures. L'évocation de Chaï et de Chepeset s'explique par l'aspect ambivalent de ces termes qui désignent des divinités tutélaires, mais aussi le (mauvais) sort et la mort.[17] Enfin, la locution *r-ḫrw=f* après la signature (l. x + 8), si elle renvoie bien à un « ordre » reçu du père, pourrait exprimer la volonté de ce dernier, énoncée non pas de son vivant, mais depuis l'au-delà, peut-être sous la forme d'un songe.

10. Voir *supra* note 6.

11. Voir, par exemple, Brian Muhs, « Demotic Ostraca in Amsterdam », *Enchoria* 30 (2006/2007) : 60–62 et pl. 30.

12. On notera qu'Isis est mentionnée ici devant Osiris, comme sur le serment BM EA 43611 (= Ursula Kaplony-Heckel, *Die demotischen Tempeleide*, ÄgAbh 6 [Wiesbaden : Harrassowitz, 1963], 240–41 n° 141) qui est l'un des rares exemples où ces deux divinités figurent comme garantes d'un serment.

13. Depauw, *Demotic Letter*, 281–83.

14. Pour la difficulté à déterminer le sens précis de *qse.t*, qui varie en fonction du contexte, voir la bibliographie citée dans la note (d) de la ligne x + 1. Le fait d'enterrer son père est non seulement une obligation de piété filiale (cf. l'extrait 11 de Régen, « À propos du sens de *qrs*, 'enterrer' », 394–95), mais aussi un requis pour hériter et/ou succéder au père, cf. Sandra Lippert, « Inheritance », *UCLAEE*, https ://escholarship.org/uc/item/30h78901, 2 et 4. Ces questions font parfois l'objet de lettres adressées aux morts, cf. Sylvie Donnat Beauquier, *Écrire à ses morts : Enquête sur un usage rituel de l'écrit dans l'Égypte pharaonique* (Grenoble : Millon, 2014), 70, 151–52, 163 et 214.

15. Voir, en dernier lieu, la liste établie par Julia Troche, « Letters to the Dead », dans *UCLAEE*, https ://escholarship.org/uc/item/6bh8w50t : le papyrus Brooklyn 37.1799 E en hiératique anormal, publié par Jasnow et Vittmann, « Abnormal Hieratic Letter to the Dead », 23–43, est, à ce jour, l'exemplaire le plus tardif du genre. Toutefois, le ton ici est très différent puisque, du moins dans la partie conservée, on ne relève aucune forme de plainte du vivant auprès du défunt : au contraire, il s'agit d'une promesse (faite par le passé ou après le décès du père), peut-être à la suite de difficultés rencontrées ou pour des questions de succession. Donnat Beauquier, *Écrire à ses morts*, 164–66, s'interroge, à la suite de plusieurs spécialistes, sur une possible filiation entre lettres aux morts et lettres aux dieux. Notre document pourrait aller dans son sens et montrer que cette pratique a perduré sporadiquement au moins jusqu'à l'époque ptolémaïque.

16. Il est peu vraisemblable que ce texte ait été rédigé sur une jarre complète, vu la forme irrégulière de l'ostracon et le fait que les lignes conservées, à l'exception de l'une d'entre elles, le sont dans leur intégralité ; en revanche, on peut imaginer que ce tesson de belles dimensions a été déposé près de la momie du père ou dans un lieu de culte.

17. Quaegebeur, *Le dieu égyptien Shaï*, 126–29.

Toutefois, une interprétation différente pourrait aussi être envisagée, comme nous l'a suggéré Mark Smith : le tesson conserverait un texte rituel prononcé par le fils devant la dépouille de son père, une situation qui rappellerait celle du papyrus Harkness.

Pour conclure, nous publions en annexe de ce commentaire deux ostraca de Deir el-Medineh mentionnés par le passé[18] qui contiennent des injonctions à « accomplir la *qe(re)set* » *(ỉr q(r)s.t)* : celles-ci sont adressées à un agent funéraire du nom de Paynefer (= Pinouphis)[19] fils de Pamont (= Pamônthès), vraisemblablement chargé d'effectuer ces rites « conformément à la prescription d'Isis »[20] ; bien que ces documents soient de nature différente[21], il nous a paru utile de les présenter ici.

Figure 2. Ostracon démotique Deir el-Medineh 5-1. © Institut français d'archéologie orientale du Caire / Alain Lecler.

Figure 3. Ostracon démotique Deir el-Medineh 5-2. © Institut français d'archéologie orientale du Caire / Alain Lecler.

O. dém. DelM 5-1[22]
(1) *ỉ-ỉr-ḥr Pꜣy-nfr sꜣ Pa-Mnṯ*
(2) *my ỉr=w qs.t n Pꜣ-šr-Mnṯ r-ẖ(.t) pꜣ ḥn*
(3) *(n) Ỉs.t*
« À l'attention de Paynefer (= Pinouphis) fils de Pamont (= Pamônthès) : fais qu'on accomplisse la *qeset* de/pour Pachermont (= Psenmônthès) conformément à la prescription d'Isis ».

18. Didier Devauchelle, « Notes sur l'administration funéraire égyptienne à l'époque gréco-romaine », *BIFAO* 87 (1987) : 151. Nous remercions l'IFAO et ses directeurs successifs pour l'autorisation de publier ces documents.

19. Le nom Paynefer (= Pinouphis) n'est pas autrement attesté en démotique (pour le grec, voir Trismegistos Nam_ID 11622), mais il faut le rapprocher de Panefer (= Panouphis).

20. Comme relevé par Mark Smith, « A Demotic Formula of Intercession for the Deceased », *Enchoria* 19/20 (1992/1993) : 139, il faut voir ici une allusion à l'« ordre » (*ḥn*) que donne Isis de faire une *q(r)s.t* (*nfr.t*), cf., notamment, pap. Rhind I, 3h,5 = I 3d,4–5 (*ḥn s Ỉs.t wr.t mw.t-ntr r ỉr qs.t nfr.t*) et II 4 h/d1 (*ḥn s Ỉs.t r ỉr qs.t*) ; voir aussi les remarques rassemblées par Jan Quaegebeur, « Diodore I, 20 et les mystères d'Osiris », dans *Hermes aegyptiacus : Egyptological Studies for BH Stricker on his 85th Birthday*, éd. Terence DuQuesne, Discussions in Egyptology Special Number 2 (Oxford : DEPublications, 1995), 162–65.

21. À rapprocher de certaines étiquettes de momies hermonthites, cf. Nur el-Din et Pestman, « Demotic Mummy Labels », 171–89, et Devauchelle, « Notes sur l'administration funéraire égyptienne », 148.

22. Numéro de séquestre 13493 ; terre cuite brun foncé ; l. 10,5 cm, h. 7,7 cm, ép. 1 cm.

O. dém. DelM 5-2[23]
(1) *i-ir-ḥr Pꜣy-nfr sꜣ Pa-Mnṯ*
(2) *my ir=w qs.t n Tꜣ-šr.t-ỉmn*
(3) *r-ẖ(.t) pꜣ ḥn (n) ỉs.t*
« À l'attention de Paynefer (= Pinouphis) fils de Pamont (= Pamônthès) : fais qu'on accomplisse la *qeset* de/pour Tacheretimen (= Senmônthès) conformément à la prescription d'Isis ».

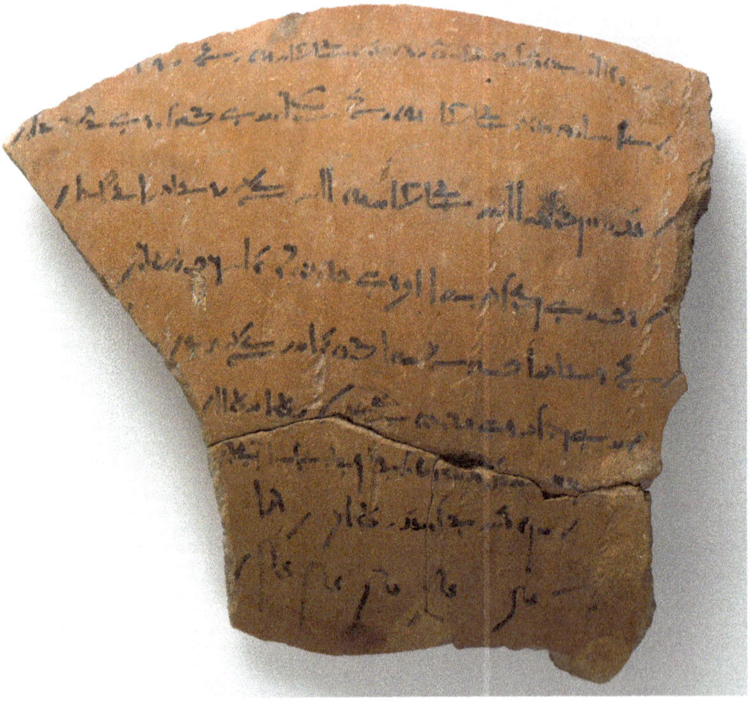

Figure 4. Ostracon démotique Louvre E 11037, recto. © Musée du Louvre, dist. RMN-Grand Palais/Christian Décamps.

Figure 5. Ostracon démotique Louvre E 11037, verso. © Musée du Louvre, dist. RMN-Grand Palais/Christian Décamps.

23. Numéro de sequestre 13520 ; terre cuite marron clair ; l. 9,3 cm, h. 7,6 cm, ép. 0,9 à 1,2 cm.

Some Observations on the Demotic Lease P. Tebtynis dem. 5944

CHRISTINA DI CERBO

In October 2000 two extensive Demotic leases were excavated by the Italian-French Mission to Tebtynis, only days before their season ended.[1] As is the case with the vast majority of the papyri, these were found east of the Soknebtynis temple,[2] an area where the temple workers discarded their unwanted papyri.[3]

I would like to present some observations on this rather confusing lease (P. Tebtynis dem. 5944),[4] together with an overview of the text to Richard Jasnow with whom I share many years of "quarreling" about Demotic texts and graffiti.

When excavated, P. Tebtynis dem. 5944 was lying flat in the sand with the lower quarter[5] of it folded back. The right side of the text was still in rather good condition, but its left side was badly broken, although the various fragments were mostly attached to each other (fig. 1).

After the papyrus was cleaned and preserved, the inscription on the recto was for the most part well preserved, but the inscription on the verso was very puzzling. At first, I thought it was a palimpsest with the right side cut off, but the text, obviously Demotic, didn't "look right." Only after some time did I finally realize that the Demotic inscription was reversed.

In figure 2 I tried to show how the papyrus was folded originally when it had an "accident." At some point, when the papyrus was still partially rolled, the lower 2/3 of it had become wet and the water caused the ink on the recto to bleed into the mostly blank verso of the papyrus, leaving a negative imprint on it.[6] The white squares show some of the signs on the recto and verso which can be most easily identified.

As shown in fig. 2c (original recto), strips 1 and 2 were not affected at all by the water, but the recto (lines 14–28) of strips 3, 4, and 5 left an exact imprint on the verso. The following strips were not folded properly, so there is only a partial imprint of strip 6, nothing(?) of strip 7[7] and then again a clear imprint of strip 8. Also strip 10 at the beginning of the text was folded on top of strip 9, leaving a distinctive imprint of the first signs (lines 18–26) on the recto (fig. 2c–d). The water damage to the text happened while the papyrus was still well preserved, since the imprint on the verso is intact and does not show any signs of holes. It is intriguing to speculate that the papyrus was still being used, perhaps lying on a table, when a careless person spilled some water over it. In any case, the water damage happened

---

1. I am very grateful to Claudio Gallazzi for letting me study and photograph the Demotic papyri found in the years 1997–2000 in Tebtynis and to Kim Ryholt who is managing the publication of these texts.
2. This implies that the lease was stored in the temple property and was not in the possession of the lessor or lessee.
3. Claudio Gallazzi, "Lo scavo di una discarica a Umm-el-Breigât (Tebtynis), ovvero, le sorprese del pattume," *NAC* 27 (1998): 185–207.
4. A full publication of this text and another lease (P. Tebtynis dem. 5939), which was found at the same time, will be part of the Franco-Italian series at the Institut français d'archéologie orientale.
5. The papyrus was folded along line 24.
6. By folding a paper copy of the papyrus one can easily see how the recto was imprinted on the verso.
7. The bottom of strip 7 is too damaged to be certain about any traces.

Figure 1. P. Tebtynis dem. 5944 in October 2000. Photograph by the author.

before the papyrus was buried with sand, since the position in which the text was found does not account for this kind of damage.

In order to make the reversed imprint on the verso more understandable, I will give an overview with a preliminary transcription and translation of the text.

This long text[8] is a lease drawn up between the half-brothers *rpꜥy m-ntry* ...[9] *Ḥr-pꜣ-ẖm* son of *Pꜣ-mꜣj*, his mother *ꞽIs.t-rnpy* and *Pa-n-ꞽIs.t*, the second, son of *Pꜣ-tj-Ḥr-pꜣ-šr-n-ꞽIs.t*, his mother *ꞽIs.t-rnpy* as lessors on one side and the farmer and servant of Sobek *Pꜣ-tj-ꞽIs.t* (son of) *Pꜣ-mꜣj*, his mother *ꞽIs.t-rnpy* as the lessee on the other side. Since party B is also a son of *ꞽIs.t-rnpy*, one can assume that he is a half-brother to party A1 and a full brother to party A2. These three brothers seem to own a large field, from which the two parties A1 and A2 lease their share of the field (line 10 *pꜣj=n wn ꜣḥ*) to party B for two years (lines 12–13). Unlike in other texts from Tebtynis[10] it is not mentioned that the field was inherited,[11] which seems possible since the three parties are siblings.

8. The dimensions of the papyrus are 29.0 × 29.0 cm. The recto has twenty-eight lines and the verso eight witness signatures plus a notation.

9. See Cary J. Martin, "Ptolemaic Demotic Land Leases," in *Law and Legal Practice in Egypt from Alexander to the Arab Conquest*, ed. James G. Keenan, Joseph G. Manning, and Uri Yiftach-Firanko (Cambridge: Cambridge University Press, 2014), 346: "the lessors invariably belong to the priesthood."

10. Wilhelm Spiegelberg, *Die demotischen Denkmäler II: Die demotischen Papyrus; Tafeln, CGC Nos. 30601–31270, 50001–50022* (Strasbourg: Dumont Schauberg, 1908): P. Cairo CG 30617a,3, 300628,16 and 31254,14, see *pḥ*, "to inherit" (Pieter W. Pestman, Jan Quaegebeur, and R. Vos, *Recueil de textes démotiques et bilingues*, vol. 2: *Traductions* [Leiden, 1977], 97 n. r).

11. Joseph G. Manning, "Demotic Law," in *A History of Ancient Near Eastern Law*, ed. Raymond Westbrook, HdO 72 (Leiden: Brill, 2003), 2:839–40.

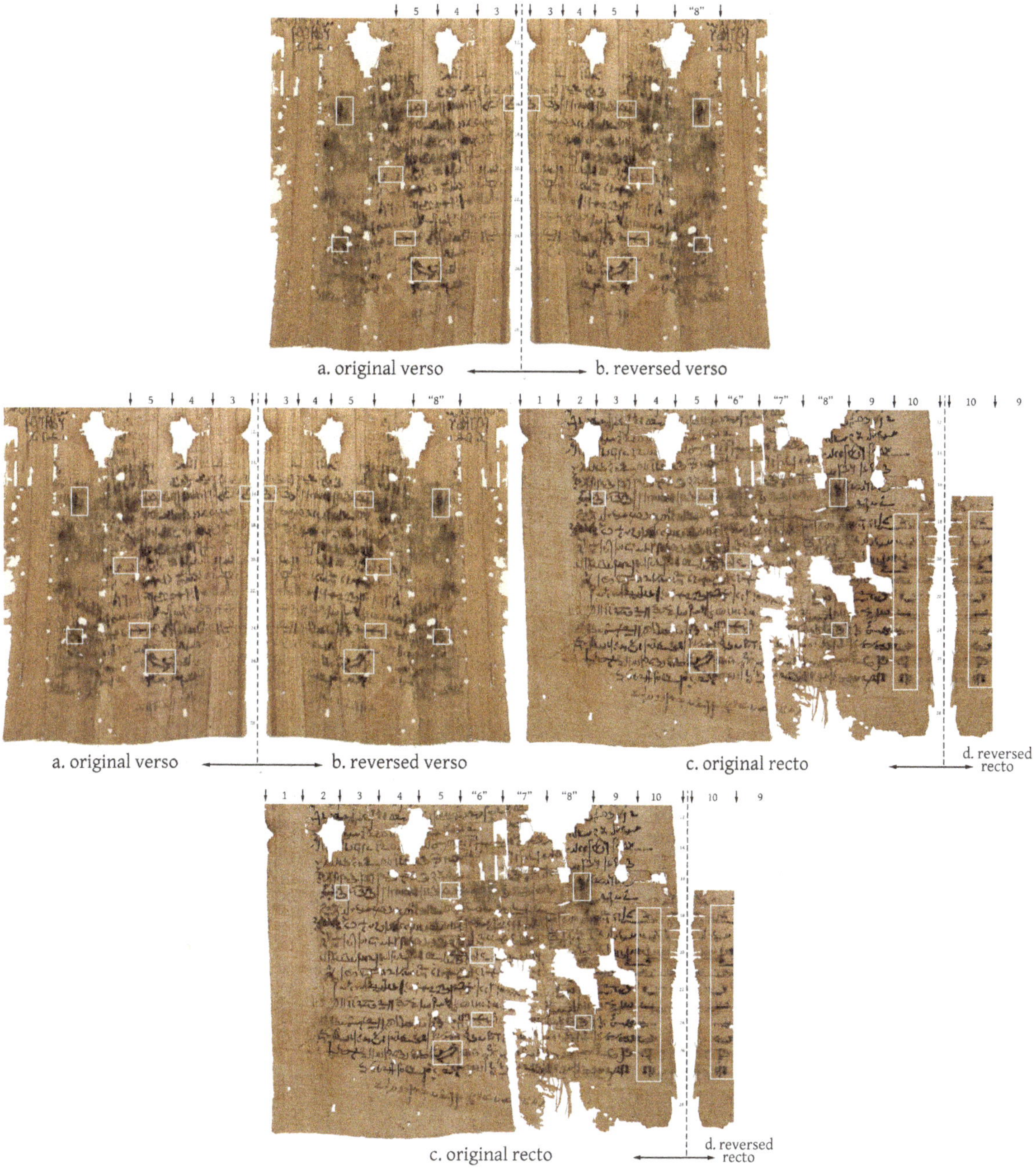

Figure 2. Two mirrored images of the verso and recto showing the water damage of P. Tebtynis dem. 5944, with squares highlighting some of the imprints.

As common in leases, the neighboring plots are given (lines 13–14) and it is specified that the lessee is required to do the necessary farmwork and provide all needed equipment (lines 14–16). Party B has made a prepayment for the lease. Parties A1 and A2 acknowledge that they have received the payment (line 18) for the first year of the lease and that they will receive the payment for the second year of the lease in the month Payni of year 39 (June/July 131 BCE). In this text we can see that the document was drawn up in August during the inundation in the summer (June to September) and that it ended after the Nile started to flood the fields again.

Transliteration, recto	Translation, recto
1. *ḥꜣ.[t-s]p 37.t ibt 3 šmw sw 29(?) nꜣ pr-ꜥꜣ Ptlwmys irm Ḳlwptrꜣ irm nꜣ ntr.w mnḫ i.ir*	Reg[na]l year 37, month 3 of the *šmw* season, day 29(?) of the Pharaohs Ptolemy (VIII) and Cleopatra (III) and the gods Euergetai, being
2. *P⸢t⸣[l]⸢w⸣mys irm Ḳlwptrꜣ irm nꜣ ntr.w (ntj) prj tꜣ pr-ꜥꜣ Ḳlwptrꜣ tꜣj=f sn(.t)-ḥm.t tꜣ ntr.t mnḫ⸢.t⸣ wꜥb*	P⸢t⸣⸢o⸣[l]emy (VIII) and Cleopatra (II) and the gods Epiphaneis, the queen Cleopatra (II), his sister-wife, the goddess Euerge⸢tis⸣, (and) the priest (of)
3. *ꜣlgsꜣntrws irm nꜣ ntr.w ntj nḥm nꜣ ntr.w sn.w nꜣ ntr.w mnḫ nꜣ ntr.w mrj it.ṯ(=w) nꜣ ntr.w ntj prj pꜣ ntr ⸢r⸣ tny it.ṯ(=f)*	Alexander and the gods Soteres, the gods Adelphoi, the gods Euergetai, the gods Philopatores, the gods Epiphaneis, the god ⸢E⸣upator
4. *irm pꜣ ntr mrj mw.t=f irm nꜣ ntr.w mnḫ Ptlwmys pꜣ šr mḥ-2 pr-ꜥꜣ Ptlwmys irm tꜣ pr-ꜥꜣ Ḳlwptrꜣ*	and the god Philometor and the gods Euergetai (being) Ptolemy, the second son of Pharaoh Ptolemy and the queen Cleopatra (II)
5. *tꜣj=f sn(.t)-ḥm.t tꜣ ntr.t mnḫ s.ḥm.t Tꜣmwnꜣsꜣs ta ꜣplwnyꜣs tꜣ fꜣy.t šp kn m-bꜣḥ Br-*	his sister-wife, the goddess Euergetis, the lady *Tꜣmwnꜣsꜣs* daughter of *ꜣplwnyꜣs* (being) Athlophoros before Ber-
6. *ꜣnygꜣ tꜣ ntr.t mnḫ s.ḥm.t ꜣysytwrꜣ ta Ḳypylws tꜣ fꜣy.t tn nwb m-bꜣḥ ꜣrs-*	enike, the goddess Euergetis, the lady *ꜣysytwrꜣ* daughter of *Ḳypylws* (being) Kanephoros before Ars-
7. *ynꜣ tꜣ mr sn s.ḥm.t ꜣrtꜣmw ta Sꜣlwḳws tꜣ w⸢ꜥb.t ꜣ⸣rsynꜣ tꜣ mrj it.ṯ dd rpꜥy*	inoe Philadelphos (and) the lady *ꜣrtꜣmw* daughter of *Sꜣlwḳws* (being) the pr⸢iestess of A⸣rsinoe Philopator. Said the prince
8. *m-ntry irm nꜣ ntr.w ntj nḥm nꜣ ntr.w sn.w nꜣ ntr.w mnḫ nꜣ ntr.w mrj it.ṯ nꜣ ntr.w ntj prj pꜣ ntr tny it.ṯ*	(and) prophet and the gods Soteres, the gods Adelphoi, the gods Euergetai, the gods Philopatores, the gods Epiphaneis, the god Eupator
9. *⸢irm pꜣ ntr mrj mw.t=f⸣ [irm nꜣ ntr.w mn]⸢ḫ⸣ Ḥr-pꜣ-ḫm (sꜣ) Pꜣ-mꜣj [mw.t]⸢=f⸣ Ỉs.t-rnpy ḥnꜥ Pa-n-Ỉs.t mḥ-2 (sꜣ) Pꜣ-tj-Ḥr-pꜣ-šr-n-Ỉs.t mw.t=f Ỉs.t-rnpy*	⸢and the god Philometor⸣ [and the gods Euerget]⸢ai⸣ (being) *Ḥr-pꜣ-ḫm* (son of) *Pꜣ-mꜣj*, ⸢his⸣ [mother] *Ỉs.t-rnpy* and *Pa-n-Ỉs.t*, the second, (son of) *Pꜣ-tj-Ḥr-pꜣ-šr-n-Ỉs.t*, his mother *Ỉs.t-rnpy*
10. *r rmt ⸢s-2 wꜥ rꜣ⸣ [n wyꜥ] bꜣk Sbk Pꜣ-tj-Ỉs.t (sꜣ) Pꜣ-mꜣj ⸢mw.t=f⸣ Ỉs.t-rnpy sḥn=n n=k pꜣj=n ⸢wn⸣ ꜣḥ ntj ḫn*	amounts to ⸢two men together⸣ [to the farmer] (and) servant of Sobek *Pꜣ-tj-Ỉs.t* (son of) *Pꜣ-mꜣj*, ⸢his mother⸣ *Ỉs.t-rnpy*. "We leased to you our ⸢section⸣ of field, which is in
11. *Twtrs ⸢ntj(?)⸣ [... ḥtp-ntr(?)] Sbk-nb-Tn ntj ḫn tꜣ sḫ.t [...] Sbk-Tꜣ-nb-tꜣ-tn ntj ḫn tꜣ tnj.t*	*Twtrs* ⸢which(?)⸣ [... tempel domain of(?)] Soknebtynis, which is in the field of [...] Soknebtynis, which is in the division of
12. *Pwlmn ntj [ḥr ꜥt rsj tꜣ ḥ]ny [Mꜣ]-⸢wr*[12] *pꜣ⸣ [tš ꜣrs]ynꜣ pꜣ rt [ḥꜣ.t-sp 38.]⸢t⸣*	Polemon, which is [on the south side of the Mo]⸢eris⸣ [ca]nal in the [nome of Ars]inoe (Arsinoites) for the growth [of regnal year 38] (and)

12. Katelijn Vandorpe, "The Henet of Moeris and the Ancient Administrative Division of the Fayum in Two Parts," *APF* 50 (2004): 61–78.

13. *pꜣ rt ḥꜣ.t-sp 39 r rnp.t* [2].⸢*t*⸣ [*r*] ⸢*š*⸣*mw 2.t nꜣ* ⸢*hyn*⸣*.w nꜣ ꜣ*⸢*ḥ.w*⸣ *ntj ḥrj rsj* [*ḥn*]*y tw mḥṯ* [...] ⸢...⸣	the growth of regnal year 39, amounts to [2] years, [amounts to] 2 ⸢har⸣vests. The ⸢boundarie⸣s of the aforementioned fie⸢lds⸣: south, the [can]al of the mountain(?); north, [...] ⸢...⸣ of
14. *Sbk-m-ḥb* (*sꜣ*) *Pa-Ḫꜥpj iꜣbt.ṯ imnṯ nꜣ ḥtp-ntr nꜣ s*[...] ⸢...⸣ ... *m*[*tw=k i*]⸢*r*⸣ *nꜣ ꜣḥ.w ntj ḥrj wp.t nb* (*n*) *wyꜥ*	*Sbk-m-ḥb* son of *Pa-Ḫꜥpj*; east (and)(?) west of the tempel domain properties of the ... [...] ⸢...⸣ .... Y[ou are to carry] ⸢out⸣ (for) the aforementioned fields all the farmwork.
15. *mtw=k ir=w sm* (*n*) *pꜣ* [*mw*] *ḥꜣ.t-sp* ⸢*38*⸣ *m*[*tw=k ir=w sw pꜣ mw*] *ḥꜣ.t-sp 39 mtw=k tj.t grg sm grg sw r.r=w*	You are to cultivate them with fodder crops (from) the [inundation] of regnal year ⸢38⸣, yo[u are to cultivate them with wheat from the inundation] of regnal year 39. You are to give equipment for the fodder crop (and) equipment for the wheat,
16. *m*[*tw*]*=k skꜣ=w* ⸢*m*⸣[*tw=k m*]⸢*ḥ(?)*⸣*=w mt*⸢*w*⸣*=k* ..[.]*=w nꜣj=k* ⸢*rmt*⸣[*.w*](?) *nꜣj=k grg.w nꜣj=k iḥ.w rmt-nmḥ mtw=k*	y[o]u are to plough them, ⸢y⸣[ou are to fi]⸢ll(?)⸣ them (and) you ar⸢e⸣ to eq[uip(?)] them (with) your ⸢me⸣[n](?), your equipment, your oxen, as a free man. You may
17. *ṯꜣj pꜣ šn* [*wtḥ ntj iw=w r*] *ḫpr* ⸢*n=k ẖn nꜣ ꜣḥ.w ntj ḥrj pꜣ rnp.t 2.t ntj ḥrj* ⸢*pꜣ*⸣ *šmw pꜣ rt ḥꜣ.t-sp 38.t*	take the wood [(and) the fruit] which will] accrue for yo⸢u⸣ in the aforementioned fields (for) 2 the aforementioned years. (Concerning) ⸢the⸣ harvest for the regnal year 38,
18. *tj=k st n=n* [*ḥ.t-ḥꜣ.t*] ⸢*pꜣ hrw*⸣ ⸢*šp=n*⸣ *st n tr.t=k pꜣ* ⸢*hrw*⸣ *ḥꜣ.ṯ=n mtr n.im=w iw=w mḥ iwṯ ntj nb* ⸢*nkt nb*⸣	you have given it to us, [the prepayment] ⸢today⸣. ⸢We have received⸣ it from you ⸢today⸣. Our heart is satisfied with it, they being paid in full, without any⸢thing (lacking) at all⸣.
19. *pꜣ rt ḥꜣ.t-sp* ⸢*3*⸣[*9.t* ...] *mtw=k tj.t s n=n ḥꜣ.t-sp 39 ibt 2 šmw ꜥrḳy*[13] ⸢*s*⸣*w nfr iw=w wꜥb iwṯ sn.w*	(Concerning) the growth of regnal year ⸢3⸣[9 ...], you will give it to us in regnal year 39, month 2 of *šmw*, day 30, (meaning) good ⸢wh⸣eat which is pure, unadulterated,
20. *iw=w ẖꜣ*[*j=*]⸢*w*⸣ [*iw=w fꜣj=w iw=w*] ⸢*swṯ r pꜣj=n*⸣ *ꜥ.wj tmy Sbk-Tꜣ-nb-tꜣ-tn tꜣ ipt pꜣ 1/10 ntj wḏꜣ*	me[asur]⸢ed,⸣ [transported (and) de]⸢livered to our⸣ house (in) the town of Soknebtynis. The correct oipe of the 1/10
21. [*pꜣ tmy*] ⸢*ntj ḥrj*⸣ [...] ⸢*tj.t(?)*⸣ [...] *tj.t st* ⸢*i.ir=k*⸣ *tj.t st n=n n.im=w ẖn kj hrw 5*	[of the] ⸢above-mentioned⸣ [town ...] ⸢give(?)⸣ [...] give it. ⸢You are⸣ to give it to us within another 5 days,
22. *m-sꜣ pꜣ ibt r*[*n*]⸢*=f ... bn-iw=n*⸣ [*rḫ*] ⸢*ḏ*⸣[*d tw=*]⸢*n n=k sw*⸣ *n.im=w(?) iwṯ iw* ⸢*mtw=n*⸣ *tj.t* ⸢*w*⸣*j mt pr-ꜥꜣ nb pꜣ tꜣ*	after the men[tion]⸢ed⸣ month. ⸢... we will not⸣ [be able to] ⸢s⸣[ay: W]⸢e⸣ [have] ⸢given to you thereof(?) the wheat⸣ without receipt. ⸢We are to re⸣move every matter (of) pharaoh on earth
23. *ntj iw=w r pḥ* ⸢*nꜣ ꜣḥ*⸣*.w* (*ntj*) *ḥrj* ⸢*ḥnꜥ*⸣(?) *mtw=n* [*wj(?)* ...] ⸢...⸣ *yꜣs nb pꜣ tꜣ ntj iw=w pḥ r.r=w iw=n nḥm nꜣ ꜣḥ.w ntj ḥrj*	which will accrue to ⸢the⸣ aforementioned ⸢fiel⸣ds ⸢and⸣(?) we will be [far(?)] from every [...]⸢...⸣*yꜣs* on earth which will accrue to them. If we hold back the fields that are above

13. Heinz Felber, *Demotische Ackerpachtverträge der Ptolemäerzeit: Untersuchungen zu Aufbau, Entwicklung und inhaltlichen Aspekten einer Gruppe von demotischen Urkunden*, ÄA 58 (Wiesbaden: Harrassowitz, 1997), 212: "Das Ende der Pachtzeit ist in mehreren Texten auf einen Tag im Juni festgelegt, nämlich auf den 30. Pachons." I believe it should be Payni and not Pachons.

24. *ḫr.r=k g3* ⸢*mtw rmt nb p3 t3*⸣ [*nḥm=w ḫr.r=k iw=n*] ⸢*tm tj.t wꜥb=w*⸣ *n=k g3* ⸢...⸣ *mt.w ntj ḥrj iw=n tj.t n=k ḥt 1500*	from you, or if ⸢any man on earth⸣ [holds them back from you, (and) if we] ⸢do not clear them⸣ for you or ⸢...⸣ matters that are above, we will give to you silver, 1,500 (deben),
25. *ntj ir krkr 5 ḥmt tbꜥ 2*[*4 r ḥt kt 2 iw=n tj.t n=k*] *kt ḥt 1500 (r) n3 kll.w n3 wtn.w n3 ꜥby.w n3 pr-ꜥ3.w*	makes 5 talents, 2[4] copper obols [to 2 silver kite, (and) we will give] another silver, 1,500 (deben) to the burnt offerings, libations (and) offerings to the kings,
26. *ꜥnḫ ḏ.t* ⸢*ḥ*⸣[*n hrw*] ⸢*5 iw.iw=k*⸣ [*m-s3=n*] ⸢*r-ḫ nkt nb ntj ḥrj*⸣ *ꜥn ntj nb nkt nb ntj mtw=n ḥnꜥ n3 ntj iw=n (r) tj.t ḫpr=w*	living forever, ⸢with⸣[in] ⸢5⸣ [days]. You have a [claim on us] ⸢in accordance with everything aforementioned⸣, again, (and) all and everything which belongs to us together with what we will acquire, is
27. *iwj.t p3 hp p3* ⸢*sḥn ntj ḥrj ...*⸣ [...]⸢... *n ḥtr iwṯ mn*⸣ *sḫ Sbk-m-ḥb (s3) ꜣIr.t-Ḥr-r.r=w*	(the) security of the right of the ⸢aforementioned lease. ...⸣ [...]⸢..., compulsorily and without delay⸣. Written by *Sbk-m-ḥb* son of *ꜣIr.t-Ḥr-r.r=w*
28. [*sḫ Ḥ*]*r-p3-*[*ḫ*]*m (s3) P3-m3j* *sḫ Pa-n-ꜣIs.t p3 ḫm (s3) P3-tj-Ḥr-p3-šr-ꜣIs.t*	[*Ḥ*]*r- p3-*[*ḫ*]*m*, the younger (son of) *P3-m3j* [wrote this]. *Pa-n-ꜣIs.t*, the younger)son) of *P3-tj-Ḥr-p3-šr-n-ꜣIs.t* wrote this.

Notes, Recto

Line 1

- *ḥ3.t-sp 37.t šmw sw 29(?)* (= August 16(?), 133 BCE[14]): Most of the leases were drawn up "in the period between the end of August and the beginning of November, i.e., just before work on the land was to begin." Martin, "Ptolemaic Demotic Land Leases," 345. Therefore, this lease starts slightly earlier, giving the farmer more time to prepare the field.

Lines 1–2

- Ptolemy VIII was married to his niece and stepdaughter Cleopatra III and to his sister Cleopatra II (mother of Cleopatra III); at this time they held the epithet *n3 ntr.w mnḫ.w.*[15]

  In the regnal year 37 (134–133 BCE) reigned:
- Ptolemy VIII: son of Ptolemy V and Cleopatra I, married to his sister Cleopatra II and his niece Cleopatra III,
- Cleopatra II: daughter of Ptolemy V and Cleopatra I, mother of Cleopatra III, married to her brothers Ptolemy VI and Ptolemy VIII,
- Cleopatra III: daughter of Ptolemy VI and Cleopatra II, married to her uncle Ptolemy VIII.

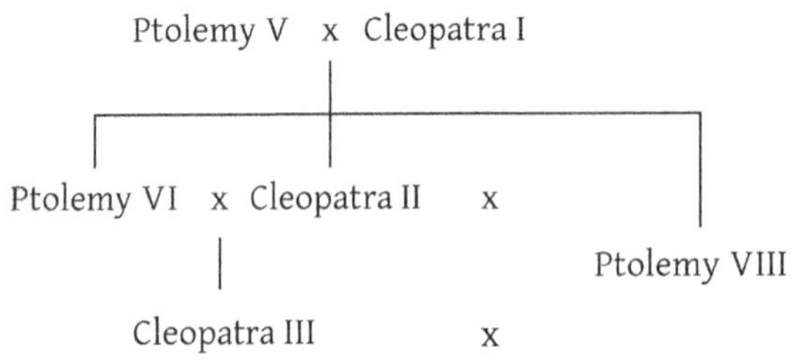

14. http://aegyptologie.online-resourcen.de/ptolemies
15. Pieter Pestman, *Chronologie égyptienne d'après les textes démotiques (332 av. J.C.–453 ap. J.C.)*, PLB 15 (Leiden: Brill, 1967), 62.

Lines 3–5

- At the end of the line is a long vertical stroke (not shown in facsimile). The significance of it is unclear.

Lines 2–7

In the dating formula of the text four eponymous priests of regnal year 37 are named—they are, except for the priestess of Arsinoe Philopator, unattested. The name of the Alexander priest is mentioned after the title, while the names of the following priestesses appear before the title.

- Priest of Alexander and the deified Ptolemies: Ptolemy, the second son of the Pharaoh Ptolemy and the Queen Cleopatra. This priest is possibly the later Pharaoh Ptolemy X Alexander I.[16]
- Athlophore before Berenike, the goddess Euergetis: the woman *T3mwn3s3s*, daughter of *3plwny3s*,
- Kanephore of Arsinoe Philadelphos: the woman *3ysytwr3*, daughter of *Ḳypylws*,
- Priestess of Arsinoe Philopator: the woman *3rt3mw*, daughter of *S3lwḳws*.

Line 4

- Who is Ptolemy, the second son of the Pharaoh Ptolemy and the queen Cleopatra, his sister-wife, the goddess Euergetis? On the one hand, it seems that he is a second son of Ptolemy VIII and Cleopatra II. However, they had only had one son, Ptolemy Memphites. He was brutally murdered by his father Ptolemy VIII in the year 130.[17] On the other hand, Ptolemy VIII and his second wife Cleopatra III had two sons (Ptolemy IX Soter II and Ptolemy X Alexander I), but Cleopatra III was his niece and step-daughter, not his wife-sister. Since both of these two explanations are flawed, one must assume that the scribe made a mistake and confused Cleopatra II with III. Considering their multiple relationships to Ptolemy VIII, this is not surprising. So it seems most likely that Ptolemy, the second son of Pharaoh Ptolemy (VIII) must have been the younger son of queen Cleopatra (III), who became Ptolemy X Alexander I in 107 BCE. The epithet Alexander reinforces the assumption that it was indeed Ptolemy X Alexander I who was the priest of Alexander in the regnal year 37.[18]

Line 5

- The small stroke in front of *s.ḥmt* belongs to *ntr.w* in line 4.

Lines 5–7

- In this lease the name of the three eponymous priestesses is preceded by *s.ḥmt*; in other texts from Tebtynis the priestesses generally remain anonymous.

---

16. Ptolemy, the second son of the Pharaoh Ptolemy, clearly points to Ptolemy X and not Ptolemy IX, see Christina Di Cerbo, "Neue demotische Texte aus Tebtynis, Überblick zu den demotischen Papyri der italienisch/französischen Ausgrabung in Tebtynis aus den Jahren 1997–2000," in *Res severa verum gaudium: Festschrift für Karl-Theodor Zauzich zum 65. Geburtstag am 8. Juni 2004*, ed. Friedhelm Hoffmann and Heinz-Josef Thissen, StudDem 6 (Leuven: Peeters, 2004), 116.

17. Thomas Schneider, *Lexikon der Pharaonen: Die altägyptischen Könige von der Frühzeit bis zur Römerherrschaft* (Zürich: Artemis, 1994), 340.

18. In the Greek text P. Tebt. III 810 a Ptolemy, son of king Ptolemy, was priest of Alexander in the regnal year 36. Was he Ptolemy Memphites or perhaps Ptolemy X Alexander I? See W. Clarysse and G. van der Veken, *The Eponymous Priests of Ptolemaic Egypt*, PLB 24 (Leiden: Brill, 1983), 32–33, 67.

Line 7

- The priestess of Arsinoe Philopator, the lady *3rt3mw*[19] daughter of *S3lwḳws*, is the only known eponymous priest from this year.
- The title *rpʿy m-ntry* occurs in several texts from Tebtynis, see Andreas Winkler, "Collecting Income at Kerkesoucha Orous: New Light on P. Cairo CG 30625," *JEA* 96 (2010): 161–74.
- The title *rpʿy m-ntry* can stand by itself,[20] be followed by *ḥrj-šy-Ḳm3 ḥrj-šy-Rs-nb-ʾImnṯ* alone,[21] or accompanied by a list of deified kings,[22] by *nb wʿb.w ḥrj šy-Wt-wr ʾIs.t-n3.w-nfr-ir-šty.t*,[23] or *rpʿy m-ntry* is followed directly by a list of deified Ptolemies.[24]

Line 8

- *m-ntry*: Joachim Quack, "Zu einigen demotischen Gruppen umstrittener Lesung oder problematischer Ableitung," in *Aspects of Demotic Orthography*, ed. Sven P. Vleeming, StudDem 11 (Leuven: Peeters, 2013), 111–16.

Line 9

- Party A1: *Ḥr-p3-ẖm* son of *P3-m3j*, his mother *ʾIs.t-rnpy*.
- *P3-m3j*, *DemNb*, 186. The father's name of party A1 and party B is probably identical, which means that they are full brothers, while party A2 is their half-brother. The writing of the father's name *P3-m3j* varies slightly in line 9[25] 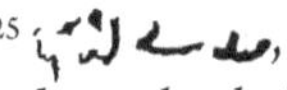, line 10  and line 28 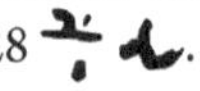. His name in the notation on the verso, written by the scribe is clearly *P3-m3j* .
- *ʾIs.t-rnpy* (*DemNb*, 79) is the mother of all three parties.
- Party A2: *Pa-n-ʾIs.t*, the second, son of *P3-tj-Ḥr-p3-šr-n-ʾIs.t*, his mother *ʾIs.t-rnpy*.

Line 10

- *P3-tj-ʾIs.t*: The writing of the name (cf. *DemNb*, 290) is identical with that in P. Cairo CG 30619,I,6.
- *wʿ r3*: CDD *R* (2001), 3 "together."
- Party B: *wyʿ b3k Sbk P3-tj-ʾIs.t* (*s3*) *P3-m3j*, his mother *ʾIs.t-rnpy*.
  wyʿ b3k: Joseph G. Manning, "Land and Status in Ptolemaic Egypt: The Status Designation 'occupation titles + *B3*k + Divine Name,'" in *Grund und Boden in Altägypten: Rechtliche und sozio-ökonomische Verhältnisse; Akten des internationalen Symposions, Tübingen 18.–20. Juni 1990*, ed. Schafik Allam (Tübingen: self-published, 1994), 147–76.
- *wn 3ḥ*: Party A1 and A2 leased their part of a field without giving the dimensions of the field, see P. Cairo CG 31079,12–13: *sḥn=y n=k t3j=y* (*st3*) *2.t 3ḥ*. One can assume that the field (inherited[26] from their common mother) had been divided up and then one part was leased to the one brother (*wyʿ b3k*) who wanted to farm it.
- *sḥn=n*: As is common in the Fayum the lease was drawn up by the lessor, see Manning, "Demotic Law," 848; Cary J. Martin, "A Third-Century Demotic Land Lease (P. BM EA 10858)," in *Illuminating Osiris: Egyptological Studies in Honor of Mark Smith*, ed. Richard Jasnow and Ghislaine Widmer, MVCAE 2 (Atlanta: Lockwood, 2017), 255; and Felber, *Demotische Ackerpachtverträge*, 118.

19. Clarysse and van der Veken, *The Eponymous Priests of Ptolemaic Egypt*, 35.
20. See P. Cairo CG 30612, 30617, 30620, 31250.
21. See P. Cairo CG 30612, 30615, 30620, 30625, 31079, 31254.
22. See P. Cairo CG 30608, 30609, 30612, 30628, 30632.
23. See P. Cairo CG 30626.
24. See P. Cairo CG 30607, JdE 34662.
25. The diagonal in line 9 above the second sign could be a "flaw" in the papyrus.
26. Manning, "Demotic Law," 841–42.

Line 11

- *Twtrs*: *DemNb*, 1276, 1294 (*thwtwrs*). The reading of this Greek name seems certain, but it is unclear if this belongs to an individual or if it is a place name.
- I am doubtful of what needs to be added in the lacunae. The Tebtynis papyri in the Cairo Museum have very similar passages, but none of them helps entirely to reconstruct the missing sections of this lease. See P. Cairo CG 3015,5 *ntj ḥr tꜣ ḫyꜣ.t ꜥꜣ.t pꜣ ḥtp-ntr Sbk-nb-Tn pꜣ ntr ꜥꜣ tꜣ sḫ.t Tꜣ-nb-Tn*, or P. Cairo CG 31079,13 *ntj ḥr tꜣ ḫyꜣ.t ꜥꜣ.t tꜣ sḫ.t Tꜣ-nb-Tn*.

Lines 11–12

- P. Cairo CG 31254,13–14 (*ḫft-ḥr Sbk-tꜣ-nb-Tn ẖn tꜣ tnj.t Plwmn ntj ḥr pꜣj=f ꜥt rsj [tꜣ] ḥny Mr-wr pꜣ tš ꜣrsynꜣ*), see also P. Cairo CG 30612,4–5 (*ḫft-ḥr Sbk-nb-Tn pꜣ ntr ꜥꜣ ntj n tmy Sbk-tꜣ-nb-Tꜣ-Tn ntj ẖn tꜣ tnj.t Plwmn ḥr ꜥt rsj tꜣ ḥny Mꜣ-wr*), 30617a,2–3 and 30621,3.
- See Felber, *Demotische Ackerpachtverträge*, 127.

Line 13

- *šm*: CDD Š (2010), 143.
- [*ḥn*]*y tw*: The reading of these words seems certain. The traces with the water sign at the end fit well *ḥny* (see *ḥny* in P. Cairo CG 30612,4 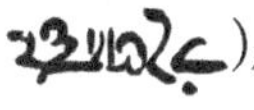), but the connection to *tw*, "mountain, desert plateau", CDD *T* (2012), 105–6 is unclear.

Line 14

- *Pa-Ḥꜥpj* is written as *Pa-m-ḥb*, the last part being the same as in *Sbk-m-ḥb*; see *DemNb*, 399.
- *wp.t nb n wyꜥ*: Felber, *Demotische Ackerpachtverträge*, 135.

Line 15

- *ir sm*: *DG*, 430 "heuen"; see Martin, "Third-Century Demotic Land Lease," 248.
- *grg*: It also can have the meaning "seed," see CDD G (2004), 49 n.pl. "seed."
  Usually the lease is from the inundation of year x to the (inundation) of year y, see Martin, "Ptolemaic Demotic Land Leases," 345.
  m[*tw=k … pꜣ mw*] *ḥꜣ.t-sp 39*: There is not enough space for a repetition of the previous *mtw=k ir=w sm* (*n*) *pꜣ* [*mw*] *ḥꜣ.t-sp ⸢38*, but something similar must be expected here.
- It seems that the lessor was supposed to plant *sm*, "fodder crops" in one year and *sw*, "wheat," in the next.

Line 16

- *skꜣ*: Felber, *Demotische Ackerpachtverträge*, 166.
- In the lacuna one would expect *mtw=k mḥ=w*, which frequently occurs in leases,[27] but the space for it is rather large and the traces do not fit *mḥ* very well. A comparable phrase in P. Tebtynis dem. 5939,11 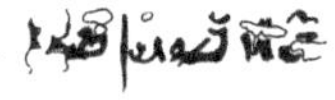 is unfortunately also damaged.

27. See Martin, "Ptolemaic Demotic Land Leases," 360: "I am to plough them; I am to fill them with cattle, seed, men, (and) all agricultural equipment for sowing (and) for harvest, as a free man"; P. Erbstreit 6,7: Katelijn Vandorpe and Sven P. Vleeming, *The Erbstreit Papyri: A Bilingual Dossier from Pathyris of the Second Century BC*, StudDem 13 (Leuven: Peeters, 2017), 79.

- *mtw=k ..[.]=w*: The reading of this word is unclear to me. It describes what needs to be done with the items which are listed in the following, but transliterations such as *mḥ* or *grg* (line 15 , , line16 ) are not possible and other readings like *ẖl*, *qr*, or *ẖr* do not provide any acceptable solution.

  A similar phrase also occurs in P. Tebtynis dem. 5939,11 , but there it seems to be spelled *ꜣl*, see *DG*, 67 *ꜥl* and CDD *ꜥ* (2003), 107–10. See Cary Martin, "A Demotic Land Lease from Philadelphia: P. BM 10560," *JEA* 72 (1986): 161.
- *rmt-nmḥ*: Maren Schentuleit and Günter Vittmann, *"Du hast mein Herz zufriedengestellt…": Ptolemäerzeitliche demotische Urkunden aus Soknopaiu Nesos*, Corpus Papyrorum Raineri 29 (Berlin: de Gruyter, 2009), 18; H. Felber, "Augustus Ζεὺς ἐλευθέριος im Demotischen und die Etymologie von PWME," *GM* 123 (1991): 34n31.

Line 17
- See a very similar passage in P. Cairo CG 31079, 16–17 *mtw=k ṯꜣj pꜣ šn pꜣ wtḥ ntj iw=f ḫpr ẖn=w* and P. Mil. Vogl. dem. Inv. 24,7 (Felber, *Demotische Ackerpachtverträge*, 155).

Line 18
- *ḥt ḥꜣ.t* can be restored after P. Cairo CG 31079,18, see CDD *Ḥ* (2009), 336–37.
- *pꜣ hrw*:[28] This literally means "today," but it probably does not indicate that the payment took place on this very day but that an earlier payment was in place from "today" on. For *pꜣ hrw*, see also P. Cairo CG 30613,11, [30615,8], and 31079,19.
- Water damaged this area badly, but the reading *iw=w mḥ iwṯ ntj nb* **nkt nb** (CDD *N* [2004], 136) seems certain, although *iw=w mḥ iwṯ* **sp nb**, "they being paid in full, without any remainder" is more common in Tebtynis, see P. Cairo CG 30630,13.

Line 19
- *iwṯ sn.w*: CDD Numbers (2014), 15 "w/out foreign particles (lit., 'seconds'), w/out chaff."

Line 20
- *iw=w ẖꜣj=w iw=w fꜣj=w iw=w swṯ*: A parallel in P. Tebtynis dem. 5939,13  helps to fill the lacuna.

Lines 20–21
- *tꜣ ip.t pꜣ 1/10 ntj wḏꜣ pꜣ tmy ntj ḥrj*: CDD *Ꜣ*, 102 "the correct oipe of the 1/10 of the above-mentioned town". See P. Tebtynis dem. 5939,13-14: 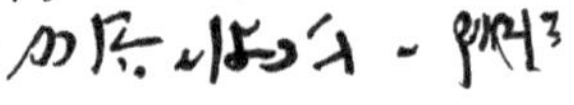 and P. Mil. Vogl. dem. Inv. 24,12–13.

Line 21
- *ẖn kj hrw* 5: Usually this phrase is *n wꜥ hrw ẖn hrw 5* "on one day within five days" (CDD *H* [2001], 70), as in P. Mil. Vogl. dem. Inv. 24,11.

Line 22
- *m-sꜣ pꜣ ibt rn=f*: *=f* is written almost as a vertical line as in line 4 (*pꜣ ntr mrj mw.t=f*). The missing section is completed with the help of P. Tebtynis dem. 5939,15 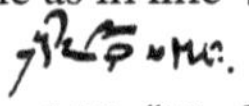.
- *bn-iw=n rḫ ḏd*: Felber, *Demotische Ackerpachtverträge*, 159: "Nachweis der Zahlung."

28. Felber, *Demotische Ackerpachtverträge*, 209.

- *ỉwṯ ỉw*: P. Mil. Vogl. dem. Inv. 24,10; Felber, *Demotische Ackerpachtverträge*, 160: "ohne Quittung."
- *mtw=n tj.t wj mt pr-ꜥꜣ*: The lessor is responsible for paying the taxes (Martin, "Ptolemaic Demotic Land Leases," 348). In the Fayum the lessor paid the taxes,[29] indicating that he was the "weaker party."[30]
- *mt pr-ꜥꜣ*: Taxes, see Felber, *Demotische Ackerpachtverträge*, 143, 149.

Lines 22–23

- This badly damaged section can be restored based on P. Tebtynis. dem. 5939,15. 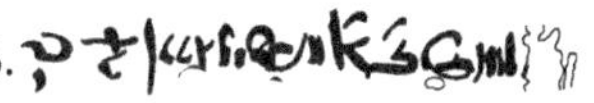
- *pḥ*: CDD *P* (2010), 143 "to accrue to, to devolve upon (someone)." See Pestman, Quaegebeur, and Vos, *Recueil de textes démotiques et bilingues*, 2:97.
- *mt pr-ꜥꜣ nb pꜣ tꜣ ntj ỉw=w pḥ*: This phrase appears twice in these two lines.

Line 23

- Unfortunately this complete passage does not occur in P. Tebtynis dem. 5939, but this papyrus does at least help to restore the first missing section  (P. Tebtynis dem. 5939,16).
- In the lacuna one could expect some other kind of tax or contribution. Could therefore the foreign name [...] ⸢...⸣*yꜣs* 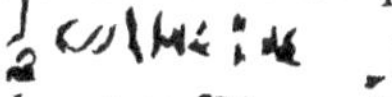 possibly be read as Ptolemy and indicate a tax raised by Ptolemy? In P. Tebtynis dem. 5939 only *mt pr-ꜥꜣ* is mentioned.

Lines 23–24

- *ỉw=n nḥm nꜣ ꜣḫ.w ntj ḥrj ẖr.r=k gꜣ mtw rmt nb pꜣ tꜣ nḥm=w ẖr.r=k*. The same phrase occurs in Martin, "Third-Century Demotic Land Lease," 248. There it continues *n nꜣ ss.w nty ḥrj m-sꜣ mt pr-ꜥꜣ ỉw=k (r) tj.t n=y ḥt*.

Line 24

- Cairo CG 30615,22: *[ỉw]=y nḥm nꜣ ꜣḫ.w ntj ḥrj [ẖr].r=k gꜣ ỉw=y tm tj.t wꜥb=w n=k ỉw=y tj.t n=k ḥt 3000*.
- *tj.t wꜥb*: CDD *W* (2009), 43–44 "to clear (property of legal encumbrances)."
- *gꜣ ⸢...⸣ mt ntj ḥrj*: None of the other leases seems to offer any parallels.

Lines 24–25

- *ḥt 1500 ntj ỉr krkr 5 ḥmt tbꜥ 24 r ḥt ḳt 2*: See Richard H. Pierce, "Notes on Obols and Agios in Demotic Papyri," *JEA* 51 (1965): 155. There are two payments, one half to party B and the other half to the state (Felber, *Demotische Ackerpachtverträge*, 186, calls it "Fiskalmult") for the offerings of the king. In other texts from Tebtynis, such as P. Cairo CG 30613, 30615, 30628,20, 30631, 31079 (*ỉw=y tj.t n=k ḥt 3000 ntj ỉr krkr 10 ḥmt tbꜥ 24 (ḳt 2) pꜣ bnr tj.t s n=y pr-ꜥꜣ ꜥn*), the penalty amounts to 3,000[31] deben, to be paid by the lessor to the lessee and the state. The amount is not split up into two equal halves as in P. Tebtynis dem. 5944. In leases from Tebtynis, first the lessee is mentioned as receiving the penalty reward and only then the king is mentioned, while in other leases it is the other way around, see P. Erbstreit 9,12, Felber, *Demotische Ackerpachtverträge*, 186–87.

---

29. In the sale contract P. Cairo CG 30612, 13–14 party B had to pay the taxes since the property went into his possession permanently and not only for a short time.

30. George R. Hughes, *Saite Demotic Land Leases*, SAOC 28 (Chicago: University of Chicago Press, 1952), 31–34 and George R. Hughes, "Notes on Demotic Egyptian Leases of Property," *JNES* 32 (1973): 152 first made this assumption, which was adopted by others (Manning, "Demotic Law," 848).

31. Three thousand deben seems to be the most common amount of penalty in Tebtynis, but also 6,000 deben can be found (P. Cairo CG 30254,21).

Line 25

- *nꜣ kll.w nꜣ wtn.w nꜣ ꜥby.w nꜣ pr-ꜥꜣ.w*: CDD G (2004), 60–61.

Line 26

- The badly preserved section is completed with the help of P. Tebtynis dem. 5939,19

Line 27

- - *Ỉr.t-Ḥr-r.r=w*: *DemNb*, 72–73.

Line 28

- At the end of the lease the parties A1 and A2 signed the document. While in line 9 party A2 is called *Pa-n-Ỉs.t mḥ-2* 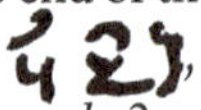, he himself signs as *Pa-n-Ỉs.t pꜣ ḫm* 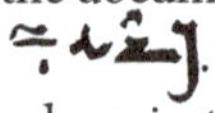. The scribe has a preference for calling the younger son *mḥ-2*, as seen in the designation of the Alexander priest *Ptlwmys pꜣ šr mḥ-2*.

Notation

Figure 3. Notation on verso of P. Tebtynis dem. 5944.

Pꜣ-tj-Ḥr-pꜣ-šr-n-Ỉs.t sꜣ Pꜣ-mꜣj	*Pꜣ-tj-Ḥr-pꜣ-šr-n-Ỉs.t* son of *Pꜣ-mꜣj*

Witness List

The eight witnesses signed the lease on the verso of the papyrus.

1. *Sbk-m-ḥb* (*sꜣ*) ⸢*Pa*⸣*-Ḥꜥpj*	*Sbk-m-ḥb* (son of) ⸢*Pa*⸣*-Ḥꜥpj*
2. *Sbk-*⸢*m-ḥ*⸣*b* (*sꜣ*) *Sbk-m-ḥb*	*Sbk-*⸢*m-ḥ*⸣*b* (son of) *Sbk-m-ḥb*
3. *Ḥr* (*sꜣ*) *Sbk-m-ḥb*	*Ḥr* (son of) *Sbk-m-ḥb*
4. *Py* (*sꜣ*) *Py*	*Py* (son of) *Py*
5. *Pa-n-Ỉs.t* (*sꜣ*) *Ḥr*	*Pa-n-Ỉs.t* (son of) *Ḥr*
6. *Pꜣ-*⸢*wn*⸣*(?)-nfr* (*sꜣ*) *ꜥnḫ-Ḥr*	*Pꜣ-*⸢*wn*⸣*(?)-nfr* (son of) *ꜥnḫ-Ḥr*
7. *Pa-*⸢*Ḥ*⸣*ꜥpj(?)* (*sꜣ*) *Pa-Ḥꜥpj*	*Pa-*⸢*Ḥ*⸣*ꜥpj(?)* (son of) *Pa-Ḥꜥpj*
8. ⸢*Ḥr*⸣*-wn-nfr(?)* (*sꜣ*) *Ḥr*	⸢*Ḥr*⸣*-wn-nfr(?)* (son of) *Ḥr*

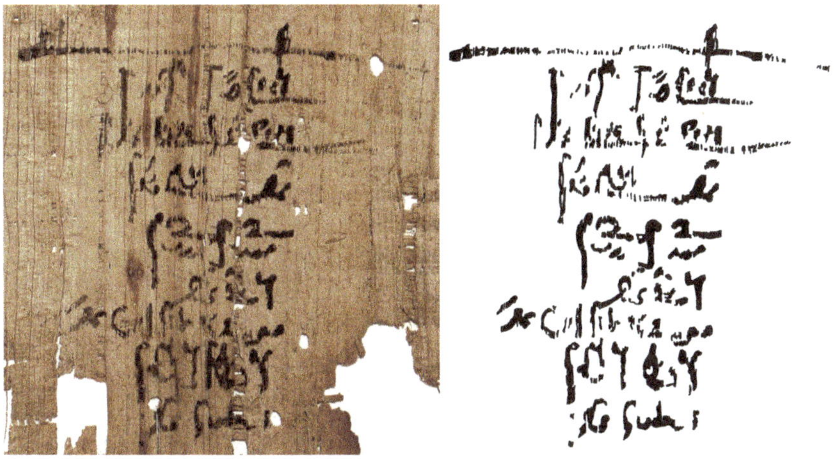

Figure 4. Witnesses' signatures on the verso of P. Tebtynis dem. 5944.

Papyri Cited

P. BM EA 10858	Martin, "Third-Century Demotic Land Lease," 247–58, pl. 16.
P. Cairo CG 30612	Spiegelberg, *Die demotischen Denkmäler II*.
P. Cairo CG 30613	Spiegelberg, *Die demotischen Denkmäler II*.
P. Cairo CG 30615	Spiegelberg, *Die demotischen Denkmäler II*.
P. Cairo CG 30617	Spiegelberg, *Die demotischen Denkmäler II*.
P. Cairo CG 30619	Spiegelberg, *Die demotischen Denkmäler II*.
P. Cairo CG 30621	Spiegelberg, *Die demotischen Denkmäler II*.
P. Cairo CG 30625	Andreas Winkler, "Collecting Income at Kerkesoucha Orous: New Light on P. Cairo CG 30625," *JEA* 96 (2010): 161–74.
P. Cairo CG 30628	Spiegelberg, *Die demotischen Denkmäler II*.
P. Cairo CG 30630	Spiegelberg, *Die demotischen Denkmäler II*.
	Andreas Winkler, "Swapping Lands at Tebtunis in the Ptolemaic Period: A Reassessment of P. Cairo CG 30630 and 30631," in *Acts of the Tenth International Congress of Demotic Studies: Leuven, 26–30 August 2008*, ed. M. Depauw and Y. Broux, OLA 231 (Leuven: Peeters, 2014), 331–90.
P. Cairo CG 30631	Spiegelberg, *Die demotischen Denkmäler II*.
	Winkler, "Swapping Lands at Tebtunis."
P. Cairo CG 30632	Spiegelberg, *Die demotischen Denkmäler II*.
P. Cairo CG 31079	Spiegelberg, *Die demotischen Denkmäler II*.
P. Cairo CG 31254	Spiegelberg, *Die demotischen Denkmäler II*.
P. Cairo JdE 34662	Erich Lüddeckens, "Eine wiederentdeckte demotische Zahlungsschrift: Nachtrag zu den 'Ägyptischen Eheverträgen,'" *AcOr* 25 (1960): 238–49.
P. Erbstreit	Vandorpe and Vleeming, *Erbstreit Papyri*.
P. Mil. Vogl. dem. Inv. 24	Edda Bresciani and Pieter Pestman, "Testi demotici nn. 1–7," in *Papiri della Università degli studi di Milano* 3, ed. A. Vogliano, T. Orlandi, C. Gallazzi, M. Vandoni, and D. Foraboschi (Milan: Cisalpino, 1965).
P. Tebtynis dem. 5939	Unpublished.

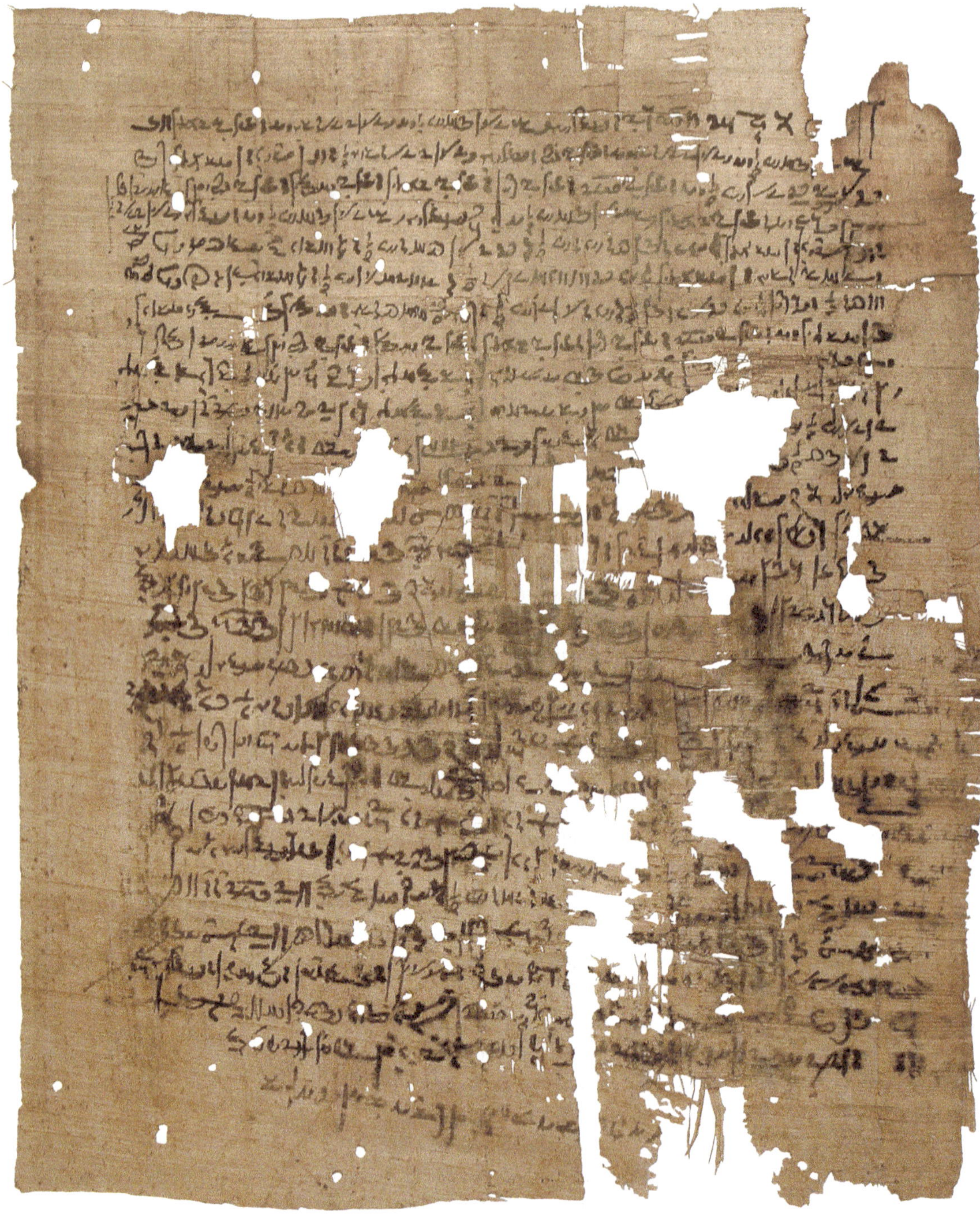

Figure 5. P. Tebtynis dem. 5944. Photograph by the author.

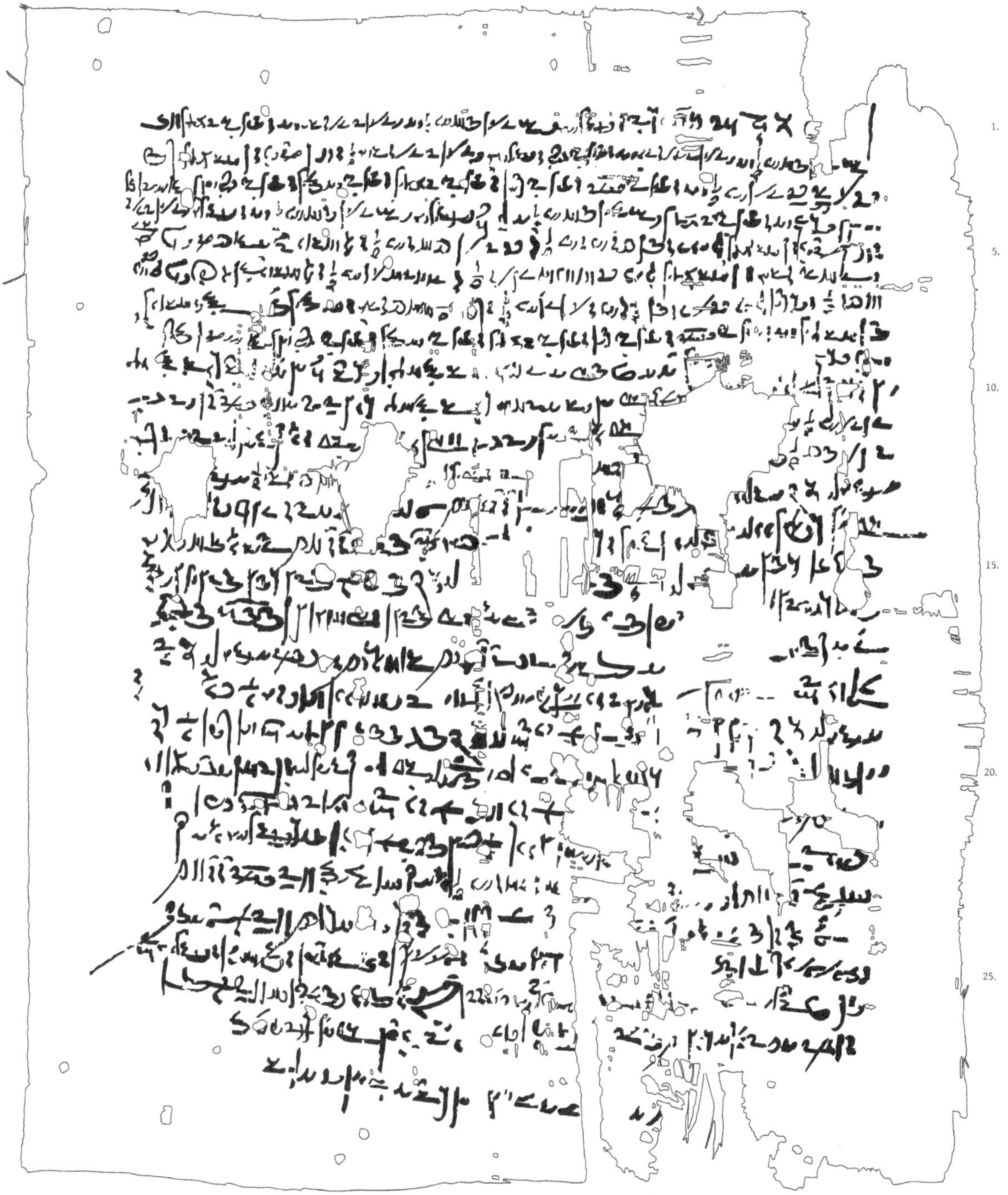

Figure 6. P. Tebtynis dem. 5944.

A Demotic Administrative Papyrus from the Tuna el-Gebel Necropolis (P. el-Ashmunein Magazine Inv. No. 1455-B)

Mahmoud Ebeid and Cary J. Martin

Richard Jasnow has the well-deserved reputation for editing and interpreting some of the most difficult and obscure Demotic texts. It is, therefore, with great pleasure that we offer to him this small enigmatic papyrus from the Tuna el-Gebel necropolis. In both reading and meaning this text still contains numerous problems, which we hope he will enjoy solving.

Between 1931 and 1952 Sami Gabra, together with other colleagues from Cairo University, including Alexander Badawy, Anwar Shoukry, Naguib Mikhail, and Zaki Aly, undertook the first official excavations of the University in the Tuna el-Gebel necropolis. A team from Munich University, led by Dieter Kessler, continued the work in 1979, and this was resumed in 1989 under the directorship of the Joint Mission of the Cairo and Munich Universities.[1] During these excavations, many Demotic texts were found in different parts of the necropolis. These texts were written on various materials: papyri, ostraca, limestone stelae, pottery and wooden coffins, limestone sarcophagi, wooden and limestone statuettes, bronzes and linen. Many of them are now stored in the galleries of the Tuna el-Gebel Magazine. Some have been moved to the el-Ashmunein Magazine, the Mallawi Museum, the Museum of the Faculty of Archaeology at Cairo University, the Museum of the Central Library at Cairo University, the Grand Egyptian Museum (GEM), and the Cairo Museum, while other pieces are scattered in various museums and private collections around the world.[2]

For their help during their leadership of the Joint Mission we would like to give our thanks to the late Prof. Dr. M. A. A. Nur el-Din, the former head of the Joint Mission of Cairo and Munich University in the Tuna el-Gebel necropolis, and to Prof. Dr. Dieter Kessler, head of the German side of the Mission. We are grateful to Dr. Mostafa Waziri, Secretary General of the Supreme Council of Antiquities in the Ministry of State for Antiquities, and the members of the Permanent Committee in the Ministry of State for Antiquities, who kindly reconfirmed the official permission to publish this papyrus. We are grateful to our colleagues in the Antiquities Department of the Inspectorate of Mallawi and el-Ashmunein, Mahmoud Salah, Ali el-Bakri, Fathi Awad, and Sayed Abd el-Malek. We would also like to thank our colleagues in the el-Ashmunein Magazine, Atta Makramalla, Director of the Magazine, Edwar Roshdy, Ahmed Anwar, Saber Tagy, Yaser el-Gebaly, and Ishak Yagoubi, for their help during the work in the Magazine. For the photographs of the papyrus, we thank Frank Steinmann (Leipzig University) and Patrick Brose (Munich University). The papyrus has recently been rephotographed by S. Abd el-Mohsen (Egyptian Museum Cairo). The authors are also grateful to Prof. Dr. Dieter Kessler and Prof. Dr. Günter Vittmann who kindly offered many helpful suggestions on the papyrus.

1. For résumés of the excavation work in the necropolis, see Günter Grimm, "Tuna el-Gebel 1913–1973: Eine Grabung des deutschen Architekten W. Honroth und neuere Untersuchungen in Hermopolis-West (Tanis Superior)," *MDAIK* 31 (1975): 221–36; Dieter Kessler, unter Mitarbeit von Partick Brose, Mahmoud Ebeid, Abd el-Halim Nur el-Din, and Frank Steinmann, *Die Oberbauten des Ibiotapheion von Tuna el-Gebel: Die Nachgrabungen der Joint Mission der Universitäten Kairo und München 1989–1996*, Tuna el-Gebel 3 (Haar: Patrick Brose, 2011), 1–7; Mélanie C. Flossmann-Schütze, "40 ans de recherches menées par l'Institut d'égyptologie de Munich à Touna el-Gebel: La nécropole animale et son association religieuse," *BSFE* 190 (2014): 9–22; Katrin Schlüter, *Die Kultstellen im Tierfriedhof von Tuna el-Gebel in frühptolemäischer Zeit: Der Gang C-B und die Kammer C-B-2*, Tuna el-Gebel 7 (Vaterstetten: Patrick Brose, 2017), 1:3–6, with earlier references.

2. Mahmoud Ebeid, "A New Demotic Private Letter from Hermopolis," *JEA* 98 (2012): 214nn3–5; Mahmoud Ebeid, "Seven

P. el-Ashmunein Magazine Inv. No. 1455-B

The papyrus (el-Ashmunein Magazine inv. no. 1455-B) published here belongs to the large collection of objects that were found during the excavations of Gabra and his successors. Gabra did not provide any detailed information on the papyri in his brief reports or in the register book of his excavations, *Fouilles de l'Université Égyptienne à Touna*

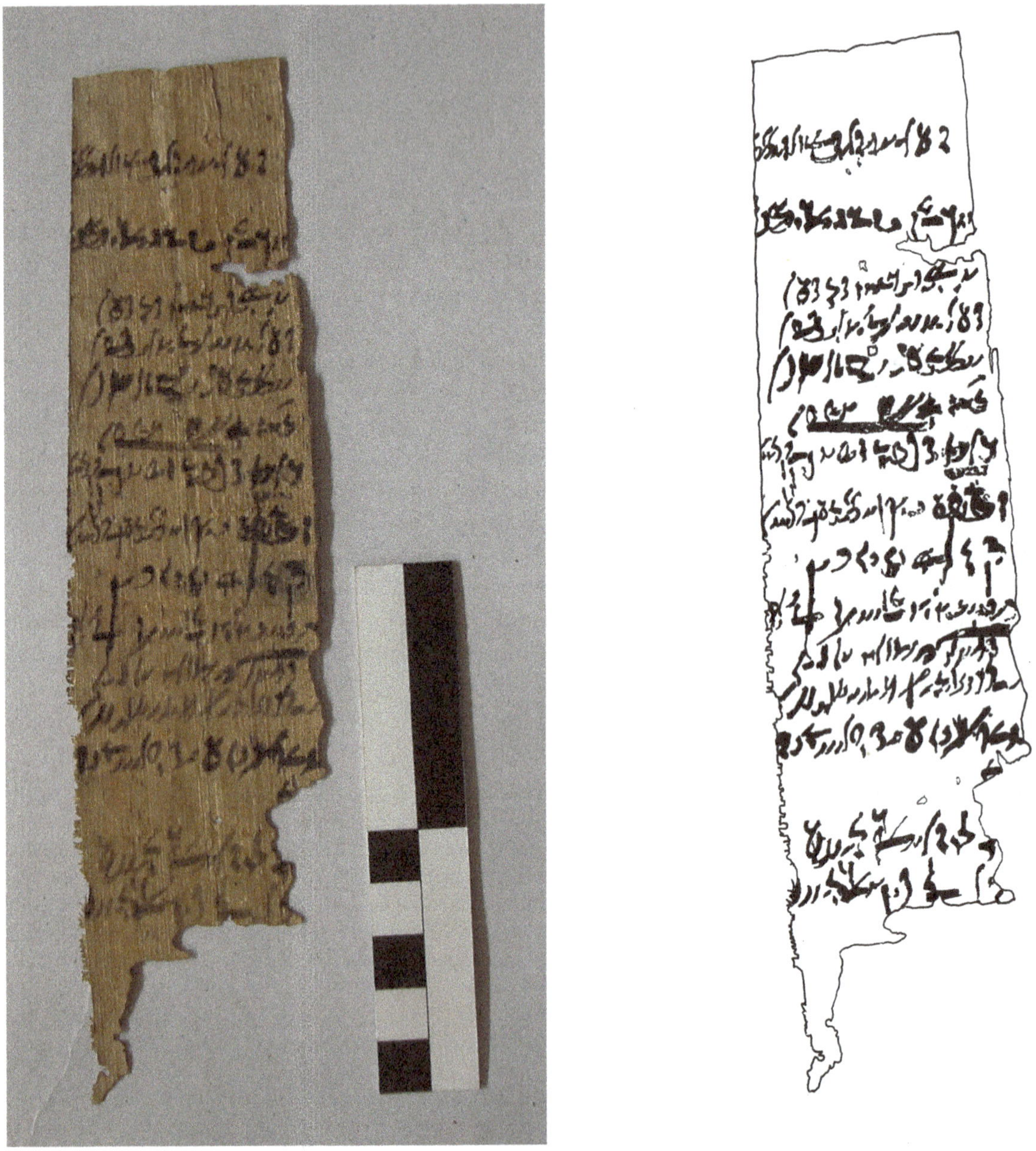

Figure 1. Front of P. el-Ashmunein Magazine Inv. No. 1455-B. Photograph © P. Brose.

Demotic Votive Inscriptions on Various Objects from the Tuna al-Gebel Necropolis," *ZÄS* 141 (2014): 41; Mahmoud Ebeid, "Two Early Demotic Letters from the Tuna al-Gebel Necropolis, P. Al-Ashmunein Magazine Inv. Nr. 1093 (P. Hormerti-1) and P. Mallawi Museum Inv. Nr. 486 C (P. Hormerti-4)," in *Sapientia felicitas: Festschrift für Günter Vittmann zum 29. Februar 2016*, ed. Sandra L. Lippert, Maren Schentuleit, and Martin A. Stadler, CENiM 14 (Montpellier: Équipe "*Égypte Nilotique et Méditerranéenne*," 2016), 123–24.

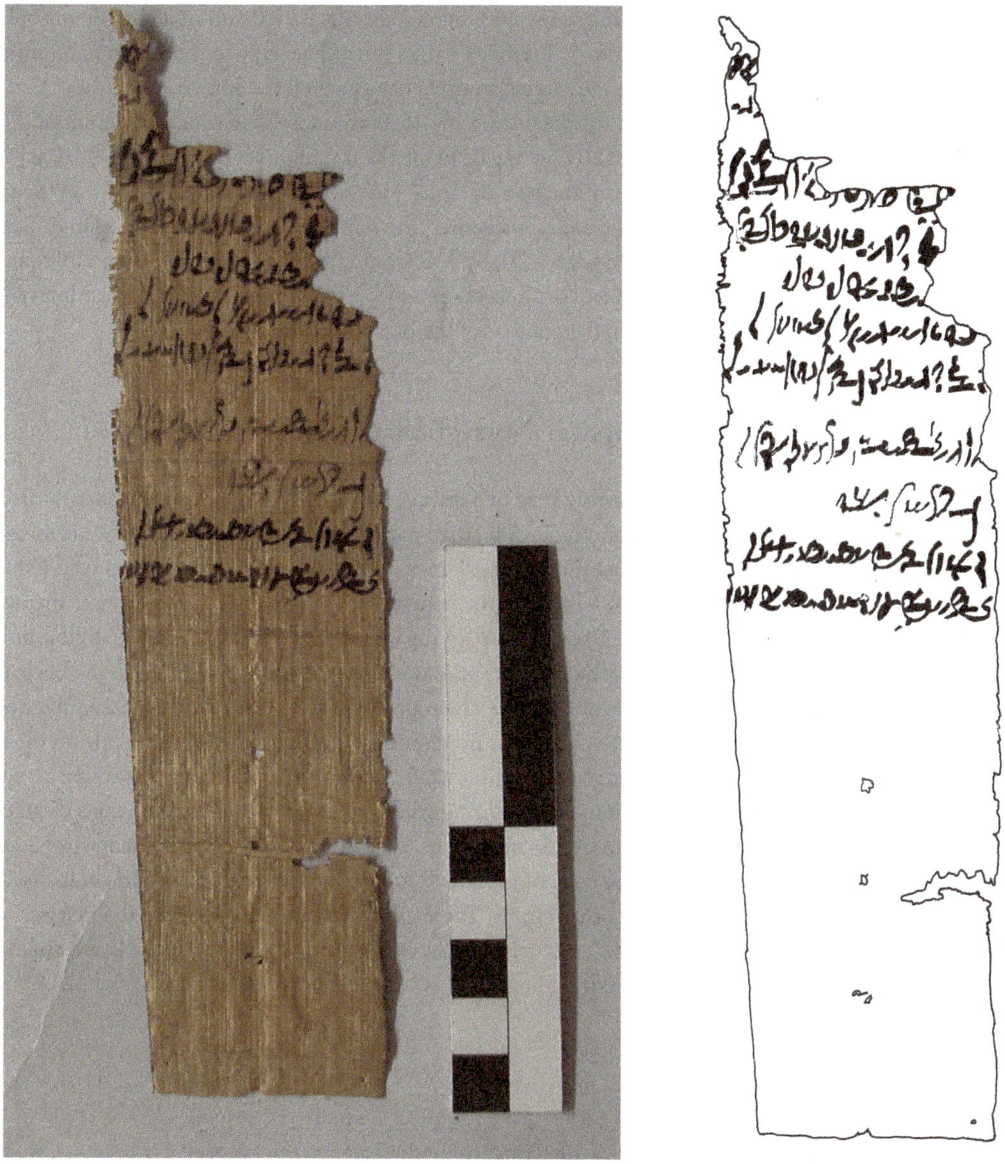

Figure 2. Back of P. el-Ashmunein Magazine Inv. No. 1455-B. Photograph © P. Brose.

el-Gebel (Hermopolis Ouest) (unpublished). Nor is there any information in the official register book of the el-Ashmunein Magazine. All we know is that some papyri were found in the subterranean galleries and in the area to the east of the galleries. This is mentioned in Gabra's register book,[3] his reports[4] and his *Adorateurs du Trismegiste.*[5] The papyrus

3. Sami Gabra, Register Book: *Fouilles de l'Université Égyptienne* à *Touna el-Gebel (Hermopolis Ouest)*, 80–81, 90–91, 152–53, 156–61, 174–75.

4. Sami Gabra, "Touna el-Gebel—Hermopolis ouest: Fouilles de l'Université Fouad; Campagne de 1939–1940," *CdÉ* 20 (1945): 93; Sami Gabra, "Tounah el Gebel: Fouilles de l'Université Fouad," *CdÉ* 22 (1947): 264; Sami Gabra, "Fouilles de l'Université Fouad Ier, à Hermopolis ouest Tounah el-Gabal et Meir, saison 1946–1947," *BFA* 9.1 (1947): 133.

5. Sami Gabra, *Chez les derniers adorateurs du Trismegiste: La necropole d'Hermopolis, Touna el Gebel (Souvenir d'un Archéologue)* (Cairo: General Egyptian Authority for Compilation and Publishing, 1971), 170.

is now kept in a glass frame in the el-Ashmunein Magazine with other Demotic papyri and small fragments of hieratic papyri. The glass frame as a whole bears the inventory number 1455 in the official register book. To differentiate our papyrus from the previously published text from the same frame, we have given it the Inv. No. 1455-B.[6]

A first reading of the papyrus was made from the original in the el-Ashmunein Magazine by Mahmoud Ebeid in the 2009 season. Ebeid returned to the papyrus in 2017 when he made the facsimile of the text. In 2018, Cary Martin checked the old transliteration and translation from the photographs. He provided some suggestions on the content and many new readings and translations. In addition, he presented the papyrus at the Demotic Summer School in Munich (Demotische Sommerschule 27. bis 30. August 2018). We would like to thank Friedhelm Hoffmann, Joachim F. Quack, and Mélanie C. Flossmann-Schütze for their comments at the conference. Adrienn Almásy-Martin also kindly added fruitful ideas and comments on the content of the papyrus.

Physical Description

Dimensions: H. 20.5 cm × W. 5.0 cm. This is a narrow strip of papyrus. It is torn at the bottom and there is also some damage on the lower right-hand side (as seen from the Front), with partial loss of text. There are sixteen lines of text on the Front (↔), written parallel to the fibers, but further short lines may be missing at the bottom where the papyrus is badly torn at the right-hand side. It is also possible that the papyrus was originally much longer, as the height of a papyrus roll would be considerably greater than 20 cm.[7] The papyrus was turned over, from bottom to top, and there are x+11 lines of text on the Back (↕). Because of the damage, little remains of the first two lines on the Back and the next six have suffered some loss of text. On the Front there is a margin of 1.5 cm at the top and, assuming no text is missing on the right-hand side, 3.5 cm at the bottom. There is no margin on the right-hand side, while on the left the scribe has squashed the writing right up to the edge of the papyrus. In fact, it looks as though the scribe actually cut through some of the signs at the edge after he had finished writing (the edge is very straight, showing a clean cut and no damage). On the Back there is a bottom margin of 9.5 cm, but no side margins. Here also, the final word on the last line looks as though it had continued just past the edge of the sheet, suggesting that the scribe had cut it after he had finished writing. The text appears to be divided into sections. There are spaces of 1 cm between the first and second lines and between the second and third. Line 14 is a very short line. On the Back, there is a space between lines x+7 and x+8. Lines x+5 and x+9 are short. The handwriting in general is large, neat, and practiced.

Provenance

Although, as mentioned above, there is no information concerning the original find-spot of the papyrus, we think it likely that it may have come from the area of the administrative buildings (the "tower houses") to the east of the animal galleries; see the discussion in the Commentary below. This is based on the content of the text and the similarity with the handwriting of other Demotic documents from the same area.[8]

6. Ebeid, "New Demotic Private Letter," 211n1.

7. See the discussion by Mark Depauw, "The Royal Format of Early Ptolemaic Demotic Papyri," in *Acts of the Seventh International Conference of Demotic Studies, Copenhagen, 23–27 August 1999*, ed. Kim Ryholt, CNIP 27 (Copenhagen: Museum Tusculanum Press, 2002), 85–100.

8. This was to be the subject of a paper that Ebeid was preparing at the time of his death.

Date

Although the text is not dated, the hand is certainly Ptolemaic. On the basis of the handwriting and the suggested provenance of the piece, a date in the Early or Middle Ptolemaic period (late fourth to early second century BCE) seems likely. A comparison with other papyri found in the area of the tower buildings, especially the famous Legal and Mathematical Papyrus from Hermopolis (P. Mattha),[9] the unpublished Family Archive of *Ḏd-ḥr* son of *Ḥr*,[10] and P. el-Ashmunein Magazine Inv. No. 1455, would also support this date.[11]

The Text

Front

	Transliteration	Translation
1	*nꜣ šs.w / ḥbs.w n Pꜣ-hb r di͗.t di͗=w s (r) pꜣ rḫṱ (n)*	The linen / cloth of The Ibis to have it given (to) the washerman (at)
	Space	
2	*pꜣ sḫn n tꜣ s.t (n) sḫt*	the table in the place of weaving.
	Space	
3	*Pꜣy-kꜣ sꜣ Pa-nfr (?) di͗.t i͗r=f nꜣ šs.w / ḥbs.w*	Pikos son of Panouphis (?) to cause that he makes the linen / cloth.
4	*nꜣ šs.w / ḥbs.w n Pꜣ-Ḥr sꜣ Ṯꜣy-n.i͗m=w r.ḏbꜥ=w*	The linen / cloth of Pauris son of Samaus, which has been sealed.
5	*pꜣ rḫṱ r . . . . . .*	The washerman . . . . . .
6	*Ḏd-ḥr <sꜣ> Ḳrr* (space) *ḥt 8 (ḳd.t) 9 wp-st*	Teos <son of> Krouris: silver, 8 deben 9 (kite). Specification:
7	*swn tꜣ šnt (r) ṯꜣy.ṱ=w I͗nḥy (?)*	price of the cloak / the linen piece (in order) to take them (to) Inhy (?);
8	*tꜣ tm nty n-tr.t pꜣ rḫṱ I͗nḥy (?)*	the mat which is in the hand of the washerman Inhy (?);
9	*wꜥ ḫm ꜥꜥm*	a small (quantity) of *ꜥꜥm*-plant.

9. The Front was originally published by Girgis Mattha and George R. Hughes, *The Demotic Legal Code of Hermopolis West*, BdÉ 45 (Cairo: Institut français d'archéologie orientale, 1975). The whole papyrus, front and back, has recently been reedited by Birgit Jordan, *Die demotischen Wissenstexte (Recht und Mathematik) des pMattha*, Tuna el-Gebel 5 (Vaterstetten: Patrick Brose, 2015), with new color photographs. See pp. 33–45 for a detailed discussion of the date of the text, which is generally accepted to be the third century BCE.

10. For further details on this family archive from the second century BCE, see Erich Lüddeckens, "Ein demotischer Urkundenfund in Tuna el-Gebel mit einer genealogischen Skizze," in *Akten des 13. Internationalen Papyrologenkongresses, Marburg/Lahn, 2.–6. August 1971*, ed. Emil Kiessling and Hans-Albert Rupprecht, MBPF 66 (München: Beck, 1974), 235–39; Erich Lüddeckens, "Papyri, Demotische, Kairo, aus der äg. Grabung in Tuna el-Gebel," *LÄ* 4:831; Erich Lüddeckens, "Urkundenarchive," *LÄ* 6:881; Adel Farid, "Two Demotic Annuity Contracts," in *Studies in Honor of A. Radwan*, ed. Khaled A. Daoud, Shafia Bedier, and Sawsan Abd el-Fatah, CASAE 34/I (Cairo: Supreme Council of Antiquities, 2005), 323–46; Adel Farid, "A Demotic Sale Contract of the Whole Property," in *The Horizon: Studies in Egyptology in Honour of M. A. Nur el-Din (10–12 April 2007)*, ed. Basem Samir El-Sharkawy (Cairo: Supreme Council of Antiquities, 2009), 3:261–76; Mahmoud Labib El-Bokl, "Miscellanies Demotic and Greek Documents from Tuna el-Gebel Necropolis: Philological, Palaeographical and Cultural Study" (PhD diss., Helwan University, 2017), 2–8.

11. Ebeid, "New Demotic Private Letter," 211–23. Some Demotic inscriptions written on the pottery and wooden coffins and limestone sarcophagi (the ibis inscriptions) found in the Ptolemaic galleries *in situ* are consistent with this date.

10	*hm.t ꜥḳ ỉt bny.w ṯꜣy=w s*	Transport (of) bread, barley, (and) dates. They were taken
11	*[r] pr-ḥḏ (n) Hry=w <sꜣ> Pꜣ-šr-tꜣ-ỉḥ.t*	[to] (the) storeroom (of) Herieus <son of> Psentaes.
12	*Stꜣ.ṱ=w-wty <sꜣ> Pa-sy sꜣ Ḥr*	Stoetis <son of> Pasis son of Horos is
13	*[pꜣ] ⸢nty⸣ glꜥ ⸢r dỉ.t⸣ ḥwy<=w> ⸢s⸣ (?)*	[the] one who wraps to cause that <they> apply it
14	*[r] ⸢bnr⸣*	outside (?)
	Space	
15	*[Pꜣ]-⸢šr⸣-ta-Ỉmn pꜣ sẖṱ (n)*	[P]sentamounis, the weaver (of)
16	*[nꜣ] šs.w / ḥbs.w (n) rn (n) <nꜣ> rmt(.w) (n) pꜣ sẖṱ*	[the] linen / cloth, (in the) name (of) <the> people (of) the weaver.

Back

x+1	[. . . . .] ⸢. .⸣	[. . . . .] . .
x+2	[. . . . . *ḳnḥ*](*.t*)	[. . . . . chap]el.
x+3	*[nꜣ nt]r.w nty ỉw bw-ỉr-tw=w ṯꜣy.ṱ=w*	[The go]ds which they have not yet taken
x+4	*[r tꜣ ḳn]ḥ(.t) nty ỉ.ỉr-ḥr nꜣ ntr.w*	[to the] chapel, which is in front of the gods
x+5	*[n pꜣ š]ym ỉmnt mḥt*	[in the] north-west passage
x+6	*r-ḏbꜣ.ṱ(=w) r ḥḏ (ḳd.t) 2 wp-st Gm=w-Ḥp (ḳd.t) 1.t*	concerning them, makes 2 silver (kite). Specification: Komoapis, 1 (kite);
x+7	*tꜣ knḥ(.t) (n) Ḥr-Ḥp 1.t*	the chapel (of) Horhap . . . . ., 1 (kite).
	Space	
x+8	*[pꜣ] ꜥ.wy (n) ỉr wpy(.t) (n) Ỉs.t-m-ḥꜣ.t ta Ḏḥwty-ms*	[The] place (of) carrying out work (for) Esemhat daughter of Thotmosis,
x+9	*Ỉnḥy (?) ḳd.t 2 1/2*	Inhy (?), kite 2 1/2;
x+10	*dỉ.t dỉ=w ꜥn pꜣ šym (n) Ỉꜥḥ-ms*	(for) causing that they cause the passage (of) Amosis to be attractive;
x+11	*ỉr wpy(.t) (n) gḏ n pꜣ šym ỉmnt mḥt*	(for) carrying out the plastering in the north-west passage.

Textual Notes

Front

Line 1

– When written only with the cloth determinative-sign, the signs 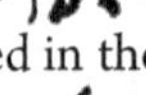 could be read as either *nꜣ ḥbs.w*, "the cloth," or *nꜣ šs.w*, "the linen."[12] Both words are regularly attested in the embalming texts, although *šs* usually appears as *šs-nsw*, "king's linen," "byssus;"[13] see lines 3  and 4  (there is also a fragmentary writing in line 16).

12. See CDD *Ḥ* (2009), 95–97; *Š* (2010), 206; *DG*, 300–301, 522.

13. See Rene L. Vos, *The Apis Embalming Ritual: P. Vindob. 3873*, OLA 50 (Leuven: Peeters, 1993), 372–73 no. 375, 398–99 no. 534; Susanne Töpfer, *Das Balsamierungsritual: Eine (Neu-)Edition der Textkomposition Balsamierungsritual (pBoulaq 3, pLouvre 5158, pDurham 1983.11 + pSt. Petersburg 18128)*, SSR 13 (Wiesbaden: Harrassowitz, 2015), 384.

- *pꜣ hb*: The *b* is very abbreviated, but similar writings of the word as a personal name are plentiful.[14] Given the context *pꜣ hb* must be the Ibis god here, rather than the name of a person. This linen/cloth of the ibis would have been used for wrapping not only the mummified sacred ibis but also the coffins and sarcophagi with the mummified sacred animals inside, parts of the sacred animals such as the feathers and the eggs and statues and statuettes of the divinities that were stored in the subterranean galleries.[15] The linen/cloth could also be deployed for wrapping the papyrus rolls[16] and for sealing pottery coffins with a thin layer of gypsum.[17] In addition, painted linen cloth was used for closing the cult shrines of the mummified sacred ibises and baboons in the animal galleries.[18] During Gabra's excavation in the galleries, some pottery coffins with a narrow rim were found containing only cloth bundles.[19]
- The following group must be *di.t di=w*, followed by a very thin third person singular dependent pronoun (which is also required by the grammar).
- The title  *pꜣ rḫṯ*, "the washerman," is damaged at the end here, but there are clear writings in lines 5  and 8 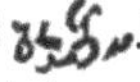.[20] The definite article *pꜣ* is very squashed between the *s* and the *rḫt*. The title appears frequently in the ibis inscriptions.[21] The duties of the washerman included the fabrication of the cloth for the deceased (in our text this would also mean the sacred animals).[22]

Line 2

- *pꜣ sḫn* presumably is a "table" here rather than the extended meaning "the bank." The word appears in both masculine and feminine forms in Demotic.[23] While our translation assumes that "the table" is the indirect object of the verb in the preceding line, the noticeable space between the two lines could argue for a translation as separate sentences.
- 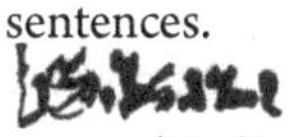 *tꜣ s.t (n) sḫt*: "the place (of) weaving." For the reading of *sḫt*, see the clearer writings (with the strong *ṯ*) in lines 15 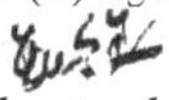 and 16 .[24] The term will refer to a place that was used for preparing the wrappings for the sacred animals. To date, we have no information on its precise location in the necropolis, but it is highly probable that there was a central administration and production area for linen somewhere near the *tar-*

14. *DemNb* I. 1, 202–3. The alternative would be to read it as a writing of the personal name *Pꜣ-šr-Ḏḥwty*, with the lower horizontal/oblique stroke of *Ḏḥwty* touching the *šr* sign.

15. Naguib Mikhail, "The Cult of Thoth in Hermopolis West in the Saite Period and the Roman Period" (PhD diss., Cairo University, 1943), 190–91 (in Arabic); Angela von den Driesch, Dieter Kessler, Frank Steinmann, Véronique Berteaux, and Joris Peters, "Mummified, Deified and Buried at Hermopolis Magna: The Sacred Birds from Tuna el-Gebel, Middle Egypt," *ÄgLev* 15 (2005): 227–28; Dieter Kessler, "Einwickeln und unterirdische Ablage von Bronzen im Tierfriedhof von Tuna el-Gebel," in *"Zur Zierde gereicht…": Festschrift für Bettina Schmitz zum 60. Geburtstag am 24. Juli 2008*, ed. Antje Spiekermann, HÄB 50 (Hildesheim: Gerstenberg, 2008), 153–63.

16. See Zaki Aly, "Egypt's Contribution towards the Promotion of Papyrological Studies," in *Proceedings of the IX International Congress of Papyrology, Oslo, 19th–22nd August, 1958*, ed. Leiv Amundsen and Vegard Skånland (Oslo: Norwegian Universities Press, 1961), 329–30.

17. Driesch et al., "Mummified, Deified and Buried," 208–9; Ebeid, "Seven Demotic Votive Inscriptions," 51–53.

18. Mikhail, "The Cult of Thoth," 149–50; for further details, see Schlüter, *Die Kultstellen im Tierfriedhof*, 1:244–320.

19. Mikhail, "The Cult of Thoth," 204.

20. For other writings of the title, see CDD *R* (2001), 59–62.

21. Mahmoud Ebeid, *Demotic Inscriptions from the Subterranean Galleries of the Sacred Animals in the Tuna al-Gebel Necropolis I*, Tuna el-Gebel 10 (Vaterstetten: Patrick Brose, 2021).

22. Mark Smith, *Papyrus Harkness (MMA 31.9.7)* (Oxford: Griffith Institute, 2005), 103, line 9 (C) note.

23. CDD *S* (2013), 386, for references.

24. For the writing of *sḫt*, see CDD *S* (2013), 392–94.

icheion, "the mummification place," which will not have been far away from the burial place.[25] The title of weavers is, incidentally, also found connected to the Buchis bull at Hermonthis.[26]

Line 3

- *Pa-nfr* (?): The name appears to be written without the divine determinative, which is unusual but not unprecedented.[27]
- The reading of the group  *dỉ.t ỉr=f* is certain, although the typical writing of the group *ỉr=f* in the necropolis is usually with a long tail of the *=f* at the end.

Line 4

- *Pꜣ-Ḥr sꜣ Ṯꜣy-n.ỉm=w*: The proper name *Pꜣ-Ḥr* is found as a variant writing of *Pa-Ḥr*.[28] The oblique upper stroke of the *Ḥr* has run into the *sꜣ* sign. For another example of *Pꜣ-Ḥr* in the necropolis, cf. the pottery coffin TG 3695 (no. 246. II) .[29]
- Reading the group  *r ḏbꜥ=w*, "which has been sealed," as a relative clause or "in order to seal them,"[30] makes better sense than interpreting the group as a proper name, that is, *sꜣ NN*.[31]

Line 5

- The writing at the end of the line is rather blotchy and no plausible reading suggests itself. The first group looks like the verb *wḏꜣ*, but it is difficult to understand the meaning.[32] A personal name, *Wḏꜣ=f*, could be considered,[33] but what precedes it looks like the preposition or infinitival subordinator *r*, which would rule out this possibility. The final group might be a writing of *Ḥr*, with an elaborate oblique stroke that descends below the line, but equally a name does not really work here either and other interpretations should be considered (e.g., *n.ỉm=w*).

Line 7

- *swn*: There appears to be a horizontal stroke beneath *swn*, which is difficult to explain. While the possessive of *swn* is written with the suffix pronoun, the stroke here could only be the second person singular *=k*, and this makes no sense at all. Consequently, we can only suggest that it should be seen as extraneous.
- (*r*) *ṯꜣy.ṯ=w*: The reading is uncertain and, as Vittmann pointed out, we would not expect the strong *ṯ* before the suffix pronoun in a relative clause.[34] What we take to be *ṯ=w* looks more like a writing of the definite article *pꜣ*, but this makes the reading of the following enigmatic group even more complicated.
- The word 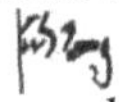 is a real crux. It also appears in lines 8 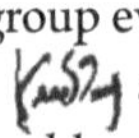 and Back, x+9 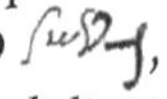, the latter being the clearest writing. It may be a personal name, but the reading is problematic. One possibility is to take the first three signs as the uniliteral signs *ỉ*, *n*, and *ḥ*, followed by the divine determinative and then the group *ỉw*, "to come." However, this requires the first part to be a theonym for which there is no obvious candidate.[35] Equally problematic

25. The small room above the Ptolemaic entrance of the galleries, which was mistakenly called "*atelier d'embaumement*" by Sami Gabra, "Fouilles de l'Université 'Fouad el Awal' à Touna el-Gebel (Hermopolis ouest)," *ASAE* 39 (1939): 491, was in fact used for the opening of the mouth ritual; see Kessler et al., *Die Oberbauten des Ibiotapheion*, 90–96.

26. O. Bucheum no. 30, no. 67; Robert Mond and Oliver H. Myers, *The Bucheum*, EES EM 41 (London: Oxford University Press, 1934), 2:57–63, 64.

27. *DemNb* I. 1, 388 ex. 1, 3, 5, 21, 26, 27.

28. *DemNb* I. 1, 400 ex. 5.

29. Ebeid, *Demotic Inscriptions*, 257–58.

30. For sealing the packages with linen and clothes, see Peter Kaplony, "Siegelung," *LÄ* 5:933–37, especially 934. We owe the reading and the reference to Günter Vittmann (pers. comm., June 13, 2019).

31. For the writing of *ḏbꜥ*, "to seal," see CDD *Ḏ* (2001), 30.

32. Neither the verb "to be sound," "healthy" (*DG*, 108) or hieroglyphic "to go," "proceed" (*Wb.* I:403), makes sense in the context.

33. The name can be written both with and without the divine determinative; see *DemNb* I. 1, 130, I. 3, *Korrekturen und Nachträge*, 141.

34. Pers. comm., 26 October 2018.

35. There is a deity whose name appears to be written *Ỉnḥ* in P. Cairo 31169, Ft V, 15, but the reading is uncertain and, even if correct,

is the interpretation of the central vertical sign as the divine determinative. On the Back, line x+9, this would be acceptable, but in the first two writings on the Front it looks exactly like the letter *ḥ* and is not at all similar to the divine sign (see the writing of this, for example, in *Pꜣ-hb* in line 1). If it is the letter *ḥ*, then this automatically rules out *-iw* for what follows. For these final strokes a reading as the letter *y* would also be quite acceptable, although how to interpret the determinative is not as obvious. It looks like the fallen warrior in the writings on the Front, but on the Back this is less convincing. Equally, the writing on the Back has a slight angle to it, unlike the divine determinative in other personal names in the text. Another problem with reading the first part as three uniliterals is that we would expect the *ỉn*-group rather than just the separate signs *ỉ* and *n*.[36] An alternative approach, however, would be to take the second and third signs together as a writing of the *nḥ* group. Identical writings of this can be found, for example, in *nḥb.t*, "neck,"[37] and *nḥḥ*, "eternity."[38] If this possibility is correct, then the following *ḥ* sign could be either a phonetic complement as, for example, in writings of *nḥb.t*, "neck," or a separate letter. On balance, we think the former is the more likely, and would, therefore, suggest, with all reservation, reading the word as *Ỉnḥy*. While this might give us a satisfactory reading, the meaning still remains an enigma. There is a name *Ỉnḥ.t* in RPN but this is only attested in the Middle Kingdom and can hardly be taken as a valid comparison. Another problem we have with taking the word as a personal name, however, is in line 8, where it is preceded by *pꜣ rḫt*, "the washerman." In Demotic, if a title precedes a personal name, then no article is written; if it follows the personal name, then the article is written.[39] Here the article is clearly written before the occupational title. But if it is not a personal name, then what is it? A topographical name seems improbable because it lacks the appropriate determinative. Equally, while a place-name would work in lines 7 and 8, the context of Back line x+9 seems to require a personal name.

Line 8

-  *tꜣ tm*: "the mat."[40] The scribe had too much ink on his brush and the word is very blotchy. It is written with two determinatives—the usual plant sign and the bundle of cloth.

Line 9

- 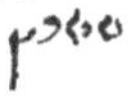 *ꜥꜥm*: there is a word *ꜥꜥꜣm* that is attested as a medicinal plant but with uncertain meaning.[41] As such its presence here would be rather unexpected, but the reading *ꜥꜥm*, with the plant determinative, is clear.[42] Alternatively, this may be a Demotic writing of the hieroglyphic word  *ꜥꜣmw.t*, "field

it differs from our word in that it has the *ỉn* group after the *Ỉ*; see Christian Leitz, ed., *Lexikon der ägyptischen Götter und Götterbezeichnungen*, OLA 110 (Leuven: Peeters, 2002), 1:400.

36. As for example in the words listed in *DG*, 34–35.

37. *DG*, 223.

38. *DG*, 224, in particular the first four Roman writings.

39. As noted by Kurt Sethe, *Demotische Urkunden zum ägyptischen Bürgschaftsrechte vorzüglich der Ptolemäerzeit*, AAWL 32 (Leipzig: Teubner, 1920), 7 n. § 5 a.

40. CDD *T* (2012), 196–97.

41. Hildegard von Deines and Hermann Grapow, *Wörterbuch der ägyptischen Drogennamen,* Grundriß der Medizin der alten Ägypter 6 (Berlin: Akademie-Verlag, 1959), 91–94; Renate Germer, *Handbuch der altägyptischen Heilpflanzen*, Philippika 21 (Wiesbaden: Harrassowitz, 2008), 38–39 (*ꜥꜣmw* / *ꜥꜥm*).

42. It is quite rare in Demotic texts. To the examples in the CDD *ꜥ* (2003), 43–44, can be added two ostraca: one from Abydos, published by Richard Jasnow and Mary-Ann Pouls Wegner, "Demotic Ostraca from North Abydos," *Enchoria* 30 (2006–2007): 49–50, and the other possibly from Kus, for which see Sten V. Wångstedt, "Demotische Ostraka: Varia II," *OrSuec* 30 (1981): 20–21 (corrections to the reading by Vittmann in TLA).

plant,"[43] which could have been a food source for animals or the priests as Kessler has pointed out.[44] During Gabra's excavations in the galleries, pottery coffins were found containing several plants such as olives, olive leaves, dum-palm fruits, sycamore, and wheat,[45] so it may also have had a religious purpose.

Line 10

- The reading of *hm.t*, "freight," "cargo," "freight / transport charges," is certain, but we would expect the definite article *tꜣ*, which may have been lost in the torn edge of the papyrus. We take the final sign to be a rather flattened letter *.t*.[46]
- *ꜥḳ it*: The first of these two words must be of *ꜥḳ*, "bread," given how the beginning is written.[47] Were it not for this, we would also be inclined to read the second  as *ꜥḳ*, as this writing is very similar to other examples of the word.[48] However, as this has to be excluded, we have to consider whether what is written should be read *it* or *bd.t*. These two words are often hard to differentiate, but the fact that here there is a dot with an oblique stroke above it makes us inclined to prefer *it*, "barley," rather than *bd.t*, "emmer," which is usually written with two oblique strokes.[49]

Line 11

- *pr-ḥḏ*: Given the context, the meaning here must be the "storehouse/storeroom" of Herieus rather than "treasury."[50] This would have been used for the storage of grain and other foodstuffs; see the Commentary below. Herieus will have been the official responsible for the distribution of the foodstuffs to the priests.

Line 12

- *Stꜣ.ṯ=w-wty*: The beginning of the name is slightly damaged, but the reading is supported by the clear *wty* at the end. It is not certain whether the sign immediately preceding the *wty* should be interpreted as *tꜣ* or *=w*, but, as the definite article is regularly omitted, we assume that it is not written here.[51]
- *Pa-sy*: The reading is by no means certain, but because of the following *sꜣ Ḥr* it must be a personal name, even though this means that we then have the name of the grandfather. Mention of the names of both father and grandfather is unexpected in such a document.[52]

---

43. *Wb.* I:168, 4; Rainer Hannig, *Ägyptisches Wörterbuch, Vol. 2: Mittleres Reich und Zweite Zwischenzeit*, Hannig-Lexica 5, Kulturgeschichte der antiken Welt 112 (Mainz: von Zabern, 2006), 487. The Demotic word is masculine, but there are other cases of changes of gender between hieroglyphs and later stages of the language; see Sethe, *Demotische Urkunden zum ägyptischen Bürgschaftsrechte*, 216 n. § 18 b.

44. Pers. comm., 7 May 2019.

45. Mikhail, "The Cult of Thoth," 204–5.

46. See the writings in CDD *H* (2001), 52–55.

47. For the variations in the writing of *ꜥḳ*, see Michel Malinine, "Graphies démotiques du mot *ꜥḳ* 'nourriture, ration', etc.," *JEA* 35 (1949): 150–52; Sven P. Vleeming, *The Gooseherds of Hou (Pap. Hou): A Dossier Relating to Various Agricultural Affairs from Provincial Egypt of the Early Fifth Century B.C.*, StudDem 3 (Leuven: Peeters, 1991), 204 § 37. For another example from Tuna el-Gebel, albeit in a slightly different writing, see Mahmoud Ebeid, "A Ptolemaic Demotic Account of Bread on an Ostracon (O. Al-Ashmunein Magazine Inv. Nr. 1130)," *ASAE* 84 (2010): 160 n. e.

48. See, e.g., the writing in Ank A. den Brinker, Brian P. Muhs, and Sven P. Vleeming, *A* Berichtigungsliste *of Demotic Documents*, StudDem 7-B (Leuven: Peeters, 2005), 816 § 20; Sven P. Vleeming, "Some Notes on the Artabe in Pathyris," *Enchoria* 9 (1979): 96.

49. For identical writings of *it*, see Michel Malinine, "Un prêt des céréales à l'époque de Darius I (Pap. dém. Strasbourg no 4)," *KÊMI* 11 (1950): 12 no. 27e; Vleeming, "Some Notes on the Artabe," 93 B3, 95 I.

50. For the range of meanings, see Günter Vittmann, *Der demotische Papyrus Rylands 9*, ÄAT 38 (Wiesbaden: Harrassowitz, 1998), 2:468–69.

51. See the examples in *DemNb* I. 3, 945–46.

52. Three generations are, however, attested in some other texts from the necropolis; e.g., O. el-Ashmunein Inv. No. 1129 col. II. 5, for which, see Mahmoud Ebeid, "Two Demotic Ostraca from al-Ashmunein Magazine," *BIFAO* 109 (2009): 98–101; Ebeid, *Ibis Inscriptions*, for example, nos. 160.I, 207.I, 214, 272, 281.

Line 13

- [*pꜣ*] ⸢*nty*⸣: The reading of this line is problematic. At the Demotic Summer School, it was suggested that the sign preceding *glʿ.ṯ-s* should be read *pꜣy* and that we have here a writing of the article with prothetic *r*, introducing a relative clause. While paleographically this is quite acceptable, grammatically it presents us with a problem, as the subject of the clause in the line above is Stoetis and we would therefore expect *pꜣ i.ir glʿ*. The past tense relative form *pꜣy.glʿ* (= *pꜣ r.glʿ*) requires the subject pronoun or noun to follow the verb. Either we assume that the scribe intended to write the past participle *pꜣy.ir glʿ* (*pꜣ i.ir-glʿ*), "Stoetis … is the one who wrapped," or we have to reconsider the reading. The beginning of the line is slightly torn, but the sign immediately preceding *glʿ* might be a writing of *nty*, with a small *pꜣ* missing in the lacuna (the edge of *pꜣ* is just visible ligatured with the *nty*). Vittmann, however, said that he found the reading *nty* rather unlikely, but no alternative explanation offers itself.
- *glʿ*: Note the use of *glʿ* (written *gyl*) in the Demotic Embalmers' Agreement, line 20, *pꜣ rmt nty iw=f gyl*.[53] We wanted to read this *glʿ.ṯ=s*, but Vittmann pointed out that the *.ṯ=s* is quite different from the writing later in the line. An alternative is *r di.t*, which is paleographically quite acceptable but presents a problem with the grammar of the rest of the line. We would expect *ḥwy=w s*, but what is written looks like *ḥwy.ṯ=s*. Perhaps we should read the final signs as a writing of *s* rather than *.ṯ=s* (rather than seeing *.ṯ=s* as in error for *s*).
- 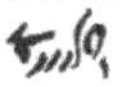 *ḥwy*: Here with the meaning "to apply" an ointment; see the Apis Embalming Ritual Text (P. Vindob. 3873, vo. II a. 10; II b. 7).[54] It is also found with the meaning of "to put" in connection with mummy-bandages (London-Leiden Magical Papyrus IX, 23).[55]

Line 14

- [*r*] ⸢*bnr*⸣: The writing is very damaged, but *bnr* is consistent with the traces. The verb *ḥwy*, however, is sometimes mentioned followed by *r-bnr* (Coptic: ϩⲓⲟⲩⲉ ⲉⲃⲟⲗ).[56]

Line 15

- Based on the context, we suggest that a proper name is written here before the title "the weaver." The beginning of the name is damaged, but it ends in *ỉmn* . A reading *Ta-ỉmn* is out of the question in the context, as there appears to be a very tiny *pꜣ* before *sḫṯ* further along the line. At the Summer School it was suggested that rather than *pꜣ* before the title, it could be the future marker *r*, but closer inspection confirms the reading of the definite article. In fact, the traces before *Ta-ỉmn* would fit a writing of the *šr*-sign, which would suggest the proper name [*Pꜣ*]-⸢*šr*⸣-*ta-ỉmn*.[57]

Line 16

- (*n*) *rn* (*n*): The *rn* is problematic because it means that the sign that looks like *nꜣ* must be the determinative and the *nꜣ* omitted by haplography (or the second stroke of *rn* has been omitted). The alternative would be to read the sign as *tn*, "each," "every," that is, "for each of the men," but this use seems to be confined to denoting periods of time.[58]

---

53. A. F. 'Peter' Shore and Harry S. Smith, "A Demotic Embalmers' Agreement (Pap. dem. B.M. 10561)," *AcOr* 25 (1960): 277–94.
54. As corrected by Joachim F. Quack, "Zwei Handbücher der Mumifizierung im Balsamierungsritual des Apisstieres," *Enchoria* 22 (1995): 127; see also Lorelei H. Corcoran, *Portrait Mummies from Roman Egypt (I–IV Centuries A.D.) with a Catalog of Portrait Mummies in Egyptian Museums*, SAOC 56 (Chicago: The Oriental Institute of the University of Chicago, 1995), 41–42.
55. G&T, 72–73.
56. Wilhelm Spiegelberg, *Demotische Grammatik* (Heidelberg: Winter, 1925; 2nd ed., Heidelberg: Winter, 1975), 178 § 400.
57. For other writings of this name, see *DemNb.* I. 1, 270.
58. CDD *T* (2012), 226.

Back

Line x+2

- The text here is practically all in lacuna except for the house determinative at the end, preceded by a very small trace of an oblique stroke . Although the writing is far from clear, it could well be the last part of *t3 ḳnḥ(.t)* (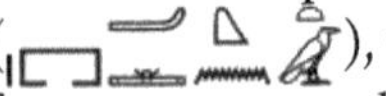), which occurs again in a clearer writing in line x+7 below 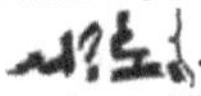. There is also another fragmentary example in line x+5 . The word can mean "the shrine" or "the chapel,"[59] but also "the vault."[60] In our text it would be an appropriate term for the "cult places" and "cult chambers" of the archaeological reports, hence our preferred translation. It could refer to either (a) the new cult chambers and shrines that were erected in the reigns of Ptolemy I and Ptolemy II and dedicated for the burial of the named deified sacred ibises and baboons and for the cult practices such as the oracle questions and the daily worship;[61] and/or (b) the larger niches for the baboon burials and rows of smaller rectangular and rounded niches for limestone sarcophagi in the walls of the main passages and the side branches of the subterranean galleries.

Line x+5

- The writing of the group  is incomplete here, but for clearer examples cf. lines x+10  and x+11 , where it is written with the masculine definite article. For the reading, both *p3 šym* and *p3 šyš* are possible, although in line x+11 the final letter looks more like an *m* than *š* (with the house determinative there written more or less on top of it). *šym* can mean a "row" of connected rooms, that is, a "corridor" or "ambulatory," or a "series of stalls,"[62] and would accordingly be a most suitable word for the galleries and passages in the necropolis. While *šyš*, on the other hand, does in fact mean "aviary," "bird farm," or similar,[63] this is used with reference to the temple poultry and not to the breeding grounds for the sacred ibises, which in Demotic is *t3 ʿẖy(.t)*.[64] While the presence of both breeding grounds and cultic installations for the living sacred ibis at Tuna el-Gebel is to be expected,[65] we think that, given the context (see the discussion in the Commentary), it is

59. CDD Q (2004), 48–50.

60. See the discussion in Cary J. Martin, *Demotic Papyri from the Memphite Necropolis: In the Collections of the National Museum of Antiquities in Leiden, the British Museum and the Hermitage Museum*, PALMA 5 (Turnhout: Brepols, 2009), 57–58; Vittmann, *Der demotische Papyrus Rylands 9*, 2:422–23.

61. Mikhail, "The Cult of Thoth," 148–62; Angela von den Driesch, Dieter Kessler, and Joris Peters, "Mummified Baboons and Other Primates from the Saitic-Ptolemaic Animal Necropolis of Tuna el-Gebel, Middle Egypt," *Documenta Archaeobiologiae: Jahrbuch der Staatssammlung für Anthropologie und Paläoanatomie München* 2 (2004): 236–37; Dieter Kessler and Abd el-Halim Nur el-Din, "Tuna al-Gebel: Millions of Ibises and other Animals," in *Divine Creatures: Animal Mummies in Ancient Egypt*, ed. Salima Ikram (Cairo: American University in Cairo Press, 2005), 144; Katrin Maurer, "Der Tierfriedhof von Tuna el-Gebel in frühptolemäischer Zeit: Zwischenergebnisse der Untersuchungen zur Ausgestaltung des Ibiotaphei," in *Archäologie und Ritual: Auf der Suche nach der rituellen Handlung in den antiken Kulturen Ägyptens und Griechenlands*, ed. Joannis Mylonopoulos and Hubert Roeder (Vienna: Phoibos, 2006), 116; Schlüter, *Die Kultstellen im Tierfriedhof*, 1:55–126; Mahmoud Ebeid, "Wooden Boards with Religious Texts, Written in Hieroglyphic, Hieroglyphic-Hieratic and Hieratic, from the Tuna Al-Gebel Necropolis in the Al-Ashmunein Magazine," in *Hieratic, Demotic and Greek Studies and Text Editions: Of Making Many Books There Is No End; Festschrift in Honour of Sven P. Vleeming*, ed. Koenraad Donker van Heel, Francisca A. J. Hoogendijk, and Cary J. Martin, PLB 34 (Leiden: Brill, 2018), 102–3; Ebeid, *Demotic Inscriptions*, 4–7.

62. CDD Š (2010), 19.

63. For the meaning of the word, see Heinz-Josef Thissen, "Verkauf eines Geflügelhofs (P. Loeb 87 + 63)," in *Texte—Theben—Tonfragmente: Festschrift für Günter Burkard*, ed. Dieter Kessler, Regine Schulz, Martina Ullmann, Alexandra Verbovsek, and Stefan Wimmer, ÄAT 76 (Wiesbaden: Harrassowitz, 2009), 409–10, who also rejects any connection with *šʿš* (409n16).

64. This point is emphasized by Thissen, "Verkauf eines Geflügelhofs," 412–13. For the breeding-grounds of the sacred ibises, see the discussion by Katelijn Vandorpe, "Les villages des Ibis dans la toponymie tardive," *Enchoria* 18 (1991): 115–22. The CDD ʿ (2003), 129–130, translates *t3 ʿẖy(.t)* by "chapel-with-aviary."

65. The feeding place of the ibis at Hermopolis is, in fact, mentioned in three early Demotic letters to Thoth, CUL Michael.Textile Fragment (5), P. Wien D 12026 and L. BM EA 73784. CUL Michael.Textile Fragment (5) and P. Wien D 12026 were published by Günter Vittmann, "Zwei demotische Briefe an den Gott Thot," *Enchoria* 22 (1995): 169–81. For Linen BM EA 73784, see Abd-el-Gawad Migahid and Günter Vittmann, "Zwei weitere frühdemotische Briefe an Thot," *RdÉ* 54 (2003): 47–59.

more likely that we should read *šym* here and translate it as a term for the underground galleries.[66] The designation of the *šym* as "west(ern)" and "north(ern)" could mean "west(ern)" and "north(ern)," that is, two corridors, or, alternatively, "northwest(ern)." In describing directions in Egyptian texts, the regular order is south, north, west, east,[67] but here the scribe has written on both occasions "west," "north." Although in Demotic, when two neighbors of a house or plot of land are the same, the scribe would simply place the words together, as here,[68] we also have examples where they are juxtaposed and mean, for example, "northwest(ern)," and so on.[69] As far as we can tell, however, the "north" or "south" is always placed first, unlike the construction in our text; see the discussion in the Commentary below. Incidentally, combinations like "southwest" or "northeast" are also found in the Wilbour Papyrus.[70]

Line x+6

- *r-ḏbꜣ.ṯ(=w)*: The signs that look like the house determinative are taken to be part of *r-ḏbꜣ.ṯ(=w)*.

Line x+7

- What follows *Ḥr-Ḥp* is uncertain. A name ⸢*Kꜣ-nfr*⸣ was one possibility, but after the almost uncial writing of the *kꜣ*-group, there appears to be something, which is not *aleph*, before the possible *nfr*,[71] which makes the reading problematic. As an alternative, we could perhaps read the group 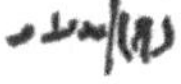 as *r-ḏbꜣ.ṯ* (?), with the signs that look like the house determinative at the end belonging to the prepositional phrase. The writing is, however, slightly different to its form in the line above.

Line x+8

-  [*pꜣ*] *ꜥ.wy*: There is only space for a very small definite article (or it may have been omitted entirely). The writing of *ꜥ.wy* would be very abbreviated.[72] The same is also attested in the ibis inscriptions, nos. 67 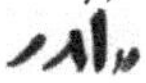 and 180 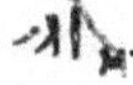.[73]
- On the image there appears to be a short vertical stroke above the line immediately in front of the *ir*-sign in *ir wpy(.t)* , which could suggest that this might be the letter *w*. In line x+11 , however, the writing is certainly just *ir* and, given the context, we certainly have the same phrase in both places. In addition, the *ir* looks rather cramped (cf. line x+11) and was perhaps added afterwards. *ir wpy(.t)*, "carrying out work," appears frequently in the Mother of the Apis inscriptions from the Sacred Animal Necropolis of North Saqqara.[74] In the Demotic texts from the necropolis we sometimes encounter titles and professions related to the construction work, for example, *ḫr-nṯr n pꜣ ꜥ.wy-ḥtp n pꜣ hb pꜣ ꜥꜥn nty pꜣ imnt n Ḫmnw*, "stonemason of the resting place of the ibis and the baboon, which is in the west of Hermopolis,"[75] and *pꜣ ḳd / pꜣ i.ḳd (?) / pꜣ r.ḳd*, "the builder,"

66. The underground necropolis as a whole is the *pꜣ ꜥ.wy-ḥtp*, "the place-of-rest," so if the word is to be read *šym* it would be used to refer to the actual corridors or galleries running in the necropolis.

67. See Dieter Kessler, "Himmelsrichtungen," *LÄ* 2:1213–15. In some Demotic texts we do find the order of west and east reversed, but they always follow south and north (in that order); see, e.g., P. Hauswaldt 1, lines 3–4 in Joseph G. Manning, *The Hauswaldt Papyri: A Third Century B.C. Family Dossier from Edfu*, DemStud 12 (Sommerhausen: Gisela Zauzich Verlag, 1997).

68. See, e.g., P. BM Andrews 22, line 11, *mḥṯ iꜣbṯ nꜣy(=y) wrḥ.w* in Carol A. R. Andrews, *Ptolemaic Legal Texts from the Theban Area*, CDPBM 4 (London: British Museum Publications, 1990), 62–63.

69. See, e.g., the examples in CDD *M* (2010), 208, and CDD *R* (2001), 66–67.

70. Alan H. Gardiner, *The Wilbour Papyrus II: Commentary* (London: Oxford University Press, 1948), 26.

71. For writings of the name, see *DemNb* I. 3, 1004.

72. For examples of such writings, see *DG*, 53.

73. Ebeid, *Demotic Inscriptions*, 83, 198–99.

74. Harry S. Smith, Carol A. R. Andrews, and Sue Davies, *The Sacred Animal Necropolis at North Saqqara: The Mother of Apis Inscriptions*, EES TEM 14 (London: Egypt Exploration Society, 2011), 260–61.

75. P. Cairo 24/11/62/4 ro., lines 4–5; see Farid, "A Demotic Sale Contract," 262–63.

mentioned in the ibis inscriptions (text nos. 120, 168, 200).[76] In his dissertation, Mikhail examined how the galleries were dug based on a study of the unfinished parts.[77]

- *ỉs.t-m-ḥ3.t ta Ḏḥwty-ms*: "Esemhat daughter of Thotmosis." Three of the five examples of *ỉs.t-m-ḥ3.t* in the *DemNb* are in the unpublished Family Archive of *Ḏd-ḥr* son of *Ḥr* from Tuna el-Gebel (P. Cairo TR no. 24/11/62/6, 4; P. Cairo TR no. 24/11/62/7, 7; P. Cairo TR no. 24/11/62/8, 7).[78]

Line x+9

- For the possible reading of the personal name as *ỉnḥy*, see line 7 above.
- *ḳt 2 1/2*: The number 2 is written at a slight angle, as in line x+6, and ligatured with the following 1/2, which makes it look like a writing of 1/8.

Line x+10

- *di.t di=w ˁn*: The expression is rather awkward, but the reading seems to be clear. "To give beauty," presumably means "to improve the appearance of" or "to make more attractive."[79] It is, of course, possible that we should read this as a subjunctive *sḏm=f* of the adjective verb, in which case the translation would read, "to cause that they make the gallery (of) Amasis attractive." Although the edge of the papyrus is torn, given the length of the lines above, it does not appear that any text is lost.

Line x+11

- *gḏ*: This at first sight strange writing is the letter *g* ligatured with the end of the preceding *wpy(.t)*, followed by the letter *ḏ* (less likely *b* or the heart sign) and then a rather blotchy determinative, which looks like the stone sign. There are two possible translations. The first is that it is a writing of *gḏ* / *gyḏ*, "hand" > Coptic ϭⲓϫ.[80] In this case *wpy(.t)-(n)-gḏ* would be "work-of-hand," referring to the physical digging of the passages and perhaps contrasted with the work of decoration mentioned in the line above (which would explain the stone determinative). In the dictionaries one of the translations given for Coptic ϭⲓϫ is "manual work" or similar. The second possibility, which we prefer, is that this is hieroglyphic *ḳḏ*, "gypsum," which is attested, written *gḏ*, in two other Demotic texts.[81] Gypsum was used for plastering the surfaces of a tomb prior to the decoration.[82] In the context of dealing with work in the underground passages, a translation by "carry out the plastering," literally "carry out the work of gypsum," makes excellent sense.[83] In his PhD dissertation, Mikhail mentioned that gypsum plaster was used to cover the ceilings of some cult chambers in the galleries before painting them with religious scenes.[84] He also

76. Ebeid, *Demotic Inscriptions*, 134–36, 186–87, 217.

77. Mikhail, "The Cult of Thoth," 144–48.

78. *DemNb* I. 1, 77, I. 3, *Korr. und Nach.*, 133.

79. For *ˁn* as a noun, see CDD ˁ (2003), 76.

80. Not in the *Wb.*, but hieroglyphic writings are given in Wolfhart Westendorf, *Koptisches Handwörterbuch* (Heidelberg: Winter, 1965/1977), 472; Werner Vycichl, *Dictionnaire étymologique de la langue copte* (Leuven: Peeters, 1983), 350. For the Demotic, see *DG*, 595; CDD *G* (2004), 78–79.

81. *Wb.* V:82, 7. For the Demotic, see Vos, *Apis Embalming Ritual*, 191 ro. VI b, 19; Heinz-Josef Thissen, "Ein Vertrag über Gipsfabrikation," in *". . . vor dem Papyrus sind alle gleich!": Papyrologische Beiträge zu Ehren von Bärbel Kramer (P. Kramer)*, ed. Raimer Eberhard, Holger Kockelmann, Stefan Pfeiffer, and Maren Schentuleit, AfP Beiheft 27 (Berlin: de Gruyter, 2009), 238–39, with a discussion of the origin of the word (loanword from Akkadian). The Demotic example of the word from P. Phil. 30, I. 40 that is cited by Thissen has subsequently been reinterpreted as a writing of *gḏ(.t)*, "ear-ring"; see Heinz-Josef Thissen and Karl-Theodor Zauzich, "Ein thebanisches Grab und seine Restaurierung," in Donker van Heel, Hoogendijk, and Martin, *Hieratic, Demotic and Greek Studies*, 153.

82. Jaroslav Černý, *The Valley of the Kings: Fragments d'un manuscrit inachevé*, BdÉ 61 (Cairo: Institut français d'archéologie orientale, 1973), 35–41.

83. The papyrus published by Thissen mentioned above also refers to *ir t3 wp.t n psy gḏ*, but there we are dealing with the making of the gypsum (by heating, *psy*) rather than the plastering work.

84. Mikhail, "The Cult of Thoth," 149.

added that the walls of some early Ptolemaic branches such as C-B were also covered with gypsum plaster before they were painted.[85]

Commentary

This unusual papyrus appears to be a list or, perhaps, a series of notes by, or for, the managers of the central administration of the Tuna el-Gebel necropolis. Cut as a tall, thin strip, it is not dissimilar to a typical "high format" Demotic letter in its appearance, and equally enigmatic. The topics that it covers are:

- Linen/cloth for the mummification of the sacred ibis;
- Linen products for the temple/necropolis priests;
- Provision of food products for the temple/necropolis priests;
- Payment for organising the burial of and cult for the sacred animals;
- Payment for carrying out work in the catacombs of the sacred animals.

The first line seems to act as a sort of introduction to the rest of the text on the Front, as there is a short space beneath it before line 2 after which there is also a small gap. Lines 3–14 are structured as one section, which is separated from lines 15–16, the final sentence on the Front (as preserved—an additional short line, or lines, may be lost). The beginning of the text on the Back is lost, the papyrus having been turned over from bottom to top, but the content appears to be unrelated to that on the Front. There is a connection, however, in that the same problematic personal name, perhaps to be read *ỉnḥy*, appears on both sides. On the Back there is a short space after line x+7. This separates the section on the burial of the sacred animals from the second part that deals with work in the galleries.

Lines 1–2 on the Front are concerned with the instructions for the people responsible for providing the linen and/or wrapping the mummies for the sacred ibis. They refer to the fabrication of the wrappings by the "washermen" in the place of weaving,[86] which might be located besides the place of mummification in the necropolis, not far from the animal necropolis. Lines 3–14 deal with the provision of linen/cloth and with the transportation of foodstuffs. The importance of linen for the wrapping of the sacred animals and for the priesthood is well documented.[87] The evidence from Tuna el-Gebel shows that not only were the dead animals and related organic material wrapped but also the statues and statuettes made of stone or wood and every bronze figure.[88] The storage facilities for the linen and for the foodstuffs will have been within the administrative buildings to the east of the subterranean galleries and to the north of the tomb of Petosiris, above the subterranean galleries, about 150 m opposite the temple of Osiris-Baboon.[89] These buildings (the "tower houses") were erected on both sides of a long processional way that runs from the ancient eastern settlement of Kom el-Loli at the eastern edge of the desert to the main entrance of the temple of

85. Mikhail, 155–56.

86. For the tasks that the washermen performed, see the relevant note to line 1.

87. Gillian Vogelsang-Eastwood, "Textiles," in *Ancient Egyptian Materials and Technology*, ed. Paul T. Nicholson and Ian Shaw (Cambridge: Cambridge University Press, 2000), 294–96. For the requirement of linen among the priesthood, see Herodotus 2.37.

88. Kessler and Nur el-Din, "Tuna el-Gebel," 151; Driesch et al., "Mummified, Deified and Buried," 239.

89. For further details on these buildings, see Gabra, *Chez les derniers adorateurs du Trismegiste*, 170; Aly, "Egypt's Contribution," 329–30; Kessler et al., *Die Oberbauten des Ibiotapheion*, 6–7; Mélanie C. Flossmann-Schütze, "Grabungsbericht Tuna el-Gebel: Die Turmhäuser von Tuna el-Gebel; Zu den Anlagen der ptolemäerzeitlichen Tempel- und Friedhofsverwaltung," *Thots* 6 (2011): 26–37; Mélanie C. Flossmann-Schütze "'Manhattan in der Wüste': Tierkult und Turmhäuser in Tuna el-Gebel," *aMun* 46 (2013): 4–11; Mélanie C. Flossmann-Schütze, "Les maisons-tours de l'association religieuse de Touna el-Gebel," in *Les maisons-tours en Égypte durant la Basse-Époque, les périodes Ptolémaique et Romaine: Actes de la table-ronde de Paris, Université Paris-Sorbonne (Paris IV), 29–30 novembre 2012*, ed. Séverine Marchi, NeHeT 2 (Paris: Sorbonne Université; Brussels: Université libre de Bruxelles, 2014), 9–31; Jörg W. E. Fassbinder, Lena Kühne, and Mélanie C. Flossmann-Schütze, "The Hellenistic Settlement of Tuna el-Gebel," *Archaeologia Polona* 53 (2015): 276–80.

Osiris-Baboon and the subterranean galleries. They date from the Early Ptolemaic to the Early Roman period and are related to the ancient settlement of Kom el-Loli.[90] Evidence of food preparation and storage has been found within them.[91] These complexes usually consisted of between one and three tower houses surrounded by smaller annex buildings, as well as numerous production units like bakeries and storage areas, an administrative center, and cult places. The tower houses were where the priests and their families lived. The priests were probably organized in local religious associations dedicated to the main deities of the animal cemetery, namely Osiris-Baboon and Osiris-Ibis. Their main tasks were to arrange the burial for the thousands of animal mummies each year and to organize and maintain the cult in the chapels and the cult places in the animal cemetery. Some of these houses will also have functioned as administrative centers.[92]

The beginning of the text on the Back refers to a *ḳnḥ(.t)*, a chapel or cult place (see line x+2 note a) and the transportation of the mummified ibises, "the gods," there. This section of the text will be concerned with work in the underground galleries. *pꜣ šym* would then be the word for one of the main galleries or side passages in the catacombs. These often contain wall niches and adjacent chambers and shrines for the burial of the sacred animals, in particular the baboons and ibises. When the text refers to a *ḳnḥ(.t)* in lines x+2 and x+7, it will be these cult places or cult chambers that are intended.[93]

The *šym* is described as "west" and "north" (i.e., "northwest"; see line x+5 note above). Defining exactly what is meant by this is problematic. The animal catacombs form a vast subterranean region. Four to five meters below the ground, they consist of long main galleries, with chambers of varying sizes carved out of the rock for the burial of baboons, and with numerous passages branching off on the sides, filled with pottery jars containing mummified ibises and other sacred animals.[94] Gallery D, the oldest passage that dates to the Saite period, runs in a north–south direction; in the Persian period, the gallery system extended in the eastern direction (Gallery C-D); in the Thirtieth Dynasty, the galleries turn to the north (Gallery C-C). The entrance to this long main gallery (C-C) was integrated into the new main temple building that dates to the beginning of the Ptolemaic period. Probably as the result of a ceiling collapse restricting access, a new entrance to the galleries was then built to the north of the earlier one during the reign of Ptolemy II. If our papyrus dates to the early Ptolemaic period, we would suggest that one of the left-hand side—that is, western—passages off the main gallery C-C that runs northwards from the main Ptolemaic temple building could fit the "west" "north" statement in the text: that is, interpreting the Demotic text to mean the "west" passage off the "north" gallery.[95] If the date of the papyrus is later, then it could be that it refers to passages off the northernmost parts of Gallery B (Gallery G-B-A or G-B-C). The last phase of the ibis burials was in Gallery A, for

90. Kessler et al., *Die Oberbauten des Ibiotapheion*, 12–15.

91. Flossmann-Schütze, "Grabungsbericht Tuna el-Gebel," 34–35; Flossmann-Schütze, "'Manhattan in der Wüste,'" 8; Flossmann-Schütze, "Les maisons-tours," 21.

92. In the recent excavations of the Joint Mission in the area between 2002 and 2012, a group of Demotic ostraca were excavated in these houses that refer to grain deliveries and food rations with some lists of personal names.

93. For images of these chambers and niches, see Mikhail, "The Cult of Thoth," 149–52; Kessler and Nur el-Din, "Tuna el-Gebel," pl. 6.2 (opposite p. 162); Schlüter, *Die Kultstellen im Tierfriedhof*, 2:pls. 27, 33, 36, 38 and *passim*. These cult chambers and shrines were closed with mud-brick slabs, wall paintings (pieces of painted linen) and limestone slabs, often with scenes of a king or a priest in adoration before a seated ibis or baboon.

94. Kessler and Nur el-Din, "Tuna el-Gebel," 133–47, for a description of the development of the galleries. For a map of the animal galleries, see Kessler and Nur el-Din, "Tuna el-Gebel," 122–23; Schlüter, *Die Kultstellen im Tierfriedhof*, 2:plan 1.

95. For further information on Gallery C, see Dieter Kessler, "Die Galerie C von Tuna el-Gebel," *MDAIK* 39 (1983): 107–24; Dieter Kessler, "Die Galerie C von Tuna: Forschungsstand bis 1983; Vorbericht über die Kampagnen Frühjahr und Herbst 1983," in *Tuna el-Gebel I: Die Tiergalerien*, ed. Joachim Boessneck, HÄB 24 (Hildesheim: Gerstenberg, 1987), 3–36.

which another entrance far to the north was built, but our papyrus was probably written before this gallery and the accompanying passages were constructed.[96]

The text on the back of the papyrus therefore appears to concern three payments related to the burial of the sacred animals in the catacombs and to work carried out there. Payment of two kite was made for taking the "gods" to the cult place: to Komoapis, one kite, and for the cult chapel of Horhap, one kite. A payment of two-and-a-half kite was made to Inhy for work "in the place of Esemhat, daughter of Thotmosis," for "making attractive" the gallery/corridor of Amosis and for carrying out the plastering in the western and northern galleries. We assume by "making attractive" the scribe means decorating one of the chambers.[97] Inhy is therefore being paid for first preparing the surface to be decorated with gypsum and then the actual decoration.

What is particularly noticeable about the text on this side is that the places are ascribed to named individuals. That these are not the names of the sacred animals buried there is self-evident.[98] Equally, they do not refer to the workmen, for they are the recipients of the payment. The most likely possibility is that these are the administrators who were responsible for organizing the work in the designated areas and whose names were therefore used as a reference point to identify specific places in the catacombs. The ibis inscriptions refer to officials who were responsible for organizing the mummified sacred animals inside these passages and their adjacent chambers.[99] So, Horhap and Amosis mentioned here would be officials responsible for these passages and corridors. One of the individuals, interestingly, is a woman, Esemhat daughter of Thotmosis. Women are regularly found holding important priestly positions and owning property in Ptolemaic Egypt, but it is perhaps unexpected to see a female in such a senior administrative role.[100] We do, however, find other evidence for the involvement of women in the management of the activities in the Tuna el-Gebel necropolis. There are two recently published Demotic ostraca from the site in which women appear to be collectors of sums of money paid presumably by members of the priesthood, both men and women.[101] There is another ostracon, O. el-Ashmunein magazine Inv. No. 1130, which refers to a certain *Ta-Ỉy-m-ḥtp*, who received priestly rations of bread during the period in which she served in the necropolis.[102] In addition, from the ibis inscriptions we find women as dedicators of sacred animals and they are also mentioned among the officials responsible for depositing the mummified ibises inside the galleries.[103] We should also not rule out the possibility that there was

96. Gallery A is unfinished. The presence of Roman oil lamps and pottery suggests that it was used in the last phase of ibis burials; see Kessler and Nur el-Din, "Tuna el-Gebel," 147.

97. See, e.g., the scenes reproduced from Chamber C-B-2 in Schlüter, *Die Kultstellen im Tierfriedhof*, 2:pls. 42–52.

98. The names are neither prefaced by *Wsir*, "Osiris," nor bear any relationship to those attested for the individual baboons or ibises; see the list of names in Schlüter, *Die Kultstellen im Tierfriedhof*, 1:322–45.

99. Mahmoud Ebeid, "*N-trt* (*m-ḏr.t*) in the Demotic Inscriptions on the Ibis Coffins and Sarcophagi from the Galleries of Tuna el-Gebel Necropolis," in *Scribe of Justice: Egyptological Studies in Honor of Schafik Allam*, ed. Zahi A. Hawass, Khaled A. Daoud, and Ramadan B. Hussein, CASAE 42 (Cairo: Ministry of State for Antiquities, 2011), 134–35.

100. On the occupations held by women and their ownership of property, see Janet H. Johnson, "Women, Wealth and Work in Egyptian Society of the Ptolemaic Period," in *Egyptian Religion, The Last Thousand Years: Studies Dedicated to the Memory of Jan Quaegebeur*, ed. Willy Clarysse, Antoon Schoors, and Harco Willems, OLA 85 (Leuven: Peeters, 1998), 2:1393–1421; Koenraad Donker van Heel, *Mrs. Tsenhor: A Female Entrepreneur in Ancient Egypt* (Cairo: The American University in Cairo Press, 2014). For the role of priestesses in the Egyptian cult and their membership of cult associations, see Françoise de Cenival, "Deux papyrus inédits de Lille avec une révision du P. dém. Lille 31," *Enchoria* 7 (1977): 21–23, 29–31; Frédéric Colin, "Les prêtresses indigènes dans l'Égypte hellénistique et romaine: Une question à la croisée des sources grecques et égyptiennes," in *Le rôle et le statut de la femme en Égypte hellénistique, romaine et byzantine: Actes du colloque international, Bruxelles – Leuven 27–29 Novembre 1997*, ed. Henri Melaerts and Leon Mooren, StudHell 37 (Paris: Peeters, 2002), 41–122.

101. Ebeid, "Two Demotic Ostraca," 95–104. See also Kessler et al., *Die Oberbauten des Ibiotapheion*, 178–79. In the first ostracon, Inv. No. 1128, a woman *Tꜣ-ʿnn.t*, perhaps a senior member of a cult guild, receives money from sixteen individuals, four of whom are female. In the second ostracon, Inv. No. 1129, three women appear as recipients of payments.

102. Ebeid, "A Ptolemaic Demotic Account of Bread," 161.

103. Ebeid, *Demotic Inscriptions*, section 6: Appendices.

private financing involved in the construction of the necropolis and the establishment of the cult there.[104] In this case the people named could be the benefactors, but again we are faced with the unexpected presence of a woman. The participation of women in such dedications, other than members of a family group, is practically nonexistent.[105] There may, of course, be other explanations and perhaps the publication of further Demotic material from the necropolis will help to shed further light on their role here.

In memoriam—Mahmoud Ebeid

On July 4, 2020, after this article had been completed and sent to the editors, my co-author, Mahmoud Ebeid, a professor of Egyptology at Cairo University, tragically passed away, a victim of the COVID-19 virus. After finishing his PhD in 2006, Ebeid's work had focused on the Demotic material from Tuna el-Gebel, where he had been involved for many years as a member of the Joint Archaeological Mission of Cairo and Munich Universities. The fruits of this were a major volume, *The Demotic Inscriptions from the Subterranean Galleries of the Sacred Animals in the Tuna el-Gebel Necropolis*, which appeared posthumously in 2021, and an extensive series of publications of Demotic papyri, ostraca, inscriptions, and votive objects, as well as hieratic and hieroglyphic material, from the site.

Ebeid was an inspirational teacher, widely respected by his students and held in great esteem by his colleagues. I will also remember him, in particular, for his kindness and his thoughtfulness. As the pandemic raged across the planet, he used to regularly email me to check that Adrienn and I were okay. The last email was sent in mid-June, just a few days before he fell ill. This article was to have been the first of a number of collaborations that we had planned to write together. Sadly, it will also be the last.

Cary J Martin

104. For the involvement of private individuals in the financing of temple projects, see in particular Christophe Thiers, "Égyptiens et Grecs au service des cultes indigènes: Un aspect de l'évergétisme en Égypte lagide," in *Les régulations sociales dans l'antiquité: Actes du colloque d'Angers 23 et 24 mai 2003*, ed. Michel Molin (Rennes: Press universitaires de Rennes, 2006), 275–301; Christophe Thiers, "Observations sur le financement des chantiers de construction des temples à l'époque ptolémaïque," in *7. Ägyptologische Tempeltagung: Structuring Religion, Leuven, 28. September–1. October 2005*, ed. René Preys, Königtum, Staat und Gesellschaft früher Hochkulturen 3,2 (Wiesbaden: Harrassowitz, 2009), 231–44; Christelle Fischer-Bovet, *Army and Society in Ptolemaic Egypt*, Armies of the Ancient World (Cambridge: Cambridge University Press, 2014), 329–62; Joanna Wilimowska, "Benefactions toward Temples in the Ptolemaic Fayum," *JARCE* 54 (2018): 187–202.

105. Thiers, "Égyptiens et Grecs," 281.

“Black Is Her Hair, More Than the Black of the Night”: The Tale of the Herdsman and the Origins of Egyptian Love Poetry

Marina Escolano-Poveda

Richard is no doubt one of the best scholars of Demotic in his generation, and his attention to detail and insightful ideas are known to all those who work in this field.[1] However, Richard is more than just a Demoticist. He could be better described as an “omnivorous Egyptologist,” a scholar with a great interest not only in every period and aspect of the study of ancient Egypt, but also in other Near Eastern and classical civilizations, and in areas such as biography and music, which he has brought masterfully into his Egyptological work.[2] The essay that I am offering him here does not deal with Demotic, but with yet another area that he has also examined with his usual keen eye: the transmission of the Egyptian literary tradition. This study derives from my work on P. Mallorca I, which I started while I was Richard’s graduate student at Johns Hopkins. With this essay I want to honor the wisdom he has passed on to me in innumerable hours of conversation and discussion, and his patience and *savoir faire* as a mentor. I hope he finds the ideas I propose here interesting, or at least intriguing.

1. Reinterpreting the Tale of the Herdsman: P. Mallorca I

In 2017, I published the *editio princeps* of P. Mallorca I and II, which I identified as new fragments of the papyrus roll P. Berlin 3024, corresponding to both the Debate Between a Man and His Ba and the Tale of the Herdsman.[3] Together with the edition and commentary of the fragments and an analysis of their materiality, origin, and placement within the original manuscript, I proposed new interpretations of the two poems based on the insights provided by the previously unknown text sections. I also connected the text on P. Mallorca I frags. 2-4, which describes the physical appearance of the goddess of the Tale of the Herdsman, with the description of princess Mutirdis on the Third Intermediate period stela S. Louvre C100, identifying the latter as deriving directly from the former. In the present study I offer a new edition of P. Mallorca I frags. 2-4 and lines 3–4 of S. Louvre C100 and contextualize the transmis-

1. I want to wholeheartedly thank John Baines (University of Oxford), Roland Enmarch (University of Liverpool), Diego M. Santos (Universidad Pedagógica Nacional [UNIPE]), and Mason Wilkes (Johns Hopkins University) for reading drafts of this paper and making very useful suggestions to improve its clarity and correctness, and for checking my English. I have acknowledged their contributions at the pertinent locations in the footnotes. I also would like to thank Vincent Rondot, director of the Department of Egyptian Antiquities of the Musée du Louvre, for generously allowing me to use the image of S. Louvre C100 in this paper (fig. 2).

2. His reference to Paco de Lucía’s masterpiece “Entre Dos Aguas” in the title of his study of Greco-Egyptian interaction is my favorite; see Richard Jasnow, “Between Two Waters: The Book of Thoth and the Problem of Greco-Egyptian Interaction,” in *Greco-Egyptian Interactions: Literature, Translation, and Culture, 500 BCE–300 CE*, ed. Ian Rutherford (Oxford: Oxford University Press, 2016), 317–56.

3. Marina Escolano-Poveda, “New Fragments of Papyrus Berlin 3024: The Missing Beginning of the Debate between a Man and his Ba and the Continuation of the Tale of the Herdsman (P. Mallorca I and II),” *ZÄS* 144 (2017): 16–54.

sion of this passage of the Tale of the Herdsman within the literary phenomenon of Egyptian love poetry and the oral tradition of pastoral narratives.

The Tale of the Herdsman has come down to us in a single manuscript, as a section of a papyrus roll attached to the end of the only copy of another very important work of Middle Egyptian literature, the Debate Between a Man and His Ba. These two sections constitute the roll that we now identify as P. Berlin 3024, which is part of the so-called "Berlin Library," a collection of four papyrus rolls containing one copy of Sinuhe (P. Berlin 3022) and two almost complementary copies of the Eloquent Peasant (B1: P. Berlin 3023; B2: P. Berlin 3025). The papyrus section corresponding to the Tale of the Herdsman is 95 cm long and contains twenty-five legible columns of text, with eight columns having been erased, four at the beginning and four at the end. We therefore lack both the beginning and the end of the poem, and we do not know how much longer it would have originally been. In the preserved twenty-five columns an unnamed herdsman refers to a first encounter with a goddess in the marshes, where he was tending his animals. Rather enigmatically, he says that the goddess made him a proposal, but that he could never do what she asked him. Significantly shaken by this encounter, he commands the other herdsmen to cross back with the herd in order to spend the night in a safer area, and the wise men among the herdsmen then recite a water spell, which is quoted in full. After this, the story returns to an external narrator and moves on to the next morning. The goddess approaches the herdsman for a second time as he is going down to the water, taking off her clothes and loosening her hair.[4] This is the end of column 25, so we do not know what the reaction of the herdsman was in this second encounter, or the ultimate nature of the goddess's intentions.

To my knowledge, all the interpretations of the Herdsman prior to my 2017 *editio princeps* of P. Mallorca I and II have understood the interest of the goddess in the herdsman to be of a sexual character. This, however, is never indicated in the story, and it does not make sense with the herdsman's reaction to the first encounter: crossing the cattle and protecting it with a water spell. The motivation of the goddess in her two encounters with the herdsman does not seem to be sexual in nature, but instead she uses erotic appeal only in the second encounter as a means rather than a goal.[5] Therefore, I have proposed that the goddess's intention in her interactions with the herdsman is to take possession of the cattle[6], which is supported by a later tradition preserved in a medieval Arabic narrative by Murtaḍā ibn al-ʿAfīf.[7] In this narrative a king called Gebir (Alexander the Great) is building Alexandria for Queen Charoba (Cleopatra).[8] Charoba gives him a herd of a thousand goats to provide milk for the royal kitchen. These goats are tended by a handsome shepherd and his subordinates. While he is with the animals, a young lady comes out from the sea and, in a very polite way, proposes him to wrestle her. If he were to win, she would do to him, and let him do to her, whatever he desired, but if she were victorious, he would have to give her one of the animals from the herd. The

4. Mathieu has recently proposed a new interpretation of the text in which he considers that the companions of the herdsman refuse to abandon the place where they are, after he asks them to do so, and to leave him alone. Like all the other scholars who have examined the poem, Mathieu here considers that the goddess's intentions in the first encounter are of a sexual nature, and from this he proposes to see in this encounter an antecedent of the theogamy texts. For Mathieu's analysis, which includes corrections to the reading of different signs and a new French translation, see Bernard Mathieu, "Le conte du Pâtre qui vit une déesse (P. Berlin 3024, verso)," in *And the Earth is Joyous … Essays in Honour of Galina A. Belova*, ed. Sergey Viktorovich Ivanov (Moscow: CES RAS, 2015), 196–204. The Tale of the Herdsman, however, is not located on the verso of the roll, but on the recto of a different section of papyrus attached to the roll of the Debate. I want to thank Mathieu for bringing this article to my attention and sending me a copy of it.

5. It is important to remark that there is no reference to a sexual proposal in either of the two encounters. The hypothetic use of erotic means to achieve her goal is entirely based on her description in cols. x+24–x+25: "She came shedding her clothes and messing up her hair," translation from James Peter Allen, *Middle Egyptian Literature: Eight Literary Works of the Middle Kingdom* (Cambridge: Cambridge University Press, 2015), 366.

6. For this interpretation, see Escolano-Poveda, "New Fragments of Papyrus Berlin 3024," 37–40.

7. For more details on this narrative, see Escolano-Poveda, 39–40; and section 6.

8. On the Arab traditions concerning Alexander and Cleopatra, see Okasha El Daly, *Egyptology: The Missing Millennium* (London: University College London Press, 2015), which contains abundant references to the later traditions on both monarchs throughout.

woman wins the fights over and over, taking the animals with her to the sea and thus diminishing the size of the herd, until Gebir comes to know of the situation and impersonates the shepherd, defeating the woman. As I have proposed before, following Maspero's suggestion,[9] this narrative, which mixes elements from different previous ancient traditions, may derive from an oral transmission of the Tale of the Herdsman. This point will be very significant for my argument and will be examined in detail in section 6.

My new interpretation of the Tale of the Herdsman is further reinforced by a suggestion that Bernard Mathieu has kindly made to me.[10] He proposes to read the end of P. Mallorca I frag. 3 col. 2 as *rḫ.t*, "count" (*Wb.* II:448, 19–21), with the resulting phrase being *jw dbḥ.n=s rḫ.t* ⸢*jḥ(.w)*⸣, "She requested the count of the cattle."[11] This new reading, which I gladly adopt, makes the interest of the goddess in the size of the herd explicit.

2. The Description of the Goddess: P. Mallorca I frags. 2-4 and S. Louvre C100 ll. 3–4

What follows is an updated transliteration and translation of P. Mallorca I frags. 2-4, which should replace the one I published in the *editio princeps*.[12] The commentary notes refer to new readings or observations relevant to the present analysis and should be considered in parallel to the full commentary in the *editio princeps*.[13] After this, I present a new transliteration, translation, and commentary of lines 3–4 of S. Louvre C100, incorporating the insights provided by P. Mallorca I frags. 2-4.

2.1. *P. Mallorca frags. 2-4* (fig. 1)[14]

1. [...] ⸢*n(j)*⸣ *grḥ j3rr.wt d3b.w* {⸢*s*⸣}
2. [...] ⸢*ṯs.wt*⸣ *=s r dq.w r q3ḥ*

1. [...] of the night, and grapes and figs [...]
2. [...] her teeth more than flour and more than gypsum

1. ⸢*n(j)*⸣ : In my first edition of P. Mallorca I, I identified the traces on top of fragment 2 as ⸢*r*⸣, noting that they could correspond to either *m*, *r*, or *n*.[15] I correct this reading here to the genitive adjective *n(j)* in parallel with the text on S. Louvre C100, l. 3: *km n(j) grḥ* "the black of the night."

9. See Escolano-Poveda, "New Fragments of Papyrus Berlin 3024," 39–40; and Gaston Maspero, "Fragments d'un conte fantastique remontant à la XIIe dynastie," in *Études égyptiennes I*, ed. Gaston Maspero (Paris: Imprimerie Nationale, 1886), 79–80.

10. Pers. comm. of Bernard Mathieu via email of 07/19/2017. In this email, Mathieu corrects my reading of frag. 7-5 to *ḥr-s3 jn.n n=f* ⸢*3tw jw*⸣, "after the supervisor of the livestock had brought to him," which I accept and adopt. The label of the third image on p. 45 should be changed from frag. 7-9 to frag. 7-5. I want to thank Bernard Mathieu for these insightful suggestions.

11. Instead of my original translation: "She requested to know the cattle(?)," see Escolano-Poveda, "New Fragments of Papyrus Berlin 3024," 27.

12. Escolano-Poveda, 25–27.

13. For a complete commentary of P. Mallorca I, see Escolano-Poveda, 25–29.

14. For a material description of P. Mallorca I, see Escolano-Poveda, 16–18.

15. See Escolano-Poveda, 25–26.

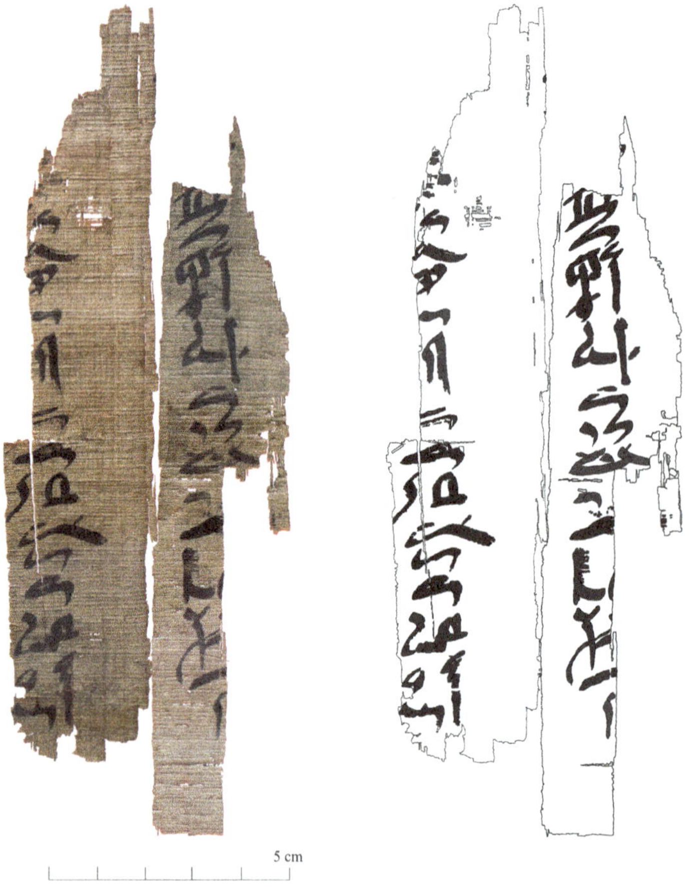

Figure 1. P. Mallorca I frags. 2-4. Photography by Sergio Carro Martín, facsimile by Marina Escolano-Poveda.

⸢*s*⸣ : According to my reconstruction of the text on frags. 2-4 in comparison with the stela Louvre C100 (see fig. 2), this ⸢*s*⸣ would be spurious, an error resulting from the possessive suffix pronoun ⸗*s* located at the end of the previous column: *šn.w⸗s*.

2. *ṯs.wt*: In my *editio princeps* of the fragments I did not read the first signs on frag. 2, and I interpreted the tooth-sign (F18) as an abbreviated writing of *jbḥ* "tooth" (*Wb.* I:64, 2–4).[16] A new inspection of the fragment suggests the reading of the traces above the tooth-sign as sign U40. The lower horizontal trace of the sign is slanted upwards towards the right, as in P. Berlin 3025 l. 111 (Eloquent Peasant B2), *wṯsw* "complainer, accuser,"[17] which appears as an example for the sign in Möller (405): 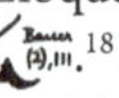.[18] Although the vertical trace has not been preserved in frag. 2, a small tick of the diagonal upper trace is still visible. The *t* of *ṯs.t* has been inserted into the sign, perhaps

16. Escolano-Poveda, 25–26.

17. For a photograph of the papyrus, see Richard Bruce Parkinson and Lisa Baylis, *Four 12th Dynasty Literary Papyri (Pap. Berlin P. 3022–5): A Photographic Record* (Berlin: Akademie-Verlag, 2012), Photo 10 P. 3025 E(2) = Peasant B2 109-25. Hieroglyphic transcription in Richard B. Parkinson, *The Tale of the Eloquent Peasant* (Oxford: Griffith Institute, Ashmolean Museum, 1991); commentary in Richard B. Parkinson, *The Tale of the Eloquent Peasant: A Reader's Commentary*, LingAeg SM 10 (Hamburg: Widmaier, 2012), 301.

18. The upwards orientation of the horizontal trace is not as pronounced in Möller's copy as it is in the original papyrus.

as a later addition. The faint traces above the U40 sign fit those of a bolt-*s* (O34) and a *ṯ*-sign (V13). The *Wörterbuch* and Bardinet record attestations of *ṯs.t* meaning "tooth" starting in the Eighteenth Dynasty.[19] Bardinet notes the orthography with U40 as peculiar, attested for the first time in the Nineteenth Dynasty in P. Leiden I 348, rto. 2.3.[20] However, Leitz has indicated to me that the word *ṯs.t*, with the orthography 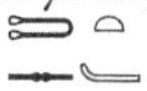 appears in the Cuve de Coptos, side 2 (west) col. 18, which dates to the Twenty-Second Dynasty, but the text of which is considered to have been composed in the Middle Kingdom.[21] P. Mallorca I frag. 2 would therefore be the oldest attestation of this word used for "tooth"[22] and for its orthography with U40. The conflation of the orthographies of the verb *ṯs* "to tie" and *ṯsi* "to elevate" is attested since the Pyramid Texts.[23]

dq.w r qꜣḥ: The version in S. Louvre C100 connects both nouns with the indirect genitive. The parallelism with the previous line, in which we find a double comparison, suggests in this case the consideration of *dq.w* and *qꜣḥ* as two elements that are being compared to the whiteness of the goddess's teeth, as the black of the night and the tandem of grapes and figs[24] are compared to the blackness of her hair.[25] The text in S. Louvre C100 adds another comparison after these, so perhaps the presence of *r* and *n(j)* in P. Mallorca I and S. Louvre C100 respectively is in both cases a correction from an original in which both terms appeared grouped together without a linking element, as in the case of *jꜣrr.wt dꜣb.w* "grapes and figs." The poem may have originally had a chiastic structure:

km n(j) grḥ – jꜣrr.wt dꜣb.w	black of the night – grapes and figs
dq.w qꜣḥ – ḫb(ꜣ) m ḥn(j)	flour and gypsum – slice in a papyrus stem[26]

2.2. *S. Louvre C100 ll.* 3–4 (fig. 2)

S. Louvre C100 is a limestone round-top stela that measures 43.5 by 40.3 cm. Under a winged sun disk, a ritual scene depicts a king wearing a diadem and a headdress composed of two high plumes, facing the goddess Mut, mistress of Isheru, who directs life, stability, and dominion towards his nose. Behind the king stands the king's daughter Mutirdis, prophetess (*ḥm.t-nṯr*) of Mut and Hathor. She wears a diadem and holds a sistrum in her right hand, presenting it towards the goddess, and a *menit* necklace in her left hand. The bottom half of the stela contains four horizontal lines of hieroglyphic text.[27] The stela was intentionally damaged in antiquity, and four of the cartouches of the king have been erased,[28] while the surviving ones identify him as Menkheperre. A close examination of the erased cartouches reveals two clear reed leaves in the last section of all of them. The vertical cartouche on the left part of the scene shows

19. *Wb.* V:409, 9–12; Thierry Bardinet, *Dents et mâchoires dans les représentations religieuses et la pratique médicale de l'Égypte ancienne*, Studia Pohl: Series Maior 15 (Rome: Editrice Pontificio Istituto Biblico, 1990), 12–26.

20. Bardinet, *Dents et mâchoires*, 26. Bardinet indicates that the date is according to Borghouts. For the attestation in P. Leiden I 348, see Bardinet, 16–17.

21. Christian Leitz, pers. comm. For the Cuve de Coptos, see Jean Yoyotte, "Conférence de M. Jean Yoyotte," in *AnnEPHE* 90 (1981–1982), 189–96.

22. Bardinet points out that the use of *ṯs.t* with the meaning of teeth probably goes back to at least the Middle Kingdom, see Bardinet, *Dents et mâchoires*, 25.

23. *Wb.* V:396, 12.

24. The tandem of grapes and figs appears in other Middle Kingdom texts with the nuance of bountifulness, such as Sinuhe B 81 and the Shipwrecked Sailor cols. 47–48.

25. This corrects my previous reading in Escolano-Poveda, "New Fragments of Papyrus Berlin 3024," 25–26.

26. Perhaps originally *ḫb n(j) mḥn* "slice of papyrus"; for this reading, see commentary to *ḫb(ꜣ) m ḥn(j)* in the edition of S. Louvre C100 ll. 3–4, infra.

27. The original inscription may have been longer, since evidence of a fifth line is visible on the left side of its bottom edge.

28. All the erased cartouches correspond to the *sꜣ-Rʿ* name of the king.

Figure 2. S. Louvre C100. © 2015 Musée du Louvre, dist. RMN-Grand Palais_Christian Décamps.

the legible traces of the sign *jn*, the *nw*-pot over two legs (see fig. 2). This confirms Yoyotte's attribution of the stela to an obscure king of the Third Intermediate period called Iny.[29] The erasure of the king's name, uncommon during the Libyan period, and the name of his daughter, Mutirdis, have led scholars like Kitchen to date the reign of this king and therefore the stela to the early Twenty-Fifth Dynasty.[30]

29. Jean Yoyotte, "Pharaon Iny: Un roi mystérieux du VIIIe siècle avant J.-C.," *CRIPEL* 11 (1989): 113–31.
30. Kitchen first read the name of the king as Khmuny, see Kenneth A. Kitchen, *The Third Intermediate Period in Egypt (1100–650*

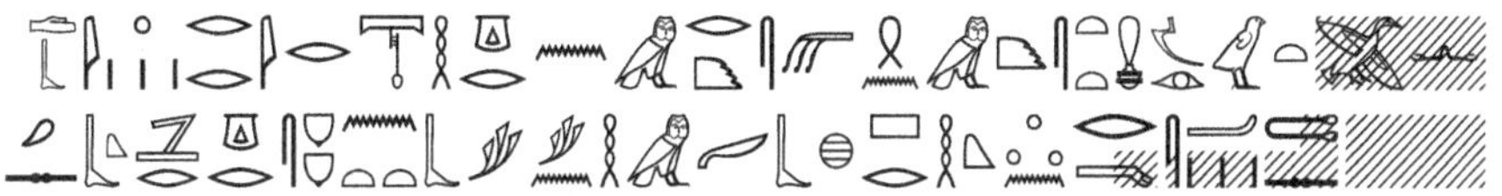

3
4

3. ⸢*n pꜣ*⸣ *.tw mꜣ(ꜣ) mj.tt=s km šnw=s r km n(j) grḥ r j(ꜣ)rr(.wt) {j}d(ꜣ)b(.w)*
4. [*ḥḏ*] *ṯs.wt=s r dq.w n(j) q(ꜣ)ḥ r ḫb(ꜣ) m ḥn(j) bn.tj=s grg(.wj)*[31] *r q(ꜣ)b(.t)=s*

3. Her like has not been seen. Black is her hair, more than the black of the night, more than grapes and figs.
4. [White] are her teeth, more than gypsum powder, more than a slice in a papyrus stem. Her breasts are (well) established upon her chest [...]

3. *j(ꜣ)rr(.wt)*: The word is only determined by the pupil (D12) and the plural strokes.[32] Despite its unusual orthography, the word was already identified as *jꜣrr.wt* "grapes" in Pierret's first translation of the text.[33] This reading is confirmed by the full writing in P. Mallorca I frag. 2.

{j}d(ꜣ)b(.w): *Wb.* V:417, 9–15. No orthographies with initial *yod* seem to be attested,[34] so this writing appears to derive from a corruption of the text.[35] The word as it stands has no determinative, which could have been located at the beginning of line 4. As in the case of *j(ꜣ)rr(.t)*, this may have been just the pupil (D12) and the plural strokes, without any specific visual connection with its original meaning as fruit (indicated in P. Mallorca I frags. 2-4 by means of the M43 sign). The combination of this orthography and the confusion between the pupil (D12) and the grain of sand (N33) determinatives could have led to the conflation with the word *jdb*

B.C.) (Warminster: Aris & Phillips, 1973), 137 and 371. In his monograph on Egyptian poetry he is more inclined to read it as Piankhy, see Kenneth A. Kitchen, *Poetry of Ancient Egypt* (Jonsered: Åström, 1999), 459.

31. I reconstruct here the 3rd person plural ending of the stative, even though the subject is the feminine dual *bn.tj=s*, since dual endings were generally replaced in Middle Egyptian by the 3rd masculine form. However, examples of these dual endings are attested in texts such as P. Ebers, or the Hymns to the Crowns, as noted by Gardiner. See Alan Gardiner, *Egyptian Grammar: Being an Introduction to the Study of Hieroglyphs*, 3rd ed. (Oxford: Griffith Institute, 1957), 234, and nn. 11–15. I want to thank Roland Enmarch for pointing out the later instances of the dual ending to me.

32. Notice the different size of this sign with the tripled N33-sign of *dq.w* in line 4, which indicates the care of the scribe in distinguishing both signs. I want to thank Diego M. Santos for pointing out to me that the determinative in *jꜣrr.wt* is D12 and not N33, noting that this word also means "pupil" even in Coptic, ⲉⲗⲟⲟⲗⲉ; see Walter E. Crum, *A Coptic Dictionary* (Oxford: Oxford University Press, 1939), 55. The word *dꜣb*, "fig" is also known with the D12 determinative, as noted in the Wörterbuch Digitized Slip Archive, Document DZA 31.329.350 (Diego M. Santos, pers. comm., email of October 9, 2019).

33. Paul Pierret, *Recueil d'inscriptions inédites du Musée Égyptien du Louvre: Deuxième Partie* (Paris: Vieweg, 1878), 105–7. Later on, however, Maspero and Max Müller translated it as "berries": Gaston Maspero, "Notes sur quelques points de grammaire et d'histoire," *ZÄS* 17 (1879): 53; Wilhelm Max Müller, *Die Liebespoesie der alten Ägypter* (Leipzig: Hinrichs, 1899), 44. Hermann returned to the reading as "grapes" ("Weintrauben"), which has been the predominant one since then: Alfred Hermann, *Altägyptische Liebesdichtung* (Wiesbaden: Harrassowitz, 1959), 127.

34. See Renate Germer, "Untersuchung über Arzneimittelpflanzen im alten Ägypten" (PhD diss., University of Hamburg, 1979), 109–10.

35. On this issue, Diego M. Santos has suggested to me that the initial yod may be an error of *j* */a/ for *r* */a/, indicating that the text would have been composed from memory instead of looking at a written copy, reflecting the pronunciation of a hypothetical *r km nj grḥ r jꜣrr.wt r db.w*. Santos suggests that if the text in P. Mallorca I is not corrupt, the text of the stela (or an earlier intermediate copy) would have been corrected because the repetition of the comparative *r* was considered as better Middle Egyptian, or because the text had been updated according to the language of the time/place. It is important to note that in S. Louvre C100 an extra comparative *r* has been introduced between *grḥ* and *jꜣrr.wt* (Diego M. Santos, pers. comm., email of October 9, 2019).

"riverbank" (*Wb.* I:153, 2–10), as translated by scholars such as Kitchen and Mathieu.[36] The reading as "figs" was already proposed by Hermann in 1959 and has been followed by many scholars since.[37]

4. *dq.w n(j) q(ꜣ)ḥ*: Both *dq.w* and *qꜣḥ* are written phonetically in P. Mallorca I frags. 2-4. This parallel corrects the reading of S. Louvre C100 from *qꜣw*[38], proposed by scholars like Kitchen,[39] Bardinet,[40] or Popko,[41] to *dq.w*,[42] both words meaning "flour, powder." The distinction between *qꜣw* and *dq.w* was discussed by Harris, who indicated that *dq.w* might be the most satisfactory reading for the group when dealing with minerals.[43] The word *dq.w* had not been attested so far before the Second Intermediate period,[44] so the attestation in P. Mallorca I would then be the earliest one for this word. The full writing of *qꜣḥ* in P. Mallorca I frags. 2-4 suggests the reading *qꜣḥ* also in S. Louvre C100. Harris included two separate entries for *qꜣḥ* and *qḥ* in his lexicographical analysis, translating the former as "earth, clay" and the latter as "(gypsum) plaster" based on its use in S. Louvre C100 as a material characteristic for its white color.[45] As I have previously remarked, the orthography *qꜣḥ* in P. Mallorca I frags. 2-4 suggests that these should be taken as two orthographies of the same word,[46] with a range of meanings from clay to mortar/gypsum plaster.[47] Bardinet has indicated that "dents blanches et petites dents sont bien les deux principes immuables de l'esthétique dentaire."[48]

   ẖb(ꜣ) m ḥn(j): I follow here Bardinet's reading, who translates the phrase as "entaille dans le roseau."[49] I take *ẖb* as a noun related to the verb *ẖbꜣ* "to destroy, to cut off"[50] (*Wb.* III:253, 2–11). I have translated *ḥn(j)* as papyrus in a broad sense (genus *Cyperus*), referring to a marshy reed plant whose section appears white when

36. Reading *ỉd*[*bw*], although the *b* is present in the stela: Kitchen, *Poetry of Ancient Egypt*, 460–61; reading *jdb*[*wy*]: Bernard Mathieu, *La poésie amoureuse de l'Égypte ancienne: Recherches sur un genre littéraire au Nouvel Empire*, BdÉ 115 (Cairo: Institut français d'archéologie orientale, 1996), 36n34. Mathieu also suggests the reading *j.dꜣb*[*.w*], "figues."

37. Hermann, *Altägyptische Liebesdichtung*, 127. For example, Schott, Bardinet, and Mathieu (see n. 36 supra) also read "figs": Siegfried Schott, *Altägyptische Liebeslieder* (Zürich: Artemis, 1950), 100; Bardinet, *Dents et mâchoires*, 86: "le fruit du figuier," he did not recognize the word *jꜣrr.wt*, "grapes."

38. *Wb.* V:8, 2–5; Hildegard von Deines and Hermann Grapow, *Wörterbuch der ägyptischen Drogennamen*, Grundriss der Medizin der alten Ägypter 6 (Berlin: Akademie-Verlag, 1959), 512–13.

39. Kitchen, *Poetry of Ancient Egypt*, 460.

40. Bardinet, *Dents et mâchoires*, 86.

41. Lutz Popko in TLA (October 2012).

42. *Wb.* V:494, 15–495, 5; von Deines and Grapow, *Wörterbuch der ägyptischen Drogennamen*, 582–83.

43. John R. Harris, *Lexicographical Studies in Ancient Egyptian Minerals*, VIO 54 (Berlin: Akademie-Verlag, 1961), 221. See also von Deines and Grapow, *Wörterbuch der ägyptischen Drogennamen*, 609–10.

44. This statement is based on the attestations of the word collected in the database of the TLA (http://aaew.bbaw.de/tla/) as of October of 2019. The *Wörterbuch* document DZA 31.463.360 lists a series of cognates of *dq.w*. I want to thank Diego M. Santos for pointing them out to me. A thorough inspection of the nuances of these cognates would perhaps clarify the early meaning of *dq.w*, but it falls outside of the purposes of the present study.

45. *qꜣḥ*: Harris, *Lexicographical Studies*, 205–6; *ḳḥ*: Harris, 90.

46. See Werner Vycichl, *Dictionnaire étymologique de la langue copte* (Leuven: Peeters, 1983), 91, s.v. ⲕⲁϩ. I want to thank Diego M. Santos for this reference, and for his erudite discussion of this word with me.

47. Escolano-Poveda, "New Fragments of Papyrus Berlin 3024," 27. On mortar and plaster, see Alfred Lucas, *Ancient Egyptian Materials & Industries*, 3rd rev. ed. (London: Arnold, 1948), 93–98; Barry Kemp, "Soil (Including Mud Brick Architecture)," in *Ancient Egyptian Materials and Technologies*, ed. Paul T. Nicholson and Ian Shaw (Cambridge: Cambridge University Press, 2000), 92–93. I thank Diego M. Santos for this reference.

48. Bardinet, *Dents et mâchoires*, 87.

49. Bardinet, 86. This reading is also followed by Popko in TLA (October 2012); and Mathieu, who translates "entame d'un roseau": Mathieu, *La poésie amoureuse*, 87n276. *ẖb* was already translated as "entame" by Maspero: Maspero, "Notes sur quelques points," 53.

50. Quack translates *ẖb* as "fibers (?)": Joachim Friedrich Quack, "Where Once Was Love, Love Is No More? What Happens to Expressions of Love in Late Period Egypt?," in *WdO* 46 (2015): 65n19.

freshly cut.[51] Other scholars have read *m(ꜣ)ḥ*[52] "wreath" or *mḥ*[53] "flax" instead, ignoring the *n*-sign below the first M2 sign. This reading further connects the description of the goddess in the Tale of the Herdsman to a marshy environment. The common words for papyrus (*Cyperus papyrus*) are *mḥj.t* and *mnḥ*. This word appears as *mnḥ.j* in P. Mallorca I frag. 48.[54] Another possibility is to read here *ḫb mḥn*, with a metathesis *mnḥ* > *mḥn* "papyrus slice."[55]

2.3. Comparison of Both Texts and Reconstruction

The comparison of P. Mallorca I frags. 2-4 and S. Louvre C100 lines 3–4 clearly shows that we are dealing with the same text. However, the orthographies of some of the words differ from one text to the other. The first main difference appears in the writing of *jꜣrr.wt* and *dꜣb.w*. While P. Mallorca I has full orthographies for both words, in S. Louvre C100 both the phonetic writing of the words and their determinatives have been abbreviated, and in the case of *dꜣb.w* no determinative is present. If this determinative was located in the beginning of line 4, it would probably have been the material-sign (N33) with plural strokes, as in *jꜣrr.wt*. As I have noted above, these orthographies have hindered the identification of these words, especially *dꜣb.w*, until now. Another of the main orthographic differences concerns the word for "teeth," which may have been spelled with the sign U40 in P. Mallorca I, and the expression *dq.w r/n qꜣḥ*, where once more the writings in S. Louvre C100 are more abbreviated. These differences indicate that the text in S. Louvre C100 is not a direct copy from P. Mallorca I but was derived from an intermediate attestation of the text, either copied at some point from P. Mallorca I or from another manuscript of the Tale of the Herdsman. The fact that the fragment from P. Mallorca I seems to have been preserved with the rolls of the Berlin Library may indicate that it played some role in the later transmission of the text, as I will discuss below.

Using both copies we can reconstruct what the text in P. Mallorca I would have looked like. The first section of the description in S. Louvre C100 may not have been part of the original text, which may have started either with *n pꜣ.tw* or directly with *km*. For this reconstruction I chose the first option. The text in the gray box corresponds to the section preserved in P. Mallorca I. For the orthographies of the words only present in S. Louvre C100, I opted for Middle Kingdom orthographies.[56]

51. See *Wb.* III:100, 1–9; von Deines and Grapow, *Wörterbuch der ägyptischen Drogennamen*, 351.

52. Max Müller, *Die Liebespoesie der alten Ägypter*, 44 and n. 10.

53. Quack, "Where Once Was Love, Love Is No More?," 65n19. He labels the translation as uncertain.

54. See Escolano-Poveda, "New Fragments of Papyrus Berlin 3024," 29 and 46. For *mḥj.t*, see Germer, "Untersuchung über Arzneimittelpflanzen," 138–40.

55. I want to thank Diego M. Santos for this suggestion.

56. For the orthography of *ḫbꜣ* in col. 4 I followed the orthography in P. Berlin 3023 col. 174, which includes the knife determinative, present in S. Louvre C100.

As for the continuation of the text beyond this point, it is possible to make a suggestion. Bardinet connects the text on S. Louvre C100 with the "Chants du Verger".[57] In one of them we have a talking pomegranate tree saying: "A ses dents mes grains sont semblables, et mes fruits ressemblent à ses seins." Here we also see the succession teeth-breasts in the description, which might indicate that the comparison that followed on S. Louvre C100 would have been of Mutirdis's breasts with pomegranates or other fruits, like the fruits of the mandrake that we see in love poems.

3. The Stela S. Louvre C100 and New Kingdom Love Poetry

The stela S. Louvre C100 was acquired in 1826 by the Department of Egyptian Antiquities of the Musée Charles X, later the Louvre Museum, as part of the Salt Collection.[58] The first record of it appears in the catalog of the collection made by Champollion, in which he did not include a provenance for the stela but dated it to the reign of Thutmose III based on the preserved cartouches.[59] The first image of it was published by Prisse d'Avennes in 1847,[60] and the first translation was made in 1878 by Paul Pierret,[61] curator of the Department of Egyptian Antiquities of the Louvre at the time. This translation was improved upon, with suggestions for the reading of some of the broken and unclear areas, by Maspero a year later.[62] The connection of the text on the stela with New Kingdom love poetry, a corpus that was being edited at the same time, was first suggested by Maspero in 1883 in an article about the poems in the col-

57. Bardinet, *Dents et mâchoires*, 87.

58. Yoyotte, "Pharaon Iny," 117 and n. 30.

59. Jean-François Champollion, *Notice descriptive des monuments égyptiens du Musée Charles X* (Paris: Imprimerie de Crapelet, 1827), 57n31.

60. Émile Prisse d'Avennes, *Monuments égyptiens, bas-reliefs, peintures, inscriptions, etc., d'après les dessins executes sur les lieux* (Paris: Didot, 1847), pl. IV, 1.

61. Pierret, *Recueil d'inscriptions*, 105–7. The translation of the section that parallels P. Mallorca I frag. 2-4 goes as follows: "Le noir de sa chevelure est au dessus du noir de la nuit, au dessus des grappes de la vigne ... les ... du fruit-qaḥs'a. Coupés ... ses seins, l'amour réside dans ses bras."

62. Maspero, "Notes sur quelques points," 54: "Noire sa chevelure plus que le noir de la nuit, plus que les baies du prunelier. [Rouge]

lection of the Turin Museum and P. Harris 500.[63] In 1899 Max Müller published the first German translation of the stela and with brilliant intuition noted in his introduction that he thought the text had been borrowed from an older composition, dating to the Middle Kingdom.[64] The stela has since then been included in most studies of Egyptian poetry, such as those of Schott,[65] Hermann,[66] and Kitchen,[67] as well as in analyses of Egyptian love poetry in connection with the biblical *Song of Songs*,[68] and in various analyses of other topics.[69] Vernus does not include the stela in his book on ancient Egyptian love songs,[70] and although Mathieu leaves it out of his corpus, which he restricts to the New Kingdom material, he refers to it in several notes offering the transliteration and translation of some passages.[71] The most recent translation of the text of the stela is that of Quack in an analysis of the expression of love in Egyptian literature in the first millennium BCE.[72]

The description of princess Mutirdis in S. Louvre C100 presents a series of double comparisons of parts of her body with different natural elements, organized from the top down. First, the color of her hair, and perhaps its lushness and sheen, is compared to the darkness of the night and to grapes and figs. Then the whiteness of her teeth is

---

sa [joue] plus que les grains du jaspe, plus que l'entame d'un régime de palmes, Les pointes de sa gorge séduisent plus encore que son flanc!"

63. Gaston Maspero, "Les chants d'amour du papyrus de Turin et du papyrus Harris no. 500," *Journal Asiatique* 8 (1883): 45–46: "Je crois, quant à moi, que l'inscription de la stèle C. 100 du Louvre est un fragment détaché de l'un d'eux [scil. New Kingdom love poems]. Cette stèle, dédiée par un roi à sa fille Moutiritis, renferme, au lieu du proscynème ordinaire, une description des beautés de la princesse," and "C'est là évidemment un morceau de poésie populaire que le rédacteur de la stèle a cru pouvoir appliquer à la princesse. Malheureusement l'exemple qu'il avait donné ne paraît guère avoir été suivi; je ne connais aucune stèle qui renferme un texte analogue au texte de la stèle du Louvre." In this article Maspero offers a translation of the text that does not differ substantially from that published in 1879.

64. Max Müller, *Die Liebespoesie der alten Ägypter*, 44 and pl. 16, 18: "Zum Schluss ein merkwürdiges Fragment aus einem alten Liebesgedicht, das uns, wie Maspero zeigte, im Epitaph einer Frau erhalten ist. Dies wurde eingemeisselt unter einem Äthiopenkönig, aber die Stelle ist gewiss einem älteren Text entnommen. Ich vermute ein Original des mittleren Reiches." His translation of the section with the description of the princess is the following: "Schwärzer war ihr Haar – als das Dunkel der Nacht, als die Beeren des Adeb(-Strauches?). [Weisser waren?] ihre Zähne (?) als der Splitter von Feuerstein an (?) der Säge (?) Zwei Kränze waren ihre Brüste, festgesetzt (?) an ihren Arm."

65. Schott, *Altägyptische Liebeslieder*, 100: "Schwärzer ist ihr Haar als die Schwärze der Nacht, als Weintrauben und Feigen. Ihre Zähne sind schöner gereiht als … Kerne, als (die Kerben des Feuerstein)messers. Ihre Brüste stehen fest an ihrem Leib."

66. Hermann, *Altägyptische Liebesdichtung*, 127, who borrows Schott's translation.

67. Kitchen, *Poetry of Ancient Egypt*, 460–61, including transliteration: "More raven is her hair than the black of night, than the grapes of the river-[bank], [Whiter are] her [teeth], than flakes (?) of plaster, than a slice of papyrus(-pith). Her breasts are firm on her bosom […]."

68. John Bradley White, *A Study of the Language of Love in the Song of Songs and Ancient Egyptian Poetry* (Missoula, MT: Scholars Press, 1975), 189–90: "Blacker is her hair than the blackness of the night, than the grapes of the *idb*-vines. [Whiter (are) her teeth] than flakes of (white) stone at cutting. (Two) wreaths are her breasts settled at her arm." Michael V. Fox, *The Song of Songs and the Ancient Egyptian Love Songs* (Madison: University of Wisconsin Press, 1985), 349 and 408 for hieroglyphic copy: "Blacker her hair than the black of night, than grapes of the riverbank. [Whiter] her teeth than bits of plaster, than---in a *ḥn*-plant. Her breasts are set firm on her bosom."

69. The hieroglyphic text without translation is part of Jansen-Winkeln's catalog of Late period inscriptions: Karl Jansen-Winkeln, *Inschriften der Spätzeit, Teil II: Die 22.–24. Dynastie* (Wiesbaden: Harrassowitz, 2007), 382–83. Bardinet incorporates the stela into his analysis of teeth in ancient Egypt, providing a hieroglyphic transcription, transliteration, and translation of lines 3 and 4, with some commentary. Bardinet, *Dents et mâchoires*, 85–87: "Sa chevelure est noire plus que le noir de la nuit, plus que le fruit du figuier… sa denture <est blanche> plus que la poudre de gypse, plus que l'entaille dans le roseau; ses dents seins sont fermes sur sa poitrine."

70. Pascal Vernus, *Chants d'amour de l'Égypte antique* (Paris: Imprimerie Nationale, 1992).

71. Mathieu, *La poésie amoureuse*, 36n34: "*km šnw.w⸗s r km n grḥ r j(ꜣ)rr(.t) jdb*[*.wy*] (*qu j.dꜣb*[*.w*]), ses cheveux sont plus noirs que le noir de la nuit, que les raisins des Deux-Rives (ou que les raisins et les figues)," and 87n276: "[*ḥḏ ṯs.t*]*⸗s r dḳ*{*r*} *n ḳḥ r ẖb m ḥn*(*.t*) *bn.ty⸗s grg*(*⸗w*) *r ḳb⸗s* […], sa denture est plus blanche que la poudre de gypse, que l'entame d'un roseau, ses seins sont bien droits sur sa poitrine […]."

72. Quack, "Where Once Was Love, Love Is No More?," 64–65: "Blacker is her hair than the black of the night, than grapes of the …, [whiter] are her teeth than gypsum powder(?), than the fibers(?) of flax(?). Her breasts are set firm on her bosom. […]"

correlated with that of powder for gypsum mortar, and to the color of a freshly sliced papyrus stem. The next body part described are her breasts, which are said to sit firm on her chest. Unfortunately, the comparisons that probably followed this statement are lost.

The poetical character of the description was recognized very early, as I have noted above, and its structure was compared to that of some of the other Egyptian love poems. In his monograph on Egyptian love poetry, Alfred Hermann presented a classification of the surviving Egyptian poems into three genres: "Beschreibungslied," "Tagelied," and "Türklage" (the Greek *paraklausíthyron*).[73] Hermann borrowed the name of the first genre from the Arabic poetical tradition, where it is known as *waṣf* (plural *awṣāf*). It consists in a description of the parts of the body of the girl comparing them to other elements, normally taken from the rural environment. Hermann classified under this category the poems in P. Harris 500 recto 1.11–2.1,[74] P. Chester Beatty 1 C1 1.1–1.5,[75] and our praise of princess Mutirdis in S. Louvre C100.

Although the text on S. Louvre C100 shares characteristics with the love poetry of the New Kingdom, it differs from it in two main aspects. The first one is its language: while the New Kingdom love poems are written in Late Egyptian, the idiom of the period, the language of S. Louvre C100 is Middle Egyptian. Secondly, the corpus of texts that we designate as New Kingdom love poetry is limited chronologically to the second half of the thirteenth and the twelfth century BCE, consisting of three papyri and about a dozen ostraca.[76] S. Louvre C100 lies outside of this chronological frame, dating to the Third Intermediate period.[77] Because of these two characteristics, its language and chronology, S. Louvre C100 has heretofore been seen as a problematic fit in this tradition, being considered as a late development of the New Kingdom poetical corpus.[78]

4. Connections between the Tale of the Herdsman and New Kingdom Love Poetry

The identification of the description of the goddess in the Tale of the Herdsman, as preserved in P. Mallorca I, with the praise of Mutirdis in S. Louvre C100 has significant implications for the chronology of the New Kingdom love poetry tradition and offers a firmer basis upon which to search for antecedents of this tradition. Many scholars have

73. Hermann, *Altägyptische Liebesdichtung*, 124–30. These genres were translated by White as "descriptive song," "day song," and "lament at the door," see White, *Study of the Language of Love*, 114. Fox named the "Beschreibungslied" "Praise of the Beloved," see Fox, *The Song of Songs*, 269. His classification is not the same as Hermann's, since he only considers as part of this theme P. Chester Beatty I, C1 1–8 and O. Gardiner 304 recto. Fox only considers the New Kingdom poems under his designation "Praise of the Beloved," see Fox, *The Song of Songs*, 269.

74. In this poem, the fourth one of the first collection in the papyrus, the mouth, breasts, arms, forehead and hair of the girl are compared to flowers and fruits, and to tools for fowling, while the lover identifies himself with a wild goose being trapped by the beloved. For a recent translation and commentary, see Mathieu, *La poésie amoureuse*, 57 and notes.

75. The body parts listed in this poem are the girl's complexion, the look in her eyes, the speech of her lips, her nape, chest, hair, arms, fingers, buttocks, waistline, and hips. Some of the elements used in the comparisons in this poem are lapis lazuli and gold (for her hair and arms, respectively), which are substances associated with the divine and therefore approximate the beloved girl to a goddess. Translation and commentary in Mathieu, *La poésie amoureuse*, 26–27 and notes.

76. For a brief summary of the characteristics of Egyptian love poetry, see Waltraud Guglielmi, "Die ägyptische Liebespoesie," in *Ancient Egyptian Literature: History and Forms*, ed. Antonio Loprieno (Leiden: Brill, 1996), 335–47.

77. For the dating, see section 2.2 above.

78. Quack has acknowledged the problems in the understanding of this textual tradition, see Quack, "Where Once Was Love, Love Is No More?," 65: "What makes the text more special are the final preserved phrases. They clearly stand in the tradition of the description of bodily beauty as attested in New Kingdom Egyptian texts (pChester Beatty I, vs. C, 1–8), as well as the Song of Songs. Even if we accept the Louvre stela as evidence that some memory of love poetry was still living around 700 BCE, the problem remains that the quite substantial Demotic literary remnants from the Ptolemaic and Roman periods do not include any single piece of love poetry resembling the New Kingdom compositions or the Song of Songs."

attempted to contextualize the extremely time-restricted phenomenon of New Kingdom love poetry. Hermann proposed that the genre of the Beschreibungslied in particular had derived from the cultic descriptive hymns in which parts of the body of the deceased king were equated with those of the gods.[79] Fox responded that the similarities ended in the listing of parts of the body: "Nowhere in the love songs are the parts of the girl's or boy's body identified with gods or anything belonging to gods. Furthermore, the predications in the cultic hymns are not meant to praise the dead man's body but rather to bestow upon it the protective power of divinity".[80] Loprieno sees two genres in the origins of Egyptian love poetry: a type of text that "combines mythical and pastoral traits and praises the joys of life in the countryside," in which he classifies the Tale of the Herdsman and the Pleasures of Fishing and Fowling; and the genre of the harpers' songs.[81] More recently, Darnell connected the Herdsman with other compositions like the Pleasures of Fishing and Fowling and some New Kingdom poems in the frame of the return of the goddess in the New Year.[82] He also examined the pastoral setting of the love poems.[83] For his part, Baines acknowledges that love poetry may have originated before the New Kingdom and that its appearance in written form at this point may be due to a change in decorum more than in cultural practice. He considers its closeness to the harpers' songs and to magical texts, with both of which it was grouped together by the scribe of P. Harris 500.[84]

These interpretations highlight three elements in the love poems: a pastoral environment, connection with hymns to deities, and closeness to magical texts. The same elements also happen to be present in the Tale of the Herdsman. Concerning the first one, many of the poems are set in the world of the marshes, for example with the tools used for fishing and fowling incorporated to the description in P. Harris 500 recto 1.11–12. We also find what Hermann called "Hirten-Travestie," in which the lover assumes the identity of a herdsman or shepherd.[85] White highlighted the erotic aspect of the "woman in the swamp," present in the Middle Kingdom already in the Tale of the Herdsman, and continuing into the New Kingdom with the "erotic adventure" of a boat trip to the marshes for papyrus-gathering.[86] The second element, the connection with hymns to deities, has been further analyzed by Mathieu, who identified the hymn to Mut in ostracon O. DM 1055 as the source for the Chester Beatty cycle.[87] Furthermore, according to my proposal here, the model for the praise of princess Mutirdis in S. Louvre C100, and the earliest attestation of the Beschreibungslied known so far, is the description of the goddess in the Tale of the Herdsman preserved in P. Mallorca I. Thus, Fox's aforementioned affirmation that the descriptions in love poems are not connected to anything belonging

79. Hermann, *Altägyptische Liebesdichtung*, 130: "Anderseits hat sich zeigen lassen, daß dieser literarische Typ in der religiösen Literatur Ägyptens eine Art Vorläufer besaß in Gestalt der kultischen Beschreibungshymne. Diese beruhte auf der Vorliebe des archaischen Denkens, ein körperliches Ganzes, z. B. eine Gottesgestalt, sich in ihre Glieder zerlegt vorzuführen, um die Einheit aus der Aneinanderfügung der Teile erstehen zu lassen."

80. Fox, *The Song of Songs*, 271.

81. Antonio Loprieno, "Searching for a Common Background: Egyptian Love Poetry and the Biblical Song of Songs," in *Perspectives on the Song of Songs*, ed. Anselm C. Hagedorn (Berlin: de Gruyter, 2005), 112.

82. John Coleman Darnell, "A Midsummer Night's Succubus—The Herdsman's Encounters in P. Berlin 3024, The Pleasures of Fishing and Fowling, The Songs of the Drinking Place, and the Ancient Egyptian Love Poetry," in *Opening the Tablet Box: Near Eastern Studies in Honor of Benjamin R. Foster*, ed. Sarah C. Melville and Alice Louise Slotsky (Leiden: Brill, 2010), 99–140. On pp. 126–27 Darnell points out that the boat mentioned in P. Harris 500 B1, line 10 is called *smḫ*, the same word used in the Tale of the Herdsman, col. x+11. As I noted in my edition of P. Mallorca I, *smḫ* also appears in frag. 3 col. 1, and the Tale of the Herdsman is the only Middle Kingdom attestation of the word.

83. See John Coleman Darnell, "The Rituals of Love in Ancient Egypt: Festival Songs of the Eighteenth Dynasty and the Ramesside Love Poetry," *WdO* 46 (2016): 22–24.

84. John Baines, "Classicism and Modernism in the Literature of the New Kingdom," in Loprieno, *Ancient Egyptian Literature: History and Forms*, 167–68.

85. See Hermann, *Altägyptische Liebesdichtung*, 119–24.

86. See White, *Study of the Language of Love*, 73–74.

87. Mathieu, *La poésie amoureuse*, 240.

to a deity would not be accurate.[88] On the one hand, the model for them seems to be the description of a goddess, and on the other hand, the elements used in the description in P. Chester Beatty 1 C1 1.1–1.5, gold and lapis lazuli, assimilate the girl to the ideal of a goddess. The goddess in the Tale of the Herdsman has been identified with a Hathor-like goddess,[89] and Hathor is in fact the goddess who appears more frequently in the corpus of Egyptian love poetry.[90] It is relevant to remark here that Mutirdis was a priestess of Hathor and Mut. The connection with magical texts involves the way the Tale of the Herdsman has come down to us, and thus I proceed to its discussion in the following section.

5. Transmission: The Water Spell and the Description of the Goddess

The reason why the section containing twenty-five columns of the Tale of the Herdsman was attached at the end of the roll of the *Debate* remains a mystery, but it might have been connected to the presence, around the middle part of the preserved text (cols. 14–22), of the water spell. This spell is also known from Coffin Texts 836, only attested once, in the coffin of Mentuhotep called Buau (CG 28027), which according to Morenz should be dated to the mid-Twelfth Dynasty.[91] Scholars have long debated the connection between these two attestations.[92] Ogdon's hypothesis that the spell was originally part of the Tale of the Herdsman, from where it was incorporated into the Coffin Texts, seems likely to me.[93] I propose that the fragmentary way in which this narrative has come down to us is connected to the deliberate preservation of the section with the spell and its context, in order to be used in the Coffin Texts and perhaps in magical handbooks that have not survived. The preservation of the fragments of the Herdsman now in Mallorca may also have been connected to an intentional preservation of the description of the goddess and its context[94] for future use.[95]

A closer look at the use of water spells provides a connection between this magical formula and New Kingdom love poetry, linking the later potential context of use of the water spell and the description of the goddess in the

---

88. However, as John Baines points out to me (pers. comm., 24 May 2020), the origin of the genre would be in performed social practice, invisible to us. Here, humans were the ultimate model for the physical description of deities.

89. See my discussion with references in Escolano-Poveda, "New Fragments of Papyrus Berlin 3024," 38–39.

90. Mathieu indicates that Hathor (or Goddess of Gold) appears a total of five times, while Amon appears twice or three times, Ptah twice, Night personified twice, and Re, Nun, Sothis, Sekhmet, Iadet, Nefertum, and Menqet once. Hathor is especially prominent, since she is the one who assigns the girl to her lover. See Mathieu, *La poésie amoureuse*, 233.

91. Ludwig D. Morenz, *Beiträge zur Schriftlichkeitskultur im Mittleren Reich und in der 2. Zwischenzeit* (Wiesbaden: Harrassowitz, 1996), 136 and n. 585.

92. This connection was first noted by Gilula, see Mordechai Gilula, "Hirtengeschichte 17–22 = CT VII 36a-r," *GM* 29 (1978): 21–22, and has been the subject of several analyses by Ogdon (Jorge Roberto Ogdon "CT VII, 36i-r = Spell 836," *GM* 58 [1982]: 59–64; Jorge Roberto Ogdon, "A Hitherto Unrecognized Metaphor of Death in Papyrus Berlin 3024," *GM* 100 [1987]: 73–80; Jorge Roberto Ogdon, "Return to Coffin Texts Spell 836 and the Hirtengeschichte," *CCdE* 6 [2004]: 117–35), who thinks that the spell in the Coffin Texts was borrowed from the Herdsman. Baines considered this hypothesis uncertain, see John Baines, "Myth and Literature," in Loprieno, *Ancient Egyptian Literature: History and Forms*, 368. Mathieu agrees with Ogdon's interpretation in Mathieu, "Le conte du Pâtre," 201. Morenz proposed in 1996 that Buau may have been the owner of the Berlin Library, see Morenz, *Beiträge zur Schriftlichkeitskultur*, 124–41. This interpretation has not been generally accepted, since there is not enough evidence to support such a claim.

93. Below, I propose an interpretation that may indicate that this specific spell was composed originally for the Tale of the Herdsman. These water spells to ward off crocodiles existed already in the Old Kingdom, where we find them inscribed next to scenes of herdsmen crossing canals and marshy areas with their cattle. For these, see Robert Kriech Ritner, *The Mechanics of Ancient Egyptian Magical Practice*, SAOC 54 (Chicago: Oriental Institute of the University of Chicago, 1993), 225–29.

94. Part of this context may have been the transformation of the goddess into human form in P. Mallorca I frag. 3.

95. The scribe who put together P. Berlin 3024 as it stands now does not seem to have attached the P. Mallorca I fragments to it, but he seems to have decided to preserve them together with the four rolls of the Berlin Library. For my reconstruction of how P. Mallorca I and II and P. Berlin 3024 came to be in the state in which they have come down to us, see Escolano-Poveda, "New Fragments of Papyrus Berlin 3024," 30–33.

Herdsman. Scholars like Hermann and Mathieu noted the connections between some love poems and magical practices.[96] A reference to a water spell is mentioned in the love poem preserved in O. DM 1266, 11–13.[97] In this poem the lover has to cross a river in order to reach his beloved. In order to do so he says that his love is as effective as magic, and in particular, as a *ḥs.t-mw*, a "water spell." This is the same designation used in the Herdsman. This reference thus further connects the pastoral context and the magic performed for protection from evil forces in this environment to the love poetry of the New Kingdom. It is relevant to note that the Harris Magical Papyrus (P. Harris 501 = P. BM EA 10042) contains a series of spells to ward off crocodiles.[98] This papyrus appears to have been found together with P. Harris 500 (= P. BM EA 10060), one of the main compilations of Ramesside love poems, although the circumstances of the find are not entirely clear.[99] If the information provided by Harris about the origin of the papyri is indeed correct, and the papyri were originally buried together in a hole inside a tomb on the mountains behind Medinet Habu,[100] this may indicate that the last owner of the texts had an interest both in magic and in love poetry.

6. Transmission: Orality, Literacy, and "Archaism"

The use of the water spell in the Tale of the Herdsman, which is recited by the wise men among the herdsmen (*rḫ.w-ḫ.wt n.w mn.jww*, cols. 12–13), has some bearing upon the interactions between orality and literacy in the transmission of the description of the goddess in the Herdsman and its incorporation into the praise of princess Mutirdis in S. Louvre C100. The inclusion of the water spell in the Herdsman brings into this narrative the lived reality of herdsmen who tended their animals in the marshes, and the dangers they faced there. The spell could have originally been used and transmitted orally already in the Old Kingdom, being put into writing later and incorporated into the Herdsman,[101] and subsequently into the Coffin Texts. The reference to a water spell in O. DM 1266 and the collection in the Harris Magical Papyrus attest to the continuation of the belief in the effectiveness of these spells in the New Kingdom.

The description of the goddess in the Herdsman, as we have seen, follows a very similar structure to that found in several New Kingdom love poems. Its attestation in S. Louvre C100 indicates that it survived beyond the New Kingdom, to be used again in the Third Intermediate Period. I have proposed previously that the papyrus fragments that preserve it were intentionally kept together with the rolls of the Berlin Library.[102] A hint as to how this may have

96. See Hermann, *Altägyptische Liebesdichtung*, 84–88; Mathieu, *La poésie amoureuse*, 230–32.

97. For the text, see Mathieu, *La poésie amoureuse*, 231–32.

98. Latest edition in Christian Leitz, *Magical and Medical Papyri of the New Kingdom*, Hieratic Papyri in the British Museum 7 (London: British Museum Press, 1999), 31–51. See also Joanna Alexandra Kyffin, "'Every Golden Scale': Scribal and Rhetorical Strategies in the Harris Magical Papyrus" (PhD diss., University of Liverpool, 2009). I thank Roland Enmarch for the latter reference.

99. For the different accounts of the origin of these papyri, see Kyffin, "'Every Golden Scale,'" 77–108.

100. For Harris's account and Birch's more polished retelling of it, see Kyffin, "'Every Golden Scale,'" 85–87.

101. But see a possible alternative explanation below in this section. Ritner has explored the social context of these spells in Ritner, *Mechanics of Ancient Egyptian Magical Practice*, 222–31. Here he connects the water spell to the finds from the tomb of the Ramesseum, in particular to the ivory figurine of a herdsman carrying a calf and to the female figure with leonine head. The latter in particular has been related to the goddess of the Tale of the Herdsman, see Darnell, "A Midsummer Night's Succubus," 117; Richard Bruce Parkinson, *Reading Ancient Egyptian Poetry among Other Stories* (Oxford: Wiley-Blackwell, 2009), 144–45.

102. Escolano-Poveda, "New Fragments of Papyrus Berlin 3024," 33. The remaining fragments of the roll of the Tale of the Herdsman, now P. Mallorca I, may have been preserved rolled up over one of the other rolls, perhaps P. Berlin 3024 itself, which would explain their state of preservation. We have evidence of manuscripts rolled up together from other papyrus ensembles, such as P. St Petersburg 1116A and 1116B and P. Anastasi 3 and 3A, see Roland Enmarch, The Dialogue of Ipuwer and the Lord of All (Oxford: Griffith Institute, 2005), 3. Enmarch indicates that "P Anastasi 3A is only a single sheet and may have been rolled up with P Anastasi 3 for protection," Enmarch, *The Dialogue of Ipuwer*, 3. This may have been the case of P. Mallorca I with respect to P. Berlin 3024 or another of the rolls of the Berlin Library.

happened can be found in P. Chester Beatty I 16.9, which introduces a poem as "Beginning of the sweet verses (*ṯs.w nḏm*) found in a book container (*ṯꜣy-drf*) and written by the scribe of the Necropolis Nakhtsobek."[103] Although the finding of a book is a literary *topos*,[104] this reference may actually describe how some of these poems were kept and transmitted in written form, including P. Mallorca I frags. 2-4.[105]

Despite their similarities in structure, the New Kingdom Beschreibungslied-type poems were composed in Late Egyptian, and thus they do not depend directly on the Middle Egyptian description of the goddess in the Herdsman. This observation seems to point towards a strand of transmission parallel to the written tradition. The same was already indicated by Baines, as I noted above, who suggested that the appearance of the love poems in written form in the New Kingdom may respond to a change in decorum.[106] Thus, a tradition of love poetry, and in our case of poetical descriptions of the female body in particular, connected to Hathor-like goddesses and their cult, may have existed before the New Kingdom. It seems to have filtered into written form at just a few times in history.[107] We only have written attestations for it in the Middle Kingdom with the Herdsman, in the New Kingdom with the Beschreibungslied-type poems, and in the Third Intermediate period with the praise of Mutirdis.[108] While the transmission from the Herdsman to S. Louvre C100 seems to have been in written form, since despite some orthographic variations the text remained the same, the New Kingdom attestations seem to correspond to a recording of oral practice, and thus they were written in the idiom of the period, Late Egyptian.

The Tale of the Herdsman probably had a parallel oral transmission as part of the folklore of the marshy areas, as its attestation in medieval times in the story told by Murtaḍā ibn al-ʿAfīf might indicate.[109] From the original Tale of the Herdsman as preserved in P. Berlin 3024 and in P. Mallorca I, we only have a section of the whole story, but we may use Murtaḍā's narrative in order to reconstruct the parts that are missing, chiefly the story's conclusion. As I noted above, at the end of Murtaḍā's story, once the shepherd has been defeated several times and has lost a significant part of the royal herd, the king Gebir (Alexander the Great) intervenes and defeats the goddess. If we consider that the Tale of the Herdsman may have had a similar plot, with the intervention of a king who finally defeats the goddess after she has won against a nameless herdsman/shepherd repeatedly, perhaps we can try to identify who this king was by means of hints in the Middle Kingdom story itself. The water spell inserted in the narrative refers to a goddess called *Wsr.t*.[110] Mathieu has highlighted that the name of this goddess—which is one of the names of the goddess Mut—is also a constituent part of the names of several kings of the Twelfth and Thirteenth Dynasties, Senwosret, which could point to a Theban origin for the Herdsman.[111] We can argue that the inclusion of the *Wsr.t* in the narrative was also meant to connect it

103. For the text, see Mathieu, *La poésie amoureuse*, 32 and 47.

104. For this literary topos, see Wolfgang Speyer, *Bücherfunde in der Glaubenswerbung der Antike: Mit einem Ausblick auf Mittelalter und Neuzeit* (Göttingen: Vandenhoeck & Ruprecht, 1970).

105. The Ramesseum papyri of the Middle Kingdom were found in a box with some figurines and tools that may have belonged to a practitioner of magic, see n. 101 above.

106. Baines, "Classicism and Modernism in the New Kingdom," 167–68.

107. On the issue of orality and literacy in ancient Egypt, see John Baines, "Literacy and Ancient Egyptian Society," John Baines and Christopher Eyre "Four Notes on Literacy," and John Baines, "Orality and Literacy" in *Visual and Written Culture in Ancient Egypt*, ed. John Baines (Oxford: Oxford University Press, 2007), 33–62, 63–94, and 146–78 respectively. More recently, see Jacqueline E. Jay, *Orality and Literacy in the Demotic Tales* (Leiden: Brill, 2016).

108. I am not discussing in this paper the Near Eastern transmission of this kind of poetical description that led to the Song of Songs.

109. Furthermore, Schneider has pointed out that the story seems to have survived also as a Berber legend that features an ogress or lioness who tempts herdsmen with gentle requests in order to devour them, see Thomas Schneider, "Contextualising the Tale of the Herdsman," in *Egyptian Stories: A British Egyptological Tribute to Alan B. Lloyd on the Occasion of His Retirement*, ed. Thomas Schneider and Kasia Szpakowska (Münster: Ugarit-Verlag, 2007), 317–18.

110. See Herdsman col. x+21 (in the Coffin Texts CT VII 36q).

111. Mathieu, "Le conte du Pâtre," 201.

specifically with the first of the kings of this name, Senwosret I, who is connected to another of the poems found in the Berlin Library: the Tale of Sinuhe. The text of the spell says *r ꜣkt nšnj n Wsr.t*,[112] "until the storm of the Powerful One has perished," which may relate to king Senwosret's defeat of the goddess in the narrative. This point could also be used to argue that the water spell was specifically composed for the Tale of the Herdsman, since it would refer directly to king Senwosret I and his intervention in the conclusion of the narrative. This would highlight his capacity to pacify and defeat the dangerous powers of nature, embodied here in the Hathoric-like goddess of the Herdsman. From the Herdsman, the spell would have been incorporated into the Coffin Texts. As I noted above, the only attestation of the spell as part of the Coffin Texts appears in the coffin of Buau, dated to the mid-Twelfth Dynasty, which makes this interpretation chronologically plausible. On the connection between the original king Senwosret I of the Herdsman and the Gebir (Alexander the Great) of Murtaḍā's narrative, it is interesting to highlight that both kings were conflated in later literature.[113] In summary, the Tale of the Herdsman could be considered as part of the series of compositions written in the early Middle Kingdom as a legitimizing device for the Twelfth Dynasty, focused on the figure of Senwosret I, together with the previously mentioned Tale of Sinuhe and the Instruction of Amenemhat I.

These interpretations are highly hypothetical, since they deal with a tradition of which actual evidence is rather sparse. Nevertheless, I believe that they offer some interesting ideas for the study of oral and written transmission in the literature of ancient Egypt. Before concluding this essay, I would like to make a further proposal as to why the scribe who composed the text on S. Louvre C100 decided to use an old description written in Middle Egyptian. According to Yoyotte's interpretation of the erased cartouches, king Iny, the father of princess Mutirdis, who probably commissioned the stela, was a Theban contemporary of and probably also opponent to the Kushite kings of the Twenty-Fifth Dynasty.[114] This king chose the coronation name Menkheperre, building a connection with the New Kingdom. The choice of the poetical description of the goddess in the Herdsman may also have been a conscious connection with the classical literary past, which together with his name can be connected with the artistic and literary phenomenon known as "archaism."[115] It is not possible to ascertain whether the author of the text for the stela was aware of the origin of the description, or if it had already arrived to him independently from the narrative. Jasnow and Der Manuelian[116] have attested the transmission of some classical Middle Egyptian literary texts into the first millennium, so it is not completely unlikely that this connection was still known.

Conclusion

The connection between the sections of the Tale of the Herdsman preserved in P. Mallorca I and the stela of princess Mutirdis has allowed us to reevaluate the status of the latter as a solitary epilogue to New Kingdom love poetry, and to establish it as a crucial key to the understanding of the origins and evolution of what seems to be a parallel oral and written literary tradition. The story of the Herdsman may have been originally part of the legitimatory program of king Senwosret I and had itself an oral transmission as a folk narrative in the environment of the marshes that survived at least until the Middle Ages. The sources and interpretations presented here demonstrate the complexity and

112. *nšnj nj Wsr.t* might have been reminiscent of the name of the king, *Z-nj-wsr.t*.

113. See Kim Ryholt, "Imitatio Alexandri in Egyptian Literary Tradition," in *The Romance between Greece and the East*, ed. Tim Whitmarsh and Stuart Thomson (Cambridge: Cambridge University Press, 2013), 60–62. The legendary Sesostris is a fusion of several kings of this name.

114. See Yoyotte, "Pharaon Iny," 126–31.

115. For a brief introduction with updated bibliography, see Jochem Kahl, "Archaism," in *UCLAEE*, https://escholarship.org/uc/item/3tn7q1pf.

116. See Richard Jasnow, "Remarks on Continuity of Egyptian Literary Tradition," in *Gold of Praise: Studies on Ancient Egypt in Honor of Edward F. Wente*, ed. Emily Teeter and John A. Larson, SAOC 58 (Chicago: Oriental Institute, 1999); Peter Der Manuelian, *Living in the Past: Studies in Archaism of the Egyptian Twenty-Sixth Dynasty* (London: Kegan Paul International, 1994), 6–18.

interconnectedness of the Egyptian literary tradition and warn us about treating concepts such as orality, literacy, or genre reductively.

Making an Impression: How to Seal an Ur III Period Administrative Tablet in Nippur

Marian H. Feldman

During the Third Dynasty of Ur (or Ur III for short, ca. 2112–2004 BCE),[1] the number of administrative documents, in the form of clay tablets inscribed in the cuneiform script, increases exponentially from preceding periods. Many of these are simple documents recording basic economic transactions. Part way into the period, at the very end of the reign of Amar-Suen through the following reign of Šu-Suen, these simple administrative documents begin to be sealed with increasing frequency and extraordinary consistency.[2] In the last twenty years or so, scholars have focused on studying the practices of sealing Ur III documents, linking the apparent standardization of sealing practices to the emergence of a centralized territorial state under the Ur III rulers. Major archives associated with the state administration have been recovered, mostly illicitly, from several southern Mesopotamian cities, including Ur, Umma, Girsu, Drehem (ancient Puzriš-Dagan), and Garšana. It is against this backdrop of state archives and centralizing administration that this paper explores the sealing of a single tablet in the University of Pennsylvania Museum of Archaeology and Anthropology, UM 29-15-893, excavated from the site of Nippur at the end of the nineteenth century (figs. 1 and 2).[3]

The corpus of Ur III documents from Nippur presents a slightly different picture from other archives as many do not belong to the state apparatus despite the fact that individuals known from the texts have close associations with the state administration.[4] Indeed, the relationship of the individuals at Nippur to the Ur III state complicates notions

---

1. For a comprehensive overview of the Ur III period, see Walther Sallaberger, "Ur III-Zeit," in *Mesopotamien: Akkade-Zeit und Ur III-Zeit*, Walther Sallaberger and Aage Westenholz, OBO 160.3 (Fribourg: Presses Universitaires; Göttingen: Vandenhoeck & Ruprecht, 1999), 121–390. My thanks to Paul Delnero and Jake Lauinger for commenting on drafts of this article; they are, however, in no way responsible for any mistakes that remain.

2. In the earlier part of the Ur III period, tablets are more often encased in envelopes, and the envelopes are sealed. See, Piotr Steinkeller, *Sale Documents of the Ur-III-Period*, FAS 17 (Stuttgart: Steiner, 1989), 113. Overall, during the Ur III period, there is a large increase in the use of seals on administrative documents, with approximately 20% of the known corpus (more than 120,000) bearing seals, see Christina Tsouparopoulou, *The Ur III Seals Impressed on Documents from Puzriš-Dagān (Drehem)*, HSAO 16 (Heidelberg: Heidelberger Orientverlag, 2015), 17.

3. CDLI no. P121340 (https://cdli.ucla.edu/search/search_results.php?SearchMode=Text&requestFrom=Search&PrimaryPublication=&Author=&PublicationDate=&SecondaryPublication=&Collection=&AccessionNumber=&MuseumNumber=&Provenience=&ExcavationNumber=&Period=&DatesReferenced=&ObjectType=&ObjectRemarks=&Material=&TextSearch=&TranslationSearch=&CommentSearch=&StructureSearch=&Language=&Genre=&SubGenre=&CompositeNumber=&SealID=&ObjectID=P121340&ATFSource=&CatalogueSource=&TranslationSource=).

4. For example, tablets from Nippur tend to use the Nippur calendar and conventions of the Nippur scribal traditions. See, Steven J. Garfinkle, *Entrepreneurs and Enterprise in Early Mesopotamia: A Study of Three Archives from the Third Dynasty of Ur (2112–2004 BCE)*, CUSAS 22 (Bethesda, MD: CDL, 2012), 110, 112. The archaeological findspots of the Nippur tablets are not entirely clear. Their archaeology is discussed in Atsuko Hattori, "Texts and Impressions: A Holistic Approach to Ur III Cuneiform Tablets from the University

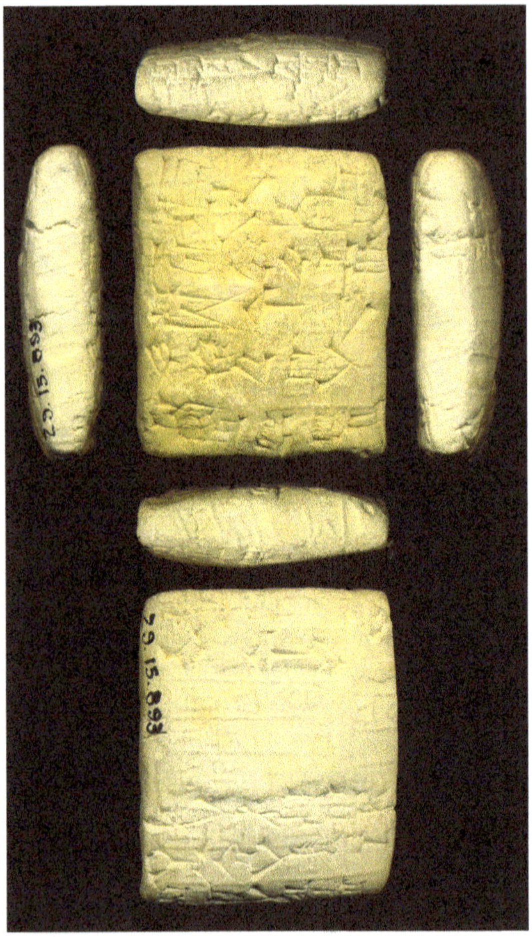

Figure 1. Scan of tablet UM 29-15-893 (NATN 642; CDLI P121340). Reproduced courtesy of Penn Museum.

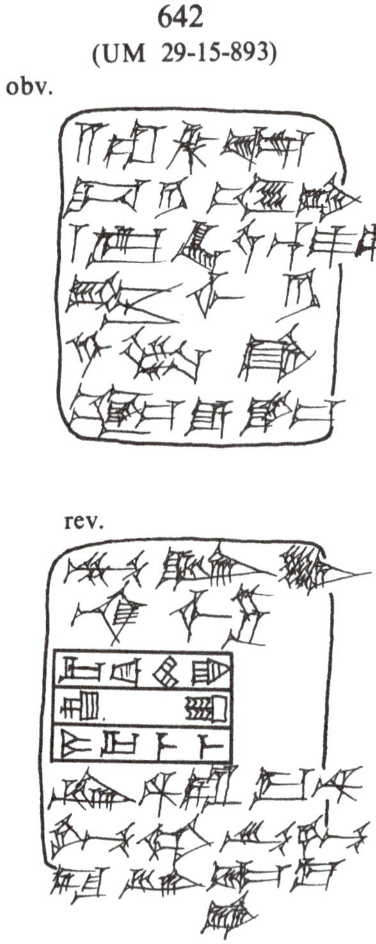

Figure 2. Hand copy of tablet UM 29-15-893 (NATN 642). Reproduced courtesy of David I. Owen.

of public versus private.[5] The sealed tablets from Nippur, therefore, provide an intriguing case for examining practices in relation to intersecting communities, both institutional (state) and noninstitutional. For instance, there appears to be a high number of "actors" involved in sealing the transactions found at Nippur. At Puzriš-Dagan, a major administrative center of the Ur III state and where around one-seventh of the tablets are sealed (2,110 out of more than 14,000), almost 300 are sealed by the same four officials.[6] At Nippur, in contrast, of 544 sealed tablets (out of 1,372 total) examined by Atsuko Hattori, 489 different seals were identified, while only 41 seals were used more than once.[7]

of Pennsylvania Expeditions to Nippur" (PhD diss., University of Pennsylvania, 2002), 7–36. On Nippur archaeological contexts of Ur III archives, see also Garfinkle, *Entrepreneurs and Enterprise*, 110–12.

5. Garfinkle argues for a flourishing noninstitutional economy during the Ur III period that worked symbiotically with the state. Garfinkle, *Entrepreneurs and Enterprise*.

6. Tsouparopoulou, *The Ur III Seals*, 19.

7. Atsuko Hattori, "Sealing Practices in Ur III Nippur," in *Proceedings of the XLVe Rencontre Assyriologique Internationale: Pt. II, Seals and Seal Impressions*, ed. William W. Hallo and Irene J. Winter (Bethesda, MD: CDL, 2001), 73.

Thus, it appears that at Nippur there was a much more dispersed group of individuals who participated in administrative and/or commercial transactions, perhaps indicative of the noninstitutional nature of their social structures.

In the seminal 1977 volume, *Seals and Sealings in the Ancient Near East*, Piotr Steinkeller presents an overview of sealing practices in the Ur III period.[8] He divides the Ur III administrative texts into three main groups: standard administrative texts (ration lists, receipts, disbursements, etc.); bullae; and letter orders. He notes that among the standard administrative texts, seal impressions occur almost exclusively on receipts and disbursements.[9] They appear most frequently on receipts characterized by certain keywords: šu ba-ti ("he received" + inanimate entities), i_3-dab_5 ("he received" + animate entities) and kišib ("seal [of PN]"). Hattori's study of the sealed tablets from Nippur includes receipts, which formed the majority of sealed tablets (227 of the 544 she examined), loans (151 out of 544), sale texts (25), other legal documents of various natures (36 total), letter orders (12), and a few other miscellaneous texts.[10] In general, across all the types of sealed documents, the sealer is typically the receiver of goods, or in the case of loans, the receiver of the loan (i.e., the debtor); in other words, it is the individual who has taken on a thing or an obligation who seals. Christina Tsouparopoulou, in her study of the Puzriš-Dagan sealed tablets, notes that sealings served multiple, sometimes nonoverlapping, purposes during the Ur III period: to identify the responsible individual in a transaction, to identify the tablet writer, to prevent tampering with the text, and to confirm receipt of goods.[11] Hattori classifies the text under study here, UM 29-15-893, as a legal document, recording the purchase of two copper hoes on credit.[12] It is sealed with the seal of Ur-du_6-ku_3, son of Ur-me-me.

According to her study of tablets from Girsu, Claudia Fischer proposes that there was a change in sealing practices at the end of the reign of Amar-Suen when a decline in the use of envelopes resulted in an increase in sealing the tablet itself.[13] This shift in sealing practices is evident among the Puzriš-Dagan tablets, according to Tsouparopoulou, and appears to hold also for the Nippur tablets based on Hattori's catalog.[14] The tablet under consideration in this article unfortunately is not dated. However, the fact that it is sealed all over, and that two other tablets sealed with the seal of Ur-du_6-ku_3, son of Ur-me-me are dated to the fourth and fifth years of Šu-Suen, suggests that this tablet also belongs to the later time when tablets were typically sealed themselves and the use of envelopes had fallen out of favor.

It has been known for some time that the administrative documents of the Ur III period were produced in standardized forms and that the method of sealing appears related to the contents of the texts.[15] In her 2002 University of Pennsylvania dissertation, Hattori examines the practices involved in sealing tablets from Nippur.[16] She documents a standard way of impressing the seals vertically from top to bottom, often—but not always—with the legend parallel

8. Piotr Steinkeller, "Seal Practice in the Ur III Period," in *Seals and Sealings in the Ancient Near East*, ed. McGuire Gibson and Robert D. Biggs (Malibu: Undena, 1977), 41–53.

9. Steinkeller, 42.

10. Hattori, "Sealing Practices in Ur III Nippur," 74–76.

11. Tsouparopoulou, *The Ur III Seals*, 19, 80–81.

12. Hattori, "Texts and Impressions," SI#102, 348; David I. Owen, *Neo-Sumerian Archival Texts Primarily from Nippur in the University Museum, The Oriental Institute and the Iraq Museum* (NATN) (Winona Lake, IN: Eisenbrauns, 1982), no. 642.

13. Claudia Fischer, "Siegelabrollungen im British Museum auf Ur-III-zeitlichen Texten aus der Provinz Lagaš: Untersuchung zu den Verehrungsszenen," *BaM* 28 (1997): 99–100. The shift in sealing practices corresponds to a broader shift in administrative practices (Tsouparopoulou, *The Ur III Seals*, 83; Marcel Sigrist, *Drehem* [Bethesda, MD: CDL, 1992]).

14. Tsouparopoulou, *The Ur III Seals*, 80, 83–84; Hattori, "Texts and Impressions," 50. Tsouparopoulou (*The Ur III Seals*, 80n194) notes that tablets from Girsu and Umma "are sealed at a consistent rate during all reigns." However, Di Ludovico sees an increasing importance in the use of the seal on Umma texts beginning with the end of Shulgi's reign (Alessandro Di Ludovico, "Symbols and Bureaucratic Performances in the Ur III Administrative Sphere: An Interpretation Through Data Mining," in *From the 21st Century B.C. to the 21st Century A.D.: Proceedings of the International Conference on Sumerian Studies Held in Madrid, 22–24 July 2010*, ed. Steven Garfinkle and Manuel Molina [Winona Lake, IN: Eisenbrauns, 2013], 132).

15. Hattori, "Texts and Impressions," 51.

16. Hattori, "Texts and Impressions"; also Hattori, "Sealing Practices in Ur III Nippur."

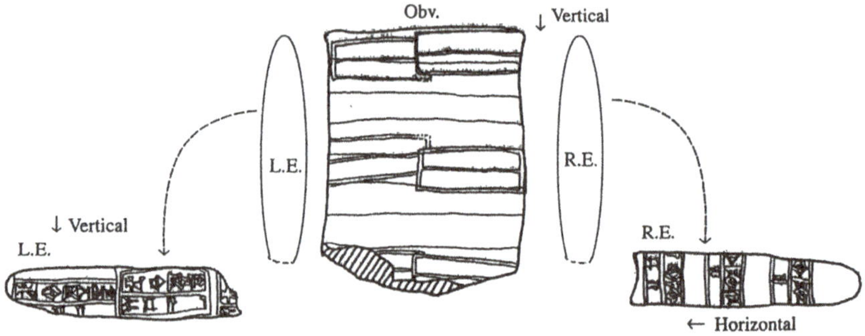

Figure 3. Drawing of process of sealing Ur III tablets. From Hattori, "Sealing Practices in Ur III Nippur," fig. 1. Reproduced courtesy of Atsuko Hattori.

Figure 4. Ur III cylinder seal and impression, with two-line inscription "Aḫa-nīšu, the servant of Nūr-Šulgi." Black stone (hematite?). Johns Hopkins Archaeological Museum FIC.07.178. Image courtesy of the Johns Hopkins Archaeological Museum.

to the writing on the tablet.[17] The seals are applied in vertical columns in order to cover the entire obverse and reverse of the tablet and are impressed over the writing. Usually three of the four edges were also sealed, either vertically or horizontally (fig. 3).

Ur III period seals also follow standardized patterns in their content and composition, which have for a long time now been understood as the result of their widespread use in the expanding state administration.[18] By far the most common design depicted shows a seated god, goddess, or ruler, before whom comes a standing individual, often accompanied by one or more divine figures (the so-called presentation scene; fig. 4). There are several variations of

17. Hattori, "Sealing Practices in Ur III Nippur," 80.

18. See Irene J. Winter, "The King and the Cup: Iconography of the Royal Presentation Scene on Ur III Seals," in *Insight through Images: Studies in Honor of Edith Porada*, ed. Marilyn Kelly-Buccellati, Bibliotheca Mesopotamica 21 (Malibu: Undena, 1986); and Irene J. Winter, "Legitimation of Authority through Image and Legend: Seals Belonging to Officials in the Administrative Bureaucracy of the Ur III State," in *The Organization of Power: Aspects of Bureaucracy in the Ancient Near East*, ed. McGuire Gibson and Robert D. Biggs, SAOC 46 (Chicago: Oriental Institute of the University of Chicago, 1987).

the motif, but the overall scene remains highly consistent throughout the period, and the large majority of Ur III seals depicts some form of this presentation scene before either a god/goddess or king.[19] The seal imagery, overlooked for a long time in glyptic studies, received important attention by Irene Winter in the 1980s, who argued that they convey information regarding the seal owner's position.[20]

To the side of the scene on the seal, running perpendicular to the scene itself (which extends horizontally across the seal) is an inscription, almost always enclosed in a rectangular field (or cartouche) divided into lines. The inscription, of two or more lines, names the seal owner and, typically, his occupation and/or a patronym, and sometimes the father's occupation.[21] Longer inscriptions tie the seal owner to their superiors, including the king. The seal legends thus identify the seal owners as members of various social and economic circles, often connected to large institutions, but not always. The legends document the widespread ownership of seals and the centrality of seals in a broad community of individuals both within and outside of the major state institutions. Within the Nippur corpus, the legends tend to be short (two or three lines), providing the owner's name, occupation, and patronym.[22] Longer seal inscriptions are associated with higher officials and those closely connected to the king, and thus the shorter inscriptions on the Nippur sealings align with other evidence for the noninstitutional nature of the corpus.[23]

In a 2001 article, Hattori summarized the sealing practices she encountered on the Nippur tablets that she studied for her 2002 dissertation.[24] My own research on a select subset of these Nippur tablets confirms the general validity of her observations, although it also has noted interesting patterns within the larger set of parameters that she describes.[25] Seals are applied to the obverse and reverse of tablets so that the seal legend runs parallel with the inscribed text; this means that the seal was applied in a vertical direction, perpendicular to the flow of the tablet's text, with the top edge of the seal aligned parallel to the left edge of the tablet. The tablet edges present some variation and could be sealed with the seal legend text either parallel to the long sides of the edge, or—more frequently in the instance of my subsets—perpendicular to the long sides of the edges. When parallel to the long sides, an entire line of the seal legend would be visible; when perpendicular, only a few signs from adjacent lines of the legend appear. In this latter case, and also in the multiple applications of the seal to the obverse and reverse, it appears that the seal is more "stamped" or pressed than actually rolled. Hattori demonstrated that most of the Nippur tablets were written first and then sealed, a proposal made earlier by Fischer and confirmed for many of the Puzriš-Dagan tablets.[26]

Scholars have long noted that the seal legend was privileged over the seal imagery when impressing the seal on a tablet, and the Nippur tablets are no exception.[27] Hattori records that, of 488 individual seals impressed on tablets (identified as individual seals by their legends), 162 do not display enough of the seal image for the scene to be classified.[28] Hattori further notes that, "Ur III documents commonly have an additional special space reserved for sealing in the center of the reverse."[29] Tsouparopoulou, however, argues that the space on the reverse was not specifically intended for sealing, because blank spaces occur on tablets that, according to her, "were certainly not destined to

19. For an overview of seal imagery, see Tsouparopoulou, *The Ur III Seals*, 27–36.

20. Winter, "King and the Cup," and Winter, "Legitimation of Authority."

21. For the Drehem seal legends, see Tsouparopoulou, *The Ur III Seals*, 22; for Nippur, see Hattori, "Texts and Impressions," 165–78.

22. Hattori, "Sealing Practices in Ur III Nippur," 76–77.

23. Hattori, 77.

24. Hattori, 80–83.

25. This is part of a larger project, from which this short article on one of the tablets derives. My sincere thanks to Phil Jones of the Penn Museum Tablet Room for facilitating this study.

26. Hattori, "Sealing Practices in Ur III Nippur," 98; Fischer, "Siegelabrollungen," 98–100; Tsouparopoulou, *The Ur III Seals*, 82–83.

27. Hattori, "Sealing Practices in Ur III Nippur," 76.

28. Hattori, 78.

29. Hattori, 80.

be sealed."[30] Tablet UM 29-15-893 contributes to this question, and I would suggest that the blank space left on the back of the Nippur administrative documents did serve an important function in legibly presenting the seal legend.

UM 29-15-893 bears the seal of Ur-du$_6$-ku$_3$, the scribe and son of Ur-me-me. His seal is found on three other tablets from Nippur (CBS 8388, UM 29-13-796, and UM 29-15-631).[31] CBS 8388 and UM 29-15-631 are legal documents like UM 29-15-893, while UM 29-13-796 is a šu ba-ti receipt. In all three legal documents, Ur-du$_6$-ku$_3$, as the sealer, appears as the debtor.[32] Tsouparopoulou proposes that—at least among her Drehem tablet corpus—the person who sealed the tablet was usually the one who wrote it as well, perhaps even shaping the tablet, too.[33] In many cases this would have been the recipient of the goods.[34] If this is also the case for the Nippur tablets, and at least in the case of Ur-du$_6$-ku$_3$, who is identified as a scribe, it seems likely, then we can look at a tablet bearing the seal of Ur-du$_6$-ku$_3$ and examine it from the perspective of him making the tablet, inscribing it, and finally sealing it.

Here, I briefly describe the sealing practices evident in my close study of UM 29-15-893, and I propose that a "correction" to the sealing process indicates the importance of the legibility of the seal legend, which in turn sheds light on the significance of the use of the blank space on the reverse. The tablet measures 3.5 cm wide by 4.2 cm high, making it slightly taller than many of the Nippur documents, which tend to be between 3.5 cm and 3.8 cm high. It is of a yellow-green clay and is complete and well preserved, with edges that are sealed flat. Its method of sealing conforms closely to the others that I have examined and to Hattori's general schema. The tablet had clearly been written before it was sealed. On the obverse, two columns of sealings are visible: the left-hand column appears to have been impressed first and shows most of the height of the seal (the seal having been impressed so that the top of the seal imagery would be aligned with the left side of the tablet); a second column to the right preserves less of the height of the seal. In both columns, the seal was impressed so that the seal legend is the primary part of the seal visible. Several impressions of the legend are evident in each column, indicating that the seal was pressed down and picked up from the tablet several times, rather than rolled continuously.

All four edges are sealed. In each case, the seal has been impressed so that the lines of the legend run perpendicular to the long sides of the edge. This is the case whether it is a top/bottom or a side edge. Thus, it is clear that the seal was not impressed continuously from obverse to reverse, but instead each side and each edge was separately impressed. Similar to the multiple impressions seen on the obverse, the edges all display multiple impressions of the seal legend, demonstrating that the seal was pressed down and picked up several times.

The reverse follows the standard sealing practice seen in the other Nippur tablets, which is a variation on how the obverse was sealed. Where there is inscribed text on the reverse, in this case, two lines at the top and three lines at the bottom (going onto the bottom reverse edge), the seal legend is impressed into the tablet in two unequal columns so that all the inscribed text is fully sealed. However, what makes UM 29-15-893 interesting is that after the tablet was inscribed and sealed, the area of the blank space between the top and bottom lines of text was "corrected" with the addition of new clay on the left two-thirds side of the blank space. Tsouparopoulou, noting that scribal mistakes are fairly common among the Drehem tablets, cites Taylor and Cartwright regarding the need to scrape away the tablet in order to erase signs, because it is not possible to simply smooth out the surface.[35] Adding a new layer of clay also

30. "While officials naturally preferred to roll their seal on any space left on the reverse after the writing of the text was completed, for then it would be more legible, that space had certainly not been left for a seal impression." Tsouparopoulou, *The Ur III Seals*, 82.

31. See Hattori, "Texts and Impressions," SI#102.

32. In the receipt, UM 29-13-796, the receiver is a ^{d}En-lil$_2$-la$_2$-al-sig$_5$, with Ur-du$_6$-ku$_3$ serving as a proxy sealer. Hattori, "Texts and Impressions," 348.

33. Tsouparopoulou, *The Ur III Seals*, 47–48, 68, 79, 84.

34. Tsouparopoulou sees it as the recipient's responsibility to write up the receipt, seal it, and then send it to the dispenser as confirmation of receipt of the goods. Tsouparopoulou, *The Ur III Seals*, 79. In this respect, the four tablets sealed by Ur-du$_6$-ku$_3$ did not reside in his archive but rather in the archive(s) of the lender.

35. Tsouparopoulou, *The Ur III Seals*, 55–56; Jon Taylor and Caroline Cartwright, "The Making and Re-Making of Clay Tablets," *Scienze dell'Antichità* 17 (2011): 313.

Figure 5. Reverse of tablet UM 29-15-893. Photograph by the author; reproduced courtesy of Penn Museum.

Figure 6. Detail of corrected area on reverse of tablet UM 29-15-893. Photograph by the author; reproduced courtesy of Penn Museum.

offered a way to correct a tablet that had dried too much. However, on UM 29-15-893, we appear to be dealing not with the need to correct the text inscribed on the tablet, but instead the need to correct the impression made of the seal legend in the blank space. Such a correction indicates that there was an agreed-upon sense of how the sealing should be done and, furthermore, suggests that the sealing of the blank space was considered important enough to be executed according to a specific protocol (figs. 5 and 6).

Looking closely at the corrected area, one can see that an oval-shaped bit of clay has been spread over the blank space; its edges, especially on the bottom and right sides, are visibly higher than the tablet itself. It is clear that the clay was added after the tablet was inscribed and the two columns of seal impressions were made; the added clay encroached on the inscribed text, necessitating the reinscription of parts of the signs of the first line of text below the blank space, most visible in the upper wedges of the r a and m a signs. The seal was then reimpressed over the newly added clay in order to make visible the seal legend. It appears that the space left blank was just a little bit too narrow to easily fit the three-line inscription of Ur-du$_6$-ku$_3$'s seal, but his name and profession (d u b s a r) are clearly visible, as is the beginning of his patronymn (d u m u u r - m e - m e). It seems likely that, because of the narrow space left blank, it was difficult to impress the legend cleanly, requiring a correction and reimpression.

According to the observed practices and the sense of protocol indicated by the correction, the preserved legend in the blank space provides two different functions. First, it provides clear recognition of the seal owner, the person who is taking on the responsibility recorded by the text (even if that person is serving as a proxy for someone else).[36] Second, it provides an easier identification of the seal impressions made elsewhere on the tablet. These other sealings were clearly meant to ensure the integrity of the inscribed text. They cover all parts of the written tablet, impressed in such a way that they closely abut one another in multiple columns. The legend is the identifiable part of the seal, and it is the legend that is impressed over all the text. When some of the seal scene imagery appears, it is on either side of the

36. It has been noted that proxies are usually closely related to the person taking on the responsibility, such as a son sealing on behalf of his father. Hattori, "Texts and Impressions," 191.

legend.[37] In my own examinations of the tablets, I found that I was able to pick out the seal legend impressed over the inscribed text much more easily once I had seen the full seal legend impressed in the blank space. Although it was not always possible to read the legend in full, enough signs were visible to be able to match them to the complete legend in the blank space. It appears, therefore, that it was critical to make sure the seal legend impressed in the blank space was largely legible. UM 29-15-893 seems to have needed amending in order to ensure that this was the case. Why some tablets remain unsealed, including those with blank spaces on their reverses, remains a question.

This brief paper has looked closely at the sealing practices evident on one particular tablet, UM 29-15-893. We do not know much about Ur-du_6-ku_3, but from the four tablets bearing his seal, he appears to have belonged to the large, educated population at Nippur that was engaged in a variety of transactions.[38] His seal legend describes him as a scribe, and he may well have written the tablet in addition to using his seal on it. The tablets are, however, somewhat unusual among the known corpus of sealed Nippur documents, most of which are receipts. Three of them document legal transactions that appear to show Ur-du_6-ku_3 in debt, including the purchase on credit recorded in UM 29-15-893, a possible agreement to repay barley (CBS 8388), and a possible statement of payment due with a penalty clause (UM 29-15-631).[39] On the fourth sealed tablet, Ur-du_6-ku_3 served as a proxy on a standard šu ba-ti receipt of barley as wages for plowing. While legal documents make up only a small portion of the corpus of sealed tablets during this period, and the texts appear to record transactions occurring outside of state institutions, the exhibited sealing practices align well with those seen across Nippur, as well as across many of the Ur III state documents.

By situating this tablet in the larger context of Nippur, and beyond, of the Ur III state, the specific sealing practices speak to at least two conclusions. First, although the individuals involved in these transactions appear to have been operating outside of state institutions, they were clearly familiar with and practiced in the accepted protocols employed by the state. The complicated imbrication of institutional and noninstitutional players during the Ur III period has already been suggested based on the shared use of relatively standardized administrative vocabulary across both "private" (noninstitutional) and state/institutional texts.[40] Recognizing that "private" individuals like Ur-du_6-ku_3 were fully versed in the minute details of sealing practices performed by state officials further confirms this conclusion. Second, as has already been proposed, the impression of the seal legend was the first priority of the sealer. This observation, however, can be further elaborated from the study of UM 29-15-893. The corrected "blank space" area on the reverse, with a newly impressed seal legend, demonstrates that the legibility of the legend in this space was considered critical. I have suggested that it served two purposes: first, to identify the sealer and second, to help later tablet readers see and recognize the same legend when impressed over the written text.

37. This appears to be particularly the case for the sealings made by seals belonging to lesser officials and "private" individuals. When higher officials, owning seals with longer legends linking them to the king and higher administration, impress tablets, more of the scene seems to be included. This is certainly the case for the one subset of sealed tablets that I examined, which are sealed by Lugal-ma_2-gur_3-re, who has an $arad_2$-zu seal (Hattori, "Texts and Impressions," SI#354; see also in Hattori, "Texts and Impressions," 199). On the four tablets surviving with his seal, all of them include extensive evidence of the presentation scene before a seated goddess.

38. His legend says that he is the son of Ur-me-me. Ur-me-me is the name of a powerful local family at Nippur, the patriarch of which—Ur-me-me—was the chief administrator of the temple of Inanna (see Richard Zettler and Martha T. Roth, "The Genealogy of the House of Ur-Me-me: A Second Look," *AfO* 31 [1984]: 1–9). It seems unlikely, however, that Ur-du_6-ku_3 belonged to this family, because his texts date later in the Ur III period (based on the genealogy of Ur-me-me's family, Ur-du_6-ku_3 would probably have belonged to the fourth generation, making Ur-me-me his grandfather or great-grandfather) and because Ur-me-me is usually identified in seal legends as the ugula e_2 ^{d}Inanna (the chief administrator of the temple of Inanna), whereas on Ur-du_6-ku_3's seal no title is provided for his father Ur-me-me.

39. Owen, NATN, nos. 139, 621, and 642.

40. Garfinkle, *Entrepreneurs and Enterprise*; Steven J. Garfinkle, "Ur III Administrative Texts: Building Blocks of State Community," in *Texts and Contexts: The Circulation and Transmission of Cuneiform Texts in Social Space*, ed. Paul Delnero and Jacob Lauinger (Boston: de Gruyter, 2015), 146n11.

Göttlich, nicht königlich: Ein neuer Thot-Hymnus aus Deir el-Medineh

Hans-W. Fischer-Elfert

Philologen innerhalb der ägyptologischen Zunft eignet eine besondere Affinität zum altägyptischen Sachwalter u.a. von Schrift und Schreiben namens Thot. Richard Jasnow bildet hier keine Ausnahme, ganz im Gegenteil. Spätestens seit Erscheinen der 1. Ausgabe seines mit Karl-Theodor Zauzich rekonstruierten *Book of Thoth* im Jahre 2005 ist diese Beziehung evident und manifestiert sich in Folgepublikationen zum gleichen Text.[1] So erscheint es Verf. eine passende Gabe zu seinem 65. Wiegentag, einen für geraume Zeit unter dem Label „Königshymnus" laufenden Text als tatsächlich an eben diesen Thot gerichtete Lobpreisung in seiner Festschrift zu offerieren.

Ganz erheblich trägt eine im Ägyptischen Museum –Georg Steindorff– aufbewahrte Variante zu deren weiterer Rekonstruktion bei.[2] Die übrigen und bislang bekannten Textzeugen sind ODeM 1100, ODeM 1644 und ODeM 1799. Sie finden sich in den von Georges Posener und Annie Gasse herausgegebenen Bänden der literarischen und religiösen Ostraka des IFAO.[3] Grund für die frühere Klassifizierung als Königshymnus war der lange Zeit fehlende Anfang bzw. Titel des Textes. Wie noch zu zeigen, trägt das Leipziger Stück ÄMUL 3957 (Abb. 1–2) entscheidend zu seiner annähernd vollständigen Rekonstruktion bei, unterstützt des Weiteren durch eine hier erstmalig präsentierte Variante im Ashmolean Museum Oxford aus der ehemaligen Gardiner-Sammlung (ANAsh Mus. H.O. 398 = Abb. 3).[4] Dabei kann dieser „neue" Thot-Hymnus mit einer Reihe anderweitig nicht standardmäßig bezeugter Epitheta des Gottes aufwarten, wie eine entsprechende Suche im *LGG* erweist.

Das Leipziger Ostrakon ÄMUL 3957 besteht aus Kalkstein und mißt 14 × 16,2 × 2,0 cm, es ist beidseitig und mit fortlaufendem Text beschriftet, unter Verwendung von roter und schwarzer Tusche. Eine vor Beschriftung erfolgte Glättung der Oberfläche kann nicht nachgewiesen werden. Dieser Umstand spricht für eine eher flüchtige Kopie seitens des dafür verantwortlichen Schreibers, was sich auch an seiner Handschrift ablesen läßt, die alles andere als

1. Richard Jasnow und Karl-Theodor Zauzich, *The Ancient Egyptian Book of Thoth*, Bd. 1: *Text;* Bd. 2*: Plates* (Wiesbaden: Harrassowitz, 2005), und Richard Jasnow and Karl-Theodor Zauzich, *Conversations in the House of Life: A New Translation of the Ancient Egyptian Book of Thoth* (Wiesbaden: Harrassowitz, 2014).

2. Dieser Text wird nebst allen übrigen hieratischen Ostraka des Ägyptischen Museums Leipzig auch in dem in Bearbeitung befindlichen Band *Hieratika et Demotika* erscheinen. Weitere Ko-Autoren sind Anke Blöbaum, Charlotte Dietrich, Christine Greger, Katharina Stegbauer, Billy Böhm und Johannes Jüngling. Robert Demarée wird sich insbesondere den administrativen Texten aus Deir el-Medineh widmen und Franziska Naether den demotischen Quellen. Ich danke Charlotte Dietrich ganz besonders für die kritische Lektüre meiner Transkription von ÄMUL 3957 und die Übertragung meiner Synopse in Vector Office-Hieroglyphen.

3. Georges Posener, *Catalogue des ostraca hiératiques littéraires de Deir el-Médineh T. I*, FIFAO I (Kairo: Institut français d'archéologie orientale du Caire, 1938), Taf. 52/*a*; Georges Posener, *Catalogue des ostraca hiératiques littéraires de Deir el-Médineh T. III*, FIFAO XX (1977–1978–1980), Taf. 68/*a*; Hans-W. Fischer-Elfert (Bearb.), *Lesefunde im literarischen Steinbruch von Deir el-Medineh*, Kleine Ägyptische Texte (Wiesbaden: Harrassowitz, 1997); Hans-W. Fischer-Elfert, „Vermischtes III", *GM* 143 (1994): 41–50; Annie Gasse, *Catalogue des ostraca littéraires de Deir al-Médîna T. V*, DFIFAO XLIV (Kairo: Institut français d'archéologie orientale du Caire, 2005), 49–50 (dort bereits als Beginn des Thot-Hymnus ediert).

4. Für die Publikationsgenehmigung danke ich Herrn Dr. Liam McNamara (Ashmolean Museum Oxford) sehr herzlich.

Abbildung 1. © ÄMUL 3957 recto.

Abbildung 2. © ÄMUL 3957 verso.

Abbildung 3. ANAsh Mus. H.O. 398. © Ashmolean Museum, University of Oxford.

elegant oder geübt wirkt. Einige der Textlücken können weitgehend mithilfe der anderen Versionen geschlossen werden, auch wenn dabei stets zu berücksichtigen ist, daß es im Verlaufe der Traditionsgeschichte des Hymnus zu varianten Lesungen gekommen sein mag, die erst durch besser erhaltene Exemplare bestätigt oder widerlegt werden können. Insofern eignet der hier präsentierten Rekonstruktion eine gewisse Vorläufigkeit.

Das Leipziger Exemplar wurde im Winter 1928/29 von Georg Steindorff im Antikenhandel von „Theben" erworben, es hat keine verbriefte archäologische Provenienz. Die Annahme seiner ursprünglichen Verfertigung und anschließenden Verwendung qua Rezitation im Thotkult von Deir el-Medineh ist deshalb gleichfalls nichts weiter als pure Spekulation. Ebenso wenig hat das Oxforder Exemplar eine entsprechende Herkunftsangabe. Lediglich die archäologisch dokumentierten Parallelen aus den Deir el-Medineh-Grabungen des IFAO in Kairo legen diese lokale und kultische Einbindung nahe.

Die paläographisch verlässliche Datierung literarischer Ostraka aus Deir el-Medineh steckt bekanntlich noch in den Kinderschuhen, auch wenn in den letzten Jahren hier gewisse Fortschritte erzielt worden sein mögen. Verf. bleibt aber sehr skeptisch, hier auf absehbare Zeit sicheren Boden unter die Füße zu bekommen. In diesem Beitrag soll deshalb nur eine grobe Zeitmarge in die Ramessidenzeit veranschlagt werden.

Die Anordnung der Textzeugen in H.-W. Fischer-Elfert, *Lesefunde im literarischen Steinbruch*, 58–59, könnte sich durch das auf Ostr. ÄMUL 3957 Überlieferte grundlegend ändern insofern, als die eine Seite (hier = a) den Beginn eines Thot-Hymnus enthalten hat ([*ỉnḏ-ḥr*]=*k Ḏḥw.ty* ...), während die andere Seite dazu die Fortsetzung bilden dürfte. Diese Reihung der beiden Seiten des Ostrakons würde dann mit dem erhaltenen Textbestand in der auf den Ostraka DeM 1100 und 1644 gegebenen Sequenz übereinstimmen. Die scheinbar individuellen Handschriften auf der Leipziger Variante sprechen m.E. nicht dagegen. Der auf der Seite a) unterhalb der 4. Zeile fehlende Textbestand könnte dann auf ODeM 1100 rt. 4 – vs. 3 und ODeM 1644 rt. 4–6 repräsentiert sein. Seite b) geht nämlich mit ODeM 1100 vs. 4 und ODeM 1644 vs. 4 parallel. Dazu kommt, daß das unpubl. Ostr. ANAsh Mus. H.O. 398 nicht unwesentlich zur Vervollständigung mehrerer Verse beiträgt (hier Vv. 17–24[?]).

Diese Lesefolge hätte demzufolge gravierende Auswirkungen auf die Gesamtinterpretation insofern, als auch die von Posener edierten Exzerpte zusammen genommen einen *Thot*-Hymnus und eben keinen *Königs*-Hymnus darstellen würden, wie noch in meinen *Lesefunde* angenommen. Auf dieser Prämisse wird die weitere Arbeit am Text im Folgenden beruhen, da sich sämtliche der Epitheta bestens zur Prädikation dieses Gottes fügen.[5]

Zu dieser neuen Interpretation fügt sich ferner der archäologische Befund recht gut, daß die beiden von G. Posener edierten Varianten ODeM 1100 und 1644 nördlich des Grabes des Thothermeketef (TT 357) gefunden wurden, konkret ODeM 1100 am 5.1.1929 und 1644 am 9.2.1929. A. Gasse hat diese Fundgeschichte aus den Tagebüchern Bernard Bruyères rekonstruiert.[6] Diese archäologischen Indizien sollten in jedem Fall bei aller weiteren Beschäftigung mit diesem bislang als „Königs-Hymnus" gelesenen Text gebührend berücksichtigt werden.

Transkription, Transliteration und Übersetzung

1)

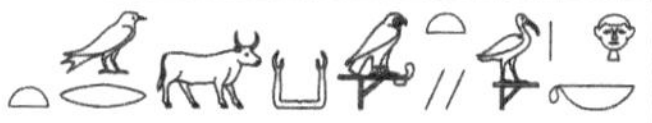	ÄMUL 3957
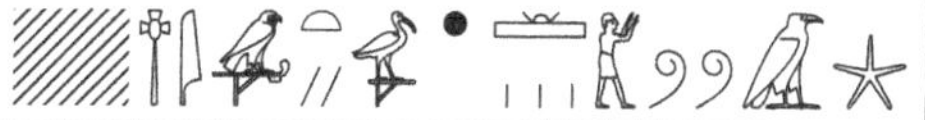	DeM 1799

3957a 1) [*ỉnḏ*]-*ḥr*=*k Ḏḥw.ty kꜣ-wr*

1799 1) *dwꜣ.w-Ḏḥw.ty ỉnḏ*-[*ḥr*=*k*]

[Sei gegrüß]t, Thot, Großer Stier!
Verehrung des Thot: Sei [gegrüßt]!

5. Ein weiterer und bislang nicht erschlossener Hymnus an Thot auf einem vermutlich ebenfalls ramessidischen Ostrakon liegt vor auf der Kalksteinscherbe Hildesheim PM 5572. Das Objekt mißt H 12,6 × B 10,0 × T 2,9 cm, trägt die Reste von sieben Zeilen, und wurde 1985 in der Züricher *Galerie Nefer* erworben. Nach seiner Eröffnung durch *jꜣw n-Ḏḥw.ty* – „Lobpreis dem Thot" fährt der Text u.a. in Z. 1 und Z. 3 fort mit *jr-pꜣ-mnꜥ*{*.t*} – „Was angeht den Erzieher [...]" und *jr-pꜣ-*[...] resp. Das Epitheton *pꜣ-mnꜥ* ist m.W. von Thot bislang nicht bekannt, zumindest nicht nach Ausweis des *LGG*. – Für ihre Recherche, alle Auskünfte und ein Photo des Ostrakons danke ich Antje Spiekermann, Pelizaeus-Museum Hildesheim, sehr herzlich.

6. A. Gasse, „Le K2, un cas d'école?", in *Deir el-Medina in the Third Millennium AD: A Tribute to Jac. J. Janssen*, hg. Robert J. Demarée und A. Egberts, EU 14 (Leiden: Nederlands Instituut voor het Nabije Oosten, 2000), 112 und 115; s.a. 119; Karte auf 120; A. Gasse, Review: Fischer-Elfert, *Lesefunde im literarischen Steinbruch*, *BiOr* 55 (1998): 745, benennt sie deren Fundort als „sur le même site, le «K 2», un *kôm* situé à l'est de la chapelle 121". Sie notiert ferner, daß „le culte de Thot, par ailleurs, est réputé relativement présent dans ce secteur"; Gasse, „Le K2", 118 mit Anm. 26 = Bernard Bruyère, *Rapport sur les fouilles de Deir el-Médineh (1929)*, FIFAO 7/2 (Le Caire: L'Institut français d'archéologie orientale, 1930), 17, etc.

2)

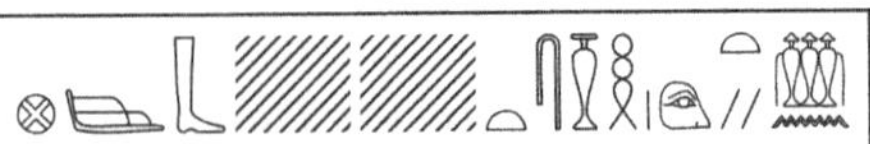	ÄMUL 3957
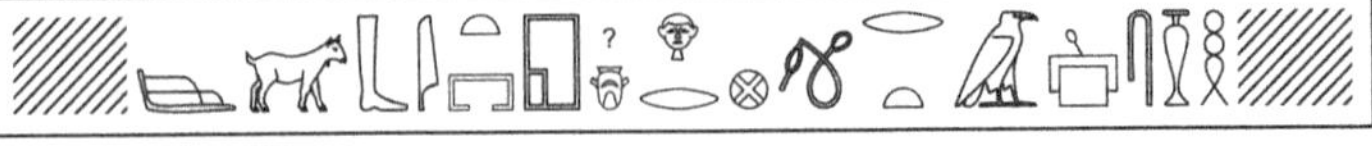	DeM 1799

3957 *ḫnti-Ḥsr.t* (2) [… … *i*]*b*(*ṯ.t*)
1799 [*ḫnti-*](2)-*Ḥsr.t ḥri-ib-ḥw.t-ib*(*ṯ.t*)

Prominentester von Hesret [… Vogel]falle
[Prominentester] von Hesret, inmitten des Hauses-der-Vogelfalle

3)

	ÄMUL 3957
	DeM 1799

3957 *nb-Ḫmnw wḏꜥ-*…(?)[…]
1799 [… … … … … … …]

Herr von Hermopolis, der […] richtet / trennt
[… … …]

4)

	ÄMUL 3957
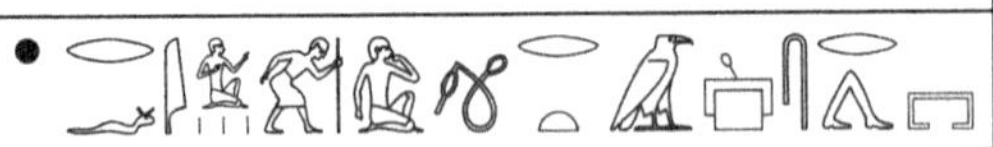	DeM 1799
	DeM 1100

3957 [… … … … (3) … *wr*(?)](3).*w-r=f*
1799 3) *pr* <*m*>*-sꜣr.t wr.w-ir=f*
1100 rt. 1) *pr m-sꜣr.t*(?) [… …]

[… … … grö]ßer(?) als er
Der <als> Weiser / mit Weisheit hervorgekommen ist, …(?)
Der als Weiser / mit Weisheit hervorgekommen ist [… …]

5)

	ÄMUL 3957
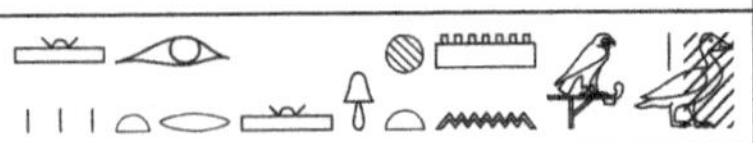	DeM 1799
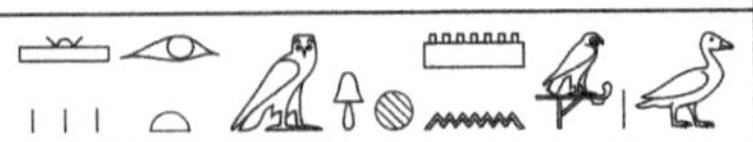	DeM 1100

3957 *zꜣ mn*[…]
1799 *zꜣ mnḫ-jr.t*
1100 *zꜣ mnḫ m-jr.t*

ein Sohn, der wirksam ist in dem/durch das Geschaffene
[...] Sohn [...]
ein Sohn, wirksam an(?) Geschaffenem

6)

	ÄMUL 3957
	DeM 1799
	DeM 1100

3957 *ir-*[... ... ...]
1799 [... ... ...]
1100 *ir-ẖr*[*.t*(?) ... ...]

Der [... ... ...] sorgt [... ... ...]
[... ... ...]
Der für den Unterhalt sorgt [...]

7)

	ÄMUL 3957
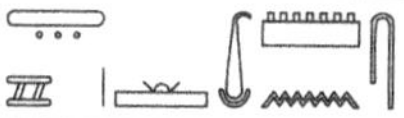	DeM 1799
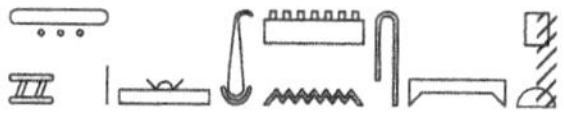	DeM 1100
	DeM 1644

3957 [... ... ...]
1799 [... ...] *smn-tꜣ*
1100 (3) [*ꜥḫi*(?)]*-p.t smn-tꜣ*
1644 (2) [... ... ... *s*]*mn-tꜣ*

[... ... ...]
[... ...], der die Erde auf Dauer gestellt hat
Der den Himmel [erhoben hat(?)], der die Erde auf Dauer gestellt hat
[... ... der] die Erde auf Dauer [ge]stellt hat

8)

	ÄMUL 3957
	DeM 1799
	DeM 1100
	DeM 1644

3957 (4) [... *ḫ*]*ḏ šꜣꜥ<.t>.n=f*
1799 *n-ḫḏ šꜣꜥ<.t>.n=f*
1100 3) *n-ḫḏ šꜣ*[*ꜥ<.t>.n=f*]
1644 *n-ḫḏ šꜣꜥ<.t>.n=f*°

[... ... ... zer]stört/mißachtet werden, was er begonnen hat
Nicht kann zerstört/mißachtet werden, was er begonnen hat
Nicht kann zerstört/mißachtet werden, [was er] begonnen(?) [hat]
Nicht kann zerstört/mißachtet werden, was er begonnen hat

9)

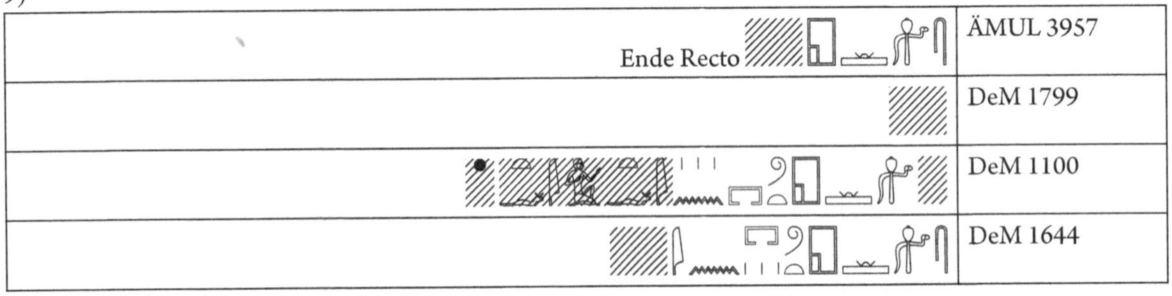

3957 *swꜣḏ/swḏ*(?) [... ...] ENDE von Seite a)
1799 [... ... ...]
1100 4) [*s*]*wꜣḏ-ḥw.wt n-iti-iti.w*[*=f*(?)]°
1644 *swꜣḏ-ḥw.wt n-i*[*ti*(?) ...]

Der gedeihen läßt/anordnet(?) [... ... ...]
[... ... ...]
Der die Tempel des Vaters [seines(?)] Vaters(?) gedeihen [läßt]
Der die Tempel des Va[ters(?) ... ...]

10)

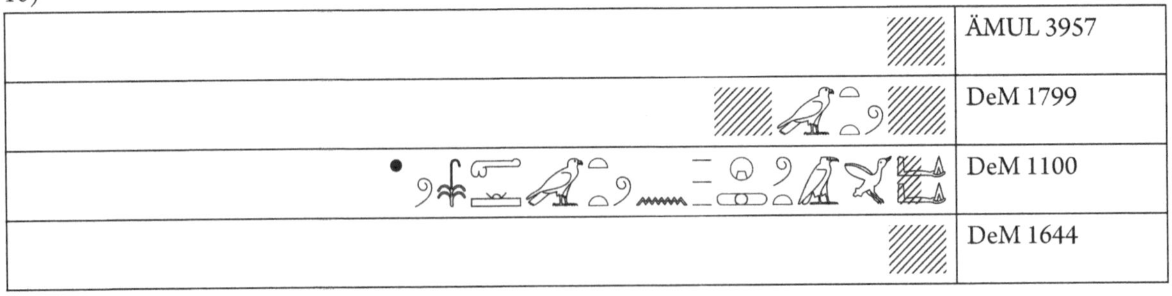

3957 [... ... ...]
1799 [... ... ...](5)-*wtṯ*-[...]
1100 *ḏd*-(5)-*pꜣw.t* <*n*>-*wtṯ-sw*°
1644 [... ... ...]

[... ... ...]
[... ... ...] Erzeuger [...]
Der Opferbrote spendet dem, der ihn erzeugt hat
[... ... ...]

11)

	ÄMUL 3957
ENDE 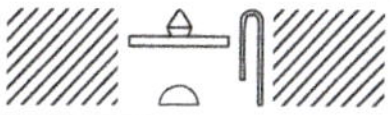	DeM 1799
	DeM 1100
	DeM 1644

3957 [… … …]
1799 [… …] *sḥtp*[7] °[… …] ENDE
1100 6) … (?) *sḥtp-Ḥrw Stḫ* […]
1644 [… … …]

[… … …]
[… …], der befriedet (hat) [… …]
… (?), der Horus und Seth befriedet (hat)
[… … …]

12)

	ÄMUL 3957
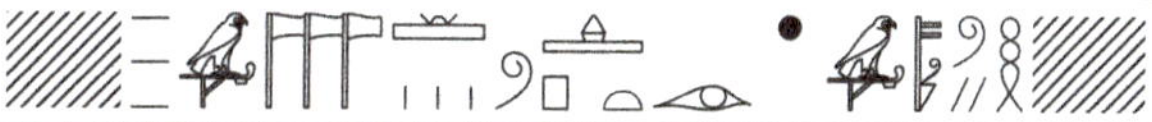	DeM 1100
	DeM 1644

3957 [… … …]
1100 [*wp/wḏꜥ-r*](vs.1)*ḫ.wi ir-ḥtp-nṯr.w*
1644 [… … …]

[… … …]
[Der] die Beiden [Streit]hähne [trennt], der den Götterfrieden bewirkt
[… … …]

13)

	ÄMUL 3957
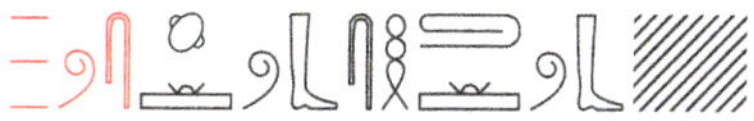	DeM 1100
	DeM 1644

3957 [… … …]

7. Ich meine die Spuren von Z. 5 Ende so deuten zu dürfen, auch wenn der rote Punkt dann deplatziert wäre, aber das ist er schließlich schon in Z. 1 nach *dwꜣ.w*.

1100 [...] (2) [*wḏ*]*b ḥs*<*b-sw*>[8]
1644 [...]*y.w-wḏb ḥsb-sw*°

[... ... ...]
[...] ... (?), der ihn/es/sie berechnet(?)
[ih]re(?) ... (?), der ihn/es/sie berechnet(?)

14)

	ÄMUL 3957
	DeM 1100
	DeM 1644

3957 [... ... ...]
1100 *ꜥnn-sw r-sṯz-sẖr.*(3)*n=f*
1644 *ꜥnn-sw sẖr=f* [...]

[... ... ...]
Der sich (wieder) dem zuwendet, um aufzurichten den er zu Fall gebracht hat
Der sich (wieder) zuwendet, wenn(?) er niederwirft [...]

15)

	ÄMUL 3957
	DeM 1100
	DeM 1644

3957 [... ... ...]
1100 *pẖr-ib sẖf-šsr.w=f*°
1644 [... ... ...]

[... ... ...]
Der mit umkreisendem Herzen, der seine Pfeile (wieder) löst
[... ... ...]

16)

	ÄMUL 3957
	DeM 1100
	DeM 1644

8. „Alphabetisch" in rot supralinear nachgetragen.

3957b[9] 1) *nb-ḥtp.w wḥꜥ-dꜣis<.t>.n=f*
1100 4) *nb-ḥtp.w wḥꜥ.n=f*[10]*-ḏꜣis<.t>.n=f* °
1644 [... ... ...]

Herr der Gnade, der das löst, was er verknotet hatte
Herr der Gnade, nachdem er gelöst hat das, was er verknotet hatte
[... ... ...]

17)

	ÄMUL 3957
	DeM 1100
	DeM 1644
	HO 398

3957 *mi-ꞽItmw sḫm m-ir*[...]
1100 *mi-ꞽItmw sḫm m-ir.w=f* °
1644 [... ... ...]
398 [*sḫm m-jr.w=f(?)*] *nb*

gleichwie Atum, mächtig in [seinen(?)] sichtbaren Erscheinung[en]
gleichwie Atum, mächtig in seinen sichtbaren Erscheinungen
[... ... ...]
[... ... ...]-seine-sichtbaren-Erscheinungen

18)

	ÄMUL 3957
	DeM 1100
	DeM 1644
	HO 398

3957 [... ...] (2) *mrw.t-r=f*
1100 *iwti-ḫsf=f m-mrw.t.n=f* °
1644 [...](4)*-ḫsf=f m-mrr.w.n=f* °
398 [... ... ...]

[... ...]
Dessen Ablehnung dessen, den/was er schätzen gelernt hat, es nicht gibt
Dessen Ablehnung dessen, der/was ihm lieb und teuer ist, [es nicht gibt(?)]

9. Hier beginnt das Verso.
10. *n=f* ist durch DA überschrieben!

[… …]

19)

	ÄMUL 3957
	DeM 1100
	DeM 1644
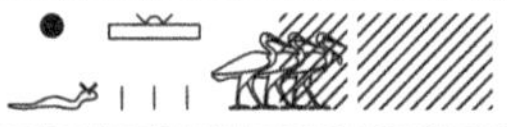	HO 398

3957 *spd-šsr.w ꜥꜣ-bꜣw* […]
1100 *spd-*[…] (6) *ꜥꜣ-bꜣw* […]
1644 *spd-šsr.w ꜥꜣ-bꜣw* […]
398 [… … …] *bꜣw=f* °

Der mit spitzen Pfeilen, gewaltig an [seinem] Machterweis
Der mit spitzen […], gewaltig an [seinem] Machterweis
Der mit spitzen Pfeilen, gewaltig an [seinem] Machterweis
[… … … … … … … … … …] an seinem Machterweis

20)

	ÄMUL 3957
Ende 	DeM 1100
	DeM 1644
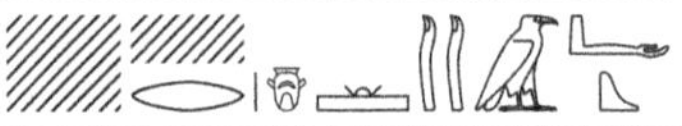	HO 398

3957 *ꜥḳꜣ-*[…] (3) […]*-p.t*(?)
1100 *ꜥ*[*ḳꜣ*]*-ib ḏsr imi-*[… …] ENDE
1644 [… … …]
398 *ꜥḳꜣ-ib* … [… …]

Der Recht[schaffene … …] Himmel(?)[11]
Der Re[cht]schaffene, Abgeschirmter, der im [Himmel(?) …] ENDE
[… … …]
Der Rechtschaffene … [… …]

21)

	ÄMUL 3957
	DeM 1644

11. An diesem Punkt scheint mir die Versgrenze ausgesprochen unsicher, zumal ÄMUL 3957 keine Punkte setzt.

	HO 398

3957 *mrw.t(y)-Ꞽtmw m-mꜣꜣ-n=f*
1644 [… …]
398 [… … … …](3)=*f*

Der Geliebte Atums, wenn (der) seiner ansichtig wird(?)
[… …]
[… … … …] seiner [… …]

22)

	ÄMUL 3957
	DeM 1644
	HO 398

3957 *ir-mꜣꜥ.t n-w*[*tṯ-sw*(?)]
1644 [… … …]
398 *ir-mꜣꜥ.t n-wtṯ-sw*(?)

Der Ma'at ins Werk setzt für den, der [ihn] er[zeugt hat(?)]
[… … …]… ,
Der Ma'at ins Werk setzt für den, der ihn erzeugt hat.

23)

	ÄMUL 3957
	DeM 1644
	HO 398

3957 4) […] *sbbi.w nw-Nb-r-ḏr*
1644 […] (5) … (?) *sbbi.w ḥr-Nb-r-ḏr* [o]
398 [… …]
[…] Rebellen des Allherrn
[…] … (?) rebellieren gegen den Allherrn
[… …]

24)

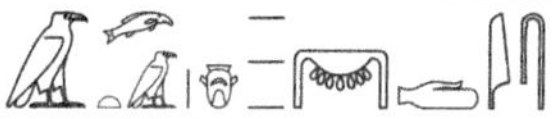	ÄMUL 3957
	DeM 1644
	HO 398

3957 *sid-ib* <*n*>*-ḫ3*[*k*(?) …]
1644 *sid-ib* <*n*>*-ḫ3.wt* … (?) *r=f*°
398 4) […]-*ib n-ḫ3w.t-ib-r=f*°
Der das Herz der Krumm[herzigen(?) …] zur Raison bringt
Der das Herz der Krumm … (?) gegen sich zur Raison bringt
[Der das] Herz der Krummherzigen gegen sich [… …]

25)

	ÄMUL 3957
	DeM 1644
	HO 398

3957 5) [… …]*w n-nṯr-nb*
1644 … (?) […] (6) […]
398 *ḏr-s3*[… …]
[… … … … … … … … …] eines jeden Göttes
[… … …]
welcher vertreibt … [… …]

26)

	ÄMUL 3957
	DeM 1644
	HO 398

3957 *di=sn-n=k i3w.t rꜥ-nb*°
1644 [… … …]
398 [… …] (4') *rꜥ-nb*° *grḥ*
Sie mögen dir Lobpreis spenden einen jeden Tag
[… … …]
[… … …] einen jeden Tag – *Pause*

27)

	ÄMUL 3957
	DeM 1644
ENDE 	HO 398

3957 *t3ty* [… … …]
1644 [… … …]
398 *t3ty wp-m3ꜥ.t*° ENDE
(du) Wesir, [… … …]

[... ... ...]
(du) Wesir, der die Ma'at eröffnet

28)

	ÄMUL 3957
ENDE 	DeM 1644

3957 (6) *ḥḏ-wsfꜣ{.t} mꜣꜣ=f-ḥr=f*
1644 (6) *ḥḏ-wsfꜣ{.t} mꜣꜣ.n=f-ḥr=f*[12] [o] ENDE[13]
Der den Nachlässigen vernichtet, wenn er seiner ansichtig wird
Der den Nachlässigen vernichtet, nachdem er seiner ansichtig wird

29)

	ÄMUL 3957

3957 *ir-sw mi-nty-nn-ms*(?)
Der ihn macht wie/zu einer/m, der nicht geboren wurde(?)

30)

	ÄMUL 3957

3957 7) *[s]ḫtm-bꜣ=f m-ẖr.t-nṯr*
[Der] seinen Ba in der Nekropole [aus]löscht

31)

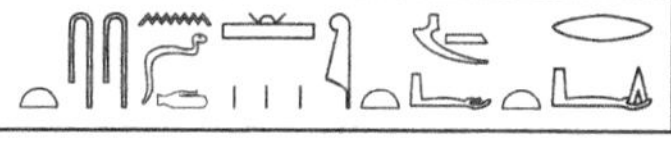	ÄMUL 3957

3957 *rd-mꜣꜥ.t n-ḏd-s-*(8)*-s.t*[sic]
Der Ma'at spendet dem, der sie ausspricht

32)

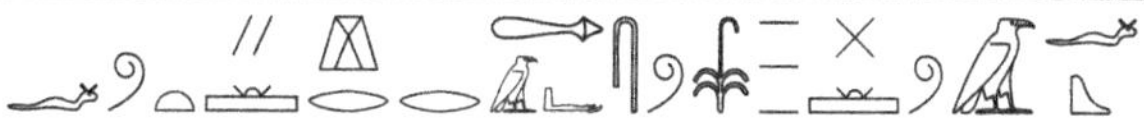	ÄMUL 3957

3957 *fkꜣ-sw sꜥꜣ-ẖr.t=f* ENDE
Der ihn belohnt, der seinen Besitz vergrößert.

12. Spuren in Poseners Facsimile sprechen klar für die Lesung *ḥr=f*.
13. In Z. 8 zu Anfang noch blasse Spuren + Gliederungspunkt, dann Ende. Da die Zeile 6 aber noch Platz geboten hätte, eventuell nicht mehr zum Hymnus gehörig.

Bemerkungen

1) Mit der Leipziger Hs liegt ein varianter Textanfang vor, sicher erkennbar ist am Original noch der Rest von [*ind-ḥr*]=*k*, von *ḥr* ist noch das obere Ende erhalten, der Logogrammstrich und der Anfang des Suffixes /=*k*/. ODeM 1799 hat eine kürzere Version mit seinem *dwꜣ.w-Ḏḥw.ty*.[14]
2) Diese Sequenz von Epitheta ist Standard in Bezug auf Thot. Das komplizierte Determinativ der Bügelfalle von defektiv notiertem *ib*<*t.t*> hat beiden Kopisten sichtlich gewisse Mühe bereitet.[15]
3) Zu dem mit *wḏꜥ* beginnenden Beiwort vgl. auch das dem Thot beigelegte auf Ostr. Petrie 41, Z. 7: *wḏꜥ.n=f-mwt r-ꜥnḫ°* – „nachdem er den Verdammten vom Lebenswerten getrennt hat". Jener Text ist laut Subskriptum ein *dwꜣ-Ḏḥw.ty*, bislang aber m.W. nirgends bearbeitet.[16]
4) Zu *pr m-sꜣr.t* vgl. *pr.n-sꜣr.t m-nṯry=f r-smsw-wḏ*, dort aber nicht von Thot.[17] Die Hss werden wohl sämtlich zu **sꜣr* – „Weiser" zu verbessern sein, denn „der aus der Weisheit hervorgegangen ist" ergibt kaum Sinn. In jedem Fall sind die Spuren auf ODeM dank der Leipziger Variante nun eindeutig als *sꜣr.t* zu lesen.
5) Eine Lesung *zꜣ-mnḫ* ist bislang hauptsächlich von Osiris bezeugt[18]. Vom König belegt z.B. als *iwꜥ n-ꜥꜥn zꜣ-mnḫ n-Ỉsdn* – „Erbe des Pavians, wohltätiger Sohn des Isden"[19].

   Eine Verteilung der beiden Wörter auf zwei Kola – *zꜣ mnḫ* – mit der Bedeutung „ein Sohn, der wirksam ist durch ..." würde gut zu folgendem *m-jr.t* – „in dem/durch das Geschaffene" o.ä. passen. In jedem Falle ist das von Posener in ODeM mit Fragezeichen gelesene *smnḫ* eindeutig als Falke-auf-Standarte + *mnḫ* zu lesen, und die Zeichen davor als *zꜣ* + Strich. ÄMUL 3957 und ODeM 1100 tragen also in diesem Vers den gleichen Text.
6) *nṯr.w nṯr.wt m-hj-hnw ir.n=f-ḫr.t-im=s n-dwꜣ-sw*[20] – „Götter und Göttinnen sind in frenetischem Jubel, nachdem er den Bedarf durch sie (= die vorweg genannte Ma'at) für den, der ihn lobpreist, geschaffen hat".

   Auf dem Turiner Papyrus CG 54053 aus der 19. Dyn. lautet eines der Epitheta des Thot innerhalb einer Kette von *ind-ḥr=k*-Invokationen: *ind-ḥr=k ir-ḫr.t-tꜣ.wy sḥḏ-sw wn-kk.ty*(?) *nn-wn-m-itn-im=f*(?). Lesung und Verständnis meinerseits basieren ganz wesentlich auf einer Transkription J. Černýs in seinem notebook 151.58–59, deren Kopie ich der Freundlichkeit J. Máleks verdanke: „Sei gegrüßt, der den Bedarf der Beiden Länder geschaffen hat, der sie erhellt, wenn sie dunkel sind, ohne daß es eine (Mond-)Scheibe an ihm gibt(?)"[21].
7) Die Ergänzung zu *ꜥḫi-p.t* in diesem Text schlägt Joachim F. Quack vor.[22] Nach Berlandini ist das Verbum *ꜥḫi* speziell „retenu plus que tout autre pour qualifier la faculté créatrice du démiurge memphite" (S. 11); s. aber

---

14. Zu Thot als „Großer Stier", s. *LGG* VII, 110–16, 129, 254 A) h).

15. Zu Thot als „Vorderstem des Hauses der Bügelfalle," s. Dagmar Budde, „Das ‚Haus-der-Vogelfalle'. Thot und eine seltsame Hieroglyphe auf einem Obelisken Nektanebos' II. (BM EA 523)", *GM* 191 (2002): 19–25, mit einer besonders reizvollen Schreibung des Zeichens der Falle (T 26) aus der Zeit Nektanebos' II. Ein „Haus der Bügelfalle" gleichen Namens ist jetzt auch von Geb bezeugt, wozu s. D. Meeks, *Mythes et legendes du Delta d'après le papyrus Brooklyn 47.218.84*, Mémoires publiés par les membres de l'Institut français d'archéologie orientale 125 (Kairo: Institut français d'archéologie orientale, 2006), 82 Anm. 194 und bes. 219–20 § 14b.

16. *Hieratic Ostraca I*, hg. J. Černý und A. H. Gardiner (Oxford: Oxford University Press, 1957), Taf. XXA.1.

17. *LGG* III, 81c–82a.

18. *LGG* VI, 80c–81a

19. Émile Chassinat, *Le temple de Dendara I* (Kairo: Imprimerie de l'Institut français d'archéologie orientale), 60.10, kurz besprochen bei Maria-Th. Derchian-Urtel, *Thot à travers ses épithètes dans les scènes d'offrandes des temples d'époque gréco-romaine,* Rites égyptiens 3 (Brüssel: Fondation Égyptologique Reine Elisabeth, 1981), 55–56.

20. Günther Roeder, *Ägyptische Inschriften aus den Königlichen Museen zu Berlin* (Leipzig: Hinrichs, 1924), 2:40.

21. Willem Pleyte and Francesco Rossi, *Papyrus de Turin* (Leiden: Brill, 1869–1876), Taf. XXV.6

22. Joachim F. Quack, Buchbesprechung *Lesefunde im literarischen Steinbruch von Deir el-Medineh*, von Hans-W. Fischer-Elfert, *WdO* 30 (1999): 139. Zu diesem Festritus, am 1. Phamenoth für Ptah zelebriert, s. aber ausführlich Jocelyne Berlandini, „Ptah-demiurge et l'exaltation du ciel", *RdÉ* 46 (1995): 9–41.

auch Joachim F. Quack zum memphitischen Hintergrund dieses Festes und seiner Bezeugung im Esna-Tempel.[23]

Danach scheint Thot nicht der geeignete Kandidat für dieses Prädikat zu sein und die Ergänzung zu *ꜥḫi* alles andere als gesichert. Immerhin kann zur Rolle von Thot als „Himmelsstütze" auf Belege aus den Tempeln von Edfu und Denderah und in spätzeitlichen Totenbuch-Papyri verwiesen werden, die Dieter Kurth kurz in seinem Buch *Den Himmel stützen*[24] behandelt. Doch auch die vier Träger an den Ecken des 4. Schreines Tutanchamuns haben mit Kurth eine Beziehung zu Thot. Von daher mag das Epitheton des Thot *smn-tꜣ* konkret auf diese Eigenschaft des Gottes hinweisen.

smn-tꜣ als negierte Aussage über Fremdländer, die dem bloßen Hören des Namens von Ramses III. nicht „standhalten" in seiner Inschrift vom 8. Jahr in Medinet Habu:[25] *bw-smn-tꜣ-nb n-sḏm-rn=i*.

8) *n-ḥḏ šꜣꜥ.n=f* ist ein Vers, der auch in der Lehre eines Mannes für seinen Sohn (§ 3.4) verwendet wird, dort allerdings mit Bezug auf das von den beiden Göttinnen Renenet und Mesechnet gesetzte Schicksal. Allerdings kann die Übersetzung des einheitlich *šꜣꜥ* geschriebenen Verbums kaum anders denn durch „Es gibt keinen, der mißachten könnte, was er begonnen hat" übersetzt werden. „Er" kann aber dort schwerlich auf die Göttinnen zielen, sondern sollte den König als Referenten haben.

9) Zu Thot als *s:wꜣḏ-pr.w grg-ḥw.wt* – „der die Tempeldomänen gedeihen läßt und die Kapellen ausstattet" s. Stadler den kurzen Hymnus auf der Berliner Statue 2293 des *Ḫri.w=f*, Kol. 3.[26]

12) Die Ergänzung zu [*wp/wḏꜥ-r*]*ḥ.wy* liegt mehr als nahe; zu den verschiedenen Verben vor *rḥ.wy*.[27] Die Trennung von Horus-dem-Älteren und Seth und deren Zuständigkeit samt Kronen über Unter- und Oberägypten, sowie die endgültige Übergabe Gesamtägyptens an Horus-den-Jüngeren findet im unteräg. Hermopolis (i.a. *pr-Ḏḥw.ty*) statt.

jr-ḥtp-nṯr.w – „der den Götterfrieden herstellt" oder „der-für-die-Götteropfer-Sorge-trägt"?[28] Das korrekte Verständnis des Kolons ist abhängig von der Interpretation des Determinativs nach *ḥtp.w*, ob Buchrolle oder Opferbrot. ODeM 1100 vs. 1 entscheidet zugunsten ersterer. Leider entziehen sich die Zeichenspuren des 1. Wortes des folgenden Kolons einer eindeutigen Lesung.[29]

13) Ist mit *wḏb* das „Uferland" gemeint, das Thot den beiden Antipoden Horus und Seth „berechnet", also letztlich die Beiden Ufer und damit Ober- und Unterägypten? Diese Deutung s. Vernus hängt an der korrekten Ergänzung des vorangehenden Wortes, dessen Reste recht unspezifisch bleiben.

---

23. Joachim F. Quack, „Fragmente memphitischer Religion und Astronomie in semidemotischer Schrift (pBerlin 14402 + pCarlsberg 651 + PSI Inv. D 23)", in *Res severa verum gaudium. Festschrift für Karl-Theodor Zauzich zum 65. Geburtstag am 8. Juni 2004*, hg. Friedhelm Hoffmann und Hans J. Thissen, StudDem 6 (Leuven: Peeters, 2004), 495–96.

24. Dieter Kurth, *Den Himmel stützen. Die «Twꜣ pt»-Szenen in den ägyptischen Tempeln der griechisch-römischen Epoche*, Rites Égyptiens 2 (Brüssel: Fondation Égyptologique Reine Elisabeth, 1975), 85–86; s.a. Ursula Verhoeven, *Das saitische Totenbuch der Iahtesnacht. P. Colon. Aeg. 10207*, mit einem Beitrag von Peter Dils, 3 Bde., Papyrologische Texte und Abhandlungen (Bonn: Habelt, 1993), zu Tb 161, Kol. 146–47: vier Figuren des Thot mit Himmelsstütze.

25. Kenneth A. Kitchen, *Ramesside Inscriptions Historical and Biographical V* (Oxford: Blackwell, 1983), 41.16.

26. Roeder, *Aegyptische Inschriften*, 41; *Urk.* IV:1875; vgl. auch *s:wꜣḏ-ḥw.t-bjk* in *LGG* VI, 211b.

27. Martin A. Stadler, *Weiser und Wesir. Zu Vorkommen, Rolle und Wesen des Gottes Thot im ägyptischen Totenbuch*, Orientalische Religionen des Altertums 1 (Tübingen: Mohr Siebeck, 2009), 337; Dimitri Meeks, *Mythes et légendes du delta*, 26 § 28; dazu weiterer Kommentar auf den Seiten 119–20 und 266–27.

28. Vergleiche *LGG* I, 476c–477a.

29. Vergleiche a. PT § 1465b.

14) Zu ꜥnn-GN r-NN – „Gott NN wendet sich (wieder) um zu NN“[30] Eine exakte Parallele zu dieser Phrase verzeichnet er nicht. Das Verbum ꜥnn benennt nach Vernus eine essentielle Eigenschaft von Gottheiten, *ḥtp* – „gnädig sein“ dagegen eine circumstantielle.
Thot als „Niederwerfender(?)“ (*sẖr*) eventuell des Urfeindes von Re und seiner Barke auf OPetrie 41 Z. 7-8.[31] Das Verbum *sṯz* „aufrichten“ ist dann aber nicht ganz korrekt determiniert.[32] Der vermeintliche Eintrag *sṯs* auf S. 362.4 ist von Schweitzer[33] in *srs* – „aufwecken“ korrigiert worden.

15) *pẖr-jb* – „Der-mit sich-umwendendem-Herzen“ knüpft an die Persönliche Frömmigkeitsphrase *ꜥnn-sw* in V. 14 direkt an. Daß die Wendung *pẖr-jb* auch der Terminus für den sog. „Liebeszauber“ darstellt, wird spätestens aus dem Lemma-Eintrag auf einer aus TT 34 stammenden Holztafel deutlich, die eine Reihe von Verben der Bewegung lexikographisch abhandelt; dazu mehr Verf., *Laufende Lemmata: Studien zu Verben der Bewegung nach zwei römerzeitlichen Holztafeln* (i.Vb.). Die Angaben in *Wb.* I sind nicht erschöpfend.[34]
Die Graphie von *sfẖ* – „lösen“ in Gestalt von *sẖf* ist wohlbekannt, auch vom Simplex *fẖ*[35]: zu *fẖ* für *ẖf* – „zerstören“ in *Wb.* I:578.
Ein Epitheton *sfẖ-sšr.w=f* – „der-seinen-Pfeil-(wieder)-lost“ scheint von Thot bislang nicht bezeugt zu sein, zumindest listet das *LGG* VI keinen solchen Eintrag auf.[36]

16) *wḥꜥ-ṯzz.t* – „Der-das-Verknotete-löst“ in der jüngeren Ausprägung – hier als *ḏꜣis* – als Epitheton des Thot z.B. schon auf der Kopenhagener Stele Ny Carlsberg Inv. 1241, Z. 4, des Siegelbewahrers Antef, Sohn der Myt, aus der späten 11. Dynastie.[37]

17) Epitheton des Sonnengottes, hier Atum.[38] Von daher ist J. F. Quacks Emendationsvorschlag zu *sḫm-ir=f*, „Machthaber“, weniger wahrscheinlich.[39]
Rein graphisch verdient die herausgehobene Größe des *sḫm*-Szepters in ODeM 1100 vs. 4 Erwähnung und mag ihren Grund in einer besonderen Betonung dieses Wortes gehabt haben. Vielleicht hat aber der Schreiber auch nur die Form des Zeichens geschätzt und es deshalb nur geringfügig „hieratisiert“.
ODeM 1100 vs. 5 und Ostr. ANAsh Mus. H.O.398 x+1 schreiben *jrw.w=f*, also „seine-sichtbaren-und-durch-Attribute-erkennbaren-Erscheinungsformen“, wenn die Ausführungen zu diesem Terminus durch Dimitri Meeks so zusammengefaßt werden dürfen.[40] ÄMUL 3957 vs. 1 bricht leider nach den ersten zwei Zeichen ab.

18) *jwty-ḫsf=f* – „Dessen-Abwehr-es-nicht-gibt“ scheint der 1. Beleg dieses Epithetons für Thot zu sein, denn der bislang einzige ist belegt in *Dendera* X.[41] Nachfolgendes *m-mrr.n=f* in ODeM 1644.4 und *m-mrw.t.n=f* in ODeM 1100 vs. 5 und vielleicht so auch in ÄMUL 3957 vs. 2 ist dagegen originell für diesen frühen Beleg.

---

30. Siehe Pascal Vernus, „La piété personnelle à Deir el-Medineh: La construction de l'idée de pardon“, in *Deir el-Médineh et la Vallée des Rois*, hg. Guillmette Andreu (Paris: Khéops, 2003), 322–25 und 332–34.
31. Černý and Gardiner, *Hieratic Ostraca I*, Taf. XXA.1.
32. Vergleiche *Wb.* IV:360–61 und 361.6: „Lobpreisung, Erhebung mit Worten“.
33. Simon D. Schweitzer, „Aus der Arbeit am Ägyptischen Wörterbuch. Einige Ghostwords (III)“, *GM* 230 (2011): 66.
34. *Wb.* I:544, 14–515, 3.
35. Günter Vittmann, *Der demotische Papyrus Rylands 9, Teil II Kommentare und Indizes*, ÄAT 38 (Wiesbaden: Harrassowitz, 1998), 332 Anm. 357.
36. Siehe allenfalls Stadler, *Weiser und Wesir*, 337, zu *sfẖ* in Bezug auf Horus von Seth.
37. Jacques J. Clère and Jacques Vandier, *Textes de la première période intermédiaire*, BiAe 10 (Brüssel: Fondation Égyptologique Reine Élisabeth 1948), § 32. Zur Ergänzung, Wolfgang Schenkel, *Memphis – Herakleopolis – Theben*, ÄgAbh 12 (Wiesbaden: Harrassowitz, 1965), 232 n. f; s.a. Boyo Ockinga, *Die Gottebenbildlichkeit im alten Ägypten und im Alten Testament*, ÄAT 7 (Wiesbaden: Harrassowitz, 1984), 83 (88) und 88.
38. *LGG* VI, 527b.
39. Quack, Buchbesprechung Fischer-Elfert, 139.
40. Dimitri Meeks, *La vie quotidienne des dieux égyptiens* (Paris: Hachette, 1993), 84–90 und passim.
41. *Dendera* X, 58.2; s. *LGG* I, 162c–163a.

19) *spd-sšr.w* – „Mit-spitzen-Pfeilen" von Upuaut[42], von Thot hingegen scheint es mit diesem Hymnus erstmalig bezeugt zu sein.

ꜥꜣ-bꜣw ohne folgendes Suffix *=f* in dem Hymnus an Iah-Thot auf der Ramses II-zeitlichen Stele Kairo JE 72025 eines Penamun aus Deir el-Medineh.[43] Dieses Epitheton ist dank der inzwischen bekannten Versionen auf ODeM 1644 und ÄMUL 3957 nun auch auf ODeM 1100 vs. 6 klar zu rekonstruieren.

20) *ꜥḳꜣ-jb* – „Rechtschaffener" oder „Geradherziger" ist von Thot laut (*LGG* II, 236) erstaunlicherweise bisher unbekannt. Auch dieses Epitheton ist nun dank der Parallelen auf ODeM 1100 vs. 6 eindeutig identifizierbar. Dieses Epitheton hat bekanntlich Jacques J. Clère, „[âka-ib] "honnête, loyal"[44] insbesondere anhand von Belegen aus der Spätzeit, näher untersucht. Auf Nr. 6 führt er dazu eine Stelle aus dem Grab des Petosiris in Hermopolis an, in der die „Rechtschaffenheit" des Grabinhabers mit der des Thot, Herrn von Hermopolis, gleichgesetzt wird: *jb=k-ꜥḳꜣ mj-nb-ḫmnw*: „Deine R. ist wie die des Herrn von Hermopolis".[45] Von daher wäre es umso erstaunlicher, wenn dieses Beiwort nicht schon früher auf Thot gemünzt worden sein sollte.

jmy-p.t von Thot-Iah auf der bereits ad V. 12 zit. Statue Berlin 2293, vorn Z. 2, bei Günter Roeder.[46]

21) Eine Konstruktion *m-sḏm.n=f*, noch dazu mit redupliziertem Verbum sec. gem. *mꜣꜣ*, vermag ich in den Grammatiken des Mitteläg. nicht zu finden. S. aber immerhin die redupl. *sḏm=f*: Relativform nach *m*.[47]

Die wohl eleganteste Lösung wäre aber die Annahme eines Infinitivs + Präpositionalverbindung *n=f* nach vorangehender Präp. *n* statt *m*. Dann läge die Wendung *n-mꜣꜣ-n=f* vor: „blicken auf jemand; auf etwas.[48] Auch: sich freuen, jemand zu sehen. Wahrscheinlich nur für *n mꜣ.f*, das damit wechselt". Es wäre also nur die Präp. *m* in *n* zu emendieren, was durch den Einfluß des Neuäg. evoziert sein könnte. Es ist aber auch zu beachten, daß das *m* mit frischer Tusche und wie nachträglich in den Text buchstäblich hineingequetscht worden zu sein scheint. Das hätte zur Folge, daß Atum als untergehender Sonnengott beim Anblick von Thot diesen als seinen Stellvertreter in der Nacht wertschätzen (*mrw.ty*) würde.

22) OBM EA 65602 rt. 2 hat ähnlich unserem Vers *shrr-tꜣ.wy n-wtṯ-sw°* - „der die Beiden Länder beruhigt für den, der ihn erzeugt hat".[49] Jener Thot-Hymnus dürfte auf dem Verso seine Fortsetzung finden, dafür sprechen mindestens die letzten zwei Zeilen, von denen x+6 zu [*tm-rd*] *ḥr-gs* – „[Der nicht] parteiisch ist", lit. „der nicht auf eine Seite legt", zu restituieren sein dürfte.

23) In der Lücke ist ein Verbum aus dem Bedeutungsspektrum „vernichten" gefordert.[50]

24) Trotz des von der Wurzel *iꜣd.t* > *id* – „Tau" geborgten Determinativs des tropfenden Himmels dürfte hier *s:id* – „zur Ordnung bringen (von Feinden u.ä.)" anzusetzen sein.[51] Eine schöne Parallele liegt vor in dem Hymnus an die 7 Uräen des Sonnengottes in TT 27: *s:id=s-n=k ḫꜣk.w-ib* – „sie schüchtert für dich die Krummherzigen

42. *LGG* VI, 285–86.
43. *KRI III* 732.10; s. *LGG* II, 20c.
44. Jacques J. Clère, „[âka-ib] ‚honnête, loyal'", *BIFAO* 89 (1989): 68–71.
45. Clère, „[âka-ib]", 68 (Nr. 6).
46. Roeder, *Ägyptische Inschriften*, 40.
47. James P. Allen, *Middle Egyptian: An Introduction to the Language and Culture of Hieroglyphs* (Cambridge: Cambridge University Press, 2000), 25.3.1.
48. *Wb.* II:9, 1–4.
49. Robert J. Demarée, *Ramesside Ostraca* (London: British Museum Press, 2002), Taf. 165.
50. Nr. 230.12 bei Jan Assmann, *Sonnenhymnen aus Thebanischen Gräbern* (Mainz: von Zabern, 1983), 324, hat *ḥtm* als Aktion des Lichtauges zugunsten des Chepre-Harachte; der Thot-Hymnus Haremhebs in New York formuliert *sḫr-sbi* (Z. 8 = *Urk. IV* 2092.10). ÄMUL 3957 vs. liest aber nicht *ḥr-Nb-r-ḏr*, sondern klar genitivisch *nw-Nb-r-ḏr*. Zur Kollokation *sbi-ḥr* s. noch die Anmerkungen bei Harco Willems, „The Social and Ritual Context of a Mortuary Liturgy of the Middle Kingdom (*CT* Spells 30–41)", in *Social Aspects of Funerary Culture in the Egyptian Old and Middle Kingdoms*, hg. Harco Willems, OLA 103 (Leuven: Peeters, 2001), 309 Anm. 229.
51. *Wb.* IV:41, 8.

ein."[52] Das in Ostr. ANAsh Mus. H.O. 398.4 oberhalb der Zeile nachgetragene Genetiv-*n* ergänze ich entsprechend auch in den Varianten. Die Parallele auf Ostr. ANAsh Mus. H.O. 398 macht die Ansetzung als *ẖ3w.t-ib-r=f* sicher, wobei *ẖ3w.t* wohl zu **ẖ3k.w* emendiert werden darf. Zur Verbindung *ẖ3k r-* „feindlich, listig, verschlagen gegen jemand sein".[53]

25) Die Ergänzung dieses Epithetons fällt nicht leicht, zumal das *LGG* kein *dr-s3*[...] anbietet. Auf dem großen Ostr. ANAsh Mus. H.O. 303 vs. begegnet ein *dr-ẖnꜥ* (mit dem Seth-Tier determiniert), was immer das heißen mag.[54] Immerhin ist der Vergleich mit unserem Leipziger Ostrakon so hinkend nicht, denn die Eulogie auf den anonymen Wesir auf Ostr. ANAsh Mus. H.O. 303, so die beiden Editoren, liest sich wie ein einziger großer Hymnus auf den Gott Thot, je weiter man sich dem Textende nähert.

26) Im Thot-Hymnus Haremhabs auf seiner New Yorker Statue soll die Neunheit in der Nachtbarke ihm *i3w*: „Lobpreis" spenden.[55]

Auf dem noch unbearbeiteten Ostr. Petrie 41 fordert ein – anonymes – Kollektiv zu diversen Aktionen zugunsten des Gottes Thot auf. Aus dem Subskriptum in Z. 9 innerhalb einer Rezitationsanweisung gehen Gattung und Adressat des vorangehenden Rezitativs spätestens hervor: *dw3.w-Ḏḥw.ty*.[56] Auf der aus der frühen 18. Dyn. datierenden Holztafel BM EA 5646 in London werden die Götter aufgefordert: *dw3-sw sḳ3-sw imi-n=f i3w* – „preist ihn, rühmt ihn, spendet ihm Lobpreis!" (Z. 3), und in Z. 4 heißt es: *ist-nṯr-nb nṯr.t-nb.t rdi=sn-i3w n-Ḏḥw.ty*:[57] „Jeder Gott nun und jede Göttin, sie mögen dem Thot Lobpreis spenden".

27) Dieser Vers überwiegend nur auf Ostr. ANAsh Mus. H.O. 398, aber auf ÄMUL 3957b.5 ist an der linken Bruchkante immerhin noch der rubrizierte *ṯ3*-Vogel von *ṯ3.ty* zu erkennen. An dieser Stelle gehen der Oxforder (Z. 5) und der Leipziger Textzeuge zusammen. Am Beginn der Zeilen müßte auf ÄMUL 3957b.3–7 doch mehr fehlen als zunächst erwartet. Exakt quantifizieren läßt sich das natürlich nicht, da niemand sagen kann, inwieweit diese Version an diesen Stellen von den übrigen Varianten abweicht. Da jedoch noch mindestens fünf Verse auf dem Leipziger Stück folgen, kann angesichts des leer belassenen Raumes auf der Oxforder Version notiert werden, daß diese es bei ihrem Vers- und stropheneinleitenden *ṯ3.ty wp-m3ꜥ.t* beläßt und damit nur eine partielle Kopie des gesamten Hymnus vorliegt. *ṯ3.ty wp-m3ꜥ.t* fungiert als Scharniervers zur finalen Strophe.[58]

28) *ḥḏ-wsf3{.t} m33=f-ḥr=f* u.ä. ist m.W. von Thot anderweitig nicht belegt.[59]

29) Dieses Epitheton ist in *LGG* I nicht verzeichnet. Ich möchte bezweifeln, daß *ir-sw* in diesem Vers „der sich machte (zu ...)" bedeutet, sondern daß *sw* sich auf einen Antipoden des Gottes bezieht, genauso wie derjenige, dessen Ba er laut V. 30 in der Nekropole vernichtet.

---

52. Text Nr. 27.17 bei Assmann, *Sonnenhymnen in Thebanischen Gräbern*, 36 (TT 27).

53. *Wb.* III:363, 12; Zu *id* / *s:id* s. ferner Jürgen Osing, *Hieratische Papyri aus Tebtunis I*, CNIP 17 (Copenhagen: Museum Tusculanum Press, 1998), 215 Anm. 1052. Seinem Verweis auf CT I 320b (speziell 75) verdanke ich auch die alternative Determinierung von *idd.w* mit dem „regnenden Himmel" (sign-list N4) in der Var. B2L: *ink-gr-idd.w=f-p.t t3*: „Ich bin doch derjenige, der Himmel und Erde zur Ruhe bringt".

54. Černý und Gardiner, *Hieratic Ostraca I*, Taf. XCII.1

55. *Urk.* IV:2092, 12; s. dort auch 2093.7 in der Selbstaufforderung der Adoranten.

56. Černý und Gardiner, *Hieratic Ostraca I*, Taf. XII/A.1. Auf Ostr. ANAsh Mus. H.O. 321.3 hinwiederum „spendet ihm (bzw. dem *Iꜥḥ*, „Mond") die Götterneunheit Lobpreis", Fischer-Elfert, *Lesefunde im literarischen Steinbruch*, 103–7.

57. Richard B. Parkinson, *Cracking Codes: The Rosetta Stone and Decipherment* (London: British Museum Press, 1999), 148–49 Nr. 64.

58. Zu Thot als Wesir s. noch Derchain-Urtel, *Thot à traves ses épithètes*, 95–106, sowie Stadler, *Weiser und Wesir*, passim.

59. *LGG* V, 610.

Die Lesung *ms* und Deutung als *msi* – „gebären" ist angesichts der Bruchkante nicht über jeden Zweifel erhaben. In der Reihe von zehn *jnḏ-ḥr=k*-Invokationen des Thot auf Pap. Turin CG 54053 ist in vs. 2.4 u.a. auch von seiner Autogenese die Rede: *ms-sw ḏs=f*.[60]

30) Auf der zitierten New Yorker Statue Haremhebs soll Thot den Ba des Rebellen *sḏ* – „zerbrechen".[61]

32) Vom *fḳꜣ*, „Extra-Lohn; Bonuszahlung" für die *mꜣꜥ-ib* „Rechtschaffenheit", oder den „Rechtschaffenen"(?), ist auch am Ende des Sonnenhymnus Nr. 189 die Rede.[62]

Die Verwendung dieses aus der Administration von Deir el-Medineh gut bekannten Terminus verdient in jedem Fall eine zumindest kurze Annotation. Aus einschlägigen Listen über Auszahlungen an die Handwerker geht hervor, daß es sich bei *fḳꜣ*, wie auch bei *mkw* und *ḥtr*, um Sonderzahlungen oder -zuwendungen handelt, die in besonderer Anerkennung von Arbeitsleistungen ausgeteilt werden.[63] So ist für deren Übergabe insbesondere der Wesir zuständig, z.B. dann, wenn er den Fortgang der Arbeiten am jeweiligen Königsgrab inspiziert. Ausgehend von diesem Umstand könnten wir uns also fragen, ob der Gott Thot in diesem letzten Vers des Hymnus nicht auch gezielt als Wesir agiert, als welchen ihn V. 27 ja ausdrücklich deklariert.

Die unverzichtbare Buchrolle nach *s:ꜥꜣ* scheint zu einem /*r*/ mißraten zu sein. Ich vermute hinter *s:ꜥꜣ* in Bezug auf den *ẖr.t* – „Unterhalt; Besitz" die gleiche Bedeutung wie in dem Wortspiel zwischen diesen beiden Wörtern in der Ausdeutung des Traumbildes in Pap. Ch. B. III 2.11: *ꜥꜣ n-ḥnn=f – nfr: ꜥšꜣ n(?)-jḫ.t=f-pw* – „Ist sein Penis groß: Gut: Das bedeutet, daß er über reichlich Besitz verfügt."

Fortlaufende Übersetzung (im Wesentlichen nach ÄMUL 3957):

1) [Sei gegrüß]t, Thot, Großer Stier!
2) [Prominentester] von Hesret, inmitten des Hauses-der-Vogelfalle
3) Herr von Hermopolis, der [...] richtet
4) Der <als> Weiser/ <mit> Weisheit hervorgekommen ist ...
5) ein Sohn, der wirksam ist in dem/durch das Geschaffene
6) Der für den Unterhalt sorgt [...]
7) Der den Himmel [erhoben hat], der die Erde auf Dauer gestellt hat
8) Nicht kann zerstört werden, was er begonnen hat
9) Der die Tempel des Vaters [seiner(?)] Väter gedeihen [läßt]
10) Der Opferbrote spendet dem, der ihn erzeugt hat
11) ... (?), der Horus und Seth befriedet (hat)
12) [Der trennt] die Beiden [Streit]hähne, der den Götterfrieden bewirkt
13) [ih]re(?) ... (?), der ihn/es berechnet(?)
14) Der sich (wieder) dem zuwendet, um aufzurichten den er niedergeworfen hat
15) Der mit umkreisendem Herzen, der seine Pfeile (wieder) löst
16) Herr der Gnade, der das löst, was er verknotet hatte
17) gleichwie Atum, der mächtig in [seinen(?)] sichtbaren Erscheinung[en] ist
18) Dessen Ablehnung dessen, den/was er schätzen gelernt hat, es nicht gibt
19) Der mit spitzen Pfeilen, gewaltig an [seinem] Machterweis
20) Der Recht[schaffene ... ...], Abgeschirmter, der im Himmel(?)

60. Alessandro Roccati, *Magica Taurinensia: Il grande papiro magico di Torino e i suoi duplicati* (Rome: Gregorian & Biblical Press, 2011), 44.

61. *Urk.* IV:2092, 19.

62. Assmann, *Sonnenhymnen aus Thebanischen Gräbern*, 268–69.

63. Benedict G. Davies, *Life within the Five Walls: A Handbook to Deir el-Medina* (Wallasey: Abercromby, 2018), 263 und 267, nennt dafür Beispiele.

21) Geliebter Atums, wenn der seiner ansichtig wird(?)
22) …, der Ma'at ins Werk setzt für den, der [ihn] er[zeugt hat(?)]
23) [der vernichtet o.ä.] den Rebellen des/gegen den Allherrn
24) Der das Herz der Krumm[herzigen(?) …] einschüchtert
25) welcher vertreibt … [… …] eines jeden Gottes
26) Sie mögen dir Lobpreis spenden einen jeden Tag
27) (du) Wesir, der die Ma'at eröffnet
28) Der den Nachlässigen vernichtet, wenn er seiner ansichtig wird
29) Der ihn macht wie/zu einer/m, der nicht geboren wurde(?)
30) [Der] seinen Ba in der Nekropole [aus]löscht
31) Der Ma'at spendet dem, der sie ausspricht
32) Der ihn belohnt, der seinen Besitz vergrößert.

Umfang, Themen und Struktur des Hymnus

In Anbetracht von noch immer fehlendem Textbestand sind alle folgenden Ausführungen als vorläufig zu betrachten, angefangen bei der Zahl der Verse und endend beim Verständnis so manch eines Epithetons. In jedem Fall darf der auf den hier synoptisch zusammengestellten Ostraka rekonstruierte Text nunmehr als Hymnus an den Gott Thot klassifiziert werden, der in Deir el-Medineh nach Ausweis seiner drei dort gefundenen Exemplare ODeM 1100, 1644 und 1799 bekannt war und tradiert wurde. Dies geschah sicher nicht nur zu reinen Studienzwecken, sondern auch für den praktischen Gebrauch im Kult dieses Gottes. Der Leipziger Textzeuge steht im Verdacht, einst den gesamten Wortlaut getragen zu haben, was sich bei keiner der anderen Versionen mit Sicherheit sagen läßt. Allein deswegen kommt ÄMUL 3957 eine kapitale Bedeutung für die textuelle Rekonstruktion dieses anderweitig bis heute nicht belegten Hymnus an Thot zu.

Unter der Voraussetzung, daß die Vers- und Kolonabtrennung hier korrekt vorgenommen worden ist, haben wir 32 Verse insgesamt zu veranschlagen. Diese Zahl mag auf purem Zufall – oder Wunschdenken! – beruhen, in Anbetracht des theologischen Bezugs von Thot zu Hermopolis als „Stadt der 8 (Urgötter)" scheint mir das aber mehr als unwahrscheinlich. 32 ist das Vierfache von 8 und ausgehend von V. 3 mit seinem Epitheton *nb-ḫmnw* – „Herr-der-Stadt-der-Acht" kann diese Gesamtverszahl durchaus intendiert sein.[64] Eine Gesamtzahl der Hebungen für diesen Hymnus zu bestimmen verbietet sich aufgrund des noch immer unvollständigen Wortlautes.

Der Hymnus ist – soweit schon jetzt erkennbar – klar strukturiert und handelt mehrere Facetten des Wesens von Thot in Strophen von unterschiedlicher Länge ab. Erwartungsgemäß sind einige der inkorporierten Epitheta eher dem Standardrepertoire vergleichbarer Thot-Hymnen zuzurechnen, andere dafür aber umso weniger. Dieser Befund macht den Text zu einer kleinen Fundgrube für neue Einträge im *Lexikon der Götter und Götterbezeichnungen*.

64. Zur Rolle von – symbolischen – Vers- und Kolonzahlen in der Metrik hat Gerhard Fecht sich in verschiedenen einschlägigen Arbeiten geäußert. Dabei ist seine eher beiläufige Bemerkung hierzu in seinem Aufsatz „Die Form der altägyptischen Literatur. Metrische und stilistische Analyse", *ZÄS* 91 (1964): 57, vergleichsweise wenig hilfreich: „Es ist nicht selten, daß ein aus recht verschiedenen Elementen bestehender, in seiner allgemeinen Zweckbestimmung aber einheitlicher Text insgesamt eine so runde, in sich abgeschlossen wirkende Anzahl von Versen ergibt." Etwas konkreter wird er dann in seinem Beitrag „Stilistische Kunst", in *Ägyptologie: Literatur*, hg. Bertold Spuler (Leiden: Brill), 26: „Beliebt sind als Gesamtzahl von Versen (in Gesamttexten oder in Strophen) neben den runden Zahlen des Dezimalsystems die Zahlen sieben, acht, neun, sei es einfach, addiert oder multipliziert"; s.a. Gerhard Fecht, *Literarische Zeugnisse zur „Persönlichen Frömmigkeit" in Ägypten. Analyse der Beispiele aus den ramessidischen Schulpapyri*, AHAW Phil.-hist. Kl. (Heidelberg: Heidelberger Akademie der Wissenschaften, 1965), 16–17 (u.a. Qadesch-Gedicht aus 7 × 70 Versen); und seine Bearbeitung des Qadesch-Gedichts in der Festschrift für Wolfgang Helck: Gerhard Fecht, „Das ‚Poème' über die Qadeš-Schlacht", *SAK* 11 (1984): 281–333; zu den Zahlenverhältnissen s. dort 329–33.

Versuchen wir zunächst die Themen bzw. Motive der Epitheta zu identifizieren. Dies geschehe in tabellarischer Form:

Vers	**1. und letztes Epitheton, soweit erhalten und identifizierbar**	**Motivik**
1–3	*kꜣ-wr – wḏꜥ-[…]*	Herr von Hermopolis
4–5	*pr m-sꜣr – smnḫ m-jr.t*	Weiser und Wirksamer im Geschaffenen
6	*jr-ẖr.t – […(?)]*	Garant von Unterhalt und Versorgung
7–8	*[ꜥḫ]-p.t – n-ḥḏ-šꜣꜥ<.t>.n=f*	Schöpfer von unzerstörbarem Himmel und der Erde
9–10	*swꜣḏ-ḥw.wt – n-wtṯ-sw*	Versorger von Tempeldomänen und -kapellen
11–12	*[…] sḥtp-Ḥrw – jr-ḥtp-nṯr.w*	Schlichter zwischen Horus und Seth
13–18	*[…] wḏb – m-mrw.t.n=f*	Herr von Gnade und Vergebung
19–20	*spd-šsr.w – jmj-p.t(?)*	Von großen Machterweisen im Himmel
21–22	*mrw.ty-Jtmw – n-wtṯ-sw*	Statthalter seines Schöpfers Atum und Garant der Maꜥat
23–24	*[…] dr-s3.w – ẖꜣ<k>.w-jb-r=f*	Vernichter von Rebellen
25–26	*ḏr-sꜣ[…] – […]*	(unklar)
27–32	*ṯꜣ.ty – sꜥꜣ-ẖr.t=f*	Wesir, der den Trägen vernichtet und den Ma'at-Praktizierenden versorgt

Neue Epitheta des Thot, nach Versnummern:

4) *pr m-sꜣr.t(?)*
5) *zꜣ mnḫ m-jr.t*
8) *n-ḥḏ šꜣꜥ<.t>.n=f*
9) *[s]wꜣḏ-ḥw.wt n-ỉtỉ-ỉtỉ.w[=f(?)]*
10) *dd-pꜣw.t <n>-wtṯ-sw*
12) *ỉr-ḥtp-nṯr.w*
13) *[…]y.w-wḏb ḥsb-sw*
14) *ꜥnn-sw r-sṯz-sḫr.n=f*
15) *pẖr-ỉb sḫf-šsr.w=f*
16) *wḥꜥ.n=f-ḏꜣis<.t>.n=f*
17) *mi-ỈItmw sḫm m-ỉr.w=f*
18) *ỉwtỉ-ḫsf=f m-mrw.t.n=f*
19) *spd-šsr.w*
20) *ꜥḳꜣ-jb*
21) *mrw.t(y)-Ỉtmw m-mꜣꜣ-n=f*

22) *i͗r-mꜣꜥ.t n-wtṯ-sw*(?)
23) [...] *sbbi.w nw-Nb-r-ḏr*
24) *sid-i͗b <n>-ẖꜣ*[*k*(?) ...]
25) *dr-sꜣ*[... ...]
28) *ḥḏ-wsfꜣ{.t} mꜣꜣ=f-ḥr=f*
29) *i͗r-sw mi͗-nty-nn-ms*(?)
30) [*s*]*ḥtm-bꜣ=f m-ẖr.t-nṯr*
31) *rd-mꜣꜥ.t n-ḏd.ti-s.t*
32) *fḳꜣ-sw sꜥꜣ-ẖr.t=f*

Der inhaltliche Kommentar zu diesem Thot-Hymnus konnte eine stattliche Reihe an Epitheta zu Tage fördern, die nach Ausweis des Materials im *LGG* anderweitig für Thot nicht bezeugt sind, oder – wie im Falle von V. 17 – erstmalig in diesem Text. Auch wenn sich in dem einen oder anderen Fall ähnliche Prädikate finden lassen, so bleibt die Tatsache unbestritten, daß deren Anordnung und damit auch die thematische Gliederung dieses Hymnus in der Thot-Lyrik bislang ihresgleichen suchen.

Möge es damit vorläufig sein Bewenden haben, und möge Richard als Kenner und Kollege des Thot seine Freude an dieser kleinen Festgabe haben, als Zeichen des Dankes für all seine eigenen Arbeiten und für seine Freundschaft.

Black Spread over Mummy Cases and Tomb Walls in Dra Abu el-Naga

José M. Galán

The color black is associated with the rebirth of vegetation through the fertile dark soil and with humans that identify themselves with the god Osiris seeking to share his fate.[1] The rebirth power of the color black may explain its use as background color on wooden coffins, common during the Twenty-Second Dynasty, but attested since the Twelfth Dynasty.[2] A Seventeenth Dynasty *rishi*-coffin found by the Spanish archaeological mission at Dra Abu el-Naga shows clearly the association between black soil and the human hope for rebirth: while the lid is decorated with a feather pattern and the face has a bright yellow color, the outer side of the box is completely painted in black (fig. 1).[3]

During the Twenty-Second Dynasty, at the same time black coffins were in vogue, it also became common practice among the Theban elite to deposit the mummified body of the deceased inside a human shaped cartonnage case, which in turn would be placed inside the coffin. The mummy case was covered with a layer of plaster and then profusely decorated with a colorful combination of images of gods, daemons, emblems, amulets, and hieroglyphic texts. The raw materials used as basis would be considered inexpensive, or at least affordable for most members of the scribal class within the civil and/or religious service. In addition to these, the quality of the work carried out by the draftsmen and painters on the outer layer must have required a variety of pigments and a knowledge of religious themes and current trends, adding time to the manufacture and a significant increase in the price. However, once the mummy case was resting inside the coffin awaiting to be delivered into a burial chamber or a similar shelter, a black thick substance was poured on top of it, spreading over most of its surface and hiding its elaborate, polychrome decoration under a black and opaque crust.[4] What may seem an odd practice today was most probably not perceived

---

This article is part of the research project HAR2014-52323-P within the Spanish National Program for Scientific Research, Technology and Innovation.

1. Jacques Connan, "La momification dans l'Égypte ancienne: Le bitumen et les autres ingrédients organiques des baumes de momies; ou Les ingredients organiques des baumes de momies égyptiennes: Bitumen, cire d'abeille, résines, poix, graisse, huile, vin, etc.," in *Encyclopédie religieuse de l'Univers vegetal: Croyances phytoreligieuses de l'Égypte ancienne*, ed. Sydney H. Aufrère, Orientalia Monspeliensia 15 (Université Paul Valéry: Montpellier, 2005), 3:176–79; Salima Ikram and Aidan Dodson, "A Twenty-Second Dynasty Mummy-Cartonnage in the Gayer-Anderson Museum," in *Another Mouthful of Dust: Egyptological Studies in Honour of Geoffrey Thorndike Martin*, ed. Jan van Dijk, OLA 246 (Leuven: Peeters, 2016), 321; Ute Rummel and Stéphane Fetler, "The Coffins of the Third Intermediate Period from Tomb K93.12 at Dra Abu el-Naga: Aspects of Archaeology, Typology, and Conservation," in *Proceedings First Vatican Conference*, ed. Alessia Menta and Hélène Guichard (Vatican City: Edizioni Musei Vaticani, 2017), 455.

2. John H. Taylor, "Patterns of Colouring on Ancient Egyptian Coffins from the New Kingdom to the Twenty-Sixth Dynasty: An Overview," in *Colour and Painting in Ancient Egypt*, ed. W. Vivian Davies (London: The British Museum Press, 2001), 166, 168; Ikram and Dodson, "A Twenty-Second Dynasty Mummy-Cartonnage," 321.

3. José M. Galán and Ángeles Jiménez-Higueras, "Three Burials of the Seventeenth Dynasty in Dra Abu el-Naga," in *The World of Middle Kingdom Egypt (2000–1550 BC)*, ed. Gianluca Miniaci and Wolfgang Grajetzki, Middle Kingdom Studies 1 (London: Golden House Publications, 2015), 109, 111, fig. 13, pl. XVIII.

4. On the composition of the black coating, see Andrzej Niwinski, "Ritual Protection of the Dead or Symbolic Reflection of His Special Status in Society?," in *The Intellectual Heritage of Egypt: Studies Presented to László Kákosy by Friends and Colleagues on the Occasion*

Figure 1. *Rishi*-coffin of Neb, Seventeenth Dynasty, with the box painted black.

as such by the ancient Egyptians, since decorated coffins ended up being buried and removed from the sight of the living in any case. It becomes clear, therefore, that it is the magical power conveyed by the scenes and inscriptions that the owner of the coffin and/or the mummy case was pursuing and paying for.

The pouring of a black paste over a decorated surface, however, adds to the nuance of the color black itself, prompting a series of questions concerning the time and space of the act: How did it happen? When? Where? Why were some mummy cases blackened and others were not? It seems that the best way to tackle these questions is to analyze the issue on a case-by-case basis.

In 2016, the Spanish mission working at Dra Abu el-Naga southwest of the open courtyard of Djehuty's tomb-chapel (TT 11) excavated a Seventeenth Dynasty funerary shaft of larger proportions than any other of the twenty shafts unearthed to date in the area. It was associated with a mud-brick offering chapel also larger than the other three that have been excavated. The chapel was enlarged a short time after it was built, which seems to indicate that its owner must have been a highly respected member of the Theban elite. The burial chamber ends just below the chapel, and measures 3.10 × 2.00/1.35 m and 1.70 m high. There is a recess in the middle of the floor, 2.20 × 1.04 m and 1.90 m deep, which was intended for a large coffin. The latter was found filled with debris, while fragments of cartonnage and mud bricks were piled around its mouth. Before reaching the burial chamber there is a corridor or antechamber that measures 5.70 × 1.60 m and 1.75 m high, which was found filled with debris almost to the ceiling.

From its possible original owner, fragments of a linen shroud with a few Book of the Dead chapters written in cursive hieroglyphs and hieratic were retrieved from the shaft, but little more.[5] The shaft was robbed in antiquity and reused in the Twenty-Second Dynasty, as attested by a set of wax figurines in the shape of the four sons of Horus, eight sets of mud and baked-clay *shabtis*, and fragments of eight cartonnage mummy cases,[6] which seem to have been intentionally smashed into hundreds of small pieces.

of His 60th Birthday, ed. Ulrich Luft, Studia Aegyptiaca 14 (Budapest: Chaire d'Égyptologie de l'Université Eötvös Loránd de Budapest, 1992), 466–68; Natalie C. McCreesh, A. P. Gize, and A. R. David, "Pitch Black: The Black Coated Mummies, Coffins and Cartonnages from Ancient Egypt," in *Proceedings of the Tenth International Congress of Egyptologists*, ed. Panagiotis Kousoulis and Nikolaos Lazaridis, OLA 241 (Leuven: Peeters, 2015), 1731–37; Connan, "La momification dans l'Égypte ancienne," 163–91; Rummel and Fetler, "Coffins of the Third Intermediate Period" 453.

5. Lucía Díaz-Iglesias Llanos, "Glimpses of the First Owners of a Reused Burial: Fragments of a Shroud with Book of the Dead Spells from Dra Abu el-Naga North," *BIFAO* 118 (2018): 83–126.

6. John H. Taylor, "Theban Coffins from the Twenty-Second to the Twenty-Sixth Dynasty: Dating and Synthesis of Development," in *The Theban Necropolis: Past, Present and Future*, ed. Nigel Strudwick and John H. Taylor (London: The British Museum Press, 2003),

Two of the mummy cases are inscribed and their texts allow for a partial reconstruction of two different family trees. One of them belonged to a woman, whose name is lost, daughter of Iwes-nehes-Mut and of the scribe and *wab*-priest of Amun, Pa-di-Iset, son of Nes-er-Amun. The second belonged to a man called Pa-setjenfy, who was a servant in the temple of Amun. He was the son of a man who acted before him as servant in the house of Amun, called Pa-di-iset (different from the one mentioned above), who was married to Djed-iset-iwes-ankh, daughter of a fourth prophet of Amun called Djed-khonsu-iwef-ankh.

Inscribed *shabtis* were found for Pa-di-iset[7] and for Djed-iset-iwes-ankh,[8] but also for two other people named Iry[9] and Nes-pa-kaef,[10] who also seem to have lived and died during the Twenty-Second Dynasty. The human remains found in the shaft seem to indicate that at least nine individuals were buried in the shaft in the Twenty-Second Dynasty. Their bodies were all violently beheaded and dismembered by ancient robbers.

The eight mummy cases are presently being reconstructed and studied by Lucía Díaz-Iglesias and Charlotte Hunkeler. Two of them have already been reassembled with the aid of the restorer Pía Rodríguez Frade. Among the mummy cases, only one had a black substance poured over it (SMDAN 1357) while it was lying horizontally and facing up. The basic component of the substance seems to be amorphous charcoal, mixed with organic materials that remain unidentified. When cooled, the substance turned into a very hard crust and stayed like that; but when it was poured it had a viscose texture and, therefore, must have been warm if not hot. It could never have been too hot as it never fully became liquid, as most of the drippings sliding down the sides did not reach the base of the case and did not stain its back (figs. 2–3).

The thick coating covered the whole front side of the mummy case (1.66 m in height), completely hiding its painted decoration, which is only visible on the back and partially on the sides (figs. 4–5). The backside has an unusual register design, which alternates friezes of geometrical patterns with *uraei* on a white background.[11] The arrangement in registers seems to be the pattern also on the front, which may be associated with Taylor's Design I, dated by him to the early Twenty-Second Dynasty, ca. 900 BCE.[12] The mummy case has a brief offering formula written around the feet, but unfortunately only a few signs may be read: "[...] may he grant an invocation offering of bread and beer, beef and fowl [...]." There is no trace of the owner's name, title, or gender.

The backside of the mummy case was not varnished, but it seems plausible that at least parts of the front received some varnishing. Most probably being made of some kind of organic substance(s),[13] such as pistacia resin, the varnish, together with the still present mummy smell, must have attracted some of the sweet tooth flies flying around when it was still fresh, and their legs and wings got glued to the sticky surface. The dipterous have been identified as *Lucilia* and *Chrysomya*, two species of the Calliphoridae family which are active during the whole year and are known

103–13; David Aston, *Burial Assemblages of Dynasty 21–25: Chronology—Typology—Developments*, DÖAWW 56 (Vienna: Austrian Academy of Sciences, 2009).

7. Sixty-six *shabtis* were found bearing his name, made of grey mud and painted in light green/blue. They were all intentionally broken in half.

8. Her *shabtis* were made of blue faience; twenty-five were found complete and fourteen broken at different heights.

9. Eighteen complete red mud *shabtis* painted in green/blue.

10. Forty-six complete red mud *shabtis* painted in green/blue.

11. Taylor, "Patterns of Colouring," 172–73.

12. Taylor, "Theban Coffins," 104–5.

13. Margaret Serpico and R. White, "Resins, Amber and Bitumen," in *Ancient Egyptian Materials and Technology*, ed. Paul T. Nicholson and Ian Shaw (Cambridge: Cambridge University Press, 2000), 459–60; Margaret Serpico and R. White, "The Use and Identification of Varnish on New Kingdom Funerary Equipment," in Davies, *Colour and Painting in Ancient Egypt*, 33–42; Taylor, "Patterns of Colouring," 166; Elisabeth Geldhof, "Painting Techniques of the Leiden Coffins," in *The Coffins of the Priests of Amun: Egyptian Coffins from the 21st Dynasty in the Collection of the National Museum of Antiquities in Leiden*, ed. Lara Weiss, Papers on Archaeology of the Leiden Museum of Antiquities 17 (Leiden: Sidestone, 2018), 63–65.

Figure 2. Lucía Díaz-Iglesias working on the backside of the cartonnage mummy case (SMDAN 1357).

Figure 3. Detail of the black substance sliding down the sides of the mummy case.

for having a remarkable sight and even better smell.[14] When the black substance was poured, it was considered irrelevant that there were flies around the face, on the wig and down to the foot end of the mummy case. The flies were covered by the black paste, and so they became part of the mummy case forever.

14. I am grateful to the entomologist Carolina Martín for the identification and comments.

Figure 4. Part of the face and wig of the mummy case, coated with the black substance.

Figure 5. Detail showing the flies trapped and a testimony of the gilded face under the black coating.

The action of pouring a black substance over a mummy case, a coffin, or another item of the funerary furniture has been commonly understood as being part of a ritual conducted at the time of the funeral.[15] However, the number of flies agonizing or dead on top of the object to be sanctified would have certainly dimmed the charm of the performance. Moreover, only around ten percent of mummy cases and coffins were blackened,[16] which is close to the rate within the assemblage found in the shaft by the Spanish mission, being one out of eight. This low percentage implies that it was not a general practice but instead took place only under certain circumstances. Which circumstances could these have been? Apparently, the only physical feature that makes the blackened mummy case SMDAN 1357 different from the rest of the group is that it has a gilded face. The orpiment may be seen in a few spots where the black coating is detached from the surface (see figs. 4, 5). However, in other cases the opposite approach was adopted, and the gilded face, hands, and feet were the only body parts left uncovered by the coating.[17] It is difficult to identify a pattern that would explain the choice of pouring the black substance over a decorated mummy case.

Keeping in mind this still open question about the use of the black substance as coating over a decorated surface, it might be of interest to broaden the survey and look for other objects and monuments that were intentionally blackened in a similar way[18] by using amorphous charcoal as its basic ingredient. Within the Spanish concession at Dra Abu el-Naga, the walls of the rock-cut tomb-chapels of Djehuty and Hery (TT 11 and TT 12) were blackened at some

15. Niwinski, "Ritual Protection of the Dead," 457; McCreesh, Gize and David, "Pitch Black;" Ikram and Dodson, "A Twenty-Second Dynasty Mummy-Cartonnage," 318, 322.

16. Rummel and Fetler, "Coffins of the Third Intermediate Period," 456. Niwinski, "Ritual Protection of the Dead," 469, also asked himself, "why only some cartonnages," and tried to connect the black coating "with the status of the deceased in the Theban society."

17. Niwinski, "Ritual Protection of the Dead," 466; Ikram and Dodson, "A Twenty-Second Dynasty Mummy-Cartonnage," 318. Concerning the percentage of mummy cases that were blackened, as well as which parts were left uncovered, it has to be taken into account that the black substance could have been removed in their host museums, as pointed out by Ikram and Dodson, "A Twenty-Second Dynasty Mummy-Cartonnage," 319, fig. 11.

18. Taylor, "Patterns of Colouring," 168; Connan, "La momification dans l'Égypte ancienne," 175–76; McCreesh, Gize and David, "Pitch Black."

point, not by smoke coming from fires lit inside when they were reused for other purposes but by a substance that was spread with a still unknown intention when the tomb-chapels were being built and decorated. The black substance is no longer easy to spot on the rock walls, but it is still well preserved on the stone blocks that were attached to them as repairs to fill gaps of considerable size. These blocks eventually became detached, fell down, and were recovered in the excavation on the open courtyard.

The attached blocks only have black on the side that was carved and exposed, while the other sides remained perfectly neat and bright in their original color. This fact seems to indicate that the black substance must have been spread when the blocks were already inserted and tightly embedded into the wall, since the edges present a sharp contrast in the coloration. However, while the surface of the embedded pieces shows a thin crust of black, the area of the walls around them has no significant traces of black. It seems, then, that the walls were somehow washed and the black was removed from the surface after the block had fallen down from its place. In this way, the block preserved the black substance on the carved side while the rest of the wall did not.

A second possible reconstruction of the events that may explain this intriguing situation is that the black coating was carefully spread only over the attached blocks. This could have been related to their condition as additions to an original structure and decorative tableau. When and why could this have happened is uncertain.

Hery was overseer of the granaries of the king's mother and royal wife, Ahhotep, in the early Eighteenth Dynasty.[19] Most likely, he reused an unfinished and undecorated tomb of the Eleventh/early Twelfth Dynasty. He then enlarged the tomb and carved the walls in relief.[20] The tomb-chapel TT 12 has no transverse hall and, due to the poor condition of the rock, the right wall of the central corridor suffered large losses when it was being recut and carved. The edges of the gaps were carved straight so that the new blocks would be easier to cut and attach to the wall. The repair blocks fell down and were found by the Spanish mission in the excavation of the courtyard. At least those coming from the scene of fishing and fowling in the marshes were coated with a black substance that, when it cooled and dried, formed a thin and lustrous crust. One of the blocks that fell down broke into pieces and each fragment underwent different environmental circumstances that washed the surface in various degrees: one fragment preserves a glossy black, while another shows the limestone as white as it could be, and the other two fragments that join together attest for the middle stages of the black being washed out (figs. 6–8).[21]

Djehuty, owner of TT 11, was overseer of the treasury under the joint reign of Hatshepsut and Thutmose III.[22] His monument penetrates horizontally into the hill eighteen meters and has a transverse hall that is almost eleven meters wide. The blackened blocks that were found in the excavation outside come from the right wall of the central corridor. The two most illustrative examples are part of the Opening of the Mouth panel. The blackened blocks preserve the reliefs in a much sharper condition than the area of the wall from where they come, which means that they fell down quite soon, avoiding most of the erosion that happened later in the corridor (figs. 9–14). The black on the surface looks matte compared to the shiny crust of Hery's blocks, but the final result is broadly similar, as the darkness of the attached block strikes out from the wall. Awaiting complementary analysis, the contrast may be due to the different environmental conditions to which the corridors of TT 11 and TT 12 were exposed. On the one hand, Djehuty's walls suffered for centuries the effect of wind and rainwater flowing through the tomb-chapel, which gradually eroded the reliefs and could have also dimmed the original brightness of the black coating. On the other hand, Hery's corridor remained segregated and protected from most of the destructive human activities that happened when the

19. José M. Galán and Gema Menéndez, "The Funerary Banquet of Hery (TT 12), Robbed and Restored," *JEA* 97 (2011): 143–66.

20. José M. Galán, "The Tomb-Chapel of Hery (TT 12) in Context," in *Mural Decoration in the Theban New Kingdom Necropolis*, ed. Betsy M. Bryan and Peter F. Dorman, SAOC (Chicago: Chicago University Press, in press).

21. I am most grateful to the restorer Miguel A. Navarro for his comments on the phases of use and the wall damages in the tomb-chapel of Hery.

22. José M. Galán, "The Inscribed Burial Chamber of Djehuty (TT 11)," in *Creativity and Innovation in the Reign of Hatshepsut*, ed. José M. Galán, Betsy M. Bryan, and Peter F. Dorman, SAOC 69 (Chicago: Chicago University Press, 2014), 247–72.

Figure 6. Right wall of the tomb-chapel of Hery (TT 12), showing in red attached blocks.

Figure 7. Detail of one of the blocks with different stages of the black coating.

Figure 8. Detail of one of the blocks with different stages of the black coating.

monument was reused down to the second century BCE.[23] It also remained sheltered from wind and rainwater, so that the reliefs did not suffer almost any erosion and the black substance preserved its original glossy appearance.

Considering the blackening of the walls, particularly in the tomb-chapel of Djehuty, another possibility to be taken into account is that a varnish or a similar treatment of the surface darkened with the passing of time. This possibility has been considered for coffins and mummy cases, and it seems to be the case in some painted Theban tomb-chapels.[24] However, the fact that the surface has traces of charcoal seems to exclude this possibility.[25] Due to the large gaps still present in the walls, it is hard to say if only the blocks from the corridor were blackened or if all the blocks attached as repairs were once blackened.

The inner walls and ceilings of the tomb-chapels of Djehuty and Hery, and those of a third tomb chapel between them (numbered "399"),[26] were intentionally broken to connect them and to likewise connect them to other tomb-chapels nearby. The alteration of the structures probably happened in the Ramesside or Third Intermediate period, so that when they were reused in the second century BCE to deposit animal mummies, and the priests in charge of the rituals and storage wrote Demotic graffiti on the walls, the rock surface in Djehuty's corridor was already badly eroded by the wind and rainwater that came in through the holes. By the second century BCE at least, the

23. Galán, "Tomb-Chapel of Hery (TT 12)."

24. A very interesting case study is brought up by Alexis Den Doncker and Huges Tavier, "Scented Resins for Scented Figures," *Egyptian Archaeology* 53 (2018): 16–19.

25. A portable Raman spectrometer was used in the tomb-chapels for preliminary analysis by Santiago Sánchez-Cortés and Mercedes Iriarte.

26. Frederike Kampp, *Die Thebanische Nekropole: Zum Wandel des Grabgedankens von der XVIII. bis zur XX. Dynastie*, Theben 13 (Mainz: von Zabern, 1996). See also Galán, "Tomb-Chapel of Hery (TT 12)."

Figure 9. Right wall of the central corridor of the tomb-chapel of Djehuty (TT 11) showing a missing block.

Figure 10. Blackened repair block found in the excavation outside and placed back in the Opening of the Mouth tableau.

Figure 11. Blackened block from Djehuty's Opening of the Mouth tableau in the process of being placed back.

Figure 12. The block back in its original place, around which there are no traces of fire or any black coating.

Figure 13. View of the block's front.

Figure 14. View of the block's back.

connections between adjoining tomb-chapels were carefully finished, and staircases were cut into the rock or built in mud bricks to save the difference in height between them. Therefore, with little effort, by turning down part of the separating walls (0.5/1 m thick) and adding staircases when necessary, this area of the hillside of Dra Abu el-Naga was turned into a catacomb, which included burial chambers at the bottom of funerary shafts and several levels of tomb-chapels up the hill (figs. 15–16).

Above the tomb-chapels of Djehuty, Hery, and –399–, there is a large cavity that probably formed part of the catacomb, although today its supposed connection with the lower level is blocked by and hidden under the debris that fill most of its rooms. The Spanish mission gained access into it in 2010 through a tomb-chapel that belonged to an overseer of the weavers under Ramesses II, called Ramose. It is hard to produce an accurate plan and get a coherent idea of the complex with the partial information that is visible today after excavation. Six rooms are accessible today, while at least three more remain blocked. It seems that the walls were never decorated, but this observation needs to be confirmed. Two of the rooms, the larger ones, have a central pillar, and from each of them a dead-end-room opens to the north, which corresponds to the ideal west (fig. 17). The whole complex has been intentionally blackened—walls, pillars, and ceiling—with the only exception of the dead-end-room at the end of the gallery (letter F in figures 15, 16), which was left pristine white. Not only do its walls and ceiling preserve the white color of the original limestone, but the surface of an area above the entrance to the room was peeled off and left clean, acting as a lintel,

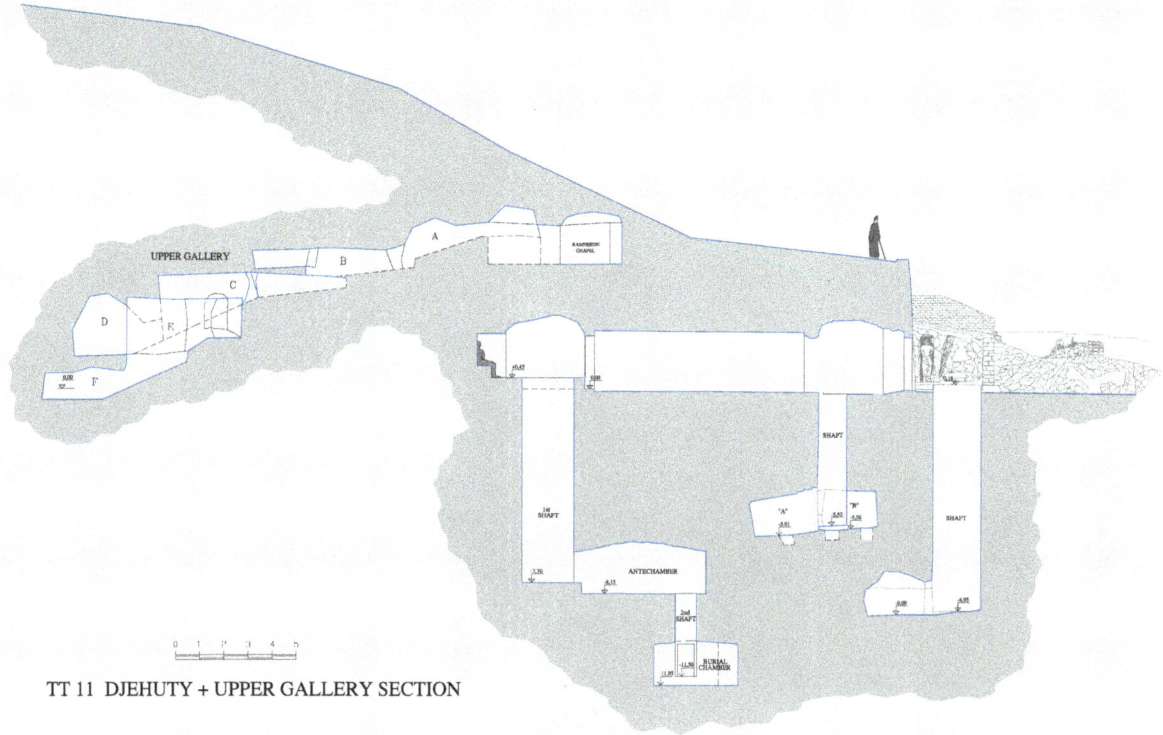

Figure 15. Section of Djehuty's tomb-chapel (TT 11) and upper gallery.

on which two Demotic graffiti were written in red ink (fig. 18).[27] The contrast between this room and the rest of the complex seems to indicate that the blackening of the catacomb gallery was carried out intentionally.

Walls and ceilings were blackened mostly by smoke, but not accidentally, that is, as the side effect of lighting bonfires inside the rooms, but actually it seems to have been produced with the aim of blackening an entire space.[28] The intentionality seems to be confirmed by a few drippings of a black substance on the floor near the base of the pillar in room E (fig. 19). Similar drippings were found also in a small niche that was opened in the inner most room of the tomb-chapel of Hery. A couple of meters from the latter, within a disturbed layer but associated with material culture dating to the Ptolemaic Period, a broken vessel was found containing a piece of solidified black substance (fig. 20). It could be the bottom of a small flask, with a rounded flat base of 7 cm diameter and very fine walls, made of silty clay similar to the fine cooking wares recorded in the Ptolemaic period.[29] The content is most probably the remains of the substance that was spread over the walls of the upper gallery and the neighboring tomb-chapels that were also blackened. Amorphous charcoal and a bituminous substance were mixed with vegetable and animal oils, castor oil, and

27. The Demotic graffiti have been studied by Christina Di Cerbo and Richard Jasnow, published under the title *On the Path to the Place of Rest: Demotic Graffiti relating to the Ibis and Falcon Cult from the Spanish-Egyptian Mission at Dra Abu el-Naga (TT 11, TT 12, -399- and Environs)* (Atlanta: Lockwood Press, 2021).

28. I am in dept to Francisco Bosch and Salima Ikram, who are responsible for the excavation and study of this intricate underground structure. The comments and interpretations here expressed are, nevertheless, my responsibility.

29. I am grateful to Zulema Barahona for her expertise.

Figure 16. Plan of the tomb-chapels TT 11, TT 12 and -399-, overlapped by the upper gallery.

Figure 17. View of the central pillar of room E of the upper gallery.

Figure 18. Entrance to room F, where Salima Ikram and José M. Parra are taking notes. Two Demotic graffiti are written over a clean surface above the entrance.

Figure 19. Drippings of black substance next to the pillar in room E.

Figure 20. Ptolemaic vessel with black substance solidified inside.

beeswax. The mixture is, therefore, very similar to the substance spread over the Twenty-Second Dynasty mummy cases more than seven hundred years before.[30]

Other Demotic graffiti, all dating to the mid-second century BCE, were written on the walls over the already blackened surface, what may be used as an *ante quem* dating for the blackening of the complex. The religious idea behind the practice of blackening most of the rooms of the Ptolemaic catacomb in this area of Dra Abu el-Naga, and/or its practical purpose, remains hypothetical. It seems reasonable to think that there was an association with Osiris and an attempt to generate an appropriate atmosphere for rebirth through the use of the black color. But there could have been also a connection with the circumstance that an already sanctified space was being reused after a lapse of time, and it was considered appropriate to purify it for the benefit of the ritual actions that would take place there from then on, associated with the deposition of animal mummies. This interpretation would link the blackening of the walls in the Ptolemaic Period with one of the possible interpretations of the blackened repair blocks attached to the walls of the Hery and Djehuty monuments mentioned above.

The varied casuistry of circumstances in which a black substance was spread over an element of the funerary equipment or an architectural structure matches the long span of time during which this practice is attested. Each case has its idiosyncrasies and needs to be analyzed individually, within its own context. However, there is a chance that a small step towards a better understanding of the idea underlying this action and of the purpose pursued by it may be obtained by broadening the perspective and taking into consideration other cases that, despite their differences, share a common denominator, which is the spreading of a black substance.

I hope that the collection of peculiar cases presented above from within the Spanish mission at Dra Abu el-Naga will inspire curiosity and new ways of looking at certain well-known objects, as well as monuments repaired and reused in antiquity. Despite the abundance of images, I very much hope that such a great "lover of Demotic graffiti," as Richard is, will accept this contribution as a token of admiration and friendship. Luckily, his heart is as big as his thirst for challenging handwritings and texts (figs. 21–22).

30. See n. 4 above.

Figure 21. The author showing to Christina Di Cerbo and Richard Jasnow the flies trapped under the black coating poured over the mummy case.

Figure 22. Looking at Demotic graffiti in a blackened tomb-chapel parallel to Hery's corridor.

Funerary Shrouds from Dendera in the Oriental Institute Museum of the University of Chicago. Part II: Shroud OIM E4789

François Gaudard

> Silence—the perfume was stifling. …
> A voice, seeming to come from a great distance, cried: "On your knees to the Book of Thoth!"
> Sax Rohmer, *Brood of the Witch Queen*

"On your knees to the Book of Thoth!" Such must have been the admiring exclamation uttered by the scholarly community upon the masterful publication of this major composition.[1] Richard Jasnow, however, is not only one of the interpreters of this fascinating text but also a skillful explorer of many other arcane matters, as reflected in his varied and numerous contributions to the field of Egyptology. Due to our alma mater, the University of Chicago, and our work for both the Chicago Demotic Dictionary and the Epigraphic Survey, Richard and I have much in common. It is therefore with all the more pleasure that I would like to present this much-appreciated colleague with this study of a Denderite funerary shroud as a token of friendship.

I would like to thank the Oriental Institute of the University of Chicago: Gil Stein and Jack Green for giving me permission to publish the present shroud, Emily Teeter for providing access to the records, Helen McDonald and Susan Allison for providing access to the shrouds, and Laura D'Alessandro for her restoration work and technical information. Special thanks go to Robert Ritner and Christina Riggs for their useful comments.

See also François Gaudard, "Funerary Shrouds from Dendera in the Oriental Institute Museum of the University of Chicago. Part I: Shroud OIM E4786," in *Sur les pistes du désert: Mélanges offerts à Michel Valloggia*, ed. Sandrine Vuilleumier and Pierre Meyrat (Gollion: Infolio, 2019), 63–70.

NB: The shrouds' left corresponds to the viewer's right and vice versa. The symbols used in the transliteration and translation are as follows: [ ] lacuna in the text or restoration, ⸢ ⸣ partial restoration, ( ) scribal omission reconstructed or addition made by the present writer for the sake of greater clarity, { } superfluous characters to be skipped by the reader.

1. Richard Jasnow and Karl-Theodor Zauzich, *The Ancient Egyptian Book of Thoth: A Demotic Discourse on Knowledge and Pendant to the Classical Hermetica*, 2 vols. (Wiesbaden: Harrassowitz Verlag, 2005, 2020 [2nd ed.]); Richard Jasnow and Karl-Theodor Zauzich, *Conversations in the House of Life: A New Translation of the Ancient Egyptian Book of Thoth* (Wiesbaden: Harrassowitz, 2014).

Provenance, Date, and Description

Shroud fragment OIM E4789[2] is part of a lot of four shrouds[3] discovered during W. M. Flinders Petrie's excavations at Dendera in the winter of 1897–1898[4] and offered to the Haskell Oriental Museum of the University of Chicago by the Egypt Exploration Fund. Although these shrouds were found in a necropolis now dated to the early Roman period,[5] during which shrouds tend to combine Greek and Egyptian influences, these ones are truly Egyptian in style. Their design is reminiscent of some Third Intermediate period cartonnage coffin decoration with columns of text in the center and protective deities on the sides.[6] The style, the paint colors, and the level of detail of their inscriptions seem more in keeping with an earlier rather than a later date, which would favor a Ptolemaic dating. It would not be surprising, however, to find such a style as late as the early Roman period. All of them are made of linen with a thin layer of gesso applied directly to the textile. They were selected by Petrie specifically for their inscriptions, which include some good examples of sportive and unusual writings characteristic of the Ptolemaic and Roman periods,[7] such as that of the word *ḥnq(.t)* "beer" occurring in the present shroud as . From an iconographic point of view, this fragment also provides us with an interesting depiction of Anubis as a falcon.

Text

Shroud OIM E4789. Linen, gesso, pigment. 71.3 × 36.3 × ~ 0.1 cm (fig. 1)
Dendera. Late Ptolemaic/early Roman period

This shroud fragment includes three registers and a main text of two vertical columns in retrograde writing[8] running in the center and crossing a painted *wesekh* collar, which consists of five rows of various beads (tubular and amygdaloid) alternating with papyrus blooms, lotus flowers, and daisies. Unlike those of Shrouds OIM E4786 and OIM E4788, the hieroglyphs of the two central columns have been left unpainted. Only part of the decoration, which depicts the four sons of Horus and various protective deities as birds of prey, is preserved. The text placed in front of the heads of the birds continues between the wings. The sons of Horus and the deities depicted on the same register, on either side of the central columns, always form matching sets of gods or goddesses mirroring each other. The colors used are black, brown, blue, green, red, and pink.

---

2. For further information, see Gaudard, "Funerary Shrouds from Dendera, Part I," 63–65.

3. That is, Shrouds OIM E4786, OIM E4787, OIM E4788 (= OIM E42046), and OIM E4789. Shroud OIM E4788 has been published as OIM E42046 because it was re-registered before the museum staff was able to identify its original registration number. See François Gaudard, "Fragment of a Funerary Shroud (OIM E42046)," in *Visible Language: Inventions of Writing in the Ancient Middle East and Beyond*, ed. Christopher Woods, Emily Teeter, and Geoff Emberling, 2nd ed., OIMP 32 (Chicago: Oriental Institute of the University of Chicago, 2015), 176–77, no. 86. Shrouds OIM E4787 and OIM E4788 will be the subject of future publications by the present writer.

4. W. M. Flinders Petrie, *Dendereh 1898*, MEEF 17 (London: The Egypt Exploration Fund, 1900), 32, §36.

5. See Sven P. Vleeming, *Demotic and Greek-Demotic Mummy Labels and Other Short Texts Gathered from Many Publications (Short Texts II 278–1200): A. Texts*, StudDem 9 (Leuven: Peeters, 2011), 28n4; cf. Jan Moje, *Demotische Epigraphik aus Dandara: Die demotischen Grabstelen*, IBAES 9 (Berlin: Golden House Publications, 2008), 2–3.

6. For additional examples of the use of cartonnage coffin decoration in shrouds, see, e.g., Shrouds UC36209 (Dyn. 21) and UC45845 (TIP) in the Petrie Museum (Jónatan Ortiz-García, pers. comm.).

7. For further discussion on Ptolemaic hieroglyphs, see, e.g., François Gaudard, "Ptolemaic Hieroglyphs," in Woods, Teeter, and Emberling, *Visible Language*, 173–75.

8. Judging by the context, and in comparison to the similar texts of Shrouds OIM E4786 (see Gaudard, "Funerary Shrouds from Dendera, Part I") and OIM E4788 (= OIM E42046) (publication forthcoming), we are dealing here with an inscription in retrograde writing. For references, see Gaudard, "Funerary Shrouds from Dendera, Part I," 65n13.

1) Center
column 1:

Hy Wsir ḫnt(y) ỉmnt.t nṯr ꜥꜣ n⸢b⸣[1a] *ꜣbḏ⸢w⸣ ỉwn(y) wr*[b] *ḫnt(y) Tꜣ-Tꜣ-rr*[c] *ꜣs.t ⸢wr⸣.t mw.t-nṯr nb(.t)*[d] *ỉꜣ.t-d⸢ỉ⸣*[e] [... *ḥr(y)-ib*][f]

"Hail Osiris, foremost of the West, the great god, lor⸢d⸣ of Abyd⸢os⸣, the great Heliopolitan, foremost of the Land of Ta-rer, Isis, ⸢the grea⸣t one, the god's mother, lady of Iat-d⸢i⸣, [..., who dwells in][9]

Notes

[a] *nb.w* is used as a writing of *nb*; cf. n. d, infra.

[b] For *ỉwny wr,* "the great Heliopolitan," as an epithet of Osiris in Dendera, see, for example, Sylvie Cauville et al., *Le Temple de Dendara: Les chapelles osiriennes, Index,* BiÉtud 119 (Cairo: Institut français d'archéologie orientale, 1997), 28, s.v. "*ỉwny.*" For a possible identification of this epithet with *ỉwn wr,* "the great pillar," see *LGG* I, 189, s.v. "*ỉwny-wr.*" For an alternate reading of this epithet as *ỉwn wr,* "the great pillar," see, for example, Herman de Meulenaere, "Trois stèles inédites des Musées Royaux d'Art et d'Histoire," *ChronÉg* 48 (1973): 56 (S. Brussels MRAH E. 8242, l. 1); cf. *PtoLex,* 51–52, s.v. "*ỉwn.*" For *ỉwn,* "the pillar," as an epithet of Osiris, see, for example, *Wb.* I:53, 20; Bruno H. Stricker "Osiris en de obelisk," *OMRO* 34 (1953): 45–46. For the feminine ending, see, for example, Dieter Kurth, *Einführung ins Ptolemäische: Eine Grammatik mit Zeichenliste und Übungsstücken* (Hützel: Backe, 2007), 1:84–85, §3 and 88, §7.4; cf. Hermann Junker, *Grammatik der Denderatexte* (Leipzig: Hinrichs, 1906), 52, §69.

[c] In Shrouds OIM E4786, OIM E4788 (= OIM E42046), and OIM E4789, the toponym *Tꜣ-rr,* "Ta-rer," a designation of Dendera, occurs always as (with the sign [N17] written twice) instead of , , , and so forth (see Henri Gauthier, *DG* 6:26); compare the similar writing in Statue Cairo 690 (JE 27837), column 1 (see Ludwig Borchardt, *Statuen und Statuetten von Königen und Privatleuten im Museum von Kairo, Nr. 1–1294, Teil 3: Text und Tafeln zu Nr. 654–950,* CGC [Berlin: Reichsdruckerei, 1930], 34–35, pl. 127), which Georges Daressy ("Statues de basse époque du Musée de Gizéh," *RecTrav* 15 [1893]: 159–61, no. 8) reads "Taui-rert" (= *Tꜣ.wy-rr.t*), but which Gauthier (*DG* 6:38) reads "ta Tarer (?)" (= *Tꜣ-Tꜣ-rr*) and takes to be a variant of *Tꜣ-n-Tꜣ-rr,* "Land of Ta-rer" (*DG* 6:23, 26), itself being a less common form of *Tꜣ-rr,* "Ta-rer." In light of this, we would expect the writing , where the dung beetle stands for the sign *tꜣ,* also to be read *Tꜣ-Tꜣ-rr,* although listed under *Tꜣ-rr* in Gauthier (*DG* 6:26) and Cauville et al. (*Les chapelles osiriennes, Index,* 603 [116, 3]). Indeed, the initial sign is unlikely to be a phonetic complement reading *t* because writings of the word *tꜣ,* "land" including *t* as phonetic complement are early and occur rarely (see, e.g., *Wb.* V:212). Compare also the toponym which Gauthier (*DG* 1:49) reads "âou tarer" (= *ỉw-Tꜣ-rr*), "Island (?) of Ta-rer," also attested as and read as *ỉw-Tꜣ-rr,* "Island of Ta-rer," by Cauville et al. (*Les chapelles osiriennes, Index,* 25 [222, 13]), but see *LGG* V, 871–72, s.v. "*Ḫnty-Tꜣ-rr*" (no. 29). Alternatively, we could also consider that in the writings , , and *tꜣ.wy* is used inaccurately for *tꜣ* (see, e.g., *Wb.* V:219) and read this toponym *Tꜣ{.wy}-rr.* For *Tꜣ-rr,* "Ta-rer," as a designation of Dendera, see, for example, *Wb.* V:226, 1; Gauthier, *DG* 6:26; François Daumas, *Dendara et le temple d'Hathor: Notice sommaire,* RAPH 29 (Cairo: Institut français d'archéologie orientale, 1969), 12; Cauville et al., *Les chapelles osiriennes, Index,* 603; Holger Kockelmann, *Edfu: Die Toponymen- und Kultnamenlisten zur Tempelanlage von Dendera nach den hieroglyphischen Inschriften von Edfu und Dendera,* Die Inschriften des Tempels von Edfu, Begleitheft 3 (Wiesbaden: Harrassowitz, 2002), 52, 65–66; René Preys, "La terre tentyrite: *tꜣrr* et *tꜣ-n-jtm,*" *RdÉ* 64 (2013): 177–87. For the epithet *ḫnty Tꜣ-Tꜣ-rr,* "foremost of the Land of Ta-rer," attributed to Osiris, cf. *LGG* V, 871–72, s.v. "*Ḫnty-Tꜣ-rr.*"

9. For discussion, see n. f, infra.

[d] For  *nb.w* used as a writing of  *nb.t* in the texts from Dendera, see, for example, Sylvie Cauville, *Le Temple de Dendara: La Porte d'Isis* (Cairo: Institut français d'archéologie orientale, 1999), 298; cf. n. a, supra.

[e] For *Ꜣ.t-di*, "Iat-di," as a designation of Dendera, see, for example, Gauthier, *DG* 1:35; Cauville et al., *Les chapelles osiriennes, Index*, 18. More precisely, this toponym, which means "the Mound-of-Giving" (figuratively "the Mound-of-Birth," referring to the birth of Isis), designates both the small temple of Isis to the southwest of the great temple of Hathor in Dendera and the Denderite nome. For discussion, see, for example, Gauthier, *DG* 1:35; François Daumas, *Les mammisis des temples égyptiens*, Annales de l'Université de Lyon, troisième série, Lettres, fascicule 32 (Paris: Les Belles Lettres, 1958), 31nn2–3 and 197–98n4; Daumas, *Dendara et le temple d'Hathor*, 11–12; Kockelmann, *Die Toponymen- und Kultnamenlisten*, 52, 60–64; Preys, "La terre tentyrite," 177–78. For the epithet *nb.t Ꜣ.t-di*, "lady of Iat-di," attributed to Isis, see, for example, Cauville et al., *Les chapelles osiriennes, Index*, 18, s.v. "*Ꜣ.t-di*," 256, s.v. "*nb.t*"; *LGG* IV, 7. For the group 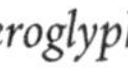 (N97) (here written as ), which reads *Ꜣ.t-di*, see, for example, François Daumas et al., *Valeurs phonétiques des signes hiéroglyphiques d'époque gréco-romaine* (Montpellier: Publications de la Recherche-Université de Montpellier, 1990), 3:463, nos. 531, 533; Kurth, *Einführung ins Ptolemäische*, 1:323, no. 69; Dieter Kurth, *A Ptolemaic Sign-List: Hieroglyphs Used in the Temples of the Graeco-Roman Period of Egypt and Their Meanings* (Hützel: Backe-Verlag, 2010), 138, no. 69.

[f] This restoration is based on Shroud OIM E4786, center, column 2 (see Gaudard, "Funerary Shrouds from Dendera, Part I," 66). An alternate restoration could be *ḥr(y.t)-ib*. It would be tempting to restore the full titulary of Isis in Dendera as follows: (column 1) ... *Ꜣs.t* ⸢*wr*⸣*.t mw.t-nṯr nb(.t) Ꜣ.t-d*⸢*i*⸣ [*ḥr(y.t)-ib*] (column 2) ⸢*I*⸣*w*⸢*n*⸣*.t* ..., "Isis, ⸢the grea⸣t one, the god's mother, lady of Iat-d⸢i⸣, [who dwells in] ⸢I⸣u⸢n⸣et." However, with such a restoration, there would apparently not be enough space left at the end of column 2 to complete the traditional offering formula and to mention the name and filiation of the deceased (see n. r, infra). Alternatively, we could restore the full titulary of Isis only in column 1 and take the mention of *Iwn.t*, "Iunet," at the beginning of column 2, to be part of the epithet of another deity (see n. g, infra), perhaps Horus, son of Isis and son of Osiris (cf. n. 20, infra). Compare Shroud OIM E4786, center, column 1, where we have the same options. On Isis's titulary, see, for example, René Preys, "Jeux de titulatures dans le temple de Dendera," in *Proceedings of the Ninth International Congress of Egyptologists, Grenoble, 6–12 septembre 2004*, ed. Jean-Claude Goyon and Christine Cardin, OLA 150 (Leuven: Uitgeverij Peeters en Departement Oosterse Studies, 2007), 2:1551–57; Preys, "La terre tentyrite," 178.

column 2:

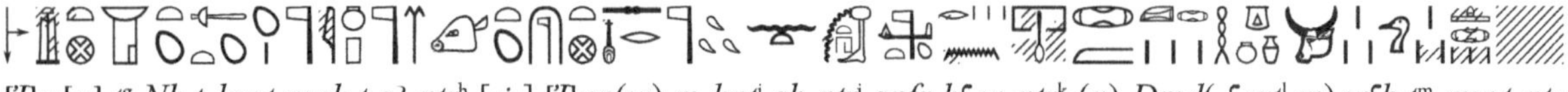

⸢*I*⸣*w*⸢*n*⸣*.t*[g] *Nb.t-ḥw.t mnḫ.t sꜣ-nṯr*[h] [*sic*] ⸢*I*⸣*np(w) m-ḫnt*[i] *sḥ-nṯr*[j] *snfr ḥꜥ.w-nṯr*[k] (*n*) *Dmḏ(-ꜥ.wt*[l] *m) wꜥb.t*[m] *mw.t-nṯr* [*sic*] ...(?)*.w n* [*sic*][n] ⸢*prt-ḫrw*⸣[o] *m t ḥnq(.t)*[p] *kꜣ.w Ꜣpd.w* ⸢*ḥtp*⸣[*.w*[q] ...][r]

⸢I⸣u⸢n⸣et,[10] Nephthys, the excellent one, the god's sister,[11] ⸢A⸣nubis within the god's booth,[12] who restores the divine body of the One (whose limbs are) reassembled (in) the *wabet*,[13] that they may give[14] ⸢invocation-offerings⸣ consisting of bread (and) beer, oxen (and) fowl, ⸢*ḥtpw*-offering⸣[s ...]."[15]

10. For discussion, see n. f, supra and n. g, infra.

11. For discussion, see n. h, infra.

12. For a brief discussion and references on the term *sḥ-nṯr*, "god's booth, hall of god," see, e.g., *PtoLex*, 890 and 739, s.v. "*ḫnty(w)-sḥ*."

13. Literally, "who restores the divine body of the Reassembled One (of limbs in) the *wabet*." For discussion, see n. l, infra. For discussion and references on the *wabet* as the place where embalming was performed, see, e.g., *Wb.* I:284, 4; Raymond O. Faulkner, *A Concise Dictionary of Middle Egyptian*, 4th ed. (Oxford: Griffith Institute, Ashmolean Museum, 1981), 57; *PtoLex*, 214.

14. For discussion, see n. n, infra.

15. For discussion, see n. r, infra.

Notes

[g] For *ỉwn.t*, "Iunet," as a designation of Dendera, see, for example, *Wb.* I:54; Gauthier, *DG* 1:56; Daumas, *Les mammisis des temples égyptiens*, 31n2; Cauville et al., *Les chapelles osiriennes, Index*, 28–29; Kockelmann, *Die Toponymen- und Kultnamenlisten*, 52–59; Preys, "La terre tentyrite," 177–78. For the epithet *ḥry-ỉb ỉwn.t* (fem. *ḥry.t-ỉb ỉwn.t*), "who dwells in Iunet," and for various deities to whom it can be attributed, see, for example, Cauville et al., *Les chapelles osiriennes, Index*, 29, s.v. "*ỉwn.t*," 390, s.v. "*ḥry-ỉb*"; *LGG* V, 315–16, 413–14. For discussion, see n. f, supra.

[h] The expected epithet should be *sn.t-nṯr*, "the god's sister," as attested in similar texts from Dendera such as that of S. Brussels MRAH E. 8242, l. 2 (see de Meulenaere, "Trois stèles inédites," 56–57 [fig. 3]; Luc Limme, *Stèles égyptiennes*, Guides du département égyptien 4 [Brussels: Musées Royaux d'Art et d'Histoire, 1979], 52–53, no. 20). For this epithet attributed to Nephthys, see also *Wb.* IV:151, 18; Cauville et al., *Les chapelles osiriennes, Index*, 500; *LGG* VI, 372, A, e. The same error occurs in the text of the lower register, left side, between the wings (see infra).

[i] For *m-ḫnt*, "within, inside," see, for example, *Wb.* III:302, 11; Junker, *Grammatik der Denderatexte*, 160, §218, a; Cauville et al., *Les chapelles osiriennes, Index*, 195 (for a similar writing, see 71, 6 [14]); *PtoLex*, 737. For another epithet of Anubis which includes *m-ḫnt*, see, for example, *LGG* I, 396, s.v. "*Inpw-m-ḫnt-ḥwt-Nt*."

[j] Note the writing of *sḥ-nṯr* with the town determinative. Compare the epithet *ỉnp(w) ḫnt(y) sḥ-nṯr* in S. Brussels MRAH E. 8242, l. 2 (see de Meulenaere, "Trois stèles inédites," 56–57 [fig. 3]; Limme, *Stèles* égyptiennes, 52–53, no. 20); in S. Cairo (unnumbered), ll. 2–3 (see Georges Daressy, "Inscriptions tentyrites," *ASAE* 18 [1919]: 184; Maria-Theresia Derchain-Urtel, *Priester im Tempel: Die Rezeption der Theologie der Tempel von Edfu und Dendera in den Privatdokumenten aus ptolemäischer Zeit*, GOF 4.19 [Wiesbaden: Harrassowitz, 1989], 41); and in Shroud Moscow I, 1a, 5763, fourth register, right scene, inscriptions [I A, 2.4 b], l. 2 (see Dieter Kurth, *Materialen zum Totenglauben im römerzeitlichen Ägypten* [Hützel: Backe-Verlag], 20).

[k] In the passage *snfr ḥꜥ.w-nṯr*, it is likely that the upper sign (F51B) does double duty, both as part of the writing of *ḥꜥ.w-nṯr* and as the letter *f* in *snfr* with a permutation of the signs and (D21). For the sign used with the value *f*, see, for example, François Daumas et al., *Valeurs phonétiques des signes hiéroglyphiques d'époque gréco-romaine* (Montpellier: Publications de la Recherche-Université de Montpellier, 1988), 1:286, no. 649 and 287, no. 651; Sylvie Cauville, *Dendara: Le fonds hiéroglyphique au temps de Cléopâtre* (Paris: Cybèle, 2001), 96; Kurth, *Einführung ins Ptolemäische*, 1:228, no. 93; Kurth, *A Ptolemaic Sign-List*, 82, no. 93. For Greco-Roman writings of *snfr*, "to restore," with the sign , see, for example, *Wb.* IV:163; Cauville et al., *Les chapelles osiriennes, Index*, 503 (223, 7; 413, 12). For inversions and permutations of signs, see, for example, Cauville, *Dendara: Le fonds hiéroglyphique*, 7; Kurth, *Einführung ins Ptolemäische*, 1:89, §7.8; cf. Serge Sauneron, *L'écriture figurative dans les textes d'Esna*, Esna VIII (Cairo: Institut français d'archéologie orientale, 1982), 87–89; Alan H. Gardiner, *Egyptian Grammar: Being an Introduction to the Study of Hieroglyphs*, 3rd rev. ed. (Oxford: Griffith Institute, Ashmolean Museum, 1982), 51, §56.

[l] For the epithet *Dmḏ*, "the Reassembled One," see, for example, *LGG* VII, 541–42, s.v. "*Dmḏ*" (der Vereinigte), 542, s.v. "*Dmḏ*" (der Vollständige). However, we would rather expect Osiris to be referred to as *Dmḏ-ꜥ.wt*, "the One whose limbs are reassembled" (see, e.g., *Wb.* V:460, 1; Cauville et al., *Les chapelles osiriennes, Index*, 637; *LGG* VII, 542–43); compare the epithet *Dmḏ-ḥꜥ.w* (see Cauville et al., *Les chapelles osiriennes, Index*, 638, s.v. "*Dmḏ-ḥꜥ*"; *PtoLex*, 1197; *LGG* VII, 545). The epithet *snfr ḥꜥ.w-nṯr n Dmḏ-ꜥw.t*, "who restores the divine body of the One whose limbs are reassembled," attributed to Anubis, occurs in S. Brussels MRAH E. 8242, ll. 2–3 (see de Meulenaere, "Trois stèles inédites," 56–57 [fig. 3], 58nb; Limme, *Stèles* égyptiennes, 52–53, no. 20; *LGG* VI, 383). If one assumes that *ꜥ.wt*, "limbs," should not be restored, an alternate reading of this passage could be *snfr ḥꜥ.w-nṯr dmḏ* (*m*) *wꜥb.t*, "who restores the divine body, it being reassembled (in) the *wabet*," or, if one assumes that the preposition *m*, "in," is not missing, one could read *snfr ḥꜥ.w-nṯr* (*n*) *Dmḏ*(*-ꜥ.wt*) *wꜥb.t*, "who restores the divine body of the Reassembled One (of limbs) of the *wabet*."

[m] Compare the epithet *ỉnpw m wꜥb.t* (see *LGG* I, 395). Note the use of the sign (O4) as the determinative of the word *wꜥb.t* instead of the usual sign (O1). For the confusion between these two signs, see, for example,

Cauville, *Dendara: Le fonds hiéroglyphique,* 255 (*Dend.* VII, 66, 4). For writings of *wꜥb.t, "wabet,"* with the determinative placed inside the sign (D60) in Dendera, see, for example, Cauville et al., *Les chapelles osiriennes, Index,* 112 (135,14); Cauville, *Dendara: Le fonds hiéroglyphique,* 62 (D340); Filip Coppens, *The Wabet: Tradition and Innovation in Temples of the Ptolemaic and Roman Period* (Prague: Czech Institute of Egyptology, Faculty of Arts, Charles University in Prague, 2007), 56.

[n] The passage is corrupt: *mw.t-nṯr* is written mistakenly with (D37) instead of (D39) (cf. n. 33, infra), and the identification of the sign rendered here as (D21) is problematic. Judging by the context, it is obvious that the scribe meant to write *di=sn*, "that they may give"; compare S. Brussels MRAH E. 8242, l. 3 (see de Meulenaere, "Trois stèles inédites," 56–57 [fig. 3]; Limme, *Stèles* égyptiennes, 52–53, no. 20). For a similar corrupt passage in a text from Dendera, see S. Cairo (unnumbered), l. 4, which has , translated as "don du" by Daressy ("Inscriptions tentyrites," 184), but read as *di.n=i* and emended to *di=sn* by Derchain-Urtel (*Priester im Tempel,* 41n35).

[o] We are dealing here with a damaged writing of *prt-ḫrw,* "invocation-offerings," with the sign (X4A) as determinative; compare S. Brussels MRAH E. 8242, l. 3, where *prt-ḫrw* is written as , with the same determinative followed by the plural strokes (see de Meulenaere, "Trois stèles inédites," 56–57 [fig. 3]; Limme, *Stèles* égyptiennes, 52–53, no. 20).

[p] Note the unusual writing of *ḥnq(.t),* "beer," as instead of, for example, , the latter being a Greco-Roman variant of the common writing (see *Wb.* III:169). The sign (W11), which usually reads *g,* is used here with the value *q* (see, e.g., Junker, *Grammatik der Denderatexte,* 29, §37, b; François Daumas et al., *Valeurs phonétiques des signes hiéroglyphiques d'époque gréco-romaine* [Montpellier: Publications de la Recherche-Université de Montpellier, 1995], 4:794, nos. 359, 365; Kurth, *Einführung ins Ptolemäische,* 1:426, no. 24; Kurth, *A Ptolemaic Sign-List,* 202, no. 24. Note that *q* and *g* are interchangeable: see, for example, Kurth, *Einführung ins Ptolemäische,* 1:534, §27), while the sign (W24), which usually reads *nw,* is used here with the value *n* (see, e.g., Daumas et al., *Valeurs phonétiques,* 4:805, nos. 515, 517; Cauville, *Dendara: Le fonds hiéroglyphique,* 235; Kurth, *Einführung ins Ptolemäische,* 1:428, no. 37; Kurth, *A Ptolemaic Sign-List,* 203, no. 37). Moreover, we are dealing with a permutation of the signs and . For inversions and permutations of signs, see n. k, supra.

[q] Although very damaged, the sign (R4) is still recognizable; compare S. Brussels MRAH E. 8242, l. 3 (see de Meulenaere, "Trois stèles inédites," 56–57 [fig. 3]; Limme, *Stèles égyptiennes,* 52–53, no. 20), which also has . For *ḥtp.w* as a general word for offerings, see, for example, *PtoLex,* 687.

[r] For a restoration of this passage as ⸢*ḥtp*⸣[*.w ḏf3.w ḫ.t nb.t nfr.t* ...], "⸢*ḥtpw*-offering⸣[s, *ḏf3.w*-offerings, all things good ...]," see S. Brussels MRAH E. 8242, ll. 3–4 (see de Meulenaere, "Trois stèles inédites," 56–57 [fig. 3]; Limme, *Stèles* égyptiennes, 52–53, no. 20) and S. Cairo (unnumbered), l. 4 (see Daressy, "Inscriptions tentyrites," 184; Derchain-Urtel, *Priester im Tempel,* 41). For *ḏf3.w* as a general word for food offerings, see, for example, *PtoLex,* 1234.

2) *Upper register* (uninscribed)

a) left side:

The scene depicts two sons of Horus, namely, Imsety, whose head is damaged, and Hapy[16] as mummiform figures wearing a tripartite wig and a sash-kilt, which "consists of a length of linen wrapped around the hips and tied so that

16. For discussion and references on the sequence Imsety-Hapy-Duamutef-Qebehsenuef, see Kurth, *Materialen zum Totenglauben,* 12–13.

the ends hang decoratively in front, forming a sort of apron."[17] Their hands, protruding from the wrappings, hold a loop of cloth.[18]

b) right side:
The scene, which once depicted the other two sons of Horus, namely, Duamutef and Qebehsenuef, is now lost and only the extremity of a sash-kilt is visible.

3) Central register
a) left side: Horus, son of Isis and son of Osiris, as a falcon wearing the solar disk on his head
in front of the head:

	*Ḥr sꜣ ꜣs.t*	Horus, son of Isis (and)

between the wings:

	*sꜣ ⸢W⸣sir*[19] *nṯr ⸢ꜥ⸣ꜣ ⸢ḥr(y)-ib⸣*[20]	son of ⸢O⸣siris, the ⸢gr⸣eat god, ⸢who dwells in⸣.[21]

b) right side: Anubis as a falcon[22]
in front of the head:

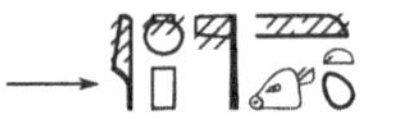	*⸢Ỉn⸣p(w) ⸢m⸣-ḫnt*[23]	⸢Anu⸣bis ⸢with⸣in

17. See Lyn Green, "Clothing and Personal Adornment," in *The Oxford Encyclopedia of Ancient Egypt*, ed. Donald B. Redford (Oxford: Oxford University Press, 2001), 1:275–76. On the sash-kilt, see also Gillian Vogelsang-Eastwood, "Textiles," in *Ancient Egyptian Materials and Technology*, ed. Paul T. Nicholson and Ian Shaw (Cambridge: Cambridge University Press, 2000), 287–88; Gillian Vogelsang-Eastwood, *Pharaonic Egyptian Clothing*, Studies in Textile and Costume History 2 (Leiden: Brill, 1993), 64–69.

18. For similar examples, see François Gaudard and Janet H. Johnson, "Six Stone Mummy Labels in the Oriental Institute Museum," in *Honi soit qui mal y pense: Studien zum pharaonischen, griechisch-römischen und spätantiken Ägypten zu Ehren von Heinz-Josef Thissen*, ed. Hermann Knuf, Christian Leitz, and Daniel von Recklinghausen, OLA 194 (Leuven: Uitgeverij Peeters and Departement Oosterse Studies, 2010), 198–99. For the loop of cloth as a sign of transfiguration after death, see Christina Riggs, *The Beautiful Burial in Roman Egypt: Art, Identity, and Funerary Religion*, Oxford Studies in Ancient Culture and Representation (Oxford: Oxford University Press, 2005), 60, fig. 21. For the funerary uses of linen, see, e.g., Vogelsang-Eastwood, "Textiles," 294–96.

19. For *Ḥr sꜣ ꜣs.t sꜣ Wsir*, "Horus, son of Isis (and) son of Osiris," see *LGG* V, 284–85.

20. The scribe left this epithet incomplete due to the lack of space (cf. n. 24, infra). It was perhaps *ḥry-ib Ỉwn.t*, "who dwells in Iunet" (cf. n. f, supra). For this epithet attributed to Horus, son of Isis and son of Osiris, see, e.g., *LGG* V, 315–16.

21. For discussion, see preceding note.

22. Compare the gods Anubis-Horus (see *LGG* I, 396, s.v. "*Ỉnpw-Ḥr*"), Anubis-Harsiese (see *LGG* I, 396, s.v. "*Ỉnpw-Ḥr-sꜣ-ꜣst*"), and Horus-Anubis (see Cauville et al., *Les chapelles osiriennes, Index*, 381, s.v. "*Ḥr-Ỉnpw*"; *LGG* V, 245, s.v. "*Ḥr-Ỉnpw*"; Jacques Vandier, *Le Papyrus Jumilhac* [Paris: Centre national de la recherche scientifique, 1962], 32; Brigitte Altenmüller, "Anubis," *LÄ* 1:330; Michel Malaise, "Documents nouveaux et points de vue récents sur les cultes isiaques en Italie," in *Hommages à Maarten J. Vermaseren: Recueil d'études offert par les auteurs de la Série Études préliminaires aux religions orientales dans l'Empire romain à Maarten J. Vermaseren à l'occasion de son soixantième anniversaire le 7 avril 1978*, ed. Margreet B. de Boer and T. A. Edridge, EPRO 68 [Leiden: Brill, 1978], 2:672); compare also *Ḥr m Ỉnpw* (see Cauville et al., *Les chapelles osiriennes, Index*, 47, s.v. "*Ỉnpw*," 380, s.v. "*Ḥr*"; *LGG* II, 692, s.v. "*Bꜣ-Ḥr-m-Ỉnpw*") and *Ḥr m qd Ỉnpw* (see Cauville et al., *Les chapelles osiriennes, Index*, 47, s.v. "*Ỉnpw*").

23. The sign (Aa15) is written mistakenly from left to right. For inversions and permutations of signs, see n. k, supra.

between the wings:

⸢s⸣ḥ-n⸢ṯ⸣r s.t [*sic*][24] — the g⸢o⸣d's ⸢b⸣ooth ...[25]

4) Lower register

a) left side: Nephthys as a vulture[26]

in front of the head:

Nb.t-ḥw.t ⸢*ꜥ*⸣*ꜣ(.t)*[27] — Nephthys, ⸢the gr⸣eat one,

between the wings:

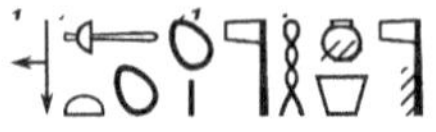

mnḫ.t sꜣ-nṯr[28] [*sic*] — the excellent one, the god's sister,[29]

ḥnw.t nṯ⸢*r*⸣*(.w)* (?)[30] — the mistress of the go⸢d⸣(s) (?).[31]

b) right side: Isis as a vulture[32]

in front of the head:

ꜣs.t wr.t — Isis, the great one,

24. At first sight, the interpretation of the signs  is problematic. However, when comparing this passage with the one concerning Anubis in column 2 (see supra), it can be inferred that the scribe likely meant to write the epithet *snfr ḥꜥ.w-nṯr (n) Dmḏ(-ꜥ.wt m) wꜥb.t*, "who restores the divine body of the One (whose limbs are) reassembled (in) the *wabet*," but he could only write the initial *s* of *snfr* due to the lack of space. He then added the group 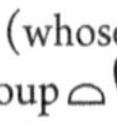 (feminine ending; see n. b, supra) probably as a filler (see, e.g., Cauville, *Dendara: Le fonds hiéroglyphique*, 7 [hiéroglyphes superfétatoires]). For another incomplete epithet in the present shroud, see n. 20, supra.

25. For discussion, see preceding note.

26. Compare, e.g., Shroud OIM E4786, central register, left side (see Gaudard, "Funerary Shrouds from Dendera, Part I," 68n36).

27. For the epithet *ꜥꜣ.t*, "the great one," attributed to Nephthys, see, e.g., Cauville et al., *Les chapelles osiriennes, Index*, 76; *LGG* IV, 99, s.v. "*Nbt-ḥwt-ꜥꜣt*."

28. For discussion, see n. h.

29. For discussion, see n. h.

30. The first two signs of this passage are faded, and the ink is smudged. However, after a careful examination of the original shroud, I was able to identify the group 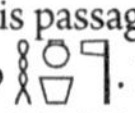. Note that the *nw*-vase used in the writing of *ḥnw.t*, "mistress," has a long neck, as in the writing of *Inp(w)*, "Anubis," in Shroud OIM E4786, center, column 2 (see Gaudard, "Funerary Shrouds from Dendera, Part I," 66, 70 [fig. 1]). If the scribe meant to write *ḥnw.t nṯr.w* "the mistress of the gods" (see, e.g., *LGG* V, 188–89), he wrote the word *nṯr* without the plural strokes, as seems to be the case with *nṯr.t* in the epithet *ḥnw.t nṯr.(w)t*, "the mistress of the goddess(es)," in Shroud OIM E4786, lower register, right and left sides, in front of the head and between the wings (see Gaudard, "Funerary Shrouds from Dendera, Part I," 68–69), but this may also be due to the lack of space. For an example of *nṯr* missing the plural strokes, see, e.g., *LGG* V, 189, s.v. "*Ḥnwt nṯrw nbw*" (no. 101). For an occurrence of *ḥnw.t*, "mistress," written as , see, e.g., *LGG* V, 164, s.v. "*Ḥnwt-Iwnw*" (no. 14). For the same writing with a determinative or a feminine ending, see *LGG* V, 179, s.v. "*Ḥnwt-pr-nfr*" (no. 7); 193, s.v. "*Ḥnwt-rnnwt*" (no. 1); 203, s.v. "*Ḥnwt-smyt-m-imntt*" (no. 1); 209, s.v. "*Ḥnwt-m-ḳsw*" (no. 1); 217, s.v. "*Ḥnwt-m-ḏt.s*" (no. 1). An alternate reading of the group  as *ḥnw.t*, "the mistress," with the sign  (R8) as the divine determinative, is less likely since we would rather expect a determinative such as the egg, the seated woman, or the cobra (see, e.g., *Wb.* III:107; Cauville et al., *Les chapelles osiriennes, Index*, 376; *PtoLex*, 652; *LGG* V, 161); compare, however, *LGG* V, 178, s.v. "*Ḥnwt-Pr-mrt*" (no. 1); 188, s.v. "*Ḥnwt-nṯrw*" (no. 1); 196, s.v. "*Ḥnwt-ḥmwt*" (no. 1); 216, s.v. "*ḥnwt-nt-dmi-nb*" (no. 1); 217, s.v. "*Ḥnwt-ḏsrt*" (no. 1), where *ḥnw.t* is written with the determinative 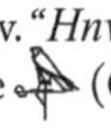 (G7).

31. For discussion, see preceding note.

32. Compare, e.g., Shroud OIM E4786, central register, right side, with a depiction of Isis as a vulture wearing the solar disk on her head (see Gaudard, "Funerary Shrouds from Dendera, Part I," 67, 70 [fig. 1]).

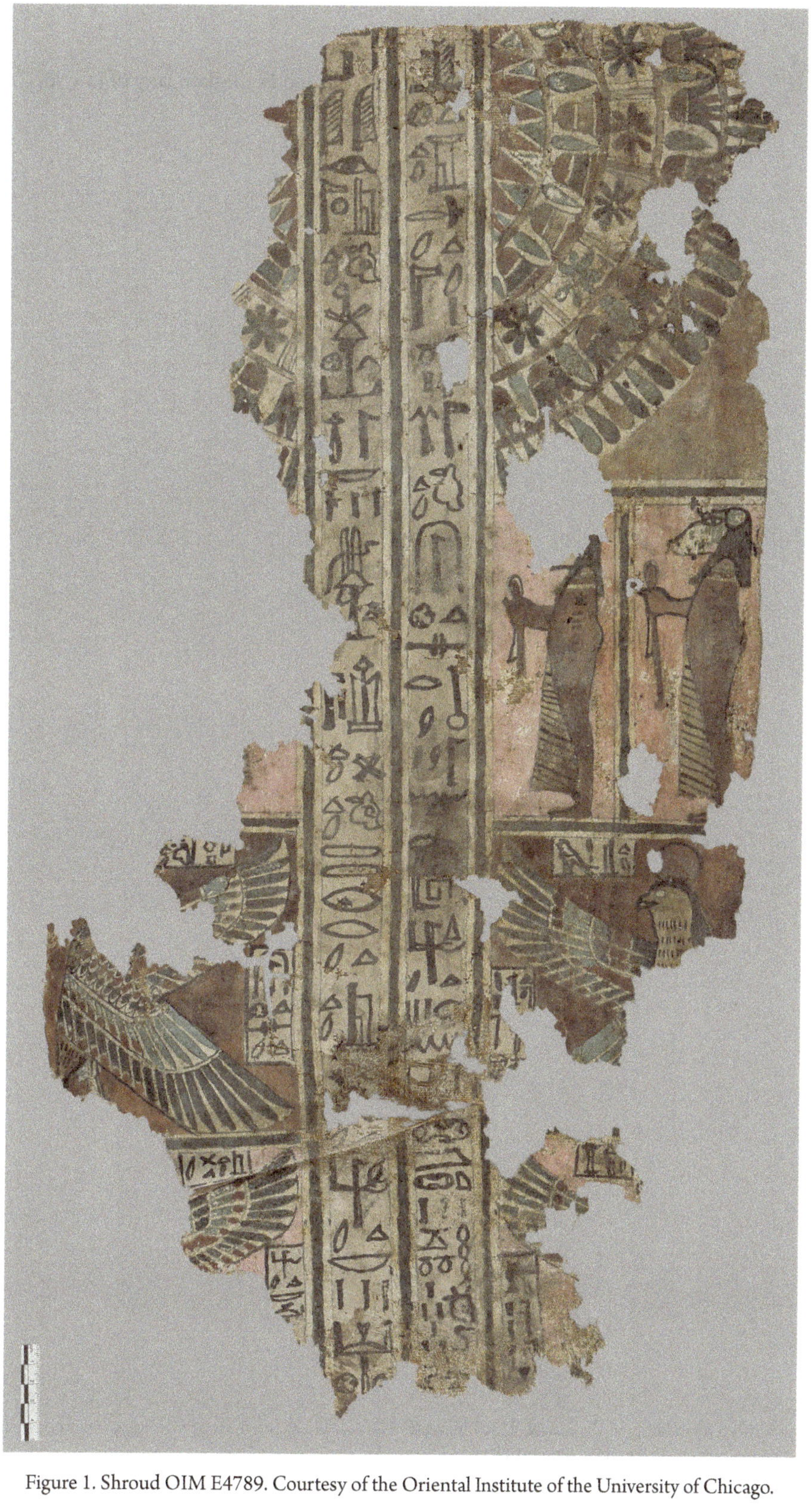

Figure 1. Shroud OIM E4789. Courtesy of the Oriental Institute of the University of Chicago.

between the wings:

mw.t-nṯr[33] *nb(.t) Ỉꜣ˹.t˺-ḏ[ỉ]*[34] the god's mother, lady of Ia˹t˺-d[i].

33. *Mw.t-nṯr* is written mistakenly with (D36) instead of (D39) (cf. n. n supra). For similar confusions between signs, see, e.g., Cauville, *Dendara: Le fonds hiéroglyphique*, 253.

34. For the unusual writing of the group (N97), see n. e supra.

Anmerkungen zu P. Loeb 2

Friedhelm Hoffmann

Diese Zeilen widme ich Richard Jasnow und danke ihm von ganzem Herzen für alles, was ich von ihm über viele Jahre lernen durfte. Er war einer meiner Lehrer, als ich im Wintersemester 1986/87 Ägyptologie in Würzburg zu studieren begann. Viele begeisternde Veranstaltungen konnte ich bei ihm besuchen. Immer habe ich ihn offen, interessiert und nachsichtig helfend erfahren. Richard hat sich stets auch für schwierige Texte interessiert. Daher hoffe ich, daß mein Beitrag zu seinen Ehren ihm nicht nur gefällt, sondern daß Richard mir die vielen ungelösten Probleme, die ich mit P. Loeb 2 noch habe, nachsieht. Ich gratuliere ihm zu seinem Geburtstag und wünsche ihm alles Gute!

Der beidseitig beschriebene Papyrus von 15 auf 37 cm[1] (Abb. 1 und 2) stammt vielleicht noch aus der ausgehenden Argeadenzeit.[2] Man erkennt unschwer, daß es sich um eine Abrechnung handelt – die vielen Zahlen machen das deutlich. Die Frage aber, was den Gegenstand der Rechnungen bildet, ist deutlich schwieriger zu beantworten. Spiegelberg hat in seiner Edition der Loeb-Papyri zwar gesehen, daß P. Loeb 2 Abrechnungen enthält, hat auch einige Personennamen gelesen, muß aber gestehen: „Worauf sich die Rechnung bezieht, ist mir unklar geblieben."[3] Diese Aussage bezieht sich eigentlich sogar nur auf die Rückseite. Zur anderen Seite äußert sich Spiegelberg noch vorsichtiger: „Auf der Vorderseite stehen Zahlen gelegentlich in Verbindung mit Personennamen, darunter ..." – er zählt dann einige Namen auf. Die *Berichtigungsliste* führt lediglich einige Korrekturen zu Spiegelbergs Namenlesungen auf.[4] Trismegistos[5] listet abgesehen von Spiegelbergs Ausgabe keine anderen Editionen auf und bezieht aus der DAHT-Datenbank als Inhaltsangabe lediglich „account".[6] In den *Thesaurus Linguae Aegyptiae* ist P. Loeb 2 nicht aufgenommen worden.[7] So bietet der Papyrus auch mehr als 90 Jahre nach seiner Erstpublikation noch erhebliche

Die Idee zur hier vorgestellten Deutung des P. Loeb 2 kam mir in meinem demotischen Lektürekurs im Wintersemester 2015/16 an der Universität München und betraf zunächst die Zeilen I 1–3 (zur Zählung s. unten). Ich danke allen Teilnehmerinnen und Teilnehmern dafür, daß ich meine Beobachtungen mit ihnen besprechen durfte. Am 7. September 2017 konnte ich auf dem Internationalen Demotistenkongreß in Leipzig meine Auffassungen zu noch mehr Stellen des P. Loeb 2 vorlegen. Auch für diese Gelegenheit und die dabei empfangenen Hinweise bin ich sehr dankbar.

1. Wilhelm Spiegelberg, *Die demotischen Papyri Loeb*, Papyri der Universität München 1 (München: Beck, 1931), 7 und Taf. 3.

2. Das ist der Datierungsvorschlag von Spiegelberg, *Papyri Loeb*, 7 („Zeit des jungen Alexander?"). Eine explizite Jahreszahl enthält der Papyrus nicht. P. W. Pestman, *Chronologie égyptienne d'après les textes démotiques (332 av. J.-C. - 453 ap. J.-C.)*, PLB 15 (Leiden: Brill, 1967), 13 hat P. Loeb 2 daher nicht und führt ihn auch S. 182 im Index der benutzten Papyri nicht auf. Mark Depauw, *A Chronological Survey of Precisely Dated Demotic and Abnormal Hieratic Sources*, Trismegistos Online Publications 1, Version 1.0 (Köln: Trismegistos, 2007) hat den P. Loeb 2 ebenfalls nicht aufgenommen. Das Papyrusformat würde insofern zu der vorgeschlagenen Datierung passen, als von 240 v. Chr. an die Blatthöhe deutlich geringer wird: Mark Depauw, „The Royal Format of Early Ptolemaic Demotic Papyri", in *Acts of the Seventh International Conference of Demotic Studies, Copenhagen, 23–27 August 1999*, hg. Kim Ryholt, CNI Publications 27 (Kopenhagen: Museum Tusculanum Press, 2002), 85–100, bes. 89–90.

3. Spiegelberg, *Papyri Loeb*, 7.

4. A. A. Den Brinker, B. P. Muhs und S. P. Vleeming, *A* Berichtigungsliste *of Demotic Documents*, Papyrus Editions, StudDem 7 (Leuven: Peeters, 2005), 270.

5. Trismegistos, https://www.trismegistos.org/. Die TM-Nr. des P. Loeb 2 ist 46038.

6. https://www.trismegistos.org/daht/detail.php?tm=46038.

7. http://aaew.bbaw.de/tla/servlet/s0?f=0&l=0&svl=%25Loeb%25.

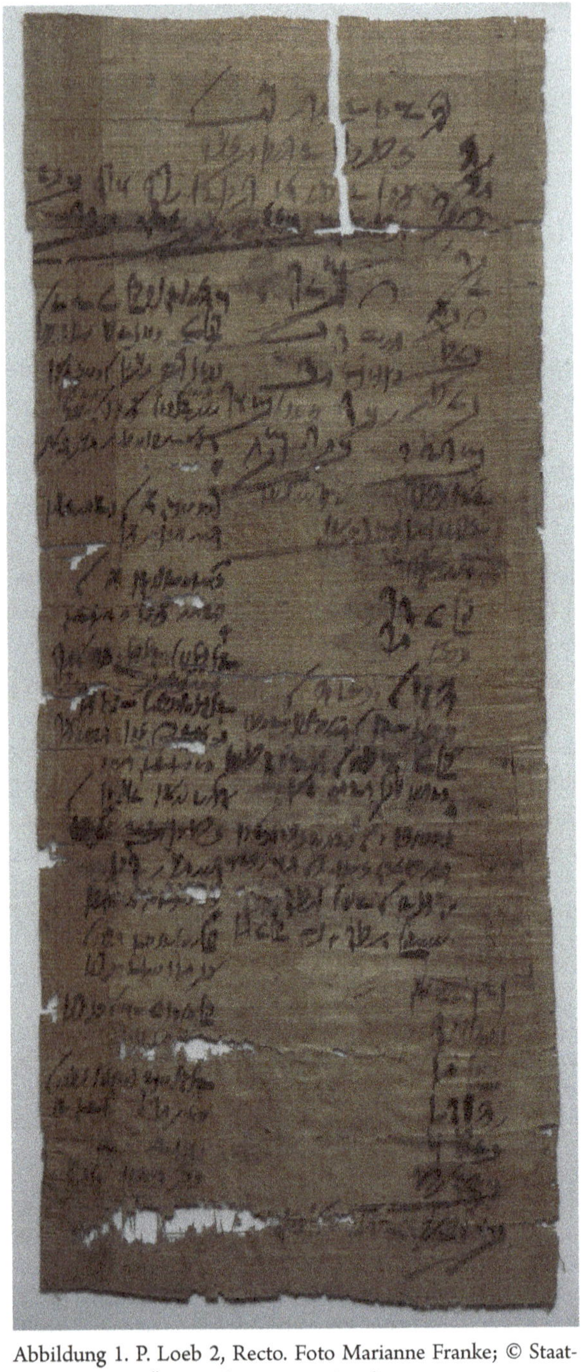

Abbildung 1. P. Loeb 2, Recto. Foto Marianne Franke; © Staatliches Museum Ägyptischer Kunst, München.

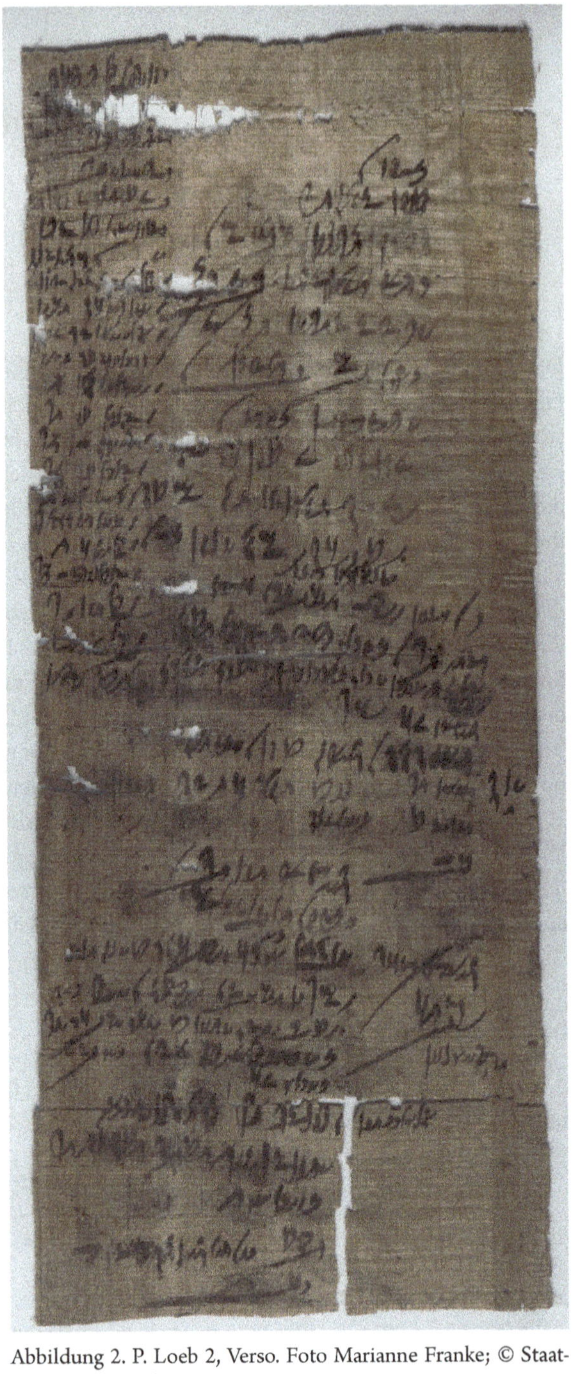

Abbildung 2. P. Loeb 2, Verso. Foto Marianne Franke; © Staatliches Museum Ägyptischer Kunst, München.

Probleme. Bis heute hat, soweit ich sehe, niemand eine zündende Idee zum Inhalt des P. Loeb 2 publiziert. Lediglich diese Frage, wovon der Papyrus eigentlich handelt, möchte ich hier behandeln. Ich lege keine Neuedition und keine vollständige Übersetzung des Papyrus vor und bin mir der Vorläufigkeit meiner Bemühungen sehr bewußt.

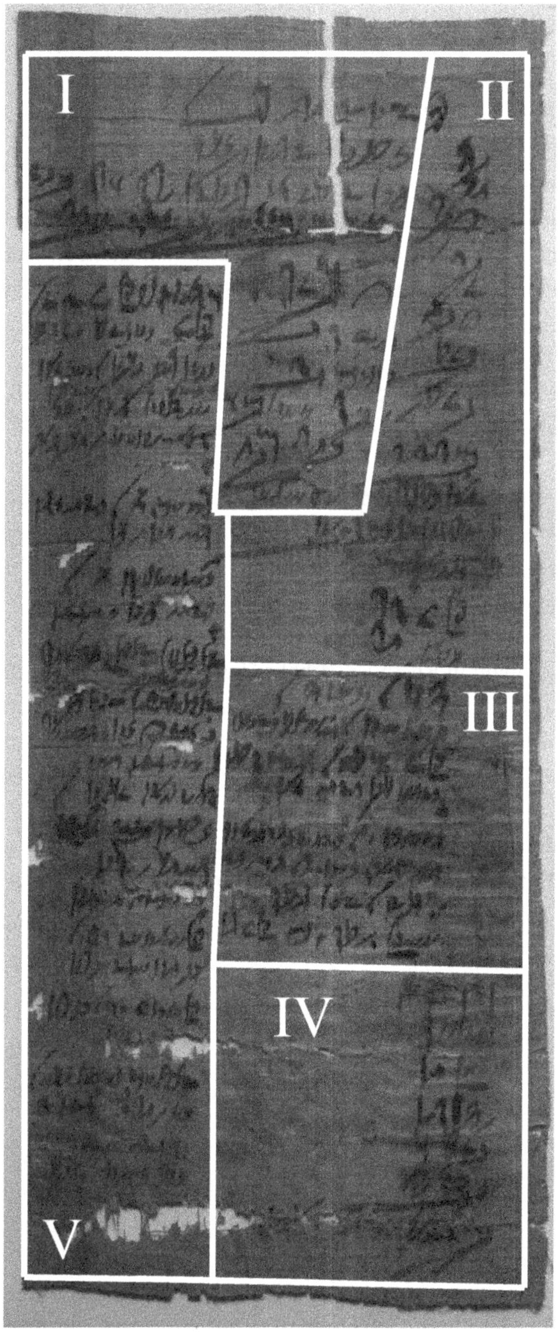

Abbildung 3. P. Loeb 2, Recto mit Markierung der Teiltexte. Foto Marianne Franke, Bildbearbeitung Friedhelm Hoffmann; © Staatliches Museum Ägyptischer Kunst, München.

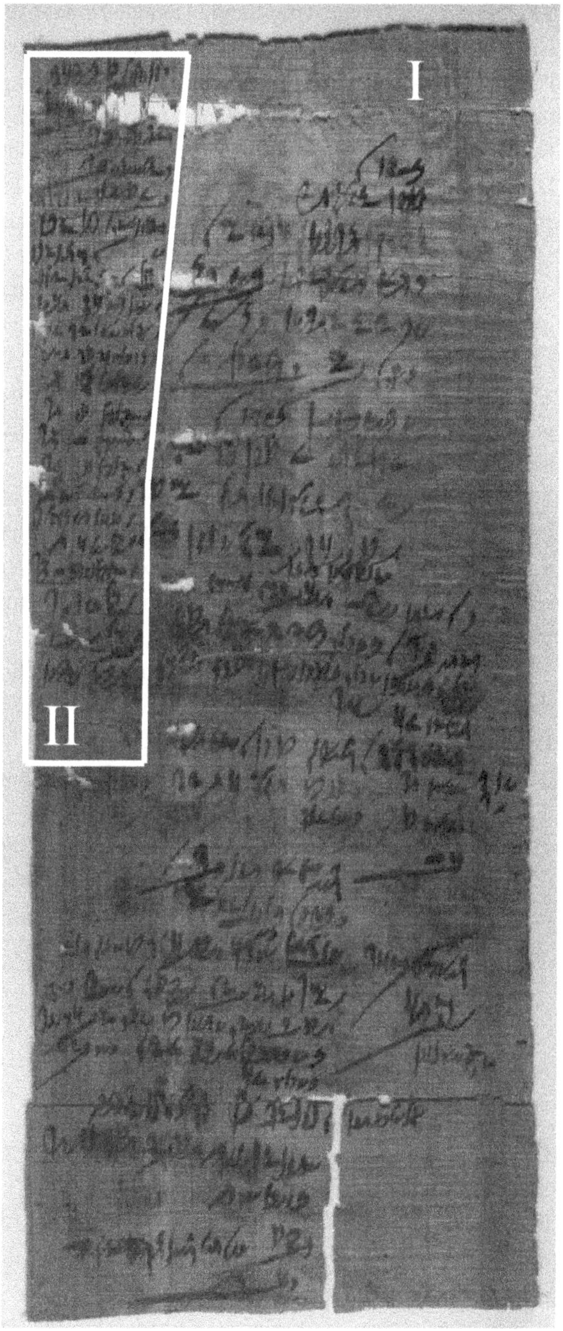

Abbildung 4. P. Loeb 2, Verso. Foto Marianne Franke, Bildbearbeitung Friedhelm Hoffmann; © Staatliches Museum Ägyptischer Kunst, München.

Man bemerkt vielleicht erst auf den zweiten Blick, daß der Papyrus keinen zusammenhängenden Text enthält, sondern aus einer Vielzahl kleinerer Einheiten besteht, die ich auf der Vorderseite von I bis V durchzähle (s. Abb.

3)[8]. Den Charakter unzusammenhängender Notizen erkennt man an den mitunter verspringenden Zeilen, an ihrer Gruppierung zu kleinen Untereinheiten, an unterschiedlicher Schwärze der Tinte usw. Ich glaube einen vergleichsweise breit geschriebenen Text ganz oben absetzen zu können, der später in schmalere Zeilen übergeht, wo der „Rest" behandelt wird – das Wort *sp* erkennt man gut in Z. 5 (Abschnitt I). Rechts außen befindet sich eine ganz schmale Kolumne, die vor allem aus Zahlen besteht (Abschnitt II). Eine Zeile dieses Blocks weiter unten ist etwas länger. Dann schließt sich ein etwa quadratischer Eintrag an (Abschnitt III). Ganz unten rechts, nochmals nach rechts ausgerückt, findet sich eine weitere Abrechnung, die, wenn ich ihr erstes Wort richtig lese, sogar als *ip* bezeichnet wird (Abschnitt IV). Links auf dem Blatt steht eine schmale Kolumne, die recht hoch ist und viele Personennamen enthält (Abschnitt V). Manche dieser Teilkolumnen tendieren zu einer kleinen flüchtigen Schrift und sind über weite Strecken schwer lesbar. Sie alle aber sind Abrechnungen oder vorsichtiger: Rechnungen – die vielen Zahlen sprechen, wie schon gesagt, klar dafür.

Der Schreiber hat an mehreren Stellen korrigiert, indem er Textpartien ausgelöscht und neu geschrieben hat, z.B. in I 4–5; II 2–3; IV 4; V 19. Auch Nachtragungen kommen vor, so in V 4 und 14, die in sehr kleiner Schrift geschrieben sind.

Die dunklen Verfärbungen, die stellenweise verlaufene Tinte bzw. die kleine Schrift tragen nicht zur besseren Lesbarkeit des Papyrus bei. Man gewinnt jedenfalls den Eindruck, daß P. Loeb 2 schriftliche Rechnungen, Notizen und Nebenrechnungen enthält; dazu kommen gelegentliche Korrekturen und Ergänzungen. Aber der Bezug der einzelnen Einträge zueinander wird kaum explizit gemacht, so daß mir der Zusammenhang vieler Rechnungen unklar bleibt.

Die Tatsache, daß die langen „Schwänze" dreier Hunderterzahlen in Recto I 3–4 links abgeschnitten sind, zeigt, daß der Schreiber das Recto zunächst auf einem größeren Papyrus begonnen, später aber das Blatt, das heute den P. Loeb 2 bildet, vom Rest der Rolle abgetrennt hat.[9] Die Einträge auf dem Verso (der Papyrus wurde nach oben gewendet) scheinen mir dann nämlich auf den entstandenen linken Blattrand Rücksicht zu nehmen (s. besonders Abschnitt II des Verso).

Nun zum Inhalt. Ich habe zunächst nach Beziehungen unter den Zahlen selbst gesucht. Denn die Zahlzeichen scheinen mir immer noch das am deutlichsten Lesbare im P. Loeb 2 zu sein. Rechts unten kann ich folgende Zahlen erkennen:

IV 4.	/ *71* (aus *72* korrigiert) *1/2*	/ *1*
5.	*143*	*2*
6.	*286*	/ *4*
7.	/	
8.	*3⸢5⸣7* … ⸢… … …⸣	

Das ist einfach eine ägyptische Multiplikation von 71 1/2 mal 5 mittels Verdoppelungsreihe: 71 1/2 mal 2 sind 143, das mal 2 ergibt 286. Markiert sind mit einem Schrägstrich die Zeile mit der 71 und die mit der 286. Addiert man die 71 1/2 und die 186, erhält man eigentlich 357 1/2. Die 1/2 fehlt aber in der Summe, es sei denn, man nimmt den langen Schrägstrich hinter der *3⸢5⸣7* als Zeichen für 1/2 Arure. Dann würde die Rechnung 71,5 × 5 korrekt aufgehen, und der P. Loeb 2 würde Felder betreffen. Der Schreiber hätte lediglich in der Notation zwischen normalem Bruchzahlzeichen und Arurenbruchzahl geschwankt. Die Rechnung könnte sich übrigens natürlich auch als Division 357 1/2 : 71 1/2 = 5 verstehen lassen.

Was wie eine Verlegenheitslösung klingt, wenn ich ein Nebeneinander von normalen Bruchzahlen und Arurenbruchzahlen annehme, könnte aber doch an Wahrscheinlichkeit gewinnen. Ich verweise auf die obersten drei Zeilen

8. Für die Rückseite s. S. 204–5.

9. Zu diesem Phänomen vgl. jüngst Kim Ryholt, „A Phyle Roster from Tebtunis with a Note on Offset Cutting, Traces, and Loss", *Enchoria* 36 (2018–2019): 145–50.

des Recto. Die schmale Spalte rechts gehört, wie oben bereits gesagt, schon wieder nicht mehr dazu. Ich meine lesen zu können (Anmerkungen füge ich gleich in die Umschrift, wenn sie für die Argumentation wichtig sind.):

I 1. *60 ꜣḥ* – Das Wort ist recht flüchtig und verkürzt geschrieben.[10] Jedenfalls gibt es den Gegenstand des P. Loeb 2 an: Es sind Rechnungen zu Feldern! – *tn 15 r 900 wp-s.t*

2. *24 1/2* – als langer Schrägstrich, also als Arurenbruchzahl geschrieben, was die Annahme, es gehe um Felderberechnungen noch einmal bestätigt – (*sṯꜣ.t*)[11] *ꜣḥ tn 5 sṯꜣ.t ꜣḥ 122 1/2* – als normale Bruchzahl; das Ergebnis der Berechnung sind also keine Aruren; daher gehört meiner Meinung nach das vorangehende *sṯꜣ.t ꜣḥ* nicht mit der *122 1/2* zusammen. –

3. *30 ꜣḥ tn 3 r 90 5 1/2* (*sṯꜣ.t*) *ꜣḥ tn 1 r 5 1/2* – wieder als normale Bruchzahl; das Ergebnis der Berechnung sind demnach keine Aruren. – *95 1/2 218*

1. 60 Acker(aruren), je 15, macht 900. – Spezifikation:
2. 24 1/2 Acker(aruren), je 5 (pro) Ackerarure, (macht) 122 1/2;
3. 30 Acker(aruren), je 3, macht 90; 5 1/2 Acker(aruren), je 1, macht 5 1/2. – (Zwischensumme aus dieser Zeile am linken Rand:) 95 1/2. – (Gesamtsumme der Z. 2 und 3, ebenfalls am linken Rand:) 218.

Zunächst wird für 60 Ackeraruren ausgerechnet, wieviel Einheiten – ich weiß nicht, wovon – sich ergeben, wenn jeder Arure 15 dieser Einheiten zugeordnet werden. Das sind 900. Im folgenden schließt sich eine differenziertere oder alternative Betrachtung an: Die 60 Aruren werden in drei unterschiedlich große Gruppen eingeteilt: 24 1/2, 30 und 5 1/2. Jeder dieser Gruppen wird nun wieder etwas zugeordnet, das aber je nach Gruppe variiert: je 5 oder 3 Einheiten oder je 1 Einheit. Entsprechend ergeben sich unterschiedliche Beträge (122 1/2, 90 und 5 1/2). Die letzten beiden werden zu 95 1/2 addiert, ehe die Gesamtsumme mit den 122 1/2 aus Z. 2 zusammen als 218 angegeben wird.

Der Rechenweg selbst ist damit klar. Aber es bleibt die Frage nach der Bedeutung der ersten Zeile: Angenommen, es werden den Flächen unterschiedliche Erträge (z.B. 5, 3 und 1 Artabe je Arure?) zugeordnet: Welche Funktion hätte die Rechnung in Z. 1? Es müßte dann ja um 15 (Artaben?) gehen. Dieser Wert ist aber um ein Vielfaches höher als die anderen Zahlen (5, 3, 1). Die Berechnung eines Durchschnittes, der dann je nach Feldertyp aufgeschlüsselt würde, kann es also nicht sein. Dazu würde auch das Ergebnis 900 in der ersten Zeile gar nicht passen. Dennoch muß Z. 1 mit den beiden folgenden zusammenhängen: Es geht um insgesamt 60 Aruren. Ich hatte zunächst angenommen, daß sich die Zahlen nach dem *tn* „je“ (Z. 2 und 3) als 15 = 5 × 3 × 1 miteinander in Beziehung setzen lassen und mit der 15 in Z. 1 zusammenhängen. Dann war ich erst einmal steckengeblieben.

W. Wegner verdanke ich die Idee, daß man hier doch weiterkommt, wenn man hinsichtlich der 15 einen bloßen Zufall annimmt. In der ersten Zeile könnte beispielsweise ein erwarteter Gesamtertrag der 60 Aruren angegeben sein. Denn die glatte Zahl von 900 Einheiten spricht dafür, daß es sich um ein Ideal, eine Prognose, einen Überschlag o.ä. handelt. In den nächsten Zeilen wären je nach Feld, Feldertyp oder Besitzer oder sonstwie differenziert z.B. Abgaben von der Ernte notiert. Dabei scheinen die Arurenzahlen festzustehen, aber die davon abgeleiteten Zahlen wären wieder schematisch ermittelt, etwa so:

> 60 Aruren liefern pro Arure 15 Einheiten einer Feldfrucht (vielleicht, wie schon vermutet, in Artaben angegeben), macht zusammen 900 (Artaben?).

Die 60 Aruren werden aber z.B. unterschiedlich hoch besteuert:

10. Vergleiche W. Erichsen, *Demotisches Glossar* (Kopenhagen: Munksgaard, 1954), 9, zweiter Eintrag *ꜣḥ*.

11. So wie hier setze ich hinter eine Bruchzahl „(*sṯꜣ.t*)“, wenn es sich um ein Arurenbruchzahlzeichen handelt (vgl. Erichsen, *Glossar*, 706).

24,5 Aruren mit je 5 Einheiten (auch Artaben?; 5 von 15 entsprächen einer Abgabenrate von 1/3), ergäben 122,5 Einheiten Abgaben.
30 Aruren mit je 3 Einheiten (von 15, entspräche 1/5), ergäbe 90 abzuführende Einheiten.
5,5 Aruren mit je 1 Einheit (von 15, entspräche 1/15), ergäbe 5,5 Einheiten.

Wir hätten es unter dieser Annahme mit 60 Aruren mit insgesamt 900 Einheiten erwartetem Ertrag, von denen 218 Einheiten (= 24 2/9 %) als Abgabe berechnet werden, zu tun.

Diese Vermutung würde gut zu dem passen, was man bisher z.B. von der Besteuerung von Weizenfeldern in der Ptolemäerzeit weiß:[12] Normalerweise wurde eine Artabe pro Arure ausgesät, der Ertrag betrug das Zehn- bis Zwölffache oder noch mehr.[13] Im P. Loeb 2 wäre, wenn die hier angestellten Überlegungen stimmen, ein Ertrag von 15 Artaben pro Arure zugrunde gelegt worden (Z. I 1). Die unterschiedliche Abgabenhöhe von 5, 3 oder 1 Artabe würde ins normale Bild passen, galten doch keine festen Raten für das gesamte Ackerland. Vielmehr wurden die Abgaben u.a. nach der Höhe der Nilflut und der Landqualität bestimmt.[14] Im Fajum schwankten sie typischerweise von 4 bis 6 Artaben Weizen pro Arure, doch die königlichen Bauern in Kerkeosiris zahlten beispielsweise etwa 1 bis knapp 5 Artaben Weizen-*ekphorion* pro Arure, in Oberägypten sind Raten von 3 bis 8 Artaben gängig.[15] Die Zahlen des P. Loeb 2 sind also insgesamt mit diesen Werten vergleichbar.

Der gesamte Abgabenertrag, nämlich 218 Artaben von 60 Aruren, d.h. durchschnittlich knapp 3 2/3 Artaben pro Arure, läge freilich deutlich unter den für die Ptolemäerzeit bekannten Weizenabgaben, die z.B. 5,3 in Oberägypten und 5,9 im Fajum betrugen.[16] Aber natürlich könnte es sich im P. Loeb um eine andere Feldfrucht handeln, die Abgabensätze könnten zudem in der Argeadenzeit, in die der P. Loeb vielleicht zu datieren ist, oder in Mittelägypten anders gewesen sein. Vielleicht ist zu diesem Zeitpunkt im Textverlauf aber auch noch nicht die gesamte Abgabenlast ermittelt (vgl. im folgenden).

Der Abschnitt I des P. Loeb 2 würde sich aber tatsächlich gut als eine überschlagsmäßige Prognose zu den erwarteten Erträgen und Abgaben von 60 Ackeraruren Land verstehen lassen. Dabei handelt es sich, wie die vielen Korrekturen zeigen, jedenfalls um ein Konzept mit den schriftlichen Überlegungen und Nebenrechnungen, nicht um die Reinschrift.[17]

Mit der Summe 218, die sich ganz am Ende der dritten Zeile befindet, wird anschließend wohl weitergerechnet. Z. 4, die stärker zerstört ist, enthält sowohl Hunderter- als auch Zehnerzahlen, am Ende steht 255. Vielleicht kamen irgendwie 37 Einheiten zusammen, die zu den 218 noch addiert wurden und eben 255 ergaben. Doch vermutlich ist auch das nur ein weiterer Zwischenschritt, denn es folgt in Z. 5 die Angabe eines Restes (*sp*) von 245[18]. Mit dem nachfolgenden *wp-s.t* „Spezifikation" findet wieder eine Zerlegung (einer aus der 245 gewonnenen 250?) in 100 und 150 statt:

---

12. Die folgenden Angaben nach Andrew Monson, *From the Ptolemies to the Romans: Political and Economic Change in Egypt* (Cambridge: Cambridge University Press, 2012), 162–72, wo sich nicht nur eine knappe Zusammenfassung findet, sondern auch viel weiterführende Literatur angegeben wird.

13. Monson, *Ptolemies to Romans*, 172.

14. Monson, 169.

15. Monson, 170–71.

16. Auch diese Angabe nach Monson, *Ptolemies to Romans*, 170–71.

17. Meiner Meinung nach spricht zudem die formale Uneinheitlichkeit der vier Einträge in den Zeilen I 1–3 für den Entwurfcharakter des Textes (x, y und z stehen für Zahlen):

I 1	x *ꜣḥ*	*tn* y	*r* z
2	x *ꜣḥ*	*tn* y *sṯꜣ.t ꜣḥ*	z
3	x *ꜣḥ*	*tn* y	*r* z
	x *ꜣḥ*	*tn* y	*r* z

18. An der 200 ist korrigiert worden.

I 6.	Saatgetreide(?)[19]	50	100
7.	die Leute …	150 (Ist das die Summe der beiden vorangehenden Zahlen?)	
8.	macht	250 (Wird hier die 100 noch einmal zur 150 addiert?)	
	… (ein Name?)	395	

Die 395 kommt unerwartet, aber mit ihr wird weitergerechnet:

9.	215	macht(?) 610.

610 ist als Summe von 395 (Z. 8) und 215 (Z. 9) verstehbar. Es scheint sich, wie man sieht, um Rechnungen zu handeln, bei denen immer wieder Größen neu kombiniert werden. Und vielleicht sind die 610 Einheiten die, die am Schluß von den 900 übrigbleiben – nach Abzug der Abgaben, des zurückzulegenden Saatgutes für das nächste Jahr, der Bezahlung für die Erntearbeiter[20] und wohl noch anderer Posten, die ich nicht recht erkennen kann. Wenn tatsächlich nur noch 610 Einheiten von 900 übrig bleiben sollten, 290 also abgeführt würden, bedeutete das eine Abgabenlast von 290 Artaben(?) auf 60 Aruren, also ca. 4,8 Artaben pro Arure, was den oben genannten Sätzen der ptolemäischen Weizenabgaben von 5,3 und 5,9 Artaben pro Arure schon recht nahe käme.

Die übrigen Einträge des Papyrus sind unterschiedlicher Art. So gibt es etwa rein numerische Notizen, z.B.:

II 8. *143*
9. *1/2 (sṯꜣ.t)*
10. *143 1/2 (sṯꜣ.t)*

Das ist rechnerisch banal. Aber die Tatsache, daß die Rechnung hier steht, beweist meiner Meinung nach, daß sowohl die 143 als auch die 1/2 (Arure) irgendwoher kamen und irgendwie zu berücksichtigen waren. Der Text sagt uns aber nicht, wie. Es muß gewissermaßen in der realen Welt außerhalb der vorliegenden Rechnung einen Grund dafür gegeben haben, daß die beiden Zahlen und ihre simple Addition hier schriftlich festgehalten werden.

Mit *dmḏ* werden Textabschnitte abgeschlossen, so z.B. mehrfach in der linken Spalte. Hier teilt der Schreiber offenbar ein paar Mal größere Beträge auf. Einer der Einträge lautet:

V 7. *dmḏ* – das schließt den vorangehenden Eintrag ab –
8. *ḥ* … – ein Name? – *30 wp-s.t nty? ẖn? 21 ꜣḥ?*
9. … *10 ꜣḥ r 31*
10. *ḏd-ḥr (sꜣ?) pꜣ?-… 30* – ist das die *30* von Z. 8? – *wp-s.t*
11. *nty ẖn 30 ꜣḥ* …
12. *dmḏ*

7. Summe (= Ende des vorigen Eintrags).
8. *ḥ* … : 30; Spezifikation: Was(?) in(?) 21 Acker(?)(aruren) ist:
9. … 10 Acker(aruren), macht 31.

Aus dem Text wird mir nicht klar, warum ausgerechnet die 21 und die 10 zu 31 kombiniert werden, während mit der 30 offenbar erst einmal nichts weiter passiert. Es folgt:

10. Djedher, (Sohn[?]) des(?) Pa(?)-… : 30; Spezifikation:
11. was in 30 Acker(aruren) ist …

19. Die Lesung *pr.t* haben J. Korte und W. Wegner vorgeschlagen.

20. Einen Eindruck von Kosten für die Felderbestellung bietet der frühptolemäische P. Brooklyn 37.1647E, D(1)/2, ed. Steve Vinson, „P. Brooklyn 37.1647E, D(1)/2: An Early Ptolemaic Agricultural Account", in *Res severa verum gaudium: Festschrift für Karl-Theodor Zauzich zum 65. Geburtstag am 8. Juni 2004*, hg. F. Hoffmann und H. J. Thissen, StDe 6 (Leuven: Peeters, 2004), 595–611. Im Brooklyner Papyrus wird Geld abgerechnet.

12. Summe.

Wenn hier 30 als 30 „umgerechnet" bzw. erklärt wird, dann zeigt das, daß die mathematische Routine einer *sachlich* begründeten, also einer außerhalb des Textes selbst liegenden Notwendigkeit folgt.

In vielen weiteren Einträgen wird eine zu Beginn genannte größere Zahl in kleinere zerlegt, z.B.:

V 27. *wsir-ḫʿ (sꜣ) pꜣ-di-ꜣs.t ḥnʿ? iy-m-ḥtp 23 ꜣḥ wp-s.t*
28. *... 15 ... 8*

27. Usircha, (Sohn) des Padiaset, und(?) Iiemhetep: 23 Acker(aruren); Spezifikation:
28. ... 15 ... 8

Auch wenn ich in dieser Zeile nur die Zahlen lesen kann, scheint mir der Zusammenhang klar: 23 = 15 + 8.

Wie schon erwähnt, hat der Schreiber des P. Loeb 2 an mehreren Stellen korrigiert, stellenweise auch ganze Rechnungen ausgelöscht. Insofern mag man erwarten, daß nicht alle Rechnungen in der Weise aufeinander zu beziehen sind, daß sie „aufgehen". Vielleicht ist zumindest stellenweise davon auszugehen, daß der Schreiber Alternativen durchprobiert hat. Dafür könnten neben den Tilgungen auch die Nachtragungen sprechen. Damit läßt sich der Charakter des Textes als Sammlung von vielen Einzelrechnungen jedenfalls gut zusammenbringen.

Werfen wir noch einen Blick auf die Rückseite (s. Abb. 4), für deren Beschriftung das Blatt nach oben umgewendet wurde. Der generelle Eindruck ist ähnlich wie der der Vorderseite: Wieder findet sich eine Vielzahl von kleineren Einträgen mit Rechnungen und Auflistungen. Ihren Zusammenhang habe ich noch nicht verstanden. Schon ihre Abgrenzung voneinander finde ich schwierig. Vermutlich sind es mehr Einheiten als auf Abb. 4 festgehalten. Die größer geschriebenen Partien enthalten ganz überwiegend Zahlen, die immer wieder durch *wp-s.t*-Zeichen gegliedert sind. Übrigens scheint mir in I 16 und 17[21] das normale Zeichen für „1/2" benutzt zu werden, nicht der spezielle Bruch für „1/2 Arure".

Recht bemerkenswert ist die in die linke obere Ecke gequetschte Tabelle (II). Ihr Zweck entgeht mir zwar, aber ich verstehe wenigstens ihren Aufbau. Einige Auszüge mögen ihn verdeutlichen. Mit Z. 7 endet eine vorangehende Zusammenstellung; das Wort *dmḏ* zeigt das wieder an. Doch noch in derselben Zeile setzt der Schreiber mit *wp-s.t* neu ein. Die nachfolgenden Zeilen sind jeweils mit einem Schrägstrich am Anfang markiert. Nun folgt pro Zeile die Nennung einer Person, gefolgt von jeweils zwei Zahlen. Zum Beispiel:

9.	*/ ...*	*2 1/2*		*12 ꜣḥ*
10.	*/ ḏḥwty-iw?*	*8 1/2*		*42* [*1/2*]
11.	*/ ...*	*3 1/2*		*17 1/2*
12.	*/ pꜣ-di-wsir-ḥp?*	*6*		*30*
13	*/ wsir-ḫʿ*	*3 1/2*		*15*
14.	*/ ḥ...*	*7*		*35*
15.	*/ wsir-ḫʿ*[22]	*3*		*15*
...				
18.	*/ sbk-iw*	*2*		*10*
19.	*/ wsir-ḫʿ ḥnʿ? ...*	*7*		*35*
20.	*/ sbk-...*	*1*	*r?*	*5*

21. Die Zählung ist ganz vorläufig. Ich habe Block I als eine Einheit durchgezählt. Tatsächlich handelt es sich aber wohl um eine Hauptrechnung mit rechts von ihr notierten Nebenrechnungen.

22. Deutlich flüchtiger geschrieben als vorher.

Wie man sieht, ist die zweite Zahl jeweils das Fünffache der ersten. Nur Z. 13 stimmt nicht dazu, weil 3 1/2 mal 5 nicht 15, sondern 17 1/2 ergibt. Liegt hier einfach ein Rechenfehler vor? Oder ist die 1/2 zu tilgen? Denn 3 mal 5 ist ja 15. Die letzte Zeile würde jedenfalls wieder zum sonstigen Schema paßt:

22. */ 14 r 70 ꜣḥ* „/ 14 macht 70 Acker(aruren)"

Die Zahl 14 und entsprechend auch die 70 sind allerdings nicht die Summen zur ganzen Liste; dafür sind sie zu klein. Auffällig ist dennoch ihre Höhe und das Fehlen eines Namens in der Zeile.

Wie auch immer. Ich belasse es bei diesen Andeutungen zum P. Loeb 2. Sicher ist meiner Meinung nach jetzt zumindest, daß er Felder betrifft. Klar ist auch ein Bezug zu dem „Opfergut des Sobek" (*ḥtp-nṯr sbk*), das schon Spiegelberg „über dem Schlußabsatz" des Verso gelesen hat.[23] Teile der Vorderseite stellen wohl speziell Ertrags- und Abgabenberechnungen dar. Auch sehe ich immerhin, daß mehrfach größere Flächen in kleinere unterteilt und Zahlen unterschiedlich miteinander kombiniert werden. Vielleicht wurde Land in Felder eingeteilt. Doch welcher Art die Berechnungen sind, entgeht mir. Ich muß es Berufeneren überlassen, sich intensiver mit P. Loeb 2 zu beschäftigen.[24]

23. Spiegelberg, *Papyri Loeb*, 7.
24. Eine Neubearbeitung des Papyrus durch A. Monson und J. F. Quack ist in Vorbereitung.

A Statue of Ptah-Sokar-Osiris in the Archaeological Collection of The Johns Hopkins University

Fatma Ismail

A statue of a standing mummified human figure is now displayed in the newly renovated Archaeological Collection of the Johns Hopkins University, collection #JHU 2911 (figs. 1–2). James Teackle Dennis, a native Baltimorean, donated to Johns Hopkins several Egyptian objects, including this statue, that he acquired while visiting Egypt from 1905 to 1918 with the Egypt Exploration Fund, as an appreciation for the university's funding.[1] The statue has been recently cleaned, restored, and displayed at an exhibition on ancient Egypt at Washington College.[2] However, the original location of the piece and how Dennis acquired it remains a mystery.

The statue is made of two separate pieces of a miniature anthropoid casket and coffin lid. The body of the figure is 61 cm long, 14 cm wide, and 9 cm thick, and the separate headdress is 23 cm long, 17.5 cm wide, and 2.8 cm deep. Both pieces are carved from single flanks of wood and covered by a thin layer of gilding or paint. The interior surface of the body shows some chisel marks. The figure wears a tripartite wig with double lappets exposing the ears. The headdress contains a *šwty* crown of two ostrich plumes encircling a sun disk and horizontal ram's horns. A cobra is depicted at the forehead. A false beard curling at the end is attached to the face. The shrouded body has no hands. The back is curved slightly to suggest calves and buttocks. Below the feet a small plinth becomes a wooden peg. The statue must originally have been inserted into a rectangular base that is now missing. Eight wooden tenons join the casket and lid, two in the head and six around the outline of the body. A long, narrow and hollow core is formed by the two statue parts.

At the front of the statue, gilding appears on the headdress, face, neck, ears, cobra, wide collar, and on vertical pillars inscribed with two lines of hieroglyphs. The elaborate *wsḫ n bik* collar terminates in two falcon's heads on the shoulders and has seven concentric rows of lotuses, rosettes, and geometric shapes. Between the collar and the two vertical lines of inscription, a shrine-shaped pectoral shows three seated divinities—Osiris, Isis, and Nephthys—with their names inscribed above their heads. The rest of the body is painted, applied directly without plaster in some places. The surface of the statue has been restored and repainted in modern times making it hard to distinguish the original colors from the modern alterations. Traces of "Egyptian Blue" pigment emanated from many of the dark-colored surfaces of the statue when illuminated with visible light and captured in infrared.[3] The facial features, horizontal horns, wig, and divine beard are outlined in black. The body and feet are painted red. The feathers on the headdress

1. Ellen R. Williams, *The Archaeological Collection of the Johns Hopkins University* (Baltimore: Johns Hopkins University Press 1984), 5–6.

2. The exhibition, "For Now and Forever: Funerary Artifacts from Ancient Egypt," was curated by this author at the Kohl's gallery of Washington College, from September 9 to December 2, 2011.

3. This process is called photo-induced luminescence and is currently being developed by the British Museum. See Glenn Alan Gates, "Discovering the Material Secrets of Art: Tools of Cultural Heritage Science," *American Ceramic Society Bulletin* 93.7 (2014): 20–27; https://ceramics.org/wp-content/uploads/2014/08/Cover-story_sept141.pdf; The author thanks Sanchita Balachandran, curator/conservator of The Johns Hopkins Archaeological Museum for her help in using this technique.

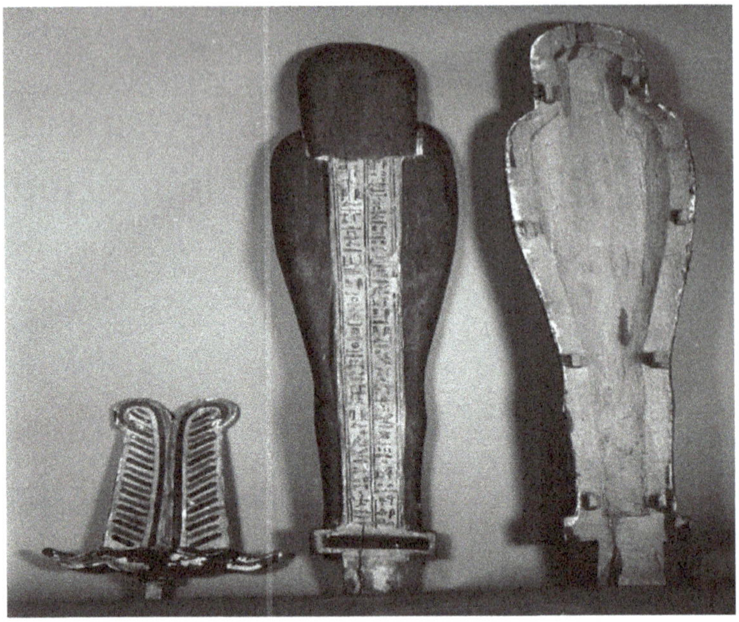

Figure 2. Statue of Ptah Sokar Osiris, JHU 2911, showing back view of all separate parts. Image courtesy of the Walter's Art Museum.

Figure 1. Statue of Ptah Sokar Osiris, JHU 2911, front view. Image courtesy of the Johns Hopkins Archaeological Museum. Photograph by Jay Van Rensselaer.

are alternately red, black, and yellow. At the back of the statue, a slightly raised pillar contains two long vertical lines of inscription painted black against a yellow background, perhaps imitating gold foil or papyrus roll. The small plinth below the feet is painted yellow except for a thick horizontal blackish-green line on each of the four sides. Noticeably, the colors and hieroglyphs differ on both parts; on the back the colors are lighter and less saturated (for example, they are greenish-black on the back but dark black on the front), and the hieroglyphs are better inscribed on the front. This could be the result of more care being given to the front of the statue, perhaps for economical reasons.

Since at least the Middle Kingdom, the funerary ensemble of Egyptian tombs usually included mummiform statuettes representing the deceased. They developed into various types distinguished by their date, inscription, numbers, stylistic features, or functions. During the middle of the New Kingdom, a new type of mummiform funerary statuette was introduced: a hollow Osiris or Osiris papyrus sheath, made of wood in the likeness of Osiris and typically used as a magical storage case for funerary papyri.[4] In the Third Intermediate period and well into the Ptolemaic period, this type of statuary became what is called Ptah-Sokar-Osiris statuary,[5] of which our figure is an example.

The earlier Osiris papyrus sheath and the later Ptah-Sokar-Osiris statues had stylistic variations but mainly differed in that the features of the god Sokar were added. The Ptah-Sokar-Osiris statues often had an anthropomorphic head with the *šwty* crown of Sokar, a human body with the falcon head of Sokar, or an anthropomorphic figure with an additional miniature falcon on the statue's base.[6] Ptah-Sokar-Osiris statues are also characterized by the inclusion of the inscription of long or short versions of the Atum hymn among the hieroglyphic inscriptions on the back, front, or base of the statues. The inscriptions frequently associate the deceased with Osiris or Osiris-Sokar and less commonly with the syncretistic god Ptah-Sokar-Osiris.[7] Perhaps it is more appropriate to refer to these figurines as Sokar-Osiris rather than Ptah-Sokar-Osiris, especially when the inscriptions mention Sokar-Osiris, as in our statue.

Although Ptah, Sokar, and Osiris were amalgamated in texts since the Middle Kingdom,[8] they began to be pictorially depicted as one entity only in the New Kingdom.[9] Their iconography varied considerably, sometimes taking features from Osiris or Sokar or combining all three. The same is true for Sokar-Osiris, so we can never be certain whether such figurines represent Sokar-Osiris or Ptah-Sokar-Osiris. We can be certain at least of the Sokar-Osiris combination especially because of the *šwty* headdress of Sokar, and we can also be certain that these gods are associated with Atum due to the hymn that is so often used in such objects.[10]

This Sokarization of the earlier Osiride statuettes coincides with the increasing popularity of Sokar in the Late and Ptolemaic periods when the god became the center of the Osirian celebration during the month of Khoiak.[11] Unfortunately, our statue is missing its cavity contents, but generally Ptah-Sokar-Osiris statue cavities included not only

4. The main study for these objects is still Maarten J. Raven, "Papyrus-Sheaths and Ptah-Sokar-Osiris Statues," *OMRO* 59–60 (1978–1979): 258–62. See also David A. Aston, "Two Osiris Figures of the Third Intermediate Period," *JEA* 77 (1991): 95–106; Edith Varga, "Statues funéraires en bois dans la Collection Égyptienne de Budapest," *Bulletin de Musée Hongrois des Beaux-Arts* 83 (1995): 3–20; Carlo Rindi Nuzzolo, "An Unusual Group of Ptah-Sokar-Osiris Figures: Some Reflections on Typology and Provenance," *JARCE* 49 (2013): 193–204. Nuzzolo supplements Raven's typologies by adding type VI, based on a study of a group of unusual Greco-Roman Ptah-Sokar-Osiris statues from Middle Egypt.

5. Raven, "Papyrus-Sheaths and Ptah-Sokar-Osiris Statues," 263–71; Julia Budka, "Ptah-Sokar-Osiris-Statuetten aus Grab VII im Asasif," in *Das alte Ägypten und seine Nachbarn: Festschrift zum 65. Geburtstag von Helmut Satzinger, mit Beiträgen zur Ägyptologie, Koptologie, Nubiologie und Afrikanistik*, ed. Monika Hasitzka, Johannes M. Diethart, and Günther Dembski (Krems: Österreichisches Literaturforum, 2003), 32–42; Julia Budka, "Einige Bemerkungen zu Ptah-Sokar-Osiris-Statuetten," *GM* 193 (2003): 99–101; Kate Bosse-Griffiths, "Problems with Ptah-Sokar-Osiris Figures: Presented to the 4th International Congress of Egyptology, Munich, 1985," in *Amarna Studies and Other Selected Papers*, by Kate Bosse-Griffiths, OBO 182 (Fribourg: Presses Universitaires, 2001), 181–88; Christiane Müller-Hazenbos, "Eine Ptah-Sokar-Osiris-Statuette des *Ṯ3j-ḥ*ʿ*pj-n-im.w*," in *Begegnungen: Antike Kulturen im Niltal; Festgabe für Erika Endesfelder, Karl-Heinz Priese, Walter Friedrich Reinecke, Steffen Wenig*, ed. Caris-Beatrice Arnst and Angelika Lohwasser (Leipzig: Wodtke und Stegbauer, 2001), 365–72. The Ptah-Sokar-Osiris statues became a standard item in the burials of the Egyptian private tombs of Ptolemaic time, usually one statue per burial; Raven, "Papyrus-Sheaths and Ptah-Sokar-Osiris Statues," 254 and 257n24.

6. For example, Christiane Desroches-Noblecourt and Jean Vercoutter, *Un siècle de fouilles françaises en Égypte 1880–1980: À l'occasion du centenaire de l'École du Caire (IFAO)* (Paris: Musée du Louvre 1981), 322; Nigel Strudwick, *Masterpieces of Ancient Egypt* (London: British Museum, 2012), 296–97; Eleni Vassilika, *Masterpieces of the Museo Egizio in Turin* (Turin: Fondazione Museo delle antichità egizie di Torino, 2009), 115.

7. Only one example is known to the author, Raven, "Papyrus-Sheaths and Ptah-Sokar-Osiris Statues," 275.

8. Mostly on funerary stelae, Maj Sandman Holmberg, *The God Ptah* (Lund: C. W. K. Gleerup, 1946), 138; Edward Brovarski, "Sokar," *LÄ* 5:1055–58 and 1060.

9. Holmberg, *The God Ptah*, 139; Brovarski, "Sokar," 1061.

10. For this Atum Hymn, see Raven, "Papyrus-Sheaths and Ptah-Sokar-Osiris Statues," 276–81.

11. Katherine J. Eaton, "The Festival of Osiris and Sokar in the Month of Khoiak: The Evidence from Nineteenth Dynasty Royal Monuments at Abydos," *SAK* 35 (2006): 75–101; Louis B. Mikhail, "The Festival of Sokar: An Episode of the Osirian Khoiak Festival," *GM* 82 (1984): 25–44. See also Wolfgang Helck, "Zu Ptah und Sokar," in *Religion und Philosophie im alten Ägypten: Festgabe für Philippe Derchain zu seinem 65. Geburtstag am 24. Juli 1991*, ed. Ursula Verhoeven and Erhart Graefe, OLA 39 (Leuven: Department Orientalistiek, 1991), 159–64.

funerary papyri but also wrapped bundles of mummified body parts or soil with germinating grains of corn.[12] Germinating seeds are perhaps connected to the growing regard for the grain-Osiris figures which reached their zenith in the Ptolemaic period in both tomb and temple settings.[13] According to Aston, changing burial customs at Thebes from circa 750 to 675 BCE might have influenced the transition from Osiris figures to Ptah-Sokar-Osiris statues.[14]

The Johns Hopkins example can be classified under type IV of Raven's typology of "Ptah-Sokar-Osiris Statues with gilded face," closest to his IV E and IV F types, most dating to the Ptolemaic Period.[15] Dating based on stylistic features is less reliable, but the design of casket and coffin lid with a cavity in between is Ptolemaic.[16] The inscription on the front of the statue[17] identifies the owner as Horudja and his father as Pashermehet, who was probably the priest of Min represented on a stela from Akhmim.[18] During the Ptolemaic period, the cult of the gods Min and Osiris flourished in Akhmim, generating many stelae and funerary objects dedicated to them.[19] At the front of the statue, his mother is identified as Tasheretmin, indicating once more an association with the god Min of Akhmim. While the name Horudja is relatively common at many sites, at least among the owners of the Ptolemaic stelae gathered by Kamal and Munro, the name Tasheretmin occurs more frequently in Akhmim and the name Pashermin is attested only in Akhmim.[20] The style of the hieroglyphic inscription on the back pillar can be compared with a similar Ptah-Sokar-Osiris figure of a priest named Hor, son of Djedher. The inscriptions on the back pillar of that figure, located in the National Gallery of Victoria, exhibits similar orthography and strong indications of Akhmim provenance. [21] The unique combination of the gilded front and the polychrome back seems to be a feature of Akhmim manufacture.[22]

The overarching concept behind most ancient Egyptian funerary artifacts was resurrection and rebirth. These Ptah-Sokar-Osiris figures are no exception; undoubtedly, they were to ensure that the deceased would be resurrected. However, the physical appearance and textual evidence of such objects reveals in-depth information about the complex ideas underlying Egyptian resurrection beliefs. Although Osiris was obviously considered essential for rebirth and its eternal recurrence, the deceased was also associated with Sokar, a primarily chthonic god in close proximity to the Memphite necropolis of Ptah, which may have influenced his nature as a mortuary god at an early date.[23] This chthonic aspect is associated with the power of transfiguration or generative processes occurring underground.[24] These Ptah-Sokar-Osiris statues perhaps incorporate several conceptions of creation: Ptah's vertical creation/reani-

12. Raven, "Papyrus-Sheaths and Ptah-Sokar-Osiris Statues," 253n101.

13. Eaton, "Festival of Osiris and Sokar," 75–101; John H. Taylor, *Death and Afterlife in Ancient Egypt* (Chicago: University of Chicago Press, 2001), 212; Maartin Raven, "Corn-Mummies," *OMRO* 63 (1982): 7–38.

14. Aston, "Two Osiris Figures," 106; David A. Aston, "Tomb Groups from the End of the New Kingdom to the Beginning of the Saite Period" (PhD diss., University of Birmingham, 1987), 638–40.

15. Raven, "Papyrus-Sheaths and Ptah-Sokar-Osiris Statues," 269–71 and 276.

16. Raven, 287n261; Colin A. Hope, "A Head of Nefertiti and a Figure of Ptah-Sokar-Osiris in the National Gallery of Victoria," *Art Bulletin of Victoria* 24 (1983): 51.

17. See translation below.

18. RPN, 118; Alimal Kamal, *Stèles ptolémaiques et romaines (Catalogue général du Musée du Caire, 22001–22208)* (Cairo: Institut français d'archéologie orientale, 1905), 8–9. The stela is now in the Egyptian Museum, JE 26910= CG 22007.

19. Kamal, *Stèles ptolémaiques*, 1–5.

20. Peter Munro, *Die spätägyptischen Totenstelen*, ÄF 25 (Glückstadt: Augustin, 1973), 117–54 and 358–72; Kamal, *Stèles ptolémaiques*, 275–77.

21. Hope, "Head of Nefertiti," 51–52. The owner of that figure carried important titles such as stolist (of Min), the *imy-is* priest, the *ḥsk*-priest (of Osiris), stolist of Coptos, and the rare title of oracle-scribe, see Hope, "Head of Nefertiti," 49; Colin A. Hope, *Gold of the Pharaohs: An Exhibition Provided by the Egyptian Antiquities Organisation* (Melbourne: Museum of Victoria, 1989), 72–73. Also compare the inscriptions on the back of the damaged Swansea Ptah-Sokar-Osiris statue, Bosse-Griffiths, "Problems with Ptah-Sokar-Osiris Figure," fig. 2, 184–86, which specifically mentions Akhmim.

22. Theban models either showed the Ptah-Sokar-Osiris figures with painted front and back. If gilded, the foil covers only the face, sundisk, and collar.

23. Holmberg, *The God Ptah*, 124.

24. Brovarski, "Sokar," 1055–56. Even Osiris is said to be buried in the temple of Sokar, Holmberg, *The God Ptah*, 138n23.

mation aboveground and Sokar's horizontal creation/transfiguration belowground. The hymn further associates the deceased with the initial moment of creation of the cosmos from the primeval waters, thus associating with another creation aspect.

The size, intricate details, and the unique hymn to Atum suggest that these figures underwent a ritual before interment. The merging of Ptah, the divine artist and craftsman god, into the funerary realm might have guaranteed the successful reanimation and physical revival of the deceased. In the Coffin Texts, Ptah and Horus are responsible for the Opening of the Mouth Ritual and starting from the New Kingdom, Sokar replaces Horus in the Books of the Dead.[25] Ptah, and more specifically Ptah-Sokar, is responsible for the magical reanimation of the deceased's body parts. In funeral texts, Ptah-Sokar gives the deceased his two arms[26] and in another instance, Ptah-Sokar enables the deceased to "hold food in his hands."[27] In the Book of Breathing, Ptah "opens the eyes of the deceased just like he did for Sokar-Osiris in the House of Gold."[28] Ptah-Sokar empowers deceased individuals to use their hands to lift the mummy-masks from their faces or to join the mask together.[29] In the Book of the Dead, the deceased wishes that his feet could be like those of Ptah to "walk on water and tread on earth."[30]

This formidable syncretistic god of resurrection manifested in a three-dimensional coffin-like sculpture probably indicates that it may well have undergone a ritual similar to the Opening of the Mouth ceremony performed on the mummy to allow it to revive. The change from the Osiris papyrus sheath statuettes to Ptah-Sokar-Osiris figures also included a change in the design of the base, from trapezoid to consistently rectangular, perhaps reflecting the design of the magical bricks or the mound of Sokar.[31] The Ptah-Sokar-Osiris figures include representations of water on the four sides of the plinth and show evidence that some contained germinating seeds of grain inside.[32] This may perhaps imply that there was also a water ritual.

The introduction of the Ptah-Sokar-Osiris figures into the Late and Ptolemaic Egyptian burial assemblage is significant not only because the physical design was innovative but also because the figures illustrate the syncretic capabilities of Egyptian religion. The ancient Egyptians combined a wide spectrum of symbolic imagery to provide protection-by-invocation of a god encompassing all stages of death and rebirth. Both metaphorically and literally, the ancient Egyptians imbued such figures with the necessary information to guide the deceased in the afterlife.

Translation

Inscription on the front two columns (fig. 3)

1. *ḏd mdw in wsir ḥm-nṯr sš-nsw 1r-wḏ3 m3ˁ ḫrw s3 n wsir ḥm-nṯr sš-nsw P3-šr-Mḥt m3ˁ ḫrw*

Words spoken by the Osiris, the prophet, royal-scribe Horudja, true of voice, son of the Osiris, prophet, royal-scribe Pashermehet, true of voice,

25. Holmberg, 95–100.
26. Holmberg, 96.
27. Holmberg, 99.
28. Papyrus Berlin 3052, III, I; J. Claude Goyon, *Rituels funéraires de l'ancienne Égypte: Le rituel de l'embaumement, le rituel de l'ouverture de la bouche, les livres des respirations* (Paris: Éditions du Cerf, 1972), 253; Leitz, *LGG* VI, 667.
29. Holmberg, *The God Ptah*, 99–100.
30. Holmberg, 103–4.
31. For example, see the magical bricks among the burial assemblage of Henutmehyt, Strudwick, *Masterpieces of Ancient Egypt*, 214–16.
32. Raven, "Papyrus-Sheaths and Ptah-Sokar-Osiris Statues," 271 and 287.

Figure 3. Two vertical columns of Hieroglyphic inscription on the front of the statue. Image courtesy of the Johns Hopkins Archaeological Museum. Photograph by Lorraine Trusheim.

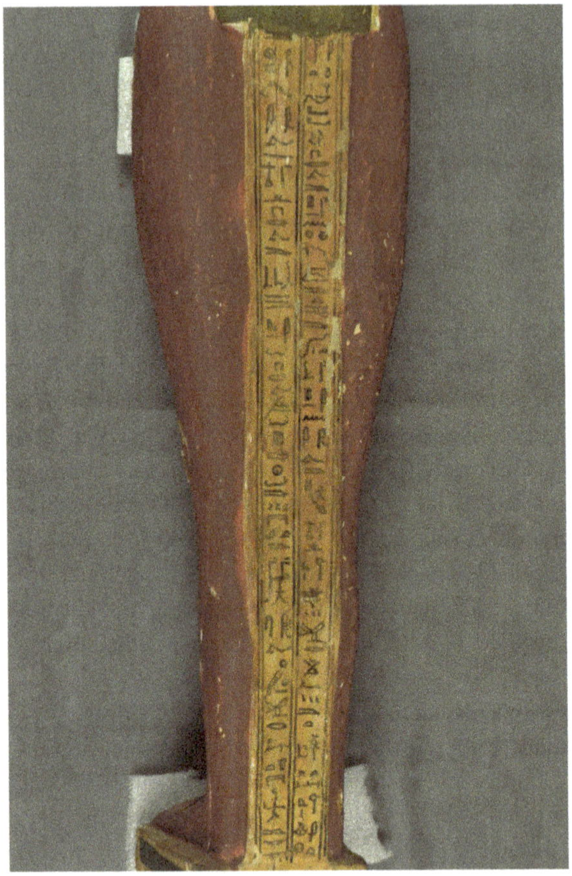

Figure 4. Two vertical columns of Hieroglyphic inscription on the back of the statue. Image courtesy of the Johns Hopkins Archaeological Museum. Photograph by Lorraine Trusheim.

2. *[ỉr n] nb.t pr ṯꜣ-sr.t-Mn mꜣꜥ ḫrw m-bꜣḥ wsỉr [ḫnty] ỉmntyw nṯr nfr nb ꜣbḏw*[33] *skr wsỉr nṯr nfr*

born to lady of the house, Tasheretmin, true of voice, in the presence of Osiris (foremost) of the westerners, good god, lord of Abydos, Sokar Osiris, the good god.

Inscription on the back two columns (fig. 4)

1. *ỉnḏ ḥr.k ỉwꜥ pr m nṯr pn nẖẖ*[34] *[p]r m m ṯm ḏ.t nṯr ỉpn*[35] *n ỉỉ.(tỉ) m wḥm nṯr nfr ḥḳꜣ tꜣ-wr(.t)*[36] *ḫꜥ m ỉꜣbtt ḥḳꜣ ꞌIg(r)t* [37]

33. The first sign of *ꜣbḏw* is puzzling; it resembles sign W8 in Gardiner's Sign List but it is not attested in the writing of *ꜣbḏw*.

34. *nẖẖ* for *nẖẖ*, "spittle," *Wb.* II:319, 4; Penelope Wilson, *A Ptolemaic Lexikon: A Lexicographical Study of the Texts in the Temple of Edfu*, OLA 78 (Leuven: Peeters, 1997), 543.

35. *nṯr ỉpn n* is awkward here. It could be understood as a variant for *nṯr pn ỉn* with *ỉn*.

36. *tꜣ-Wr(.t)* for *tꜣ-wr*, *Wb.* V:353, 5. The *t* sign is auxiliary.

37. A very common title of Osiris, *Wb.* I:141, 3–6; Wilson, *A Ptolemaic Lexikon*, 118.

Hail to you, heir who went forth from this god, spittle/fluid, which went forth from Atum from this divine body by returning again,[38] good god, ruler of Ta-Wer, who appeared in the East, the ruler of *Igrt* (the realm of the dead),

2. *m iḫḫ*[39] *ii.n nṯr nfr pr m ḥbb.t*[40] *iḳr.f pr dp.t.f psḏ.f m Nw.t*[41] *m s3ḥ šmsw iḫm- wrḏ*[42] *pt ḥ*ʿ*(ti)*[43] *m nb.s*[44]

in the twilight. The good god has arrived, he having gone forth from the primeval waters. He was effective when his boat went forth so that he might shine within Nut as Orion. The circumpolar stars follow, and the sky is joyful about her lord.

38. *m wḥm*= again, Wilson, *A Ptolemaic Lexikon*, 253.
39. The walking legs sign is a mistake for Gardiner sign N3, *Wb*. I:126, 4.
40. *Wb*. III:63, 3–5.
41. *Wb*. II:214, 1 and 215, 18.
42. *Wb*. I:125, 13–16 and *Wb*. III:279, 10.
43. Ha(ti), a stative, *Wb*. III:40, 2; 41, 2, with m= 41, 6.
44. The standard ending of the hymn (*imyw m hy s3-t3 n k3 n Wsir N. s3 nb s3.f*) is missing from our statue. The same is true for the inscription on the back pillar of the Ptah-Sokar-Osiris at the National Gallery of Victoria, C. Hope, "Head of Nefertiti," 50–51.

Richard at the Well

MICHAEL JASNOW

Very deep is the well of the past. Should we not call it bottomless?
Thomas Mann, *Joseph and His Brothers*[1]

When Richard's friend and colleague, Dr. Betsy Bryan, asked if I would write a few lines in honor of my brother, I of course said yes, I would be pleased, more than pleased, to do so. A wedding? A funeral? Aside from these, how often are you invited to honor your beloved brother? But how to honor him in a meaningful way? How to say something worthy of him, to speak alongside his colleagues who, after all, are so much better able to discuss his professional accomplishments, his life as teacher, mentor, and scholar? What can I say that will not descend into platitude? This difficulty is especially acute given the essential nature of Richard. As I know very well, and as his colleagues must also understand, Richard is the most modest of men. He avoids being the center of attention. He is almost certainly upset that I am writing about him at all. I will, however, assert the privilege belonging to older brothers and ignore his objections. Still, the problem remains. What can I say about Richard that will not morph into a best man's toast? His family loves and honors him? Yes, but that is to be expected. We are in awe of his scholarly attainments and the unceasing energies he applies to Demotic? Certainly, but there is nothing new to be learned in that direction.

However, in thinking about Richard, I understand there is no danger of falling into platitude. Yes, he is brilliant; it would be false modesty to deny this. I recall how surprised our very smart father was, when Richard, age ten, began to beat him at chess. But to acknowledge Richard's cognitive capacities is only a beginning, necessary but not sufficient. When we, his family, think of Richard, it is sometimes in his guise as an initiate, one who, having endured the rites, emerges from the temple to share his wisdom with the rest of us. My brother has the unusual gift of drawing from time's deep well and passing round the cup.

This sounds like hyperbole. I do not mean to be hyperbolic. I mean to convey what I know about my brother. Thinking about Richard, I think about time and love. Time sets the frame for human experience, and love is the capacity to resonate with the world. Human beings must learn to use time just as we learn to walk and talk. Time is the soil into which we sink our roots, and from which we thrust upward to the sky. In the 1930s, the Russian psychologist Lev Vygotsky described the steps that the child takes to break free from the present. The young child, around five years old, steps back from the present moment and, like a chick pecking through its shell, shatters the chains of the perceptual instant and begins to master the temporal field: time past, time present, and time future. It is only with this conquest of time that we become human.

This first conquest of time, this child's step, is only the necessary starting point. In thinking about Richard, I reflect upon what happens when daily life requires an entry into deep time. I know from my own work as a psychoanalyst that people relate to time in ways that are vastly different. And these differences are not trivial. Some people, for ex-

The author wishes to acknowledge with gratitude the valuable assistance of Benjamin Jasnow, Daniel Jasnow, and Jody Bolz.

1. Thomas Mann, *Joseph and His Brothers*, trans. H. T. Lowe-Porter (New York: Knopf, 1934).

ample, work very hard to live only in the present. The past is too disturbing, the future too frightening. But the more we make a feast of time, the more active our relationship to time, the higher the mountain of life, the further we see. What brings me up short, what is magical to me, is Richard's loving connection to what has been, his perspective on human experience as it has been lived in the deep past.

In Thomas Mann's Joseph tetralogy, it is the character's relationship to the past, to the present, and to the future that is key. There is particular time and there is mythic time, and they will not be kept apart; they are tangled like vines so grown together they can no longer be separated. Joseph and Jacob and all the many others are not pinned in particular time. They move back and forth between time past and time present. It is this special relationship to the deep well of time that nourishes the characters, gives them power, and endows them with a richness they could never attain if they moved only in the narrowly compassed present. Mann's characters shelter beneath the shadow of the past, resonate with it. There is nothing mystical in this, but there is much that is psychological.

Twenty-five years ago, as we sat together in an almost empty theater waiting for the movie to begin, Richard turned to me and in a strong voice called out "One god, one pot!" He then told me the story of the scribe's distress. The feathered god, Sacred Ibis, must be treated with reverence, not jammed one upon the other into a single pot like so many cheap trinkets. Every god merited its own pot. Amusing and tender was my brother's concern for the scribe—a scribe whose hand he could tell apart from all others. To reach back thousands of years and revive a fragment of a fragment of human experience is no small thing.

I also spoke of love. Love in its most expansive sense, love long as a great river. Richard's capacity for love is the source of his intellectual mastery. It is love that has channeled his mind and enlivened his career as teacher, mentor, and scholar. Just as it was Pygmalion's love for Galatea that brought the statue to life, that transformed a formal but lifeless beauty into a living being, it is Richard's capacity for love that must be given its due and celebrated here—Richard's love that gives rise to his generosity, his kindness, his lack of artifice, and his playfulness.

Such love does not come into the world unbidden. I was asked by Dr. Bryan to write a few lines in honor of Richard, but as I worked on this task, I came to understand that I was only the spokesman for his family, past and present, which wishes to join in celebrating him. Richard's capacity to touch the past with sympathy, to retrieve what is valuable, to animate what has been lost to time, is an outcome of being loved. Thus, those who shaped Richard are also present and crowd round, joyful in the honor you do him. Our grandmother Nina, indomitable and loving even with Cossacks in the living room, and her husband, our fabled grandfather Mischa, the gentle dentist turned sad-eyed candy-store owner. And of course, our parents: our father, Alexander, who taught Richard how to range over time's broad field—and then, our mother.

A true story. Richard and I are standing together surrounded by hundreds of people. It is a celebration, a graduation. Richard's nephew, my son, has graduated from college, and we, the family, are standing in Washington Square. Time to eat. The graduate knows a good place, and we take off with him in the lead. Heading east along Eighth Street, we cross Astor Place and pass The Cooper Union. My son leads on. Richard and I look at each other and tell the graduate that soon we will reach St. Mark's Place. Our mother, the graduate's grandmother, was born and raised in this neighborhood.

We cross Second Avenue and take a few more steps. Here, we are told, is where we will lunch. Richard and I are standing alongside each other in front of the three-story brownstone that houses the restaurant. We look, and, as we look, it becomes clear as the lustrous sky that the restaurant inhabits the same building where our mother was born, the building in which she lived until, in 1949, she married our father. It is the building in which her mother, Grandma Bea, a milliner, kept her hat shop. As Richard and I stand there, I picture the pressed tin ceiling sheltering hats with beautiful feathers. We go down the stairs and enter the restaurant. The sheltering ceiling is still there. Instead of hats, now, there is hummus.

We take our seats, unsettled by the strangeness of the moment. Richard takes charge of the proceedings. He takes his pen, a pen with a very fine point, and a piece of paper. Soon, the paper is graced with flowing script. The scribe writes in New Kingdom hieroglyphs. First, the scribe recites in the old tongue and then in English. The scribe requests that the gods, perhaps Thoth himself, keep the name of the scribe's mother, Eleanor, alive for all time.

The manager is asked for. We explain our need. He takes hold of the paper and disappears behind a curtain and down a flight of stairs. In the basement there is a wall. The wall is brick. There is a loose brick in this wall. Behind this loose brick, in the back where brick touches earth, the scribe's prayer is nestled. The cup is returned to the well.

Idrimi's Aunts at Emar: On Line 5 of the Idrimi Inscription

Jacob Lauinger

This chapter focuses on a passage in the Idrimi inscription in which the future king of Alalah and his brothers flee from their home city of Aleppo to the city of Emar on the Middle Euphrates. At Emar, the refugees stay with their maternal aunts (literally, "sisters of my mother"), who, curiously, are described as "men of Emar." In the seventy years since the inscription was first published,[1] scholars have offered various solutions for resolving this perceived contradiction. As shown in a review of the literature, however, none of these proposed solutions is entirely satisfactory. In this chapter, I argue that the description of Idrimi's aunts as "men of Emar" identifies them as resident aliens at that city. This interpretation, which derives from cuneiform texts from Middle and Late Bronze Age Syria, including Emar itself, shows how the Idrimi inscription reflects the sociopolitical reality of its time. As I discuss, it also fits well with a larger narrative strategy that is at work in this literary text. It is an honor to be able to offer this chapter in homage to my colleague Richard, who has been a mentor to me at Hopkins—both officially and unofficially! In the weight that the chapter considers a single word can carry, I hope it does justice to the spirit of inquiry that Richard has always modeled in both his research and teaching.

The text called the Idrimi inscription actually comprises two inscriptions that are carved onto the statue of a man that was found by Sir Leonard Woolley in 1939 at the site of Alalah, modern Tell Atchana, a site located near the great bend of the Orontes westward to the Mediterranean. One inscription of three lines in Akkadian cuneiform on the statue's cheek identifies the man as a king and requests blessings for him; another 101-line inscription on the statue's body, also in Akkadian cuneiform, identifies him as Idrimi, who is known from archival texts from Alalah as city's earliest historically attested king in the Late Bronze Age. This longer inscription tells a story in the first person of this king's life: How, as young refugee prince, he won a kingdom and then placed it on firm footing.[2] The narrative, however, seems to be pseudo-autobiographical. While the historical Idrimi most likely lived in the mid-fifteenth century BCE,[3] a reevaluation of Woolley's excavations records has shown that the findspot of the statue should be dated to the fourteenth century—that is, from fifty to one hundred years after the historical Idrimi.[4] Even though it is still possible that the inscription was composed and carved onto the statue during or shortly after Idrimi's lifetime, seven decades of scholarship have made clear that the narrative of Idrimi's life must nonetheless be considered a literary construction.[5]

---

1. Sidney Smith, *The Statue of Idri-mi*, Occasional Publications of the British Institute of Archaeology in Ankara 1 (London: British Institute of Archaeology in Ankara, 1949).

2. On the interaction between the two inscriptions, see Jacob Lauinger, "Discourse and Meta-discourse in the Statue of Idrimi and its Inscription," *MAARAV* 23 (2019): 19–38.

3. Eva von Dassow, *State and Society in the Late Bronze Age: Alalaḫ under the Mittani Empire*, SCCNH 17 (Bethesda, MD: CDL, 2008), 42

4. Amir Fink, *Late Bronze Age Tell Atchana (Alalakh): Stratigraphy, Chronology, History*, BAR-IS 2120 (Oxford: Archaeopress, 2010).

5. On this point, see, in particular, Gary Oller, "The Autobiography of Idrimi: A New Text Edition with Philological and Historical Commentary" (PhD diss., University of Pennsylvania; Philadelphia, 1977), 191–200; and Mario Liverani, "Leaving by Chariot for the Desert," in *Myth and Politics in Ancient Near Eastern Historiography* (Ithaca, NY: Cornell University Press, 2004).

Over the decades, the Idrimi inscription has received a great deal of scholarly attention, including many refinements to our understanding of its difficult text. Nonetheless, interpretive difficulties abound. Line 5 of the inscription presents one such difficulty. I give here the wider context of the line together with a literal translation:

3. *i-na* ^{uru}*ha-la-ab*^{ki} E$_2$ *a-bi-ia*	In Halab, my father's house,
4. *ma-ši-ik-tu*$_2$ *it-tab-ši u*$_3$ *hal-qa*$_3$*-nu* / IGI[6]	a criminal act occurred, so we fled before
5. LU$_2$-HA$_2$ ^{uru}*e-mar*^{ki} *a-ha-te*-HA$_2$	men of Emar, sisters
6. [*š*]*a um-mi-ia u*$_3$ *aš-ba-nu a-na* ^{uru}*e-mar*^{ki}	of my mother, and we stayed at Emar

The difficulty lies in the fact that, taken literally, the inscription seems to describe Idrimi's maternal aunts (*ahhāte ša ummiya*) as men from the city of Emar (*amīlī Emar*). Scholars have offered various solutions for resolving this perceived contradiction that approach it from either end of the equation; i.e., by arguing either that the "men" are not men or that the "sisters" are not sisters. I begin this chapter by discussing literature on the end of the line, the "sisters," before moving to the "men," and then offer my own interpretation, one that attempts to harmonize the social and political reality of the Late Bronze Age Syria with a literary understanding of the text.

One approach to resolving the seeming difficulty of Idrimi's mother's sisters being identified as men from Emar has been to read the string of signs *a-ha-te*-HA$_2$ not, as expected, as *ahhāte*, the plural oblique form of *ahātu*, "sister," but as an unusual form of the cognate noun *ahu*, "brother" (plural *ahhū*), so that that it is Idrimi's maternal uncles and not aunts who were "men of Emar." To my knowledge, the first scholar to make such an attempt was Matitiahu Tsevat. While he admitted that the word in question was formally *ahhāte*, "sisters," nonetheless, he understood it to refer to "the male population of the City of Emar" because the scribe "writes an elegant West Semitic style, pairing a masculine noun with a masculine noun and a feminine noun with another feminine noun."[7] This approach was taken still further by the *CAD*, whose editors claimed that the string actually was the lexeme *ahu*, "brother" with the suffix -*āte* being a West Semitic plural.[8] Not surprisingly, *CAD*'s suggestion is taken up in the translation of A. Leo Oppenheim, the editor-in-charge of the *CAD* at the time ("the people of Emar, brothers of my mother").[9]

However, Edward Greenstein and David Marcus objected to both Tsevat's and the *CAD*'s interpretations in their 1976 edition of the inscription.[10] Regarding the *CAD's* booking of the word as *ahu*, "brother," with a putative West Semitic plural suffix, they observed that the form "does not reflect West Semitic morphology ... since in WS 'brothers" is expressed *ʾahîm*." And regarding Tsevat's interpretation, they acknowledged more generally the stylistic feature to which he appealed but continued on to remark, "[u]nfortunately this feature does not apply in Idrimi since here we do not have a pairing of nouns according to gender, but a feminine noun *ahāte* in place of an expected masculine form."

---

6. The scholarship is evenly divided as to whether the IGI written at the end of l. 5 should be read logographically and understood to be a prepositional use of *pānu* that has run over from l. 4 (as transliterated above; i.e., *halqānu pān amīlī Emar ahhāte ša ummiya*, "We fled before the men of Emar, the sisters of my mother") or whether it should be read syllabically as -*ši*, taken at the end of l. 5, and understood to be the 3fs possessive pronominal suffix attached to *ahhāte* in a pleonastic genitive construction (i.e., *halqānu amīlū Emar ahhāteši ša ummiya*, "We fled. The men of Emar were sisters of my mother"). The reader will see both positions in the literature quoted below. This note is not the space to present a complete argument for the former, logographic, reading, but in my opinion, the strongest evidence in its favor has not yet been raised: In general, the line rulings in this quadrant of the Idrimi inscription match closely to the length of the lines themselves. However, in l. 5, the ruling very clearly terminates immediately above the plural determinative HA$_2$, implying that this sign marked the end of the line for the scribe and that the following IGI should be a continuation of the previous line that has run over.

7. Matitiahu Tsevat, "Alalakhiana," *HUCA* 29 (1958): 111.

8. *CAD* A/1 s.v. *ahu* A heading and mng. 1a–2′.

9. A. Leo Oppenheim, "The Story of Idrimi, King of Alalakh," in *The Ancient Near East in Texts and Pictures Relating to the Old Testament*, 3rd edition with supplement by James Pritchard (Princeton: Princeton University Press, 1969), 557.

10. Edward Greenstein and David Marcus, "The Akkadian Inscription of Idrimi," *JANES* 8 (1976): 67.

Other scholars have attempted to interpret the sign string *ah-ha-te*-HA_2 not as some form of *ahu*, "brother," but as a different cognate word. This approach is the one that was taken by Sidney Smith in his pioneering first edition of the text. Smith translated the string as "relatives" and parsed the form in his glossary to the text as "either n.f.s.coll., 'relations', or adj.f.pl. in error for m., 'related'."[11] Smith, then, understood the string as either an otherwise unattested collective noun or as a scribal mistake. More recently, Jean-Marie Durand argued that the string is "un mot nouveau" that is constructed off of the plural of *ahu*, "brother," with the feminine case ending used to form an abstract noun: "Il s'agit d'un vocable *ahhâtum* (plutôt qu'*ahhatum*?) abstrait en *-atum*, construit sur le thème de pluriel, qui affirme que tous ces gens sont des *ahhû*."[12] He considered this word to mean something like "fraternity, brotherly relations" and suggested that it was synonymous with *athūtu*, another cognate of *ahu*, "brother," that is fairly well attested in the second millennium. For a parallel to his proposed **ahhātu*, Durand pointed to the word *abbūtu*, "fatherhood, patronage," which is built off *abbū*, the plural of *abu*, "father," though with the abstract suffix *-ūtu*(*m*). This parallel, though, also highlights a potential difficulty with Durand's proposal in that abstracts formed with the feminine case ending are generally derived from adjectives; e.g., *damiqtu*, "favor, good fortune," < *damqu*, "good," or *kīnātu*, "truth, justice" < *kīnu*, "true."[13] In the end, both Smith's and Durand's interpretations of the sign string as something other than *ahhātu*, "sisters," require us to posit otherwise unattested words, and so neither interpretation is entirely satisfying.

A third attempt to see the sisters as something other than sisters was put forward by Albrecht Goetze in his review of Sidney Smith's edition of the inscription.[14] Goetze translated *a-ha-te*-HA_2 *ša um-mi-ia* as "my mother's side," adding the remark, "*ahāte* for *ahiāti(m)*." By this comment, Goetze evidently meant to communicate that he understood the string *a-ha-te*-HA_2 not to be a form of the noun *ahātu*, "sister," or even *ahu*, "brother," but rather to be a different word altogether, *ahītu*, "side," that is attested in the plural with the meaning "acquaintances, dependents."[15] Goetze's suggestion seems unlikely, however, because the majority of the attestations of the word with this meaning date to the Old Babylonian Period/Middle Bronze Age, (and so all display an uncontracted form of the plural, *ahiātu*(*m*), not a contracted form **ahâtu*(*m*) as the string would have to be interpreted in this line). Furthermore, as Durand has remarked, the interpretation also seems "invraisemblable sémantiquement" within the larger context of the passage, as "c'est la mère qui devrait plutôt être dite appartenir à la population d'Émar."[16]

Finally, a number of scholars have translated the string as "relatives" without any comment, and so it is impossible to know whether they are following Smith, Goetze, or have some other justification in mind.[17]

None of the suggestions offered to explain the string *a-ha-te*-HA_2 as referring to anything other than the sisters (*ahhāte*) of Idrimi's mother is convincing. Indeed, the various suggestions that have been put forward seem to be driven primarily by a feeling about what the text should say. Even Greenstein and Marcus, who raised the objections

---

11. Sidney Smith, *The Statue of Idri-mi*, 15, 95. In the glossary of his study of the Akkadian dialect of Alalah, George Giacumakis simply provided the lexeme *ahātu*, "sister," with a sense "relatives," though he cited under it only this attestation from the Idrimi inscription; see George Giacumakis, *The Akkadian of Alalah* (Paris: Mouton, 1977), 65.

12. Jean-Marie Durand, "La fondation d'une lignée royale syrienne. Le geste d'Idrimi d'Alalah," in *Le jeune héros: Recherches sur la formation et la diffusion d'un thème littéraire au Proche-Orient ancien*, ed. Jean-Marie Durand, Thomas Römer, and Michael Langlois (Fribourg: Academic Press; Göttingen: Vandenhoeck & Ruprecht, 2011), 114.

13. *GAG* § 60a and 61p

14. Albrecht Goetze, Review of *The Statue of Idri-mi*, by S. Smith, *JCS* 4 (1950): 227.

15. *CAD* A/1 s.v. *ahītu* mng. 5; see now also *AbB* 13 78 note b and the texts cited there. This meaning does not appear to be in *AHw* (pp. 20b–21a) but has been added to the *CDA*'s updated English-language translation of *AHw*'s entries; see *CDA* s.v. *ahītu* mng. 3.

16. Durand, "La fondation d'une lignée royale syrienne," 114n68.

17. Three examples that attempt to be somewhat chronologically and linguistically representative: Giorgio Buccellati, "La 'carriera' di Davide e quella di Idrimi, re di Alalac," *Bibbia e Oriente* 4 (1962): 95 ("parenti di mia madre"); Marie-Joseph Seux, "L'inscription d'Idrimi (vers 1550–1500 av. J.-C.)," in *Textes du Proche-Orient ancien et histoire d'Israël* (Paris: Cerf, 1977), 43 ("relations de ma mère"); Edward Greenstein, "Autobiographies in Ancient Western Asia," in *Civilizations of the Ancient Near East*, vol. 4., ed. Jack M. Sasson (New York: Scribner' Sons, 1995), 2426 ("relatives of my mother").

to the interpretations of Tsevat and the *CAD* discussed above, continued in their note to the line, "Tesvat is probably correct that the text intends to denote the male population," translating, evidently *ad sensum*, "'My mother's relatives,' lit., 'my mother's sisters.'"[18] But since there is no compelling reason, either external or internal to the text, to interpret the string *a-ha-te*-HA_2 as anything other than *aḫḫāte*, "sisters," it seems sensible for the moment to follow those scholars who have done just that.[19] At the end of this chapter, we will see that a literary approach to the passage lends additional support to this reading.

For now, let us turn to the first half of the line, the logogram LU_2-HA_2, to be normalized as *amīlī* or, perhaps, *amīlūti* under the influence of West Semitic.[20] Although Smith translated *amīlī* as "men," in which he was followed by Buccellati,[21] many subsequent editors have understood the plural form more generally as "people, population" (even as they simultaneously translated *a-ha-te*-HA_2 with the gender-neutral word "relatives" and thus obviated any need to avoid translating *amīlī* as "men").[22] The translation of *amīlī* as "people, population" reflects a common pairing in Akkadian of *amīlu/ū* with a toponym as a way of indicating the relationship of a person or group of people to a place. However, a general translation "people, population of Emar" overlooks that this phrase frequently carried with it some political sense.

One such sense found throughout Akkadian texts of the second millennium is the use of the phrase *amīl* + toponym to designate the ruler of a city,[23] and beginning with Albrecht Goetze in 1957, a number of scholars have attempted to see the phrase *amīlī* Emar in the Idrimi inscription as an example of this sense.[24] One immediate difficulty with this interpretation, though, is that the word *amīlu* is invariably in the singular when it is paired with a toponym to designate the toponym's ruler, yet *amīlu* is plural in the Idrimi inscription. To be sure, one senses some awareness of this problem in the scholarship, with concomitant attempts to navigate around it. For instance, Manfried Dietrich and Oswald Loretz translated, "Die Herren von Emar stammten von des Schwestern ...," thus understanding the

---

18. Greenstein and Marcus, "The Akkadian Inscription of Idrimi," 71.

19. William Foxwell Albright, "Some Important Recent Discoveries: Alphabetic Origins and the Idrimi Statue," *BASOR* 118 (1950): 16; Rykle Borger, "Die Statueinschrift des Idrimi von Alalach (um 1400 v. Chr.)," in *Textbuch zur Geschichte Israels*, ed. Kurt Galling (Tübingen: Mohr Siebeck, 1968), 22; Oller, *The Autobiography of Idrimi*, 9, 24–25; Manfried Dietrich and Oswald Loretz, "Die Inschrift des Königs Idrimi von Alalah," *UF* 13 (1981): 204, 210; Manfried Dietrich and Oswald Loretz, "Historisch- Chronologische Texte aus Alalah, Ugarit, Kamid el-Loz/Kumidi und den Amarna Briefe," in *Historisch- Chronologische Texte* II, ed. Otto Kaiser, TUAT 1/5 (Gütersloh: Gütersloher Verlagshaus, 1985), 502.

20. Dietrich and Loretz, "Die Inschrift des Königs Idrimi von Alalah," 210, pointing to the syllabic spellings of *abu*, "father," in the plural later in the inscription as *a-bu-te*-HA_2 (ll. 47–48).

21. Smith, *The Statue of Idri-mi*, 15; Buccellati, "La 'carriera' di Davide e quella di Idrimi, re di Alalac," 95.

22. E.g., Goetze, " Review of The Statue of Idri-mi, by S. Smith," 227; Tsevat, "Alalakhiana," 111; Mario Liverani, "Il fuoroscitismo in Siria nella tarde età del bronzo," *Rivista storica italiana* 77 (1965): 322; Oppenheim, " The Story of Idrimi, King of Alalakh," 557; Greenstein and Marcus, " The Akkadian Inscription of Idrimi," 67; Oller, The Autobiography of Idrimi, 9; Greenstein, " Autobiographies in Ancient Western Asia," 2426; Tremper Longman, *Fictional Akkadian Autobiography: A Generic and Comparative Study* (Winona Lake, IN: Eisenbrauns, 1991), 216; Daniel Snell, *Flight and Freedom in the Ancient Near East*, CHANE 8 (Leiden: Brill, 2001), 109; Jordi Vidal, "Summaries on Young Idrimi," *Scandinavian Journal of the Old Testament* 26 (2012): 82; Mario Liverani. *The Ancient Near East: History, Society, Economy* (Hoboken: Taylor & Francis, 2013), 332.

23. *AHw* 90b; *CAD* A/2 s.v. *amīlu* mng. 4d.

24. Albrecht Goetze, "The Syrian Town of Emar," *BASOR* 147 (1957): 22n2; Rykle Borger, "Die Statueinschrift des Idrimi von Alalach (um 1400 v. Chr.)," 22; Aaron Kempinski and Nadav Na'aman, "The Idrimi Inscription Reconsidered," in *Ḥafirot u-meḥkarim*, ed. Yohanan Aharoni (Tel Aviv: Hotsaʾat ha-Makhon le-arkheʾologyah ʿal yedei Karṭa, 1973) 211; Marie-Joseph Seux, "L'inscription d'Idrimi (vers 1550–1500 av. J.-C.)," 43; Dietrich and Loretz, "Die Inschrift des Königs Idrimi von Alalah," 204; Horst Klengel, "Historisch Kommentar zur Inschrift des Idrimi von Alalah," *UF* 13 (1981): 273–74; Dietrich and Loretz, "Historisch-Chronologische Texte aus Alalah," 502; Daniel Fleming, "A Limited Kingship: Late Bronze Emar in Ancient Syria," *UF* 24 (1991): 70–71; Jean-Marie Durand, "La fondation d'une lignée royale syrienne," 135.

plurality of rulers to exist in time and not space.[25] But the verb *stammen*, on which this understanding depends, is not actually in the Akkadian text. Daniel Fleming, on the other hand, noted "th[e] absence of Imar kings in the 18th century" and "the impression from the 13th-century archives that kingship is there a relatively new feature of Emar society," and thus saw the Idrimi inscription as evidence of a transitory stage in the fifteenth century in the development of Emar's monarchy: "The word LÚ (*awīlu*) commonly refers to the city ruler in western Akkadian texts from the second millennium, and here the plural gives the impression of a leading family more than a single dominant (so, named) king."[26] In the absence of any additional evidence on Emar's monarchy in the early Late Bronze Age, though, Fleming's speculation can only remain such, and one cannot shake the suspicion that its trajectory may be overly evolutionary.

With his translation of *amīlī Emar* as "des nobles d'Emar," Durand seems to stand with this subset of scholars.[27] In fact, though, his discussion of Idrimi's sojourn at Emar provides the key to seeing the phrase with a different political sense. To understand how, we must proceed a few lines further into the inscription to a point where Idrimi, still at Emar, has the realization that motivates him to leave the city and begin his quest to gain a kingdom. Even if the lines in question, 10–12, are among the more difficult in the entire inscription, their overall sense is clear: Idrimi contrasts a person who stands in some positive relation to his patrimonial inheritance (literally, "the house of his father," E_2 *a-bi-šu*, l. 10) with his own present condition ("Who is indeed a slave to the sons of Emar?" *ma-an-nu-um a-na* DUMU-HA_2 ^{uru}*e-mar*^{ki} *lu-u*$_2$ ARAD, ll. 11–12).

For Durand, the contrast between these two persons that Idrimi draws is ultimately one of citizenship: "lorsque Idrimi réfléchit au sort de la personne, c'est bien d'avoir une place dans la société ... il faut néanmoins appartenir à un *bît abi*, car on est alors un citoyen, un «dumu» (*mâru* = «fils»), de la cité."[28] In contrast, a "slave" is "plutôt de «celui qui est venu proposer localement ses services» et qui correspond au *wardum*, le « descendu» (de *warâdum* «descendre») au service de quelqu'un. Il n'a pas le statut de «dumu» de la ville (*mâru* en termes babyloniens) et ne participait donc pas aux instances politiques ni aux décisions qu'elles prenaient. »[29] Having lost Aleppo, his patrimonial inheritance, and fled to Emar, then, Idrimi will forever be an outsider dependent on others, a "slave" ((*w*)*ardu*), in the eyes of the "sons" of that city (*mārī Emar*).

It is this contrast between a "slave" and the "sons of Emar" in ll. 10–12 that suggests another political sense for the description of Idrimi's mother's sisters as "men of Emar" only a few lines earlier. Texts from Middle and Late Bronze Age Syria-Palestine show a careful differentiation between the "sons" of a city and the "men" of a city, with the former term designating the citizenry who participated in collective decision making and the latter designating any inhabitant of the place. In his analysis of collective governance at Middle Bronze Age Mari, Fleming originally suggested the opposite, being led in this direction by letters that describe "sons" of various cities as "human resources" used for work crews "who must be counted in a census and who likewise swear a loyalty oath."[30] But being counted in a census and required to take a loyalty oath are political acts of belonging par excellence and mark the "sons" of the city as its citizenry much more than as simply human resources to be deployed. I have found a similar use of terminology in texts from Middle Bronze

25. Dietrich and Loretz, "Die Inschrift des Königs Idrimi von Alalah," 204; so also Dietrich and Loretz, "Historisch-Chronologische Texte aus Alalah," 502.

26. Daniel Fleming, "A Limited Kingship," 70–71.

27. Unless he means by "des nobles" to give *amīlu* the meaning "freier Bürger" (*AHw*, 90b) or "free man, gentleman" (*CAD* A/2 s.v. *amīlu* mng. 3) with which it is most famously found in the Code of Hammurabi? But this meaning is temporally restricted to the early second millennium; see Eva von Dassow, "Freedom in Ancient Near Eastern Societies," in *The Oxford Handbook of Cuneiform Culture*, ed. Karen Radner and Eleanor Robson (Oxford: Oxford University Press, 2011), 213.

28. Durand, "La fondation d'une lignée royale syrienne," 111.

29. Durand, 112–13.

30. Daniel Fleming, *Democracy's Ancient Ancestors: Mari and Early Collective Governance* (Cambridge: Cambridge University Press, 2004), 189.

Age Alalah, and Brendan Benz has recognized it in the Amarna Letters, where it reflects the sociopolitical conditions of the Late Bronze Age Levant.[31]

And one of the clearest examples of the indigenous division of a city's population into its "sons," who could participate in civic decision making, and the other residents, who could not, comes from Emar itself. As is well known, the archival cuneiform documentation at Emar falls into one of two types, the so-called Conventional and Free-Format traditions.[32] While originally the reason for the presence of two traditions at the city was thought to be simply the result of a chronological development, in fact the traditions overlapped and coexisted. In a perceptive study, Sophie Démare-Lafont and Daniel Fleming have explained the reason for this coexistence: "The people of Emar consciously distinguished between a population identified with the city as such and others who were resident without belonging to the city and enjoying the prerogatives of that status."[33] The former population group, whom Démare-Lafont and Fleming refer to as "townsmen," were named "sons" of Emar in the texts and had recourse to tablets of Conventional format to record their economic activity; the latter population group, whom Démare-Lafont and Fleming refer to as "peregrines," had recourse to Free Format tablets.

I suggest that the phrase *amīlī Emar* in l. 5 identifies Idrimi's aunts as belonging to this latter population group. To my knowledge, the peregrines or resident aliens are not given a specific designation in the extant documentation at Emar surveyed by Démare-Lafont and Fleming, and herein might lie an objection to extending this understanding to the *amīlī Emar* in l. 5: It runs the risk of being an *argumentum ab absentia*, in that it derives as much from the fact that Idrimi's maternal aunts are not described as "sons of Emar" as from the fact that they are described as "men" of that same city. But this risk is mitigated if not avoided by the passage in ll. 10–12, especially as elucidated by Durand, discussed above, where Idrimi's description of his current status as a "slave" of the "sons of Emar" directs us to a reading of *amīlī Emar* as residents at the city who cannot participate in civic life. Presumably, if *amīlī Emar* signified that his aunts were among the city's elite, he would have had this access.

Indeed, understanding *amīlī Emar* in l. 5 to mean "resident aliens at Emar" fits well with the passage's larger literary context. A set of positive : negative binaries runs through Idrimi's early history, before he embarks on his adventure:

father : mother

Aleppo : Emar

inheritance : no inheritance

A contrast between the "sons of Emar," who participate in the city's civic life, and the "men of Emar," the resident aliens who cannot, maps readily onto this set:

citizen : resident alien.

Idrimi, of course, is the hero who, in ll. 10–12, recognizes this binary—in contrast to his brothers:

Idrimi : his brothers

and so leaves Emar to reclaim his inheritance:

action : inaction.

Indeed, recognizing the binaries at work in this part of the inscription actually provides another compelling reason to interpret the string *a-ha-te*-HA_2 as the expected *ahhāte*, "sisters," since it creates a further binary in the text:

brothers : sisters.

31. Jacob Lauinger, *Following the Man of Yamhad: Settlement and Territory at Old Babylonian Alalah*, CHANE 75 (Leiden: Brill, 2015), 129–31; Brendan Benz, *The Land before the Kingdom of Israel: A History of the Southern Levant and the People who Populated It*. History, Archaeology, and Culture of the Levant 7 (Winona Lake, IN: Eisenbrauns, 2016), 72.

32. Frequently called "Syrian" and "Syro-Hittite"; for arguments against these designations, see Daniel Fleming and Sophie Démare-Lafont, "Tablet Terminology at Emar: 'Conventional' and 'Free Format'," *AuOr* 27 (2009): 19–26.

33. Sophie Démare-Lafont and Daniel Fleming, "Emar Chronology and Scribal Streams: Cosmopolitanism and Legal Diversity," *RA* 109 (2015): 60.

By staying at Emar—by their inaction—Idrimi's brothers remain in the realms of sisters, heightening the contrast with Idrimi. We might even say that, to some extent, they transform into sisters, for, tellingly, the next time we meet these brothers in the inscription, Idrimi has won his kingdom, and they have joined him as his dependents ("My brothers heard and came to me. My brothers labored with me, and I protected my brothers," ŠEŠ.MEŠ-*ia iš-mu-*u_2-*ma* u_3 *a-na mah-ri-ia il-li-ku-*u_2 *ah-he-*HA_2*-ia it-ti-ia-ma in-na-hu-*u_2 *ah-*he_2-HA_2*-ia aṣ-ṣur-šu-nu*, ll. 39–42).

For our part, recognizing the binaries at work in the inscription helps us understand why Idrimi's aunts, his mother's sisters, are identified as *amīlī Emar*. They are outsiders at the city, and this identification serves as part of a larger narrative strategy of the inscription to cast Idrimi into the role of "fugitive hero," thereby helping to justify his rule over Alalah.[34] Of course, the existence of this narrative strategy means that we cannot mine the inscription for historical nuggets.[35] For instance, we cannot conclude that the historical Idrimi was a younger brother—or even that he had brothers at all—because the inscription states it. However, such an awareness does not mean the inscription has no historical value. On the contrary, it is of enormous value for studying the cultural matrix in which the inscription was created. In the case of Idrimi's aunts at Emar, we see the great importance placed on citizenship and belonging in the social and political world of Late Bronze Age Syria.

34. For Idrimi as fugitive hero, see Edward Greenstein, "The Fugitive Hero Narrative Pattern in Mesopotamia," in *Worship, Women, and War: Essays in Honor of Susan Niditch*, ed. John Collins, T. M. Lemos, and Saul Olyan, Brown Judaic Studies 357 (Providence: Brown Judaic Studies, 2015), 22–24.

35. The position is not new; see n. 5 above.

Gift Giving, Generosity, and the Etymology of Manna

THEODORE J. LEWIS

As they wandered in the desert, the hungry "riffraff" (*hāʾsapsup*) mentioned in Numbers 11, rather than being grateful for their liberation, felt an "intense craving" (*hitʾawwuˆ taʾăwāh*) for a particular Egyptian food about which Richard Jasnow has often (he says daily) remarked with disfavor: fish! Numbers 11:5–6 reads:

> We remember the fish we ate in Egypt for nothing, the cucumbers, the melons, the leeks, the onions, and the garlic; but now our gullets are dried up. There is nothing at all! Nothing but this *manna* (*mān*) to look to!

What is this fish alternative called *manna*?

A Tale of Divine Providence Found in Exodus 16

The nature and etymology of manna has long been a concern for scholars with Paul Maiberger even devoting two volumes to the subject.[1] This is understandable because a folk (or literary[2]) etymology in Exodus 16 teases the reader to want to know more.

> 4Then the LORD said to Moses, "Behold, I will rain food from heaven for you; and the people shall go out and gather a day's portion every day ..." 8Moses said (to the people): "It is the LORD who will give you meat to eat in the evening and bread in the morning, abundant in nature (*lāśōbaʿ*) ..." The LORD spoke ... 12"By evening you shall eat meat, and in the morning you shall have your fill (*tiśbĕʿuˆ*) of bread that you may know that I the LORD am your God ..."
>
> 13In the evening quail came up and covered the camp; and in the morning there was a fall of dew[3] about the camp. 14And when the fall of dew lifted, there was on the surface of the wilderness a fine, flake-like substance, as fine as frost on the ground. 15When the Israelites saw it, they said to one another, "What is it?" (*mān hūʾ*)—for they did not know what it was (*mah hûʾ*). And Moses said to them, "It is the food which the LORD has given you to eat ..."

---

1. Paul Maiberger, *Das Manna: Eine literarische, etymologische und naturkundliche Untersuchung*, ÄAT 6/1, 6/2 (Wiesbaden: Harrassowitz, 1983). A condensed version can be found in Paul Maiberger, "*mān*," *TDOT* 8:389–95.

2. Houtman observes that it is more helpful to think of such usages as examples of literary etymologies rather than the commonly used category of folk etymology. See Cornelis Houtman, *Exodus, Vol. 1*, Historical Commentary on the Old Testament (Leuven: Peeters, 1993), 72–73 and Cornelis Houtman, *Exodus, Vol. 2: Chapters 7:14–19:25*, Historical Commentary on the Old Testament (Leuven: Peeters, 1996), 339n83.

3. The translation of *šikbat haṭṭal* as "a fall (or outpouring) of dew" follows those translations (e.g., JPS, RSV) and scholars (e.g., Houtman, *Exodus*, 2:45, 336) who see the root *škb* with the meaning of "'(the act of) lying down,' [extended to a] 'deposit,' 'discharge.'" See Harry M. Orlinski, "The Hebrew Root *škb*," *JBL* 63 (1944): 36–39. An alternative is to translate "a layer of dew" with dew "lying" on the ground as does Propp. See William H. C. Propp, *Exodus 1–18*, Anchor Bible 2 (New York: Doubleday, 1999), 583, 586. The former is to be preferred due to the motif of how dew descends (√*yrd*; √*npl*; Num 11:9; 2 Sam 17:12; Ps 133:30) from the heavens (Gen 27:28, 39; Deut 33:13, 28; Prov 3:20; Zech 8:12; Dan 4:12, 20, 30; 5:21). See B. Otzen, "*ṭal*,"in *TDOT* 5:323–26.

> [31]The house of Israel named it *manna* (*mān*); it was like coriander seed, white, and the taste of it was like wafers (?) (made) with honey. [32]And Moses said, "This is what the LORD has commanded: 'Let one *omer* of it be kept throughout your generations, that they may see the food with which I fed you in the wilderness, when I brought you out from the land of Egypt.'"
>
> Exod 16:4, 8, 12–15, 31–32

Even though the immediate context five times defines manna as a divine gift of food (*hûʾ halleḥem ʾăšer nātan yhwh lākem lĕʾoklāh*) in a time of need, scholars have looked far and wide for the etymology and botanical nature of manna. The lure is the folk (or literary) etymology that has the people responding, "what is it?" (*mān hūʾ*) in their initial deliberations about the unknown substance that they subsequently call "*manna*" (*mān*). Other biblical traditions in Deut 8:3, 16 also stress the unknown nature of the *manna* substance that God fed their ancestors.

Whether the expressions *mān hūʾ* ... *mah hûʾ* in Exodus 16:15 were meant to be perplexing, poetic, or playful, there is one thing *mān* is not: It is not a precise horticultural term. The taxonomic details come in two other verses where the author felt the need to describe the physical properties of the unknown *mān*-substance in detail together with how it tasted (Exod 16:14, 31; cf. Num 11:7–8). These physical properties were not inherent to the word itself whose meaning must have been generic. Hence the need for additional descriptors by our author. Curiously, modern interpreters have consistently privileged finding a botanical explanation for *mān* that would correlate with the descriptions of its physical properties rather than looking at the author's rhetoric. And the rhetoric is crystal clear: the author chose a word whose etymology perfectly fit his context of divine gift giving.

Three Primary Approaches to the Etymology of Manna

There is no need to provide an inventory of the many proposals for the etymology of Hebrew *mān, mann-*, and Aramaic *mannāʾ* as Maiberger has collected these for us.[4] What is fascinating to observe though is how the search for etymologies tells us much more about reception history. Of the many etymologies, three deserve consideration, one from the root *mnh*, two from the root *mnn*.

One of the earliest etymological roots suggested was *mnh*, "to count, allot, remit" with the related nouns *mānāh*, "share, portion, choice portion" and *māneh*, "*mina*-measurement." Maiberger traces this understanding back to the Amoraim of the fifth century and suggests that it could go back as early as the first century BCE (Wis 16:20). The notion of *manna* as a portion or gift from God, according to Maiberger, received wide support among Jewish medieval exegetes (Rashi, Ibn Ezra, Qimhi) and "was accepted by almost all Christian theologians and predominated into the past century."[5] (Maiberger highlights Martin Luther.) Despite such a lengthy reception history, the frequent (though not universal) doubling of the *n* in the word *manna* (easily seen in Targumic Aramaic *mannāʾ*, Syriac *manĕnāʾ*, Arabic *manna*, LXX *manna*) argues against a final weak root (*mnh*; but cf. *manĕkā* in some mss of Neh 9:20 as opposed to *mannĕkā* in others) and in favor of a geminate root (*mnn*).

Along a similar benevolent line of thinking, a second suggestion looks to the root *mnn* to underscore the nature of *manna* as a divine gift. Morphologically, Hebrew *man*/*mān*, Aramaic *mannāʾ*, and Arabic *manna* constitute a regular monovocalic **qall* noun pattern used of geminate roots.[6] As noted by Maiberger, connecting the Hebrew and Aramaic words for *manna* to the Arabic root *manna* (and divine benevolence) dates back as early as 1661.[7] The Qurʾanic

4. Maiberger, *Das Manna*, 280–308; Maiberger, "*mān*," 389–93. For a dedicated study of the Targumic Aramaic *mannāʾ* traditions, see Bruce J. Malina, *The Palestinian Manna Tradition: The Manna Tradition in the Palestinian Targums and Its Relationship to the New Testament Writings*, Arbeiten zur Geschichte des Spätjudentums und Urchristentums 7 (Leiden: Brill, 1968).

5. Maiberger, "*mān*," 390; Maiberger, *Das Manna*, 280–81.

6. See Joshua Fox, *Semitic Noun Patterns*, HSS 52 (Winona Lake, IN: Eisenbrauns, 2003), 126, 132; Hans Bauer and Pontus Leander, *Historische Grammatik der hebräischen Sprache des Alten Testamentes* (Tübingen: Niemeyer, 1922), 453.

7. Maiberger, *Das Manna*, 282–83; Maiberger, "*mān*," 390–91.

manna passages (Q Baqarah 2:57; Q Aʿraf 7:160; Q Taha 20:80–81) had laid the foundation for this view with their language of God providing good food to eat. As can be seen from early (e.g., Jawhari, Ibn Manzur, Firuzabadi, Zabidi) to modern (e.g., Wehr) Arabic lexica, the verb *manna* means "to be benevolent, gracious, kind" as well as "to bestow, confer, or grant benevolence or benefits." Related nouns and adjectives include *manna* (gift, favor, blessing, gracious bestowal), *minna* (benevolence, kindness, benignity), *mannān* (benign, generous), *mamnūn* (indebted, grateful, thankful), *mamnūnīya* (indebtedness, gratitude), *mumtann* (indebted), and *imtinān* (indebtedness, gratitude). To underscore its ancient pedigree, as we will show below, the root *mnn* is also attested from Late Bronze Age sources (Amarna Canaanite, Western Akkadian, Ugaritic).

The third etymological option for *manna* is a subset of the second, looking again to the Arabic root *mnn*, but specifically to a plant named *mann*. Maiberger (citing Šihāb al-Nuwairī [1279–1332]), notes how early Arabic understandings "enumerate[d] thirteen different kinds of *manna* ... which [due to the natural products having a thin layer] ... were assumed to have fallen from heaven."[8] Among these, the tamarisk-*manna* has captured the attention of modern interpreters from the early nineteenth century to the present, especially those looking to posit a naturalistic explanation underlying the miraculous biblical narrative.[9] Whereas Heinrich Friedrich Wilhelm Gesenius's 1833 Latin edition of his famous Hebrew lexicon has a brief reference to the tamarisk tree, subsequent editions of his lexicon (e.g. in 1846 and 1857 published after Gesenius's death in 1842) elaborated noting that "some British naturalists [quoting Hardwick] have *proved* that certain insects ... aid in producing the manna" and this claim "has since been more exactly *confirmed* by Ehrenberg" (emphasis mine).[10] Such language of "proving" and "confirming" a naturalistic explanation for the biblical manna struck a nerve, as the following bracketed editorial addition (author not listed) is appended in these same editions: "[No one who simply credits the inspired history of the giving of manna can doubt that it was something *miraculously* given to the Israelites, and that it differed in its nature from anything now known"] (emphasis original).[11]

Enter Edward Robinson. Robinson's name is well known for his work in Greek and Hebrew lexicography.[12] As to the latter, Robinson was a student and close friend of Gesenius and was the person responsible for translating the 1833 Latin version of Gesenius lexicon into English in 1836 and editing the 1854 revision. The 1833 Latin version has come down to us today as it served as the basis for the Brown, Driver, Briggs (BDB) version of Gesenius, a stan-

---

8. Maiberger, "*mān*," 392; Maiberger, *Das Manna*, 300–304.

9. The extensive literature, dating back to Josephus, has nicely been gathered by Maiberger, *Das Manna*, 356–409; Maiberger, "*mān*," 392–93. Josephus's mention of manna existing in the Sinai in his day (*Ant.* 3.1.6) had previously been noted by Edward Robinson, *Biblical Researches in Palestine, Mount Sinai and Arabia Petraea: A Journal of Travels in the Year 1838 Undertaken in Reference to Biblical Geography*, vol. 1 (Boston: Crocker & Brewster, 1841), 590 n. xv.

10. The two authors being referred to are: Thomas Hardwick, "Description of a Substance called Gez or Manna, and the Insect Producing It," *Asiatic Researches* 14 (1822): 182–86; Christian G. Ehrenberg, "Über die Manna-Tamariske nebst allgemeinen Bemerkungen über die Tamariscineen," *Linnaea. Ein Journal für die Botanik in ihrem ganzen Umfange* 2 (1827): 241–82, esp. 241; Christian G. Ehrenberg, *Symbolae physicae seu icones et descriptiones corporum naturalium novorum aut minus cognitorum quae ex itineribus per Libyam, Aegyptum, Nubiam, Dongalam, Syriam, Arabiam et Habessinam publico institutis sumptu Friderici Guilelmi Hemprich et Christiani Godofredi Ehrenberg studio annis 1820–1825 redierunt. 1–2 Zoologica, 2a Icones et descriptiones insectorum* (Berolini Mittler, 1830). For the latter, Robinson (*Biblical Researches*, 590 n. xv) refers to "Insecta, Dec I. Tab 10" and "Plantae, Dec I. Tab. 1,2." See too Maiberger, *Das Manna*, 397–98. For a 1947 update of Ehrenberg, see F. S. Bodenheimer, "The Manna of Sinai," *BA* 10 (1947): 1–6 on which Houtman (*Exodus*, 1:143–44) relies.

11. This bracketed remark, along with Robinson's similar words in the 1854 edition of Gesenius (see below) were removed from subsequent editions that have come down to today's BDB.

12. Francis Brown, S. R. Driver and Charles A. Briggs praise Robinson's lexicographic skills calling him a "broad-minded, sound, and faithful scholar [who] added to the successive editions of the book in its English form the newest materials and conclusions in the field of Hebrew word-study." See Francis Brown, S. R. Driver, and Charles A. Briggs, *A Hebrew and English Lexicon of the Old Testament with an Appendix Containing the Biblical Aramaic Based on the Lexicon of William Gesenius as translated by Edward Robinson* (Oxford: Clarendon Press, 1907), v.

dard in the field. In addition to his work with lexicography, Edward Robinson's second claim to fame is his influential *Biblical Researches in Palestine, Mount Sinai and Arabia Petraea: A Journal of Travels in the Year 1838 Undertaken in Reference to Biblical Geography.*[13] As is clear in the subtitle, Robinson was intent on correlating bedouin Arabic place names with their biblical cognates. Though not his intention, Robinson's[14] description of the tamarisk-*manna* and related incest secretions that quoted Ehrenberg proved irresistible for those who wanted to find further support for a naturalistic explanation for the nature of the biblical manna, correlating the biblical term *mān* and the bedouin Arabic term tamarisk-*manna* just as Robinson had done with toponyms. Yet Robinson himself was very skeptical. Robinson wrote that "of all the characteristics of manna [described in the biblical narratives] not one is applicable to the present [tamarisk/insect-related] manna."[15] Thirteen years later, when it came to editing the 1854 edition of Gesenius's lexicon (which included an even more expanded naturalistic section), Robinson again felt the need to object with a bracketed editorial addition. Referring to his influential 1841 volumes where he described the small quantities, scarcity, and intermittent supply of tamarisk manna, he penned: "[Of all the characteristics ascribed in Scripture to the manna, not one belongs to the present [tamarisk/insect-related] manna; nor could there ever have been a supply of it sufficient for the consumption of a host like that of Israel."[16]]

Despite Robinson's protestations (and the reference to manna as grain [*dāgān*] in Psalm 78:24–25; cf. Numbers 11:8), today the tamarisk-*manna*/insect secretions option for the etymology of Hebrew *mān* has reached a near-consensus to judge from the Maiberger's conclusion and the entries in major lexica (e.g., BDB, 577; KB^{1}, 564; KB^{3}, 564; Holladay, 200; *HALOT*, 596; *DCH*, 336), commentaries (e.g., Houtman *Exodus*, 1:143–44) and encyclopedia (e.g., ABD 4:511; cf. NIDB 3:790). Maiberger confidently asserted that "the author of Ex. 16:14 knew perfectly well what notions lay behind [*mān*] ... [and] he is doubtlessly thinking here of the Sinaitic tamarisk manna."[17]

A Different Approach: Gift Giving, Generosity, and the Semitic Root *mnn*

The history of biblical Hebrew lexicography in the nineteenth century needs to be contextualized with the emergence at that time of the critical study of the Hebrew Bible and its understandable desire to find naturalistic explanations due to the *Zeitgeist* of the times, especially nineteenth century biblical studies in Germany. Yet, paying closer attention to the narrative at hand reveals a simple observation already noted above: Lexicographers, spurred on by tales of travelers encountering exotic bedouin customs, have mistakenly concentrated on a taxonomic botanical etymology for a generic word designating a generous provision of food. They have also failed to recognize the literary nature of the narrative at hand. The author of Exodus 16 is certainly making a rhetorical word play having the speakers ask, "What is it?" (*mān hūʾ*) for the unknown (*mah hû*)—to which Moses replies that the *mān* is a provision of food.

13. The full three-volume work that has been called "epoch making" by John A. Dearman earned Robinson the Royal Geographical Society's Gold Medal and subsequent election into the American Academy of Sciences, not to mention the epithet "the Father of Biblical Geography." See John A. Dearman, "Robinson, Edward (1794–1863)," in *Dictionary of Biblical Interpretation*, ed. John H. Hayes (Nashville: Abingdon, 1999), 407.

14. Robinson, *Biblical Researches,* 109–10, 170–71, 590, n. xv. Due to the later reprints with varying pagination, it is helpful to note that Robinson's comments on manna are in his diary entries of March 20 and March 28, 1838.

15. Robinson, *Biblical Researches,* 170–71.

16. Edward Robinson, *A Hebrew and English Lexicon of the Old Testament including the Biblical Chaldee from the Latin of William Gesenius* (Boston: Crocker & Brewster, 1854), 579–80. Robinson goes on to exaggerate the number of Israelites to be two million(!), yet his point still stands within the narrative, that a scarce and intermittent supply would be an insufficient food source to feed very many people on a daily basis. See similarly Nahum Sarna, *Exodus = Shemot: The Traditional Hebrew Text with the New JPS Translation* (Philadelphia: Jewish Publication Society, 1991), 89.

17. Maiberger, "*mān,*" 392. See too Maiberger, *Das Manna,* 435–38.

Moreover, this provision is suitably then called *mān*, a **qall* geminate noun pattern from the root *mnn*, designating a benevolent bestowal of generosity—which is the very point of the narrative!

To get a different perspective to challenge the current consensus, it is helpful to return to the core meaning of the root *mnn* and to explore unrecognized examples of the root that are at home within an ancient Near Eastern perspective. The central meaning of the verb *manna* in Arabic means "to be benevolent, gracious, kind" as well as "to bestow generously, confer, or grant benevolence or benefits." Sources from Amarna Canaanite, Western Akkadian, and Ugaritic reveal that this meaning for the root *mnn* has an ancient pedigree.

The term *maninnu* occurs in western Akkadian to designate a most generous gift (a necklace of the very finest quality made of gold, lapis lazuli, and other precious stones) that was used in international diplomacy and as a royal gift to the gods. Luca Peyronel, building on the formative works of Zaccagnini, Liverani, and Feldman, highlights how "the highest level in the [Late Bronze Age] exchange system is that of ceremonial gift exchange ... mainly gold ... and lapis lazuli."[18] Such benevolence (and the underlying ideology of prestige) is best attested in the Amarna archive where *maninnu* exchange gifts promoted "well-being" (*šulmānu*) between kings.[19] Consider EA 21 where Tushratta, the king of Mittani, hopes that the *maninnu*-necklace he is sending will rest on the neck of Amenhotep III for 100,000 years. Consider too Tushratta's wedding gifts that accompany the giving of his daughter Tadu-Hepa to Amenhotep III to be his wife. One text alone (EA 25) repeatedly mentions 19 *maninnu*-necklaces (see too EA 22). A *maninnu* gift carried such cultural, ideological, and symbolic weight that at Late Bronze Age Qatna it appears as a prestige object that the royal dynasty presented to the gods.[20]

At Ugarit we have a so-called myth and ritual text (KTU 1.23) written to promote the interests and vital necessity of god, king, and state with particular emphasis on agricultural sustenance.[21] KTU 1.23 promotes the god ʾIlu's life-giving sovereignty as it buttresses the royal power of the Late Bronze Age kingdom of Ugarit. King (*mlk*) and queen (*mlkt*) are described as reigning over the proceedings (KTU 1.23.7). Though set against the backdrop of viticulture, KTU 1.23 is essentially about God and king. I concur with Mark S. Smith who insightfully writes: "[KTU] 1.23 expresses royal power by connecting the cosmic origins in the figure of El with the present reality in the person of the king ... [KTU] 1.23 further reinforces the identification of god and king."[22]

I have written elsewhere of how a central part of the myth describes the benevolence of the deity using the root *mnn*.[23] Using synonymous parallelism together with double entendre, the poet describes how the god ʾIlu is "generous" with his royal scepter/staff/penis (*ḫṭ* // *mṭ*) to two women who become his wives. ʾIlu lowers his scepter/staff

18. Luca Peyronel, "Between Archaic Market and Gift Exchange: The Role of Silver in the Embedded Economies of the Ancient Near East during the Bronze Age," in *Gift Giving and the "Embedded" Economy of the Ancient World*, ed. Filippo Carlà and Maja Gori (Heidelberg: Winter, 2014), Pages 355–75 (357).

19. On the importance of luxury objects as *šulmānu* greeting gifts for royal diplomacy (including *maninnu*-necklaces), see Marian H. Feldman (*Diplomacy by Design: Luxury Arts and an "International Style" in the Ancient Near East* [Chicago: University of Chicago, 2006], 105–14) to whom I am indebted.

20. See Jean Bottéro, "Les inventaires de Qatna," *RA* 43 (1949): 158–59; Feldman *Diplomacy by Design*, 109. Feldman astutely points out how "the Qatna inventories share certain formal aspects with the Amarna archive inventories, in particular EA 22 and 25 ... deriving from Mitanni."

21. Due to the abuses of past "myth and ritual" scholarship, this phrase needs to be qualified in order to shed any notion of a putative *hieros gamos* mythology. For a full analysis of KTU 1.23 with emphasis on royal cult, see Theodore J. Lewis, "God [ʾIlu] and King in *KTU* 1.23," in *"Like ʾIlu are You Wise": Studies in Northwest Semitic Languages and Literatures in Honor of Dennis G. Pardee*, ed. H. H. Hardy, Joseph Lam, and Eric D. Reymond (Chicago: Oriental Institute of the University of Chicago, forthcoming).

22. Mark S. Smith, *The Rituals and Myths of the Feast of the Goodly Gods of KTU/CAT 1.23*, Resources for Biblical Study 51 (Atlanta: Society of Biblical Literature, 2006), 162–63.

23. This passage is notoriously difficult. For a full discussion of the various proposals and the defense of what is presented here in brief, see Lewis, "God [ʾIlu] and King in *KTU* 1.23."

to the women in an act of royal benevolence well known from passages such as Esther 8:3–5.[24] The poetic bicola reads:

ʾil ḫṭh nḥt	ʾIlu lowers his scepter,
ʾil ymnn mṭ ydh	ʾIlu is generous with the staff in his hand. [KTU 1.23.37][25]

The use of the verb *mnn* to express generosity between god as king and the women resonates with the entire text that emphasizes how the blessings of agriculture are ordained from time immemorial, from the hand of the god ʾIlu, and of royal patronage. KTU 1.23 is tantalizing for our present discussion of manna as a divine provision of food (*leḥem*) for one's hungry children[26] in the steppe-land/wilderness (*midbār*) in Exodus 16 and Numbers 11, as its capstone (KTU 1.23.68–76) describes the hunger of ʾIlu's children in the steppe-land/wilderness (*mdbr, šd//pʾat mdbr*). ʾIlu as "the Guardian/ Protector" (*nǵr*) benevolently comes to aid of his hungry and thirsty sons in the desert, generously providing not just bread and water, but bread and wine (*lḥm, yn*), the abundant fruits of sown agriculture over which he serves as guardian (*nǵr mdrʿ*).[27] Analogously, one could call to mind the Deuteronomic tradition whose vocabulary echoes that of KTU 1.23 with El protecting (*nṣr*) his child in the wilderness (*midbār*) as he nurses him with honey and feeds him with the produce of the field (*śādāy*) where he drinks fine wine (*tišteh ḥāmer*) made of grapes (*ʿēnāb*) (Deut 32:6, 10, 13–14). Psalm 146:9 has Yahweh watching over sojourners, orphans, and widows. Psalm 107:4–9 beautifully articulates the broad motif of wandering famished and parched in the steppe-land and crying out to one's deity who then leads to an inhabited town and amply satisfies thirst and hunger.[28]

---

24. Esther 8:3–5 (cf. 5:1–3) reads: Now Esther spoke again to the king, fell down at his feet, and implored him with tears to counteract the evil of Haman the Agagite, and the scheme that he had devised against the Jews. *And the king extended (= lowered) the golden scepter toward (the bowed) Esther.* So Esther arose and stood before the king, and said, "If it pleases the king, and if I have found favor in his sight and the thing seems right to the king and I am pleasing in his eyes, let it be written ..."

25. My vocalization of this bicola would be:
ʾilu ḫaṭṭahu naḥḥita (D suffixal form 3 m sg)
ʾilu yumānin maṭṭâ yadihu (L prefixal form 3 m sg)
A parallel bicola occurs in KTU 1.23 lines 40, 43–44. Options for vocalizing these lines include:
naḥḥuta-ma/nuḥata-ma/naḥūtu-ma ḫaṭṭuka "lowered is your staff"
(Dp suffixal form 3 m sg + enclitic *m*/Gp suffixal form 3 m sg + enclitic *m*/G pss ptc m sg + enclitic *m*)
mumānin-ma/mumannanu-ma maṭṭû yadihu "generous is the staff of your hand"
(L ptc m sg + enclitic *m*/Dp ptc m sg + enclitic *m*)

26. Exodus 16 and Numbers 11 preserve varying nuances to the basic motif of food provision in response to the people's "murmurings" (Exod 16:2–3, 7–9, 12; Num 11:1–6, 10–15). Exodus 16 (mostly the P source) additionally blends in sabbath motifs (Exod 16:22–30) while Numbers 11 (non-P) blends in judgment motifs (Num 11:1–3, 18–20, 33–34) as well the sharing of Moses authority among elders and prophets (Num 11:16–17, 24–30). For further source and redactional analysis, see Propp, *Exodus 1–18*, 588–92.

The notion of the hungry people being one's own children is emphasized in Numbers 11, not Exodus 16 apart from its minor reference to preserving the story for future "generations" (*dōrōt*; Exod 16:32–33). Numbers 11:12 preserves the remarkable reference (albeit via a frustrated Moses's penchant for the dramatic) to God as a mother conceiving, birthing and nursing her suckling child in the wilderness.

Deuteronomy takes the hunger and manna tradition in an altogether different direction equating the eating of manna with sustaining oneself by the divine word (Deut 8:3).

27. For my defense of ʾIlu as the *nǵr mdrʿ*, see Lewis, "God [ʾIlu] and King in *KTU* 1.23."

28. The Hebrew Bible contains extensive *midbār* traditions that need not detain us here. The *midbār* can represent a place of hunger and thirst and thus potential death (Exod 16:3; 17:1; Num 20:1–4; Jer 2:6). As such, like *mdbr qdš* in KTU 1.23.65b, it is often a sacred place of sacrifice and offerings (Exod 3:18; 5:1, 3; 8:27–28; Lev 7:38; Num 9:5; 1 Chr 21:29) and a place where theophanies (Exod 16:10; Ps 29:8) and divine oracles were thought to occur (Num 1:1; 3:14; 9:1).

Thus in biblical lore, the *midbār* provides the perfect opportunity for God to meet people in their need for sustenance, feeding them (Exod 16:32; 1 Kgs 19:4–8) even with overflowing Edenic bounty (Deut 2:7; Isa 51:3) and security (Ezek 34:25). Though the contexts are different, Hosea 2:16–17 [Eng 2:14–15] has Yahweh alluring (√*pth*; cf. √*pty* in KTU 1.23.39b) the young woman he loves whom

In addition to KTU 1.23.37, 40, 44, the root *mnn* also occurs in the onomastic record from Ugarit. Thanks to the research of Wilfred G. E. Watson, we can document several individuals at Ugarit who bore the name *mnn* as well as at Emar.[29] That a single text includes three different individuals with the name *mnn* may attest to the popularity of the name marking one who has received benevolence from a deity.[30] What is of note is that all of these names occur in economic texts and one wonders if any individuals were so named due to their "indebted" status. Several Ugaritic texts from Ras ibn Hani are tantalizing in this regard for they attest to a creditor, perhaps appropriately named Muninuya ("benevolent, debt lender"?), who loans silver to twelve debtors (see KTU 3.10, 4.783, 4.791, 4.792, 4.401).[31]

Manna: A Benevolent and Generous Provision

When we add these examples of the use of the root *mnn* from Amarna, Qatna, and especially Ugarit with its thematic provision-of-food-for-one's-hungry-children-in-the-wilderness motif, to the prevalent use of the root *mnn* to designate benevolence and generosity in our cognate Arabic sources, a solid case can be made for understanding the etymology of Hebrew (and Aramaic) manna along these lines rather than privileging a narrow botanical definition. Manna (Hbw *mān, mann-*, Arm *mannāʾ*, Syr *manĕnāʾ*, Arb *manna*, LXX *manna*) and its Semitic cognates (Arb *mnn*, Akk *maninnu*, Ugr *mnn*) constitute a generous provision (be it a prestige good to god or king, food to the hungry, an economic transaction between creditor and debtor producing gratitude and indebtedness, or the generosity a superior extends to the favored) given by a benevolent party or, in diplomatic discourse, by a party who desired to be viewed as benevolent in order to promote economic well-being between nations. The biblical manna traditions echo a motif known elsewhere from Late Bronze Age Ugarit—that gods were thought to be viewed as royally and parentally providing for their children in a time of need, especially when it came to the vulnerability of hunger in semi-arid steppe-lands lacking in dependable food sources.[32] Once again, we should emphasize the agrarian nature of such benevolence in these Ugaritic and biblical traditions. The manna story in Exod 16:4 describes how Yahweh "rains down bread from heaven" (*mamṭîr*; cf. Neh 9:15). This is echoed by the tradition preserved in Ps 78:23–25 of how God "rained down manna to eat" (*wayyamṭēr ... mān leʾĕkōl*) which synonymously parallels how God gave "grain of heaven" (*dĕgan-šāmayīm*) also called "the bread of the powerful/strong" (*leḥem ʾabbîrîm*),[33] which was abundant in nature (*lāśōbaʿ*; cf. Ps 105:40).

---

he then leads through the *midbār* and presents with vineyards (cf. KTU 1.23.73–76). In a similar metaphorical vein, Jeremiah 2:2 tells of Yahweh's youthful bride loving him as she followed him in the *midbār*, even though it was a "land not sown" (*ʾereṣ lōʾ zĕrûʿâ*). The Deuteronomic tradition has Yahweh carrying his young son in the *midbār* (Deut 1:31), caring, guarding, feeding and nursing the son whom he begat (Deut 32:6b, 10, 13–14).

29. The names are variously vocalized in the Akkadian syllabic spellings. See Wilfred G. E. Watson, "Ugaritic Onomastics (4)," *AuOr* 13 (1995): 224–25; Wilfred G. E. Watson, "Ugaritic Onomastics (5)," *AuOr* 14 (1996): 101.

30. The three different people are *mnn bn krmn*, *mnn bn qqln*, and *mnn bn ṣnr* in KTU 4.35.5,13,16 [RS 8.183 + 201]). See Kevin M. McGeough, *Ugaritic Economic Tablets: Text, Translation and Notes*, ANES 32 (Leuven: Peeters, 2011), 501–3.

31. For the texts and the reconstruction of the timeline of when the loans were made and repaid, see Pierre Bordreuil and Dennis Pardee, *A Manual of Ugaritic*, Linguistic Studies in Ancient West Semitic 3 (Winona Lake, IN: Eisenbrauns, 2009), 278–82; McGeough, *Ugaritic Economic Tablets*, 599–603.

32. On the available food sources of the *mdbr*, "desert/steppe-land" (e.g., seasonal "shrub-steppe" and "dry" vegetation that led to the predominance of sheep and goat pastoralism that was supplemented by hunting activity), see Lewis, "God [ʾIlu] and King in *KTU* 1.23."

33. Due to five occurrences of God being called *ʾăbîr yaʿăqōb*, "the Mighty One of Jacob" (Gen 49:24; Isa 49:26; 60:16; Ps 132:2, 5)—but note the single *b* in *ʾăbîr*—most interpreters see the plural *ʾabbîrîm* here as a reference to the preternatural, hence *leḥem ʾabbîrîm*, "the bread of angels" in line with the later explicit tradition found in Wis 16:20. Yet, the way in which kings emulated divinity

Benevolence and generosity. This brings us back to where we began, with this volume being a tribute to Richard Jasnow. Richard may shun fish (unlike the hungry *hāʾsapsup* of Numbers 11), but he has no equal when it comes to the generosity he extends to colleagues and students alike. The gracious, daily provision of his humanity is manna to us all.

---

especially with providing agricultural sustenance, makes one wonder if an earlier understanding of "the bread of the powerful/strong (bull-like)" (*leḥem ʾabbîrîm*) had a royal flavor.

Papyrus Berlin P. 7056: Division of a *kleros* between Members of a Priestly Family from Roman Soknopaiou Nesos

Sandra Lippert and Maren Schentuleit

Papyrus Berlin P. 7056 has been published with a phototype image and a very succinct description by Spiegelberg in his catalogue of Demotic papyri at Berlin.[1] He gave a preliminary and rather lacunary translation of lines 1 to 5, followed by the admission "Die entscheidenden Ausdrücke der nächsten Zeilen sind mir unbekannt," before resuming with the translation of the imperial protocol and dating in lines 9 to 10. On the basis of this short overview, Spiegelberg labeled the document a "Teilungsvertrag,"[2] gave the origin as "Fajiûm" and the date (incorrectly) as February 8, 112 CE. The papyrus has since been mentioned by Seidl, as an example of a typical Demotic division document still attested in the Roman period,[3] and in the list of Demotic papyri in the *LÄ* as "Besitzteilung aus dem Fajjum."[4] It has also been used by the Chicago Demotic Dictionary (CDD) and was entered in the database *Demotic and Abnormal Hieratic Texts* (*DAHT*) under the number TM#45753, where the content is classified as "contract, division of property" and the date is corrected to March 13, 112 CE—Spiegelberg's calculation had seemingly been based on the assumption of a continued use of the ancient Egyptian calendar without leap years, instead of the Alexandrian calendar, for Demotic legal documents in the Roman period.[5]

Surprisingly, in the over one hundred years since it has been made accessible for the scholarly community by Spiegelberg, P. Berlin P. 7056 has never been fully edited. One of the reasons for this could be the handwriting: the light to medium brown papyrus (fig. 1) is inscribed on the recto in the highly idiosyncratic and sometimes puzzling ductus used by persons educated in the scribal school of Roman Soknopaiou Nesos/Dime; the verso is blank.

During our work for the research project "Soknopaiu Nesos nach den demotischen Quellen römischer Zeit" under the direction of Karl-Theodor Zauzich at Würzburg, we collected and classified texts from Dime and initially planned on including this papyrus into the volume on legal documents from Roman Soknopaiou Nesos.[6] However,

1. Wilhelm Spiegelberg, *Demotische Papyrus aus den Königlichen Museen zu Berlin* (Leipzig: Giesecke & Devrient, 1902), 24, pl. 59.

2. Spiegelberg, *DPB*, 24: "Also mehrere Parteien teilen sich in (sic!) ein Besitztum auf die Dauer von vier Jahren. Nach dieser Zeit kann sich jeder unter gewissen Bedingungen von den Vertragsverpflichtungen frei machen. Mehr kann ich der Urkunde zur Zeit nicht entnehmen."

3. Erwin Seidl, *Rechtsgeschichte Ägyptens als römische Provinz (Die Behauptung des ägyptischen Rechts neben dem römischen)* (Sankt Augustin: Richarz, 1973), 86, 232.

4. Karl-Theodor Zauzich, "Papyri, Demotische, Berlin," *LÄ* 4:767 (no. 13 d).

5. For the introduction of the Alexandrian calendar in 22 BCE, see Dieter Hagedorn and Klaas Worp, "Das Wandeljahr im römischen Ägypten," *ZPE* 104 (1994): 244. For the occasional continued use of the Egyptian calendar in documentary sources with a religious contexts, see Sandra Lippert, "Au clair de la lune – The organisation of cultic service by moon calendar in Soknopaiou Nesos," in *Actes du IXe congrès international des études démotiques. Paris, 31 août – 3 septembre 2005*, ed. Ghislaine Widmer and Didier Devauchelle, BdÉ 147 (Cairo: Institut français d'archéologie orientale, 2010), 186–87.

6. Sandra Lippert and Maren Schentuleit, *Demotische Dokumente aus Dime, Vol. 3: Urkunden* (Wiesbaden: Harrassowitz, 2010).

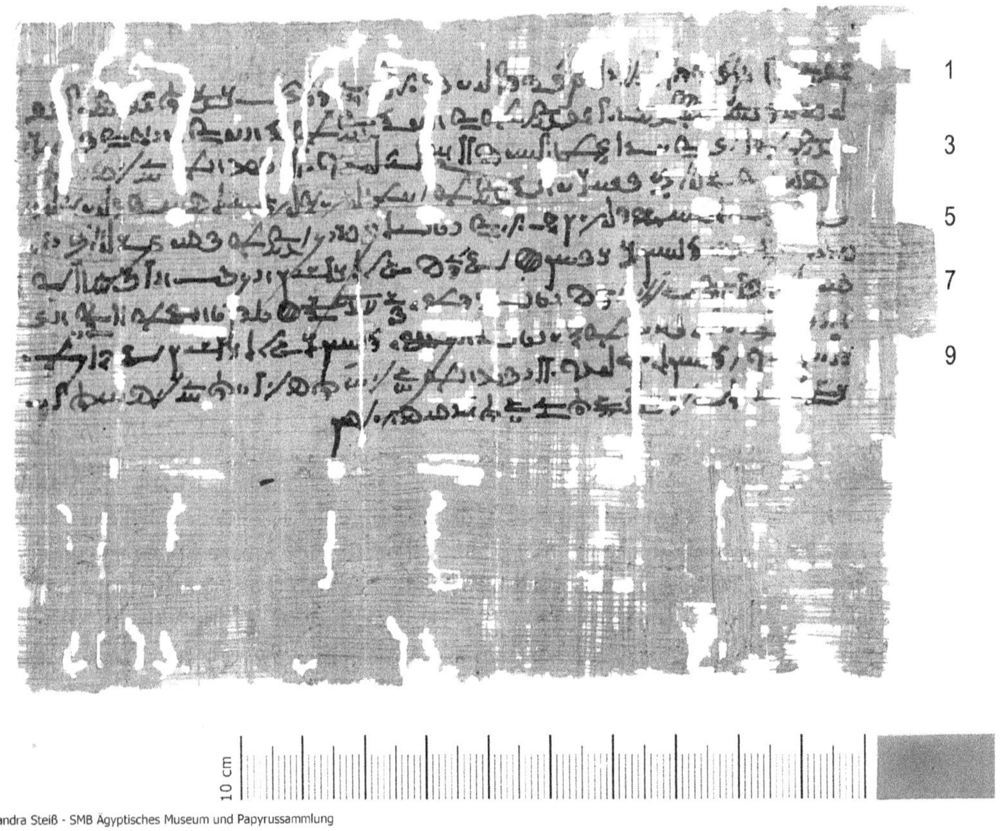

Figure 1. © Staatliche Museen zu Berlin, Ägyptisches Museum und Papyrussammlung, P. 7056 (photograph by Sandra Steiß).

we finally limited our choice to notarial documents, that is, those following the formal requirements of a *sẖ*-document,[7] and left aside for later publications those which, like P. Berlin P. 7056, are *šʿ.t*-documents.[8] The invitation to contribute to this volume is a welcome opportunity to finally edit this interesting and, in some ways, unusual document in honor of Richard Jasnow.

1. Physical Description of the Papyrus

Papyrus Berlin P. 7056 measures only 10.4 cm in height by 14.9 cm in width; its right-hand margin is 1.3 cm large, but the one on the left is much narrower, and the writing occasionally even touches the edge of the papyrus. The lines descend slightly to the left, the top margin is therefore 0.8 cm on the right side and about 1–1.2 cm on the left side. The bottom margin measures 3.5 to 4.3 cm.

7. For the term, see Mark Depauw, *A Companion to Demotic Studies*, PapBrux 28 (Brussels: Fondation Reine Élisabeth, 1997), 123–24; Sandra Lippert, *Einführung in die altägyptische Rechtsgeschichte*, EQÄ 5 (Münster: LIT, 2008), 138–39.

8. For a discussion of the type and legal phraseology of the text, see section 4 below.

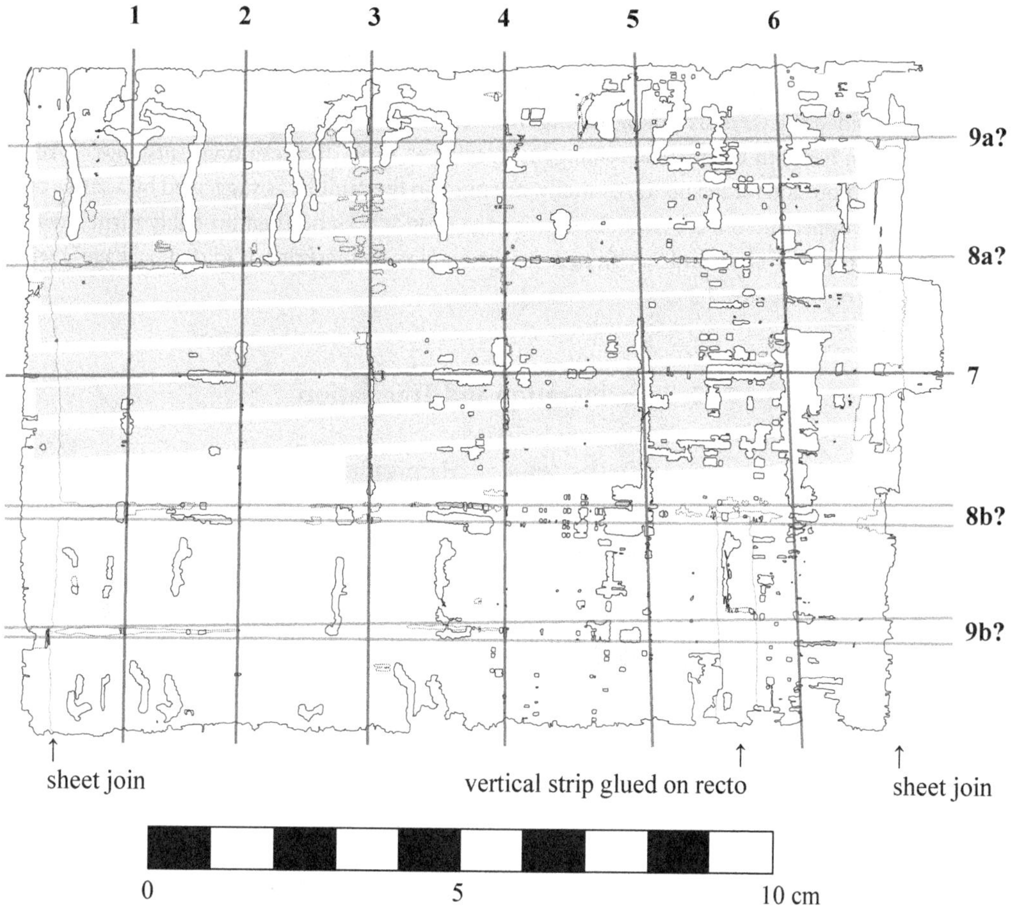

Figure 2. Schematic drawing of the recto of papyrus Berlin P. 7056, indicating the folds (Lippert and Schentuleit).

The sheet shows some damage from insects which left roundish holes and elongated "galleries," sometimes just in one of the two layers of fibres. The upper, horizontal layer is also missing on the right-hand edge and at the upper left corner. The original (i.e., cut) edges are well preserved at the top and left-hand sides, largely also at the bottom, but only a small portion has survived on the right-hand side. Two vertical sheet joins are visible (fig. 2): they are glued right over left, as is common for papyri inscribed in Demotic. On the right, the papyrus was cut off from the scroll just to the right of a join, and another join is visible 0.5–0.7 cm from the left margin. The distance between sheet joints therefore measured just about 14 cm; *collêseis* of similar width are also attested for the papyri used for temple receipts at Soknopaiou Nesos in the late first to early second centuries CE,[9] while earlier papyri had somewhat wider

9. E.g., P. Berlin P. 15668+23515+30003, 71 CE (TM#100226; Sandra Lippert and Maren Schentuleit, *Demotische Dokumente aus Dime, Vol. 2: Quittungen* [Wiesbaden: Harrassowitz, 2006], 32, no. 3): 14.2 cm; P. Vienna D 4898+6785, 87 CE (TM#100228; *DDD* 2:41, no. 5): 13.3 cm and 13.5 cm; P. Vienna D 6831, 107/8 CE (TM#100230; *DDD* 2:55, no. 8): 14.6 cm; P. Vienna D 6344, 111 CE (TM#47539; *DDD* 2:68, no. 13): 13 cm.

intervals.[10] The papryus was also cut off horizontally, probably to about a third of the original scroll height.[11] On the lower part of the sheet, about 3 cm from the right-hand edge, a rectangular strip of about 0.5 cm in width and 3 cm in height, with vertical fibres, was glued on the top layer, perhaps in order to repair a tear.

The papyrus was folded sideways six times, starting from left to right, as shown by the repeating damage patterns and increasing distance between the vertical folding lines (folds n° 1–6). The resulting *Faltstange*[12] ("rod-folding") was flipped over once more and folded up horizontally, not quite in the middle, as suggested by a series of horizontal holes 4.8 cm from the upper and 5.5 cm from the lower edge (fold n° 7), and then probably turned over again and folded up again twice (folds n° 8a+b and 9a+b), so as to form a tiny *Faltpäckchen* ("folded package") with a simple outer folding (type I), of about 2 by 2.3 cm.

2. Transliteration and Translation

1	*Ḥr-p⸢yt⸣ (sꜣ) Pa-Ḥꜥpy ⸢ḥnꜥ⸣ Hr=w (sꜣ) ⸢Pa-Ḥ⸣ꜥpy ḥnꜥ pꜣ ⸢sp⸣ nꜣy=f ⸢sn⸣.w ⸢nꜣ nty⸣ ḏd (n) Pa-gš (sꜣ) Hr-⸢p⸣yt (sꜣ) ⸢Ḥr⸣*	Harpagathes, (son) of Paopis, and Herieus, (son) of Paopis, and the rest of his siblings are the ones who say (to) Pekysis, (son) of Harpagathes, (son) of Horos,
2	*ḥnꜥ Sṯꜣ.ṱ⸢=w⸣-tꜣ-wty (sꜣ) sp(-2) (sꜣ) ⸢T⸣še-nfr (sꜣ) Ḥr pše=n i͗rm=tn pše=tn i͗rm=n ⸢ḥꜣ.ty⸣=n m[tr]e.t (n)*	and Stotoetis, (son) of the like-named, (son) of Tesenouphis, (son) of Horos: "We have divided with you, you have divided with us, our heart is content (with)
3	*[nꜣ] pše.w(t) r.i͗r=n (n) pꜣ ꜥ-n-(sṯꜣ.t-)20.t (n) Nsw$^{\text{ꜥ.w.s.}}$-tꜣ.wy (n) ṯꜣy (n) ḥꜣ.t-sp ⸢1⸣5 (n) pꜣ nṯr [nty] mḥe Tyln⸢s⸣*	[the] divisions which we have made (of) the 20-(aroura-)*kleros* (in) Sentheus, from regnal year 15 (of) the conquering god Trajan
4	*(r-)[h]n (r) ḥꜣ.t-sp [1]⸢8⸣ rnp.t 4.t mtre pꜣy=tn pše r pꜣ rsy pꜣ i͗mn.ṱ (n) tꜣ ḥny(.t) ḥnꜥ pꜣ ⸢i͗mn.ṱ⸣ pꜣ*	until regnal year [1]8, 4 years, (more) precisely, your segment being (situated) towards the southwest (of) the canal and the northwest
5	*⸢m⸣[ḥ.ṱ] (n) ⸢tꜣ⸣ ḥny(.t) pꜣ rmṯ nb n-i͗m=n {nty-} nty i͗w ḥn n=f sṯꜣ.ṱ=f r pše {m}m-sꜣ tꜣy rnp.t 4.t mtw⸢=f⸣*	(of) the canal. Any man of us who wants to withdraw himself from (the) division after these 4 years, shall
6	*⸢sṯꜣ.ṱ=f {nty-}nty-i͗w=f ḫꜣ⸣ ꜣḥy (sṯꜣ.t) 2.t (n) sme sp(-2) r-bnr tꜣ dni͗.t (r) šꜥd swb i͗w=f ḫpr i͗w=w qty=w{w} r i͗n⸢=w⸣*	withdraw himself. He (*scil.* any man of us) shall set apart 2 (arouras) of radish field from the part, (for) cutting green fodder. When they bring them (back) again

10. E.g., P. Vienna D 6839, 11 BCE (TM#100267; *DDD* 2:189, no. 56): 17.3 cm; P. Vienna D 6859 (TM#46343; DDD 2:195, no. 58): 16.2 cm; P. Vienna D 6845, 10/9 BCE (TM#47533; *DDD* 2:198, no. 59): 15.7 cm and 17.5 cm; P. Vienna D 6819, 42 CE (TM#47528; *DDD* 2:153, no. 45): 19 cm.

11. The standard height of papyrus scrolls in Roman Soknopaiou Nesos seems to have been 3 ½ to 4 palms or approximately 26–30 cm, with most measuring 28–29 cm in height (*DDD* 3:3). Occasionally, scroll heights of about 32–33 cm (P. Vienna D 6845, see n. 10 above. P. Vienna D 6857: TM#47529; *DDD* 2:205–9, no. 61; P. Vienna D 10084: TM#46342; *DDD* 2:214–17, no. 64. P. Vienna D 6049 + D 6936: TM#58204; *DDD* 3:125–38, no. 2. P. Oxford EES D L/92: TM#109366; *DDD* 3:431–38, no. 39) and exceptionally, even 40 cm (P. Berlin P. 8932 vso: TM#45598; *DDD* 2:105–8, no. 26) are attested.

12. See for the terminology Myriam Krutzsch, "Kniffen, Knicken, Falten. Was Objekte erzählen," in *KulturGUTerhalten: Restaurierung archäologischer Schätze an den staatlichen Museen zu Berlin*, ed. Uwe Peltz and Olivia Zorn (Mainz: von Zabern, 2009), 111.

7	*m-sꜣ[=s] ⸢nty-iw=w⸣ ḥwy qll r tꜣ dni.t {nty-}nty iw ⸢bn-pw⸣=s šm n=w ky sp nty-iw=w bꜣk=w gpe i.ir*	later, they shall cast lots for the part which had not gone to them the other time. They shall work them diligently in order to accomplish
8	*y⸢ꜥ⸣b⸢y⸣-w⸢ꜥ⸣⸢y⸣ nb pꜣ {nty-}nty iw bn-iw=f ẖꜣꜥ ꜣḥy (sṯꜣ.t) 2.t (r) šꜥd swb r-bnr <m>tw=f di.t {n}*	all farmwork. The one who will not set apart 2 (arouras) of field (for) cutting green fodder shall give
9	*swꜥ ⸢rtb⸣ 5 r ꜣḥy (sṯꜣ.t) wꜥ.t.t sẖ ḥꜣ.t-sp 15 (n) pꜣ nṯr nty mḥe Qsls Nlwꜥ Tylns*[ꜥ.w.s.]	5 artabas of wheat per one (aroura) of field." Written in regnal year 15 (of) the conquering god Caesar Nerva Traian[l.p.h.]
10	*Sbt⸢st⸣ Ql⸢mnq⸣s Ttqꜥ ibd 3 pr.t sw 17*	Augustus Germanicus Dacicus, month 3 of the peret-season, day 17.

3. Palaeographical and Philological Commentary

line 1:

The use of *nꜣy=f sn.w*, "his siblings" instead of *nꜣy=w sn.w*, "their siblings" is at first glance surprising: the preceding *pꜣ sp (n)*, "the rest (of)" implies that Harpagathes and Herieus are also brothers.[13] But since this is a *šꜥ.t*-document,[14] the first-mentioned Harpagathes is himself the scribe and therefore, even though the introduction is stylized objectively in the 3rd person, writes from his personal, that is, singular perspective.

line 3:

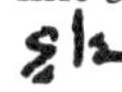 *ꜥ-n-(sṯꜣ.t-)20.t*: this is a shortened version of the expression *ꜥ-n-sṯꜣ.t-..-n-ꜣḥ*, generally explained as "chief (*ꜥ(ꜣ)* "great one") of .. arouras of field," corresponding to the Greek ... ἀρουρος κληροῦχος.[15] Its use in papyrus Berlin P. 7056 to designate not a person, but the piece of land itself, is therefore somewhat surprising: either the scribe left out *ꜣḥ* just before or he might have understood  as *ꜥ.wy (n)*[16] instead of *ꜥ(ꜣ)-n-*, "chief of." For a clear case of *ꜥ.wy* not meaning "pair," but "portion, piece, part" and perhaps even specifically "piece of land, plot," see P. BM EA 69532,[17] l. 6: *wn-nꜣ.w ꜥšꜣ nꜣ ꜥ.wy.w (n) pꜣ ḥtp-nṯr r.wn-nꜣ.w [s]ḥn n=f*, "Numerous were the parts/plots (of) the god's domain that were entrusted to him." For the history of this *kleros* of 20 arouras within the family, see section 6.2 below.

 *Nsw*[ꜥ.w.s.]*-tꜣ.wy*: the first part of this toponym is clearly the word *nsw* "king" with a divine determinative and the abbreviated writing of *ꜥnḫ wḏꜣ snb* that is also used after the name Trajan in l. 9. The second part also occurs in other religious papyri from Roman Soknopaiou Nesos, like P. Strasbourg dem. 31[18] and P. Berlin

13. For the reconstruction of the family tree of the involved persons, see figure 3 below.

14. See section 4 below.

15. Sven Vleeming, "Two Unrecognized Greek Concepts in Demotic P.BM 10597," *CdÉ* 58 (1983): 97–98.

16. *DG*, 52 "Portion, Paar."

17. John Tait, "Pa-di-pep Tells Pharaoh the Story of the Condemnation of Djed-her: Fragments of Demotic Narrative in the British Museum," *Enchoria* 31 (2008/2009): 116–17; Günter Vittmann, "Demotische Texte," in *Weisheitstexte, Mythen und Epen*, ed. Bernd Janowski and Daniel Schwemer, TUAT NF 8 (Gütersloh: Gütersloher Verlagshaus, 2015), 442–44.

18. TM#48899. Wilhelm Spiegelberg, *Die demotischen Papyrus der Strassburger Bibliothek* (Strasbourg: Schlesier & Schweikhardt, 1902), 49, pl. 15; Ghislaine Widmer, "Sobek Who Arises in the Primaeval Ocean (PBM EA 76638 and PStrasbourg Dem. 31)," in *New Archaeological and Papyrological Researches on the Fayyum: Proceedings of the International Meeting of Egyptology and Papyrology, Lecce, June 8th–10th 2005*, ed. Mario Capasso and Paola Davoli, Papyrologica Lupiensia 14/2005 (Lecce: Congedo, 2007), 345–54.

P. 6750,[19] in exactly the same writing ,[20] which Widmer read *tꜣ.wy*: the first element of this is the word *dni.t*, "part" (cf. also *dni.t* in P. Berlin P. 7056, l. 6 and l. 7), which is used as an unetymological writing to phonetically express /to(e/i)/ or /ta(i)/,[21] and thus the dual of *tꜣ*.[22] Widmer explains the following *nṯr*-group ()—or according to her, two *nṯr* signs ()—as indications of the dual *tꜣ.wy*, but as she points out, in the majority of cases this word is actually used in P. Berlin P. 6750 as an unetymological writing of *dwꜣ*, "hymn."[23] We therefore would prefer to see in this *nṯr*-group, as well as the following determinatives (plural strokes over lotus determinative and divine determinative), the means for clearly indicating the intended reading as *dwꜣ*, "hymn" instead of *tꜣ.wy*, "two lands," even though they were kept in those rarer cases in P. Berlin P. 6750 where actually a reading *tꜣ.wy*, "two lands" was intended—as in P. Berlin P. 7056, l. 3. For a more detailed discussion of this toponym see section 6.1 below.

line 4:

For *mtre*, "(more) precisely," see *Wb.* II:174 *r mtr* and section 4, commentary to clause 2 below.

line 5:

At its second occurrence, the scribe at first wrote *ḥny(.t)*, "canal" with the determinative of the grain with plural strokes underneath, as if it were *ḥny(.t)*, "incense; food offering, ritual activity,"[24] before correcting this to the large and small canal signs he used in the preceding line.

pꜣ rmṯ nb: The combination of the definite article and the definer *nb*, which are generally deemed mutually exclusive, is rather common in Roman Soknopaiou Nesos.[25]

{nty-}nty iw ḥn n=f: That this is one of the rare attestations of the Demotic precursor of the Coptic verb (ⲉ)ϩⲛⲁ= has already been remarked by Zauzich[26] who saw this example as proof that Černý's[27] interpretation as a verb ϩ or ϩⲛ joined to the preposition ⲛⲁ= was correct—an idea in principle already raised by Sethe.[28] The consistent writing as *ḥn* in Demotic[29] shows, however, that Sethe's proposition to trace (ⲉ)ϩⲛⲁ= back to earlier *ꜣḫ n=*, "it is agreeable to …"[30] is incorrect, as Černý had already deduced on phonetic grounds.[31] Finally, it has to be stressed

19. TM#55938. Ghislaine Widmer, *Résurrection d'Osiris - Naissance d'Horus: Les papyrus Berlin P. 6750 et Berlin P. 8765, témoignages de la persistance de la tradition sacerdotale dans le Fayoum à l'époque romaine*, ÄOP 3 (Berlin: de Gruyter, 2015).

20. Col. x+1, l. 8; col. x+2, l. 9, 14; col. x+3, l. 3, 22; col. x+5, l. 1; col. x+7, l. 14, 18, 22; col. x+9, l. 16, 21. Facsimile by the authors, taken from Widmer, *Résurrection d'Osiris*, 448 (col. x+2, l. 9).

21. Cf. Coptic ⲧⲟⲉ, ⲧⲟ, ⲧⲁ, ⲧⲟⲓⲉ, ⲧⲁⲉⲓ etc., "part, share" (*KHw*, 219; *CD*, 396a). For another example of this use in Roman Soknopaiou Nesos, see Sandra Lippert, "Die Abmachungen der Priester: Einblicke in das Leben und Arbeiten in Soknopaiou Nesos," in *New Archaeological and Papyrological Researches on the Fayyum: Proceedings of the International Meeting of Egyptology and Papyrology Lecce, June 8th–10th 2005*, ed. Mario Capasso and Paola Davoli, Papyrologica Lupiensia 14/2005 (Lecce: Congedo, 2007), 149.

22. See Wilhelm Spiegelberg, *Aegyptische und griechische Eigennamen aus Mumienetiketten der römischen Kaiserzeit auf Grund von grossenteils unveröffentlichetem Material* (Leipzig: Hinrichs, 1901), 41* (who, however, assumes that this group was used for the plural, *tꜣ.w*).

23. See Widmer, *Résurrection d'Osiris*, 134–35.

24. *DG*, 312, s.v. *ḥnj* "Spetzereien. Auch Weihrauch"; CDD *Ḥ* (2009), 155–56, s.v. *ḥny(.t)*, "spices, aromatics"; 156–57 s.v. *ḥny(.t)*, "food offering (ceremony)."

25. *DDD* 3:28.

26. Karl-Theodor Zauzich, "Spätdemotische Papyrusurkunden IV," *Enchoria* 7 (1977): 152.

27. Jaroslav Černý, "Coalescence of Verbs with Prepositions in Coptic," *ZÄS* 97 (1971): 46.

28. Kurt Sethe, "Über einige sekundäre Verbformen im Koptischen," *ZÄS* 47 (1910): 136–41.

29. Other examples: P. Harkness, col. 4, l. 24 (TM#54058; Mark Smith, *Papyrus Harkness (MMA 31.9.7)* (Oxford: Griffith Institute, 2015), 76 and 207, commentary a) to l. 24); P. Carlsberg 207, col. x+2, l. 3 (TM#56084; W. John Tait, "P. Carlsberg 207: Two Columns of a Setna-Text," in *The Carlsberg Papyri 1: Demotic Texts from the Collections*, ed. Paul J. Frandsen, CNIP 15 (Copenhagen: Museum Tusculanum Press, 1991), 23, 27, 31; see also Mark Smith, review of *The Carlsberg Papyri I: Demotic Texts from the Collection*, by Paul J. Frandsen, *JEA* 80 (1994): 259; P. London-Leiden, col. 9, l. 10 and perhaps also l. 3 (TM#55955; Francis Llewellyn Griffith and Herbert Thompson, *The Demotic Magical Papyrus of London and Leiden* (London: H. Grevel&Co., 1904–1909), 1:68–69; 2:pl. 9).

30. Sethe, "Sekundäre Verbformen," 139.

31. Černý, "Coalescence of Verbs," 46.

that the attestation in P. Berlin P. 7056 seems for the moment to be the only one in Demotic that actually writes out a separate *n* between *ḥn* and the suffix, while the above-mentioned attestations join the suffix referring to the logical subject directly to the verb.

 *{m} m-sꜣ*, "after": For the simple form, see l. 7 ( *m-sꜣ*[=*s*]); writings with an additional *m*, whether for the purpose of clarity or for phonetic reasons, are well attested in texts from Dime.[32]

line 6:

For better preserved writings of *{nty-} nty-iw* see for example l. 7 ()—the "rolled up" bottom of the first vertical stroke of *iw* is *nty*, which is commonly ligatured with *iw* in Roman Soknopaiou Nesos. Perhaps because this might be mistaken for *b* or the *bw*-group, some Dime scribes chose to add a horizontal *n*,[33] another *nty* (as here)[34] or even *nty-n-*[35] before this whole group. While in l. 5, 7 (middle) and 8 true relative forms (*{nty-} nty iw*) are meant, *{nty-} nty-iw=* is here, as *nty-iw=* at the beginning of line 7,[36] used as a phonetic rendering of the conjunctive *mtw=*.[37]

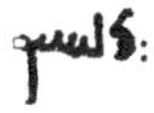: The word *ꜣḥy* "field" also occurs in P. Vienna D 12006[38] col. 5, l. 13 and 15 (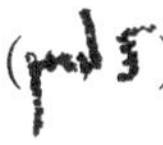).[39]

The unwritten feminine unit used in connection with *ꜣḥy* "field" is *sṯꜣ.t* "aroura," as in *ꜥ-n-(sṯꜣ.t-)20.t* in line 3.

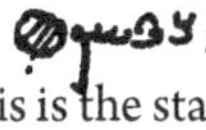 *sme sp(-2)*, "radish": the use of the *sp*-sign for *sp-2* is not unusual in Roman Soknopaiou Nesos,[40] where this is the standard way to express filiation with a like-named father.[41] The expressions 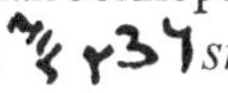 *sm sp-2* in P. Vienna D 6257[42] and 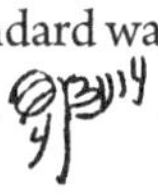 *sym sp-2* in P. Leiden RMO Inv. No. F 1974/7.52 B[43] have been understood as *sm (m) sm*,

32. For example, P. Vienna D 12006, *passim* (Martin Stadler, *Isis, das göttliche Kind und die Weltordnung: Neue religöse Texte aus dem Fayum nach dem Papyrus Wien D. 12006 recto*, MPER NS 28 [Vienna: Österreichische Nationalbibliothek, 2004], 296), with the exception of two of the four attestations with suffix pronoun, (col. 3, l. 22; col. 4, l. 31), which use the simple form instead.

33. See the unpublished *ḥnw*-agreement P. Vienna D 971+etc. recto (frequently, although not exclusively). The edition of this and other agreements from Soknopaiou Nesos is currently in preparation by the authors, as *Demotische Dokumente aus Dime, Vol. 4.1: Agreements: Text Edition.*

34. See the unpublished *ḥnw*-agreement P. Berlin P. 15661+15666 col. 1, l. 13; col. 2, l. 2, 13, 15, 19.

35. See the unpublished *ḥnw*-agreement P. Berlin P. 15580 col. 2, l. 5.

36. For the special writing *nty-iw=w* in line 7, see the commentary below.

37. See also Karl-Theodor Zauzich, "Die Bedingungen für das Schreiberamt von Soknopaiu Nesos," *Enchoria* 12 (1984): 87; Lippert, "Die Abmachungen der Priester," 150.

38. TM#80211. Stadler, *Isis*.

39. Facsimile by the authors, taken from Stadler, *Isis*, pl. 11. Stadler understood it as a plural *ꜥq.w* "breads, provisions" (Stadler, *Isis*, 70; 142; 288). The supposed attestation in the singular in col. 5, l. 5 is much damaged and does not seem to belong to the same word. Instead, Stadler reads the word  that actually is *ꜥq* "bread, ration" (and both times occurs just before), as *nkt*: Stadler, *Isis*, 32–33, who refers to Zauzich, "Schreiberamt," 88 (commentary to line 5). However, the reading *ꜥq* is also the correct one in P. Vienna D 4852 l. 5: *mtw=f ṯꜣy pꜣ ꜥq nty i.ir nꜣ mr-mšꜥ(.w) nꜣ wꜥb.w r ṯꜣy-ṯ=f(...)* "He shall take the (same) ration which the *lemeisa* of the priests will be taking (...)." The same writing is used in the expression *ꜥq r-ꜥ-wꜥb.t* "ration/bread of purification" (most likely referring to the food consumed by priests during – and perhaps in preparation for – their service time in order to remain in a state of ritual purity) for which wheat is receptioned by the acting phyle from the temple granary in two receipts for offering wheat, cf. *DDD* 2: no. 47 and 48 and p. 183.

40. See also Widmer, *Résurrection d'Osiris*, 417.

41. Karl-Theodor Zauzich, "Spätdemotische Papyrusurkunden I," *Enchoria* 1 (1971): 31, 36, 42.

42. TM#55973. Eva A. E. Reymond, *From the Contents of the Temple Libraries of the Suchos Temples in the Fayyum. Part I. A Medical Book from Crocodilopolis. P. Vindob. D. 6257*, MPER NS 10 (Vienna: Österreichische Nationalbibliothek, 1976), 104–5 (col. x+IX, l. 18), where Reymond transliterates *sm sp-2* but translates "herbs of any kind" (see also her entry in the glossary, 276, no. 138, where the passage is transliterated *sm nb*); 122–23 (col. x+XIV, l. 17). Facsimile by the authors, taken from Reymond, pl. VI (col. x+XIV, l. 17).

43. TM#102069. Brian Muhs and Jacco Dieleman, "A Bilingual Account From Late Ptolemaic Tebtunis," *ZÄS* 133 (2006): 58, 61 (col. 2 rto, l. 4, 5 and col. 3 rto, l. 2). Facsimile by the authors, taken from Muhs and Dieleman, "Bilingual Account," pl. 15 (col 3 rto, l. 2).

"herb as herb" = "real herb" by Reymond[44] and *symsym*, "sesame" by Muhs and Dieleman[45]; the latter reading and translation has also entered the CDD.[46] However, according to Hoffmann,[47] who prepares a reedition of P. Vienna D 6257, the "real *sm*(*y*)-plant" (*sm*(*y*) *sp-2*) is most likely to be understood specifically as radish (*Raphanus sativus*),[48] as opposed to the generic term *sm*(*y*), "herb, plant, vegetable,"[49] because twice in papyrus Vienna D 6257 the roots of this plant are used.[50] This translation is also to be preferred in P. Leiden RMO Inv. No. F 1974/7.52B, where *sym sp-2* is bought several times over a short period of time, a practice better suited to a vegetable that one consumes fresh, like radish, than to a commmodity with long term storage potential like sesame. For the cultivation of radish in Roman Egypt, see section 6.4 below.

 *šꜥd*: The same writing also occurs in other texts from Roman Soknopaiou Nesos, for example, in P. Vienna D 12006 col. 3, l. 21 (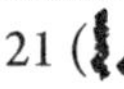)[51] and col. 5, l. 27, where Stadler read the word as *wš*;[52] he also proposed this reading for  in P. Vienna D 10000,[53] instead of *wš ms*[54] or *wš šr*.[55] However, while the first sign,  / , is indeed very similar to the hair lock sign of *wš*, "hole, gap etc.[56]"—which, as Stadler points out, actually does occur simply as  in P. Vienna D 12006[57]—and the determinative of the dying warrior would fit such a reading as well, the final metal determinative makes it more likely that the first sign of 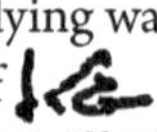 is in fact the knife[58] and that the whole word therefore should be read *šꜥd*, "to cut, cut short, abridge, diminish."[59] This would also fit the cited attestations:

44. Reymond, *Medical Book*, 277, no. 140. This was followed by Wolfgang Brunsch, review of *From the Contents of the Temple Libraries of the Suchos Temples in the Fayyum, Part I: A Medical Book from Crocodilopolis*, by Eva A. E. Reymond, *WZKM* 72 (1980): 157, referring to Pieter W. Pestman, "A Note Concerning the Reading *ḥḏ sp-2*," *Enchoria* 2 (1972): 35–36.

45. Muhs and Dieleman, "Bilingual Account," 58, 59 note g, 61 with note a.

46. CDD *S* (2013), 240–41 (N.B.: P. Leiden RMO Inv. No. F 1974/7.52 is there called "pLeiden 752").

47. Pers. comm. 3 August 2019; see also his translation of parts of P. Vienna D 6257; Friedhelm Hoffmann, "Rezepte aus einer medizinischen Sammelhandschrift (pWien D 6257)" in *Texte zur Heilkunde*, ed. Bernd Janowski and Daniel Schwemer, TUAT NF 5 (Gütersloh: Gütersloher Verlagshaus, 2010), 300–305.

48. Cf. Coptic, *CD*, 334a, s.v. ⲥⲓⲙ, "a *grass, fodder, herbs* in general," "b *radish*" and *CD*, 240b, s.v. ⲛⲉϩ, oil": ⲛⲥⲓⲙ of "radish"; see also *KHw*, 185 and *CED*, 152. See however Gérard Charpentier, *Recueil de matériaux épigraphiques relatifs à la botanique de l'Égypte antique* (Paris: Trismégiste, 1981), 564–65 (no. 910), attestation 4 "*nḥi n sym* huile d'herbes," but commented "= ῥαφάνινον Diosc. I 37" and "la référence 4 de Dioscoride I. 37 se rapporte à l'huile de raifort (*sic!*)." For the use of radish oil in Roman Egypt, see also section 4, commentary to clause 4 below.

49. *DG*, 430; CDD *S* (2013), 207–11; see also *Wb*. IV:119–120; Charpentier, *Recueil de matériaux*, 564–65 (no. 910); 588–89 (no. 953).

50. *nny sm sp-2*, "radish root": col. 3, l. 18 (corresponds to Reymond, *Medical Book*, 104–5, col. x+IX, l. 18, who read *kꜣpy* instead of *nny*); *bnny sm sp-2*, "radish tap-root?": col. 4, l. 17 (corresponds to Reymond, *Medical Book*, col. x+XIV, l. 17, who understood *bnny* as "pill(s)?"). Hoffmann, pers. comm. 6 August 2019.

51. Authors' facsimile, taken from Stadler, *Isis*, pl. 7.

52. Stadler, *Isis*, 59, 72, 123.

53. TM#48888. Col. 1, l. 12 in the edition by Karl-Theodor Zauzich, "Das Lamm des Bokchoris," in *Festschrift zum 100-jährigen Bestehen der Papyrussammlung der Österreichischen Nationalbibliothek Papyrus Erzherzog Rainer (P.Rainer Cent.)*, (Vienna: Österreichische Nationalbibliothek, 1983), 165–74, corresponds to col. 2, l. 12 in the revised edition by Michel Chauveau, "L'*Agneau* révisité ou la révélation d'un crime de guerre ignoré," in *Illuminating Osiris: Egyptological Studies in Honor of Mark Smith*. ed. Richard Jasnow and Ghislaine Widmer, MVCAE 2 (Atlanta: Lockwood, 2017), 37–69. Facsimile by the authors, taken from Zauzich, "Das Lamm des Bokchoris," pl. 2.

54. Zauzich, 166.

55. Chauveau, "L'*Agneau* révisité," 40, 43.

56. *DG*, 101.

57. Stadler, *Isis*, 48, 123, 165–67.

58. Occuring both with and without the oblique stroke, see Wolja Erichsen, *Demotische Lesestücke. 3. Heft Schrifttafel* (Leipzig: Hinrichs, 1937), 38 no. LL.8, contrary to the hair determinative, which does not have the oblique stroke; see p. 38, no. LL.9.

59. *DG*, 492–93: "schneiden, abschneiden;" CDD *Š* (2010), 49–51: "to cut," "to subtract," "to deduct, withdraw," "to diminish."

P. Vienna D 12006 col. 3, l. 21: *ỉn-nꜣ.w ỉw=y rḫ šꜥd pꜣ ḏtḥ r tỉ=y šm n=y*, "Will I be able to abridge the captivity so as to allow myself to go away?"[60]

While this does not essentially change the understanding of the phrase, reading *šꜥd*, "to cut short, abridge, diminish" has the advantage of not needing to postulate a new, hitherto unattested transitive verb *wš*, "to end sth."

P. Vienna D 12006 col. 5, l. 27: *ỉw=k (r) ṯꜣy ḥmt (n-)ḏr.ṯ=k ḫn št[ꜣ].w ỉw=k šꜥd (n-)ḥꜣ(.t)*[61]*=k ỉw=k dỉ.t hꜥy m-sꜣ=k*, "You will grasp (a) bronze (tool)[62] in your hand in the woods, while cutting down before you and letting drop behind you."[63]

Stadler saw this as a reference to Horus attacking Seth and his minions in the marshes with a harpoon, and assumed another new transitive sense, "to not know sth.," for *wš*, explained as an expression for "running berserk."[64] Reading *šꜥd*, "to cut (down)" instead of *wš* and restoring *št[ꜣ].w*, "woods"[65] instead of *št[y].w*, "ponds"[66] clarifies that this passage, which continues "You will hit and they fall, you will collect them while they are scattered" and is in l. 28 glossed "It is Pre who has felled the *nbs*-trees" refers to a mythological episode of Re chopping down trees, presumably with a hatchet. This seems indeed intentionally equated with cutting down enemies with a battle ax—an association probably inspired by the red sap the *nbs*-tree (*Zizyphus spina-christi*)[67] "bleeds" when its bark is cut.[68]

P. Vienna D 10000 col. x+2, l. 12: [.....] *r-r=f ỉw=w (r) šꜥd nꜣy[=f(?)* .....] "[.....] than/against/towards him, they will cut/diminish his(?) [.....]."[69]

The context remains fragmentary, but it looks like this line still treats the subject of scarce supplies (see l. 9, [...] *ḥqꜣ n ꜥq* [...] "hungry for bread") as symptom of the coming dystopia.

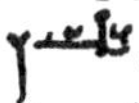 *swb*: The word (see also l. 8) is not listed in the *DG* but appears with the translation "weed" in several recent dictionaries.[70] By contrast, its Fayumic successor, ⲥⲁⲩⲃⲟⲩ, like the Bohairic counterpart ⲥⲱⲟⲩⲃⲉⲛ, is listed in Coptic dictionaries with the meaning "grass, hay"[71] and appears in Biblical contexts where this is used as animal feed: Sahidic translations of the Bible use ⲬⲞⲢⲦⲞⲤ < χόρτος "green fodder" in its place.[72] The diverging translations of Demotic *swb* in the CDD and the *TLA* seem based on Spiegelberg's assumption that there was a fixed expression

60. Versus Stadler, *Isis*, 59 "Werde ich die Gefangenschaft beenden können, so daß ich mich fortgehen lasse?," 123–24.

61. For the similarity of *(n/r-)ḥꜣ.t=* "before" and *ḥꜥ=* "self," see P. Vienna D 12006, col. 7, l. 18 (Stadler, *Isis*, 80; pl. 14–15; glossary 307).

62. The preceding title of the paragraph, l. 26, as well as a gloss in l. 28 mentions *ḥmt qnqn*, "bronze (for) hitting/fighting."

63. Versus Stadler, *Isis*, 72: "Du wirst Erz <mit> deiner Hand ergreifen in den T[ei]<ch>en. Du wirst dich selbst nicht kennen, während du hinter Dir zugrunde gehen läßt."

64. Stadler, *Isis*, 154: "... drückt den besinnungslosen Kampf aus." See also Martin Stadler, *Théologie et culte au temple de Soknopaios: Études sur la religion d'un village égyptien pendant l'époque romaine; Quatre séminaires à l'École Pratique des Hautes Études, Section des Sciences religieuses, Mai-juin 2015* (Paris: Cybèle, 2017), 80.

65. *DG*, 527, s.v. *štꜣ*, "der Wald."

66. Not attested in the *DG*; see Stadler, *Isis*, 154 who connects this with earlier *šdy.t*, "body of water." The presumed water-determinative in the first occurence at the beginning of l. 27, is simply the plural determinative: the second ocurrence ends with two long vertical strokes, i.e., wood sign and vertical plural mark.

67. Renate Germer, *Handbuch der altägyptischen Heilpflanzen*, Philippika 21 (Wiesbaden: Harrassowitz, 2008), 365–66. Charpentier, *Recueil de matériaux*, 384–87 (no. 609).

68. Amots Dafni, Shay Levy, and Efraim Lev, "The Ethnobotany of Christ's Thorn Jujube (Ziziphus spina-christi) in Israel," *Journal of Ethnobiology and Ethnomedicine* 1.8 (2005), DOI: 10.1186/1746-4269-1-8.

69. Versus Zauzich, "Lamm," 166–67 (col. 1): "[.....] als er, wenn sie kein Kind haben. Diese [.....]" and similar Chauveau, "L'*Agneau*," 40 (col. 2); 48: "[.....] contre lui, alors qu'ils seront sans enfant, ses [.....]."

70. CDD *S* (2013), 72–73, s.v. *swb*, "weed;" Charpentier, *Recueil de matériaux*, 574–75 no. 924 "mauvaise herbe?"; TLA lemma no. 5958: *swb* "Unkraut."

71. *CD*, 369a, s.v. ⲥⲱⲟⲩⲃⲉⲛ (B), ⲥⲁⲩⲃⲟⲩ (F) "grass;" *KHw*, 203 "Heu, Gras." Charpentier (*Recueil de matériaux*, 592–93, no. 960) suggests a (phonetically hardly convincing) connection between ⲥⲱⲟⲩⲃⲉⲛ and *snb*, a fibrous aromatic plant (perhaps Sweet flag, *Acorus calamus*?).

72. *CD*, 369a.

(*n-*)*wš swb* "without weed" in land leases and similar texts,[73] and the CDD lists a number of supposed attestations for this, including P. Berlin P. 7056 l. 6 and l. 8 for which we just established that *šꜥd* should be read instead of *wš*. However, on closer examination of the other four texts cited by the CDD, dating from the Ptolemaic period, the word preceeding *swb* turns out to be always written with a clear knife sign (i.e., including the oblique stroke) and should therefore not be read (*n-*)*wš* either, but always *šꜥd*.

Lease offer P. Ox. Griffith 46[74] (Soknopaiou Nesos, 138 BCE): ... *mtw=y tꜣy* (11) *dni.t ꜣḥ r šꜥd* ()[75] *swb ḫn=f* (12) *ḥr rnp.t* ..., "... To me belongs this part of a field in order to cut fodder in it, yearly ..."[76]

Land lease P. Cairo CG 31079[77] (Tebtynis, 105 BCE): *mtw=k di.t-st n=y* (28) *n ḥꜣ.t-sp 18 nꜣ ꜣḥ.w* ⸢*nty ḥry*(?)⸣ *ḫr šꜥd* (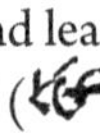)[78] *swb*, "and you will give them (back) to me in year 18, the fields which are (mentioned) above(?), for the purpose of cutting fodder."[79]

In two other land leases from Tebtynis, P. Cairo CG 30613[80] and P. Cairo CG 30615,[81] the beginning of the phrase is missing, but the context seems similar to P. Cairo CG 31079: each time *šꜥd* (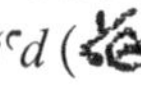;[82] 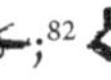[83]) *swb* is to take place in the growth period of the year *after* the lease ends. Thus, the expression (*n-*)*wš swb*, "without weed" is in fact a "ghost phrase," and the translation "weed" for *swb* has to be abandoned altogether. What is meant here is crop rotation by using land, perhaps specifically land previously cultivated with wheat, for *šꜥd swb*, "cutting green fodder." For the attestation of this practice in Greek documents see section 4, commentary to clause 4 and section 6.4 below.

iw=f ḫpr: Although the protasis is grammatically conditional, it refers to a future event that is almost certainly going to happen (see section 4, commentary to clause 5 and section 6.3 below), so a temporal translation "when (it will happen)" is preferred here. A similar interpretation of *iw=f ḫpr* as a quasi-temporal protasis seems preferable also in some letters (where, however, editors hitherto tended to stay with a purely conditional translation)[84]—perhaps this was a feature borrowed from spoken language.

---

73. Wilhelm Spiegelberg, *Die demotischen Denkmäler II. 30601–31270. 50001–50022. Die demotischen Papyrus*, Catalogue Général des Antiquités du Musée du Caire (Strasbourg: Schauberg, 1908), 256–57.

74. TM#45606. Edda Bresciani, *L'archivio demotico del tempio di Soknopaiu Nesos nel Griffith Institute di Oxford, Vol. 1: P. Ox. Griffith nn. 1–75* (Milan: Cisalpino-Goliardica, 1975), 60–61, pl. 26.

75. Facsimile by the authors, taken from Bresciani, *Archivio demotico*, pl. 26.

76. Versus Bresciani, *Archivio demotico*, 60–61: *mtw-j ḫpr*(?) (11) ... *1/2 5/6*(?) *r wš sw ḫn-f* (12) *ḥr rnp.t*, "e sarà a mio carico (?) .... di deficit di grano in essa per anno."

77. TM#43415. Spiegelberg, *Demotische Denkmäler II*, 254–57; pl. 102.

78. Facsimile by the authors, taken from Spiegelberg, *Demotische Denkmäler II*, pl. 102.

79. Spiegelberg, *Demotische Denkmäler II*, 255, 256–57: "Du gibst sie mir (zurück) im Jahre 18, die obigen Äcker, ohne Unkraut(?)."

80. 94 BCE. TM#43281. Spiegelberg, 43–45; pl. 23.

81. 98 BCE. TM#43283. Spiegelberg, 47–50; pl. 24.

82. Facsimile by the authors, taken from Spiegelberg, pl. 23 (30613, l. 16).

83. Facsimile by the authors, taken from Spiegelberg, pl. 24 (30615, l. 14).

84. E.g., P. Berlin P. 13579 (TM#46487; Karl-Theodor Zauzich, *Demotische Papyri aus den Staatlichen Museen zu Berlin: Lieferung I Papyri von der Insel Elephantine* [Berlin: Akademie Verlag, 1978]), l. x+18; P. Saq. 71/2 DP 145 (TM#46814; Harry S. Smith, "Sunt Lacrimae rerum. A. F. Shore honoris causa," in *The Unbroken Reed: Studies in the Culture and Heritage of Ancient Egypt in Honour of A. F. Shore*, ed. Chris Eyre, Anthony Leahy, and Lisa Montagno Leahy. EES Occasional Publications 11 [London: The Egyptian Exploration Society, 1994], 282–88; pls. 37–38), l. 4; P. Berlin P. 15622+23668 (TM#46458; Karl-Theodor Zauzich, *Demotische Papyri aus den staatlichen Museen zu Berlin – Preussischer Kulturbesitz – Lieferung III Papyri von der Insel Elephantine* [Berlin: Akademie-Verlag, 1993]), l. 6; P. BM EA 10498 (TM#622; Michel Chauveau, "La correspondence bilingue d'un illettré: Petesouchos fils de Panobchounis," in *La lettre d'archive: Communication administrative et personelle dans l'antiquité proche-orientale et égyptienne; Actes du colloque de l'Université de Lyon 2, 9–10 juillet 2004*, ed. Laure Pantalacci, Topoi. Orient-Occident. Suppl. 9. Bibliothèque Générale 32 [Cairo: Institut français d'archéologie orientale, 2008], 34–37), l. 8–9.

For the reflexive use of *qty*, "turn" with *r* + infinitive in the sense of "to repeat doing something, to do something again," not yet attested in Demotic, compare the Coptic ⲔⲞⲦ= (refl.) ⲉ- + infinitive[85] (rarely also with the qualitative, ⲔⲦⲞ= (refl.) ⲉ- + infinitive).[86]

line 7:

 *ḥwy qll*, "to cast lots": The loan word *qll*, not listed in the *DG*, is derived from the Greek term κλῆρος.[87] The practice is also attested in the division document P. Berlin P. 3118[88] where it is stipulated that, once the co-heirs decide to physically split up the liturgies falling to them from their father, they do so by assigning them by lot. For the mechanism most likely used in P. Berlin P. 7056, see section 4, commentary to clause 5 below.

šm n=, "to fall to, devolve to" (of real estate) might be a localism: it is used in a version of the inheritance clause of Demotic sales documents that is for the moment not attested outside Soknopaiou Nesos.[89]

ky sp: While (*n-*)*ky-sp*, literally "another time, on another occasion" (cf. Coptic ⲚⲔⲈⲤⲞⲠ, "another time, again; already"),[90] can, in a negative sentence, mean "not again," here the negation refers not to the adverbial, but to the verb. The "other time" is the last time when the shares of the *kleros* were distributed, see section 4, commentary to clause 5.

 *nty-iw=w*: This writing is the standard form in Roman Soknopaiou Nesos.[91]

 *gpe*: Since a translation "secretly"[92] yields no sense in this context, we propose to link this word to Coptic ϬⲈⲠⲎ, "hasten (σπεύδειν); be eager, be busy (σπουδάζειν)" and the derived adverb ϬⲈⲠⲎ, "quickly, readily."[93] See also section 4, commentary to clause 6 below.

i.ir is understood as a phonetic writing for *r ir*.

line 8:

  *y*⌜ʿ⌝*b*⌜*y*⌝: For the reading compare the complete writing of the word 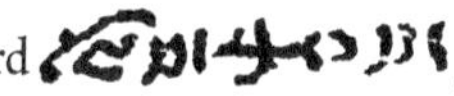 *yʿby* in P. Vienna D 12006 col. 7, l. 12.[94] The translation "sickness, fever, hardship, plight"[95] obviously does not yield much sense here. However, the common use of unetymological writings in Roman Soknopaiou Nesos[96] makes another solution conceivable, that is, understanding *yʿby* as a phonetically close writing for *wp.t*, "work" (cf. the Bohairic form ⲒⲈⲂ, "work"),[97] but with an added layer of meaning: the scribe could have chosen *yʿby* specifically in order to underline the strenuousness of the work in question. *yʿby-wʿy* therefore expresses the composite noun *wp.t-wʿy*,

85. *KHw*, 71–72: "etwas wiederholen;" *CD*, 124b–125a: "turn self, repeat."

86. *KHw*, 70: "etwas wiederholen."

87. Cf. CDD *Q* (2004), 65, s.v. *qrr*(*e*) "lots" and *ḥwy qrr* "to cast lots"; *CD*, 735a: ϩⲒ ⲔⲖⲎⲢⲞⲤ "cast lots."

88. 116 BCE. TM#48272. *DPB*, 14, pl. 29; Pieter W. Pestman, *The Archive of the Theban Choachytes (Second Century B.C.): A Survey of the Demotic and Greek Papyri Contained in the Archive*, StudDem 2 (Leuven: Peeters, 1993), 166–69.

89. *DDD* 3:20.

90. *CD*, 91a, 350b.

91. Karl-Theodor Zauzich, "Das Ende der Form *ḥr-nꜣ=w-stm* – eine Selbstkorrektur," *Enchoria* 27 (2002): 207–8.

92. See CDD *Q* (2004), 26–27, s.v. *qp*(*e*), "to hide, be hidden," also *n qp*, "in secret, secretly."

93. *CD*, 825a–b.

94. Authors' facsimile, taken from Stadler, *Isis*, pl. 15.

95. *DG*, 48, s.v. *jʿb*: "Krankheit, Fieber o.ä. … Auch in der Bedeutung Not, Leid, Kummer o.ä.."

96. Cf. Martin Stadler, *Einführung in die ägyptische Religion ptolemäisch-römischer Zeit nach den demotischen religiösen Texten*. EQÄ 7 (Münster: LIT, 2012), 118–22. For examples in documentary texts from Soknopaiou Nesos see, e.g., Sandra Lippert and Maren Schentuleit, "Stoetis in geheimer Mission: Der Brief pBerlin P 8092," in *Honi soit qui mal y pense: Studien zum pharaonischen, griechisch-römischen und spätantiken Ägypten zu Ehren von Heinz-Josef Thissen*, ed. Hermann Knuf, Christian Leitz and Daniel von Recklinghausen. OLA 194 (Leuven: Peeters, 2010), 364–65, 370.

97. *KHw*, 49. See also Fayumic ⲒⲈⲂⲒ, "sickness."

"agricultural activity, farmwork,"[98] and the modifier *nb* refers to the whole expression and not just *wꜥy*. For the parallel of this clause in Greek lease documents, see section 4, commentary to clause 6 below.

The *m* of *<m>tw=f* is not rubbed off but was left out erroneously.

At the end of the line, there is a small, probably accidental dot.

line 9:

The typical Fayumic lambdacism concerns the whole imperial titulature (ll. 9–10). The inversion of *r/l* and *y* in the name Trajan is also attested in other texts from Soknopaiou Nesos.[99]

line 10:

 *Sbt⌜st⌝*: While notarial documents from Roman Soknopaiou Nesos show only minor, nondeforming variations in their rendering of Σεβαστός,[100] several erroneous writings occur in documentary texts from the Soknopaios temple: although no identical form has yet come to our attention, one might compare 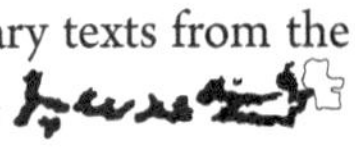 *Sbtṯs*[101] and 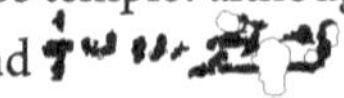 *Sbtsṯ*.[102]

 *Ttqꜥ*: The same doubling of *t* instead of *q* for the honorific *Dacicus* also occurs in the temple receipt P. Vienna D 6344, l. 5  *Ttqs*.[103] The final letter, which looks like the ꜥ-sign in *Nlwꜥ* in l. 9, is therefore hardly a phonetic indication, but seems to have been caused by accidentally leaving out the horizontal stroke of a bolt-*s*.

4. Structure and Legal Clauses of the Document

The introduction *A nꜣ nty ḏd n B* qualifies P. Berlin P. 7056 as a *šꜥ.t*-document, that is, a legal document not written by a notary, but by the first party himself.[104] Other typical elements of a *šꜥ.t*-document are the dating at the end (instead of the beginning, as was common for notarial, i.e., *sẖ*-documents) and the lack of a scribal signature in the ideal, and here actually occuring, case that the first party is able to pen the text himself.

The body of the document consists of seven clauses, the first three belonging to (or inspired by) the model of notarial property divisions of the second type (i.e., those establishing physical division of formerly jointly owned property, mainly between co-heirs),[105] while the rest are more in line with stipulations of lease documents. Similar agreements between associates that start off as property divisions are also attested in Greek.[106]

---

98. *DG*, 79, 86 (*wp.t n wyꜥ*, "Landarbeit, Landwirtschaft"); for attestations, see P. Berlin P. 13608 (91/90 BCE. TM#308. Wilhelm Spiegelberg, "Eine neue Erwähnung eines Aufstandes in Oberägypten in der Ptolemäerzeit," *ZÄS* 65 (1930): 54, 55 n. VIII; see for this text also Ursula Kaplony-Heckel, "Demotische Verwaltungsakten aus Gebelein: Der großer Berliner Papyrus 13608," *ZÄS* 121 (1994): 75–91, for the term in question 79, 86, and 88) and ostracon Berlin P. 6528, l. 2 and 3. 95 BCE. TM#43540. Wilhelm Spiegelberg, *Demotica II*, SAWM 1928.2 (Munich: Verlag der Bayerischen Akademie der Wissenschaften, 1928), 50. See also the Coptic forms ⲉⲓⲉⲡⲟⲩⲉⲓⲉ (S); ⲓⲉⲫⲟⲩⲱⲓ (B), "farmwork": *KHw*, 50; *CED*, 47; *CD*, 81b.

99. Cf. P. Vienna D 6344 (see n. 9 above), l. 5: *Tylns*; P. Vienna D 6787 (TM#100234; *DDD* 2: no. 14), B l. 5 and P. Berlin P. 15691 (TM#100239; *DDD* 2: no. 21) l. 6: *Tyrns*; P. Berlin P. 8932 vso (see n. 11 above), l. 9: *Tyrwns*.

100. See *DDD* 3:476.

101. P. Vienna D 6817 (TM#100261; *DDD* 2: no. 49), F l. 6. Facsimile by the authors. See also P. Berlin P. 15596+23711 (TM#100240; *DDD* 2: no. 22), l. 4.

102. P. Berlin P. 15595 (TM#100241; *DDD* 2: no. 23), l. 4. Facsimile by the authors.

103. See n. 9 above.

104. Depauw, *Companion to Demotic Studies*, 124–25; Lippert, *Einführung in die altägyptische Rechtsgeschichte*, 139–40.

105. For the terminology see Lippert, *Einführung in die altägyptische Rechtsgeschichte*, 155. For examples from Roman Soknopaiou Nesos, see *DDD* 3:59–65.

106. See Andrea Jördens, *Griechische Papyri aus Soknopaiu Nesos (P. Louvre I)*, PTA 43 (Bonn: Habelt, 1998), 58.

Demotic notary documents disappear in the last quarter of the first century CE,[107] so it is not surprising that this is not a *sẖ*-document. However, since the parties to this agreement were, as will be shown below, members of a priestly family, and, as such, were literate in Demotic, they probably did not feel the need to have the village notary draw up a Greek document. All eventually arising disputes would have been settled before a tribunal of their peers anyway; the extensive use of Demotic *hnw*-agreements between the priesthood of the Soknopaios temple as a group and various individual office holders and contractors[108] shows that in the first and second centuries CE, the temple was largely legally self-regulating when it came to internal matters.

1) The division clause

> *pše=n irm=tn pše=tn irm=n* ⸢*ḥꜣ.ty*⸣ *=n m[tr]e.t (n)* (3) *[nꜣ] pše.w(t) r.ir=n (n) pꜣ* ꜥ*-n-(stꜣ.t-)20.t (n) Nsw*ꜥ.w.s.*-tꜣ.wy (n) ṯꜣy (n) ḥꜣ.t-sp* ⸢*1*⸣*5 (n) pꜣ nṯr [nty] mḥe Tyln*⸢*s*⸣ (4) *(r) [h]n (r-)ḥꜣ.t-sp [1]*⸢*8*⸣ *rnp.t 4.t*
> We have divided with you, you have divided with us, our heart is content (with) (3) [the] divisions which we have made (of) the 20-(aroura-)*kleros* (in) Sentheus, from regnal year 15 (of) the conquering god Trajan until regnal year [1]8, 4 years.

The first part of the clause underlines the mutuality of the division; it is (depending on the parties, also with singular pronouns) the standard division clause in documents of this type from at least the third century BCE onwards.[109] The second part, ⸢*ḥꜣ.ty*⸣*=n m[tr]e.t* (3) *[nꜣ] pše.w(t) r.ir=n (n)* ..., does not seem to be attested in this form in other division documents of the second type, although some do contain a phrase stressing the contentedness of the parties, either instead of the first part—in which case the phrase takes over the aspect of mutuality usually present there[110]—or, like in P. Berlin P. 7056, after it.[111]

The division clause introduces the description of the object that is to be divided. This can contain clauses explaining how the division partners came into its possession (e.g., through inheritance) and, especially in the case of houses, more or less elaborate indications about the location following the pattern well established for object descriptions in sales documents.[112] In comparison, the description in P. Berlin P. 7056 is quite succinct, giving simply the object type and surface size and the locality: as will be shown below, the joint ownership went already back about forty-five years, and all involved persons knew exactly which property was meant. An unusual feature in P. Berlin P. 7056 is the indication of a time period (four years) for which the physical division is valid: normally, divisions of the second type are permanent.

2) The clause specifying the individual part

> *mtre pꜣy=tn pše r pꜣ rsy pꜣ imn.ṱ (n) tꜣ ḥny(.t) ḥn*ꜥ *pꜣ* ⸢*imn.ṱ*⸣ *pꜣ* (5) ⸢*m*⸣*[ḥ.ṱ] (n)* ⸢*tꜣ*⸣ *ḥny(.t)*
> (more) precisely, your segment being (situated) towards the southwest (of) the canal and the northwest (of) the canal.

---

107. The last known Demotic notarial document, P. Vienna D 10086 (TM#93264), dates to the year 85 CE; Maren Schentuleit and Günter Vittmann, "Eine spätdemotische Abtretungsurkunde aus Athribis (P. Wien D 10086)," in *Ripple in Still Water Where There Is No Pebble Tossed: Festschrift in Honour of Cary J. Martin*, ed. Adrienn Almásy-Martin, Michel Chauveau, Koen Donker van Heel and Kim Ryholt, GHP Egyptology 34 (London: Golden House), in press.

108. See Lippert, "Die Abmachungen der Priester."

109. E.g., P. Berlin P. 3089+P. BM EA 10426a, 230 BCE (TM#2709; Günter Vittmann, "Eine demotische Teilungsurkunde aus dem Jahr 230 v. Chr.," *ZÄS* 109 [1982]: 166–71, pls. 5–8), l. 2. See also *DDD* 3:60.

110. E.g., P. Louvre E 9415, 190 BCE (TM#46158; Didier Devauchelle, "Le papyrus démotique Louvre E 9415: Un partage de biens," *RdÉ* 31 [1979]: 29–35, pl. 5), l. 6: *mtr=n (n) pš(.t) irm=t mtr=t (n) pš(.t) irm=n* ..., "We are agreed (to) dividing with you, you are agreed (to) dividing with us ... ."

111. P. Vienna KHM dem. 3872 (TM#3569; Eugène Revillout, *Nouvelle Chrestomathie. Mission de 1878: Contrats de Berlin, Vienne, Leyde, etc.* [Paris: Ernest Leroux, 1878], 89): *mtr=n irm=k n* ..., "We are in agreement with you regarding ... ."

112. See *DDD* 3:60.

This clause introduces the specification of the physically distinct part of the property that falls to the adressees of the document: it is lacking in the earlier divisions of the second type, and in its hitherto earliest attestation in P. Vienna KHM dem. 3872, it does not use the key word *mtr*, "(more) precisely," which is the common feature of the later phrasing.[113] Again, the description is only understandable for persons who know the lay of the land, and does not even include the size—for a reconstruction; see section 6.3 and fig. 5 below.

3) The retraction clause

pꜣ rmṯ nb n-ỉm=n {nty-}nty ỉw ḥn n=f sṯꜣ.ṱ=f r pše {m}m-sꜣ tꜣy rnp.t 4.t mtw⸢*=f* ⁽⁶⁾ *sṯꜣ.ṱ=f*⸣
Any man of us who wants to withdraw himself from (the) division after these 4 years, shall withdraw himself.

Retraction clauses are a common feature of legal documents with reciprocal commitments and therefore also occur regularly in division documents of the second type, at least from the second century BCE onwards.[114] The only significant difference in the phrasing of the protasis in P. Berlin P. 7056 is the use of the auxiliary *ḥn* where most known texts simply say, "whoever of us retracts himself."

The normal retraction clause basically prohibits withdrawal from the agreed-upon physical division by stipulating in the apodosis a heavy fine, payable mainly to the royal cult, to the co-associates, or both. Even after paying the fine, this standard clause still does not allow the revocation of the arrangement. Conversely, P. Berlin P. 7056 does not specify what would happen if one of the partners tried to go back on the division agreement, but explicitly allows retraction from the division after the four years are up. This reflects the fact that the arrangement here does not permanently split the jointly owned field, in which case one party might eventually feel they had been disadvantaged by getting stuck with a smaller or lower-yielding share, but merely temporarily distributes the shares that were switched between the parties every few years anyway; see the commentary to clause 5 below.

While Spiegelberg, probably on the basis of his knowlegde of other division documents, deduced that the next lines should contain the conditions under which the retraction is possible,[115] these are mainly obligations pertaining to the cultivation of the part during the four years of the agreed-upon division (clauses 4, 6 and 7), and only one, clause 5, actually regulates what happens after the four-year period is up. Therefore, the third person singular of the conjunctive *{nty-}nty-ỉw=f* (i.e. *mtw=f*) in the immediately following clause (4) refers back to *pꜣ rmṯ nb n-ỉm=n* "any man of us = whoever of us," not to *pꜣ rmṯ nb n-ỉm=n {nty-}nty ỉw ḥn n=f sṯꜣ.ṱ=f r pše* "any man of us who wants to withdraw from the division." This lack of clarity is unfortunately not a singularity: from the moment when the scribe could no longer use the notarial model for his text, his suffix references become ambiguous and the order in which the clauses are presented loses coherence.

4) Clause about crop rotation

⸢*{nty-}nty-ỉw=f ẖꜣ*ʿ⸣ *ꜣḥy (sṯꜣ.t) 2.t (n) sme sp(-2) r-bnr tꜣ dnỉ.t (r) šʿd swb*
He shall set apart 2 (arouras) of radish field from the part, (for) cutting green fodder.

Due to the elliptic nature of the document, the syntactic role of the various elements in this phrase is not easy to identify. However, the shorter phrasing in clause 7, which refers to the penalty in case of nonobservance (see below), helps to clarify this: thus, *sme sp-2*, "radish" seems to have been considered as the main crop, but two arouras of this "radish field" should be reserved for fodder plants instead. Similar clauses indicating that all or part of a field is used εἰς σπορὰν χόρτου καὶ κοπῆς (or εἰς σπορὰν χόρτου κοπῆς καὶ ξηρασίας) "for sowing, cutting (and drying)

113. See *DDD* 3:60: "Teilzuweisungsklausel."
114. See *DDD* 3:62: "Rückzugsstrafklausel."
115. *DPB*, 24.

of fodder" also occur in Greek land leases and lease offers from the Fayum.[116] For this practice of crop rotation, see section 6.4 below.

5) Clause about the redistribution of thc shares by casting lots

iw=f ḫpr iw=w qty=w{w} r in⸢*=w*⸣ (7) *m-s3*[*=s*] ⸢*nty-iw=w*⸣ *ḥwy qll r t3 dni.t* {*nty-*}*nty iw* ⸢*bn-pw*⸣*=s šm n=w ky sp*

When they bring them (back) again later, they shall cast lots for the part which had not gone to them the other time.

This clause refers to the time after the four-year period of the division is up and the parties therefore "bring" their shares back in order to redistribute them. Given that there were only three shares, situated in a triangle (see also fig. 5 below), the easiest way to redistribute them without anyone getting the same share as last time would have been for each party to move to the next share either clockwise or counterclockwise. If they always moved in the same direction, then each party would get the same share again on every third redistribution. In that case, no casting of lots would have been necessary after the initial distribution and the choice of the direction of the rotation. The fact that the parties still stipulated a redistribution by lots in 112 CE implies that this regular one-way rotation, although it looks at first glance the fairest method, was deemed undesirable: its great disadvantage is in fact that each party always takes over their new share after it has been cultivated by the same person, meaning that the party who succeeded someone who was notoriously negligent always received their new share in a bad state. Therefore, casting lots at each redistribution in order to decide whether it would be made by moving clockwise or counterclockwise was indeed more equitable. For indications that this or a similar practice had already been used by the co-heirs of the *kleros* before 112 CE, see section 6.3 below.

6) Clause about correct cultivation

nty-iw=w b3k=w gpe i.ir (8) *y*⸢ʿ⸣*b*⸢*y*⸣*-w*ʿ⸢*y*⸣ *nb*

They shall work them diligently in order to accomplish all farmwork.

This clause is comparable to a version of the "Bewirtschaftungsklausel" found in some Ptolemaic period and early Roman Demotic land leases: *mtw=y ir=w n wp.t nb n wy*ʿ *n pr.t šmw*, "and I shall work them with all farmwork, in the *pr.t* and *šmw* seasons" (and similar).[117] However, the more elaborate phrasing here might be influenced by contemporary Greek lease documents and lease applications in which a clause obliges the lessee to accomplish (ἐπιτελεῖν) all agricultural work (τὰ γεωργικὰ ἔργα πάντα) on the leased fields:[118] the addition of *gpe*, "diligently" could be an attempt to convey the impression that ἐπιτελεῖν implied more intensity than simple τελεῖν, which of course already means "to fulfill, accomplish." The inclusion of this clause, like the crop rotation clause 4 above, is motivated by the fact that, under the previously discussed redistribution mechanism, one of the two shares allotted in 112 CE to Pekysis and Stotoetis would necessarily fall to Harpagathes and his siblings at the next redistribution: they therefore had an interest in obliging their co-shareholders to treat their shares with care.

---

116. E.g., BGU II 526 (86 CE, Soknopaiou Nesos); P. Kron. 10 (116 CE, Tebtynis), BGU I 166 (157 CE, Fayum), BGU XI 2036 (162–163 CE, Herakleia); P. Mil.Vogl. III 142 (165? CE, Tebtynis).

117. Heinz Felber, *Demotische Ackerpachtverträge der Ptolemäerzeit: Untersuchungen zu Aufbau, Entwicklung und inhaltlichen Aspekten einer Gruppe von demotischen Urkunden*, ÄA 58 (Wiesbaden: Harrassowitz, 1997), 135 (unfortunately without a complete list of texts). Other examples are P. Turin Suppl. 6107, Djeme, 109 BCE (TM#45114; Pieter W. Pestman, "Bail à fermer de la terre « La Pointe »," in *Textes grecs, démotiques et bilingues*, ed. Ernst Boswinkel and Pieter W. Pestman, PLB 19 (Leiden: Brill, 1978), 3–12) and P. Botti I, l. 8–9, Tebtynis, 4 CE (TM#46032; Giuseppe Botti Jr., "Papiri demotici dell'epoca imperiale da Tebtynis," in *Studi in onore di Aristide Calderini e Roberto Paribeni* 2, Studi di papirologia e antichitè orientali (Milan: Casa Editrice Ceschina, 1957), 75–86).

118. See the above-mentioned BGU II 644 (69 CE), l. 29. The clause is common in Fayumic documents from the second half of the first century CE to the first quarter of the third century, see, e.g., BGU II 526 (86 CE), l. 17–19; P. Mich. IX 564 (150 CE), l. 13–14; BGU II 633 (221 CE), l. 12–14.

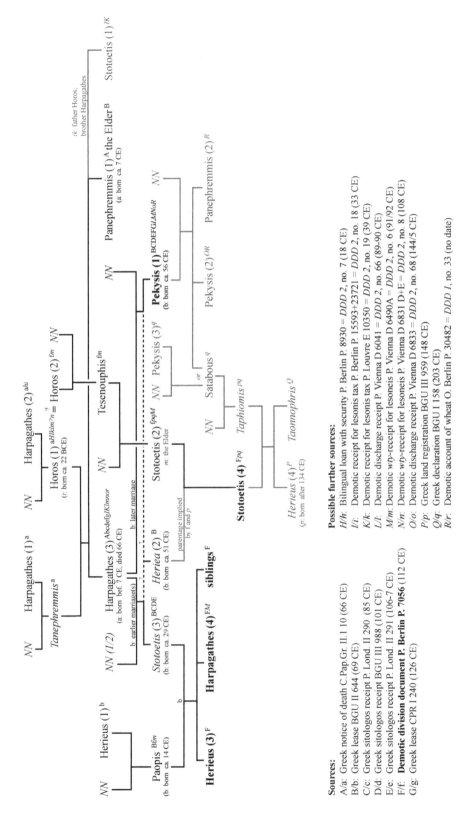

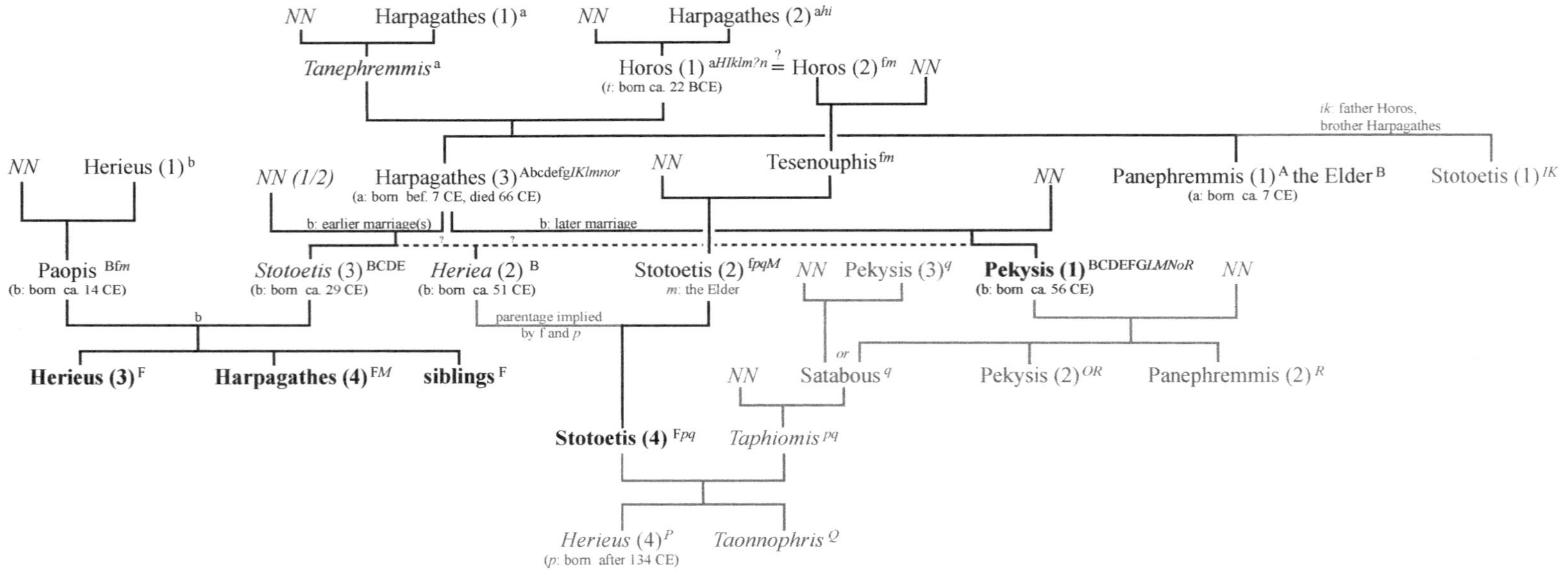

Sources:

A/a: Greek notice of death C.Pap.Gr. II.1 10 (66 CE)
B/b: Greek lease BGU II 644 (69 CE)
C/c: Greek sitologos receipt P. Lond. II 290 (85 CE)
D/d: Greek sitologos receipt BGU III 988 (101 CE)
E/e: Greek sitologos receipt P. Lond. II 291 (106-7 CE)
F/f: **Demotic division document P. Berlin P. 7056** (112 CE)
G/g: Greek lease CPR I 240 (126 CE)

Possible further sources:

H/h: Bilingual loan with security P. Berlin P. 8930 = *DDD 2*, no. 7 (18 CE)
I/i: Demotic receipt for lesonis tax P. Berlin P. 15593+23721 = *DDD 2*, no. 18 (33 CE)
K/k: Demotic receipt for lesonis tax P. Louvre E 10350 = *DDD 2*, no. 19 (39 CE)
L/l: Demotic discharge receipt P. Vienna D 6041 = *DDD 2*, no. 66 (89-90 CE)
M/m: Demotic *wty*-receipt for lesoneis P. Vienna D 6490A = *DDD 2*, no. 6 (91/92 CE)
N/n: Demotic *wty*-receipt for lesoneis P. Vienna D 6831 D+E = *DDD 2*, no. 8 (108 CE)
O/o: Demotic discharge receipt P. Vienna D 6833 = *DDD 2*, no. 68 (144/5 CE)
P/p: Greek land registration BGU III 959 (148 CE)
Q/q: Greek declaration BGU I 158 (203 CE)
R/r: Demotic account of wheat O. Berlin P. 30482 = *DDD 1*, no. 33 (no date)

In the family tree, upper case letters are used to indicate that the person him/herself is mentioned in a document, while additional information that can be deduced through it, like the dates of birth and decease, filiations, marriages or other parentage links, are referenced through lower case letters. The names of women are given in italics. Persons only attested in sources with potential links to this family are printed in gray.

Figure 3. Family tree (Lippert/Schentuleit)

7) Clause about compensatory payment

> *pꜣ {nty-}nty iw bn-iw=f ḫꜣꜥ ꜣḥy (sṯꜣ.t) 2.t (r) šꜥd swb r-bnr <m>tw=f di.t {n}* (9) *swꜥ ⸢rtb⸣ 5 r ꜣḥy (sṯꜣ.t) wꜥ.t.t*
>
> The one who will not set apart 2 (arouras) of field (for) cutting green fodder shall give 5 artabas of wheat per one (aroura) of field.

This clause seems to have been added as an afterthought: it is the penalty clause for failure to comply with the injunction of clause 4 to practice crop rotation by using part of the field for green fodder. The beneficiary of the penalty, payable in grain, is not specified: either it was Harpagathes and his siblings, or the whole group of joint owners who would have received it.

5. The Family

Joint inheritance is the main reason for the establishment of division documents of the second type,[119] but the scant information given in P. Berlin P. 7056 does not, by itself, allow us to understand whether or how the four named persons are related to each other and thus, how they came to be associates in this division. Luckily, it is possible to securely attribute six other documents to this same family, five of which also mention the *kleros* or parts of it, while ten further texts might also concern members of the family.[120] The resulting family tree (fig. 3) would cover six generations and over two hundred years.

In BGU II 644 (doc. B), a Greek lease dated 69 CE, Pekysis (1) and his paternal half-sisters Stotoetis (3) and Heriea[121] (2) lease the 20-aroura *kleros*[122] to a certain Papeis, son of Stotoetis, for three years. Since this document has been somewhat misunderstood by the first editors, who thought that Pekysis and a certain Haplous, son of Ekysis, were the lessors and the sisters, together with a certain Apeis, son of Stotoetis, were the lessees, the relevant part of the document is reedited here:

(...) ἐμίσθωσεν Πεκυσις Ἁρπα-
γα̣θου ὡς ἐτῶν δέκα τριῶν ἄσημος μετὰ ἐπιτρό-
που τοῦ πατ̣ρ̣ὸ̣ς̣ ἀδελφοῦ {ἀδελφοῦ} Πανεφριμμις
πρεσβυτέρου τοῦ Ὥρου ὡς ἐτῶν ἑξήκοντα δύο
οὐλὴ μετώπωι ἐξ ἀριστερῶν, καὶ ⟨τοῦ⟩ ἄλλου Πεκ̣υσιος
ὁμοπατρίαι ἀδελφαὶ Στοτοητι ὡς ἐτῶν τεσ-
σαράκοντα̣ οὐλὴ καρπῶι δεξιῶι, καὶ Ἑριεα ὡς
ἐ̣τῶν̣ δ̣έκα ὀκτὼ οὐλὴ μετώπωι μέσωι μετὰ
κυριοῶν ἀ̣μ̣φ̣οτέρων τοῦ τῆς Στοτοητιος ἀνδρὸς
Π̣αωπιος τοῦ Ἑριεως ὡς ἐτῶν πεντήκοντα
πέντε, οὐλῆι δακτύλῳ μικρῷ χ̣ε̣ιρὸς ἀ̣ρ̣ι̣σ̣τε(ρᾶς),
Παπειτι Στοτοητιος Πέρσηι τῆς ἐπιγονῆς ὡς
ἐτῶν τριάκοντ̣α̣ π̣έ̣ν̣τ̣ε οὐλὴ ὑπὸ ἀντικνήμιον
δεξιόν, τὰς ὑπαρχούσας αὐτοῖς περὶ Φιλοπάτορα

119. See for the document type section 4 above.

120. In the following sections the different documents are referred to by capital letters. A list is given with the family tree in fig. 3.

121. The Demotic unisex name *Ḥr=w* is generally rendered in Greek papyri as Ἑριευς regardless of gender, but this reading seems not possible here.

122. For detailed information concerning this *kleros* see section 6 below.

Ἀπιαδος Θ̣ε̣μ̣ί̣στου μερίδος κλήρου κατοικικοῦ ἀρου-
ρων̣ εἴκοσι ἢ ὅσων ἐὰν ὦσι ἐν δυσὶ [σ]φρα̣γῖσι εἰς ἔτη τρῖ-
α ἀπὸ τοῦ ἐνεστῶτος ἔτους (...)

7 Πανεφριμμις l. Πανεφριμμεως 8 καὶ ⟨τοῦ⟩ ἄλλου Πεκ̣υσιος ed.pr. καὶ Ἀπ̣λ̣οῦς Ἐκύσιος 9 ἀδελφαὶ ed.pr. l. ἀδελφῇ; Στοτοητι ed.pr. Στοτοητις 12 κυ̣ριοῶν l. κυρίου ed.pr. κυρίων 14 οὐλῇι l. οὐλή 15 Παπειτι ed.pr. καὶ Ἀπεῖτι 18–19 ἀρου|ρων l. ἀρού|ρας

(...) Pekysis, son of Harpagathes, about 13 years old, without a mark, with as his tutor his father's brother, Panephremmis the Elder, son of Horos, about 62 years old, with a scar on the left side of his front, and the sisters of the other one, (namely) Pekysis, from the same father, Stotoetis, about 40 years old, with a scar on the right wrist, and Heriea, about 18 years old, with a scar in the middle of her front, with as the *kyrios* of both the husband of Stotoetis, Paopis, son of Herieus, about 55 years old, with a scar on the little finger of the left hand, have leased to Papeis, son of Stotoetis, Persian of the *epigonê*, about 35 years old, with a scar on the right shin, their 20 arouras of a catoeicic cleros, or however many there are, situated near Philopator Apiados in the *Themistou meris*, in two plots, for three years from this year on. (...)

The reason why Panephremmis the Elder acts as a tutor to his underage nephew Pekysis (1) becomes clear from C.Pap.Gr. II.1 10 (doc. A), dated 66 CE, being the notice of the death of Pekysis's (1) father, Harpagathes (3), son of Horos, grandson of Harpagathes (2) and of the mother Tanephremmis, daughter of Harpagathes (1) (who might have been the same as Harpagathes [2]),[123] submitted by his brother Panephremmis. This text also gives us the information that both were priests at Soknopaiou Nesos and that Panephremmis was born about 7 CE. Harpagathes (3) was certainly older, and either the first- or second-born son, because he bears his paternal and/or maternal grandfather's name. At the death of Harpagathes (3), the *kleros* fell to his three children who owned it jointly and at first leased it out together.

That the sisters are referred to as Pekysis's (1) ὁμοπατρίαι ἀδελφαί, "sisters of the same father" in doc. B implies that the three siblings had at least two, and perhaps even three different mothers. This is not surprising given the age difference of about twenty-seven years between Stotoetis (3) and Pekysis (1). We can also presume from the fact that no other children of Harpagathes (3) are mentioned that Pekysis (1) was the only surviving male child, although he was certainly not the first-born son (in which case he should have been called Horos after his paternal grandfather);[124] likewise, Stotoetis (3), the eldest surviving daughter, was probably not the first-born one, which should have been called Tanephremmis like her paternal grand-mother. The mention of Stotoetis's (3) husband Paopis also resolves the question of how Harpagathes (4) and Herieus (3), sons of Paopis, come to be involved in the division in P. Berlin P. 7056: by 112 CE, Stotoetis (3), born in about 29 CE, had probably passed away, and her and Paopis's children—Pekysis's (1) nephews, although probably about the same age as him or even a bit older—had inherited.

Stotoetis's (3) death might have happened not long before 112 CE: a series of *sitologos* receipts for the *kleros* from the years 85 CE (P. Lond. II 290, doc. C), 101 CE (BGU III 988, doc. D) and 106/7 CE (P. Lond. II 291, doc. E)[125] mention Pekysis (1) and his half-sister Stotoetis (3), who therefore was still alive and active at about 77/8 years old. These receipts also show that later, the *kleros* was cultivated by the three siblings (and later their descendants) themselves, each of them getting one share. Heriea probably also died before 112 CE—the seemingly unrelated Stotoetis (4), son of Stotoetis (2), grandson of Tesenouphis, great-grand-son of Horos (2) mentioned together with Peky-

123. For sibling marriage in Roman Egypt, see Jane Rowlandson and Sandra Lippert, "Family and Life Cycle Transitions," in *A Companion to Greco-Roman and Late Antique Egypt*, ed. Katelijn Vandorpe (Medford, MA: Wiley Blackwell, 2019), 336.

124. For this practice, see Rowlandson and Lippert, "Family and Life Cycle Transitions," 332.

125. The link between these three receipts and BGU II 644 has already been pointed out by Deborah Hobson, "The Village of Apias," *Aegyptus* 62 (1982): 85. For more information see section 6.3 below.

sis (1) as the adressees of P. Berlin P. 7056, is best explained as Heriea's son. The last certain mention of Pekysis (1) appears in the Greek lease CPR I 240 (doc. G) of 126 CE: Pekysis (1), said to be "about [6]5" (or [7]5?) years old—according to doc. B, he should have been about 70—leases his part of the *kleros* to a certain Stotoetis, who could have been this same son of Heriea and Stotoetis (2), but could obviously also be someone completely unrelated.

Other documents that might mention members of the family are the bilingual loan P. Berlin P. 8930 (doc. H) from 18 CE in which a Horos, son of Harpagathes with a not preserved lengthy (and therefore most likely priestly) title is the creditor. His age, about 40 years, means that he was born in about 22 BCE, which could well correspond to Pekysis's (1) grandfather Horos (1), who had his eldest son Harpagathes (3) some time before 7 CE.

A Demotic receipt for the *lesonis* tax, P. Berlin P. 15593+23721 (doc. I) of 33 CE, mentions a Horos, son of Harpagathes, and his sons Harpagathes and Stotoetis, followed by eight other persons as *lesoneis* of Soknopaios for the year 19 of Tiberius, and another one, P. Louvre E 10350 (doc. K) of 39 CE, enumerates at least eleven *lesoneis* of Isis Nepherses (the main female deity of Soknopaiou Nesos) for the year 3 of Caligula, and the list starts again with Harpagathes, son of Horos and his brother Stotoetis. If these are Horos (1) and Harpagathes (3) with a hitherto unknown brother Stotoetis (1), Horos (1) would have been about 55 in doc. I, and perhaps deceased, or at least retired, six years later in doc. K. Harpagathes (3) would have been in his late twenties or early thirties in doc. I, and his brother Stotoetis (1) somewhat younger.

Pekysis (1) himself might be mentioned in three other Demotic temple receipts: a Pekysis, son of Harpagathes, grandson of Horos, signs among the representatives of the priests on the discharge receipt P. Vienna D 6041 (doc. L) of 89–90 CE. If this was our Pekysis (1), he would have been about 33 years old. However, the receipt for *wty* tax P. Vienna D 6831 D+E (doc. N) of 108 CE mentions not only a Pekysis, son of Harpagathes, grandson of Horos, but also a Pekysis, son of Harpagathes, grandson of Horos, great-grandson of Satabus, which shows that the identification in doc. L is by no means unequivocal. A similar problem arises with the receipt for *wty* tax P. Vienna D 6490A (doc. M) of 91/2 CE: there, a Pekysis, son of Harpagathes, grandson of Harpagathes is mentioned, and the fact that the second "Harpagathes" is written out instead of indicating it by *sp-2*, as was the norm in Soknopaiou Nesos, suggests that this could be a mistake for Horos—but then, this might again be either Pekysis (1) or the like-named great-grandson of Satabus mentioned in doc. N. However, doc. M also mentions a Harpagathes, son of Paopis who could be Pekysis's (1) nephew (and most likely the scribe of P. Berlin P. 7056) Harpagathes (4), as well as a Stotoetis the Elder, son of Tesenouphis, grandson of Horos, who could have been Stotoetis (2), the father of the Stotoetis (4) and thus, if our reconstruction is correct, Pekysis's (1) brother in law.

Two Demotic temple documents might refer to Pekysis's (1) children: on the discharge receipt P. Vienna D 6833 (doc. O) of 144/5 CE, a Pekysis, son of Pekysis, son of Harpagathes signs; if this was a son of Pekysis (1), he might have been anything between 40 and 65 years old. The ostracon Berlin P. 30482 (doc. R, undated), listing priests receiving grain, mentions a Pekysis, son of Harpagathes and his sons Pekysis and Panephremmis. If the identification of the first with Pekysis (1) is correct (and again, this might also be the other Pekysis, son of Harpagathes from doc. N), this ostracon would assign all the members of this family descending from Harpagathes (2) to the first phyle, which might explain why Horus (1) and his sons had been put at the beginning of the lists in docs. I and K.

In BGU III 959 (doc. P), 148 CE, a female underage Herieus, daughter of Stotoetis, granddaughter of Stotoetis, and of the mother Taphiomis, registers her three aroura of catoeicic land near Apias formerly belonging to a certain Chrysaria. Herieus is assisted by a tutor who was probably a relative (an elder brother or an uncle?) named Panephremmis, son of Stotoetis. She could be the eldest granddaughter of Heriea (2) and Stotoetis (2). Her father, Stotoetis (4), would have been at least 45 and potentially as old as 60 years old at her birth, and probably had died by 148 CE. Taonnophris, daughter of Stotoetis and grand-daughter of Stotoetis and of the mother Taphiamis (another Greek transcription of *Ta-pꜣ-ym*, Taphiomis), daughter of Satabous, granddaughter of Pekysis (who might even have been the same as Pekysis [1]!), who addressed the *strategos* and the village scribe of Herakleia in 203 CE through the Greek declaration BGU I 158 (doc. Q), is most likely the sister of this Herieus (4) mentioned in doc. P.

6. The *kleros*

6.1. Location

Papyrus Berlin P. 7056 locates the whole *kleros* at , a toponym that does not appear in other published Demotic texts from Roman Soknopaiou Nesos that we are aware of.[126] The first reading would naturally be *Nsw-tꜣ.wy*, but this is not listed in *Trismegistos Places*. However, a toponym 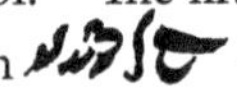 [127] occurs in P. Lille I 5 (verso l. 17), a third-century BCE letter found at Ghoran, where Cenival[128] read it as *Smꜣ-tꜣ.wy*, despite the divine determinative after the first sign, and it is under this name that it has entered *Trismegistos Places*.[129] Cenival thought that the whole action of the letter took place in the Memphite area, based on the assumption that the toponym *Tꜣ-rswṯy*, "the watch," to the south of which the addressee is said to have come recently (recto l. 11), referred to the Memphite quarter Φυλακή,[130] and therefore interpreted  as "Junction (*smꜣ*) of the Two lands," a name that would indeed be suited for a toponym at the entrance of the Fayum, at the northern end of the Nile Valley, close to the apex of the Delta.[131] How a letter sent to a person supposedly at Memphis would end up at Ghoran, on the western end of the *Themistou meris* in the Fayum, remains unexplained. Monson[132] proposed this 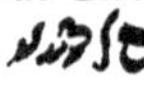 to be the same place as 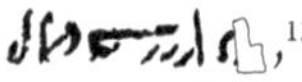,[133] 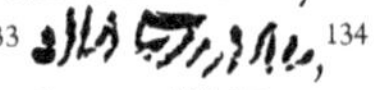,[134] which he read *Pꜣ-ʿ.wy-Smꜣ-tꜣ.wy*, attested in several Ptolemaic land surveys and accounts from Tebtunis.[135] *Trismegistos Places* accepts this identification and accordingly attributes *Pꜣ-ʿ.wy-Smꜣ-tꜣ.wy* the same reference number TM_Geo 11560.

It has long been recognized that the distinction between Demotic writings of *Nsw-tꜣ.wy* and *Smꜣ-tꜣ.wy*, theoretically hinging on the presence or absence of a divine determinative, was not always so clear-cut;[136] the problem is compounded by a possible phonetic convergence of both *nsw* and *smꜣ* towards /se/ or /so/. Moreover, *Nsw-tꜣ.wy* is a common epithet of Herishef, while *Smꜣ-tꜣ.wy* is the name of the child god (Greek Σεμθευς) of Herishef's triad at Heracleopolis. Therefore, even the supposedly clear writing 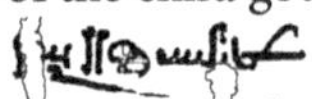 in P. Berlin P. 7056, with abbreviated *ʿnḫ wḏꜣ snb* after the divine determinative, is not an absolute guarantee that *Nsw-tꜣ.wy* was meant. In any case, it is possible or even likely that the toponym in P. Berlin P. 7056 refers to the same Fayumic place as 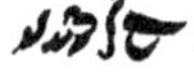 in P. Lille I 5, but whether it is to be understood as *Nsw-tꜣ.wy* or *Smꜣ-tꜣ.wy* and whether this is identical to the place *Pꜣ-ʿ.wy-Smꜣ-tꜣ.wy* in the P. Agri. papyri, which might potentially also be understood as *Pꜣ-ʿ.wy-Nsw-tꜣ.wy*, cannot be ascertained.

---

126. The toponym is, however, also attested in the account P. Vienna D 5c verso, col. 17, l. 5 which is currently being edited for an online publication in the context of the French-German research project DimeData (ANR-17-FRAL-0004-01 and 02 - DFG 389429869).

127. Facsimile by the authors, taken from Françoise de Cenival, "Lettre demandant la libération d'un prisonnier (P.dém. Lille 5) Provenance: Ghoran (Fayoum) - Date: 20 août 245 avant notre ère," *CRIPEL* 13 (1991): pl. 5.

128. Cenival, "P.dém. Lille 5," 41.

129. TM_Geo 11560.

130. Cenival, "P.dém. Lille 5," 40.

131. Cenival, 45.

132. Andrew Monson, *Agriculture and Taxation in Early Ptolemaic Egypt. Demotic Land Surveys and Accounts (P.Agri)*, PTA 46 (Bonn: Habelt, 2012), 3.

133. P. Agri. 4 (TM#44346), col. 4, l. 1. Facsimile taken by the authors from Monson, *Agriculture and Taxation*, pl. 15.

134. P. Agri. 6 (TM#46250) recto, col. 4, l. 1. Facsimile taken by the authors from Monson, pl. 20.

135. Monson, 169: other attestations in P. Agri 1, col. 1, l. 4 (*op.cit.*, 41) and perhaps also P. Agri. 9, verso l. 11, although there one might also simply read *pꜣ ʿ.wy Smꜣ-tꜣ.wy*, "the house of (the man) Semtheus," since this is a list of real estate (Monson, 136–37).

136. Wilhelm Spiegelberg, *Aegyptische und griechische Eigennamen aus Mumienetiketten der römischen Kaiserzeit auf Grund von grossenteils unveröffentlichtem Material* (Leipzig: Hinrichs, 1901) 41*–43*; Jan Quaegebeur, "Études démotiques et égyptologie: Quelques titres et noms de métier," in *Acta Demotica: Acts of the Fifth International Conference for Demotists. Pisa, 4th–8th September 1993*, EVO 17 (Pisa: Giardini, 1994), 241; Günter Vittmann, *Der demotische Papyrus Rylands 9*, ÄAT 38 (Wiesbaden: Harrassowitz, 1998), 424–25.

Concerning the localization of this place, there are two leads that we can pursue. On the one hand, there exists a Greek toponym Σενθευς[137] in the Fayum, which Clarysse had already linked to the personal name *Sm3-t3.wy*,[138] but which could equally well be a phonetic transcription of *Nsw-t3.wy*. According to *Trismegistos Places*, this village is mentioned in three papyri from the archive of Epagathos, estate manager of Gemellus,[139] two of which also mention Apias[140] in the *Themistou meris*, a testamentary division from Soknopaiou Nesos[141] bequeathing land both in Sentheus and Philopator Apiados[142] (a village probably situated so close to Apias that it merged with the latter in the mid-first century CE),[143] and a letter of the early third century CE mentioning a "phrontistes of the villages of Apias and Sentheus."[144] We can now add a sixth attestation, because the lease BGU II 644 (doc. B), which refers to the same 20-arouras *kleros* as P. Berlin P. 7056 43 years earlier, describes its situation as "near Philopator Apiados," but later it is stipulated that the rent, taxes and storage fees payable in grain are to be measured μέτρ[ῳ] δρόμῳ τετραχοινίκ(ῳ) (25) θησαυροῦ Συνθεως, "with the four-choinix *dromos*-measure of the granary of Syntheus."[145] This toponym has entered *Trismegistos Places* under the reconstructed nominative form Συνθις (TM_Geo 53110), but in the light of the preceeding remarks, Συνθεως should rather be interpreted as the genitive of an alternative writing of the toponym Σενθευς (gen. Σενθεως).

On the other hand, in BGU III 988 (doc. D), the second of the three surviving *sitologos* receipts acknowledging tax payments from the co-heirs for their shares of the same *kleros*, only two shares are said to be on the territory of Philopator Apiados and the third on that of Herakleia,[146] and this is confirmed by the lease G, which concerns only the share that Pekysis (1) held at that moment, again said to be "near Herakleia." The close proximity of Herakleia and Apias is also well known from other sources:[147] in SPP XXII 50, land is described as being situated "near the villages of Apias and Herakleia," and according to P. Lond III 842, their territories actually touched. Therefore, even though we know from doc. B that the *kleros* consisted of two plots (l. 19: ἐν δυσὶ [σ]φραγῖσι), the indications in P. Berlin P. 7056, ll. 4–5 make it likely that these were not far apart, but adjacent and simply separated by the canal mentioned in P. Berlin P. 7056, which probably at the same time was the boundary between the territories of Philopator Apiados/Apias and Herakleia.

And here we can close the circle: the god Herishef, whose main epithet was *Nsw-t3.wy*, "king of the two lands," as well as the child god *Sm3-t3.wy* of the Heracleopolitan triad were, through *interpretatio graeca*, identified with

137. TM_Geo 2121. N.B.: The name is never attested in the nominative, but always appears as Σενθεως.

138. See also the Greek renderings of the personal name *Sm3-t3.wy* as Σομτους in the Theban region and as Σεμθευς, Σενθευς, Σοντευς, Συντευς etc. in the Fayum and Herakleopolite region (*Trismegistos People*, TM_namID 1044.

139. P. Fay. 102, l. 12; P.Fay. 111, l. 22–23 (damaged); P. Fay. 112, l. 20. For the archive, see most recently Ruben Smolders, "Epagathos, estate manager," Leuven Homepage of Papyrus Collections, ArchID 134. Version 2 (2013), https://www.trismegistos.org/arch/archives/pdf/134.pdf.

140. TM_Geo 240.

141. SB XXII 15705, l. 16, 90 CE.

142. TM_Geo 1775. Emanuela Battaglia, "Philopator Kome," *Aegyptus* 62 (1982): 124–35; Emanuela Battaglia, "Ancora su Philopator Kome," *Aegyptus* 63 (1983): 181.

143. Hobson, "The Village of Apias," 84–87; see also Francisca Hoogendijk, "Parachoresis von Katökenland," in *Papyri in honorem Johannis Bingen octogenarii (P. Bingen)*, ed. Henri Melaerts, Studia Varia Bruxellensia ad Orbem Graeco-Latinum Pertinentia 5 (Leuven: Peeters, 2000), 257–58, and Cornelia E. Römer, *The Fayoum Survey Project: The Themistou Meris, Vol. A: The Archaeological and Papyrological Survey*, Collectanea Hellenistica KVAB VIII (Leuven: Peeters, 2019), 317–19.

144. P. Lond III 851(b), col. 2, l. 11–12, 217 CE.

145. For the different types of authoritative *choinix* measures (of private, village, or temple granaries) mentioned in Greek papyri, see Rachel Mairs, "An Early Roman Application for Lease of a Date Crop (P. Duk. inv. 85) and the Six-Choinix Measure of the Hermeneus," *ZPE* 172 (2010): 186–89.

146. TM_Geo 772. Deborah W. Hobson, "The Village of Heraklia in the Arsinoite Nome," *BASP* 22 (1985): 101–15; Römer, *Fayoum Survey Project*, 315–17.

147. Hobson, "The Village of Heraklia," 103; Römer, *Fayoum Survey Project*, 318.

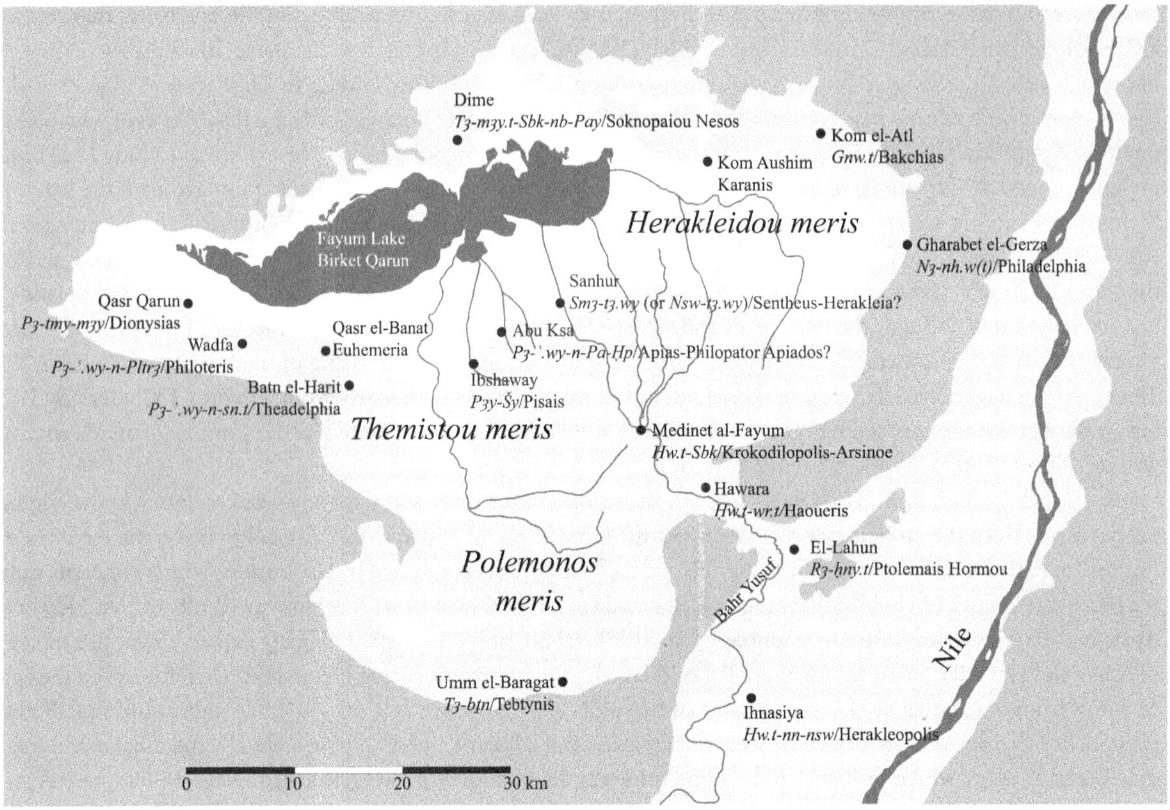

Figure 4. Map of the Fayum (Lippert and Schentuleit).

Heracles[148]—hence the translation of their main cult place, *Ḥw.t-nn-nsw* "House of the royal child," as Ἡρακλέους πόλις. It seems therefore reasonable to assume that the Demotic toponym , whether it is to be read as *Smꜣ-tꜣ.wy* or *Nsw-tꜣ.wy*, was in Greek occasionally transcribed phonetically as Σενθευς/Συνθευς, but mainly translated as Ἡράκλεια.

Römer[149] recently proposed to identify Herakleia with Abu Ksa, some 4 km to the northeast of Ibshaway (ancient Pisais),[150] and Apias/Philopator Apiados with Sanhur, another 6 km to the north-east, and there are indeed multiple indications that both villages must have been in this area of the *Themistou meris*, not far from Pisais, close to the lake and right across from Soknopaiou Nesos. However, the descriptions of the shares of the 20-arouras *kleros* on the edge between the two territories that we were able to glean from the various documents mentioning it raise the question whether it might not have been the other way round (see also section 6.2 and figs. 4 and 5): if the canal mentioned in P. Berlin P. 7056 corresponds in fact to the boundary between the territories of the two villages, as seems likely, the

148. Jan Quaegebeur, "Somtous l'Enfant sur le lotus," *CRIPEL* 13 (1991): 113, 121; Jan Quaegebeur, "Une statue égyptienne représentant Héraclès-Melqart?" in *Studia Phoenicia V: Phoenicia and the East Mediterranean in the First Millennium B.C.; Proceedings of the Conference Held in Leuven from the 14th to the 16th of November 1985*, ed. Edward Lipiński, OLA 22 (Leuven: Peeters, 1987), 160–63; Gisèle Clerc, "Héraklès et les dieux du cercle isiaque," in *Hommages à Jean Leclant III. Études isiaques*, ed. Catherine Berger, Gisèle Clerc, and Nicolas Grimal, BdÉ 106.3 (Cairo: Institut français d'archéologie orientale, 1994), 98. See also Maren Schentuleit, "Herischef und Herakles," in *Herischef – Metamorphosen eines Gottes*, ORA, forthcoming.

149. Römer, *Fayoum Survey Project*, 315–18. See also the map p. 398 and pl. XV.

150. Römer, 314–15.

plot west of this canal, falling to Pekysis (1) and Stotoetis (4) in the division of 112 CE and therefore corresponding to two of the three shares, should match the shares I and II, situated according to docs. C, D, and E in the area of Philopator Apiados. The remaining plot, falling in 112 CE to Harpagathes (4), Herieus (3), and the rest of the children of Stotoetis (3) and Paopis,[151] should be share III which, according to docs. D and G, lay in the area of Herakleia. This would also explain why Harpagathes (4), the scribe of P. Berlin P. 7056, situated the whole *kleros* in Sentheus/Herakleia.

6.2. Size and Origin of the kleros *as Property of the Family*

In docs. B and F, the whole *kleros* is said to be 20 arouras large, although the former adds the conventional ἢ ὅσων ἐὰν ὦσι, "or however many there are." Twenty arouras would equal 55,125 m^2 or just over 5 ½ ha[152]; if square, this would correspond to a field of about 235 m by 235 m. Twenty arouras is the *kleros* size allotted to indigenous cavalry officers (*machimoi hippeis*) in the second and first century BCE.[153] Therefore, either one of the forebears of Pekysis (1) and his co-heirs was such a *machimos hippeus* in the Ptolemaic army (which is rather unlikely, given that this was a priestly family), or an ancestor—probably their father Harpagathes (3)—had bought the *kleros* in the Roman period, when the transfer of catoeicic land outside the family line or even the group of *katoikoi* became possible.[154] This opportunity to enlarge their land holdings seems to have been taken by many inhabitants of Soknopaiou Nesos, which had notoriously poor agricultural land,[155] and as a consequence one finds many persons with typically soknopaiounesiotic names as holders of land, and specifically catoeicic land, in the region of Apias/Philopator Apiados[156] and Herakleia.[157]

6.3. Size, Location, and Redistribution of the Shares

The lease doc. B explicitly states that the *kleros* consisted of two plots (ἐν δυσὶ [σ]φραγῖσι), that is, two separate parcels of land, and this is also implied in P. Berlin P. 7056, where the plot falling to Pekysis (1) and Stotoetis (4) is said to lie "to the southwest of the canal and the northwest of the canal." The curious phrasing implies that the canal in question made a bend in the middle of the *kleros*, and the second plot lay most likely just to the east of that same canal (fig. 5).

Neither of these two texts gives us the exact size of the two plots. However, catoeicic land was taxed at one artaba per aroura,[158] so the three surviving *sitologos* receipts (docs. C, D, and E) concerning the three shares of Pekysis (1) and his co-heirs give us some information about the way the *kleros* was split between the parties: the amount of wheat

---

151. For the redistribution of the shares, see section 4, commentary to clause 5 above and section 6.3 below.

152. 1 aroura = 100 ground cubits (*mḥ-ỉtn*) = 10,000 square cubits (*mḥ-ḫty*, = 52.5cm×52.5 cm = 0.275625 m^2). 1 aroura therefore corresponds to 2756.25 m^2 (Sven P. Vleeming, "Demotic Measures of Length and Surface, Chiefly of the Ptolemaic Period," in *Textes et études de papyrologie grecque, démotique et copte*, ed. Pieter W. Pestman, PLB 23 [Leiden: Brill, 1985], 220–22.)

153. Edmond Van 't Dack, *Ptolemaica Selecta: Études sur l'armée et l'administration lagides*, StudHell 29 (Leuven: Orientaliste, 1988), 12; Christelle Fischer-Bovet, *Army and Society in Ptolemaic Egypt*, Armies of the Ancient Word (Cambridge: Cambridge University Press, 2014), 164–65, 218; Christelle Fischer-Bovet and Patrick Sänger, "Security and Border Policy: Army and Police," in *A Companion to Greco-Roman and Late Antique Egypt*, ed. Katelijn Vandorpe (Medford, MA: Wiley Blackwell, 2019), 167, 169.

154. Andrew Monson, *From the Ptolemies to the Romans. Political and Economic Change in Egypt* (Cambrigde: Cambridge University press, 2012), 94–95.

155. Hoogendijk, "*Parachoresis*," 249.

156. Hobson, "The Village of Apias," 88–91.

157. Deborah W. Hobson, "The Inhabitants of Heraklia," *BASP* 23 (1986): 99–123.

158. Monson, *Ptolemies to Romans*, 183.

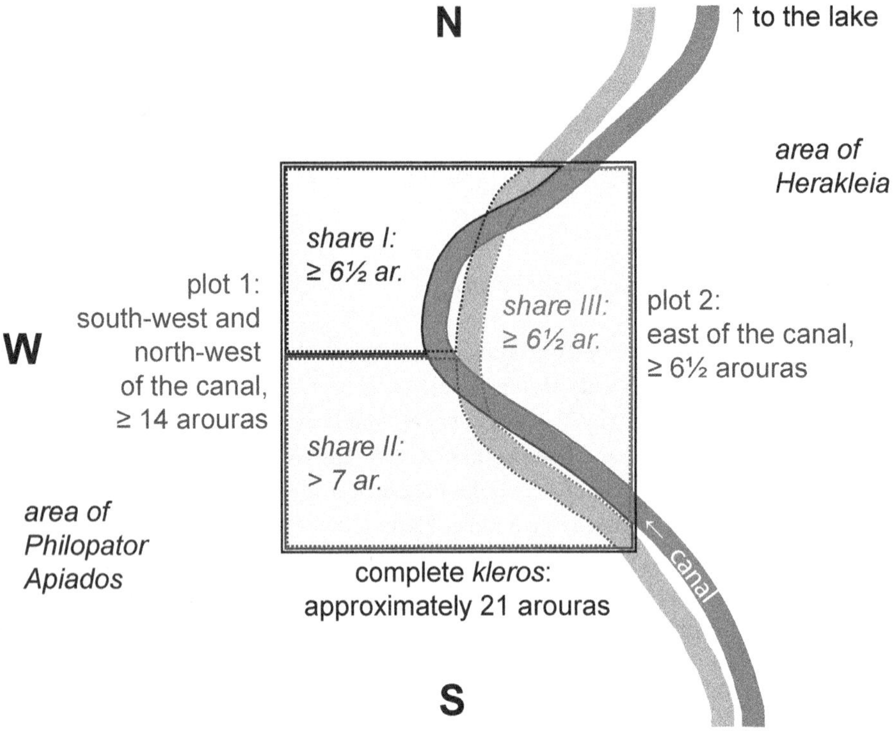

Figure 5. Schematic drawing of the *kleros* (Lippert and Schentuleit)

in artabas paid by each (without the προσμετρούμενα surtax)[159] should therefore reflect the size of their shares in arouras—with the *caveat* that the artaba is traditionally subdivided into forty-eighths,[160] while the aroura is subdivided into sixty-fourths,[161] so occasionally some rounding occurred.

Doc. C (85 CE): Pekysis (1) pays 7 ⅓ ¹/12 artabas for his share in Philopator Apiados, Stotoetis (3) pays 6 ½ ¹/12 artabas also in Philopator. Of the third payment, the name of the payer, the amount and the situation of the share are lost, but at least the first and last can be reconstructed with certainty: because ranking of persons in Egypt generally followed the rule "male before female, older before younger,"[162] the third payer should have been Heriea (2) herself and not a man, and her share would have been the one situated on the Herakleia side.

Doc. D (101 CE): Pekysis (1) pays 7 ⅓ ¹/24 artabas for a share in Philopator Apiados, another 6 ½ ⅓ artabas for a share in Herakleia and finally ¹/6 ¹/24 artabas for a certain Pappion, but the latter payment has probably nothing to do with the *kleros*; Stotoetis (3) pays [x] ½ ⅓ artabas for her share in Philopator Apiados. So it looks like that at least in 100/1 CE, Pekysis (1) had taken over and cultivated also the share that should have fallen to Heriea (2), or perhaps already to her son Stotoetis (4), but we do not know how this came about.

159. For this tax, see Ture Kalén, *Berliner Leihgabe griechischer Papyri* (Uppsala: AB Lundequistska bokhandeln, 1932), 231–35. S. L. Wallace, *Taxation in Roman Egypt from Augustus to Diocletian* (Princeton: Princeton University Press, 1938), 38–41.

160. John Shelton, "Artabs and Choenices," *ZPE* 24 (1977): 63–65.

161. Vleeming, "Measures of Length and Surface," 223–29.

162. Rowlandson and Lippert, "Family and Life Cycle Transitions," 332. For application of this rule in succession, see Sandra Lippert, "Inheritance," in *UCLAEE*, 3, https://escholarship.org/uc/item/30h78901.

Doc. E (106/7 CE): Pekysis (1) pays [x] artabas for a share whose location is lost (but should have been the one in Herakleia); the name of the second payer is lost, but it must have been either Pekysis again or Stotoetis (4), the son of Heriea, who pays 6 ½ artabas for a share in Philopator Apiados, and finally Stotoetis (3) pays [x] artabas also for a share in Philopator Apiados; the overall sum, without προσμετρούμενα, is said to be 21 $^{1}/_{24}$ artabas. Unless there is, again, a payment for another person included that has nothing to do with the *kleros*, it looks like its real size was not 20 arouras (about 5.5 ha) after all, but a little over 21 arouras (probably something between 21 $^{1}/_{32}$ and 21 $^{1}/_{16}$ arouras, i.e., about 5.8 ha). A total tax payment of 21 $^{1}/_{24}$ artabas works also very well for doc. D, where just the integer in the payment of Stotoetis (3) is missing: the two payments by Pekysis (1) and the ½ ⅓ artabas preserved from her payment add up to 15 $^{1}/_{24}$ artabas, she therefore must also have paid [6] ½ ⅓ artabas. For doc. C, an overall tax sum of 21 $^{1}/_{24}$ artabas would mean that the third payment, i.e. the one for the Herakleia share made by Heriea, amounted to 7 $^{1}/_{24}$ artabas. Finally, the Greek lease doc. G of 126 CE gives the size of the share in Herakleia which Pekysis (1) leases out for three years as 6 ½ arouras.

Therefore, tax payments per share varied between at least 6 ½ artabas and at the most 7 ⅓ $^{1}/_{12}$ artabas, and at no observable moment all three share-holders paid exactly the same amount, meaning that the size of their shares was unequal (although in doc. D, two were identical in size, while the third was larger). Moreover, it becomes clear that the size of a specific share could vary over time—this is especially obvious for the single share (III) situated on the territory of Herakleia, for which 6 ½ ⅓ artabas were paid in 101 CE, but probably 7 $^{1}/_{24}$ in 85 CE, and which was said to measure only 6 ½ arouras (and therefore would have been taxed at 6 ½ artabas) in 126 CE. The Philopator plot, comprising two shares, was not divided equally either: it seems to have consisted of a larger part (share II, over 7 arouras) and a smaller part (share I, under 7 arouras),[163] with the larger one slightly shrinking between 85 CE and 101 CE and the smaller one first getting larger, and by 106/7 CE smaller again. The easiest explanation for these changes is that, while the outer limits of the *kleros* stayed the same, the canal, which according to P. Berlin P. 7056 seems to have separated the two plots, shifted its course over time, cutting off land from one side and adding it to the other. While this seems unlikely for a straight, man-made irrigation canal, the description of the plot falling to Pekysis (1) and Stotoetis (4) as lying "to the southwest of the canal and to the northwest of the canal" implies that it made a curve in its preponderantly south–north course where it traversed the *kleros*, which makes it look much more like a natural rivulet or drainage gully anyway.

The unequal and changing size of the shares probably was the reason why the co-heirs decided to establish some sort of periodical swapping of shares that prevented anyone from feeling slighted. According to clause 5 in P. Berlin P. 7056, this was done by casting lots (*ḥwy qll*) and in a way that precluded a share falling to the same party twice in a row (see section 4 above). That this, or a similar technique, was also in vigor before and after 112 CE becomes clear from the fact that Stotoetis (3) had the smaller Philopator share (I) in 85 CE and 101 CE, but the larger one (II) in 106/7 CE, and her descendants received the Herakleia share (III) in 112 CE. Heriea had the Herakleia share (III) in 85 CE, but in 112 CE, her son Stotoetis (4) received one of the two Philopator shares (I or II). We do not know whether the system continued when all of the original three heirs had been replaced by their descendants.

6.4. Crop Plants

Three different crop plants are mentioned in P. Berlin P. 7056: radish (*sme sp-2*), green fodder (*swb*), and wheat (*sw3*).

Pliny (*Nat.* 15.7.30 and 19.26.79) reports that radish was widely cultivated as an oil crop in Roman Egypt (see *Raphanus sativus* var. *oleiferus*), and radish oil (ἔλαιον ῥαφάνινον) appears regularly in Greek papyri of the Roman

163. The location of the the smaller share I to the north and the larger share II to the south in fig. 5 is arbitrary.

period, although rarely before that time.[164] Radish oil (*nḥḥ sm*) is explicitly mentioned alongside olive oil (*nḥḥ ḏyt*) and safflower(?) oil (*nḥḥ ḏḏš*) in the regulations for the scribe of the priests from Soknopaiou Nesos, P. Vienna D 4852 l. 12 (95/6 CE),[165] as well as in various still unpublished accounts and *hnw*-agreements from Roman Dime. The seeming scarcity of references to radish seed in Greek papyri had already been remarked on by Mayerson[166] who tentatively suggested that the reason might be that it was referred to in the papyri as λαχανόσπερμον, "vegetable seed," although he accepted, in what looks like a last-minute addition,[167] Bagnall's identification of λαχανόσπερμον as sesame on the basis of an inscripton in the monastery of Phoibammon containing a Greek-Coptic word list.[168] However, in view of the Demotic evidence, Bagnall's argumentation is not compelling: the word ⲚⲤⲈⲘⲤⲘ that is equated in the word-list with ⲤⲠⲈⲢⲘⲀ ⲖⲀⲬⲀⲚⲞⲨ can more convincingly be explained as *n3 (n) sm (m) sm*, "those (i.e., the seeds) of real *sm*-herb (= radish)."[169] Moreover, while sesame can hardly be described as a λάχανον, "vegetable," since no part of the plant, besides the grains, has any value for human consumption, radish furnished edible leaves and roots and was considered "the" vegetable/herb (*sm*) *par excellence*. One can therefore safely assume that the disappearance of σήσαμον and the appearance of λαχανόσπερμον in the Roman period is not a shift in terminology, as Bagnall presumed, but a shift in actual crop preferences: sesame oil (ἔλαιον σησάμινον / *nḥḥ n 3qy*) is replaced by radish oil (ἔλαιον ῥαφάνινον / *nḥḥ n sm*) at the same time that the crop plant sesame (σήσαμον / *3qy*) is replaced by oil-seed radish (ῥάφανος / *sm (m) sm, sm sp-2*), whose oleiferous seeds are called in Greek texts λαχανόσπερμον as a calque on the Demotic term *sm*. If this equation is correct, it is possible that radish was at least occasionally planted on this *kleros* already before 112 CE: in BGU II 644 (doc. B), a fragmentary clause in lines 37 to 39 indicating the crop to be grown (in a certain year of the three-year lease?) on half of the kleros mentions λαχα-[, which has to be restored as a form of either λάχανον or, given the available space, more likely λαχανόσπερμον, although we do not know in which case, because the verbal form is missing.

As mentioned above,[170] *swb*, "green fodder" is the Demotic equivalent of χόρτος. Both appear in clauses stipulating crop rotation, often in alternation with cereals,[171] and in some documents covering several years, it is even specified at which intervals this is to happen.[172] Occasionally, texts allow alternatives for χόρτος, and these are always legumes, such as ἄρακος (fodder peas, *Lathyrus annuus*) or τῆλις (fenugreek, *Trigonella foenum-graecum*).[173] This shows, on the one hand, that ancient Egyptian farmers had, by experience, learned that legumes act as a natural fertilizer by fixing nitrogen in the soil and thus counteract soil depletion by other, nitrogen consuming crops like cereals. On the other hand, it makes it likely that *swb*/χόρτος[174] was not simply "grass," but consisted mainly or entirely of protein-rich legumes[175] like the *bersim* clover (*Trifolium alexandrinum*) that is still widely used in modern Egypt

164. Maria Mossakowska, "Les huiles utilisés pour l'éclairage en Égypte (d'après les papyrus grecs)," *JJP* 24 (1994): 121, 126–27 (erroneously referring to *Raphanus sativus* as "rave" [beet] instead of "radis" [radish]); Philip Mayerson, "Radish Oil: A Phenomenon in Roman Egypt," *BASP* 38 (2001): 109.

165. TM#45643. Edda Bresciani, "Un documento demotico dell'anno 15° di Domiziano dall'archivio templare di Dime," in *Festschrift zum 100-jährigen Bestehen der Papyrussammlung der Österreichischen Nationalbibliothek Papyrus Erzherzog Rainer (P.Rainer Cent.)* (Vienna: Österreichische Nationalbibliothek, 1983), 180–84, pl. 6. For the interpretation of *ḏḏš* as safflower, see Lippert and Schentuleit, *Agreements: Text Edition*, forthcoming.

166. Mayerson, "Radish Oil," 114n8.

167. Mayerson, 109n1.

168. Roger Bagnall, "Vegetable Seed Oil is Sesame Oil," *CdÉ* 75 (2000): 133–35.

169. See the commentary to l. 6 above.

170. See the commentary to l. 6.

171. Michael Schnebel, *Die Landwirtschaft im hellenistischen Ägypten*, MBPR 7 (Munich: Beck, 1935), 218–28.

172. E.g., P.Mich. III185 (122 CE, Fayum): fourth year of a four-year lease; P. Mil.Vogl. III 144 (166 CE, Tebtynis) and P. Mil.Vogl. IV 238 (143/4 CE, Tebtynis): second and fourth years of a four-year lease.

173. E.g., P. Tebt. I 106 (Tebtynis, 101 CE), l. 3; SB XIV 11279 (Theadelphia, 44 CE), l. 28.

174. Schnebel, *Landwirtschaft im hellenistischen Ägypten*, 211–18.

175. See also Schnebel, 212–13, and Felber, *Demotische Ackerpachtverträge der Ptolemäerzeit*, 137.

as forage crop, because it is more nutritious for animals than grass or hay.[176] A probably partial and/or temporally restricted sowing of χόρτος on the share that Pekysis (1) leases out is also stipulated in doc. G (ll. 26–27), but the clause is unfortunately much damaged.

Wheat is mentioned in P. Berlin P. 7056 only in the context of the penalty clause 7, so we do not know whether, and how much of, the *kleros* was actually sown with cereals during the four-year division. It is quite likely that this was simply the default: the three-year leases docs. B and G specify that the rent and taxes are to be paid in wheat even though we have seen that doc. B might already have allowed or even demanded that radish should be grown in certain years or on certain parts of the *kleros*, while doc. G had a crop rotation clause about χόρτος. The *sitologos* receipts docs. C, D, and E also simply state that the tax for the *kleros* was paid in wheat, at the rate of one artaba per aroura, but again this does not necessarily mean that all and every part of the shares were used to grow cereals in these years.

7. Conclusion

The small papyrus Berlin P. 7056—no larger than a postcard!—has yielded surprisingly plentiful new information about the prosopography of Roman Soknopaiou Nesos, the toponymy and topography of the *Themistou meris* as well as agricultural practices in the Fayum. Furthermore, as we were able to bring together a dossier consisting of up to seventeen documents, we can keep track of this priestly family over at least five generations and more than two hundred years. The interplay between Greek and Demotic texts reveals social, economic, and legal details, and, last but not least, brings new lexicographical insights. This shows once more what treasures can still be raised from sources that have been known for a long time.

176. Fouad N. Ibrahim and Barbara L. Ibrahim, *Egypt: An Economic Geography* (New York: Tauris, 2003), 134.

Speaking Clearly through the Canaanite Amarna Letters: How to Connect with an Audience in Cuneiform

ALICE MANDELL

What Is Canaano-Akkadian, and Why Do We Care?

In this paper, I offer several case studies from the Canaanite Amarna Letters that demonstrate how cuneiform scribes tried to speak clearly to their scribal peers in Egypt through the medium of their scribal craft.[1] This corpus dates to the Amarna Age (the mid-fourteenth century BCE)—a period that resonates with Egyptologists and scholars of the Levant alike. The letters from Canaan offer us a glimpse of what was most certainly a substantial body of diplomatic letters between the Egyptian royal court and southern Levantine rulers.[2] Direct communication between these courts was made possible by cuneiform-trained scribes working at both ends of this communicative chain. During this period, cuneiform scribes in the Near East (including Egypt) were trained to write Middle Babylonian, the contemporary written dialect of Akkadian.[3] Those scribes writing for Canaanites rulers, however, produced a strikingly different work product—one characterized by a lexicon and orthography derived from Old Babylonian, an earlier phase of Akkadian (an East Semitic language), and verbal inflections and syntax from their own West Semitic languages (e.g., the ancestor dialects of Aramaic, Hebrew, and Phoenician, etc.).[4]

1. When I was asked to write a piece in honor of Richard Jasnow, I thought about some of his characteristics that I most admire and settled on his kindness and humor. Both of these qualities are expressed in Richard's speeches, particularly those in honor of past or present scholars. His speeches are hilarious, thoughtful, and always generous; he has the rare gift of connecting with his audience in a profound way that leaves them laughing and smiling. With this in mind, I decided to contribute a piece on ancient Canaanite scribes and the ways that they, too, sought to better connect with their audiences in Egypt. This seemed a fitting topic for a paper meant to bridge the study of the Levant and Egyptology in honor of an Egyptologist.

2. See Jana Mynářová, "Discovery, Research, and Excavation of the Amarna Tablets—The Formative Stage," in Anson F. Rainey, *The El-Amarna Correspondence: A New Edition of the Cuneiform Letters from the Site of El-Amarna Based on Collations of All Extant Tablets*, ed. William M. Schniedewind and Zipora Cochavi-Rainey (Leiden: Brill, 2015), 37–54.

3. See Anson F. Rainey, "The Hybrid Language Written by Canaanite Scribes in the 14th Century BCE," in *Language in the Ancient Near East: Proceedings of the 53rd Rencontre Assyriologique Internationale (Moscow, Russia, July 23, 2007)*, ed. Leonid Kogan, Natalia Koslova, Sergey Loesov, and Serguei Tishchenko, Babel und Bibel 4/2 (Winona Lake, IN: Eisenbrauns, 2010), 851–61; Anson F. Rainey, *Canaanite in the Amarna Tablets: A Linguistic Analysis of the Mixed Dialect Used by Scribes from Canaan*, 4 vols. (Atlanta: Society of Biblical Literature, 1996), 2:1–32; for a more recent survey of the verbal system see Krzysztof J. Baranowski, *The Verb in the Amarna Letters from Canaan* (Winona Lake, IN: Eisenbrauns, 2016).

4. Canaano-Akkadian forms are first attested in the Taanach Letters (late fifteenth century). This corpus of letters includes letters from an Egyptian official (or at least someone having an Egyptian name), who hired a scribe based at Megiddo (Taanach 5-6). See the discussion in Wayne Horowitz, Tayakoshi Oshima, and Seth L. Sanders, *Cuneiform in Canaan: Cuneiform Sources from the Land of Israel in Ancient Times* (Jerusalem: Israel Exploration Society, 2006), 139–42; and in the revised publication Wayne Horowitz, Takayoshia Oshima, and Seth L. Sanders, *Cuneiform in Canaan: The Next Generation*, 2nd ed. (University Park, PA: Eisenbrauns, 2018), 132–55.

Scholars of Canaano-Akkadian debate how to classify it (e.g., as a dialect of Akkadian; an alloglottography, whereby Canaanite was written using the cuneiform script; or a hybrid, mixed, or interlanguage).[5] In this study, I step back from these debates, and instead focus upon the scribal communities making and receiving these tablets.[6] Throughout the lifecycle of a tablet, any orthographic variation, scribal marks, or shifts in language variety would have been neutralized when the message was read aloud and translated.[7] Identifying these forms and their origins in these two language families (West or East Semitic) is of course important, but it does not really tell us much about how the intended audiences understood these letters. Such forms do, however, inform us about the strategies that Canaanite scribes used to connect with scribes in Egypt through their shared knowledge of cuneiform.

We can reconstruct the following scenario beginning with a meeting between a ruler and a cuneiform trained scribe in the southern Levant:

(1) A speech or set of directives was spoken to a local cuneiform scribe in a local West Semitic dialect. This scribe worked for the local court, or was based at a nearby polity, or was an itinerant scribe working within a bounded geographic district.[8]

(2) This message, or its approximation, was encoded into a clay tablet in cuneiform taking the form of the local scribal system, Canaano-Akkadian.[9] Through this process it was altered to fit the conventions of diplomatic epistolary protocol; its written form was impacted by the scribe's training and their own linguistic and scribal idiosyncrasies.[10]

---

5. For a range of views, see Shlomo Izre'el, "Canaano-Akkadian: Linguistics and Socio-linguistics," in *Language and Nature: Papers Presented to John Huehnergard on the Occasion of His 60th Birthday*, ed. Rebecca Hasselbach and Na'ama Pat-El, SAOC 67; Chicago: Oriental Institute of the University of Chicago, 2012), 171–218; Eva von Dassow, "Canaanite in Cuneiform," *JAOS* 124 (2004): 643–44; Alexander Andrason and Juan-Pablo Vita, "From Glosses to the Linguistic Nature of Canaano-Akkadian," *FolOr* 51 (2014): 155–75; Baranowski, *The Verb in the Amarna Letters from Canaan*; and Alice Mandell, "Scribalism and Diplomacy at the Crossroads of Cuneiform Culture" (PhD diss., University of California; Los Angeles, 2016), 42–53.

6. For another such approach, see Juan-Pablo Vita, *Canaanite Scribes in the Amarna Letters* (Münster: Ugarit-Verlag, 2015).

7. By neutralized, I mean that the differences between verbs written using a "more" Akkadian vs. Canaanite orthography, although visually striking, would have been eliminated in translation. By way of example, the 1cs prefixed verb *a-⸢na⸣ṣa-ru* "I am guarding," from *naṣāru* "to protect, guard," in EA 296:3 is written in a way that more resembles the Akkadian 1cs G durative *anaṣṣar*; and yet, the final *-u* marks this verbal form as an imperfect and the work product of a Canaanite trained scribe. We can contrast this orthography with one that is doubly marked in its orthography as a West Semitic form. The verbal form *i-na-⸢ṣa⸣-ru* in EA 331:13 derives from the same verbal root, yet with a "more" West Semitic inflection marking the 1cs imperfective through both the use of *i-* to mark an initial *'aleph* and a final *-u* vowel to mark this verb an imperfect. The variation between prefixed forms serving as preterite and suffixed forms acting as perfects in the same letter would also have been neutralized in translation. For example, the introduction of EA 63 features both the 1cs suffixed form *ma-aq-ta-⸢ti⸣* (operating as a Canaanite perfect) and the 1cs G prefixed verb *⸢am⸣-⸢qú-ut* (an Akkadian preterit) in the prostration formula of this letter; both verbs are performatives in this context and are translated in the same way: "I now fall." The alternation between Akkadian word order (SOV) and West Semitic word order (VSO) in these letters would also have been neutralized in the translation of these texts. This word order shift typically occurs after the introductions of letters, which largely follow Middle Babylonian grammar, whereas the content sections of letters tend to transition to West Semitic syntax. For a discussion that highlights the origins of this variation in secondary language acquisition through scribal training exercises see Baranowski, *The Verb in the Amarna Letters from Canaan*, 115–23.

8. Two key works have clarified the loci of tablet making and scribal production: First, Yuval Goren, Israel Finkelstein, Nadav Na'aman, and Michal Artzy, *Inscribed in Clay: Provenance Study of the Amarna Tablets and Other Ancient Near Eastern Texts* (Tel Aviv: Emery and Claire Yass Publications in Archaeology, 2004), offers a petrographic analysis that identifies the regions where tablets were created. Second, Vita's study of the paleography of the letters identifies the individual scribes (or scribal schools) that produced specific letters (*Canaanite Scribes in the Amarna Letters*).

9. See also the description of the *chaîne opératoire* of these tablets in Diane H. Cline, "The Amarna Letters: A Web of Interaction," *JAEI* 7.4 (2015): 58–60.

10. Jacob Lauinger contributes a valuable discussion of the relationship between the layout of the letters, the influence of individual scribes, and regional tablet-making practices (Jacob Lauinger, "Contributions to a Diplomatics of the Amarna Letters from the Levant:

3) The tablet was carried to the Egyptian court. Some letters were also written (or recopied) at Egyptian bases in the Levant by Canaanite scribes who traveled with a diplomatic envoy, and then taken to Egypt.[11]
4) The tablet was delivered, processed, and at some point read and (most probably) translated into Egyptian. Some letters were read to the Pharaoh, or to a key official(s) dealing with Levantine affairs;[12] and, in some cases, a reply was drafted and sent out. While the extant evidence speaks to those letters processed, stored, and discarded at Tell el-Amarna (ancient Akhetaten),[13] it is reasonable to assume that important letters followed the movement of the royal court.[14]

This background reminds us that *the vocalization of the text in its spoken linguistic form—its pace, register, and any gestures or bodily movement that accompanied its reading—were largely determined by the scribes in Egypt.* This is why there seems to be such a concern from the scribes transmitting these missives in the postscripts of certain letters for securing a positive response. These tablets are wishes—from one scribe to another—that the main points expressed would be read, discussed, and addressed promptly and favorably. In what follows, I will outline several strategies that Canaanite scribes used to speak clearly to their counterparts in Egypt within the constraints of the cuneiform writing system. These letters reflect learned scribal practices, but also speak to the ingenuity of individual Canaanite scribes as they anticipated a breakdown in communication.

To better isolate the rote from the innovative, I propose two key strategies: (1) to approach these tablets as multimodal things that communicated in material, linguistic, and metadiscursive ways; and (2) to use the terminology of "community of practice" in order to conceptualize the people making, receiving, and reading this correspondence.[15] Viewing the Canaanite Amarna Letters as crafted scribal products highlights several strategies that would have been noticed by other cuneiform scribes, but not necessarily by a person hearing a translation or retelling of these messages. Such strategies included departure from the expected epistolary formulae and varying use of scribal marks to structure and highlight key thematic demarcations. Moreover, the clustering of visual, linguistic, and stylistic strategies added texture to these letters and guided their reading.[16]

<<La Mise en Page>>," in *De l'argile au numérique: Mélanges assyriologiques en l'honneur de Dominique Charpin,* ed. Grégory Chambon, Michaël Guichard, Thomas Römer, Anne-Isabelle Langlois, and Nele Ziegler [Peeters: Leuven, 2019], 566–80.)

11. For example, EA 97, a letter for the ruler of Beirut, was written on a tablet formed from sandy clay from the area of Gaza, which was a major Egyptian base at this time (Goren et al., *Inscribed in Clay,* 323).

12. We cannot assume that all letters were read to the Pharaoh. The slew of complaints about the lack of response suggest that the zeal with which Canaanite kings reached out to the Pharaoh was not reciprocated. See Nadav Na'aman, "The Egyptian-Canaanite Correspondence," in *Amarna Diplomacy: The Beginnings of International Relations,* ed. Raymond Cohen and Raymond Westbrook (Baltimore: Johns Hopkins University Press, 2000), 127–33, 137–38.

13. The refences to past correspondence in numerous Amarna Letters suggest that scribes would have had access to past letters as a point of reference. Letters from the same sender were most likely stored together and arranged according to their chronological order and/or point of origins. For example, at least 16 tablets included an ink, hieratic label that was added to the tablet, presumably when the letters arrived to Tell el-Amarna. These marks appear to relate to the storing of these letters. EA 254, for example, appears to have originally included a hieratic date: "year 12" or "year 32" (William. L. Moran, *The Amarna Letters* [Baltimore: Johns Hopkins University Press, 1992], xxxvii); see more recently Jana Mynářová, "Expressions of Dates and Time in the Amarna Letters," *ÄgLev* 21 (2011): 123–24.

14. The cuneiform letters discovered at Tell el-Amarna come from about the thirthieth year of Amenhotep III's reign until the abandonment of the city after Akhenaten's death. Those letters dating to the reign of Amenhotep III were brought to Akhenaten's new capital from Thebes. See Philippe Abrahami and Laurent Coulon, "De l'usage et de l'archivage des tablettes cuneiformes d'Amarna," in *La lettre d'archive: Communication administrative et personnelle dans l'antiquite proche-orientale et égyptienne; Actes du colloque de l'Université de Lyon 2, 9–10 Juillet 2004, ed. Laure Pantalacci,* Topoi Supplément 9 (Cairo: Institut français d'archéologie orientale, 2008), 10–11.

15. Past studies have framed the discussion of Canaano-Akkadian (sometimes implicitly) as the language of scribal speech communities, including in a more restricted educational context. See, e.g., Izre'el, "Canaano-Akkadian: Linguistics and Socio-Linguistics."

16. By texture, I mean that these strategies worked together in a manner akin to the ways in which paralinguistic cues in speech (e.g., gesture, volume, tone, stress, and bodily distance etc.) add the nuance, emotion, and emphasis needed to better express a speaker's

Methodology: Thinking about the Canaanite Amarna Letters as Scribal Things, Made by Scribes for Scribes

Past studies have addressed the reception of these letters by royal advisors to the Pharaoh or by the Pharaoh himself.[17] To this, I contribute a discussion of the cuneiform scribes working in Egypt as the first (and perhaps primary) audience of the Canaanite Amarna Letters. I analyze EA 147, 252, 286, 287, 288, and 316 as crafted scribal "things."[18] I consider these tablets as linguistic envelopes that reflect a limited materialization of these communications—the phase in which they were accessed by scribes mediating between these powers.[19] This approach pays homage to individual scribes who crafted texts that spoke to scribal and royal audiences.[20] Such strategies show a concern and "awareness of the reader and his or her need for elaboration, clarification, guidance and interaction."[21] This perspective considers the ways in which these tablets articulated meaning to members of a professional class: *cuneiform scribes writing diplomatic letters meant to be read by other cuneiform scribes.*[22] Such scribes were the gatekeepers who determined which letters merited a royal audience, which were to be stored for a later reading, and which were to be thrown into a scrap heap.

Multimodality

The first step in my approach is inspired by recent work that considers the act of writing in terms of design, whereby the creation of a text is tethered to conventions of visual representation.[23] Most of the information encoded in the Canaanite Amarna Letters was only accessed by people who were trained in the cuneiform writing system and were

---

attitude. For example, when a speaker takes a step back, raises one eyebrow, makes a grimace, and says "that's interesting," we know that they are expressing disapproval.

17. For a discussion of the important role of the Pharaoh's advisors in these exchanges, see Jana Mynářová, "Communicating the Empire, or How to Deliver a Message of the King," in *There and Back Again – the Crossroads II: Proceedings of an International Conference Held in Prague, September 15–18, 2014*, ed. Jana Mynářová, Pavel Onderka, and Peter Pavúk (Prague: Charles University in Prague, 2015), 150–54.

18. The approach to these tablets as scribal "things" draws upon the study of the materiality, affordances, and agency of things and their entanglement in human networks in such works as Arjun Appadurai, ed. *The Social Life of Things: Commodities in Cultural Perspective* (Cambridge: Cambridge University Press, 1986); Bill Brown, "Thing Theory," *Critical Inquiry* 28.1 (2001): 1–22; Ian Hodder, ed., *The Meaning of Things: Material Culture and Symbolic Expression* (London: Unwin Hyman, 1989); Lorraine Daston, *Things That Talk: Object Lessons from Art and Science* (New York: Zone Books, 2004); Daniel Miller, ed., *Materiality* (Durham, NC: Duke University Press, 2005); see also the approach to the presentation and display of curated things in Laurel Thatcher Ulrich, Ivan Gaskell, Sara J. Schechner, and Sarah Anne Carter, ed., *Tangible Things: Making History through Objects* (Oxford: Oxford University Press, 2015).

19. For analysis that considers the extra-linguistic aspects of inscriptions, see Kathryn E. Piquette and Ruth D. Whitehouse, eds., *Writing as Material Practice: Substance, Surface and Medium* (London: Ubiquity Press, 2013); Paul Delnero and Jacob Lauinger, ed., *The Circulation and Transmission of Cuneiform Texts in Social Space*, SANER 9 (Boston: de Gruyer, 2015); see also Emily Cole and Alice Mandell, eds., *Communicating through the Material in the Ancient World*, [special issue] *Maarav* 23.1 (2019).

20. See for example, Jacob Lauinger, "Discourse and Meta-discourse in the Statue of Idrimi and Its Inscription," *MAARAV* 23 (2019): 19–38; Juan-Pablo Vita, "On the Lexical Background of the Amarna Glosses," *AoF* 39 (2012): 278–86; and Mandell, "Scribalism and Diplomacy," 485–505.

21. Ken Hyland, *Metadiscourse: Exploring Interaction in Writing* (New York: Continuum, 2005), 17.

22. Anthony Eastmond reminds us that "inscriptions are not just disembodied words that can be studied in isolation. Instead, they must be considered as material entities, whose meaning is determined as much by their physical qualities as by their contents ("Introduction: Viewing Inscriptions," in *Viewing Inscriptions in the Late Antique and Medieval World*, ed. Anthony Eastmond [Cambridge: Cambridge University Press, 2015], 2).

23. See the discussion in Debra A. Myhill, "The Ordeal of Deliberate Choice: Metalinguistic Development in Secondary Writers," in *Past, Present, and Future Contributions of Cognitive Writing Research to Cognitive Psychology*, ed. Virginia Wise Berninger (New York: Psychology Press, 2012), 249.

familiar with Canaanite scribal practices.[24] Each tablet in this corpus was "an act of selection, choice, shaping, reflection, and revision."[25] Some of the choices made in the creation of these tablets included decisions about the clay; size and shape of the tablet; its language, style, register; its orientation, and layout; as well as the signs, orthography, and any use of scribal marks (or decisions to leave them out). This perspective highlights the processes of text-making and text-accessing. Thinking about the materiality of text moves us to consider the choices that scribes made about the physical form and presentation of their work product. How could a scribe make their letter stand out from the Pharaoh's other correspondence—in particular, from that of their Canaanite scribal peers?[26] This perspective moves the people making, reading, and storing these letters to the forefront of our analyses, in contrast to the ongoing tendency to focus on the relationships between the rulers, the named officials, or the broader geographic or political entities that these letters are thought to represent.[27]

Scribal Communities of Practice

Once we approach these texts as multimodal objects produced by scribes for scribes, we must more seriously consider the scribes creating and receiving them. Since we know very little about their origins, we are on safer ground making informed statements about their professional training and the strategies that they used to craft letters for their employers. Cuneiform scribes were members of a professional class, but were not necessarily a monolithic linguistic or cultural block. Some cuneiform scribes were part of diplomatic missions and traveled extensively; and some scribes wrote for multiple polities.[28] Certain cuneiform scribes navigated between different orthographic traditions in the same letter (e.g., using Middle Babylonian orthographies as well as those unique to their own scribal tradition, or those more aligned with Egyptian cuneiform practices).[29] This all speaks to the important role that a scribe's craft

24. Other aspects may have been accessible to people who were unable to read the content but were familiar with the protocols of diplomatic letter writing in cuneiform. For example, the size, shape, and clay color of a tablet might have been identified as the work of a scribe writing from a particular place or for a specific ruler; seeing a clay tablet held by a royal messenger (i.e., as a royal or "important" letter) or the use of cuneiform (wedges in clay) might have signaled the larger political and social backdrop of what these tablets meant. In some cases, the execution might have spoken to the skill of the scribe, and differentiated the work product of a professional scribe at a major court (Tell el-Amarna) from one from a more provincial court (a small polity in Canaan). Moreover, the use of scribal marks, in particular horizontal lines, might have informed even those unable to read about the way that a tablet should be held, accessed, or read.

25. Myhill, "The Ordeal of Deliberate Choice," 253.

26. In Jacob Lauinger's study of the size and layout of a range of Canaanite letters, he makes the important point that even the size of a tablet and orientation of the writing may have impacted its reception in Egypt. For example, EA 202's unusual "landscape" orientation may have been a deliberate strategy to make this letter stand out from other letters from the Bashan region (Lauinger, "Diplomatics of the Amarna Letters from the Levant," 579–80).

27. A recent analysis of the networks in contact uses these letters as a means of recreating the levels of intimacy between individuals and royal households. While this is an invaluable contribution to the study of diplomacy during this period, key people left out of this study are the very scribes who wrote these tablets. See Diane H. Cline and Eric H. Cline, "Text Messages, Tablets, and Social Networks: The 'Small World' of the Amarna Letters," in Mynářová, Onderka and Pavúk, *There and Back Again*, 17–44.

28. The twenty-two letters written at Egyptian sites in the Levant, or sites with a strong Egyptian administrative presence, suggest that royal scribes traveled along with diplomatic envoys to confer with Egyptian officials before sending a letter to the court at Tell el-Amarna. See the discussion in Goren et al., *Inscribed in Clay*, 323. The prolific scribes working for the royal family of Gezer also wrote for other rulers in the region. See Juan-Pablo Vita, "Scribes and Dialects in Late Bronze Age Canaan," in *Proceedings of the 53e Rencontre Assyriologique Internationale, Vol. 1: Language in the Ancient Near East*, edited by Leonid E. Kogan, Natalia Koslova, Sergey Loesov and Serguei Tishchenko (University Park, PA: Penn State University Press, 2021), 863–94; and more recently in Vita, *Canaanite Scribes*, 75–84.

29. See the discussion in Mandell, "Scribalism and Diplomacy," 348–49, 360–97. For a sociolinguistic analysis of the linguistic and orthographic variation in the Idrimi Statue as an act of identity, see Kathryn McConaughy Medill, "The Idrimi Statue Inscription in Its Late Bronze Age Scribal Context," *BASOR* 382 (2019): 243–59.

played in their own identity performance, as scribes, as members of a linguistic and socio-political group, and as individuals.[30]

For these reasons, rather than focusing upon the faceless speech communities behind these texts, I advocate that we consider the scribal "communities of practice" that crafted and read them.[31] A community of practice is a group of people united by a learned activity that, in turn, impacts their linguistic practice.[32] Using the "community of practice" as an object of study places emphasis on a group's activities and the transmission of its practices.[33] This shift in perspective factors in the scribes' situational use of language, such as the act of creating a tablet meant to be read by foreign cuneiform scribes vs. their engagement with local scribes in a professional setting vs. their speech practices at home with their families. This approach also considers the broader technical aspects of scribalism and the mix of spoken *and* written *and* performed language reflected in this corpus.[34] In addition, it moves the scribal audiences in Egypt, who were the true audience of these messages in their written-down form, into the spotlight.

Linguistic and Nonlinguistic Scribal Cues in the Canaanite Amarna Letters

I now offer a selection of examples that demonstrate the linguistic *and* nonlinguistic strategies that Canaanite scribes used to reach across the aisle to their scribal colleagues in Egypt. I will both describe these strategies and analyze how they are used to attract the attention of the scribes receiving and processing the Pharaoh's correspondence from Canaan.

30. It is important to note that this perspective is not accepted by all. For example, Eva von Dassow ("Canaanite in Cuneiform," 649) writes, "certainly Canaano-Akkadian was used almost exclusively by members of a distinct group, namely, Canaanite scribes, but they did not use it as a symbol of their distinctive identity, simply as their job." Baranowski (*The Verb in the Amarna Letters from Canaan*, 39–40 and 40n31) also minimizes the "high sociolinguistic complexity" of this corpus, and attributes the internal variation to "second language acquisition phenomena (learning errors, partial acquisition, creation of new forms etc.)." However, these views minimize the complexity of language use, which even in writing can express a range of social identities.

31. A community of practice is defined as "an aggregate of people who come together around mutual engagement in an endeavor. Ways of doing things, ways of talking, beliefs, values, power relations—in short, practices—emerge in the course of this mutual endeavor. As a social construct, a community of practice is different from the traditional community, primarily because it is defined simultaneously by its membership and by the practice in which that membership engages" (Penelope Eckert and Sally McConnell-Ginet, "Think Practically and Look Locally: Language and Gender as Community-Based Practice," *Annual Review of Anthropology* 21 [1992]: 464). For an early discussion of the community of practice and the transmission of group knowledge, see Jean Lave and Etienne Wenger, *Situated Learning: Legitimate Peripheral Participation* (Cambridge: Cambridge University Press, 1991).

32. By way of example, we can think about football fans sitting in an airport bar watching a match during the Euro-cup; while they might be speakers of different languages or members of different cultural communities, during the course of the experience of watching a match together they are participants in a community of practice. This shared activity (and passion for the sport) may condition their dress, hairstyle, vocabulary, facial expressions and bodily gestures; depending on the game, they may verbalize or express emotion in similar ways. For an application of the "community of practice" to a sociolinguistic context, see Anna de Fina, "Code-Switching and the Construction of Ethnic Identity in a Community of Practice," *Language in Society* 36 (2007): 371–91.

33. For a comparison of the speech community, social identity theory, and community of practice models, see Janet Holmes and Miriam Meyerhoff, "The Community of Practice: Theories and Methodologies in Language and Gender Research," *Language in Society* 28 (1999): 177–82, esp. 179, table 1.

34. We must also consider the complex relationship between speech and writing, which is a growing subfield at the crossroads of sociolinguistics, linguistic anthropology, and visual media studies. See the recent works by Peter Unseth, "Sociolinguistic Parallels Between Choosing Scripts and Languages," *Written Language & Literacy* 8 (2005): 19–42; Mark Sebba, *Spelling as a Social Practice* (Cambridge: Cambridge Press, 2007); Mark Sebba, "Iconicity, Attribution, and Branding in Orthography," *Written Language & Literacy* 18 (2015): 208–27; Alexandra Jaffe, Jannis Androutsopoulos, Mark Sebba, and Sally Johnson, eds., *Orthography as Social Action: Scripts, Spelling, Identity and Power* (Boston: de Gruyter, 2012); Mark Sebba, Shahrzad Mahootian, and Carla Jonsson, eds., *Language Mixing and Code-Switching in Writing: Approaches to Mixed-Language Written Discourse* (New York: Routledge, 2012).

The Air Kiss: EA 147, A Letter from Tyre

My first example, EA 147, a letter from Tyre, is what I call an "air kiss" letter.[35] It makes a stark contrast with the "snub" letter, EA 252 (discussed below)—EA 147 is flattering, hyperbolic, obsequious, and seemingly intimate. The introduction of this letter includes expressions of subservience additional to the usual formulae and refers to Akhenaten's religious reform.[36]

First Greeting:[37]
Obv: 01–05a) *a-na* LUGAL EN-*lí-ia* DINGIR.MEŠ-⸢*ia*⸣ ⸢^{d}⸣⸢UTU⸣-*ia um-ma A-bi*-LUGAL ÌR-*ka* 7 *u* 7 *a-na* GÌR.MEŠ LUGAL EN-*lí-ia am-qut*[38] *a-na-ku ep-ru iš-tu ša-pa-li ši-ni* LUGAL EN-*lí-ia*
To the king, my lord, my god, my sun god, a message of Abi-Milki, your servant:
Seven times and seven times I now fall to the feet of the king, my lord. I am dirt beneath the sandals of the king, my lord.

Extended Greeting:
05b–15 Obv.) *be-li* ^{d}UTU *ša it-ta-ṣí i-na muḫ-ḫi* ^{KUR}*ma-ta-ti i-na* u_4*-mi ù* u_4*-mi-ma ki-ma ši-ma-at* ^{d}UTU *a-bu-šu* SIG_5 *ša i-ba-li-iṭ i-na še-ḫi-šu* DU_{10}(!).GA *ù i-sà-ḫur i-na ṣa-pa-ni-šu ša it-ta-ṣa-ab*[39] *gáb-bi* KUR-*ti i-na pa-ša-ḫi i-na du-ni* ZAG: *ḫa-ap-ši ša id-din ri-ig-ma-šu i-na sa-me ki-ma* ^{d}IŠKUR *ù* ⸢*tar*⸣*-*gu_5*-ub gáb-bi* KUR-*ti* ⸢*iš*⸣*-tu ri-ig-mi-šu*
My lord is the sun god,
who has come out over the lands day by day,
in the manner of the sun god, his wonderful father
who gives life with his sweet breath,
and returns with his north wind,
who has established all of the lands in peace,
by the strength of (his) arm,
who thundered in the heavens like the storm god,
and all of the land quaked from his voice.[40]

35. According to Vita's paleographic analysis, it is the work of "Tyre Scribe 2," who also wrote all but one of the Tyre Amarna Letters (namely, EA 165; Vita, *Canaanite Scribes*, 58–59).

36. For a list of Egyptian features in the Tyre Amarna Letters, see Luis R. Siddall, "The Amarna Letters from Tyre as a Source for Understanding Atenism and Imperial Administration," *JAEI* 2 (2012): 26.

37. The transliterations largely follow Anson F. Rainey, *The El-Amarna Correspondence: A New Edition of the Cuneiform Letters from the Site of El-Amarna Based on Collations of All Extant Tablets*, ed. William M. Schniedewind and Zipora Cochavi-Rainey (Leiden: Brill, 2015); the translations are my own unless specified otherwise.

38. The verb of prostration in this context acts as a performative. See Baranowski, *The Verb in the Amarna Letters*, 181–83, esp. 181n23 and 183n24.

39. The analysis of this verb follows the analysis proposed by William L. Moran (*The Amarna Letters*, 233–34) rather than that of Anson F. Rainey ("A New Translation of the Amarna Letters—After 100 years," *AfO* 36/37 [1989/1990]: 65).

40. My translation reflects my understanding that the image created here is one of the storm god thundering in the heavens, which frightens the inhabitants of the earth. The phrase *iddin rigma* evokes the imagery and bivalent use of the word *qōl*, which meant "voice" but also "thunder" in biblical Hebrew (e.g., in the theophany in Exod 19 and Deut 5; and in 2 Sam 22:14/Ps 18:14 and Isa 29). The CAD cites EA 147:13 *iddin rigma* as a potential scribal error; the verb *iddin* (the 3ms preterit of *nadānu*) is seen to be an error for *iddi*, the 3ms preterite of *nadû*, which is the verb commonly used to describe Adad thundering. However, cognate evidence suggests that *iddin rigma*, might simply be a Northwest Semitic calque. In later Iron Age Hebrew, for example, the pairing of *ntn* and *qōl* is used to describe YHWH thundering. See, e.g., the image of YHWH as a storm god (or at least a god that speaks in a way that marshals the elements of storms)

In this letter, a hymn praising the Pharaoh is appended to the prostration formula beginning in line 5b. Throughout this tablet, this scribe shows off their familiarity with Egyptian language and culture in a way unparalleled in the rest of the Canaanite corpus.[41] The poetic language compares both the current Pharaoh and his father to the solar disk crossing the heavens. In particular, the description of the "sweet breath" of the king and solar imagery in this passage appear to refer to the worship of Aten.[42] Later, the Pharaoh is compared to the West Semitic storm god. Past works proposed that this letter was the work of an Egyptian scribe working in Byblos. However, as Moran notes, this letter "exhibits no typically Egyptian features."[43] Moreover, it demonstrates the scribe's mastery of features of local Canaanite scribalism both in the use of Canaano-Akkadian and in the use of Canaanite words rendered in syllabic cuneiform.[44] This suggests that we are looking at the work of a local scribe working in Tyre who showcased their knowledge of Egyptian culture in order to gain favor with the Pharaoh's staff.[45] Through this flowery introduction (the "air kiss") and references to events in Egypt, Abimilki's scribe presented themselves as a cosmopolitan professional to their scribal counterparts in Egypt.

The Snub: EA 252, a Letter from Shechem

EA 252, one of three letters written to the Pharaoh on behalf of Lab'ayu of Shechem, has attracted much scholarly attention because it features a Canaanite parable about an angry ant. The introduction in EA 252 also offers an example of a scribal "snub"—it has an abbreviated introduction, which omits key politeness formulae.[46] In what follows, I build upon past observations about this letter and offer a key difference in methodology: I approach EA 252 as a

in Exod 9:23; 1 Sam 12:17–18; 2 Sam 22:14; Jer 10:13, 25:30, 51:16; Joel 4:16; Amos 3:4; Ps 18:13, 46:6, 68:33, and 77:17). See also CAD N s.v. *nadānu* 2, under the subentry *rigmu*; also CAD R s.v. *rigmu* 4.

41. For example, the scribe uses an Egyptian term in the following gloss in line 12: *du-ni* ZAG: *ḫa-ap-ši*, "strength of his arm." The reference to the breath of the king as a life-giving force in lines 25–26 is also an appeal to an Egyptian literary trope. Moreover, the fronted references to the Pharaoh as solar disk suggest an awareness of the religious transition in Egypt. For this reason, Albright originally proposed that this scribe was an Egyptian working in Tyre (William F. Albright, "The Egyptian Correspondence of Abimilki, Prince of Tyre," *JEA* 23 [1937]: 190–203, at 196). Other studies have similarly focused on the identity of the scribe. Stanley Gevirtz contended that they may have been a Canaanite who was versed in Egyptian culture (Stanley Gevirtz, "On Canaanite Rhetoric: The Evidence of the Amarna Letters From Tyre," *Or* 42 [1973]: 162–77, at 177). Cecilia Grave, however, has highlighted that there are many Canaanisms in this corpus (Cecilia Grave, "The Etymology of the Northwest Semitic *ṣapānu*," *UF* 12 [1980]: 221–29; Cecilia Grave, "On the Use of an Egyptian Idiom in an Amarna Letter from Tyre and in a Hymn to the Aten," *OrAnt* 19 [1980]: 205–18; Cecilia Grave, "Northwest Semitic *ṣapānu* in a Break-Up of an Egyptian Stereotype Phrase in EA 147," *Or* 51 [1982]: 161–82).

42. See Siddall, "The Amarna Letters," 27.

43. William L. Moran, *Amarna Studies: Collected Writings*, ed. John Huehnergard and Shlomo Izre'el (Winona Lake, IN: Eisenbrauns, 2003), 249n3.

44. For example, in this letter, the Pharaoh seemingly speaks in Canaanite: EA 147:35–38 *e-nu-ma iq-bi* LUGAL *be-li-ia*: *ku-na a-na pa-ni* ÉRIN.MEŠ GAL *ù iq-bi* ÍR-*du a-na be-li-šu*: *ia-a-ia-ia*, "When the king, my lord said: 'Prepare for the arrival of the great army,' then (his) servant said to his lord: 'Yes!'"

45. Siddall has argued that the references to Egyptian religion were a strategy to draw attention to Abimilki's letters; he sees the ruler himself as playing a greater role in the composition choices. He writes, "Abimilki wrote his letters in a shrewd manner, using West Semitic and Egyptian elements in order both to attract the attention of Canaanite officials in the Egyptian administration and to delight the pharaoh" ("The Amarna Letters," 30). Hanadah Tarawneh examines EA 147 as part of a larger discussion of scribal strategies used to communicate effectively in this corpus: "Amarna Letters: Two Languages, Two Dialogues," in *Egypt and the Near East – the Crossroads: Proceedings of an International Conference on the Relations of Egypt and the Near East in the Bronze Age, Prague, September 1–3, 2010*, ed. Jana Mynářová (Prague: Charles University, 2011), 279.

46. See Richard S. Hess, "Smitten Ant Bites Back: Rhetorical Forms in the Amarna Correspondence from Shechem," in *Verse in Ancient Near Eastern Prose*, ed. Johannes Cornelis Moor and Wilfred G. E. Watson, AOAT 42 (Neukirchen-Vluyn: Neukirchener Verlag, 1993), 98–103.

crafted scribal product aimed first and foremost at a scribal audience in Egypt.[47] I also consider the visual display of this letter as a part of the scribe's communicative strategy.

The Lab'ayu letters are all made from local clays of the central hill country, but are the work of two different scribal hands.[48] EA 253 and 254 are the work of one scribe, whereas EA 252, "the snub," appears to be that of a different person.[49] The introductions of all three Lab'ayu letters comprise (1) a heading and (2) salutations and prostration formulae, conforming to Jana Mynářová's Type 12A (that of 70% of the Amarna Letters).[50] When we take a closer look, however, EA 252 stands out—the title used to introduce the Pharaoh is abbreviated and the prostration formula is shortened to a bare reference to Lab'ayu prostrating once. The scribe also omits the reference to Lab'ayu's inferior status (dirt beneath the Pharaoh's feet). While such lapses in diplomatic protocol may not have been expressed when the tablet was read, they would not have gone unnoticed by recipient scribes. We can contrast the sparse introduction to EA 252, with the more deferential greetings in EA 253 and 254, which were also written for Lab'ayu but by a different scribe.

EA 252: 1–4 Obv.
a-na ^{I}LUGAL-*ma bé-lí-ia qí-bí-ma um-ma* ^{I}*La-ab-a-yu* ÌR-*ka a-na* GÌR.MEŠ-⸢*pí*⸣ *be-lí-ia am-qú-ut*
Speak to the king, my lord: a message of Labʾayu, your servant. I now fall at feet of my lord.

EA 253: 1–6 Obv.
[*a-na šà*]*r-ri* [EN-*ia*] ⸢*ù*⸣ [^{d}UTU]-⸢*ia*⸣ *um-ma* [^{I}*La-a*]*b-a-ya* [ÌR]-*ka ù e*[*p-ru*] [*ša*] *ka-bá-*⸢*še*⸣-[*ka*][*a-n*]*a* GÌR.MEŠ *š*[*àr-r*]*i* ⸢EN⸣-*ia* ⸢*7*⸣-⸢*šu*⸣ *7-ta-a-an am-qut*
[To the ki]ng, [my lord] and my [sun god]: a message of [La]bʾayu, your [servant] and the di[rt on which] you tread. I now fall seven times and seven times [a]t the feet of the k[in]g, my lord.

EA 254: 1–6a Obv.
a-na šàr-ri EN-*ia ù* ^{d}UTU-*ia um-ma La-ab-a-yu* ÌR-*ka ù ep-ru ša ka-bá-ši-ka a-na* GÌR.MEŠ *šàr-ri* EN-*ia ù* ^{d}UTU-*ia 7-šu 7-ta-a-an* ⸢*am*⸣-*qut*
To the king, my lord and my sun god: a message of Labʾayu, your servant and the dirt on which you tread. I now fall seven times and seven times at the feet of the king, my lord, my sun god.

Additionally, there are two key differences in how the scribe refers to the Pharaoh when transitioning to the main core of the message. The scribe who wrote EA 253 and 254 included an additional layer of deference through the use of the phrase *iš-te-me a-wa-te.*MEŠ *ša šàr-ru* "I have heard (obeyed) the words of the king." The verb *iš-te-me* "to hear/obey" frames the subsequent content of these letters as a statement of compliance with the Pharaoh's previous

47. Hess's study of EA 252 ("Smitten Ant Bites Back," 111) focused on its rhetorical characteristics, as a statement of Lab'ayu's defiance. He writes, "Labaya and his scribe are more than Canaanites struggling with the international Akkadian language of their day. They represent rhetoricians who use poetical devices in these prose texts in order to convey their message with the maximum effect." In this work, Lab'ayu is described as an author who expresses his defiance through the omission of key formulae in the introduction, through the use of Canaanite linguistic forms, and the final ant parable in lines 16–22, while the Pharaoh is the audience and "reader" of this tablet.

48. EA 252 and 254, though written by different scribes, are characterized by soils from the Motza and 'Amminadav Formations; EA 253 uses soil that is different from EA 252 and 254, being a mix of rendzina and terra rossa, which are both found at the site of Shechem (see Goren et al., *Inscribed in Clay*, 262–65, at 264–65).

49. Vita, *Canaanite Scribes*, 74–75.

50. See Jana Mynářová, *Language of Amarna—Language of Diplomacy: Perspectives on the Amarna Letters* (Prague: Czech Institute of Egyptology, 2007), 105–6.

orders. In EA 252, however, the scribe omits the statement of obedience found in EA 253 and 254, and moves right into Lab'ayu's grievance.

EA 252: 5–6 [omission of *iš-te-me a-wa-te*.MEŠ *ša šàr-ru*] *i-nu-ma šap-ra-ta a-na ia-a-ši*
Regarding what you wrote me....

This is followed by a quotation of the Pharaoh's past message: *ú-ṣur-mì* LÚ.MEŠ *ša ṣa-ab-tu* URU, "Protect the men that attacked the city!" The rest of the letter goes on to undermine the Pharaoh's order as being ridiculous and harmful to Lab'ayu's cities.

EA 253 and 254, on the other hand, both begin the content section of the letters with a statement of obedience. Both letters also make reference to a past message from the Pharaoh, but they make clear that Lab'ayu has "heard" (that is obeyed) the order that he was given. While EA 253 is fragmentary, it uses the same statement of obedience as EA 254.

EA 253: 7–10 [*iš*-]*te-me a-wa-te*.MEŠ [*ša*] ⸢*šàr*⸣*-ru* EN-*ia* [*i*-]*na lìb*-[*bi*] *ṭup-pí* ⸢*iš*⸣*-tap-ra*-⸢*an*⸣*-ni*
[I have] heard the words [which] the king, my lord, sent to me [i]n a tablet.

EA 254: 6–7 *iš-te-me a-wa-te*.MEŠ ⸢*ša*⸣ *šàr-ru iš-tap-ra-an-ni*
I have heard the words that the king has sent to me.

There is also a key difference in the verb used to describe the Pharaoh's incoming letters. The scribe who wrote EA 252 structures this clause as though Lab'ayu is speaking directly to the Pharaoh. The verb here is a 2ms G perfect form of *šapāru* with the meaning "you sent" (*šap-ra-ta*); it is followed by a 1cs independent dative pronoun, "to me" (*a-na ia-a-ši*). This verb would have flagged this letter as one that could only be the work of a Canaanite scribe.[51] In this same context, the scribes who wrote EA 253 and 254 use a more standard Akkadian form in reference to the Pharaoh sending a message to Lab'ayu. The form *iš-tap-ra-an-ni*, "he has sent to me," is a 3ms G perfect of this same verbal root; it is marked by a ventive followed by the 1cs enclitic pronominal suffix (**am+ni>anni*).[52] This is a verbal form more akin to what we would expect in the work product of a scribe employed by Egypt. We thus have this key difference, which would have been perceptible to a scribe, but not necessarily to a person hearing the message once it was translated into Egyptian.[53] All of this suggests that the abbreviated introduction in EA 252 is an intentional snub meant draw attention to this letter and to express Lab'ayu's frustration with the orders that he has been given.[54]

Clustering, EA 252

In the previous section, I argued that the abbreviated introduction in EA 252 marks this letter as distinct from the other Lab'ayu letters that use a fuller and more respectful greeting. EA 252 also challenges us to think about how scribes used a mix of linguistic and visual strategies to draw attention to their work. While past studies have focused on the individual features (a gloss and/or gloss mark, or the use of Canaanite word or expression), when we think

51. See the discussion of the distinctions between Canaanite *qatal* and *qatil* and the Akkadian stative, which is also a suffixed verbal form in Baranowski, *The Verb in the Amarna Letters from Canaan*, 62–73; Rainey, *Canaanite in the Amarna Tablets*, 2:281–316.

52. See Rainey, *Canaanite in the Amarna Tablets*, 2:73–75.

53. For a broader discussion of this phenomenon see, Mandell, "Scribalism and Diplomacy," 376–78, 392; see also Izre'el, who describes this process as governed by "discourse triggers" ("Canaano-Akkadian: Linguistics and Socio-linguistics," 187–89).

54. For a different interpretation of this shortened prostration formula see Ellen F. Morris, "Bowing and Scraping in the Ancient Near East: An Investigation into Obsequiousness in the Amarna Letters," *JNES* 65.3 (2006): 188–89.

about these tablets as multimodal objects, we have to consider how these strategies worked together within the space of a text. Such "clustering" functioned as a type of metalinguistic signaling, akin to the combined use of a bookmark, a highlighter, underlining, and scribbled handwritten notes on the margins of a book to mark an important passage.

The layout of EA 252 is striking and sets it apart both from the other two Shechem letters and from other Canaanite Amarna Letters.[55] The scribe (or person who made the tablet) drew vertical line around the outer, left edge of the obverse and reverse of the tablet and numerous single, horizontal line rulings, on the obverse under lines 1–12 and 14–15, and on the reverse under lines 19–21, and 31. The other two Shechem letters, however, do not use scribal marks in this way.[56] If we think about the use of scribal marks in terms of visual design, the contrast between lined and unlined space becomes significant as a mode of communication. The empty space on this tablet is found in the portion of the letter where we find the infamous ant parable and the main contention in this letter, on the reverse. This suggests that perhaps we should view the use of scribal marks as a strategy of visual presentation. That is, the use of horizontal lines was a deliberate strategy to lead the eye of a viewer to the most important part of this letter, where Lab'ayu complains that the Pharaoh's orders are endangering him and his cities.

While the introduction of EA 252 stands out because it is a snub, its conclusion is also striking both rhetorically and linguistically. The letter ends in a Canaanite parable, featuring several West Semitic forms.

EA 252: 16–17 Obv; 18–22 Rev.
⸢*ša*⸣*-ni-tam*
> *ki-i na-am-lu tu-um-ḫa-ṣú la-a ti-ka-pí-lu*[57] *ù ta-an-*⸢*šu*⸣*-*⸢*ku*⸣ *qa-ti* LÚ*-lì ša yi-ma-ḫa-aš-ši*
> *ki-i a-na-ku i-ša-ḫa-ṭú*[58] *ú-ma a-nu-ta*$_5$ *ù ṣa-ab-ta-at-mì* 2 URU*-ia*

Furthermore,
> When an ant is smitten, it does not curl up, but it bites the hand of the man who struck it.
> Likewise, I am being attacked this day. Another of my cities has been captured.

This is followed by another statement of submission in lines 23–30, which features another cluster of Canaanite forms.

55. For an overview of the use of scribal marks in this corpus see Fred Mabie, "Ancient Near Eastern Scribes and the Mark(s) They Left: A Catalog and Analysis of Scribal Auxiliary Marks in the Amarna Corpus and in the Cuneiform Alphabetic Texts of Ugarit and Ras Ibn Hani" (PhD diss., University of California; Los Angeles, 2004).

56. EA 253 and 254 do not employ scribal line rulings in this way. EA 253 has one line ruling that concludes the space of the reverse of the tablet (this is based on prior studies, as I was unable to confirm this ruling); 254 preserves the trace of a vertical line ruling on the far-left edge of the tablet obverse, which is barely visible but is clear in the images of this tablet available from The West Semitic Research Project's image bank on Inscriptifact, http://www.inscriptifact.com.

57. This analysis follows Rainey's proposal that this verb derives from *kapālu*, "to curl up," a cognate of the Northwest Semitic *kpl*, "to fold, double." Albright analyzed this as *tiqabbilu*, a D stem and cognate to the Northwest Semitic verb *qbl* "to receive." Today, most scholars follow Avi Hurwitz's proposal (adopted first by Moran) that this verb should be read as *ti-qà-bi-lu*, related to the substantive *qablu*, with the general meaning "to be in opposition to, to fight." However, as Rainey points out, the verb *qubbul* is otherwise unattested for this period. See William F. Albright, "An Archaic Hebrew Proverb in an Amarna Letter from Central Palestine," *BASOR* 89 (1943): 31n16; William L. Moran, "Amarna Glosses," *RA* 69 (1975): 149n1; Baruch Halpern and John Huehnergard, "El-Amarna Letter 252," *Or* 51 (1983): 229; and Rainey, *Canaanite in the Amarna Tablets*, 1:148; and Anson F. Rainey, "New Translation of the Amarna Letters—After 100 Years," *AfO* 36–37 (1989/1990): 68–69.

58. I follow Rainey's suggestion that is an 1cs N imperfect form of *šaḫāṭu* A, "to jump up, attack" (*Canaanite in the Amarna Tablets* 2:119). See also the entries in the CAD Š-1 s.v. *šaḫāṭu* A and B; and *AHw* 1130. An alternative analysis is that this verb is a 1cs imperfect form of *šaḫātu* (*u*-class), "to fear, to be afraid" (u/u/) (see *AHw* 1129b; CAD Š-1 s.v. *šaḫātu* B). This latter reading understands the line to express Lab'ayu's passivity or fear.

ša-ni-tam

šum-ma ti-qa-bu ap-pu-na-ma nu-pu-ul-mì ta-aḫ-ta-mu ù ti-ma-ḫa-ṣú-ka i-bi ú-ṣur-ru-na LÚ.MEŠ *ša ṣa-ab-tu*$_4$ URU *i-li šu-sú-mì ṣa*[!]-*bi-ia*[59] *ù ú-ṣur-ru-šu-nu*

Furthermore,

Even if you were to say, "Fall under them so that they can strike you," I would protect my enemy. As for the men who captured the town, I am able expel my enemies, but I will protect them.[60]

This passage is also marked linguistically as a striking display of Canaanite identity, since this section of the letter departs from the Middle Babylonian lexicon.[61] The verbal form *tu-um-ḫa-ṣú* is an internally marked passive (a Gp imperfect), a form not found in Akkadian; *ta-an-*⌜*šu*⌝-⌜*ku*⌝ derives from the West Semitic verbal root **nšk*. The 2ms imperative *nu-pu-ul-mì*, "fall down" derives from the West Semitic root **npl*, whereas the Akkadian verb with this meaning that we see most in the Canaanite Amarna Letters is *maqātu*. For example, the verb of prostration earlier in this letter is a standard Akkadian 1cs preterite, *amqut*; the form *ta-aḫ-ta-mu* in the Pharaoh's command "fall under them" derives from a West Semitic preposition *tḫt*; it is further marked as a Canaanite form by a Canaanite 3pl suffix.[62]

This cluster of Canaanite forms both visually and linguistically differentiates the act of falling described here (which implicitly ends in violence) from the act of prostration described in the introduction of letters to the Pharaoh. It is also striking that we have a Canaanite verb spoken by the Pharaoh, whereas in other letters there seems to be a concerted effort by scribes to use forms more akin to the Middle Babylonian forms that they saw in letters from Egypt. That is, they employed a "higher" register of written language when quoting or referring to the Pharaoh.[63]

All of this suggests that the clustering of linguistic and visual markings in this letter are part of a strategy to draw attention to this tablet. While these elements of scribal craft may not have be accessible to the pharaoh, they would have stood out to a scribe trained in Middle Babylonian working at the royal court. Moreover, this scribe's ability to navigate between a more classical register of Akkadian, in the introduction of this letter, the Canaanite-inflected Akkadian used in the Cis-Jordan, and the syllabic writing of Canaanite in this letter (ll. 16–26), speak as well to their mastery of their craft. Together, these visual and linguistic strategies mark EA 252 as a masterpiece of Canaanite scribal training, language, and rhetoric—a veritable scribal snub.

59. I adopt Mario Liverani's proposal that *a-bi-ia* is a scribal error for *a-<ai>-bi-ia*, "my enemies" ("The Father of Lab'aya," *NABU* no. 4 [1997 (December)]: 121). Baruch Halpern and John Huehnergard propose a different scribal error; they read this word as *ṣa*[!]-*bi-ia* and translate the concluding line "I am able to send out my troops, and I will protect them" ("El-Amarna Letter 252," 228 and n. 7). However, Liverani's proposal best accords with the rhetorical function of the ant parable (I am a weaker and smaller ruler, but I not passive— I can fight back) and the following statement of obedience in lines 23–30 (even if you ask me to do something that will harm me, I will do it). In this letter, Lab'ayu demonstrates that he can strike back at his enemies, but is choosing not to. He is compliant with the Pharaoh's orders, but not out of weakness.

60. Several translations follow Albright and analyze this verb as a G mp participle form of *šsy*, "the plunderers" (**šāsû>šōsû*, written as *šu-sú*, reflecting the Canaanite shift), as a description of the raiding of Lab'ayu's family god. My translation of *šūṣû* follows the suggestion made in Halpern and Huehnergard ("El-Amarna Letter 252," 227–330) that this is a Š infinitive form of *(w)aṣû*: *ili šūṣû*, "I can expel (them)."

61. William F. Albright went as far as to write, "Disregarding the particle u, 'and,' we count only about 90% of his words in these lines as pure Accadian, with 40% mixed or ambiguous, and no less than 40% pure Canaanite. No wonder the letter has proved baffling!" ("An Archaic Hebrew Proverb in an Amarna Letter from Central Palestine," *BASOR* 89 [1943]: 29).

62. We might expect Akkadian *šaplānu*, which is also written in this corpus logographically as KI.TA.

63. Mandell, "Scribalism and Diplomacy," 357, 376–78, 392, 417–18.

The Postscript, EA 286, 287, 288, and 316

In the Amarna corpus, there are a handful of "postscripts" (i.e., letters within letters) that directly address the scribe(s) on the receiving end of these diplomatic exchanges.[64]

EA 286: 61–64 Rev.
[a-n]a ⸢*ṭup*⸣*-šar* ⸢LUGAL⸣ EN-*ia um-ma* ^{I}⸢ÌR⸣-⸢*ḫé*⸣-⸢*ba*⸣ [Ì]R-*ka-ma še-ri-ib a-wa-ti.*⸢MEŠ⸣ ⸢*ba*⸣*-na-ta a-na* LUGAL EN-*ia ḫal-qa-at* ⸢*gáb*⸣*-bi* KUR.ḪI.A LUGAL EN-*ia*
[T]o the scribe of the king, my lord, a message of ʿAbdi-Ḫeba, your [ser]vant: Present eloquent words to the king, my lord. "[Al]l of the lands of the king, my lord are lost!"

EA 287: 64–70 Rev. and Edge
a-na ṭup-šar šàr-ri EN-*ia qí-bi-ma um-ma* ^{I}ÌR-*ḫe-ba* ÌR-*ka-ma a-na* 2 GÌR.MEŠ-*<ka> am-qut-mi* ÌR-*ka a-nu-ki še-ri-ib a-wa-ta*$_5$.MEŠ *ba-na-ta a-na šàr-ri* EN-*ia* ⸢LÚ⸣ ⸢*ú*⸣-⸢*e*⸣-⸢*é*ʾ⸣ ⸢*šàr*⸣-⸢*ri*⸣ *a-*⸢*nu*⸣-⸢*ki*⸣ *ma-at-ti a-na ka-ta*$_5$!
To the scribe of the king, my lord, speak a message of ʿAbdi-Ḫeba, your servant: I now fall at your two feet. I am your servant. Present eloquent words to the king, my lord. "I am a soldier of the king. I die for you!"

EA 288: 62–66 Rev. and Edge
[a-na] ⸢LÚ⸣ *ṭup-šar šàr-ri* EN-*ia [um-ma]* ⸢^{I}⸣⸢ÌR⸣-*ḫe-ba* ÌR-*ma a-na* 2 GÌR.MEŠ *[am-qut-]mi še-ri-ib a-wa-ta*$_5$.M[EŠ] *ba-na-ti a-na šàr-r[i]* [xxx LÚ] ÌR[-*ka ù* LÚ.]⸢DUMU⸣-*ka a-na-ku*
[To] the scribe of the king, my lord: [a message of] ʿAbdi-Ḫeba, <your> servant: I now fall at <your> two feet. Present eloquent words to the king [xxx] I am your servant and your son.

EA 316: 16–25 Rev.
[a-n]a ^{I}*ša-aḫ-ši-ḫa-ši-*⸢*ḫa*⸣ [EN-*ia*] *um-ma* ^{I}*Pu-*⸢^{d}⸣⸢IŠKUR⸣ ⸢*a*⸣-⸢*na*⸣ ⸢2⸣ ⸢GÌR⸣.⸢MEŠ⸣-*ka* ⸢*am*⸣*[-qú-ut]*⸢*i*⸣*-ia-*⸢*nu*⸣ ⸢*mi*⸣-⸢*im*⸣-⸢*ma*⸣ ⸢*i*⸣*-[n]a* ⸢É⸣-*ia i-n[a] [i]-re-[-bi-]*⸢*i*⸣*a a-[na]* ⸢*ša*⸣-⸢*šu*⸣⸢*u*⸣ ⸢*ki*⸣*-na-na la-[a] uš-ši-ir-[t]i*$_7$ KASKAL-*ra-*⸢*na*⸣ *a-na k[a-ta]*$_5$ *a-nu-ma i-*⸢*šu*⸣*[-ši-]ru* KASKAL-*ra-na dam-*⸢*qá*⸣*-ta* ⸢*a*⸣-⸢*na*⸣ *ka-ta*$_5$
[T]o the letter writer [of my lord], a message of Pu-Baʿlu: "I now fall at your two feet. There was nothing i[n] my house when I entered it, therefore I did not send a caravan to you. Now I am sending fine caravan to you."

Such postscripts were visually and organizationally separated from the main content of the primary royal letter. All four postscripts are placed at or near the end of the primary message; they begin with a new introductory formula addressed to the scribe, which marks the following content as a separate text. Additionally, scribes did at times separate postscript messages from the main body message with a scribal mark, typically a line ruling.[65] The titles referring to the Egyptian scribe suggests a degree of familiarity with the inner workings of the cuneiform scribal depot at the Egyptian capital.[66] The last example in EA 316 infers that such scribes were rewarded for their cooperation in these

64. EA 286, 287, and 288 are written on behalf of ʿAbdi-Ḫeba of Jerusalem; EA 316 is a letter written for Pu-Baʿlu of Yurzu.

65. The postscripts in EA 286 and EA 289 blend visually with the rest of the letter; only the second introduction marks them as separate messages. In EA 287, the scribe used two horizontal lines to bracket the postscript (in lines 64-70); the letter continues in lines 71–78 with what appears to have been an addition to the original message. This letter also concludes with a prostration formula, which is unusual. The main message in EA 316 ends on the obverse of the tablet with a horizontal ruling. Even though there is room for a line of text on the obverse, the postscript is placed on the other side of the tablet. This layout seems to demarcate the primary and secondary letters inscribed on this tablet.

66. EA 316 uses an approximation of the Egyptian scribe's title: ^{I}*ša-aḫḫ-ši-ḫa-ši-*⸢*ḫa*⸣ = *sš š*ʿ*.t*, "letter writer;" in the Jerusalem

transactions. References to "eloquent words" in EA 286–288 reflect a concern with the transmission of the message, most likely its translated Egyptian version.[67]

Conclusion

In this paper, I have presented strategies used by scribes writing in Canaan to communicate more effectively with their scribal counterparts in Egypt. When we approach the Canaanite Amarna Letters as messages mediated by scribes, we must address characteristics of these letters that would have stood out to the scribes. These cuneiform-trained scribes were not part of a monolithic speech community; however, because of their ongoing engagement in similar material and intellectual practices, we can consider these scribes to be part of a community of practice. Over time, through their exchange of letters, Canaanite scribes developed linguistic and nonlinguistic strategies to speak clearly to their peers in Egypt, and perhaps to show off their professional skills.

Unpeeling the layers of meaning that Canaanite scribes encoded into the clay tablets that they sent to Egypt calls for an approach that balances analysis of their physical form with their words. To do this, I highlighted several key strategies: the contrast between shortened and extended greetings (the snub and air kiss); the clustering of scribal marks, code-switching, and use of a local rhetorical style to highlight key content (clustering); and reliance on messages within royal letters that directly addressed recipient scribes (postscripts). How might these strategies have impacted how these letters were read and transmitted to the Pharaoh or to key Egyptian officials? Thinking about the reading of these letters as a performance is helpful: we can assume an audience including Egyptians and perhaps members of a Canaanite diplomatic mission, as well as local cuneiform scribes or other officials who were tasked with processing the letters. This reminds us that letter writing and reading was not a "solitary activity," but a social practice that entailed "group discussion and what needs to be said."[68] Seen in this light, perhaps the use of a Canaanite proverb and the influx of Canaanite verbal forms in EA 252 may have inspired a shift in the spoken register of Egyptian which was being used, or may have led the person transmitting this message to gesture or even act out this part of the letter. At the very least, we can imagine a relationship of sorts developing as scribes on both ends of this communicative chain learned to recognize each other's work, and noted changes in formulae, style, or the execution and layout of the tablets that they exchanged.

---

letters, the title *tupšar šarri*, "royal scribe," seems to be a calque for the Egyptian title *sš nswt (m3ˁ.t)*, "royal scribe," or "true royal scribe" (William F. Albright, "Cuneiform Material for Egyptian Prosopography 1500–1200 B.C.," *JNES* 5 [1946]: 20–21).

67. As Seth L. Sanders writes, "Those pleasing words were spoken on behalf of the Canaanite ruler of Jerusalem but whether the message was imagined in Egyptian or Canaanite, they could not have been in the same Babylonian words as the letter itself.... This cosmopolitan writing system connected with local languages by encoding it, translating it into writing rather than copying it and fully representing it" (*The Invention of Hebrew* [Urbana, IL: University of Illinois Press, 2009], 82).

68. David Barton and Nigel Hall, ed. *Letter Writing as a Social Practice* (Amsterdam: John Benjamins, 2000), 4. See also Andrea R. Fishman, "Because This Is Who We Are: Writing in the Amish Community," in *Writing in the Community*, ed. David Barton and Roz Ivanič, Written Communication Annual 6 (Newbury Park, CA: Sage, 1991), 14–37.

"Let the Ibis Be Consulted": Letters Mentioning Cult Practices or Containing Possible Allusions to Literary Texts

Franziska Naether

This quotation in the title of this essay originates from a private letter of a certain Herieus, an ibis curator from Hermoupolis Magna.[1] During the end of the fourth and the early third century BCE, Herieus traveled to a temple of Thoth in the nome of Prosopis.[2] In his letter to an unnamed addressee, maybe an authority of some sort, he complained about the miserable treatment of an ibis, a bird held in captivity for oracular purposes. Apparently, Herieus's investigations were unwanted: he even received death threats by members of the local priesthood. Herieus ended his accusatory letter with a claim for truth, saying: *mj šn=w pꜣ hb*, "Let the ibis be consulted!"

Opening with this example, it is obvious that the contents of letters inform us about religious matters, a topic that I would like to explore in this contribution. It is dedicated to Richard Jasnow, an eminent scholar of literature and religion in the Greco-Roman world, especially in the field of Demotic studies. His editions of texts such as the monumental Book of Thoth (together with Karl-Theodor Zauzich) and a treatise on ecstatic rituals at a festival of Mut (together with Mark Smith) are just two examples of how Richard helped us to understand cult practices of the ancient world. Together with his wife Tina, he is an avid decipherer of graffiti, and should his demotist's eagle eye need help, he is making use of technology from the digital age.[3] All the best to our jubilarian and many happy returns! I hope Richard will find these humble musings interesting and thought provoking.

Ending his letter with a plea for asking a sacred bird for a justification of his statements, Herieus's writings point to an oracular consultation, most likely through a ticket oracle, a processional oracle, or an oracle by the movements and the behavior of the ibis. All these divinatory techniques are attested in the cult of Thoth.[4]

1. P. Louvre E 3334, l. 30. If not stated otherwise, all editions of texts have been accessed through the Thesaurus Linguae Aegyptiae (TLA), available online: http://aaew.bbaw.de. The main bibliography of the editions and corrections can also be found there. wish to thank the editors and their team, in particular Mark Smith, for his critical reading of a former version of this contribution.

2. As identified by Richard Jasnow, "The Fourth Lower Egyptian Nome in Demotic," *Enchoria* 11 (1982): 112.

3. Christina Di Cerbo and Richard Jasnow, "Building Dipinti at Medinet Habu (with an Appendix on Remains of Color Decoration in the Palace)," in *En détail – Philologie und Archäologie im Diskurs: Festschrift für Hans-W. Fischer-Elfert*, ed. Marc Brose, Peter Dils, Franziska Naether, Lutz Popko, and Dietrich Raue, BZÄS 7 (Berlin: de Gruyter, 2019), 239–59.

4. For an overview, see Franziska Naether, *Die Sortes Astrampsychi: Problemlösungsstrategien durch Orakel im römischen Ägypten*, ORA 3 (Tübingen: Mohr Siebeck, 2010).

Letters and Other Text Types Bearing Letter Formulae

This contribution deals solely with letters from ancient Egypt and their value for the study of ritual phenomena, mainly oracular inquiries. For this, I have looked through a good number of corpora of Egyptian letters and selected a few examples.[5]

Letters are a special genre. No matter how well scholars are able to decipher their words, contextualize the senders and the addressees in their respective social networks, ascertain the archaeological findspots of the letters between their places of writing, their ways to the addressees, and further stations of archiving, reuse, and abandonment as well as background information on the letter's contents, there will always remain one or more mysteries in studying them. Sometimes, the true meaning behind the lines as only recognizable to the people that mattered: the sender and the addressee. This is the universal crux with this genre; the same is true for emails and messages of modern services on digital devices: texts can be misunderstood for reasons of secrecy, brevity, intercultural communication codes—no matter if on an ostracon or in a modern WhatsApp message.

During my research on cult practices in Egyptian literary texts, I first wanted to include letters, graffiti and related genres to analyze their potential for the study of religion, rituals, divination and magic.[6] Very early on, I decided to leave out these genres for the sake of length of the study. Letters, no matter if exchanged between private individuals or among professionals in the administration or priestly ranks, offer insights into ancient Egyptian daily life. Studying this genre can facilitate the understanding of ritual instruments, handbooks or depictions on temple walls—when the letter writer mentions ritual action. By this means, cult practices can receive a "face," a practitioner and maybe his or her name. We are informed about festivals, animal cults, offerings, prayers, and further practices (cf. parts 2 and 3 in this paper). What I will leave out of the discussion are the numerous "pious" wishes at the beginnings and the ends of letters which make use of greetings and well-wishes in the name of the god(s).[7]

Oracle questions as written up in ticket oracles have certain similarities to letters. Mark Depauw in his *Demotic Letter* has already pointed to the similarities of the genres,[8] and I continued on this track in my book on the *Sortes Astrampsychi*.[9] The way petitioners ask questions to divinities is written in a form of letter format. Both text types belong to the group of documentary texts (or "applied formulae" as used in magic and as opposed to literary texts). The same could be said about the text type "letters to the gods", the successor of the phenomenon of the "letters to the dead".[10]

For this purpose, I have compiled the following list, roughly sorted according to date and location:

---

5. I basically centered my research on letters available in the TLA. Thanks are due to Karl-Theodor Zauzich for sharing his upcoming edition of letters from Elephantine with me, the fourth installment of the series Demotische Papyri aus den Staatlichen Museen zu Berlin, Papyri von der Insel Elephantine, forthcoming.

6. Naether, *Kultpraxis in der altägyptischen Literatur*, forthcoming.

7. "Initial" and "final courtesy"; see, e.g., Mark Depauw, *The Demotic Letter: A Study of Epistolographic Scribal Traditions against Their Intra- and Intercultural Background*, DemStud 14 (Sommerhausen: Gisela Zauzich Verlag, 2006).

8. Depauw, *The Demotic Letter*, 301–14.

9. Naether, *Die Sortes Astrampsychi*, 359–410.

10. Newer treatments of these text types are Kata Endreffy, "Business with Gods: The Role of Bargaining in Demotic Letters to Gods and Graeco-Roman Judicial Prayers," in *Commerce and Economy in Ancient Egypt: Proceedings of the Third International Congress for Young Egyptologists, 25–27 September 2009, Budapest*, ed. András Hudecz and Máté Petrik, BAR-IS 2131 (Oxford: Archaeopress, 2010), 49–54; Chrysi Kotsifou, "Prayers and Petitions for Justice: Despair and the 'Crossing of Boundaries' between Religion and Law," *Tyche* 31 (2016): 167–99; Sylvie Donnat Beauquier, *Écrire à ses morts: Enquête sur un usage rituel de l'écrit dans l'Égypte pharaonique* (Grenoble: Jérôme Millon, 2014). See also the ongoing project "Magic in Context: Defixiones and the Communication with Ancient Gods" by Giuditta Mirizio at Heidelberg University, SFB 933.

No.	Cult Practice / Temple Business Mentioned	Source	Date, Script, Provenance
1	Processional oracle of Hathor in Dendera: "When they came ... they wanted to see (= ask in an oracle) Hathor, the lady of Dendera, your mistress ... and we sailed downstream because of the task on which you sent us. So we stood like a group of people (with Hathor, in procession)." (ll. 5–8: *jwi=st [...] =tn ꜥḥꜥ.t ptr Ḥw.t-Ḥr nb.t-Jwn.t tꜣy=k ḥn.wt [...] jw=n ḫd m-sꜣ tꜣ wpw.t j:hꜣb=k n=n ḥr=s st [tw]=n ꜥḥꜥ m ꜥḥꜥ*)	P. Valencay 2, letter of Pa-hen and Sah-nefer to their superior	Ramesses IX, hieratic, provenance unknown
2	Processional oracle of the divinized Amenhotep I (quoted): "I will protect you, I will bring you back safely and you will fill your eyes with my temple forecourt." (vo., l. 4: *jw=j zꜣ=k jw=j jni.t=k jw=k [w] ḏꜣ.tj jw=k mḥ jr.tj=k m pꜣ wbꜣ=j*)	P. BM EA inv. 10417, letter of Djehuty-Mes to the absent priest of Amenhotep I	Ramesses XI, hieratic, from Deir el-Medina
3	Processional oracle; the general has positive feedback on what happened after an oracle (probably of Amenhotep I; quoted): "I have laid the documents/scrolls in front of this great god so that he can judge them in good judgement" (ll. 3–4: *wꜣḥ=j nꜣ mḏꜣ.t m-bꜣḥ pꜣj nṯr-ꜥꜣ wḏꜥ=f sn m wḏꜥ nfr*)	P. Turin inv. 1975 = LRL 22, letter of the pharaoh's general to the scribe of the necropolis Tjaroy (Djehuty-Mes)	Ramesses XI, hieratic, from Deir el-Medina
4	Processional oracle of Chnum in Elephantine, most probably about the well-being of a relative (the father or the son of the writer): "Now, I have caused it (the matter) be laid before Chnum (for an oracle) (and) he replied, saying: 'He will be safe and sound', so he said to the singer of Amun Tuja and the scribe Hori." (ll. 5–6 vo.: *ḫr di= {t}j wꜣḥ.tw=f m-bꜣḥ Ḫnm.w ḏd=f r-ḏd jw=f wḏꜣ ḫr=f n šmꜥ.yt-n-Jmn ṯwjꜣ zḫꜣ Ḥr*)	P. BN 196.III = LRL 31, letter of Pa-en-ta-hut-resu (in Elephantine) to Bu-teh-Imen (in Deir el-Medina)	Ramesses XI, hieratic, from Deir el-Medina
5	Letter with a reply from an oracular session of Imhotep-Asclepius with a recipe to cure a fever of the patient Teos	O. PSBA 35, pl. 27, letter from Imhotep to Horos	fourth–third century BCE, Demotic, from Thebes
6	Ticket oracle; the sender reminds the addressee to take care of the correct cult practices (*ir ꜥrš*) until the god grants an oracle (*sḥn-nfr*); ll. 19–20 mentions a dispute of officials and the god (maybe involving a selection procedure?), in ll. 23 ro.–5 vo. the sender requests that Hartoph-nakhthes ask Isis in a ticket oracle if he should marry Tayris or Tareshy (this would mean two questions to the god = four tickets)	P. Berlin P. dem. 13538, letter of an unknown sender to Hartoph-nakhthes	fourth–third century BCE, Demotic, from Elephantine

7	Ticket oracle(?); election of priests, probably verified through a ticket oracle; the god agrees with the suitable candidate Pahet-neter: "The god agrees with him as well." (ll. 17–18: *pꜣ nṯr mtr r.r=f ꜥn*)	P. Berlin P. dem. 13549, letter of Hartophnakhthes to Eschnompmetis	fourth century BCE, Demotic, from Elephantine
8	Ticket oracle; letter with a request to present a ticket oracle to Isis: "Is it to my good fortune to go to the nome on the day of reception of money(?) for seed or is it better to remain here in Elephantine?" (ll. x+2–7 *pꜣj=(j) ꜥš-sḥn nfr šm r pꜣ tš (n) pꜣ ssw (n) šsp [ḥḏ] n pr.t gr ỉn nꜣ.w-nfr=[s] ḫpr dj n jb*)	P. Berlin P. dem. 15637 + 15803, no names mentioned	fourth–third century BCE, Demotic, from Elephantine
9	Ticket oracle; letter with a reply from a ticket oracle by Chnum from Elephantine to the prophet about the well-being of a woman (maybe the same one who is mentioned in his letter as pregnant)	P. Berlin P. dem. 23601: letter of *Ḫnm-m-ꜣḫ.t* to the prophet *Ns-ḫnm-mtr*	fourth–third century BCE, Demotic, from Elephantine
10	Ticket oracle; letter with a request to ask a ticket oracle about the marital faithfulness of the sender	P. Cairo JE 95205 = P. Qasr Ibrim 1, letter from Primhi to Kolanthion (first letter of the papyrus)	fourth–third century BCE, Demotic, from Qasr Ibrim
11	Ticket oracle; letter with a request to ask a couple of questions by ticket oracle to Amun (after the correct cult practices – *ir tꜣ md.t n šms*) about a certain imprisoned Psenamunis: "Will he get out of the circumstances in which he is in? Will they be far from him? All the sad things in which he is—is it you (= Amun) who finds fault in him? Will he live (= survive) or will he die in the imprisonment in which he is (currently) in?" Questions about a certain Teos: "Should he work with the sheep? Will he go back there again (into katoche)?" (Psenamunis, ll. 12–23: *ỉn ỉw=f r ỉr-bnr n nꜣ md.wt ntj-ỉw=f ẖn=w; ỉn ỉw=w r wj r.r=f; tḥꜣ nb ntj-ỉw=f ẖn=w ỉn {n} mtw=k (pꜣ) ntj gm n=f bwꜣ; ỉn ỉw=f r ꜥnḫ ḫn ỉw=f r mwt n pꜣ ḏdtḥ ntj-ỉw=f n.ỉm=f;* Theos, ll. 25–29 *ỉw=f bꜣk ẖn nꜣ ỉswe.w; ỉn ỉw=f r šm r-n.ỉm=w ꜥn*	P. Cairo JE 95206 = P. Qasr Ibrim 2, letter from Abesenehi to Kolanthion	fourth–third century BCE, Demotic, from Qasr Ibrim
12	Unknown oracular practice: request to ask a sacred ibis bird in an oracle to verify the truth	P. Louvre E 3334, letter of the ibis curator Herieus to an unnamed official	early third century BCE, Demotic, from Hermoupolis Magna
13	Ticket oracle? letter with mention of an oracle (l. 14: *pꜣ ꜥš pꜣ nṯr*, "the calling of the god"), maybe in connection with the request that Tesenuphis and the priests not leave for Nilopolis the next morning	Bresciani, Archivio, no. 26, letter of the lesonis Petesuchos to priests and to Tesenuphis	around 133 BCE, from Soknopaiou Nesos

Commentary

At first glance, most of the sources originate from corpora of well-attested archaeological sites: late Ramesside hieratic letters from Deir el-Medina and early Demotic letters from Elephantine. Both locations were known for their temples with their respective oracular practices. In New Kingdom Deir el-Medina, the deceased pharaoh Amenhotep I was venerated as a divinity who gave processional oracles during festivals. For this, the public had access to the forecourt of the temple and could ask questions. Those were put by a few keywords or short sentences on ostraca and laid down in the processional route of the boat that contained a chapel with the god's processional image. According to the movement of the priests carrying the boat, the answer to the question could have been affirmative (a movement forward), negative (a movement backwards/withdrawing) or noncommittal (sideways movements). The implications of these oracular answers to the petitioners were later interpreted by priests who also helped in formulating and writing the questions and put them into the temple's archives. Letter no. 1 from the list refers to the setting of the processional oracle: a festival of Hathor in Dendera, with a crowd of spectators on the main *dromos*. Nos. 3 and 4 show that the petitioner himself put down his questions on the floor of the *dromos*. It is hard to say if this was always the rule since in the case of no. 3 we are dealing with a cult official who himself asked a question. *Nota bene*, a couple of the sources presented here show that priests themselves made use of the various oracular methods. This is an argument against the expressed view that priestly fraud was common in the consultation of oracles: in fact, it confirms that these practices that were used through millennia also "worked" to keep the sacralized kingdom and the political ideology of the empire together, albeit with changing foci —such as the "Priestly State" of the Twenty-First Dynasty onwards where many decisions, including the selection of appointees to the highest offices, were made by ordeals. Letter no. 7 is such an example: in this, a candidate for a priestly position has been confirmed as suitable. The letter writer uses this oracle to enhance his own position on the matter, that is, agreeing with the god. Reinforcing the truth of one's words is also the intention of Herieus the ibis curator in letter 12. Both men use oracle questions in a rhetorical way to strengthen their arguments.

According to no. 3, several questions were asked, presumably on one occasion. We have no evidence of official restrictions on how many questions could have been asked at festivals. The letter does not state if the sender went to more than one procession. More likely, he asked two questions via two ostraca at the same time. In no. 11, the addressee is requested to ask four questions on behalf of a prisoner who might already be executed and two more about the future of a former *katochos*. This catalogue of questions implies a highly worried letter writer, who uses these questions to press the addressee to action due to the urgency of the matter. Six questions by one party on a single occasion strikes me as an unusually high number. The content of the letter implies that the petitioners are very worried and hope for the survival of Psenamunis, but cannot rule out the possibility that he is guilty of the accused crimes—hence the fourth question of whether Amun finds him at fault.

The ticket oracle, attested from the Twentieth/Twenty-First Dynasties until the eighth century CE and partly replacing the processional oracle, works differently from the processional oracle.[11] For this, the petitioners or their stand-ins (see letter no. 4) prepared the questions with priests, but were not present when the priests let the gods decide. This happened in the sanctuary; once again, the gods decided by movement or another mode of sortition picking up options from an array of choices (see letter nos. 6 and 7). The ticket oracle questions were written up in an affirmative and in a negative version on a small papyrus ticket—hence the name—and then handed in to the divinity. The examples in letters 6, 10, and 11 do not bear the usual formulas but list simple questions to be asked. However, in no. 8, the sender shows a certain familiarity with the formulas and process: "Is it to my good fortune to go to the nome on the day of reception of money(?) for the seed or is it better to remain here in Elephantine?" This would be the affirmative version of the two questions, as opposed to "Is it to my good fortune. . . ." The second question, howev-

11. Naether, *Die Sortes Astrampsychi*, 43–44.

er, was abbreviated as in the other letters. With the knowledge about the tripartite formulae of the ticket oracles—(1) invocation of the divinities and identification of the petitioner; (2) introduction of the question in protasis-apodosis form; and (3) request to bring back the ticket and scribal remark—it is possible for us to draw up all the questions mentioned in the letters of nos. 6, 8, 10, and 11.

Whereas some letters deal with questions be put to an oracle, others mention answers of the divine. In letter no. 2, the priest Amenhotep, who worked far from home, is promised by the god Amenhotep I that he will one day return safe and sound to Deir el Medina. Most probably, the priest requested this oracle in an earlier letter. No. 5 contains a recipe to cure a patient—not unlike what is found in medical and magical handbooks of the *Papyri Graecae et Demoticae Magicae* attributed to the healer god Imhotep-Asclepius from Deir el-Bahari, for example, in P. Oxy. 11, 1381. In this case, one can only speculate about how this oracular answer was delivered: perhaps through a divinatory method other than ticket oracles such as incubation or another revelatory practice.[12] It would, however, not be uncommon to ask the divinity through the ticket oracle if a certain medical potion is recommendable for certain symptoms.[13]

It has been supposed that oracular practices were accompanied by certain rituals—perhaps prayers and chants, offerings, purification, abstinence from food, sex, and so on.[14] The letters do not shed any light upon such matters; they only state in no. 6 and 11 that the cult practices have to be performed in a proper way and at the right time.

It cannot be ruled out that priests had the option to ask the gods questions apart from festivals—as the pharaoh Petubastis did in the narrative The Fight for the Prebend of Amun during the conflict (which took place during the Festival of the Valley).[15] The timespan between question, letter, and reaction is very short in no. 13—maybe only a few hours—if the divine ordeal mentioned by the writer of the letter is cited to dissuade the recipients from leaving for Nilopolis the next morning. The verb *ʿš* used in the text to signify "calling" the god reminds me of the "Platz des Flehens" (*s.t-sbḥ*), situated at the rear of a god's sanctuary adjacent to the outer enclosure wall, where the deity was invoked for help.[16] Perhaps Petesuchos referred not only to oracles but to possible prayers and offerings at the rear of the temple as well? For certain, all parties in letter no 13 must have lived very close to each other to allow the messages being posted.

The topics raised in the questions fit very well with the general trends: most frequently, people asked about health (especially during travel or about those on the road), issues relating to property, marital life, and business-/job-related questions. A special case is the supposed trial marriage in P. Qasr Ibrim 1; the matter could also have been solved through the more common temple oaths because a huge number of the over eight-hundred sources deal with the faithfulness of men and women during wedlock.[17]

---

12. Gil Renberg, *Where Dreams May Come: Incubation Sanctuaries in the Greco-Roman World*, RGRW 184 (Leiden: Brill, 2017).

13. See the Coptic ticket oracles P. Antinoe? B = P. Donadoni 2 = Florenz, Istituto Papirologico G. Vitelli PSI inv. Ant.; and P. Antinoe inv. N 66/115/A = Florenz, Istituto Papirologico G. Vitelli PSI inv. Ant.; P. Antinoe inv. NN 06 – Kôm Ost – C4 – II – 23.01.2006; P. Antinoe inv. NN 07 – Kôm Ost – A4 – II – 28.01.2007, all found in Antinoopolis in which the petitioners ask if they should take a certain medical prescription. See Naether, *Die Sortes Astrampsychi*, 401–2.

14. See Naether, *Die Sortes Astrampsychi*, 87–91, 98, 128. The medieval version of the *Sortes Astrampsychi* lists a couple of rules but all the manuscripts date to the thirteenth–sixteenth centuries. They might be derived from ancient codices and scrolls.

15. Wilhelm Spiegelberg, *Der Sagenkreis des Königs Petubastis nach dem Strassburger demotischen Papyrus sowie den Wiener und Pariser Bruchstücken*, DemStud 3 (Leipzig: Hinrichs 1910)

16. The topic will be explored in the PhD project of Julia Dorothea Preisigke, Munich, "Bittplätze – Orte des privaten Gebets – an Tempeln der westlichen Oasen Ägyptens vom 7. Jh. v. Chr. bis zum 4. Jh. n. Chr.: Ihre Architektur, ihre Darstellungen und ihre Bedeutung."

17. Franziska Naether and Tami Schmidt-Gottschalk, "Die Tempeleide: Kulturelle und rechtshistorische Kontextualisierung einer Textsorte; Mit einer Edition vom O. Lips. ÄMUL dem. inv. 340," in *Hieratic, Demotic and Greek Studies and Text Editions: Of Making Many Books There Is No End: Festschrift in Honour of Sven P. Vleeming*, ed. Koenraad Donker van Heel, Francisca Hoogendijk, and Cary J. Martin, PLB 34 (Leiden: Brill 2018), 288–97.

For sure, more can be said by taking into account the social networks of the correspondents and the archaeological contexts of temples, houses, routes, and messaging services. For now, I would like to conclude that most of the letters mentioning oracular and other cult practices were written by (elite) men, often involved in temples and higher administration, some of them temporarily away on business. The letters confirm the procedures of the respective oracular practices and add additional information about the practitioners, locations, and times when the rituals were performed. Moreover, they deal with the interpretation of divine ordeals and therefore reveal more of the social drama behind the simple protasis-apodosis framework.

Letters with Reference to Cult Practices and Temple Business

There are of course many other cult practices mentioned in Egyptian letters. People cared for their families while away from their hometown and asked others to pray for their good health[18]—similar to the oracle questions asked on behalf of others mentioned above. Perhaps a prayer is also the context of the request, "Do not leave this god outside his town!"[19]

Frequent are the mentions of offerings to gods or to the deceased. Letter writers report on what they have done or give instructions for others to do things.[20] In one case, there is a request to put money in front of the god.[21]

Certain events mark the cultic calendar, among them festivals[22] and burials.[23] For such events, statues of gods would be procured.[24] In other letters, the addressees are informed about the openings of tombs,[25] business with dead spirits,[26] the procurement of amulets,[27] and other cult practices[28]—some of them explicitly happening at night.[29]

Naturally, not everything went well. A good number of issues reported in the communications from the priests of Elephantine contain reports of sacrilege against the gods.[30] We look forward to the upcoming publication by

18. P. Leiden 1, 370, letter of Djehuty-Mes to Bu-teh-Imen and Shed-em-duat; P. Turin inv. 1971, letter of Bu-teh-Imen, Shed-em-duat and Hemet-sheri to Djehuty-Mes with the wish to pray before the gods against a disease.

19. P. Loeb 08, 34 = vo., l. 1: *m-ir ḫ3ʿ p3j nṯr p3-bnr(-n) p3j=f dmj.*

20. P. BN 199.5–9 + 196.V + 198.IV; P. Turin (without no.)/1; O. Cairo 25667; P. Geneva D 191; O. Michaelides 85; P. Berlin P. dem. 15522; P. Berlin P. dem. 15500+23678+15813; P. Berlin P. dem. 23551; P. Berlin P. dem. 23570.

21. P. Saq. H5–DP 18 [1616] (mentioned twice).

22. O. BM EA inv. 5627, P. Berlin P. dem. 23553 (on plants used in the festival for the Epagomenai), P. Berlin P. dem. 13565 (a priest from Elephantine attended a religious festival in Alexandria but was detained in Alexandria on his way back).

23. P. Mallawi inv. 482 and 483 mention the burial of sacred animals.

24. O. BM 65933 = O. Nash 11 (on a temple statue); P. Loeb 10 (on a crocodile figure).

25. P. BM EA inv. 10375; O. BM EA dem. inv. 5679.

26. P. BM EA inv. 75021.

27. P. BM EA inv. 10411; P. Saq. H5–DP 265 [1863].

28. Bresciani, Archivio, no. 13.

29. P. Berlin P. dem. 15527 (order of the sender that the addressees should not fail to come to the Abaton at night and should not cause the god to punish him (l. 22 ro.–2 vo.: *m-ir ir wš n ij r pr-wʿb n p3 grḥ m-ir dj.t ẖdbṯ=(j) p3 nṯr r wʿ gj*); P. Loeb 5 (drinking for Sobek at night).

30. P. Berlin P. dem. 13548 (perhaps containing a warning of sacrilege), P. Berlin P. dem. 23552 (on stolen[?] cups from the sanctuary); P. Berlin P. dem. 15645+15649+23666 (on disputes among the priesthood).

Karl-Theodor Zauzich of letters which will shed valuable light on issues such as temple economy,[31] administration,[32] and priests and politics.[33]

I would like to end this section with a letter of rather mysterious contents: In Bresciani, Archivio, no. 16: "You put Psais, son of Marres, in our hand in the temple of Demeter, which is [in the temple of] Sobek to come with us to the island (= Soknopaiou Nesos) because(?) of the things which the priests will tell him. When he did not (= will not have?) agree to it (the things?), and he comes to the temple of Demeter [...] and he returns(?) to the temple of Demeter..." Perhaps Psais committed a bad deed that had to be addressed with the other priests. Possibly, he lived in the temple in some form of asylum or as a *katochos* like the man Teos mentioned in letter no. 11.

Letters with Quotations of Works of Fiction and Proverbs

Some Egyptian letters are famous for bearing quotations of or allusions to well-known works of fiction.[34] It is not uncommon for letter writers to add instructions to teach their maxims of normatively good, *maat*-style conduct of life. Others expressed situations in a metaphorical way, for example, through parables. The most famous example of this is possibly the Teaching of Menena, a wisdom text in letter form.[35] Menena, a high-ranking official from Deir el-Medina, tried to teach his rather notorious son, who was known for impregnating a married woman and intermingling with foreigners (of course, both were considered unacceptable behavior). This text bears two modified quotations of the narration of The Shipwrecked Sailor, the Teaching of Ptahhotep and the lamentation of the Eloquent Peasant.[36]

31. P. Berlin P. dem. 13542; P. Berlin P. dem. 13552 (including disputes among the priesthood of Chnum in Elephantine); P. Berlin P. dem. 13569 (on the distribution of the syntaxis tax); P. Berlin P. dem. 15501; P. Berlin P. dem. 15502; P. Berlin P. dem. 15503; P. Berlin P. dem. 23561; P. Berlin P. dem. 23594 (wages for builders, masons, a sealer(?), the first lector priest, a prophet); P. Berlin P. dem. 23586; P. Berlin P. dem. 23593; P. Berlin P. dem. 23603; P. Berlin P. dem. 23612 (orders and accounts of food such as meat, oil, bread, emmer); Günter Vittmann, "An Abnormal Hieratic Letter from Dakhleh Oasis (ostracon Amheida 16003)," in *A True Scribe of Abydos: Essays on First Millennium Egypt in Honour of Anthony Leahy*, ed. Claus Jurman, Bettina Bader, and David A. Aston, OLA 265 (Leuven: Peeters 2017), 491–503 (letter of a prophet of Seth, ca. 700–650 BCE, from Amheida, on temple business).

32. P. Berlin P. dem. 15615 + 23670; P. Berlin P. dem. 15801+23682a/b.

33. P. Berlin P. dem. 15614+23677+23707 (on a visit of a high official, e.g., of the Osiris temple(?) during a festival); P. Berlin P. dem. 23562 (on informing the priests on political events at war).

34. See Ursula Verhoeven, "Funktionen und Wiederholung und Abweichung in ägyptischen Erzähltexten," in *Das Erzählen in frühen Hochkulturen, I. Der Fall Ägypten*, ed. Hubert Roeder, Ägyptologie und Kulturwissenschaft 1 (Munich: Fink, 2009), 315–34. She explores the question how Egyptians practiced quoting literary texts. In general, there were no one-to-one quotations of an *Urtext*. This is especially true for parts of plots that are repeated within narratives, for example, to inform other protagonists of new developments, such as in Sinuhe when he heard about the demise of Pharaoh Amenemhat I (Verhoeven, 316–19). Ursula enumerated six such cases. One of her results is that passages that are repeated in works of fiction are especially ones that have "ritualhaften Charakter," that serve to inform third parties, and that function as key moments or turning points in a narrative. The "true" sequence of the plot in these situations is apparently crucial to the author(s), especially in ensuring that the audience knows how to judge third parties who might want to alter the truth in order to use it for their evil purposes. Last but not least, if confronted with facts central to a story in a repeated way, the audience will more easily remember them, and thus also the main conflict of a narrative (Verhoeven, 331–33).

35. To this genre, perhaps add the letter of P. Anastasi 9 of a certain Hori to Ra-mesu. In ll. 1–3, we read: "Another message to my lord, as follows: I have heard the words of dispute about which you have written me. It is the wisdom of life from a man's father to his son that you wrote/sent to me, and not a matter of death." (*ky swḏꜣ-jb n pꜣy=j nb r-ntj sḏm.n=j nꜣ md(w).t ꜥḥꜣ hꜣb=k n=j ḥr=w ẖr jw mꜣꜥ pš j.ḏd=k wj m-bꜣḥ=j dgi=w n ꜣnḫ n jtj n r(m)ṯ n pꜣy=f šrj nꜣ hꜣb=k n=j ḥr=w bn md(w).t n mwt jwnꜣ*). The passage reminds one of the Teaching of a Man for His Son.

36. Hellmut Brunner, "Zitate aus Lebenslehren," in *Studien zu den altägyptischen Lebenslehren*, ed. Erik Hornung and Othmar Keel, OBO 28 (Fribourg: University Press; Göttingen: Vandenhoeck & Ruprecht, 1979), 105–71; Waltraud Guglielmi, "Zur Adaption und Funktion von Zitaten," *SAK* 11 (1984): 347–64; Hans-Werner Fischer-Elfert, "Synchrone und diachrone Interferenzen in literarischen Werken des Mittleren und Neuen Reiches," *Orientalia* 61 (1992): 354–72; B. van de Walle, *La transmission des textes littéraires égyptiens*, (Brussels: Fondation égyptologique Reine Elisabeth, 1948).

Another problematic genre that should be mentioned here is the model letters of the Late Egyptian Miscellanies, a rather heterogeneous Late Egyptian collection of texts chiefly containing passages of wisdom texts for training lower- and middle-ranking officials. Also worth mentioning are P. Anastasi 2, 5, 6–6, 4 with a eulogy on the king in letter format,[37] and a couple of poetic compositions collected by Deborah Sweeney.[38]

The identification of such sayings and allusions is far from easy to detect for modern scholars[39] because we lack the knowledge about traditions in applying quotations and proverbs (paremiology) from about five thousand years ago. Letters, often reflecting oral communication, are notoriously hard to understand. Judging alone from written evidence, quotations and proverbs can often hardly be reconstructed and explained, but it is possible to make observations.[40] While looking through ancient Egyptian letters, I came across a couple of examples that have been suspected to contain allusions to works of fiction or at least proverbs:[41]

- "Everything belongs to me, and one says: 'half a life is better than a complete death.'"—*jnk (j)ḫt nb r-ḏd nfr gs n ꜥnḫ r mwt m zp wꜥ*, Hekanakhte letter, P. MMA Hekanakhte 2, col. 2 ro, l. 26
- "So it will fall down on your skull like a sand dune"—*mtw=f hꜣ.y ḥr tbn=k mj wꜣb.t-n-šꜥ*, P. Anastasi 4, col. 10, l. 8
- "Oh, I do not dip my feet in the (Nile's) mud … and I do not stand in the dust of the harvest, because I am surrounded (by) […] and I stand on pebbles and sit on the mountains […] the petals of the greenery are his satiety. (?)"—*jꜣ bn tw=j ḥr tḫ<b> rd.wy m tꜣ ꜥmꜥ.t n* […] *ḫr bn tw=j ḥr ꜥḥꜥ n pꜣ ḫm šm.w tw=j j⸢nḥ⸣ k* […] *ꜥḥꜥ=j ḥr ꜥr ḥmsi=j nꜣ ḏw.w n pꜣ gꜣb wꜣḏwꜣḏ pꜣy=f sꜣ.w*, letter to Ramses IV concerning the cult of a statue, P. Turin inv. 1879 vs.(E), col. 2, ll. 2–5[42]
- "One knows the strong one, who is here/exists(?)."—*st ir-rḫ pꜣ nḫt.ṯ ⸢ntj⸣ ḫpr*, P. Berlin P. dem. 13585, ll. x+7–8[43]
- "Also nothing exists except the work of the (personal) god"—*bw-ir gr ḫpr m-sꜣ tꜣ wp.t pꜣ nṯr*, P. Berlin P. dem. 15617, l. 5[44]
- "Painful is the offence against (the) gods."—*mr nfy r nṯr.w*, letter to a dead person on a bowl from Qau, outside, l. K6
- "He speaks words with his mouth which are not in his heart"—*ḫr ḏd=f hjn md(.t) n rꜣ=f iw bn-iw st n ḥꜣtj=f in*, P. Berlin P. dem. 13544, ll. 14–17[45]

---

37. In a student's hand, a copy of the same text is P. Anastasi 4, 5, 6ff. See Adolf Erman, *Die ägyptischen Schülerhandschriften*, APAW 2 (1924), 25 with a list.

38. Deborah Sweeney, *Correspondence and Dialogue: Pragmatic Factors in Late Ramesside Letter Writing*, ÄAT 49 (Wiesbaden: Harrassowitz, 2001), 16–17n105.

39. As well as humor. See, e.g., Richard Jasnow, "'And Pharaoh Laughed …': Reflections on Humor in Setne 1 and Late Period Egyptian Literature," *Enchoria* 27 (2001): 62–81.

40. See the research project of Camilla di Biase-Dyson: "Grounded in Space? Diachronic and Cognitive Approaches to Spatial Metaphors in Written Egyptian" (Forschergruppe C2, Excellence Cluster 264: TOPOI. The Formation and Transformation of Space and Knowledge in Ancient Civilizations). On methods of citation in letters see also Sweeney, *Correspondance and Dialogue*, 3–4; esp. 25–26 on the corpus of late Ramesside Letters (Jaroslav Černý, ed., *Late Ramesside Letters*, BiAe 9 [Brussels: Fondation Égyptologique Reine Elisabeth, 1939]).

41. See also Černý, ed., *Late Ramesside Letters* 41, 13–16; Sweeney, *Correspondance and Dialogue*, 223, where the proverb is introduced by *<j>n bw-pw=k sḏm … sḏd*, "Haven't you heard … the proverb."

42. Ingelore Hafemann suspects this to be a proverb; see her comment in the TLA, *ad locum*.

43. Günter Vittmann thought of a proverb; see his comment in the TLA, *ad locum*. The editor of the text, Karl-Theodor Zauzich, translated "Man kennt den Sieg(?), der entstanden ist."

44. See also Heinz Josef Thissen, "Annotationes Demoticae," *Enchoria* 28 (2002/2003): 101 for a similar passage in one part of the refrain of P. Insinger.

45. According to Günter Vittmann's comment in the TLA, *ad locum*, this passage bears similarities to P. Rylands 9 where the word

Texts thaat might be proverbs include short, gnomic sayings, often containing comparisons of some sort—metaphors, allegories, or parables. The "half-life" (vs. death) and the falling sand dune would fit in these categories, while short, parenomic sayings on the power of the gods could be treated like isolated maxims from a wisdom text. The role of the personal god is very strong in a couple of teachings.[46] The same is true of the motif of divine justice as referred to in the bowl with the letter to the dead.[47] The "strong one" could also refer to a god, a demon or another very powerful person whose malevolent forces might have been common knowledge at the time.

The do-ut-des principle of the teachings (also dubbed substitute actions or reciprocal solidarity, that is, doing something for the gods/the king/the dead in order to benefit from these actions), is of course a well-known feature of the letters to the dead. In a small stele from Cairo, ll. 1–5 (number and present location unknown),[48] Mer-irtief says to the deceased Nebet-itief: "How are you? Does the Great One (= the goddess of the West, probably Hathor) take care of you as you wish? See, I am the one whom you loved on earth. Take care of me (and) for my name. I did not garble any saying before you, (but) I cause your name to be remembered on earth. Keep the disease far from my limbs. Oh—may you be a spirit for me (and) in front of me, so that I may see in a dream (how) you take care of me. I will lay down the offerings [... until the sun?] sets, while I set up the offering table for you."

Even though letters and religious texts such as the letters to the gods contain largely formulaic language, this example gives us a hint towards the grief of the husband Mer-irtief, who lost his wife. He asks for her wellbeing in the afterlife, and if she receives nourishment by Hathor and is faring well. The husband also reassures her that he is properly taking care of bringing her offerings to the offering table at her tomb. The text does not mention what his offerings comprise of—at least water and burnt incense—but he might also have brought other goods such as meat and vegetables for a burnt offering and liquids other than water for a libation. Probably through prayers, setting up written evidence at the tomb and through good behavior, Nebet-itief tries to ensure that he will keep the name of his late wife in good standing among the living and the gods. But for all these investments of time and property, he wants something in return: staying healthy and in good standing with his name in front of the gods and the living. Those are the standard wishes of people, expressed for example in letter formulae wishing the addressee well, or formulated as concerns of oracles, in graffiti at healing centers in temples or listed among the dangers in the Oracular Amuletic Decrees (not being remembered, being struck by an illness).[49] This being insufficient, the husband also requests proof of Nebet-itief's actions, to be sent to him in a dream.

Conclusion

In my overview, I could only discuss a few sources in detail—the ones referring to oracular practices—and mentioned a couple of other papyri and ostraca with reference to cult practices. New editions of texts such as the upcoming volume of letters from Elephantine by Karl-Theodor Zauzich will offer new insights, as they feature correspondence chiefly among priestly ranks and inform us about practical aspects of the daily business of running a temple.

---

hjn is also used; see Günter Vittmann, *Der demotische Papyrus Rylands 9*, ÄAT 38 (Wiesbaden: Harrassowitz, 1998), 375 (commentary for *hjn*) and 359n501.

46. Winfried Barta, "Der anonyme Gott der Lebenslehren," *ZÄS* 103 (1976): 79–88 and Naether, *Kultpraxis in der altägyptischen Literatur*, ch. 3.

47. Quack, "Göttliche Gerechtigkeit und Recht am Beispiel des spätzeitlichen Ägypten," in *Recht und Religion: Menschliche und göttliche Gerechtigkeitsvorstellungen in den antiken Welten*, ed. Heinz Barta, Robert Rollinger, and Martin Lang, Philippika 24 (Wiesbaden: Harrassowitz Verlag 2008), 135–53 and Naether, *Kultpraxis in der altägyptischen Literatur*, ch. 4.

48. See Edward Wente, "A Misplaced Letter to the Dead," in *Miscellanea in Honorem Josephi Vergote*, OLA 6/7 (Leuven: Dept. Oriëntalistiek, 1975/1976), 595–600; Edward Wente, *Letters from Ancient Egypt*, WAW 1 (Atlanta: Society of Biblical Literature, 1990), 215, no. 349.

49. Alina Grams, "Der Katalog von Gefahren in den Oracular Amuletic Decrees," *SAK* 46 (2017): 55–100.

Greek and Coptic letters would help to elucidate the picture even further. However, it is important to integrate the knowledge about chronological and local peculiarities and developments in the cult practices, as well as recognize the fact that letter writers were sometimes misinformed about certain matters or tried deliberately to mislead their addressees. As with literary sources, there is always the caveat to take the facts *cum grano salis*: as authors, letter writers had their agendas and intentions in drawing up their texts. Nevertheless, the prominence of religious practices in letters shows that ritual and divinatory methods must have been a widespread and well-discussed topic in the daily lives of the Egyptians.

A New Inscription From Taharqo's "Cattle Road"

Jeremy Pope

The "cattle road" of Taharqo has long been an enigma in Nubiology. In 1906 and 1908, Arthur Weigall discovered two nearly identical graffiti carved into boulders on the west bank of the Nubian Nile—the first between Kalabsha and Tafa in the Khor Hanush and the second immediately inland of Tafa itself (fig. 1). Both contained five lines of hieroglyphic text, were dated to the third month of Inundation in Taharqo's nineteenth regnal year, and made reference to "the cattle road," *t3 mi(.t) n iḥ.w*. Noting that each of the graffiti faced northward, Weigall speculated that they would have been written during Taharqo's "headlong flight" from the Assyrian army.[1] Just a few years later, Günther Roeder published the first translation of the Khor Hanush and Tafa graffiti, highlighting several grammatical and orthographic issues in the texts and proposing that they instead marked a local footpath to transport cattle around the granite cliffs of the Bab el-Kalabsha.[2] In 1959, Fritz Hintze published a third graffito of the same date and content that faced *southward* at Ambarkab between Tafa and Qirtas, opining that it commemorated Taharqo's march to retake Thebes from the Assyrians.[3] The three graffiti were then included in Pawel Wolf's 1990 doctoral thesis on the reign of Taharqo, but Wolf did not offer his own interpretation of the texts.[4] By contrast, Klaus Dallibor's 2005 book, *Taharqo: Pharao aus Kusch,* hypothesized that the graffiti commemorated Taharqo's movement of troops in *anticipation* of the Assyrian threat, presumably because the dateline of the graffiti actually *pre*ceded the Assyrian conquest of Egypt.[5] In 2007, I studied the three graffiti at Johns Hopkins University under the direction of my graduate advisor, Richard Jasnow, and we were especially intrigued by the scribe(s) use of compound prepositions and the possible influence of a hieratic original upon the graffito's hieroglyphic orthography; these links to contemporary grammar and hieratic bookkeeping differentiated the Lower Nubian graffiti from the more archaizing style favored in most of Taharqo's other hieroglyphic inscriptions. In my 2014 book, *The Double Kingdom under Taharqo,* I provided a synoptic translation of the three graffiti (fig. 2) and weighed the published explanations. Since the graffiti contained no militaristic references or epithets and coincided with no known military campaigns, I questioned Weigall's, Hintze's, and Dallibor's attempt to connect them to dramatic events in international warfare. Observing that all three graffiti described a "cattle road" and were located within just a few kilometers of one another along the same local footpath, I defended Roeder's theory that these inscriptions marked said path.[6]

1. Arthur Weigall, "Upper Egyptian Notes," *ASAE* 9 (1908): 105–12 (106). For the chronology of these events, see Jeremy Pope, *The Double Kingdom under Taharqo: Studies in the History of Kush and Egypt c. 690–664 BC* (Leiden: Brill, 2014), 186n196.
2. Günther Roeder, *Les temples immergés de la Nubia: Debod bis Bab Kalabsche*, vol. 1 (Cairo: Institut français d'archéologie orientale du Caire, 1911), 211–12, 215–16, Taf. 94, 127a–b.
3. Fritz Hintze, "Eine neue Inschrift vom 19. Jahre König Taharqas," *MIO* 7 (1960): 330–33.
4. Pawel Wolf, "Die archäologischen Quellen der Taharqozeit im nubischen Niltal" (PhD diss., Humboldt-Universität; Berlin, 1990), 19–20, 103.
5. Klaus Dallibor, *Taharqo, Pharao aus Kusch: Ein Beitrag zur Geschichte und Kultur der 25. Dynastie* (Berlin: Achet, 2005), 81. For the date, see Pope, *Double Kingdom under Taharqo*, 186n196.
6. Pope, 181–91.

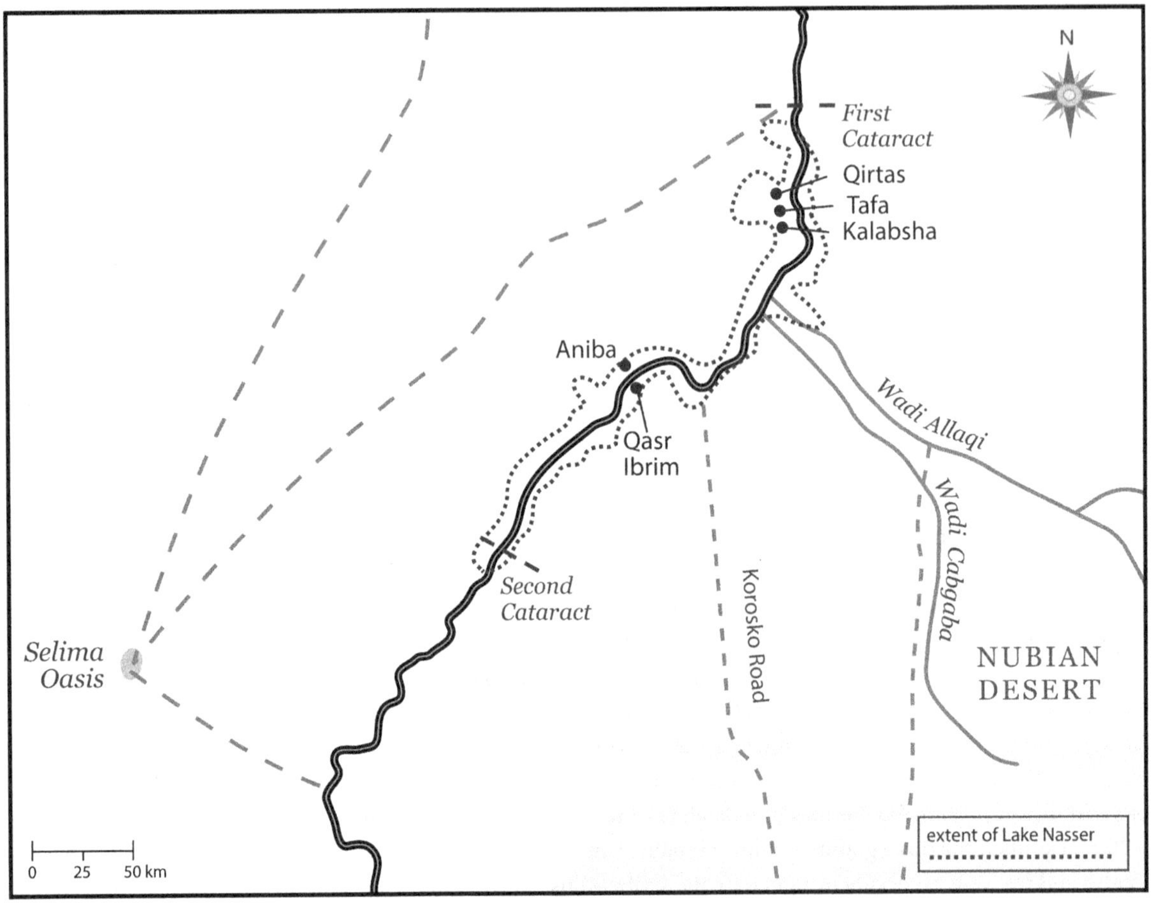

Figure 1. Map of Lower Nubia. Courtesy of the University of Wisconsin-Madison Cartography Laboratory.

Yet it seems that Wolf, Dallibor, and I missed a crucial piece of unpublished evidence. In Mark Horton's 1991 summary of work at Qasr Ibrim, he mentioned in a single sentence that a "newly-discovered rock-cut inscription near to Ibrim records the construction of a cattle road at the time of Taharka."[7] Horton's team had found the graffito during a 1988 regional survey, and Peter French had transcribed it onto a site card now stored in the EES archive,[8] but he did not publish it or attempt a translation. I first became aware of the Ibrim graffito when David Edwards kindly brought it to my attention in 2015, during our service together for Mahmoud Beshir's disputas at the University of Bergen.[9]

The Ibrim graffito necessarily affects interpretation of the other three. After all, each graffito in this ensemble of four was commissioned by the same pharaoh during the same month of the same year, and they each describe a "cattle road" with nearly the same wording throughout. Yet the Ibrim graffito did not share the same local footpath as the other three. In fact, it is located more than 100 kilometers south of them and on the other side of the river (see

7. Mark Horton, "Africa in Egypt: New Evidence from Qasr Ibrim," in *Egypt and Africa: Nubia from Prehistory to Islam*, ed. W. Vivian Davies (London: British Museum Press, 1991), 265–77 (273).

8. I thank Mark Horton for providing this information (pers. comm., 6 August 2019), and Julie Anderson of the British Museum for permitting me to access the site card and photographs.

9. I thank also Pam Rose for generously granting me permission to publish Taharqo's Qasr Ibrim graffito.

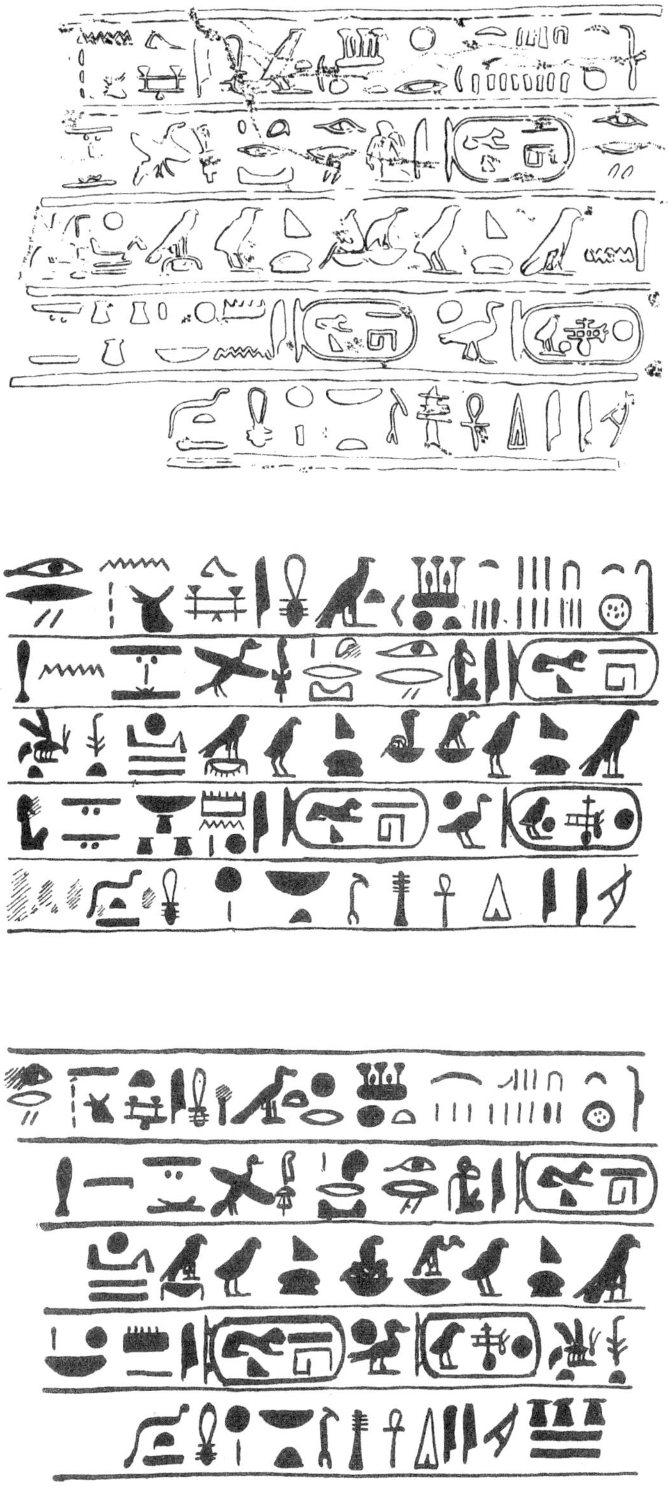

Figure 2. Comparison of Taharqo's graffiti in the Kalabsha region. From top to bottom: Ambarkab, Tafa, Khor Hanush. Ambarkab transcription after Hintze, "Eine neue Inschrift vom 19. Jahre König Taharqas," 331. Tafa and Khor Hanush transcriptions after Roeder, *Debod bis Bab Kalabsche*, Taf. 127a–b.

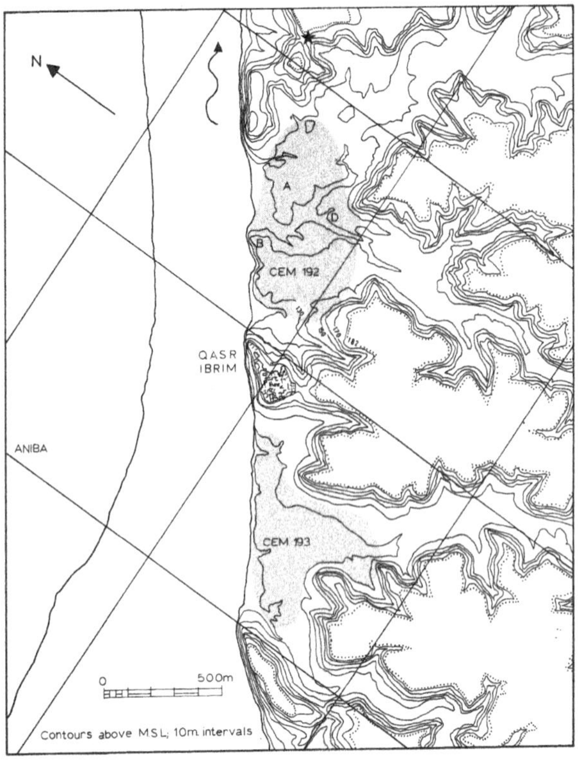

Figure 3. Topographical map of Ibrim and its headlands, with black star inserted by the author to indicate the location of Taharqo's graffito. After Mills, *Cemeteries of Qasr Ibrim*, pl. III.

Figure 4. North headland at Ibrim, with rectangle inserted to show the location of Taharqo's graffito. Photograph Mark Horton, Egypt Exploration Society Archive, courtesy of the Trustees of the British Museum. I thank Pam Rose for indicating the exact location of the graffito: pers. comm., 28 May 2019.

again fig. 1). Either Taharqo's cattle road was very long, or there was more than one. The opportunity to revisit the Khor Hanush, Tafa, and Ambarkab graffiti in the new light cast by the fourth at Ibrim has also revealed fresh clues and implications for the peculiar details of syntax and orthography that so fascinated Richard and me years ago.

The Findspot

When Horton's team arrived at Qasr Ibrim for the 1988 season, Lake Nasser had recently subsided in the area by approximately ten vertical meters, exposing parts of the headlands that had previously been under water—perhaps submerged for decades since the construction of the Aswan High Dam.[10] While surveying a headland on the east bank about one kilometer downstream of Qasr Ibrim (figs. 3–4), they encountered a "five line inscription incised into a vertical face to the right of a hewn approach to a hilltop on which are, to left and right, walled enclosures containing graves and various drystone monuments."[11] Upon further study, the drystone monuments were associated with a Roman siege camp used during the famous attack of 23 BCE.[12] By contrast, the hillside graffito clearly bore a cartouche of Taharqo from nearly seven centuries prior, but other parts of the text were not so legible (fig. 5). In the description recorded at the time by Peter French, lines 3–5 were "much damaged, especially 5, apparently by weathering rather than water," whereas the first two lines had been protected by an overhanging cornice.[13] Working either without copies or without awareness of the Khor Hanush, Tafa, and Ambarkab parallels, in situ transcription of the weathered Ibrim graffito was challenging (figs. 6–7), and a full translation was not attempted. The only published result was the aforementioned one-sentence allusion to the graffito in Horton's 1991 article.[14] The rising waters of Lake Nasser subsequently covered the graffito, so that it can no longer be inspected or copied (fig. 8).[15]

Unbeknownst to Horton's team in 1988,[16] the Ibrim graffito had actually been documented once before. In 1899, Somers Clarke had explored the same headland and noted "a tablet cut in the rock face" measuring approximately forty-three inches tall and fifty-five inches wide and containing "five lines of hieroglyphics, the lower much defaced by exposure," because "the sandstone here is very coarse & friable and quickly loses its fine surface."[17] Clarke's transcription (fig. 9), now stored at the Griffith Institute, further confirms French's judgment that weathering had already severely damaged the text long before the rising waters of Lake Nasser. Although Clarke accurately transcribed the cartouche of Taharqo at the beginning of the graffito's second line, he attempted neither translation nor commentary and did not announce his find in any article or book of which I am aware. Thus, while the Ibrim graffito has never been published, it was actually the first record of Taharqo's cattle road to be discovered by an Egyptologist.

Clarke's and French's transcriptions (figs. 9 and 6–7, respectively) are valuable evidence for the graffito's condition over time, but the translator who attempts to read it in the twenty-first century enjoys the distinct advantage of easy comparison with the parallel texts at Khor Hanush, Tafa, and Ambarkab (fig. 2). Now submerged under the waters of Lake Nasser, the Ibrim graffito is ironically more legible today than it was when first discovered.

10. David Edwards, pers. comm., 25 May 2015; Mark Horton, pers. comm., 6 August 2019.
11. Qasr Ibrim site card 88.1.7/1 (EES Archive).
12. Horton, "Africa in Egypt," 268-271. Pam Rose, pers. comm., 26 May 2019; Mark Horton, pers. comm., 7 August 2019.
13. Qasr Ibrim site card 88.1.7/1 (EES Archive).
14. Horton, "Africa in Egypt," 273.
15. David Edwards, pers. comm., 25 May 2015; Mark Horton, pers. comm., 6 August 2019.
16. Mark Horton, pers. comm., 6 August 2019.
17. Entry dated 25 January 1899 in Somers Clarke Notebook O (Griffith Institute, Oxford). I thank Pam Rose for directing me to this source, pers. comm., 26 May 2019.

Figure 5. Taharqo's graffito at Ibrim. Photograph Mark Horton, Egypt Exploration Society Archive, courtesy of the Trustees of the British Museum.

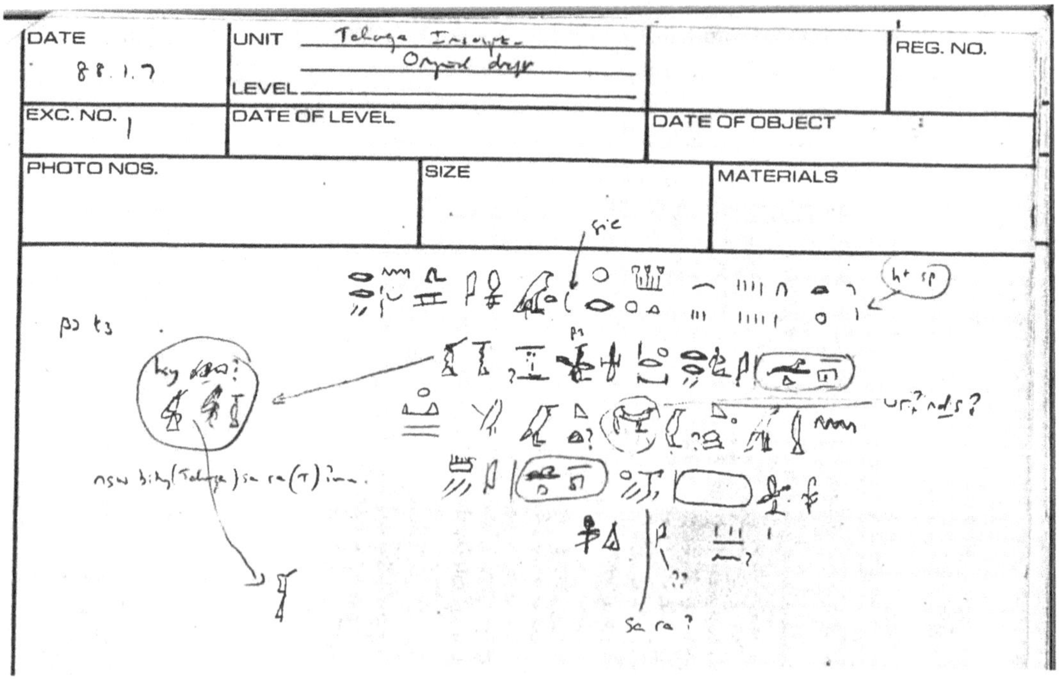

Figure 6. Site card containing Peter French's transcription of the Ibrim graffito in 1988. Egypt Exploration Society Archive, courtesy of the Trustees of the British Museum.

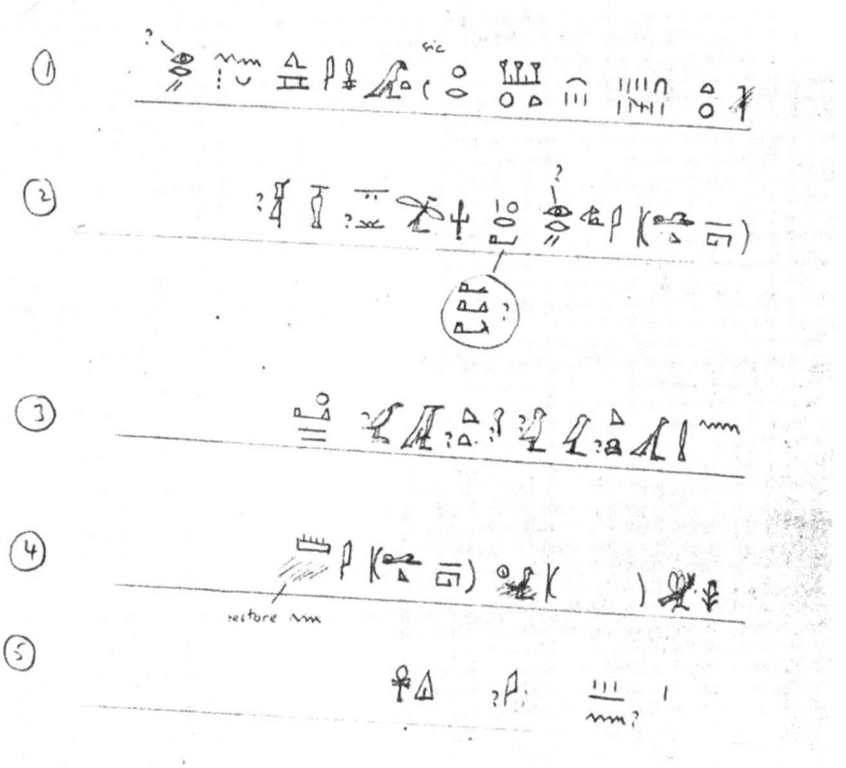

Figure 7. Verso of the site card shown in figure 6, containing Peter French's second attempt to transcribe the Ibrim graffito in 1988. Egypt Exploration Society Archive, courtesy of the Trustees of the British Museum.

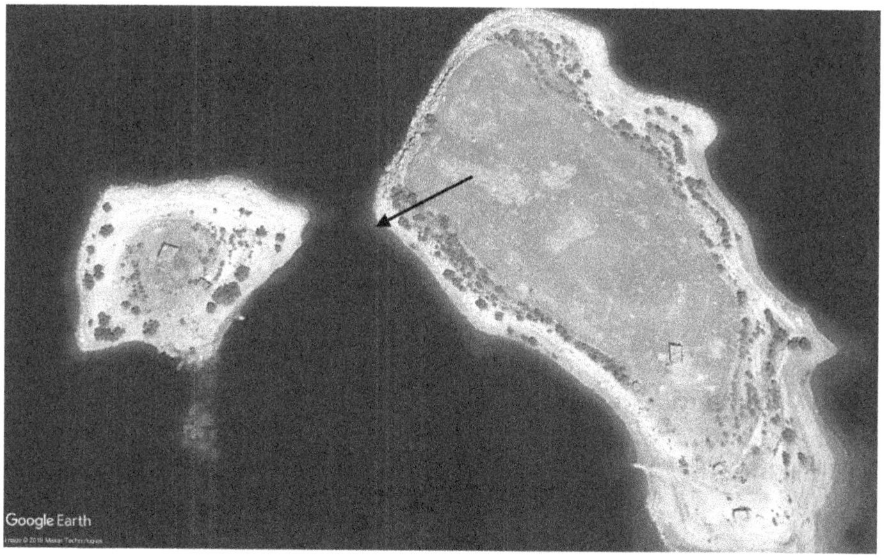

Figure 8. Aerial photograph of headland north of Qasr Ibrim, with arrow showing location of Taharqo's graffito (now underwater). © Google Earth 2009 (with better contrast than more recent photographs). I thank Mark Horton for indicating the exact location of the graffito on the headland: pers. comm., 6 August 2019.

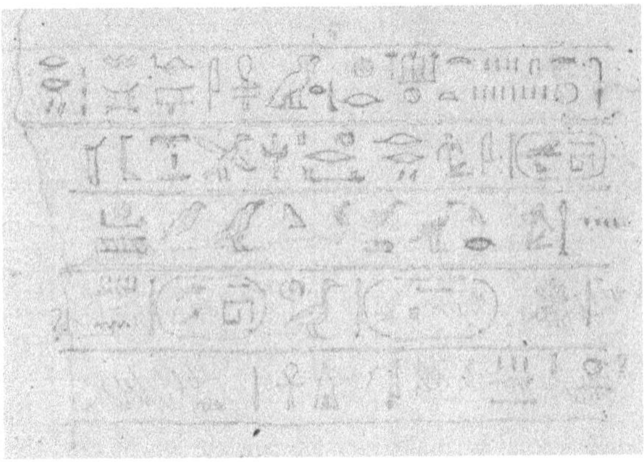

Figure 9. Somers Clarke's transcription of the Ibrim graffito in 1899. Somers Clarke notebook O, page 88. Copyright Griffith Institute, University of Oxford.

Figure 10. Author's JSesh transcription of Taharqo's Ibrim graffito.

Translation and Commentary

As a proper epigraphic tracing is no longer possible, I have instead provided here a standardized hieroglyphic transcription (fig. 10) by comparing Clarke's and French's hand copies with Horton's fifty-seven photographs and the published Khor Hanush, Tafa, and Ambarkab graffiti. In the commentary below, attention is focused only upon those passages of the Ibrim graffito that shed new light on the three parallel texts; for a fuller discussion of the orthography and grammar of those texts, readers may consult my 2014 book.[18] The Ibrim graffito reads as follows:

> *1| ḥꜣ.t-sp 19 i͗bd 3 ꜣḫt ⸢sw⸣ 1 tꜣ mi͗(.t) n i͗ḥ.w i͗ry 2| Tꜣ-h-r-q i-i͗ry-tp rꜣ ḏw i͗ꜣb pꜣ tꜣ ⸢ḥs(y) mꜣꜥ⸣ 3| n Ḥm Ḥr Qꜣ-ḫꜥ.w Nb.ty Qꜣ-ḫꜥ.w Ḥr-nb Ḫw-tꜣ.wy 4| nsw.t bi͗t.y Ḫw-Nfrtm-Rꜥ sꜣ-Rꜥ Tꜣ-h-r-q mry ꞽImn- 5| Rꜥ nb ns.wt tꜣ.wy di͗ ꜥnḫ ḏd wꜣs nb{t} mi͗ Rꜥ ḏ.t*
>
> Regnal year 19, month 3 of Inundation, day 1[a]: the cattle road which Taharqo made[b] at the entrance of the eastern mountain(ous region)[c] of the land[d] ⸢truly favored⸣[e] of the Majesty of Horus: Exalted-of-Epiphanies; Two-Ladies: Exalted-of-Epiphanies; Golden-Horus: Protector-of-the-Two-Lands; King-of-Upper-and-Lower-Egypt: Re-is-the-Protector-of-Nefertem; Son-of-Re: Taharqo, beloved of Amun-Re, Lord of the Thrones of the Two Lands, given all life, stability, and dominion like Re forever.

(a) In Hintze's publication of the Ambarkab parallel text in 1959, he assumed that the scribe had not understood the conventional Egyptian dating formula, because the date given in line 1 was not immediately followed by the king's names. Hintze therefore proposed that the scribe had made an error in all three copies, writing in lines 3–5 the royal titulary that he had intended to include in lines 1–2.[19] In my 2014 commentary, I questioned this theory,[20] and further reflection over the past five years has deepened my skepticism about Hintze's sweeping emendation of the text. After all, during the Twenty-Fifth Dynasty scribes were accustomed to omitting the king's names from the date

18. Pope, *Double Kingdom under Taharqo*, 181–91.
19. Hintze, "Eine neue Inschrift vom 19. Jahre König Taharqas," 330.
20. Pope, *Double Kingdom under Taharqo*, 188, 190.

formulae of private hieratic documents,[21] and there are multiple indications that Taharqo's Lower Nubian graffiti had been copied from a hieratic original (see c, d, and e below). Devoting the entirety of lines 3–5 to the king's titulary would seem to have been sufficient to distinguish the text as a royal commission.

The dateline of each graffito has proven more enigmatic. The mason(s) responsible for carving the Khor Hanush graffito and this new Ibrim graffito inserted 𓐍𓂋 immediately after *3ḫt*, whereas in the Ambarkab graffito the same pair of hieroglyphs appears instead before *3ḫt*,[22] and the Tafa example omits 𓐍𓂋 altogether.[23] No previous translation (including mine in 2014) has convincingly explained the presence of 𓐍𓂋 in three of the four cattle road graffiti. Yet its similar positioning in the Ibrim graffito and Khor Hanush graffito does now suggest an explanation: following specification of the season in the date formula, one would expect 𓇳 *sw* ("day"),[24] a hieroglyph whose hieratic rendering a stonemason could easily confuse with the hieratic rendering for 𓐍.[25] Moreover, when written in immediate succession the phonetic complements 𓐍 and 𓏏 of *3ḫt* were equally similar in hieratic appearance to 𓐍𓂋 *ḫr*, and they could be included or not at the scribe's discretion.[26] The mason responsible for carving the scribe's work onto stone at Ambarkab may very well have mistaken those complements for 𓐍𓂋, just as the mason(s) at Khor Hanush and Ibrim mistook 𓇳 for 𓐍𓂋.

In the Ibrim, Ambarkab, and Tafa graffiti, the date formula ends with a horizontal caret that seems best read as a "1," whereas the Khor Hanush graffito does not specify a day at all.[27] I am inclined to interpret "day 1" as the date when Taharqo approved (or perhaps finished) improvements to the cattle roads as an ensemble (see b below), but, given the distance between Ibrim and the other sites, "day 1" was not necessarily the date when each graffito was copied from hieratic papyrus onto stone.

It remains unclear whether the same stonemason would have been responsible for carving the graffiti at all four sites: the confused insertion of 𓐍𓂋 in three of the graffiti might be taken to suggest so, but the inconsistent sequencing of hieroglyphs in the four date formulae undermines any assumption that they would all have been executed by the same hand.

(b) When Hintze surveyed the landscape around Taharqo's Ambarkab graffito in 1959, he could discern no visible evidence that the path had been cleared for traffic, so he chose to interpret the verb *iry* as a statement that the king

21. Sven P. Vleeming, "La phase initiale du démotique ancient," *CdÉ* 56 (1981): 31–48 (39 E 1 and n. 3); Koenraad Donker van Heel, "Papyrus Louvre E 7852: A Land Lease from the Reign of Taharka," *RdÉ* 48 (1997): 81–93 (83); Koenraad Donker van Heel, *An Abnormal Hieratic Reading Book, Fascicle II: Papyri from Paris* (Leiden: Het Leids Papyrologisch Instituut, 2013), 19.

22. Hintze, "Eine neue Inschrift vom 19. Jahre König Taharqas," 331 Abb. 1.

23. Roeder, *Debod bis Bab Kalabsche*, Taf. 127b.

24. E.g., also from the reign of Taharqo: pLouvre E 7856 vo. l. 1, ro. l. 1, in Koenraad Donker van Heel, "Papyrus Louvre E 7856 Verso and Recto: Leasing Land in the Reign of Taharka," *RdÉ* 49 (1998): 91–102 (93, 99, pls. XII–XIII); P. Louvre E 7851 vo. l. 1, ro. l. 1, in Koenraad Donker van Heel, "Papyrus Louvre E 7851 Recto and Verso: Two More Land Leases from the Reign of Taharka," *RdÉ* 50 (1999): 135–44 (138, 143, pls. XIII–XIV).

25. Ursula Verhoeven, *Untersuchungen zur späthieratischen Buchschrift*, OLA 99 (Leuven: Peeters, 2001), 158–59, 208–9; Georg Möller, *Hieratische Paläographie*, vol. 3 (Osnabrück: Zeller, 1936), 28; Georg Möller, *Hieratische Paläographie*, vol. 4 (Osnabrück: Zeller, 1936), 55.

26. Cf. P. Leiden F 1942/5.15, l. 1, in Koenraad Donker van Heel, *An Abnormal Hieratic Reading Book, Fascicle I: Papyri from London, Brooklyn, Cairo and Leiden* (Leiden: Het Leids Papyrologisch Instituut, 2013), 31–32; P. Louvre E 7856 vo. l. 1, in Koenraad Donker van Heel, *An Abnormal Hieratic Reading Book II*, 19–20; P. Vienna D 12002, col. I, l. 1, in Koenraad Donker van Heel, *An Abnormal Hieratic Reading Book, Fascicle III: Papyri from Oxford, Turin, Vienna & Tablets from Egypt & Leiden* (Leiden: Het Leids Papyrologisch Instituut, 2014), 9–10. Note also that no less an authority than Jaroslav Černý appears to have once mistaken the phonetic complements of *3ḫt* for the sun-disc *sw* and a numeral; see John C. Darnell and Colleen Manassa, "A Trustworthy Sealbearer on a Mission: The Monuments of Sabastet from the Khephren Diorite Quarries," in *Studies on the Middle Kingdom: In Memory of Detlef Franke*, ed. Richard Parkinson and Hans-Werner Fischer Elfert (Wiesbaden: Harrassowitz, 2013), 55–92 (77n108).

27. The possibility cannot be excluded that the Khor Hanush graffito deliberately contained no day at all. For examples of hieratic lapidary inscriptions that include a regnal year, season, and month, but no day, see Cairo JE 59499 lunette and ll. 9, 12, and Cairo JE 59484, l. 1, in Darnell and Manassa, "A Trustworthy Sealbearer on a Mission," 55–92 (62–63, 75–77, figs. 2–3, 4–6).

had traveled a cattle road, not that he had actually cleared or constructed one.[28] I concurred with Hintze's judgment in my 2014 book, electing to translate *tꜣ mi.t n iḥ.w iry Tꜣ-h-r-q* as "the cattle road which Taharqo traveled." In fact, I minimized the significance of the distinction: "Whether the road was actually 'made' (*ỉr*) or simply 'traveled' (*ỉr*) may be immaterial, for the king's claim to have traveled the road through the entrance of the western mountain was likely tantamount to its royal 'construction,' even if not a single boulder was moved in the process."[29]

Yet this new graffito at Ibrim was associated with unmistakable evidence of road clearance by human hands. When Clarke visited it in 1899, he noted on both the "rock saddle" and "lower down" on the slope that "tool marks are seen where pieces of the rock have been cut away to improve the road,"[30] and Horton's team in 1988 likewise described the path as a "hewn approach to a hilltop."[31] Taharqo's statement that he had actually "made" the road on this headland at Ibrim may therefore be compared to Tjauti's earlier assertion on a desert road west of Thebes: *ỉr=ỉ nn n mrw.t ḏꜣt ḫꜣs.t tn*, "I have made this for the purpose of traversing this gebel."[32] Both the Gebel Tjauti and Ibrim graffiti marked difficult paths up very steep hillsides, and thus the Darnells' proposal about the former is suggestive for the latter:

> If the road in its natural state were always so treacherous, only a few determined travelers could have used it and the track would have been impassable to pack animals ... Tjauti may have built artificial ramps in the washed-out areas in order to make the road viable for large groups and animals[, but] ... Tjauti's improvements may have fallen into disrepair at the end of the New Kingdom.[33]

Similar evidence for the excavation of a road by Taharqo's crews is visible only at Ibrim, but the possibility cannot be excluded that the graffiti at Khor Hanush, Tafa, and Ambarkab may have commemorated the erection of transitory ramps or other improvements to the path that have not survived the millennia. If this hypothesis proves justified, then Taharqo's intervention in the Lower Nubian landscape may have been more substantial than I first surmised from the incomplete evidence of the other three graffiti.

The possibility that Taharqo actually made or improved the cattle roads at Ibrim and in the Kalabsha region naturally raises the question of why he would have done so. Certainly, roads made for the movement of domesticated animals are attested in Egyptian texts—for example, the "road of horses" described on a stela from the Twenty-First Dynasty.[34] However, the specific purpose for which Taharqo would have facilitated the movement of cattle in Lower Nubia is not immediately obvious. Thus, Horton interpreted the Ibrim graffito as evidence that "Nubia continued to supply Egypt with agricultural produce during the XXVth Dynasty."[35] Under this scenario, the cattle road might conceivably be a single and very long route crossing the Nile at least once and connecting the agricultural basins of Nubia with one or more storehouses in Egypt.

While this hypothesis is reasonable, it is not necessarily preferable to the simpler inference that the cattle road may have been designed to supply Egypt with *cattle* during the Twenty-Fifth Dynasty. Across the millennia, herds have occupied a central position within the economy of Lower Nubia as portable insurance against agricultural cri-

28. Hintze, "Eine neue Inschrift vom 19. Jahre König Taharqas," 332–33.

29. Pope, *Double Kingdom under Taharqo*, 191.

30. Entry dated 25 January 1899 in Somers Clarke Notebook O (Griffith Institute, Oxford).

31. Qasr Ibrim site card 88.1.7/1 (EES Archive).

32. John C. Darnell and Deborah Darnell, *Theban Desert Road Survey in the Egyptian Western Desert, Vol. 1: Gebel Tjauti Rock Inscriptions 1–45 and Wadi el-Ḥôl Inscriptions 1–45*, OIP 119 (Chicago: Oriental Institute of the University of Chicago, 2002), 31, 36–37.

33. Darnell and Darnell, *Theban Desert Road Survey 1*, 36–37.

34. John C. Darnell and Deborah Darnell, "Opening the Narrow Doors of the Desert: Discoveries of the Theban Desert Road Survey," in *Egypt and Nubia: Gifts of the Desert*, ed. Renée Friedman (London: British Museum Press, 2002), 132–55 (132–34, 136 fig. 3).

35. Horton, "Africa in Egypt," 273

sis—"bank on the hoof."[36] In fact, Taharqo enumerated cattle and antelope among his donations to the Temple of Karnak,[37] and he listed red Nubian gazelle among his gifts at that temple's Edifice by the Sacred Lake.[38]

Even simpler still is the possibility that Nubia may have had *more than one* cattle road and that these were designed to supply *local Nubian* temples with cattle during the Twenty-Fifth Dynasty—as attested, for instance, among Taharqo's donations to the Temple of Amun-Re, Bull of the Land of the *St*-Bow, at Sanam in Upper Nubia.[39] In this regard, it is noteworthy that a study of cattle bones from the Napatan and Meroitic periods found specifically at Ibrim concluded that these animals had been raised and then slaughtered in the summer in order to provide meat for the priests of a neighboring temple.[40] An alternative, but by no means mutually exclusive, explanation would posit cattle wealth as a source of *milk* for the well-documented Nubian practice of ritual milk libation;[41] indeed, Taharqo's successor, Tanutamani, boasted of having built for Amun "another portal for going outside to make his milk from his many herds, being tens of thousands, thousands, hundreds, and tens, without reckoning the number of yearling calves of their mothers."[42] The purpose of the cattle road at Ibrim might therefore be connected with Taharqo's construction of a temple at the same site, but this explanation is less convincing for his cattle road in the Kalabsha region, where no temple construction can yet be attributed to that king.[43]

(c) Whereas the Khor Hanush, Tafa, and Ambarkab graffiti (fig. 2) on the west bank of the Nile describe a cattle road "at the entrance of the western mountain," this new Ibrim graffito more than 100 kilometers upstream on the *east* bank of the Nile predictably describes a cattle road "at the entrance of the *eastern* mountain" (figs. 5, 10). One obvious but significant consequence of this textual distinction is that the four graffiti cannot all be describing the same mountain, so we can no longer assume that the term *ḏw* was intended to reference a singular landmark in *any* of these graffiti.[44] An alternative is to interpret *ḏw* as a more generic reference to the "mountainous *region*"—that is, the deserts east and west of the Nubian Nile. During the first millennium BCE and first millennium CE, *ḏw* was increasingly treated in this fashion as a synonym of *ḫ3st*,[45] a tendency attested in Taharqo's own inscriptions elsewhere: while Ramesses II had been described as *ptpt ḫ3s.wt*, "the one who tramples the hill-countries," Taharqo became

36. Bruce Trigger, *History and Settlement in Lower Nubia*, Yale University Publications in Anthropology 69 (New Haven: Yale University Press, 1965), 21–22; William Y. Adams, *Nubia: Corridor to Africa* (Princeton: Princeton University Press, 1977), 54; Kevin C. MacDonald, "Before the Empire of Ghana: Pastoralism and the Origins of Cultural Complexity in the Sahel," in *Transformations in Africa: Essays on Africa's Later Past*, ed. Graham Connah (London: Leicester University Press, 1998), 71–103; A. H. Thompson et al., "Stable Isotopes and Diet at Ancient Kerma, Upper Nubia (Sudan)," *Journal of Archaeological Science* 35 (2008): 376–87.

37. Pascal Vernus, "Inscriptions de la Troisième Période Intermédiaire (I): Les inscriptions de la cour péristyle nord du VIe pylône dans le temple de Karnak," *BIFAO* 75 (1975): 1–66 (7 fig. 6, 10 fig. 9).

38. Richard Parker, Jean Leclant, and Jean-Claude Goyon, *The Edifice of Taharqa by the Sacred Lake of Karnak*, BES 8 (Providence: Brown University Press, 1979), 66nn16–17, pl. 26.

39. Francis Llewellyn Griffith, "Oxford Excavations in Nubia VIII–XVII: Napata, Sanam Temple, Treasury and Town," *Liverpool Annals of Archaeology and Anthropology* 9 (1922), 67-124, pls. IV-LXII (pl. XL frag. 16).

40. Mark S. Copley et al., "Short- and long-term foraging and foddering strategies of domesticated animals from Qasr Ibrim, Egypt," *Journal of Archaeological Science* 31 (2004), 1273–86 (1274, 1283).

41. Copley, "Domesticated animals from Qasr Ibrim," 1274; Janice Yellin, "The Use of Abaton-Style Milk Libations at Meroe," *Meroitica* 6 (1982): 151–55.

42. Cairo JE 48863, ll. 22–24, in Nicholas-Christophe Grimal, *Quatre stèles napatéennes au Musée du Caire* (Cairo: Institut français d'archéologie orientale du Caire, 1981), pls. III a, III.

43. Pope, *Double Kingdom under Taharqo*, 178.

44. Contra Pope, 189.

45. *DG*, 611; *CD*, 440–41; Francis Llewellyn Griffith, *Catalogue of the Demotic Graffiti of the Dodecaschoenus*, vol. 1 (Oxford: Oxford University Press 1937), 115–18; Jeremy Pope, "The Demotic Proskynema of a Meroïte Envoy to Roman Egypt," *Enchoria* 31 (2008/2009): 68–103 (76); Jeremy Pope, "Meroitic Diplomacy and the Festival of Entry," in *The Fourth Cataract and Beyond: Proceedings of the 12th International Conference for Nubian Studies*, ed. Julie Anderson and Derek Welsby, British Museum Publications on Egypt and Sudan 1 (Leuven: Peeters, 2014), 577–82 (578–80).

instead *ptpt ḏw.w*, "the one who tramples the mountains."[46] This semantic interchange may have resulted from a palaeographic one—namely, a confusion of hieratic writings that differed by just a single stroke of the reed.[47] In fact, the substitution of a three-peaked mountain for a two-peaked one occurs during the Twenty-Sixth Dynasty,[48] and the reverse substitution appears again centuries later upon a stela commissioned by the Kushite king Nastasen.[49] The generic translation of *ḏw* as "mountainous region" fits the Ibrim graffito particularly well, because this inscription marked a pathway descending into the Khôr Meḥeigar and trailing eastward toward the desert routes that brought pastoralists seasonally to the Nile.[50] According to Hans Fischer-Elfert, unpublished Abnormal Hieratic documents from Qasr Ibrim specifically name Libyans who had "arrived" (*ỉw*) at the site.[51]

(d) In the first published translation of the Khor Hanush and Tafa graffiti in 1911, Roeder noted that *tꜣ* "land" was written with the papyrus-roll determinative in a position where one would expect instead a canal determinative for that word: . Citing his personal communication with Adolf Erman, Roeder proposed that the scribe in both cases had copied from a hieratic original and had therefore mistaken the hieratic rendering of the canal determinative for the very similar hieratic rendering of the papyrus-roll determinative.[52] When Hintze discovered the Ambarkab graffito in 1959, it too featured the surprising papyrus-roll determinative for *tꜣ*, so he adopted Roeder's explanation.[53] My own 2014 commentary introduced the additional possibility that the scribe could have intended to signify "*dmḏ*, 'united,' an adjective frequently appended to *tꜣ*," but my translation ultimately deferred to Roeder's explanation as the most probable.[54] The new Ibrim graffito does not resolve this question on its own; it merely provides a fourth, redundant example of the same unusual orthography.

Yet, the eight years that have passed since my 2014 study have brought to my attention some compelling support for Erman's interpretation, because this same unusual orthography for *tꜣ* appears four times in a later Kushite text that was clearly influenced by the cursive ductus of a hieratic document. In lines 5, 11, and 12 of the annals of Harsiyotef, the toponym *tꜣ-nḥst*, "Land of the Neḥeset," is written as , , and , respectively. In each case, the first two graphemes and the final four are written as hieroglyphs, whereas the Sennar guinea fowl (G 21) sandwiched between these groups is unmistakably hieratic in form: or .[55] Line 13 of

46. See Ramesses II's 'Rhetorical' Stelae, Tanis III, Face C, main text l. 1, in Kenneth Kitchen, *Ramesside Inscriptions, Vol. 2: Ramesses II, Royal Inscriptions* (Oxford: Blackwell, 1999), 294 l. 10; cf. Khartoum SNM 2678 (Kawa IV = Merowe Museum 52), l. 4, in Miles F. L. Macadam, *The Temples of Kawa, Vol. 1: The Inscriptions* (London: Oxford University Press, 1949), pls. 7–8. Pierce would translate *ḏw.w* as "evil," but the determinatives would suggest instead "mountains" or "mountainous region"; at most, a pun was perhaps intended. Tormod Eide et al., eds., *Fontes Historiae Nubiorum: Textual Sources for the History of the Middle Nile Region between the Eighth Century BC and the Sixth-Century AD, Vol. 1: From the Eighth to the Mid-Fifth Century BC* (Bergen: Klassisk Institutt, Universitetet i Bergen, 1994), 138.

47. Verhoeven, *Untersuchungen zur späthieratischen Buchschrift*, 162–63; Möller, *Hieratische Paläographie* 3, 30–31.

48. Statue of Psamtik-sa-Neith, 22, 6 (twice), in Peter Der Manuelian, *Living in the Past: Studies in Archaism of the Egyptian Twenty-sixth Dynasty* (New York: Kegan Paul, 1994), 78.

49. See Berlin ÄMP 2268, viewer's left side of lunette, second column from right above king's mother, in Heinrich Schäfer, *Die aethiopische Königsinschrift des Berliner Museums: Regierungsbericht des Königs Nastesen des Gegners des Kambyses* (Leipzig: Hinrichs, 1901), Taf. I, with commentary in Carsten Peust, *Das Napatanische: Ein ägyptischer Dialekt aus dem Nubien des späten ersten vorchristlichen Jahrtausends: Texte, Glossar, Grammatik* (Göttingen: Peust & Gutschmidt, 1999), 44, 107.

50. Ricardo A. Caminos, *The Shrines and Rock-Inscriptions of Ibrim* (London: Egypt Exploration Society, 1968), pl. 2; cf. modern patterns of pastoral migration in: Hans Barnard, "The Desert Hinterland of Qasr Ibrim," in *Qasr Ibrim, Between Egypt and Africa: Studies in Cultural Exchange (NINO Symposium, Leiden, 11–12 December 2009)*, ed. Jacques van der Vliet and J. L. Hagen (Leuven: Peeters, 2013), 83–103 (90, fig. 3).

51. I thank Hans Fischer-Elfert for sharing with me this information: Hans Fischer-Elfert, pers. comm., 27 August 2019.

52. Günther Roeder, *Debod bis Bab Kalabsche*, 212. Cf. Verhoeven, *Untersuchungen zur späthieratischen Buchschrift*, 162–63, 204–5; Möller, *Hieratische Paläographie* 3, 30–31, 52–53.

53. Hintze, "Eine neue Inschrift vom 19. Jahre König Taharqas," 333n9.

54. Pope, *Double Kingdom under Taharqo*, 186, 190.

55. For G 21, see Alan Gardiner, *Egyptian Grammar*, 3rd ed. (Oxford: Griffith Institute, 1957), 469.

the same text then demonstrates that the word *tꜣ* was patterned after a hieratic original even when *nḥst* was not attached.[56] The confusion between hieratic and among the determinatives of *tꜣ* is understandable, but I have not yet succeeded in locating any text in *Egypt* that used the same substitution in hieroglyphic transcription.[57]

The recurrence of this rare orthography multiple times in the graffiti of Taharqo and again multiple times in the annals of Harsiyotef centuries later may be purely coincidental, but other explanations should at least be explored. After all, this orthography is not the only distinction shared by these texts: Taharqo's four graffiti and Harsiyotef's annals also revealed further hieratic influences (see a and c above, as well as e below) and utilized orthographies and compound prepositions typical of Demotic syntax,[58] and they were all displayed in a specifically Nubian setting at the behest of a Kushite king. One conceivable explanation of these shared traits would be that Harsiyotef's court in the fourth century BCE could have witnessed a sudden influx of Egyptian (or Egyptian-trained) scribes from the very same Theban or Memphite milieu that presumably staffed Taharqo's earlier administration.[59] The hieroglyphic inscriptions commissioned by the Twenty-Fifth Dynasty in Egypt do reveal several traces of hieratic influence.[60] Moreover, the Napatan royal corpus does manifest a decisive turn during the reign of Harsiyotef, a movement away from the archaizing Classical Middle Egyptian that had been cultivated by his Kushite predecessors and toward the Late Egyptian favored in contemporaneous Egypt.[61] This scenario might not satisfactorily explain the absence of the peculiar orthography among Egyptian documents across the intervening centuries, but that orthography is admittedly a lone example and may well surface in the Egyptian evidence during future research.

However, an alternative explanation would instead attribute the shared features of Taharqo's graffiti and Harsiyotef's annals to a shared *Kushite* scribal milieu. There are indeed multiple signs of continuity in Kushite literacy during those three centuries. I have observed elsewhere on onomastic grounds that the administration of Kush seems to have consisted largely of Kushite individuals across this span,[62] and László Török's meticulous analysis of the surviving Kushite lapidary inscriptions has convincingly inferred the existence of an impermanent paper trail in the Kushite temples consisting of literary works, funerary texts, inventory lists, royal daybooks, and annals.[63] It would not be surprising if a small Kushite scribal community responsible for the maintenance of archives and scriptoria in Kush then developed scribal practices that were occasionally distinctive from those employed in distant Egypt. In this regard, Carsten Peust and Giuseppina Lenzo have each cataloged in "la période napatéenne ... plusiers spécificités graphiques qui s'expliquent facilement par leur origine géographique koushite ... [et] l'éloignement géographique de l'Égypte."[64] Interestingly, these peculiar distinctions between Kushite and contemporaneous Egyptian texts are more

56. Cairo JE 48864, ll. 5, 11, 12, 13, in Grimal, *Quatre stèles napatéennes*, pls. XIa–XII.

57. I thank Giuseppina Lenzo and Peter Der Manuelian for their consultation on this issue; any errors of interpretation are entirely my own. Interestingly, the papyrus-roll determinative was employed with particular frequency in Abnormal Hieratic texts of the same era; see Koenraad Donker van Heel, *A Very Easy Crash Course in Abnormal Hieratic* (Leiden: Het Leids Papyrologisch Instituut, 2013), 33.

58. Peust, *Das Napatanische*, 274–83; Cara Sargent, *The Napatan Royal Inscriptions: Egyptian in Nubia* (PhD diss., Yale University; New Haven, 2004), 9, 344, 346n54, 348n61.

59. Derek Welsby, *The Kingdom of Kush: The Napatan and Meroitic Empires* (Princeton: Wiener, 1996), 189.

60. Giuseppina Lenzo, *Les stèles de Taharqa à Kawa: Paléographie* (Cairo: Institut français d'archéologie orientale, 2015), ix–xi; Giuseppina Lenzo, "L'écriture hiératique en épigraphie à l'Époque napatéenne," in *Ägyptologische 'Binsen' – Weisheiten I-II: neue Forschungen und Methoden der Hieratistik: Akten zweier Tagungen in Mainz im April 2011 und März 2013*, ed. Ursula Verhoeven (Mainz: Akademie der Wissenschaften und der Literatur, 2015), 271–95.

61. Sargent, *Napatan Royal Inscriptions*, 344.

62. Pope, *Double Kingdom under Taharqo*, 145–48.

63. László Török, *The Image of the Ordered World in Ancient Nubian Art: The Construction of the Kushite Mind (800 BC–300 AD)* (Leiden: Brill, 2002), 335–38; see also Jeremy Pope, "History and the Kushite Royal Inscriptions," in *The Oxford Handbook of Nubia*, eds. Geoff Emberling and Bruce Williams (London: Oxford University Press, 2020).

64. Lenzo, *Les stèles de Taharqa à Kawa*, ix; see also Peust, *Das Napatanische*, 85 *passim*.

frequently orthographic and palaeographic rather than grammatical; for the seventh through fifth centuries BCE, Cara Sargent identified "few, if any linguistic anomalies in the Classical Egyptian Napatan texts that do not also occur in contemporary Egyptian texts," so she proposed that throughout the era "Napatans were 'keeping pace' linguistically with their northern neighbors."[65] The rare survival of a Kushite judicial text from the sixth century BCE serves as a valuable reminder that Kushite scribes were sufficiently familiar with the spoken Egyptian of their day to utilize it in texts of the appropriate register,[66] even if they preferred more archaic grammar for coronation accounts and battle narratives. It would therefore appear that while Egyptians and bilingual Kushites were speaking very similar forms of the Egyptian language, their respective scriptoria were writing that language with slightly different hieroglyphs or graphically distinct forms of the same hieroglyphs.

At present, the evidence is still too thin to exclude any of the hypotheses mooted above about scribal milieux, but they constitute an intriguing prospectus for future research. If the graffiti on Taharqo's cattle road do provide a rare glimpse of Kushite scribal practice and its continuity over the centuries, then they become increasingly significant beyond the ambit of pastoral and agrarian history.

(e) The pair of hieroglyphs (fig. 11) at the end of the second line in the Ibrim graffito is not present in any of the parallel texts from Khor Hanush, Tafa, and Ambarkab (fig. 2), and in the Ibrim graffito these hieroglyphs appear in the middle of a phrase that was already regarded as enigmatic for the other graffiti: "the land ... of the Majesty of Horus . . . ."[67] Moreover, the two hieroglyphs are some of the best-preserved in the whole text at Ibrim. As a result, this passage of the Ibrim graffito would seem especially promising for the translator.

Unfortunately, the passage has also proven especially challenging for the epigrapher. When Clarke first transcribed the graffito in 1899, he rendered the first hieroglyph as a foot and lower leg (D 58) with an unusual line projecting horizontally from its top (fig. 9), but Horton's 1988 photograph (fig. 11) draws this interpretation into question. The sloping indentation that Clarke viewed as the arch of a foot does not end convincingly in toes; instead, it fades indistinctly into a weathered streak of the rock face. For the second hieroglyph, Clarke drew a narrow vertical rectangle with a thin line inclining away from its upper right corner, a shape that matches no hieroglyph of which I am aware.

By contrast, French (figs. 6–7) proposed in 1988 to read two hieroglyphs that are attested in other texts and consistent with Horton's photograph. For the first hieroglyph, French recognized the flat top, curved sides, and flared base of a tall water-pot (W 14). For the second hieroglyph, French experimented with several shapes on the Ibrim site card but eventually settled upon the feather with a stroke at its side (H 6*). This is a commendable hypothesis, because the exaggerated stroke is attested for this hieroglyph in late forms of hieratic ,[68] and other hieroglyphs in the graffito do suggest that the mason was copying from a hieratic original (see a, c, and d above). Moreover, a feather would match well the peculiar contour of the hieroglyph's left edge as shown in Horton's photograph (fig. 11) and especially that photograph's negative (fig. 12). French appended a question mark after his transcription of this hieroglyph, and indeed other transcriptions of the second hieroglyph should not be foreclosed prematurely. Yet, my examination of the photograph and the available repertoire of Egyptian hieroglyphs has suggested no alternative superior to that which French perceived in situ.

The difference between the Ibrim graffito and those at Khor Hanush, Tafa, and Ambarkab suggests two logical possibilities for translation: either the additional hieroglyphs inserted a detail applicable only to Ibrim and not to the other sites, or those two hieroglyphs conveyed a detail that was considered expendable to the text when it was reproduced at those sites. Remarkably, French's reading fits both of these possibilities. Taken together, the two hieroglyphs

65. Sargent, *Napatan Royal Inscriptions*, 8.

66. Louvre C 257 (Aspelta's Dedication Stela) and the Dukki Gel Stela in: Sargent, *Napatan Royal Inscriptions*, 331; Dominique Valbelle, *Les stèles de l'an 3 d'Aspelta* (Cairo: Institut français d'archéologie orientale, 2012), pls. 3A–3B, 5A–5B.

67. Pope, *Double Kingdom under Taharqo*, 190.

68. Verhoeven, *Untersuchungen zur späthieratischen Buchschrift*, 146–47.

Figure 11. Left end of line 2 in Taharqo's Ibrim graffito. Photograph Mark Horton, Egypt Exploration Society Archive, courtesy of the Trustees of the British Museum.

Figure 12. Negative image of figure 11, showing the left end of line 2 in Taharqo's Ibrim graffito. Photograph Mark Horton, Egypt Exploration Society Archive, courtesy of the Trustees of the British Museum.

that he transcribed would produce a phrase well-known from other texts—*ḥs*(*y*) *mꜣ*ʿ, "truly favored"[69]—suggesting either that this distinction was accorded only to Ibrim or that it was a mere platitude omitted from the other graffiti. French's aforementioned hesitation about the second hieroglyph might derive from the fact that the resultant phrase, *ḥs*(*y*) *mꜣ*ʿ, and its variants are typically epithets of individuals, not of lands.[70] Again, however, my own exploration of other possible translations has suggested no alternative superior to that which French's transcription would produce.

Summary

The new inscription is located on the east bank of the Nile about one kilometer downstream of Qasr Ibrim, but it is currently submerged under the waters of Lake Nasser. Despite remaining unpublished until now, this graffito was actually the first record of Taharqo's cattle road to be discovered by an Egyptologist. The Ibrim graffito is very similar but not quite identical to the parallel texts already known from Khor Hanush, Tafa, and Ambarkab, and its archaeological context and historical content clarify those other graffiti in three valuable ways. First, tool marks on the adjacent path at Ibrim show that it had been cleared for traffic, suggesting that Taharqo's crews did not merely *travel* the cattle road as previously assumed; rather, they actually *hewed* it as a public works project. If the other three graffiti accompanied a similar project in the Kalabsha region, then Taharqo's intervention into the Lower Nubian landscape was more substantial than I first surmised. Second, differences between the Ibrim graffito and the other three suggest that the "mountain" referenced in each was not a singular landmark but instead a more generic reference to the mountainous regions east and west of the Nile. Among the available explanations for Taharqo's cattle road, I have favored here the theory that there were several such roads in Nubia and that the road at Ibrim was designed to transport cattle from the east to a local Nubian temple for meat provisions and/or milk libations. Third, the opportunity to revisit the roads' graffiti as an ensemble has cast new light on the influence of hieratic script upon the hieroglyphic text, and some of the graffiti's most unusual features may provide a rare glimpse into the ways in which successive generations

69. Lit. "true praised one" (passive participle followed by adjective). See El-Bersheh Tomb 8, main chamber, inscription on left-hand wall, col. 8, in Archibald Sayce, "Gleanings from the Land of Egypt," *RecTrav* 13 (1890): 187–94 (190, 193); Francis Llewellyn Griffith and Percy E. Newberry, *El Bersheh: Part 2* (London: Egypt Exploration Fund, 1895), 39–40, pl. xxi.

70. Cf. *Wb.* III:157, 4; Dmitri Meeks, *Année lexicographique: Égypte ancienne*, Tome 3 (Paris: Cybele, 1998), 201.

of Kushite scribes wrote and conceptualized Egyptian hieroglyphs. Their experience in learning and interpreting the details of Egyptian writing systems will be familiar to any Egyptologist who had the pleasure of doing the same as a student of Richard Jasnow.

New Studies on the Greek Version of the Demotic Myth of the Sun's Eye: An Additional Fragment (P. Vindob. G 29357) and an Analysis of the *kwf*/*lynx*-Monkey

Luigi Prada

My first (electronic) meeting with Richard dates back to December 2009, when, as an MPhil student, I was preparing applications for doctoral programmes in Egyptology in Europe and the USA. I eventually remained in Oxford for my doctorate, but the contact had been established, and ever since I have thought of Richard as a mentor across the pond. Over the years, in conversations via email, at conferences and workshops, or simply through his publications, he has always been a supportive and inspiring presence, a model of how to be an Egyptological .[1]

I am therefore delighted to have the opportunity to offer this essay to Richard, as a small token of my esteem and friendship. We all know how much not only Egyptology, but also cognate disciplines in the study of the ancient Mediterranean owe him, thanks to his research into cultural transmission between Egypt and the classical world. This is why I trust that he will enjoy the topic of this short paper, which gathers together a number of fresh observations on the Greek version of the Demotic Myth of the Sun's Eye, a text with which Richard has had several dealings throughout his career.[2] To quote his own words, "[w]ithout a doubt, Mythus will long provide Egyptologists with an

---

I should like to thank a number of individuals and institutions who have assisted me with this article. I am grateful to the Papyrussammlung of the Österreichische Nationalbibliothek, Vienna, specifically Bernhard Palme and Claudia Kreuzsaler, for facilitating my search for and study of P. Vindob. G 29357 and giving me permission to publish it. The British Library, London, provided me with digital images of P. Lond. Lit. 192. The Museo Archeologico Nazionale of Palestrina (Polo Museale del Lazio) kindly allowed me to take new photographs of the Nile Mosaic. The Palestine Exploration Fund, London—namely, Felicity Cobbing—allowed me to republish a photograph from their archive. Here in Oxford, Paul D. Wordsworth assisted me with the preparation of all images for this article, and Stephanie West discussed with me aspects of the Vienna fragment. Mark de Kreij (Nijmegen) gave feedback on my draft text edition. Last but not least, I am deeply grateful to the editors of this Festschrift—especially Marina Escolano-Poveda—for their invitation to join them, alongside many other friends and colleagues, in celebrating Richard. This paper was written during the tenure of a British Academy postdoctoral fellowship.

1. Facsimile from P. Vienna D 6343, col. 3, l. 16, after Richard Jasnow and Karl-Theodor Zauzich, *The Ancient Egyptian Book of Thoth: A Demotic Discourse on Knowledge and Pendant to the Classical Hermetica* (Wiesbaden: Harrassowitz, 2005), pl. 62.

2. Such dealings include a painstaking analysis of the Demotic text, as testified in Richard Jasnow, review of *Le Mythe de l'oeil du soleil: Translittération et traduction avec commentaire philologique*, by Françoise de Cenival, *Enchoria* 18 (1991): 205–15. They also comprise studies of the Greek translation, exemplified by a seminar paper from his student days titled *A Study of the Greek Version of Mythus* (Chicago, 1979)—an important essay, which, although never published, Richard has generously shared with several colleagues over the years; see already Heinz-Josef Thissen, "'Lost in Translation?': 'Von Übersetzungen und Übersetzern,'" in *Literatur und Religion im alten Ägypten: Ein Symposium zu Ehren von Elke Blumenthal*, ed. Hans-Werner Fischer-Elfert and Tonio S. Richter, AAWL 81/5 (Leipzig: Sächsische Akademie der Wissenschaften zu Leipzig and S. Hirzel, 2011), 126–63, at 132.

abundant supply of [...] literary problems."[3] Perhaps these few pages will provide him with a good excuse to turn his attention again to this fascinating text and its problems, further helping advance our understanding of it.

Introduction

The primary aim of the present article is to publish a number of observations about the Greek version of the Myth of the Sun's Eye, tying up a few loose ends of my research on this text. In an article from 2012, first highlighting how badly neglected the materiality and provenance of P. Lond. Lit. 192 was, I published the first complete physical description of the manuscript, discussed its date (second to mid-third century CE), presented unpublished archival evidence about the history of its acquisition (via Theodor Graf in Vienna), and advanced suggestions about its provenance (the Fayum).[4] One of my conclusions was that, given the modern history of the manuscript, additional fragments of it may have been left behind in Vienna, as was known to be the case with other papyri belonging to the same lot put up for sale by Graf. This hypothesis has since been confirmed by research in the Viennese Papyrussammlung, and a small, additional fragment of this manuscript is what I am publishing in the first part of this article.

The second section focuses instead on the male protagonist of the tale, the representative of the god Thoth and Tefnut's companion in her adventures, that is, the Greek (λυκό)λυγξ—Demotic (*wnš-*)*kwf*—the simian nature of which I have proven in another study.[5] Specifically, I discuss here in further detail the terms *kwf* and λύγξ, arguing that the Greek noun, like its Egyptian equivalent, designates a guenon, and not a baboon. After this follows the examination of a likely iconographic specimen of the oft-misunderstood *lynx*-monkey, which I believe can be found in the famous Nile Mosaic of Palestrina (so far misidentified, yet again, as a feline lynx), and which offers a welcome parallel from the visual arts furthering our appreciation of the tale of the Myth of the Sun's Eye.

It remains to be noted that all of the material here presented will eventually be integrated in a multiauthored publication of all manuscripts of the Myth of the Sun's Eye, in both Demotic and Greek, which is currently underway.[6] The sheer size of the corpus, however, means that more years, realistically, will be needed to complete this enterprise. In light of the growing interest in this text, it therefore seems useful, in the meantime, to publish these notes, for the use of colleagues and any interested readers.[7]

---

3. Jasnow, review of *Le Mythe de l'oeil du soleil*, 215.

4. Luigi Prada, "For a New Edition of P.Lond.Lit. 192: Current Research on the Greek Version of the *Myth of the Sun's Eye*," in *Actes du 26ᵉ congrès international de papyrologie: Genève, 16–21 août 2010*, ed. Paul Schubert, RR 30 (Geneva: Droz, 2012), 627–34.

5. Luigi Prada, "Translating Monkeys between Demotic and Greek, or Why a Lynx Is Not Always a Wildcat: (λυκό)λυγξ = (*wnš-*) *kwf*," *ZPE* 189 (2014): 111–14.

6. About this project, see Prada, "For a New Edition of P.Lond.Lit. 192," 631n29 (with a list of the Demotic manuscripts identified up to 2010); and Frank Feder, "The Legend of the Sun's Eye: The Translation of an Egyptian Novel into Greek," in *Cultures in Contact: Transfer of Knowledge in the Mediterranean Context: Selected Papers*, ed. Sofía Torallas Tovar and Juan Pedro Monferrer-Sala, SSA 1 (Córdoba: CNERU, CEDRAC, and Oriens Academic, 2013), 4–12, at 7n26 (with a list of the project members, which I also have since joined). The casual statement by Martin A. Stadler, *Einführung in die ägyptische Religion ptolemäisch-römischer Zeit nach den demotischen religiösen Texten*, EQÄ 7 (Berlin: Lit, 2012), 64n302, bemoaning that this research project is not a collective enterprise, is as baffling as it is uninformed.

7. In recent years, a number of significant contributions have appeared concerning the Greek translation of the Myth of the Sun's Eye. These include overall studies, such as Feder, "The Legend of the Sun's Eye"; Stephanie West, "Divine Anger Management: The Greek Version of the *Myth of the Sun's Eye* (*P.Lond.Lit.* 192)," in *The Romance between Greece and the East*, ed. Tim Whitmarsh and Stuart Thomson (Cambridge: Cambridge University Press, 2013), 79–90; and, most recently, Marie-Pierre Chaufray, "Les «traductions» grecques des textes littéraires égyptiens," in *Curiosité d'Égypte: Entre quête de soi et découverte de l'autre, de l'Antiquité à l'époque contemporaine*, ed. Michel Chauveau, Jean-Luc Fournet, Jean-Michel Mouton, and Antonio Ricciardetto, HEMGR 59 (Geneva: Droz, 2020), 45–63, at 58–60. Particularly noteworthy is a new, annotated translation of the text into German, in Andrea Jördens, "Griechische Texte aus Ägypten," in *Weisheitstexte, Mythen und Epen*, ed. Bernd Janowski and Daniel Schwemer, TUAT NF 8 (Gütersloh: Gütersloher Ver-

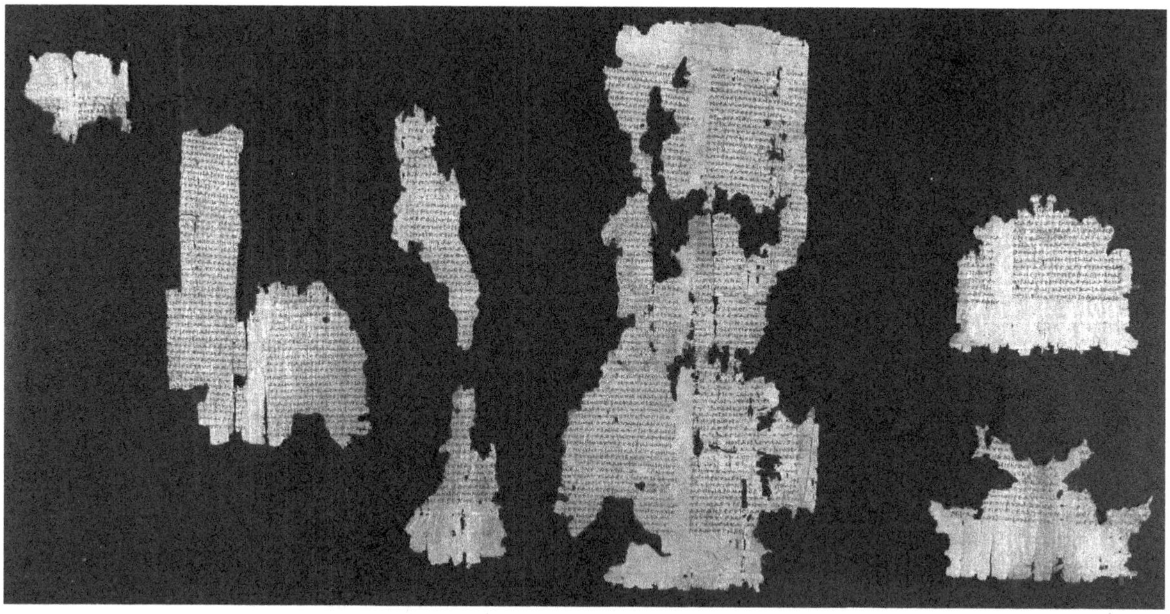

Figure 1. P. Lond. Lit. 192 in its current mounting (courtesy of The British Library, London).

A New Fragment of P. Lond. Lit. 192 in Vienna: Edition of P. Vindob. G 29357

P. Lond. Lit. 192 (Mertens-Pack[3] no. 2618) was purchased in 1893 by the British Museum from a collection assembled by Theodor Graf, which was eventually split between London and Vienna (fig. 1).[8]

Since London had the first choice, while the remainder was kept in Vienna, it is sometimes the case that fragments might still be found in the Österreichische Nationalbibliothek that pertain to some of the manuscripts now in the collection of the British Library. This is already known to be the case for four literary manuscripts originating from this purchase.[9] The Greek Myth of the Sun's Eye can now be added to this group of *disiecta membra*, since I was able to identify one additional fragment of it in Vienna: P. Vindob. G 29357 (fig. 2).[10]

The fragment is quite small and bears little writing. However, its material and palaeographical features make the attribution to our manuscript certain. Like the seven other fragments that constitute P. Lond. Lit. 192, it bears writing on one side only (along the fibres), being blank on the other. Its maximum dimensions are 6.5 × 2 cm (height

lagshaus, 2015), 479–518, at 481–90 (no. 2). This considerably adds to the body of modern translations available for this text, which previously included one in German (with synopsis of the Greek and Demotic parallels) by Thissen, "Lost in Translation?," 144–63, and another in Spanish by María Paz López Martínez and Sofía Torallas Tovar, "La versión griega de la leyenda demótica del Ojo del Sol," *Lucentum* 23–24 (2004–2005): 185–95, at 192–94.

8. On this and the details of the modern history of P. Lond. Lit. 192, see Prada, "For a New Edition of P.Lond.Lit. 192," 627–30.

9. Mertens-Pack[3] nos. 1039 (*Odyssea*), 0115 (Aratus, *Phaenomena*), 2531 (anonymous imperial panegyric), and 0293 (Demosthenes, *De falsa legatione*). For more details, see Prada, "For a New Edition of P.Lond.Lit. 192," 630n23.

10. I identified this fragment in 2011, during a visit to the Viennese Papyrussammlung, when I surveyed the microfilms of the Greek papyri between and around the inventory numbers borne by the Viennese fragments of the aforementioned four manuscripts (that is, P. Vindob. G 26700s and 29200s–29800s), as per the plan I had outlined in Prada, "For a New Edition of P.Lond.Lit. 192," 630. More fragments of this manuscript may remain to be found in Vienna: only a more extended survey will tell. Notwithstanding my intention to expand the search for more fragments in the future, and despite the scantiness of P. Vindob. G 29357, it seems nevertheless appropriate not to delay its publication any further.

Figure 2. P. Vindob. G 29357 (courtesy of the Papyrussammlung der Österreichischen Nationalbibliothek, Vienna).

by width), with no apparent traces of a *kollesis*. Most of it consists of an *intercolumnium*, which has a width of approximately 1.2 cm and thus matches the intercolumnar spaces of P. Lond. Lit. 192.[11] The size of the writing, the spacing in between the lines, and the scribal hand are also identical to those of the London papyrus. The presence of a *paragraphos* (at col. x+2, l. x+9) is remarkable, and is yet another shared feature with the British Library manuscript.[12] The fragment bears the scant remains of just over ten lines from two columns of text. Hardly anything survives of the first one. As for the latter, only the first couple of letters from part of its lines are preserved. Not one word can be read from it with any degree of certainty, for none is likely to be fully preserved—unless we should assume to be dealing with negations (οὐ) or definite articles (ὁ, ἡ). Here below, I therefore simply provide a diplomatic transcription of P. Vindob. G 29357. It is not possible to determine whether the fragment preserves the top of the two columns, and therefore includes part of the scroll's upper margin (with l. x+1 being the original first line), or if it comes from a lower point of the *intercolumnium*. No joint with any of the seven London fragments can be identified.

When it comes to the date of the manuscript, the Vienna fragment does not add any new element to the discussion, and I here maintain the second to mid-third century CE dating that I discussed in my earlier study (with a preference for the late second century, as opposed to the absolute attributions to the third century that still dominate the relevant literature).[13] As for its provenance, I still believe it very probable that this manuscript was originally unearthed in the Fayum, as I have already argued.[14] Remarkably, when I inspected P. Vindob. G 29357, the fragment came in an old paper folder which bore the following handwritten note: "Aus S. Nesos." Of course, albeit tantalizing, such an isolated and otherwise unsubstantiated archival note cannot be used as a proper argument for a provenance from Soknopaiou Nesos/Dime. In fact, it is not unlikely that this note was added simply as a record of the fact that this fragment came from the 1893 sale of Graf's collection, that is, from the so-called III. Papyrusfund, a large collection of material from the Fayum traditionally assigned to Soknopaiou Nesos, but which, in fact, stems from other Fayumic sites too.[15] It is worth noting in this respect that the small Vienna fragment that complements another London manuscript from this same find is also preserved in an old envelope which bears a similar provenance note (Mertens-Pack[3] no. 0293 = P. Lond. Lit. 127 + P. Vindob. G 29775, bearing Demosthenes's *De falsa legatione*).[16]

The Fayumic provenance of the manuscripts from the III. Papyrusfund and the fact that only a fraction of them can positively be attributed to Soknopaious Nesos has been discussed by several scholars, primarily with regard to the

11. These variate between 1 and 1.5 cm. On all the material features of P. Lond. Lit. 192, see Prada, "For a New Edition of P.Lond. Lit. 192," 628.

12. On this diacritic, see discussion below.

13. Prada, "For a New Edition of P.Lond.Lit. 192," 628.

14. Prada, 629–30.

15. Prada, 629.

16. The note, in this case, reads "P III," referring to the aforementioned III. Papyrusfund. See Marco Perale, "Un nuovo frammento della 'membrana Grafiana' (P.Vindob. G 29775: Demostene, *Sulla falsa ambasceria*, 16, 18)," *ZPE* 172 (2010): 22–26, at 25. According to Perale, this note was added by Carl Wessely in or after 1899, when he joined the staff of Vienna's then Imperial Court Library. It is possible that Wessely might be the author of the note on the folder containing P. Vindob. G 29357 too (as I did not see the envelope with Demosthenes's fragment, I could not compare the handwriting).

material in Greek.[17] However, it should not be forgotten that this papyrus find did not include only Greek papyri and parchments. Papyrological material also in Demotic stemmed from it, part of which is currently being investigated, and is revealing its connections not only with the Fayum, but also, specifically, with Soknopaiou Nesos. This is the case with P. Lond. II 264, the *recto* of which contains an important Demotic liturgical text for the cult of Sobek in Soknopaiou Nesos.[18] Such ritual and religious Demotic material from Soknopaiou Nesos or the wider Fayum pertaining to this group of manuscripts should not be ignored when investigating the original context of our papyrus, nor should its relevance to the Greek Myth of the Sun's Eye be underestimated. This is especially true when one remembers that the Myth of the Sun's Eye itself, far from being a "novel," represents an important mythological text from Egyptian religious tradition, and its Greek version might have been used by members of the Egyptian priesthood who were more at ease reading Greek than Demotic.[19] Admittedly, all evidence concerning the origin of our papyrus remains, in the end, circumstantial, but the elements pointing at the Fayum—if not at Soknopaiou Nesos itself—can hardly be dismissed.

Col. x+1	Col. x+2
– –	– – –
]α̣	[
]	[
] ̣	[
]	̣[
]	̣[
]	επ̣[
]	ου[
] ̣	εc ̣[
]	ε̅π̅ ̣[
]	ηυ[
]	κα[
]	μα ̣[
]	πω ̣[
– –	– – –

Palaeographical notes

Col. x+1, l. x+3. Faint trace of a horizontal stroke, likely the extended middle hasta of end-of-line ε (compare numerous specimens in P. Lond. Lit. 192, frag. d, cols. 1–2).

Col. x+1, l. x+8. End of a descending oblique stroke, from α or λ, perhaps μ.

Col. x+2, l. x+12. Beginning of an ascending oblique stroke, probably from λ, but δ or μ are also possible; perhaps, but less likely, even χ.

Despite the scanty nature of the surviving text, one general observation can be made about its original content, thanks to the presence of a *paragraphos* at col. x+2, l. x+9. *Paragraphoi* are found in the London fragments of this manuscript too, and are used exclusively in dialogues to indicate a change in speaker, marking the start and/or the

17. For a recent overview, see Perale, "Un nuovo frammento della 'membrana Grafiana,'" 25–26.

18. Martin A. Stadler, "Eine neue Quelle zur Theologie des Sobek aus Dimê: Papyrus British Library 264 recto," in *Auf den Spuren des Sobek: Festschrift für Horst Beinlich zum 28. Dezember 2012*, ed. Jochen Hallof, SRaT 12 (Dettelbach: J.H. Röll, 2012), 265–73, at 265. Incidentally, note that P. Lond. Lit. 192 originally appeared in the same P. Lond. catalogue, as P. Lond. II 274.

19. On this, see Prada, "For a New Edition of P.Lond.Lit. 192," 632.

end of a character's direct speech.[20] Namely, they can be observed in P. Lond. Lit. 192, frag. a, col. 2, l. 50 (start of Hermes's speech), and frag. d, col. 2, ll. 24 (start of goddess's speech), 35 (end of goddess's speech), 39 (start of Hermes's speech), and 42 (start of goddess's speech). Therefore, given the presence of a *paragraphos*, it is clear that the portion of text included in the second column of P. Vindob. G 29357 must originally have contained a dialogic section.[21]

The Simian Protagonist of the Myth of the Sun's Eye: Between a Baboon and a Guenon, between Text and Image

The animal identity of the male protagonist of the Myth of the Sun's Eye, that is, the representative of the god Thoth, has been puzzling modern interpreters for over a century. Labeled as *wnš-kwf* and as *kwf* in the Demotic text, this misunderstood creature has been subjected to all types of interpretations and translations, with perhaps the most bizarre of all identifying it with a squirrel.[22] In more recent times, agreement has been reached on understanding these Demotic zoological terms as types of monkeys: a *kwf*-monkey and a dog-snouted variant (*wnš*, literally "wolf") of the same. Doubts have however persisted about the way the Greek Myth of the Sun's Eye translates the Demotic nouns, with the terms λύγξ and λυκόλυγξ respectively—and understandably so, since the standard translation of Greek λύγξ is a felid, the lynx wildcat.[23] This misunderstanding has been cleared only lately, by a study that showed how Greek λύγξ can also indicate a type of monkey. The Greek version of the male protagonist's names is therefore faithful to its Demotic original, and all terms in each language refer exclusively to species of monkeys.[24]

But with what types of monkeys are we exactly dealing? It is generally agreed that Egyptian *kwf* (originally, *gif/gwf*) indicates a guenon (genus *Cercopithecus*).[25] However, it appears that in later phases of the Egyptian language the term could also be used in a more indiscriminate and unmarked fashion, to designate not only the guenon, but any kind of monkey—even the baboon (genus *Papio*; Egyptian *iʿny*, *ʿʿn*, vel sim.).[26] This is confirmed by iconographic evidence, in which this noun appears correctly associated with guenons in early representations, but in later times can also be observed as a label for figures that clearly portray baboons. One can compare, for instance, the Middle

20. Stephanie West, "The Greek Version of the Legend of Tefnut," *JEA* 55 (1969): 161–83, at 162.

21. With regard to diacritics in P. Lond. Lit. 192, their presence has been used to suggest that this manuscript was intended for use by Egyptian speakers in order to learn Greek ("una copia di lettura per Egiziani che apprendevano il greco")—so Guglielmo Cavallo, quoted in Antonio Stramaglia, "Fra 'consumo' e 'impegno': Usi didattici della narrativa nel mondo antico," in *La letteratura di consumo nel mondo greco-latino: Atti del convegno internazionale: Cassino, 14–17 settembre 1994*, ed. Oronzo Pecere and Antonio Stramaglia (Cassino: Università degli Studi di Cassino, 1996), 97–166, at 138. This view is not only over-simplistic in its tracing of a clear-cut ethnic/linguistic/cultural divide in second/third century CE Egypt or in its implicit assumption that the Myth of the Sun's Eye had a role in Egyptian culture and education comparable to that of the Homeric poems in Greek *paideia*, it is also untenable based on what we know about teaching practices in Roman (as well as Hellenistic) Egypt. On the latter, see recently Luigi Prada, "Egyptian Education in Hellenistic and Roman Egypt: A Take from the Fayum—School Textbooks and *P.Schulübung* Revisited," in *Le Fayoum: Archéologie – Histoire – Religion: Actes du sixième colloque international: Montpellier, 26–28 octobre 2016*, ed. Marie-Pierre Chaufray, Ivan Guermeur, Sandra Lippert, and Vincent Rondot (Wiesbaden: Harrassowitz, 2018), 101–28, at 102–5.

22. Eugène Revillout, "Leçon d'ouverture du 2 décembre 1901 sur l'apologue dans le Koufi et dans un autre traité philosophique contemporain," *RdÉ* 10 (1902): 69–85, at 70: "le Koufi, le petit chacal-singe—un simple écureuil."

23. For a recent example, see Stadler, *Einführung in die ägyptische Religion*, 65 ("eine Art Luchs").

24. Prada, "Translating Monkeys between Demotic and Greek." I refer to this study for more details.

25. See, e.g., Pascal Vernus and Jean Yoyotte, *Bestiaire des pharaons* (Paris: Agnès Viénot Éditions and Éditions Perrin, 2005), 615–16; Joachim F. Quack, "The Animals of the Desert and the Return of the Goddess," in *Desert Animals in the Eastern Sahara: Status, Economic Significance, and Cultural Reflection in Antiquity: Proceedings of an Interdisciplinary ACACIA Workshop Held at the University of Cologne: December 14–15, 2007*, ed. Heiko Riemer, Frank Forster, Michael Herb, and Nadja Pöllath, CA 4 (Cologne: Heinrich-Barth-Institut, 2009), 341–61, at 342; Ingrid Bohms, *Säugetiere in der altägyptischen Literatur*, Ägyptologie 2 (Berlin: Lit, 2013), 11.

26. Vernus and Yoyotte, *Bestiaire des pharaons*, 620.

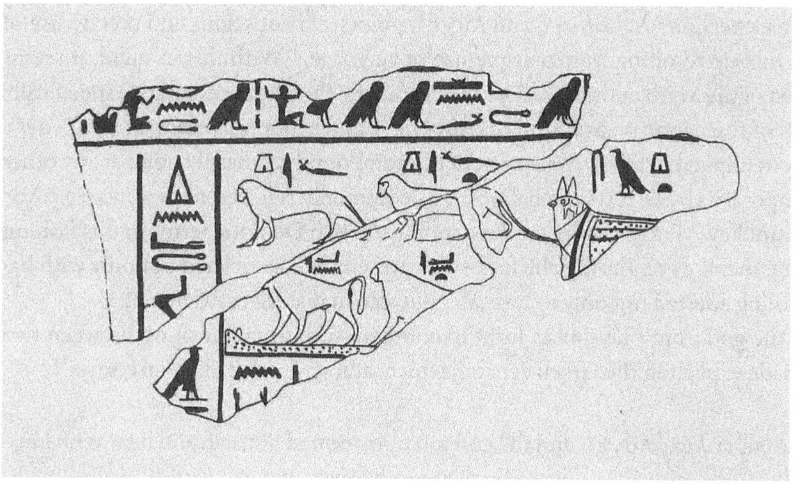

Figure 3. Guenons (top row) and baboons (bottom row), from the Middle Kingdom tomb of Neheri, Deir el-Bersha (after Griffith and Newberry, *El Bersheh*).

Kingdom representation of a couple of guenons, labeled as *gif* and *gif.t* ("he-" and "she-guenon"), in the tomb of Neheri in Deir el-Bersha (fig. 3),[27] with a relief from the time of Augustus in the forecourt of the temple of Hathor at Philae, which depicts a baboon, and yet is still accompanied by the caption *py kwf* ("the *kwf*-monkey"; fig. 4).[28]

It is perhaps on account of this lexical blurring that, in the Demotic text of the Myth of the Sun's Eye, the rescuer of Tefnut is also indicated as a *kwf*, despite the fact that—by virtue of his association with the baboon-god Thoth—one would rather expect him to have the animal hypostasis of a baboon than that of a guenon.[29]

But there is an alternative interpretative avenue which is worth exploring. The fact that the Demotic text names the monkey in one of two specific ways (*wnš-kwf* and

Figure 4. Baboon as a musician, from the temple of Hathor, Philae (after Daumas, "Les propylées du temple d'Hathor").

27. Francis L. Griffith and Percy E. Newberry, *El Bersheh: Part II*, ASEg 4 (London: Egypt Exploration Fund, 1895), pl. xi. The guenons are in the upper row. In the row beneath, note instead a couple of baboons, captioned *iꜥn* and *iꜥn.t* ("he-" and "she-baboon").

28. François Daumas, "Les propylées du temple d'Hathor à Philae et le culte de la déesse," *ZÄS* 95 (1968): 1–17, pl. 3 (bottom).

29. On the expected Thoth/baboon association, see already, e.g., Françoise de Cenival, "Lyco-lynx et chacal-singe dans le *Mythe de l'œil du soleil*," *BIFAO* 99 (1999): 73–83, at 73; and Joachim F. Quack, "Die Rückkehr der Göttin nach Theben nach demotischen Quellen," in *Documents de théologies thébaines tardives (D3T 1)*, ed. Christophe Thiers, CENiM 3 (Montpellier: Université Paul Valéry (Montpellier III) - CNRS, 2009), 135–46, at 138. Note, incidentally, that in one passage of the Demotic text the goddess assimilates her interlocutor, the *kwf*-monkey, to a *ꜥꜥn*, "baboon" (P. Leiden I 384, col. 9, l. 6); for the original Demotic text, see Wilhelm Spiegelberg, *Der ägyptische Mythus vom Sonnenauge (der Papyrus der Tierfabeln – „Kufi") nach dem Leidener demotischen Papyrus I 384* (Strasbourg: Straßburger Druckerei und Verlagsanstalt, 1917), 28, pl. viii.

kwf), as accurately reflected by the Greek version (λυκόλυγξ and λύγξ), points at a conscious and precise use of terminology, rather than a haphazard mix-up resulting from a vague use of language.[30] With this in mind, it seems possible to understand the Demotic text of the Myth of the Sun's Eye as referring to Thoth's representative specifically as a guenon (*kwf*) and, in earlier parts of the narrative, as a kind of baboon, or as a baboon-like simian (*wnš-kwf*). Indeed, the reference to the canine snout implied in the *wnš*-element of the compound can hardly point at any other type of primate; to be sure, in contemporary Greek texts the baboon was commonly referred to as κυνοκέφαλος (Latin *cynocephalus*), a "dog-headed" monkey.[31] Furthermore, understanding the two Demotic terms in this fashion allows us to identify parallels within the theology of Thoth, which can also present him associated not only with baboons, but also with guenons—something attested not only in textual,[32] but also in material evidence.[33]

In our tale, the metamorphosis of the god from one simian form to another—clearly, a transition between two visibly distinct types of simians—is made explicit in the Greek version, which, at frag. f, col. 2, ll. 59–61, says:[34]

με[τέ]βα[λε δὲ καὶ ὁ θεὸς] | καὶ οὐκέτι λυκόλυγξ α̣[λλὰ] | λὺγξ ἦν ὁρᾶσθαι.	and the god too transformed himself, and he was no longer to be seen as a *lykolynx*, but as a *lynx*.

It is striking how closely the translator decided to stick to the Egyptian letter. As the original text did not use the standard noun for baboon, *ꜥꜥn*, his translation also avoided a plain option in Greek, like κυνοκέφαλος. Instead, he likely himself concocted the neologism λυκόλυγξ, a perfect calque of the Demotic *hapax wnš-kwf*. Such a choice confirms the importance that the translator clearly attached to the observance of correct terminology, as well as his ease with Demotic Egyptian and Greek likewise: if the Demotic had *wnš-kwf*, then his Greek translation had to reflect the original compound and prefix the monkey's name with λυκο- ("wolf," Demotic *wnš*), not κυνο- ("dog," Demotic *iwiw*). As for the name of the monkey itself, that was maintained in the compound as λύγξ, chosen as the Greek equivalent of Demotic *kwf*. It is perhaps especially this choice of translating *kwf* with the very rare simian term

30. The switch in the name used for the character from *wnš-kwf* to *kwf* is deliberate and occurs close to the end of the Demotic text (early on in col. 21 in the copy of P. Leiden I 384), when he and Tefnut reach Egypt, and in correspondence with the metamorphosis of the goddess herself. Occurrences of the phrase *wnš-kwf* in this final section are retrospective, referring to earlier events in the narrative (see, e.g., P. Leiden I 384, col. 21, l. 15, and col. 22, l. 8).

31. On the baboon/*cynocephalus* equivalence, see William C. McDermott, *The Ape in Antiquity*, JHUSA 27 (Baltimore: The Johns Hopkins Press, 1938), 104 (no. 2).

32. Besides the internal parallel in the Myth of the Sun's Eye already quoted above (see n. 29), with the monkey being also associated with a *ꜥꜥn*, see, for example, the invocations to Thoth in the liturgical text preserved in the Ptolemaic hieratic P. BM EA 10569, and specifically col. 22, l. 4, which reads: 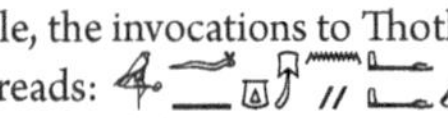 *Ḏḥwty ꜣꜥꜥny gf*; edition in Raymond O. Faulkner, *An Ancient Egyptian Book of Hours (Pap. Brit. Mus. 10569)* (Oxford: Griffith Institute, 1958), 15, 35*. While Faulkner translates it "Thoth the Baboon and Ape," it may be possible to better understand it as a compound, "Thoth the baboon-guenon," as originally suggested by Mark J. Smith, "Sonnenauge, Demotischer Mythos vom," *LÄ* 5:1082–87. The presence of only one divine determinative at the end of the whole sequence better suits, in my opinion, such an interpretation (compare, for instance, writings of the compound *wnš-kwf* in P. Leiden I 384, also with only one final divine determinative—in standardized hieroglyphic transcription: 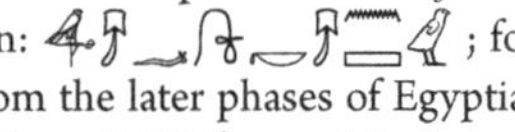 ; for the Demotic original, see Spiegelberg, *Der ägyptische Mythus vom Sonnenauge*, 106 [no. 173]). Still from the later phases of Egyptian religion, the Roman magical text *PDM Suppl.* 163, with its mention of *pꜣ qwf n Bḥt(.t)* ("the *qwf*-monkey of Edfu"), possibly also associates Thoth with a guenon, though note that here the name of Thoth is not mentioned, hence the association in this case remains uncertain (mostly relying on the epithet just preceding ours, *p(ꜣ) hb šps*, "the noble ibis"). See Hans D. Betz, ed., *The Greek Magical Papyri in Translation: Including the Demotic Spells* (Chicago: University of Chicago Press, 1986), 329n33; for the original Demotic text, see Janet H. Johnson, "Louvre E3229: A Demotic Magical Text," *Enchoria* 7 (1977): 55–102, at 64, pl. 15 (col. 6, l. 20).

33. The study of ancient animal remains from sacred animal burials connected with the cult of Thoth has confirmed that the simian mummies there deposited do not belong exclusively to baboons, but also include guenons. For cases from Saqqarah and Thebes, see Alain Charron, "Taxonomie des espèces animales dans l'Égypte gréco-romaine," *BSFE* 156 (2003): 7–19, at 11.

34. Greek text from West, "The Greek Version of the Legend of Tefnut," 181. The transformation of the monkey, which directly follows that of the goddess into a gazelle, is not dwelt upon in the Demotic text; see Thissen, "Lost in Translation?," 162.

λύγξ—rather than with a more common and/or generic Greek noun for monkey—that confirms the importance placed on this noun in both versions. The translator must have been aware of the fact that *kwf* was not used in the original text as a loose term for any sort of monkey, let alone a baboon.

But let us now look closer into what type of monkey a simian *lynx* could typically designate in Greek. Unfortunately, the available data is very scarce. In contrast with its more common use to indicate a wildcat, the term is employed to describe a monkey only in a handful of Greek and Latin authors from the imperial period. Typically, hardly anything specific is said about this species. Thus, the polymath Pliny the Elder (*Nat.* 8.72) mentions the *lynx*-monkey in a chapter dealing with the fauna of ancient Ethiopia, in combination with the *sphinx* (another kind of African monkey), while the dream interpreter Artemidorus of Daldis (*Onir.* 2.12) lists it within a section discussing dreams about monkeys.[35] Some more information, however, comes from the physician Galen, who discusses various types of monkeys in two of his works, *De anatomicis administrationibus* and *De usu partium*, also offering some anatomical information about them. A passage in the latter tract (11.2) is particularly informative, for it discusses, among others, both the λύγξ and the κυνοκέφαλος (baboon). The former simian is grouped with other types of monkeys, for, according to Galen, they all share an oral setup similar to that of humans: a short mandible, weaker temporal muscles, and smaller teeth. The κυνοκέφαλος is instead set somewhat aside, "for this is by nature between a monkey and a dog" (μεταξὺ γάρ τοι τὴν φύσιν οὗτός ἐστι πιθήκου καὶ κυνός), very much according to its name.[36] Consequently, Galen remarks, its jaws are different from those of other, more human-like monkeys, as the κυνοκέφαλος/baboon displays a longer mandible, stronger temporal muscles, and larger teeth. Based on Galen's words, we can thus conclude that, to a Greek author of the second century CE like him (one contemporary, *nota bene*, to the date of the Greek Myth of the Sun's Eye's papyrus), a simian *lynx* was a kind of African monkey clearly distinct from a baboon. Any zoological classification more specific than this is hardly possible, however, based on this sole evidence.[37]

It is only the translingual evidence stemming from the Greek version of the Myth of the Sun's Eye that enables us to better define what simian was meant by the Greek noun λύγξ. Since the compounds *wnš-kwf*/λυκόλυγξ clearly indicate a baboon or baboon-like simian, and since *kwf* is patently used in contrast to it, that is, in its etymological meaning as guenon, it is an inescapable conclusion that its Greek counterpart, the λύγξ, must also indicate a species of guenon. This is clearly how the translator understood the noun λύγξ—and who would have been better suited to precisely identify and name a guenon, an African monkey commonly imported into Egypt, than the Greek translator of the Myth of the Sun's Eye, a learned bilingual inhabitant of Egypt equally versed in Demotic and Greek?[38] It should also not surprise that the translator did not render *kwf* with κῆβος/κῆπος, a common Greek word for monkey which is related to—and most likely derives from—Egyptian *kwf*.[39] In the first place, the noun λύγξ must have indi-

35. Perhaps unsurprisingly, Pliny's passage is still commonly misunderstood to this day, with his mention of *lynxes* being mistaken for a reference to wildcats. See, e.g., Ragnar Kinzelbach, *Tierbilder aus dem ersten Jahrhundert: Ein zoologischer Kommentar zum Artemidor-Papyrus*, APFB 28 (Berlin: de Gruyter, 2009), 99. Artemidorus's passage is instead generally overlooked; it is, for instance, missed by McDermott, *The Ape in Antiquity*. Incidentally, the mention of a λύγξ in the magical invocations of PGM 13.880 (the only such mention in this corpus) is rather ambiguous. Given the solar context of this spell, it seems possible to understand it as a simian *lynx*; however, no element speaks necessarily against a feline identification either (with thanks to Korshi Dosoo, Würzburg, for discussing this passage with me). See Betz, *The Greek Magical Papyri in Translation*, 192.

36. The quote is from *De usu partium* 11.2 (= Kühn III, 844). Galen's text is also discussed in McDermott, *The Ape in Antiquity*, 95–96.

37. See already McDermott, *The Ape in Antiquity*, 72 ("the *lynx* [...] is probably some species of monkey rather than a baboon"), 95–96 ("the lynx was an ape, probably one with a tail"), 105 ("[t]he λύγξ of Galen is probably a monkey, but no species can be given").

38. I have already discarded as heavily flawed past suggestions that the translation of the Myth of the Sun's Eye might have been a two-stage process, with a rough translation by a native Egyptian scribe being later embellished by a Greek writer with literary skills. See Prada, "For a New Edition of P.Lond.Lit. 192," 632.

3 . See, e.g., *DG*, 562 (s.v. *kf*); Wolfhart Westendorf, *Koptisches Handwörterbuch* (Heidelberg: Winter, 1965–1977), 462 (s.v. ϭⲁⲡⲓ, ϭⲁⲡⲉⲓ); Vernus and Yoyotte, *Bestiaire des pharaons*, 620. The noun is also found in biblical Hebrew, as קוֹף (*qoph*), and remains today

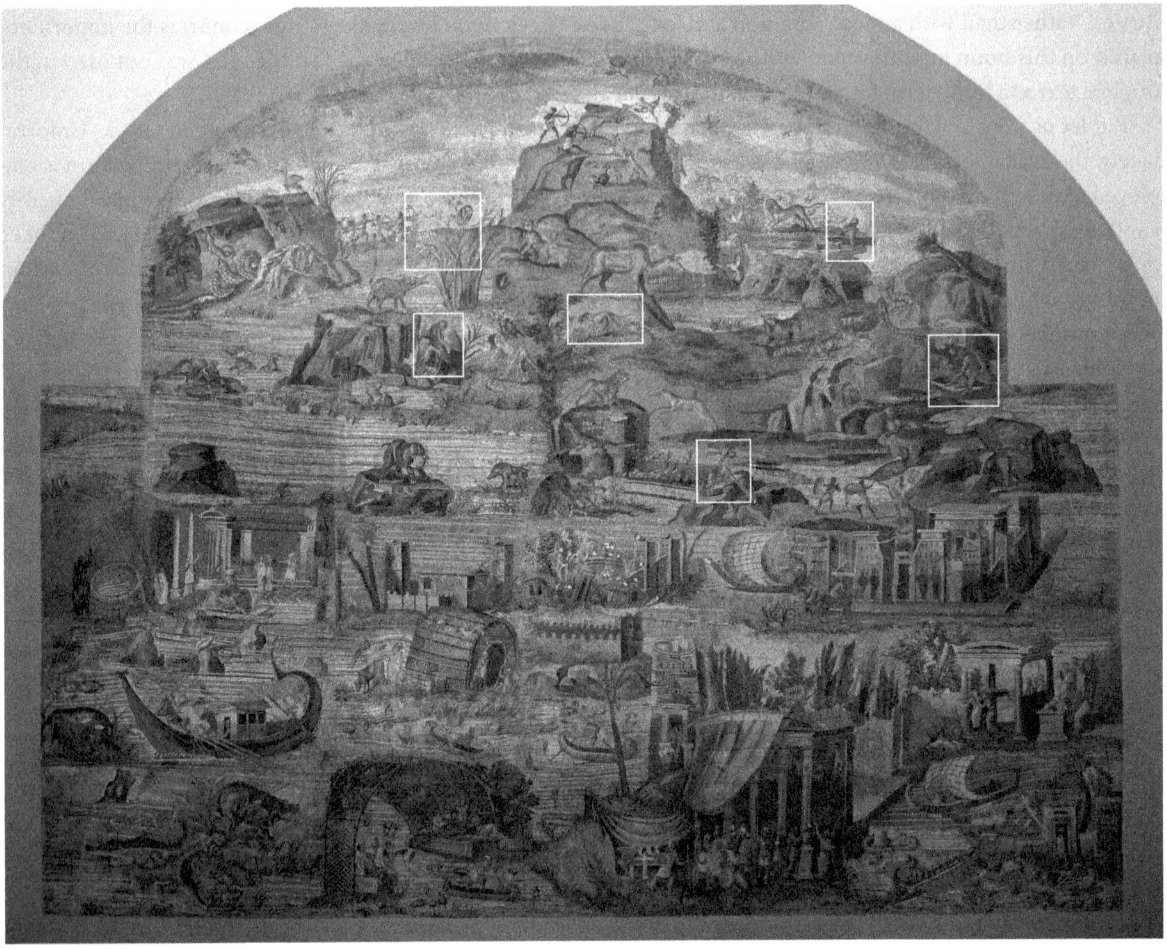

Figure 5. The Nile Mosaic, Museo Archeologico Nazionale, Palestrina, with indication of the monkeys featured in it (courtesy of Polo Museale del Lazio, Rome).

cated an exact species of guenon, the one intended by the translator (which one, it will probably remain impossible for us to say), while κῆβος was often used as a generic noun to indicate any type of simian with a tail, and was thus less relevant to our translator's needs.[40] In the second place—and more importantly—some Greek authors describe the κῆβος as having features resembling those of a baboon.[41] This naturally disqualified this word in the eyes of our translator, who was looking for a type of guenon that was clearly distinguished from a baboon (or a baboon-like monkey, depending on the exact value of λυκόλυγξ). Hence, regardless of the affinity between the two words, our translator never really had the option to translate Demotic *kwf* with κῆβος.

the main word for "monkey" in modern Hebrew. It is, however, more plausible that it came to Greek from Egyptian, and not Hebrew; see Heinrich Lewy, *Die semitischen Fremdwörter im Griechischen* (Berlin: Gaertners, 1895), 6. But see now also the comparative analysis, taking into consideration a wider pool of ancient languages, in Francis Breyer, *Tanutamani: Die Traumstele und ihr Umfeld*, ÄAT 57 (Wiesbaden: Harrassowitz, 2003), 325–26.

40. See McDermott, *The Ape in Antiquity*, 68–69.

41. An example is Aelian (also an author from the second–third century CE), who, in *Nat. an.* 17.8 says of the κῆπος: "and as for the shape of its face, you will be right if you compare it to that of a baboon" (προσώπου δὲ μορφή, κυνοκεφάλῳ παραβαλὼν αὐτὴν ἀληθεύσεις).

Moving now beyond the boundaries of textual evidence, one further attestation of a simian *lynx*—and one that could corroborate its proposed identification with a guenon—is possibly found in the visual arts of antiquity. For I believe that the representation of a disputed animal in the renowned Nile Mosaic of Palestrina might be the earliest attestation of a *lynx*-monkey (fig. 5).

This colossal mosaic, which probably dates to the end of the second century BCE and has a Ptolemaic, Alexandrian model, famously depicts an idealized bird's-eye view of the Nile, extending from its Delta up to the wilderness of Sudanese Nubia or classical Ethiopia.[42] The upper section of the mosaic, with its Nubian landscapes, includes numerous scenes of wildlife, in which plenty of African animals are depicted, often accompanied by captions in Greek. Among these animals, a number of monkeys also appear. Table 1 gathers all simians clearly featured in the scene.[43]

Table 1. Monkeys in the Nile Mosaic of Palestrina.

Type of monkey	Greek caption	Action depicted	Location within mosaic	Image
guenon	n/a	sitting on rock	section 1	
guenon (red monkey?)	CΦINΓIA *lege* σφιγγία = *sphinx*-monkeys (× 2)[44]	on shrub/tree: one sitting, the other scampering along branch	section 2	

42. On this artifact and related issues, including its dating, I refer the reader to Paul G. P. Meyboom, *The Nile Mosaic of Palestrina: Early Evidence of Egyptian Religion in Italy*, RGRW 121 (Leiden: Brill, 1995). By a serendipitous coincidence, the honorand of this Festschrift has also busied himself with this masterwork of ancient musive art: see Richard Jasnow, review of *The Nile Mosaic of Palestrina: Early Evidence of Egyptian Religion in Italy*, by Paul G. P. Meyboom, *JAOS* 119 (1999): 165–66.

43. For the type of monkey, I only offer the identification suggested by Meyboom, *The Nile Mosaic of Palestrina*, 21–22, 25–26, 48. As for the location of the figures within the mosaic, I refer to its sections according to the numbering in Meyboom, *The Nile Mosaic of Palestrina*, fig. 7. The position of all these monkeys (as well as the *lynx*) is also highlighted in the general view of the Nile Mosaic given as fig. 5 here. All images of the mosaic included in the present article were taken by Paul D. Wordsworth, with the kind assistance of the museum staff, during a visit to Palestrina in July 2020.

44. This is the plural of neuter σφιγγίον, a diminutive of standard σφίγξ (as already suggested by Meyboom, *The Nile Mosaic of Palestrina*, 22), and surely not a feminine singular variant of that word (as instead argued by McDermott, *The Ape in Antiquity*, 284, who also erroneously discerns here only one monkey, instead of two—see n. 52 below). The existence of a neuter singular word σφιγγίον in Greek (and not a feminine σφίγγια, which is a ghost word) is confirmed by Latin borrowings attested in Pliny the Elder, *Nat.* 6.184 and 6.173 (singular, *animal sphingion*, and plural, *sphingia*, respectively). The use of a plural here for the *sphinx*-monkeys also matches the

guenon (green monkey?)	n/a	sitting on rock	section 2	
baboon	ΚΗΠΙΕΝ[45] *lege* κηπίον = small *kepos*-monkey	on tree, scampering along branch	section 6	
baboon (Anubis baboon?)[46]	[CATTYOC][47] *lege* σάτυρος = *satyros*-monkey	sitting on rock	section 7	

conventions of the mosaic: for the animal names that it provides are given in the plural, in those cases in which more than one specimen of the same species are depicted. Compare, for instance, the two spotted hyaenas in section 1, which are labeled as ΘΩΑΝΤΕC—that is, θώαντες, a plural form from singular θώς—and the two cheetahs in section 7, which are accompanied by the caption ΤΙΓΡΙC—clearly not a writing for the singular τίγρις, but for the plural τίγρεις (misspelt through iotacism). On these two couples of animals, see Meyboom, *The Nile Mosaic of Palestrina*, 21–22, 115–18, and 26, 122–24, respectively.

45. My reading (also of McDermott, *The Ape in Antiquity*, 285). Meyboom, *The Nile Mosaic of Palestrina*, 25, reads the even odder ΚΗΙΥΙΕΝ (still understanding it as a diminutive of κῆπος). Note also how this monkey, which is labeled as a sort of κῆπος, seemingly displays the features of a baboon. This is another confirmation of the possible overlap between guenon and baboon species that can characterize the use of this term, on which, see n. 41 above.

46. Following Meyboom, *The Nile Mosaic of Palestrina*, 25. I need not discuss here the possible mismatch between the simian portrayed (seemingly, a baboon) and the name assigned to it (a *satyros* is a guenon), about which, see Meyboom, *The Nile Mosaic of Palestrina*, 48, 227–28n19, 240n62.

47. The caption is now lost, but is recorded in early modern copies, the Dal Pozzo watercolors (on which, see n. 64 below): Meyboom, *The Nile Mosaic of Palestrina*, 26. For images of the Dal Pozzo drawings that include the simians here under discussion, see Helen Whitehouse, *Ancient Mosaics and Wallpaintings*, PMCDPA 1 (London: Harvey Miller, 2001), 88–91 (nos. 1–2), 98–101 (nos. 6–7).

Overall, the mosaic displays an impressive catalogue of African simians, with at least six specimens of probably five different species.[48] But it is possible that there may be one further monkey, hiding in plain sight, to be spotted in this mosaic: a *lynx*. Found in section 6, placed halfway between the small *kepos* and the *satyros*, but at a somewhat lower level within the composition, a curious creature is sitting on a rock. It looks in the direction of a group of Nubian hunters, towering above one of them, who is busy shooting his arrows across a marshy area to the left, in the direction of the water-hogs (fig. 6).

Figure 6. The *lynx* in the Nile Mosaic (section 6), Museo Archeologico Nazionale, Palestrina (courtesy of Polo Museale del Lazio, Rome).

The animal's coat has two shades: a lighter one, of a beige hue, on its tummy and face, and a darker brown color on its back and limbs. It also shows a spotted or speckled pattern. The face is curiously flat, with just the two eyes and a large, protruding nose. The animal is identified by the caption ΛΥΝΞ (*lege* λύγξ).

Needless to say, studies of the mosaic categorize this animal as a feline lynx, pointing out that this is, of course, not the Eurasian lynx, but an "African lynx" (an inexact, but often still used, designation), that is, a caracal (*Caracal caracal*) or a serval (*Leptailurus serval*).[49] Such an identification is often presented in contemporary studies as self-evident, undoubtedly because of the presence of the Greek caption. But, if one is to look at it more closely, things appear to be more problematic. For starters, not all of the literature on the topic has been equally univocal or unproblematic in its dealing with this animal. Earlier studies—in fact, even some of the earliest antiquarian publications on the Nile Mosaic—saw in this creature a monkey.[50] Such is their conviction in seeing in this figure a simian, they go as far as to assign the caption λύγξ (which, of course, they also understand as referring to a felid) to the running animal above it, while matching the simian with the Greek caption to its right, ΑΓΕΛΑΡΥ (or ΑΓΕΛΑΡΧ, *lege*

48. It has been suggested that the mosaic might have originally included yet another monkey, labeled as a κυνοκέφαλος, the figure of which would now be completely lost. This, however, is a highly dubious conjecture, which is based on a suggested restoration to [κυνοκ]έφαλος of a caption in section 6, which reads ΕΦΑΛΟC; see Helen Whitehouse, *The Dal Pozzo Copies of the Palestrina Mosaic*, BAR-SS 12 (Oxford: British Archaeological Reports, 1976), 90–91n21. It is in fact much more plausible that this caption should be supplied and emended into [χοιρ]έλαφος, and matched with the image of the warthog located just beneath it, in section 10; see Meyboom, *The Nile Mosaic of Palestrina*, 25, 237–38n55. Note, also, that the conjecture about the κυνοκέφαλος seems to have recently been discarded by its original deviser too, in favor of the χοιρέλαφος; see now Whitehouse, *Ancient Mosaics and Wallpaintings*, 98 (no. 6). On a related note, the animal in section 9, with the caption ΧΟΙΡΟΠΙΘΙΚ (*lege* χοιροπίθηκος), is a water-hog of sorts. Its name, a compound of πίθηκος, should not mislead one into believing it a type of monkey. See Meyboom, *The Nile Mosaic of Palestrina*, 26, 125–26.

49. Among many others, see Meyboom, *The Nile Mosaic of Palestrina*, 25. Given the Nubian setting, these two large species of felids would be the most obvious candidates; not so much the domestic cat-sized African wildcat (*Felis silvestris libyca*), which was common throughout Egypt. On lynxes and wildcats in Egypt, see De Cenival, "Lyco-lynx et chacal-singe dans le *Mythe de l'œil du soleil*" (bearing in mind, however, that parts of her study ought to be used with caution, and that her core thesis—trying to justify why the Greek version of the Myth of the Sun's Eye should replace the simian creature of the Demotic original with a feline lynx—is now superseded). Specifically, on Egyptian wildcats, see Jaromir Malek, *The Cat in Ancient Egypt* (London: British Museum Press, 1993), 15–44.

50. See, e.g., Jean-Jacques Barthélemy, *Explication de la mosaïque de Palestrine* (Paris: H.L. Guérin & L.F. Delatour, 1760), 37–38 ("une espece de Singe"); Sante Pieralisi, *Osservazioni sul musaico di Palestrina* (Rome: Tipografia Salviucci, 1858), 31 ("un gagliardo vecchio della specie delle scimmie"); Orazio Marucchi, "Il grande mosaico prenestino ed il 'lithostroton' di Silla," DPAA S. II 10/1 (1910): 149–90, at 174 ("un'altra specie di scimmia"), an identification repeated in Orazio Marucchi, *Guida archeologica della città di Palestrina l'antica Preneste* (Rome: Enzo Pinci, 1932), 83. In more recent times, see Salvatore Aurigemma, "Il restauro di consolidamento del mosaico Barberini, condotto nel 1952," *RAR* S. III 30–31 (1957–1959): 41–98, at 86 ("una scimmia").

ἀγελάρχης), "leader," hence believing it to be described as the head of its troop of fellow monkeys.[51] Of course, such a reshuffling of the legends is untenable. The darting beast above is clearly an equine, surely an onager, and has nothing to do with the caption λύγξ, which does pertain to our problematic animal. Conversely, the caption read as ἀγελάρχης must refer to the leader of the Nubian hunters, and not to an animal. This being said, the confirmation that our animal is indeed to be matched with the *lynx* caption surely does not help solve the uncertainty about its feline versus simian identity. This is proven by the fact that a number of those scholars who do believe it to be a wildcat still point out its unsettling similarity with a monkey.[52]

Let us look at this animal's appearance in further detail. It is quickly evident that, even if we were to accept the identification of it as a large wildcat, it can hardly be a caracal. This felid's fur is uniform in color, without spots, and is radically different to the one seen in the mosaic. If anything, we would need to think of another African wildcat with a spotted coat, such as a serval.[53] There remains, however, a major issue with this identification, as well as with any other wildcat-related proposals: the evident lack of ears in the mosaic's portrayal of our beast.

Indeed, one of the most obvious characteristics of both the caracal and the serval are their conspicuous ears. In the case of the caracal, these are very pointy, ending in tufts of hair. Such hairy ears are regularly featured in depictions of caracals from classical art, sometimes with almost grotesque outcomes, as in the case of the "African lynx" (explicitly captioned as ΛΥΝΞ) in the famous hunting scene of Tomb I from the rock-cut necropolis of Marisa/Maresha, in modern-day Israel (fig. 7).[54] The painted frieze of Marisa dates from approximately the late third century BCE, at a time when the region was under Ptolemaic control.[55] Its style thus pertains to the same artistic *koine* that produced the Palestrina mosaic, one with strong Alexandrian connections.

Figure 7. The lynx (caracal) in the hunting frieze of Tomb I, Marisa (courtesy of the Palestine Exploration Fund, London).

Another, somewhat later depiction of a lynx is on the *verso* of the Artemidorus Papyrus (dating from around the turn of the first century BCE and CE), included among its famous animal sketches.[56] Here, what is clearly also a caracal, accompanied by the label ΛΥΓΞ,

51. See Meyboom, *The Nile Mosaic of Palestrina*, 238–39nn56–57.

52. See, e.g., Otto Keller, *Die antike Tierwelt: Erster Band: Säugetiere* (Leipzig: Wilhelm Engelmann, 1909), 84: "[d]ieser Luchs ist ohne Zweifel schlecht restauriert; er sieht mehr einem Menschenaffen gleich als einem Luchs" (the problem of modern restorations in the mosaic is treated further on in my discussion). See also McDermott, *The Ape in Antiquity*, 285: "a lynx [...] which has been taken for a monkey [...] does at first glance look a little like a monkey [...] but is surely a real lynx of the cat family." Note, however, that McDermott is extremely cautious, if not miserly, in his identification of monkeys in the Nile Mosaic, for he also rejects the simian classification of one of the *sphinx*-monkeys (which he wrongly describes as being "on the ground," rather than on a tree branch) and of the small *kepos* (McDermott, *The Ape in Antiquity*, 284–85). Instead, he sees in them two felids—surely, mistakenly so.

53. So already Meyboom, *The Nile Mosaic of Palestrina*, 25.

54. David M. Jacobson, *The Hellenistic Paintings of Marisa*, PEFA 7 (Leeds: Maney and The Palestine Exploration Fund, 2007), 35 (no. 17), pls. 26, 28, xv.

55. On the possibility of a slightly later, Seleucid date for Tomb I—which, nevertheless, would not detract from the Ptolemaic "artistic fashions" inspiring its paintings—see Dov Gera, "Some Dated Greek Inscriptions from Maresha," *PEQ* 149 (2017): 201–22, at 211–12.

56. I am aware of the notorious debate about the disputed authenticity of this manuscript. A good overview of it (concluding in favor of the papyrus's genuineness) remains that by Giambattista D'Alessio, "On the 'Artemidorus' Papyrus," *ZPE* 171 (2009): 27–43.

is attacking a "wild goat" (αἴγαγρος).[57] The ears with their tufts of dark hair are perfectly reproduced (fig. 8).

Even when we move beyond depictions of caracals in classical art and look at earlier examples from pharaonic Egypt, the same is true: in pharaonic art conventions, too, the animal's distinctive ears are faithfully portrayed.[58]

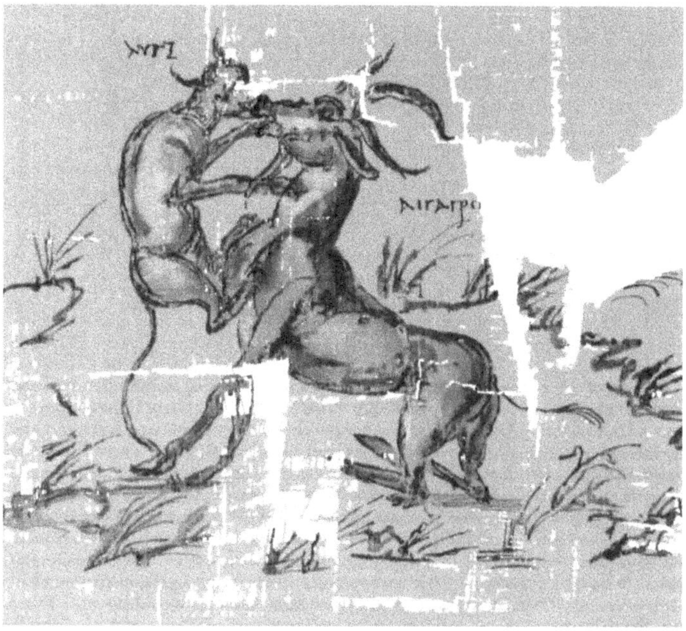

Figure 8. The lynx (caracal) in the Artemidorus Papyrus (after Gallazzi *et al.*, *Il papiro di Artemidoro*).

Thinking of our *lynx* as a serval—which, as we already saw, would be a better match with its spotted coat—is also of little help. The ears of a serval have no zany tufts of hair, to be sure. Yet, they are still are very noticeable and clearly stand out, for they appear somewhat disproportioned, if not oversized, with respect to the animal's head. No doubt, had the artist intended to portray a serval, its distinctive ears could not have been left out.[59] This is confirmed by the depiction of a couple of cheetahs in section 7 of the mosaic, identified in the caption as τίγρεις (fig. 9).[60] Quite the opposite of a serval, cheetahs are large cats with relatively small ears, yet these are clearly portrayed in the mosaic.[61] Overall, it therefore appears impossible to me that this *lynx* should be a wildcat, whether caracal, serval, or even another type of wild felid. The omission of ears in its depiction is, on its own, incompatible with such an interpretation.

The Palestrina mosaic in its current form differs significantly from the original ancient artwork, due to losses and rearrangements of sections within it, and, most importantly, heavy restorations that have taken place over the centuries.[62] Before coming to any conclusions concerning the image of the *lynx*, it is hence necessary to check whether it has been restored and, if so, whether its current aspect matches the original one.

57. Claudio Gallazzi, Bärbel Kramer, and Salvatore Settis, eds., *Il papiro di Artemidoro (P.Artemid.)* (Milan: LED, 2008), 447–50 (no. V38), pls. xvi, lx. See also Kinzelbach, *Tierbilder aus dem ersten Jahrhundert*, 99–100 (V38a), pl. xl.

58. See two fine examples from the Old and Middle Kingdoms in Louis Keimer, "*Inb*, le caracal (*Caracal caracal* Schmitzi Matsch.) dans l'Égypte ancienne," *ASAE* 48 (1948): 373–407, at 376 (fig. 1), pls. i, viii. Vernus and Yoyotte, *Bestiaire des pharaons*, 168, lament the general lack of diagnostic features between different types of wildcats in Egyptian art, but this is clearly not the case with the caracal, as the examples in Keimer's study show.

59. When it comes to depictions of the serval in classical art, it is difficult to tell this species apart from other felids sporting a spotted coat. Whatever the exact nature of the (wild) cat depicted, the ears are, however, always reproduced. Somewhat less problematic to identify, though still far from straightforward, is the portrayal of servals in Egyptian pharaonic art; see Pierre Meyrat, "*Miw ꜥ3*: Grand chat ou serval?," *GM* 224 (2010): 87–92.

60. Meyboom, *The Nile Mosaic of Palestrina*, 26, 122–24. With regard to these animals' original caption, see n. 44 above.

61. The same attention to ears applies also to nonfelids in our mosaic. See, for instance, the spotted hyaenas in section 1, the lovely bear in section 7 (visible, to the left of the cheetahs, here in fig. 9), or the rhinoceros in section 9; Meyboom, *The Nile Mosaic of Palestrina*, 21–22, 26.

62. On the modern history of the mosaic, the restorations it underwent starting with the seventeenth century, and its reconstruction, see Meyboom, *The Nile Mosaic of Palestrina*, 3–7, to which add Whitehouse, *Ancient Mosaics and Wallpaintings*, 76–78.

Figure 9. The *tigreis* (cheetahs) in the Nile Mosaic (section 7), Museo Archeologico Nazionale, Palestrina (courtesy of Polo Museale del Lazio, Rome).

As it happens, our figure is indeed partly, if not largely, the result of modern restorations.[63] However, the reproduction of our *lynx* in the Dal Pozzo set of watercolors—early copies of the mosaic dating from approximately 1627, just before it underwent a first, large-scale restoration in Rome—shows that our animal in its current form is original, and the seventeenth century restoration did not redesign it (fig. 10).[64] If anything, the Dal Pozzo copy of the *lynx* slightly misrepresents some of its features (as sometimes is also the case with other watercolors from this set): most remarkably, it does not mark the animal's spotted coat, giving it, instead, a sort of mane similar to that of the lioness (*sic*, λέαινα) to its left.[65] But what matters most here is that the Dal Pozzo copy also gives our animal no ears. Hence, one can confidently conclude that these were never present, and surely were never lost in a maladroit early restoration attempt.[66]

63. How much of this part of the mosaic is original, and how much restored, can be seen in the images provided in the two main studies on the topic: Giorgio Gullini, *I mosaici di Palestrina*, SArchClass 1 (Rome: Archeologia Classica, 1956), pl. xxiv; and Aurigemma, "Il restauro di consolidamento del mosaico Barberini," 85 (fig. 46). Note, however, that Gullini's and Aurigemma's respective assessments differ quite significantly, with regard to both the *lynx* and other parts of the mosaic; on this problem, see also Meyboom, *The Nile Mosaic of Palestrina*, 198n12.

64. The copy is in Windsor Castle, Royal Library, inv. no. 19206, published in Whitehouse, *Ancient Mosaics and Wallpaintings*, 99 (fig. 6, in color) = Whitehouse, *The Dal Pozzo Copies of the Palestrina Mosaic*, 36 (fig. 6a, in black and white). Specifically, on the date of the Dal Pozzo drawings, see Whitehouse, *Ancient Mosaics and Wallpaintings*, 74–76.

65. Note that the *lynx*'s spotted coat is unquestionably genuine, as it is preserved in the surviving original section of the mosaic (according to both Gullini and Aurigemma; see n. 63 above). The mane too is clearly an artistic licence by the modern copyist, which is not reflected in the original figure.

66. To play devil's advocate, even if a "creative" restoration had taken place on our *lynx* in the earlier 1600s (and we know, in fact,

Figure 10. The *lynx* in the Dal Pozzo copy of the Nile Mosaic (after Whitehouse, *Ancient Mosaics and Wallpaintings*).

Figure 11. A baby of De Brazza's monkey (*Cercopithecus neglectus*), a guenon with a characteristically speckled coat (© Lynne Gorrie, Blackpool Zoo).

On account of all of the above, I believe that the *lynx* depicted in the Nile Mosaic is a simian *lynx*. As previously argued, the most telling feature is its head, especially the lack of protruding ears. As regards its body, the appearance of its hindquarters, which has been understood as feline, is in fact compatible with the representation of other monkeys in the mosaic. A good comparison is with the small *kepos* in section 6, scampering along a branch, the body of which also shows a slender waist, and which indeed has also been occasionally mistaken for a large cat.[67] The straight, fully extended arms of the *lynx* also find parallels in the posture of yet another monkey, this time in the *satyros* of section 7, which also sits on a rock, and whose left arm is in the same position. Finally, the remarkable spotted coat of our *lynx* can also be understood as a simian feature, so depicted in order to reproduce the speckled coat that characterizes many species of guenons (fig. 11). Indeed, when we consider the physical features of this simian—the flat face (as opposed, for instance, to the protruding snout of baboons) and the speckled coat—they all point at its identification with a guenon, as we would indeed now expect from the name given in the caption, λύγξ.

As for which exact type of guenon may be represented in the Nile Mosaic, this is a question that I do not think can be answered satisfactorily. A survey of various species of guenons attested in East Africa can produce various plausi-

---

that no such thing happened before the Dal Pozzo copies were made), one would still expect a Renaissance restorer to give the animal visible ears, for this is how contemporary European depictions typically represent such a wildcat (in this case, based on the Eurasian lynx, whose ears are similar to the caracal's). A good example is, for instance, the lynx depicted in 1521 by Albrecht Dürer in a drawing now at the Sterling and Francine Clark Art Institute, Williamstown MA, inv. no. 1955.1848 (online at: https://www.clarkart.edu/ArtPiece/Detail/Sketches-of-Animals-and-Landscapes). Even closer in space and time to our mosaic, in Rome, in 1603, the newly founded Accademia dei Lincei (today, Accademia Nazionale dei Lincei) adopted as its emblem the lynx: its logo, since its first 1603 incarnation, has always depicted a wildcat with large ears (a historical overview of the Lincei's logo is online at: http://www.lincei-celebrazioni.it/istoria_lince.html).

67. See n. 52 above.

ble options, but none can be offered, in my opinion, with any actual degree of certainty. As in the case of our lexicographical study concerning what monkey a simian *lynx* is, here too in the field of the visual arts we must acknowledge the limits of the evidence available to us, and be satisfied with recognizing in this depiction a guenon, *tout court.*

Epilogue

In conclusion, I hope that the present publication of a new, small fragment of the papyrus containing the Greek translation of the Myth of the Sun's Eye will provide further impulse to studies on this fascinating composition, from both a textual and a material perspective. Its identification sheds further light on the manuscript's modern history and can further help corroborate a provenance of the papyrus from the Roman Fayum—perhaps, even more specifically, from Soknopaiou Nesos. At the same time, the study of the animal identity of the male protagonist of the tale, with his simian hypostases precisely defined in both Demotic and Greek, clarifies his association with two specific genera of monkeys, while showing, at the same time, remarkable parallels with lesser-known aspects of the theology of Thoth as attested in other Egyptian sources. Namely, the simian protagonist is pictured as a kind of baboon, or baboon-resembling species, in the first part of the tale (under the name of *wnš-kwf*/λυκόλυγξ), to then transform himself into a guenon (a *kwf*/λύγξ). The Nile Mosaic of Palestrina, which originally stems from a Hellenized Egyptian milieu as much as our Greek translation, probably even offers us a unique visual representation of what a *lynx*-guenon looked like.

Hopefully, these sundries will also have served the purpose of reminding the reader of a lesson that I, alongside many others, have learnt from Richard's publications: namely, that the later phases of Egypt's history still offer us invaluable and fascinating material aplenty to explore, perhaps even more so when we turn our attention to the junction between the ancient Egyptian and other Mediterranean cultures.

Ein frühdemotischer Weisheitstext: Papyrus Berlin 23504

Joachim Quack

Wenn ich die vorliegende Edition[1] Richard Jasnow widme, so hat dies insofern eine spezielle Note, als er selbst die erste gedruckte Erwähnung dieses Papyrus geliefert hat.[2] Er kennt ihn also sicher bereits gut, und ich kann nur hoffen, daß er sich darüber freut, wenn er für die Forschung insgesamt zugänglich wird. Vielleicht kann ich zudem zumindest die eine oder andere Nuance beisteuern, die er als bereichernd empfindet.

Über die Herkunft des Fragments ist leider kaum etwas bekannt. Das Inventarbuch bietet lediglich die Angabe „Ankauf 1966 (87/66)".

Technische Beschreibung

Heller Papyrus, 20,4 × 19,1 cm. Die Rückseite ist schlechter als die Vorderseite gearbeitet. Eine erhaltene Klebung ca. 8,0 cm vom rechten Rand, wohl ca. 2 cm breit. Unten ca. 5 cm freier Rand; darin eine unklare kleine Tintenspur. Im Bereich der Klebung fehlt auf dem rechten Blatt auf einem kleinen Bereich von ca. 2,4 cm Höhe etwa 1,5 mm Rektofaser; die Beschriftung sitzt hier direkt auf freiliegenden Vertikalfasern. Dieser Befund deutet auf eine vierlagige Klebung hin. In einigen Teilen fallen die Fasern des vorderen Blattes zur Klebung hin deutlich ab.

Auf dem unteren Rand befindet sich eine deutliche vertikale Linie, etwas darüber Reste, die eventuell zum Kopf desselben Zeichens gehören und dann als Seitenzahl 5 zu verstehen sein könnten. Die möglichen Implikationen dieser Deutung sollen unten weiter verfolgt werden.

Die Schrift ist sorgfältig und kalligraphisch mit relativ viel Freiraum zwischen den Zeilen; auch angesichts des breiten unteren Randes ist die Handschrift als großzügige, qualitätvolle Buchrolle zu betrachten. Es gibt zwei auffällige dünne Linien, einmal von Z. x+4 (das *g* von *gy*) bis x+5 (der oberste Teil von *ḥꜣ.tỉ*), und ein anderes Mal von Z. x+9 (das *ꜣ* von *ꜣšw*) bis x+10 (durch den vorderen Teil von *ẖbt*).

Auf dem Verso sind stark verwischte und kaum lesbare Schriftreste vorhanden; das Material ist stark grau, mutmaßlich Palimpsest. Es gibt insbesondere rechts oben viele kleine Oberflächenabsplitterungen, die hellweiß hervorstechen. Solche Phänomene kenne ich insbesondere von Texten, die in der Schülerausbildung eingesetzt wurden.[3]

Vom äußeren Erscheinungsbild macht der Papyrus den Eindruck, zerrissen worden zu sein. Besonders deutlich ist dies an der Kante oben rechts, die schräg zu den Fasern läuft, was bei Bruchkanten unüblich ist. Auffällig sind auch die fallweise längeren Einzelfasern, die über den sonstigen Rand hervorstehen.

1. Für ein gutes Photo des Papyrus und die freundlich gewährte Publikationsgenehmigung danke ich Verena Lepper. Das Bild stammt von Sandra Steiß.

2. Richard Jasnow, *A Late Period Hieratic Wisdom Text (P. Brooklyn 47.218.135)*, SAOC 52 (Chicago: University of Chicago Press, 1992), 40 Anm. 63.

3. Joachim Friedrich Quack, „A Text Says More Than a Thousand Words", in *The Idea of Writing: From Scribbles to Master Scribe*, hg. Alex de Voogt und Reinhard Lehmann (Leiden: Brill, in Druck); Joachim Friedrich Quack, „Eine Liste von Formen des Mond-Thot", in *Hieratic Texts from Tebtunis Including a Survey of Illustrated Papyri*, hg. Kim Ryholt (Kopenhagen: Museum Tusculanum Press, 2020), 19–24, dort 23–24.

Datierung

Eine Datierung des vorliegenden Papyrus ist nur anhand der Paläographie möglich, wobei die relativ geringe verfügbare Menge an Zeichen die Möglichkeiten einschränkt. Bei der ersten Erwähnung wurde der Papyrus als möglicherweise ins 5. Jahrhundert v. Chr. datiert angegeben.[4] Friedhelm Hoffmann hat dagegen vorgeschlagen, die Hand ins 4. Jahrhundert v. Chr. zu setzen.[5] Dies steht bei ihm im Rahmen eines größeren Modells, daß nach einer Unterbrechung bzw. rein oralen Phase die demotische Literatur in demotischer Schrift nach dem Ende der ersten Perserherrschaft einsetzt. Als Argument für die vorgeschlagene Datierung dient ihm insbesondere die große Nähe zur Schrift des pChicago OI 17481 = pChicago Hawara I, der auf das Jahr 17 des Nektanebes (I.), 2. Monat der Überschwemmungszeit (365/364 v. Chr.) datiert ist.[6]

Die Heranziehung dieser Urkunde für die paläographische Datierung wirft allerdings Fragen von grundsätzlicher Bedeutung für die Methodik von Datierungen auf: pChicago Hawara 1 wirkt, verglichen mit anderen demotischen Handschriften dieser Zeit, insgesamt „archaisierend" bzw. wohl besser „retardierend".[7] Ist der Zustand seiner Schrift damit punktuell genau für den Zeitpunkt seiner Niederschrift ein maßgeblicher Anker (wie Hoffmann offenbar angenommen hat), oder kann man für eine zunächst unbestimmte Menge vorangehender Jahre von der Existenz eines ganz ähnlichen Duktus ausgehen? Beispielhaft für die lange Beharrung kann man z.B. den römerzeitlichen Duktus von Soknopaiou Nesos erwähnen, der sich über mehr als 100 Jahre so wenig entwickelt, daß man allenfalls anhand weniger spezieller Zeichen unterschiedliche Schreiberhände unterscheiden kann.[8] Für Hawara speziell hat man das Problem, daß es von diesem Ort keine älteren Handschriften zum Vergleich gibt. Hinzu kommt das generelle Problem, daß die zweite Hälfte des 5. Jhdts. v. Chr. sehr schlecht mit datierten demotischen Texten dokumentiert ist.[9]

Auch in ptolemäerzeitlichen Urkunden aus Memphis können relikthaft ältere Zeichenformen nachgewiesen werden, aber meist im selben Dokument mit jüngeren Formen variierend.[10] Für eine Datierung sollten somit weniger die archaisch wirkenden Zeichenformen ausschlaggebend sein, sondern diejenigen, die vergleichsweise am jüngsten sind. Der hier publizierte Papyrus ist immerhin im erhaltenen Bereich sehr regelmäßig und konsistent in seinen Formen.

Besonders auffällig sind die ausführliche Form von *ỉrm* Z. x+7, von *gmi̯* Z. x+9, von *sr* Z. x+9 und von *rmč* Z. 9 und 11; keine davon ist in Chicago Hawara I belegt. Die Pluralstriche werden mit nach rechts gehenden kleinen Elementen oben geschrieben (Z. x+11). Auch das Buchrollendeterminativ (mit vorangehendem Einheits-Element)

4. Jasnow, *Late Period Hieratic Wisdom Text*, 40 Anm. 63.

5. Friedhelm Hoffmann, „Die Entstehung der demotischen Erzählliteratur. Beobachtungen zum überlieferungsgeschichtlichen Kontext," in *Das Erzählen in frühen Hochkulturen, I. Der Fall Ägypten*, hg. Hubert Roeder (München: Fink, 2009), 351–84, dort 362 und 377.

6. Publikation George Robert Hughes and Richard Jasnow, Oriental Institute Hawara Papyri: Demotic and Greek Texts from an Egyptian Family Archive in the Fayum (Fourth to Third Century B.C.), OIP 113 (Chicago: Oriental Institute of the University of Chicago, 1997), 9–15, Taf. 1–7.

7. Ich definiere hier „archaisierend" als bewußte Wiederaufnahme von zwischenzeitlich außer Gebrauch gekommenen Zeichenformen, „retardierend" dagegen als Beharrung auf bestimmten etablierten Formen im Kontrast zu einer sonst vonstatten gehenden Weiterentwicklung.

8. Sandra L. Lippert und Maren Schentuleit, *Demotische Dokumente aus Dime I. Ostraka* (Wiesbaden: Harrassowitz, 2006), 5–7; Sandra L. Lippert und Maren Schentuleit, *Demotische Dokumente aus Dime II. Quittungen* (Wiesbaden: Harrassowitz, 2006), 6–8; Sandra L. Lippert und Maren Schentuleit, *Demotische Dokumente aus Dime III. Urkunden* (Wiesbaden: Harrassowitz, 2010), 75–78.

9. Vergleiche die Liste vorptolemäischer demotischer Papyri bei Heinz-Josef Thissen, „Chronologie der frühdemotischen Papyri", *Enchoria* 10 (1980): 105–25 sowie P. W. Pestman, *Les papyrus démotiques de Tsenhor (P. Tsenhor): Les archives privées d'une femme égyptienne du temps de Darius Ier*, StDe 4 (Leuven: Peeters 1994), 171–73.

10. Cary J. Martin, „Memphite Palaeography: Some Observations on Texts from the Ptolemaic Period", in *Aspects of Demotic Orthography: Acts of an International Colloquium Held in Trier, 8 November 2010*, ed. Sven P. Vleeming, StudDem 11 (Leuven: Peeters, 2013), 41–62.

wird stets sehr ausführlich gezogen, so in *nfr* (x+5), *gm+* Z. x+9, *č̣bꜣ* (x+10); strukturell ähnlich auch in *čꜣw* (x+7). In *pꜣy=f* (Z. x+10) sind die Schilfblätter sehr detailliert mit seitlichem schrägen Strich ausgearbeitet. Das Determinativ von *mnḫ* (Z. x+5) ist detailliert ausgearbeitet (und an das Herz-Zeichen angeglichen, aber ausführlicher als bei *ḥꜣ.tỉ* in Z. x+5.11). Dagegen ist bei *rn* bereits der ursprünglich von *n-rn* stammende horizontale Strich oben generalisiert (Z. x+9).

Andererseits können für die Frage der Datierung potentiell auch die Schriftreste auf dem Verso herangezogen werden. Was davon noch erkennbar ist, zeigt nicht denselben Typ besonders eleganter Zeichenformen wie das Rekto, wohl aber manche ebenfalls recht altertümlich wirkenden Züge, z.B. die seitlichen schrägen Striche der Schilfblätter in *pꜣy=ỉ*.

Insgesamt möchte ich es vorerst bei einer provisorischen Datierung ins 5. oder frühe 4. Jhdt. v. Chr. belassen; für eine präzisere Datierung sind weitere Detailarbeiten zur Paläographie der betreffenden Epoche erforderlich. Vorptolemäisch, sogar vorargeadisch ist die Handschrift ganz sicher.

x+1 …]⸢…⸣[…
x+2 …]⸢.⸣ ..*n=f*⸢.⸣[..]⸢*=f* ..⸣[…
x+3 …]⸢*=f* …*=w*⸣ *n wꜥ rn ꜥn*⸣ *ḫr šm nꜣ* ⸢…⸣ […
x+4 …]⸢..⸣ *šꜥ pꜣ-hrw nꜣ-sḫ (?) pꜣ gy n č̣i̮.t* ⸢*ḫpr (?)*⸣ […
x+5 …]⸢..⸣ *ỉw=f r mnḫ n=f bw-ỉri̮=f nfr n ḥꜣ.tỉ n wpy* ⸢*bw*⸣-[…
x+6 … *m-ỉri̮ ḥ]pḥp n ḥꜣ.tỉ n rsṯy bw-ỉr.rḫ=k nꜣ ntỉ ỉw=w r* ⸢*ỉyi̮*⸣ […
x+7 …]⸢*=k*⸣ *pꜣ ntỉ.ỉw nꜣ-ꜥ nkt ỉrm čꜣw nm pꜣ ntỉ bw* […
x+8 …]. *n-č̣r.ṯ=w st tn nꜣ nkt.w ỉ:ỉri̮ ḫpr n nꜣ pr-ꜥꜣ.w* […
x+9 … *ỉ:ỉri̮]=f č̣i̮.t gmi̮=w rn=f r ꜣšw (?) nꜣ sr.w nꜣ rmč.w* [*ꜥꜣy.w* …
x+10 … *ḫr*] *č̣i̮ pꜣ nčr mḥr=s n pꜣy=f ḫbt (r)-č̣bꜣ č̣i̮.t ḫpr* […
x+11 …] ⸢*pꜣ*⸣ *rmč rḫ ntỉ.ỉw pꜣ mri̮.ṯ n pꜣ nčr pꜣ ntỉ ỉw=f r č̣i̮.t s n ḥꜣ.tỉ*[*=f* …

x+1 …]…[…
x+2 …]. sein /ihn … .[..]..[…
x+3 …] … ihn … für einen Namen wiederum. Es gehen die Jäger (?) […
x+4 …].. bis heute. Bitter (?) ist die Art, […] zu erwerben […
x+5 …] …, er wird wohltätig zu ihm sein. Er ist nicht freundlichen Herzens bei einer Arbeit; nicht […
x+6 … Sei nicht be]trübt im Herzen für Morgen; du weißt nicht, was kommen wird […
x+7 …]. du den, <bei dem> Besitz wie Wind groß ist (??). Wer ist es, der nicht […
x+8 …] bei ihnen. Wo sind sie, die Besitztümer, die den Königen zuteil wurden? […
x+9 …] Für was läßt er sie seinen Namen finden? Die Fürsten und die [bedeutenden] Leute […
x+10 …] Der Gott läßt es für den von ihm Verdammten schmerzhaft sein wegen des Erwerbens/Erzeugens […
x+11 …]. Der Weise, welcher der Geliebte des Gottes (ist), ist es, dem er es ins Herz eingeben wird […

x+2: Es gibt Reste des Buchrollendeterminativs, davor wohl zwei kleine Striche als Reste von  sowie  unter einem anderen Zeichen.

x+3: Am Anfang sind wohl Buchrollendeterminativ und Pluralsuffix erhalten; darunter Reste vom Abstrich eines *f*. Am Ende ist eventuell die *nw*-Gruppe zu erkennen.

x+4: Am Anfang liegt entweder die Pluralgruppe oder das Suffix *=n* vor. Es gibt ein in der Lesung unsicheres Wort mit dem Determinativ des schlechten Vogels. Vermutlich liegt ein Eigenschaftsverb mit *nꜣ*-Präfix vor. Am vorderen Zeichen scheint korrigiert zu sein, ohne daß die letzte Intention wirklich ersichtlich ist. Möglich ist, das der Schreiber zunächst direkt den schlechten Vogel geschrieben hat, also eine knappe Schreibung für *nꜣ-ḫm* „klein ist" vorliegt, anschließend jedoch *nꜣ-sḫ* „bitter ist" ohne Tilgung des ursprünglichen Zeichens geschrieben wurde, und zwar wohl

Figure 1. Text recto.

im Moment der Erstniederschrift selbst, da andernfalls die nachfolgenden Wörter in ihrer Position hätten korrigiert werden müssen.

x+5: Am Zeilenanfang gibt es Reste wohl des Buchrollendeterminativs.

x+5: Die Spuren am Zeilenende sehen am ehesten wie nochmals die Negation aus.

Figure 2. Text verso.

x+6: Im Textfluß plausibel ist am Anfang die Ergänzung des negierten Imperativs, für den ich hier bewußt neutral die normale Form *m-ỉrỉ̱* wähle; im Lichte der unten geführten Diskussion wäre auch denkbar, stattdessen die im Großen Demotischen Weisheitsbuch übliche Ausdrucksweise mit *tm* anzusetzen.[11]

---

11. Für deren Deutung vgl. Joachim Friedrich Quack, *Einführung in die altägyptische Literaturgeschichte III. Die demotische und gräko-ägyptische Literatur*, 3., erneut veränderte Aufl., Einführungen und Quellentexte zur Ägyptologie 3 (Berlin: LIT Verlag, 2016), 126.

x+7: Am Anfang des erhaltenen Bereichs ist wohl das Determinativ des Mannes mit Hand am Mund über *=k* zu lesen; weniger wahrscheinlich ist *ỉnk* „ich". Die Konstruktion *pꜣ ntỉ.ỉw nꜣ-ꜥ nkt ỉrm čꜣw* ist syntaktisch unklar. Ob *pꜣ ntỉ.ỉw nꜣ-ꜥ<=s> nkt ỉrm čꜣw* „was bedeutend ist, sind Besitz und Lebensodem"? Am Zeilenende dürfte *ntỉ bw* und nicht *ntỉ.ỉw* zu lesen sein, da diese Schreiberhand bei *bw* stets einen bei *ỉw* fehlenden Punkt auf der Grundlinie folgen läßt (Z. x+5.6).

x+8: Gegen ein alternatives Verständnis von *st tn nꜣ nkt.w* als „man zählt/schätzt die Besitztümer" spricht, daß in diesem Falle im Präsens I vor determiniertem Objekt ein *n* zur Anknüpfung erforderlich wäre. Bei der von mir favorisierten Deutung dürfte inhaltlich ein *Vanitas*-Konzept intendiert sein.

x+9: Paläographisch kann wohl nur *r ꜣšw* gelesen werden. Ein dem *ꜣšw* entsprechendes Wort ist jedoch in den gängigen Nachschlagewerken nicht zu finden. Potentiell am ähnlichsten ist pHeidelberg D 5, rt. x+2, 16 (unveröffentlicht)[12] *ỉš* in einer seinerseits nicht ganz einfachen Passage. Konkret steht dort *ỉw=w čṭ n=k ỉš ⸢pꜣỉ⸣ ꜣIyi̱-m-[ḥtp]*, was ich als „Sie werden dir sagen: ‚Was ist das, Im[hotep]?'" deuten würde. Ich vermute, daß es sich um eine etwas irreguläre phonetische Weiterentwicklung der aus dem Neuägyptischen stammenden Fragepartikel *ỉč* handelt.

x+10: Bei *pꜣy=f ẖbṭ* (auf den Gott bezogen) ist mit blasserer Tusche ein *k* eingetragen, so daß man auch *pꜣy=k ẖbṭ* „dein Feind" (auf den Empfänger der Lehre bezogen) verstehen kann. Bei *č̣i̱.t ẖpr* ist eventuell die in Weisheitstexten auch sonst bezeugte Vorstellung gemeint, daß der Gott sein Ansehen dadurch erhöht, daß er seine Frevler straft; vgl. z.B. pBrooklyn 47.218.135, x+4, 11.[13] Vergleiche etwas ähnlich auch pLouvre N 2414 1,2.

Gattungsbestimmung

Ich habe schon früher kurz angedeutet, daß ich das Fragment als Weisheitstext ansehe.[14] Daß es kein narrativer Text ist, sollte offensichtlich sein. Textlinguistisch markant ist die Häufigkeit genereller Aussagen. Die Ansetzung einer negierten Aufforderung in Z. x+6 ist lediglich eine von mir vorgenommene Ergänzung, allerdings im Textfluß einsichtig; sie würde letzte Zweifel am grundsätzlichen Inhalt zerstreuen.

Mit einer solchen Identifizierung der Textsorte verliert das Fragment in jedem Falle an Relevanz für die Diskussion über die Verschriftlichung demotischer Erzählliteratur, die ihm in früheren Diskussionen gegeben wurde. Umso relevanter wird es jedoch für die Frage der Chronologie demotischer Weisheitstexte. Hier lohnt eine genauere Diskussion.

Sofern es sich um einen weisheitlichen Text handelt, wäre die primäre Frage, welchem konkreten Typ man ihn zuweisen will. Es gibt in der demotischen Weisheitsliteratur grundsätzlich zwei Typen.[15] Der erste gibt zwar die Maximenstruktur älterer ägyptischer Weisheitstexte auf, kennt aber noch inhaltlich relativ kohärente Abschnitte, die auch als Kapitel mit Überschrift organisiert werden. Am bekanntesten hiervon ist das Große Demotische Weisheitsbuch,

12. Für eine kurze Beschreibung s. Joachim Friedrich Quack, „Imhotep – der Weise, der zum Gott wurde", in *Persönlichkeiten aus dem Alten Ägypten im Neuen Museum*, hg. Verena Lepper (Petersberg: Imhof, 2014), 43–66, dort 58–60.

13. Jasnow, *Late Period Hieratic Wisdom Text*, 84–85

14. Quack, *Einführung*, 1 und 153.

15. Quack, 120–21.

das am vollständigsten im Papyrus Insinger erhalten ist;[16] daneben gibt es noch einen weitgehend unpublizierten weiteren Text dieser Art.[17]

Der zweite Typ zeigt eine lose, allenfalls assoziativ verbundene Abfolge von Einzelsätzen, die keine klare thematische Strukturierung aufweisen. Der am besten bekannte Vertreter dieses Typs ist die Lehre des Chascheschonqi,[18] aber auch eine Reihe kleinerer Kompositionen wie pLouvre N 2414, pLouvre N 2377 vs. und pLouvre N 2380 vs.[19] Vergleichsweise umfangreich, aber bislang noch unpubliziert, ist pBerlin P 15709 rt.[20] Diese Handschriften zeichnen sich auch dadurch aus, daß sie fallweise für Einzelsprüche enge Parallelen zeigen.

Bislang ist ein zwar graphisch hieratischer, sprachlich jedoch bereits demotischer Weisheitstext in einer Handschrift (pBrooklyn 47.218.135) bekannt, die noch in die Saitenzeit datieren könnte.[21] Er stellt einen Übergangstypus dar, bei dem die thematische Strukturierung nur noch bedingt erkennbar ist. Weitere Handschriften, die Parallelen zu Sprüchen der Lehre des Chascheschonqi bieten, somit zum Typ der lose assoziierten Texte gehören, setzen etwa in der frühen Ptolemäerzeit ein.[22] Vom Großen Demotischen Weisheitstext ist die älteste Handschrift mutmaßlich[23] der pInsinger, der entweder spätptolemäisch oder frührömisch datiert.[24] Jedoch sollte man sich davor hüten, die Datierung der erhaltenen Handschriften mit der Entstehung der Komposition als solcher gleichzusetzen. Bereits Aksel Volten hat vorgeschlagen, daß der Verfasser des Textes mehrere Jahrhunderte vor Christus, wahrscheinlich sogar schon in vorptolemäischer Zeit gelebt habe.[25] Man muß allerdings einräumen, daß sein Hauptargument, nämlich die zahlreichen Korruptelen in der Textüberlieferung, von allenfalls bedingtem Wert für die Einschätzung der Länge der

---

16. Vergleiche Quack, *Einführung*, 122–34 mit weiteren bibliographischen Angaben sowie die neueste Übersetzung in Friedhelm Hoffmann und Joachim Friedrich Quack, *Anthologie der demotischen Literatur*, 2., neubearbeitete und erheblich erweiterte Auflage, Einführungen und Quellentexte zur Ägyptologie 4 (Berlin: LIT, 2018), 272–308 und 417–21 sowie die (Neu)edition vieler Parallelhandschriften in Joachim Friedrich Quack, „Neue Fragmente des demotischen Weisheitsbuches. Mit einer Kollationierung der alten Fragmente", in Joachim Friedrich Quack und Kim Ryholt, *The Carlsberg Papyri 11: Demotic Literary Texts from Tebtunis and Beyond* (Kopenhagen: Museum Tusculanum Press, 2019), 421–88. In Joachim Friedrich Quack, „Fragmente demotischer Weisheitstexte", in *Mélanges offerts à Ola El-Aguizy*, hg. F. Haikal, BdÉ 165 (Kairo: IFAO, 2015), 331–47, dort 333–34, ist ein möglicherweise ebenfalls zu dieser Komposition gehöriges Fragment publiziert worden.

17. Quack, *Einführung*, 134.

18. Quack, *Einführung*, 138–48; Hoffmann und Quack, *Anthologie*, 308–35 und 422–25.

19. Quack, *Einführung*, 148–55; Hoffmann und Quack, *Anthologie*, 335–39 und 426–27. Für noch weitere potentiell in diese Kategorie gehörige Fragmente s. Quack, „Fragmente demotischer Weisheitstexte". Auflistung der Parallelen zum pBM EA 10508 in Damien Agut-Labordère, *Le sage et l'insensé: La composition et la transmission des sagesses démotiques*, Bibliothèque de l'École des hautes études, sciences historiques et philologiques 347 (Paris: Champion 2011), 327–42.

20. Kurze bibliographische Angaben in Quack, *Einführung*, 148.

21. Edition Richard Jasnow, *Late Period Hieratic Wisdom Text*. Zur Frage der Datierung s. Ursula Verhoeven, *Untersuchungen zur späthieratischen Buchschrift*, OLA 99 (Leuven: Peeters, 2001), 319–28. S. den Überblick in Quack, *Einführung*, 134–38. Neueste Übersetzung in Hoffmann, Quack, *Anthologie*, 263–71 und 416–17.

22. Serge Rosmorduc, „145: Fragment de sagesse", in *Papyrus de la Sorbonne (P. Sorb. IV No 145–160)*, hg. Marie-Pierre Chaufrey and Stéphanie Wackenier (Paris: Presses de l'université Paris-Sorbonne, 2016), 25–28 (dort ist m.E. in Fragment A+C, rt. 8 statt *m-ỉr ꜣs r* vielmehr *m-ỉr ỉ ḥms ỉ n* zu lesen, was die vorgeschlagene Parallele zu Chascheschonqi 9, x+18 definitiv absichert); Joachim Friedrich Quack, Rezension zu *Demotic Ostraca and Other Inscriptions from the Sacred Animal Necropolis, North Saqqara*, von J. D. Ray, *Orientalia* 84 (2015): 110–17, dort 113.

23. Aksel Volten, *Kopenhagener Texte zum Demotischen Weisheitsbuch (Pap. Carlsberg II, III verso, IV verso und V)* (Kopenhagen: Munksgaard, 1940), 7–8 wollte den pCarlsberg 4 vs. (eine Parallelhandschrift zum pInsinger) in die letzten vorchristlichen Jahrhunderte datieren, s. dagegen Quack, „Neue Fragmente", 435.

24. Zur Frage der Datierung vgl. Friedhelm Hoffmann, „Neue Fragmente zu den drei großen Inaros-Petubastis-Texten", *Enchoria* 22 (1995): 27–39, dort 38–39; Joachim Friedrich Quack, „Ein Formular für Eheurkunden. Papyrus Heidelberg D 688", demnächst in einer Festschrift.

25. Aksel Volten, *Das demotische Weisheitsbuch. Studien und Bearbeitung* (Kopenhagen: Munksgaard, 1941), 123. Diese Datierung hat eine Rolle gespielt, was die Bewertung von Parallelen zwischen dem Großen Demotischen Weisheitsbuch und der Lehre des Jesus Sirach betrifft, s. Jack B. Sanders, *Ben Sira and Demotic Wisdom*. SBL Monograph Series 28 (Chico: Society of Biblical Literature, 1983),

Textgeschichte ist, zumal die meisten davon mehr spezifisch für den pInsinger als für die restlichen (chronologisch späteren) Handschriften relevant sind.

Mein eigener Vorstoß, die ursprüngliche Komposition der Lehre des Chascheschonqy und des Großen Demotischen Weisheitsbuches anhand inhaltlicher und sprachlicher Kriterien in die Saitenzeit zu datieren,[26] ist nicht überall auf Gegenliebe gestoßen.[27] Heinz-Josef Thissen äußert sich einerseits skeptisch hinsichtlich der Lehre des Chascheschonqi und meint, in einer Sammlung von Sprichwörtern sei älteres Spruchgut zu erwarten, dies ändere aber nichts an der Datierung der Handschrift.[28] Zumindest in dieser Formulierung geht diese Kritik an meinem Ansatz jedoch komplett vorbei, da es mir ja gar nicht um die Datierung der konkreten Handschrift ging, sondern um die Frage nach der Komposition als solcher – wobei ich bereits auf das methodische Problem hingewiesen habe, daß bei einem derart fluiden Textbestand kaum ein einzelner Zeitpunkt als Kompositionsdatum festgesetzt werden kann.[29]

Andererseits hat Thissen hinsichtlich meiner Datierung der Rahmenerzählung in die Saitenzeit eingewandt, dort sei die Steuer für die Zulassung zum Priesteramt (*tn*) erwähnt, diese sei aber erst ab der Ptolemäerzeit belegt.[30] Dieser Einwand ist jedoch methodisch problematisch, weil die Steuer für die Einsetzung als Priester vorrangig in literarischen Texten (Setne I, 3, 16; pBerlin P 13588, 2, 7 u. 8)[31] und daneben noch der Rosettana (Z. 9) belegt ist, nicht jedoch in dokumentarischen Texten, was kaum eine ausreichende Basis darstellt, um die reale historische Laufzeit der dahinterstehenden administrativen Praxis festzulegen.[32] Von diesen Texten ist zudem die Erzählung des pBerlin P 13588 nicht nur der Eigenbehauptung nach in die Saitenzeit datiert, sondern zeigt auch präzise Kenntnis einer

70, 80, 91 und 99–100 und kritisch dazu Heinz-Josef Thissen, Rezension zu *Ben Sira and Demotic Wisdom*, von Jack B. Sanders, *Enchoria* 14 (1986): 199–201, dort 200–201

26. Joachim Friedrich Quack, „Zur Chronologie der demotischen Weisheitsliteratur", in *Acts of the Seventh International Conference of Demotic Studies, Copenhagen, 23–27 August 1999*, hg. Kim Ryholt, CNIP 27 (Kopenhagen: Museum Tusculanum Press 2002), 329–42.

27. Vergleiche immerhin Kim Ryholt, „A New Version of the Introduction to the Teaching of *o*Onch-Sheshonqy (P. Carlsberg 304 + PSI Inv. D 5 + P. CtYBR 4512 + P. Berlin P. 30489)", in *The Carlsberg Papyri 3: A Miscellany of Demotic Texts and Studies*, hg. Paul J. Frandsen und Kim Ryholt, CNIP 22 (Kopenhagen: Museum Tusculanum Press 2000), 113–40, Taf. 16–22, dort 119–20, der argumentiert, die Parallelhandschrift pCarlsberg 304 hinge von einer hieratischen Vorlage ab und deshalb sei eine Entstehung vor dem 3. Jhdt. v. Chr. anzunehmen.

28. Heinz-Josef Thissen, „Achmim und die demotische Literatur", in *Perspectives on Panopolis: An Egyptian Town from Alexander the Great to the Arab Conquest; Acts from an International Symposium, Held in Leiden on 16, 17 and 18 December 1998*, hg. A. Egberts, Brian P. Muhs und Jacques van der Vliet, PLB 31 (Leiden: Brill 2002), 249–60, dort 250 Anm. 5.

29. Quack, „Zur Chronologie", 342.

30. Thissen, „Achmim und die demotische Literatur", 250 Anm. 7.

31. Wolja Erichsen, *Eine neue demotische Erzählung*, Akademie der Wissenschaften und der Literatur (Mainz): Abhandlungen der Geistes- und Sozialwissenschaftlichen Klasse 1956 (2) (Mainz: Verlag der Akademie der Wissenschaften und der Literatur 1956), 59 und 66; Steve Vinson, *The Craft of a Good Scribe: History, Narrative and Meaning in the First Tale of Setne Khaemwas*, HES 3 (Leiden: Brill 2018), 115 und 137.

32. Derzeit gibt der TLA für *pꜣ tny (n) wꜥb* „die Priesterabgabe" pBerlin P 15619, rt. 4 als Beleg an, einen Brief, der ins 4. Jhdt. v. Chr. datiert, und zwar mutmaßlich in die 30. Dynastie, s. Karl-Theodor Zauzich, *Papyri von der Insel Elephantine*. Demotische Papyri aus den Staatlichen Museen zu Berlin 3 (Berlin: Akademie-Verlag 1993); dort Seite V zur mutmaßlichen Datierung, was Thissens Argument sachlich aushebeln würde. Allerdings liegt dort eindeutig die Gruppe für *ṭnꞽ.t* „Anteil" vor; und ich würde eher *⸢tꜣ⸣ ṭnꞽ.t nꜣ wꜥb.w* „der Anteil der Priester" lesen, so daß die Stelle als Beleg für die in Rede stehende Abgabe ausfällt.

tatsächlichen Mondfinsternis im Zusammenhang mit dem Tod Psammetichs I.,[33] was es plausibel macht, daß hier zumindest ein Kern der Handlung zeitgenössisch ist.[34]

Auch zu meiner Datierung des Großen Demotischen Weisheitsbuches äußert sich Thissen kritisch, ohne jedoch spezifische Argumente zu nennen.[35]

Andreas Blasius meint für das Große Demotische Weisheitsbuch und die Lehre des Chascheschonqi, die Erwähnung des vorptolemäisch unüblichen „Geldes" spräche mindestens für eine Aktualisierung der Inhalte.[36] Dieses Argument scheint mir so nicht zutreffend.[37] „Geld" in Form von Silberwerten normierten Gewichts ist schon in der Saiten- und Perserzeit in ägyptischen Verträgen ganz normal,[38] z.B. erscheint die Phrase *č̣i̯=k mtỉ ḥꜣ.tỉ(=ỉ) n pꜣ ḥč̣* „du hast mein Herz mit dem Geld zufriedengestellt" bereits im pRylands I, rt. 3–4, also dem derzeit ältesten bekannten demotischen Urkundentext überhaupt (Psammetich I, Jahr 21 = 644 v. Chr.).[39] Weiterhin wendet Blasius im Hinblick auf die Lehre des Chascheschonqi ein, die Belegsituation mit drei Textzeugen aus ptolemäischer Zeit, zwei dem Text nahestehenden Lehren ebenfalls aus der Ptolemäerzeit und einem Zeugen des 2. Jhdts. n. Chr. mache gegenüber der Frühdatierung stutzig.[40] Aber es hat sich inzwischen in der Ägyptologie gut genug gezeigt, daß Lücken der Überlieferung von mehreren hundert Jahren nachweisliche Realität[41] und Datierungsversuche, welche bei literarischen Texten die Entstehungszeit nahe bei der ältesten erhaltenen Handschrift sehen, oft fehlerträchtig sind.[42]

Der hier veröffentlichte Papyrus, der auf jeden Fall einen demotischen Weisheitstext in vorptolemäischer Zeit dokumentiert, dürfte dem Modell einer frühen Entstehung der demotischen Weisheitsliteratur tendenziell Auftrieb geben.[43] Kann man noch etwas weiterkommen? So schlecht erhalten das vorliegende Fragment ist, bleibt es doch deutlich, daß seine Aussagen vorrangig um das Thema von Erwerbsleben und Besitz kreisen. Angesichts des über etliche Zeilen konsistenten Themas dürfte es somit der ersten und nicht der zweiten Kategorie der demotischen Weisheitstexte zuzurechnen sein. Hier muß sich insbesondere die Frage stellen, ob es sich um eine bislang ganz unbekannte Komposition handelt, oder um bislang verlorene Teilbereiche einer an sich bekannten Komposition.

---

33. Mark Smith, „Did Psammetichus I Die Abroad?", *OLP* 22 (1991): 101–9; Dan'el Kahn, „Revisiting the Date of King Josiah's Death", in *In the Shadow of Bezalel: Aramaic, Biblical, and Ancient Near Eastern Studies in Honor of Bezalel Porten*, hg. Alejandro F. Botta, CHANE 60 (Leiden: Brill 2013), 255–64, dort 257–61. Der Einwand von Rolf Krauss, „Die Bubastiden-Finsternis im Licht von 150 Jahren Forschungsgeschichte", *MDAIK* 63 (2007): 211–23, dort 219–20, der Text sei unhistorisch, weil er das erst in der Ptolemäerzeit entstandene Buch vom Atmen erwähne, ist, wie bereits Kahn zeigt, doppelt unzutreffend. Einerseits geht es in der Erzählung um einen Funerärtext für einen König, so daß man Befunde für die Ausstattung von Privatpersonen nicht einfach darauf übertragen kann, zum anderen weicht die Terminologie für den in der Erzählung genannten Text, nämlich *tꜣ.wỉ n snsn* „Anbetung zum Atmen", von den für die Bücher vom Atmen real verwendeten Titeln eindeutig ab.

34. Quack, *Einführung*, 77–78

35. Thissen, „Achmim und die demotische Literatur", 251 Anm. 12.

36. Andreas Blasius, *„It was Greek to me ..."* – Die lokalen Eliten im ptolemäischen Ägypten", in *Lokale Eliten und hellenistische Könige. Zwischen Kooperation und Konfrontation*, hg. Boris Dreyer und Peter Franz Mittag, Oikumene 8 (Berlin: Verlag Antike 2011), 132–90, dort 169 Anm. 116.

37. Kritik bereits in Quack, *Einführung*, 123–24 Anm. 265.

38. Vergleiche z.B. Sven P. Vleeming, The Gooseherds of Hou (Pap. Hou): A Dossier Relating to Various Agricultural Affairs from Provincial Egypt of the Early Fifth Century B.C., StudDem 3 (Leuven: Peters, 1991), 87–89.

39. Griffith, volume 1, 46 und 203, volume 2, Taf. 4, volume 3, Taf. I–VIII.

40. Blasius, *„It was Greek to me ..."*, 167 Anm. 113.

41. Joachim Friedrich Quack, „Irrungen, Wirrungen? Forscherische Ansätze zur Datierung der älteren ägyptischen Literatur", in *Dating Egyptian Literary Texts*, hg. Gerald Moers, Kai Wiedmaier, Antonia Giewekemeyer, Arndt Lümers und Ralf Ernst, LingAeg SM 11 (Hamburg: Widmaier, 2013), 405–69, dort 420–23.

42. Karl Jansen-Winkeln, „Zur Datierung der mittelägyptischen Literatur", *Or* 86 (2017): 107–34.

43. Hinweisen kann man auch auf den bislang noch nicht bearbeiteten Weisheitstext pSommerhausen 2, Photo in Karl-Theodor Zauzich, *Hieroglyphen mit Geheimnis. Neue Erkenntnisse zur Entstehung unseres Alphabets* (Darmstadt: Wissenschaftliche Buchgesellschaft, 2015), Taf. 3, der paläographisch ins 4. Jhdt. datieren dürfte. Die gleichartigen Textanfänge mit *hmy* in den ersten sechs Zeilen sprechen für eine Zuordnung zum zweiten Typ demotischer Weisheitslehren mit assoziativer Komposition.

Vom Großen Demotischen Weisheitsbuch ist der Anfang ja nur sehr bruchstückhaft bekannt, weil die zum pInsinger selbst gehörenden Bruchstücke, die heute auf verschiedene Sammlungen verteilt sind, noch größere Lücken aufweisen,[44] und von den Parallelhandschriften nur wenige kleine Fragmente sicher diesem Bereich zugewiesen werden können.[45] Hier wäre potentiell noch Raum, die auf dem pBerlin P 23504 rt. überlieferten Textreste unterzubringen. Konkret denkbar wäre die 2. Lehre des Großen Demotischen Weisheitsbuches, in der es um den Erwerb des Lebensunterhalts geht, was sich mit der Thematik der hier erhaltenen Sätze vorzüglich deckt. Diese Lehre dürfte mit 82 Sprüchen die längste der Komposition überhaupt gewesen sein,[46] und mehr als eine ganze Kolumne davon ist bislang noch völlig verloren.[47] Da wäre also reichlich Platz vorhanden, um den Text des pBerlin P 23504 unterzubringen.

Hier ist auch die Option nochmals aufzugreifen, daß unten auf dem Rand von pBerlin P 23504 die Zahl 5 zu lesen und als Seitenzahl zu verstehen ist. Eine Kalkulation ist insofern schwierig, weil die genaue Länge des Prologs des Großen Demotischen Weisheitsbuches unsicher ist.[48] Zudem gibt es keine belastbaren Werte für den Schriftspiegel des pBerlin P 23504. Aber die hier vorgeschlagene Identifizierung als Teil der zweiten Lehre des Großen Demotischen Weisheitsbuches wäre mit einer Deutung der Schriftreste als Seitenzahl 5 prinzipiell kompatibel.

Anhang: Zum Verso-Text

So schlecht lesbar die Reste auch sind, seien hier zumindest einige versuchsweise Lesungen geboten. Dabei ist bereits die korrekte Zitierkonvention der Zeilen mit einigen Problemen verbunden, da die jetzt noch erkennbaren Schriftzeichen zu mindestens zwei unterschiedlichen Palimpsestierungsstufen gehören dürften. Ich differenziere hier zwischen den Bereichen A und B. A ist auf den rechten Bereich der Handschrift beschränkt und geht tiefer; B geht über die ganze Breite und liegt teilweise oberhalb von A, ist also die spätere Beschriftung. Ich gebe hier ohne Übersetzung zumindest die Umschrift dessen, was ich zu erkennen meine; vorrangig, um damit eine Zielscheibe für Kritik abzugeben.

Bereich A
1–5 *Komplett unentzifferbar*
6 [...] ... *=f*
7 [...] ... *ꜥnḫ (?) n-č̣r.ṱ=w*
8 [...] ... ... *⌜pꜣ kỉỉ⌝*
9 [...] ... . *⌜ṱ=tn⌝*
10 [...]*.ṱ=w ỉw=f ⌜č̣ṭ⌝ r*
11 [...] *⌜rmč ỉw=f⌝ rḫ ỉri̭ pꜣy=ỉ ꜥrš*
12 [...]*⌜.⌝y rḫ č̣i̭.t s ỉ.ỉri̭=k šm (?)*

44. Philippe Collombert, „Contribution à la reconstitution des premières pages du Papyrus Insinger", in *Sapientia Felicitas. Festschrift für Günter Vittmann zum 29. Februar 2016*, hg. Sandra L. Lippert, Maren Schentuleit und Martin A. Stadler, Cahiers „Égypte Nilotique et Méditerranéenne" 14 (Montpellier: Équipe „Égypte Nilotique et Méditerranéenne", 2016), 51–65.

45. Vergleiche zuletzt Joachim Friedrich Quack, „Neue Fragmente des demotischen Weisheitsbuches. Mit einer Kollationierung der alten Fragmente", in Quack und Ryholt, *Carlsberg Papyri 11*, 421–88, dort 430–31, 438–40 und 461–63.

46. Für die korrekte Lesung der Zahl s. Collombert, „Contribution à la reconstitution", 52–53.

47. Vergleiche die Rekonstruktionsskizze bei Collombert, 62.

48. Die Schätzung von Collombert, 58 und 62, dafür mindestens eine Kolumne anzusetzen, ist tendenziell allenfalls zu niedrig, da PSI Inv. D 98 + pFlorenz Museo Archeologico 11928 Reste dieses Prologs auf dem unteren Rand einer Seite zeigen, daneben weitere Fragmente, die ebenfalls zu diesem Prolog gehören, aber bereits auf der zweiten Seite gestanden haben müssen, und diese Handschrift mutmaßlich mehr Text als pInsinger auf einer Seite unterbringen konnte, vgl. Quack, „Neue Fragmente", 438.

Bereich B

x+1 …
x+2 … *ỉw=f* …
x+3 …
x+4 … … *n=f* … *mtw=n*
x+5 … … …*=f ỉ:ỉr=w (?) tꜣy=k mṭ(.t (?) hwn-nꜣỉ*
x+6 … … … *=f wpi̭*
x+7 *č̣ṭ ỉ:ỉri̭=k wẖꜣ/ẖꜣꜥ* […]… … *č̣ṭ=w*
x+8 ⸢…⸣*=k n.ỉm=f rẖ* ⸢… …⸣ [*h*]*b r ḥw.t-nčr* ⸢*rẖ*

Die wenigen auch nur tentativ deutbaren Reste lassen nicht so leicht eine Textsorte erkennen. Der Irrealiskonverter könnte in einem Brief vorkommen,[49] daneben auch in einem literarischen Text, nicht jedoch in einem Vertrag oder einer Abrechnung. Auch die Verwendung der 1. Person Plural paßt zu derartigen Textsorten. Die Erwähnung des „Kultdienstes" (*ꜥrš*) würde zu einer Verortung im Tempelbereich passen. Das würde potentiell zumindest gewisse Schlüsse hinsichtlich der sozialen Situierung demotischer Literatur ergeben.[50]

49. Da hier dem Layout nach sicher kein Originalbrief vorliegt, könnte es sich dann nur um eine Abschrift handeln.

50. Vergleiche für einen anderen Fall, wo Notizen auf dem Verso eines literarischen Textes Rückschlüsse dieser Art erlauben, Joachim Friedrich Quack, „Eine weise Stimme der Autorität (Papyrus Amherst Eg. XLIII.1 rt.). Mit Anhängen über Abrechnungen (Papyrus Amherst Eg. XLIII.1 vs. und XLIII.2)", in *Illuminating Osiris: Egyptological Studies in Honor of Mark Smith*, hg. Richard Jasnow und Ghislaine Widmer, MVCAE 2 (Atlanta: Lockwood, 2017), 303–18, Taf. 19–22, bes. 311–18.

Jubilating Baboons and the Bes Pantheos

Robert K. Ritner†

As co-editor of the Demotic Book of Thoth, with its complex symbolism and often arcane mythological allusions, Richard Jasnow has repeatedly encountered sacred baboons in varying contexts: as forms of the gods Thoth, Osiris, and Bebon, "angelic" souls (*ba*-spirits) of the East and West, speakers of divine language, and groups within which the initiate desires to participate.[1] Thoth is visualized as "the baboon who has joined with the snake, who has judged the earth with his scale."[2] In company with dogs, jackals, and snakes, baboons "prophesize according to their utterances,"[3] while the creator "knew the form of the speech of the baboons and ibises."[4] In association with the underworld boats of the excellent spirits, a baboon gives the initiate a spear and even speaks the Egyptian language.[5]

Jubilating baboons are particularly associated with the company of the solar bark, and it is probably in this context that the initiate proclaims: "I shall act as a baboon among them (or therein)."[6] The proclamation may derive directly from Book of the Dead spell 100: "I have sung (*šmꜥ*) and praised (*dwꜣ*) the sun disk, I have joined those among the jubilating baboons, and I am one of them."[7] As recognized by Assmann, in funerary contexts the deceased can become a member of the baboon cohort aboard the solar craft, and clearly becoming a baboon (*ỉr* + office/role) can be the case for a living initiate as well.[8] The phraseology "among them" specifically recalls the later preferred epithet of these choral baboons: *imy.w-ḥt.t*, "those who are among the jubilating baboons," designating the animals that praise

1. See the general discussion in Richard Jasnow and Karl-Theodor Zauzich, *The Ancient Egyptian Book of Thoth* (Wiesbaden: Harrassowitz, 2005), 38–39, and 16n5 (Osiris as baboon), 346 (Bebon as baboon), and the many examples gathered in *DG*, 502 (*ꜥꜥn*). But note that some examples in the *DG* have been reread as the phonetically similar "donkey"; see Richard Jasnow and Karl-Theodor Zauzich, *Conversations in the House of Life: A New Translation of the Ancient Egyptian Book of Thoth* (Wiesbaden: Harrassowitz, 2014), 62.

2. Jasnow and Zauzich, *Book of Thoth*, 39 and 241–42, l. 16 = Jasnow and Zauzich, *Conversations*, 122–23, statement 419.

3. Jasnow and Zauzich, *Book of Thoth*, 39 and 268–69, l. 3 = Jasnow and Zauzich, *Conversations*, 132–33, statement 456: "which prophesy with their mouths."

4. Jasnow and Zauzich, *Book of Thoth*, 39, 261, 262 and 265, l. 8 = Jasnow and Zauzich, *Conversations*, 130–31, statement 445.

5. Jasnow and Zauzich, *Book of Thoth*, 306 and 309, l. 6 = Jasnow and Zauzich, *Conversations*, 65, statement 524: "A baboon gave to me a spear of 60 cubits. He said to me: 'It is their wooden post of trapping.'"

6. Jasnow and Zauzich, *Book of Thoth*, 372 and 384 (BO6, 1/16) = Jasnow and Zauzich, *Conversations*, 65, statement 44: "I shall be a baboon among them."

7. The text is frequently quoted; it opens the study by Herman Te Velde, "Some Remarks on the Mysterious Language of the Baboons," in *Funerary Symbols and Religion*, ed. Jacques H. Kamstra, H. Milde and Kees Wagtendonk (Kampen: J. H. Kok, 1988), 129–37; and is quoted in Jan Assmann, *Liturgische Lieder an den Sonnengott*, Münchner ägyptologische Studien 19 (Berlin: Hessling, 1969), 209, and in Alexandra von Lieven, "'The Soul of the Sun Permeates the Whole World': Sun Cult and Religious Astronomy in Ancient Egypt," in *Sun Worship in the Civilizations of the World*, ed. Adalbert Gail (Prague: Triton), 54.

8. Jan Assmann. *Egyptian Solar Religion in the New Kingdom: Re, Amun and the Crisis of Polytheism* (London: Kegan Paul, 1995), cited in Jasnow and Zauzich, *Book of Thoth*, 56n166. The latter authors follow Hornung here in denying in principle ultimate union between deity and practitioner, but I would disagree. Expressions of divine union are both explicit and numerous in the so-called funerary texts that are used also by the living. See Robert K. Ritner, "Divinization and Empowerment of the Dead," in *Book of the Dead: Becoming God in Ancient Egypt*, ed. Foy Scalf, OIMP 39 (Chicago: Oriental Institute of the University of Chicago, 2017), 109–15; and Edward F. Wente, "Mysticism in Pharaonic Egypt?," *JNES* 41 (1982): 161–79. For the common *ỉrỉ* + office to indicate "act in the capacity of," see Raymond O. Faulkner, *A Concise Dictionary of Middle Egyptian* (Oxford: Griffith Institute, 1981), 26.

the sun at its rising or setting.[9] In recent additions to the Book of Thoth, the initiate seems to reverse the process, celebrating the celebrants by "praising the jubilating baboons."[10] I have had the pleasure of knowing Richard since our days as students together at Chicago, and am pleased to offer him some additional "baboonic"[11] praise for his well-deserved Festschrift.

The "form/manner of speech" (*gy n mt*, Coptic ϬΙΝΜΟΥΤЄ[12]) of baboons and sacred animals is a repeated concern in the Book of Thoth, and Jasnow and Zauzich have suggested that in a passage mentioning the creation of hieroglyphs, this "speech" of the baboons and ibises refers less to actual animal vocalizations but rather "is perhaps the sound values of hieroglyphic signs," an idea advanced on multiple occasions.[13] In the symbolic extensions of the "Ptolemaic" hieroglyphic system, the figure of a sitting baboon does acquire a relevant value as *ḏd*, "to say/speak," but the nuance probably derives from the animal's distinctive cries.[14] Indeed, "baboonic" sounds are surely intended when the creatures are said to "prophesy with their mouths" or be found "worshipping in a mode of speech."[15] That form of speech is made explicit in the Greco-Egyptian magical papyri (PGM) in an invocation to the solar god:

> I call upon you as the three baboons call upon you, who speak your holy name in a symbolic fashion, A EE ÊÊÊ IIII OOOOO YYYYYY ÔÔÔÔÔÔÔ (speak as a baboon).[16]

While Jasnow and Zauzich hesitate to identify the "speech of the ibises,"[17] the "Eighth Book of Moses" in the PGM gives examples of "birdglyphic," contrasted with hieroglyphic, Hebraic, Egyptian, "baboonic," "falconic," and hieratic: "I call upon you, lord, in "birdglyphic"; ARAI, in hieroglyphic: LAILAM; … in Egyptian: ALDABAEIM; in "baboonic": ABRASAX, in "falconic": CHI CHI CHI CHI CHI CHI CHI TIPH TIPH TIPH; in hieratic: MENEPHÔIPHÔTH CHA CHA CHA CHA CHA CHA CHA."[18]

Here the phonetics imitate bird and falcon cries,[19] while the baboons invoke the sacred name Abrasax. Notably, these are contrasted with written hieroglyphs and hieratic as well as with contemporary Egyptian (Demotic), however garbled. In variants following later in the spell, the baboon appears in a traditional context, and his greeting is explained by the numerological value of the Greek alphabet: "Now he who appears on the boat rising together with you is a clever baboon; he greets you in his own language, saying 'You are the number of [the days of] the year, ABRASAX.'"[20]

---

9. See *Wb.* II:504, an expansion of the designation *ḥtt*, "jubilating baboons," attested from the Pyramid Texts onwards.

10. Jasnow and Zauzich, *Conversations*, 166–67, statement 609.

11. I owe the term to Morton Smith, who used it in his translation of PGM XIII, discussed below. See Hans Dieter Betz, ed., *The Greek Magical Papyri in Translation including the Demotic Spells*, 2nd ed., (Chicago: University of Chicago, 1992), 174. The term has now been adopted from the same source in Christian H. Bull, *The Tradition of Hermes Trismegistus*, RGRW 186 (Leiden: Brill, 2018), 346–51.

12. See Jasnow and Zauzich, *Book of Thoth*, 265, with reference to *DG*, 572; Te Velde, "Some Remarks"; and add *CD*, 192b.

13. Jasnow and Zauzich, *Conversations*, 20 and 130, nos. 445–48.

14. *Wb.* V:618 (note also the use of a quacking goose head for the same value); François Daumas, *Valeurs phonétiques des signes hiéroglyphiques d'époque gréco-romaine*, 4 vols. (Montpellier: Université de Montpellier, 1988), 1:244–46, nos. 547, 548, and 601; for the bird head, see 2:342, nos. 51 and 55.

15. Jasnow and Zauzich, *Conversations*, 132–33, no. 456; and 158–59, statement 565: "I found six rowers sitting, they being complete, they worshipping in a mode of speech." Though unidentified, the rowers are either baboons or comparable to them.

16. PGM IV.1004–1006; Karl Preisendanz, *Papyri Graecae Magicae*, vol. 1, 2nd ed.(Stuttgart: Teubner, 1973–1974 [repr. of 1928–1931]), 107; and Betz, *The Greek Magical Papyri*, 58 with my note 140.

17. Jasnow and Zauzich, *Book of Thoth*, 265.

18. P. Lugd. Bat. J 395 (IV century) = PGM XIII.80–87; in Preisendanz, *Papyri Graecae Magicae*, vol. 2, 2nd ed. (Munich: Saur, 2001), 91; Betz *The Greek Magical Papyri*, 174.

19. Cf. Jasnow and Zauzich, *Book of Thoth*, 306, l. 5: "I understood their falcons."

20. For the three variants; see PGM XIII.149–161 (baboon ll. 153–156); in Preisendanz, *Papyri Graecae Magicae*, 2:94; Betz, *The*

Figure 1. Naos Cairo 70028: baboons adore the rising sun. Photo by the author.

Figure 2. Graffito at Ptah temple in Karnak, south external wall: baboons adore the rising sun. Photo by the author, 1996.

Despite the novelty of the recorded sounds in these texts, the morning greeting of the sun by baboons is a recurrent feature in Egyptian literature and iconography, deriving from observed actions by the hamadryas baboon: "sunning" in the early morning, with arms raised during morning grooming, and emitting grunts that "sound considerably like human vowels."[21] Representations of baboons adoring the rising sun appear throughout the formal repertoires of temple design, obelisk bases, naoi (fig. 1), coffin decoration, and pyramidions,[22] as well as in popular graffiti (fig. 2).[23] Where labeled, the scenes can be designated simply *dwꜣ rꜥ*, "Praising Re" or *dwꜣ nṯr*, "Praising God."[24] By virtue of the daily cycle of the so-called Solar-Osirian unity, the baboons can adore the risen *djed*-column of Osiris as well.[25] As noted by Christopher Faraone, adoring baboons continue to appear on Roman-era gems, but they are hardly "some superficial nods to Egyptian tradition" whose morning praises are dependent upon Greek sources.[26] On these gems

Greek Magical Papyri, 176; PGM XIII.454–470; in Preisendanz, *Papyri Graecae Magicae*, 2:109–10; Betz, *The Greek Magical Papyri*, 184; and PGM XIII.593–600; in Preisendanz, *Papyri Graecae Magicae*, 2:115; Betz, *The Greek Magical Papyri*, 187.

21. Elizabeth Thomas, "*Papio Hamadryas* and the Rising Sun," *Bulletin of the Egyptological Seminar* 1 (1979): 91–94 and pl. 4 (captions for 4a and 4d reversed); Bull, *The Tradition of Hermes Trismegistus*, 348 (with references).

22. Cf. the façade of Abu Simbel, illustrated in Thomas ("*Papio Hamadryas* and the Rising Sun," pl. 4c); the remaining Luxor temple obelisk base, Naos Cairo 70028 in Günther Roeder (*Naos*, Catalogue Genéral des Antiquités Égyptiennes du Musée du Caire No. 70001–70050 [Leipzig: Breitkopf & Härtel, 1914], 110 and pl. 38a); Heidelberg coffin Ägyptisches Institut Inv. No. 1015, in Steffen Wenig (*The Woman in Egyptian Art* [Leipzig: Edition Leipzig, 1989], 52 and 89); Pyramidion Leningrad 2260, in Herman de Meulenaere, "Pyramidions d'Abydos," *JEOL* 20 (1967–1968): 5–7 and pl. II. Note the quotation from Book of the Dead spell 100 on the north face of Pyramidion Glasgow 13.176, in de Meulenaere, "Pyramidions d'Abydos," 3 and pl. I: "I have praised (*dwꜣ*) the sun disk, I have joined those among the jubilating baboons, and I am one of them."

23. Graffito on the south face of the Ptah temple at Karnak. Photograph by the author, 1996.

24. De Meulenaere "Pyramidions d'Abydos," 5 and pl. II, east face (pyramidion of Rer and Nitocris): *dwꜣ rꜥ*; Wenig, *The Woman in Egyptian Art*, 89: *dwꜣ nṯr sp-4*.

25. See the two examples in Edda Bresciani, Sergio Pernigotti, and Maria Paola Giangeri Silvis, *La tomba di Ciennehebu, capo dell flotta del Re*, Biblioteca di studi antichi 7 (Pisa: Giardini, 1977), pls. 32, 33 and 63. For the complexity surrounding the term Solar-Osirian unity, see Mark Smith, *Following Osiris: Perspectives on the Osirian Afterlife from Four Millenia* (Oxford: Oxford University Press, 2017), *passim*.

26. Contra Christopher A. Faraone, "Protective Statues for Home and Workshop: The Evidence for Cross-Cultural Contact in the Greek Magical Papyri," in *Languages, Objects and the Transmission of Rituals: An Interdisciplinary Analysis on Ritual Practices in the Graeco-Egyptian Papyri (PGM)*, ed. Sabina Crippa and Emanuele M. Ciampini, Antichistica 11 (Venice: Foscari, 2017), 67–68. Faraone does not illustrate an example, but see Paolo Vitellozzi, "Relations between Magical Texts and Magical Gems: Recent Perspectives," in *Bild und Schrift auf "magischen" Artefakten*, ed. Sarah Kiyanrad, Christoffer Theis, and Laura Willer, (Berlin: de Gruyter, 2018), 219 §2.37, fig. 29 (Florence: Museo Archeologico Nazionale Fi 72).

a single baboon adores Hermes, who in this context is not a solar deity[27] but the equivalent of *Thoth*, and the baboon is his appropriate sacred animal. The Egyptian connection is specific and meaningful.

The Egyptian terminology for the form of praising by baboons has been the subject of several discussions and presents a classic case of a suggestion becoming a "fact" by repetition and poor reasoning. In his 1969 study of liturgical hymns to the sun god, Jan Assmann examined the role of baboons,[28] and in particular two facing parallel texts on the east wall of the Re chapel of the small temple of Medinet Habu:

> The baboons who announce Re when this great god is born at the hour in the Underworld, they appearing for him after he has come into being. They are on *both* sides of this god when he shines in the eastern horizon of heaven, as they dance (*ỉb*) for him, as they chant (*šmꜥ*) for him, as they sing (*ḥsỉ*) for him, as they *tỉꜣ* for him.[29]

This analysis varies from Assmann's as he wrongly inserted an extra term for "dance" (*ẖbỉ*) not present in the Medinet Habu text, and he transliterated the critical term *tỉꜣ* in an alternate, and rarer, spelling *ṯỉꜣ*.[30] With no discussion, Assmann suggests a translation "sie kreischen(?)" ("they screech[?]") for the phrase.[31]Assmann does note a questionably relevant passage from Aelian, *Nat. an.* 6.10, that in Ptolemaic times Egyptians taught baboons *to dance*, but he does not suggest that any Egyptian term for "dance" is baboon specific, and all such terms have a human, not a baboon, determinative.[32] In Aelian baboons are imitating human activity, not the reverse.

Thirty years later, Joachim F. Quack revived Assmann's suggestion in a presentation for the Fifth Ägyptologische Tempeltagung, but now deprived of the significant question mark. Published in one of Quack's many unverifiable articles on suggested elements in the unpublished and never depicted "Book of the Temple," a section said to describe the promotion of priestly candidates to the place of their fathers requires that each one chosen be taught "das Kreischen (*tỉꜣ*)."[33] Now it is supposedly priests who imitate the shrieks of baboons. Quack's paragraph of justification[34] for his translation "Kreischen" is nothing more than a reference to the unsupported suggestion of Assmann (1969) and Te Velde's 1988 note that has no specific mention of the term, but translates Assmann's Medinet Habu verbs as "danced … shouted, jubilated and *sang*" and as "jump gaily … sing .. sing praises … *shout out*" (emphasis added).[35] Clearly, there is no consensus on the term in question. In any case, until there is a proper scholarly publication of at least some part of the so-called Book of the Temple, nothing said about it can be considered established.

---

27. Contra Faraone, "Protective Statues," 68: "it [the baboon] probably refers to some solar aspect of Hermes in Late Antiquity."

28. Assmann, *Liturgische Lieder an den Sonnengott*, 208–14.

29. The Epigraphic Survey, *Medinet Habu VI: The Temple Proper, Part II*, OIP 84 (Chicago: Oriental Institute of the University of Chicago, 1963), pl. 420B.

30. Assmann, *Liturgische Lieder an den Sonnengott*, 208. The only term for "dance" in the Medinet Habu text is *ỉb*, variant *ỉbꜣ* (*Wb.* I:62, 8–14), not *ẖbỉ* (*Wb.* III:250, 5–16). Assmann's text and transliteration are based on the later Taharqa version (cited on the same page), a modified parallel. For *tỉꜣ*, see *Wb.* V:241, 6–10. The *Wb.* "Zetteln" (slips of paper) for 241 give only three spellings with *t* (including the two Taharqa spellings), three with *d* (vocalized t in contemporary pronunciation and one punning with *tỉ.t*, "image"), and seven with *t* (including the two Medinet Habu writings). Leonard Lesko (*A Dictionary of Late Egyptian*, vol. 4 [Providence, RI: Scribe, 1989], 73) adds the phrase from P. Chassinat I, col. x +2, l. x+ 12: see Georges Posener, "Le Conte de Néferkaré et du Général Siséné," *RdÉ* 11 (1957): 126 and 128: *tỉꜣ tỉꜣ.w*, "clamer les acclamateurs" (linked with *ḥsỉ*, *šmꜥ*, and *gwꜣ*, all with human determinatives). The most extensive discussion of the term appears in Penelope Wilson, *A Ptolemaic Lexikon: A Lexicographical Study of the Texts in the Temple of Edfu*, OLA 78 (Leuven: Peeters, 1997), 1123–24.

31. Assmann, *Liturgische Lieder an den Sonnengott*, 209.

32. Assmann, 208–9n95. The passage is also cited in Te Velde, "Some Remarks," 132.

33. Joachim F. Quack, "Die Dienstanweisung des Oberlehrers aus dem Buch vom Tempel," in *5. Ägyptologische Tempeltagung: Würzburg 23.–26. September 1999*, ed. Horst Beinlich (Wiesbaden: Harrassowitz, 2002), 161.

34. Quack, "Die Dienstanweisung des Oberlehrers," 163 and n. 15.

35. Te Velde, "Some Remarks," 130 and 136nn6–7.

The final devolution of the discussion of the term is reached in a 2010 article by A. von Lieven,[36] who parrots—and expands upon—Quack's statement as *proved*. The only citation is to Quack 2002:[37]

> That this monkey screeching was indeed imitated by priests in the cult is proven by the Book of the Temple, a handbook of the Egyptians on how an ideal temple should be built and run.... In the entry on the head teacher it is also prescribed which styles of singing he has to teach the priests-in-training. Among them figures the song technique "screeching." The word used is indeed the same as the one used for the noise made by the jubilating baboons and this surely is not by chance.

Despite the expressed certainty, serious problems with this interpretation remain, as little philological diligence has been expended on the term *tἰȝ*. Notably, the determinative of each linked verb in the relevant Medinet Habu inscription (*ἰb, šmʿ, ḥsj,* and *tἰȝ*) has a human, not a baboon, determinative, so that each represents an adaption for a baboon of an activity appropriate for *people*. For the first three verbs, this is unquestionable as they are quite common in multiple contexts without reference to the activities of baboons. The situation is in sharp contrast to terms such as *ḳnd* or *ḫʿr*, "to rage," which do employ a monkey determinative and so explicitly compare human "raging" to the fury of primates.[38] For *tἰȝ*, only two determinatives are ever attested: the "man with hand to mouth," usually accompanied by the "tusk/tooth" determinative as is common with verbs of human speech, and, in the Ptolemaic era, the "kneeling woman with tambourine" where the term appears in the Edfu mammisi and is applied to the goddess Hathor, who strikes a tambourine before her son Horsomtas.[39] Not a single example among the thirteen gathered by the *Wb.* includes a baboon, and it is highly unlikely that Hathor was imitating a baboon. The New Kingdom through Ptolemaic examples are preceded by an identically written MK term, directly linked in the *Wb.* files: the Kahun Medical Papyrus, col. 3/25 (*Wb.* V:241, 6), where it is a sound produced by a patient with toothache, and so suggested to be "groaning," "crying," or similar. A most likely interpretation that covers the notions of "wailing musically" would be "ululation," a standard feature of musical expression in Egypt and a reasonable *human* action that could be applied to *primate* "singing." The situation is actually the inverse of that posited by Quack and von Lieven. In employing a term extended from human to primate behavior, the term thus parallels the most common expression for the baboons' activity, "praising" (*dwȝ*) the solar creator.

Figure 3. P. Turin 1778. Creator transformed through Amduat imagery, after Niwinski, *Studies on the Illustrated Theban Funerary Papyri*, 187, fig. 63.

36. Von Lieven, "The Soul of the Sun," 54.

37. She cites Joachim Friedrich Quack, "Die Dienstanweisung des Oberlehrers aus dem Buch vom Tempel," in *5. Ägyptologische Tempeltagung: Würzburg, 23.–26. September 1999*, ed. Horst Beinlich, Jochen Hallof, Holger Hussy, and Christiane von Pfeil (Wiesbaden: Harrassowitz, 2002). 159–71.

38. *Wb.* V:56–57 and III:244; Daumas, *Valeurs phonétiques*, 1:244, no. 543. As noted above, the baboon hieroglyph can read *ḏd*, "to speak" in Ptolemaic hieroglyphs, but the following speech is in *Egyptian*, not "baboonic." Nor has the sign been given the phonetic value *tἰȝ*. Contrast this with animal-specific onomatopoetic terms for hissing reptiles (*ḏdft*, "one who says *ft*"), the speech of dogs ("The dog says *whwh*") or the term for *miw* for cats, etc., discussed in Janet H. Johnson, "The Demotic Dictionary Project: 'Onchsheshonqy Had a Farm,'" *The Oriental Institute Annual Report 1984–1985* (Chicago: Oriental Institute of the University of Chicago, 1985), 55–57, https://oi.uchicago.edu/sites/oi.uchicago.edu/files/uploads/shared/docs/ar/81-90/84-85/84-85_CDD.pdf (accessed 23 July 2019). The *whwh*, "barking" of dogs is specifically mentioned in company with the speech of the ibises and baboons in the *Book of Thoth*; see Jasnow and Zauzich, *Book of Thoth*, 260–62 and 266; and Jasnow and Zauzich, *Conversations*, 130–31, nos. 445–447.

39. *Wb.* V:241, 6–10 and Zetteln. For the mammisi writing, see Émile Chassinat, *Le Mammisi d'Edfou*, MIFAO 16 (Cairo: Institut français d'archéologie orientale, 1910), 117 (reign of Ptolemy IX); and Daumas, *Valeurs phonétiques*, 1:90, no. 191.

Figure 4. (a) Penn Museum E387. (b) Penn E387, top.

The visual form of that creator can vary, as in P. Turin 1778 (fig. 3), where a motif transformed from royal Amduat texts depicts two flanking baboons adoring a winged, double headed serpent wearing crowns of Upper and Lower Egypt with the scarab of Khepri rising above him.[40] The identity of the compound deity is confirmed by presence of the adoring baboons and the solar scarab issuing from him. A further, better-attested variant is directly pertinent to the ongoing discussion of the Bes Pantheos.[41] I am indebted to Jennifer Wegner, assistant curator in the Egyptian Section of the Penn Museum, for calling my attention to three interesting, and unpublished, scarabs in the Philadelphia collection. Penn Museum E387, made of steatite with yellowish faience glaze (L: 1.5 cm W: 1.1 cm), is decorated on its base with an image of Bes flanked by two Cynocephalus baboons, their arms raised in adoration (fig. 4).[42] Two ovals carved above the baboons' upraised arms are intended as circular sun disks, so that the flanking compositions can be read as "Adoring Re" (*dwꜣ rꜥ*). Museum records establish that the scarab was excavated by Sir William M. Flinders Petrie at Lahun, purchased from him in 1890, and dated to the Twenty-Second Dynasty. The transfer of some Lahun finds to the University of Pennsylvania is noted in Petrie's *Lahun II*, with reference to tombs 608 and 906, but with no explicit mention of this scarab.[43] Although this Third Intermediate period object is not illustrated in Petrie's publications, a "rude square plaque" with comparable imagery is drawn and briefly noted in his 1891 report on Lahun ("Illahun"). The simplified drawing shows two baboons with arms raised adoring a central Bes figure. It omits the two small sun disks, though that is most likely an error by the nineteenth-century copyist rather than by the ancient artist. On the reverse side of the plaque is the royal name Menkheperre (fig. 5). Petrie assigns it to Dynasty 22.[44] The plaque would thus be contemporary with Penn E387 and reinforce its assigned date.

44

Figure 5. After Petrie, *Illahun Kahun and Gurob*, pl. XXIX, no. 44.

40. Andrej Niwinski, *Studies on the Illustrated Theban Funerary Papyri of the 11th and 10th Centuries B.C.*, OBO 86, (Freiburg: Universitätsverlag; Göttingen: Vanderhoeck & Ruprecht, 1989), 187, fig. 63 (papyrus identification on p. II, no. 63).

41. For discussion and bibliography, see Robert K. Ritner, "Pantheistic Figures in Ancient Egypt," in *Illuminating Osiris: Egyptological Studies in Honor of Mark Smith*, ed. Richard Jasnow and Ghislaine Widmer, MVCAE 2 (Atlanta: Lockwood, 2016), 319–24; *contra* Joachim Quack, "The So-Called Pantheos: On Polymorphic Deities in Late Egyptian Religion," in *Aegyptus et Pannonia III*, ed. Hedvig Györy (Budpest: MEBT – ÓEB, 2006), 175–90.

42. See Penn Scarab E387 online http://www.penn.museum/collections/object/15773. I thank David Silverman, Chief Curator of the Egyptian Section, for permission to publish the Penn scarabs.

43. Sir William M. Flinders Petrie, Guy Brunton and M. A.Murray, *Lahun II*, BSAE 33 (London: British School of Archaeology in Egypt, 1923), 43–44 and pl. XLIX. A scarab is attributed to tomb 608.

44. Sir William M. Flinders Petrie, *Illahun Kahun and Gurob*,(Warminster: Aris & Philips, 1974 [repr. of 1891]), 25 and pl. XXIX, no. 44. Note that only the left baboon's tail is drawn and the border obscures whether the end rises behind him. All objects on the plate

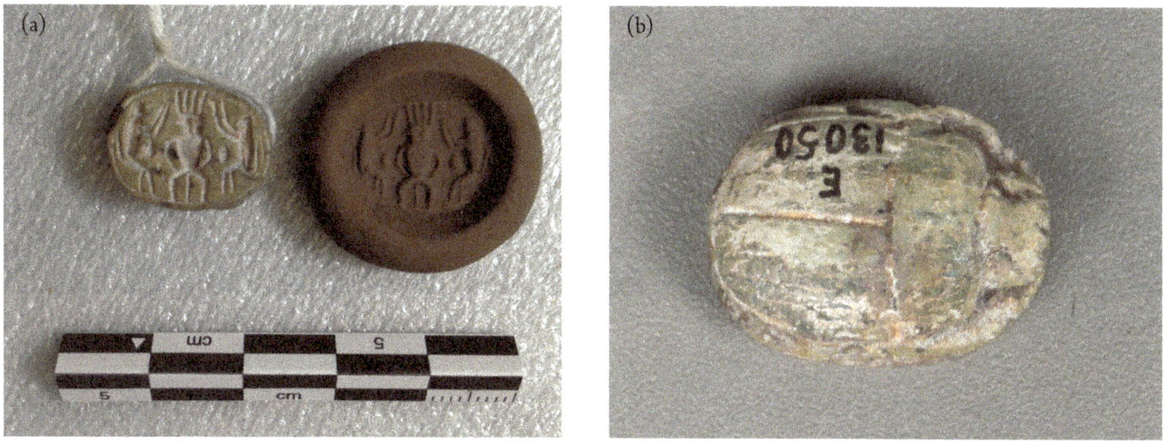

Figure 6. (a) Penn 13050. (b) Penn 13050, top.

A second Philadelphia scarab, Penn Museum E13050 (fig. 6), is similar to E387 except that the ovals are carved between Bes and the primates, placed below the baboons' upraised arms. Made of whitish glazed steatite, the scarab (L: 1.7 cm × W: 1.3 cm) is recorded as a gift of Maxwell Sommerville.[45] A third example, Penn Museum 38-28-24 (L: 2.1 cm × W: 1.5 cm) also of steatite and originally glazed was presented by John F. Lewis in December 1938 (fig. 7). The baboons' lips are elongated and only a single sun disk is carved—above the lips of the left baboon.

Figure 7. Penn 38-28-24.

A fourth unpublished Philadelphia-area example is found in the Glencairn Museum in Bryn Athyn, Pennsylvania.[46] Scarab 15.JW.233 (fig. 8) is now strung on a necklace with beads, other scarabs, and a falcon amulet and was part of an Egyptian and Classical collection belonging to Raymond Pitcairn, who acquired it from the dealers Azeez and Victor Khayat, probably during the 1920s.[47] As noted by curator Ed Gyllenhaal, the current arrangement is not ancient: "The Khayats were known to string together beads from a variety of excavations in a way that was pleasing to their clients, so I would assume nothing about the relationship between the Bes scarab and the other scarabs/bead on that string."[48] The Glencairn scarab (L: 2.0 cm × W: 1.4 cm) is more roughly carved. The baboons have no tails, their lips are elongated (as on Penn Museum 38-28-24), and the oval solar disks are placed above the lips.

are designated "XXIInd Dyn.," including many with the same royal name, presumably a reference to Thutmose III rather than to the High Priest of Amon of Dynasty 21, whose kingship is questionable; see Kenneth A. Kitchen, *The Third Intermediate Period in Egypt (1100–650 B.C.)*, 2nd ed. (Warminster: Aris & Philips, 1986), 51 and 533–34.

45. Penn's only professor of glyptology; see Alessandro Pezzati, "The Eccentric Maxwell Sommerville," *Expedition* 54.3 (2012): 39.

46. I am grateful to Ed Gyllenhaal, curator of the Glencairn Museum, for information, photographs, and permission to publish scarab 15.JW.233.

47. The Khayats had offices in New York, Haifa, and Cairo. See the discussion of the Pitcairn collection in Ed Gyllenhaal, "From Parlor to Castle: The Egyptian Collection at Glencairn Museum," in *Millions of Jubilees: Studies in Honor of David P. Silverman*, ed. Zahi Hawass and Jennifer Houser Wegner, Supplément aux Annales du Service des antiquités de l'Egypte 39 (Cairo: Conseil Suprême des Antiquités de l'Egypte, 2010), 175–203, esp. 193. A jewelry list of dealer descriptions by the Khayats later transcribed by an employee of Pitcairn and now in the museum refers to the necklace in entry 233 as "From the Zakieh collection." Perhaps a local dealer/collector in Egypt, Zakieh is unknown to me.

48. Pers. comm., 28 March 2018.

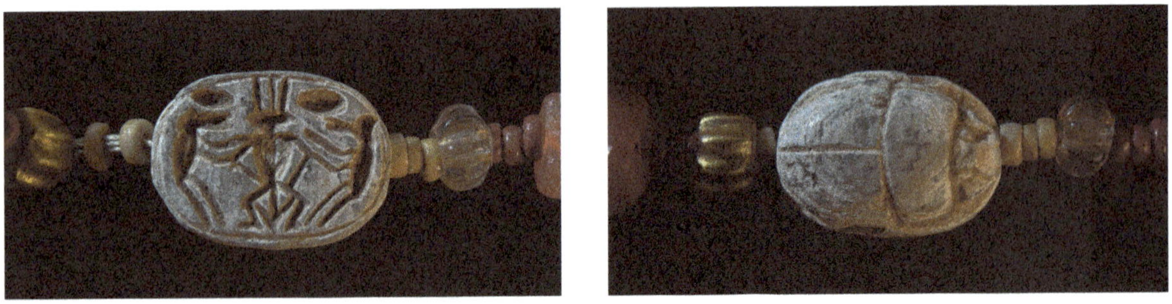

Figure 8. Glencairn scarab front and back.

Figure 9. Private collection. Photograph by permission of owner b. Top rotated.

The final example known to me (though many more may exist) was offered for sale by the on-line dealer Sands of Time, item EA1559,[49] and is now in a private collection (fig. 9). The green glazed steatite scarab, formerly in the K. Hammond collection, was mounted in the early twentieth century as a pendant in a gold braided frame (including frame L: 2.85 cm × W: 2 cm). The scarab's glaze is intact and the imagery is the best preserved. The baboons' faces are correctly proportioned, the tails droop rather than standing erect (unless that detail is obscured by the pendant frame), and the two (again oval) solar disks are placed above their raised arms (as on Penn E387, Glencairn 15.JW.233, and the one disk on Penn 38-28-24). Although the sale catalogue dated the piece to "Middle Kingdom, Dynasty 12, 1939–1760 BC," the secure parallels Penn E387 and the Lahun plaque indicate that the entire group should be dated to the Third Intermediate period and not earlier.

Despite minor differences in details and workmanship, the composition and significance are the same in all of these images. The adoring baboons with sun disks explicitly designate the revered Bes figure between them as an image of the solar creator. These Third Intermediate period representations are thus the direct antecedents of the "Bes Pantheos" figures known from papyri, statues, cippi, and gems. The later images are not simply "polymorphic" but legitimately "pathestic." The representative depiction on papyrus Brooklyn 47.218.156 is succinctly labeled Re-Khepri-Atum, the trinitarian unity who is "the one god who made himself into millions," confirmed by the addition of a figure of *ḥḥ*, "millions" above the projection of heads that issue from this "Bes of 7 faces."[50] While the Brooklyn

49. https://www.pinterest.com/pin/405886985147657098/ (accessed 25 July 2019).

50. Ritner, "Pantheistic Figures in Ancient Egypt," 321–24. For pantheos imagery on Roman-era gems, see Faraone, "Protective Statues," 59–64, but note that Faraone (62n7) accepts the erroneous conclusions of Quack, "The So-called Pantheos."

description entails the symbolic number 7,[51] a variant title for the figure from papyrus Carlsberg 475 (l. 6) names him "Bes of 9 faces on a single neck,"[52] a probable reference to the Ennead, in the Egyptian numerological system a plural of plurals (three threes). This description is echoed in a much later source of the Roman era, written in Greek but dependent upon Egyptian theology: the fourth-century "Eighth Book of Moses," cited above for its recorded "baboonic" speech. The variants of the text each invoke a pair of deities at the creation: a falcon-headed crocodile,[53] whose "popping" cries greet the solar creator, and the "Nine-formed One" who empowers him and ensures the rise of the sun.

> At each increase of the sun and diminution he (the falcon-faced crocodile) gives forth his popping noise. The Nine-formed One gives him the power to make the noise at that time, so that the sun may ascend from the sound of water, for he himself (the crocodile) appears together with him (the sun). Therefore he (the crocodile) received the forms and power of the nine gods that rise with the sun.... Accordingly, draw the two, that is the falcon-faced crocodile and the Nine-formed One standing on him.[54]

In essence, the crocodile is here comparable to the baboons with their morning greetings to the sun, recorded elsewhere in the same text. The pantheistic Nine-Formed god is both singular and plural. As a singular, "he" responds antiphonally to the crocodile's greeting, greets in turn the practitioner in hieratic speech, and is one of two figures invoked and drawn; as a plural he is the "forms and powers of the nine gods."[55] The text later reveals that his nine forms correspond to "nine names."[56]

A further, relevant image of the creator within the PGM corpus is the so-called Akephalos, or "Headless One," identified with both Osiris and, significantly, Bes.[57] An elaborate spell for revelation (PGM II.64–183) requires the drawing of two solar images, a scarab (ll. 159–160) and the Akephalos, inscribed with sacred names and vowels (fig. 10).[58] Unrecognized in previous commentary is the fact that the image is not, in fact, "headless." Issuing from his

---

51. For the symbolism of seven, see Robert K. Ritner, *The Mechanics of Ancient Egyptian Magical Practice*, SAOC 54 (Chicago: Oriental Institute of the University of Chicago, 1993, [reprinted with corrections 2008]), 161n749 and the references in the index, 310; and Jean-Claude Goyon, *Les dieux gardiens et la genèse des temples*, BdÉ 93/1 (Cairo: Institut français d'archéologie orientale du Caire, 1985), 185–88.

52. Joachim Quack, "Ein neuer Zeuge für den Text zum neunköpfigen Bes (P. Carlsberg 475)," in *The Carlsberg Papyri 7: Hieratic Texts from the Collection*, ed. Kim Ryholt, CNIP 33 (Copenhagen: Carsten Niebuhr Institute of Near Eastern Studies, University of Copenhagen: Museum Tusculanum Press, 2006), 53–64 and pls. 6–6A.

53. For the hieracocephalic crocodile, see Robert K. Ritner, "The 'God' Ptiris and the Curses of Philae," in *Guardian of Ancient Egypt: Studies in Honor of Zahi Hawass*, ed. Janice Kamrin, Miroslav Bárta, Salima Ikram, Mark Lehner, and Mohamed Megahed (Prague: Charles University, Faculty of Arts, 2020), 3:1259–370.

54. PGM XIII.390–397 and 410–15; ("nine gods" in ll. 395–396) in Preisendanz, *Papyri Graecae Magicae*, 2:107–8; Betz, *The Greek Magical Papyri*, 183, where Morton Smith translates the singular "Nine-Formed One" variously as "the nine-formed [the Ennead]," and "the nine-formed god." Drawing the "Nine-Formed One" is repeated in ll. 421–423 (Preisendanz, *Papyri Graecae Magicae*, 2:108; Betz, *The Greek Magical Papyri*, 184). For a variant of the section, see PGM XIII.40–54; in Preisendanz, *Papyri Graecae Magicae*, 2:89–90; Betz, *The Greek Magical Papyri*, 173.

55. The antiphonal greeting to the crocodile appears in ll. 45 and 415 in Preisendanz, *Papyri Graecae Magicae*, vol. II, 89 and 108; Betz, *The Greek Magical Papyri*, 173, 183. The "hieratic speech" of the Nine-formed One is in ll. 159-160 and 469-470 in Preisendanz, *Papyri Graecae Magicae*, vol. II, 94 and 110; Betz, *The Greek Magical Papyri*, 176 and 184.

56. PGM XIII.53 and 424; in Preisendanz, *Papyri Graecae Magicae*, vol. II, 90 and 108; Betz, *The Greek Magical Papyri*, 173 and 184. In a later passage, Phoebus (the sun) is given precedence of the nine gods, possession of their power and glory and a name derived from the nine gods (ll. 542-556 = Preisendanz, *Papyri Graecae Magicae*, vol. II, 113; Betz, *The Greek Magical Papyri*, 186).

57. See the discussion and PGM references in Betz, *The Greek Magical Papyri*, 335, correcting the Osiris reference to PGM V.96–172.

58. PGM II.166 in Preisendanz, *Papyri Graecae Magicae*, 1:30 and pl. I, fig. 2; Betz, *The Greek Magical Papyri*, 18. The Akephalos is earlier linked to "an infant child seated upon a lotus, O rising one, O you of many names" (Betz, 16).

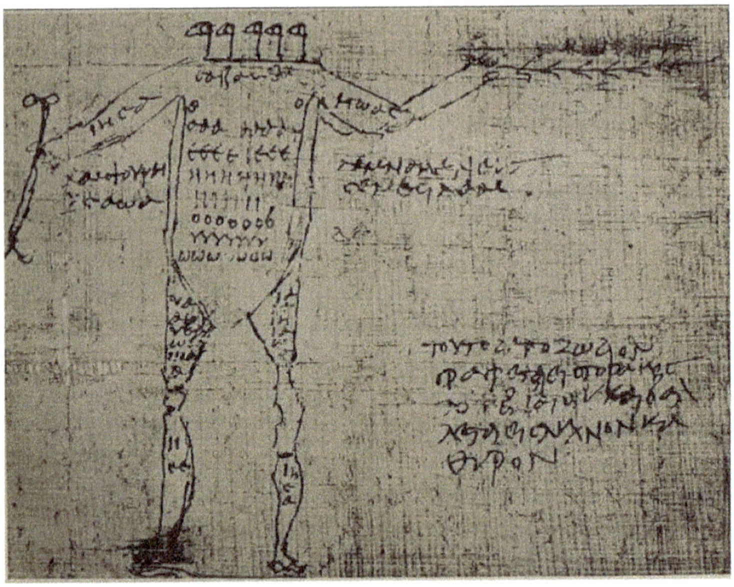

Figure 10. Akephalos – PGM vol. I pl. 1 fig. 2 1928.

neck are five summarily drawn *nṯr* signs, so that—like the Bes Pantheos—the single deity emanates a multiplicity not simply of "forms" but of "gods," not merely polymorphic, but pantheistic.

Notes on the Copenhagen Hawara Papyri

Kim Ryholt

As Richard is the publisher of about half of the known texts from the archive that forms the subject of this paper, I trust I have found a topic that will strike a note with the esteemed colleague and dear friend to whom this volume is dedicated.

On October 30, 2017, the seven largest Hawara papyri belonging to the Papyrus Carlsberg Collection at the University of Copenhagen were returned, after having been deposited off-site in the Arnamagnaean Collection (the collection of Islandic manuscripts) for more than thirty years. The transfer provided the opportunity for a closer inspection of the papyri, in the course of which a few new discoveries were made. Having also found documentation relating to their acquisition and possible archaeological context, I take this opportunity to write up the new findings.

Acquisition

Erich Lüddeckens mentions in the introduction to his *Demotische Urkunden aus Hawara*, which was published in 1998, that our group of papyri:

> wurden 1954/55 von Aksel Volten für das Ägyptologische Institut der Universität Kopenhagen bei einem Antiken-Händler im Chan el-Chalili von Kairo erworben. Noch kurz vor dem Erwerb durch Volten konnte ich die zusammengerollten Papyri, in einzelnen Blechbehältern verwahrt, sehen und den Händler über ihre Herkunft befragen. Nach dessen Aussage hatte sie ihm ein Bauer aus "einem Dorf im Fajum" gebracht, der sie auch zusammen gefunden zu haben behauptete.[1]

Since we had no records concerning this acquisition in the collection at the time, I wrote to Lüddeckens to ask if he had any further details, such as the name of the dealer. I received a very kind answer, but unfortunately, he could no longer recall the identity of the dealer and he was unable to offer any details other than those he had put in the volume.

After some searching, I was finally able to locate the relevant documentation in the archives of the Carlsberg Foundation several years later. It emerges that Aksel Volten saw the papyri in the antiquities shop of Khawam Brothers at Khan el-Khalili in November of 1954 and, through Prof. C. E. Sander-Hansen, he received funding from the Carlsberg Foundation for the acquisition.[2] The transaction was completed in December. Volten received a fixed sum of money corresponding to the asking price and, apparently having negotiated a better deal, was allowed to use the rest

I am grateful to Cary Martin for checking my English and to Ida Adsbøl Christensen who assisted me in photographing the clay sealings of P. Carlsberg 46, 47, and 48.

1. Erich Lüddeckens, *Demotische Urkunden aus Hawara*, VOHD Suppl. 28 (Stuttgart: Steiner, 1998), ix.

2. For this dealership, see Fredrik Hagen and Kim Ryholt, *The Antiquities Trade in Egypt 1880–1930* (Copenhagen: Det Kongelige Danske Videnskabernes Selskab, 2016), 81–82, fig. 62–67; 228–29, figs. 147–149, *et passim*.

of the funding to acquire further papyri. The latter purchases include material from the estate of Maurice Nahman, from Jean Tano, and from Kamel Abdallah Hammouda, all of whom were similarly based in Cairo.[3]

Archaeological Context

Regretfully, as is so often the case, the ancient archive lacks a documented archaeological context and it seems unlikely that it can ever be retrieved. Yet, for what it is worth, Wolja Erichsen—to whom the publication was originally entrusted—provides an interesting detail that must have been communicated to him through Volten and been based on information supplied by the dealer. While Lüddeckens was informed that the papyri had been brought by a peasant from a village in the Fayum, Erichsen provides some additional detail and states that "they were found in a jar under the ruins of the great temple in Hawara in the Fayum province."[4] This is noteworthy since the family to whom the archive belonged is known to have owned real estate at the site of the temple,[5] and also in view of the excellent preservation of the papyri, which indicates that they do not derive from a rubbish context. All the documents represent legal instruments (there are no letters or accounts) and such documents were typically deposited in sealed jars and carefully hidden away, sometimes even buried, to prevent accidental loss through fire, theft, or other hazards.[6] Moreover, the claim that the papyri derived from Hawara was immediately confirmed when they were unrolled and deciphered. It is similarly noteworthy that the earlier group of papyri relating to the embalmers at Hawara found in March 1911, according to Lefebvre, was discovered "non loin de la pyramide d'Amenemhat III, dans les environs de la chapelle funéraire connue sous le nom de 'Labyrinthe,'" that is, the very same general location as that provided independently for the Copenhagen papyri.[7] The information provided by Erichsen may therefore represent an accurate description of the actual circumstances of the discovery.

3. For these dealers, see Hagen and Ryholt, *The Antiquities Trade in Egypt*, 226 (Kamel Abdallah Hammouda); 253–56 (Maurice and Robert Nahman); and 266–67 (Phocion Jean Tano), et passim.

4. Lecture entitled "Et nyt Papyrusfund" ("A New Papyrus Find") presented to the Royal Danish Academy of Sciences and Letters on 20 March 1964. Erichsen speculated that the jar might have been deposited in a temple archive, but I consider this unlikely. A few years earlier, in 1961, he presented another paper on the papyri, "Neue demotische Papyri aus Hawara," at Der XV. Deutsche Orientalistentag in Göttingen, but he did not mention the discovery of the papyri on this occasion. (A Danish version of the paper, "Nye demotiske Papyri," was also presented somewhere, perhaps at the Royal Academy.) He had also discussed the Hawara papyri in 1958 at the Ninth International Congress of Papyrology in Oslo, but, as explicitly emerges from the Göttingen paper, he was at this point in time as yet unaware of the Hawara papyri in Copenhagen. The Oslo paper was published as Wolja Erichsen, "Ein neuer Typ einer demotischen ehegüterrechtlichen Urkunde," in *Proceedings of the IX International Congress of Papyrology*, ed. Leiv Amundsen and Vegard Skånland (Oslo: Norwegian Universities Press 1961), 320–27. The original manuscripts of the other papers are deposited in the Royal Library in Copenhagen.

5. P. Carlsberg 51 is a receipt for payment of *phelochicon* relating to a stone building at the Labyrinth. Since stone buildings are rare, this was perhaps a part of the ancient temple that had been converted for other use at a time when the original cultic function of the building had long since ceased.

6. On the storage of papyri in jars, with many further examples, see Kim Ryholt, "The Storage of Papyri in Ancient Egypt," in *Collect and Preserve : Institutional Contexts of Epistemic Knowledge in Pre-Modern Societies*, ed. Eva Cancik-Kirschbaum, Jochem Kahl, Eung-Jeung Lee, and Michaela Engert, Episteme in Bewegung 9 (Wiesbaden: Harrassowitz, 2021), 23–64.

7. Gustave Lefebvre, "Papyrus du Fayoum," *Bulletin de la Société d'Alexandrie* 14 (1912): 4. A note in Lefebvre's hand on the box with the Hawara papyri from 1911 in the Cairo Museum states that they were found "à l'Ouest de la pyramide": Wilhelm Spiegelberg, *Die demotischen Denkmäler III: Demotische Inschriften und Papyri*, Catalogue général des antiquités égyptiennes (Berlin: Reichsdruckerei, 1932), 82. This seems to be a slip of the pen, since the Nile flows west of the pyramid and the temple is situated to its south. It remains uncertain who actually found these papyri. Flinders Petrie had the official concession at Hawara for the season of 1910/11, but the only substantial papyri he found were Greek and dated to the Roman period: William M. Flinders Petrie, *Roman Portraits and Memphis (IV)* (London: School of Archaeology in Egypt; Quaritch, 1911), 22–23. They would therefore seem to have been discovered just after he

Storage: The Phenomenon of Compound Rolls

The papyri acquired from the Khawam Brothers are explicitly described in the application to the Carlsberg Foundation as "six unopened manuscripts." Volten must have been very pleasantly surprised when they were unrolled in Copenhagen. As it turned out, the ancient owner of the archive had in some cases rolled up together related papyri, and several of the rolls thus consisted of more than one physically separate document. The acquisition was found to consist of a total of "9 large Demotic complete documents and 4 Greek," that is, thirteen documents rather than just six.[8] These are:

Inventory no.	Editio princeps[9]
P. Carlsberg 34	P. Lüdd.Haw. I
P. Carlsberg 35	P. Lüdd.Haw. II
P. Carlsberg 36	P. Lüdd.Haw. III
P. Carlsberg 37a	P. Lüdd.Haw. IVa
P. Carlsberg 37b	P. Lüdd.Haw. IVb
P. Carlsberg 38a	P. Lüdd.Haw. Va
P. Carlsberg 38b	P. Lüdd.Haw. Vb
P. Carlsberg 39a	P. Lüdd.Haw. VIIa
P. Carlsberg 39b	P. Lüdd.Haw. VIIb
P. Carlsberg 46	Bülow-Jacobsen, *BICS* 29 (1982), 12–16, pl. 1–2
P. Carlsberg 47	Bülow-Jacobsen, 12–16, pl. 1–2
P. Carlsberg 48	Bülow-Jacobsen, 12–16, pl. 1–2
P. Carlsberg 51	Bülow-Jacobsen, 45–47, pl. 3

I have been unable to locate any notes describing precisely which papyri were rolled up together. Based on their contents, I would imagine the following situation (the roll numbers are arbitrary):

Roll 1	P. Carlsberg 34, annuity contract, 239 BCE
Roll 2	P. Carlsberg 35, annuity contract, 235 BCE
Roll 3	P. Carlsberg 36, document of cession, 233 BCE
	P. Carlsberg 46, tax receipt relating to the same property, 239 BCE
	P. Carlsberg 47, tax receipt relating to the same property, 237 BCE
	P. Carlsberg 48, tax receipt relating to the same property, 236 BCE
Roll 4	P. Carlsberg 37a, document concerning complaint about burial, 220 BCE
	P. Carlsberg 37b, document of cession relating to P. Carlsberg 37a, 220 BCE
Roll 5	P. Carlsberg 38a, document of sale, 217 BCE
	P. Carlsberg 38b, document of cession relating to P. Carlsberg 38a, 217 BCE

---

left the site, whether through illicit digging or by sebbakh diggers, or they might have been stolen during his excavations. Thefts from excavations was exceedingly common; see Hagen and Ryholt, *The Antiquities Trade in Egypt*, 30.

8. Letter from Aksel Volten to the Carlsberg Foundation dated 2 September 1960. The Demotic documents are also referred to explicitly as "nine new papyri" in Erichsen's above-mentioned lectures, "Neue demotische Papyri aus Hawara" and "Nye demotiske Papyri."

9. Lüddeckens, *Demotische Urkunden aus Hawara*; Adam Bülow-Jacobson, "Three Ptolemaic Tax-Receipts from Hawara (P. Carlsberg 46–48)," *BICS* 29 (1982): 12–16, pl. 1–2; Adam Bülow-Jacobson, "Receipt for ΦΕΛΩΧΙΚΟΝ (P. Carlsberg 51)," *BICS* 32 (1985): 45–47, pl. 3. The texts are all included in Steve Pasek, *Hawara: Eine ägyptische Seidlung in hellenistischer Zeit*, vol. 2 (Berlin: Frank & Timme, 2007).

Roll 6	P. Carlsberg 39a, document of sale, 183 BCE
	P. Carlsberg 39b, document of cession relating to P. Carlsberg 39a, 183 BCE
Uncertain	P. Carlsberg 51, tax receipt relating to some property, 235 BCE

According to this reconstruction, three pairs of related papyri were rolled up together, while three small tax receipts were rolled up within the main document to which they pertained.

The ancient owner of the documents had also rolled up several of those papyri from the archive that are now in Chicago. It is recorded that P. Chic.Haw. 4 was rolled inside P. Chic.Haw. 9, that P. Chic.Haw. 10 was rolled inside P. Chic.Haw. 2, and that the small tax receipt P. Chic.Haw. 7c was rolled up within P. Chic.Haw. 7a+b.[10] It is noteworthy that the documents that formed rolls "a" and "b" are not closely related but in fact separated by several generations. Without reliable records (assuming that the records are in fact fully accurate and that no references have been mixed up), it would have been otherwise impossible to determine that these documents were once kept together in this fashion.

Roll a	P. Chic.Haw. 4, donation document, 292 BCE
	P. Chic.Haw. 9, provisional sale, 239 BCE
Roll b	P. Chic.Haw. 2, annuity contract, 331 BCE
	P. Chic.Haw. 10, acknowledgement of repayment of loan, 221 BCE
Roll c	P. Chic.Haw. 7a+b, provisional sale and mortgage agreement, 245 BCE
	P. Chic.Haw. 7c, tax receipt relating to P. Chic.Haw. 7a+b, 245 BCE

I have recently discussed the phenomenon of rolling up related papyri elsewhere and there is no need to repeat that discussion here.[11] It will suffice to note that compound rolls represent a practical manner for keeping documents together, which is attested at least since the early second millennium BCE, and that the earlier discovery of papyri found at Hawara in 1911 included a group of no less than six documents that had been rolled up together; a photograph of the latter was published by Spiegelberg.[12]

Individual vs. Multiple-Document Papyri

The editio princeps of the Demotic Copenhagen papyri noted the possibility that the two pairs of documents of sale with corresponding documents of cession preserved in P. Carlsberg 38a and 38b and P. Carlsberg 39a and 39b had, in both cases, originally formed single papyri that were cut up in modern times.[13] This suggestion was based on the observation, by Joachim F. Quack, that the horizontal fibers of the last sheets of P. Carlsberg 38a and 39a match those of the first sheets P. Carlsberg 38b and 39b. The same was also suggested for P. Carlsberg 37a and 37b, which is more surprising—as also noted by Lüddeckens—since the texts were written three days apart, and I have myself been unable to detect any fiber match despite a thorough inspection.

While the fibers of the other two pairs of texts do match, the new documentation reveals that the individual texts had in fact already been cut into separate papyri in antiquity. The cuts are relatively sharp, but this cannot always be

10. George Robert Hughes and Richard Jasnow, *Oriental Institute Hawara Papyri: Demotic and Greek Texts from an Egyptian Family Archive in the Fayum (Fourth to Third Century B.C.)*, OIP 113 (Chicago: Oriental Institute of the University of Chicago, 1997), 5, 23, 38, 46.

11. Ryholt, "Storage of Papyri in Ancient Egypt."

12. Spiegelberg, *Die demotischen Denkmäler III*, 82, unnumbered figure.

13. Lüddeckens, *Demotische Urkunden aus Hawara*, ix.

taken to indicate that they are modern. Papyri were also cut with knives in antiquity and not all papyri have suffered from wear. A good example is provided by one of the papyri in question, P. Carlsberg 39b, where the upper and lower edges as well as the original left edge are just as sharp as the right edge that joins P. Carlsberg 39a. The fact that an extra sheet was added to the original left edge in antiquity shows—should any doubt exist—that these are not modern cuts either.

It is only natural that related texts issued on the same day and relating to the same transaction should be written on sections of papyrus with matching fibers. The explanation is purely practical. A professional scribe would write a document on a roll and, once complete, cut the finished document from the roll. He would then proceed to the next document, whether it was related or not. Hence, if he wrote two documents for the same individual, one after the other, those documents would usually have been cut from the same papyrus and the fibers of the end of one and the beginning of the other would thus inevitably match. An exception would be those situations where the scribe had reached the end of a papyrus or did not have enough space for another document, in which case he would choose a new roll.[14] The same approach is also attested for shorter texts, such as letters and oracle questions, where we often find "offset traces" due to slightly inaccurate subsequent cutting.[15]

At the same time, there are also many cases where related documents were in fact inscribed and kept together on a single papyrus. Two examples, both consisting of a document of sale followed by its corresponding document of cession, are preserved in P. BM EA 10830 and 10390, dating to 198 BCE and 136 BCE respectively.[16] In both cases, the scribe wrote one document after the other in the usual manner, but instead of making a cut after the first one and another cut after the second, he only made a cut after the second and issued the pair of documents together on a single papyrus. It hardly mattered to the scribe whether the documents formed separate manuscripts or not. They were written in a manner—with ample margins—where they could easily be divided later, and the decision whether to do so or not was left to the discretion of the owner. Having related documents on a single continuous papyrus naturally afforded a convenient way of keeping them together and they could always be cut up at some subsequent point in time, should the need arise.

Along the same lines, it was not uncommon that an original document would be brought to the relevant official and inscribed with a tax receipt, when such was required by the nature of the transaction, rather than having it issued on a separate piece of papyrus. Again, this would also help ensure that the documentation was kept together. This, of course, was not possible in the case of the type of tax receipts discussed below, which feature a rolled up and sealed interior with a (very) partial copy of the text in question.

Without conservation records, it can be difficult to ascertain whether or not papyri cut from the same roll and inscribed with related documents formed separate manuscripts in antiquity. Some of them may well represent large multiple-document papyri that were cut up in modern times to reduce their size for reasons of storage or in order that they may be sold as several separate items, instead of just one, for higher profit. A trained conservator would usually give the cut a distinct pattern, rather than a straight line, to show what belongs together and that the cut is not ancient. A good example of this is afforded by P. BM EA 10722 and 10723 (181 BCE) from the archive of Amenothes son of Harsiesis, which are—once again—inscribed with a document of sale and a document of cession respectively. Here the cut is evidently modern, and it is therefore clear that the two papyri originally formed a single manuscript

14. A possible example of a scribe reaching the end of a roll is P. Carlsberg 39b, where the scribe has added a piece of very coarse papyrus to the end of the document to provide the necessary margin for rolling it up safely.

15. Kim Ryholt, "A Phyle Roster from Tebtunis with a Note on Offset Cutting, Traces, and Loss," *Enchoria* 36 (2018/19): 149–50.

16. Carol A. R. Andrews, *Ptolemaic Legal Texts from the Theban Area*, Catalogue of Demotic Papyri in the British Museum IV (London: British Museum Publications, 1990), cat. 3 and 33, and esp. pls. 8 and 65.

inscribed with the two documents.[17] The same may also be the case with two other sets of documents of related transactions from the same archive.[18]

The Archive

It has long been recognized that the Copenhagen papyri form part of the same archive as the ten papyri in the Chicago Oriental Institute and the Rendell Papyrus, which were published by Hughes and Jasnow in 1997.[19] Most of the twenty-four papyri relate directly to the same individuals and transactions. It is almost inevitable that further documents from the archive will have ended up in other collections through their dispersal on the antiquities market, and the now missing papyri may have provided the links to those few documents where the exact relation is less obvious.

A series of other Ptolemaic-period papyri from Hawara pertain to individuals with a similar social background, that is, embalmers from Hawara, and hence presumably from the same community. These papyri do not appear to have any direct relation to the Chicago-Copenhagen-Rendell archive and the circumstances of their acquisition also suggest that they were part of a separate discovery. Accordingly, the group of documents relating to the embalmers at Hawara as a whole is likely to represent at least two if not more distinct archives discovered in the same general area.[20] This situation would be comparable to that of Pathyris, which has similarly yielded a number of contemporary but distinct archives belonging to individuals with an identical social background, some of them related by blood,[21] and to the several choachyte archives from Thebes.[22]

P. Carlsberg 47: A Greek Tax Receipt Restored

Among our four Greek tax receipts from Hawara, it has puzzled me in the past that the top part of P. Carlsberg 47, which would have contained the interior writing, apparently was missing. The papyrus was found inside one of the larger rolls and thus ought to have been intact. The point between the exterior and the rolled up interior sections of these receipts is often quite fragile, and it is precisely here that the papyrus is broken, whether in antiquity or in

17. Andrews, *Ptolemaic Legal Texts*, cat. 10, and esp. pl. 28.

18. Scil. the document of sale P. BM EA 10721 and the document of cession P. BM EA 10727 (182 BCE), and the document of sale P. BM EA 10768 + P. Brux. E 8053, the document of cession P. Brux. E 8051A+B, and perhaps also the tax receipt P. Brux. E 8054 (170 BCE): Andrews, *Ptolemaic Legal Texts*, cat. 12; Mark Depauw, "A Sale of a House in Thebes on a Complete Papyrus Roll," in *Elkab and Beyond: Studies in Honour of Luc Limme*, ed. Wouter Claes, Herman De Meulenaere, and S. Hendrickx, OLA 191 (Leuven: Peeters, 2009), 261–81.

19. Hughes and Jasnow, *Oriental Institute Hawara Papyri*. The current whereabouts of the Rendell Papyrus are unknown to me.

20. Sven P. Vleeming, "Hawara Papyri Studies," *Enchoria* 25 (1999): 128–43; see also Pasek, *Hawara: Eine ägyptische Seidlung in hellenistischer Zeit*, 2:9–49; and Inge Uytterhoeven, *Hawara in the Graeco-Roman Period: Life and Death in a Fayum Village*, OLA 174 (Leuven: Peeters, 2009), 259–88.

21. An extensive survey is provided by Katelijn Vandorpe and Sofie Waebens, *Reconstructing Pathyris' Archives: A Multicultural Community in Hellenistic Egypt*, Collectanea Hellenistica 3 (Brussels: Wetenschappelijk Comité Klassieke Studies van de Koninklijke Vlaamse Academie van België voor Wetenschappen en Kunsten, 2009).

22. The main archives are discussed by P. W. Pestman, *The Archive of the Theban Choachytes (Second Century B.C.): A Survey of the Demotic and Greek Papyri Contained in the Archive*, StudDem 2 (Leuven: Peeters,1993); Pieter W. Pestman, *Les papyrus démotiques de Tsenhor (P. Tsenhor): Les archives privées d'une femme égyptienne du temps de Darius Ier*, StudDem 4 (Leuven: Peeters, 1994); and Koenrad Donker van Heel, *Abnormal Hieratic and Early Demotic Texts collected by the Theban Choachytes in the Reign of Amasis* (PhD diss., Leiden, 1995). Three documents from a previously unknown archive, with indirect ties to that of Djekhy, were recently acquired for the Papyrus Carlsberg Collection; a preliminary report is published by Ida A. Christensen and Kim Ryholt, "Choachytter i København," *Papyrus* 39 (2019): 16–23 (Danish).

modern times. The same is the case with P. Carlsberg 51 (for which see below).

As luck would have it, the missing section of P. Carlsberg 47 turned up when I inspected the newly returned Demotic documents in 2017. The interior writing had been unrolled and, for some reason, mounted with the Demotic P. Carlsberg 35. Lüddeckens had noted the unrelated piece which he briefly refers to as "ein unabhängig von der Urkunde mitverglastes Papyrusstück mit 2,5 cm. Schrift."[23] However, he did not read the brief text nor note that it was actually written in Greek. Having joined and restored the papyrus, it is now virtually complete (fig. 1). It measures 7.3 by 22.4 cm.

The interior writing only provides the date of the document, ι Τυβι ῑ, "Year 10, Tybi 10," but this detail is significant, since the year is lost in the exterior writing and only traces of the rest of the date remain. It confirms the restoration already proposed in the *editio princeps* by Adam Bülow-Jacobson, and thus the date of the papyrus is now firmly established as 28 February 237 BCE.

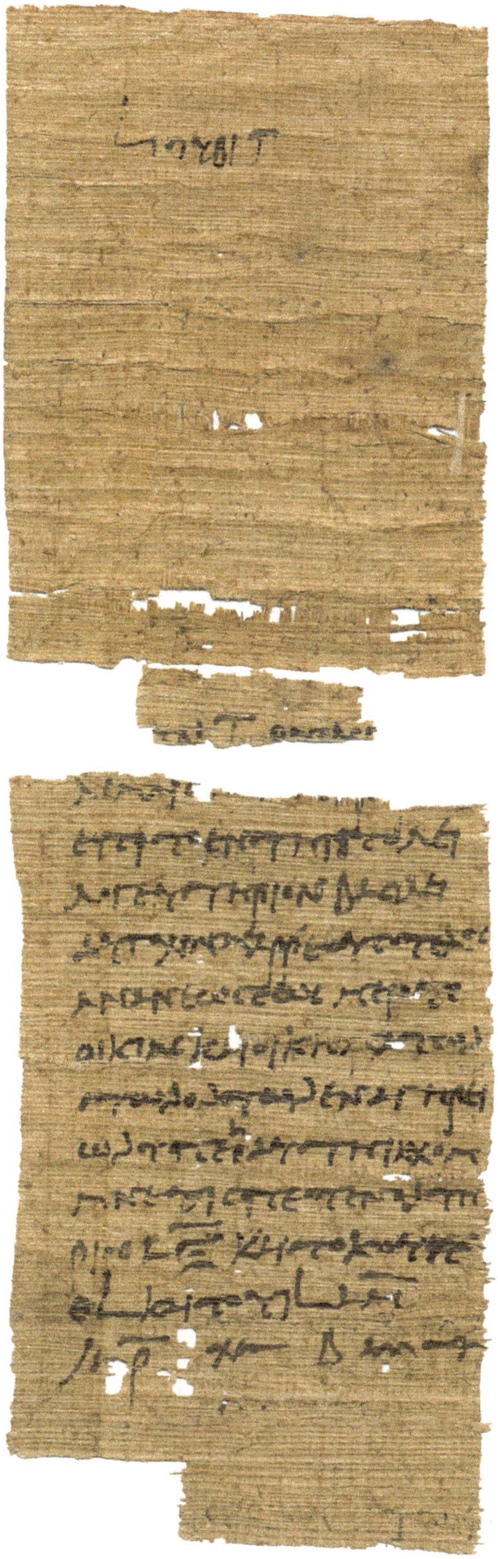

Figure. 1. P. Carlsberg 47.

The Clay Sealing of P. Carlsberg 47

Having relocated the missing interior writing of P. Carlsberg 47, it is clear that this document was discovered intact like the other documents. Since the purpose of the interior writing of a document was to remain sealed, unless an examination by the appropriate authority was required, it must once have been rolled tight and provided with a clay sealing as is customary.

Many years ago, I came across the only clay sealing in the collection that is not attached to a papyrus, and it was later designated P. Carlsberg 814 for the sake of our records (fig. 4). In view of its size and the dimensions of the preserved strings, this is almost certainly the sealing that was removed from the P. Carlsberg 47 when the interior writing was unrolled.[24] It may be no more than a coincidence that it depicts

23. Lüddeckens, *Demotische Urkunden aus Hawara*, 13.

24. The small oracle questions from Tebtunis in the collection, to which a sealing of this size could also have belonged, appear to have already been unrolled at the time of their acquisition. They are published by Wolja Erichsen, *Demotische Orakelfragen*, Kgl. Danske Vid. Sel. Hist.-fil. Med. XXVIII,3 (Copenhagen: Munksgaard, 1942); Karl-Theodor Zauzich, "Die demotischen Orakelfragen: Eine Zwischenbilanz," in *The Carlsberg Papyri 3: A Miscellany of Demotic*

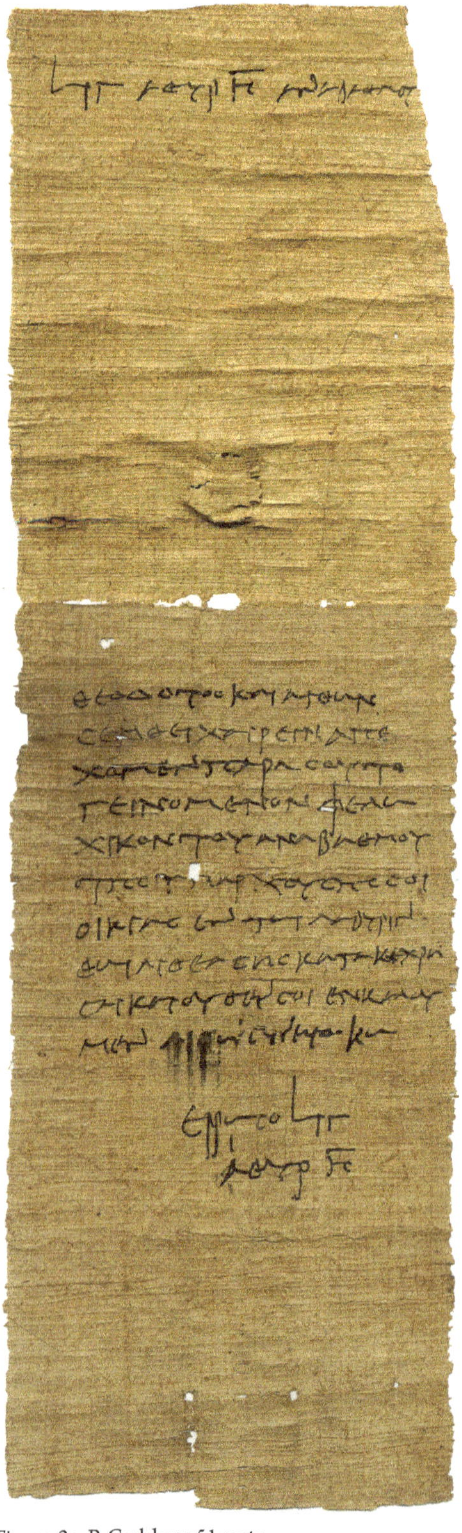

Figure. 2a. P. Carlsberg 51 recto.

Figure. 2b. P. Carlsberg 51 verso, position of sealing.

a deity with its back to an *ankh* sign, while one of the sealings from P. Carlsberg 48 similarly displays an *ankh* sign.

A close visual inspection of the papyrus has not enabled me to determine whether it originally had two sealings, like P. Carlsberg 46 and 48, or just a single one, like P. Carlsberg 51. Since only one sealing has been found, the latter was presumably the case.

P. Carlsberg 51: A Greek Tax Receipt Reunited

As in the case of P. Carlsberg 47, also the tax receipt P. Carlsberg 51 had at one point broken at the point between the exterior and the rolled up interior sections of the text, and the two halves had become disassociated—in this case twice. Bülow-Jacobsen discovered the still rolled up and sealed interior part in a box in the early 1980s and published the full text of the document. The unrolled interior part could not be located during a review of the collection in the late 1990s but turned up among the contents of the Papyrus Hauniensis Collection a few years before the two collections merged in 2013. It had presumably been brought

Texts and Studies, ed. Paul J. Frandsen and Kim Ryholt, CNIP 22 (Copenhagen: Museum Tusculanum Press, 2000), 1–25.

Figure. 3. The sealings of P. Carlsberg 46.

there for study. Since no image of the papyri has previously been published, I use this opportunity to publish a scan which shows the restored document after conservation (fig. 2). It measures 8.9 × 28.7 cm.

The Clay Sealings of the Four Tax Receipts P. Carlsberg 46–48 and 51

A noteworthy detail about the sealings of the four receipts is the different practices involved, despite their shared provenance and date.[25] One seal-impression displays a royal portrait like what might be found on a coin with the king looking right (P. Carlsberg 51). It is unlikely to actually have been made from a coin, since in that case the image would be mirrored and the king would face left. Bülow-Jacobsen argues that it might depict Ptolemy III Euergetes.[26] It is roughly 50 percent larger than the other five sealings.

Two other sealings were made from hieroglyphic seals. One displays an *ankh* sign next to the depiction of a seated male deity (P. Carlsberg 47). He appears to be wearing the double feather crown that would identify him as Amun.

25. For a survey of sealing practices in Greco-Roman Egypt, see Katelijn Vandorpe, "Seals and Stamps as Identifiers in Daily Life in Greco-Roman Egypt," in *Identifiers and Identification Methods in the Ancient World*, ed. Mark Depauw and Sandra Coussement, OLA 229 (Leuven: Peeters, 2014), 141–51.

26. Bülow-Jacobson, "Three Ptolemaic Tax-Receipts," 45n1.

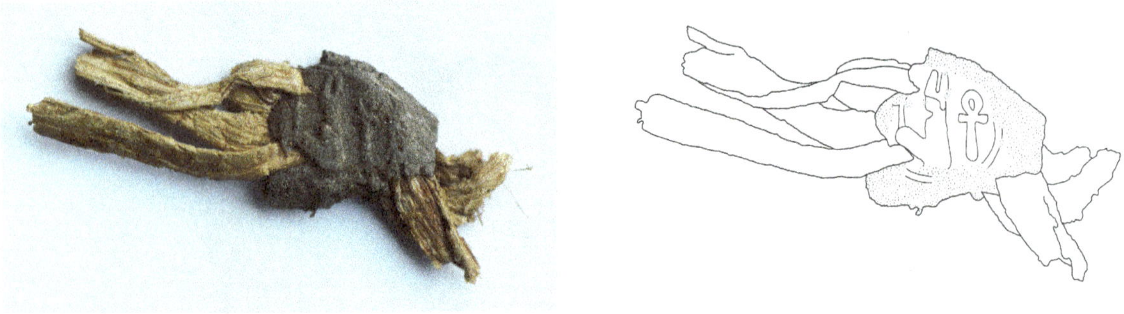

Figure. 4. The sealing of P. Carlsberg 47.

The damaged sign on his knees is presumably a small *ankh* sign. The other sealing shows only an *ankh* sign (P. Carlsberg 48 right). The impression might be incomplete, but it is certainly not from the same seal as the preceding.

The three remaining sealings have no visible imprints and are apparently blank. What may appear as a vague outline is, at least in the case of the two sealings of P. Carlsberg 46, the string against which the clay was pressed. One of the sealings has a concave surface and seems to have been pressed by the tip of a finger (P. Carlsberg 48 left) and the other two seems to have been made by pinching the clay between the tips of two fingers (P. Carlsberg 46 right and left). The two seals of a fifth Greek tax receipt from the archive, P. Chic.Haw. 7c, similarly appear to be blank.[27]

The measurements provided in the table below are made from the angle at which the sealings were photographed. It may be added that the two seals of P. Chic.Haw. 7c measure ca. h. 8.5 × w. 8.5 mm (right) and h. 9.0 × w. 7.5 mm (left) respectively, based on the published photograph.

Sealing	**Description**
P. Carlsberg 46 right h. 6.5 × w. 8.5 mm	Blank, the sealing looks as if pinched between two fingers (fig. 3)
P. Carlsberg 46 left h. 6.0 × w. 7.0 mm	Blank, the sealing looks as if pinched between two fingers (fig. 3)
P. Carlsberg 47 h. 7.0 × w. 8.5 mm	A seated male deity and an *ankh* sign (fig. 4)
P. Carlsberg 48 right h. 8.5 × w. 7.5 mm	Just an *ankh* sign is visible; complete? (fig. 5)
P. Carlsberg 48 left h. 9.0 × w. 8.5 mm	Blank, the sealing looks as if pressed by the tip of a finger (fig. 5)
P. Carlsberg 51 h. 11.5 × w. 11.0 mm	A royal portrait (fig. 6)

27. See Hughes and Jasnow, *Oriental Institute Hawara Papyri*, 46, pl. 43.

Figure. 5. The sealings of P. Carlsberg 48.

Figure. 6. The sealing of P.Carlsberg 51.

Postscript: In his research on the German papyrus cartel, Holger Essler has discovered that several intact Demotic rolls bought in 1912, alongside a number of fragments, were sent to Hamburg. The papyri form Lot 82 and were acquired from the antiquities dealer Maurice Nahman through Max Pieper on 26 October 1912. The rolls are almost certainly to be identified with the Hawara papyri in Hamburg, since there are no other groups of intact Demotic documents in that collection. Moreover, the documents in Hamburg are directly related to the Hawara documents in Cairo, the latter of which were discovered in March 1911 (see Vleeming's survey cited in note 21 above). While it seems clear that the two groups of papyri form part of the same discovery, details on the acquisition of the Hawara papyri have not previously been available, and I am grateful to Holger Essler for permission to cite his discovery here.

Postscript 2: I happened to be reading a letter from Carl Schmidt to H. O. Lange in the Royal Library, dated 9 April 1937, when I received the final proofs of this paper. As chance would have it, the letter refers to the Hawara archive here under discussion. Schmidt notes that most of the papyri has already been acquired by Edgerton from Nahman, but that there is still a set of six rolls for sale by a dealer in Cairo and another two rolls were available in Fayum. Being an active middleman in the papyrus trade, he was offering to procure these papyri for Lange, but no transaction was carried out, presumably because the latter had just spent substantial means on the acquisition of the Tebtunis papyri. It would not seem unreasonable to assume that the six papyri from the archive, which were in possession of an unnamed dealer in Cairo, are in fact identical with the six papyri later acquired by Volten in the same place. It is also noteworthy that Schmidt mentions the existence of two further rolls from the same find in the hands of a local dealer in Fayum (by which Medinet el-Fayum is usually meant). Whether or not one of them is identical with Papyrus Rendell, this information suggests that there may still be documents from the archive laying unrecognized somewhere, perhaps several in view of the fact that some of the known rolls consisted of two or more separate papyri."

Defining the *ḫ3 n ṯ3ty*; Or, Where Did the Vizier Conduct His Work?

JJ Shirley

I am honored to be asked to contribute to a Festschrift for Richard Jasnow. I hope that this small contribution, which has its origins in a question Richard asked at my PhD defense so many years ago, will be of some interest to him.

Introduction

Discussions on the vizier in ancient Egypt have most often centered around the duties and responsibilities of the office holder, and the vizier's power vis-à-vis the king. Less often has the conversation turned to the actual place in which the vizier conducted his work—his *ḫ3 n ṯ3ty*, or "office" of the vizier. In fact, there are very few textual mentions of the vizier's office, and even fewer depictions of it. While G. P. F. van den Boorn did address this topic in his excellent discussion of the sociohistorical context of the Duties of the Vizier,[1] some of his conclusions regarding the precise spatial arrangement of the buildings within the *ẖnw* have been criticized generally by David Lorton and with regard to Thebes in particular by David O'Connor.[2] These criticisms appear not to have entered the discourse of archaeologists working on royal residences, who have largely utilized van den Boorn's conclusions in identifying particular architectural features. Nor has the work of Pagliari on palace terminology been employed. This contribution will first summarize the existing textual and pictorial evidence for the *ḫ3*, and then review the relevant archaeological material from a variety of sites. By examining the evidence *in toto*, alongside the conclusions of van den Boorn, Lorton, and Pagliari, I hope to shed additional light on where this important administrative building might have resided, and what its location relative to the king's palace relays about the office and office holder.

I would like to thank Tamás Bács, Violaine Chauvet, Dimitri Laboury, Peter Lacovara, and Nadine Moeller for their comments and suggestions on earlier drafts, all of which helped to improve the final text. I would also like to thank Peter Lacovara, Nadine Moeller, Nicholas Picardo, Anna Stevens, and Josef Wegner for allowing me to use images from their own works.

1. G. P. F. van den Boorn, *Duties of the Vizier: Civil Administration in the Early New Kingdom* (London: Routledge, 1988). The date of the Duties is still under discussion, and while there is not room here to delve into this debate, for arguments against van den Boorn's early Eighteenth Dynasty dating of the text see, e.g., Stephen Quirke, "The Residence in Relations between Places of Knowledge, Production and Power: Middle Kingdom Evidence," in *Egyptian Royal Residences: 4. Symposium zur ägyptischen Königsideologie*, ed. Rolf Gundlach and John Taylor, Königtum, Staat, und Gesellschaft früher Hochkulturen 4.1 (Weisbaden: Harrassowitz, 2009), 114; Eva Pardey, "Die Datierung der Dienstanweisung für den Wesir und die Problematik von *ṯp rsj* im Neuen Reich," in *Es werde niedergelegt also Schriftstück: Festschrift für Hartwig Altenmüller zum 65. Geburtstag*, ed. Nicole Kloth, Karl Martin, and Eva Pardey, SAK Beiheft 9 (Hamburg: Buske, 2003), 323–34.

2. David Lorton, "What Was the *Pr-Nsw* and Who Managed It? Aspects of Royal Administration in the 'Duties of the Vizier,'" *SAK* 18 (1991): 291–316; David O'Connor, "Beloved of Maat, the Horizon of Re: The Royal Palace in New Kingdom Egypt," in *Ancient Egyptian Kingship*, ed. Wolfgang Helck, PdÄ 9 (Leiden: Brill, 1995), 273–74, 281–82.

Textual and Pictorial Evidence

The position of vizier is known since the Old Kingdom, and we have material relating to several holders of the job from the Old Kingdom onwards,[3] but the first textual reference to the vizier's *ḫ3* seems to appear only in the Middle Kingdom, when it is found on sealings and papyri.[4] In addition, although the tombs of some Old and Middle Kingdom viziers are known to us, and there are clearly scenes that relate to their duties as viziers, there is nothing in them to suggest that the *ḫ3* itself was in any way depicted, or even mentioned.[5] The majority of our knowledge about the *ḫ3* of the vizier comes from inscriptions and scenes found in the Theban tombs of four mid-Eighteenth Dynasty viziers: Useramun (TT131), Rekhmire (TT100), Amenemopet called Pairy (TT29),[6] and Hepu (TT66), as well that of the Ramesside vizier Paser (TT106). Within these tombs are remains of texts detailing the installation and/or the duties of the vizier, as well as other inscriptions that mention the *ḫ3* of the vizier. The physicality that the word *ḫ3* is meant to represent is immediately clear. The writing of *ḫ3* in these tombs consistently utilizes the phonetic ideogram of a columned hall (Gardiner O 27) to denote the entire word.[7] Only twice in Rekhmire's tomb is this different: in the first column of Rekhmire's Installation text, only the lotus plant (Gardiner M 12) and *pr* (Gardiner O1) signs are used to denote the vizier's *ḫ3*,[8] while in an inscription in the passage the full phonetic writing is given with the columned hall used alongside *pr* as determinatives.[9]

In addition to the paleography of the word itself, there are several textual instances in which clues to the structure of the building are given. For example, the installation texts of both Rekhmire[10] and Useramun[11] contain a brief description of the *ḫ3*:

3. For a recent analysis of the vizier in the Old Kingdom, see Miroslav Bárta, "Kings, Viziers, and Courtiers: Executive Power in the Third Millennium B.C.," in *Ancient Egyptian Administration,* ed. Juan Carlos Moreno García, HdO 104 (Leiden: Brill, 2013), 163–75 *passim*, and references therein. For the Middle Kingdom vizier, see Wolfram Grajetzki, *Die höchsten Beamten der ägyptischen Zentralverwaltung zur Zeit des Mittleren Reiches: Prosopographie, Titel und Titelreihen* (Berlin: Achet-Verlag, 2000), 9–42, 210–19, and 229–66 *passim*; Wolfram Grajetzki, *Court Officials of the Middle Kingdom* (London: Duckworth, 2009), 15–41; and Wolfram Grajetzki, "Setting a State Anew: The Central Administration from the End of the Old Kingdom to the End of the Middle Kingdom, in *Ancient Egyptian Administration*, ed. Juan Carlos Moreno García, HdO 104 (Leiden: Brill, 2013), 215–37.

4. Grajetzki, *Court Officials*, 15–17.

5. The Fifth Dynasty tomb of the vizier Nebkauhor includes mention of archives and a records office, which could suggest that a vizier's *ḫ3* existed at this time, particularly since viziers are no longer necessarily members of the royal family at this time; see Bárta "Kings, Viziers, and Courtiers," 166–67 and refences therein. Interestingly, in the Sixth Dynasty mastaba of the vizier Khentika Ikheki at Saqqara, a scene at the entrance to the tomb depicts in the second register an individual named (only) Ikheki who is overseeing the rendering of justice (including punishments). The only titles given here for Ikheki are sole companion and lector priest, which has raised the question of whether this could be a depiction of Khentika Ikhekhi fulfilling his function of vizier despite the lack of the title being mentioned; see T. G. H. James and M. R. Apted, *The Mastaba of Khentika called Ikheki*, ASE 30 (London: EES, 1953), pl. xi. I would like to thank Violaine Chauvet for bringing this to my attention.

6. See also the ostracon preserving a section of the text: Pierre Tallet, "Un nouveau témoin des « Devoirs du Vizier » dans la tombe d'Aménémopé (Thèbes, TT29)," *CdÉ* 80.159–160 (2005): 66–75.

7. Admittedly, since it is quite likely that each new vizier utilized the same text, whether from a precursor's tomb or a papyrus, consistency is perhaps expected in the texts as well as in the iconography.

8. TT100: PM I.1, 209 scene (5); Norman de Garis Davies, *The Tomb of Rekh-mi-Rē at Thebes*. 2 vols. Publications of the Metropolitan Museum of Art Egyptian Expedition 11 (New York: Metropolitan Museum of Art Egyptian Expedition, 1943), 2:xiv.

9. TT100: PM I.1, 214 scene (19); Davies, *The Tomb of Rekh-mi-Rē at Thebes*, 2:cxi–cxii, 1–2. See also *Wb*. III:221, 18–22 and 222, 1–4, which notes the variations and gives the main definition as "Hall des Königs, des Gerichts" and with another use as "Amtshalle, Büro des Viziers"

10. TT100: PM I.1, 209 scene (5); Davies, *The Tomb of Rekh-mi-Rē at Thebes*, 2:xv: col. 18.

11. TT131: PM I.1, 246 scene (12); Eberhard Dziobek, *Die Gräber des Vezirs User-Amun Theben Nr. 61 und 131*, AV 84 (Mainz: von Zabern, 1994), 77, pl. 84 col. 18 and Eberhard Dziobek, *Denkmäler des Vezirs User-Amun*, SAGA 18 (Heidelberg: Heidelberger Orientverlag, 1998), 55–66, pl. 3b, col. 18.

Figure 1. Scenes of Amenemopet (top) and Rekhmire (bottom) seated within the *ḫꜣ* of the vizier. Photographs © Dimitry Laboury, FNRS-U Liège.

ir isṯ ḫꜣ sḏm=k im=f iw wsḫ.t im=f ḫr [*sš.w*] *wḏw mdw* [*nb*(*.t*)]
Now as for the *ḫꜣ* in which you listen, there is a *wsḫ.t* therein it with the documents of all earlier judgments.

The use of *wsḫ.t* implies that at least one room of the building was a hall or court of some type. Additionally, the fact that this room is described as containing documents, possibly archives, indicates that the *ḫꜣ* had more than one room. The idea of a multiroom building is further supported by sections of the Duties where the activities of the vizier are detailed. As van den Boorn noted in his discussions concerning the *ḫnr.t wr*, a main function of this place, which has its own administrative apparatus, was as an archival storage facility. The vizier reviewed documents brought from the *ḫnr.t wr*, and then re-archived them. In dealing with issues concerning local administration rather than central, the vizier also needed to review documents brought from local archives.[12] This suggests that there was likely an area within the vizier's *ḫꜣ* where such documents could be examined and temporarily stored. The large number of officials attached to the vizier, comprising scribes, messengers, chamberlain, and so on[13] also suggests that there would have been rooms in which they would work or wait while the vizier was conducting business that did not require their presence. Finally, in both Useramun's and Rekhmire's tombs, there are scenes in which the vizier sits and inspects the *inw n ḫꜣ n ṯꜣty*.[14] The accompanying registers depict rows of individuals from the south and north of Egypt bringing goods, which scribes are shown recording. Even if the goods themselves are not paraded into the *ḫꜣ*, there would have needed to be enough room for the scribes to oversee the presentation of *inw* while the vizier looked on. This again suggests a large central space, as well as perhaps smaller rooms where the scribes could then compile and store the official records.

Within Useramun's, Rekhmire's, and Amenemopet's tombs, the vizier is depicted sitting within his *ḫꜣ* undertaking vizieral duties—as a conceptual accompaniment to the text—providing further information about the building's physical layout.[15] Although Useramun's scene is nearly completely destroyed,[16] the scene is well preserved in the other two tombs (fig. 1).[17] In these images, the vizier sits on a high-backed chair placed on a reed mat, holding his *ʿbꜣ* scepter and staff, exactly as is described in the first column of the Duties inscription.[18] Above him is a roof that extends across several registers of figures, with three fluted columns, one on either side of the vizier, and the third behind the rows of figures.[19] The roof is painted yellow, as are the support pieces that extend below the roof and connect to the column capitals. The column shafts are all painted reddish brown, with yellow bands just below the multicol-

12. Van den Boorn, *Duties of the Vizier*, 121, 125–29, 133–45, 302, 316–20.

13. Van den Boorn, 324–29.

14. Rekhmire: TT100, PM I.1, 206 scene (2) (adjacent to the Duties of the Vizier text) and 209 scene (6); Davies, *The Tomb of Rekh-mi-Rē at Thebes*, 1:33–36 and 2:xxix, xl; Usermaun: TT131, PM I.1, 246 scene (7); Dziobek, *Die Gräber des Vezirs*, 85–86, pl. 75, 87.

15. The scene which might have accompanied Hepu's text is completely lost; see TT66, PM I.1, 132 scene (6); Nina de Garis Davies, *Scenes from Some Theban Tombs (Nos. 38, 66, 162, with excerpts from 81)*, PTT 4 (Oxford: Oxford University Press, 1963), 10, pl. x. I was not able to access the 2001 tomb publication by Shaheen (Alaael-Din M. Shaheen, *The Theban Tomb of the Vizier Hepu (no. 66) at Qurneh, Egypt*, (Kuwait: Kuwait University, 2001). In Paser's tomb, which has not been published, both the text and the "scene in judgment-hall" are partially extant; see TT106, PM I.1, 221 scene (8).

16. TT131: PM I.1, 246 scenes (6)–(7); Dziobek, *Die Gräber des Vezirs*, 78–85, pl. 75, 85–86.

17. For Rekhmire's tomb, TT100, see PM I.1, 206 scene (2) and Davies, *The Tomb of Rekh-mi-Rē at Thebes*, 1:30–32 and 2:xxv–xxviii. In the tomb of Amenemopet called Pairy, TT29, the scene is described in PM I.1, 46 scenes (3)–(4). This tomb is currently being studied by Laurent Bavay and Dimitri Laboury as part of a larger project to excavate, conserve, and document both this tomb and that of Sennefer, TT96. I would like to thank both of them for allowing me to access the tomb and their photographs, as well as many useful discussions over the years.

18. Van den Boorn, *Duties of the Vizier*, 12–13, 25–29; Davies, *The Tomb of Rekh-mi-Rē at Thebes*, 1:31.

19. Despite the column distribution being compositional in nature, there is no reason to think that it did not also reflect a reality of the physical structure of the building. The three columns suggest a wide space that required roof support.

ored fluted capital, and they sit atop white bases.[20] Davies suggested that this might be an impermanent structure,[21] but it seems more likely that the roof and columns are meant to denote the reception hall where the vizier would have conducted most of his work. Indeed, the combination of roof supports and wooden columns on stone bases suggests these were permanent columns. While the columns on either side of the vizier's figure might denote a kiosk-type or baldachin area within the hall where the vizier sat, this would have been a permanent emplacement. Placing the vizier's seat near the rear of the room would also have projected the status of the vizier as akin to that of the king in his throne room. It is not clear whether the roof and column extending beyond the vizier is meant to denote an extended overhang, or perhaps a roofed hall, though given the arrangement of figures the latter seems more likely.[22] These scenes of the vizier in his *ḫ3* are identical in all the tombs that contain them, and even if these images to a certain degree drew upon scenes in the tombs of predecessor viziers, it still argues for a level of standardization of the building that suggests that it was an independent structure that each vizier utilized in his turn and not an area attached to a private residence.

An additional scene in Rekhmire's tomb provides further support for a multi-roomed building (fig. 2). In the passage Rekhmire is depicted seated within his *ḫ3 wr* while a banquet takes place to which various officials have been invited. According to the inscription accompanying Rekhmire, as well as the text associated with the officials, the activity is taking place after he returned from the temple of Amun.[23] While the grouping of the officials into multiple registers follows a standard format for this type of scene, the overlapping nature and close arrangement of several figures implies a considerable crowd, thus requiring a large space in which they could gather and eat. Rekhmire is seated at his own banquet table behind a column, indicating that this is a separate space from the main area. However, the column is not in the same fluted style as the ones that appear as part of the *ḫ3* in the scene of him performing vizieral duties. Rather, it is a very simple straight pillar, lacking a capital, and appears to have supports at the base. These features combined with the lack of a roof give a sense of impermanence and suggest that the pillar may have been brought into the room especially for this purpose,[24] or may denote some type of offering structure.[25] A parallel can perhaps be found in the Old Kingdom governor's residence at Ain Asil in the Dakhla Oasis where remains of limestone pedestals were found that apparently were used as supports for a portable wooden structure. The limestone pedestals are found in multiple rooms, suggesting they were semipermanent while the structure they supported was

20. These are likely wooden columns with either palmiform or campaniform capitals. See, e.g., J. Peter Phillips, *The Columns of Ancient Egypt* (Manchester: Peartree, 2002). I would also like to thank Franck Monnier for discussing with me this scene as well as the one described below. According to Dimitri Laboury (pers. comm, 4 April 2020), in Amenemopet's tomb (TT29) the roof, supports, capitals, and columns are all painted entirely red, without the differentiation between column and capital, because "the painter and his order-giving patron decided to avoid yellow in the decoration of the tomb. So, anything that was supposed to be painted in yellow was converted into pink or red."

21. Davies, *The Tomb of Rekh-mi-Rē at Thebes*, 1:30–31.

22. Although the portion of the scene depicting Rekhmire seated does bear similarity to scenes of officials seated under a kiosk or canopy found throughout the Theban tombs, in those scenes it is only the official who is under cover, and the wide range of activities that he can be overseeing, including those that clearly took place outdoors, indicates that this was meant to denote his status rather than any clear portion of the home or office.

23. TT100: PM I.1, 214 scene (19); Davies, *The Tomb of Rekh-mi-Rē at Thebes*, 1:66–68, 2:cxi and Norman de Garis Davies, *Paintings from the Tomb of Rekh-mi-Rēʿ at Thebes*, PMMAEE 10 (New York: Metropolitan Museum of Art Egyptian Expedition, 1935), pl. xxv. There is also a similar scene in TT29 of Amenemopet; Dimitri Laboury, pers. comm., 18 April 2020.

24. So also Davies, *The Tomb of Rekh-mi-Rē at Thebes*, 1:67.

25. Franck Monnier, pers. comm., 28 January 2020. For comparison, the "house scene" depicted in the tomb of Djhutynefer (TT104, see Abdel Ghaffar Shedid, *Stil der Grabmalereien in der Zeit Amenophis' II. untersucht an den thebanischen Gräbern Nr. 104 und Nr. 80*, AV 66 (Mainz: von Zabern, 1988), pl.5a, 36a), depicts what appears to be multiple levels with columns similar to those found in Rekhmire's two *ḫ3* scenes. In Djhutynefer's image the columns with distinct capitals are in areas where the tomb owner or his guests are shown, while the plainer columns seem relegated to stairwells and work areas. All of the rooms appear to be roofed, and an important distinction is that in Djhutynefer's scene even the plain columns have bases and lack supports, indicating they are structural and permanent features.

Figure 2. Rekhmire seated within the *ḫ3 wr*. Photograph © Dimitri Laboury, FNRS-U Liège.

moved as necessary.[26] As we will see below, multiple courts generally formed parts of large residences and palaces, and one would expect the same to be true of an important official building. While the main court of the *ḫ3* would have had the permanent seat of the vizier, as depicted in the Duties scene, secondary courts might have utilized less permanent covers or shield walls so that the vizier could be set apart from those he entertained.

Prior Suggestions for the Location of the Vizier's *ḫ3*

Van den Boorn proposed that the *ḫ3* was a portion of the official residence of the vizier, as opposed to his private one, and was situated within the official area of the king's palace.[27] This conclusion is based on his interpretation of section 1, col. 1 and section 3, cols. 5–8 of the Duties, of which the relevant portions read:

Column 1:

tp-rd n ḥms.t n imy-r niw.t ṯ3ty n niw.t rsy.t n ẖnw m ḫ3 n ṯ3.ty

Instruction for the sitting of the vizier of the Southern City, (and) of the Residence, in the *ḫ3* of the vizier[28]

26. Georges Soukaissian, "A Governor's Palace at 'Ayn Asil, Dakhla Oasis," *EA* 11 (1997): 16; Nadine Moeller, *The Archaeology of Urbanism in Ancient Egypt: From the Predynastic Period to the End of the Middle Kingdom* (Cambridge: Cambridge University Press, 2016), 206–8.

27. Van den Boorn, *Duties of the Vizier*, 54–68, 310–11, 324–35.

28. After Van den Boorn, 12–13. On pp. 18–21 he discusses his interpretation that the Southern City, i.e., Thebes, should be understood as separate from the Residence, i.e., Memphis.

Columns 5–8:

> *ʿḳ=f grt r nḏ-ḫrt nb ʿnḫ wḏ3 snb iw smi(w) n=f ḫrt t3.wy m pr=f rʿ nb ʿk=f r pr-ʿ3 ḫft imy-r ḫtm ʿḥʿ=f r snt mḥtt [ḫ]r mnmn ṯ3ty m wbn m p3 sb3 n rw.ty wr.ty ḫr*
>
> *imy-r ḫtm ii=f mḫs=f ḥnʿ smi.t n=f r ḏd ... pr-nsw ʿḏ wḏ3 ḫr ṯ3ty smi=f n imy-r ḫtm r ḏd ... st nbt n ḫnw ʿd [wḏ3] ... ḫr ir m-ḫt smi wʿ n wʿ m p3 sr 2 ḫr ṯ3ty ḫ(3)b=f*
>
> *r wn sb3 nb n pr-nsw ...*
>
> Now, he shall enter to greet the Lord, l.p.h., each day when the affairs of the Two Lands have been reported to him in his residence. He shall enter the *pr-ʿ3* when the overseer of the treasury has drawn up to his position at the northern flagstaff. Then the vizier shall move (in) from the East in the doorway of the great double-gate. Then the overseer of the treasury shall come to meet him and he shall report to him saying: "... the palace is sound and prosperous." Then the vizier shall report to the overseer of the treasury, saying: "... every department of the Residence-city is sound and prosperous ...." Now after both officials have reported to each other, the vizier shall send out to open every doorway of the palace ...[29]

In his figure 5, van den Boorn provides an illustration of the possible architectural configuration of the *ḫnw*, "residence-city," within which lay the *pr-nsw*, "palace," that was comprised of both public and private (*pr-ʿ3*) areas (fig. 3).[30] According to van den Boorn's reading of the Duties, the *pr n ṯ3ty* and *ḫ3 n ṯ3ty* lay adjacent to each other within the *pr-nsw*, to the south of the private portion of the palace. This reconstruction has already been utilized in interpretations at Tell el-Dab'a[31] and Malkata.[32] In his 1991 article, Lorton analyzed both van den Boorn's reading of the textual sections of the Duties that led to the spatial configuration just described, as well as his interpretation of the nature and management of the *pr-nsw*. According to Lorton, since the text indicates that the vizier hears reports concerning the state of the two lands while in his "official" *pr*, then reports to the *imy-r ḫtm* on the condition of the *ḫnw* at a time when the doors of the *pr-nsw* are closed but those of the *ḫnw* are open, and also receives a report on the condition of the *pr-nsw* from the *imy-r ḫtm*,

> we are left to infer that the location of the vizier's house [is] within the Residence, but not within the *pr-nsw* ... the text does not afford any clues as to the exact location of the 'bureau of the vizier'. If its workday began only after the doors of the *pr-nsw* were opened, it could conceivably have been located within it; but it could have been located elsewhere in the Residence, and perhaps even have been a part of or adjunct to the vizier's house.[33]

---

29. After Van den Boorn, 54–55, with sections omitted for brevity.

30. See Van den Boorn, 67. These terms as well as others related to the term "palace" have recently been studied by Giulia Pagliari, "Function and Significance of Ancient Egyptian Royal Palaces from the Middle Kingdom to the Saite Period: A Lexicographical Study and Its Possible Connection with the Archaeological Evidence" (PhD diss., University of Birmingham, 2012), ethesis: https://etheses.bham.ac.uk/id/eprint/3657/. See also Eva Lange-Athinodorou, "Palaces of the Ancient Mind: The Textual Record versus the Archaeological Evidence," *Palaces in Ancient Egypt and the Ancient Near East, Vol. 1: Egypt*, ed. Manfred Bietak and Silvia Prell, CAENL 5 (Vienna: Austrian Academy of Sciences Press, 2018), 39–64, which combines textual and archaeological evidence in an attempt to assign specific ancient Egyptian terms to known architectural features.

31. Manfred Bietak, "Houses, Palaces and Development of Social Structure in Avaris," in *Cities and Urbanism in Ancient Egypt, International Workshop in November 2006 at the Austrian Academy of Sciences*, ed. Manfred Bietak et al., UZK 35 (Vienna: Austrian Academy of Sciences Press, 2010), 23, and Manfred Bietak, "A Thutmosid Palace Precinct at Peru-Nefer/Tell El-Dab'A," in Bietak and Prell, *Palaces in Ancient Egypt and the Ancient Near East*, 239.

32. Peter Lacovara, "In the Realm of the Sun King: Malkata, Palace-City of Amenhotep III," *Amarna Letters* 3 (1994): 19; Peter Lacovara, *The New Kingdom Royal City*, Studies in Egyptology (London: KPI, 1997), 71–72; Peter Lacovara, "Recent Work at Malqata Palace," in Bietak and Prell, *Palaces in Ancient Egypt and the Ancient Near East*, 278.

33. Lorton, "What Was the *Pr-Nsw*," 293. The other main point of Lorton's extensive argument is that, in his view, the Duties, par-

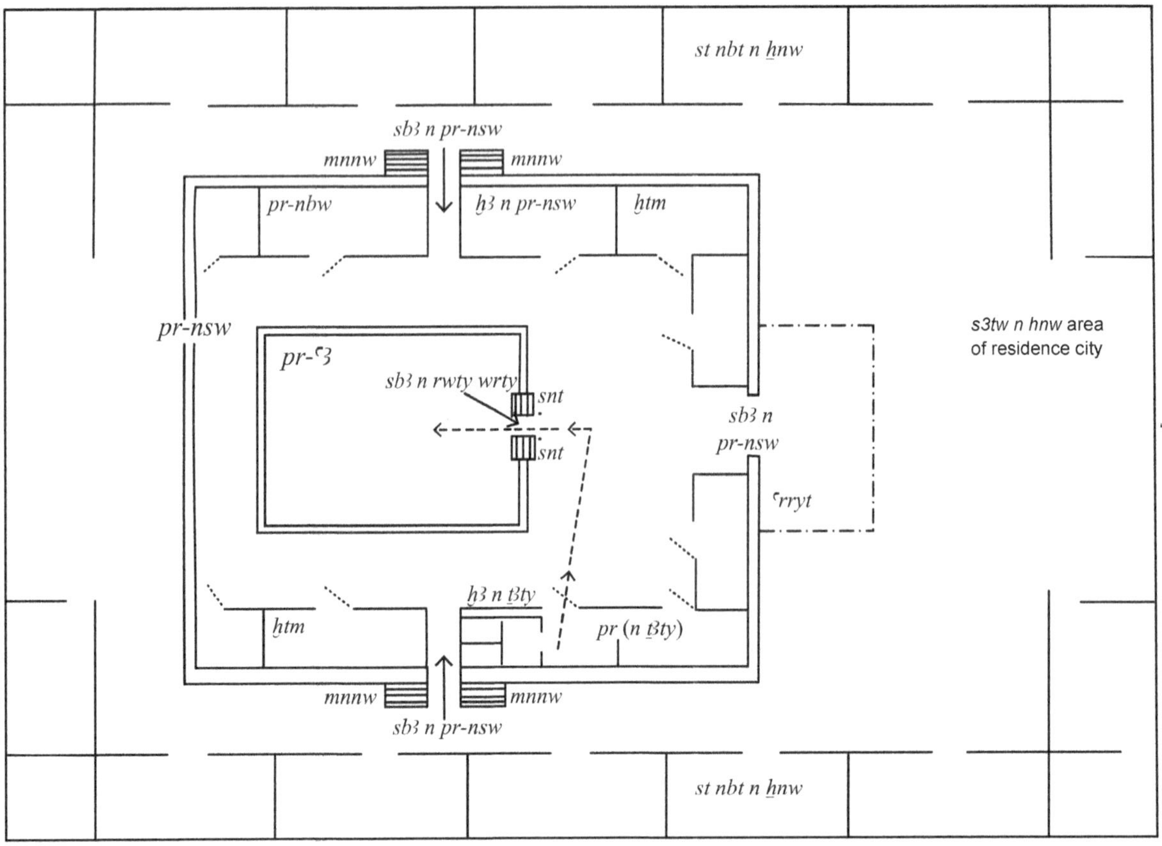

Figure 3. Suggested architectural reconstruction of the vizier's *ḫꜣ*. Drawing by Hazem Shared; after van den Boorn, *Duties of the Vizier*, 67, fig. 5.

O'Connor, in his 1995 work on New Kingdom palaces at Thebes, lays out precise arguments for locating the administrative palace of the king on the east bank, likely within or just adjacent to the Amun precinct at Karnak, and located to the north and slightly west of the main temple entrance. In so doing, he refutes van den Boorn, who views the first two lines in which the vizier mentions entering to greet the king as occurring only *after* meeting and exchanging reports with the treasurer, and thus the vizier is entering to see the king "from the East" which necessitates a reconstruction of the palace that the vizier approaches as having an east–west orientation and a flagstaff before its gate.[34] For O'Connor this cannot be possible because there is no indication of palaces having flag-staffs, only temples, and thus this building must be a temple, oriented east–west, and separate from the palace into which the vizier enters. O'Connor supports this argument by understanding the sequence of events presented at face value, and taking an alternative translation of the phrase *m wbn*, which he interprets as indicating that the vizier is appearing "in glory" after leaving the king.[35] While O'Connor's argument is sound, the verbal gymnastics involved with the phrase *m wbn* are perhaps unnecessary. It should be noted that the only phrase mentioned in relation to the vizier's location in this

ticularly sections 2–3 and 12–17, makes it clear that it is the treasurer (*imy-r ḫtm*) who was in charge of the *pr-nsw*, which should be viewed as "an entity (administrative and otherwise) separate from the administrative apparatus directed by the vizier" (309).

34. Van den Boorn, *Duties of the Vizier*, 64–65.

35. O'Connor, "Beloved of Maat," 270–79.

section is his *pr*, not his *ḫ3*. While van den Boorn presumed that this must refer to an "official" residence located within the vizier's *ḫ3*,[36] and others have followed suit, this need not be the case. It seems entirely plausible that since the events described are the first of the day, and following Lorton (above) that the vizier goes to his *ḫ3* only after greeting the king, the vizier could potentially be arriving to greet the treasurer from his actual residence, located further east from the temple and palace.[37]

The lexicographical study of Pagliari on the five principal terms used by the ancient Egyptians to mean "palace" or areas of the palace, including a review of the known architectural elements, are also relevant to this discussion. Her analysis presents a picture of the *ẖnw* as signifying the main center of kingship and administration, possibly meaning an area within the capital city, but also in reference to the capital city as a whole. As a term, Pagliari understands *pr-nswt* as largely administrative in nature, possibly comprised of its own group of buildings, or as an area within a palatial structure. She concludes that the term *pr-ʿ3* should not necessarily be understood as referring to a particular architectural area, but rather could be applied to any part of the *pr-nsw*. For Pagliari the use of *pr-ʿ3* in relation to the activities and titles of officials, particularly during the New Kingdom, suggests that it referred to the palace in a general sense, and could be used instead of *pr-nsw* to denote or imply closeness to the king. In her view, this is what led to the word transitioning from meaning palace in any respect to meaning pharaoh himself. Indeed, she seems to imply that the *pr-nsw* should in fact be understood as an area within the *pr-ʿ3*, rather than vice-versa.[38] With regard to the vizier's *ḫ3*, Pagliari reads the phrase in the Duties as indicating the physical relationship between the *ḫ3* and the *ẖnw*, and thus like Lorton also views the vizier's *ḫ3* as not necessarily being located within the *pr-nsw*.[39]

With this information laid out, I will now turn to an analysis of known architectural structures that might provide additional material relevant to determining the structure and location of the vizier's *ḫ3*, as well as his *pr*.

Archaeological Evidence

Before diving into the archaeological material, it should be noted that our modern understanding of the separation of "home" and "work" does not always apply to ancient Egypt. Indeed, given the rise in people today who "work from home," or have an "office" space within their home, perhaps this should not come as a surprise. It does however mean that in general it is perhaps a futile task to try and discern discrete working areas from residential areas within a house, except in the cases of large-scale industrial production or storage facilities.[40] Nonetheless, there are instances where we have textual evidence describing the *ḫ3* of a particular official, or a particular type of storage or administrative area. In these cases, we might reasonably assume the existence of architectural material to match it. Indeed, there is ample

36. Van den Boorn, *Duties of the Vizier*, 58.

37. Lange-Athinodorou also discusses the phrase *mnmn m wbn* in relation to palace entrances and the great double gate (*rw.ty wr.ty*), noting that while main entrances are largely located at the north or northeast, it is possible that something other than a main entrance is being referred to. She does concede that "local" north and true north might affect the understanding of the phrase and its relationship to actual architecture. See Lang-Athinodorou, "Palaces of the Ancient Mind," 45–47.

38. In a more recent analysis, Lange-Athinodorou views the *pr-nsw* less as a "palace" proper and more as an area where various administrative or economic activities took place, with the *pr-ʿ3* referring to the building which housed the actual living areas of the king; see Lange-Athinodorou, "Palaces of the Ancient Mind," 43–44.

39. Pagliari, "Function and Significance," 232–75.

40. On these issues, see the excellent discussions of Kate Spence, "Court and Palace in Ancient Egypt: The Amarna Period and Later Eighteenth Dynasty," in *The Court and Court Society in Ancient Monarchies*, ed. Antony Spawforth (Cambridge: Cambridge University Press, 2007), 302–11; Moeller, *The Archaeology of Urbanism*, 6–30; and also those found in Miriam Müller, *Household Studies in Complex Societies: (Micro) Archaeological And Textual Approaches; Papers from the Oriental Institute Seminar Household Studies in Complex Societies, Held at the Oriental Institute of the University of Chicago, 15–16 March 2013*, OIS 10 (Chicago: Oriental Institute of the University of Chicago, 2015), particularly the contributions on Egypt by Picardo, Moeller, Spence, and Spencer.

evidence from a multitude of sites and periods (e.g., Abydos, Tell el-Dab'a, Amarna, Amara West, Buhen) for the residences of governors and mayors, as well as administrative and industrial areas. For the vizier's *ḫꜣ*, as well as his *pr*, which in the context of the Duties has been interpreted as an "official" house rather than his personal or primary one, the archaeological evidence is less certain. This is in part because our knowledge of primary royal residences, where one might expect to find the vizier based, is scanty, and even our understanding of the concept of what constitutes a palace, or royal residence, is imprecise (see discussion below). Excepting Amarna, most "national capitals" have not been located, nevermind excavated, while the location of the main city of ancient Thebes is largely underneath the modern town, with only small areas near Karnak temple affording a glimpse of what the royal *ẖnw* might have looked like. In addition to Amarna, the Eighteenth Dynasty palace complex at Tell el-Dab'a and the residence-city of Malkata built on the west bank of Thebes by Amenhotep III are perhaps our best chances for archaeologically locating an actual vizier's *ḫꜣ*.

Comparative Material from Provincial Sites

Before turning to these New Kingdom sites however, it is worth examining town remains from planned settlements and provincial capitals. At sites such as *Wah-sut* at Abydos-South, Lahun near the Fayum, Tell Edfu in Upper Egypt, and Elephantine at Egypt's southern border, there is both archaeological and textual material to draw from. The remains of residential and administrative structures at these sites, as well as their locations relative to each other and other important areas of the site, may help in understanding how to reconstruct the vizier's *ḫꜣ* and official *pr*.

For example, at the town of *Wah-sut* at Abydos, the mayor's home, which was utilized by a series of mayors during the later Middle Kingdom, has been reconstructed with a private quarter including kitchen space, a roofed courtyard, and a large peristyle courtyard at the front of the house, which Wegner theorizes might have been used as a semiofficial reception space (fig. 4). Behind the house, at its southwest corner, is a separate area where thousands of sealings were found. This was the *ʿrryt*, an area specifically designed for the mayor's official business. Wegner's excavations have shown this to be "a series of multi-roomed structures and smaller areas for storage and distribution of goods."[41] Thus, the mayor's house served as a primary residence for the most important official of the town, and while it contains open areas for hosting large numbers of people, the main administrative work was centered outside the home. Also of interest is that at *Wah-sut* the mayor's residence is located in the southwest corner of the site, affording it a view over the production areas for which the mayor was in charge. Running northeast from his house are several elite homes that, based on the sealings recovered, served as "hybrid households," incorporating domestic and institutional activities of other officials of the town.[42]

At Lahun, the town is architecturally divided into two distinct areas, the "western block" of smaller homes, and the area to the east, which contained multiple large "mansions" running along the northern edge of the town. The largest of these homes is in the northwest corner and has been identified as the "mayor's residence"; given the additional large houses similar in layout to that of the mayor, it seems likely that some of these belonged to other important administrative officials connected to the town, as seen at *Wah-sut* (fig. 5).[43] The placement of the "mayor's residence"

41. Josef Wegner, "Modeling the Mayor's House at South Abydos: The Palatial Residence of *Wah-Sut*," *Expedition* 56 (2014): 30; see also Josef Wegner, "Tradition and Innovation: the Middle Kingdom," in *Egyptian Archaeology*, ed. Willeke Wendrich, Blackwell Studies in Global Archaeology 13 (Oxford: Wiley-Blackwell, 2010), 135–40, and Joseph Wegner, *The Mortuary Temple of Senwosret III at Abydos*, Publications of the Pennsylvania-Yale Expedition to Egypt 8 (New Haven: Yale Egyptological Seminar, 2007), 26–27, 291–93.

42. Nicholas Picardo, " Hybrid Households: Institutional Affiliations and Household Identity in the Town of Wah-sut (South Abydos)," in Müller, *Household Studies in Complex Societies*, 254–57, 263–74.

43. Stephen Quirke, *Lahun: A Town in Egypt 1800 BC, and the History of Its Landscape* (London: Golden House, 2005), 47, 55–73; Zoltán Horváth, "Temple(s) and Town at el-Lahun: A Study Of Ancient Toponyms in the el-Lahun Papyri," in *Archaism and Innovation: Studies in the Culture of Middle Kingdom Egypt*, ed. David P. Silverman, William Kelly Simpson, and Josef Wegner (Philadelphia: Uni-

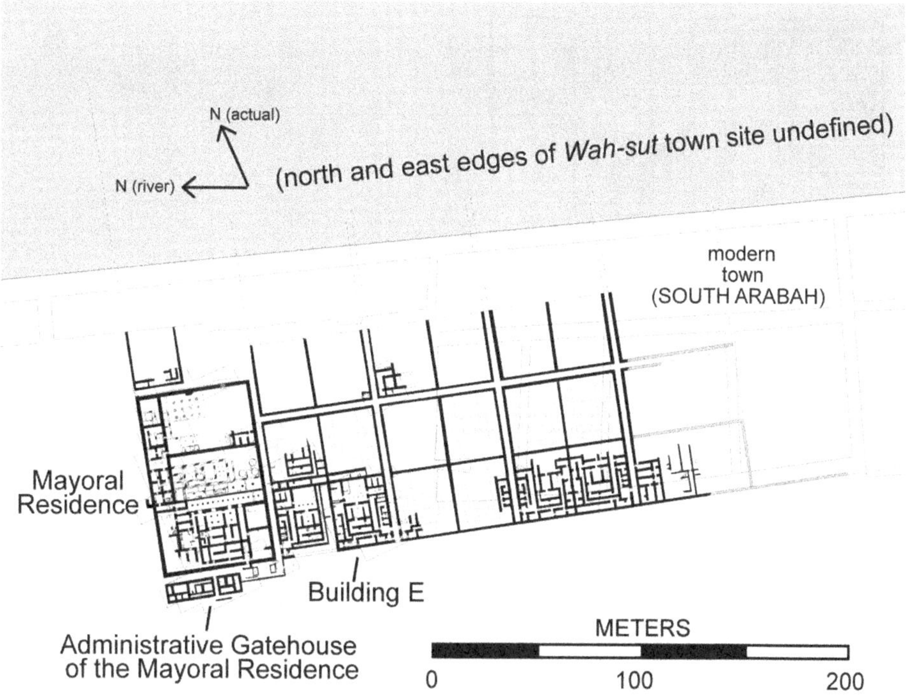

Figure 4. Mayor's home and nearby residences at *Wah-sut*. From Picardo, "Hybrid Households," fig. 11.4, with thanks also to J. Wegner.

(called "Acropolis" in fig. 5) in the northwest corner also means that it faced the pyramid of Senusret II, and was directly north of the valley temple, giving it a view towards both areas under his administrative authority. In addition to the archaeological remains, a great deal of papyri and sealings were recovered from Lahun. It is somewhat unclear where exactly the sealings were found; Quirke locates them mainly in the western area of the town,[44] while Horvath has suggested the majority came from the area of the large houses, with a secondary "dump" in the western area near the valley temple.[45] Moeller takes this one step further, interpreting the group of smaller structures just south of the enigmatic structure, perhaps a temple, that is directly opposite the mayor's house as a centralized administrative area.[46] The likelihood of an administrative area with offices for various officials is also supported by the sealings and papyri from Lahun, which contain references to scribes, messengers, and district officials, as well as the *ḫ3 n sp3.t* and *ḫ3 n ṯ3ty*. While Lahun was largely a planned settlement, it is not far from the national capital of Itj-tawy / Lisht, and the presence of seals from Lahun referring to the *ḫ3* of the vizier suggests that there was likely an administrative space that

versity of Pennsylvania Museum of Archaeology and Anthropology.; New Haven: Department of Near Eastern Languages and Civilizations, Yale University, 2009), 180–81.

44. Quirke, *Lahun*, 87.

45. Horváth, "Temple(s) and Town at el-Lahun," 180. For a more recent analysis laying out just how difficult it is to determine the find spots, see Ulrich Luft, "*Sḫm-S-n-wsr.t m3ʿ-ḫrw* versus *Ḥtp-S-n-wsr.t m3ʿ-ḫrw*. Remarks on Arguments Pro and Contra the Denomination of the Pyramid Town at El-Lâhûn," in *Florilegium Aegyptiacum: Eine wissenschaftliche Blütenlese von Schülern und Freunden für Helmut Satzinger zum 75. Geburtstag*, ed. Roman Gundacker, Julia Budka, and Gabriele Pieke, GM Beiheft 14 (Göttingen: Seminar für Ägyptologie und Koptologie der Georg-August-Universität, 2013), 235–47.

46. Moeller, *The Archaeology of Urbanism in Ancient Egypt*, 283–85.

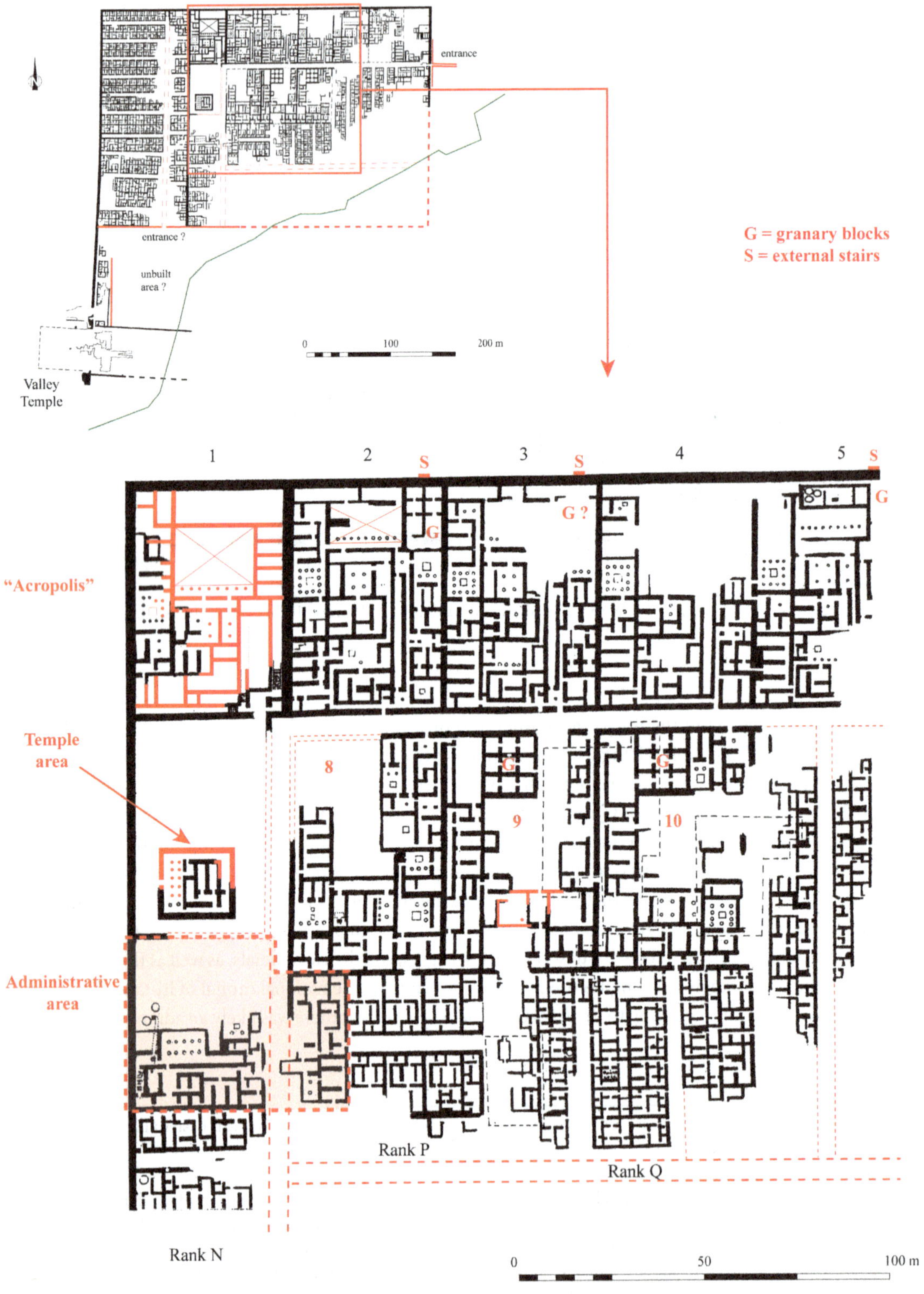

Figure 5. Town plan of Lahun. © Moeller, *The Archaeology of Urbanism in Ancient Egypt*, fig. 8-26.

could have been utilized by the vizier when visiting.[47] The records from Lahun indicate that the mayor and the temple scribe were in regular communication, and that the mayor also had some degree of administrative authority over the temple, given his title of *imy-r ḥw.t-nṯr*. According to Horvath, the documents and sealings further demonstrate that there were two distinct areas within the overall town: Hotep-Senwosret was the main town under the direct purview of the mayor, while Sekhem-Senwosret was the area attached to the cult installation where the temple scribe resided and carried out his duties. In his view, the western sector should be understood as the residential and administrative area attached to Senwosret's valley temple, thereby separate from but connected to the town proper. In this case, the residence, both primary and official, of the temple scribe would likely be located closer to the valley temple in the southern area of this sector.[48] The administrative connection between the mayor and temple scribe offers an interesting parallel to the situation of the vizier and treasurer as expressed in the Duties; they are separate but (nearly) equal officials in charge of distinct areas that nonetheless need to regularly communicate with and report to each other.

The site of Elephantine has remains dating as far back as the Early Dynastic period, with a "mayor's residence" being constructed at some point in the Old Kingdom and in use through the Middle Kingdom.[49] Here, as at Tell Edfu (see below) and Lahun, there seems to be a certain amount of mixing of administrative buildings and residences in the town area adjacent to the mayor's house. This area of the settlement is centered on the eastern portion of the island, and seems to have had a relatively stable architectural history, with expansion to the northwest only occurring in the Middle Kingdom (fig. 6).[50] While the mayor's house dominated the site architecturally, there do not at present appear to be any houses that can clearly be identified as belonging to a local "elite." In the Middle Kingdom at least, the houses all appear to be of a roughly standard size and configuration. Across from the mayor's house, hundreds of sealings were found indicating that a great deal of official business was being conducted in or around the mayor's house.[51] Given that the majority of the building has been destroyed by *sebbakhin* digging, one wonders if in fact there may have been both a residence and an "official" area attached to the residence, as seen at *Wah-sut* and Lahun. In the area of the Satet temple to the north of the mayor's house there was another large house that shows evidence of associated production areas. While not certain, it seems at least possible that the officials associated with the temple, and perhaps with the production of items for the temple, resided and worked in this vicinity.[52] At the far northwest of the site, beyond the expanding Middle Kingdom residential area, there is another building (H84) that has been identified as primarily administrative in nature. Despite the overall "domestic" character of the architecture, it has been interpreted as a large administrative complex containing storage facilities, perhaps related to the *ẖtm*, which is mentioned on several sealings recovered both here (though not in primary context), and near the mayor's residence.[53]

---

47. It is also possible that these seals came from the vizier's *ẖꜣ* at Itj-tawy, rather than being produced at Lahun. Quirke, *Lahun*, 70–71; Geoffrey Martin, *Egyptian Administrative and Private-Name Seals, Principally of the Middle Kingdom and Second Intermediate Period* (Oxford: Griffith Institute, 1971), 142; Horváth, "Temple(s) and Town at el-Lahun," 182 with references; so also Barry Kemp, *Ancient Egypt: Anatomy of a Civilization* (London: Routledge, 1989), 56. Luft implies a similar use of the buildings in this area: "the Nomarch's stay in *Sẖm-S-n-wsr.t mꜣꜥ-ẖrw* is comprehensible if he used the acropolis as a temporary residence according to his rank. Stadelmann's remark that the acropolis could have been a royal residence might be expanded to all high-ranking officials who had to visit "*Sẖm-S-n-wsr.t mꜣs-ẖrw* including the Nomarch." (Luft, ""*Sẖm-S-n-wsr.t mꜣꜥ-ẖrw* versus *Ḥtp-S-n-wsr.t mꜣꜥ-ẖrw*," 11).

48. Horváth, "Temple(s) and Town at el-Lahun," 194–99. Luft however interprets both areas of the town as two parts of a singular whole, called Sekhem-Senwosret, and views Hotep-Senwosret as another town entirely, where the Nomarch perhaps resided; see Luft, "*Sẖm-S-n-wsr.t mꜣꜥ-ẖrw* versus *Ḥtp-S-n-wsr.t mꜣꜥ-ẖrw*," 10–12. As Luft views the "acropolis" as the residence where visiting dignitaries, such as the Nomarch, could stay, his difference of interpretation regarding the name and division of the town does not match the interpretation offered here.

49. For the earlier periods as represented at Elephantine, see Moeller, *The Archaeology of Urbanism in Ancient Egypt*, 174, 220–26.

50. Moeller, 305–7.

51. Moeller, 309, 312–16.

52. Moeller, 307–9

53. Moeller, 309–12.

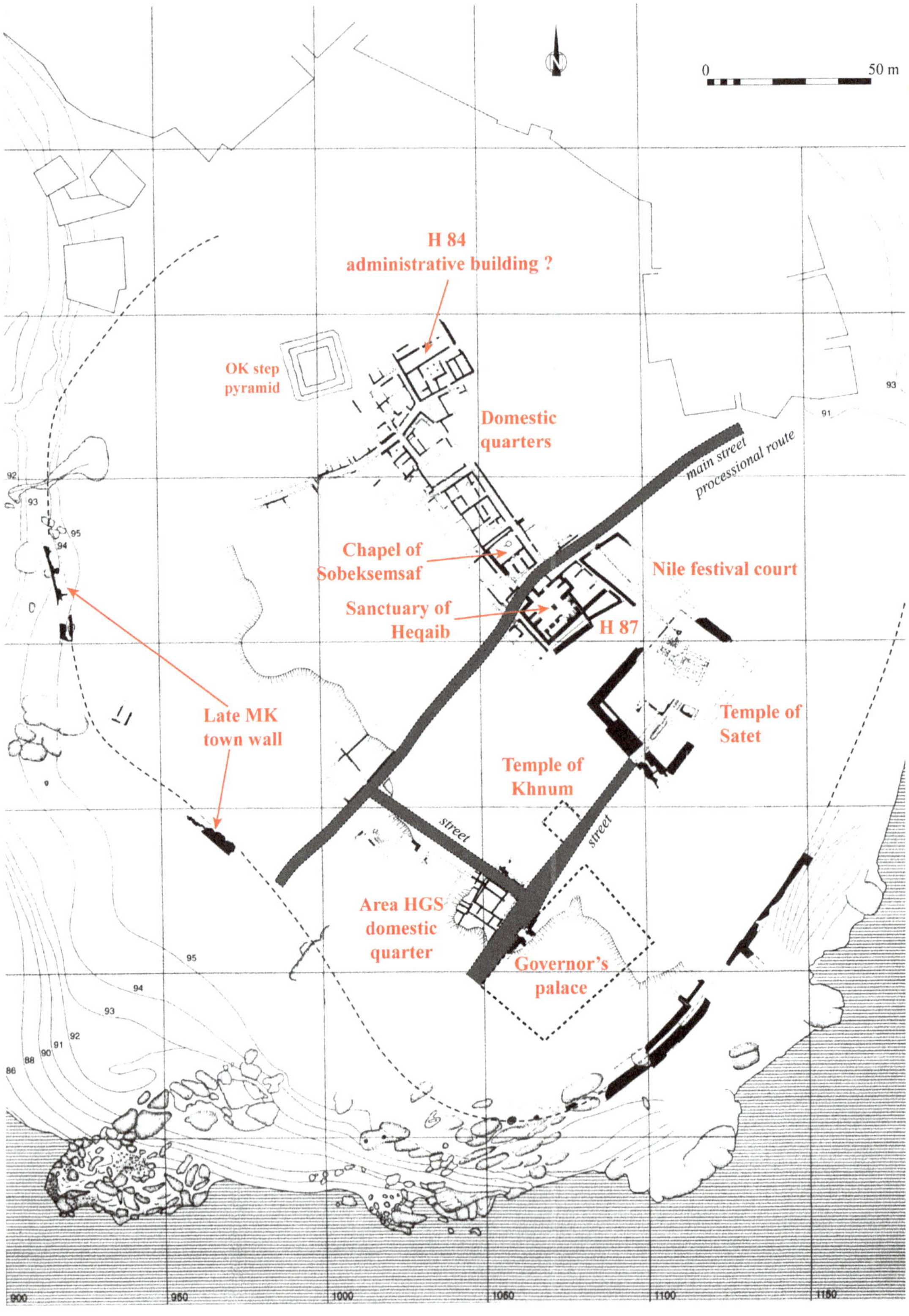

Figure 6. Town plan of Elephantine. © Moeller, *The Archaeology of Urbanism in Ancient Egypt*, fig. 8-40.

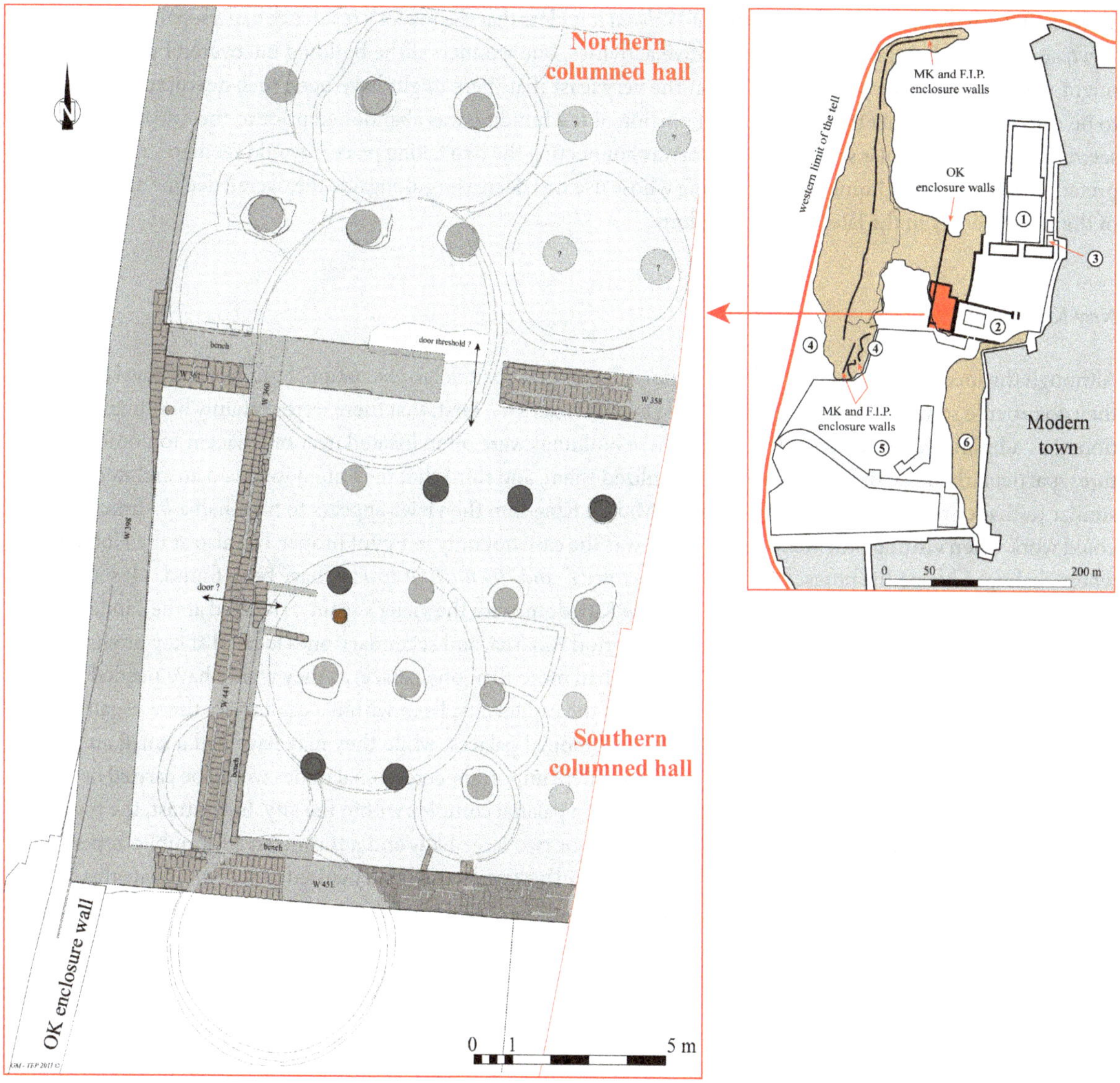

Figure 7. The mayor's residence at Edfu. © Moeller, *The Archaeology of Urbanism in Ancient Egypt*, fig. 8-45.

However, it should be noted that the architecture might also suggest that it functioned at least in part as an official residence for whomever was in charge of the administrative activities taking place nearby.

Finally, the site of Tell Edfu has recently yielded new information relevant to the discussion here. Excavations in the so-called administrative quarter of the site have uncovered the remains of two large columned halls which have been interpreted as belonging to the mayor's house (fig. 7).[54] Moeller draws parallels based on the sealing evidence to the mayor's residence at *Wah-sut*, suggesting that the additional material recovered indicates a fairly wide range of

54. Nadine Moeller, "Preliminary Report on Seasons 2005–2009," *JARCE* 46 (2010): 100–109; Nadine Moeller, "Unsealing Tell Edfu, Egypt: Who Was a Local Official and Who Was Not," *NEA* 75 (2012): 116–25, and Moeller, *The Archaeology of Urbanism*, 317–21. On the earlier levels at Tell Edfu, see Moeller, *The Archaeology of Urbanism in Ancient Egypt*, 226–31.

activities taking place. However, given that at *Wah-sut* it is clear that the mayor's residence had a separate building, the *ꜥrryt,* specifically designated for administrative activities, one wonders if the building uncovered by the excavators might perhaps belong to this structure, or at the very least that there might have been such a structure which is yet to be discovered. The fact that the southern portion of the building was abandoned prior to the northern, and there seems to have been regular sealing of the doorway connecting the two taking place,[55] would seem to support its interpretation as a separate administrative building whose use was decreasing alongside the overall decline and disruption of the site generally in the late Middle Kingdom.

New Kingdom Royal Sites

Although the local centers outlined above do not offer an exact parallel to the national capitals and royal complexes, they do provide some useful clues when looking for the vizier's *ẖꜣ*. First, that there were certainly buildings that functioned as administrative centers, second that these buildings were often located near or adjacent to domestic structures, particularly those of the local elite who utilized them, and third that they often followed an architectural plan similar to that of residences. In addition, in the Middle Kingdom the vizier appears to have had a *ẖꜣ* from which he could work when visiting provincial centers. This was the case not only in Egypt proper, but also at the Nubian forts, where sealings bearing the phrase "*ẖꜣ n ṯꜣty n niw.t rsy.t*" and "*ẖꜣ n ṯꜣty n tp-rsy*" have been found.[56] It seems likely that this would also have continued during the New Kingdom, with the vizier's main *ẖꜣ* located at the capital cities of Memphis, Thebes, and Piramesses, and for a brief period Amarna, and secondary ones located at key provincial centers. It is also important to note that kings generally had more than one palace, as they would have needed a proper setting in which to stay when they traveled outside of the capital city. Even within a capital city there usually existed multiple palaces, likely with distinct functions.[57] Ceremonial palaces, while they may have had a small area within which the king could rest, largely served as the place where important ceremonial duties would be carried out. These might be attached to a temple, but also could be part of a palatial complex within the city. In contrast, the residential palace itself, even though it would have contained one or two large halls and a throne area for public appearances, would have served as the primary residence of the king and his family and be structured to accommodate this. Finally, there is the "administrative" or "working" palace, which, like the ceremonial one, would have allowed for private areas where the king could withdraw but would also include a fair number of more public spaces designed for business use,

55. Moeller, "Unsealing Tell Edfu," 118–20.

56. Martin, *Egyptian Administrative and Private-Name Seals*, 142–43. According to Nigel Strudwick (*The Administration of Egypt in the Old Kingdom: The Highest Titles and Their Holders*, Studies in Egyptology [London: KPI, 1985], 321–28), during the late Fifth Dynasty the vizierate was split in two, with one placed in charge of the provinces and often perhaps based there, while the other continued to reside in Memphis. Thus, there was already a sense of the importance of the vizier's presence, even if occasional, outside of the capital city. It is also possible that these sealings should be understood as coming from the vizier's *ẖꜣ*, having marked an object that was sent to the provincial site from the vizier. But since we know that the vizier traveled and was sent on various missions, and that the heads of regional and local administration came under his authority, the likelihood that he had regular buildings from which to work, and perhaps reside, while outside the main city seems probable.

57. On the itinerancy of the royal court see, e.g., the work of Fredrik Hagen, "On Some Movements of the Royal Court in New Kingdom Egypt," in *Another Mouthful of Dust: Egyptological Studies in Honour of Geoffrey Thorndike Martin*, ed. Jacobus van Djik, OLA 246 (Leuven: Peeters, 2016), 155–81; and Quirke, "The Residence in Relations," 112–14. For contemplating how we should best understand what constituted a capital, or royal residence, as well as the function(s) of the palace-type buildings found there, see, e.g., Martin Raaven, "Aspects of the Memphite Residence as Illustrated by the Saqqara New Kingdom Necropolis," in Gundlach and Taylor, *Egyptian Royal Residences*, 153–64 and "Memphis: The Status of a Residence City in the Eighteenth Dynasty," in *Abusir and Saqqara in the Year 2000*, ed. Miroslav Bárta and Jaromir Krejci, Archiv Orientální Suppl. 9 (Prague: Academy of Sciences, 2000), 99–120.

and therefore might have been located in a certain area of the city.[58] It is to this type of palace that we should probably look in attempting to identify the vizier's *ḫ3*.

Tell el-Dab'a provides us with something of a link between the provincial centers described above and a capital city.[59] Although its settlement history begins in the Middle Kingdom, eventually becoming the capital of Avaris during Hyksos rule of northern Egypt in the Second Intermediate period, during the New Kingdom it took on a new function. The mid-Eighteenth Dynasty levels at Tell el-Dab'a (Phases C/3-2, Str. d-c), have been identified as the naval base of Peru-nefer, an important strategic center well known during the reigns of Thutmose III and Amunhotep II.[60] Dating to this time period is a large palatial precinct within which are four structures that have been identified as one large (G) and two smaller palaces (F [ceremonial only] and J), and a large nonpalatial building (L) (figs. 8 and 9). Building L is located at the southeast corner of Palace G, with the entrance and more public spaces, including a large court, at the southern end and what Bietak interprets as residential quarters at the northern end. Directly across from the entrance to Building L, there is an entry point through the enclosure wall of the entire palatial complex. Bietak has reconstructed a bent corridor passageway leading from the northwest side of Building L's court to Palace G, where a side entrance at the rear, residential section of the palace was located. Although the passage is indirect, this would mean that the seemingly public portion of Building L had an access point to the private section of the palace. Bietak has suggested that the entire complex resembles what one would expect for the main capital at Memphis, but here Building L, rather than belonging to the vizier as would be expected at Memphis, likely belonged to the official in charge of Peru-nefer, who at the time of Amenhotep II was one Kenamun, the *ỉmy-r pr wr n nswt m Prw-nfr* and owner of TT 93.[61] In doing so, Bietak, citing van den Boorn, draws a parallel between the function of Building L and the vizier's residence and *ḫ3* in the capital city.[62] The building is certainly large enough to have incorporated both residential and official areas, but I would argue that while it could well have functioned as the building in which the steward of Peru-nefer conducted his work, it was less likely to be his (primary) residence. Although Building L does have open and closed spaces, like a residence, the arrangement of rooms in the northern section could as easily be interpreted as work rooms and storage areas. Indeed, Bietak notes that the "spatial program of the northern half of the building ... is difficult to fathom."[63] In fact, this section of the building bears some similarity to the architectural reconstruction of the *ʿrryt* at *Wah-sut*. And this leads to a second point, which is that at *Wah-sut* an entrance in the rear, residential section of the mayor's house leads out the back of the home to the administrative building, much as is seen at Tel el-Dab'a. In addition, Bietak notes that the architectural structure of Palace J, located directly behind

58. David O'Connor, "City and Palace in New Kingdom Egypt," *CRIPEL* 11 (1989): 73–78; Rolf Gundlach, "Strukturen und Aspecten pharaonischer Residenzen," in *Hof und Theorie: Annäherungen an ein historisches Phänomen*, ed. Reinhardt Butz, Jan Hirschbiegel, and Dietmar Willoweit, Norm und Struktur 22 (Köln: Böhlau, 2004); Rolf Gundlach, "Hof - Hofgelsellschaft - Hofkultur im pharaohischen Ägypten," in *Der ägyptische Hof des Neuen Reiches – seine Gesellschaft und Kultur im Spannungsfeld zwischen Innen- und Außenpolitik*, ed. Rolf Gundlach and Andrea Klug, Königtum, Staat und Gesellschaft früher Hochkulturen 2 (Wiesbaden: Harrassowitz, 2006), 8–11; Lacovara, *The New Kingdom Royal City*, 24–41; Kate Spence, "The Palaces of el-Amarna: Towards an Architectural Analysis," in Gundlach and Taylor, *Egyptian Royal Residences*, 165–71, 186. See also Pagliari who interprets the palace located at Karnak, which is referred to primarily as an *ʿḥ*, as being largely ceremonial in nature, and therefore essentially distinct from the *pr-nsw* at Thebes, though it would have had some administrative functions; Pagliari, "Function and Significance," 233–44.

59. The same might be said of Deir el-Ballas, but in the interest of space I have chosen to focus only on Tell el-Dab'a as more has been excavated, published, and discussed. For Deir el-Ballas, see Lacovara, *The New Kingdom Royal City*, 81–90; Peter Lacovara, "Deir el-Ballas and the Development of the Early New Kingdom Royal Palace," in *Timelines: Studies in Honour of Manfred Bietak*, ed. Ernst Czerny, OLA 149 (Leuven: Peeters, 2006) and Peter Lacovara, "Deir el-Ballas," in *Palaces in Ancient Egypt and the Ancient Near East, Vol. I: Egypt*, ed. Manfred Bietak and Silvia Prell, CAENL 5 (Vienna: Austrian Academy of Sciences Press, 2018).

60. Bietak, "A Thutmosid Palace Precinct."

61. Bietak, "Houses, Palaces and Development of Social Structure in Avaris," 22–23 and Bietak, "A Thutmosid Palace Precinct," 237–39.

62. Bietak, "A Thutmosid Palace Precinct," 239 with n. 37.

63. Bietak, 237.

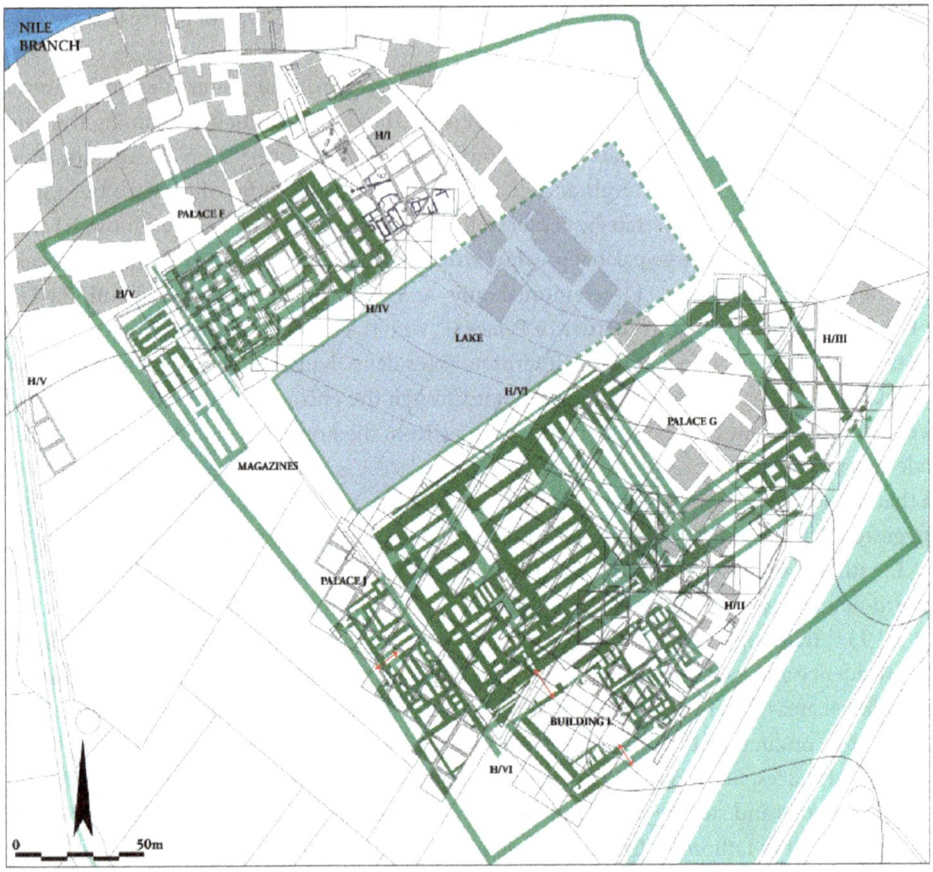

Figure 8. Eighteenth Dynasty Palace Precinct at Tell al-Dab'a with entrances/exits noted in red. After Bietak, "A Thutmosid Palace Precinct," 226, fig. 4; additions by Hazem Shared.

(southwest) of Palace G is essentially the same as the large palace, but in miniature.[64] Palace J, like Building L, also has a side entrance, in this case about halfway along the building's southwestern side. The location of the entrances to Palace J and Building L, along with the side entrance at the rear of Palace G indicates that relatively quick and direct access was required between all three buildings. Based on these observations, I would suggest that Palace G represents the primary residential palace of the king, Palace J an administrative or working palace, akin to the "King's House" at Amarna (see below), and Building L an official building where indeed the steward of Peru-nefer may have conducted his work, and perhaps occasionally rested, but which was not his primary residence.[65]

Turning to Thebes, we would certainly expect a *ẖnw*, "royal residence," to be located here, as it was a capital city during both the Middle and New Kingdoms and retained significant importance for ceremonial purposes from the Middle Kingdom onwards. Although an east bank location of the main city of Thebes, including palaces and administrative centers, is most likely,[66] the dearth of excavated area relating to where the ancient city of Thebes may have

64. Bietak, 233.

65. It is also possible that Palace J might actually be the residence of someone like Qenamun, who was also a steward and foster-brother of Amenhotep II's. Given the degree of closeness he held, the rather grand nature of the building does not seem so far-fetched for a favored official of the king who was also in charge of the naval base.

66. I follow O'Connor's theory ("Beloved of Maat, the Horizon of Re," 266–84) that the primary residence of the king would also

Figure 9. Detail of Building L in figure 8, with entrances/exits noted in red. After Bietak, “A Thutmosid Palace Precinct,” 226, fig. 14; additons by Hazem Shared.

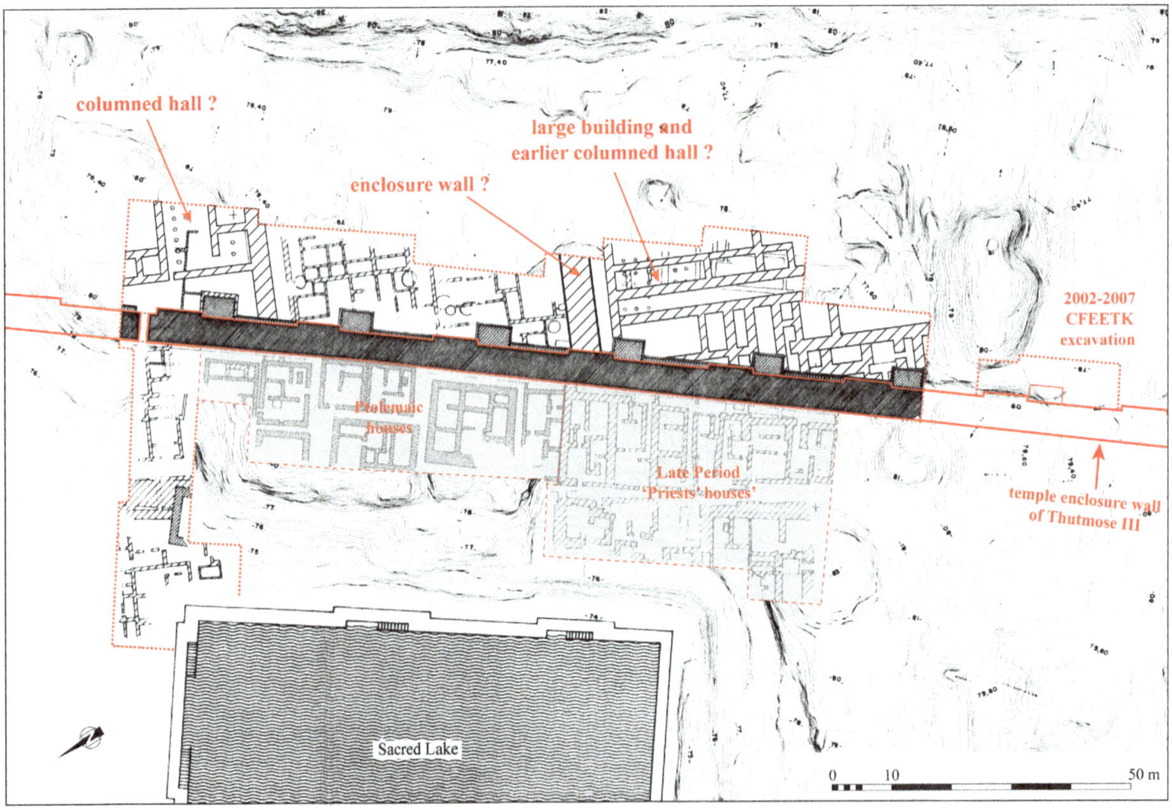

Figure 10. Remains of the Middle Kingdom city of Thebes, within the current Karnak Temple precinct. © Moeller, *The Archaeology of Urbanism in Ancient Egypt*, fig. 8-39.

been means that there is a concomitant lack of evidence for the structures associated with the royal residence. Some remains dating to the Middle Kingdom have been located near to Karnak, including what appears to be portions of a palace or elite houses with large columned halls as well as areas with baking and brewing installations on the south side of the Thutmose III enclosure wall (fig. 10).[67] Among the objects recovered from the excavations was a sealing with the label "*ḫ3* of the vizier of the southern town."[68] Although not definitive, the architectural remains and the presence of this sealing could suggest that in the Middle Kingdom the *ḫ3* of the vizier was located, perhaps along with a royal palace, in this eastern section of Karnak, just beyond the sacred lake. Indeed, as discussed above, the location of the New Kingdom palace near the Amun precinct, though to its northwest, has been suggested already by O'Con-

have been located in the main city on the eastern bank of Thebes, rather than that espoused by Stadelmann that palaces attached or near to Karnak were purely ceremonial and one must look to the west bank for the location of New Kingdom residential palaces both before and after Amenhotep III. See Rainer Stadelmann "Temple Palace and Residential Palace," in *Haus und Palast im alten Ägypten: Internationales Symposium 8. bis 11. April 1992 in Kairo*, ed. Manfred Bietak, Denkschriften der Gesamtakademie 14 (Vienna: Verlag der Österreichischen Akademie der Wissenschaften, 1996), 226–29.

67. Jean Lauffrey, "Les travaux du Centre Franco-Égyptien d'étude des temples de Karnak de 1972–1977," *Les Cahiers de Karnak* 6 (1980): 44–52; Jean Lauffrey, "Le rempart de Thoutmosis III à l'est du Lac Sacré," *Les Cahiers de Karnak* 10 (1995): 257–85; Marie Millet and Aurélia Masson, "Karnak: Settlements," *UCLAEE*, https://escholarship.org/uc/item/1q346284 (2011): 4, 6; Moeller, *The Archaeology of Urbanism in Ancient Egypt*, 304–5.

68. Lauffray, "Les travaux du Centre Franco-Égyptien," 49.

nor.[69] I would further point out that the Middle Kingdom remains and sealing, which are located to the *east* of the main temple in both the Middle and New Kingdoms, might suggest that it is in this eastern section of Karnak that we should be looking for the New Kingdom administrative buildings, including the vizier's *ḫ3* and his *pr*, since the vizier, according to van den Boorn's understanding, "moved from the East" to greet the king.[70]

The best example from Thebes of a royal residence in fact comes from the west bank, in the form of the palace complex of Malkata, which Amenhotep III built in preparation for his first jubilee, and which thereafter became his primary residence. It is this site that gives us a semblance of how a proper *ẖnw* might have appeared. Although Malkata has never been fully published, much has been written about it, particularly the area of Amenhotep III's main palace, called the "House of Rejoicing," and nearby buildings (fig. 11).[71] Adjacent to this palace on the west side are several structures. Furthest to the west appears to be a group of houses, the so-called west villas, which include a group of three large homes (collectively Ho. 3 W) as well as several smaller ones.[72] The next structure to the east appears to be larger in scale, and has been labeled as "Middle Palace" (Ho. 2 W), though this designation is tenuous at best. Finally, the structure closest to the palace, denoted as Ho. 1 W, is similarly larger in scale and apparently had access to the palace itself.[73] The entrance to the palace, which is at the northwestern side, gave access to a large court space. However, this entrance ramp led, at its other end, not out into the city but directly to Ho. 1 W where it opened into another court. Peter Lacovara has most recently interpreted Ho. 1 W as belonging to the vizier—his *ḫ3* and official *pr*. He bases this on the grand scale of the structure's architecture,[74] its direct access to the king's palace, and the discovery of wooden braces for door jambs in the corridor leading to the palace, which he interprets as the *rw.ty wr.ty* mentioned in the Duties and through which the vizier passes to greet the king, thereby moving east.[75] Yet, he also notes the similarity to the composition of buildings in the central city at Amarna (see below), where the king's palace (*pr-nsw*), is connected via a bridge to the king's house (*pr-ꜥ3*). In earlier publications this was the interpretation

---

69. O'Connor, "City and Palace," 78–80; O'Connor, "Beloved of Maat," 272–74, 278–79.

70. On the presence of Amarna palaces and other structures in the eastern part of Karnak see Dimitri Laboury, *Akhénaton, Les grand pharaons* (Paris, Pygmalion, 2010), chapter on Karnak. On the movement of the Nile, and construction of canals and basins around Karnak, all of which would have impacted what area(s) were accessible when, see Luc Gabolde, *Karnak, Amon-Ré: La genèse d'un temple, la naissance d'un Dieu*, BdÉ 167 (Cairo : IFAO, 2018), 5–86 and Mansour Boraik, Luc Gabolde, and Angus Graham, "Karnak's Quaysides: Evolution of the Embankments from the Eighteenth Dynasty to the Graeco-Roman Period," in *The Nile: Natural and Cultural Landscapes in Egypt; Proceedings of the International Symposium Held at the Johannes Gutenberg-Universität Mainz, 22 & 23 February 2013*, ed. Harco Willems and Jan-Michael Dahms (Bielefeld : Transcript, 2017), 97–144.

71. Dorothea Arnold, "The Royal Palace: Architecture, Decoration, and Furnishings," in *The Pharaohs*, ed. Christiane Ziegler (New York: Rizzoli, 2002), 270–95; Kemp, *Ancient Egypt*, 213–17; Peter Lacovara, "The Development of the New Kingdom Palace," in Gundlach and Taylor, *Egyptian Royal Residences*, 84–89; Peter Lacovara,"In the Realm of the Sun King," 6–20; Peter Lacovara, *The New Kingdom Royal City*, 25–28, 70–72; Lacovara, "Recent Work at Malqata Palace," 275–81; David O'Connor, "The King's Palace at Malkata and the Purpose of the Royal Harem," in *Millions of Jubilees: Studies in Honor of David P. Silverman*, vol. 2, ed Zahi Hawass and Jennifer Houser Wegner, Supplément aux Annales du Service des antiquités de l'Egypte 39 (Cairo: Conseil Suprême des Antiquités de l'Egypte, 2010), 55–80. For the Amun temple at Malkata, see Aikaterini Kotsilda, "A Dark Spot in Ancient Egyptian Architecture: The Temple of Malkata," *JARCE* 43 (2007): 43–57.

72. Lacovara, *The New Kingdom Royal City*, 44, fig. 40. Included among these villas is a structure labelled Ho. W3, and a "middle palace." I have been unable to find additional information about the architectural remains of these structures, though it would appear from the most recent reconstruction of the site that the "middle palace" forms part of Ho. W 1. See the plans in Lacovara, "In the Realm of the Sun King" and Lacovara, *The New Kingdom Royal City*, figs. 20, 40.

73. Lacovara, *The New Kingdom Royal City*, fig. 20.

74. In the most recent reconstruction, by Franck Monnier, it seems as though Ho. W 2 has been incorporated into Ho. W 1, thus further enlarging this structure. See Franck Monnier, "Scientific Reconstruction of the Palace of Amenhotep III at Malqata," in *Studies on the Palace of Amenhotep III at Malqata*, ed. Peter Lacovara (forthcoming), fig. 13. I would like to thank Peter and Franck for sharing their forthcoming work with me.

75. Lacovara, "In the Realm of the Sun King," 19; Lacovara, "Recent Work at Malqata Palace," 277–78; Peter Lacovara, pers. comm., 27 January 2020.

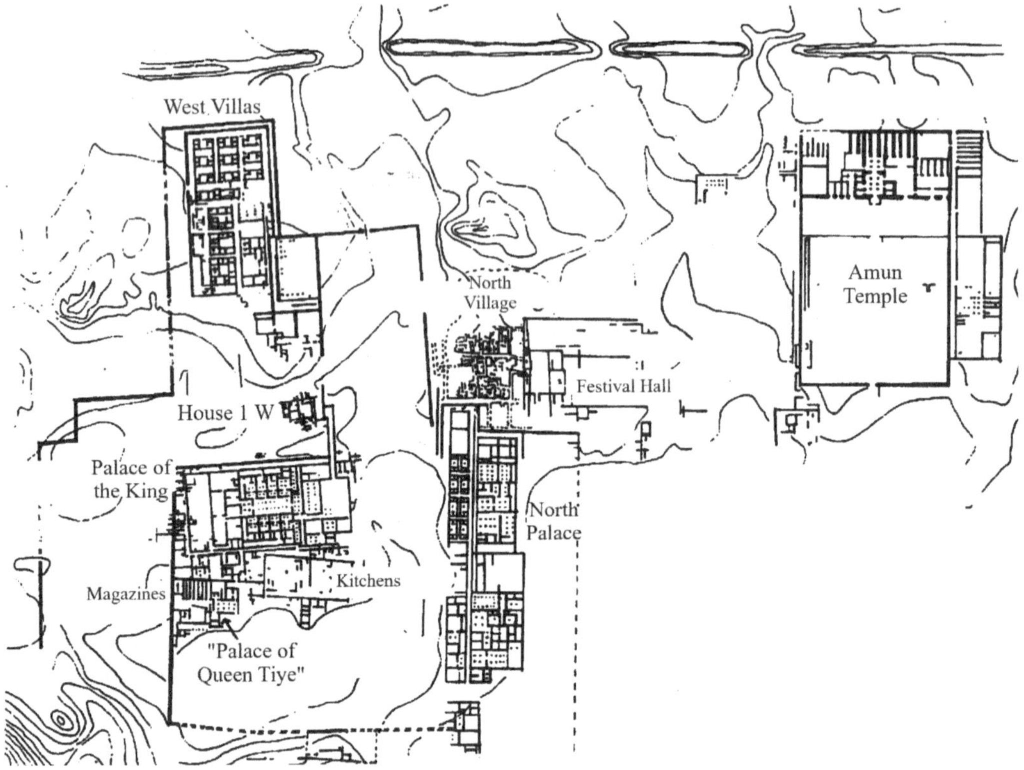

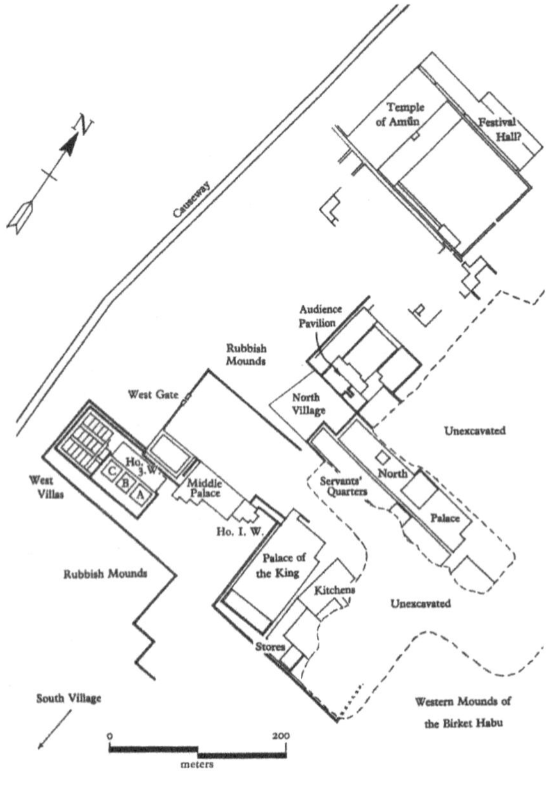

Figure 11. Site plans of Malkata with structures denoted. Above: after Lacovara, "In the Realm of the Sun King," 8, with retouching by Hazem Shared. Left: after Lacovara, "Recent Work at Malqata Palace," 275, fig. 1.

that Lacovara suggested for these two buildings at Malkata, going so far as to identify various portions of them with the terms utilized in the Duties. In addition, he draws parallels between the area of the "west villas" at Malkata and the administrative area at Amarna, located directly west of the "King's House" and incorporating a "record's office."[76]

In reexamining this material, and taking into account the critiques of van den Boorn mentioned above, it seems that Lacovara's earlier interpretation is the more accurate one. In this case, the vizier's *ḫ3* would not be Ho. 1 W, but rather should be looked for either in the area of "west villas" or, perhaps, in the area of buildings located on the palace's east side, where there is a large structure that has been labeled the "Palace of Queen Tiye" (fig. 12). Lacovara has already suggested that this "palace" would perhaps be better understood as an office space related to the buildings around it.[77] In addition, this location would give access to the king's palace: at the rear of the king's palace an entrance on its east side opens into a bent-axis corridor that leads into a short passage across the north end of a group of small structures, and directly into the "Palace of Queen Tiye." This interpretation of the structures would also resemble the suggested placement of the steward's *ḫ3* at Peru-nefer at the rear corner of the king's palace.[78] As a last note, it

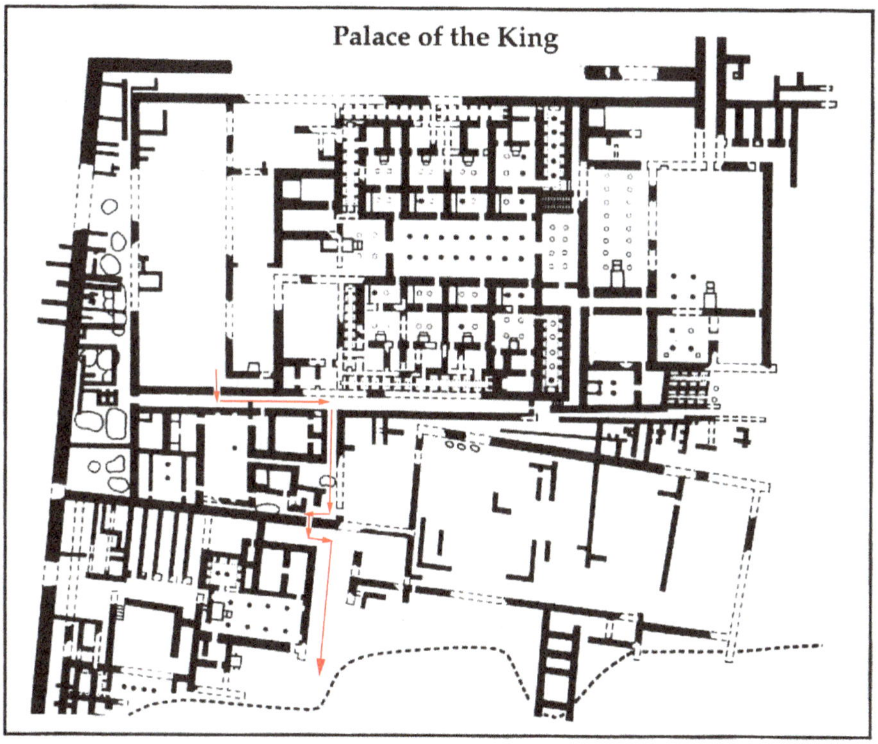

Figure 12. Detail of the "Palace of the King" and structures to the east at Malkata. After Lacovara, "In the Realm of the Sun King," 8; with retouching by Hazem Shared.

76. Lacovara, "The Development of the New Kingdom Palace," 89, 93; Lacovara, *The New Kingdom Royal City*, 28, 30, 43–44, 57, 70–72 with figs. 28, 39–40, 72.

77. Lacovara, *The New Kingdom Royal City*, 44–45, fig. 21.

78. In fact, there are at least three palaces at Malkata: in addition to Amenhotep III's main palace and the "Palace of Queen Tiye" already discussed, there is also the so-called North Palace. This building has been interpreted as perhaps being designated for the harim, given its unusual architecture and the adjacent (to the west and slightly north) "Festival" or "Audience Hall," which may have had a window of appearances. Other architectural areas at Malkata include the "North Village," what appears to be an area of small houses, storage areas, and possibly some industrial activity immediately west of the North Palace and to the north of this a large Amun temple.

is important to understand that although there likely was a *ḫ3* for the vizier located at Malkata, this is because the palace-city was Amenhotep III's primary residence after year 30. Before this time, as well as continuing afterwards, it is most likely that the vizier's *ḫ3*, as well as his primary residence, were located on the east bank, near Karnak temple.[79]

At the site of Amarna we have some of the best-preserved and best-studied architectural remains relating to a royal residence, and thus perhaps the best chance of identifying the possible location of the vizier's *ḫ3*. Based on the extensive excavations and analyses, particularly those of Kemp, Mallinson, Stevens, and Spence,[80] it is clear that the area termed the Central City at Amarna was the core administrative section of the royal residence (fig. 13). This area is bounded to the north and south by the great and small Aten temples respectively, between which are located the king's great palace and great house on the west, and numerous structures related to the administration of the city as a whole on the east. As noted above in the discussion of Malkata, the king's palace (also termed the "House of Rejoicing" as at Malkata) and house are connected to each other by a bridge, though there were also separate access points into each of the buildings from ground level. These two royal structures were largely functional in nature, containing private areas for the king, but not comprising the primary place of residence, which was at the north of the city.[81] The administrative area is located immediately behind and east of the king's house and comprised of several rows of discreet buildings along with smaller "clerks houses" to the south. The building in the first row at the southern corner is the so-called Records Office (Q 42.21), the "*ḫ3* for the king's correspondence" where the Amarna Letters were discovered. Although as yet no clear evidence has been found that points to the vizier's *ḫ3* being located in this area, it is a possible setting. Running along the north side of the king's house, between it and the Great Aten temple bakeries (Q 40.5) is another administrative area comprised of a series of storerooms and other structures likely associated with the production of items for the temple (Q 41.9, 40.10).[82] At the southwest corner of this area, almost directly across from the north gate leading into the king's house, is a structure that could perhaps also have been the vizier's *ḫ3* (P 41.3). According to Kemp, all that remains are "the foundations of a house (P41.3) with particularly massive foundations which had been severely destroyed, to the extent that no traces survived even of its floor. This arouses the suspicion that the foundations belong to the earlier building phase of the Central City."[83] While both the record's office and this enigmatic structure would place the vizier's *ḫ3* at a relative corner of the king's house, in parallel to what we have seen already at Malkata and Tell el-Dab'a, building P 41.3 seems more likely given its large size and apparent combination of official and "private" areas. It would also compare well with the place of work and "official" residence of the high priest of Aten, Panehsy (T 41.1), which is located at the southeast corner of the Great Aten temple.[84] The location of Panehsy's work residence in relation to the Aten Temple parallels the probable location of the temple scribe's official house at the outer corner of the valley temple at Lahun mentioned above. The relative locations of the

---

At the very south end of Malkata is also the Kom el-'Abd, near which are additional housing areas, and possibly an administrative zone. As noted by Lacovara, the entire layout bears a great deal of similarity to both Amarna and Deir el-Ballas. See Lacovara, "In the Realm of the Sun King," 9–12 and Lacovara, *The New Kingdom Royal City*, 36–38, 46, 48–49, 56–57, 68–72, figs. 33, 43, 48, 59, 71; O'Connor "The King's Palace."

79. It also seems possible that while the vizier may have had a *ḫ3* at Malkata, it may have been secondary to the one on the east bank.

80. A current list of the publications relating to Amarna is available at: http://www.amarnaproject.com/pages/publications/index.shtml. Of particular use are: Barry Kemp, "The Window of Appearance at El-Amarna, and the Basic Structure of this City," *JEA* 62 (1976): 82–99; Barry Kemp, *The City of Akhenaten and Nefertiti: Amarna and Its People (New Aspects of Antiquity)* (Cairo: American University in Cairo Press, 2012); Barry Kemp and Salvatore Garfi, *A Survey of the Ancient City of El-'Amarna*, Occasional Publications 9 (London: Egypt Exploration Society, 1993).

81. Kemp, "The Window of Appearance," 82–99; Kemp, *Ancient Egypt*, 287–88, figs. 89, 91; Kemp, *The City of Akhenaten and Nefertiti*, 125–35; O'Connor, "Beloved of Maat," 287–90; O'Connor, "City and Palace," 82–84; Spence, "The Palaces of el-Amarna," 171.

82. Kemp and Garfi, *A Survey of the Ancient City*, 57–65; Kemp, *Ancient Egypt*, 287–94; Kemp, *The City of Akhenaten and Nefertiti*, 125–35.

83. Kemp and Garfi, *A Survey*, 62.

84. Kemp and Garfi, 52, fig. 11.

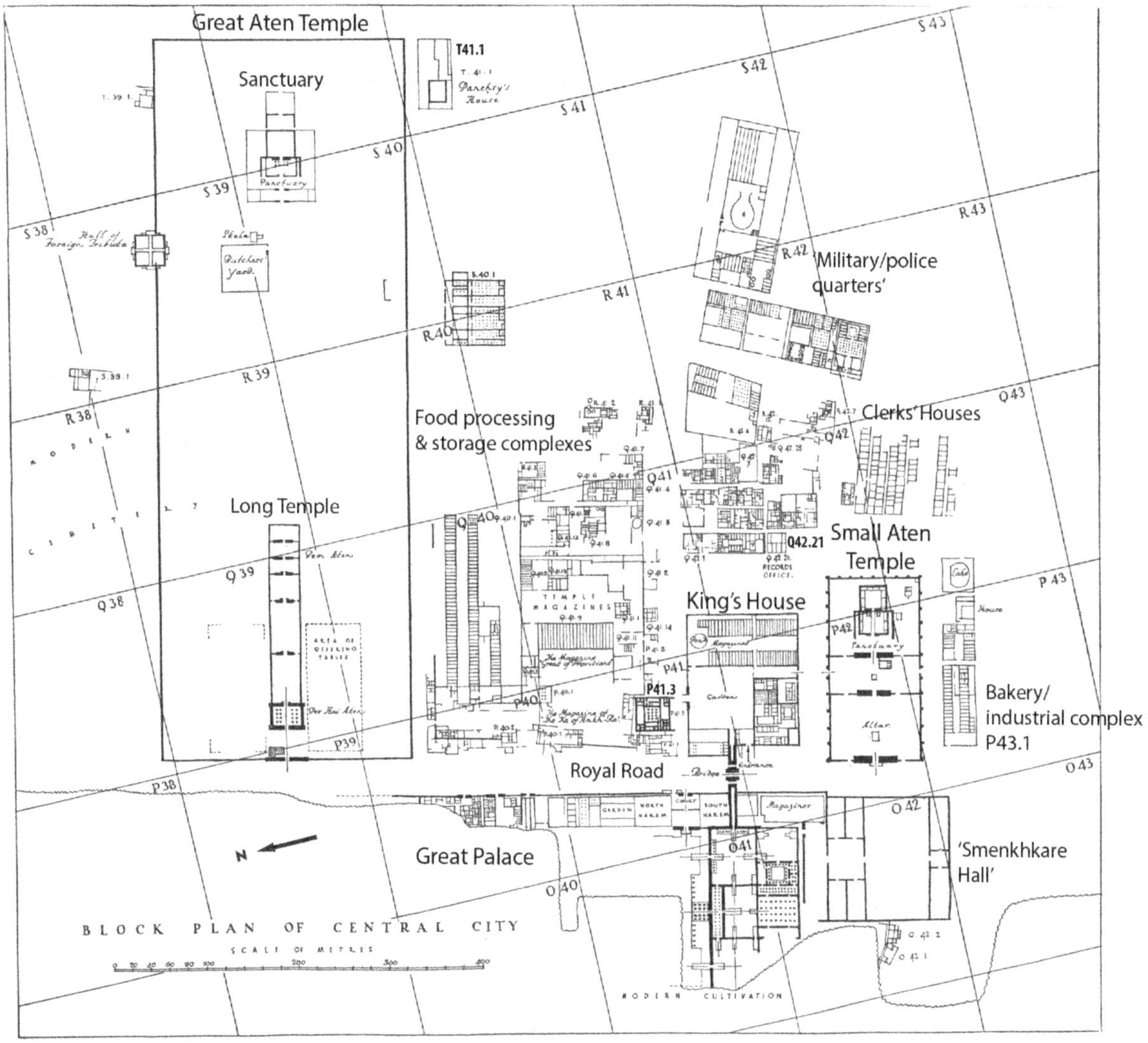

Figure 13. Plan of the "Central City" section of Amarna. After Anna Stevens, "Tell el-Amarna," *UCLAEE* (2016), fig. 12, https://escholarship.org/uc/item/1k66566f; with additions by Hazem Shared.

main residences of Panehsy and the vizier Nakht(-pa-Aten), both of which are known, are also interesting. Panehsy's house is an enormous structure located at the north end of the residential area directly adjacent to the central city (R 44.2), making it quite close to the administrative quarter. In comparison, the vizier's residence (K 50.1) is located much further away, at the north end of the "south suburb," an area not connected in any way to the central palatial or administrative center of the city. The vizier's house is quite large, and although we might presume that some official or semiofficial work might have been conducted there, it is located too far for it to have been his primary *ḫ3*.[85] While officials seem to have been in charge of building their own housing at Amarna, it is possible that this difference in

85. C. Leonard Woolley, "Excavations at Tell el-Amarna," *JEA* 8 (1922): 61–64; T. Eric Peet and C. Leonard Woolley, *The City of Akhenaten, Part 1: Excavations of 1921 and 1922 at el-'Amarneh*, EES EM 38 (London: Egypt Exploration Society, 1923), 5–9, pls. iii–v; Kemp, *Ancient Egypt*, 294.

location is also symbolic of the relative power of the high priest of Aten as compared to that of the vizier during Akhenaten's reign,[86] particularly given that Panehsy had an elaborate tomb within the larger northern group (Tomb 6) while Nakht's Amarna tomb (Tomb 12) is located within the smaller group at the southern end of the cliff.[87]

Conclusions

The above review of the textual, pictorial, and archaeological material, though brief, has nonetheless brought to light several observations. First, it seems unlikely that the vizier's *ḫ3* was actually located within the palace proper. The reading of the Duties text does not necessitate this, though it does indicate that the *ḫ3* would have been located in close proximity to the king's "administrative" palace, and in New Kingdom Thebes, probably near to the Amun temple. Second, given the overall standard nature of ancient Egyptian architecture, and an apparently preferred design for the layout of the royal palace-city,[88] one would expect there to be also a relatively conventional format for the necessary administrative areas that would accompany such a city. Third, the review of the material from Tell el Dab'a, Malkata, and Amarna has shown that at all three sites there appear to be large house-like structures located near the royal palaces that have a direct access route to the palace, and also have the columned halls and subsidiary rooms mentioned or implied in the textual and pictorial evidence presented in the viziers tombs. Since it is clear that the king had multiple palaces, it makes the most sense that the *ḫ3* of the most important official would be located closest to the main administrative palace, rather than the residential or ceremonial one. In this case, it becomes less strange that there might be access between the "private" quarters of the palace and an official building, since these were rooms used by the king when retiring from duties. Indeed, one could envisage the vizier attending on the king for the morning's report while he was in these rear chambers, before the king presented himself in the more public areas for the day, particularly when, according to the Duties, it was only after these reports are given that the palace doors are opened. This theory matches well with the buildings located adjacent to the palace at all three sites, and which at Tell el-Daba' and Malkata are also located within the overall enclosure wall surrounding the palace(s). Fourth, the vizier's *ḫ3* was clearly comprised of multiple rooms, likely resembling a house plan, though with rooms that should be understood as primarily private workspaces rather than residential ones. The "domestic" qualities of this structure should not be surprising. Large public spaces would have been needed, as well as more secluded private workspaces, not unlike a residential layout. Indeed, as has already been noted, architecture in ancient Egypt followed a basic plan that was scaled up or down as needed, and which always comprised what can be read as public and private areas. For officials whose duties required them to interact with large segments of the population, such as the vizier, a "domestic" style layout for the *ḫ3* works especially well.

---

86. If building P 41.3 was the vizier's *ḫ3*, it was likely constructed for use by Ramose, Amenhotep III's vizier and Nakht's predecessor under Akhenaten. He was a very powerful official and his Theban tomb (TT 55) showcases the change in artistic trends from the earlier years of Amenhotep IV to those of Akhenaten. As there is no indication he had a tomb at Amarna, he may have been succeed by Nakht(-pa-Aten) relatively soon after the move to Amarna. See also the recent work on the tomb of the vizier Amenhotep called Huy, who may have served alongside Ramose: Francisco J. Martín Valentín and Teresa Bedman, "The Tomb of the Vizier Amenhotep-Huy in Asasif (TT28): Preliminary Results of the Excavation Seasons 2009–2012," in *Archaeological Research in the Valley of the Kings and Ancient Thebes. Papers Presented in Honor of Richard H. Wilkinson*, ed. Pearce Paul Creasman, Wilkinson Egyptology Series I (Tucson: University of Arizona Egyptian Expedition, 2013), 181–99; Francisco J. Martín Valentín and Teresa Bedman, "The Tomb Belonging to Amenhotep III's Vizier, Asasif Tomb no. 28, Luxor-West Bank. Excavation Results: 'Vizier Amenhotep-Huy Project' (2009–2014)," in *Proceedings of the XI International Congress of Egyptologists, Florence Egyptian Museum, Florence, 23–30 August 2015*, ed. Gloria Rosati and Maria Cristina Guidotti, Archaeopress Egyptology 19 (Oxford: Archaeopress, 2017), 377–83.

87. For the tombs see Norman de Garis Davies, *The Rock Tombs of El Amarna,* 6 vols (London: Egypt Exploration Fund, 1903–1908, repr. London: Egypt Exploration Society, 2004).

88. See the overall site comparisons of Malkata, Amarna, and Deir el-Ballas in Lacovara, *The New Kingdom Royal City.*

In sum then, while we cannot be completely certain as to the precise location of the vizier's *ḫ3*, its placement close to the king's working palace seems clear. As the top government official of the country, at least in most periods, he would have required nearly constant and direct access to the king. However, we should be careful in uncritically using van den Boorn's hypothetical reconstruction, which did not take actual archaeological and architectural material into account. Indeed, as has been shown, the sites of Tell el Dab'a, Malkata, and Amarna contain remains suggestive of the vizier's *ḫ3*, and match both the textual and pictorial evidence overall, even if not van den Boorn's exact interpretation of the text. Only additional archaeological material will solve the issue entirely.

Some Egyptian-Greek Language/Script Interactions as Reflected in *Magical*

Ariel Singer and Janet H. Johnson

It is hoped that this article, which tries to highlight the knowledge of the Greek language and script possessed by the Demotic scribes who wrote *Magical*, and the Demotic Magical Papyri (DMP) in general, will be of interest to Richard, with his Greek background, deep commitment to Demotic, and years of reading and interpreting the Book of Thoth, which has so helped to illumine the higher interactions of Greek and Egyptian learning.[1] May it also help the non-Egyptologist understand and appreciate the erudition of Egyptian scribes.

As has been noted by nearly everyone who has studied the DMP, the scribes freely switched among Egyptian scripts (mostly Demotic, a fair amount of hieratic, and a small amount of [cursive] hieroglyphs). They also incorporated three new scripts. The first was a cryptic script used for writing common words and has not been found in other texts. The second was a new uniliteral (alphabetic) script,[2] whose existence and form were presumably influenced by the scribes' familiarity with the purely alphabetic form of Greek. The last new script was Old Coptic,[3] which uses Greek characters supplemented by a few signs from Demotic for sounds that do not occur in Greek to write an essentially Egyptian language. The latter two scripts were used especially for Magical Names (MN), presumably because proper indication of the vowels was vital to correct pronunciation of the names. But the scribes used both the uniliteral script and Old Coptic to write not just MN but also to incorporate originally Greek vocabulary into the Demotic/Egyptian texts.[4] It is this writing of Greek words in Egyptian scripts that is the focus of these brief comments.

---

1. It is our honor to include these thoughts in the *Festschrift* for Richard Jasnow, a fine scholar, teacher, and friend, as a token of our respect and appreciation for him and all he has done for Demotic studies specifically and Egyptology generally, in pursuing knowledge and showing wisdom, in educating younger generations, and helping, encouraging, and supporting everyone he has met. Our special thanks are due to the editors of this *Festschrift* for their willingness to accept a late manuscript. "*Magical*" refers to the "Demotic Magical Papyrus of London and Leiden," F. L. Griffith and Herbert Thompson, *The Demotic Magical Papyrus of London and Leiden*, 3 vols. (London: Grevel, 1904, 1905, 1909), hereafter referred to as G&T vol. # (year of publication). All images of text are from G&T 2 (1905).

2. Note that the spelling of magical names given here is based on the Demotic spelling supplemented by the Old Coptic spelling. If there is a disagreement between the two, the Demotic is accepted. See Janet H. Johnson, "The Dialect of the Demotic Magical Papyrus of London and Leiden," in *Studies in Honor of George R. Hughes, January 12, 1977*, ed. Janed H. Johnson and Edward F. Wente, SAOC 39 (Chicago: Oriental Institute of the University of Chicago, 1976), 105–32, for a discussion of the correlations among Greek, Old Coptic, and Demotic found in this text. Transcriptions try to maintain a one-to-one correspondence between ancient script and modern. Note the following conventions: *ō* for *ʿ3*  (the ligature used to write an o-vowel; see below); *ø* for 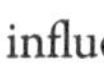, a relatively uncommon variant writing of the o-vowel, as in 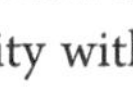 (XXI/8); *høp* (Coptic ϩⲱⲡ) for Demotic *ḥp*, the imperative of the verb *ḥp*, "to hide" (note that the use of *ø* is an arbitrary choice of a symbol and does not imply anything about pronunciation). Note also the *t3*-ligature, here transliterated t͡o, used to write "land, earth" in Demotic, is used as the phonetic group ⲦⲞ/Ⲧⲱ; similarly, the (historic) *t3w*-group is used for ⲦⲈⲨ. The entire word *ʿ.wy*, "house," with its classifier, was used occasionally to represent ⲎⲒ (Coptic for "house"). We would like to record our appreciation to Brendan Hainline for trying to make our venture into some basic linguistics comprehensible to a linguist.

3. Coptic is the stage of the Egyptian language and script that eventually replaced Demotic with the conversion of Egypt to Christianity.

4. The editors of *Magical* compiled a list of 64 Greek words that appear in the text outside of the Greek passages; however, of these,

We will concentrate on three primary aspects that help to elucidate the relationship which Egyptian scribes had with Greek and Demotic. The first is how Egyptian determinatives, or, better (perhaps), classifiers, are incorporated into the spelling of demoticized Greek words,[5] thereby bringing the Greek vocabulary into the "categorized" world which classifiers had provided for Egyptian vocabulary since the beginning of the Egyptian writing system. The second is what the Greek/Egyptian phonetic correspondences tell us about contemporary pronunciation of Greek. Finally, we will note the inclusion of Greek vocabulary in Egyptian grammatical constructions, specifically noun formations, again, as with the use of classifiers, suggesting the growing incorporation of this vocabulary into Egyptian as loanwords.[6]

We see in most dialects of Coptic extensive Greek vocabulary that has been incorporated into Egyptian, but this process had started already before Coptic became its own language. In the DMP, the incorporation of Greek vocabulary into the Demotic text shows that Demotic scribes had little or no trouble incorporating originally Greek vocabulary into Egyptian passages, while still following the rules of Demotic grammar, suggesting that such words were, or were well on their way to becoming, loanwords,[7] at least among the initiated.[8] The development of an (artificial) uniliteral (alphabetic) script allowed such words to be incorporated in the text while the text remained fully "Egyptian" grammatically. Not surprisingly for texts written, or copied, in a milieu that had been bilingual for hundreds of years, the evidence indicates how fluidly the scribes switched not only between Egyptian scripts but also between Egyptian and Greek.

This brief article cannot pretend to discuss every example in the DMP, or even in *Magical*, which falls under these rubrics; rather, we intend to discuss a sample of words written using the uniliteral Demotic and Old Coptic scripts. These examples provide information about the Egyptian scribes' use of various scripts, their fluency in switching from script to script (and language to language), and the creative ways that they merged these writing traditions.

The Use of Classifiers in Greek Words Written in the Demotic Uniliteral Script

We will start with the distinctively Egyptian use of classifiers, non-phonetic signs written at the end of a word to identify the category (or categories) to which the word belonged in the Egyptian ethos. Classifiers can fall into broad generalized categories (e.g., plant, animal, geographical location) or into more precise ones (e.g., lotus, dog, shrine) and are often used to identify more abstract concepts (e.g., an arm with a hand holding a stick for words indicating strength, a man with his hand to his mouth to indicate actions of the mouth—and by extension the head and brain). Much work has been done concerning the Egyptian worldview revealed by the choice and distribution of such classifiers.[9] What is interesting to us is that the Egyptian scribes felt that it was necessary and/or appropriate to add such

only 33 were written in Demotic (and thus had a classifier applied to them); see G&T 3 (1909), 102–4. An interesting and important question is why the scribes occasionally glossed "good Egyptian words," a question we hope to consider in the future but will not try to explicate here.

5. Such classifiers are used in *Magical* almost exclusively with nouns.

6. These processes should be compared to the processes of incorporation of Greek vocabulary attested in bilingual Demotic/Greek ostraca dating to the second half of the second century or early third century of the modern era from the village of Narmuthis in the Fayum, especially the "subarchive" of Phatres, son of Hormeinos, and the so-called school texts, including those attributed to an "apprentice librarian." For a list of texts and bibliography, see the Leuven Homepage of Papyrus Collections material on the "Temple of Narmuthis: House of the Ostraca," ArchID 534, Version I (2012), Katelijn Vandorpe and Herbert Verreth, https://www.trismegistos.org/arch/archives/pdf/534.pdf.

7. A word borrowed/imported into one language from another.

8. Or at least they had become part of the scribes' professional vocabulary to the extent they felt comfortable incorporating them into the Demotic script/passages.

9. See, inter alia, Orly Goldwasser, *From Icon to Metaphor: Studies in the Semiotics of the Hieroglyphs,* OBO 142 (Fribourg: Presses

classifiers to all Greek words written out in alphabetic Demotic.[10] Also of interest is the range of classifiers attested and how well they matched the meaning of the Greek word. Unsurprisingly, the use of classifiers by the scribes of the DMP reflects a system of categorization that is still fully functional and usually reflects the scribes' full understanding of the Greek words being classified.

The commonest use of a classifier in the DMP[11] is the use of the divine classifier (ʃ) at the end of MNs,[12] serving almost as a word-divider. However, among the demoticized Greek words, this classifier is actually quite rare (for the sole example see table 1, #1). The most frequently used types of classifiers in this set of Greek vocabulary are the broad level classifiers of the noun, specifically the plant (#2a–c) and mineral (#3) categories. There are almost no examples of classifiers for people (#4), and the two that do occur are quite generic.[13] There are no classifiers for types of animals.[14] There are a number of examples of signs that act as indicators of the type of material from which an item is made: stone (#5), wood (#6), metal (#7), and flesh (#8). Some classifiers reflect types of human production or intervention: dishes/pots (#9), and substances (minerals, etc.) that have been ground up (#10). Others reflect aspects of what can be called the political world: the geographic classifier (#11) in the DMP can indicate foreign lands, and the foreign(er) classifier (#12) is used to indicate some abstract notions borrowed from a foreign language (i.e., Greek[15]). This is not the only way that abstract concepts were marked, however; we also see the use of the classifiers for divinity (#1) and evil (#13) (the "bad" bird or dead man)—although the book roll, which is often used in Egyptian texts to classify intangible things, is not found with any of the Greek words. Finally, we see a scribal palette (#14), which is used for terms related to writing, which can be either abstract or physical. For details of the individual classifiers and their use, see table 1.

Although most words in the Egyptian writing system (especially when it reached the Demotic stage) had one classifier (or a specific grouping of classifiers) that was used most frequently and thus, presumably, was considered the most appropriate, the system was flexible. This means that a word could be written with different classifiers reflecting different aspects of the word in different contexts, or a single example of a word could incorporate more than one classifier.[16] Both of these phenomena occur in the DMP; see table 2, which includes examples with multiple classifi-

---

Universitaires, 1995); Orly Goldwasser, "A Comparison between Classifier Languages and Classifier Script: The Case of Ancient Egyptian," in *Studies in Memory of H. J. Polotsky*, ed. Gideon Goldenberg and Ariel Shisha-Halevy (Jerusalem: The Israel Academy of Sciences and Humanities, 2009), 16–39; Orly Goldwasser and Colette Grinevald, "What Are 'Determinatives' Good for?" in *Lexical Semantics in Ancient Egyptian*, ed. Eitan Grossman, Stéphane Polis, and Jean Winand, LingAeg SM 9 (Hamburg: Widmaier, 2012), 17–53; Orly Goldwasser, "What Is a Horse? Lexical Acculturation and Classification in Egyptian, Sumerian, and Nahuatl," in *Classification from Antiquity to Modern Times: Sources, Methods, and Theories From an Interdisciplinary Perspective*, ed. Tanja Pommerening and Walter Bisang (Berlin: de Gruyter, 2017), 45–65.

10. But not those written in Old Coptic; indeed, other Old Coptic texts as well as "real" Coptic do not use the system of classifiers, having become an entirely phonetic writing system. MN for which the correspondence is given in hieratic are ignored since any classifier is part of the hieratic word.

11. For a list of *normalschrift* Demotic classifiers see the *Demotische Wortliste online*, https://www.dwl.aegyptologie.lmu.de/det_hinweise.php?det=form#tab.

12. And the names of divinities; it could also be used with objects that have a divine context; see, e.g., I/27 *nꜣy ḫpš.w n nb*, "these forelegs of gold," where *ḫps.w* "forelegs" has a divine classifier because it refers to forelegs belonging to the gods.

13. We see one example each of the man with hand to mouth (#4a) and the seated man (#4b).

14. We do have a few examples of the flesh classifier (#8); however it is only once used to identify an animal.

15. Two of these words, *lōw* and *lsmṯnwṯ*, have not been identified with known Greek words. Although they may simply be Greek terms that we have not yet figured out, it is also possible that they are actually from some other ancient language.

16. The Egyptian writing system never felt it necessary to include every possible sign (classifier or phonetic [e.g., the normal writing of the Egyptian word for "beer," *ḥnq* uses only the *ḥ* and *q*, with the *n* seen only rarely in hieroglyphic or hieratic texts, although it is still preserved in Coptic ϩⲛⲕⲉ]); rather, they used enough to make the identification clear (to an Egyptian scribe, even if not to a modern scholar).

ers. We would suggest that this reflects the depth to which the scribes of the DMP had incorporated this vocabulary into their Egyptian worldview.

Some classifiers used in *Magical* have more than one form; see, for example, the three variant forms of the plant classifier (#2a–c) in table 1. Usually a given scribe used only (or primarily) one of the variant forms. Since Egyptian scribes were taught to read and write in schools,[17] it has been suggested that the different forms of individual classifiers used by a scribe may reflect his scribal training. This suggestion is reinforced in *Magical* by the fact that differences in choice of classifier may be associated with other spelling differences. The best example of this, as found in table 2, is seen in the choice between using the flesh classifier (#8) or the man-with-hand-to-mouth classifier (#4a) in writing *plege* for Greek πληγή "sting." There is a correlation between the use of a "standard" form of *g* in examples with the flesh classifier and a much rarer form of *g* with the man-with-hand-to-mouth classifier. Similarly, in *Magical* the foreign-land classifier (#12) appears in two different forms. Form #12a occurs in the transliteration of ἄφοβος, "without alarming," where the alpha privative in the Greek word is written in Demotic using an *r*, here corresponding phonetically to alpha.[18] Form #12b occurs in the transliteration of ἄψευστος "without deceiving," where the alpha privative is written in Demotic using an ayin, one of the standard correspondences with alpha. Thus, the latter Demotic spelling of the privative reflects its original grammatical usage in Greek, while the former reflects only its pronunciation[19] in Egyptian. It would have been nice to be able to argue that the use of two different forms of the foreign-land classifier reflects two different scribal traditions from which the scribe of *Magical* was copying.[20] But this becomes problematic almost immediately because both examples (from II/14) actually form part of a longer Greek phrase transcribed into Demotic where the first Greek word displays the first form of this classifier but the second and third display the second form: {Figure 25 Here}. We can, of course, continue to make the argument about scribal training; but to do so we would have to step back at least one more copyist to find the man combining the two scribal traditions.

This set of terms is also an interesting example of the phonetic information that is found in these types of words, and several noteworthy writings or pairs of writings can be seen. First, as noted above, the alpha privative in Greek is once represented by a simple ayin (standard phonetic correlation) and once by the letter *r*. The latter normally reflects a Greek rho but, as noted above, occasionally is used in glosses of actual Demotic words to indicate the a/ vocalic pronunciation of the "prothetic" (vowel) at the beginning of an imperative.[21] Second, the first word illustrates the correlation of glosses transliterated *ō* to both the short and long form of the o-vowel, reflecting the lack of distinction between long and short vowels in the Egyptian, while the last word reflects the "sibilantization" of *h* before (a long) i sound. These latter changes are discussed in part B, following.

17. Evidence for which exists throughout Pharaonic Egypt (on scribal schools in ancient Egypt, see Ronald J. Williams, "Scribal Training in Ancient Egypt," *JAOS* 92 [1972]: 214–21).

18. What looks like the letter *r* in the imperative form *r-wn* (Coptic ⲁⲟⲩⲱⲛ) "open!" is twice glossed ⲁ in I/5; for other examples of *r* in restricted situations reflecting pronunciation as an *a*, especially as a "prothetic" vowel, see Johnson, "Dialect of the Demotic Magical Papyrus," 105–32. Such use also reflects the appearance of the old "stand-alone" form of the preposition *r*, "to, towards, against, etc.," as a simple a/e-vowel in Coptic, while the pronominal form (where a suffix pronoun has been added to the end of the word and thus preserved the *r*-pronunciation) appears as ⲉⲣⲟ= / ⲁⲣⲟ=.

19. Or does it somehow reflect the "exceptional" character of an element prefixed to a noun changing its meaning?

20. Or, if the scribe of *Magical* was himself responsible for the Demotic alphabetic spelling of some words, one might attribute words with one version of the classifier to him and the other to a manuscript from which he was copying some of his text.

21. See n. 18 above.

Comments on the Uniliteral Script Developed by the Demotic Scribes and What It Reflects of Greek Pronunciation

Both Demotic and the earlier forms of Egyptian essentially did not indicate vowel sounds. The scribes of the DMP used the Egyptian consonants ayin and aleph (which did not appear in Greek) to indicate the vowel a, the "semi-vowels"/"semi-consonants" *w* and *y* for /u/ and /i/, the ligature *ꜥꜣ* for *o* and *ō*, and a "filler"[22] form for *e* and *ē*. This suggests that, at most, the Egyptian scribe was hearing only the "color" of a vowel, not its length.

Most correspondences between Demotic and Greek consonants are predictable[23] and standardized (e.g., Demotic *b*—Greek beta; Demotic *l, m, n*—Greek lambda, mu, nu).[24] The shin that occurs in Egyptian is treated in the Greek as a sigma. When transcribing MN, the Demotic scribes normally seem to have written what they heard, which did not always reflect what was written in the Greek. This discrepancy is found with letters showing "aspiration," "sibilantization," and "voicing," all of which are discussed below.

Aspiration

There is no simple /h/ (voiceless glottal fricative) in the Greek script (although some texts employ a rough breathing mark to indicate aspiration) but three of the Greek "double letters" (theta, phi, chi) appear to involve the combination of a consonant sound (t, p, or k) with an /h/. Demotic, by contrast, has five consonants,[25] which are *transliterated* as variants of *h*. The least common (*ẖ*) does not occur in MNs in the DMP. Two others (*ḫ* and *h̭*), are rare in MNs in the DMP and are written in Demotic when they do so occur. The two most guttural sounds (*h* and *ḥ*) are common in MNs and are normally glossed Ⲩ. When two of the Greek double letters involving /h/ occur next to each other, the Demotic scribe (heard and) expressed aspiration only on the second. We see this in the MN *Hrekssygthō*,[26] which is glossed ⲢⲎϨⲒⲬ·Ⲑ·Ⲱ—where the chi is rendered simply with a *g*. Similarly, Old Coptic ⲈⲔⲞⲘⲪ·Ⲑ·Ⲱ is transcribed in Demotic alphabetic script *Egōmthō*, with variant *Egōmp(ꜣ)t͡q*,[27] where the phi is rendered as a *p*, when it is even written (in which case the theta is also only a *t*).

22. This group, consisting of two small, slightly curved strokes, was used regularly in Demotic to reflect the final short vowel found at the end of most feminine nouns (and appearing in Coptic as final Ⲉ or Ⲓ, depending on dialect).

23. There is one graphic difference in the writing of glosses of Egyptian words in *Magical* worth noting. In column I (as preserved), the scribe used two forms of the letter *p* in glosses, both a standard pi (π) and a "pointed" form with the two legs of the pi joined at a point at the top (∧). The latter is used only, and consistently, for the masculine singular copula pronoun *pe* in the construction *ỉnk pe* N(P) "I am Noun (Phrase)." This writing is not noted in G&T 3 (1909), 28n282 (on the copula pronoun), although it is noted in the list of glosses (128, #383). In I/9 the copula pronoun *pꜣy/pw* in the construction NP 1 NP 2 *pꜣy/pw* (NP 1 is NP 2) is not glossed, nor are other examples of the copula pronoun throughout the text. The standard form of pi is used for the alphabetic letter *p*. It is also used in the masculine singular demonstrative *pꜣy* (initially [I/8] glossed ⲀⲠ, from right to left, but then consistently [I/9 & ff.] ⲠⲀ, from left to right), with rare variants: I/19—ⲠⲀⲈ, and VII/10—ⲠⲀⲈⲒ (these variant spellings occur in a phrase identical to one with the "normal" spelling: *pꜣy ỉw* "this youth" [I/11, and I/18 broken]) and the masculine singular possessive *pꜣy(=y)* (ⲠⲀ) (I/10). In later columns, only the standard form of pi is found (with the exception of II/12, where the pointed form of pi is used in the gloss of the copula pronoun in the nominal construction N *pe pꜣy=y rn (n mꜣꜥ.t)*, "N is my (true) name.").

24. Although note that even these had standardized variants, for example, depending on dialect; Demotic *b* and *p* could be interchanged for each other and for beta and pi, just as Demotic *r* and *l* could with rho and lambda.

25. See Janet H. Johnson, *Thus Wrote 'Onchsheshonqy*, SAOC 45 (Chicago: Oriental Institute of the University of Chicago, 2000), 3–4.

26. Verso XV/3.

27. XVII/25 and XVI/21 respectively (from *r qm(ꜣ) p(ꜣ) tꜣ* "(in order) to create the earth/land"); cf. *Qmtꜣ* glossed ⲔⲞⲘⲦⲰ in VII.6; *Etsyqmēt͡ō* glossed ⲈⲆⲒⲔⲞⲘⲦⲰ (perhaps "to cause the creation of the land") in XVI/17.

An initial *r* in a MN is frequently preceded by an *h* in the Demotic, indicating unwritten aspiration in the Greek. As noted above, *Hrekssygthō* in the Demotic alphabetic script is glossed ⲢⲎϨⲒⲬⲐⲰ, with the *h* marking aspiration omitted in the written form of the gloss. Another, albeit more complicated, example can be seen in the MN *Gōkšyrhrōn͡tōr*,[28] which is glossed ⲔⲰⲬⲒⲢ.ⲢⲞⲆⲞⲢ[29] with an aspirated *r* at the beginning of the second part of the name. This aspiration is confirmed by the indication of aspiration at the beginning of this MN when it occurs by itself: *Hrōn͡tōr*[30] in Demotic alphabetic script is glossed ⲢⲞⲆⲞⲢ.

In a few cases, a MN includes a Demotic name that begins with an *h*. There is a particularly illuminating case in which Demotic *ḥry nṯr* is written in standard Demotic script followed by *ꜣrynwte* in the Demotic alphabetic script.[31] Earlier in the text,[32] we find this name (written *Hrenwte*) glossed *k(y) ḏ(d)* ⲀⲢⲈⲚⲞⲨⲦⲈ "another (manuscript) says Arenoute." In Demotic *ḥry* means "he who is over, chief" and *nṯr* means "god"[33]; thus, this group can be translated as the title "chief god" or the like. Although the Demotic is written using the ancient group *nṯr* for "god," it is known from Coptic that this word was pronounced ⲚⲞⲨⲦⲈ (dialectical variant ⲚⲞⲨⲦⲒ).[34] Thus the compound written in traditional Demotic has been repeated in alphabetic Demotic, and the initial *ḥ* sound has been rendered *ꜣr*, while the whole group can be translated (albeit redundantly) "Chief god, Arynoute." The guttural fricative found in Demotic *ḥry nṯr* and the Demotic alphabetic rendering *Hrenwte* is lacking in the written form of the Old Coptic gloss ⲀⲢⲈⲚⲞⲨⲦⲈ. It is possible that the Ⲁ in this gloss is an attempt to represent the initial aspiration known from the Demotic and reflected in the Demotic alphabetic rendering (and embedded in the initial rho in Greek but perhaps not in the initial rho in the Old Coptic gloss). The aspiration may remain unreflected in the *writing* of the Greek. We see a similar relationship in the writing of the Demotic *ḥry tꜣ* "chief of the land" glossed ⲢⲈⲦ.[35] As in the previous example, the correspondence between initial Demotic *ḥr* and Greek rho is easily explained as the simple absence of any written mark of the aspiration of an initial *r* sound in Greek.[36]

Finally, we find a case of unexpected aspiration in a Demotic noun: *Petery* ° *Petery* ° *Pꜥter* ° *Enphe* ° *Enphe*,[37] "My father, my father, father, in heaven, in heaven." The last phrase reflects Demotic *n p.t* "of heaven" or *m p.t.* "in heaven," but *p.t* is not aspirated in Egyptian except in Bohairic Coptic. Could this phrase then come from a scribe speaking "proto-Bohairic"? This is certainly an interesting question that deserves further study beyond the limits of this article.

Sibilantization

In most cases, Greek double letters are written using the two appropriate letters of the Demotic alphabet. However, when a long i vowel follows one of these double letters ending in *h* (in the Demotic spelling), most examples are written with an *s* (rarely a *š*) instead of the *h* (thus: theta, phi, chi change from *th*, *ph*, *kh* to *ts*/*tš*, *ps*/*pš*, *ks*/*kš*). This

---

28. XXVIII/9; for the shin, which (with preceding *k*) corresponds to chi, see the discussion of sibilantization below.

29. Note that the period here represents a "verse point," which is more commonly found between words but occasionally occurs within MN as well. Presumably this was to aid in the pronunciation, but further study may prove enlightening.

30. Verso XXVI/7.

31. Verso XXVII/3.

32. I/14.

33. See the variant in XXIX.8, *ꜥrkhnwtsy*, glossed ⲀⲢⲬⲚⲞⲨⲦⲤⲈⲒ, using Greek ἀρχός, "chief" and the sibilantized version of *nṯr* discussed below.

34. Some assume this dialectical difference reflects a difference in pronunciation. Others argue that the pronunciation may have been identical (or nearly so) but different scribal conventions developed to reflect it in writing. That is, was this a dialectical difference in pronunciation or in writing conventions?

35. I/20 (twice).

36. G&T 1 (1921), 24–25, n. to l. 20, which cites additional relevant examples and refers to this as "suppressing" the aspiration.

37. XVII/13. Also in V.17 as *Petery sp-2* ° *Pater* ° *Enphe sp-2*, and glossed ⲠⲈⲦⲈⲢⲒ ⲠⲀⲦⲎⲢ ⲈⲚⲫⲈ ⲈⲚⲫⲈ ⲂⲂ̄. For discussion of *Pater* and *Petery*, see below in the section on grammar.

switch in writing from *h* to *s* presumably reflects a modification of the pronunciation of the letter in this environment.[38] There are numerous examples of this in MNs, including: *Thᶜm* ° *Thᶜmthōm* ° *Thᶜmᶜthōm* ° *Thᶜmᶜthwmthᶜm* ° *Thᶜmᶜthwtsy* (ΘΑΜ, ΘΑΜΘΟΜ, ΘΑΜΑΘΟΜ, ΘΑΜΑΘΟΜΘΑΜ, ΘΑΜΑΘΟΥΘΙ),[39] where the glosses have theta for the *th* before ᶜ, *ō*, and *w*, while the Demotic scribe transcribing these sounds evidently heard and wrote *ts+y* in the last case. *Thwts* (ΘΟΥΘΙ)[40] is glossed with thetas for both the *th+ou* and the *ts+y*. Another example can be seen in the phrase *Pysrytsy sp-2 Srytsy sp-2 Abrytsy* (ΠΙCΡΕΙΘΙ CΡΕΙΘΙ ΑΒΡΙΘΙ),[41] where all of the MN end in ΘΙ, and all are written in Demotic with *tsy*. We also see this in the Demotic alphabetic writing *epᶜletsyᶜ* (glossed ΕΠΑΛΗΘΕΙΑ)[42] for the Greek phrase ἐπ᾽ ἀληθείᾳ "truthfully." Finally, we have one example of a *š* (shin) being used rather than an *s*: *Gōkšyrhrōn̅t̅ōr*[43] is glossed ΚΩΧΙΡ.ΡΟΔΟΡ where chi is represented by *ksh* (rather than the expected *ks*) before the long i.

Similarly, but not involving the double letters, we see the MN *ᶜ.ᶜ.tsyꜣwy*[44] is glossed ΑΑΤΙΕΥΕΙ, so in this case the tau followed by the long i has been rendered as *tsy*. Another example of this is the MN *Mᶜstsynks* glossed ΜΑCΤΙΝΞ,[45] where the pronunciation of the Greek ΤΙ seems to have led to an added sibilant in the Demotic. We also see this transcription occasionally when the Demotic word *nṯr* (as noted above, pronounced noute/i) occurs: *ꜣrbethbꜣy.nwtsy*[46] in the Demotic uniliteral writing is glossed ΑΡΒΗΘΒΑΙΝΟΥΘΙ. However, this *tsy* combination could be rendered in other ways, such as Demotic *ᶜrkhnwtsy*,[47] which is glossed ΑΡΧΝΟΥΤCΕΙ.[48]

Voicing

Another difference between the Demotic phonetic inventory and the Greek includes writings indicating voicing. Although Egyptian originally had both a *d* and a *t* sound, the two had collapsed into *t* long before Demotic. If the scribe wanted to ensure a pronunciation as a *d* (i.e., with voicing), he wrote *n* + *t*.[49] Demotic had different forms of the letter *n*, including a "flat" version () and a rounded one (); the *n* used in the combination *n* + *t* → *d* was consistently the flat *n*, which could be written easily over the *t*. Examples include *Ntōntrōmᶜ* glossed ΔΟΝΔΡΟΜΑ,[50] and *Gynn̅t̅ōthwr*[51] glossed ΚΙΝΔΑΘ[...]Ρ (where, as elsewhere, the first [phonetic] *n* is the rounded *n* while the second *n*, combining with *t*, is the flat *n*). Another interesting case is the string *Semeᶜ.gᶜnṯꜣw* ° *Genṯꜣw* ° *Gōnṯꜣw* ° *Gerynṯꜣw* ° *Ntᶜrengō*, glossed CΗΜΕΑ.ΚΑΝΤΕΥ ΚΕΝΤΕΥ ΚΟΝΤΕΥ ΚΗΡΙΔΕΥ ΔΑΡΥΝΚΩ.[52] In each name the *ṯꜣw* ending is

38. This same switch is found occasionally with delta, reflected by writing an *s* before the long i.
39. XIV/11–12.
40. XIV/13.
41. XIV/26.
42. II/14. For more on this term see table 1, #12b.
43. XXVIII/9.
44. XXV/4.
45. XIV/8.
46. XVII/11.
47. XXIX/8.
48. Perhaps in this case, since the first part of the word is Greek, they chose a spelling of the Demotic word in the Greek letters that they felt more "Greek"?
49. As we have seen already in *Hrōn̅t̅ōr* glossed ΡΟΔΟΡ with n̅t̅ō representing ΔΟ, written with the Demotic word *tꜣ*, "earth, land," including the house classifier (v. XXVI.7) and *Gōkšyrhrōn̅t̅ōr*, glossed ΚΩΧΙΡ.ΡΟΔΟΡ (XXVIII/9), both cited above in the discussion of aspiration of initial *r*.
50. XXVIII/9 and v. XXVI/7, although note that the rounded *n* + *t* (the second grouping) is glossed as ΝΔ.
51. Verso XXVI/3, although note the variation in XXVIII/8: *Gynntethwr*, glossed ΚΙΝΤΑΘΟΥΡ, where the first *n* is also rounded and second is flat (over a *t*); perhaps the *e* (as opposed to the *ꜣ*) following this set of letters is indicating that it was pronounced as a *t*.
52. VII/28.

written in Demotic using a group that originally read *ṯ3w* "wind"; but this original *ṯ* had long since become a *t*. In all these names, where the *n* + *t* pronunciation was retained, the rounded *n* was used before the *t3w* group; in those cases where the *n* + *t* combined to produce a *d*, the flat *n* was used.

Similarly, very early Egyptian had distinguished between *s* and *z*, but this distinction was lost early in the written history of the Egyptian language. If the Egyptian scribe wanted to ensure pronunciation as a *z*, he wrote flat *n* + *s*; examples include Demotic alphabetic *Nsew* corresponding to Old Coptic ⲌⲈⲞⲨ[53] and Demotic alphabetic *Bwnsʿnw* corresponding to Old Coptic ⲂⲞⲨⲌⲀⲚⲀⲨ.[54] Both Demotic *g* and *k* are regularly transcribed Ⲕ in the glosses, but in some MN a flat *n* is written before the *g* and the group is rendered gamma in the gloss.[55] For example, *Hesen.myngʿ. ntōn* in Demotic alphabetic script is glossed ⲨⲤⲈⲚⲘⲒⲄⲀⲆⲰⲚ,[56] *Eresgšyngʿl*, the name of the Sumerian goddess of the Underworld, is glossed ⲈⲢⲈⲤⲬⲒⲄⲀⲖ,[57] and *Ngōngetsyk* is glossed ⲄⲰⲄⲨ ⲐⲒƷ.[58] This appears to be another conscious use of a flat *n* plus a consonant to mark voicing.[59] In another case,[60] the Demotic script writes *ʿn-gen*[61] for Greek ἀγγῖον, thereby reflecting the Greek pronunciation of *g* + *g* as *ng*.

Greek Vocabulary Becoming Egyptian "Loanwords"

It is not surprising that Greek nouns used in *Magical* appear, when required by Egyptian grammar,[62] with the appropriate Demotic masculine or feminine, definite[63] or indefinite article. For example, in III/9–10, we see the feminine

53. XVII/18.

54. XVII/25.

55. Although at least once the flat *n* was written before *k* and the group was glossed with a gamma (*Lʿrknʿnes* glossed ⲖⲀⲢⲄⲚⲀⲚⲎⲤ [VII/22]) and once a rounded *n* before a *g* was glossed with a gamma (*Sengenbʿy* glossed ⲤⲈⲄⲈⲚ ⲂⲀⲒ [XVI/10]).

56. VII/25.

57. VII/26.

58. Verso XXVI/6. But in XXVIII/9 *Ngō.ngethygs* in Demotic alphabetic script is also glossed ⲄⲰⲄⲨⲐⲒƷ. In this example, theta + iota in the gloss has been rendered *thy* in the Demotic, not the sibilant form *tsy*, which is found normally (and in v. XXVI/6); presumably, the scribe here is influenced by the written form rather than the pronunciation.

59. But note *ntʿrengō* using flat *n* + *g* but glossed ⲆⲀⲢⲨⲚⲔⲰ (VII/28).

60. XII/11.

61. Using the Demotic word-group *ʿn* ("again") rather than only uniliteral signs.

62. One interesting, and anomalous, occasion of Greek grammar being reflected in the Egyptian is the use of Greek genitival endings. Greek words were almost always rendered in the nominative (one rare exception is *epʿletsyʿ* for ἐπ' ἀληθειᾳ, see table 1, #12b); however, it appears that it was quite common to have Greek words before amounts in the genitive. A complete list of the words that appear to have genitive endings in Demotic is: κισσός (cypher: ⲔⲒⲤⲤⲞⲨ; *gyss-ʿ3-s*—ivy), ὀποβάλσαμον (ⲎⲠⲞⲂⲀⲤⲀⲘⲞⲨ; *hepwbʿlsʿmw*—juice of the balsam tree), μανδραγόρας (cypher: ⲘⲀⲚⲆⲢⲀⲔⲞⲢⲞⲨ (ⲢⲒƷⲀ); *mʿntrʿgwrw*—mandrake [root]), σατύριον (*s3terw*—orchid[?]). There is also *trymyʿmʿ-t3-s*, which G&T have suggested is from θυμιάμα(τος) (incense), which would mean the Demotic reflects the genitive, or τερμινθος (terebinth), in which case it is simply the nominative. The last perhaps final two examples are written in cypher, with the Demotic being an actual translation of the term: χηνάγριον (ⲬⲎⲚⲀⲄⲢⲒⲞⲨ; *sre.t*—young wild goose) and μαλάβαθρον (ⲘⲀⲖⲀⲂⲀⲐⲞⲨ; *hb-ir-yr*—malabathrum plant). A complete study of this phenomenon is beyond the scope of this article; yet the issue certainly merits further work.

63. The spelling of several MN suggests that the aleph of the definite article (series) *p3/t3/n3* was being lost/had already been lost, as it had been by Coptic. Several MN written in (cursive) hieroglyphs beginning with the definite article are glossed with no reflex of the aleph. Three examples (for all following, # refers to G&T 3 [1909], 2–100) show the feminine definite article *t3* before a name consisting of (or beginning with) *h3n* (#159–61). All are glossed using a theta (thus *t3 h3n* became ⲐⲀⲚ), thereby clearly indicating nothing intervened between the *t* and the *h*; the aleph was gone. Similarly, the cursive hieroglyphic writing *pitit.w* glossed ⲠⲒⲀⲦⲒⲀⲦⲈ (#387) "the father of fathers" (note that in this writing only the *p* is written, so the aleph is dropped in both versions) and *n3 by(.w)* (#324) glossed (ⲚⲂⲀⲒ) demonstrate the masculine singular and the plural articles written with no reflex of an aleph. When Demotic is used, rather than (cursive) hieroglyphs (or hieratic), the same pronunciation, without aleph, is reflected. Examples include the gloss ⲠⲒⲀⲘ for *p3 yʿm*, "the sea" (#386), the gloss ⲠⲞⲨⲈⲢⲦⲈⲒⲞⲨ for *p3 wr diw*, "the great one of 'tens'" (#398), the gloss ⲠⲚⲈⲂⲂⲀⲒ for *p3 nb b3.w*, "the lord/pos-

Greek word βατάνη "flat dish," in instructions to bring and fill (with oil) a new dish. In the first instance it is written *wʿ.t*[64] *bꜣtꜣne.t,* and in the second *tꜣ*[65] *bʿtʿne.t.*[66] Both spellings include the ending *.t,* which was used (although not always/ consistently) to mark feminine nouns. This ending was originally pronounced t but had long since been reduced in pronunciation to a final short vowel (frequently a short e, i.e., the "filler" e mentioned above). Because the Egyptian scribes did not distinguish between short and long vowels, this group also reflects the long e (eta) feminine ending of the Greek word. Another similar example of this phenomenon is found in the word *lʿmps,* the Demotic alphabetic writing of Greek λαμπάς "lamp."[67] Although this word does not end with the traditional Egyptian feminine *.t,* it does have a feminine indirect article, reflecting that the scribe understood that the Greek word was feminine (even though it does not have the standard first declension feminine eta ending—that is, the feminine ending that we most commonly see reflected in the Demotic writing). One final example of the gendering of Greek words in Demotic is slightly more complicated: *splelyn,* the Demotic uniliteral writing of the Greek σπληνίον,[68] "a compress of linen" is marked with a feminine independent pronoun, even though the Greek word is neuter. The few other neuter words that are rendered with an article in this text are read as masculine.[69] However, since some of the most common words in Egyptian (and Demotic) for linen are *ʿꜣ.t* and *pꜣq.t,* both feminine, perhaps the scribe decided that this was a more appropriate way to render a word for which Egyptian did not have an equivalent gender.

As we have seen, in most cases Greek masculine and feminine nouns are so treated in the Egyptian.[70] But in a spell invoking the moon,[71] which is a masculine noun in Egyptian but feminine in Greek, the Demotic uses the feminine pronoun for reference following an address to the moon. The directions instruct the magician to say the spell nine times *šʿ mtw=s wnḥ=s r-r=k* "until she reveals herself to you." Was the scribe translating from Greek into Egyptian and following the Greek too closely to note the need to change the pronouns? Such translation has been suggested for various spells, even spells with purely Egyptian content, and may reflect double/second translations.

We have an example that may reflect reinterpretation of a MN as incorporating the Demotic masculine definite article, even when it originally did not. The MN *Pʿn͡togrʿt͡or*[72] seems to represent Greek παντοκράτωρ "almighty"; it is followed immediately by *ꜣn͡tqgrʿt͡qr.*[73] It has been suggested that the *p* of the Greek word has been (incorrectly) reinterpreted as the Demotic masculine singular definite article and omitted.

---

sessor of *bas*" (#394). The example of Demotic *bʿ n pꜣ Rʿ* glossed ⲂⲀⲘⲠⲢⲈ (#84) reflects two changes from earlier pronunciations: the masculine definite article *pꜣ* has become *p* and the presence of *p* immediately after the genitive *n* has caused it to be pronounced as an *m.* Two examples using MN, which are not recognized as Egyptian but which appear to have the masculine singular definite article written *pꜣ* in the Demotic but *p* in the gloss, include *n pꜣ nws͡tqr* glossed ⲘⲠⲚⲀⲤⲦⲞⲢ (# 310, perhaps for the Greek ναστήρ "inhabitant") and *n pꜣ leꜣsphøt* glossed ⲘⲠⲖⲈⲀⲤⲪⲎⲦ (# 309).

64. The feminine singular indefinite article.

65. The feminine singular definite article.

66. Both spellings incorporate the pot classifier, see table 1, #9, and note the free interchange between *ꜣ* and *ʿ* to represent an alpha.

67. XXVIII/5, and see table 1, #7.

68. For more on this word, its determinative, and the use of two *l*, see table 1, #8.

69. Ex. (*pꜣ*) *ʿn-gen* for ἀγγῖον, "vessel," (*wʿ*) *ꜣrkyʿ* for ἀρκίον "chest," and *(wʿ, pꜣ) gʿwmʿ* for καῦμα "fever."

70. Note that the neuter nominative/accusative -ον ending is generally written *-wn* in Demotic (κρινάνθεμον [glossed ⲔⲢⲒⲚⲀⲐⲈⲘⲞⲚ], written *grynʿthemwn* [martagon lily], and ἀρσενικόν, written *ꜣrsenygwn* [orpiment]). When this ending has an iota before it, -ῖον, there is rather more variation in the Demotic writing. In one case we see *ʿꜣ-n* (ξηρίον, written *kser-ʿꜣ-n* [dry powder]), in another it is *-en* (ἀγγῖον, written *ʿn-gen* [vessel]), this same ending may also be written *-yn,* as we see in *splelyn* (poultice), which may be for the Greek σπληνίον; however, the Greek may have a variant written σπλήν, which is reflected here.

71. XXIII/26.

72. Verso XII/10, twice using the biliteral *tꜣ* (see n. 2 above) within the otherwise uniliteral Demotic script and the frequent correspondence of Demotic *g* with Greek kappa.

73. With the same peculiarities of writing as *Pʿn͡togrʿt͡or,* as well as the common interchange of aleph and ayin.

Not only are the definite articles used normally with Greek nouns, so are the Demotic possessive articles[74] and even the Demotic possessive pronouns. In an example of this latter case, *Pꜥter* in the string *Petery* ° *Petery* ° *Pꜥter* ° *Enphe* ° *Enphe* "My father, my father, father, in heaven, in heaven"[75] is assumed to be the Greek noun πατήρ, an interpretation supported by the seated-man classifier attached to the word. If so, then *Petery* can be explained as the Greek noun with the Demotic first-person singular personal possessive pronoun =*y*, "my" as a suffix, in good Egyptian fashion (and with the appropriate vowel reduction).[76]

Comfort Using Greek

The Egyptians not only felt comfortable rendering Greek words into Demotic, they also felt comfortable integrating them into a fully Egyptian grammatical context. This can be seen with the Greek noun θέρμος "lupine," used in a well-attested Demotic nominal formation. The construction *s* "man" plus an item that can be sold indicates the name of a profession: "seller of ..." Two examples of this construction are found in *Magical* that use θέρμος, written *trmws* in Demotic.[77] In one example the "lupine-seller" is identified with the "wreath-seller,"[78] while in the other it is said one can find flowers of the "eye of raven" plant "in the place of the lupine-seller."[79]

The impression that the scribes felt "at home" with Greek vocabulary is reinforced by the occasional use of a Greek word as a gloss to clarify an Egyptian term. Two of the Egyptian terms are common Egyptian words: one[80] was written in Demotic (*tks* meaning either "boat" or some kind of "chair" but glossed with ⲦⲢⲀⲠⲈⲤⲈⲚ, for the Greek word τραπέζιον "small table," suggesting perhaps a "stool" or similar[81]), the other[82] in hieratic (*sre.t* an unusual feminine form of a common masculine word for goose glossed ⲬⲎⲚⲀⲄⲢⲒⲞⲨ, which G&T[83] suggested was the Greek word χηνάγριον "wild goose"). A third example[84] is a phrase, written in Demotic, combining common Demotic words (*sym* "vegetable, plant" and *gyḏ* "hand") with the plant classifier but producing a plant name (lit., plant of hand) which is otherwise unattested. However, the gloss, ⲠⲚⲦⲀⲔⲦⲀⲖⲞⲤ has been identified[85] as standing for πενταδάκτυλος, lit., "five-fingered (plant)," which is also known today as potentilla or cinquefoil.[86] All of these examples would seem to suggest that the scribe thought that the Greek words would clarify the Demotic (presumably the native tongue of anyone reading this text)—pointing to a significant level of bilingualism.

74. For example, v. XXXXII/5 has *pꜣy=f swmꜥ*, "its body" with Greek σῶμα written in Demotic alphabetic characters, preceded by the Demotic possessive article using the masculine singular form *pꜣy=f* (Coptic ⲠⲈϤ).

75. V/17, VII/13.

76. For the aspiration in the final repeated word, see above.

77. V/25, XXVII/25, for more on this term see table 1, #10.

78. V/25; *pꜣ s-qlm ky d pꜣ s (n) trmws*, "the seller of wreaths (lit., the wreath-man), var. (lit., another (manuscript) says) the lupine-seller (lit., lupine-man)."

79. XXVII/25; *hyn.w ḥrr n bel n* ⲈⲂⲰⲔ *ḥr gm=k sw n pꜣ mꜣꜥ n pꜣ s (n) trmws,* "some flowers of 'eye of raven' plant. You find them in the place of the lupine-seller."

80. IV/1.

81. Perhaps glossed in the Greek because of the confusion between the two words in Demotic.

82. IV/6.

83. G&T 1 (1921), 40–41, n. to l. 6.

84. Verso VIII/7.

85. By G&T 1 (1904), 180, n. to l. 7, who cite Dioscorides 4.42.

86. The latter retaining the concept of "five" (albeit in French), but coming by way of πενταφυλλον, "five-leaved."

Conclusion

Overall, the scribes of *Magical* display mastery of all aspects of the impressively wide range of scripts and languages they incorporate in their presentation of the magical texts. This reflects not only the very long period of time (several centuries) that many Egyptians had been bilingual in Egyptian and Greek but also the sophistication of these scribes who could use their fluency in different Egyptian scripts and stages of the language to bring into their writing the loanwords from Greek that their work on the magical texts had made part of their world view/ethos.

Table 1. Classifiers Used in Demotic Transcriptions of Greek Vocabulary.

#	Sign	Demotic	Gloss (OC);[1] Cypher[2]	Context	G&T #;[3] loc.[4]	Greek	Translation
1	 - divine nature	*n͡toteg*ʿ*gyste*	ΔΟΔЄ-ⲔⲀⲔΙϹΤΗ	in a list of MN[5]	—; VII/26	δωδεκακίστη (from δωδεκακίς "twelve times")	—[6]
2a	 - plant[7]	(*p*ꜣ) *gyssōs*	— ; ΚΙϹϹΟΥ[8]	sleep medication	25; XXIV/10, 19, 22	κισσός	ivy
		*gryn*ʿ*themwn*	— ; ΚΡΙΝΑΘΕΜΟΝ[9]	list of ingredients	26; G&T 171, n. to v. II/3; v. II/3, 6	κρινάνθεμον	houseleek (a type of succulent) or martagon lily
		*m*ʿ*ntr*ʿ*gwrw*[10]	— ; ΜⲀΝΔΡⲀΚΟΡΟΥ[11]	sleep medication	33; XXIV/7, 18	μανδραγόρας	mandrake[12]
2b	 - tree[13]	*s*ꜣ*terw*	—	list of ingredients	47; G&T 187, n. to v. XIV/5; v. XIV/5	σατύριον[14]	orchid or lily[15]

1. In Old Coptic (OC).
2. In bold.
3. G&T 3 (1909), 102–4 # in "List of Words of Greek Origin" and/or discussion in G&T 1 (1904) (followed by the page number); any G&T cited without a volume number refers to G&T 1 (1904), with the page and note numbers given in the entry.
4. The column and line numbers in *Magical*.
5. Including *Eresgšyng*ʿ*l* with this divine classifier for the name of the Sumerian goddess of the Underworld (see G&T 1, 61, n. to l. 26); for discussion of the spelling, see the section on potential voicing of Greek gamma, below.
6. The DGE identifies the term δωδεκακίστη as an epithet of the moon. This presumably reflects the idea of the twelve hours of the night (in Egyptian astronomy, mythology, etc.).
7. Very similar to the writing of the late hieratic classifier for "plant" (Gardiner M2); see Möller III, #268.
8. Note that when written in Demotic, the ending appears to be the nominative (*ōs* for ός), however in the cryptic writing the ΟΥ ending appears to be the genitive. This is a rare example of Greek endings being reflected in the Demotic, although this does appear to be more common when the word is associated with a numerical amount.
9. This is written in Greek, not cypher.
10. In the phrase *nn.t n m*ʿ*ntr*ʿ*gwrw*, "root of the mandrake," all in Demotic.
11. In the phrase ΜⲀΝΔΡⲀΚΟΡΟΥ ΡΙⳄⲀ, "root of the mandrake," all in Greek.
12. See, e.g., *rrm.t*, "root of mandrake"; Lise Manniche, *An Ancient Egyptian Herbal* (London : British Museum, 1989), 117–19. It seems possible that the Greek word was used because the part of the mandrake used in this text is the root, not the flower or fruit, which is what was depicted in Egyptian art.
13. Very similar to the writing of the late hieratic tree classifier (Gardiner M1); see Möller III, #266.
14. The LSJ identifies this as a type of orchid (*man orchis, Acera anthropophora*) and the lily *Fritillaria graeca* (in the phrase σατύριον ἐρυθραϊκόν); it is also a type of water rodent, but that does not seem particularly helpful here.
15. One would assume that this classifier would be used with a plant that was a type of tree, or at least a type of bush; however, neither of these plants would fall into this category. This could mean that we have the wrong Greek word, or that the Egyptian scribe did not understand the type of plant being cited.

#	Sign	Demotic	Gloss (OC); Cypher	Context	G&T #; loc.	Greek	Translation
2c	 - plant[16]	*tphn*	—	material of a peg for hanging a lamp[17]	13; XXVII/15	δάφνη	laurel
		ꜣmwnyꜥk	TⲀMONIⲀKH	list of incense ingredients; OC = description of a plant	4; G&T 102 n. to l. 23; XIV/23, v. IV/15	ἀμμωνιακόν	ammoniacum[18]

16. For a discussion of this classifier in καῦμα "fever," see table 2, where it is read as a sail rather than a plant classifier.

17. The use of the classifier is perhaps influenced by the spelling of Demotic *ẖt*, "wood" in the same phrase. The phrase reads *wꜥ.t šmwꜣ.t n ẖt n tphn*, "a peg of wood of a laurel." It is also possible that this version was chosen because the scribe was unsure whether the δάφνη was more "flower-like" or "tree-like" (or felt that it fell somewhere in between) and thus chose the more neutral Demotic sign over the more distinctive hieratic classifier.

18. G&T translate "styrax" without an explanation, but they cite Dioscorides 3.98, who writes: "Ammoniacum is an herb whence the ammoniacan incense (comes)." (Ammonia was a region in ancient Libya.) Perhaps, as was suggested for *tphn*, "laurel," above, this classifier was used because the scribe did not want to commit to a "tree" versus a "flowering plant" category (did he not know, or was it ambiguous because it was resin-producing?), but without further examples there is simply no way to know.

#	Sign	Demotic	Gloss (OC); Cypher	Context	G&T #; loc.	Greek	Translation
3	 - mineral[19]	*g3l3g3ntsy*	ⲔⲀⲖⲀⲔⲀⲚⲐⲒ	ingredient to be put on a lamp	59; III/24	καλακάνθη (var. of χαλκάνθη)	copper sulphate
		3rsenygwn	—	in comparison to describe a stone	7; v. III/18	ἀρσενικόν	orpiment
		psymytsy[20]	—	cure "water" in a woman	64; v. VI/2	ψιμύθιον	white lead
		kʿrʿyne	—	color of a lizard[21]	20; v. IV/8	καλαίνη (from κάλαις)	chrysolite (a blue-green stone)
		mʿknesyʿ	ⲘⲀⲚⲈⲤⲒⲀ[22]	description of ores	31; G&T 172–73, nn. to ll. 8, 11, 13; v. II/8	μαγνησία	magnesium oxide
		mʿknes	ⲘⲀⲄⲚⲎⲤ	see previous	see previous; v. II/11	Μάγνης[23]	called "living maknes"
		mʿnes	ⲘⲀⲔⲚⲎⲤ	see previous	see previous; v. II/13	Μάγνης	called "human ma(k)nes"
4a	 - [24]	—	—	—	—; —	—	—

19. For more on the names and occurrence of types of minerals in Egypt, see John R. Harris, *Lexicographical Studies in Ancient Egyptian Minerals* (Berlin: Akademie-Verlag, 1961).

20. Note that the ending of this word is quite odd. One would expect some variant of *-wn*, reflecting the Greek neuter ending. We do see a similar ending in *g3l3g3ntsy*, where the last letters clearly represent -θη (as is written in the gloss). Of course, καλακάνθη is a feminine word, so this makes sense, but ψιμύθιον is clearly neuter (and indeed in the following line the masculine suffix is used to refer to the mineral). The reason for the ending remains unclear.

21. Although at first the use of the feminine ending seems odd—one would expect the gender to match *iwn*, "color," a masculine word—the word is ultimately being used to describe the color of a salamander which is feminine term in both Greek and Egyptian. Salamander is written in Greek (ⲤⲀⲖⲀⲘⲀⲦⲢⲀ) and then reiterated in the line below in Demotic (*wʿ.t ḥflelʿ.t*).

22. For this and the following two entries the OC words are not precisely glosses of the Demotic (since they do not occur directly over the Demotic), but they do appear to be acting with the same function. The section reads (with ; indicating line breaks and the variates of the term in bold): *p3 mʿknesyʿ* ; ⲘⲀⲚⲈⲤⲒⲀ ; *wʿ iny n ty iw=f km m-qty* (10) stem *iir=k nt=f iw=f km* ; ⲘⲀⲄⲚⲎⲤ *p3 mʿknes nt ʿnḫ ḥr in=w=f* ; ⲘⲀⲔⲚⲎⲤ *iir=k ḫy.ṯ=f iw=f km* ; *p3 mʿnes n rmṯ ḥr in=w=f* ; *n t3 ʿn-tsyke iir=k ḫy.ṯ=f* (15) *ḥr ir=f ti iw snf r-bnr*, "Magnesium. A stone of a type that is black like (10) galena. If you grind it, it is black. Magnes: the maknes which is living; it is brought. Maknes: If you scrape it, it is black. Human ma(g)nes: It is brought from India. If you scrape it, (15) it exudes blood."

23. This (and the next example) refer to the adjective for things that come from the region of Magnesia (in Thessaly) after which the ore magnesium is named.

24. The man-with-hand-to-mouth classifier, typically used for actions related to speaking, eating, or other actions related to the mouth; see the section on multiple classifiers, below.

#	Sign	Demotic	Gloss (OC); Cypher	Context	G&T #; loc.	Greek	Translation
4b	 - seated man[25]	*pᶜter*	—	in an epithet of a god	—; V/17, VII/13, XVII/6	πατήρ	father[26]
		ᶜbrᶜḥme	ⲁⲃⲣⲁⲭⲁⲙ	in a list of MN	—; VIII/8	Ἀβραάμ	Abraham
5	 - stone	*gᶜrbꜣnᶜ*	—	description of a stone	58; G&T 173, n. l. 6; v. III/6	χαλβάνη	galbanum (a kind of resinous sap)[27]
		sgewe	—	description of a stone	50; G&T 174, n. l. 7; v. III/7	σκευή(?)[28]	?[29]
6	 - wood	*pyngs* or *pynᶜks*[30]	—	astrological divination	42; IV/21, 22	πίναξ	a tablet or board[31] (usually for writing)—here "for reading the hours"[32]
7	 - metal	*lᶜmps*[33]	—	vessel inquiry	28; XXVIII/5	λαμπάς	lamp[34]

25. This classifier is used for almost anything related to a person (particularly a man, or any human when gender was not a factor), such as professions, abstract concepts related to human actions or emotions, familial or community relationships, and names. In both instances attested here, the classifier is stressing that this (MN) is a (deified) human.

26. For a discussion of the entire phrase see the section on grammar.

27. In the phrase "it is a bright stone like galbanum," in a remedy for "evil sleep"; Demotic iny "stone" has same classifier. G&T note that this plant is "*Bubo galbanum* L., a plant of the fennel tribe used in medicine" and cite Dioscorides 3.87.

28. There is also the far more common word σκεῦος, which is a term for a vessel or implement (but can also just mean "thing"); however this also does not make particular sense in this context (the line reads *wn ke wᶜ iw ḥr ir=w ir=f n sgewe*, "There is another one which is made into ..."

29. The *LSJ* identifies this word as "equipment, attire, apparel, dress," none of which make any sense in this context (or with this classifier). G&T: "Max Müller (*Rec. tr.*, viii. 174) suggests that σκευή may have the meaning "quick-lime," though this sense is not found in the dictionaries." Whether Müller found a source that has since been lost, or this is simply a Greek word that is not clear to us from the Demotic, it is unfortunately not possible to say without further evidence.

30. These variant spellings seem to reinforce the fact that spelling was fluid in Egyptian (see *bᶜtᶜne.t* & *bꜣtꜣne.t*) and vowels were less important than consonants.

31. The use of the wood classifier indicates the material from which the tablet was made.

32. *wᶜ pyngs n ᶜš wnw.t;* the second reference says, *mtw=k sẖ pꜣy=k ᶜš-sḥn r wᶜ ḏmᶜ n-mꜣy mtw=k wꜣḥ=f ḥr pꜣ pynᶜks*, "You should write your business on a new papyrus and put it on the tablet."

33. *n ḥmt*, "of copper." Note that the writing of the word for copper consists of this same sign followed by the granule over three strokes (classifier #10).

34. The question of why this Greek word was used rather than the more common Demotic *ẖbs* (which is found innumerable times in this text alone) does not have a clear answer. It should also be noted that this lamp is in the phrase *mtw=k ṯ rꜣ wᶜ.t lᶜmps n ḥmt,* which is translated by G&T (without a note) as "you light a bronze [now translated 'copper'] lamp." (G&T 1 [1904], 163. The translation by Johnson in Hans Dieter Betz, *The Greek Magical Papyri in Translation, including the Demotic Spells* (Chicago: University of Chicago Press, 1986), 238 has the same [with the metal identified as copper].) The translation of *ṯ rꜣ* is literally "seize (the) mouth," which is not a phrase found elsewhere. And the classifiers on *rꜣ* include the standard flesh sign, but also a brazier sign, which also does not appear to have a parallel, thus suggesting the classifier is acting for the whole phrase. The reason for the use of this phrase and any implications from this that may impact the choice of *lᶜmps* instead of *ẖbs* remain obscure.

#	Sign	Demotic	Gloss (OC); Cypher	Context	G&T #; loc.	Greek	Translation
8	 - flesh[35]	*swmꜥ*	—; ⲤⲞⲘⲀ[36]	spell to make a woman mad about a man	52; XIII/17, v. XXXII/5	σῶμα	body[37]
		gꜥlꜣ.t	—; ϭⲀⲖⲈ	list of ingredients	11;[38] [XIII/22], XXIV/25, 37	γαλῆ	weasel[39]
		splelyn[40]	—	making a poultice	51; G&T 182, n. l. 9 ; v. IX/9	σπλήν (var. of σπληνίον)	a compress of linen[41]

35. This classifier is used predominately to indicate anatomical parts (of humans or animals) or other things associated with a physical body. For examples of the flesh classifier used in conjunction with (an)other classifier, see the discussion of words with multiple classifiers, below.

36. *Nota bene*, there is another cypher a few lines above (l. 12) written ⲘⲞⲤⲈ, which G&T 1 (1921), 94–95, note to l. 12, have suggested is a misspelling for ⲤⲞⲘⲀ.

37. The reason for using the Greek word here rather than the common Egyptian word (*ẖ(e).t*) is unclear. In both instances it is the body of a shrewmouse (*ꜥmꜥme*, in cypher: ⲈⲘⲒⲘ) that is being referenced, so it seems plausible that this is an important factor. But the shrewmouse was a common animal in ancient Egypt, so there would have been no need to draw on foreign vocabulary, as if to identify an unusual term. Also of note, in neither case is σῶμα in a genitival construction (i.e., "the body of the shrewmouse"); rather, in both cases the shrewmouse is mentioned at the beginning of the spell and the body is discussed later in the spell, which rules out the use due to the borrowing of a "frozen phrase."

38. There is also a partially broken and restored example, which does not have the *.t* feminine ending but does have a flesh classifier, in XIII/22.

39. The word is found three times, always in the larger phrase "the gall of a weasel of Alexandria": XXIV/25, *sẖy n* ϭⲀⲖⲈ *n Rꜥ-qt;* XXIV/37, ⲤⲈϨⲒ *n gꜥlꜣ.t n Rꜥ-qt;* XIII/22, ⲤⲀϢⲈ *n [gꜥ]lꜣ(.t) n Rꜥ-qt.* (Note that in their list of Greek words, G&T do not include the third example, presumably because the word is partially broken.) Thus, although one might expect an animal hide classifier for this word, the flesh classifier has actually been transferred from *sẖy*, "gall" to the end of the phrase, to retain the information for the category of the whole phrase.

40. The inclusion of a second *l* in the Demotic is odd but also apparently reflected in a Coptic source (see Georgio Zoega, *Catalogus Codicum Copticorum Manuscriptorum* Leipzig: Hinrichs, 1903), 630, ⲤⲠⲈⲖⲈⲖⲒⲚ) as cited by G&T.

41. Note that σπλήν is a cognate with the far more common word for "spleen." Thus, the choice of a flesh classifier could be because of confusion with the word for spleen (which clearly would have taken such a sign), or it could be because this was a treatment to be applied to the body. The former option seems more convincing since other terms for treatments in Egyptian do not reflect the placement on the body, but generally the material from which the poultice it was made.

#	Sign	Demotic	Gloss (OC); Cypher	Context	G&T #; loc.	Greek	Translation
9	 - pot	*ʿn-gen*[42]	—	making fish oil to make a woman love a man	1; XII/11	ἀγγῖον	type of vessel
		lwps	—	for mixing ingredients	30; v. VII/4	λοπάς	flat dish
		bꜣtꜣne.t or *bʿtʿne.t*[43]	—	for collecting ingredients	10; III/9, 10	βατάνη/ πατάνη	flat dish
		hepwbʿlsʿmw	ΗΠΟΒⲀⲤⲀΜΟΥ	list of ingredients	37; XII/1	ὀποβάλσαμον	juice of the balsam tree[44]
		ꜣrkyʿ	—	storage container for ingredients	6; XXV/31	ἀρκίον	burdock,[45] but translated "box" by G&T[46]

42. For discussion of the phonetics of pronunciation of this term, see main text, section B, "voicing."

43. Note free interchange between *ꜣ* and *ʿ* to represent an *a*; also note use of final feminine *.t* as marker of feminine noun, corresponding to η in Greek; for discussion, see the main text section on phonetics.

44. The use of a vessel classifier for this ingredient surely reflects that the "juice" was stored in a vessel. Using a pot classifier for a liquid (especially one used in medical recipes) was a very common practice in Egyptian; see, e.g., *bni.w*, "date juice" (*Wb.* I:462, 4–5), *mstꜣ*, a liquid medicine (*Wb.* II:151, 1–2), or even *irt.t* "milk" (Wb. I:117, 1–6).

45. See Dioscorides 4.106–107.

46. If G&T were suggesting this was from ἄρκα, which is the Greek version of Latin *arca*, for "box," it would be the only example of a Latin word in this group. There is a poorly understood word *ʿkr* in Demotic, which has a "silver" classifier and a variety of spellings (CDD *ʿ* [2012], 151–52). It is defined as a "metal object," and associated with the Coptic word ⲀⲔⲖⲎ, a word Černy (*CED,* 3) translates simply as "vessel" (but notes association with Demotic word and "metal object"). Westendorf (*KHWb*, 485) lists a variant of this as ⲀⲖⲔⲎ. It seems possible that all of these Coptic words tie back to the Greek iteration of arca (which often was used for keeping valuables, such as silver, perhaps explaining the use of a "silver" classifier in a number of cases) and the version in the DMP is yet another example of this word (although note that arca in Greek and Latin is a feminine word, as are the different Coptic variants; however, in the DMP Arkya is given a masculine indefinite article). The use of the vessel classifier rather than the silver would then be explained by the fact that here the container is not used for holding money but rather spell ingredients, so the scribe opted for the more generic classifier.

#	Sign	Demotic	Gloss (OC); Cypher	Context	G&T #; loc.	Greek	Translation
10	 - granule over plural strokes	*tr*(ꜣ)*mws*[47]	—	source for ingredients	18; V/25, XX-VII/25	θέρμος	lupine[48]
		grwgws[49]	— ; ΚΡΟΚΟϹ	to bring in a thief to get the truth	27; III/29, v. XVIII/7	κρόκος	crocus
		trymyꜥmꜥṯqs	—	list of ingredients	53; G&T 101 and 102 n. to l. 23; XIV/23	A) τερμινθος[50] B) θυμιάμα(τος)	A) terebinth tree[51] B) incense N.B. This is paired with *ꜣmwnyꜥk* ("ammoniacum," see 2c, above)[52]
		kserōn	—	a wound treatment	35; G&T 176, n. to l. 14; v. IV/14	ξηρίον	a desiccative powder[53]
11	 - place	*ꜥntsyke*	—	origin of a mineral[54]	19; v. II/14	Ἰνδική	India

47. The Greek rho is once rendered by a simple uniliteral *r*, once by a variant form deriving from the noun ro "mouth."

48. In the phrase *pꜣ s-tr*(ꜣ)*mws* "the lupine-man," that is, "the seller of lupines"; for discussion of the use of a Greek word in this characteristic Egyptian nominal construction, see the main text, section D. The word and the phrase may be referring to the lupini seed/bean, a common food (Marie-Claire Amouretti and Georges Comet, *Des hommes et des plantes* [Aix-en-Provence: Publications de l'Université de Provence, 1993], 87–88—in fact in modern Egypt they are still quite popular and still called "termis"). In the first instance (V/25), this person is the person to whom you go to find "flowers of the Greek bean," perhaps suggesting that the flowers and the seeds are sold in the same place. In the other entries referenced for this term in the CDD (T [2012], 260–62), the standard Demotic plant classifier is used, so this may be an unusual reference to the seeds.

49. The only example of this written in Demotic is actually in the expression *ẖqe n grwgws*, "powder of crocus," where "powder" also has the granule over plural strokes classifier. This would suggest that a plant sign was eschewed because the powder form of the ingredient was what was being emphasized. (Note that this writing of "powder" is in fact a Semitic loan word itself, perhaps suggesting that the powdered ingredient was imported—this is particularly tempting since saffron comes from the crocus plant, so this whole expression may be referring to saffron powder.)

50. Nota bene, the phonetics are not a close fit for either suggestion.

51. Of which "turpentine," as G&T translate the passage, with a ?, is a product.

52. Perhaps the rare word τριμίγματος, "three-ingredient" is another option. There are three ingredients (*ꜣlbwnṯ*, "frankincense," *mrḥe*, "oil," and *ꜣmwnyꜥk*, "ammoniacum") prior to the word (which the *LSJ* cites only from Galen), so perhaps it is a reference to these, or perhaps it is a specific type of ammoniacum, although without any parallels for this it is impossible to say. However, for any of these options the granule-over-plural-strokes classifier is appropriate. All three terms have a suggestion of a resin or gummy incense, and such substances often take this group of signs in Egyptian; see, e.g., *snṯr*, "incense" (*Wb.* IV:180, 18–181, 17), *mnnn*, "pitch" (*Wb.* II:82, 9–14), and *ꜥnt.w*, "myrrh" (*Wb.* I:206, 7–207, 3).

53. Specifically for treating wounds; for parallels in Egyptian where this classifier is used for powdery substances, see, for example, *qꜣw*, "flour" (*Wb.* V:8, 2–5), *wgm*, "crushed grain" (*Wb.* I:377, 10), and *tmt.w*, "powder" (Wb. V:309, 4–5).

54. Specifically, "human ma(g)nes"—see #3.

#	Sign	Demotic	Gloss (OC); Cypher	Context	G&T #; loc.	Greek	Translation
12a	 - foreign land	*rphōbōs*	ⲁⲫⲟⲃⲱⲥ	instructions for how the god should appear to the youth	—; G&T 28 n. to l. 14; II/14	ἄφοβος	without alarming
		mʿkhōpnewmʿ	ⲙⲁⲭⲟⲡⲛⲉⲩⲙⲁ	in a vessel divination	—; XIV/16	μάχοπνεῦμα	fighting spirit(?), spirit of strife(?)[55]
		perypegʿneks	ⲡⲩⲣ[ⲓ]ⲡⲏⲅⲁⲛⲩⲝ	in a list of MN	—; v. XV/3	πυριπηγάναξ	lord of the fount of fire[56]
12b	 - foreign land	*ʿpsewstōs*	ⲁⲯⲉⲩⲥⲧⲱⲥ	instructions for how the god should appear to the youth	—; G&T 28 n. to l. 14; II/14	ἄψευστος	without deceiving
		epʿletsyʿ[57]	ⲉⲡⲁⲗⲏⲑⲉⲓ	same as above	same as above	ἐπ' ἀληθειᾳ	truthfully (lit., in truth)
		lōw[58]	ⲗⲟⲟⲩ	in a vessel inquiry	—; IX/6	perhaps from an unrecognized ancient language?	unknown
		lsmṯnwṯ	ⲗⲁⲥⲙⲁⲧⲛⲟⲩⲧ	same as above	—; IX/18	same as above	same as above
13	 - a "bad" thing	In this text always found in combination with at least one other classifier; see the discussion on multiple classifier, below.					
14	 - writing[59]	*ghʿlʿgter*	—	in a "petitioning of god"[60]	61; V/5	χαρακτήρ	character (as in a mark, sign, or alphabetic letter)

55. The compound is not found in Greek but is likely constructed from μάχομαι "to fight" and πνεῦμα, "spirit." (Although note the o seems an odd way to transition this word to πνεῦμα (one might expect an η), so it is possible that this is drawn from μαχάω, "to wish to fight.") The precise translation of this compound remains slightly unclear, and unfortunately the context provides no clues—it is after a string of Greek vowels (in the correct order) of which the meaning is also unclear.

56. From πῦρ(ι), "fire," πήγη, "running water," and ἄναξ, "lord." This was not translated by G&T 1 (1904), 189; but see *LSJ* (which includes citations only from magical texts: P. Mag. Osl. and P. Mag. Par. and a curse tablet). The word is at the end of a line, in which the two other words do not have classifiers but are clearly also from Greek and appear to be thematically related to this word. The first word in the line is *hrekssygth,* glossed ⲣⲏⲝⲓⲭⲑⲱ, clearly for the Greek ῥηξίχθων, "bursting forth from the earth." The second word is *perygtheōn,* glossed ⲡⲩⲣⲓⲭⲑⲱⲛ, presumably a compound of the words πῦρ(ι), "fire" and χθών, "earth." It seems plausible, since these three terms obviously relate to each other, that the classifier at the end is in fact for all three, perhaps something along the lines of "(the one) bursting forth from the earth, the fire (of?) the earth, the lord of the fount of fire."

57. This writing of ἀληθειᾳ appears to retain the dative ending required after ἐπι, and this is not an ending we see rendered in any of the other Greek words. This would suggest that in fact the scribe understood this as a fixed phrase and transcribed appropriately.

58. In a series of MN; rhymes with ⲧⲟⲟⲩ, "lands" later in this MN. Although this obviously looks remarkably like the verb λύω, "to release," this hardly makes any sense in the context.

59. A scribal palette.

60. For more on this translation, see Robert K. Ritner, *The Mechanics of Ancient Egyptian Magical Practice*, SAOC 54 (Chicago: Oriental Institute of the University of Chicago, 1993), 214–20.

Table 2. Examples of Multiple Classifiers in Demotic Transcriptions of Greek Vocabulary.

Demotic	Greek	Trans.	Context	Signs	G&T # ; loc.	Usage
gꜥwmꜥ	καῦμα	fever	an illness	- flesh - flesh & - evil, bad - wind[1] - flesh & | - plural	23; v. XXXIII/7[2] 23; v. XXXIII/4 23; v. XXXIII/6 23; v. XXXIII/8	standard classifier[3] adding descriptor[4] reference to context[5] adding indicator of plural noun[6]
p(ꜣ)etꜣgrwn[7]	ποδαγράω[8]	gouty man	treating gout	- flesh & - evil, bad	44; v. VIII/1, v. X/1	suggesting area effected and how it is effected[9]
plꜣge[10] *plege*[11] *plege*[12]	πληγή	sting	spell to drive out a sting[13]	- flesh - flesh & - evil, bad - man w/ hand to mouth - man w/ hand to mouth & - evil, bad	43; XX/17 43; XX/25 43; XX/15, 26 43; XX/1	standard classifier adding descriptor[14] variant[15] variant with descriptor

1. Sail serving as classifier of wind.

2. Bis.

3. It is possible that the flesh classifier is simply used because a fever impacts the body, but a brief examination of the Demotic suggests a more interesting reason. The Demotic word for fever is generally considered to be *ẖmm* (from earlier *šmm*; see *DG*, 380–81) which literally means "to be hot" and thus has a "brazier" classifier. However, when this is actually used to indicate the concept of fever, it is in the expression *ẖmm n ẖ.t*, lit., "the being hot of the body." The word *ẖ.t* "body" of course has a flesh classifier, thus suggesting that its usage with καῦμα actually reflects the whole expression in Egyptian.

4. Clearly a fever is a negative event for a person, so the "bad" classifier is simply emphasizing that here.

5. The function of this classifier is not immediately obvious; however a look at the context provides an explanation for its use. In the first instance of the term (which is only two lines above this one in the text), the passage reads: "A fever has seized me; a south wind has made me stand (still)." The full writing of the word "wind" in this passage is exactly the same as the classifier used for "fever" in the following reference. Thus by using the wind classifier, the scribe reminds the reader of the full, original context.

6. Here the extra classifier also references the context, although in a slightly different way. The multiple fevers referred to by the plural stroke are found in the line above (l. 7), which reads "the fevers of night, the fevers of day" (both written with the plural definite article so the plural stroke/classifier found in l. 8 was optional and omitted).

7. OC gloss: ΠΟΔⲀΚⲢⲀΝ.

8. Note that the version written in Demotic reflects the verb being written with a Greek participial ending (ποδαγρῶν) on the verb, lit., "to have gout." Thus the translation would be "one who has gout," that is, a "gouty man."

9. There is no known equivalent for this word in Egyptian, so we cannot assess any parallels as was possible with "fever." The "bad" classifier seems quite obvious as this is an illness (see for comparison, the other two Greek words assigned this determinative and the Demotic word *tḫr* "bitterness, suffering; illness; affliction, evil" (CDD T [2012], 281–82), which has the same classifier. The flesh classifier reflects that this is an affliction of body, just as with *gꜥwmꜥ* (i.e., we can almost understand, as we saw with "fever," an implied *n ẖ.t* "one who is gouty of the body," which would explain why this term for a disease does not have the pustule [Gardiner Aa2 or Aa3]—the more common classifier used with bodily ailments in Egyptian).

10. Using standard Demotic  for *g*.
11. Using standard Demotic  for *g*.
12. Using  for *g*.
13. For discussion of the ambiguity of the translation of this term, see G&T 1 (1904), 128, n. to l. 1.
14. The "bad" classifier is used once with the flesh sign and once with the man with hand to mouth; it was used both times, as elsewhere, to indicate something negative. The fact that it was employed only twice out of the five examples in this spell perhaps reflects no more than the options available in this writing system. The context for each usage is slightly different, although indeed the context for the instance in l. 25, with the "bad" classifier, is almost identical to the context in l. 26, which does not use it. It seems plausible that this particular spell was being drawn from a variety of sources when it was originally copied/compiled, and different sources used different spellings.
15. The man-with-hand-to-mouth classifier was perhaps used because the term referred to the wound caused by a venomous creature, such as a scorpion (which stings) or a snake (which bites)—these concepts would have been conflated, and the idea of a wound caused by a creature that injects poison would generically be associated with the mouth. Note that the choice of classifier here seems to be correlated with the phonetic spelling of the word (which sign to use for the /g/), perhaps supporting the argument for the association of variant spellings with scribal training (for more on this, see main text).

Political, Social, and Economic Aspects of Dreams in the Archive of Hor

MARK SMITH

I first met Richard many years ago when we were both working on the Chicago Demotic Dictionary. He impressed me because he was the only Egyptologist I had met up until that time who knew who Charley Patton was. He was an exemplary colleague in every way, except for a brief period after I accidentally broke one of his fingers with a line drive while we were playing baseball during our lunch break, which restricted his typing ability somewhat, albeit only temporarily. (In those days, dictionary entries were recorded on file cards using manual typewriters.) Our ways parted when I left Chicago to teach at Oxford and he went on to do research at Würzburg, but we have remained in close contact ever since. From time to time we have collaborated in editing Demotic texts. Casting an eye over our correspondence relating to these collaborative efforts, I am led to wonder how the texts ever got published, since our emails seem to consist mainly of exchanges concerning baseball and jazz, with the occasional remark about the reading of damaged traces or the translation of a problematic passage mixed in here and there. But somehow, the texts did get published in the end, by a rather circuitous method which made the collaboration all the more pleasurable for me.

In selecting a topic for my contribution to Richard's Festschrift, I felt it should be based upon a close reading of a text or group of texts, since he is renowned for his acuity as a textual critic. At the same time, it seemed appropriate to choose something which allowed scope for exploring wider issues, since he is also noted for his ability to contextualise the material which he publishes, integrating it with what we already know and explaining how it contributes to a better understanding of the ancient Egyptian society in which it was produced, while at the same time demonstrating to colleagues in related fields, for example, those who study the classical world or late antiquity, why this material is relevant to them and how knowledge of it can enhance their own research. With this in mind, I hope that Richard will enjoy reading the following discussion of dreams and prophecy in the Archive of Hor.

As is well known, the Archive of Hor is a collection of sixty-eight Demotic ostraca found at the site of Saqqara, in ancient times the chief necropolis of the city of Memphis.[1] They were written by a man called Hor, a priest and scribe who lived during the reign of Ptolemy VI (180–145 BCE). The texts on the ostraca were intended to form the basis of a petition beseeching that king to put a stop to abuses perpetrated by those in charge of the cult of the sacred ibis at Saqqara. Although focused upon the interests and concerns of one individual, these texts contain much significant information about contemporary Egyptian society as well. Among other things, they shed valuable light upon the socioeconomic and cultural role played by activities like prophecy and divination in Ptolemaic Egypt, in particular the identity, gender, ethnicity, and authority of those who practiced them, the economic impact that such activities had, and their influence on personal and cultural identity. They also enable us to investigate the historical implications of dream pronouncements by examining their reception, rejection, and manipulation by individuals, religious institu-

1. For their publication, see John Ray, *The Archive of Hor*, Texts from Excavations 2 (London: Egypt Exploration Society, 1976) (O. Hor 1–65); John Ray, "Observations on the Archive of Hor," *JEA* 64 (1978): 113–20 (O. Hor 66–68). In what follows, I cite the individual texts in the Archive by Ray's publication numbers, specifying, where an ostracon is inscribed on both sides, whether the word or passage quoted occurs on the recto or the verso.

tions, and political agents at a local, national, and international level. Finally, they allow us to explore the perception of oracles, prophecies, and divination by looking at the media used to convey divine messages and weighing the importance of the written record, language, and vocabulary in a variety of contexts and cultural frameworks.

Dreams play a prominent role in the texts of Hor's Archive because he claims that he is petitioning the king at the instigation of divinities who have appeared to him in his sleep. He also cites earlier dreams in which events foretold to him by deities actually came to pass in order to prove that he really was in communication with the divine world. The most notable of these is a dream which he said he experienced on 1 July 168 in which it was foretold to him that the Seleucid ruler Antiochus IV, who had invaded Egypt and was besieging Alexandria, would abandon his attempt to conquer the city and depart from Egypt peacefully by 30 July.[2] In one text, Hor describes vividly how he saw the goddess Isis walking on the water from Syria to Egypt, with the god Thoth standing before her and holding her hand to guide her. Upon her arrival in the harbor of Alexandria, the goddess proclaimed that the city was secure against the enemy, that the king was conducting business as usual within it along with his brethren, and that his crown would be inherited by his son and passed on in turn to future generations.[3]

Hor says that he reported his dream to a general called Eirenaios on 16 July, well before the predicted date of Antiochus's departure.[4] Eirenaios was initially sceptical of his report, and did not believe he was telling the truth until after the Seleucid king actually left Pelusium, a town on Egypt's northeastern border, on 30 July, thus fulfilling the prophecy. Later that day, or on the following one (31 July), Eirenaios wrote a letter to the rulers in Alexandria, informing them of the contents of Hor's dream, and gave it to Hor to deliver to them personally. Hor says that he handed it over to them in Alexandria on 29 August 168.[5] It is interesting to note the shift in the mode of transmission of his prophecy, from oral to written form, as it moves from the Egyptian to the Greek cultural sphere.

We have here an instance of a prophetic dream that purports to foretell matters of considerable import, affecting not just Egypt and its rulers, but the country's enemies and would-be conquerors as well. Not all the predictions delivered by deities in Hor's dreams are so far-ranging in scope, however. Some relate solely to his personal life. A good example is a dream in which he sees himself in the Memphite necropolis. A man has died, and Hor says *tw=y ꜥl=f (r)-ḏ3ḏ3=y in=y s (r)-ḥry Pr-Wsir-Ḥp*, "I picked him up and brought him up to the Sarapeum," that is, the burial place of the sacred Apis bulls.[6] When he reaches the dromos of the Sarapeum, a "great man" (*rmt ꜥ3*), possibly a ghost,[7] calls to Hor and orders him to approach. After questioning him, the great man predicts that Hor will die in Memphis and be buried in the Sarapeum there.[8] In another text, the goddess Isis makes a similar prediction, while

2. This dream is mentioned in O. Hor 1 recto, lines 9–18; O. Hor 2 recto, lines 4–10; O. Hor 2 verso, lines 6–12; O. Hor 3 verso, lines 8–14; O. Hor 4 recto, lines 1–8; O. Hor 66, lines x + 1–7; and possibly O. Hor 40, where too little is preserved to identify the contents with certainty. For the historical background and re-editions of the key sources, see Mark Smith, "History and Orthography: Reinterpreting the Demotic Evidence for Antiochus IV's Expulsion from Egypt in 168 BCE," in *Decorum and Experience: Essays in Ancient Culture for John Baines*, ed. Elizabeth Frood and Angela McDonald (Oxford: Griffith Institute, 2013), 66–71; Mark Smith, "A Further Demotic Source of Evidence for the Expulsion of Antiochus IV from Egypt: O. Hor 3 verso, lines 7–25," in *Hieratic, Demotic and Greek Studies and Text Editions: Of Making Many Books There is No End; Festschrift in Honour of Sven P. Vleeming*, ed. Koenraad Donker van Heel, Francisca Hoogendijk, and Cary J. Martin, PLB 34 (Leiden: Brill, 2018), 219–27.

3. O. Hor 1, lines 11–17. Remains of another version of this account are legible in the poorly preserved O. Hor 47.

4. For the possibility that this man is identical with the Eirenaios, son of Nikias attested in Greek inscriptions from the reign of Ptolemy VI, see Gil H. Renberg, "The Greek and Demotic Sources for the Career of Eirenaios, son of Nikias (Pros. Ptol. VI 14912/15262)," *ZPE* 188 (2014): 199–214.

5. For the chronology of these events, see Smith, "A Further Demotic Source," 219, 223–24, and 227.

6. O. Hor 8 recto, lines 13–14. The words *tw=y ꜥl=f (r)-ḏ3ḏ3=y* there could also mean "I had him mummified at my expense." For *ꜥl*, literally "go up, go on board (a ship)," as a figurative expression for "be mummified," see Mark Smith, *Papyrus Harkness (MMA 31.9.7)* (Oxford: Griffith Institute, 2005), 91. For the preposition *r-ḏ3ḏ3* with the sense "at the expense of," see *DG*, 673; cf. *CD*, 757b.

7. See John Tait, "P. Carlsberg 207: Two Columns of a Setna-Text," in *The Carlsberg Papyri 1: Demotic Texts from the Collection*, ed. Paul Frandsen, CNIP 15(Copenhagen: Museum Tusculanum Press, 1991), 30 and 34–35.

8. O. Hor 8 recto, lines 15–24.

promising that Hor will enjoy a happy life before his demise. She tells him: *i͗w=k*[9] *smne ẖn nꜣ nfr.w nꜣy=k sw.w n ꜥnḫ i͗w=k*[10] *mwt ẖn nꜣ nfr.w i͗w=w qs=k i͗w=w ti͗ ḥtp=k pꜣ ꜥwy ḥtp n Pr-Ḥp*, "You are established in a state of happiness (for) your days of life. You will die in a state of happiness, they will embalm you and cause you to rest (in) the house of rest of the House of Apis."[11] On a different occasion, Isis tells Hor that his sustenance is guaranteed for the days of his life and, when he dies, she will ensure that he is mummified.[12]

Nor are all of Hor's dreams prophetic. In some a deity appears to him to give him instructions to do something. Thus Hor says that his attempts to put a stop to the abuses being perpetrated by those responsible for the administration of the sacred ibis cult at Saqqara have been instigated by *pꜣ nṯr ꜥꜣ Ḏḥwty*, "the great god Thoth," who commanded him to do so in a dream (*ẖ rsw.t*).[13] This prompts us to ask, what was the nature of the abuses about which Hor was complaining?

In Egyptian iconography, the god Thoth was frequently represented in the form of an ibis or in anthropomorphic form with an ibis's head. Thus the ibis, particularly the sacred ibis (*Threskiornis aethiopicus*), was considered as a sort of avatar or symbol of his.[14] Two texts in the Archive of Hor explicitly refer to the ibis as the *ba*, or visible manifestation, of Thoth.[15] Accordingly, large flocks of these birds were kept alive at his temple, the *pr Ḏḥwty*, "house of Thoth," in Saqqara. When these birds died, they were mummified and buried, often in a small pot or vessel rather than a coffin. Visitors to the temple could pay for the burial of a bird as an act of pious devotion to the god. The number of ibises mummified and buried at Saqqara has been estimated to run into the millions, which shows the scale of the operation.[16]

According to Hor, those responsible for administering this cult, the "great men," had committed serious abuses. He claims the food that should have been given to the ibises was being stolen, so that the birds were dying of hunger every day.[17] Hor relates one instance when he entrusted some ibis food to a priest of Isis for safekeeping, but then learned that it had been subjected to "a million destructions."[18] Moreover, the birth-chapels of the sacred birds were being destroyed.[19]

Hor is particularly outraged by the fact that the very people who are responsible for the well-being of the ibises are the ones who perpetrate abuses against them. In one text he says: *ṯ=w gns n-ḏr nꜣ rmt.w ḏre*, "Wrong has been done by the powerful men,"[20] adding, with reference to Thoth, *ꜥsy ḥwy=w ꜣte=w r-r=f*, "Behold, they have turned their backs on him."[21] In another text he continues in a similar vein: *nꜣ.w tw=f ꜥꜣy=w*[22] *nꜣ i͗-i͗r gmꜥ r-r=f nꜣ.w i͗r=f prty nꜣ i͗-i͗r ẖꜣꜥ pꜣ myt*, "Those whom he (scil. Thoth) caused to be great are the ones who have wronged him, those

9. So and not *i͗r=k* as read by Ray.

10. See the preceding footnote.

11. O. Hor 9 verso, lines 7–9.

12. O. Hor 10 recto, lines 15–16. For Isis as guarantor of mummification, see Smith, *Papyrus Harkness*, 96.

13. O. Hor 23 verso, lines 15–16; compare O. Hor 25, lines 5–11.

14. See Patrick Houlihan, *The Birds of Ancient Egypt* (Warminster: Aris & Phillips, 1986), 28–30; Patrick Houlihan, *The Animal World of the Pharaohs* (Cairo: American University in Cairo Press, 1996), 158–60.

15. O. Hor 19 recto, line 5; O. Hor 25, line 4.

16. See Houlihan, *The Birds of Ancient Egypt*, 30; Houlihan, *The Animal World of the Pharaohs*, 159; Paul Nicholson, "The Sacred Animal Necropolis at North Saqqara: The Cults and their Catacombs," in *Divine Creatures: Animal Mummies in Ancient Egypt*, ed. Salima Ikram (Cairo: American University in Cairo Press, 2005), 48–68.

17. O. Hor 7, lines 12–13; O. Hor 27 verso, lines 9–10; O. Hor 61, lines 5–6.

18. O. Hor 26 recto, lines 11–14.

19. O. Hor 7, line 13.

20. O. Hor 16 recto, lines 11–12; similarly, O. Hor 17, line 5. In both texts, Ray wrongly translates *ṯ=w gns* as "I have been wronged," as if Hor is seeking redress for some personal injury. See Mark Smith, review of *The Archive of Hor*, by J. Ray, *JEA* 64 (1978): 180.

21. O. Hor 16 verso, lines 2–3. Ray misreads *ꜥsy i͗wt.w ꜣty.w r=f*, which he translates "Disaster in their midst! Calamity upon him!" For the correct reading, see Karl-Theodor Zauzich, review of *The Archive of Hor*, by J. Ray, *Enchoria* 8.2 (1978), 98.

22. Ray omits the clearly written resumptive pronoun *w*.

whom he honored[23] are the ones who have abandoned the path,"[24] while repeating the charge that the powerful men have turned their backs on the god.[25]

There were also serious irregularities with the burial of the ibises. Sometimes economies were made by squeezing more than one bird into a single pot or vessel, although the correct burial procedure, as Hor states repeatedly, was "One god, one pot."[26] Evidently, reforms introduced previously to put a stop to such illegal practices, including regular inspection of the ibises, their food, and their embalming place by three trustworthy priests each year,[27] had fallen into abeyance. Inspections were no longer being conducted properly.[28] This is the state of affairs that Hor seeks to rectify with his petition.

The Archive of Hor is of considerable interest for anyone who seeks to understand the socioeconomic and cultural role that dreams played in ancient Egypt. What can we say about Hor's social status and economic relations with others? The Archive reveals a considerable amount of information about Hor's personal history. He regularly refers to himself as a man from the town of Isis (*tmy ȝst*) in the twelfth Lower Egyptian nome, that of Sebennytos, and, in one text, may even say that he was born there.[29] He seems to have traveled around quite a bit, spending time in places like Heliopolis, before finally settling in Memphis, where he took up residence in the Memphite necropolis.

Little can be said about Hor's family background. One text gives the name of his father, which is Harendotes, but he does not have any titles attributed to him.[30] A few Greek ostraca were found along with the Demotic ones.[31] They refer to a Horos with the priestly title of *pastophoros*, "shrine opener." It is likely that this is the same as the Hor of the Demotic texts.[32] However, the Demotic texts never refer to him by this title. Instead they call him a scribe. The Greek texts mention the title *pastophoros* in conjunction with the town of Isis, so it may be that his period of employment as a priest came to an end when he left that place.

In one text, Hor mentions a "god's-servant" (*ḥm-nṯr*) of Isis.[33] Ray thinks that he is speaking of himself and that he actually held this priestly title.[34] However, since Hor normally uses first person singular personal pronouns to refer to himself, in preference to more oblique modes of reference, it is more probable that the priest in question is someone else. According to Quack, Hor was involved with the burials of the Apis and Mnevis bulls,[35] but the passage he cites in support of this view (O. Hor 1, lines 1–2), simply states that he "observed the habit" of spending the days in

23. For the verb *prty*, "honor," see George Hughes, "An Astrologer's Handbook in Demotic Egyptian," in *Egyptological Studies in Honor of Richard A. Parker*, ed. Leonard Lesko (Hanover, NH: University Press of New England for Brown University, 1986), 58. Ray mistranslates *prty* here and elsewhere in the Archive of Hor as "be in command, pre-eminent."

24. O. Hor 17, lines 6–7.

25. O. Hor 17, lines 9–10. Read *ʿsy ḥwy=w ȝte=w r-r=f* as in O. Hor 16 verso, lines 2–3.

26. O. Hor 19 verso, line 8; O. Hor 21 recto, line 18; O. Hor 22 recto, line 14. Evidently, not everyone was as punctilious about this as Hor was. In the sacred ibis burial galleries at Tuna al-Gebel, for example, it was normal for three or four ibis mummies to be buried in a single jar during the Ptolemaic period, and in the pre-Ptolemaic period even more. See Dieter Kessler and Abd el-Halim Nur el-Din, "Tuna al-Gebel: Millions of Ibises and other Animals," in *Divine Creatures: Animal Mummies in Ancient Egypt*, ed. Salima Ikram (Cairo: American University in Cairo Press, 2005), 156.

27. For these, see O. Hor 19 verso, lines 4–8; O. Hor 21 recto, lines 10–18; O. Hor 22 recto, lines 6–14.

28. O. Hor 61, lines 1–6.

29. See the phrase *ms pȝ tmy nt ḥry*, "born (in) the aforesaid town," which follows a reference to Hor as a "man of the town of Isis" in O. Hor 26 recto, lines 1–3. Ray restores *[tȝ ʿẖy.t] ms pȝ tmy nt ḥry*, "[the chapel of] birth (in) the aforesaid town." I assume that the third person singular feminine suffix pronouns in the ensuing sentence refer to Isis.

30. O. Hor 19 recto, line 1.

31. See Theodore Skeat and Eric Turner, "An Oracle of Hermes Trismegistos at Saqqâra," *JEA* 54 (1968): 199–208; Ray, *The Archive of Hor*, 1–6.

32. Ray, *The Archive of Hor*, 3.

33. O. Hor 12 verso, line 4.

34. Ray, *The Archive of Hor*, 52, followed by Gil H. Renberg, *Where Dreams May Come: Incubation Sanctuaries in the Greco-Roman World*, 2 vols., RGRW 184 (Leiden: Brill, 2017), 2:724.

35. Joachim Quack, "Zu einer angeblich apokalyptischen Passage in den Ostraka des Hor," in *Apokalyptik und Ägypten: Eine kritische*

their embalming places, which need not imply any form of employment, especially as Hor is noted for his custom of frequenting temples and other places of religious importance where he held no actual position.

How Hor supported himself once he had settled in Memphis is uncertain. As noted above, he refers to himself as a scribe, but his Archive never refers to any sort of scribal activity undertaken for others for which he may have received payment. Although the texts of the Archive of Hor were obviously written by him, the petition in which they were ultimately incorporated was intended purely to address his own personal concerns and was not composed at the behest or on behalf of anyone else. In one text, Hor says that he took up his papyrus roll and scribal palette in Memphis, which suggests that only there did he become a scribe.[36] Perhaps the scribal activities through which Hor actually earned his living were not considered germane to his petition and therefore are left unmentioned.

One confusing thing about Ray's original 1976 publication of the Archive is the fact that he distinguishes two different scribes called Hor: one from Sebennytos and one from Memphis. According to him, some of the texts from the Archive were written by the former and the others by the latter. He thinks that in some cases Hor of Sebennytos dictated texts to Hor of Memphis.[37] But it is clear from a careful reading of the Archive that there is only one Hor involved throughout. Most compelling is the evidence of O. Hor 12 and O. Hor 25. Both describe Hor being sent by Thoth to a particular place in a particular year. Clearly, the same experience is being related and it seems inconceivable that the narrator of the first text is not that of the second as well. Thus, Ray's Hor of Sebennytos and Hor of Memphis are one and the same person.[38]

Ray's original publication also cites alleged instances in which Hor deliberately sought to induce dreams that would inform him about the fates of others or even interpreted their dreams for them, claiming that he acted as a professional interpreter of dreams.[39] If true, this could have been a possible source of income for him. But when one examines the relevant passages more closely, it becomes clear that they make no reference to such activities. Although there was no shortage of professional dream interpreters in the Memphite necropolis,[40] Hor was not among them. Some think that *pastophoroi* were involved in dream interpretation and that he might have engaged in this activity in his capacity as a member of that group.[41] However, there is no evidence for this in the Archive and, as far as we can judge, Hor no longer functioned as a *pastophoros* after settling in Memphis.

Nor, as far as we can judge, did he himself ever consult others to obtain help in interpreting dreams. The texts of his Archive record numerous instances in which he approached or had contact with individuals who bore the title *ḥr-tb*, which Ray translates as "magician."[42] In two texts, he says that he petitioned four such individuals, but they did not render a judgement about the problems afflicting the ibis cult which he had communicated to them.[43] Ray, followed

---

Analyse der relevanten Texte aus dem griechisch-römischen Ägypten, ed. Andreas Blasius and Bernd Schipper, OLA 107 (Leuven: Peeters, 2002), 244.

36. O. Hor 1, line 3. Ray wrongly translates the words *ẖꜣꜥ=y pꜣy=y ḏmꜥ irm pꜣy=y gst n-ḏr.t=<y> Mn-nfr* there as "I abandoned my papyrus roll and my scribal palette (in) Memphis." Joachim Quack ("Demotische magische und divinatorische Texte," in *Omina, Orakel, Rituale und Beschwörungen*, ed. Bernd Jankowski and Gernot Wilhelm, TUAT NF 4 [Gütersloh: Gütersloher Verlagshaus, 2008], 378) translates "Ich ließ meinen Papyrus und meine Schreibpalette bei ihnen(?) in Memphis," apparently mistaking the tall vertical stroke at the end of *ḏr.t* for a suffix pronoun *w*. For the sense of the idiom *ẖꜣꜥ n-ḏr.t* in this passage, cf. Coptic ⲕⲱ ⲛⲧⲛ⸗, "put, keep in hand" (*CD*, 96a). For the tall vertical stroke at the end of *ḏr.t*, compare the writing of that noun in O. Hor 26 recto, line 15.

37. Ray, *The Archive of Hor*, 121–22.

38. See Smith, review of *The Archive of Hor*, 181; Ray, "Observations," 115–17, where he retracts his earlier view and accepts that the two Hors are identical.

39. Ray, *The Archive of Hor*, 132 and 135.

40. See, e.g., the Saqqara stela advertising the services of a Cretan dream interpreter reproduced in Renberg, *Where Dreams May Come*, 2:729, fig. 59.

41. Renberg, *Where Dreams May Come*, 2:719–26; John Ray, "Phrases Used in Dream-Texts," in *Aspects of Demotic Lexicography*, ed. Sven Vleeming, StudDem 1 (Leuven: Peeters, 1987), 89–91.

42. O. Hor 12 recto, lines 3–4; O. Hor 16 recto, line 8; O. Hor 22 recto, lines 3–4; O. Hor 23 verso, lines 18–19.

43. See O. Hor 16 recto, lines 8–11; O. Hor 17a, lines 3–7.

by Renberg, interprets this to mean that Hor went to the individuals in question to solicit a dream interpretation, which none of them was able to provide.[44] In fact, however, what the texts say is that Hor approached the individuals in question with his complaint about the abuses committed in the cult of the ibis and asked them to put an end to them but they did not take any steps to do so. So there is nothing supernatural about these episodes. The same is true in all other cases where Hor has contact with a so-called magician. In every instance it is to complain about the abuses in the ibis cult and not in connection with dreams or their interpretation.

Why does he go to magicians with his complaint? The answer is that the title which Ray translates as "magician" does not actually mean that in the texts of the Archive of Hor. *ḥr-tb* derives from earlier *ḥry-tp*, the basic sense of which is "chief, superior" (*Wb.* III:140, 6–15), denoting anyone, human or divine, who was in charge of something, be it a geographical district, city, group of people, institution, or activity.[45] The title could be employed to designate ritualists who exercised mastery in their particular sphere of competence (so-called magicians), but its use was by no means restricted to this category of specialists. Transliterated as φριτωβ, φριτοβ, φριτβ, or φεριτοβ, the title *pꜣ ḥr-tb* (< *pꜣ ḥry-tp*) occurs in Greek administrative papyri contemporary with the Archive of Hor, where requests to resolve disputes and complaints about wrongdoing are addressed to those who hold it, precisely as in the Archive.

A notable example is a draft of a petition written by Ptolemy, the famous recluse of the Sarapeum, in 161 BCE, seeking justice for Thaues and Taous, two sisters who have been wronged. He complains that they have been deprived of the sustenance which they were supposed to receive, just as Hor does on behalf of the ibises. The petition is addressed to the *hypodioiketes* Sarapion, but refers to earlier appeals made, not only to him, but to the king and an official identified as φεριτ[ο]β as well.[46] Similarly, a papyrus from Gebelein records that in 150 or 149 BCE, an official called Ptolemaios with the title φριτβ was asked to adjudicate a dispute between the priests of Hermonthis and Pathyris over the ownership of some land.[47]

The view that φριτοβ (with variants) is a Greek transliteration of Egyptian *pꜣ ḥr-tb* (< *pꜣ ḥry-tp*), first suggested with reserve by Spiegelberg and later taken up by Stricker, was accepted by Quaegebeur in a study published in 1987.[48] In another article published two years later, however, he changed his mind, reverting instead to another suggestion originally made by Spiegelberg, that Greek φριτοβ was a transliteration of the Egyptian title **pꜣ ḥry idb*, "master of the riverbank," which denoted an official with responsibility for administering arable land.[49]

In my view there are a number of reasons why the derivation of φριτοβ from *pꜣ ḥr-tb* (< *pꜣ ḥry-tp*) is preferable.

(1) The title is also attested in other Greek sources, not only administrative papyri. The historian Josephus applies it to the deified human being Amenhotep son of Hapu, while in a graffito in the sanatorium at Deir el-Bahri it is used to designate either Amenhotep son of Hapu or his fellow deified human, Imhotep. Both individuals bear the title *ḥry-tp* in Egyptian sources, but neither is ever called *ḥry idb*.[50]

44. Ray, *The Archive of Hor*, 62 and 65; Renberg, *Where Dreams May Come*, 1:437; Renberg, *Where Dreams May Come*, 2:725.

45. See Jan Quaegebeur, "La designation (*pꜣ-*) *ḥry-tp*: phritob," in *Form und Mass: Beiträge zur Literatur, Sprache und Kunst des alten Ägypten; Festschrift für Gerhard Fecht zum 65. Geburtstag am 6. Februar 1987*, ed. Jürgen Osing and Günter Dreyer, ÄAT 12 (Wiesbaden: Harrassowitz, 1987), 371–88.

46. Quaegebeur, "La designation (*pꜣ-*) *ḥry-tp*," 389; Ulrich Wilcken, *Urkunden der Ptolemäerzeit (Ältere Funde)* 1 (Berlin: de Gruyter, 1927), 267, no. 51, line 18. For the convoluted history of these twins and their dealings with the authorities, see Dorothy Thompson, *Memphis under the Ptolemies* (Princeton: Princeton University Press, 2012), 216–28, esp. 222–23.

47. P. BM 2188, lines 61–62. See Quaegebeur, "La designation (*pꜣ-*) *ḥry-tp*," 389–91; Theodor Skeat, *Greek Papyri in the British Museum (now in the British Library)* 7 (London: British Museum Publications for the British Library Board, 1974), 274, 280, and 289–90. As noted in Skeat, *Greek Papyri in the British Museum*, 275, two fragmentary papyri in Cairo, P. Cairo 10361 and 10362, preserve copies of part of this document. There, the title is written φριτοβ.

48. See reference cited in note 45 above.

49. Jan Quaegebeur, "*Phritob* comme titre d'un haut fonctionnaire ptolémaïque," *Ancient Society* 20 (1989): 159–68.

50. Quaegebeur, "*Phritob* comme titre," 159–61; André Bataille, *Les inscriptions grecques du temple de Hatshepsout à Deir el-Bahari*,

(2) Unlike *ḥr-tb* (< *ḥry-tp*), *ḥry idb* is never attested with a preceding definite article *pꜣ*. Nor does it ever appear in texts where the usage of the definite article is regular. Thus, there is no evidence that the form **pꜣ ḥry idb* which is alleged to underlie ϕριτοβ ever existed.

(3) In the period with which we are concerned, the use of the title *ḥry idb* is restricted to temple inscriptions and other religious texts, where it is applied to gods, most notably Shu, or to the king as their heir or deputy, but never to members of the Ptolemaic bureaucracy.[51] There is no evidence that any official working at any level of the Ptolemaic administration ever held it.

(4) Even if the office of *ḥry idb* did exist in the Ptolemaic period, it is difficult to see why someone whose specific responsibility was the administration of arable land in Egypt would be called upon to resolve a situation where two sisters living in the Sarapeum were being denied their rightful sustenance, as the ϕεριτοβ was asked to do in the instance mentioned in Ptolemy's draft petition. Conversely, as already noted above, this is precisely the sort of problem that Hor repeatedly brings to the attention of officials designated as *ḥry-tb* in the texts of the Archive and beseeches them to address.

Quaegebeur's reluctance to accept the derivation of ϕριτοβ from *pꜣ ḥr-tb* (< *pꜣ ḥry-tp*) appears to be based upon two assumptions. The first is that the title *ḥr-tb* (< *ḥry-tp*) was used solely to designate ritual specialists. Thus, those who held it could not have been involved in the sorts of activities the ϕριτοβ is said to undertake in Greek administrative papyri.[52] As we have seen, this is not the case. The Archive of Hor, to say nothing of earlier sources, provides us with numerous examples of holders of this title operating outside the ritual sphere. In any event, in ancient Egypt where the boundary between sacerdotal and secular was not as sharply drawn as it was elsewhere, there is no reason why a skilled ritualist, a person of standing in his local community, could not have been approached for assistance in civil disputes as well.

Quaegebeur's second assumption is that all holders of the title ϕριτοβ enjoyed the same elevated rank and status, which included honorific membership of the royal court, and that only one held office at a time.[53] This would rule out deriving the title from *pꜣ ḥr-tb* (< *pꜣ ḥry-tp*), since those bearing the latter designation clearly did not enjoy such exalted privileges and more than one of them exercised their functions concurrently. But there are no grounds for assuming that only one ϕριτοβ held office at a time. Moreover, as we have seen, the basic sense of *ḥr-tb* (< *ḥry-tp*) is "chief, superior," denoting anyone who is in charge of something, so one would expect to find holders of such a generic title with a range of different levels of authority and responsibility, from the *ḥry-tp n Šmꜥ Mḥw*, "chief of Upper and Lower Egypt," a title attributed to the deified Imhotep,[54] down to the "magicians" whom Hor petitioned on behalf of the sacred ibises.

When one views Hor's interactions with the *ḥry-tb.w* in this light, the Archive as a whole assumes a rather different aspect. Rather than consulting one specialist after another to solicit interpretations for his dreams, its protagonist devotes the majority of his time to seeking the intervention of those in a position of authority for the specific purpose of putting an end to the abuses in the administration of the sacred ibis cult about which he is complaining. Thus, there is much less emphasis on supernatural elements in the Archive, and more emphasis on legal and judicial ones.

Continuing our investigation into the question of how Hor might have supported himself in Memphis, one intriguing, albeit poorly preserved, text refers to Cleopatra II, the wife of Ptolemy VI. Hor says that "they brought her and left her and made petitions" (*in=w s ḫꜣꜥ=w s smy=w*), after which Isis prescribed a remedy for her but it was

Publications de la Société Fouad I de Papyrologie: Textes et Documents 10 (Cairo: Institut Français d'Archéologie Orientale, 1951), 61–62, no. 87, and pl. 7.

51. Danielle Inconnu-Bocquillon, "Les titres *ḥry idb* et *ḥry wḏb* dans les inscriptions des temples gréco-romains," *RdÉ* 40 (1989): 65–89.

52. See Quaegebeur, "*Phritob* comme titre," 168.

53. Quaegebeur, 168.

54. Quaegebeur, "La designation (*pꜣ-*) *ḥry-tp*," 373.

not used.[55] In another text, Hor says of someone, *sḥwr=f n3 pẖry.w*, "he scorned the remedies," but the ostracon is too poorly preserved to allow us to recover the context.[56] Although we are not told where the queen was brought or by whom,[57] the first passage suggests the practice of therapeutic incubation, whereby the sick were brought to a temple or other sacred place for healing, but there is nothing to indicate that Hor was in any way involved with this. Nor is there any reason to think that he prepared the remedies mentioned in the second passage. In any case, neither text makes any reference to dreams or dreaming, so there are no grounds for supposing that the prescriptions mentioned in them were obtained by that means.[58]

Where and how did Hor experience the dreams he records? Ray discusses at some length the question of whether or not Hor was a *katochos*, that is, whether he lived in the Sarapeum or another nearby sanctuary, devoting himself to the service of a deity, and voluntarily refrained from leaving the temple precinct. Ray thinks this was possible but says that the texts of the Archive provide no conclusive evidence one way or another.[59] Remarkably, in several of the texts Hor explicitly states that he slept or spent the night in a temple. Ray overlooked these references because he misread the verb *sḏr*, "sleep, spend the night," as *šms*, "follow, serve." It is of particular interest that the verb in question is always written with the eye determinative in the Archive of Hor, like the verb *nw*, "see," and other words related to the idea of sight. Thus, reference is made to a form of sleep in which something is seen. In one text, Hor says that he will sleep in the Sarapeum and discover something.[60] In another, he says that he sleeps in the Sarapeum.[61] A third text contains an injunction to sleep along with other enigmatic statements, which could be an instruction received in a dream.[62] Once, Hor describes himself somewhat enigmatically as sleeping in the "sky" (*p.t*) of Hepnebes, the name of that part of the Memphite necropolis where sacred animals and birds were buried.[63] On another occasion, he says explicitly that he had a dream while sleeping in the dromos, that is, the entrance way or forecourt, of a temple.[64] So Hor clearly practiced incubation, but this need not mean that his practice was restricted to one particular temple or temple precinct. Hor claims to have had the dream just cited while he was settled down (*w3ḥ*) in the temple where he experienced it,[65] which does seem to indicate that he was living there. On the other hand, the frequency and extent of his travels from one city to another are difficult to reconcile with the idea that he was a *katochos*, unless he was being sent forth on divine business, so the question must be left open.

Some of the ostraca in the Archive of Hor contain hymns or invocations of deities, occasionally with the injunction "come to me" addressed to the divinity in question.[66] These may have been employed by Hor to induce dreams in which a god or goddess would appear to him, although nowhere is it stated explicitly that this is their purpose. One particular text, O. Hor 18, described by Ray as an invocation to various gods to appear in a dream, is actually

55. O. Hor 28, lines 15–17.

56. O. Hor 32 recto, line 3.

57. The antecedent of the third person plural suffix pronouns in the sentences quoted is lost in a break.

58. Contrast Renberg, *Where Dreams May Come*, 1:386, 402, and 444–45, who thinks that Hor or a colleague is likely to have solicited the remedies through dreams.

59. Ray, The *Archive of Hor*, 161–63.

60. O. Hor 13 recto, line 8. Cf. O. Hor 13 recto, line 12.

61. O. Hor 37, line x + 1.

62. O. Hor 14 verso, lines 5–8.

63. O. Hor 23 recto, line 4.

64. O. Hor 59, line 3. For the correct reading of the example of *sḏr* in this passage, see Quack, "Zu einer angeblich apokalyptischen Passage," 250.

65. O. Hor 59, lines 1–2. Quack, "Zu einer angeblich apokalyptischen Passage," 248–49, followed by Renberg, *Where Dreams May Come*, 1:432, reads *ḏ w3ḥ* in line 1, which he translates "Antwort gibt." I agree with Quack that there are traces earlier in the line which resemble *ḏ*, "say," but the space between these and *w3ḥ* makes it impossible to construe them together. The space is sufficiently large to permit the restoration of the *tw=y* originally suggested by Ray. The resulting *ḏ [tw=y] w3ḥ ẖn ḥ.(t)-ntr* could be translated "saying: [I was] settled down in the temple."

66. See, e.g., O. Hor 8 verso, lines 1–5, O. Hor 10, and O. Hor 13, line 3.

something quite different. Numerous deities are invoked, but the boon requested of them is not to appear in a dream but rather to protect the Apis bull and the king.

In one invocation in this text addressed to the god Osiris, Ray reads *ỉm r rsw.t* and translates "Come for a dream."[67] If this were correct, it would be the only instance in the Archive where a deity was explicitly enjoined to come in a dream. However, the word which Ray interprets as *rsw.t*, "dream," is actually *rsṯȝw*, "necropolis."[68] Thus Osiris is exhorted "Come to the necropolis." There is no reference to a dream. As shown by Quack, this text is partially paralleled in two much earlier sources, the Ritual of Amenophis III and the Rite of Opening of the Mouth. The parallels occur in spells for fumigation with incense, of which O. Hor 18 is likely to be a further example, perhaps recited as a prelude to the presentation of food offerings.[69]

As already mentioned, one important contribution of the Archive of Hor is that it enables us to investigate the historical implications of religious pronouncements conveyed in dreams by examining their reception, rejection, and manipulation by individuals, religious institutions and political agents at a local, national, and international level. We have seen that Hor's dreams can be divided into two broad categories. The first is that of dreams that relate purely to his own personal life. In these dreams a deity appears to him and makes a prediction or gives an instruction that is only of direct relevance to him, for example, predicting that he will pass the rest of his life in Memphis and be buried there. Such dreams do not need to be reported to others.

The second category is that of dreams in which Hor receives a message that is intended to be shared with a wider audience. These dreams fall into two subcategories: prescriptive and prognostic. The first subcategory is exemplified by those dreams in which the god Thoth appears to Hor and instructs him to bring the abuses being perpetrated in the cult of the ibis to the attention of the proper authorities so that they can put a stop to them. These beg the question, why was Hor so concerned about such abuses? Was he the world's first animal rights activist? Quack claims that he actually had some responsibility for dealing with complaints concerning the chapels of the sacred ibis,[70] but I think the passages he cites in support of this view will not really bear such an interpretation. In the preamble to two texts,[71] Hor identifies himself as the one who is "concerned with" (*ḥr* or *wbȝ*) the complaint relating to the chapels. In my view, he is simply declaring his interest in the complaint, as was only natural given the fact that he was the one who made it.

The real answer to this question is provided by another text in the Archive. In this, Hor relates how he entrusted some ibis food to a priest of Isis for safekeeping, but then learned that it had been subjected to "a million destructions."[72] He goes on to say: *ip=y (r) tỉ wḏȝ=y tw=y wy ḏr.ṯ=y (r) pȝ ʿq (r)-ir=w smn ẖr-r-ḥr=y ẖn pȝ irp tw=y wȝḥ=f nȝ ʿq.w rn=f tȝ ẖr.t nȝ hb.w*, "I took thought (in order to) cause myself to be secure. I caused my hand to be distant (from) the provisions which were established under me in the temple. I caused him (scil. the priest of Isis) to lay down the provisions (in) his name, the sustenance of the ibises."[73] This sounds suspiciously as if Hor was trying to shift the blame for the loss of the food onto someone else. But the god of wisdom is not easily fooled. Hor continues: *gm n=y Ḏḥwty lwḥ ỉr=f šn r-ḏbȝ=s tw=f ỉr=s ḥty r-ḥr=y (r) smy n=k*, "Thoth found fault with me and made an enquiry about it. He caused it to be (as) a compulsion upon me (to) make a complaint to you."[74]

---

67. O. Hor 18 verso, line 18.

68. For the correct reading, see CDD *R* (2001), 73. Compare the identical writings of this noun in O. Hor 12A, line 5, and O. Hor 13, lines 4, 5, and 7. *rsw.t*, "dream," is easily distinguished from *rsṯȝw* because it has a feminine *t* ending. See e.g. O. Hor 1, line 5, O. Hor 2 recto, line 4; O. Hor 3 verso, line 9.

69. See Joachim Quack, "Eine Götterinvokation mit Fürbitte für Pharao und den Apisstier (Ostrakon Hor 18)," in *Ägyptische Rituale der griechisch-römischen Zeit*, ed. Joachim Quack, ORA 6 (Tübingen: Mohr Siebeck, 2014), 83–119.

70. Quack, "Zu einer angeblich apokalyptischen Passage," 244.

71. O. Hor 16 recto, line 1; O. Hor 17 recto, line 1.

72. O. Hor 26 recto, lines 11–14.

73. O. Hor 26 recto, lines 14–17.

74. O. Hor 26 recto, lines 17–19. Cf. O. Hor 61, lines 8–9.

The reference here to "the provisions which were established under me in the temple" is one of the few explicit indications in the Archive that Hor had any sort of official connection with the ibis cult. Evidently, he was entrusted with some of the birds' food, perhaps in his capacity as a scribe. The god Thoth found fault with him for failing to look after it properly (and perhaps for trying to conceal his negligence) and as punishment assigned him the task of putting a stop to the abuses being perpetrated in the ibis cult.

Anxiety over a failure to look after ibis food properly is also manifested in another text. Hor dreams that a superior has exempted him from work, and therefore absents himself.[75] But then he is pursued and made to come back to confront this official. A very frightened Hor is told by his superior that he is on trial. Then the superior reveals himself to be no less than the god Thoth himself. He tells Hor, "I am your superior Thoth. I have already told you before not to do the work of any god except me." Hor replies meekly, "I will not do it again."[76] In another dream recorded on the same ostracon, a "great man" orders Hor to bring the clover that has been entrusted to him, enough food for 60,000 ibises, and he has to confess that he has left it somewhere else.[77] The political turmoil of Ptolemy VI's reign, along with environmental factors like low Nile inundation levels resulting in poor harvests, which can be linked to volcanic eruptions outside of Egypt, may have reduced the available supply of clover around this time, making the task of securing a sufficient amount of it for the ibises more difficult and thus exacerbating any guilt Hor may have felt over his shortcomings as a custodian of fodder for the sacred birds.[78]

Whatever the motivation for Hor's efforts to try to end the abuses, his attempts involved him with a range of officials, both Egyptian and Greek, religious and secular, with varying levels of authority, in a number of different Egyptian towns and cities. Ultimately, they brought him into contact with the rulers of Egypt, Ptolemy VI and his siblings, since he was unsuccessful in persuading lesser authorities to take his complaints seriously. Thus, Hor's Archive offers us a good opportunity to observe the reception of his religious pronouncements, which in the majority of cases seems to have been negative. His claims were rejected by both individuals and the institutions that they represented. It would be interesting to have the point of view of officials like these about Hor and his dreams. How often were they approached by people making claims similar to his? What did they make of them? What standards of evidence did they use to evaluate them? Having only the texts of the Archive itself at our disposal, we are not in a position to answer such questions. Nor do we know the outcome of his petition, if indeed it was ever submitted.

The second subcategory of Hor's dreams intended for a wider audience, that of prophetic dreams, is best exemplified by the one described at the beginning of this article, in which Hor claims to have been informed that the Seleucid king Antiochus IV would leave Egypt peacefully by a certain date and that Egypt would remain in the possession of its Ptolemaic rulers, safe from the threats of invasion and conquest. We have here a case study in how dreams can be manipulated, since Hor actually cited this particular dream at a much later date in his plea about the sacred ibis cult. He employs the fact that the good auguries about Egypt and its royal family which were revealed to him in this earlier

---

75. O. Hor 8 recto, lines 1–2. I read *w3ḥ wᶜ ṯs nḥm=y ẖr b3k*, "A superior had exempted me from work," in the former, and *šᶜt=y bnr*, "I cut out" (i.e., absented myself), in the latter. Contrast Quack ("Demotische magische und divinatorische Texte," 379) who reads *mdw irm=y* instead of *nḥm=y* and *iw=k (r) wy* instead of *šᶜt=y bnr*.

76. O. Hor 8 recto, lines 2–6.

77. O. Hor 8 recto, lines 18–19.

78. Three major volcanic eruptions occurred in the decade between 170 and 160 BCE, in 168, 164, and 161, with a fourth around 158 BCE. The links between these and low inundation levels and political instability in Egypt are the subject of an ongoing investigation by the NSF-funded project "Volcanism, Hydrology and Social Conflict: Lessons from Hellenistic and Roman-Era Egypt and Mesopotamia" (Grant Number: 1824770). I am very grateful to two members of this project, Joe Manning and Francis Ludlow, for discussing their research with me and alerting me to its implications for our understanding of the social and economic setting in which the texts of the Archive of Hor were written. For some of their results, see Joseph Manning, Francis Ludlow, Alexander Stine, William Boos, Michael Sigl, and Jennifer Marlon, "Volcanic Suppression of Nile Summer Flood Triggers Revolt and Constrains Interstate Conflict in Ancient Egypt," *Nature Communications* 8, article 900 (DOI: 10.1038/s4147-017-00957-y).

dream subsequently came to pass as a means of strengthening the credibility of his claim that the divinely inspired dreams which have motivated his mission on behalf of the sacred ibises are genuine as well.[79]

The aforesaid dream also provides evidence for the rejection of prophecies, since as Hor himself tells us, the general Eirenaios did not believe it until the events predicted in it actually came to pass. One wonders whether Eirenaios himself did not exploit or manipulate Hor's prophecy for his own benefit. Being able to bring a figure like Hor to the attention of the rulers, with his message that they and their kingdom would be saved, especially after this had already happened, could not have failed to enhance his own status with them.

Hor's dream about the withdrawal of Antiochus IV from Egypt certainly had repercussions at the national level. These reached across the boundaries that divided the sacred from the profane, the military from the civilian, the royal from the nonroyal, and the Greek from the Egyptian. Thus, the dream's impact, if not international, was at the very least intercultural. Here perhaps we see the most significant aspect of the reception of dreams like Hor's: their power to bridge the gap between cultures. Dreams could do this because the belief that they were a medium for the transmission of divine messages was shared by both Egyptian and Greek. The fact that they provided a common ground on which the two could meet makes them a striking feature of the complex cultural landscape of Ptolemaic Egypt.

79. See especially O. Hor 2 recto, lines 13–16, and O. Hor 2 verso lines 13–15, with discussion in Smith, "History and Orthography," 70–71.

A New Version of the Beginning of the Book of Traversing Eternity: The Hieroglyphic-Demotic Funerary Stela of Pakhom, Son of Lykos, from Edfu (22 March 18 BCE [greg.])

Martin Andreas Stadler

Few people effuse such a cheerful enthusiasm when it comes to Demotic. Richard is certainly one of them. The difficulties that Demotic material pose did not turn him into a frustrated, grouchy scholar, rather into the contrary: he is still happy and loves Demotic even more. Thus, there is no need at all to explain why Richard may find interest in the following lines or how it fits to his research—simply look at his bibliography, and you know why! However, shortly before this volume went to the publisher, an article that he co-authored on a Demotic version of the offering formula appeared, and this provides an additional link between his work and my humble contribution.[1] Richard's passion for Demotic is also the reason why the Demotic version precedes the hieroglyphic throughout, although the hieroglyphic side of the stela is certainly the front.

I do not write in English because I would not trust in Richard's capabilities to read, understand, and speak German—everybody knows that he has lived and worked for some years in Würzburg. The reason is rather that the present owner of the funerary stela of Pakhom, son of Lykos, that is published here, is an American private collector who wants to understand my publication and to remain anonymous. I thank him for granting me the publication rights and giving me access to the original, as well as his hospitality during my visit.

1. Description

The round-topped stela measures 24.2 cm at the bottom, its maximum height is 53.5 cm, and its thickness is 1.8 cm. A carpenter made it from two wooden panels. At the top there is a hole into which a *ba*-bird was originally mortised.[2] The panels were covered with plaster and painted. On one side, most likely the front (fig. 1), a winged sun disc in the lunette is shown, from which three chains of triangles as sun rays connect to a *p.t*-hieroglyph that forms the base for two reclining jackals that face one another, each holding a *ḥḳꜣ*- and a *nḫꜣḫꜣ*-scepter in their paws. A turquoise *p.t*-hieroglyph is also the divider that separates this zone from the register beneath, in which an embalming scene is

https://orcid.org/0000-0001-6486-3321. I am grateful to Edward O. D. Love for polishing my English.

1. Richard Jasnow and Karl-Theodor Zauzich, "A Demotic Version of the Hieratic Offering Formula in P. BM EA 10209, 4/1–20 (Ostracon LACMA M.80.202.200)," *Enchoria* 36 (2018/2019): 67–93. Although the volume bears the years "2018/2019," it actually appeared in March 2021—too late to be exploited for the commentary below.

2. Compare, e.g., the stela BM EA 8468—British Museum Collection Database "EA8468," www.britishmuseum.org/collection, British Museum (accessed 11/07/2019), or Florence inv. no. 2489 (Sergio Bosticco, *Museo Archeologico di Firenze: Le stele egiziane di epoca tarda*, Cataloghi dei musei e gallerie d'Italia [Rome: Libreria dello Stato, 1972], 34–35, pl. 23).

found. At the center, Anubis treats the mummy lying on a lion bier. This scene is flanked by five deities on each side. To the left, two mummiform deities—human-headed Amseti and jackal-headed Duamutef—and two further striding gods each raising two knives follow Isis, who is raising her right hand. The first of them is purely anthropomorphic while the second has a bull's head. To the right Nephthys, also raising her left hand, leads the mummiform Hapi and Qebehsenuef to complete the set of the four sons of Horus, behind whom an anthropomorphic god with two knives stands and a falcon sits on a *ḥb*-basket. All stand on a turquoise band that, in all likelihood, is also a *p.t*-hieroglyph, but damage prevents us from being fully sure. The painter's palette is quite limited: white for the background, and otherwise a pale yellow, turquoise, a brownish red, and black. Beneath these images a hieroglyphic text is written in thirteen lines alternatingly on a red and white background. The bottom zone below the text shows two jackals sitting on a chest, each with one knife held in their paws. Around the jackals two lines of Demotic were inscribed:

1) *ꜥnṱ n Ḥr Bḥtt nṯr ꜥꜣ nb p.t*	(The) perfumer[3] of Horus of Edfu, the great god, the lord of the sky,
2) *Pꜣ-ꜥẖm pꜣ ꜥꜣ sꜣ Lyḳws*	Pakhom the elder, son of Lykos.

The stela's other side is covered with white plaster and inscribed with a Demotic text in twenty-one lines (fig. 2), followed by three more lines after a space that was left empty. Those three lines are in fact a colophon, and provide the following information (fig. 3):

1) *sẖ n ḥsb.t 12 ꜣbd 3 pr.t 28 Gysrs pꜣ nṯr pꜣ Hrwm⸢y⸣[s]*	Written in the regnal year 12, Phamenoth 28th (of) Kaisaros, the god, the Rhomai[os],
2) *⸢n⸣ ḫtmw-nṯr ḥry ꜥnṱ n Ḥr Bḥtt nṯr ꜥꜣ nb p.t*	for the god's sealbearer, the chief perfumer of Horus of Edfu, the great god, the lord of the sky,
3) *Pꜣ-⸢ꜥ⸣ẖm sꜣ Lyḳws*	Pakhom, the son of Lykos.

Commentary to Colophon

2) *n*: Seemingly the scribe has made a mistake and corrected it. On the front side the individual is called "Pakhom, the elder" and has a different title. The same titles, however, recur for this Pakhom in both the hieroglyphic and the Demotic text.

ḫtmw-nṯr: The writing with two *nṯr*-signs framing the *ḫtmw*-sign is not the conventional one, but CDD *Ḫ* (2006), 177 lists an example. Maria Cannata cites further attestations and discusses this writing.[4] She rightly rejects the reading *ḥry ḫtmw-nṯr* based on evidence to which Pakhom's stela is to be added because *ḥry* is written here differently (see the following paragraph). While the god's seal bearers are very prominent in Hawara,[5] the title's use is not limited to the Hawara-Memphis area. It is also attested in Middle Egypt. Maria Cannata argues that the title's appearance south of Memphis is part of the so-called disappearance of the choachytes from the textual record (despite one attestation during the Roman period), and that it may be linked to a spread of a "Fayumic" practice, first northward to Memphis, and then southward. She suggests its gradual adoption by the mortuary priests of Middle Egypt around the end of the second and the beginning of the first century BCE. Pakhom's stela is so far the only evidence for the title in Edfu. The attestation of the title at

3. For this title, see Frédéric Colin, "Les Paneia d'El-Buwayb et du Ouadi Minayh sur la piste de Bérénice à Coptos: Inscriptions égyptiennes," *BIFAO* 98 (1998): 111–13, and esp. Frédéric Colin, "Le parfumeur (*pꜣ ꜥnṱ*)," *BIFAO* 103 (2003): 73–109.

4. Maria Cannata, *Three Hundred Years of Death: The Egyptian Funerary Industry in the Ptolemaic Period*, CHANE (Leiden: Brill, 2020), 63–66. I thank Maria Cannata for sharing with me the relevant chapters of her book before publication.

5. Cf. George Robert Hughes and Richard Jasnow, *Oriental Institute Hawara Papyri: Demotic and Greek Texts from an Egyptian Family Archive in the Fayum (Fourth to Third Century B.C.)*, OIP 113 (Chicago: Oriental Institute of the University of Chicago, 1997), *passim*.

Edfu by the late first century BCE may fit into this picture.[6] Note also some evidence for a slightly longer persistence of the choachytes than generally assumed.[7] However, it does not fundamentally contradict the general picture of the choachytes' disappearance.

ḥry: At first sight the sign looks rather like an *h* that could stand for *ḥr(y)* as much it could stand for the preposition *ḥr*, but looking at some examples of *ḥry* in CDD *Ḥ* (2009), 219–26, a reading *ḥry* does not seem too bold. The title *ḥry ꜥnṯ* is not yet attested but would not be surprising for a bigger temple with more than just one perfumer, if we consider the Egyptians' hierarchical mind. The hieroglyphic writing of *ḥry* in l. 4 corresponding to the Demotic l. 7 confirms the reading.

There are some areas where the white background appears lighter than the rest. There, the black writing changes its color to a dark grayish-blue. Apparently, the ancient craftsman tried to fill holes in the wood and the thicker plaster made the ink react differently than on the thinner plaster. This cannot be a modern, somewhat unprofessional restoration because the incised guiding lines that separate each line run uninterrupted through the darker to the lighter and back to the darker areas. Therefore, the lighter areas are to be taken as just as ancient as the rest.

2. Dating and Provenance

Thanks to the colophon, the stela is precisely dated to March 22, 18 BCE (greg.). As to the provenance, we must rely on the ancient owner's titles referring to the cult of Horus of Edfu and the internal evidence of the deities whom the offering formula mentions and who are typical for the cultic landscape of Edfu.[8] Therefore, the stela is likely to be from the Late to Roman period necropolis of Edfu located near Nagꜥ al-Ḥiṣâyâ where a mission excavated between 1884 and 1888 on behalf of the Egyptian Antiquities Service.[9] Andreas Effland interprets this area as the ancient Beḥedet, the burial place of the primordial deities in the nome of Edfu and destination of an annual nautical procession during the feast of Beḥedet (*ḥb Bḥd.t*).[10] This proposition, however, remains rather hypothetical and does not fully convince me.

According to Jaume Bagot Peix, the art dealer in Barcelona who sold the stela to the present owner in 2016, the previous owner bought the object in the 1970s in London but did not move it to Spain until 1981 because he was the offspring of a republican-minded family that emigrated during the Spanish Civil War to Argentina. I was unable to retrieve any further information on the piece's history before the 1970s and, in particular, to find out how it was brought from Egypt to Britain.

---

6. Cannata, *Three Hundred Years of Death*, 98–79; Maria Cannata, "God's Seal-Bearers, Lector-Priests and Choachytes: Who's Who at Memphis and Hawara," in *Actes du IXe Congrès International des Études Démotiques: Paris, 31 août–3 septembre 2005*, ed. Ghislaine Widmer, Didier Devauchelle, BdÉ 147 (Cairo: Institut français d'archéologie orientale, 2009), 58–60, 66–67.

7. Andreas Winkler, "On the Longevity of the χοαχύται in Thebes and Elsewhere," *JAC* 29 (2014): 50–62.

8. There is another Behedet, modern day Nagꜥ al-Mašayiḫ near This. It is attested in Demotic: Mark Smith, *Between Temple and Tomb: The Demotic Ritual Texts of Bodl. MS. Egypt. a. 3(P)*, SSR 30 (Wiesbaden: Harrassowitz, 2019), 87. However, the deities listed in our stela's offering formula and their clear connection to Edfu rule out the possibility that we are dealing with this lesser known Behedet here.

9. Gaston Maspero, "Sur les fouilles exécutés en Égypte de 1881 à 1885," *BIE* 2e série 6 (1886): 78–80.

10. Andreas Effland, "Neues zur Lage von Behedet," in *"Nunmehr ein offenes Buch…"—Das Edfu-Projekt: Herausgegeben zum 160. Geburtstag des Marquis Maxence de Rochemonteix (1849–1891)*, ed. Andreas Effland, Jan-Peter Graeff, and Martin von Falck, Informationsbroschüre zum EDFU-Projekt der Akademie der Wissenschaften zu Göttingen 1 (Hamburg: Universität Hamburg, 2009), 34–52; accepted by Dieter Kurth, "Die Reliefs der großen Schiffsprozession im Tempel von Edfu: Nautische Realität oder idealisierte Darstellung?," *GM* 257 (2019): 85–96. On the feast itself: Svenja Nagel, "Das Neumond- und Behedet-Fest in Edfu: Eine Strukturanalyse von Text und Bild einer „unregelmäßigen" Soubassement-Dekoration," in *Altägyptische Enzyklopädien: Die Soubassements in den Tempeln der griechisch-römischen Zeit – Soubassementstudien I*, ed. Alexa Rickert and Bettina Ventker, SSR 7 (Wiesbaden: Harrassowitz, 2014), 607–84—remarkably ignored by Kurth, "Die Reliefs der großen Schiffsprozession im Tempel von Edfu," 85–96, and then often polemically cited by Dieter Kurth, *Edfou V*, Die Inschriften des Tempels von Edfu – Abteilung I: Übersetzungen 4.1 (Hützel: Backe-Verlag, 2019), 51–64, 247–72.

The image programme is typical for what Peter Munro classified as group Edfu III, dating—according to Munro—to the Late Ptolemaic to Roman periods.[11] For Edfu III, Munro lists six objects of which just BM EA 32199 is made of wood, while Herman de Meulenaere is more restrictive and does not accept more than six objects as Ptolemaic-Roman funerary stelae from Edfu in total.[12] The piece in the BM is no longer counted among the Edfu sources. Munro's argument for dating them to the Roman period is the "very clumsy style of the figures" ("sehr plumper Figurenstil"). Almost fifty years later, such a dating criterion would no longer be accepted. All the more, the exact date on the stela published here is a welcome anchor independent from subjective judgements on style.

Being wooden, this piece much more resembles contemporary Theban funerary stelae. Indeed, Munro has noted connections between the elite of Edfu and Thebes, and these may have led to similarities in the designs of funerary stelae here and there. However, those family connections between Thebes and Edfu date to the Late period, not to the Ptolemaic and Roman periods.[13] I even wonder whether Pakhom's stela was manufactured in Thebes. The writing of *ḥry* in *ḥry ꜥnṯ* would be an indicator because it is very similar to the form in o. Medinet Habu 3333, 2.[14] Unfortunately the date of the ostracon cannot be determined more precisely than 332–30 BCE.[15] Regardless, the material from Edfu is not abundant, and the scarcity of evidence should prevent us from drawing any definitive conclusions.

3. Edition of the Texts

3.1. The Offering Formula: Synopsis (fig. 5)

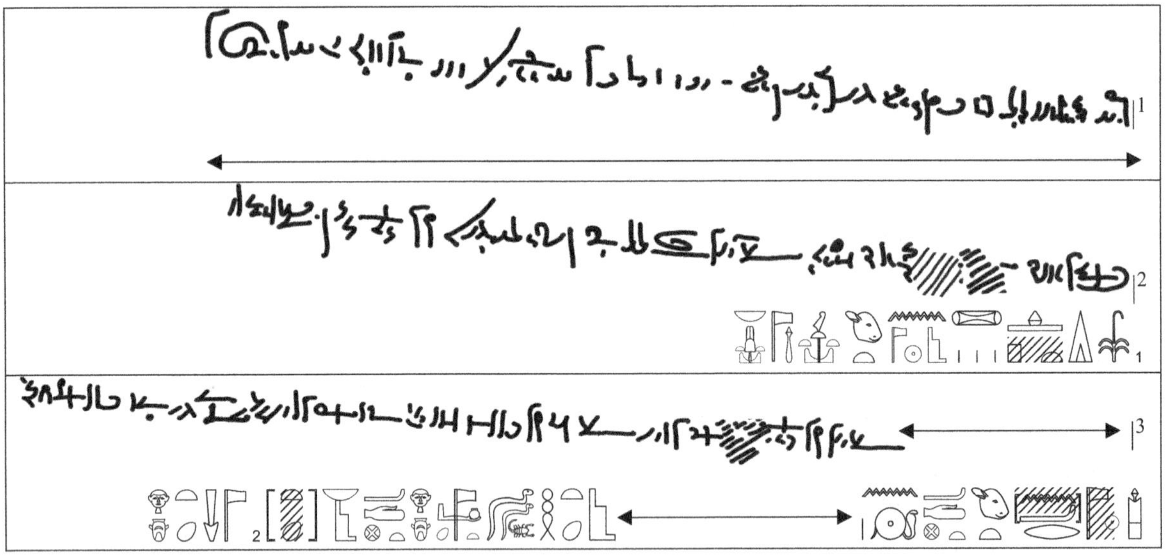

11. Peter Munro, *Die Spätägyptischen Totenstelen*, ÄF 25 (Glückstadt: Augustin, 1973), 74–75, 251–53, pl. 24.

12. Herman De Meulenaere, "Les stèles de Nag el-Hassaïa," *MDAIK* 25 (1969): 90–07, followed by Maria-Theresia Derchain-Urtel, *Priester im Tempel: Die Rezeption der Theologie der Tempel von Edfu und Dendera in den Privatdokumenten aus ptolemäischer Zeit*, GOF IV/19 (Wiesbaden: Harrassowitz, 1989), 10–11, 19–34. Further details of the discussion as to the prosopography and dating—see also Peter Munro, "Zur Chronologie der Totenstelen aus Nagꜥ el-Ḥiṣâyâ," *MDAIK* 41 (1985): 149–87—are irrelevant given my article's subject is the edition of the stela's text.

13. Munro, "Zur Chronologie der Totenstelen," 149–87.

14. Miriam Lichtheim, *Demotic Ostraca from Medinet Habu*, OIP 80 (Chicago: Oriental Institute of the University of Chicago, 1957), 69 no. 155, pl. 38.

15. Online: www.trismegistos.org/text/43712.

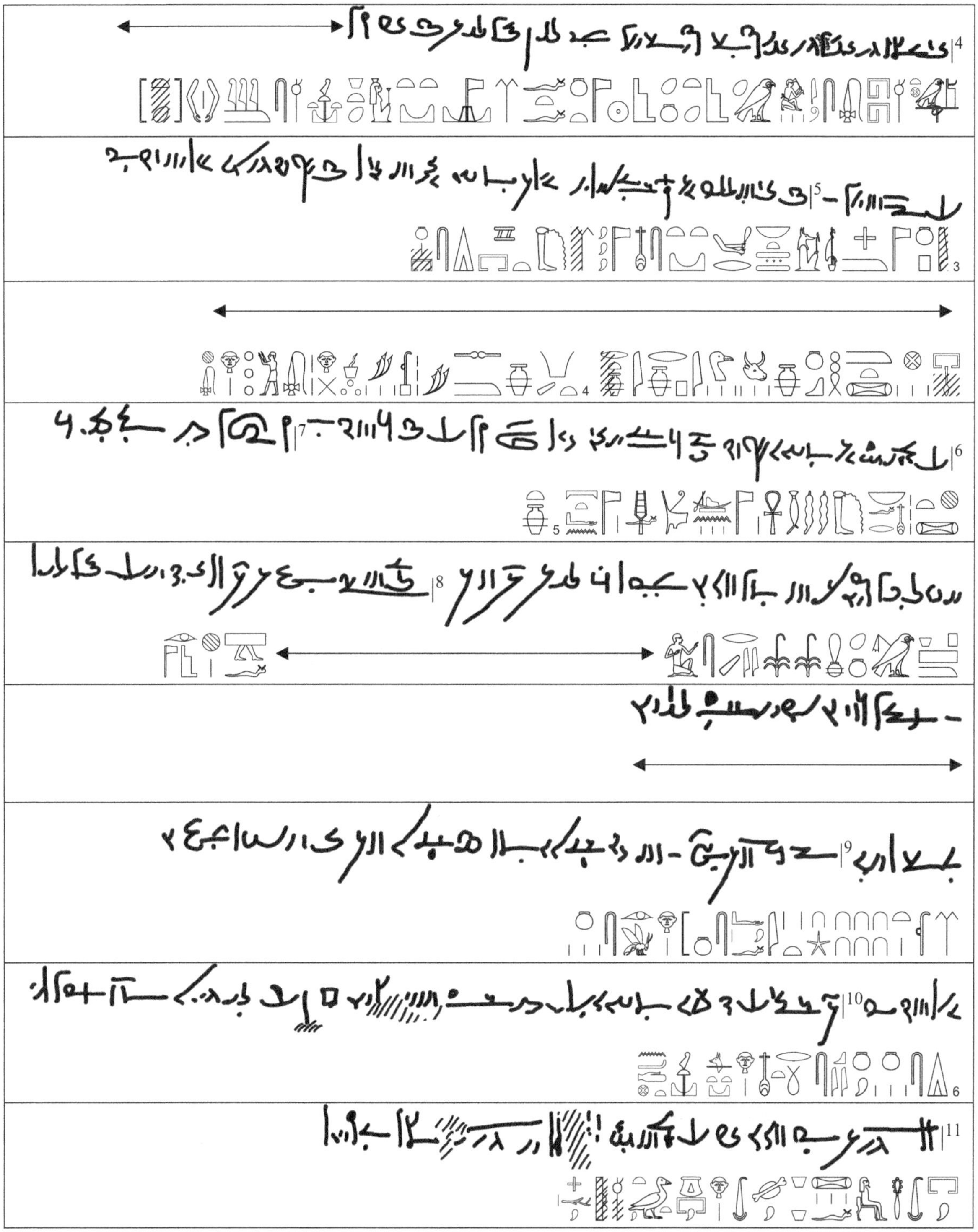

3.2. *The Offering Formula: Transliteration and Translation with Annotations*

D1	*ẖ.t pꜣ wyṱ m sẖ pr-ꜥnḫ*[16] *n Pꜣ-ꜥḫm pꜣ ꜥꜣ sꜣ Lyḳws pꜣ ḫtmw-nṯr*	The copy of the hieroglyphic stela[17] for Pakhom the elder, son of Lykos, the god's seal bearer:
H	←——→	←——→
D2	*pr-ꜥꜣ* ⸢*tꞽ*⸣ *ꜥbꜣ.wt n Wsꞽr ḫnṱ Ꞽmnṱ nṯr ꜥꜣ nb Ꞽbt*	Pharaoh gives an offering to Osiris, the foremost of the West, the great god, the lord of Abydos,
H	|[1] *ḥtp dꞽ nsw n Wsꞽr ḫnt⟨y⟩ ꞽmn.t.t nṯr ꜥꜣ nb ꜣbḏw*	An offering that the king gives to Osiris, the foremost of the West, the great god, the lord of Abydos,
D3	←——→ *Wsꞽr nṯr ꜥꜣ* ⸢*B*⸣*ḥt* *ꜣs.t mw.t-nṯr ḥr-ꞽb Bḥt Nb.t-ḥw.t ḥr⟨.t⟩-ꞽb*	←——→ ←——→ Osiris, the great god of Beḥedet, (to) Isis, the god's mother who dwells in Beḥedet, (to) Nephthys who dwells in
H	*ꞽwn [n Ḥ]r(?) ḫnty Bḥd.t n Rꜥ* ←——→ *ꜣs.t-Ḥḏḏ.t*[18] *mw.t nṯr ḥr⟨.t⟩-ꞽb Bḥd.t Nb⟨.t⟩-ḥw.t* |[2] *sn.t-nṯr ḥr⟨.t⟩-ꞽb*	the pillar,[19] [to Hor]us, the foremost of Beḥedet, to Rê, ←——→ (to) Isis-Ḥededet, the god's mother who dwells in Beḥedet, (to) Nephthys, the god's sister who dwells in
D4	*Wṯs-Ḥr*[20] ←——→ *Ḥr sꜣ ꜣs.t* *sꜣ n Wsꞽr nḏṱ ꞽṱ=f m ẖr-nṯr* ←——→ ←——→ ←——→ *Ꞽnpy n-*	the nome of Edfu, ←——→ ←——→ (to) Horus, the son of Isis and the son of Osiris, his father's protector in the necropolis, ←——→ (to) Anubis ←——→

16. See the writings in the sacerdotal decrees: Wilhelm Spiegelberg, *Der demotische Text der Priesterdekrete von Kanopus und Memphis (Rosettana) mit den hieroglyphischen und griechischen Fassungen und deutscher Übersetzung nebst demotischem Glossar* (Heidelberg: Im Selbstverlag des Verfassers, 1922), 125.

17. Lit. "stela in the script of the house of life."

18. Variant *ꜣs.t-Ḥdd.t* (*LGG* I, 76a). All attestations of this deity listed in the *LGG* are from Edfu or its environs. This Isis is even the representative of the Edfu nome according to the geographical procession that is depicted in the *soubassement* on the interior of the enclosure wall—here, the eastern half of the north wall. According to Dieter Kurth, *Edfou VI*, Die Inschriften des Tempels von Edfu Abteilung I: Übersetzungen 3 (Gladbeck: PeWe, 2014), 228, 12 (with pl. 160) she is *ꜣs.t-Ḥdd.t mw.t-nṯr ḥr.t-ꞽb Bḥd.t*, as on our stela.

19. Regarding the determination, "Osiris, lord of Dendera (*Ꞽwn.t*)" or "of Heliopolis (*Ꞽwnw*)" is unlikely. Although both are attested (*LGG* III, 576b–577b), the version given above is to be preferred (see *LGG* I, 193c–194b), the more so as the context fits the mythology of Edfu—Sylvie Cauville, *La théologie d'Osiris à Edfou*, BdE 91 (Cairo: Institut français d'archéologie orientale, 1983), esp. 186–87—and by this it complements the series of hints indicating a provenance from Edfu that the offering formula also gives.

20. See the writing of the priestly title *wṯs-Rꜥ* "carrier of Ra," CDD *R* (2001), 17–18.

H	*Wṯs.t-Ḥr wḏ⟨.t⟩ hh=s*[21] *iw sbi.w*[22]*=s Ḥr sꜣ ꜣs.t sꜣ n Wsir nḏ iti=f m ẖr.t-nṯr Nw.t*[23] *ḥnw.t imn.t.t wḏ=s gs.w-pr ḥpt[.t]*[24] |[3] *ꞽInpw*	the nome of Edfu, who puts her flame against her enemies,[25] (to) Horus, the son of Isis and the son of Osiris, who protects his father in the necropolis, (to) Nut, the mistress of the West, while commanding the temples, the embracing one, (to) Anubis,
D5	*m wyṯ nb tꜣ tsre ti=f nfr ʿʿy.w m wʿb.t ti=ysn*[26]	in Ut, the lord of the sacred land—he will make perfect the bodily parts in the embalming place—, so that they may give
H	*imy wt nb tꜣ ḏsr snfr ḥʿ.w nṯr m wʿb.t di=sn*[27]	who is in Ut, the lord of the sacred land, who perfects the god's body in the embalming place, so that they may give
D5bis	←——————→	←——————→
H	*pr.t-ḫrw m t ḥnḳ⟨.t⟩ iḥ.w ꜣpd.w irp irt⟨.t⟩* |[4] *šdḥ sm.w rnp.w snṯr ḥr sḏ.t ʿnty.w ḥr ḫ⟨.t⟩*	an invocation-offering with bread, beer, beef, fowl, wine, milk, sweet wine, fresh vegetables, incense on a flame, myrrh on a fire, and
D6	*iḫy-nb nfr.t wʿb⟨.t⟩ ntm⟨.t⟩ bne⟨.t⟩ ʿnḫ⟨.t⟩ nṯr im=ysn*	all sweet, pleasant, pure, and beautiful things on which a god lives,
H	*ḫw.t-nb⟨.wt⟩ nfr⟨.wt⟩ wʿb⟨.wt⟩ nḏm⟨.wt⟩ bnr⟨.wt⟩ ʿnḫ⟨.wt⟩ nṯr im=⟨s⟩n*	

21. The *s* is inversed as to the orientation of the rest of the text and similarly curved as the flame sign. Presumably the scribe inadvertently started a second flame, noticed his mistake, and stopped to leave the sign as a half decent *s*.

22. According to Penelope Wilson (*A Ptolemaic Lexikon: A Lexicographical Study of the Texts in the Temple of Edfu*, OLA 78 [Leuven: Peeters, 1997], 819), *ḫfty.w* would be more likely, but see the combination *wdi hh r sbi.w* that is cited in n. 25, whereas *wdi hh=s r ḫfty.w=s* is also well attested, yet just in Dendera, not in Edfu (*LGG* II, 625a).

23. As a determinative does not precede its word and as a full phonetic complementation of an ideographic writing would be strange, I assume a miswriting of  for . Or is the *nw*-pot on the head just not well done, looking instead like the bowl W10? For Nut as mistress of the West, see *LGG* V, 166b.

24. This is unattested for Nut so far, but for Neith or Hathor. However, it is easily explained, for Nut as sky goddess embraces the world as she does with the deceased in his coffin.

25. Cf. Wilson, *A Ptolemaic Lexikon*, 275, for the writing and phrase  *wd⟨.t⟩ hh r sbi.w r=k*, "putting the flame against the rebels against you" (esp. EI, 219, 5–6).

26. For the writing *=ysn*, see Martin Andreas Stadler, *Das Soknopaiosritual: Texte zum Täglichen Ritual im Tempel des Soknopaios zu Dimê*, ÄOP (Berlin: de Gruyter, 2022), 88–89. See also §4 below.

27. The *pr*-sign is, to my mind, misunderstood as two strokes that should form together with the third one above the plural determinative.

D7	⟨*n*⟩ *ḫtmw-nṯr ḥry*[28] *ʿnṯ*[29] *Pꜣ-ʿḫm sꜣ Lyḳws sṯr=f-n=f iw=f*	⟨for⟩ the god's seal bearer, the chief perfumer Pakhom, son of Lykos, so that he may go to sleep
H	*n ḫtmw-nṯr*[30] *ḥry ʿn|*[5]*.t⟨y⟩*[Kg31] *Pꜣ-ʿšm sꜣ n mi nn Ryḳs*[32]	for the god's seal bearer (?), the chief perfumer Pakhom, son of the likewise titled Lykos.
D8	*ṯḫy šm=f-n=f i.ir nꜣy=f iṭ.w n twe r tꜣy=f rsṭ* `*n*´ *rnp.t*	being drunk. He went off to his forefathers in the morning to his dawn[33] in the year
H	←→ *šm=f ḫ⟨r⟩ Wsir* ←→ ←→ *m rnp.t*	←→ He went before[34] Osiris ←→ in the year
D9	*77.t iw=f n wš n yʿb.t bn⟨.t⟩ iw=f ir pꜣy=f bꜣk ti=ysn*	77[35] being free from any evil disease and having done his service so that they gave
H	*77.t iʿi iwf=f=sn*[36] *ḥr ir⟨.t⟩ kꜣ.t=sn |*[6] *di=sn*	77. They washed his flesh, carrying out their work so that they gave
D10	*-n=f ḳsiꜣ.t nfr.t ih* ⸢*Rstꜣw*⸣ *imnṭ n Bḥt*	him a beautiful burial in the necropolis, the West of Beḥedet.
H	*-n=f ḳysr.t*[37] *nfr⟨.t⟩ ḥr ⟨Rꜣ-⟩stꜣ.w imn⟨.t.t⟩ n Bḥd.t*	
D11	*iw pr=f mne ḫr iḫy.w* ⸢..⸣[.] *iw pꜣy=f pr wḏꜣ .?.*	while his house[38] endures with property .... [..] and his house prospers ......[39]
H	*pr=f mn ḫ⟨r⟩ šps.w=f iwʿ=f mn ḥr ns.t=f sꜣ.t=f wḏ imy⟨.w⟩-ḫt=f*	His house endures with provisions. His heir endures on his seat, his daughter commands his retinue.

28. See p. 419.

29. See n. 3 above.

30. This is, to the best of my knowledge, a so far unattested writing which I fail to explain. The following *nṯr*-sign indicates that it is the same title as in the Demotic.

31. See p. 420 above with n. 3.

32. Although the *ḳ* looks like 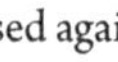 I take it as a  that became too big and that has been inversed against the general writing direction as much as in l. 6.

33. See §4 below.

34. According to the TLA, *šm ḫr* is attested abundantly in Old Egyptian. Is it an archaism here?

35. The writings for 70 known so far (CDD, numbers [2014], 157–61) look quite different from the form here. However, considering the hieroglyphic parallel there cannot be any doubt in reading it that way.

36. Apparently, something went wrong here. I suppose that the suffix pronoun =*sn* was misplaced after the nominal direct object and that the sign that looks like a square bracket should be the plural determinative. In short, I suggest emending it as: 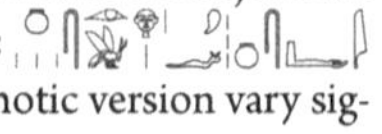 *iʿi=sn iw=f ḥr ir.t kꜣ.t=sn* (for a translation see above). However, this means that the hieroglyphic and the Demotic version vary significantly. While the hieroglyphs evoke the god's work on behalf of the deceased's corpse, the Demotic refers to what the deceased has done as a reason for why he merits an eternal life.

37. Metathesis influenced by the contemporary pronunciation of *ḳrs* as *ḳys*.

38. See §4 below.

39. I would tentatively read the final group as *twe.w*, the qualitative of *twe*, "to praise." Thus, the sentence would end "… [..] and his house prospers being praised." The tall *w*, however, has a thickening at the top towards the left which keeps me from being fully certain and leaves me with a residue of doubt. See also §4 below.

3.3. Excerpts from the Beginning of the Book of Traversing Eternity and Its Demotic Paraphrase: Synopsis

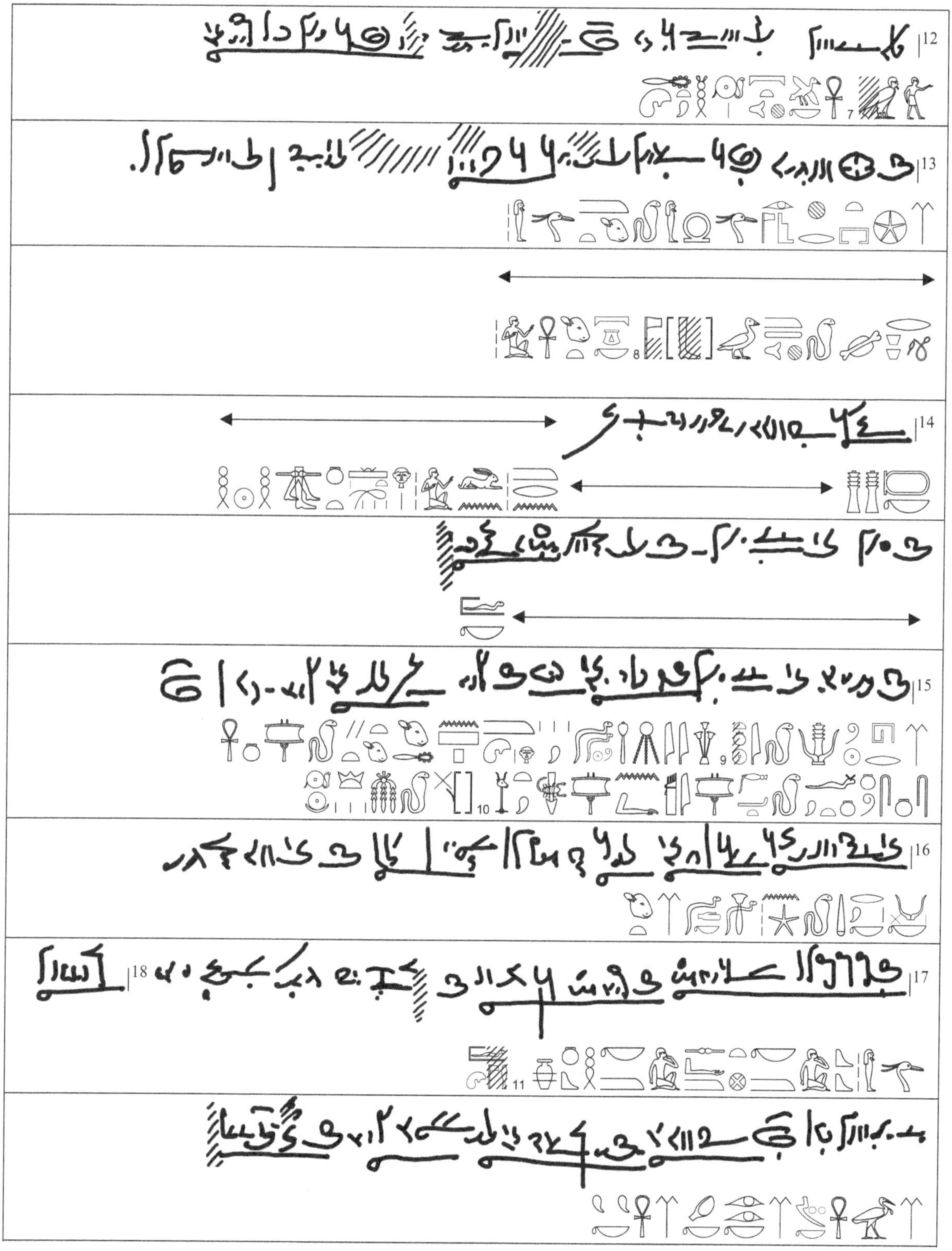

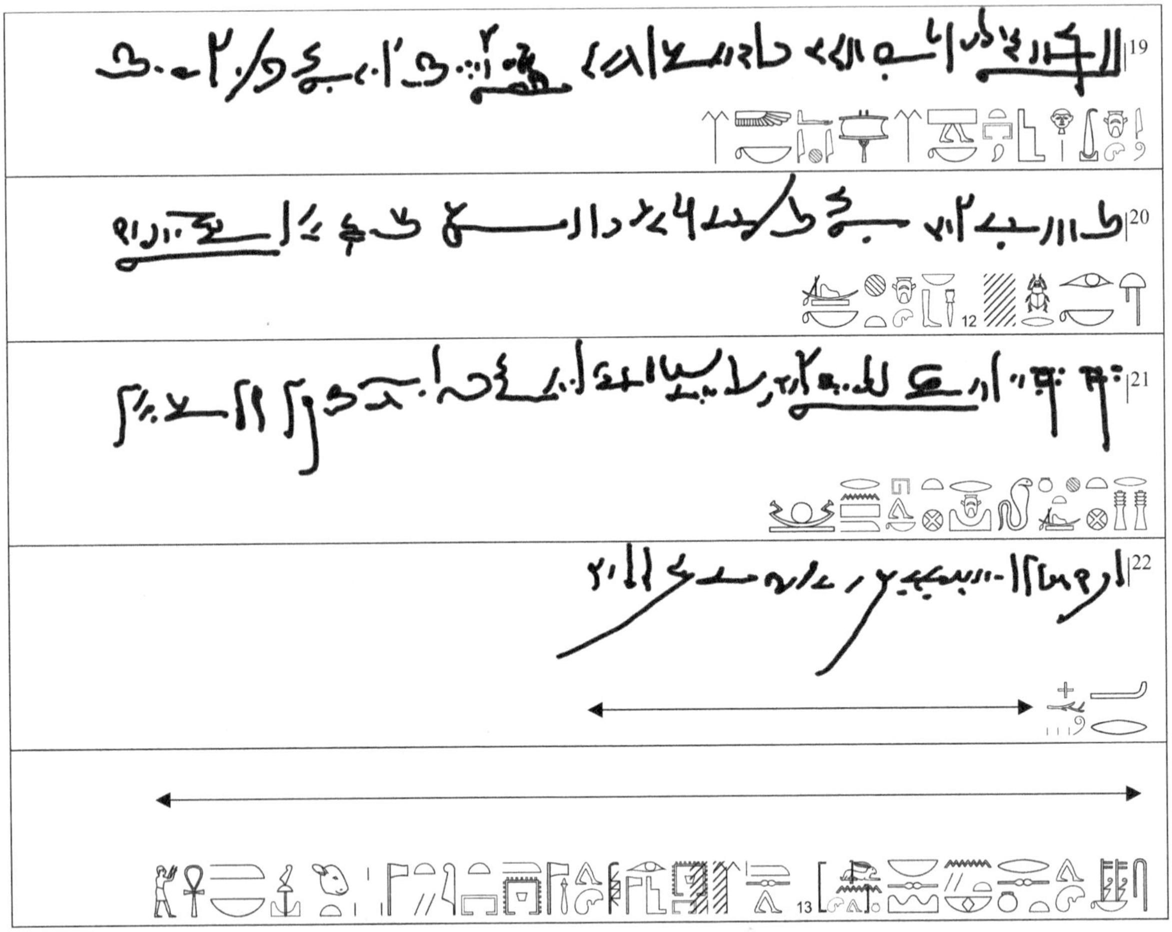

3.4. Excerpts from the Beginning of the Book of Traversing Eternity and Its Demotic Paraphrase: Transliteration and Translation with Annotations

The translation of the hieroglyphic version follows Mark Smith,[40] unless the stela's reading deviates. I comment on them only if they are not too obvious variants. Furthermore, details of understanding the Book of Traversing Eternity have not been discussed here if I have nothing new to add. For variants see the synopsis by Herbin.[41] Our stela's version omits substantial passages in comparison to what Herbin has collected.

40. Mark Smith, *Traversing Eternity: Texts for the Afterlife from Ptolemaic and Roman Egypt* (Oxford: Oxford University Press, 2009), 405–7.

41. François-René Herbin, *Le Livre de parcourir l'éternité*, OLA 58 (Leuven: Peeters, 1994), 382–411. François-René Herbin, *Books of Breathing and Related Texts*, Catalogue of Books of the Dead and Other Religious Texts in the British Museum 4 (London: British Museum Press, 2008), has published further witnesses of this composition. See also Julia Budka, Tamás Mekis, and Marie-Cécile Bruwier, "Reuse of Saite Temple Tombs in the Asasif during the Early Ptolemaic Time: The Tomb Group of *Mw.t-Mnw* from TT 414," *ÄgLev* 22/23 (2012/2013): 217–19, for another excerpt from the Book of Traversing Eternity on a Canopic box.

D12	*ỉ by-ỉypn ꜥnḫ ⸢py⸣=k r p.t ḫr Rꜥ wꜣḥ ẖe⟨.ṱ⟩=k*	"O you living ba, you shall fly up to the sky to[42] Rê. Your corpse will endure
H	*ỉ bꜣ |[7] ꜥnḫ pꜣi=k ⟨r⟩ p.t ḫr Rꜥ wꜣḥ ẖ.t=k*	
D13	*m twꜣ.t ḫr Wsỉr ỉ⸢ẖ⸣ sḥ=k [m-ḫn]ṱ ỉẖy.w*	in the underworld in the presence of Osiris. Your mummy will be magically powerful among[43] the *akh*-spirits.
H	*m dwꜣ.t ḫr Wsỉr ꜣḫ sꜥḥ=k m-ḫnt ꜣḫ.w*	
D13bis		
H	*rwḏ ỉwꜥ=k m tꜣ ḫr Gb[b] |[8] ḥr ns.t=k ḫnt ꜥnḫ.w*	On earth in the presence of Geb, your heir flourishes on your throne at the head of the living.[44]
D14[45]	*rn=k mne r nḥḥ ḏ.t m Rꜥ wbn n-m[46] ỉḫy.wt ꜥḳ=k*	Your name endures for ever and ever as Rê. Rise in radiance[47]! You will enter
H	*rn=k ḏd m rꜣ.w n wn.w ḥr mḏꜣ.wt n.t sbỉ nḥḥ prỉ=k*	Your name endures in the mouths of those who are because of the Books of Traversing Eternity.[48] You will come forth

42. For the aorist marker or the verb *ḫr*, "to speak" to write the preposition see Smith, *Between Temple and* Tomb, 140–41, 191.

43. It is also possible that *m-ḫnṱ* in the Demotic was understood as "at the head of"; see Richard Jasnow and Karl-Theodor Zauzich, *The Ancient Egyptian Book of Thoth* (Wiesbaden: Harrassowitz, 2005), 107, 256.

44. On the interpretation of this sentence, cf. the hypotheses on the origins of the Book of Traversing Eternity in a sort of coronation ritual proposed by Martin Andreas Stadler, "Prätexte funerärer Rituale: Königsliturgie, Tempelliturgie, Totenliturgie," in *Liturgical Texts for Osiris and the Deceased in Late and Greco-Roman Egypt (Liturgische Texte für Osiris und Verstorbene im spätzeitlichen Ägypten)*, ed. Burkhard Backes and Jacco Dieleman, SSR 14 (Wiesbaden: Harrassowitz, 2015), 75–90.

45. Here it is almost impossible to mark omissions and additions because the Demotic version is rather a paraphrase than a translation of the hieroglyphic one.

46. For this writing Mark Smith, "Remarks on the Orthography of Some Archaisms in Demotic Religious Texts," *Enchoria* 8.2 (1978): 22, Ghislaine Widmer, *Résurrection d'Osiris - Naissance d'Horus: Les papyrus Berlin P. 6750 et Berlin P. 8765, témoignages de la persistance de la tradition sacerdotale dans le Fayoum à l'époque romaine*, ÄOP 3 (Berlin: de Gruyter, 2015), 39, 395, and Smith, *Between Temple and Tomb*, 127.

47. See §4 below.

48. According to Joachim F. Quack ("Das Dekret des Amun an Isis," in *Auf den Spuren des Sobek: Festschrift für Horst Beinlich*, ed. Jochen Hallof, SRaT 12 [Dettelbach: Röll, 2012], 227n14 announcing a new, but still unpublished interpretation of the passage) and Joachim F. Quack ("Rohrfedertorheiten?: Bemerkungen zum römerzeitlichen Hieratisch," in *Ägyptologische „Binsen"-Weisheiten I–II: Neue Forschungen und Methoden der Hieratistik*, ed. Ursula van Verhoeven-Elsbergen, Abhandlungen der Geistes- und Sozialwissenschaftlichen Klasse / Akademie der Wissenschaften und der Literatur Einzelveröffentlichung 14 [Stuttgart: Steiner, 2015], 439n30), Book of Traversing Eternity is an inadequate title for the text. The plural here is noteworthy. It suggests that this is rather a term for a genre of texts rather than the title of a specific composition.

D15[49]	*m hrw wbn.n=w*[50] *ḥr=k ḫnm fnṯ=k ṯȝw n ꜥnḫ*	by day, after they[51] have shone on you. Your nose will breathe the breeze of life.
H	*m hrw ḫnm=k i*⸢*tn*⸣ |[9] *ḥȝy ḥdd.w=f m ḥr=k nšp ḫ⟨nm⟩.ty=k⟨y⟩ ṯȝw n ꜥnḫ snsn fnḏ=k mḥ.t is-niw srḳ.n=f*[52] *ḥty.t* |[10]*=k ms⟨.t⟩ ḫꜥ.w rꜥ-nb*	by day, when you unite with the sun disc. Its light will shine in your face, while your nostrils inhale the breeze of life and your nose breathes the north wind. The breathing air, it has opened your windpipe[53] that creates appearance every day(?).[54]
D16	*wpy=k rȝ=k mt=k ⟨n⟩ nȝ nṯr.w sḏm=w ḫrw=k m wsḫ⟨.t⟩*	You will open your mouth so that you speak to the gods, so that they hear your voice in (the) hall
H	*wpi=k rȝ=k mdw=k n nṯr.w wȝḏ ḏd=k m-ḫnt*	You will open your mouth when you speak to the two gods. Your speech will flourish among
D17	*mȝꜥ.w*[55] *wnm=k m sn*[56] *swr=k m* ⸢*ḥ*⸣*nḳ pr*	of Righteous Ones.[57] You will eat the offering bread and drink beer. Your personality of a ruler
H	*ȝḫ.w wnm=k m t*[58] *sꜥm=k m ḥnḳ⟨.t⟩* |[11] *pri*	the *akh*-spirits.[59] You will eat the offering bread and drink beer. Your majesty[60]

49. Here it is almost impossible to mark omissions and additions because the Demotic version is rather a paraphrase than a translation of the hieroglyphic one.

50. The *sḏm.n=f* would have been written with the form of a dative *n=w*. See also §4 below.

51. Who are "they"? Does the pronoun refer to the *iḫy.wt*, "rays" = "radiance"?

52. Either  is a miswriting for , or  is simply badly written. Regardless, the reading is based on the parallels as Herbin, *Le Livre de parcourir l'éternité*, 87–88, 389–91, has collected them.

53. At the beginning of the line, there are unclear relics of signs that do not fit a current determination of the word but cannot be anything else than that.

54. This participial phrase is not found in other copies of the Book of Traversing Eternity. The parallels have: *ḫnm ꜥnḫ m ḏ.t=k*"(…) so that the life unite with your body" (Herbin, *Le Livre de parcourir l'éternité*, 389).

55. On the reinterpretation of the "Hall of the Two Truths" as the "Hall of the Righteous Ones," see Martin Andreas Stadler, *Der Totenpapyrus des Pa-Month (P. Bibl. nat. 149)*, SAT 6 (Wiesbaden: Harrassowitz, 2003), 47. In P. Bibl. nat. 149, however, the righteous ones are written *mȝꜥ.ṯ.w*. See also §4 below.

56. Written like the sign in *sn*, "brother"; see Stadler, *Das Soknopaiosritual*, 217–19.

57. See §4 below.

58.  is presumably just a misreading of the graphically kind of similar 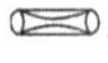.

59. See §4 below.

60. This is also a remarkable notion and better understood against the background of the Book of Traversing Eternity as a kind of coronation ritual; see n. 44.

D18	*ḥk*[61]*=k n by ꜥnḫ mne*[62]*=k n-m*[63] *ir.ṱ=k sḏm*[64]*=k m ꜥnẖ.w*[65]*=k*	will go forth as a living ba. You will see by means of your eyes. You will hear by means of your ears,
H	*ḥm=k m bꜣ ꜥnḫ mꜣꜣ=k m ir.ty=k⟨y⟩ sḏm=k m ꜥnḫ.wy=k⟨y⟩*	will go forth as a living ba. You will see by means of your eyes. You will hear by means of your ears.
D19	*iw ḥꜣ.ṱ=k smne ḥr tꜣy=f s.t ḫꜥ=k m ṯꜣw iw=k ḥl n-m*[66]	your heart being fixed in its place. You will appear as wind, while you fly up as
H	*iw ib=k mn ḥr s.t=f šm=k m ṯꜣw ꜥḫy=k m*	Your heart endures on its place. You will go as wind and fly up as
D20	*ẖyb⟨.t⟩ ir=k ẖrb-nb nt iw iw=k wḫꜣ ẖty=k ⟨r⟩*[67]	a shadow. You will assume every form that you will wish. You will fare downstream ⟨to⟩
H	*šwt iri=k ḫpr|*[12]*-nb ꜣbw ib=k ḫdi=k r*	a shadow. You will assume every form your heart is desiring. You will fare downstream to
D21	*Ḏdw ḫnṱ=k r Ꞽbt ꜥḳ.w*[68] *n nšm⟨.t⟩ nṯr Wsir*	Busiris and fare upstream to Abydos, entering[69] the divine *neshmet*-bark of Osiris
H	*Ḏdw ḫnt=k r ꜣbḏw hꜣi=k r nšm.t*	Busiris and fare upstream to Abydos. You will descend to the *neshmet*-bark
D22a	*ḥnꜥ nꜣ nṯr.w*	together with the gods
H	*ḥnꜥ imy.w-ḫt=s*	together with its retinue.
D22b	*n-irm-n-im*[70]*=f r nḥḥ ḏ.t*	with him[71] for ever and ever.
H	←——————————→	←——————————→

61. In Demotic, *ḥm*, "majesty" is rarely attested; Stadler, *Das Soknopaiosritual*, 280–81. The stela here suggests that the word was obsolescent in Demotic or even obsolete. That is why the scribe translated it with *ḥk*, "ruler." The rendering "personality of a ruler" is the attempt to accommodate the suffix as possessive pronoun without being misleading. "Your ruler" would rather mean the ruler of the addressed person rather than "your rulership" (in analogy to "your lordship") as an aspect of the addressed person. For writing earlier *ḳ* with the *kꜣ*-arms in Demotic see Günter Vittmann, "Zum Gebrauch des *kꜣ*-Zeichens im Demotischen," *SEAP* 15 (1996): 1–12.

62. For *mne*, "to see," see Mark Smith, "On some Orthographies of the Verb *mꜣ*, 'see', and *mn*, 'endure', in Demotic and Other Egyptian Texts," in *Grammata Demotica: Festschrift für Erich Lüddeckens zum 15. Juni 1983*, ed. Heinz Josef Thissen, Karl-Theodor Zauzich (Würzburg: Gisela Zauzich Verlag, 1984), 193–210.

63. See note 46.

64. The group *ṯꜣw* is likely to be written here erroneously.

65. This is a yet unattested phonetic writing. The small stroke between *n* and *ẖ* is probably just a scribal error.

66. See note 46.

67. Or is the faded oblique stroke towards the stela's margin the *r*? The distance to *ẖty=k* is admittedly big.

68. Or is the vertical stroke part of the hieraticizing walking legs determinative? The end of line 14 indicates this, where seemingly at the margin a small black stroke may be found. See further note 69.

69. I take *ꜥḳ.w* as a congealed qualitative that did not agree in gender and number anymore.

70. This is an extraordinary form, even though *n-irm* and *irm-n-im=* are attested (CDD *Ꞽ* [2011], 199–200). Possibly it is a phonetic writing to display the pronunciation ⲚⲘ̄ⲘⲀϤ with *irm* being a relic as a historical group—for this phenomenon see Joachim F. Quack, "Bemerkungen zur Struktur der demotischen Schrift und zur Umschrift des Demotischen," in *Acts of the Tenth International Congress of Demotic Studies: Leuven, 26–30 August 2008*, ed. Mark Depauw, Yanne Broux, OLA 231 (Leuven: Peeters, 2014), 207–42. Already Wilhelm Spiegelberg, *Demotische Texte auf Krügen*, DemStud 5 (Leipzig: Hinrichs, 1912), 28 no. 29, proposed this interpretation for *irm-n-im=w* in the context there. Looking at the tendency of the stela's Demotic scribe to add an *n* to the preposition *m*, the initial n here is not so surprising anymore.

71. The pronoun is presumably referring to Osiris.

D22bis	←——→	←——→
H	*s3ḥ=k r s.t {nw} n.t Ḥb-nb=s ⟨d⟩wn[=k]* |[13] *gs⟨.t⟩ m wsḫ.t Wsir šms=k nṯr ꜥ3 m wsḫ.t M3ꜥ.ty ḫnty imn.t m nb ꜥnḫ*	You will arrive at the place of Hapnebes.[72] You will hasten in the hall of Osiris so that you follow the great god in the hall of the Two Truths, the foremost of the West as "lord of life."[73]

4. On Some Noteworthy Features: Archaisms and Deviations of the Demotic Version

Apart from P. BM EA 10252[74] and the two Rhind papyri[75] this is, to the best of my knowledge, the only other source from ancient Egypt that provides the two versions of the same text in two different stages of the Egyptian language and, together with the two Rhind papyri, the only one applying two different scripts to each of the versions on one and the same object (be it a papyrus scroll or a stela). Of course, there are more translations from one stage of Egyptian to the other, but they are not on the same scroll. The first sixteen lines of P. BN 149, for instance, provide a Demotic version of several funerary texts, besides another section of the Book of Traversing Eternity spells 125 and 128 of the *Book of the Dead*,[76] albeit not on the same papyrus. The Demotic version on our stela is not a full translation of the hieroglyphic text because it omits several phrases with a very similar predication. Therefore, calling the Demotic version a "paraphrase" would be more appropriate. This raises some issues and gives us valuable insights into how the Egyptians understood their legacy of religious texts. To conclude my article, I am going to share my thoughts with the scholarly public here.

Mark Smith has described the shadings of language in Demotic funerary texts from purely Demotic to purely Middle Egyptian in Demotic script.[77] The Demotic text of Pakhom's stela is clearly an intermediate stage, that is, a text in Demotic with archaizing features, which are:

1. *nṯr ꜥ3* (D2) rather than *p3 nṯr ꜥ3*,
2. the suffix pronoun of the third person plural =*ysn* (D5, 6, and 9) vs. =*w* (D15, 16),
3. the archaizing relative form *ꜥnḫ.t* instead of *r.ꜥnḫ*,
4. the suffix pronoun in *pr=f* rather than the possessive article (D11)—in the next phrase the scribe used the Demotic possessive article (*p3y=f pr*) and returned to contemporary grammar,
5. repeating the *m3ꜥ*-sign thrice to write the plural (D17) by which the scribe chose to use a graphic archaism. I take *m3ꜥ.w* here as the plural of a nominalized participle (lit. "justified ones," rather than emending it to *m3ꜥ⟨.ṯ⟩.w*). This would be then additionally an archaizing feature on the linguistic level.

72. See the parallels that have  or similar for the name of the Abydene necropolis (Herbin, *Le Livre de parcourir l'éternité*, 405).

73. Here the stela's version is considerably abridged in comparison to all other parallels that have further sentences after *wsḫ.t M3ꜥ.ty* anyway. For this particular passage they have *sn=k Wsir m pr wr n nbw Ḫnty-Imn.t.t m nb ꜥnḫ*, "You will join Osiris in the house of gold, the foremost of the West in the 'lord of life' (i.e., the sarcophagus)." (Herbin, *Le Livre de parcourir l'éternité*, 409–11.) The version at hand is a quite mutilated version of this. The translation above tries to get as much sense as possible out of this.

74. *Urk.* VI:60–144. Pascal Vernus, "Entre néo-égyptien et démotique: La langue utilisée dans la traduction du Rituel pour repousser l'Agressif (Étude sur la diglossie I)," *RdÉ* 41 (1990): 153–208.

75. Georg Möller, *Die beiden Totenpapyrus Rhind des Museums zu Edinburg*, DemStud 6 (Leipzig: Hinrichs, 1913); Smith, *Traversing Eternity*, 302–48, with further references.

76. Stadler, *Der Totenpapyrus des Pa-Month.* For the Book of Traversing Eternity, see pp. 16–17, 27–29, 42–54. Smith, *Traversing Eternity*, 437–54, esp. 444–45; Martin Andreas Stadler, "Die Korrektur einer Korrektur: Papyrus Bibliothèque nationale 149 I 24 f. und III 7 f.," *Enchoria* 36 (2018/2019): 211–20.

77. Mark Smith, *The Mortuary Texts of Papyrus BM 10507*, CDPBM 3 (London: Published for the Trustees of the British Museum by British Museum Publications Limited, 1987), 28.

Looking at the archaisms listed above, I fail to recognize a rule. The number of interferences with old forms is higher in the Demotic version of the offering formula than in the paraphrase of the excerpt of the Book of Traversing Eternity. In translating the offering formula, however, the scribe was not consistent in choosing to render the initial sentence differently from the Middle Egyptian. Rather than formulating a headline "An offering that the king gives ..." with a Middle Egyptian relative form, he preferred to express it by using the present I ("Pharaoh gives an offering ..."), while elsewhere (no. 3 in the list of archaisms) he kept the old relative form. The strange phrase of the daughter as a commander has been rendered quite differently in the Demotic (D11). The biographical element that concludes the offering formula has a further remarkable and poetical metaphor for "death" as being the deceased's morning. Although it fits into the Egyptian world view because the sunset, the sun god's death on earth is sunrise, is the sun god's birth for the underworld, it is yet unparalleled. Thus, Pakhom's death is his birth as the sun's in the beyond.

The section of the Book of Traversing Eternity contains some exceptional renderings, such as replacing *pri*, "to come forth" with *ꜥḳ*, "to enter," which cannot be an archaism (D14). It is rather an example of a scribal variation because the translator presumably wrote the Demotic version by knowing the general lines of the funerary text by heart.[78] He mixed then the two directions of movement up, as they are a standard couple anyway.[79] A bit more surprising is why the Demotic scribe rendered hieroglyphic *šm*, "to go" as *ḫꜥ*, "to appear" (D19), for the verb *šm* is not obsolescent in Demotic and also appears in the present text. I cannot but state the fact.

The variance in graphematizing words of the roots *ꜣḫ* and *iꜣḫ* requires closer attention:

Root	Word	Hieroglyphic Writing on the Stela	Demotic Writing on the Stela	Reference
ꜣḫ	*ꜣḫ*, "to be magically powerful"		 *iẖ*	D13/H7
	ꜣḫ.w, "*akh*-spirits"	 *ꜣḫ.w*, "*akh*-spirits"	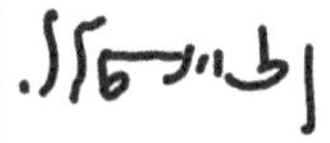 *iẖy.w*	D13/H7
iꜣḫ	 *iꜣḫ.w*, "luminous ones" according to parallels[80]		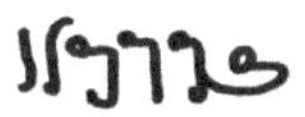 *mꜣꜥ.w*, "righteous ones"	D17/H10
	* *iꜣḫ*, "radiance"	./.	 *iẖy.wt*	D14/-

Iẖy.wt is determined like "thing, property, possessions," but I take it as phonetic writing for *iꜣḫ*. Did the scribe want to differentiate between *iꜣḫ* and *ꜣḫ*? For the latter in H7 he used *iẖ* or *iẖy* in D13. This would corroborate the distinction of the two roots as Jansen-Winkeln has carved out.[81] Regrettably, the hieroglyphic version does not give a direct parallel, and we have to rely on the context (*Rꜥ*, *wbn*) that suggests a translation as "radiance." However, later on, the distinction is blurred again because in H10 we find a writing that should be translated "*akh*-spirits," for which the Demotic corresponding word seems to be *mꜣꜥ.w*. Thus, the stela contradicts Jansen-Winkeln's rule: "Wie oben erwähnt, hat schon H. Brugsch sowohl *ꜣḫ* ‚wirksam sein' als auch *ꜣḫt* ‚Horizont' von einer Wurzel *jꜣḫ* ‚leuchten,

78. See Martin Andreas Stadler, *Weiser und Wesir: Studien zu Vorkommen, Rolle und Wesen des Gottes Thot im ägyptischen Totenbuch*, ORA 1 (Tübingen: Mohr Siebeck, 2009), 43–47.

79. Cf. *šm* – *iy*: Martin Andreas Stadler, "The Funerary Texts of Papyrus Turin N. 766: A Demotic Book of Breathing (Part I)," *Enchoria* 25 (1999): 99, but *ꜥḳ/pri* is also abundantly found.

80. Therefore, Smith, *Traversing Eternity*, 406, translates "luminous ones" for this phrase.

81. Karl Jansen-Winkeln, "'Horizont' und 'Verklärtheit': Zur Bedeutung der Wurzel *ꜣḫ*," *SAK* 23 (1996): 201–15.

strahlen' ableiten wollen, und diese Irrlehre hat sich hartnäckig bis heute gehalten.... Auch die Autoren des Wörterbuchs halten ja beide Wurzeln strikt auseinander.... Es gibt keinerlei Belege und Kontexte, in denen die Bedeutung ‚strahlen, licht sein' für *ꜣḫ* auch nur im entferntesten passend wäre."[82] Apparently, those who fashioned the stela did not see this strict distinction because *ꜣḫ.w*, "*akh*-spirits" replaces *iꜣḫ.w*, "luminous ones" and the Demotic version supports the understanding of  as *ꜣḫ* and not as a writing of *iꜣḫ*. Thus, in the hieroglyphic version, the stela's painter used a sign that connects the word with *ꜣḫ* rather than *iꜣḫ*, and the Demotic scribe (whether identical with the painter of the front side or not is open to speculation) consequently translated it with a word that corresponds to *akh*-spirits as being those who have passed the judgment and found to be righteous (see n. 55). By this, the stela reinterprets the standard version as well as it provides an example for confusing the two roots.

Looking at those deviations, they suggest that the scribe understood some notions differently from the traditional meaning. This raises of course the question whether a modern translation according to the original text of the Book of Traversing Eternity is appropriate, or whether it should be approximated to the contemporary Demotic version. In the context of this article, however, this would obscure the differences between the two versions and make the Demotic reinterpretation less obvious. That is why I refrained from approximating the hieroglyphic to the Demotic version.

82. Jansen-Winkeln, "'Horizont' und 'Verklärtheit,'" 205–6.

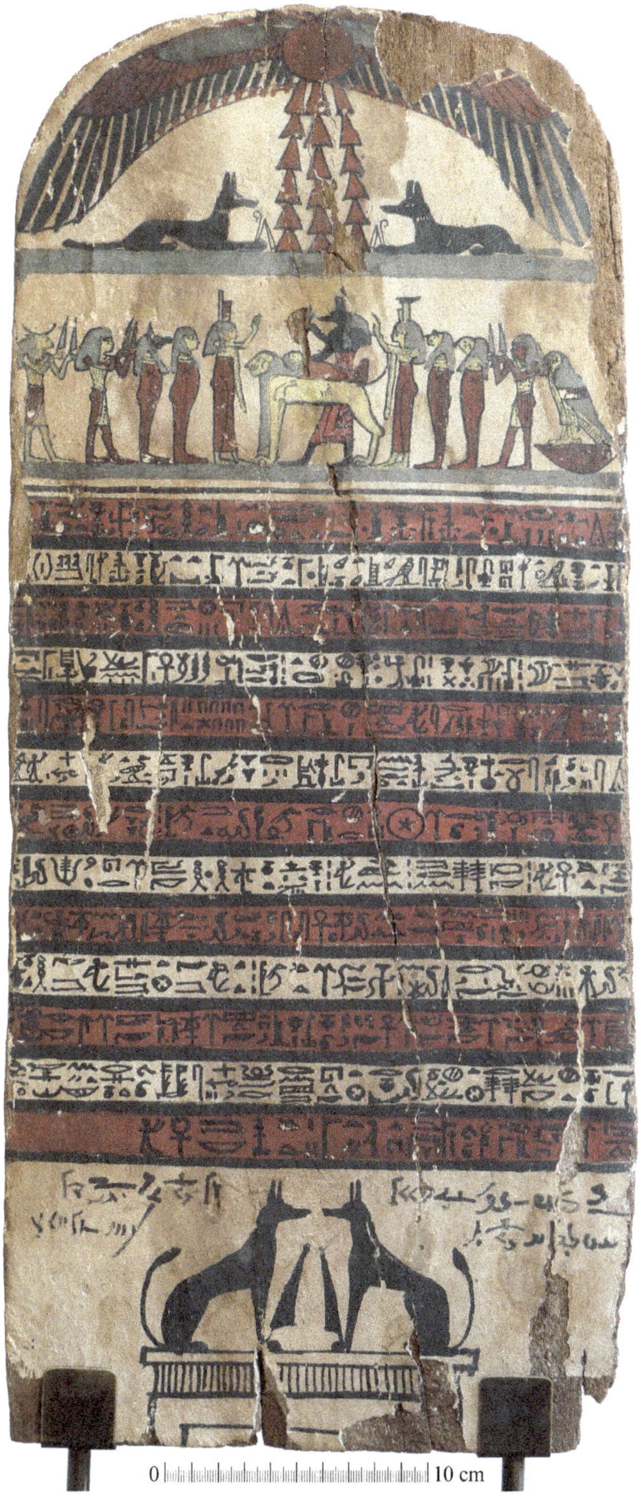

Figure 1. Stela of Pakhom, son of Lykos, from Edfu, hieroglyphic front.

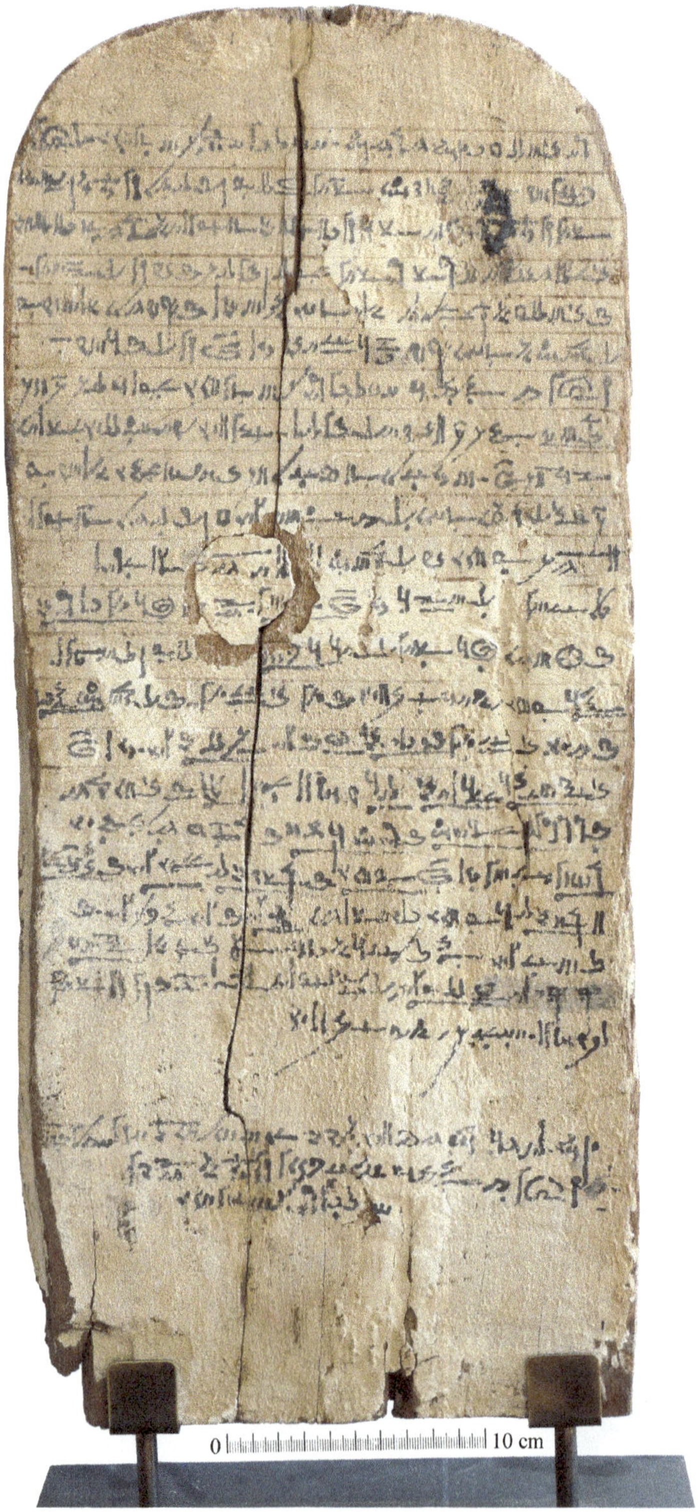

Figure 2. Stela of Pakhom, son of Lykos, from Edfu, Demotic back.

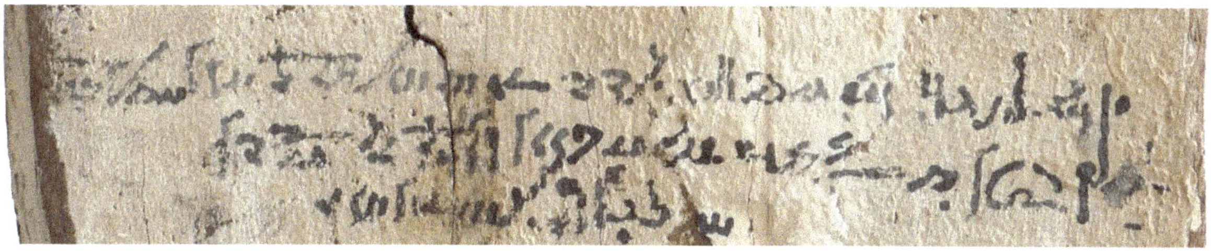

Figure 3. The stela's Demotic colophon.

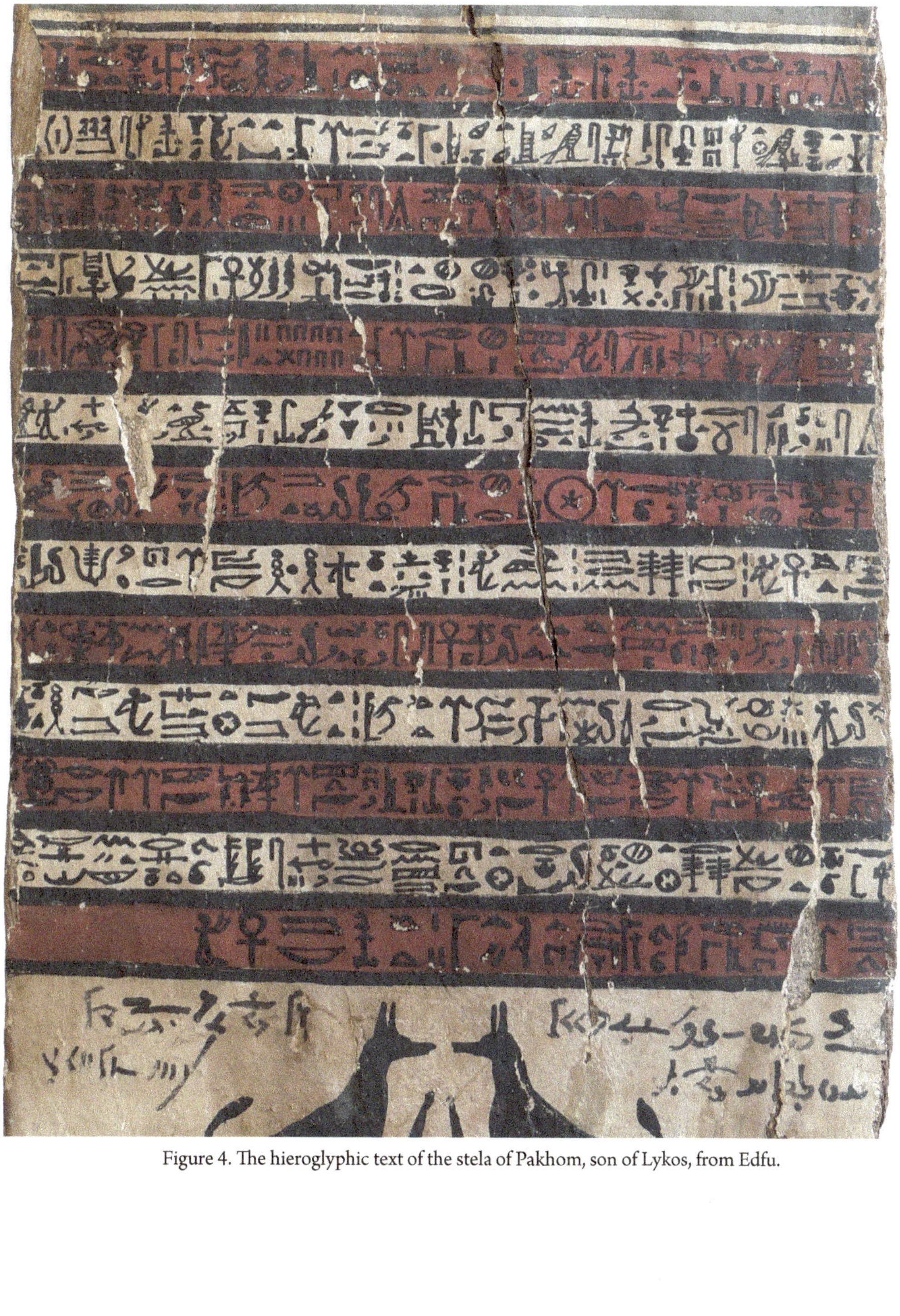

Figure 4. The hieroglyphic text of the stela of Pakhom, son of Lykos, from Edfu.

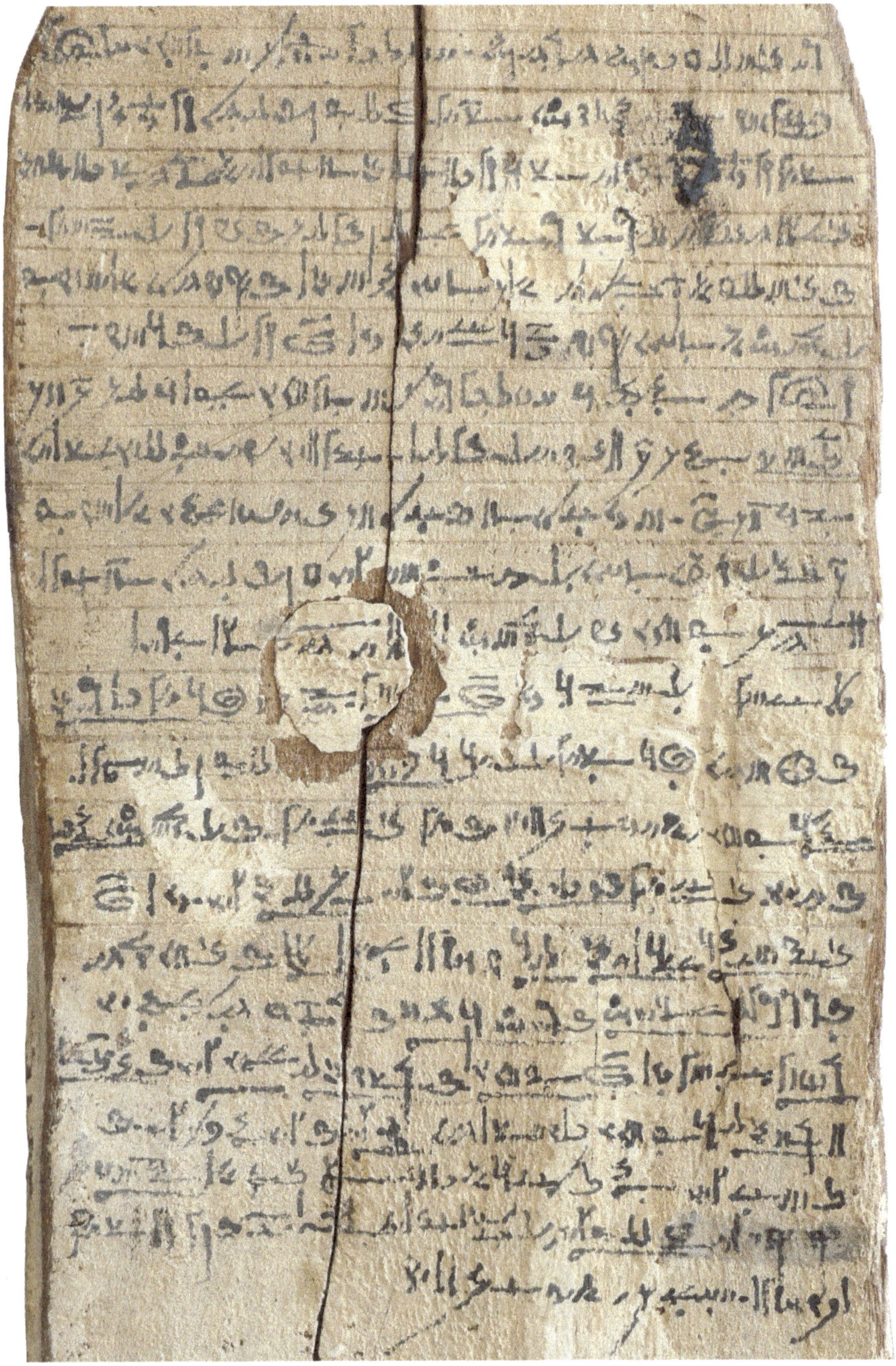

Figure 5. The demotic paraphrase of the offering formula and of the beginning of the Book of Traversing Eternity on the stela of Pakhom, son of Lykos, from Edfu.

Horus and Seth from North Saqqara: A Demotic Papyrus Fragment Excavated by the EES at the Sacred Animal Necropolis

John Tait

It is a delight to join in honoring Richard. This edition is offered to him out of respect and affection—and with the hope that he will find some appeal in the challenges posed by such a battered fragment. The varied issues that it raises lie in some of the fields to which he has made distinguished contributions: the law, the literature, and the religion of the Late, Greek, and Roman periods of Egypt.

The fragment published here was one of some seven hundred finds of papyrus fragments that came to light in the Egypt Exploration Society's Sacred Animal Necropolis excavations, when in the 1966–1967 season Professor Emery shifted the focus of the work to the north of the Central Temple Enclosure, to the area now known as the "Northern Enclosure."[1] Harry Smith and the present writer published in 1983 an EES Texts from Excavations volume,[2] which included 27 papyri,[3] chiefly from the Northern Enclosure, but also from other areas of the site. The intention there was to make available as many fragments as possible that had been identified, or might possibly be identified, as "literary,"[4] but some items had to be held over[5] and it is hoped that their piecemeal publication may soon be completed.[6]

1. For an overview of the work and of the finds, see Harry Sidney Smith, Sue Davies, and Kenneth J. Frazer, *The Sacred Animal Necropolis at North Saqqara: The Main Temple Complex: The Archaeological Report*, EES EM 75 (London: Egypt Exploration Society, 2006), 5, 8, 112–22; see fig. b, fig. 3, 5–6. The terminology and the conclusions of that work are adopted here: thus the findspot of H5-DP79 is here denoted as the "Northern Enclosure," rather than the "North Courtyard" used in some earlier accounts. Compare the comments in William John Tait, "Issues in the Dating of Saqqara Papyri," in *New Approaches in Demotic Studies: Acts of the 13th International Conference of Demotic Studies, Leipzig, September 4–8, 2017*, ed. Franziska Naether, *ZÄS* Beiheft 10 (Berlin: de Gruyter, 2019), 295–302.

2. Harry Sidney Smith and William John Tait, *Saqqara Demotic Papyri 1*, EES TEM 7; Excavations at North Saqqara, Documentary Series 5, 1 (London: Egypt Exploration Society, 1983): TM 56122–4, 56128, 56144–67; cf. 58896–7, 91019–20.

3. Strictly, 28 papyri, as "1a" is a quite separate papyrus, although the contents relate to those of 1.

4. See Smith and Tait, *Saqqara Demotic Papyri 1*, page x: "The papyri here edited are principally of literary or didactic content, though some narratives which might belong to either a literary or a documentary genre are included."

5. Harry Smith, while devoting himself to other plans for the publication of EES North Saqqara material, kindly suggested that the present writer proceed alone with the publication of the remaining literary material: over several seasons, at the Beit Emery dig house, and thereafter, we pored over all the texts together, and his contributions and encouragement are here gratefully acknowledged. Thanks are also due to the EES for their support of the present writer's work at the North Saqqara site over several years, and to Jan Geisbusch and Carl Graves at the EES office, for their help toward the production of this publication. Further debts of gratitude are owed to Richard Pierce, who first pointed out, during a study season at Saqqara, that this fragment deserved special attention, and to participants in the 8e école d'été démotique, Paris, 2015, where the Horus and Seth text was presented, for light cast both on the nature of the composition and on problems of reading, especially Sandra Lippert, Edward Love, Claudia Maderna-Sieben, Joachim Quack, and Alexandra von Lieven.

6. One such papyrus has already appeared as William John Tait, "A Date with Usima῾rē῾," in *Hieratic, Demotic, and Greek Studies and Text Editions: of Making Many Books there is no End: Festschrift in Honour of Sven P. Vleeming*, ed. Koenraad Donker van Heel, Francisca A. J. Hoogendijk, and Cary J. Martin, PLB 34 (Leiden: Brill, 2018), 157–61, pl. 33: Saq. H5-DP 444 [2365], TM 754224, registered March 1968 (found 1966–1967), from the Northern Enclosure.

Figure 1. HS-DP79, front.

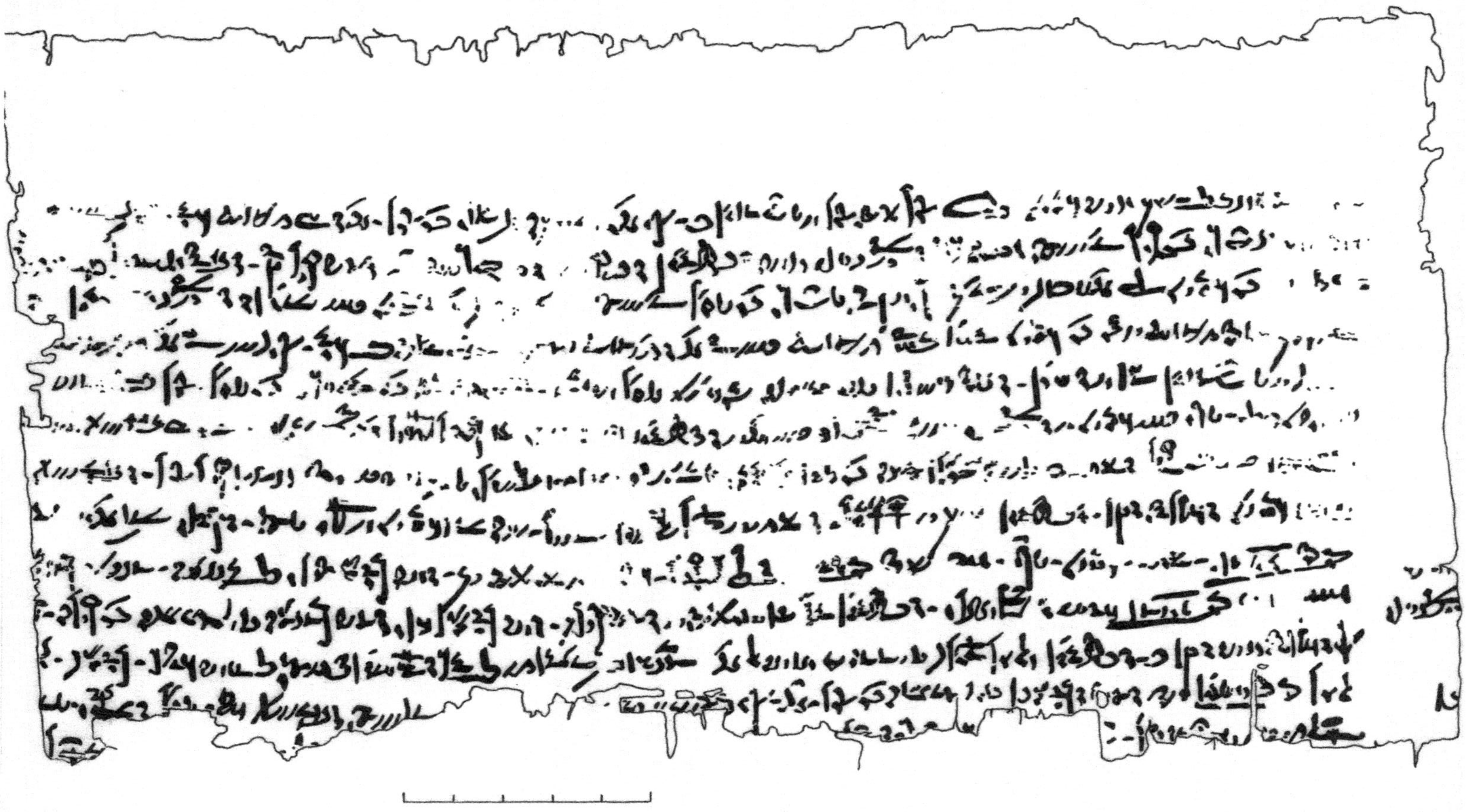

Figure 2. HS-DP79, handcopy.

Description

The fragment has the Excavators' number H5-DP79 (figs. 1 and 2).[7] The dimensions are 16.0 cm height × 29.0 cm width. The papyrus is opaque, thick, and coarse textured. Its shade is uneven: in places it is light brown, and it is generally paler where most abraded. The front (⟷) surface is very badly rubbed, and so, to a lesser extent, is the back (↕) surface. In places the papyrus is thus made translucent or is even worn completely through. It is dirty and has many grains of sand adhering. No thorough attempt has been made to remove these, for fear of causing further damage to the ink of the text.[8] The complete breadth of one sheet of papyrus is preserved (a width of about 16.0 cm is visible on the front), and parts of two others. There is one join at the right-hand edge of the fragment, 1.0–1.3 cm wide. The other is 12.5 cm from the left-hand edge, and 16.0–17.0 cm from the right-hand edge: it also is 1.0–1.3 cm wide. These joins are right-over-left, as is to be expected. The central sheet is up to 17.0 cm wide (that is, including the width of both joins).[9]

The front (⟷) surface preserves parts of two columns of continuous Demotic text. Of the first column, there are only a few traces at the ends of some of the lines. Parts of the first thirteen lines of the second[10] column are preserved. In every line, the ends of the lines are lost. The bottom edge of the fragment is irregularly torn, and a section in the middle of line 12 is missing, while several parts of line 13 are lost. The surviving line length as preserved is 27.5 cm in line 1, decreasing steadily to 26.5 cm in line 13. A top margin of 3.5 cm is preserved. Although the top edge is uneven, it presumably represents approximately the original top edge of the roll. The bottom edge is torn in a more irregular fashion.

The right-hand edge of col. x+2 is positioned just inside a sheet-join. Several literary papyri from North Saqqara consistently align the beginnings of columns with a sheet-join (P. Dem. Saq. i, **1**, **2**, **5**, and possibly also **7**).[11] If H5-DP79 similarly aligned its columns, then the amount lost from col. x+2 can be estimated. One column can hardly have occupied three (or more) sheets, as this would imply a column of unparalleled breadth. If each column occupied two sheets, and the sheet-widths were reasonably consistent, then a column-width of roughly 32.0 cm might be expected, and thus about 4.0–6.0 cm would be lost.

The back (↕) surface preserves very faint traces of a Demotic text, clearly a running account.[12] This is written the same way up relative to the text on the front. For the record, it is shown in figure 3. The present left- and right-hand edges of the fragment appear to have been cut, rather than torn: the natural assumption is that "Horus and Seth" was the original text written upon a roll that was later cut up into sections to be used for accounts. However, the piece is generally in a poorer condition than that of most of the fragments from the Northern Enclosure, and the fact that the

7. The Antiquities Service Site-Register number is 1677; the fragment was registered in April 1967. The text was at one time designated to be P. Dem. Saq. 31: this number may be worth recording here, as it has occasionally been mentioned in the past.

8. The plates here derive from photographs—of a document very difficult to photograph—taken by the late Hazel Smith. The hand-copy of col. x+2 reproduced here (fig. 2) was traced upon the original and revised over several seasons by the present writer: as ever, such a copy can serve only to record what an individual thought they saw. After discussion, it has been decided *not* to add the customary hatching to mark damage, especially as there would be few signs that did not call for extensive hatching, and (at 1:1) the result would be so cluttered as to be of very little use.

9. Sheet widths in the Saqqara papyri from the EES excavations were surveyed in William John Tait, "The Physical Characteristics of the Papyri," in *Proceedings of the XIV International Congress of Papyrologists, Oxford, 24–31 July 1974*, EES GRM 61 (London: Egypt Exploration Society for the British Academy, 1975), 262–64.

10. References here to line numbers with no mention of the column are naturally to the main column, col. x+2.

11. The use of sheet joins as guides has been discussed, and examples in other Demotic papyri cited, in William John Tait, "Guidelines and Borders in Demotic Papyri," in *Papyrus: Structure and Usage*, ed. Morris L. Bierbrier, BMOP 60 (London: British Museum, 1986), 63–89 (see esp. 69–70).

12. At the beginning of the first line of what may be taken as the second column, *sp*, "remainder" is clear, and the line probably ends *wp-st*, the abbreviation introducing a listing, "viz."

Figure 3. H5-DP79, back.

writing on both surfaces is badly rubbed suggests that it received exceptionally rough handling before it was finally discarded.

Hand

The hand of the mythological text upon the front deserves some description. At first glance, it appears rather different from the other literary hands from the North Saqqara site, but this impression is perhaps due partly to a number of individual unusual writings peculiar to the content, which are discussed below.

The hand is a comparatively small,[13] upright, rounded literary hand. It shows a limited tendency to follow a notional baseline but does not observe any upper headline. The line spacing therefore cannot be measured in any simple mechanical way; it gradually increases slightly towards the bottom of the fragment: in the first few lines the mean is perhaps 9 mm, but towards the last few lines it becomes close to 10 mm. The hand has a superficial resemblance to the hands of **4** and **5** already published from North Saqqara,[14] but it does not share their speed and their emphasis on diagonal strokes. It is not very flowing, and vertical strokes are usually made with deliberate precision. Some long strokes that are made in the direction ↙, notably the tail of *=f*, have an awkward double bend in them (e.g., *=f* in …*=f r Ḏdt* in line 8), and the extended tail of *ir=f* in line 10 is not very deftly executed. Some ligatures and freely made groups of strokes do occur, as, for example, final *y* (including suffix *=y*). Occasionally, vertical strokes show a slight curvature, or a turning flick of ink at their lower end, where the pen has started to move on to the next stroke before being lifted from the page. In very general terms, the writing has the appearance of having been made with move-

13. Small, that is, especially compared to the hands of Smith and Tait, *Saqqara Demotic Papyri 1*, 1, 2 (pls. 1–9).
14. Smith and Tait, pl. 11.

ments more of the fingers than of the whole hand. The North Saqqara hand to which, on close examination, it shows the greatest similarity is that of **1a**,[15] even though at first sight the papyri look very different. The resemblances are considerable: ultimately, however, it does not seem possible to maintain that the two texts are actually the work of the same hand. Among other considerations, the distinctive form of *ḏd* in H5-DP79 (typically )[16] is quite unlike the more familiar form found in **1a** (see lines 6, 7, 8, 9, 17, 19, 21, and 22 there).

The text contains a number of writings of words that appear elaborate, archaic, or even "hieratic." This might give rise to speculation, either that the manuscript was remarkably early in date, or that it showed signs of being copied (directly or indirectly) from a hieratic original. Some possible examples are debatable for one reason or another, but four of the more straightforward are *ḥm*, "Majesty," "Person" (col. x+2/2 bis, /7 bis, /9, /10 bis); *tꜣ Mḥw*, "Lower Egypt" (/2 bis, /6, /8, /10, /11: note the det., as well as the form of the papyrus-clump sign, and cf. *tꜣ Šmʿ* in col. x+1/x+2, col. x+2/2, /3, /6); *ḥḏt*, "White Crown" (/9); and *dšrt*, "Red Crown" (/10) (see table 1). The form of *Ḏdt* in /7 and /8 might also be considered, and some of the problematic unread groups in the second half of /6. Lengthy argument or detailed comment on individual writings would be out of place here, but two brief general observations may be offered: (1) Some of the words in question are rare or even unparalleled in Demotic—and this is not surprising, given the subject matter of the papyrus. Thus, we are not really in a position to say what "normal" writings of them would be. In a number of cases, parallels can be found. Arguably, nothing in the orthography is so out of place as to establish that the text was copied from hieratic, and the problems of the origins of the version preserved here must be debated on other grounds. (2) The manuscript of H5-DP79 may well be speculated to be a little earlier in date than such papyri as **1** and **2**, but the difference might be of the order of fifty years, or one hundred at most. The hands of the letters from North Saqqara of course form a series separate from the literary hands, but points of resemblance may be seen between literary hands such as those of **1** and **2** and those letters that are probably the latest from the site, while H5-DP79 has similarities to one or two letters that might be dated rather earlier.[17]

Table 1

ḥm		(selection only)
		Col. x+2/2
		/7
ḥm=k		
		/2
		/7

15. Smith and Tait, pl. 3.

16. The lack of the top part of the main sign might be taken as a feature of early Demotic. The final stroke at the bottom left perhaps represents a more general phenomenon: useful parallels can be seen in some of the Loeb papyri, where the presence or absence of this final stroke can be influenced by whether or not a suffix follows, and whether or not *ḏd* stands at the end of the line. See Wilhelm Spiegelberg, *Die demotischen Papyri Loeb*, Papyri der Universität München 1 (Munich: Beck, 1931); note especially papyri nos. 4, 6–9.

17. Compare the remarks in Tait, "Issues in the Dating of Saqqara Papyri," 299.

ḥm=f		
		/10
ḥm=s		
		/10
tꜣ Mḥw		
		Col. x+2/2 (second occurrence only)
		/6
		/8
		/10
		/11
tꜣ Šmʿ		
		Col. x+1/x+2
		Col. x+2/2
		/3
		/6
tꜣ ḥḏt		
		Col. x+2/9
tꜣ dšrt		
		Col. x+2/10

The hand of H5-DP79 shows a tendency to add small high dots and short strokes similar to those noted in the case of **1**, **1a**(?), and **2**. In the case of H5-DP79, these marks could more easily than in **1** and **2** be taken as an integral part of the writing, but they nevertheless seem to be of the same kind. Nothing can usefully be added here to the discussion of this feature in *Saqqara Demotic Papyri 1*, 3–4. The damaged state of the papyrus may have obscured some instances. Clear and unambiguous examples may be seen in col. x+2/3, *my d=w*, /4, *bn p̓w=w*, and /5, *nꜣ sẖ.w*.

Provenances and Date

These issues have been raised in the preceding paragraphs, and some aspects discussed elsewhere. To summarize:

For the modern findspot—the "Northern Enclosure" at North Saqqara—see note 1 above. The place of writing of the Horus and Seth text is quite uncertain, and there is only a slim possibility that this was in the Sacred Animal Necropolis itself. Even the account on the back surface could have been written elsewhere, and the fragment could subsequently have reached the Necropolis simply as scrap papyrus. The hand (see above), although distinctive, is sufficiently similar to that of other Saqqara material that the papyrus may perhaps have originated in the Memphite area.

The date of writing of the Horus and Seth manuscript can be judged only on common-sense grounds, from the context of the Northern Enclosure (thus unlikely, as a *terminus ante quem*, to fall after 355 BCE[18]), and from assessment of the palaeography, which remains as yet a rather subjective matter: around 400 BCE may be the best guess at present.

For the date of composition of the text as preserved, the usual caution is in order. Texts may, of course, be repeatedly revised whenever copied; the language is essentially Demotic, and a few peculiarities (e.g., *hr.w* as the term for "documents" in lines 1 and 4; *st*, "place," "throne" in lines 7, 8, and 9; *iw*, "came" in line 7) are not straightforward enough to hint at a pre-Demotic version.

Content

A broad spectrum of Egyptian textual material, from a wide range of dates, alludes to the "myth" of Horus and Seth. Only a small proportion of this both *concentrates* upon Horus and Seth, and is wholly or essentially narrative in nature, and among these compositions, it is usual to see some differences of genre and of purpose.[19] In hieratic, versions are found in MK fragments from Kahun,[20] in the well-preserved NK Contendings of Horus and Seth from Thebes,[21] and later

18. See Tait, 296–97.

19. Overviews include J. Gwyn Griffiths, *The Conflict of Horus and Seth from Egyptian and Classical Sources: A Study in Ancient Mythology*, Liverpool Monographs in Archaeology and Oriental Studies (Liverpool: Liverpool University Press, 1960), and Günter Burkard and Heinz Josef Thissen, *Einführung in die altägyptische Literaturgeschichte II: Neues Reich*, 2nd ed., EQÄ 6 (Münster: LIT, 2009), 35–47; several aspects have been reviewed by Mark J. Smith, "The Reign of Seth: Egyptian Perspectives from the First Millennium BCE," in *Egypt in Transition: Social and Religious Development of Egypt in the First Millennium BCE: Proceedings of an International Conference, Prague, September 1–4, 2009*, ed. Ladislav Bareš, Filip Coppens, and Květa Smolárikov (Prague: Czech Institute of Egyptology, Charles University in Prague, 2010), 396–430.

20. Petrie lot VI.2: UC32158, published by Francis Ll. Griffith, *The Petrie Papyri: Hieratic Papyri from Kahun and Gurob* (London: Quaritch, 1898), 1:4, 64–65; 2:pl. III, XXVI, a, and Mark A. Collier and Stephen G. Quirke, *The UCL Lahun Papyri: Religious, Literary, Legal, Mathematical and Medical*, BAR-IS 1209 (Oxford: Archaeopress, 2004), 20–21.

21. First published by Alan H. Gardiner, *The Library of A. Chester Beatty: Description of a Hieratic Papyrus with a Mythological Story, Love-songs, and other Miscellaneous Texts*, The Chester Beatty Papyri 1 (London: Privately printed by J. Johnson at the Oxford University Press and published by E. Walker, 1931), and included in Alan H. Gardiner, *Late-Egyptian Stories*, BiAe 1 (Bruxelles: Édition de la Fondation égyptologique reine Élisabeth, 1932). A wide-ranging study is Michèle Broze, *Mythe et roman en Égypte ancienne: Les aventures d'Horus et Seth dans le papyrus Chester Beatty I*, OLA 76 (Leuven: Peeters, 1996).

fragments from Elephantine.[22] In Demotic, Horus and Seth narratives are already well known in several collections,[23] and the myth can also be treated in other ways.[24]

The narrative presentation in the Saqqara fragment follows the manner of Demotic stories in general. There is nothing that strikingly recalls the distinctive, "formulaic" phraseology of New Kingdom narratives.[25] There is much use of direct speech, and at least once a character repeats what (they claim) another has said.[26] There is also, however, no sign of the type of standard phraseology that the present writer has suggested helps to structure many of our Demotic narratives.[27] Dates (season, month, day) occur three times in lines 7–10, but these are essential to the myth, rather than serving merely to organize the narrative. The layout of the text does not hint at any formal subdivision of the story.[28]

Apart from one passage, it would seem easy to characterize the composition as a "narrative." However, in lines 11–12, an explanation (punctuated by the verb *ḫpr*) is offered of the significance of the reactions of Isis's eyes when they look at Seth and at Horus.[29] What is not clear is whether the ancient audience would have seen some of this passage as a gloss interrupting the narrative, or simply have taken the words as a natural continuation of the speech of Isis/Wadjet in her own person. The whole of the surviving passage is surely concerned to cast light upon a number of features of cult and kingship[30]—and indeed this is surely a principal aim of all our Horus and Seth compositions.

Aside from this passage, the story shows every sign of employing the usual external narrator typical of Demotic stories, impersonal and neutral.[31] As always in the case of a mere fragment, it is impossible to be sure of this, just as it can be only an assumption that this is a fragment of a substantial, consistent, and continuous story, rather than a story-within-a-story, or a narrative passage included in a composition of quite another kind.

---

22. P. Berlin 23068: Joachim F. Quack, "Der Streit zwischen Horus und Seth in einer spätneuägyptischen Fassung," in *"Parcourir l'éternité": hommages à Jean Yoyotte*, ed. Christiane Zivie-Coche and Ivan Guermeur (Turnhout: Brepols, 2012), 907–21.

23. See Karl-Theodor Zauzich, "Der Streit zwischen Horus und Seth in einer demotischen Fassung," in *Grammata demotika: Festschrift für Erich Lüddeckens zum 15. Juni 1983*, ed. Heinz Josef Thissen and Karl-Theodor Zauzich (Würzburg: Gisela Zauzich Verlag, 1984), 275–81, pl. 38; Friedhelm Hoffmann, "Der literarische demotische Papyrus Wien D6920–22," *SAK* 23 (1996): 167–200, Taf. 3–4 (cf. Friedhelm Hoffmann, and Joachim Friedrich Quack, *Anthologie der demotischen Literatur*, 2nd, rev. and augmtd. ed., EQÄ 4 [Berlin: LIT, 2018], 205), and Kim Ryholt, "The Contendings of Horus and Seth (P. Carlsberg 676 verso)," in *Narrative Literature from the Tebtunis Temple Library*, ed. Kim Ryholt (Copenhagen: Museum Tusculanum Press, 2012), 171–80.

24. Note especially François P. Gaudard, "The Demotic Drama of Horus and Seth (P. Berlin 8278a, b, c; 15662; 15677; 15818; 23536; 23537a, b, c, d, e, f, g)" (PhD diss., University of Chicago, 2005).

25. See for example the discussions of Fritz Hintze, *Untersuchungen zu Stil und Sprache neuägyptischer Erzählungen*, 2 vols, Deutsche Akademie der Wissenschaften zu Berlin, Institut für Orientforschung, Veröffentlichung, Nr. 2, 6 (Berlin: Akademie-Verlag, 1950–1952), Jan Assmann, "Das ägyptische Zweibrüdermärchen (Papyrus D'Orbiney): Eine Textanalyse auf drei Ebenen am Leitfaden der Einheitsfrage," *ZÄS* 104 (1977): 1–25, and Günter Burkard, "Metrik, Prosodie und formaler Aufbau ägyptischer literarischer Texte," in *Ancient Egyptian Literature: History and Forms*, ed. Antonio Loprieno (Leiden: Brill, 1996), 447–63. For some such features within the NK Contendings of Horus and Seth, see Broze, *Mythe et roman en Égypte ancienne*, 157–220.

26. In line 2: probably it is Horus who repeats (in the presence of Preʿ and Thoth and others) what Preʿ had previously said to him. We cannot tell whether or not the audience of the whole story had already heard these words. Although Seth quickly raises an objection, he does not seem to challenge Horus's actual statement.

27. See William John Tait, "The Sinews of Demotic Narrative," in *Narratives of Egypt and the Ancient Near East: Literary and Linguistic Approaches*, ed. Fredrik Hagen, et al., OLA 189 (Leuven: Peeters, 2011), 397–410.

28. That is, there is no division into "paragraphs" by wider line-spacing or indentation (the beginnings of the lines in the main column are preserved, or nearly preserved).

29. Ideas relating to the eye or to eyes permeate many versions of the myth.

30. For example, the dates mentioned presumably relate to feasts and commemorations of the events.

31. In line 5, Preʿ becomes angry, but this does not show the narrator as having insight into the god's emotions: his actions are in question, his outward display of wrath; compare the remarks of William John Tait, "Anger and Agency: the Role of the Emotions in Demotic and Earlier Narratives," in *"Being in Ancient Egypt": Thoughts on Agency, Materiality and Cognition: Proceedings of the Seminar Held in Copenhagen, September 29–30, 2006*, ed. Rune Nyord and Annette Kjølby (Oxford: Archaeopress, 2009), 75–82.

The plot (the *fabula*) of the Saqqara fragment, in respect of the position of Ra as supreme authority, the nature of the character of Seth (as a chancer rather than a demonic figure),[32] and the role of Thoth, evokes the handling of the whole myth in the New Kingdom "Contendings of Horus and Seth,"[33] although the Saqqara fragment does not match any episode in the New Kingdom version, and clearly follows a different story-line. In fact, for the provisional coronations of both Seth and Horus, the obvious parallel lies in the "Memphite Theology,"[34] although there the proceedings before the Ennead are wholly directed by Geb.

Transliteration

FRONT
col. x+1

x+1.]....
x+2.] *Šmꜥ*
x+3. no trace
x+4.] ⸢*ỉr=w*⸣

col. x+2

top margin of 3.5 cm

1. *..[..] ⸢mdt⸣ nb ỉ-ỉr ḫpr n-ỉm=f ỉrm St m-bꜣḥ Ḏḥwty nw Ḏḥwty r pꜣ nẖb nty n-ḏrt Ḥr ⸢gm=f⸣ -s ⸢ỉw⸣=f wḏꜣ ḏd Ḏḥwty n Ḥr nꜣy=k hr.w st ....[*
2. *[.]…. nb ḏd ḥm=k ṯꜣy-y n=k tꜣ nty ⸢mr=k -s⸣ [n] tꜣ Šmꜥ ỉrm tꜣ Mḥw tꜣ Mḥw tꜣ ⸢nty⸣ mr=y ⸢-s⸣ ⸢tꜣy⸣ nꜣ-nfr ḥm wꜥ n nꜣ wpṱy.w .....[*
3. *…. ḏd St in Ḥr pꜣ nty ỉw=f r ṯꜣy ⸢n⸣=f [pꜣ] tꜣ r ink pꜣ nb ḏd pꜣ-Rꜥ ṯꜣy-y n=k …… ⸢ḏd⸣ ⸢St⸣ my d=w n(=y) tꜣ Šmꜥ …[.].[*
4. *…..=f ⸢ỉr⸣=w n=w hr.w r-r=w ḏd St bn-pw=w ỉr n=n hr.w my in Ḥr nꜣ hr.w ………… st n-ḏrt.ṱ=y in Ḥr ⸢nꜣ⸣ ⸢hr.w⸣ [*
5. *[..]…ṱ r pꜣ nẖb wḏꜣ r nꜣ sẖ.w n nꜣ wpṱy.w ḥr-ꜣt.ṱ=. ẖrꜥr pꜣ-Rꜥ r St …… ḏd grꜥ ḏd pꜣ-Rꜥ ⸢n⸣ Ḏḥwty m-⸢šm⸣ ….[*
6. *⸢pꜣ tꜥ⸣ḥ nty ḫpr n pꜣ tꜣ my St r tꜣ Šmꜥ ……. my Ḥr r tꜣ Mḥw ………………… tꜣy=k wty [*
7. *…. m⸢y⸣ ḏd ḥm=k tꜣ st nty ỉw=⸢y dt⸣ ẖꜥ=w n-ỉm=s ḏd pꜣ-Rꜥ ⸢Ḏdt⸣ pꜣ ẖn … ẖꜥ Šw pꜣy n ꜣbd-⸢3⸣ ꜣẖt sw 4 ỉw ḥm n Ḏḥwty n tꜣ wty [*
8. *⸢ỉrm⸣ St nꜣ nṯrw nꜣ rmṯ.w n tꜣ Mḥw …=f r Ḏdt n tꜣ st r ẖꜥ šw n … n-ỉm=s d[=f] St r Rs pꜣ bnr n tꜣ nỉwt d=f Ḥr r ⸢Mḥt⸣ [*

32. Note the observations of Smith, "The Reign of Seth," esp. 398–404, alongside the analyses of Herman te Velde, *Seth, God of Confusion: A Study of His Role in Egyptian Mythology and Religion*, PdÄ 6 (Leiden: Brill, 1967), and Alexandra von Lieven, "Seth ist im Recht, Osiris ist im Unrecht! Sethkultorte und ihre Version des Osiris-Mythos," *ZÄS* 133 (2006): 141–50.

33. In the NK composition, the status of Ra (and even his appellations: e.g., Re-Harakhty, Re-Atum, etc.) are not quite straightforward.

34. For an overview, see Hartwig Altenmüller, "Denkmal memphitischer Theologie," *LÄ* 1:1065–69. For the sections on the division of Egypt, see Kurt Sethe, *Dramatische Texte zu altägyptischen Mysterienspielen*, Untersuchungen zur Geschichte und Altertumskunde Aegyptens 10 (Leipzig: Hinrichs, 1928), 23, 27 (cols. 7–9, 10a–12a), and Hermann Junker, *Die politische Lehre von Memphis*, APAW 6 (Berlin: de Gruyter, 1941), 23–31, Taf. 1. Compare Dimitri Meeks, *Mythes et légendes du Delta d'après le papyrus Brooklyn 47.218.84*, Mémoires publiés par les membres de l'Institut français d'archéologie orientale 125 (Cairo: Institut Français d'Archéologie Orientale, 2006), 26, 266–67.

9. *ỉr=f n=w nꜥ.w n st n St n pꜣ tꜣ n ꜣbd-3 ⸢ꜣḫt⸣ sw 4 ỉr=f ⸢smn⸣ tꜣ ḥḏt n ḥm n ⸢St⸣ r ꜣst nw r-r=f n tꜣỉy=s ỉrt wnm ḫpr fṱ=s n bỉn n ḥꜣt* [
10. *ꜣbd-4 ⸢ꜣḫt⸣ sw ⸢4⸣ ỉr=f nꜥ.w smn tꜣ dšrt n tꜣ Mḥw n Ḥr ỉw ⸢ꜣst⸣ nw r ⸢nꜣ-nfr⸣ ḥm=f n tꜣỉy=s ỉrt ỉꜣbt nꜣ-nfr ḥꜣt=s ḥr-ꜣt.t.ṱ=s ḏd ḥm=s n* . [
11. *ỉ nꜣ nṯrw ỉrm nꜣ rmṯw nty n tꜣ Mḥw Wꜣḏt ḫꜥ.ṱ ḥr ḏꜣḏꜣ n pꜣy=s šr Ḥr ṯꜣty ...=f ṯꜣy ꜥwy ḫpr rn=s sp šꜥ-bnr ḫpr pꜣy=s smt n ỉrt.ṱ n* .[
12. *Wꜣḏt ỉr=f šꜥ pꜣ hrw r dt nꜣ-nfr nꜣ ỉrt.ṱ.w ḥr-⸢ꜣt.ṱ⸣=s ḏd Ḏḥwty n Ḥr n-ḏrt ⸢smn=f⸣* ....[.....] *⸢d⸣=y n=k tꜣ wty n pꜣ-Rꜥ tꜣ ỉꜣwt n p⸢ꜣy=k⸣* [*ỉt*
13. *ḥms .. pꜣ nḫb n ⸢nb⸣* [....]..........[..................]..[......]. *nb* [

Translation[35]

FRONT

col. x+1

x+1.] ....
x+2.] Upper Egypt
x+3. *no trace*
x+4.] they did

col. x+2

top margin of 3.5 cm

1. ..[..] everything which had happened to him together with Seth in the presence of Thoth. Thoth looked at the title which was in Horus's possession; he found that it was sound. Thoth said to Horus: Your documents, they are .... [
2. [.] .... Lord, Your Person has said: Take for yourself the one which you desire of Upper Egypt together with Lower Egypt. Lower Egypt is the one which I desire. The Person of one of the judges was favourable. ..... [
3. .... Seth said: Is Horus the one who shall take for himself [the] land, when I am the Lord? Preʿ said: Take for yourself ... . Seth said: Let Upper Egypt be given to me, ... [.] . [
4. .... They have made documents for them in respect of them. Seth said: They have *not* made documents for us. Let Horus bring the documents .... they are in my possession. Horus brought the documents [
5. [..] .... as the title was sound, and the writings of the judges were upon [them]. Preʿ was angry at Seth ...... speaking deceit. Preʿ said to Thoth: Go ..... [
6. the disturbance which has happened in the land. Place Seth in Upper Egypt ....; place Horus in Lower Egypt . ... your decree [
7. ..... Let your Person state the place in which I shall cause them to appear. Preʿ said: Mendes was the Residence ... of the appearing of Shu, in the 3rd month of Inundation, day 4. The Person of Thoth arrived by the decree [
8. together with Seth and the gods and the people of Lower Egypt. He ... to Mendes, in the place in which Shu appeared .... [He] placed Seth to the South, outside the city; he placed Horus to the North [

35. Nonspecialists should note that the sense of several key terms in the text is debatable. Also, it is often clear where a passage of direct speech begins, but *not* where it ends: therefore, no quotation marks have been included.

9. He made for them assemblies of enthronement for Seth in the land in the 3rd month of Inundation, day 4. He performed the setting of the White Crown upon the Person of Seth, as Isis saw him with her right eye. It happened that she was sick with evil of heart [
10. 4th month of Inundation, day 4. He performed assemblies, (and) setting the Red Crown of Lower Egypt upon Horus, as Isis saw that his Person was perfect with her left eye. Her heart was well because of it. Her Person said to . [
11. O gods together with men who are in Lower Egypt, Wadjet has arisen upon the head of her son Horus, the Vizier .... happen, her name remains henceforth, and the like has happened to the eye of . [
12. Wadjet. He has spent up to today in order to cause that eyes be well because of her/it. Thoth said to Horus when he had set .... [.....] I have given to you the decree of Preꜥ, the Office of your [father
13. sit ... the title of Lord [....] .... [..................] .. [......] . Lord [

Commentary

1. It is not evident from what survives whether in line 1 Horus is speaking privately with Thoth or before others also. By line 2, the scene may have shifted (and Ra is presumably already present), but it remains in doubt whether in lines 2–7 any of "the judges" and/or an assemblage of gods (the Ennead?) is at hand.
   — *pꜣ nḫb* 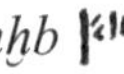 (in line 5: ): a fem. form is standard in the sense of the royal titulary, but the masc. is already attested (*DG* 225.3; CDD *N* [2004], 113.4); Joachim Quack suggests that in the present context, emphasizing legal documentation, the term may have a special meaning, perhaps of an authenticating seal. In line 13 below, *pꜣ nḫb n* ⸢*nb*⸣, "the title of Lord," if the reading is correct, there may be a similar nuance.
   — *ḥr.w*  (also four times in line 4), "documents":[36] the Demotic writing here recalls that of the verb *ḥr*, "to be content."
2. *wpṭy.w* (also in line 5) is standard in Demotic for "judges." Why "*one* of the judges" is in question here, and why they are seemingly unnamed, is unclear: possibly one of them acts as a spokesperson.
   — at end: *ḫpr* seems very probable immediately after *wꜥ n nꜣ wpṭy.w* (perhaps, "It happened ...").
3. *r ink pꜣ nb*: possibly "although I am *de facto* in charge."
4. .... *st n-ḏrt.ṯ=y*: in this much-rubbed passage, one might expect *ḏd Ḥr mdt ꜥḏ tꜣy st n-ḏrt.ṯ=y*, "Horus said: It is a lie; they are in my possession".
5. Although the reading of the suffix in *ḥr-ꜣt.ṯ=.* is doubtful, the writing of the judges would surely be upon "them," that is, *nꜣ ḥr.w*, "the documents."
6. *ḏd grꜥ*: Joachim Quack suggests the sense of misrepresentation; this would be distinct from *mdt ꜥḏ*, "lie," if that were the correct restoration in line 4.
   — *wty*: The word presents a crux, as it could be taken to represent several distinct words, including "creation" and "destruction" Although the first two writings are damaged, presumably all three had two groups as determinatives (phallus and documents), as in the third instance, and the same word is in question in all three passages.

36. Compare Francis Ll. Griffith, "The Teaching of Amenophis the Son of Kanakht: Papyrus B.M. 10474," *JEA* 12 (1926): 218n3; *Wb*. II:500, 26, *hrwj.t*, "Tagebuch"; Michel Malinine, *Choix de textes juridiques en hiératique "anormal" et en démotique (XXVe–XXVIIe dynasties), Première partie: Traduction et commentaire philologique*, Bibliothèque de l'École des hautes études, Sciences historiques et philologiques 300 (Paris: Honoré Champion, 1953), 13, n. to l. 17, 39–40, n. to l. 11, 48, n. to l. 20; Leonard H. Lesko, and Barbara S. Lesko, *A Dictionary of Late Egyptian*, rev. ed., 2 vols. (Providence, RI: Scribe, 2002–2004), 2:290, *hry*, "documents" etc.; Sandra L. Lippert, *Einführung in die altägyptische Rechtsgeschichte*, EQÄ 5 (Berlin: LIT, 2008), 62, 137.

6		*tꜣy=k wty*
7		*tꜣ wty*
12		*tꜣ wty*

If the determinatives are taken at face value, then "decree" is the most likely sense: CDD *W* (2009), 189.1, (*wt.t*), "utterance, command, decree." If this is correct, then the preposition *n* in line 7, *n tꜣ wty*, would have to bear the sense of "by," "in accordance with."[37]

7. *Ḏdt*: although *t* is clearly written, either Djedet, "Mendes" or Djedu, "Busiris" could be meant. Both have Osirian connections, and Shu is associated with both. Mendes might be suggested to be more likely, especially as its prominence through the Saite to Ptolemaic periods (particularly as the "capital" of the 29th Dynasty) make it plausible that it might be promoted as a place of coronation.[38]
   - *ỉw ḥm n Ḏḥwty*: the apparent *sḏm=f* of *ỉw* is unexpected for Demotic;[39] however this may be taken, the overall sense must be that Thoth's arrival is here narrated.
   - Unfortunately, parts of all the three dates (in lines 7, 9, 10) are damaged; it would be wrong to force readings based on their supposed significance. As matters purely of reading, it may be suggested
     - the season *ꜣḫt*, "inundation" is probably the same in line 7 and in line 9, but no judgement can be made in line 10;
     - the month number "3" is the same in line 7 and in line 9, but "4" is almost certain in line 10;
     - the day number "4" is the same in line 7 and in line 9 and could well be the same in line 10.

On purely common-sense grounds, the dates of the coronations of Seth and Horus must in some simple way echo that of Shu. The two natural possibilities are that Seth shares Shu's date, while Horus's coronation is exactly one month later (hence the need to state a separate date for the latter); or that all three share the same date (despite the difficulty of reading "3rd month" in line 10). In the context of myth, it would perhaps be inappropriate to question if both coronations could be crowded into a single day.

The Late-period traditions of listing feasts and commemorations are rich and vary from place to place. Although echoes of the Horus and Seth myth are frequent, no exact match for the possibilities in the Saqqara papyrus are apparent.[40]

37. For the writing and perhaps the phraseology, see Mark J. Smith, *The Mortuary Texts of Papyrus BM 10507*, CDPBM 3 (London: Published for the Trustees of the British Museum by British Museum Publications Limited, 1987), 117n(b).

38. For Mendes, see Herman De Meulenaere, and Pierre MacKay, *Mendes II* (Warminster: Aris & Phillips, 1976), 172–81; Herman De Meulenaere, "Mendes," *LÄ* 4:43–45; for Busiris, see Jürgen von Beckerath, "Busiris," *LÄ* 1:883–84; Kathryn A. Bard, "Busiris (Abu Sir Bana)," in *Encyclopedia of the Archaeology of Ancient Egypt*, ed. Kathryn A. Bard, with Steven Blake Shubert (London: Routledge, 1999), 179–80.

39. Janet H. Johnson, *The Demotic Verbal System*, second printing, with corrections, SAOC 38 (Chicago: The University of Chicago Press, 2004), 26, 66.

40. For overviews, see Emma Brunner-Traut, "Tagewählerei," *LÄ* 6:153–56; Alfred Grimm, *Die altägyptischen Festkalender in den Tempeln der griechisch-römischen Epoche*, ÄAT 15 (Wiesbaden: Harrassowitz, 1994); Filip Coppens, "Temple Festivals of the Ptolemaic and Roman Periods," *UCLAEE* 2009; Alexandra von Lieven, "Tagewählerei im Alten Ägypten," *Mythos* 10 (2016): 31–41.

8. *tꜣ st r ḫʿ Šw n … n-im=s*: despite the similarity, presumably *ḏšrt* is *not* to be read within this phrase, "the place where Shu appeared in *the Red Crown*," as the writing does not sufficiently match that in line 9; perhaps restore a different crown, or understand "as king/ruler" or similar.
   — *d*[*=f*]: The reading *d=f*, with no trace of the *=f* surviving, seems preferable to *d=w*, especially as *d=w* is written with an extra low dot in line 3 above.
   — *tꜣ niwt* (with article), "the city," cannot refer to Thebes, and presumably here refers to Djedet. See CDD *N* (2004), 18.3, with reference.
11. *Wꜣḏt* (or the writing could be interpreted as *Wʿtt*):[41] the first short stroke is unexpected and recalls a writing of *s-ḥmt* (which would be grammatically out of place here): the stroke is not present in the writing at the beginning of line 12.
   — *ṯꜣy ʿwy*: possibly a phrase with a sense like "to take over."
13. *pꜣ nḫb n ⸢nb⸣*, "the title of Lord," : all the signs are damaged, but seem distinctive, so that the reading is at least plausible. See n. on *pꜣ nḫb* in line 1 above.

41. For various forms, see CDD *W* (2009), 196.3, *Wt(.t)* with refs; Mark J. Smith, "The Provenience of Papyrus Harkness," in *Studies on Ancient Egypt in Honour of H. S. Smith*, ed. Anthony Leahy and John Tait (London: Egypt Exploration Society, 1999), 283–93, see p. 283–84; Christian Leitz, *Lexikon der ägyptischen Götter und Götterbezeichnungen*, 8 vols., OLA 110–16, 129 (Leuven: Peeters, 2002), 2:289; Ghislaine Widmer, *Résurrection d'Osiris – Naissance d'Horus: Les papyrus Berlin P. 6750 et Berlin P. 8765, témoignages de la persistance de la tradition sacerdotale dans le Fayoum à l'époque romaine*, ÄOP 3 (Berlin: de Gruyter, 2015), 257n(c).

Tabubue and the Menstrual Tabu

Steve Vinson

For a quarter of a century now, I've always regarded Richard Jasnow as something of a role model. Everything he did, I tried to do, but I could never do it quite as well. We both worked for a time at Chicago House, but I was there for half a season, while Richard went on to become chief epigrapher. We both studied at Würzburg with Karl-Theodor Zauzich, but I was there for only two years; Richard went on to become Prof. Zauzich's academic assistant. We both have a connection to The Johns Hopkins University, but while I got my PhD in the Hopkins Department of Near Eastern Studies, Richard went on to become a full professor there. We've even shared the mentoring of a student who attended both our Egyptology programs; but while I got this student through to the MA level at Indiana University, she's going on with Richard to earn her own PhD at Hopkins. Most important of all, as a Demotic scholar, I could never hope to even approach Richard's skill and erudition, nor his incredible knack for delivering a lecture—perhaps on the interpretation of an obscure and esoteric text like the Demotic Book of Thoth, or on some impossibly difficult problem of Demotic paleography—that is not only scholarly and substantive to the highest degree, but also delightful and actually hilarious. But Richard has also always been more than generous with advice and encouragement, and I have benefited from knowing him in ways too numerous to count. I hope that he'll enjoy this short contribution, and I look forward to hearing what he thinks of it.

With this discussion, I would like to expand on a provocative and persuasive discussion by Jens Jørgensen in the 2015 volume *Lotus and Laurel: Studies on Egyptian Language and Religion in Honour of Paul John Frandsen,* and apply it to a problematic passage in the Demotic First Tale of Setne Khaemwas (First Setne).[1] In his study "Myths, Menarche and the *Return of the Goddess,*" Jørgensen argues that the myth of the Distant Goddess—that is, the complex of goddesses who are conceived of generally as daughters and defenders of the sun god Re, who depart from Egypt, and who then return, inaugurating the new beginning of the agricultural cycle and the renewal of the cycle of life—may be rooted in rituals connected to the onset of menstruation among adolescent girls. Jørgensen himself stresses that any such rituals are otherwise unknown from ancient Egypt, and were, in his view, probably already obsolete during most of Egyptian history, as it is known to us, leaving behind only their traces in myth.

The anthropological aand sociological aspects of Jørgensen's thesis strike me as rather speculative, but they are not actually central to his overall discussion. The particular value of his discussion is the case he makes for the more general notion that the mythological and ritual texts connected to the worship of the Distant Goddess employ substantial symbolism related to menstruation. Specifically, he argues the blue-green minerals (i.e., lapis lazuli and turquoise, along with their manufactured imitation, faience) that are occasionally said to have been "scattered" in Distant Goddess ritual texts symbolize the goddess's menstrual blood, transformed from a threatening red (linked to her rage) to a blue-green that represents her pacification and her role in bringing new life to Egypt.

1. Jens J. ørgensen, "Myths, Menarche and the *Return of the Goddess,*" in *Lotus and Laurel: Studies on Egyptian Language and Religion in Honour of Paul John Frandsen*, ed. Rune Nyord and Kim Ryholt (Copenhagen: Museum Tusculanum Press, University of Copenhagen, 2015), 133–64.

For reasons of brevity, I quote only one of Jørgensen's proof texts, from P. Brooklyn 47.218.84, 9.2–3 (his translation):

> Bubastis. Concerning Bastet who is in Bubastis: This is the efflux when she came forth as Horit on the eastern mountain of Heliopolis. The blood came forth from her and it transformed into turquoise.[2]

In the discussion that follows, I would like to bring Jørgensen's suggestion to bear on First Setne 5.15–16, in which the formidable and terrifying Tabubue's salon is described in these terms:

> *ỉw=s sḥr ỉw=s nḏḫ ỉw pꜣy=s sḥre nḏḫe n ḫstb n mꜣʿ.t mfke n mꜣʿ.t*

In my own recent study of First Setne (*The Craft of a Good Scribe: History, Narrative and Meaning in the First Tale of Setne Khaemwas*), I rendered this somewhat indecisively as:

> … swept (?) and purified (?), its floor (? or, ceiling?) glittering (?) with true lapis-lazuli and true turquoise.

The immediate points of contact between this passage and the broader cultic phenomena discussed by Jørgensen are (1) the connection of blue-green minerals to a threatening, quasidivine female, and (2) the "dispersal" (to translate, for the moment, *nḏḫ/nḏḫe* as noncommittally as possible) of these minerals around Tabubue's restricted space.

In this passage, the verb *sḥr* appears to be relatively unproblematic, and in its first instance (spelled as *sḥr*) it has been all but ubiquitously taken to be the Demotic antecedent of Coptic ⲤⲰϨⲢ, "sweep" (*CD*, 386a–b); I will take this for granted in the discussion to come. Whether the variant *sḥre* actually means "floor," however, while plausible and in my view probably correct, is not absolutely certain.[3]

It is, however, considerably less clear how we should take Demotic *nḏḫ*. The word's Coptic outcome ⲚⲞⲨϪⲔ (*CD* primary dictionary form; also many variants: ⲚⲞⲨϪϬ; ⲚⲞⲨϪ; ⲚⲞⲨϪϨ; ⲚⲞⲨϪϢ; ⲚⲞⲨϢϪ) seems most often by far to be used of liquids, and to have the meaning of to "sprinkle, pour, asperge."[4] However, it is also at least sporadically attested in the meaning of "scatter" with dry substances.[5] We shall investigate this question in detail below. For the moment, the key point to make is that when—as is often the case—Coptic ⲤⲰϨⲢ, "to sweep" is paired with ⲚⲞⲨϪⲔ in a fixed expression that recalls the pairing of *sḥr* and *nḏḫ* of First Setne, the expression most often seems to have distinctly religious/cultic contexts and resonances.

We therefore have in our First Setne passage more than just a vivid visual description of Tabubue's private apartment; we also appear to have another of many hints that Tabubue is of quasidivine status—not, according to the logic of the story, actually a manifestation of the Distant Goddess, but rather a sort of reflection, or perhaps even a parody, of her. Perhaps a better way to express this would be to say that the myth of the Distant Goddess appears to provide a hermeneutic key to understanding the role of Tabubue in First Setne, and that the description of Tabubue's apartment and of Tabubue's interaction with Setne is among the passages of the tale that are most reflective of Tabubue's relationship to the Distant Goddess complex and therefore the most pregnant with meaning.

---

2. Jørgensen, "Myths, Menarche and the *Return of the Goddess*," 135.

3. For brief additional discussion, see Steve Vinson, *The Craft of a Good Scribe: History, Narrative and Meaning in the* First Tale of Setne Khaemwas, HES 3 (Leiden: Brill, 2018), 166.

4. *CD*; *DG*, 249a–b.

5. The only absolutely clear case cited in *CD* appears on p. 249b, quoting Ezek 10:2, where ⲚⲞⲨϪϢⲞⲨ "scatter them out" is used for hot coals. *nḏḫ*/ⲚⲞⲨϪⲔ is generally taken to be a Semitic loanword; see Jaroslav Černý, *Coptic Etymological Dictionary* (Cambridge,: Cambridge University Press, 1976), 119; Werner Vycichl, *Dictionnaire étymologique de la langue copte*, (Leuven: Peeters, 1983), 152a–153b; CDD N (2004), 159–60.

Background on First Setne

While the First Tale of Setne Khaemwas is among the best known of ancient Egyptian tales, and by far the best known and most important Demotic tale, students and non-Egyptologists may find an abbreviated description of the story useful, along with a brief account of (what I have argued to be) Tabubue's relationship to the Distant Goddess complex.

First Setne is known from a single manuscript now in the Cairo Museum, CGC 30646.[6] The date of the manuscript is uncertain, but it probably belongs to a point early in the Ptolemaic period. The tale revolves around a character named Setne Khaemwas, the legendary persona of a historic Khaemwas, among the most important sons of the Nineteenth Dynasty Pharaoh Ramesses II. The "Setne" element is derived from a priestly title *sm*, later spelled *stm* with an intrusive *t*, and ultimately appearing also as *stn*.[7] In the tale (and in a substantial group of related tales) it is actually treated as an element of the character's name.

In the story, Setne becomes aware of a magic book originally written by the god Thoth. He learns that the book is in the Memphite tomb of a certain Naneferkaptah, a long-dead magician and prince. Invading the tomb, he encounters not only the mummy of Naneferkaptah, but also the ghosts of Naneferkaptah's sister and wife Ihweret, and their son, Meribptah. Setne learns from Ihweret how Naneferkaptah had obtained the book in the first place, and how it had cost the entire family their lives. And we learn, incidentally, that Ihweret and Meribptah are both actually buried hundreds of miles away, in distant Koptos, near the site of their deaths. But neither Ihweret's pleas, nor a slapstick encounter with the living mummy of Naneferkaptah, dissuade Setne, who removes the book from the tomb.

Soon thereafter, Setne has an encounter with a mysterious woman named "Tabubue." His attempt to seduce Tabubue ends up in a supernatural imbroglio, both humiliating and comic; this prompts in Setne the realization that it is in his best interests to return the magic book to the tomb of Naneferkaptah at the earliest possible moment. Upon the request of Naneferkaptah, Setne then journeys to Koptos, where he exhumes the mummies of Ihweret and Meribptah, transports them to Memphis, and finally reburies them with Naneferkaptah, so that the family and the book are all reunited in eternity.

Tabubue and the Distant Goddess

The term "Distant Goddess" is actually a generic term for a mythological role, not a specific divine personality. Any one of a large number of divine females, all identified as daughters, but also (implicitly or explicitly) mothers and consorts, of the sun god Re, can and do take on the role in various textual concretizations of the myth.[8] Although many variations occur, the fundamental mythological pattern consists of a daughter of Re who departs Egypt, usually for southern regions; who rages against the enemies of Re; and who then returns to Egypt, where she is pacified. Once pacified, she takes on the benign role of consort, and it is her union with Re that guarantees the renewal of the cycle of life.

The "return" of the goddess has long been linked to an astronomical event, the heliacal rising of the star Sirius (that is, the first visible rising of Sirius after a seventy-day period of invisibility), which occurs at about the time the Nile flood typically commenced, in mid-July. Rising in the southern half of the sky just before sunrise, Sirius—the

6. In detail, see Vinson, *The Craft of a Good Scribe*, with additions and corrections in Steve Vinson, "Corrections and Additions to *The Craft of a Good Scribe: History, Narrative and Meaning in the First Tale of Setne Khaemwas*," *Enchoria* 35 (2016/2017): 200–202.

7. *Wb.* IV:119, 3–9; *DG*, 479.

8. See in detail Vinson, *The Craft of a Good Scribe*, 260–68.

brightest star in the sky—was imagined as the visible manifestation of the goddess, returned from the southland to rejoin her father the sun.[9]

As a threatening, raging entity, the Distant Goddess can blast the enemies of her father with the fire of the sun itself. But the notion of "light" is fundamental to both the raging and pacified aspects of the Distant Goddess. And it is here that we see the most important and overt link between Tabubue and the Distant Goddess complex; the name *Ta-Bwbwe* means "She of the Shining One." The Demotic word *bwbwe* lies behind Coptic ⲂⲞⲨⲂⲞⲨ (*CD*, 29a); it is a relatively rare word in Demotic that, in my view not coincidentally, occurs elsewhere only in connection with manifestations of the Distant Goddess. One of these attestations is in a Roman-period Demotic mythological narrative, the "Return of the Goddess" (P. Leiden I 384, 12.13–19; the word *bwbw* appears at 12.19), where it is used in a description of the raging Tefnut, the daughter of Re whom Re's emissaries Shu and Thoth are attempting to coax back to Egypt from Nubia:

> She changed her form into a raging lion. Six divine cubits in length[10] was she, and proportionate in breadth. She ruffled up her mane (?) before herself;[11] her fur (?) smoked with fire. Her back took on the color of blood; her face took on the glowing light of the solar disk; her two eyes burned with fire. Her glances glowed like flame. Like the sunlight of mid-summer, she projected fire. **She shone from within herself, utterly** (*ir=s bwbw n-im=s ḏr=s*).[12]

Mark Depauw and Mark Smith also called attention some years ago to the word *bwbw* in the second of a pair of Ptolemaic ostraca bearing hymns to a relatively obscure goddess, variously called Nehemanyt, Ay, and Tayt. A hymn directly addressed to her in her Ay-manifestation begins (lines 1–14):

> They say, ecstatically: **May she shine forth** (*bwbw=s*)**!** When Ay plunges them into a state of desire; (and) when they are beside themselves because of her body on a festival day; (then) may it be granted (?)—the epiphany of Ay! May he drink, may he eat, may he copulate in the presence of Tayt![13]

Beyond the *bwbwe* element of her name and its obvious connection to light, additional points of contact between Tabubue and the Distant Goddess complex include, but are not limited to, her direct connection to Bastet (villa in the Memphite Bubastieion, father a priest of Bastet), her punishing role, her overt and pronounced sexuality, and her connections to precious substances also connected to Hathor and other Distant Goddess manifestations, viz. gold, turquoise, and lapis lazuli.[14]

---

9. See Vinson, 260–61.

10. Approximately three meters. This is much larger than a typical lioness, and indeed above the typical maximum length of a mature male lion. See <https://animals.sandiegozoo.org/animals/lion>, accessed 23 July 2019.

11. On female lions with manes, see Vinson, *The Craft of a Good Scribe*, 265, n. 68.

12. Wilhelm Spiegelberg, *Der ägyptische Mythus vom Sonnenauge (Der Papyrus der Tierfabeln – "Kufi") Nach dem Leidener demotischen Papyrus I 384*, (Strassburg: Strassburger Druckerei und Verlagsanstalt, 1917), 34–35 and pl. 11; François de Cenival, *Le mythe de l'oeil du soleil*, DemStud 9, (Sommerhausen: Gisela Zauzich Verlag, 1988), 36–37; 97, n. ad loc.; pl. 11.

13. My translation; see Steve Vinson, "The Names 'Naneferkaptah,' 'Ihweret' and 'Tabubue' in the 'First Tale of Setne Khaemwas,'" *JNES* 68 (2009): 295–96; it varies on some significant points from that of Mark Depauw and Mark Smith, "Visions of Ecstasy: Cultic Revelry before the goddess Ai/Nehemanit: Ostraca Faculteit Letteren (K.U. Leuven) dem. 1-2," in *Res Severa Verum Gaudium: Festschrift für Karl-Theodor Zauzich zum 65. Geburtstag am 8. Juni 2004*, ed. Friedhelm Hoffmann and Heinz-Josef Thissen (Leuven: Peeters, 2004) 74–76.

14. For extended discussions, see Steve Vinson, "The Names 'Naneferkaptah,' 'Ihweret' and 'Tabubue' in the 'First Tale of Setne Khaemwas,'" 292–99; Vinson, *The Craft of a Good Scribe*, 254–74 (ch. 10).

Received Interpretations

Our problem passage has been variously interpreted over the years since the publication of the tale's initial decipherment by Heinrich Brugsch in 1867, but never, so far as I have been able to trace, as a description of a ritual. The following examples are in chronological order:

> Brugsch (1867): *Setna* marcha en montant par l'escalier de la maison avec *Tabubu* jusqu'à ce qu'on reonnût la terrasse de la maison. Elle était ornée et garnie, et ses ornements étaient de vrai lapis-lazuli et de vraies turquoises.[15]
>
> Brugsch (1868): das obere Stockwerk des Hauses, es war gekehrt und gesprengt, es bestand sein Kehricht und die Sprengung aus ächtem Lapis-lazuli und aus ächten Türkisen.[16]
>
> Revillout (1877): Setna monta par l'escalier de la maison avec Taboubou, afin d'en visiter l'étage supérieur, qui était incrusté de lapis vrai et de mafek vrai.[17]
>
> Brugsch (1879): Setna ging nach oben hinauf auf der Stiege des Hauses zusammen mit Tabubu, indem er Kenntnis nahm von dem oberen Stockwerke des Hauses, welches geschmückt und ausgelegt war. Sein Schmuck in ausgelegter Arbeit bestand aus dem echten Turkisen und aus echten Smaragden.[18]
>
> Revillout 1880 (revision of 1877 version): Setna monta par l'escalier de la maison, avec Tabubu, pour faire une reconnaissance de l'apparietment supérieur de la maison. Il était bien propre, peint de couleurs variées, et son intérieur était incrusté de lapis et de turquoises véritables.[19]
>
> Revillout 1882, in a comment to an article on a contract for religious service): On trouve les correspondants démotiques de ⲤⲞϨⲢ et ⲚⲞⲨϪⲔ (ainsi réunis) dans le *Roman de Setna*, p. 140 de mon edition (i.e., Revillout 1877/1880): ... *l'appartment bien belayé et bien lavé*. C'est ainsi qu'on doit traduire ce passage.[20]
>
> Hess (1888): Setne gieng hinauf auf den Treppe des Hauses mit Tabubu. Als er das oben Stockwerk des Hauses gefunden hatte, das geschmückt (?) war, das ausgelegt war, indem sein Schmuck (?) eine Auslegung von Lapis-lazuli u. Smaragd war....[21]
>
> Griffith (1900, "literary" translation): Setne ascended the steps of the house with Tabubue. And lo! He found the upper story of the house swept and garnished, the floor (?) thereof being adorned with true lapis lazuli and true turquoise.[22]
>
> Griffith (1900, "philological" translation): Setne walked up on the staircase of the house with Ta-bubue. Lo! He found the upper story of the house swept and decorated, its floor (?) being decorated with real lapis lazuli and with real turquoise....[23]
>
> Gunn (1948): The Setōm walked upstairs with Tabubu. And he found the upper part of the house cleaned and garnished, its ceiling being decorated with real lapis-lazuli and real turquoise....[24]

15. Heinrich Brugsch, "Le Roman de Setnau contenu dans un papyrus démotique du Musée égyptien à Boulaq," *RA* 16 (1867): 174.
16. Heinrich Brugsch, *Dictionnaire hiéroglyphique et démotique contenant en ordre méthodique les mots et les groupes les plus usités de la langue et de l'écriture sacrée et populaire des anciens Égyptiens*, vol. 2 (Leipzig: Hinrichs; Paris: Klincksieck), 1281.
17. Eugène Revillout, *Le roman de Setna, étude philologique et critique avec traduction mot à mot du texte démotique, introduction historique et commentaire grammatical* (Paris: Leroux, 1877), 31.
18. Heinrich Brugsch, "Setna," *Deutsche Revue über das gesammte nationale Leben der Gegenwart* 3 (1879): 15.
19. Eugène Revillout, *Le roman de Setna, étude philologique et critique avec traduction mot à mot du texte démotique, introduction historique et commentaire grammatical*, rev. ed. (Paris: Leroux, 1880), 35.
20. Eugène Revillout, "L'antigraphe des luminaires," *RdÉ* 2 (1882): 83n2.
21. Jean-Jacques Hess, *Der demotische Roman von Stne Ha-m-us, Text, Uebersetzung, Commentar und Glossar* (Leipzig: Hinrichs), 116–17.
22. Francis L. Griffith, *Stories of the High Priests of Memphis: The Sethon of Herodotus and the Demotic Tales of Khamuas* (Oxford: Clarendon), 35.
23. Griffith, 127.
24. Battiscombe Gunn, "The Story of Khamwīsĕ," in *Land of Enchanters: Egyptian Short Stories from the Earliest Times to the Present*

Lichtheim (1980): Setne walked up the stairs of the house with Tabubu. He found the upper story of the house swept and adorned, its floor adorned with real lapis-lazuli and real turquoise.[25]

Ritner (2003): Setna went up upon the staircase of the house with Tabubu. He found the upper story of the house swept, decorated, with its floor decorated with real lapis lazuli and real turquoise.[26]

Goldbrunner (2006): Setna ging nach oben auf der Treppe des Hauses mit Tabubu. Er fand das Obere des Houses, indem es gefegt und besprengt war und indem sein Boden besprengt war mit echtem Lapislazuli und echtem Malachit....[27]

Vittmann, Demotische Textdatenbank: Setne ging auf der Treppe des Hauses mit Tabubu nach oben. Er fand das obere Gemach des Hauses gefegt und besprengt, indem sein Boden mit echtem Lapislazuli und echtem Türkis ausgelegt war....[28]

Hoffmann (2007): Setne ging auf der Treppe des Hauses mit Tabubu hinauf. Er fand das obere Stockwerk gefegt und gesprengt, seinen gefegten (Boden) mit echtem Lapislazuli (und) echtem Malachit bestreut....[29]

Agut-Labordère and Chauveau (2011): Il découvrit que l'étage supérieur de la maison était nettoyé de frais, que son plancher était constellé de véritables lapis-lazulis et de véritables turquoises....[30]

Sweeping and Asperging

As the above examples indicate, the occurrences of the variant forms *nḏḫ* and *nḏḫe* have caused translators some consternation, largely occasioned by the apparent contradiction between the most common meaning of *nḏḫ*—"pour, asperge"—and the fact that the logical objects of *nḏḫe* would appear *prima facie* to be dry mineral substances. Some—including me—have opted for a more or less literal translation of *nḏḫ* in its first occurrence: Brugsch in 1868, Goldbrunner in 2006, and Hoffmann in 2007 translated "gesprengt"; Revillout in 1882 suggested "lavé"; I have "purified(?)"; while Agut-Labordère and Chauveau in 2011 rendered "nettoyé."

In its second, variant occurrence, however, this has generally not been felt to be appropriate, and authors have most opted for an extended meaning, usually something along the "decorated" or "encrusted" or my own "glittering." Few have offered a translation that suggested the literal "scattering" or "dispersal" of the lapis lazuli and turquoise: Brugsch in 1868 translated *nḏḫe* as "Sprengung," and Goldbrunner in 2006 had "besprengt"; Hoffmann in 2007 had "bestreut" but his note suggested he understood this in an extended or metaphorical sense.

It is undoubtedly significant, however, that all of the (few) attestations of Demotic *nḏḫ* (and variants) are spelled with liquid classifiers, including the two writings *nḏḫ* and *nḏḫe* in "First Setne, which use the canal classifier: 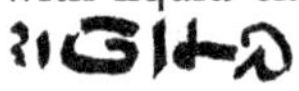 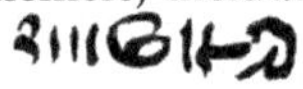 (facsimiles by William Edgerton).[31] The word, spelled *nwḏḫ*, also appears in P. Lon-

Day, ed. Bernard Lewis (London: The Harvill Press, 1948), 78. On Gunn's translation "ceiling" here, see Vinson, *The Craft of a Good Scribe*, 166 with n. 163.

25. Miriam Lichtheim, "Setne Khamwas and Naneferkaptah (Setne I)," in *Ancient Egyptian Literature*, Vol. 3: *The Late Period* (Berkeley: University of California Press, 1980), 134.

26. Robert K. Ritner, "The Romance of Setna Khaemuas and the Mummies (Setna I)," in *The Literature of Ancient Egypt: An Anthology of Instructions, Stelae, Autobiographies, and Poetry*, ed. William K. Simpson, 3rd ed. (New Haven: Yale University Press, 2003), 465. Ritner points out the literal meaning "sprinkled" here for *nḏḫ*; he adds (n. 32): "Perhaps a reference to mosaic inlay of lapis and turquoise."

27. Sara Goldbrunner, *Der verblendete Gelehrte: Der erste Setna-Roman (P. Kairo 30646)*, DemStud 13 (Sommerhausen: Gisela Zauzich Verlag, 2006), 22.

28. Günter Vittmann, Demotische Textdatenbank, < http://aaew.bbaw.de/tla/index.html >.

29. Friedhelm Hoffmann, "Die erste Setnegeschichte," in *Anthologie der demotischen Literatur*, ed. Friedhelm Hoffmann and Joachim Quack, EQÄ 4 (Berlin: Lit, 2007), 148. Hoffmann additionally notes (n. 264) that "bestreut" is being used "Wohl im Sinne von 'belegt.'"

30. Damien Agut-Labordère and Michel Chauveau, "Setné et le Livre de Thôt (Setné I)," in *Héros, magiciens et sages oubliés de l>Égypte ancienne: Une anthologie de la littérature en égyptien démotique* (Paris: Les Belles lettres, 2011), 34.

31. Complete Edgerton facsimile published in Vinson, *The Craft of a Good Scribe*, pls. XIV, XV, XVI, XVII.

don-Leiden 14.5, with an apparent *nw*-pot classifier  (Griffith handcopy), in what Griffith took with some diffidence to be a reference to a libation ritual (Griffith's translation, with modernized transliteration):

> ⲚⲦⲀ
> *hb sp-sn nwḏẖ mtw(=y) (?) nw r pꜣ nṯr ꜥꜣ i͗np pꜣ nꜥš*
> O Ibis (bis), sprinkle (?), that I may (?) see the great god Anubis, the power, … (etc.)[32]

It is interesting to note Griffith's short and suggestive, but unfortunately somewhat vague, comment to the use of *nwḏẖ* here: "*nwzẖ* is used of sprinkling of water for the reception of visitors."[33] This sounds like a reference to the usage of the word in some other text; we may perhaps conjecture that he was toying with an interpretation of *nḏẖ* in First Setne along the lines of Revillout's 1882 suggestion. However, I am unaware of any additional discussion by him in which he elaborates on the meaning of *nḏẖ*, or on what that might mean for our interpretation of the passage in question.

The only other attestation of the word recorded in the Chicago Demotic Dictionary,  (Chicago Demotic Dictionary handcopy) from P. Berlin P 13602, 4, likewise has a liquid (water) classifier.[34] And in this case, at least, the meaning of "sprinkle, pour, asperge" as of a liquid is contextually all but unmistakable: it has to do with applying a liquid preparation to the house door of a woman who is evidently undergoing a rather elaborate medico-magical procedure intended to affect her sexual desire:[35]

> *… m]⌜tw=w ti n⌝ kꜣ.ṯ=s n-im=f mtw=w nḏẖ n pꜣy=s rꜣ pꜣy=s ꜥ.wy n-im=w*
> … and th]⌜ey shall place some of it (scil., a previously-mentioned but fragmentary preparation involving a *lbs*-fish) within⌝ her vagina, and they shall asperge her door of her house therewith.

Von Lieven and Quack take the mention of "her door of her house" as object of asperging to be an example of magic by analogy ("Analogiezauber").[36] And indeed, the metaphorical equation of the patient's vagina with "her door of her house" is noteworthy, and we will return to it below. For the moment, these Demotic parallels makes it attractive to think that in First Setne, Revillout in his 1882 comment could very well have been correct, and that we could indeed be dealing with the sprinkling or pouring of a liquid. And as Revillout recognized, this conclusion is also suggested by a number of the instances in which ⲤⲰϨⲢ and ⲚⲞⲨϪⲔ with variants) occur together: in a number of these cases, it is absolutely clear that ⲚⲞⲨϪⲔ is being used of a liquid. The following examples are taken from *CD* (ⲤⲰϨⲢ and ⲚⲞⲨϪⲔ).

• In MS Copt. Bibliothèque Nationale 129^{18} 102, in an apocryphal account of the Acts of the Apostles, an idol speaks, describing how it had been placed in a temple ⲈⲨⲤⲰϨⲢ ⲈⲨⲚⲞⲨϪⲔ, "as they swept(?) and asperged."[37]

32. Francis Ll. Griffith and Herbert Thompson, *The Demotic Magical Papyrus of London and Leiden II* (London: H. Grevel & Co., 1905), pl. XIV (handcopy); Francis Ll. Griffith and Herbert Thompson, *The Demotic Magical Papyrus of London and Leiden I* (London: H. Grevel & Co., 1904), 98–99 (translit. and trans.). Griffith (1904, 99, n. *ad* l. 5) notes that while the Demotic writing of the conjunctive here might be read as *mtw=w* and understood as third-person plural (therefore logically passive), he opts for understanding *mtw(=y)* on the basis of the Old Coptic gloss ⲚⲦⲀ. Compare B. Layton, *A Coptic Grammar With Chrestomathy and Glossary*, Porta Linguarum Orientalium 20 (Wiesbaden: Harrassowitz, 2000), 276, ¶351.

33. Griffith and Thompson, *The Demotic Magical Papyrus of London and Leiden I*, 99, n. *ad nwzẖ* on l. 5.

34. CDD *N* (2004), 04:1, 159–60 (hand copy courtesy of Janet Johnson).

35. Alexandra von Lieven and Joachim Quack, "Ist Liebe eine Frauenkrankheit? Papyrus Berlin P 13602, ein gynäkomagisches Handbuch," in *Of Making Many Books There Is No End: Festschrift in Honour of Sven P. Vleeming*, ed. Koenraad Donker van Heel, Francisca Hoogendijk and Cary J. Martin (Leiden: Brill, 2018), 260–61 (text and trans.); pl. XLIV (photo).

36. Von Lieven and Quack, "Ist Liebe eine Frauenkrankheit?," 271.

37. Quoted in *CD* from Crum's personal copy of the papyrus; apparently not published.

Here, the case for the specific meaning "asperge" is at least strengthened by a Fayumic parallel in which ⲉⲩⲥⲱϩⲣ is omitted and ⲉⲩⲥⲁⲕⲃⲓ is paired with ⲉⲩⲛⲟⲩ[ϫⲕ]; there immediately follows further first-person description by the idol of having been splattered with the blood of sacrificed animals (ϣⲁⲩϭⲁϣⲅⲉϣ ⲛⲏ[ⲓ] ⲙⲡⲉⲩⲥⲛⲁϥ).[38] While Crum took ⲥⲁⲕⲃⲓ on this basis as a variant of ⲥⲱϩⲣ, Westendorf has plausibly conjectured that ⲥⲁⲕⲃⲓ is likely the outcome of *sqbb/sqb*, "to cool, to asperge."[39]

- In the Martyrdom of St. Victor the General (MS BM 7022), an individual recounts that he had done service in a temple of Apollo, ⲉⲓⲥⲱϩⲣ ⲉⲓⲛⲟⲩϫⲕ "as I swept and asperged."[40]
- In more than one contract for a child donation to a monastic community (therefore a specifically Christian context), a boy will be required to "sweep and asperge;" see, e.g., P. BM Copt. 79, ll. 37–38:

> ⲛϥⲣϩⲙϩⲁⲗ ⲙⲡⲙⲟⲛⲟⲛⲟⲥⲧⲏⲣⲓⲟⲛ ⲉⲧⲟⲩⲁⲃ ⲉⲡⲥⲱϩⲣ ⲙⲛⲡⲛⲟⲩϫⲕ ⲙⲡⲙⲟⲟⲩ ⲉⲛⲗⲟⲩⲧⲏⲣ
> "And he shall act as servant in this holy monastery, for sweeping and asperging with the water from the fountains/baptisteries (etc.);" similarly P. Cairo Copt. 8732, l. 32.[41]

In both of these cases, the meaning "asperging" is guaranteed, as the activity of ⲛⲟⲩϫⲕ is to be carried out with water.[42]

- In a Shenutian text in Vienna (MS K-9198) in reference to the "paths of the lord:"

> ⲁϥⲕⲁⲑⲁⲣⲓⲍⲉ ⲙ̄ⲙⲟⲟⲩ ⲁϥⲥⲁϩⲣⲟⲩ ⲁⲩⲱ ⲛⲟϫϭⲟⲩ ϩⲙ̄ⲡⲉϥⲥⲛⲟϥ
> "He cleansed them, and he swept them, and asperged them with his blood."

Here the occurrence of a liquid object, while evidently metaphorical, again supports the meaning of "asperge them" for ⲛⲟϫϭⲟⲩ (as spelled here) in conjunction with "sweeping."[43]

- In another text of Shenuta in a reference to cleaning a house: men are said to be customarily assigned to to ⲥⲉϩⲣ ⲡⲁⲡⲃⲟⲗ ⲁⲩⲟ ⲉⲛⲟϫ(ⲕ)ϥ, "sweep the exterior and asperge it" for the benefit of those who live there.[44]

To reiterate: most of the Coptic references suggest that, when paired together, ⲥⲱϩⲣ and ⲛⲟⲩϫⲕ typically denote activities required to keep a holy/cultic area clean and pure; the pair can be used of both Christian and pagan spaces. A number of the examples include additional lexical confirmation that ⲛⲟⲩϫⲕ in this pairing means specifically "asperge," so that the pair would appear to suggest not only complementarity, but also contrast: the one term refers to dry activities (sweeping, removing dust and debris), and the other to pouring religiously significant liquid. The very last example might be taken to suggest an extended connotation, simply "thoroughly cleaned, spick-and-span;" this is apparently how Revillout 1882 takes it in our First Setne passage. With the addition of the instrumental complements *n ḫstb n mꜣꜥ.t mfke n mꜣꜥ.t*, "with true lapis lazuli and true turquoise," however, this seems rather less likely in our context, especially given the regular cultic significance of these substances.

38. O. von Lemm, "Actes apocryphes des apôtres en langue copte," *Bulletin de l'Académie impériale des sciences de St.-Pétersbourg* N.S. I (XXXIII), (1890): 41.

39. *KHw*, 181; Vycichl, *Dictionnaire étymologique de la langue copte*, 187; cf. *Wb*. IV:304, 6–305, 13. So understood also by the Coptic Dictionary Online: TLA lemma no. C3428 (ⲥⲁⲕⲃⲓ), in: Coptic Dictionary Online, ed. by the Koptische/Coptic Electronic Language and Literature International Alliance (KELLIA), https://coptic-dictionary.org/entry.cgi?tla=C3428 (accessed 2019-08-27).

40. E. W. Budge, *Coptic Martyrdoms etc. in the Dialect of Upper Egypt* (London: Trustees of the British Museum, 1914), 263 (trans., although incorrect at this point); p. 9 (fol. 5b), text.

41. P. BM Copt. 79 = Crum and Steindorff 1912, doc. 82; P. Cairo Copt. 8732 = W. E. Crum and G. Steindorff, *Koptische Rechtsurkunden des Achten Jahrhunderts aus Djême (Theben) I. Band: Texte und Indices* (Leipzig: Hinrichs, 1912), doc. 93.

42. For ⲗⲟⲩⲧⲏⲣ, cf. λουτήρ *washing or bathing-tub* (*LSJ* 1061b). Usage of ⲉ in ⲉⲛⲗⲟⲩⲧⲏⲣ is evidently an example of "ⲉ- erroneously (phonetically) for prep ⲛ-, esp in later *S* and in *F* texts" (*CD*, 52a).

43. Karl Wessely, *Studien zur Palaeographie und Papyruskunde 9 = Griechische und koptische Texte theologischen Inhalts I* (Leipzig: Eduard Avenarius, 1909), 145a.

44. Émile Amélineau, *Oeuvres de Schenoudi: Texte copte et traduction française*, Tome premier (Paris: Leroux, 1907), 301.

If so, the instrumental *n ḫstb n m3ʿ.t mfke n m3ʿ.t* might conceivably be taken in one of two ways. We might have here a metonymic description of the vessels with which the liquid is contained during the ceremony (i.e., with the substance out of which the vessels are made substituting for the vessels themselves, like Shakespearian "steel" for "sword"). One might compare here Darnell's discovery of "a faience cup and other faience fragments near the ʿAlamant Tal Road tracks, at about the middle point of the low desert behind Qamûla," which he suggests might have been involved in a ritual welcoming the Distant Goddess on her journey back to Egypt from the south.[45] However, the text stresses that the description of Tabubue's salon with which we are dealing is focalized through Setne's personal perception; and while Setne might have been expected to recognize that an asperging ritual had recently taken place (liquid visible in a libation basin, perhaps?), it seems less likely that he would have been able to ascertain (although perhaps he could have guessed from relevant experience) the particular type of vessel that had been employed.[46]

My opinion is that, in view of the classifiers included in the writings of the words *nḏḫ/nḏḫe*, and in view of the Coptic and Demotic parallels already discussed, we more probably have to do with a description of the liquid itself. The mention that an asperging ritual is carried out "with true lapis lazuli and true turquoise" would, in this scenario, refer to a ritual liquid into which has been mixed crushed or powdered lapis lazuli and turquoise, and which would therefore presumably have a sort of a blue-green cast to it. The use of crushed minerals mixed in with ritual substances is attested in Demotic magical papyri (e.g.: P. London-Leiden 11.32 and 27.10, both of which refer specifically to crushed lapis lazuli, but other types of stones are also attested). In most cases in the Demotic magical papyri, we generally have to do with ointments to be applied to the eyes, not to a free-flowing liquid to be ritually dispensed. But there is, at P. London-Leiden 27.4, a reference to "natron water." Elaborate mélanges of crushed semiprecious minerals of all types are used for the manufacture of sacred figurines in the "Mysteries of Khoiak" in the first Osirian chapel at Dendera.[47] It is also worth noting that Jean-Claude Goyon, and also Barbara Richter, have taken it for granted that in the scattering rituals in question, the substances employed would actually have been in the form of powder, not actual chunks of lapis lazuli, turquoise, or faience.[48]

Scattering/Dispersing Minerals before the Distant Goddess

And with this we return to our point of departure: Jens Jørgensen's argument that "scattering" greenish-bluish minerals in the context of Distant Goddess worship is specifically evocative of her menstruation, and involves a transformation of her "angry" red menstrual blood into a benign substance, which resonates with the green of Egypt associated with the renewed Nile flood.

It should be noted that the image of scattering of minerals is not confined to Distant Goddess rituals, nor to the Greco-Roman period. On the contrary, the image occurs in the Pyramid Texts: PT 350 refers to the heavens being strewn (*sṯi*) with minerals including turquoise (*mfk3.t*), greenstone (*w3ḏ*), and malachite (*šsm.t*); these minerals

45. John Darnell, *Theban Desert Road Survey in the Egyptian Western Desert, Vol. 1: Gebel Tjauti Rock Inscriptions 1–45 and Wadi El-Ḥôl Rock Inscriptions 1–45* (Chicago: Oriental Institute of the University of Chicago, 2002), 66–67, with n. 276.

46. Jørgensen, "Myths, Menarche and the *Return of the Goddess*," 141–42.

47. Sylvie Cauville, *Le temple de Dendara: Les chapelles osiriennes, transcription et traduction* (Cairo: Institut français d'archéologie orientale, 1997), 19 and 27 (ref. Marina Escolano-Poveda).

48. Jean-Claude Goyon, "Répandre l'or et éparpiller la verdure: Les fêtes de Mout et d'Hathor à la néomènie d'Epiphi et les prémices des moissons," in *Essays on Ancient Egypt in Honour of Herman te Velde*, ed. J. van Dijk (Groningen: Styx, 1997), 86 (85–100) (doubting that, even when *ṯḥn.t*, "faience" is referred to, that the powder would actually have been made of faience; still, it seems possible that it would have been easy enough to collect many pieces of broken faience or "factory rejects" to use in a scattering ritual, whether in whole chunks or reduced to powder); Barbara Richter, *The Theology of Hathor of Dendera: Aural and Visual Scribal Techniques in the Per-wer Sanctuary*, Wilbour Studies 4 (Atlanta: Lockwood, 2016), 57n203.

are then identified with stars.[49] In a New Kingdom hymn to Amun (P. Leiden I 350, 2.5), we read that *tꜣ sṯy m mfk.t wbn=f ỉm=s*, "the earth is strewn with turquoise, and he (Amun) shines within it."[50] In the Ptolemaic inscriptions of the Karnak Opet temple, there is a similar image: *gs-pr.w sṯi m ṯḥn.t*, "the temples are scattered with faience"; and even *ḫt-mn r ꜣw=f sṯi m ṯḥn.t*, "the entire world is scattered with faience."[51]

Jean-Claude Goyon, however, has collected substantial material linking this sort of imagery to the Distant Goddess, even though it is clear that it is not exclusive to her.[52] It is interesting to note that among the examples he cites, most employ the verb *sṯi* with a classifier of a "throwing, scattering man."[53] However, in a Ptolemaic inscription at the Mut complex, the verb in question is written with the "spitting lips," and would therefore be, *prima facie*, read *sti*, "asperge, libate" rather than *sṯi* "scatter:" *sti tw n=s ṯḥn.t ḥr wꜣ.t.*, "faience is poured out for her on the path."[54] For the idea of asperging a path in the context of a religious ritual, we might incidentally recall the image of paths being swept and asperged in blood, in a text of Shenute quoted above.[55] A similar image, in this case possibly involving the use of wine (although without a specific mention of "sweeping"), may occur in a Coptic encomium to an Archbishop Theodore (MS BM 7030), regarding preparation of a path for festival:

> ⲦⲈϨⲒⲎ ⲆⲈ ⲈⲦ ⲞⲨⲚⲎⲨ Ⲉ ⲦⲈⲔⲔⲖⲎⲤⲒⲀ Ⲛ̄ϨⲎⲦⲤ̄ … ⲚⲤⲈⲔⲀⲐⲀⲢⲒⲌⲈ Ⲙ̄ⲘⲞⲤ ⲚⲤⲈⲚⲞⲨϪ Ⲙ̄ⲘⲞⲤ Ⲙ̄ ⲘⲞⲨⲤϮⲔⲞⲚ ⲈⲦ ⲤⲞⲦⲠ̄
> But as regards the road upon which they travel to the Church: … they clean it and they asperge it with choice muscat wine(?).[56]

In *Craft of a Good Scribe*, I had suggested that the use of the verb *sti* "asperge, libate" in the Mut inscription might suggest "a metaphorical connection to ritual asperging."[57] After reconsidering the Coptic parallels just adduced, I am now rather more inclined to take the use of the verb *sti* literally, perhaps not least since the activities of sweeping and "scattering" of dry substances (in whatever form) would appear to be at cross purposes with one another.

It therefore seems at least possible that in First Setne we should take the verb *nḏḥ* at face value, and imagine that the reference is to a purification/pacification ritual, involving the paired activity of sweeping and asperging—a ritual that appears to have made the transition to the Christian context as Egypt's pagan tradition faded away, at least in its

49. Kurt Sethe, *Die altägyptischen Pyramidentexte* 1 (Leipzig: Hinrichs,1908), 292; James P. Allen, *The Ancient Egyptian Pyramid Texts*, WAW 23 (Atlanta: Society of Biblical Literature, 2005), 79.

50. Jan Zandee, *De Hymnen aan Amon van Papyrus Leiden I 350* (Leiden: Rijksmuseum van Oudheden, 1947), 18 (trans. and commentary); pl. II (text).

51. Constant de Wit, *Les inscriptions du Temple d'Opet à Karnak I*, Bibliotheca aegyptiaca 12 (Brussels: Fondation égyptologique Reine Élisabeth, 1958), 186, l. 3; p. 250, l. 2 (text); Constant de Wit, *Les inscriptions du Temple d'Opet à Karnak III*, Bibliotheca aegyptiaca 13 (Brussels: Fondation égyptologique Reine Élisabeth, 1968), 103, 110 (trans.).

52. Goyon "Répandre l'or et éparpiller la verdure."

53. *Wb.* IV:346, 13–348, 2; Penelope Wilson, *A Ptolemaic Lexikon: A Lexicographical Study of the Texts in the Temple of Edfu*, OLA 78 (Leuven: Peeters, 1997), 955.

54. *Wb.* IV:328, 9–329, 16; Wilson, *A Ptolemaic Lexicon*, 955. See Goyon "Répandre l'or et éparpiller la verdure," 86 and fig. 1 on p. 98.

55. Again Wessely, *Studien zur Palaeographie und Papyruskunde* 9, 145a.

56. For the text, see E. W. Budge, *Miscellaneous Texts in the Dialect of Upper Egypt* (London: Trustees of the British Museum, 1915), 10, Fol. 9 a 2-9 b 1. ⲘⲞⲨⲤϮⲔⲞⲚ, clearly Greek in form, is not entered separately in *CD*, and Crum does not hazard a translation when he cites this passage in his article on ⲚⲞⲨϪⲔ; no such word appears in *LSJ* or in Friedrich Preisigke, *Wörterbuch der griechischen Papyrusurkunden* (Berlin, 1925–1931). Perhaps we have here a distortion of ⲘⲞⲨⲤⲬⲀⲦⲈⲚ (= μοσχάτον, "muscat wine"); see TLA lemma no. C9833 (ⲘⲞⲨⲤⲬⲀⲦⲈⲚ), in Coptic Dictionary Online, ed. by the Koptische/Coptic Electronic Language and Literature International Alliance (KELLIA), https://coptic-dictionary.org/entry.cgi?tla=C9833 (accessed 2019-08-01). See also μοῦστος, Latin mustum, "new wine;" *LSJ* 1149a. Budge (1915, p. 586) translates "aromatic herbs," without comment.

57. Vinson, *A Craft of a Good Scribe*, 166a.

basic form, if not in meaning. That said, the actual mode of dispersal—whether through libation or through scattering of dry material—would apparently have little bearing on the actual meaning of the ritual.

Interpretations

In sum, I think it is quite plausible that (1) Jørgensen is correct, and that the scattering of blue-green substances in the context of Distant Goddess worship—whether natural minerals like turquoise or lapis lazuli, or manufactured substances like faience—was intended to evoke her menstrual blood and its transformation into a benign substance or force; (2) the cultic/religious/ceremonial contexts in which the Coptic words ⲤⲰϨⲢ and ⲚⲞⲨϪⲔ appear together suggests that pairing of the verbs *sḥr* and *ndḫ* in First Setne in connection with the minerals lapis lazuli and turquoise likewise refer to a ritual in which these minerals are, in some manner, literally dispersed in Tabubue's salon; (3) the specific mention of lapis lazuli and turquoise here ties this dispersal ritual to the menstruation of the Distant Goddess; (4) other aspects of Tabubue's personality and portrayal, most especially her connection to light and her role in punishing Setne, confirm this connection to the Distant Goddess; (5) the usual usage of the verb *ndḫ* and its Coptic outcome ⲚⲞⲨϪⲔ, including many cases in which the Coptic word is paired with ⲤⲰϨⲢ, makes it likely that our word(s) *ndḫ/ndḫe* refers to asperging or libating, not scattering of dry minerals; and (6) this would, perhaps, also make the substance more closely parallel to the menstrual blood of the goddess.

If all of this is accepted—or at a minimum, points (1) through (4)—then there are interesting implications for how we should interpret the encounter between Setne and Tabubue. I have argued throughout *Craft of a Good Scribe* that First Setne presupposes a substantial knowledge—on both the part of the reader, and on the part of its principal characters, Setne Khaemwas, and his adversary Naneferkaptah—of Egypt's esoteric ritual tradition. This would likely include the reader's recognition of the nature and meaning of ritual involving the dispersal of blue-green minerals connected with a punishing female with strong solar associations: the insider-reader ought to have been aware of the specifically menstrual symbolism that was being forefronted in the tale.

Setne may also be presumed to understand the ritual significance of the various features of Tabubue's salon, including the dispersal of blue-green minerals within the space. But on Jørgensen's account, the "scattering" or "asperging" of turquoise and lapis lazuli (in whatever form) should suggest that Tabubue may not be in a tabu state. Relying on his knowledge of the nature of the Distant Goddess following the pacification/purification ritual of dispersal of blue-green substances, Setne might be imagined to have concluded that Tabubue's menstrual cycle has passed, along with her rage and her proclivity for punishment; she is now receptive to, indeed eager for, a sexual encounter.

However, the encounter does not go as planned. In a three-stage ordeal, Setne is required to make ever-more extreme concessions to Tabubue before she will agree to the encounter. First, he must sign over to her all of his worldly possessions. Then, he must have his children ratify this transfer, so as to forestall future lawsuits. And finally, he must agree to the murder of his children, to prevent the slightest possibility that they might renege on their approval. In other words, Setne is premature at best to conclude that Tabubue has given up her punishing role and taken on that of a renewer of life. Rather, she appears to be in a liminal zone where the danger has not yet fully passed.

Finally, all of this suggests a new possible solution to the crux of the meaning of the term *šḥyꜣ(.t)*, the mysterious object in which Setne's penis is seen to be inserted after Tabubue suddenly vanishes, leaving Setne outdoors, hot and naked.[58] In *Craft of a Good Scribe* and in an earlier discussion on translational and interpretive problems in "First Setne," I adopted a suggestion by Robert Ritner, that the term *šḥyꜣ(.t)* might refer to a chamber pot—that is, a con-

58. See Steve Vinson, "Ten Notes on the First Tale of Setne Khaemwas," in *Honi soi qui mal y pense: Studien zum pharaonischen, griechisch-römischen und spätantiken Ägypten zu Ehren von Heinz-Josef Thissen*, ed. Hermann Knuf, Christian Leitz, and Daniel von Recklinghousen (Leuven: Peeters, 2010), 461–66, esp. 461–62, for an overview of previous interpretive suggestions.

tainer for the temporary storage of human waste produced during the night, for disposal in the morning.[59] This struck me as an appropriate punchline to the cruel joke that had obviously been building all along.

Jørgensen points out, however, that there is at least some reason to believe that the "jar" hieroglyph used to write the name of Bastet—that is, not only a common manifestation of the Distant Goddess, but the very goddess of whom Tabubue's father is said to be a priest—is an image of a container for her menstrual blood.[60] And there is at least some slight real-world indication that menstrual blood might be kept, specifically for medical/magical purposes.[61] An obvious way for this to have been saved would have been to save used menstrual cloth; interesting in this connection is the regular conjecture that the *tyet*-knot amulet is emblematic of the menstrual cloth of Isis.[62] Beyond that, Paul Frandsen has adduced interesting evidence that the uterus itself could be conceptualized as a jar and a container for blood, to either nourish a fetus or to be expelled during menstruation.[63]

Could Setne's final humiliation in this encounter be that he has been magically compelled to have sex with a container of menstrual blood/used menstrual cloth? Such an interpretation might well be as shocking as the notion that his penis had been inserted into a chamber pot, but would have the advantage of being more in keeping with the sexual nature of the joke. If nothing else, we can at least say that the *šḥyꜣ(.t)* is clearly an ersatz vagina, and for the story to indicate that it has been "contaminated" with menstrual blood might well be more logical, from both a physiological and cultural standpoint, than for it to have been "contaminated" with excrement. Contact with menstrual blood is among the unpleasant features of life as a clothes washer, according to the Satire on the Trades: "He (scil., the laundryman) will place himself in the garment of a woman who is in her menstrual period."[64] For a priest, the consequences were apparently worse than simply unpleasant, as there are grounds to think that even casual and indirect contact with menstrual blood would make a man ineligible to enter sacred spaces.[65]

The one other published possible attestation of the word *šḥyꜣ(.t)* is the partly lost writing *šḥy.*[...] that occurs in the Demotic medical text P. Vindob. D. 6257, 14.6, in a fragmentary gynecological context; it apparently refers to an odor (presumably an unhealthy one) that might emanate from a female patient's *rꜣ* (as neutrally as possible, "orifice"):

> [...] *kš=f r rꜣ=s nty ỉw=s ẖnm r šḥy.* [...*n-ỉm=f*]
> [...] Pour into her *rꜣ* [from which] she smells *šḥy.* [...]

59. Vinson, "Ten Notes on the First Tale of Setne Khaemwas," 462; Vinson, *The Craft of a Good Scribe* 171; cf. Ritner, "The Romance of Setna Khaemuas and the Mummies (Setna I), 466, with n. 38.

60. Jørgensen, "Myths, Menarche and the *Return of the Goddess*," 142.

61. E.g., in P. Ebers 95, 1–3, a prescription intended to prevent excess production of breast milk; Hermann Grapow, *Die medizinischen Texte in hieroglyphischer Umschreibung autographiert*, Grundriss der Medizin der Alten Ägypter V (Berlin: Akademie Verlag, 1958), 491 (text); Hildegard von Deines, Hermann Grapow, and Wolfhart Westendorf, *Übersetzung der medizinischen Texte*, Grundriss der Medizin der alten Ägypter 4 (Berlin: Akademie Verlag, 1958), 285 (trans.).

62. Geraldine Pinch, *Magic in Ancient Egypt*, (Austin: University of Texas Press, 2006),116 (ref. Amanda Ladd); Carol Andrews, *Amulets of Ancient Egypt* (Austin: University of Texas Press; London: British Museum Press, 1994), 44–45; Willeke Wendrich, "Entangled, Connected or Protected? The Power of Knots and Knotting in Ancient Egypt," in *Through a Glass Darkly: Magic, Dreams & Prophecy in Ancient Egypt*, ed. Kasia Szpakowska (Swansea: Classical Press of Wales, 2006), 249–50 (ref. Lingxin Zhang).

63. Paul J. Frandsen, "The Menstrual 'Taboo' in Ancient Egypt," *JNES* 66 (2007): 101–3.

64. Dua-chety, 19f (trans. following P BM 29550); text, comments and trans. in Wolfgang Helck, *Die Lehre des ḏwꜣ-Ḫtjj Teil II, Kleine ägyptische Texte* (Wiesbaden: Harrassowitz, 1970), 108–11. Discussion in Frandsen, "The Menstrual 'Taboo' in Ancient Egypt," 100.

65. Frandsen, "The Menstrual 'Taboo' in Ancient Egypt," 103–4, discussing records of absences from work on the royal tombs at Deir el-Medina, and noting that male workers' absences were occasionally connected to the menstruation of women in their immediate households. From this, Frandsen concludes that contact with menstruating women rendered the men ineligible to enter the sacred space of the royal tombs on which they were employed.

While the identity of the *šḥy.*[...] of P. Vindob. D. 6257 with our *šḥyꜣ(.t)* is not absolutely certain, it does seem an attractive possibility, given the similarity of contexts. If it is, then the question arises as to what is meant by the patient's *rꜣ*—her mouth, or her vagina? The metaphorical association of the vagina with a door is well established in Egyptian literature, particularly but not exclusively in Ramesside love poetry;[66] and it is interesting to reiterate that it reappears in the passage quoted above from the medico-magical text P. Berlin P 13602, 4, in which the practitioner's instructions were to "asperge" (*nḏẖ*) "her door of her house" (*pꜣy=s rꜣ pꜣy=s ꜥ.wy*), immediately following the instruction that something is to have been "placed" (*tỉ*) within "her vagina" (*kꜣ.ṱ=s*). We noted above that von Lieven and Quack identify this as an instance of magic by analogy.[67] Whether simple, unqualified *rꜣ* might ever have been used as a technical, medical term for "vagina" cannot be confirmed through currently available material known to me, but *rꜣ* accompanied by various qualifiers does occur in the standard medical text corpus in this meaning: cf. such phrases as *rꜣ n(y) ḥm.t=s*, "opening of her uterus" from P. Ramesseum IV, C 2–3, similarly P. BM 10059, 14.5–8, or *rꜣ n(y) ẖnw ỉwf=s*, "opening of the interior of her pudendum," from P. BM 10059, 14.1–2.[68]

Here we become even more speculative; but if the *rꜣ* of P. Vindob. D. 6257 refers to the patient's vagina, then it is not impossible that the expression "smell *šḥy.*[...]" refers to an odor associated with the patient's menstrual period.[69] This in turn would at least be consistent with the notion that *šḥyꜣ(.t)* of First Setne is a container for the disposal of menstrual blood/used menstrual cloths, which might have a distinctive odor. Certainly the fact that the *šḥyꜣ(.t)* is a sort of substitute vagina; that its "pustule" classifier associates it with foul or diseased substances; that the womb could be conceptualized as a jar and that blood was thought to collect in the womb before being discharged during menstruation;[70] and that dramatically, the insertion of his penis into the *šḥyꜣ(.t)* signals Setne's final humiliation, are all consistent with this notion as well. And all of this is consistent with the meaning that Jørgensen posits for the scattering of turquoise and lapis lazuli, an image that is central to the description of Tabubue's salon in our tale. It could well be that an insider-reader would have recognized that the entire description of the encounter between Setne and Tabubue is replete with hints that she is in, or is only just concluding, her menstrual period—this latter permutation perhaps explaining why her "rage," while not having entirely abated, is nevertheless attenuated to the point that Setne's punishments and humiliations are, in the end, just an elaborate practical joke. In other words, at least for someone in Setne's exalted, priestly position, who enjoys regular access to Pharaoh himself, it could well be that sex with Tabubue is still strictly tabu.

66. Steve Vinson, "Behind Closed Doors: Architectural and Spatial Images and Metaphors in Ancient Egyptian Erotic Poetic and Narrative Literature," in *Sex and the Golden Goddess II—World of the Love Songs*, ed. Hana Navrátilová and Renata Landgráfová (Prague: Czech Institute of Egyptology, 2015).

67. Again, see von Lieven and Quack, "Ist Liebe eine Frauenkrankheit?," 271.

68. Vinson, "Behind Closed Doors", 465 with nn. 90–92. For P. Ramesseum IV, C 2–3,90, see Grapow, *Die medizinischen Texte in hieroglyphischer Umschreibung autographiert*, 476–77 (text); von Deines, Grapow, and Westerndorf, *Übersetzung der medizinischen Texte*, 277 (trans.). For P. BM 10059, 14.5–8, see Grapow, *Die medizinischen Texte in hieroglyphischer Umschreibung autographiert*, 487; von Deines, Grapow and Westerndorf, *Übersetzung der medizinischen Texte*, 283 (trans.). For P. BM 10059, 14.1–2.92, see Grapow, *Die medizinischen Texte in hieroglyphischer Umschreibung autographiert*, 482 (text); von Deines, Grapow, and Westendorf, *Übersetzung der medizinischen Texte*, 280 (trans.).

69. For possible conditions that might produce "heavy menstrual bleeding and vaginal odor," see <https://symptomchecker.webmd.com/multiple-symptoms?symptoms=heavy-menstrual-bleeding%7Cvaginal-odor&symptomids=118%7C410&locations=35%7C35> (accessed 15 August 2019).

70. Frandsen, "The Menstrual 'Taboo' in Ancient Egypt," 84–85.

Eine pseudohieratische Gefäßinschrift der Spätzeit aus Deir el-Bahari (Kairo JE 56283)

Günter Vittmann

für Richard 

§1. Einleitung

Bei den in Deir el-Bahari unter der Leitung von Herbert Winlock durchgeführten Grabungen des Metropolitan Museum wurde in der Kampagne 1930/1931 in einem späten Balsamierungsdepot 5,5 m östlich vom Grab des Djar (TT 366) auch ein großes beschriftetes Tongefäß entdeckt.[1] In seiner zusammenfassenden Grabungspublikation bietet Winlock eine knappe erste Beschreibung und das bislang einzige veröffentlichte Photo mit einer Ansicht einer von insgesamt vier durch gekrümmte Linien[2] abgetrennten Kolumnen.[3] Zur Beschriftung bemerkt er: „Many of the signs are without question Egyptian hieratic. Others are less easily identified, and the meaning of the whole has so far defied solution by anyone to whom we have shown the jar or photographs". Es handelt sich um einen sogenannten „sausage jar"[4]; das maschinschriftliche Grabungsjournal notiert dazu: „Type B. Coarse red ware, no slip. Two-thirds of the surface of the pot, from head to foot, covered with closely spaced horizontal lines of Late hieratic inscriptions written in black ink with a coarse pen. Height 55 cm. Diameter at mouth 10 cm. Maximum diameter 26 cm."[5]

Das seitdem in der Forschung nahezu völlig unbeachtet gebliebene Stück[6] gelangte ins Ägyptische Museum Kairo, wo es unter der Nummer JE 56283 registriert ist. Es wird im Magazin aufbewahrt, wo ich es im März 2017 in Augenschein nehmen und durchphotographieren lassen konnte.[7] Dabei zeigte sich, daß sich der Zustand der Inschriften vor allem in der oberen Hälfte von Kolumne III verschlechtert hatte (Abb. 7), so daß hier auf die alten

1. Erste Hinweise auf dieses Schriftzeugnis erhielt ich vor längerer Zeit von Karl-Theodor Zauzich und Mark Depauw.
2. Ähnliche Begrenzungslinien finden sich in noch unpublizierten hieratischen Gefäßinschriften der Dritten Zwischenzeit aus Mut (Dachla).
3. Herbert Winlock, „The Museum's Excavations at Thebes", *BMMA* 27 (1932): 37 und 36 fig. 40; Herbert Winlock, *Excavations at Deir el Bahri: 1911–1931* (New York: Macmillan, 1942), 221 und Taf. 96. Das Photo zeigt Kol. II und jeweils die Zeilenenden und -anfänge von Kol. I und III.
4. Vgl. hierzu die Literaturhinweise bei Günter Vittmann, „Eine kursivhieratische Gefäßinschrift aus Gurna", in *Hieratic, Demotic and Greek Studies and Text Editions: Of Making Books There Is No End; Festschrift in Honour of Sven P. Vleeming*, hg. Koenraad Donker van Heel, Francisca A.J. Hoogendijk, und Cary J. Martin, PLB 34 (Leiden: Brill, 2018), 81 Anm. 1.
5. Für die Bereitstellung der Grabungsphotos (M12C 13–17; siehe Abb. 1, 4, 8, 10, 12) sowie der einschlägigen Unterlagen (Beschreibungen im Grabungsjournal mit Angabe von jetzigem Standort und Inventarnummer; Korrespondenz zwischen Winlock und Petrie) danke ich Marsha Hill vom Metropolitan Museum sehr herzlich.
6. Erwähnungen in der Literatur sind äußerst rar; vgl. wiederholt bei Julia Budka (siehe unten Anm. 23) und Vittmann, „Gefäßinschrift aus Gurna", 82.
7. Ich danke der Direktion des Ägyptischen Museums für die Genehmigung zur Publikation und Herrn Samih Mohsen für die Anfertigung der Photos. Aus Platzgründen können nur einige davon hier reproduziert werden (Abb. 2, 3, 5–7, 9, 11).

Grabungsphotos zurückgegriffen werden muß. Der Zufall wollte es, daß mir Richard nur wenige Tage, nachdem ich das Original gesehen hatte, sein Interesse an der rätselhaften Schrift bekundete und mich zur Arbeit an der Erschließung ermutigte. Auch wenn ich den Schlüssel zum Verständnis dieses, wie ich ihn vorläufig nennen möchte, pseudohieratischen Textes leider nicht gefunden habe, hoffe ich doch, daß der Jubilar meinem Beitrag etwas abgewinnen kann und ihm der entscheidende Durchbruch gelingt!

§2. Allgemeines zum Text; Datierung

Die erste der vier Kolumnen beginnt im Unterschied zu den übrigen bereits am Gefäßhals, und zwar mit dem hieratischen Tagesdatum *ỉbd 4 pr.t sw 8* „8. Pharmuthi". Auf die nächsten sechs jeweils in sich abgeschlossenen linksläufigen Zeilen in „pseudohieratisch" folgt in I 8 der nächste Datumseintrag *ỉbd 4 pr.t sw 9* „9. Pharmuthi" mit zehn Zeilen, und so geht es kontinuierlich weiter bis zum letzten Datum *ỉbd 4 pr.t sw 18* „18. Pharmuthi" (in IV 16). Die Anzahl der den jeweiligen Datumseinträgen zugewiesenen Zeilen schwankt zwischen 6 und 14 mit Ausnahme des letzten Datums in IV 16, auf das nur eine einzige Zeile folgt, mit der die Kolumne und somit die ganze Beschriftung auf halber Höhe des Gefäßes endet.

Der Gefäßtyp („sausage jar", vgl. oben §1) weist auf eine Datierung ins 7.–6. Jh. v.Chr.[8] Die „echthieratischen" Tagesdaten (s. unten §3) tragen für eine Präzisierung wenig aus, doch scheint mir die unverbundene Schreibung von 2, 3 und 4 bei *ỉbd* eher auf die erste Hälfte des genannten Zeitansatzes hinzuweisen.

Weiteres zu Schrift sowie mutmaßlichem Inhalt s. unten §10.

§3. Die hieratischen Tagesdaten

Die nachstehende Übersicht bietet Faksimiles der hieratischen Tagesdaten; zusätzlich wird die Anzahl der jeweils anschließenden Zeilen angegeben, ebenso die „echthieratische" Kurzzeile IV 15.

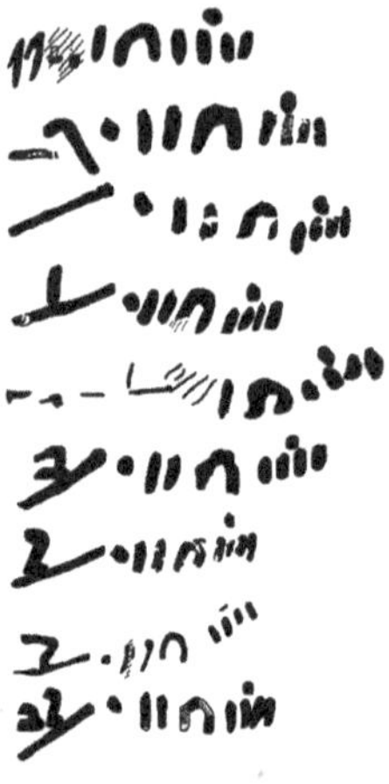

ỉbd 4 pr.t[9] *sw 8* I 1;	6 Zeilen (I 2–7)
ỉbd 4 pr.t sw 9 I 8;	10 Zeilen (I 9–18)
ỉbd 4 pr.t sw 10 I 19;	11 Zeilen (I 20–30)
ỉbd 4 pr.t sw 11 I 31;	
II 1;[10]	12 Zeilen (I 32; II 2–12)
ỉbd 4 pr.t sw 12 II 13;	10 Zeilen (II 14–23)
ỉbd 4 pr.t sw 13 II 24;	12 Zeilen (II 25–36)
ỉbd 4 pr.t sw 14 III 1;	13 Zeilen (III 2–14)
ỉbd 4 pr.t sw 15 III 15;	10 Zeilen (III 16–25)

8. Vergleiche Julia Budka, „Deponierungen von Balsamierungsmaterial und Topfnester im spätzeitlichen Theben (Ägypten). Befund, Kontext und Versuch einer Deutung", in *Archäologie und Ritual. Auf der Suche nach der rituellen Handlung in den antiken Kulturen Ägyptens und Griechenlands*, hg. Joannis Mylonopoulos und Hubert Roeder (Wien: Phoibos, 2006), 85–103, hier 92, mit weiterer Literatur.

9. Im Hinblick auf das erste Zeichen höchstwahrscheinlich so zu lesen und nicht *šmw*.

10. Das schon in I 31 notierte Tagesdatum wurde vom Schreiber im Kolumnenumbruch wiederholt.

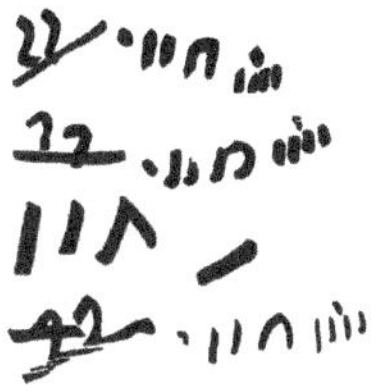

ỉbd 4 pr.t sw 16 III 26;	12 Zeilen (III 27–38)
ỉbd 4 pr.t sw 17 IV 1;	13 Zeilen (IV 2–14)
r(?) *12* „macht 12" (IV 15)	
ỉbd 4 pr.t sw 18 IV 16	1 Zeile (IV 17)

In zwei oder drei Fällen wird die Tageszahl von einem Horizontalstrich begleitet (I 8, vielleicht auch in II 1) bzw. gekreuzt (IV 16). Dieser Horizontalstrich stellt vermutlich eine Markierung dar, wie sie sich fast durchgehend an den Zeilenenden in Verbindung mit einem Vertikalstrich, in seltenen Fällen aber auch sonst, findet, vgl. unten §8b.

§4. Die Textzeilen und ihre Wiederholungen

Von den insgesamt 110 „pseudohieratischen" Zeilen werden etliche mehr oder weniger häufig wiederholt, mit einer auffallenden (scheinbaren?) Ausnahme[11] jedoch nicht im Rahmen desselben Tagesdatums. So begegnen beispielsweise Einträge [1] und [9] der nachstehenden Belegliste in neun von elf Datumseinträgen, während mehrere Einträge lediglich ein einziges Mal vorkommen. Die nachstehende Liste bietet Faksimiles und Stellennachweise für jede Zeile geordnet nach dem jeweils ersten Auftreten. Insgesamt kann man demnach 35 verschiedene, jeweils eine Zeile umfassende Zeichengruppierungen unterscheiden, wobei gewisse Abweichungen – Ersatz eines Zeichens durch ein anderes oder gelegentliche Erweiterungen – nicht mitgezählt sind (hierfür werden meist Zusatzbuchstaben verwendet).

[1] I 2. 15. 30; II 6. 18. 32; III 10. 33; IV 5

[2a] I 3. 26; II 12. 17; III 13. 36; IV 6 (hier ohne den abschließenden Horizontalstrich).

[2b] (wie 2a, aber erstes Zeichen anders) I 16; II 5. 20 (hier ohne den abschließenden Horizontalstrich). 29; III 11. 25. 32; IV 13

[3] I 4 (vgl. [28] mit weiterem Zeichen vor dem Schlußzeichen)

[4] I 5

[5] I 6 (ohne Vertikalstrich vor dem abschließenden Horizontalstrich); II 31; III 34

[6a] I 7; II 8; III 35; IV 8

[6b] (wie 6a, aber ohne das erste Zeichen) I 14. 25; III 7. 24

11. Nr. [2a] und [2b] der nachstehenden Liste kommen in fünf Fällen in denselben Datumseinträgen vor (Einträge zu Tag 11; 12; 14; 16; 17; siehe unten §9).

[7a] I 9; I 24; II 2. 14; II 28; III 2; IV 2

[7b] (statt des letzten Zeichens eine längere, anscheinend mit hieratischer *13* endende Gruppe) III 16

[7c] (wie 7a, am Ende jedoch abweichend) III 27

[8] I 10. 21; II 15. 27; III 3. 17. 30; IV 3. Die beiden ersten Zeichen auch in [19].

[9] I 11. 20; II 4. 16. 30 (hier ohne den abschließenden Horizontalstrich); III 4. 18. 29; IV 4

[10] I 12. Die ersten drei Zeichen auch in [17]; [22a+b]; [29a+b].

[11a] I 13

[11b] (wie 11a, aber mit abweichendem hinteren Teil) III 22

[11c] (= erste Hälfte von 11a + Schlußzeichen) II 23; IV 9

[12] I 17; II 7; III 6

[13a] I 18. 27; II 11; III 5. 28; vgl. [21]

[13b] IV 7 (mit zusätzlichem Vertikalstrich; vgl. [23b])

[14] I 22; II 35

[15a] I 23; II 9

[15b] II 25

[16] I 28; II 36

[17] I 29

Nota bene: Die Zeichen (inklusive Punkt) bis einschließlich ☥ auch am Anfang von [22b]; ohne Punkt in [22a]; vgl. auch oben zu [10].

[18] I 32

[19] II 3 (für den Anfang vgl. [8])

[20] II 10

[21] II 19 (die ersten beiden Zeichen mit Punkt entsprechen Gruppe [13a])

[22a] II 21. Die ersten fünf Zeichen auch in [17]. – Mit abweichender zweiter Hälfte:

[22b] II 26. Vergleiche auch oben zu [10].

[23a] II 22; IV 12

[23b] III 20 (mit zusätzlichem Vertikalstrich)

[24]  II 33;  III 31
[25] 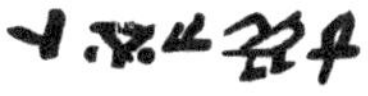 II 34
[26]  III 8
[27]  III 9
[28]  III 12;  IV 11 (vgl. [3], wo das vorletzte Zeichen fehlt)
[29a]  III 14; 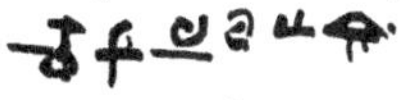 IV 14
[**29b**] (wie 29a, aber letztes Zeichen anders) 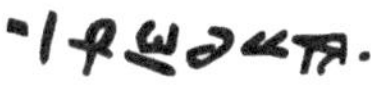 III 38
[30] 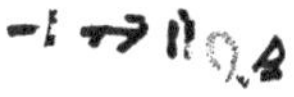 III 19
[31]  III 21
[32]  III 23
[33]  III 37
[34]  IV 10
[35]  IV 17

Oben nicht berücksichtigt wurden die einzelnen Zeichen, die sich abgesetzt am äußersten Ende von II 23–25 finden und nicht unmittelbar zum jeweils vorangehenden Text gehören dürften (vgl. Abb. 6):  II 23;  II 24;  II 25.

§5. Häufigkeit der Einträge

15×: [2a+b]
9×: [1]; [7a+b+c]; [9]
8×: [6a+b]; [8]
6×: [13a+b]
4×: [11a+b+c]
3×: [5]; [12]; [15a+b]; [23a+b]; [29a+b]
2×: [14]; [22a+b]; [16]; [24]; [28]
1×: [3]; [4]; [10]; [17–21]; [25–27]; [30–35]

§6. Zeicheninventar

Die folgende Tabelle enthält a) die vorkommenden Zeichen mit laufender Nummer sowie die Nummer der betreffenden Gruppe nach §4 in eckigen Klammern. Mehrmaliges Vorkommen eines Zeichens innerhalb einer Gruppe wird durch „2x“ gekennzeichnet; Verdoppelung eines Zeichens durch Unterstreichung „2x“[12]. Verweise auf Gruppen, die mindestens dreimal vorkommen, werden **fett** gesetzt. Die Reihe wird durch die auffallenden „kursivhieroglyphischen“ Zeichen eröffnet, die „Zahlzeichen“ 1 bis 4 stehen zum Ende hin (Nr. 28–31), und das fast in sämtlichen Zeilen erscheinende Schlußzeichen steht auch hier am Schluß. Aus Platzgründen können die Belege nicht für

12. Nur bei den Zeichen 2 und 17 belegt.

jedes Zeichen im Kontext und in extenso reproduziert werden; in verschiedener Hinsicht bemerkenswerte Zeichengruppierungen werden aber unten besprochen. Die Angabe „alle Positionen" in der letzten Spalte besagt, daß das betreffende Zeichen am Anfang, im Inneren oder am Ende einer Zeile (jedoch vor dem Schlußzeichen Nr. 32 oder ausnahmsweise Nr. 34) belegbar ist. Analog impliziert die Angabe „Ende" ohne weitere Spezifizierung, daß das betreffende Zeichen vor Nr. 32 oder 34 steht.

Nr.	Zeichen	belegt in Gruppe[13] Nr.	Bemerkungen	Position
1		[10]; [17]; [18]; [21] (2×); [22a]; [22b] (2×); [25]; [26]; **[29a+b]**; [35]	12× in 10 Gruppen	alle Positionen
2		**[7c]** (2×); [17]; [29a]; [33]		in [17] Mitte, sonst Ende vor Nr. 34 oder absolutes Ende ([33])
3		**[6a]**; **[12]**; [14]; **[15a+b]**; [26]; [33]; II 24	in [6a] / IV 8 eher , siehe oben §4 Faksimile	Anfang; im Inneren; in II 24 isoliert, s. §4 Ende
4		**[5]**; **[9]**; [17]; [20]; [34]		alle Positionen
4a		[25]		im Inneren (folgt auf )
4b		[31]		Anfang
5		**[12]**		Ende
6		[1]		Ende
7		[3]; **[12]**; [28]; [34]		im Inneren; Ende
8		**[11a–c]**; II 23 (§4 Ende)		im Inneren; Ende
9		**[23a+b]**		Anfang
10		[4]		Ende
11		[5]; [17]		im Inneren; Ende

13. „Gruppe" meint auch hier die komplette Zeile.

Nr.	Zeichen	belegt in Gruppe Nr.	Bemerkungen	Position
12		[27]		Ende
13		[**1**]; [**2a+b**]; [3]; [4]; [**5**]; [**7a–c**]; [9]; [**11a–c**]; [14]; [16]; [17]; [20]; [**22a+b**] (2×); [25]; [27]; [28]; [**29a+b**]; II 23 (§4 Ende)	18× in 17 Gruppen	Anfang; im Inneren
14		[**8**]; [19]		im Inneren; Ende
15		[**2a**]; [18]; [22a]; [28]		alle Positionen
16		[5]; [10]; [**12**]; [14]; [25]		alle Positionen
17		[**2b**]; [**13a+b**] [2×]; [17]; [19]; [21] (2×); [22a+b]; [**29a–c**]; II 25	9× in 7 Gruppen	meist am Anfang (und dann gern doppelt); einmal am absoluten Ende [22b], einmal im Inneren [19]; einmal (II 25) isoliert, s. §4 Ende
18		[**7a–c**] [2×]; [**9**]; [10]; [11a] (2×); [11b+c]; [**15a+b**]; [17]; [21]; [22a+b]; [**23a+b**]; [**29a+b**]; [34]	14× in 12 Gruppen	im Inneren; Ende
19		[**2a+b**]; [**6a+b**]; [11b]; [**15a+b**]; [**23a+b**]; [24]; [33]		im Inneren; in allen Belegen geht eines der „Zahlzeichen" Nr. 28 bis 31 voraus
20		[7a–c]; [**9**]; [**11a–c**]; [20]		im Inneren; mit Ausnahme von [20] stets in Verbindung  (Nr. 13-20-18)
21		[**7a–c**]; [10]; [17]; [19]; [21]; [22a+b] (2×); [26]; [**29a+b**]; [35]	11× in 9 Gruppen	Anfang; im Inneren; öfters 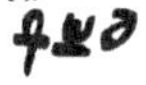 (Nr. 21-18-1)
22		[8]; [19]; [21]		Anfang; Ende
23		[34]		im Inneren

Nr.	Zeichen	belegt in Gruppe Nr.	Bemerkungen	Position
24		[7b]; [35]		[7b] vor hieratisch am Ende stehender *13*; [35] vor Nr. 32+34
25		[4]; **[15a+b]**		Anfang
26	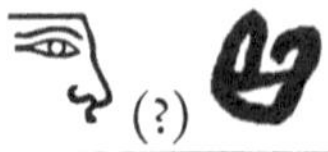	[18]; [22b]; [26] (2×); [35]	Siehe unten §10	im Inneren; Ende
27		[24]		Anfang
28		**[6a+b]**	Zu Zeichen 28 bis 31 siehe unten §8c.	Anfang; im Inneren; es folgt Nr. 19
29		[11b]; **[23a+b]**; [24];		im Inneren; es folgt Nr. 19
29a		[10]; [11a]; [11b]; [21]; [22a+b]; [30]; 34]		im Inneren (Nr. 19 folgt nie)
30		[15a]; [33]		im Inneren; es folgt Nr. 19
31		**[2a+b]**; [15b]		zusammen mit folgender Nr. 19 am Ende
32	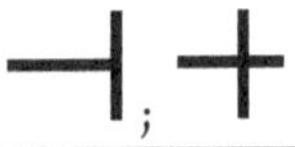	passim	Kombination aus 33+34	fast durchgehend am Zeilenende, s. §8b
33		[2a]; [2b]; [9]; II 23 (§4 Ende)	In [2a] / [2b] / [9] nur in jeweils einem von 7 / 8 / 9 Belegen; alle übrigen haben stattdessen Zeichen Nr. 32. Vgl. dagegen Zeichen Nr. 20, wo der Vertikalstrich integrierender Teil sein muß.	am absoluten Ende; in [13b] und [23b] vor Zeichen Nr. 32
34		[7c]	wie 32, aber ohne Kombination mit Vertikalstrich	am absoluten Ende
35–37		[10]	Alle Zeichen treten nur an einer Stelle (I 12) auf.	Ende
38		[11a]		im Inneren

Nr.	Zeichen	belegt in Gruppe Nr.	Bemerkungen	Position
39		[16]		Ende
40–41		[18]	beide Zeichen nur an einer Stelle (I 32)	im Inneren
42		[30]		Ende

Wie aus der Tabelle zu ersehen, steht an der Spitze der Zeichen, die am häufigsten in *verschiedenen* Gruppen (also nicht am absolut häufigsten) vorkommen, Nr. 13 (), gefolgt von Nr. 1 (), Nr. 18 (), Nr. 17 (), Nr. 21 () und Nr. 19 ().

§7. Länge der Zeilen; öfter vorkommende Zeichengruppierungen

Bei mehrfachem Vorkommen wird nur eine Schreibung als Beispiel ausgewählt; für detaillierte Belegnachweise und Faksimiles siehe oben §4. Numerierung der einzelnen Zeichen nach §6.

a) Gruppen mit 2(?) Zeichen (1)

[31]  4b-32 (1×)

b) Gruppen mit 3 Zeichen (7)

[1]  13-6-32 (9×)
[3]  13-7-32 (1×)
[6b] 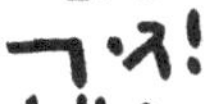 28-19-32 (4×)
[8] 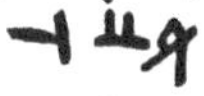 22-14-32 (8×)
[13a]  17-17-●[14]-32 (5×); s. auch unten unter b und i
[16]  13-39-32 (2×)
[27]  13-12-32 (1×)

c) Gruppen mit 4 Zeichen (5)

[4]  25-13-10-32 (1×)
[6a] 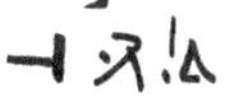 3-28-19-32 (4×)
[13b]  17-17-●-33-32 (1×); s. auch oben unter b und unten i [21]
[24] 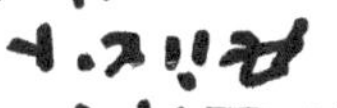 27-29-19-32 (2×)
[28] 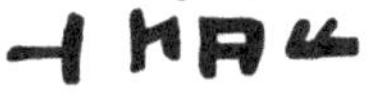 13-7-15-32 (2×)

14. Ich zähle den Punkt nicht als eigenes Zeichen mit; vgl. §8a.

d) Gruppen mit 5 Zeichen (9)

[2a]  15-13-31-19-32 (7×)
[2b]  17-13-31-19-32 (8×)
[5]  16-13-4-11-32 (3×)
[9]  4-13-20-18-32 (9×)
[12]  3-16-7-5-32 (3×)
[14]  13-8-3-16-32 (2×)
[23a]  9-29-19-18-32 (2×)
[25] 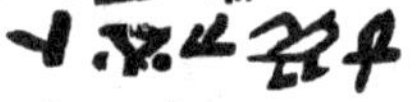 1-4a-13-16-32 (1×)
[30] 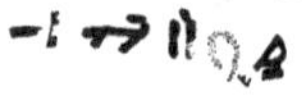 4-?-29a-42-32 (1×)

e) Gruppen mit 6 Zeichen (11)

[7a]  21-18-13-20-18-32 (7×)
[11c]  13-20-18-13-8-32 (2×); vgl. unten unter h
[15a]  25-3-18-30-19-32 (2×)
[15b]  25-3-18-31-19-32 (1×)
[18]  15-40-41-26-1-32 (1×)
[20]  13-8-20-13-4-32 (1×)
[23b]  9-29-19-18-33-32 (1×)
[29b]  ●-17-13-21-18-1-32 (1×)
[33]  3-13-30-19-8-2 (1×)
[34] 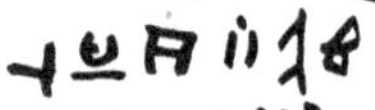 4-23-29a-7-18-32 (1×)
[35] 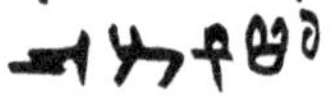 21-26-1-24-32-34 (1×)

f) Gruppen mit 7 Zeichen (2)

[26] 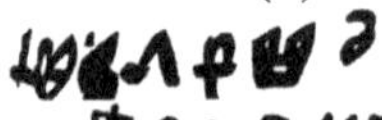 21-26-1-3-⸢?⸣-26-32 (1×)
[29a] 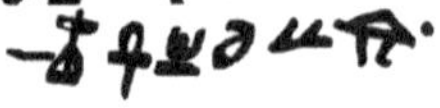 ●-17-13-21-18-1-2-34 (2×)

g) Gruppen mit 8 Zeichen (1)

[19]  22-14-32(?)-●-17-13-21-18-32 (1×)

h) Gruppen mit 9 Zeichen (2)

[7c]  21-18-13-20-18-33-2-2-34 (1×)
[11a] 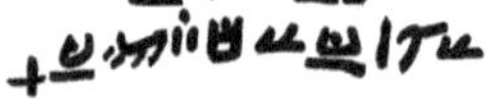 13-20-18-13-8-29a-38-18-32 (1×)

i) Gruppen mit 10 Zeichen und darüber (6)

[10]  21-18-1-13-16-29a-35-36-37-32 (1×)

[21]  17-17-●-29a-21-18-1-13-1-22-32 (1×)
[11b]  13-20-18-13-8-29a-?-13-29-19-32 (1×)
[17]  ●-17-13-21-18-1-2-?-?-4-11-?-13 (1×)

Die Zeichenfolge 17-13-21-18-1 kehrt in den zwei nächsten Gruppen wieder.

[22a]  17-13-21-18-1-29a-15-21-?-13-10-32 (1×)
[22b]  ●-17-13-21-18-1-29a-21-26-13-17 (1×)

§8. Kommentar zu einzelnen Zeichen

a) Funktion des Punktes ●:

In einigen Fällen sind ein oder zwei Punkte offensichtlich integrierender Bestandteil eines Zeichens (Nr. 16; Nr. 19; bei den „Zahlzeichen" Nr. 28–31, s. unten c), vor und nach (Nr. 17) erscheint jedoch gelegentlich ein Punkt, dessen Bedeutung unklar ist.

b) zum Schlußzeichen:

Nahezu jede Zeile wird durch ein zweiteiliges Zeichen (Nr. 32) beendet, das in den Formen , , und ähnlich erscheint und im Zeileninneren nicht üblich ist.

In II 20 (Variante von Gruppe [2b]); II 30 (Variante von [9]); IV 6 (Variante von [2a]) fehlt im Unterschied zu den Parallelen der Horizontalstrich. Umgekehrt fehlt in I 6 (Variante von [5]) im Unterschied zu den Parallelen der Vertikalstrich. Ebenfalls nur mit Horizontalstrich endet III 27 (= [7c]). Zu bemerken ist, daß [29a] (III 14; IV 14) auf endet, wo [29b] (III 38) das normale Schlußzeichen hat.

IV 17 (= [35] hat die Kombination Schlußzeichen + (zusätzlichen) Horizontalstrich.

Die langen Gruppen [17] (= I 29) und [22b] (= II 26) enden abrupt ohne Schlußzeichen oder einzelnen Horizontal- oder Vertikalstrich.

c) Zu den „Zahlzeichen": Die Zeichen , , , , (Nr. 28–31) erinnern an hieroglyphische bzw. hieratische Zahlzeichen, für die sie Petrie tatsächlich gehalten hat (s. unten §11 Appendix), doch bliebe der ausnahmslos gesetzte Punkt erklärungsbedürftig. Die Beobachtung, daß das relativ häufige Zeichen Nr. 19 () ausschließlich mit vorangehendem „Zahlzeichen" vorkommt, hilft leider nicht weiter. Auch hier gilt, daß die äußere Ähnlichkeit nicht unbedingt etwas über die tatsächliche Bedeutung besagen muß.

§9. Anstelle einer Umschrift

Anstelle einer – mit Ausnahme der Datumsangaben und der Kurzzeile IV 15 – derzeit nicht möglichen Umschrift werden einfach die Nummern der Liste in §6 angegeben. Die am Ende von II 23–25 abgesetzten Zeichen (s. oben §4 Ende) werden nach dem Zeicheninventar in §6 numeriert.

Col. I (Abb. 1–3, 12)
[1]*ỉbd 4 pr.t sw 8* [2][1] [3][2a] [4][3] [5][4] [6][5] [7][6a]
[8]*ỉbd 4 pr.t sw 9* [9][7a] [10][8] [11][9] [12][10] [13][11a] [14][6b] [15][1] [16][2b] [17][12] [18][13a]
[19]*ỉbd 4 pr.t sw 10* [20][9] [21][8] [22][14] [23][15a] [24][7a] [25][6b] [26][2a] [27][13a] [28][16] [29][17] [30][1]

[31]*ỉbd 4 pr.t sw 11* [32][18]
Col. II (Abb. 4–6)
[1]*ỉbd 4 pr.t sw 11* [2][7a] [3][19] [4][9] [5][2b] [6][1] [7][12] [8][6a] [9][15a] [10][20] [11][13a] [12][2a]
[13]*ỉbd 4 pr.t sw 12* [14][7a] [15][8] [16][9] [17][2a] [18][1] [19][21] [20][2b] [21][22a] [22][23a] [23][11c] Spatium 13-8-33
[24]*ỉbd 4 pr.t sw 13* Spatium 3 [25][15b] Spatium ●-17 [26][22b] [27][8] [28][7a] [29][2b] [30][9] [31][5] [32][1] [33][24] [34][25]
[35][14] [36][16]
Col. III (Abb. 7–9, 11, 12)
[1]*ỉbd 4 pr.t sw 14* [2][7a] [3][8] [4][9] [5][13a] [6][12] [7][6b] [8][26] [9][27] [10][1] [11][2b] [12][28] [13][2a] [14][29a]
[15]*ỉbd 4 pr.t sw 15* [16][7b[15]] [17][8] [18][9] [19][30] [20][23b] [21][31] [22][11b] [23][32] [24][6b] [25][2b]
[26]*ỉbd 4 pr.t sw 16* [27][7c] [28][13a] [29][9] [30][8] [31][24] [32][2b] [33][1] [34][5] [35][6a] [36][2a] [37][33] [38][29b]
Col. IV (Abb. 10–12)
[1]*ỉbd 4 pr.t sw 17* [2][7a] [3][8] [4][9] [5][1] [6][2a] [7][13b] [8][6b] [9][11c] [10][34] [11][28] [12][23] [13][2b] [14][29a] [15]*r 12*
[16]*ỉbd 4 pr.t sw 18* [17][35]

§10. Vergleichendes und Zusammenfassendes zu Schrift und Text

Von den Schriftzeichen sind nur wenige eindeutig an (mehr oder weniger kursiven) Hieroglyphen orientiert, am klarsten Nr. 1 ( ), 2 ( ), 3 (bzw.), recht deutlich aber auch Nr. 4 ( ) und das lediglich ein einziges Mal (als Variante des vorigen?) belegte Zeichen 4a , das in Verbindung mit dem vorangehendem (II 34, = Gruppe [25]) in wohl trügerischer Weise an den Namen *ʿnḫ-ḥr* denken läßt. Analoge Ableitungen sind etwa auch für Nr. 5 ; Nr. 7 (< ?); Nr. 13 (< ?); Nr. 26 (< ?[16]) denkbar. Es ist aber äußerst zweifelhaft, daß diese – und eventuell andere – Zeichen denselben Wert haben wie im möglichen hieratisch-hieroglyphischen Vorbild. Die überwiegende Mehrheit der Grapheme wie Nr. 17–22 läßt sich weder aus dem Hieratischen noch einer mir bekannten nichtägyptischen Schrift zwanglos und überzeugend herleiten: Könnte man für das häufige (Nr. 18) zur Not noch eine Anregung durch (kursives) vermuten, läßt sich für das ebenso häufige (Nr. 21) kein auch nur entfernt passendes hieratisches Zeichen ausfindig machen.

Ein erster flüchtiger Blick auf die Beschriftung läßt an die sogenannten „funny signs" denken, wie sie vor allem aus Deir el-Medineh und dem Tal der Könige bekannt sind.[17] Freilich sind die Zeichen hier wie dort bei näherer Betrachtung mit wenigen Ausnahmen grundverschieden, wie dies in Anbetracht des zeitlichen Abstandes von mehreren Jahrhunderten ja auch kein Wunder ist. Außerdem besteht auch formal kein erkennbarer Zusammenhang zwischen der Beschriftung des Kruges aus Deir el-Bahari und den „duty rosters" aus Deir el-Medineh einerseits und anderweitig bezeugten Markierungen andererseits, von dem sämtliche Zeugnisse mit „funny signs" um ein Vielfaches übersteigenden Umfang ganz zu schweigen. Es scheint sich also um eine eigenständige Neuschöpfung zu handeln, für die bis jetzt keine direkt vergleichbare Parallele bekannt ist. Für eine mehr oder weniger reine Alphabetschrift ist die Anzahl der verwendeten Zeichen zu groß, auch die relativ hohe Anzahl von Zeilen mit nur drei Zeichen, von denen das letzte (Nr. 32 der obigen Liste) mit Sicherheit keinen einzelnen Konsonanten bezeichnet, sondern viel-

15. III 16 endet, wie oben §4 [7b] angegeben, offenbar mit der in Klarschrift geschriebenen Zahl *13*.

16. Für einen (allerdings viel jüngeren) demotischen Beleg, der dem aus Deir el-Bahari sehr ähnlich ist, vgl. Pieter W. Pestman, *Les papyrus démotiques de Tsenhor (P. Tsenhor): Les archives privées d'une femme égyptienne du temps de Darius Ier*, StudDem 4 (Leuven: Peeters, 1994), II, 9* D20.

17. Vergleiche bahnbrechend Ben Haring, „Towards Decoding the Necropolis Workmen's Funny Signs", *GM* 178 (2000): 45–58; Daniel Soliman, „Of Marks and Men: The Functional and Historical Context of the Workmen's Marks of the Royal Theban Necropolis" (Dissertationsschrift, Universität Leiden, 2016); Ben Haring, *From Single Sign to Pseudo-Script: An Ancient Egyptian System of Workmen's Identity Marks*, CHANE 93 (Leiden: Brill, 2017) mit weiterer Literatur.

leicht eine Zahl (*1* mit spezieller Markierung?), spricht gegen eine derartige Annahme. Ob wir es dann eher mit einer Mischschrift aus Ein- und Mehrkonsonantenzeichen, vielleicht sogar mit Anreicherung durch einige „Ideogramme", zu tun haben, ist bis auf weiteres nicht zu entscheiden. Daß jedoch ein womöglich weitgehend illiterater „Schreiber"[18] auf seine Weise mit (fast?) jedem Zeichen einen eigenen konkreten Begriff für Lebensmittel, Kleidung, Geräte oder was auch immer ausdrücken wollte, halte ich in Anbetracht dafür m.E. allzu langer Zeilen, teils mit mehrfachem Vorkommen derselben Zeichen, für unwahrscheinlich.

Die Annahme, daß es sich um irgendeine Art von Abrechnung handeln dürfte, lag von Anfang an nahe (vgl. unten §11), ein endgültiger Beweis für diese Klassifizierung steht aus evidenten Gründen jedoch aus, und man fragt sich natürlich, warum eine Abrechnung in einer Art Geheimschrift verfaßt worden sein sollte. Immerhin lassen sich für die Verwendung großer Krüge als Schriftträger für Abrechnungen zeitgenössische (kursiv)hieratische und jüngere demotische Parallelen anführen.[19] Daß die Einträge in dem Krug aus Deir el-Bahari durchwegs Personennamen enthalten wie z.B. der erwähnte „sausage jar" aus Gurna oder der protodemotische pKöln 5432,[20] darf wohl ausgeschlossen werden: Die sieben aus drei bzw. unter Abzug des Schlußzeichens (§6 Nr. 32) aus lediglich zwei Zeichen bestehenden verschiedenen Gruppen (§7b) können unmöglich allesamt Namen enthalten, ganz zu schweigen davon, daß dann in der Regel auch der Vatersname oder ein Titel angegeben sein sollte. Theoretisch könnte das vor allem in längeren Gruppen, und nie am Anfang oder Ende, vorkommende Zeichen 29a (|̇|) für *s3* stehen und somit zwei Personennamen verbinden, aber ein wirklich überzeugender Nachweis hierfür ist mir nicht möglich.

Bei der Suche nach Personennamen und der Frage, ob es sich um eine Abrechnung handelt, sind nicht zuletzt zwei Umstände zu beachten:

1.) Die Zeichen |̣, |̣|, |̣||, und ||̣|| (§6, Nr. 28–31) erscheinen ausschließlich in Kombination mit folgendem •ʎ (Nr. 19), das seinerseits nie anderen Zeichen als den eben genannten folgt. Der Umstand, daß sich diese Kombinationen bereits in kurzen Gruppen mit drei und vier Zeichen einschließlich des Schlußzeichens finden (vgl. §7), schließt eine Auffassung als Personenname bzw. Teil davon sicher aus. Auch eine auf den ersten Blick naheliegende „wörtliche" Interpretation als Zahlzeichen führt nicht weiter, da sich für das erwähnte obligatorische Begleitzeichen keine passende Erklärung anbietet.

2.) Falls es sich tatsächlich um eine Abrechung handelt, sollte das Schlußzeichen Nr. 32 eine Zahl bezeichnen, dann also vermutlich eine mit einer Kontrollmarkierung versehene *1*. Für eine Abrechnung wäre es freilich recht ungewöhnlich, daß die Zahl immer *1* sein sollte, auch wenn man es natürlich nicht strikt ausschließen kann.[21] In der Tat enthält eine demotische Liste von Personennamen bei jedem Eintrag, soweit erhalten, den Vermerk *1*, womit in diesem speziellen Fall vielleicht jede einzelne Person als Teil einer Mannschaft „gezählt" wird.[22]

Grundsätzlich ist auch mit Winlock (unten §11) zu fragen, ob die Beschriftungen sachlich mit der Verwendung des Gefäßes zur Deponierung von Balsamierungsmaterialien zusammenhängen (oben §1) oder ob die genannte

---

18. Zu der in manchen Ostraka zu Tage tretenden mangelnden Vertrautheit mit dem ägyptischen Schriftsystem vgl. Haring, *From Single Sign to Pseudo-Script*, 233. Kurioserweise sind an der dort behandelten Stelle die Tagesdaten unorthodox geschrieben, während gerade diese in unserem Falle standardmäßig geschrieben sind.

19. Vittmann, „Gefäßinschrift aus Gurna", 82 mit Anm. 13–15.

20. Günter Vittmann, „Eine ‚protodemotische' Abrechnung aus der Dritten Zwischenzeit (pKöln 5632)", in *Ein Kundiger, der in die Gottesworte eingedrungen ist. Festschrift für den Ägyptologen Karl Jansen-Winkeln zum 65. Geburtstag*, hg. Shih-Wei Hsu et al., ÄAT 99 (Münster: Zaphon, 2020), 317–43.

21. In der bei Edward R. Ayrton, Charles T. Currelly und Arthur E. P. Weigall, *Abydos, Part III*, EEF 25 (London: Egypt Exploration Fund, 1904), Taf. XXXA faksimilierten kursivhieratischen Gefäßinschrift mit einer Abrechnung in mehreren Kolumnen ist die Zahl am Zeilenende meist *1*.

22. Harry S. Smith und Cary J. Martin, „Demotic Papyri from the Sacred Animal Necropolis of North Saqqara: Certainly or Possibly of Achaemenid Date", in *Organisation des pouvoirs et contacts culturels dans les pays de l'empire achémenide*, hg. Pierre Briant und Michel Chauveau (Paris: Boccard, 2009), 23–78, hier 44–46, Text Nr. 8.

Verwendung sekundär ist und die Aufschriften bereits früher angebracht worden waren, als das Gefäß für andere Zwecke genutzt wurde.

Die bisher unbemerkten fortlaufenden Tagesdaten dürften jedenfalls einen magischen Zusammenhang, wie er auch schon vermutet worden ist,[23] unwahrscheinlich machen.

§11. Appendix

Am 4. Mai 1932 teilte Petrie Winlock brieflich seine Einschätzung der Inschriften mit (vgl. Anm. 5); nicht zuletzt im Hinblick auf das Interesse des Jubilars für die Geschichte unseres Faches lohnt es sich, Petries Stellungnahme hier bekanntzumachen:

> I was shown a copy of it some time ago, but refrained from working at it, as it was in your hands. Now I send you my impressions in hopes that you may see some use in them.
>
> It is clearly an account list of items paid or received, for persons or things.
>
> Each line ends with ⊣ a sign of value (qedet?) or can ⊢ drachma[24] be as early? Before that are 9 different signs, some duplicates with ● added. This suggests finger counting +5 perhaps

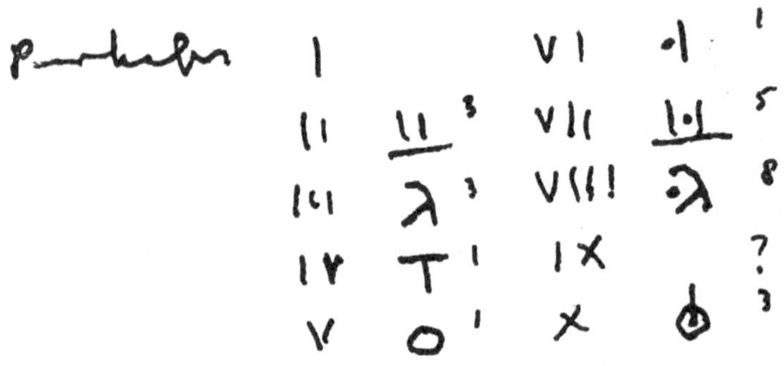

> Arabic numbers = repeats (frequency)
>
> I does not occur because the unit ⊣ does not need it.
>
> Before the numeral there may be only a single sign or or or this (*sic?*) cannot be goods. So probably names or titles of persons. So personal payments seem the most likely, but not wages as the numerals vary so much. Rather payments for goods, or receipts of goods delivered by persons.
>
> However, the whole needs to be classified before concluding anything.

In seiner vom 25. Mai 1932 datierten Antwort an Petrie schrieb Winlock:

23. Budka, „Deponierungen", 96; Julia Budka, *Bestattungsbrauchtum und Friedhofsstruktur im Asasif. Eine Untersuchung der spätzeitlichen Befunde anhand der Ergebnisse der österreichischen Ausgrabungen in den Jahren 1969–1977*, UZK 34 (Wien: Verlag der Österreichischen Akademie der Wissenschaften, 2010), 453 („vielleicht mit einem apotropäischen Zauber zu assoziieren") und 669 (Kat. 614). Die an allen drei Stellen sowie auf S. 421 erwähnte Scherbe K02/108 mit angeblicher Parallele ist jedoch nach einer mir freundlicherweise von der Verfasserin übermittelten Abbildung offenbar ein – wegen des schlechten Erhaltungszustands freilich kaum lesbarer – demotischer Text.

24. Petrie meinte die in griechischen Papyri belegte Abkürzung ⊢ = δράχμη, vgl. Pieter W. Pestman, *The New Papyrological Primer* (Leiden: Brill, 1990), unpaginierte Seite am Ende des Buches.

> We all felt that the inscription was some sort of an account, and your suggestion of numerals appears to be very enlightening. One of the things that puzzled me was to know whether the account belonged to the first or the second use of the pot. Almost all of the pots used for embalming material seem to be domestic vessels originally intended for very ordinary purposes. Some were surely wine jars, and others originally contained pickled fish. (…)
>
> We were, and still are, uncertain as to whether this account belongs to the domestic or the embalmer's use of the pot. If we knew we might have a clue as to the meaning. In any case it is very curious.

Petries ingeniöser Vorschlag, die von ihm zusammengestellten Zeichen als Zahlen zu deuten, ist unhaltbar, ganz zu schweigen davon, daß die Zahl *nach* der Einheit stehen sollte und nicht davor. Seine (und Winlocks) Annahme, daß es sich um eine Abrechnung („account list") handelt, ist an sich naheliegend, gerade auch im Hinblick auf die von beiden noch nicht wahrgenommenen Tagesdaten, aber – wie oben ausgeführt – einstweilen nicht zu erhärten und wegen des offenkundigen Fehlens unterschiedlicher Zahlenangaben fraglich. Nebenbei sei daran erinnert, daß sich Petrie durchaus auch für vergleichende Schriftgeschichte interessiert und diesem Thema sogar ein eigenes Buch gewidmet hat.[25]

25. William Matthew Flinders Petrie, *The Formation of the Alphabet*, BSAE 3 (London: Quaritch, 1912); vgl. zu Petries Auffassungen Haring, *From Single-Sign to Pseudo-Script*, 15–20, passim; Ludwig Morenz, *Sinai und Alphabetschrift. Die frühesten alphabetischen Inschriften und ihr kanaanäisch-ägyptischer Entstehungshorizont im Zweiten Jahrtausend v.Chr* (Berlin: EB Verlag, 2019), 33–34.

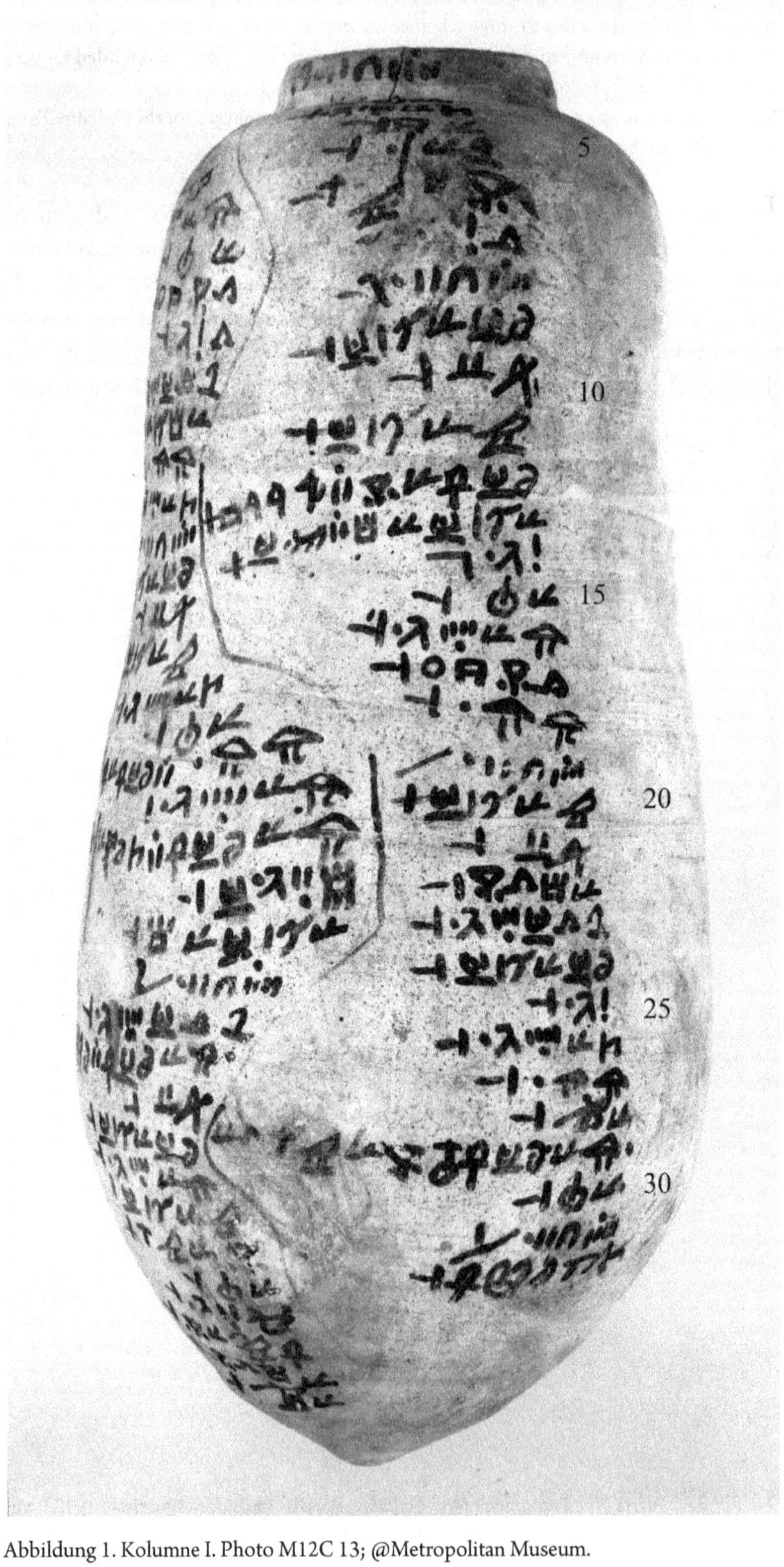

Abbildung 1. Kolumne I. Photo M12C 13; @Metropolitan Museum.

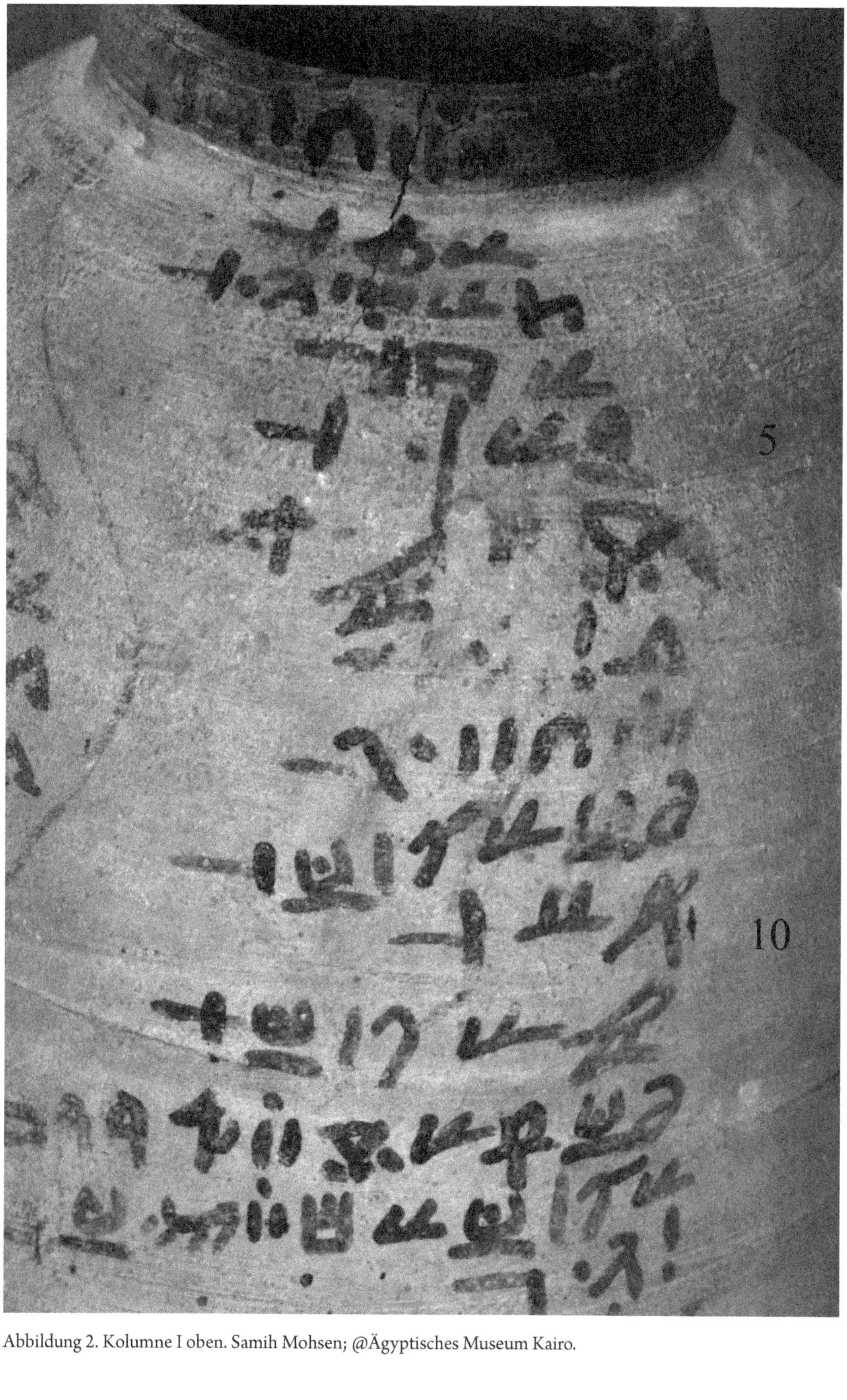

Abbildung 2. Kolumne I oben. Samih Mohsen; @Ägyptisches Museum Kairo.

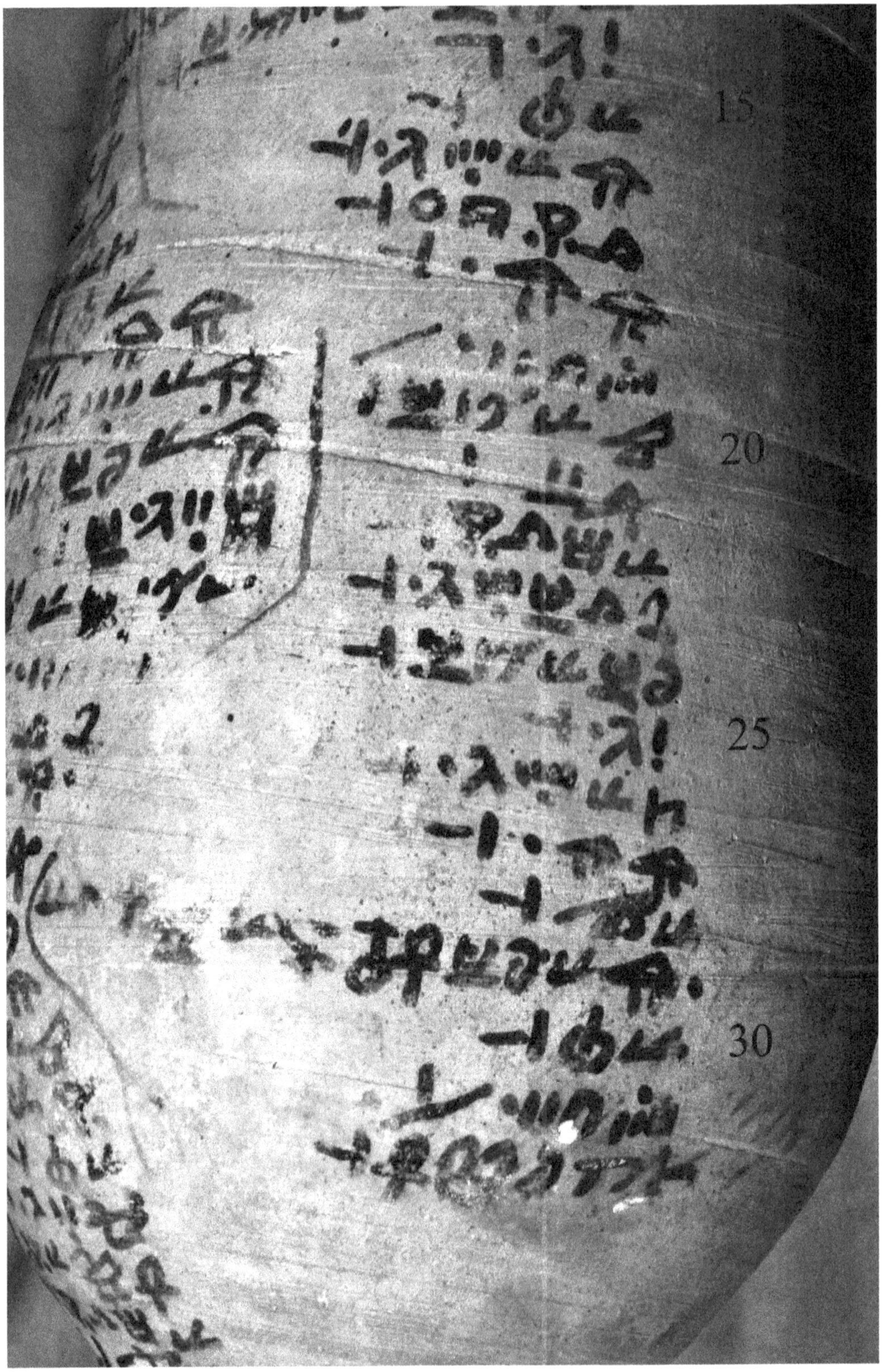

Abbildung 3. Kolumne I unten. Samih Mohsen; @Ägyptisches Museum Kairo.

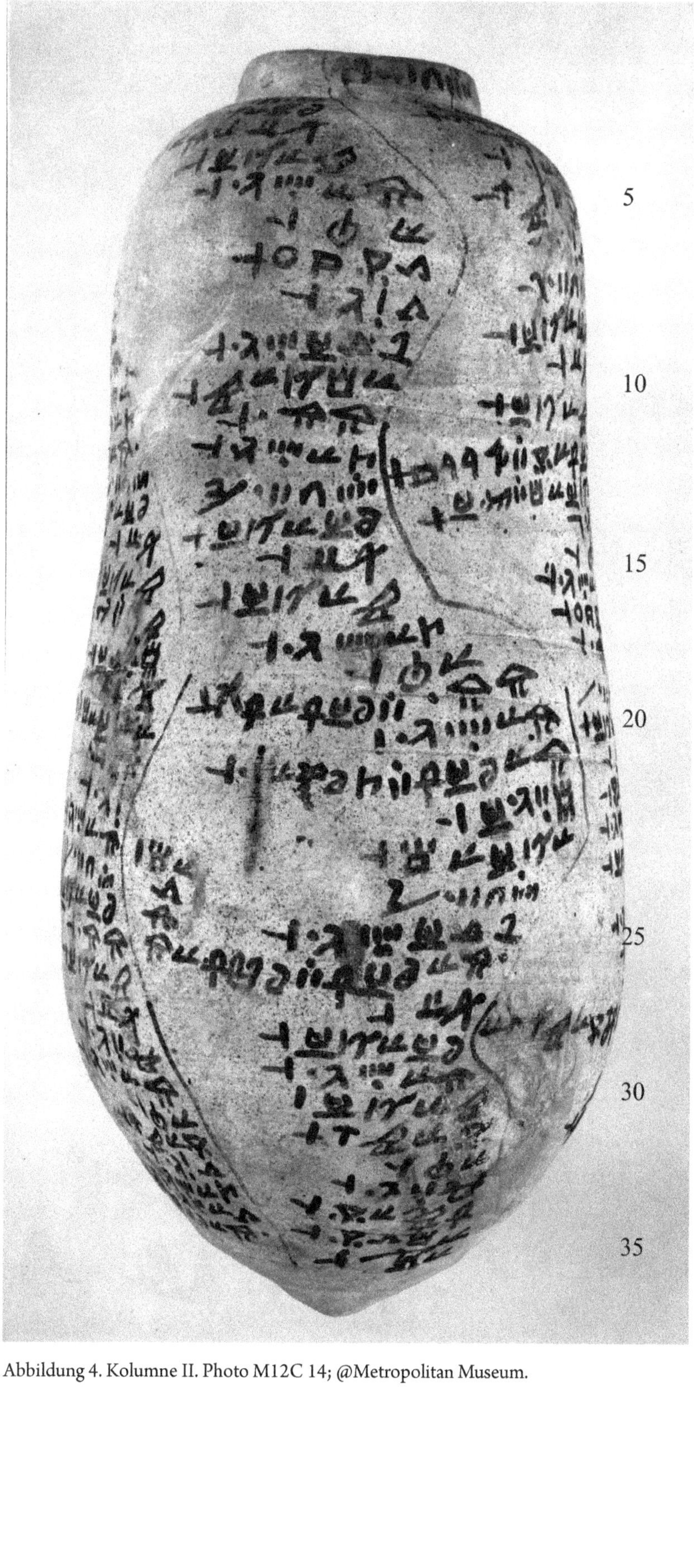

Abbildung 4. Kolumne II. Photo M12C 14; @Metropolitan Museum.

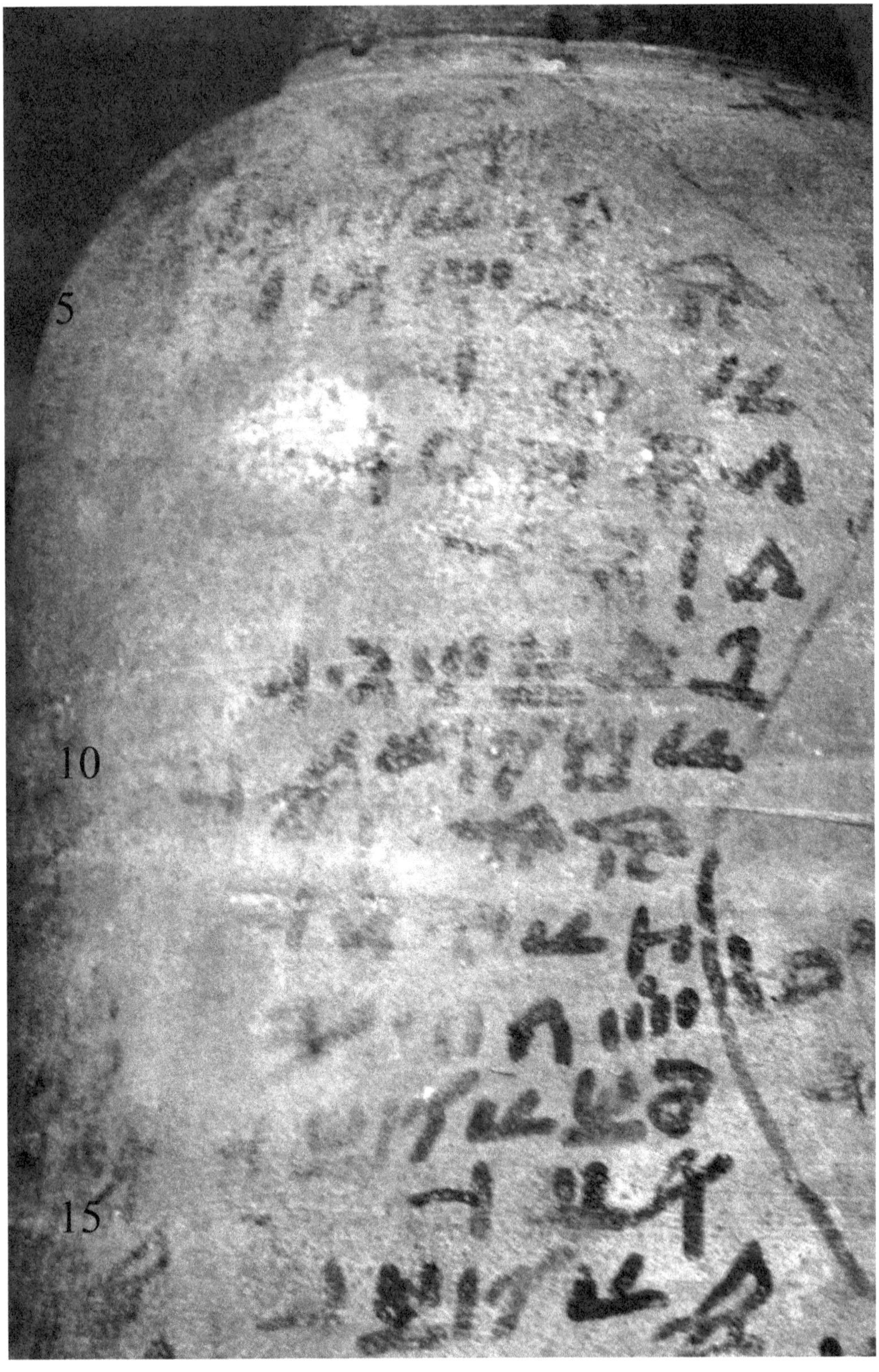

Abbildung 5. Kolumne II oben. Samih Mohsen; @Ägyptisches Museum Kairo.

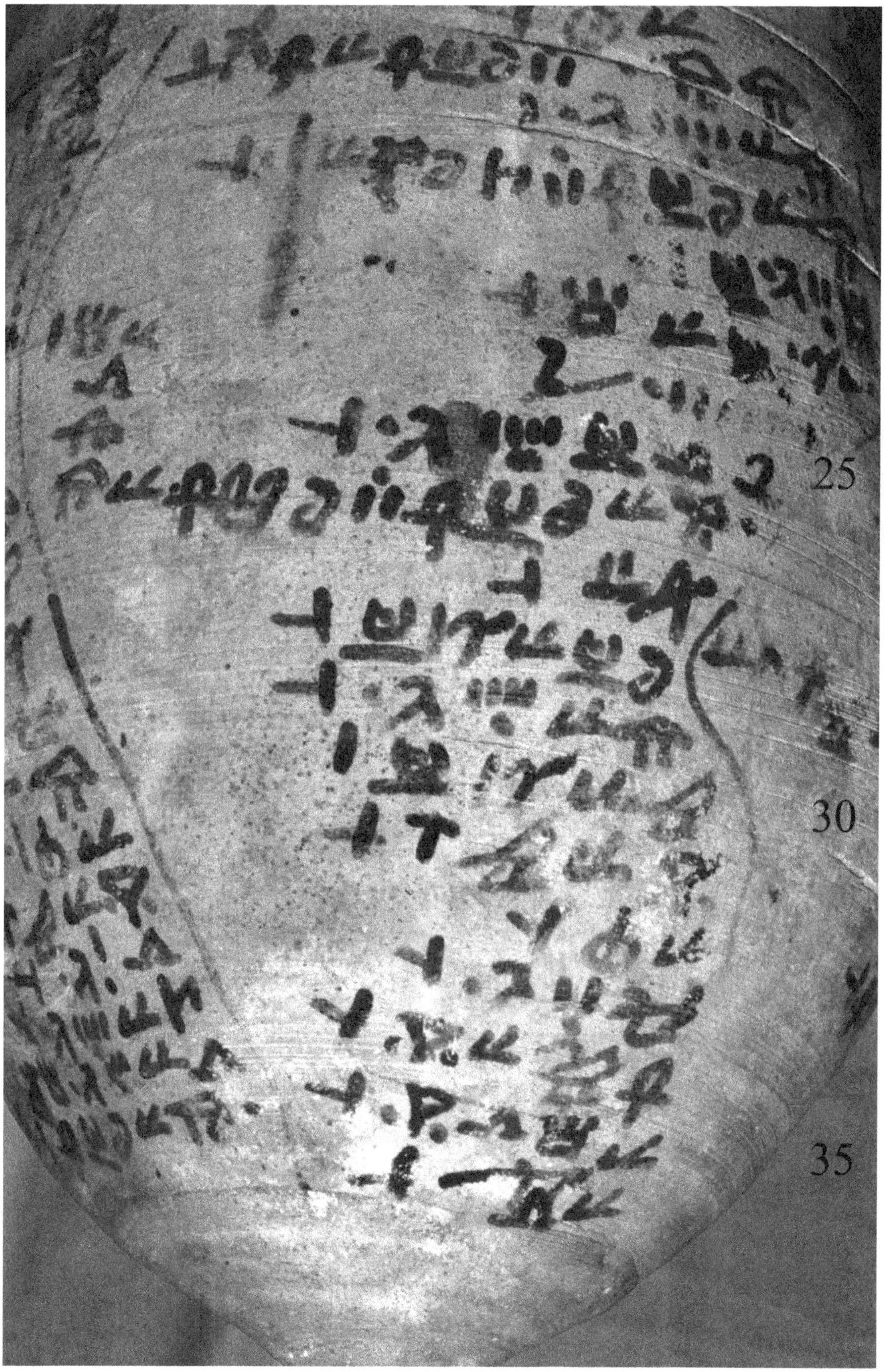

Abbildung 6. Kolumne II unten. Samih Mohsen; @Ägyptisches Museum Kairo.

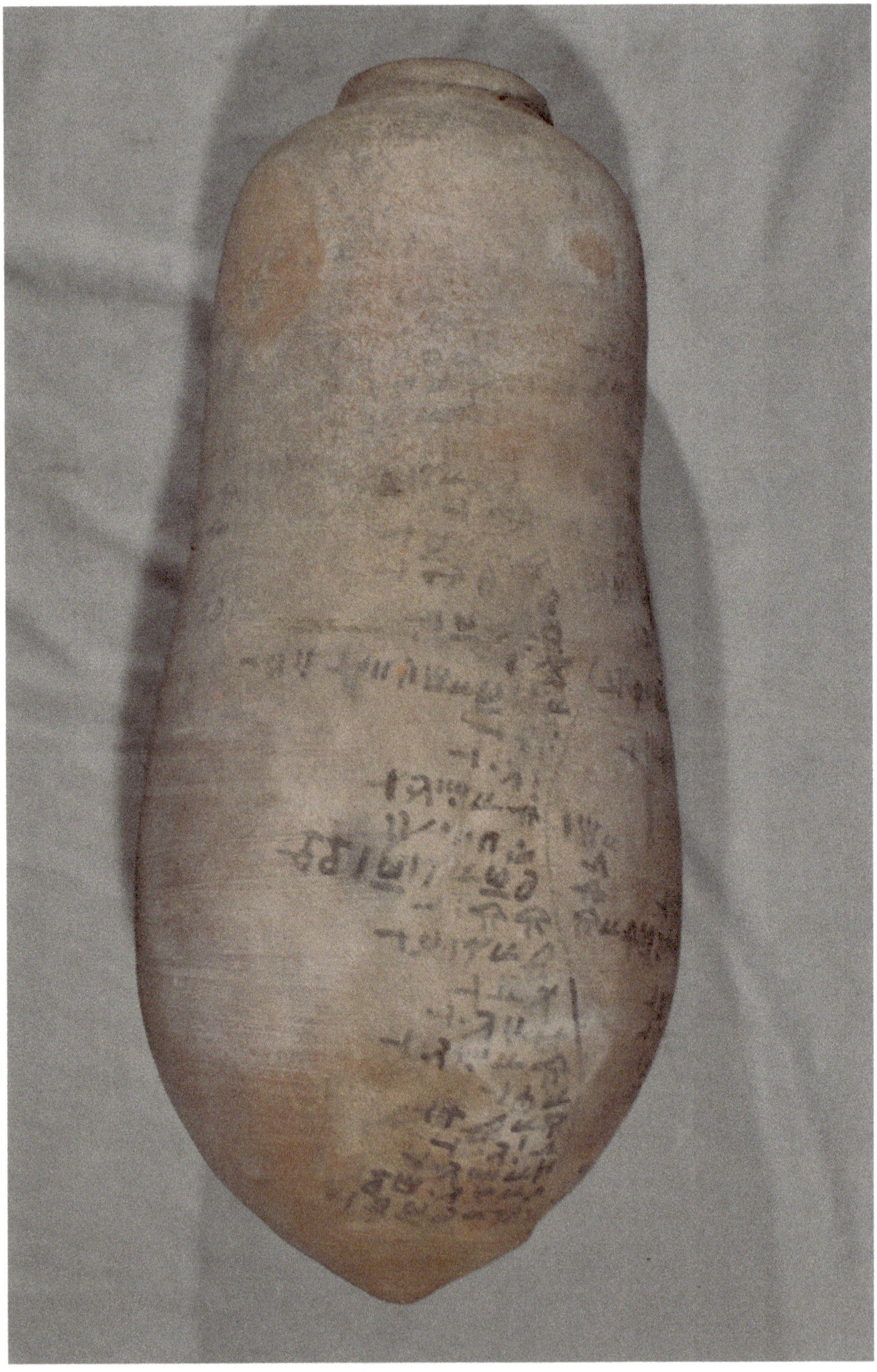

Abbildung 7. Kolumne III. Samih Mohsen; @Ägyptisches Museum Kairo.

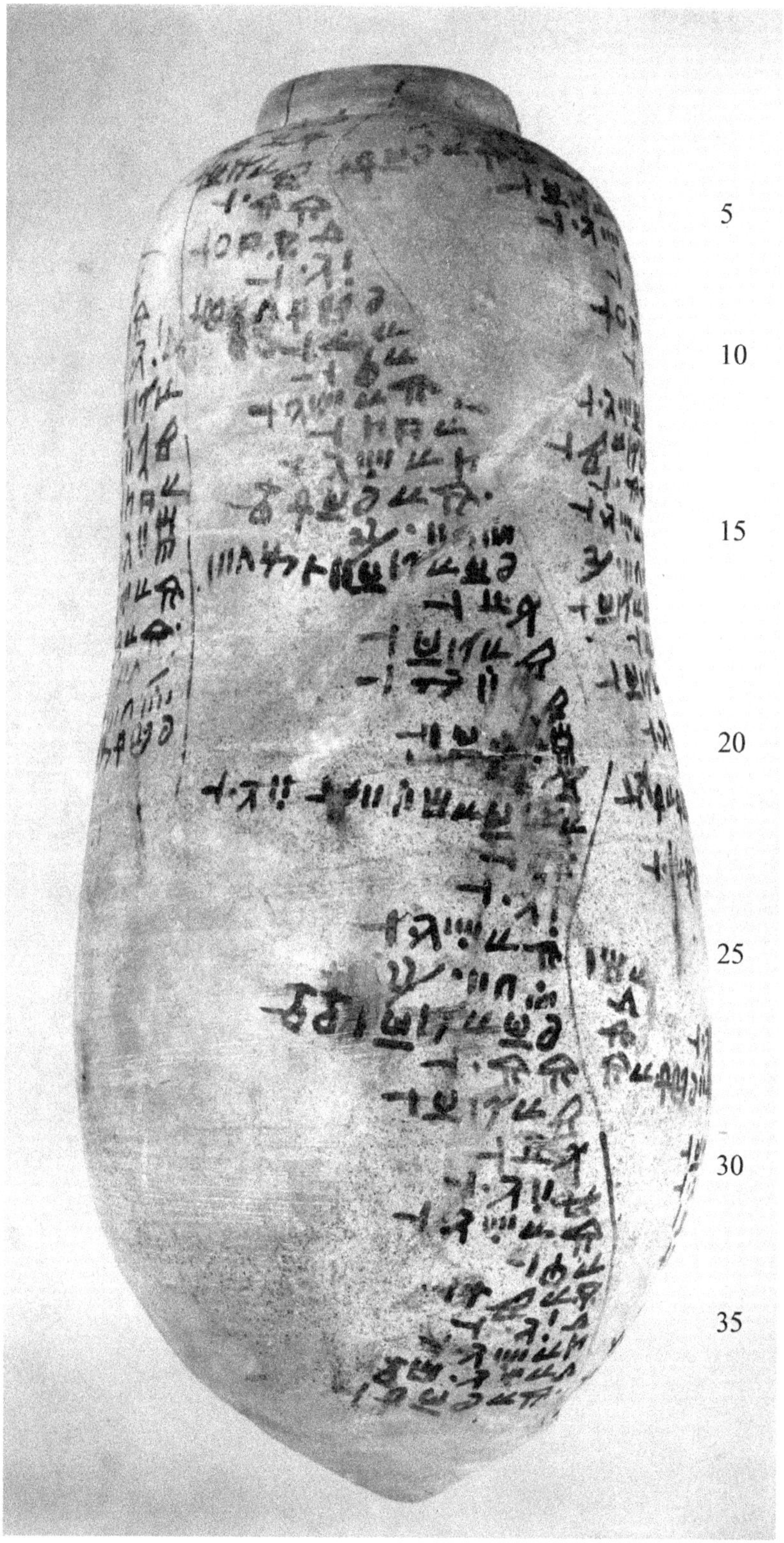

Abbildung 8. Kolumne III. Photo M12C 15; @Metropolitan Museum.

Abbildung 9. Kolumne III unten. Samih Mohsen; @Ägyptisches Museum Kairo.

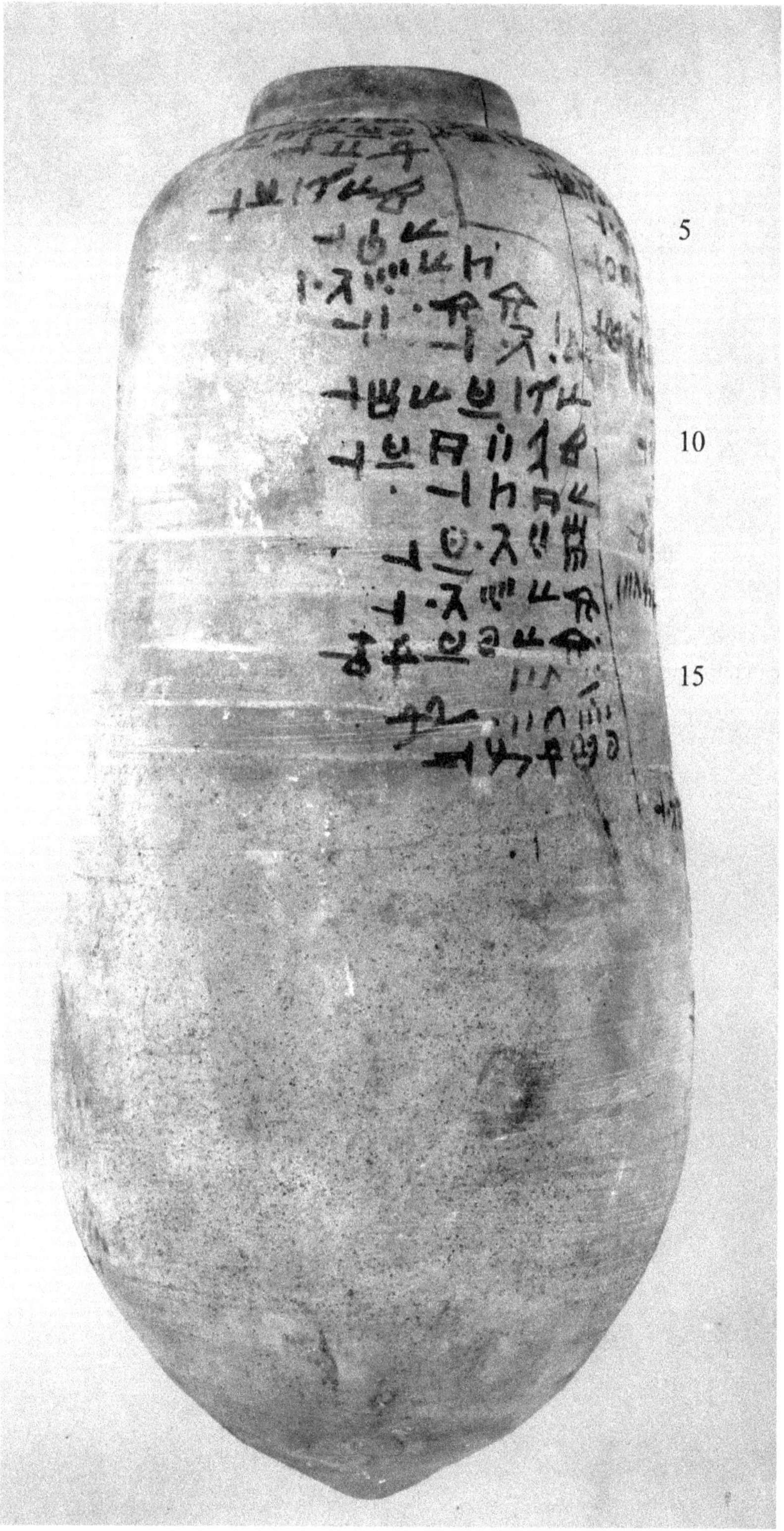

Abbildung 10. Kolumne IV. Photo M12C 16; @Metropolitan Museum.

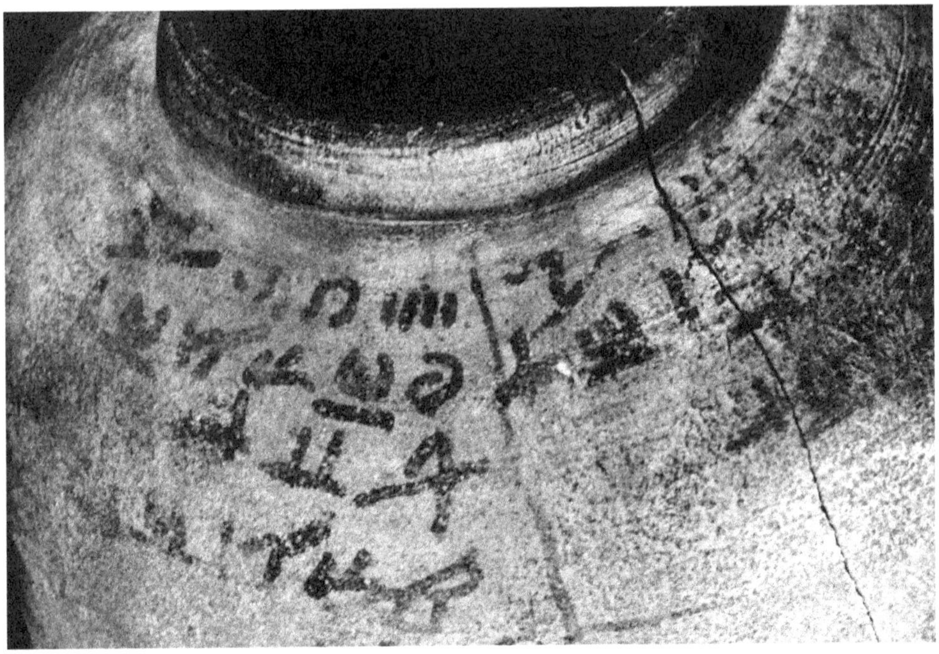

Abbildung 11. Kolumne III–IV oben. Samih Mohsen; @Ägyptisches Museum Kairo.

I II

IV III

Abbildung 12. Kolumne I–IV Anfang. Photo M12C 17; @Metropolitan Museum.

The Name of the Teacher in the Ritual for Entering the Chamber of Darkness, alias "Book of Thoth"

Alexandra von Lieven

It is a pleasure to write something for Richard, as he has always been a very friendly colleague and in particular, this is a little thanks for all he has done for me.[1] In principle, it is of course completely unnecessary to write in English, as Richard is perfectly able to read, write and speak German fluently.

Richard has done much of interest to Egyptology in general and Demotic studies in particular. However, the one publication of his (together with his former teacher Karl-Theodor Zauzich) that will probably forever be linked with his name is the edition of the text the two editors called "Book of Thoth."[2] As this text is of major interest in many respects, also in circles widely surpassing Egyptology, it is only fitting that I should contribute something on this, even if it is just a trifle.

The so-called Book of Thoth, or, as I would prefer to call it with Joachim Quack,[3] the "Ritual for Entering the Chamber of Darkness," is a discursive text. What is typical for such texts is that they envelop more or less philosophical reflections in a dialogue between two or more protagonists.

Thus, at the heart of the reflection is not another text that also could—and does indeed—exist without commentary, but rather the facts themselves.[4] These facts are then discussed within the basic text and interpreted by named interlocutors in a dialogue. It is this very dialogue that constitutes the basic text, which is then elaborated on.

As examples for true commentaries, one could mention those to the Fundamentals of the Course of the Stars or the Book of the Fayum. As examples for discursive texts, the so-called Myth of the Sun's Eye, the herein treated Ritual for Entering the Chamber of Darkness, or the Dialogue between Pharaoh and Imhotep come to mind.[5]

---

1. Here, I think of things like, e.g., his review of my MA thesis (Richard Jasnow, review of *Der Himmel über Esna: Eine Fallstudie zur Religiösen Astronomie in Ägypten am Beispiel der kosmologischen Decken- und Architravinschriften im Tempel von Esna*, by Alexandra von Lieven, *JANER* 2 [2002]: 161–64) or his friendly comments on my PhD thesis on the ICE 2008 in Rhodes (eternalized by Christian Leitz, "Zu einigen astronomischen Aspekten im sogenannten Nutbuch oder Grundriß des Laufes der Sterne," *Enchoria* 31 [2008/2009]: 21), as well as his willingness to act as a referee for me for several international applications in the past.

2. Richard Jasnow and Karl-Theodor Zauzich, *The Ancient Egyptian Book of Thoth: A Demotic Discourse on Knowledge and Pendant to the Classical Hermetica* (Wiesbaden: Harrassowitz, 2005); Richard Jasnow and Karl-Theodor Zauzich, *Conversations in the House of Life: A New Translation of the Ancient Egyptian Book of Thoth* (Wiesbaden: Harrassowitz, 2014), Richard Jasnow and Karl-Theodor Zauzich, *The Ancient Egyptian Book of Thoth II. Revised Transliteration and Translation, New Fragments, and Material for Future Study* (Wiesbaden: Harrassowitz, 2021).

3. Joachim Friedrich Quack, "Die Initiation zum Schreiberberuf im Alten Ägypten," *SAK* 36 (2007): 261–62; Joachim Friedrich Quack, "Ein ägyptischer Dialog über die Schreibkunst und das arkane Wissen," *ARG* 9 (2007): 260; and now most clearly Joachim Friedrich Quack, review of *Conversations in the House of Life: A New Translation of the Ancient Egyptian Book of Thoth*, by Richard Jasnow and Karl-Theodor Zauzich, *Enchoria* 35 (2016/17): 226–29.

4. See Alexandra von Lieven, "Commentaries and Discursive Texts in Ancient Egypt," *Abgadiyat* 15 (2020): 22–42; for the Ritual for Entering the Chamber of Darkness, in particular 33–35.

5. Fundamentals of the Course of the Stars: Alexandra von Lieven, *Grundriß des Laufes der Sterne: Das sogenannte Nutbuch*. The Carlsberg Papyri 8. CNIP 31 (Copenhagen: Museum Tusculanum Press, 2007).

The latter unfortunately is still unpublished. Of the former two, especially the Ritual for Entering the Chamber of Darkness is highly obscure, a fact that is not exactly helped by the sad state of preservation of all surviving manuscripts. The Myth of the Sun's Eye also is not easy to understand, nor is it perfectly preserved.

Both works rely on a text-internal communication situation; however, it is a bit different in each of these texts. In the Myth of the Sun's Eye, it is two animals impersonating deities, a little ape for Thoth or his son and a cat (changing in anger into a lioness) for Tefnut. They discuss different theological issues, sometimes illustrating a moral by adducing a fable.

In the Ritual for Entering the Chamber of Darkness, there are at least two interlocutors, in some parts even more, although the state of preservation makes a correct assessment very difficult. As this text indeed seems to be designed after the model of an initiatory interview, or, rather, it might also itself be the model for such, it is a dialogue between a teacher figure and a pupil. The main teacher is labeled *ḫr=f n Ḥsr.t*, *"Thus he spoke in Heseret" or as a variant *ḫr=f n ḥs i̯-rḫ*, "Thus spoke he as the one who praises knowledge."[6] Likely, the two designations are in principle identical and related by wordplay. As is of course well-known, "wordplay" is one of the favorite hermeneutical tools of Egyptian scholars to establish relationships between entities.

The first editors of the Ritual for Entering the Chamber of Darkness preferred the designation *ḫr=f n Ḥsr.t*, although strictly speaking this version is grammatically not very plausible. After *ḫr=f*, there should normally come a substantive subject "namely X" indicating the speaker, not a preposition plus substantive. This makes the translation *"Thus he spoke in Heseret" problematic, yet nothing better is forthcoming. Heseret is a known cult center of the god Thoth, the divine lord of wisdom, science, and knowledge of every description. The editors, who took this text to be a precursor of the Greek Hermetica, therefore labeling it Book of Thoth, rooted for this version, claiming this figure to be Thoth himself,[7] although some parts of the text show that Thoth is different from the teacher. While Quack clearly stated this in his introductions to his new translations and his more recent review,[8] he did not make a proposal as to which of the two designations of the teacher should be preferred.

I however think it is more plausible that the teacher's hypocoristic designation mirrors the designation of the pupil, who is called *mr-rḫ*, "The one who loves knowledge." Of course, for the latter's designation, a Greek equivalent *philosophos* would be possible.[9]

At any rate, it is clear that in this text it is not the god Thoth himself talking to a human pupil, but a human teacher talking to a human pupil in an entirely worldly situation. Nevertheless, the questions posed and answered do touch on all sort of esoteric and religious matters. Yet, in one way or the other, the dialogue is centered on writing and the acquisition of knowledge related to written texts. As far as the state of preservation allows to check, it is most likely

---

Book of the Fayum: Horst Beinlich, *Der Mythos in seiner Landschaft: das ägyptische „Buch vom Fayum"*, SRaT 11 (Dettelbach: Röll, 2013–2017) (note that the Demotic version of that text in vol. 3 is also due to Richard).

Myth of the Sun's Eye: Françoise de Cenival, *Le mythe de l'œil du soleil: translittération et traduction avec commentaire philologique*. DemStud 9 (Sommerhausen: Gisela Zauzich Verlag, 1988); Françoise de Cenival, "Les titres des couplets du Mythe." *CRIPEL* 11 (1989): 141–46; Luigi Prada, "For a New Edition of P.Lond.Lit. 192: Current Research on the Greek Version of the *Myth of the Sun's Eye*," in *Actes du 26e Congrès international de papyrologie: Genève, 16–21 août 2010*, ed. Paul Schubert (Genève: Droz, 2012), 627–34.

Ritual for Entering the Chamber of Darkness: Jasnow and Zauzich, *Book of Thoth*, Jasnow and Zauzich, *Conversations*, Jasnow and Zauzich, *Book of Thoth II*.

Dialogue between Pharaoh and Imhotep: Mentioned in Joachim F. Quack, "Vom Dekret des Neferkasokar zum Dialog des Imhotep: Ägyptische Textquellen zum idealen Tempel," *Sokar* 27 (2013): 80; Joachim F. Quack, „Imhotep – der Weise, der zum Gott wurde," in *Persönlichkeiten aus dem Alten Ägypten im Neuen Museum*, ed. Verena Lepper (Petersberg: Imhof, 2014), 54–57.

6. Jasnow and Zauzich, *Conversations*, 30; Jasnow and Zauzich, *Book of Thoth II*, 551–52.

7. Jasnow and Zauzich, *Book of Thoth*, 9–12; Jasnow and Zauzich, *Conversations*, 31; the question is now discussed again in detail in Jasnow and Zauzich, *Book of Thoth II*, 11–16.

8. Quack, "Die Initiation zum Schreiberberuf," 250; Quack, "Ein ägyptischer Dialog über die Schreibkunst," 259, with a concrete reference 289, Quack, review of *Conversations in the House of Life*, 228.

9. As already stated by Jasnow and Zauzich, *Book of Thoth*, 13–15, and later Jasnow and Zauzich, *Conversations*, 31.

that this is an initiatory dialogue situated at the end of scribal training in the context of a temple scriptorium. Therefore, quite fittingly, there are some parts within the text that clearly seek to establish a link between writing and related intellectual activities on the one hand and other culturally important activities like agriculture or hunting.

Therefore, I myself would advocate for *ḫr=f n ḥsi̯-rḫ*, "Thus spoke he as the one who praises knowledge" as the original and correct name of the teacher figure in this text. It is absolutely thinkable that already the Egyptian copyists themselves did not fully understand that name later on or—maybe more likely, and fully in line with the Esoteric view on writing, thus fully on purpose—changed or maybe just graphically seemed to change the name to a form implying the god Thoth. Unfortunately, we do not really know how close the two versions of the name might have been in their original pronunciation.

At any rate, *He-who-praises-knowledge* as teacher is a good opposite to *The One-who-loves-knowledge* as student. I therefore hope, Richard, who is a *mr-rḫ* himself, will enjoy this short note despite its brevity.

Überlegungen zu einigen libyschen Personennamen

Karl-Theodor Zauzich[†]

Diesen Aufsatz widme ich gern meinem früheren Studenten, Assistenten und jetzigen Kollegen und lieben Freund Richard Jasnow, der etwa 1983 mit einem Stipendium des Deutschen Akademischen Austausch-Dienstes (DAAD) an die Universität Würzburg gekommen ist, um mehr über die demotische Literatur zu erfahren. Anfangs hatte er die Vorstellung, er könne über die Beziehungen zwischen der demotischen und der griechischen Literatur forschen, doch konnte ich ihn schnell davon überzeugen, daß die Zeit für solche Untersuchungen angesichts der damaligen Publikationslage der demotischen literarischen Texte noch längst nicht gekommen war. Eines Tages fragte er mich, ob ich wisse, was das „Thotbuch" sei. Er hatte wohl in Černýs *Coptic Etymological Dictionary*[1] (z.B. S. 156) oder aus Unterlagen im Archiv des Oriental Institute Chicago den Hinweis auf dessen Existenz gefunden. Meine Antwort wird ihn gewiß enttäuscht haben; sie lautete: „Ja, das weiß ich, aber ich sage es Ihnen nicht." Ich hatte nämlich schon während meiner Studienzeit durch die Arbeit für die „Katalogisierung der Orientalischen Handschriften in Deutschland" von diesem sehr langen Papyrus in Berlin (P. 15531) Kenntnis erhalten und sogleich erkannt, daß dessen Publikation ganz vordringlich war. Ja, ich wunderte mich als Student darüber, daß sich anscheinend niemand von den Spezialisten der demotischen Schrift und Sprache für einen so umfangreichen Text interessierte. Bei meinen eigenen Entzifferungsversuchen erkannte ich dann sehr bald, daß der Text erhebliche Schwierigkeiten bot und daß ich allein damit nicht zurechtkommen würde. Also überraschte ich Richard Jasnow eines passenden Tages mit einer Kopie des Pap. Berlin P. 15531 und dem Angebot zu einer gemeinsamen Bearbeitung. Was als Geschenk für ihn gedacht war, erwies sich recht bald als ein Geschenk für mich selbst, denn keinen besseren Mitarbeiter hätte ich gewinnen können als ihn, der schließlich viel mehr für unsere Bücher über diesen dunklen Text beigetragen hat als ich selbst. Dafür kann ich Richard gar nicht genug danken.

Der folgende Aufsatz geht von zwei Entdeckungen aus, die ich in einem Artikel für eine Festschrift und in einem eigenen Buch publiziert habe und die zusammen anscheinend einige libysche Personennamen verständlich machen.

1. In einem Beitrag zu der Festschrift für Bezalel Porten[2] habe ich den Nachweis geführt, daß in demotischen Texten ptolemäischer Zeit die Wendung *rmt Jhw* der Name der Juden ist. Das heißt, es entsprechen sich

demotisch *rmt Jhw*	hebräisch/aramäisch *Jhw-dj*
„Mann (von) Jhw"	„(Mann) von Jhw" = griech. Jou-dai(os)

Die Schlußfolgerung erscheint zwingend, daß das hebräisch-aramäische Element -dj eine Zugehörigkeit zum vorhergehenden Nomen bedeutet und damit einer Nisbe-Endung vergleichbar ist. Über die Frage, ob Jhw ursprünglich der Name eines Ortes / einer Landschaft oder eines Gottes war, gibt es eine lange Diskussion, die mit Giveon, Goedicke, Görg begonnen hat und die ich hier nicht fortsetzen will, zumal beide Meinungen nicht unvereinbar er-

1. Jaroslav Černý, *Coptic Etymological Dictionary* (Cambridge: Cambridge University Press, 1976).

2. Karl-Th. Zauzich, „Der ägyptische Name der Juden", in *In the Shadow of Bezalel: Aramaic, Biblical, and Ancient Near Eastern Studies in Honor of Bezalel Porten*, Hg. Alejandro F. Botta, CHANE 60 (Leiden: Brill, 2013), 409–16.

scheinen.[3] Es sei nur angemerkt, daß im Demotischen die Verbindung *rmt + ntr* in der Bedeutung „frommer Mann" vorkommt,[4] die Verbindung *rmt* + Gottesname aber durchaus ungewöhnlich ist, während *rmt* mit folgendem Namen eines Ortes oder eines Landes sehr häufig ist.[5]

2. In dem in Fußnote 3 genannten Buch habe ich den „verborgenen" (*jmn*) Namen des Gottes Amun (*Jmn*) als Mitglied der Achtheit von Hermupolis als *JJ* (Doppelschilfblatt) erkannt, dessen dualische Lesung *J.wj* > *Ja.wʾj* [6] > *Jaȝ.waȝ* die wirkliche Etymologie des jüdischen Gottesnamens JHWH ist.[7] In abgekürzter Weise erscheint der Gottesname in hiero-glyphischen und hieratischen Texten als *Jw*,[8] in demotischen Namen als *Jw* und *Jw=j-jw*[9] und in deren griechischer Entsprechung als -ιευ-ς sowie in koptischen Texten als ⲓⲉⲩ. Wegen dieser griechischen und koptischen Entsprechung werde ich den Urgott *JJ* im folgenden als Jeu bezeichnen.

In dem genannten Aufsatz habe ich in einer Fußnote die Frage gestellt, ob vielleicht das Bildungselement *-tj* einiger libyscher Personennamen die gleiche Funktion wie in *Jhw-dj/tj* hat. Die Frage habe ich in dem genannten Buch auf den Seiten 112–14 wiederholt, gerade weil es seit einem Aufsatz von O. Rößler[10] als sicher gelten kann, daß die libysche Sprache zu den semitischen Sprachen gehört. Wenn wir diese Frage versuchsweise positiv beantworten, scheint sich tatsächlich eine Möglichkeit zu ergeben, etliche libysche Personennamen zu verstehen.

Die libyschen Personennamen werden überwiegend in einer Art alphabetischer bzw. syllabischer Schrift geschrieben, die gegenüber der syllabischen Schrift des Neuen Reiches stark vereinfacht ist. Durch die Zusammenstellung dieser Namen bei F. Colin in seiner Dissertation *Les Libyens en Egypte*[11] kann man sich leicht einen Überblick verschaffen. Tatsächlich verfügt diese Schrift nur über etwa 30 verschiedene Zeichen.[12] Laryngale scheinen weitgehend zu fehlen. In den Zusammenstellungen von Colin habe ich nur einen einzigen Beleg für den Buchstaben *ẖ* gefunden, nämlich im demotisch geschriebenen Namen *Wjlẖny* des Pap. Krall.[13] Aber diese vermeintliche Ausnahme beruht auf einer irrigen Lesung von Edda Bresciani,[14] die Friedhelm Hoffmann[15] in seiner Bearbeitung des Textes korrigiert hat. Das *ẖ* gelesene Zeichen ist tatsächlich ein *h*.

Durch die beiden neuen Erkenntnisse lassen sich viele libysche Personennamen neu segmentieren, wobei sich oft semitische oder ägyptische Wurzeln erkennen lassen.

Im folgenden Text werden einige Abkürzungen benutzt, nämlich:

---

3. Kurze Zusammenfassung dieser Diskussion bei Karl-Th. Zauzich, *Siebzehn ägyptische Götter – ein jüdischer Gott. Die ägyptischen Wurzeln des Monotheismus* (Sommerhausen: Gisela Zauzich, 2017), 158–59, Nachtrag zu S. 31.

4. Zum Beispiel in einem noch unveröffentlichten Brief aus Elephantine (Pap. Berlin P. 13620,8).

5. Das *Chicago Demotic Dictionary* listet unter *rmt* etwa 50 verschiedene Beispiele auf.

6. Vergleiche hierzu Clemens Alexandrinus, *Stromata* 5.6.34: Ιαουαι und Ιαουε.

7. Zauzich, *Siebzehn ägyptische Götter*, 19–42. Ägyptisches Aleph am Silbenende wird im Hebräischen regelmäßig mit Aleph oder He wiedergegeben.

8. Zauzich, *Siebzehn ägyptische Götter*, 19–23.

9. Karl-Th. Zauzich, „Der verborgene Name des Gottes Amun in demotischen Texten", in *New Approaches in Demotic Studies: Acts of the 13th International Conference of Demotic Studies*, Hg. Franziska Naether, ZÄS Beiheft 10 (Berlin: de Gruyter, 2019), 303–8.

10. Otto Rößler, „Der semitische Charakter der libyschen Sprache", *ZAVA* 50 (1952): 121–50.

11. Frédéric Colin, *Les Libyens en Egypte (XVe siècle a.C.–IIe siècle p.C.): Onomastique et histoire*, 2 Bde. (Dissertationsschrift, Université Libre de Bruxelles, 1996). https://tel.archives-ouvertes.fr/tel-00120038.

12. Auch die von mir vermutete syllabische Vorstufe unseres Alphabets scheint mit etwa 10 Konsonanten in Verbindung mit den Vokalen a, i und u ausgekommen zu sein, s. Karl-Th. Zauzich, *Hieroglyphen mit Geheimnis. Neue Erkenntnisse zur Entstehung unseres Alphabets* (Darmstadt: von Zabern, 2015), 112.

13. Colin, *Les Libyens en Egypte*, 2:10.

14. Edda Bresciani, *Der Kampf um den Panzer des Inaros (Papyrus Krall)*, MPER NS Folge 8 (Wien: Prachner, 1964), 130.

15. Friedhelm Hoffmann, *Der Kampf um den Panzer des Inaros. Studien zum P. Krall und seiner Stellung innerhalb des Inaros-Petubastis-Zyklus*, MPER NS Folge 26 (Wien: Hollinek, 1976), 249 Anm. 1328.

RPN = Ranke, *Personennamen;*[16] CLE = Colin, *Les Libyens en Egypte*, Bd. 2;[17] *DemNb* = Lüddeckens u.a., *Demotisches Namenbuch;*[18] IPN = Noth, *Israelitische Personennamen.*[19]

Die Untersuchung beginnt mit Namen, die das Element *t̠kr* enthalten:

1.	RPN	CLE	*DemNb*	*Name*[20]	*hebr.*	*ägypt.*	*Wortbedeutung*	vermutete Bedeutung des PN
a. *T̠kr-t̠*	394.25	106–13	1308?	Takelothis (griech.)	זכר		erinnern	Der zu dem Bekannten gehört
b. *T̠kr-bʿr*	394.23			Zekar-baʿal	זכר עַלבַ		erinnern Baal	Bekannter des Baal
c. *T̠kr-m*	394.24				זכר עַם		erinnern Volk	Bekannter des Volkes
d. *Tꜣ-kꜣ-rꜣ-nꜣj=w*	431.12				זכר	*nꜣj=w*	erinnern die von	Bekannter derer von (...)

Ranke (RPN 394.3–5) verzeichnet drei mit *T̠kr* beginnende Namen, nämlich *T̠kr-bʿr, T̠kr-m* und *T̠kr-t̠.* Nur für den ersten wird dort eine semitische Erklärung als Zekar-baʿal vorgeschlagen, welche Hoch (*Semitic Words*)[21] unter Nr. 556 übernimmt und mit „He who is remembered by Baʿal" übersetzt. Zu weiteren mit זכר gebildeten Personennamen wie Zacharias u.ä. s. Noth, IPN, 187.[22]

Für *T̠kr-m* ist m.W. noch keine Deutung vorgeschlagen worden, doch scheint es mir naheliegend, in *m* das semitische Wort עַם „Volk" zu sehen, zumal die libysche Sprache kein Ajin kannte.[23] Wie gleich zu zeigen sein wird, macht diese Erklärung von *m* (ohne Ajin) auch in den Namen *Pꜣ-wr-m* (Nr. 3c), *Krm-m* (Nr. 4b), *M-shr-t̠* (Nr. 4c) u.a. guten Sinn. Ob auch der bei Ranke im Nachtrag (RPN 431.12) verzeichnete Name *Tꜣ-kꜣ-rꜣ-nꜣj=w* hierher gehört, bleibt wegen der abweichenden Schreibung des ersten Bestandteiles und der fehlenden Ergänzung zum letzten Bestandteil fraglich; vgl. unten unter 6. Nimrod.

Es folgen Namen, die vermutlich mit dem semitischen Wort *zer* (RPN 392.16–18) gebildet sind:

16. Hermann Ranke, *Die ägyptischen Personennamen*, 2 Bde. (Glückstadt: Augustin, 1935 und 1952).

17. S. Fußnote 11.

18. Erich Lüddeckens u.a., *Demotisches Namenbuch* (Wiesbaden: Reichert, 1980–2000).

19. Martin Noth, *Die israelitischen Personennamen im Rahmen der gemeinsemitischen Namengebung*, Beiträge zur Wissenschaft vom Alten und Neuen Testament 3.10 (Stuttgart: Kohlhammer, 1928; Nachdruck Hildesheim: Olms, 1966).

20. In dieser Spalte habe ich nur Namen notiert, die in der Literatur üblich oder griechisch belegt sind.

21. James E. Hoch, *Semitic Words in Egyptian Texts of the New Kingdom and Third Intermediate Period* (Princeton, NJ: Princeton Unversity Press, 1994).

22. Um das sprachlich unkorrekte Partizip „Erinnerter" ebenso wie eine umständliche Formulierung zu vermeiden, weiche ich auf das annähernd gleichwertige Wort „Bekannter" aus.

23. Otto Rößler, „Der semitische Charakter der libyschen Sprache", 127.

2.	RPN	CLE	*DemNb*	*Name*	*hebr.*	*ägypt.*	*Wortbedeutung*	*vermutete Bedeutung des PN*
a. *Ṯr-ṱ*	–	104			זֵר	*ṯrj*	Saat	Der zur Saat Gehörende
b. *Ṯr-jw-jj*	392.19,21,22			Tjaroy	זֵר	*ṯrj* *Jw*	Saat Gott Jeu	Saat des Jeu
c. *Ṯr-rꜣ-jj* *Ṯr-rw-jj*	393.6				זֵר אֵל	*ṯrj*	Saat Gott	Saat Gottes
d. *Ṯr-wꜣ-sꜣ*	393.4				זֵר	*ṯrj* *Wꜣs.t*	Saat Göttin Waset	Saat der Waset

In *Ṯr* möchte ich das Element זֵר erkennen, das auch im Namen Zorobabel steckt und vermutlich auf babylonisch zēr zurückgeht, s. Noth, IPN, Nr. 441, S. 63. Das Wort ist auch *ägyptisch bewahrt*, s. Lesko, *A Dictionary of Late Egyptian* 4:111.[24] Alternativ ist zu erwägen, ob nicht das hebräische Wort zar „Fremder" gemeint ist.

Zu 2b: Die gleiche Zusammensetzung sehe ich auch im Namen des bekannten Schreibers der Nekropole *Ṯr-jw-jj*.[25]

Zu 2c. Eine Bestätigung dieses Vorschlages scheint der folgende Name zu bieten, da in ihm der neu erkannte Gottesname Jeu durch die ägyptisch syllabische Schreibung von El ersetzt ist. – Zu weiteren Namen, die mit hebr. El gebildet sind, s. weiter unten sowie RPN 43.8 und 43.16.

Zu 2d: Ob auch *Ṯr-wꜣ-sꜣ* hierher gehört, ist fraglich.

Es folgen nun einige Namen, die anscheinend das ägyptische Element *wr* in syllabischer Schreibung enthalten:

3.	RPN	CLE	*DemNb*	*Name*	*hebr.*	*ägypt.*	*Wortbedeutung*	*vermutete Bedeutung des PN*
a. *Wr-ṱ*	82.8					*wr*	Großer	Der zum Großen Gehörende
b. *Jw-wr-ṱ*	18.10	9		Iuwelot		*Jw* *wr*	Gott Jeu groß	Der zum großen Jeu Gehörende
c. *Pꜣ-wr-m*	104.8[26]	120	180	Pulēmis (gr.)	עם	*pꜣ* *wr*	der groß Volk	Der Große des Volkes
d. *Wr-k ṱ r*	83.12				כרתי	*wr*	Kreti(?)	Großer der Kreti(?)

24. Leonard H. Lesko, *A Dictionary of Late Egyptian*, 4 Bde. (Berkeley, CA: B.C. Scribe Publications, 1982–1989).

25. Zum Namen s. Zauzich, *Siebzehn ägyptische Götter*, 112–13.

26. Weitere Belege: 131.6–7, 2:357.

Zu 3b: Für diesen Namen gibt es zwei Lesungsvorschläge, den von Ranke, dem sich auch Colin anschließt und den ich hier übernommen habe. Dagegen will Graefe[27] das vorletzte Zeichen des Kanals (Gardiner N36) als *pjt* „Libyen" verstehen.

Zu 3c: Das hebräische Wort עַם *ʿam* „Volk" ist in vielen semitischen Sprachen bekannt. Das „Eta" der griechischen Entsprechung Pulēmis scheint der Vokalisierung des hebräischen Wortes zu widersprechen. Aber das ist nicht wirklich so, weil der ursprüngliche phonetische Wert des Buchstabens, der in seiner Form und seinem Namen von der hieratischen Schreibung der Hieroglyphe des Hauses (Gardiner O6)[28] abgeleitet ist, ein langes ā gewesen ist.[29] Weitere Namen mit dem Bestandteil *-m* unter Nr. 4.

Zu 3d: Wegen der Metathese ist der Vorschlag zweifelhaft. Eigentlich sind mit den sprichwörtlichen „Krethi und Plethi" Stämme der Philister gemeint, aus denen König David seine Leibwache bezog, vgl. 2. Samuel 8,18 (u.a.). Es kommen mehrere andere Wörter zur Erklärung von *kṯr* in Frage, s. Hoch, *Semitic Words*, Nr. 487–492.

Nach den Namen mit *wr* folgen einige Namen mit (ʿ)*m*:

4.	RPN	CLE	*DemNb*	*Name*	*hebr.*	*ägypt.*	*Wortbedeutung*	*vermutete Bedeutung des PN*
a. *Ṯkr-m*	394.4				זכר עם	–	erinnern Volk	Bekannter des Volkes
b. *Krm-m*	347.10	96–99		Karomama	כרם עם		Weinberg Volk	Weinberg(?) des Volkes
c. *M-shr-ṯ*	165.22	46–48		Masaharta	עם סחר		Volk umherziehen	zum Volk der Umherziehenden(?) Gehörender
d. *M-škn*					עם שָׁכֵן		Volk Einwohner	zum Volk der Einwohner(?) (Gehörender)
e. *M-škb*					עם שׁכב		Volk sich legen	Volk der sich Lagernden(?)
f. *M-šwš*	*Wb.* II:157, 3			Meschwesch	עם	*š*(ʿ)*s*	Volk Hirte	Volk der Hirten(?)
g. *M-ḏꜣj*	*Wb.* II:186			Medjai	עם	*ḏꜣj*	Volk durchziehen	Volk der Durchziehenden

Zu 4a: Zum Element *Ṯkr* s. oben unter Nr. 1.

Zu 4b: Ob es in den libyschen und berberischen Sprachen ein Wort *krm* „Garten" gegeben hat, weiß ich mangels eigener Kenntnis dieser Sprachen nicht. Aber es ist in mehreren semitischen Sprachen mit dieser Bedeutung vorhanden, wie Hoch, *Semitic Words*, 350–51 unter Nr. 479 nachweist. Die gemeinsemitische Wurzel *krm* mit der Grundbedeutung „zurückhalten" (und wohl auch „einhegen") ist jedoch in libyschen Sprachen erhalten, wie O. Rößler gezeigt

27. Erhart Graefe, „Der libysche Stammesname *p(j)d(j) / pjt* im spätzeitlichen Onomastikon", *Enchoria* 5 (1975): 13–17.

28. Alan Gardiner, *Egyptian Grammar: Being an Introduction to the Study of Hieroglyphs*, 3. Aufl. (London: Oxford University Press, 1957), 493.

29. Vergleiche zum Buchstaben, Eta Zauzich, *Hieroglyphen mit Geheimnis*, 48–49.

hat.[30] Auch Gärten mit süßen Früchten hegt man gern ein und bewacht sie, um Diebe abzuhalten. Die gedankliche Verbindung zwischen Garten und jungen Frauen ist seit der Antike ein Thema der Literatur, vom Hohenlied des Alten Testaments bis zu einem Gedicht, das durch die Vertonung von Johannes Brahms unvergeßlich bleibt: „Erlaube mir, feins Mädchen, in den Garten zu gehn, daß ich dort mag schauen, wie die Rosen so schön. Erlaube sie zu brechen, es ist die höchste Zeit; ihre Schönheit, ihr' Jugend hat mir mein Herz erfreut." Zu 4c: Das hebräische Wort *saḥar* bedeutet auch „reisender Handelsmann".

Zu 4d: Vielleicht als Gegensatz zum vorherigen Namen gemeint.

Zu 4e: Dies ist kein Name, sondern ein häufiger Titel in syllabischer Schreibung, den Hoch, *Semitic Words*, auf den Seiten 160–63 unter Nr. 209 ausführlich diskutiert hat. Dabei lehnt er Helcks Vorschlag einer Verbindung zu semitischen Wörtern *škb* m.E. zu leicht ab. Ich verweise auf eine Notiz von R. Hannig zum Wort *mškb* „Lageroffizier" mit folgendem Text: „viell(eicht) ursprünglich e(ine) ausländische Bevölkerungsgruppe".[31]

Zu 4e: Schließlich sei erwähnt, daß der Name der libyschen Bevölkerungsgruppe der Meschwesch vielleicht ebenfalls mit dem Wort *M* (= *ꜥm*) beginnt. Was sich aber hinter *šwš* verbirgt, ist zur Zeit ganz offen. Zu viele Wörter kommen in Frage, wie z.B. *Wšš* (Name eines Seevolkes); *wšwš* = kopt. ⲟⲩⲟϣⲟⲩⲉϣ „zerschlagen", „aufbrechen", auch „einbrechen". Am wahrscheinlichsten ist mir, daß *š(ꜥ)s* = kopt. ϣⲱ(ⲱ)ⲥ „Hirte" gemeint ist, wozu man meinen Beitrag „Eine bisher unverständliche Berufsbezeichnung" in *Enchoria* 26 (2000): 187–88 vergleiche. Dieses Wort geht auf ägypt. *šꜣs* „durchziehen" und *šꜣsw* „Schasu-Beduine" zurück.[32] Die Erklärung des Wortes Hyksos als „Herrscher der Hirten" durch Josephus[33] beruht auf diesem Wort. Es ist auch im Namen *Pꜣ-šꜣs* „Der Hirte" (RPN 117.24) bewahrt, vgl. auch die syllabische Schreibung *B-pꜣ-šꜣ-sw* bei Colin, *Les Libyens en Egypte*, 41.

Interessant ist, daß sich auch *ꜥꜣm* > ⲁⲙⲉ, das andere demotische > koptische Wort für „Hirte", von einer Bezeichnung für Ausländer (Asiaten, Semiten, Kanaanäer) herleitet. Der ursprüngliche Unterschied der beiden Wörter ist, daß die Hirten verschiedene Tiere betreuten. Der *ꜥꜣm* hütete Großvieh wie Rinder, der *šꜣs* hütete Kleinvieh wie Schafe. Später scheinen beide Wörter ohne Unterschied gebraucht worden zu sein, was die neuen demotischen/koptischen Wörter mit *mn-n-*... / ⲙⲁⲛ-... „Hirte von (Tier) ..." erforderlich machte. Das demotische Wort *š(ꜥ)s* wird regelmäßig mit dem gleichen Stoffdeterminativ versehen, das auch das Wort *mdqn* > ⲙⲁϫⲁⲕⲓⲛ[34] trägt, welches demnach wohl ursprünglich den „Wollweber" bezeichnet. Das demotische Wort kommt oft in spätdemotischen Urkunden aus der Tempelwirtschaft von Soknopaiu Nesos vor und kann dort kaum mehr auf Weber von Wolle beschränkt gewesen sein,[35] da den Priestern wollene Kleidung als unrein galt.[36]

Im folgenden werden weitere Namen mit dem Gott Jeu besprochen:

30. Otto Rößler, „Der semitische Charakter der libyschen Sprache", 134, Nr. 26.

31. Rainer Hannig, *Die Sprache der Pharaonen. Großes Handwörterbuch Ägyptisch – Deutsch (2800–950 v. Chr.)*, Kulturgeschichte der Antiken Welt 64 (Mainz: von Zabern, 1995), 369.

32. Westendorf, *Koptisches Handwörterbuch*, 327.

33. Flavius Josephus, *Contra Apionem* 1.82.

34. Vergleiche hierzu Karl-Th. Zauzich, „Spätdemotische Papyrusurkunden II", *Enchoria* 2 (1972): 77.

35. Die griechische Entsprechung γέρδιος ist nicht auf Schafhirten beschränkt.

36. Das wissen wir durch Herodot, *Historien* 2.37 und den Pap. Berlin P. 7059, den S. Lippert, M. Schentuleit und ich gemeinsam in dem in Vorbereitung befindlichen 4. Band der Reihe „Demotische Dokumente aus Dime" publizieren wollen.

5.	RPN	CLE	*DemNb*	*Name*	*hebr.*	*ägypt.*	*Wortbedeutung*	*vermutete Bedeutung des PN*
a. *Jw-pwt*	24.2 / 24.4	5–9		Iupet		*Jw pꜣwtj*	Jeu urzeitlich	Jeu der Urzeitliche
b. *Jw-ksr*	18.19	13			כשר	*Jw*	Jeu tauglich	Jeu ist tauglich
c. *Jw-ṯk*	18.32	13			זך	*Jw*	Jeu rein	Jeu ist rein
d. *Jw-rhn*	55.21	10–12	Ind.[37]			*Jw rhn*	Jeu stützen	Jeu stützt
e. *Mr-jw*	163.2	44–45				*mr Jw*	lieben Jeu	geliebt von Jeu
f. *Bw-jw-wꜣ-wꜣ*	393.17	38				*Jw wꜣwꜣ*	Jeu Böses ersinnen	Jeu ersinnt nichts Böses

Zu 5a: Beim zweiten Bestandteil des Namens hatte ich zunächst an *Pjt* „Libyen" gedacht, aber dazu scheint das syllabische Zeichen *wꜣ* nicht zu passen.[38] *Pwt* dürfte vielmehr eine syllabische Schreibung für *pꜣw.tj* „urzeitlich" (*Wb.* I:496–97) sein, welche auch im Demotischen syllabisch bzw. unetymologisch geschrieben wird, z.B. im Namen *Ns-pꜣi=w-tꜣ.wi* und *Ns-pꜣ-wt* (*DemNb* 672–73). In einem Ostrakon des Los Angeles County Museum of Art, das Richard Jasnow und ich demnächst publizieren wollen (*Enchoria* 36 [2018/2019]: 67 –94), steht gar *pꜣ wt tpi* für die Urgötter in einer Schreibung, die man ohne Zusammenhang wie „der erste Beschluß" lesen müßte.

Zu 5d: Auch für diesen Namen gibt es eine Variante, bei der Jeu durch Re ersetzt ist, nämlich *Rj-rhn* (RPN 217,3; CLE 57). Wahrscheinlich ist der Name *Wjlẖnj* des Pap. Krall eine Variante zu *Jw-rhn*, wie auch schon von anderen erwogen wurde, s. F. Hoffmann, *Der Kampf um den Panzer des Inaros*, 349 Anm. 1328 sowie ausführlich Colin, *Les Libyens en Egypte*, 10–13.

Zu 5e: Der Vergleich dieses Namens in der syllabischen Schreibung *M(ꜥ)-rꜣ-jw-jj* u.ä. mit dem hieroglyphisch geschriebenen Namen *Mrj-jj-jj* (RPN 162.3) u.ä. legt den Schluß nahe, daß die syllabische Schreibung *m(ꜥ)-rꜣ* nichts anderes als das ägyptische Verb „lieben" meint. Der Name RPN 56.5 *Jw-m(ꜥ)-r* ist wohl nur eine Umstellung des gleichen Namens. – Die Bedeutung „lieben" scheint auch im Namen *Ṯꜣwt-m(ꜥ)-rꜣ* (RPN 389.6) zu passen, der vermutlich als „Geliebter Nestling" zu verstehen ist.

Zu 5f: Ob dieser Name ebenfalls hierher gehört, bleibt mir fraglich, da er aber ausdrücklich als Name eines Libyers markiert ist, kann er nicht ausgelassen werden. Er scheint nach dem Muster von Namen wie *Bw-thꜣ-jmn* (RPN 94.20) „Amun übertritt nicht" oder *Bw-ir-ḥꜥr-mw.t* „Mut zürnt(?) nicht" (RPN 94.3; vgl. auch 95.2, wo doch wohl *Bw-ḥꜥr-ẖnsw* gemeint ist,)[39] gebildet zu sein. Problematisch ist die Wortstellung, die womöglich wegen der Kürze des Gottesnamens *Jw* geändert ist.

Abschließend sei darauf hingewiesen, daß bei vielen mit Doppelschilfblatt beginnenden Namen (RPN 55f. und RPN 2:268 sowie Hoch, *Semitic Words*, 50–58) der Verdacht naheliegt, daß sie den Gottesnamen Jo- (bzw. Jeu-) ent-

37. Günter Vittmann, *Demotisches Namenbuch. Namen-Indices, Verzeichnis der bibliographischen Abkürzungen, Publikationen und Quellen sowie Korrekturen und Nachträge* (Wiesbaden: Reichert, 2000), 131, Korr. zu S. 61.

38. Der alten Diskussion, ob biblisches Puṭ für Libyen oder Pu(n)t steht, kann ich hier nicht nachgehen.

39. Es ist fraglich, ob *ḥꜥr* für *ḫꜥr* „zürnen", oder für *ḥwrꜥ* „rauben" steht.

halten, wie Ranke selbst bei einigen erwogen hat. Zum Namen *Jw-m(ʿ)-sw-r3* (RPN 56.6; Hoch, *Semitic Words*, Nr. 53) verweist sogar schon das Hebräische Wörterbuch von Gesenius[40] auf *mšl* „Herrscher" (S. 470).

* * * * *

Etymologien sind für Sprachwissenschaftler manchmal das, was Kunstwerke für Kunsthistoriker sein können, ein Anlaß zu langen Diskussionen und widersprechenden Meinungen. Da es in beiden Fällen selten Beweise gibt, die nur annähernd so überzeugend wie in den Naturwissenschaften sind, bleiben manche Vorschläge für lange Zeit in einem störenden Zwielicht, das erst nach langer Zeit geklärt wird. Dabei zeigt sich oft, daß die Zeitgenossen in ihrer Erkenntnis so befangen sind, daß die nächste Generation das gar nicht mehr verstehen kann. Jeder Ägyptologe kennt wohl solche Fälle, über die man sich wundert oder bei denen man ein ungutes Gefühl hat. Die Erkenntnisfähigkeit auch von Wissenschaftlern ist durchaus an die Zeit gebunden, in der sie leben.

Ich komme abschließend zu einem Fall, der mir anfangs ganz unproblematisch erschien, den ich jetzt aber für recht kompliziert halte. Gehört der Name Nimrod hierher? Ist der Name des „tüchtigen Jägers vor dem Herrn" (Gen. 10,9) vom hebräischen Wort für „Leopard" abgeleitet?

6.	RPN	CLE	*DemNb*	*Name*	*hebr.*	*ägypt.*	*Wortbedeutung*	*vermutete Bedeutung des PN*
a. *Nmr-ṱ*	204.11	50–55	725	Nimrod / Namilt[41]	נמר		Leopard	Der zum Leopard Gehörende(?)

So passend diese Ableitung zunächst erscheinen mag, so fragwürdig ist sie aber. Ein Nimrod kommt mehrmals in der Bibel vor, zuerst in Genesis 10,6 als Enkel Noahs und Sohn Hams, sodann auch 1. Chronik 1,10 als „erster Held der Erde". Wie ich in meinem Buch *Siebzehn ägyptische Götter* auf den Seiten 84–86 zu beweisen versucht habe, beruhen die Namen Noahs und seiner drei Söhne auf den ägyptischen Himmelsrichtungen, die wie eine Überschrift vor der Völkertafel stehen, nämlich Noah für Westen, Ham für Süden, Sem für Osten und Japhet für Norden. Daß Hams Nachkommen südliche Länder sind wie Kusch, Ägypten und Puṭ (Libyen oder durch Verwechslung vielleicht Punt), ist daher sehr verständlich. Unerwartet wird jedoch Kanaan als Sohn Hams bezeichnet. Aber in der Völkertafel gibt es auch andere Stellen, die vermuten lassen, daß der Text nicht überall korrekt überliefert ist. So wundert man sich darüber, daß zwar die Nachkommen von Kusch (10,8–12), von Ägypten (10,13–14) und Kanaan (10,15–20) aufgezählt werden, die Nachfolger des Puṭ aber nicht erscheinen. Über Kusch heißt es in Genesis 10,8–12 (Einheitsübersetzung): „Kusch zeugte Nimrod; dieser wurde der erste Held auf der Erde. (9) Er war ein tüchtiger Jäger vor dem Herrn. Deshalb pflegt man zu sagen: Ein tüchtiger Jäger vor dem Herrn wie Nimrod. (10) Kerngebiet seines Reiches war Babel, Erech, Akkad und Kalne im Land Schinar. (11) Von diesem Land zog er nach Assur aus und erbaute Ninive, Rehobot-Ir, Kelach (12) sowie Resen, zwischen Ninive und Kelach, das ist die große Stadt."

Man hat viel darüber nachgedacht, welcher reale Herrscher des Orients diesem Nimrod zum Vorbild gedient haben könnte. Die Vorschläge reichen von Gilgamesch über Tukulti-Ninurta, Marduk bis zu Alexander dem Großen(!).[42] Aber sollte man nicht an einen historischen Libyerkönig mit diesem Namen denken, zumal sein Name durch assyrische Propaganda im Orient verbreitet worden ist (akkadisch Lamintu)?[43] Freilich passen alle Informa-

40. Wilhelm Gesenius, *Hebräisches und aramäisches Handwörterbuch über das Alte Testament.* 17. Aufl. (Leipzig: Vogel, 1921).

41. Zu den vielen „fälschlichen Umschreibungen" des Namens s. Thomas Schneider, *Lexikon der Pharaonen. Die altägyptischen Könige von der Frühzeit bis zur Römerherrschaft*, 2. Aufl. (Düsseldorf: Artemis & Winkler, 1997), 165.

42. Gute Zusammenstellung im Artikel „Völkertafel" von Markus Witte: https://www.bibelwissenschaft.de/ stichwort/34251/.

43. Tonprisma aus Ninive A I 90–113 (644 oder 642 v. Chr.), s. Katsuji Sano, „Die Eroberungen von Ägypten durch Asarhaddon und Aššurbanipal", *UF* 47 (2016): 251–63, speziell S. 261 Nr. 9. Kenneth A. Kitchen, *The Third Intermediate Period in Egypt (1100–650 BC)*, 2., neu bearb. Aufl. (Warminster: Aris & Phillips, 1986), 397 § 358 (Nimlot E).

tionen der Bibel über Nimrod nicht zu einem unter assyrischer Duldung herrschenden Kleinkönig von Hermupolis. Aber wenn es derselbe Name wäre, der in der Völkertafel steht, so stünde er dort ohnehin an falscher Stelle, denn er sollte nicht ein Sohn des Kusch, sondern ein Sohn des Puṭ (Libyen) sein, dessen Nachkommen in der Völkertafel fehlen. Die Redakteure der Genesis haben viele ägyptische Namen lautlich genau oder in hebräischer Übersetzung vermutlich aus ägyptischen Onomastika übernommen.[44] Da bei lautlicher Übernahme die Namen im hebräischen Text unverständlich wurden, hat man gern „Erklärungen" aus hebräisch anklingenden Wörtern beigegeben, wie zum Beispiel für Eva als „Mutter aller Lebendigen" in Genesis 3,20 oder für Seth in Genesis 4,25 (Einheitsübersetzung): „Sie gebar einen Sohn und nannte ihn Set; denn sie sagte: Gott setzte mir anderen Nachwuchs ein für Abel, weil Kain ihn erschlug." In gleicher Weise scheint die in Genesis 10,9 geradezu sprichwörtliche Beschreibung des Nimrod als „tüchtiger Jäger vor dem Herrn" den Namen als „Zugehöriger zum Leoparden" verstanden zu haben.

Für den libyschen Namen, der im deutschen Schrifttum gewöhnlich „Nimrod" geschrieben wird,[45] läßt sich eine Etymologie vorschlagen, die nichts mit dem hebräischen Wort für Leopard zu tun hat. Wenn man den Anfang des Namens mit der häufigen Schreibung *n3i=w* ernst nimmt, dann kann diese nur für das pluralische „Possessivpräfix" (Till) bzw. „Possessivpronomen" (Plisch) stehen,[46] wie es in den Ortsnamen *N3i=w-t3-ḥ.t* Natho oder *N3i=w-qrḏ* Naukratis erscheint. Für *mrṯ* drängt sich dann eine Herleitung vom See Μαρεωτις λίμνη oder Μαρεια λίμνη bzw. von der ganzen Gegend Mareotis auf, die noch in koptischer Zeit ⲘⲀⲢⲒⲰⲦⲎⲤ oder ⲠⲀⲒⲀⲦ (d.h. Libyen) hieß. Vergleiche hierzu die Ausführungen von Carsten Peust.[47]

Wie eng die Verbindung von Mareotis und Paiat ist, zeigt der letzte hier zu erwähnende Name Nimrod-pat.

6.	RPN	CLE	*DemNb*	*Name*	*hebr.*	*ägypt.*	*Wortbedeutung*	*vermutete Bedeutung des PN*
b. *Nmrṯ -pt*	204.11	55–56		Nimrod-pat		*n3i=w mrwṯ Pjt*	die von Mariotes Libyen	Nimrod von Libyen

Zum vermutlich ursprünglich libyschen Wort *Pjt* vgl. Erhart Graefe, „Der libysche Stammesname *p(j)d(j) / pjt* im spätzeitlichen Onomastikon", *Enchoria* 5 (1975): 13–17. Eine für Libyen typische Pflanze und in antiker Zeit ein Hauptausfuhrartikel der Kyrenaika war das Silphium, das vor allem wegen seiner Heilkräfte begehrt war. Seit ich im Studium dessen lateinischen, etymologisch dunklen Namen *lasarpicium*[48] durch Catulls 7. Gedicht (*„Quaeris quot mihi basiationes"*)[49] gelernt habe, denke ich, daß darin auch dieses Wort *Pjt* verborgen ist. Als Etymologie sei vorgeschlagen *ns-r3-pjt* „(Zungen)kraut vom Eingang Libyens" oder *ns-irj-pjt*[50] „Kraut zu Libyen gehörend".

Wenn auch nur ein paar der hier erwogenen Etymologien Bestand haben sollten, so ergeben sich von selbst neue Aufgaben, denn dann müßten viele andere Namen, die in der syllabischen Schrift dieser Zeit geschrieben sind, etymologisch untersucht werden, vor allem natürlich die Königsnamen Scheschonk und Osorkon. Es wäre vermutlich auch nützlich, die „libysch-syllabischen" Schreibungen mit der Auswahl der Zeichen in der frühdemotischen Schrift zu vergleichen, deren vermeintliche Einkonsonantenzeichen ja in vielen Fällen aus ehemals syllabischen Zeichen

44. Vergleiche Zauzich, *Siebzehn ägyptische Götter*, 172–82, These 5, 11, 13, 18–23.
45. Diese Vokalisierung beruht gewiß auf der hebräischen Schreibung in Genesis 10,6 und 1. Chronik 1,10.
46. Ariel Shisha-Halevy, „What's in a Name? On Coptic {pa-} '{the} of-' ", *Enchoria* 13 (1985): 97–102.
47. Carsten Peust, *Die Toponyme vorarabischen Ursprungs im modernen Ägypten. Ein Katalog*, Göttinger Miszellen Beihefte 8 (Göttingen: Seminar für Ägyptologie und Koptologie der Universität Göttingen, 2010), 61–62, unter Buḥayrat Maryūṭ.
48. Wird von anderen Autoren auch *laserpitium* geschrieben.
49. Catull wünscht sich so viele Küsse von Lesbia, *„Quam magnus numerus Libyssae arenae Lasarpiciferis iacet Cyrenis"*.
50. Zum Wort *ns* „Art Pflanzen" s. Hannig, *Großes Handwörterbuch*, 431.

abgeleitet sind, so wie auch die Buchstaben unseres Alphabets.[51] Auch die besondere demotische Schrift des aramäischen Papyrus Amherst 63 wäre bei solchen Studien zu berücksichtigen.[52]

An dieser Stelle hatte ich den Aufsatz beenden wollen, als mir eine Idee zum Namen Scheschonk[53] einfiel, die ich noch zur Diskussion stellen möchte. Sobald man sich von der Vorstellung gelöst hat, daß die Namen der libyschen Könige ganz aus libyschen Wörtern bestehen, wird es denkbar, daß die griechische Wiedergabe von Scheschonk als Σεσ-ογχ-ις bzw. Σεσ-ονχ-ις (*DemNb* 970) zu segmentieren ist und daß im Mittelteil das ägyptische Wort *ꜥnḫ* „leben" steckt. Man vergleiche hierzu den Namen *Ḥr-ꜥnḫ* („Das Gesicht lebt", *DemNb* 793), griech. Ἁ-υγχ-ις / Ἁ-ωνχ-ις (u.ä.) sowie andere Namen mit *ꜥnḫ* wie Ἀρ-υνχ-ις (*DemNb* 793), Ἀπ-υγχ-ις (*DemNb* 60), Ὠγχ-ις (*DemNb* 98), Βι-ηγχ-ις (*DemNb* 136), Νεβ-ωγχ-ις (*DemNb* 636), Τα-υγχ-ις (*DemNb* 1168).

Da die libysch-syllabische Schrift weder über ein Ajin noch ein *ḫ* verfügte, könnte die Schreibung *-nq* durchaus für ägyptisch *ꜥnḫ* stehen. Auch die assyrische Wiedergabe *Šus-ꜥnqu* widerspricht diesem Voschlag nicht.

Akzeptiert man ihn, liegt die Erklärung für den ersten Teil des Namens auf der Hand: er kann kaum etwas anderes als *šꜣs* „Hirte" bzw. „wandernder Fremdling" sein (s. oben zu 4e). Genau dieser Name *Šꜣs-ꜥnḫ* ist als Name eines ägyptischen Gottes aus den Sargtexten bekannt, vgl. *LGG* VII, 27c: „Der lebende Wanderer". Ob das ein Zufall ist oder ob die ägyptischen Berater des Königs libyscher Abstammung ihm eine ägyptische Gottheit sozusagen als Vorfahren empfohlen haben, bleibt vorläufig offen.

Daß in der griechischen Entsprechung zweimal der gleiche S-Laut steht, ist kein Widerspruch, sondern liegt daran, daß die griechische Schrift wie die phönizische und unpunktierte hebräische nur e i n Zeichen für /s/ (San < *sn*) und /š/ (Sigma < Šimga < *šnw-wa*) hat, weil in der 19. Dynastie die hieratischen Schreibungen von *sn* und *šn* zusammengefallen sind.[54]

Lieber Richard, ich lege Dir hier einen Artikel vor, von dem ich selbst nicht weiß, ob er neue Wege öffnet oder eher abwegig ist. Ich wage das mit der Zuversicht, daß Du meinen Mut zu würdigen weißt, den ein pensionierter Greis eher aufbringen kann als ein junger Mensch. Aber ich nehme mir vor, an anderer Stelle noch einen kleinen demotischen Aufsatz für Dich zu schreiben, der dann ganz unproblematisch sein wird.

51. Zauzich, *Hieroglyphen mit Geheimnis*, 175–76.

52. Karl-Th. Zauzich, „Abrakadabra oder Ägyptisch? Versuch über einen Zauberspruch", *Enchoria* 13 (1985), 119–32, besonders S. 129; Karel van der Toorn, *Papyrus Amherst 63*, AOAT 448 (Münster: Ugarit-Verlag, 2018).

53. RPN 330.6 und CLE 61–88.

54. Vergleiche Zauzich, *Hieroglyphen mit Geheimnis*, 78–79. Aus dem gleichen Grund schreibt man in deutscher Sprache für /š/ die merkwürdige Kombination s-c-h.

In memoriam—Karl-Theodor Zauzich

While this volume was in the final stages of preparation, we heard the sad news that Professor Karl-Theodor Zauzich, the author of the two articles that follow, had passed away on 23 March 2021. His death is a great loss to demotic studies, in which he was one of the leading figures. As a teacher, editor, publisher, organiser, and indefatigable researcher, he was one of the key figures responsible for the renaissance of demotic studies that began in the 1970s and continues to this day. Professor Zauzich had a particularly close relationship with Richard, who studied with him, served as his *Wissenschaftlicher Assistent* at Würzburg between 1986 and 1989, and replaced him as a Visiting Professor there during the Summer Semester of 1999. The two of them collaborated frequently. Although their best known joint publication is *The Ancient Egyptian Book of Thoth*, which is described elsewhere in these pages, they edited and published other demotic texts together as well. Their most recent collaborative effort, an edition of a difficult religious text preserved on an ostracon in the Los Angeles County Museum of Art, appeared shortly before Professor Zauzich's death, and I understand from Richard that only the week before he died, Zauzich had sent him further unpublished demotic papyri with 'nuts to crack'. As his contributions to this *Festschrift* show, Professor Zauzich retained his love for demotic and his delight in the puzzles that ancient texts can sometimes pose for us up to the very end.

Mark Smith

Jüdische Namen in einer demotischen Bier- und Weizenzuteilung aus Elephantine

Karl-Theodor Zauzich†

Entgegen jeder Erwartung gibt es in den demotischen Papyri von der Insel Elephantine, die durch die Ausgrabungen von Otto Rubensohn und Friedrich Zucker (1906–1908) in die Berliner Papyrussammlung gelangt sind,[1] nur sehr wenige Hinweise auf die jüdische Bevölkerung auf der Insel, obwohl diese doch zeitweise ganz beträchtlich gewesen sein muß, wie die große Zahl aramäischer Papyri gleicher Herkunft lehrt. Um so überraschender ist daher eine kleine Liste über eine Bier- und Weizenzuteilung, weil in ihr drei jüdische Personennamen sowie ein jüdischer bzw. babylonischer Monatsname erscheinen. Gerade deswegen kommt dem eher unscheinbaren Papyrus Berlin P. 15625 erhebliche Bedeutung zu, so daß ich seine Publikation hier einer geplanten Sammlung von Berliner Papyri mit Abrechnungen aus Elephantine vorausgehen lassen will. Für die Publikationserlaubnis, die mir am 27. September 2019 erteilt wurde, danke ich Frau Prof. Dr. Verena Lepper vielmals. Ebenso danke ich Frau Diplom-Restauratorin Myriam Krutzsch für die abschließende Restaurierung des kleinen Blattes, die sie auf meine Bitte hin auch im Hinblick auf die geplante Widmung sehr bald besorgt hat. Auch Frau Sandra Steiß hat die hier abgedruckten Fotos schnell nach der Restaurierung geschaffen, wofür ihr ausdrücklich gedankt sei. Ich widme diesen Aufsatz meinem lieben Freund Richard Jasnow als relativ sichere Ergänzung zu dem ziemlich und vielleicht unziemlich spekulativen Artikel, den ich für seine Festschrift geschrieben habe. Daß ich diese Ergänzung direkt meinem ersten Beitrag anfügen darf, ist ein großes Entgegenkommen der Herausgeber dieser Festschrift, für das ich ihnen überaus dankbar bin.

P. Berlin P. 15625

Beschreibung

Kleines und bis auf den fehlenden rechten Rand von knapp 1 cm Breite in den Zeilen 1–6 anscheinend komplett erhaltenes Papyrusblatt, zwei kleine Lücken am linken Rand der Zeilen 7 und 9–10 (ohne Informationsverlust), sonst kaum beschädigt. 7,5 cm breit × 11,5 cm hoch. Recto 11 Zeilen von 9 verschiedenen Händen in frühdemotischer Geschäftsschrift, Verso 3 Zeilen (davon 2 sehr blaß) sowie geringe Spuren einer früheren Beschriftung. Schrift auf der Vorderseite gegen die Faser. Bisher unpubliziert, beschrieben im VOHD XIX,2[2] unter Nr. 122. Trismegistos ID 46237. Rubensohn-Bibliothek ID 100314.

1. Eine Übersicht aller bisher inventarisierten Elephantine-Papyri in Berlin findet sich im VOHD 19.2, s. Fußnote 2; neuerdings auch im Internet als „Rubensohn-Bibliothek“: https://elephantine.smb.museum.

2. *Ägyptische Handschriften, Teil 2, Verzeichnis der Orientalischen Handschriften in Deutschland,* Band 19. 2, herausgegeben von Erich Lüddeckens, beschrieben von Karl-Theodor Zauzich (Wiesbaden: Steiner, 1971).

Umschrift		Übersetzung	
1	*Ns-mtr sꜣ Ns-pꜣ-nti-sn*	1	Esmethis, Sohn des Espetensenis.
2	*Ns-mtr sꜣ Pꜣ-ti-wsir*	2	Esmethis, Sohn des Petosiris.
3	*[Ỉ]-ḥr sꜣ Ns-ḥr*	3	[A]os, Sohn des Esyris.
4	*[N]s-mtr sꜣ Ỉ-ꜥ-ṭi.t pꜣi=f sꜣ*	4	[E]smethis, Sohn des Jeʿddj, (und) sein Sohn.
5	*[W]n-nfr sꜣ Brgy*	5	[O]nnophris, Sohn des Barachias.
6	*Ỉw-šꜥ ~~sꜣ Ḥr-tꜣi=f-nḫt~~*	6	Josua, ~~Sohn des Hartephnachthes~~.
7	*Pa-sny sꜣ Ỉꜥḥ-i.ir-ṭi.t-s pꜣi=f sꜣ*	7	Pasenis, Sohn des Artais, (und) sein Sohn.
8	*Ns-ḫnm-mtr sꜣ Ns-mtr*	8	Eschnummethis, Sohn des Esmethis.
9	*tn ḥ(n)q 1 r 1 rmt sw 1/3*	9	Je 1 (Krug) Bier für 1 Mann (und) 1/3 (Maß) Weizen.
10	*tmt ḥ(n)q 10 sw* ⸢*3 1/3*⸣	10	Summe Bier (Krug) 10, Weizen (Maß) ⸢3 1/3⸣.
11	*ṭmṭs sw 25*	11	Tammus Tag 25.

Rückseite			
1	⸢*tmt sw 3 1/3*⸣	1	⸢Summe⸣ Weizen (Maß) 3 1/3
2	⸢*Ḏd-ḥr sꜣ Pꜣ-ḥ...*⸣	2	⸢Teos(?)⸣, Sohn(?) des *Pꜣ-ḥ...*
3	*[N]s-ḫnm-pꜣ-mtr*	3	[E]schnummethis

Wenn man sich den Text der Vorderseite sorgfältig anschaut, merkt man bald, daß er von mehreren verschiedenen Personen geschrieben worden ist. In den Zeilen 1–8 stehen acht verschiedene Personennamen, jeweils mit Hinzufügung von *sꜣ NN* „Sohn des NN". Nur der Jude Joshua in Zeile 6 hat den ägyptischen Namen seines Vaters wieder gelöscht. Diese acht Zeilen sind ganz offensichtlich von den jeweiligen Personen eigenhändig als Quittierung der Zuteilung von Bier und Weizen geschrieben. Man erkennt das gut an den sehr unterschiedlichen Schreibungen von *mtr* in den Zeilen 1, 2, 4 und 8 (*bis*) und auch schon in den kleinen Varianten in der Schreibung des Wortes *sꜣ*. Dagegen sind die Zeilen 9–11 sehr gleichmäßig wohl von der Hand dessen geschrieben, der den Vorgang der Zuteilung überwacht hat: *[N]s-ḫnm-pꜣ-mtr*.

Bemerkungen

(1) Entgegen meiner ersten Annahme ist das zweite Zeichen der Zeile nicht als *pꜣ* zu lesen, weil der Artikel im Vatersnamen deutlich geschrieben ist. Man muß das zweite Zeichen als verkürzte Schreibung für ein *m* halten, das das Wort *mtr* einleitet, ebenso in den Zeilen 2, 4 und 8 (*bis*).

(3) Das eigentümliche Determinativ bei dem ersten Namen kennzeichnet ihn als unägyptisch, vgl. auch die Namen *Brgy* (Z. 5) und *Ỉw-šꜥ* (Z. 6). Deshalb ist eine Ergänzung zu *[Ḏd]-ḥr* kaum anzunehmen. Da nur sehr wenig am Namensanfang fehlt, läßt sich eine Ergänzung zu *Ỉ-ḥr* (*DemNb* 55) vorschlagen, was vielleicht wie *[Ḏd]-ḥr* als „Das Gesicht hat gesprochen" zu verstehen ist. Der Schreiber hat den seltenen ägyptischen Namen wohl als

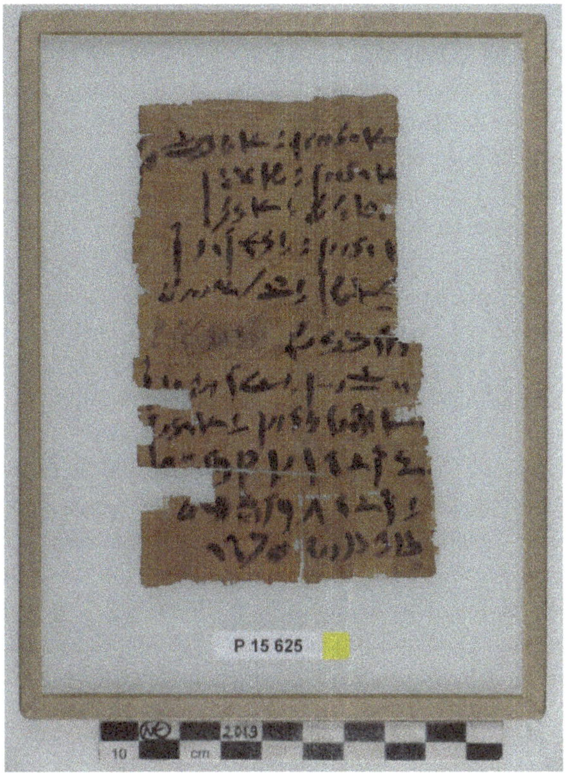

Abbildung 1. Papyrus Berlin P. 15625. Foto: Sandra Steiß; © Staatliche Museen zu Berlin, Ägyptisches Museum und Papyrussammlung, Inv. Nr. P. 15625.

Abbildung 2. Papyrus Berlin P. 15625. Foto: Sandra Steiß; © Staatliche Museen zu Berlin, Ägyptisches Museum und Papyrussammlung, Inv. Nr. P. 15625, verso.

aramäisch angesehen. Hat er womöglich an einen Namen wie *Jōḥaꜣ* יוֹחָא (Noth, *IPN*, 627)[3] gedacht? Ob eine Beziehung zum vieldiskutierten Gottesnamen *ꜣ-ḥr* im P. Amherst 63[4] besteht, bedarf noch der Klärung.

(4) Der alphabetisch bzw. syllabisch geschriebene Vatersname ist bisher unbekannt. Von den vier Zeichen ist das zweite mehrdeutig. Es sieht zwar wie ein *f* aus, aber dazu sollte es tiefer in der Zeile stehen. Daher lese ich Jod (Schilfblatt), ʿAjin, *ti.t* sowie Gottesdeterminativ, das hier eine ganz unübliche Unterlänge hat, die aber auch im Namen *Pꜣ-ti-wsir* in Zeile 2 zu sehen ist. Der Name entspricht daher dem von Noth, *IPN* unter Nr. 686 verzeichneten Namen *Jeʿddi* יֶעְדִּי, der nach ihm (S. 204) zum Stamm *ʿdh* „angenehm sein" gehört. – Am Ende der 4. und 7. Zeile steht *pꜣi=f sꜣ*, was als „(und) sein Sohn" zu verstehen ist. Nur durch diese beiden Söhne wird die Zahl von 10 (Krügen) Bier (für 10 Männer) erreicht, die in Z. 10 steht. – Die syllabische Schreibung des Namens stimmt nicht mit dem Schriftsystem des P. Amherst 63 überein.

(5) Das erste Zeichen des ersten Namens hatte ich anfangs *Ns-* gelesen, obwohl der Schrägstrich eigentlich zu weit rechts ansetzt. Dann bleibt aber der kleine waagerechte Strich unter dem ersten Zeichen ohne Erklärung. Nimmt

3. Martin Noth, *Die israelitischen Personennamen im Rahmen der gemeinsemitischen Namengebung*, Beiträge zur Wissenschaft vom Alten und Neuen Testament 3.10 (Stuttgart: Kohlhammer, 1928); Nachdruck Hildesheim: Olms, 1966.

4. Karl-Th. Zauzich, „Der Gott des aramäisch-demotischen Papyrus Amherst 63", *GM* 85 (1985): 89–90. Zuletzt Karel van der Toorn, *Papyrus Amherst 63*, AOAT 448 (Münster: Ugarit-Verlag, 2018), 127, Kommentar zu Z. 7.

man diesen ernst und ergänzt die Verbindung zu dem Schrägstrich des vermeintlichen Zeichens *Ns-*, erkennt man das halbzerstörte Zeichen [*W*]*n-* und den ganzen Namen als *Wn-nfr* „Onnophris".

Der unägyptische Name *Brgy* ist als jüdisch Berech-jah (בֶּרֶכְיָה, Barachias, Noth, *IPN*, Nr. 316; Porten, *Archives from Elephantine*, 139)[5] zu erklären, so wie der Vater des Propheten Zacharias hieß.

(6) Erneut ein jüdischer Name, der mit dem Gottesnamen *ỉw* beginnt, nämlich *ỉw-šʿ*, worin sich leicht Josua (יְהוֹשֻׁעַ, Noth, *IPN*, Nr. 614; Porten, *Archives from Elephantine*, 143) erkennen läßt. Zu weiteren demotisch überlieferten Namen mit *ỉw* vgl. meinen Aufsatz „Der verborgene Name des Gottes Amun in demotischen Texten", in *New Approaches in Demotic Studies: Acts of the 13th International Conference of Demotic Studies*, Hg. Franziska Naether, ZÄS Beiheft 10 (Berlin: de Gruyter, 2019), 303–8. – Der Vatersname ist ausgewaschen, so als hätte der Sohn sich seiner ägyptischen Herkunft geschämt. Die schwachen Spuren lassen vermuten, daß der Vater *Ḥr-tꜣỉ=f-nḫṭ* hieß.

(9) Die beschädigten Wörter am Zeilenende hatte ich erst *rmt* ⸢*Swn 10*⸣ „10 Männer aus Syene" gelesen, diese Lesung nach Vergleich mit Zeile 10 aber verworfen. Es steht tatsächlich *r 1 rmt sw 1/3* „pro 1 Mann, Weizen 1/3" da, vgl. die Anmerkung zur nächsten Zeile.

(10) Das Wort *tmt* sieht hier genau so aus, wie das Wort *sꜣ* in Z. 5. – Nach *sw* „Weizen" (man beachte das altertümliche Getreide-Determinativ [Gardiner U9]) stehen die Zeichen, die ich vor vielen Jahren als Bruchteile eines Getreidemaßes bestimmt habe, nämlich 3 1/3 Hekat(?), s. Zauzich, „Unerkannte demotische Kornmaße", in *Form und Maß. Beiträge zur Literatur, Sprache und Kunst des alten Ägypten. Festschrift für Gerhard Fecht*, ÄAT 12 (Wiesbaden: Harrassowitz, 1987), 462–71, bes. 465. Die *Berichtigungsliste*[6] hat meine paläographische Herleitung der Zeichen akzeptiert, aber sie dahingehend korrigiert, daß es sich immer um Oipe und Bruchteile des Oipe-Maßes handelt. Ob das auch für unseren Text gilt, erscheint zweifelhaft, sofern es sich wirklich, wie hier vorgeschlagen wird, um die Zuteilung für 10 Tage handelt.

Die Summe von 3 1/3 oder 10/3 zeigt, daß pro Person 1/3 Maß Weizen angewiesen worden ist. Es läßt sich vermuten, daß der dritte Teil eines Getreidemaßes (Artabe?) als Zuteilung für 10 Tage = 1/3 Monat gilt. Zur üblichen Monatsration von 1 Artabe Weizen s. Porten, *Archives from Elephantine*, 81 mit Anm. 88.

(11) Die Zahl *sw 25* „Monatstag 25" erfordert einen Monatsnamen vor sich. Dieser ist *ṯmṯs* geschrieben, was natürlich der jüdisch-babylonische *Monat* Tammus (תַּמּוּז) ist, der hier zum ersten Mal in demotischer Schrift erhalten ist. (In dem von Parker publizierten Wiener Papyrus über Mondomina[7] ist der Name an zwei Stellen ergänzt.) Interessant ist die Wiedergabe des aramäischen Zajin durch die Konsonanten *ṯ* und *s*. – Unser Beleg ist erst der zweite, bei dem ein babylonischer Monatsname in einem demotischen administrativen Text erscheint. Zum ersten Beleg dafür s. Cary J. Martin, „A Persian Estate in Egypt", in Naether, *New Approaches in Demotic Studies*, 178 Anm. 17.

(Verso 1) Die vorgeschlagene Lesung ist ganz fraglich, da die Schrift sehr blaß und nicht sicher lesbar ist. Wenn *tmt* die richtige Lesung ist, weicht die Schreibung des Wortes von der in Z. 10 des Rectos ab.

(Verso 2) Die Zeile ist sehr blaß und stammt vielleicht wie die vorhergehende aus einer früheren Beschriftung. Das 1. Zeichen ist nicht, wie ich zuerst erwogen hatte, eine 10, weil der vermeintliche Schrägstrich von links oben nach rechts unten wohl keine Schrift, sondern eine Verschmutzung ist. Der Anfang der Zeile ist vielleicht als Name *ḏD-ḥr* (Teos) zu lesen. Was danach kommt, könnte der Vatersname des Teos sein, der sich aber einer sicheren Lesung entzieht.

(Verso 3) Diese Zeile ist als einzige des Versos sicher zu lesen und ist vielleicht die Unterschrift des Mannes, der die Zuteilung von Bier und Weizen und deren Quittierung veranlaßt hat.

---

5. Bezalel Porten, *Archives from Elephantine: The Life of an Ancient Jewish Military Colony* (Berkeley: University of California Press, 1968).

6. A. A. den Benker, B. P. Muhs, und S. P. Vleeming, *A* Berichtigungsliste *of Demotic Documents*, StudDem 7-B (Leuven: Peeters, 2005), 805–6.

7. Richard A. Parker, *A Vienna Demotic Papyrus on Eclipse and Lunar Omina*, BES 2 (Providence, RI: Brown University Press, 1959).

Inhalt

Nach Auskunft der letzten drei Zeilen dürfte es sich um die Quittierung einer Zuteilung von Bier und Weizen an zehn Personen handeln. Acht dieser Personen bestätigen den Empfang mit ihrer anscheinend eigenhändigen Unterschrift. Zwei davon (in Z. 4 und 7) fügen dem Namen *pꜣi=f sꜣ* „(und) sein Sohn" hinzu, wodurch die 10 Personen zusammenkommen, die nach Zeile 10 zusammen 10 (Krüge) Bier und 3 1/3 (Maß) Weizen erhalten. Von den insgesamt 15 Namen – ein Mann in Zeile 6 hat seinen Vatersnamen gelöscht – sind 11 mit den ägyptischen Götternamen Osiris, Onnophris, Horus, Chnum, (Espeten)senis, Mond (*iꜥḥ*) und heiliger Stab (*mtr*) gebildet. Vier Namen sind unägyptisch, wenigstens drei davon in den Zeilen 4–6 sind jüdisch. Zunächst möchte man vermuten, daß diese Männer Soldaten waren, die ihren Sold teilweise in Bier und Weizen erhielten und den Empfang auf diesem kleinen Papyrus-Zettel quittiert haben. Aber würden sie dann nicht aramäisch geschrieben haben? Da sie demotisch quittieren, und durchaus nicht in unsicher erscheinender Schrift, muß man annehmen, daß sie in Ägypten vergleichsweise gut assimiliert waren. Das geht auch daraus hervor, daß 4 Männer (in den Zeilen 1, 2, 7, 8) nicht nur selbst einen ägyptischen Namen tragen, sondern auch ihre Väter. Die Vermutung liegt daher nahe, daß sie im Dienst eines ägyptischen Tempels standen und daher ihren Anspruch auf Besoldung in Bier und Weizen hatten. In der Quittung, die am 25. des jüdischen Monats Tammus geschrieben wurde, wird nicht mitgeteilt, für welchen Zeitraum die Zuteilung gedacht ist. Nach der Weizenmenge läßt sich jedoch vermuten, daß sie für 1/3 Monat, also für eine Dekade reichen sollte.

Das eigentlich Interessante an diesem Text sind die jüdischen Namen einiger Empfänger der Bierzuteilung, die in demotischer Schrift und allem Anschein nach eigenhändig geschrieben sind. Wenn jemand seinen eigenen Namen in einer fremden Schrift schreiben kann, bedeutet das natürlich noch nicht, daß er diese Schrift wirklich beherrscht. Aber die Unterschriften der nach Ausweis des Determinativs unägyptischen Personen in Z. 3 und Z. 6 sind flüssig und sicher geschrieben und lassen durchaus geübte Schreiber vermuten.

Die Frage liegt nahe, in welcher historischen Situation es für Juden auf Elephantine ratsam sein konnte, nicht aramäisch, sondern demotisch zu schreiben. Die Antwort erscheint zwingend: Kurz vor oder nach der Vertreibung der Perser aus Ägypten, die mit dem Aufstand des Amyrtaios (404 v. Chr.) begann. Der letzte aramäische Papyrus aus Elephantine datiert auf das 5. Regierungsjahr des Amyrtaios (399 v. Chr.).[8] Spätestens seit der Zerstörung des jüdischen Tempels auf Elephantine im Jahre 409 v. Chr. muß den Juden deutlich geworden sein, daß ihre Existenz in Ägypten ohne den Schutz der Perser in Gefahr geraten würde. Auch früher schon war es gewiß für Immigranten in Ägypten attraktiv, die demotische Schrift als leichteste ägyptische Schrift zu erlernen, denn nur die Kenntnis der Sprache und Schrift des Gastlandes kann zugewanderten Ausländern Chancen des Aufstiegs geben. Das war in der Antike nicht anders als in heutiger Zeit. Die zunehmende Feindschaft der Ägypter gegen die Perser muß aber den Anreiz, die demotische Schrift zu erlernen, für Ausländer sehr verstärkt haben, damit sie nicht schon durch ihre Schrift als Perserfreunde erkennbar waren. Am Ende dieser Entwicklung steht anscheinend der berühmte P. Amherst 63 mit seiner großen Sammlung aramäischer Texte in demotischer Schrift.[9]

8. P. Cowley 35 = P. TAD A3.9 (Bezalel Porten und Ada Yardeni, *Textbook of Aramaic Documents from Ancient Egypt*, Bd. 1: *Letters* [Winona Lake, IN: Eisenbrauns, 1986], 46).

9. Letzte umfassende Behandlung durch van der Toorn, *Papyrus Amherst 63*.

In What Ways Do the Gods Know You? A Bilingual Letter Revisited (Cairo mus. Inv. Nos. 10313, 10328, 30961)

Lingxin Zhang

It is my great honor and pleasure to work with Professor Richard Jasnow as a doctoral student. Not only is he a renowned expert in Demotic studies, but he is also a patient, kind, and supportive mentor. This article derives from a term paper for his Middle Egyptian class in 2016, to which Professor Jasnow offered valuable insights. He also commented "A very thoughtful paper! May be worth pursuing as an article or thinking more about." Years later, I find myself again following his very wise advice.

A Bilingual Letter concerning a Dream

This article is based on a bilingual letter reedited jointly by Gil Renberg and Franziska Naether. The letter is dated to the third century BCE,[1] from a certain Ptolemaios to some Achilles, with a possible provenance from Gebelein. The text consists of three nonjoining fragments: Cairo Mus. Inv. Nos. 10313, 10328, and 30961.[2] The papyrus was written on the recto and verso. On the recto, eighteen full lines and one incomplete line of Greek are followed by three lines of Demotic. The verso is completely written in Demotic, except for some traces of a date in Greek.[3] The last five lines on the verso were illegible, scribbled by a different hand.[4]

The Greek and Demotic parts of this letter were first published separately. Their connection was not established until Wilhelm Spiegelberg, who pointed out insightfully that the woman Ταύγχις appearing on the recto was certainly the *Ta-ʿnḫ* on the verso. The link is further strengthened considering that Ptolemaios, the sender of the letter, wrote: Αἰγυπτιστὶ δὲ ὑπέγραψα ὅπως ἀκριβῶς εἰδῆις, "I wrote in Egyptian below so you might know

I thank Steve Vinson and Marina Escolano-Poveda for their insightful feedback.

1. Ludwig Mitteis and Ulrich Wilcken, *Grundzüge und Chrestomathie der Papyruskunde*, vol. 1 (Leipzig: Teubner, 1912), 74.
2. The publication history: Gil Renberg, *Where Dreams May Come: Incubation Sanctuaries in the Greco-Roman World*, RGRW 184 (Leiden/Boston: Brill, 2017), 505–6; Gil Renberg and Franziska Naether, "'I Celebrated a Fine Day': An Overlooked Egyptian Phrase in a Bilingual Letter Preserving a Dream Narrative," *ZPE* 175 (2010): 49–71; Mitteis and Wilcken, *Grundzüge und Chrestomathie der Papyruskunde*, 50; Wilhelm Spiegelberg, *Die Demotischen Denkmäler*, vol. 2 (Strassburg: M. Dumont Schaeberg, 1908), 199–201; Edgar Goodspeed, *Greek Papyri from the Cairo Museum, Together with Papyri of Roman Egypt from American Collections* (Chicago: University of Chicago, 1902), 7–8. The Cairo bilingual letter is also mentioned in Stephen Kidd, "Dreams in bilingual papyri from the Ptolemaic Period," *BASP* 48 (2011): 113–30; Luigi Prada, "Dreams, Bilingualism, and Oneiromancy in Ptolemaic Egypt: Remarks on a Recent Study," *ZPE* 184 (2013): 85–104.
3. Renberg and Naether, "I Celebrated a Fine Day," 50–51.
4. Wilhelm Spiegelberg, *Die demotischen Denkmäler*, vol. 2 (Leipzig: Drugulin, 1904), 201.

precisely."[5] A century later, a revised edition with a more thorough commentary was brought forth by a joint effort of Renberg and Naether.[6] Renberg delves into pharaonic Egypt to contextualize some oddly phrased Greek in this letter, referencing Egyptian traditions such as the Festival of Drunkenness, the Oracular Amuletic Decrees (abbreviated as OAD below), and incubation. More precisely, Renberg's discussion concentrates on the following phrases: κἀγὼ ἡμέραν καλὴν ἤγαγον, "I too celebrated a fine day"[7] and ὃν τρόπον οἱ θεοί σε οἴδασιν "in what way the gods know you."[8]

In this article, I will make a few suggestions with regard to the translation of the Demotic dream account in the Cairo bilingual letter and recontextualize this letter within the Greco-Roman divinatory corpus, particularly with respect to the newly published dream manuals in the Tebtunis Temple Library.

The partially preserved dream account in the Cairo bilingual letter is enigmatic to say the very least. I will tentatively reconstruct the sequence of dream events below. The dream narrative begins in the lower portion of P. Cairo inv. 30961 recto. This section is fairly straightforward and sets the background for the rest of the dream. In this section, Ptolemaios saw himself standing at the doorway of a temple, looking at a priest who was surrounded by many people. The fragment breaks here. It is unclear how much of P. Cairo inv. 30961 is lost, since it constitutes the bottom piece of the letter. Regardless, when finished writing on the recto, Ptolemaios flipped the papyrus and started writing from the bottom of the back of the very papyrus, which is labeled as P. Cairo inv. 30961 verso.[9]

In P. Cairo inv. 30961 verso lines 1–2, Ptolemaios conversed with the priest at the temple in his dream. He asked the latter who the man of Pamoun[10] was; to which the priest answered, she was Nebwotis.[11] The text then offered an interpretation to the priest's response by identifying this "man of Pamoun" as a certain Paunchis (*Pꜣ-ꜥnḫ*), who is fur-

5. Spiegelberg, 200. The fact that the letter's sender, Ptolemaios, switched to Demotic for the dream account has been taken as evidence for Ptolemaios's Egyptian ethnicity. Parallels have been drawn with the dream accounts in the archive of Ptolemaios of the *enkatochoi*, within which, the dreams of the Egyptian twins, Taous and Tawe, along with those of Apollonius, an Egypt-born Greek, are written in Demotic; John Ray, "The Dreams of the Twins in St Petersburg," in *Through a Glass Darkly: Magic, Dreams and Prophecy in Ancient Egypt*, ed. Kasia Szpakowska (Swansea: Classical Press of Wales, 2006), 194. Recently, the method of taking the dream accounts' languages as evidence for the dreamers' ethnicity has been challenged by Stephen Kidd. Meanwhile, Kidd's counterargument is thoroughly evaluated by Luigi Prada. Kidd, "Dreams in Bilingual Papyri from the Ptolemaic Period," 117–19; Prada, "Dreams, Bilingualism, and Oneiromancy," 85–87.

6. Renberg and Naether, "I Celebrated a Fine Day," 49–71.

7. P. Cairo inv. 30961 recto, lines 2–3. Renberg contextualizes this phrase within the Festival of Drunkenness, where excessive drinking is a key element, see Renberg and Naether, "I Celebrated a Fine Day," 59–62. For the Demotic cultic revelries about this festival, see Richard Jasnow and Karl-Theodore Zauzich, "Another Praise of the Goddess Ait (O. Sommerhausen 1)," in *Illuminating Osiris: Egyptological Studies in Honor of Mark Smith*, ed. Richard Jasnow and Ghislaine Widmer (Atlanta: Lockwood, 2017), 155–62; Richard Jasnow and Mark Smith, "New Fragments of the Demotic Mut Text in Copenhagen and Florence," in *Joyful in Thebes: Egyptological Studies in Honor of Betsy M. Bryan*, ed. Richard Jasnow and Kathlyn Cooney (Atlanta: Lockwood, 2015), 239–82; Mark Depauw and Mark Smith, "Visions of Ecstasy: Cultic Revelry before the Goddess Ai/Nehemanit Ostraca Faculteit Letteren (K. U. Leuven) dem. 1–2," in *Res Severa Verum Gaudium: Festschrift für Karl-Theodor Zauzich zum 65. Geburstag am 8. Juni 2004*, ed. Friedhelm Hoffmann and Heinz-Josef Thissen (Leuven: Peeters, 2004), 67–93.

8. P. Cairo inv. 30961 recto, lines 3–4.

9. This practice is very common in Egyptian epistolary but is also found in Greek letter writing; see Prada, "Dreams, Bilingualism, and Oneiromancy," 86n6.

10. Naether suggests that *pꜣ rmṯ n Pa-Ỉmn(?)* could be a hitherto unattested name, see Renberg and Naether, "I celebrated a fine day," 57, notes on frag. 3 verso line 1.

11. P. Cairo inv. 30961 verso lines 1-2; Naether translates *Nb(.t)-wḏy tꜣy* as "It is Nebwotis." Clearly the genders of *pꜣ rmt n Pa-Ỉmn* and the copula *tꜣy* in line 2 do not agree. The confusion might be intentional given the dream's focus on gender binary. For the name Nebwotis, see Renberg and Naether, "I Celebrated a Fine Day," 57, L5; Erich Lüddeckens, *Demotische Namenbuch* (Wiesbaden: Reichert, 1980), 638.

ther equated with Taunchis (*Ta-ꜥnḫ*). The appearance of the word "answer, interpretation" (*wꜣḥ*) [12] in line 2 indicates that Ptolemaios's enquiry to the priest is oracular in nature.

Next (lines 4-5), Ptolemaios reiterated his conversation with the priest before revealing its true meaning: "the one within whom he is, namely, she is a woman." What remains ambiguous is the identity of "he" in the clause above. Considering that the woman, Nebwotis, was identified as "the man of Pamoun/that of Amun," it is possible that "he" could refer to Pamoun or Amun. I prefer the explanation of Amun.

Below are my transliteration and translation of P. Cairo inv. 30961 verso. The formatting reflects the *spatia* in the original text:

(1) ⸢*mtw=y*⸣ [*n pꜣ wꜥb*] (*n*)-*rn=f ḏd* ⸢*pꜣ rmṯ n Pa-Ỉmn*   *nm pꜣy*⸣
(2) *ḏd=f* [...] ⸢*Nb*(.*t*)-⸣*wḏy tꜣy*   *twy=s pꜣ wꜣḥ*
(3) *r-ḏd=w n=y*   *ẖr-ḥr=y*   ⸢*pꜣ rmṯ n Pa-Ỉmn*⸣ *r-ḏd=f Pꜣ-ꜥnḫ pꜣy*
(4) *ỉw=f ḏd Ta-ꜥnḫ*   *pꜣy ḏd r-ỉr=y pꜣ rmṯ* [*n Pa-Ỉmn*]
(5) *nm pꜣy ỉw=f ḏd*   *Nb.*(*t*)-*wḏy tꜣy ḏd n-ỉm=f*
(6) *pꜣ nty-ỉw=f n-ỉm=f ḏd sḥm.t tꜣy*   (*n*)*? pꜣ bnr n? pꜣ dj.t s*...

(1) ⸢I talked⸣ [(to) the priest] above, saying: ⸢"The man of Pamoun,[13]   Who is he?"⸣
(2) He (the priest) said [...] She is ⸢Neb⸣wotis.[14]   Behold, the answer
(3) which was said to me concerning me[15]:   ⸢The man of Pamoun,⸣ whom he (the priest) mentioned, he is Paunchis[16];

12. *wꜣḥ*, "interpretation," CDD *W* (2009), 14–15. Online: https://oi.uchicago.edu/sites/oi.uchicago.edu/files/uploads/shared/docs/CDD_W.pdf; this word appears in the phrase *ḏ* (*pꜣ*) *wꜣḥ*, "to answer, give an oracle." *wꜣḥ* is also attested in the Archive of Ḥor as oracular response, promising the enquirer longevity and a proper burial, John Ray, *The Archive of Ḥor* (London: Egypt Exploration Society, 1976), Text 9 verso and Text 14.

13. Despite of the fact that *Pa-Ỉmn*, "Pamoun" is attested as a Demotic personal name, its hieroglyphic counterpart *pꜣ-*(*n*)*-Ỉmn* is known to denote a sanctuary in Nubia, *LGG* III, 10. Considering the particular phrase in the Cairo bilingual letter, *pꜣ rmṯ n Pa-Ỉmn* "the person of he/that of Amun," it seems reasonable to interpret Pamoun as the name of a sanctuary. For Pamoun as a person name, see Renberg and Naether, "I Celebrated a Fine Day," 57, note of frag. 3 verso L 1. For the equation between *pa* and *pꜣ n*, see Janet Johnson, *Thus Wrote 'Onchsheshonqy: An Introductory Grammar of Demotic*, 3rd ed., SAOC 45 (Chicago: Oriental Institute of the University of Chicago, 2000), ¶66.

14. *Nb.*(*t*)*-wḏy* "Nebwotis" is an attested female name, Erich Lüddeckens, *Das Demotische Namenbuch* (Wiesbaden: Reichert, 1980), 638; Renberg and Naether, "I Celebrated a Fine Day," 57, note of frag. 3 verso L. 5. The masculine form, *Nb-wḏy*, is attested as a divine epithet for the god of a quarry in Theban graffito 3446, *LGG* III, 617; Richard Jasnow, "Demotic Graffiti from Western Thebes," in *Grammata Demotika: Festschrift für Erich Lüddeckens zum 15. Juni 1983*, ed. Heinz-J. Thissen and Karl-Th. Zauzich (Würzburg: Gisela Zauzich Verlag, 1984), 93–95.

15. *ẖr*, prep. "under, for, concerning," CDD *H̱* (2001), 51. Online: https://oi.uchicago.edu/sites/oi.uchicago.edu/files/uploads/shared/docs/CDD_H4.pdf.

16. Naether translates this sentence as "He is/That is Life"; Renberg and Naether, "I Celebrated a Fine Day," 54. Naether's translation has a minor problem with the definite article *pꜣ*, which requires the translation "He/It is *the* life." I suggest reading *Pꜣ-ꜥnḫ* as the name Paunchis, Lüddeckens, *Demotische Namenbuch*, 357. In Lüddeckens's examples, the name Paunchis does not always end with a seated man determinative. Similarly, the writing of Paunchis in the Cairo bilingual letter also lacks determinatives.

(4) It means,[17] Taunchis.[18] This speech which I made:[19] "The person [of Pamoun,]
(5) who is he?" he saying[20]: "She is Nebwotis." Meaning by it(?),[21] the one within whom he (Amun/Shai/Pamoun?) is,[22] namely, she is a woman. Apart from giving her ... ?

Gender binary seems to be a theme in this dream, which consists of at least two layers. First, the so-called man of Pamoun (masc.) is equated to Paunchis (masc.) and then Taunchis (fem.). Second, in the oracle, the priest identified "the man of Pamoun," a masculine entity, as "Nebwotis," the latter being a woman's name.[23] In line 6, Ptolemaios explicitly addressed the gender confusion by saying that a masculine entity (Amun/Shai/Pamoun?) is within a woman.

The wordplay between Paunchis (*Pꜣ-ꜥnḫ*) and Taunchis (*Ta-ꜥnḫ*) is worth commenting. As Spiegelberg observed, this Taunchis (*Ta-ꜥnḫ*) is likely the Ταύγχις in the Greek section of the letter. In P. Cairo inv. 10328 recto line 9, Ptolemaios writes that before he had the dream, he had written two letters, one concerning Taunchis the other concerning Teteimouthis (ἓν μὲν περὶ Ταύγχιος τῆς ἐκ Θερμούθιος, ἓν δὲ περὶ Τετεϊμούθιος τῆς Ταυῆτος...).[24] One wonders to what extent a comparison could be drawn between this Ptolemaios and Ptolemaios the *katochos*.[25]

17. *iw=f ḏd*, "it means..." is a present tense main clause. When *ḏd* appears in an oracular context, it can be translated as "to mean," providing explanations and glosses to the oracles. Compare this phrase to Demotic Chronicle Col. 2.5: *iw=f ḏd (r) pꜣ ḥry nty iw=f (r) iy m-sꜣ=w r šn r nꜣ mt.w(t) (n) Mn-nfr*, "It means, the ruler who will come after them will investigate concerning the matters (in) Memphis." The transliteration and translation of Demotic Chronicle follow Richard Jasnow's forthcoming anthology of Demotic literature. I thank Dr. Jasnow for this observation. I believe *iw=f ḏd* marks the beginning of the interpretation section for two reasons. First, the phrase follows the statement *twy=s pꜣ wꜣḥ*... "Behold the interpretation...;" second, the clause breaks away from past tense, in which the dream has been narrated.

18. *Ta-ꜥnḫ*, Lüddeckens, *Demotische Namenbuch*, 1168; according to the *Namenbuch*, this name ends with a seated man determinative.

19. The reading of *pꜣy* "this" (*DG*, 128) is not certain. However, compared to *iw=s*, which is suggested by Spiegelberg and Naether, *pꜣy* fits better within the context. I thank Dr. Jasnow for this reading.

20. I treat this sentence as a circumstantial clause.

21. My translation "meaning by it" treats *ḏd* as an infinitive and draws parallels with the Demotic Chronicle, col. 4.4: *iir=f ḏd n-im-s* ... "That is (by which is meant)..." Nevertheless, when *ḏd* is used in glosses, it often has a dummy subject "it" (*=f*), as demonstrated by the example above. Unfortunately, such is not the case in the Cairo bilingual letter, thus adding uncertainty to my translation. My transliteration and translation of the Demotic Chronicle follow Richard Jasnow's forthcoming anthology of Demotic literature. Naether transliterates and translates this phrase as *Nb.(t)-wḏy tꜣy-ḏd n-im=f*, "Nebwotis is it, who has said it," by treating *tꜣy-ḏd* as an articled past participle. However, this type of coalesced writing appears primarily with past relative forms rather than past participles; Johnson, *Thus Wrote 'Onchsheshonqy: An Introductory Grammar of Demotic*, ¶90.

22. I treat *pꜣ nty iw=f n-im=f* as a present tense relative clause "within whom he is." For the structure of present tense relative clause, see Johnson, *Thus Wrote 'Onchsheshonqy: An Introductory Grammar of Demotic*, ¶88. For the translation of *n*, see *n* preposition, "in, through, with, by means of," CDD *N* (2004), 3–4. Online: https://oi.uchicago.edu/sites/oi.uchicago.edu/files/uploads/shared/docs/CDD_N.pdf. I tentatively suggest that the "he" in this phrase refers to Amun/Shai, inferring from the phrase *pꜣ rmṯ n Pa-ỉmn* and the evocation to Psais at the end of this letter (P. Cairo inv. 10328 verso line 2). For the connection between Amun and Shai, see Jan Quaegebeur, *Le Dieu Égyptien Shaï dans la Religion et l'Onomastique*, OLA 2 (Leuven: Leuven University Press, 1975), 76–80.

23. P. Cairo inv. 30961 verso, line 2 and line 5.

24. For Renberg's interpretation that these letters are petitionary letter to a god before one conducts incubation, see Renberg, *Where Dreams May Come*, 506n58. Renberg's hypothesis is certainly possible and provides a good reason for Taunchis's appearance in the dream. However, judging from the letter itself, it is hard to say with certainty if incubation is involved. It is also noteworthy that both Taunchis and Teteimouthis are identified by metronymics, a phenomenon associated with heavy Egyptian influences in the Ptolemaic period; Mark Depauw, "The Use of Mothers' Names in Ptolemaic Documents: A Case of Greek-Egyptian Mutual Influence?" *JJP* 37 (2007): 21–29. This detail is in keeping with Prada's opinion that Ptolemaios and Achilles were ethnically Egyptian, Prada, "Dreams, Bilingualism, and Oneiromancy," 86–87.

25. Ptolemaios the *katochos* is an Egypt-born Greek who lived in the *enkatochoi* at the Sarapeum in the second century BCE. An overview of his life and dream accounts can be found in Bernard Legras, *Les Reclus Grecs du Sarapieion de Memphis*, StudHell 49 (Leuven: Peeters, 2011), 256–58; John Ray, "The Dreams of the Twins in St Petersburg," 189–203; Dorothy Thompson, *Memphis under the Ptolemies* (Princeton: Princeton University Press, 1988), 197–246.

We know from the latter's archive that he was the main caregiver for the twin sisters. Ptolemaios the *katochos* wrote profusely to authorities on the matters of the twins;[26] and the two sisters feature heavily in his dream accounts.[27]

Dream Manuals and Accounts

In this section, I will expand Renberg's discussion on the phrase ὃν τρόπον οἱ θεοί σε οἴδασιν, "in what way the gods know you." Renberg observes that the language "does not appear to reflect a typically Greek theological concept"[28] and contextualizes it in the traditions of OAD; more specifically, with respect to the following verses: "we (the gods) shall make every dream, which... any person... will see for her, good."[29] Although these verses in OAD convey a similar concept to that in the letter, with regard to the way in which a person's dream portends the fate of somebody else, considering that Ptolemaios lived in the early Ptolemaic period, it seems more likely that his point of reference lies in the Demotic divinatory corpus.

In the corpus of Demotic Dream Books, it is not uncommon to see dreams carrying significance to people other than the dreamer.[30] Two examples come to mind. One is P. Carlsberg 13b, 14–41, a section on dreams about women.[31] According to the recently revised edition by Joachim F. Quack, the section title should read: "Die Arten von Dingen, von denen ein Mensch träumt, wenn [eine Frau] davon träumt."[32] The text continues to list the different dream scenarios where women are concerned, followed by the corresponding prognostication for her. Essentially, the dreamer's vision regarding a certain woman is considered to be predictive of the woman's future.[33]

26. For instance, UPZ 23: Ptolemaios writes to the *hypodioiketes* concerning the issuing of the twins' oil; UPZ 17–41: the twins' appeals to Philometer and his queen written by Ptolemaios.

27. UPZ 77–79.

28. Renberg and Naether, "I Celebrated a Fine Day," 63.

29. Renberg and Naether, 62.

30. Nevertheless, the majority of dream manuals' predictions relate only to the dreamer, Kim Ryholt and Joachim Quack, *Demotic Literary Texts from Tebtunis and Beyond*, The Carlsberg Papyri 11, CNIP 36 (Copenhagen: Museum Tusculanum Press, 2019), 194.

31. Quack suggests that P. Gießen D 102 recto has a similar content to that of P. Carlsberg 13b, 14-41, see Joachim F. Quack, "Ein neues demotisches Traumbuch der Ptolemäerzeit (Papyrus Gießen D 102 rekto)," in *Sapientia Felicitas: Festschrift für* Günter *Vittmann zum 29. Februar 2016*, CENiM 14, ed. Sandra Lippert, Maren Schentuleit, and Martin Stadler (Montpellier: Université Paul Valéry, 2016), 489–505.

32. P. Carlsberg 13b, II. 14: *n3 ẖ(.t) nk{t} mtw rmṯ nw r-[r=w ...] sḥm.t nw r-r=w*, Ryholt and Quack, *Demotic Literary Texts*, 219–21; Joachim Quack, "Demotische magische und divinatorische Texte," in *Omina, Orakel, Rituale und Beschwörungen*, ed. Bernd Janowski and Gernot Wilhem, TUAT NF 4 (Gütersloher: Gütersloher Verlagshaus, 2004), 360. Compare Quack's translation to that of Volten and Spakowska, which reads *n3 ẖ nkt.w [sic] mtw rmṯ nw r[.r=w r wʿ.t] sḥjm.t nw r.r=w*, "The kinds of copulation, about which one dreams if one is a woman"; Kasia Szpakowska, "Flesh for Fantasy: Reflections of Women in Two Ancient Egyptian Dream Manuals," in *Egyptian Stories: A British Egyptological Tribute to Alan B. Lloyd on the Occasion of His Retirement*, ed. Thomas Schneider and Kasia Szpakowska (Münster: Ugarit-Verlag, 2007), 402. Note that *nkt* has been read and translated differently by Volten and Quack here. In the papyrus, the surviving traces fit the heiraticized writing of *nkt* "things" (*DG*, 229–30). Volten suggests that although this word appears to be *nkt*, "things," it should really be read as *nk*, "copulation" (*DG*, 229); Askel Volten, *Demotische Traumdeutung: Pap. Carlsberg XIII and XIV verso*, Analecta Aegyptiaca 3 (Copenhagen: Munksgaard, 1942), 85, n. for l. 14.

33. P. Carlsberg 13 frg. e is perhaps written with a similar structure. Ryholt and Quack revised Volten's reading of the word *b3st.t.* "knee" (*DG*, 110) to *k3y.t*, "vulva." P. Carlsberg 13 frag. e contains a series of protases concerning the vulva followed by predictions given to a woman. Unfortunately, not much of the protases are preserved and we do not know whether a man is dreaming about a vulva himself or if he sees a woman acting with respect to her vulva; Ryholt and Quack, *Demotic Literary Texts*, 224; Volten, *Demotische Traumdeutung*, 98–99, pl. 6.

The second example also comes from the Tebtunis Temple Library.[34] P. Carlsberg 490 + PSI inv. D 56 is a dream manual comprising 9 fragments. The best-preserved piece contains dreams and predictions about Pharaoh.[35] Intriguingly, some dream scenarios are described in a way akin to the aforementioned women's section, for example frg.1 line 9 reads: "[If he] sees Pharaoh fighting against the …"[36] Unfortunately, the prediction of this line does not survive. However, judging from the extant portion, the predictions seem to be a mixture of those for Egypt, for the dreamer, and for Pharaoh; for instance, frg.1 line 10 reads: "[If he is] upon a donkey: the water will come this year …" and frg.1 line 15 reads: "[If he is upon a] dog: Pharaoh will capture the foreign lands …"[37]

The editors suggest that P. Carlsberg 490 + PSI inv. D 56 might be related to the tradition of state divination, a practice most widely attested in Sothis and eclipse omina.[38] However, it is still uncommon to see a mix of prognoses for individuals (the dreamer, Pharaoh) along with those for the state, as they are in the case above.[39] Be that as it may, P. Carlsberg 490 + PSI inv. D 56 is certainly an example where dreams' impact reaches beyond the dreamers themselves.

In What Ways Do the Gods Know You?

To answer the question I raised in the title: "*In what ways* do the gods *know* you," I turn to dream manuals, the divinatory corpus, and narratives from Greco-Roman Egypt. After surveying the materials, it seems to me one potential explanation for this expression is the divine wrath and favor in the Demotic divinatory corpus.[40]

Unsurprisingly, divine wrath and favor are frequently attested themes. One prediction in the women's dream manual (P. Carlsberg 13b 2, 20) reads: "Sie wird wegen großen Gotteszornes flehen, man wird…"[41] Likewise, a manual of

34. The bulk of the Tebtunis Temple Library consists of the manuscripts from The Papyrus Carlsberg Collection. Theses texts are dated approximately to the second century CE and were presumably discovered in two underground cellars within the Soknebtunis temple complex at Tebtunis, a village at the southern edge of the Fayum. For an overview of the Tebtunis Temple Library, see Kim Ryholt, "On the Contents and Nature of the Tebtunis Temple Library: A Status Report," in *Tebtynis und Soknopaiu Nesos: Leben im römerzeitlichen Fajum; Akten des Internationalen Symposions vom 11. bis 13. Dezember in Sommerhausen bei Würzburg*, ed. Sandra Lippert and Maren Schentuleit (Wiesbaden: Harrasowitz, 2005), 141–70. Recently, the Franco-Italian excavation in Tebtunis has unearthed a Ptolemaic rubbish dump outside the temple precinct. Concerning the materials recovered from the Ptolemaic pit, Ryholt observed a continuity between them and those of the Tebtunis Temple Library; see Kim Ryholt, "Demotic Papyri from the Franco-Italian Excavations at Tebtunis, 1988–2016," in *Le Fayoum: Archéologie -Histoire -Religion; Actes du Sixième Colloque International, Montpellier, 26–28 Octobre 2016*, ed. Marie -Pierre Chaufray, Ivan Guermeur, Sandra Lippert, and Vincent Rondot (Wisbaden: Harrassowitz, 2018), 141–70.

35. Ryholt and Quack, *Demotic Literary Texts*, 186–94.

36. [*ỉw=f nw*]*e r pr-ꜥꜣ ỉw=f mẖy r pꜣ* […], Ryholt and Quack, *Demotic Literary Texts*, 87 and 189.

37. Frag. 1 line 10: [*ỉw=f*] *ḥr ꜥꜣ r pꜣ mw r ỉy n tꜣy* ˹*rnp.t*˺ frg. 1 line 15: [*ỉw=f ḥr ỉw*]*ỉw r pr-ꜥꜣ ḥḳ* ˹*nꜣ ẖꜣs.tw*˺, Ryholt and Quack, 187 and 189.

38. Ryholt and Quack, 194. There are several unpublished Sothis omina in the Tebtunis Temple Library which are concerned with the state. A published example of this kind of text is P. Cairo 31222 in George Hughes, "A Demotic Astrological Text," *JNES* 10 (1951): 256–64. For the eclipse astrological text, see Richard Parker, *A Vienna Demotic Papyrus on Eclipse- and Lunar-Omina*, BES 2 (Providence, RI: Brown University Press, 1959).

39. In dream books, occasional references to "Egypt" and "Pharaoh" are not uncommon, e.g., PSI inv. D 61, 5; Ryholt and Quack, *Demotic Literary Texts*, 217–18.

40. Through personal correspondence, Steven Vinson has made the observation that the phraseology in the bilingual letter resembles the opening of Odyssey and the choice of words could be intentionally Homeric. This is indeed possible, especially considering Luigi Prada's interpretation that Ptolemaios and Achilles were well-educated Egyptian men competent in their Greek language skills; Prada, "Dreams, Bilingualism, and Oneiromancy," 85–88. However, I will limit my discussion to the Demotic material in this article.

41. …*ỉw=s sbḥ n bwꜣ ꜥꜣ* …, Quack, "Demotische magische und divinatorische Texte," 360. My transliteration follows Ryholt and Quack, *Demotic Literary Texts*, 220. For the original publication, see Volten, *Demotische Traumdeutung*, 86–87.

terrestrial omina dated to the first century CE, the so-called the *Book of the Gecko*,[42] contains several similar prognoses concerning divine rage. For instance, col. X+II, 5 reads: "ihr Götter ihr zürnen,"[43] while col. X+II, 27 states: "Ihre Götter werden einen Vorwurf für sie finden."[44]

The same idea is elaborated in much more detail in the story of "Nectanebo's dream." This tale is preserved in Greek and Demotic versions.[45] Although in a fragmentary state, the beginning of the Greek text conserves an episode where Onuris complains to Isis about Nectanebo not finishing his temple.[46] Onuris's fury is expounded through the following accusation: Ἐκτὸς τοῦ ἑαυτοῦ ἱεροῦ εἰμει καὶ τὰ ἐν τῷ ἀδύτωι ἱμιτέλεστά ἐστειν διὰ τὴν τοῦ πρωεστῶτος κακίαν, "I am outside my temple and the incompleteness of the sanctuary is on account of the vice of the chief."[47]

Nectanebo wakes up from the dream and calls in Petese to complete the inscriptions in the temple of Onuris. Nevertheless, the sculptor succumbs to a premature death before accomplishing the assignment. Ryholt suggests that the failure to finish the temple incurred divine wrath and led to the demise of Nectanebo.[48]

Not coincidentally, the prognostications from the aforementioned *Book of the Gecko* are followed by exhortations to make offerings or to deposit to the gods, in order to appease the divine wrath.[49] These gestures, together with Nectanebo's effort in finishing the temple decorations, should be understood in a similar way, namely, pious acts intended to pacify a deity or to curry divine favor.

As far as the Cairo bilingual letter is concerned, Renberg has appropriately suggested that Ptolemaios wrote the letter so that "Achilles might take steps to correct the future."[50] Therefore, it seems to me highly likely that the answer to "in what ways do the gods know you" is divine wrath or favor regarding Achilles as revealed by the dream of Ptolemaios.

---

42. Karl-Theodore Zauzich, "Das demotische 'Buch des Geckos' und die Palmomantik des Melampus," in *Forschung in der Papyrussammlung: Eine Festgabe für das neue Museum*, ed. Verena Lepper (Berlin: de Gruyter, 2012), 355–73. There are several copies of the Book of the Gecko, one of which belongs to the Tebtunis Temple Library and is published in Ryholt and Quack, *Demotic Literary Texts*, 269–72.

43. *…n3y=s nṯr.w ḫʿly r-r=s*, Zauzich, "Das demotische 'Buch des Geckos,'" 357.

44. *n3y=s nṯr.w gm n=s lwḥ…*, Zauzich, 358.

45. The Greek text is published in UPZ 81, forming part of the archive of *enkatochoi*. The Demotic fragments are published in Kim Ryholt, "Nectanebo's dream or the prophecy of Petesis," in *Apokalyptik und Ägypten: Eine kritische Analyse der relevanten Texte aus dem griechisch-römischen Ägypten*, ed. Andreas Blasius and Bernd Schipper (Leuven: Peeters, 2002), 240–41.

46. …ἕως τοῦ νῦν ἐμοῦ τὴν πᾶσαν ἐπιμέλειαν πεποιημένου Νεκτοναβῶι τοῦ βασιλέως Σαμαῦτος ὑπὸ σοῦ κατασταθὶς ἐπὶς τῆς ἀρχῆς ἠμέληκεν τοῦ ἐμοῦ ἱεροῦ καὶ τοῖς ἐμοῖς προσσάγγμασιν ἀντιπέπτωκεν. Ἐκτὸς τοῦ ἑαυτοῦ ἱεροῦ εἰμει καὶ τὰ ἐν τῷ ἀδύτωι ἱμιτέλεστά ἐστειν διὰ τὴν τοῦ πρωεστῶτος κακίαν, "… und während ich nun bis jetzt meine ganze Sorge zuwandte dem König Nektanebos, dem Sohn des Königs-(Neffen?) Samaus, hat er, der von dir in die Herrschaft eingesetzt wurde, mein Heiligtum vernachlässigt und hat meinen Anordnungen nicht Folge geleistet. Ich bin nun außerhalb meines eigenen Tempels und das Werk im Allerheiligsten ist nur halbvollendet wegen der Schlechtigkeit des Tempelvorstehers." My translation follows Jörg-Dieter Gauger, "Der 'Traum des Nektanebos'—Die griechische Fassung," in *Apokalyptik und Ägypten: Eine kritische Analyse der relevanten Texte aus dem griechisch-römischen Ägypten*, ed. Andreas Blasius and Bernd Schipper (Leuven: Peeters, 2002), 195–97. On the historical background of Onuris's complaint, see Ryholt, "Nectanebo's Dream," 221–41.

47. The "chief" has been conventionally understood as the king, but an alternative interpretation is proposed by Ryholt, who suggests that the πρωεστῶτος (from προίστημι, "to stand in front") likely refers to the chief of temple, hence, Petese; see Ryholt, "Nectanebo's Dream," 240; Ludwig Koenen, "The Dream of Nektanebos," *BASP* 22 (1985): 185.

48. Ryholt, "Nectanebo's Dream," 240. For the theory regarding how the story's development could be part of the "Greek propaganda," see Koenen, "Dream of Nektanebos," 192–94.

49. Col. X+II, 5: … *my* (*ir*)=*s* ⸢*ʿby*⸣ *m-b3ḥ nre*(?), "möge (sie) opfern vor…," and col. X+II, 27: …*my ir*=*s* [*gy*]*l m-b3ḥ*= {*w*} *ḥri*=*w*, "Möge sie (sich) anvertrauen dem (Gott) Herieus"; Zauzich, "das demotische 'Buch des Geckos,'" 357–58.

50. Renberg and Naether, "I Celebrated a Fine Day," 63.

As a side note, from the point of view of a modern reader, it seems more conventional to express the same idea by saying "what the gods know about your future."[51] However, when it comes to the "future," ancient Egyptian evidence seems to be more concerned with the gods' abilities to "speak" or "proclaim" it. For instance, the Egyptian word *ḏd* features heavily in the oracles from the Third Intermediate period and has a rich connotation of direct contact with the divine through oracles or visions.[52]

This tradition became more prevalent in the Greco-Roman period. On the statue of Harkhebi the astrologer, the planets are evoked as "gods who foretell (*sr*) the future."[53] In a dream of Ḥor, he reports that: "Harpocrates the great god [...] speaks every matter which shall come before you (Ḥor)...."[54]

Some astrological text frames the divinatory content of the composition in the monologue of a god. For instance, PSI inv. D 35 + P. Carlsberg 684, an astrological treatise for women, writes in its opening lines: "Imhotep the Great, son of Ptah, the great god. He speaks about the manner [which ... the good (as to) fa]te and the bad (as to) fate together with the issues which happen (to) the wome...."[55] This statement implies that the composition is written in accordance with the monologue of the healing god Imhotep, which the author probably gained access to through a vision or a dream. In fact, this is exactly the situation recorded in the introduction to the Hermetic herbal treatise *De Virtutibus Herbarum*, which claims that the composition is dictated by Ascleipius to Thessalus in a vision.[56] The abundant attestation of a god speaking or proclaiming the future is probably rooted in the nature of texts preserved. After all, one purpose of the divinatory corpus is to receive messages directly from the gods.

In summary, gods know individuals favorably or adversely, the knowledge of which can be gleaned from dreams and visions. Priests claim to have access to divine knowledge (oracles, dream interpretations) and laymen rely on this

---

51. Perhaps, the epithets associated with divine foreknowledge are those related to *sỉꜣ*, "to know, to recognize," *Wb.* IV:30. For instance, *sỉꜣt-nfrt-n-wn-ḥr-smꜣty=s*, "She who knows the good for the ones on her way," an epithet for Hathor.

52. According to Krutchen, divine utterance is such a prominent feature in oracles, that the single phrase "Amon said" should imply oracular settings in New Kingdom and Third Intermediate period texts. For the use of terms such as *ḏd*, "say" and *wḏ*, "command" in oracles, see Jean-Marie Krutchen, "La terminologie de la consultation de l'oracle de l'Amon Thébain à la Troisième Période Intermédiare," in *Oracles et Prophéties dans l'Antiquité: Actes du Colloque de Strasbourg, 15–17 Juin 1995*, ed. Jean Heintz (Paris: de Boccard, 1997), 62–64. Coexisting with such words, are *hn*, "comply" and *nꜣy n ḥꜣy*, "walk backwards" in processional oracles; see Jaroslav Černý, "Egyptian Oracles," in *A Saite Oracle Papyrus from Thebes in the Brooklyn Museum (Papyrus Brooklyn 47.218.3)*, ed. Richard Parker (Providence. RI: Brown University Press, 1962), 43–45.

53. Ptolemaic period (second century BCE), Buto. *ḥnꜥ nṯr.w sr ḥn... sr,* "vorhersagen, verkünden," *Wb.* IV:189, 15–190, 17; *ḥn,* "eilen, gehen, such begeben," *Wb.* III:103, 6–21. For a recent edition of Harkhebi's biography, see Jacco Dieleman, "Claiming the Stars: Egyptian Priests Facing the Sky," in *Basel Egyptology Prize 1: Junior Research in Egyptian History, Archaeology, and Philology*, ed. Susanne Bickel and Antonio Loprieno (Basel: Schwabe & Co., 2003), 285–86; Phillip Derchain, "Harkhébis, le psylle-astrologue," *ChronÉg* 64 (1989): 74–89; Otto Neugebauer and Richard Parker, *Egyptian Astronomical Texts*, vol. 3, BES 5 (Providence, RI: Brown University Press, 1969), 214–16; Georges Daressy, "La Statue d'un Astronome," *ASAE* 16 (1916): 1–4; Ahmed Kamal, "Rapport sur quelques localités de la Basse-Égypte," *ASAE* 7 (1906): 239–40.

54. *Ḥr-pꜣ-ẖrd pꜣ nṯr ꜥꜣ [...] ḏd mdt nbt nty ỉw.w ỉy ỉ.ỉr.ḥr.k...*, Ray, *The Archive of Ḥor*, Text 9 lines 3–4.

55. PSI inv. D 35 frg. A col.1 lines 2-3: *Ỉy-m-ḥtp wr sꜣ Ptḥ pꜣ nṯr ꜥꜣ ỉw=f sḏy n(?) pꜣ gyꜣy [...tꜣ nfr (n) šꜣ]y ỉrm tꜣ bꜣn (n) šꜣy ỉrm nꜣ mt.wt nty ḫpr (n) nꜣ sḥm.wt....* This unpublished papyrus dates to the second century CE and belongs to the Tebtunis Temple Library. A provisional translation of its beginning can be found in Joachim Quack, "Imhotep, der Weise, der zum Gott wurde," in *Persönlichkeiten aus dem Alten Ägypten im Neuen Museum*, ed. Verena Lepper (Berlin: Imhof, 2014), 43–66. Similar phraseology about Imhotep is found in a parallel astrological treatise for men (P. Carlsberg 66 + P. Lille, unpublished). For a general overview of the men's treatise, see Michel Chauveau, "Un traité d'astrologie en écriture démotique," *CRIPEL* 14 (1994): 101–5.

56. Garth Fowden, *The Egyptian Hermes: A Historical Approach to the Late Pagan Mind* (Princeton, NJ: Princeton University Press, 1993), 162–64. The practice of inducing a vision such as that Thessalus experienced has been compared to spells of "god's arrival" in the London-Leiden Magical Papyri in Ian Moyer, *Egypt and the Limits of Hellenism* (Cambridge: Cambridge University Press, 2011), 252–53. (I thank Marina Escolano-Poveda for this reference.) For instance, PDM XIV 93-114 (PGM XIVa 1-11) states: *ḫr=f sḏy wby=k n rꜣ=f wby rꜣ=k n mt.t-mꜣꜥ.t ḥr hb nb ỉỉr=k*, "He (Imhotep) usually converses with you; his mouth against your mouth, in truth, concerning every dispatch which you did." This scenario aligns with Thessalus's vision of Asclepius and the opening of the Women's Astrological Manuals. For a translation of PDM XIV 93–114 (PGM XIVa 1–11), see Dieleman, "Claiming the Stars," 286–87.

channel of communication.[57] However, when the promised future does not arrive, recourse to oneiromancy could easily lapse into rejection of both the priests and the gods.[58]

In conclusion, I have provided a few modifications in translation as an attempt to better clarify the dream sequence in the Cairo bilingual letter (Cairo mus. Inv. Nos. 10313, 10328, 30961). I have also contextualized the text in the divinatory corpus from Greco-Roman Egypt. I believe that not only can the ideas about dream interpretation find their ground in Demotic dream books, but the Demotic divinatory corpus can also provide explanations for some oddly phrased expressions in the Cairo bilingual letter.

57. For an analysis of the use of magic, private ritual, and divination in Roman Egypt, see Jacco Dieleman, "Coping with a Difficult Life: Magic, Healing, and Sacred Knowledge," in *The Oxford Handbook of Roman Egypt*, ed. Christina Riggs (Oxford: Oxford University Press, 2012), 337–61.

58. In a letter from the Archive of *enkatochoi* (UPZ 70), Apollonios, the younger brother of Ptolemaios, accused his elder brother of blindly following dream omens. Apollonios writes in lines 11–13: κἄ[[ια]] ἴδῃς ὅτι μέλλομεν σωθῆναι, τότε βαπτιζώμεθα, "And whenever you see that we are to be saved, then we sink." The context makes it likely that Ptolemaios's sightings were in dreams, since the verb "to see" is widely employed to describe the action of dreaming in Egypt, e.g., το ἐνύπνειον, ὃ εἶδεν Ταγῆς, "the dream which Tages saw" (UPZ 77, col. I lines 1–2) and *ir m33 sw s m rsw.t*, "If a man sees himself in a dream" (P. Chester Beatty IIIr. 1.12).

Apollonios goes on to blame the family's destitution on πλανόμενοι ὑπο τῶν θεῶν καὶ πιστεύοντες τὰ ἐνύπτα, "being misled by gods and trusting dreams." (lines 28–30) The tirade doesn't stop there. On how the πλανᾶν "misdirection" was carried out, Apollonios said: ὅτι ψεύδῃ πάντα καὶ οἱ παρὰ σὲ θεοί ὁμοιως, "because you (Ptolemaios) lied in everything, and the gods with you likewise" (lines 6–8). Again, we should note the direct communicative aspect of ψεύδειν.

INDEXES

Subjects

Personal Names

Divine Names

Place Names

Ancient Sources

Ostraca

Stelae, Statues, and Other Objects

Cuneiform Tablets and Seals

Hebrew Bible

Classical Sources

Qu'ran